edition **3**

Auditing and Assurance Services
in Australia

Grant Gay
Monash University

Roger Simnett
university of New South Wales

McGraw-Hill
Irwin

Boston   Burr Ridge, IL   Dubuque, IA   Madison, WI   New York   San Francisco   St. Louis
Bangkok   Bogotá   Caracas   Kuala Lumpur   Lisbon   London   Madrid   Mexico City
Milan   Montreal   New Delhi   Santiago   Seoul   Singapore   Sydney   Taipei   Toronto

McGraw-Hill
Irwin

Reprinted 2005
Copyright © 2005 McGraw Hill Australia Pty Limited
Additional owners of copyright are named in on-page credits.

National Library of Australia Cataloguing-in-Publication Data

Gay, Grant E.

   Auditing and assurance services in Australia

   3rd edn

   Includes index.

   For tertiary students.

   ISBN 0 07 471563 1.

   1. Auditing – Australia. 2. Textbooks. I. Simnett, Roger. II. Title.

657.450994

Published in Australia by
McGraw-Hill Australia Pty Ltd
82 Waterloo Road, North Ryde, NSW 2113, Australia
Sponsoring Editor: Luisa Cecotti
Developmental Editor: Valerie Reed
Publishing Services Manager: Jo Munnelly
Permissions Editor: Jane Brimacombe
Editor: Megan Maniscalco
Cover and Internal Design: DiZign
Typesetter: Midland Typesetters
Indexer: Marjorie Flood
Printed in China through World Print

CONTENTS IN BRIEF

CONTENTS IN FULL

PART ONE — THE AUDITING AND ASSURANCE SERVICES PROFESSION

CHAPTER 1: Assurance and auditing: an overview — 3

CHAPTER 2: The structure of the profession — 49

CHAPTER 3: Ethics, independence and corporate governance   81

CHAPTER 4: The legal liability of auditors   141

PART TWO   PLANNING AND RISK

CHAPTER 5: Overview of elements of the financial report audit process   183

CHAPTER 6: Planning, knowledge of the business and evaluating business risk — 235

CHAPTER 7: Assessing specific business risks and materiality — 295

CHAPTER 8: Understanding and assessing internal control — 335

CHAPTER 9: Tests of controls 395

CHAPTER 10: Substantive tests of transactions and balances 449

CHAPTER 11: Audit sampling 513

PART FOUR — COMPLETION AND COMMUNICATION

CHAPTER 12: Completion and review   561

CHAPTER 13: The auditor's reporting obligations   601

PART FIVE — OTHER ASSURANCE SERVICES

CHAPTER 14: Other assurance services   651

FOREWORD

I am indeed pleased to have been given the opportunity by Grant Gay and Roger Simnett to write the foreword to the third edition of their leading textbook *Auditing and Assurance Services in Australia*.

The last two years have been marked by a number of crucial changes in the environment within which the auditing profession operates. The Australian Government's *Corporate Law Economic Reform Program (CLERP) 9*, the increased internationalisation of auditing standards, and the impact of the US *Sarbanes-Oxley Act*, have all had a tremendous impact on the financial reporting system and the auditing profession. A range of reform activities were and continue to be undertaken to promote public interest and increase public confidence in auditing and corporate governance.

Given the broad spectrum of changes and the new challenges facing the auditing profession, a new edition of this textbook is certainly welcomed. This will ensure that students and readers generally, are aware of the ongoing and basic principles of auditing as well as kept well informed of the changes in the last two years and the implications for the profession, regulators, governments, investment community and public in general.

The recent *CLERP 9* reforms have pivotal implications for the auditing profession. From 1 July 2004, the Australian Auditing and Assurance Standards Board (AUASB), which is the national standard-setting body, became a statutory body under the oversight of the Financial Reporting Council (FRC). With effect from 1 July 2006, the Auditing Standards issued by the AUASB will have the force of law. The textbook incorporates the strategies implemented up to 2005 and discusses the impact of such regulatory reforms on the profession.

In the previous edition, the authors made reference to the work of the International Auditing and Assurance Standards Board (IAASB) of the International Federation of Accountants (IFAC). Given Australia's increasing convergence with the IAASB standards on auditing and the increasing importance of globalisation, the new edition has been updated to reflect the fundamental role of the IFAC. Where relevant, the textbook refers to the standards on auditing issued by the IAASB alongside the Australian Auditing Standards.

The textbook also refers to the recently amended IFAC *Code of Ethics* and the amended *Code of Professional Conduct* Australia, which discusses the ethical responsibilities, including independence of the profession and the ethical and leadership responsibilities of management. To further stress the importance of corporate governance structures in place in organisations and the independence of the boards of directors, the Australian Stock Exchange (ASX) Corporate Governance Council has developed guidelines and the IAASB and the AUASB are currently working on a joint project on Communications with those charged with Governance.

The second edition previously discussed the concepts of auditing and assurance services, and the assurance framework. In 2004, a new framework that covers assurance engagements was developed providing a frame of reference for the auditing profession and others. In addition, a new Auditing Standard that establishes basic principles and essential procedures for assurance engagements other than audits or reviews of historical financial information was issued. This new edition of *Auditing and Assurance Services in Australia* recognises the importance of such developments by expanding on this aspect.

The concept of strategic business risk was introduced in the previous edition. Given the changing business environment and the need for an improvement in the quality of audits, a set of new audit risk standards were issued last year. The new Auditing Standards deal with the core of an audit— the auditor's assessment of the risk that the financial report could be wrong, and the way in which the auditor designs the rest of the audit in response to the identified risks. These new Auditing Standards have important implications for the audit profession and are fully and comprehensively incorporated in this new edition.

To promote transparency and comparability of auditor's reports internationally, the IAASB recently issued a new auditing standard on the form of an auditor's report for financial report audits. With globalisation, this will prove to be an important auditing standard as it sets the requirements for auditors that conducts audits in accordance with the international standards on auditing and expands the requirements needed in specific jurisdictions. The new edition of the textbook discusses the proposed changes to audit reports arising from the new auditing standard and the reasons for such changes.

The business and regulatory environments are subject to continuous change. Likewise, the reporting requirements and auditing practices are also changing. National standard-setters and the auditing profession need to be proactive and ensure that auditing practices remain appropriate in such a dynamic environment and continue to meet the public interest. The coming years will be particularly important to the auditing profession as Australia moves to the legal backing of Auditing Standards and increases convergence with the IAASB standards on auditing. This new edition of *Auditing and Assurance Services in Australia* addresses these and other changes that have occurred in the last few years and their implications for the auditing profession.

Richard Mifsud
Principal Executive
Australian Auditing and Assurance Standards Board

ABOUT THE AUTHORS

GRANT GAY, MEc *Monash,* FCA, is an associate professor in the Department of Accounting and Finance at Monash University, specialising in auditing and financial accounting. He is a former audit partner with KPMG and has extensive Australian and international audit experience. Grant is a former member of the Australian Auditing and Assurance Standards Board, as well as being an experienced facilitator in the CA Program and an author in the CPA Program. He researches actively in the audit area and has published numerous refereed articles.

ROGER SIMNETT, PhD *UNSW,* is a Professor in the School of Accounting at The University of New South Wales. He is a former auditor with Ernst & Young and teaches and researches in the auditing area. In 2002 he became the first academic appointed as a member of the reconstituted International Auditing and Assurance Standards Board (IAASB), a position he continues to hold since 2002. He has been actively involved in the development of many of the recently released auditing and assurance standards, including the assurance framework and the new audit risk standards. Roger has a background in standard setting, including his time spent on the Australian Auditing and Assurance Standards Board from 1995 to 1999.

ACKNOWLEDGMENTS

We would like to express our appreciation to all those individuals who made contributions to this book. First, our thanks to the following, who have reviewed the manuscript and enriched our book with their comments and suggestions:

THIRD EDITION

- Sandra Chapple (University of Wollongong)
- Hermant Deo (University of Wollongong)
- Greg Ellis (La Trobe University)
- Medhat Endrawes (University of Western Sydney)
- Evelyn Hogg (Murdoch University)
- James Hazelton (Macquarie University)
- Soheila Mirshekary (Central Queensland University)
- Ruvendra Nandan (James Cook University)
- Jim Psaros (University of Newcastle)
- Philip Ross (University of Western Sydney)
- Philip Saj (University of Adelaide)
- Robert Shannon (University of New England)
- Sandra Van Der Laan (University of Sydney)

SECOND AND FIRST EDITIONS

- Tracie Arkley-Smith (Charles Sturt University)
- Ross Bloore (Bond University)
- Peter Carey (Monash University)
- Kathie Cooper (University of Wollongong)
- Phillip Cobbin (University of Melbourne)
- Roe Cupido (Curtin University)
- Graeme Dean (University of Sydney)
- Bruce Diggins (University of Western Sydney)
- Paul Dunmore (Victoria University, Wellington)
- Greg Ellis (La Trobe University)
- Medhat Endrawes (University of Western Sydney)
- Colin Ferguson (University of Queensland)
- David Hay (Auckland University)
- Evelyn Hogg (Murdoch University)
- Sue Hrasky (University of Tasmania)
- Rod Johnson (Deakin University)
- Christine Jubb (University of Melbourne)
- Christopher Kelly (Deakin University)
- Susan Lambert (Flinders University)
- Margaret Lightbody (University of Adelaide)
- Joanne Moores (Victoria University, Wellington)
- Jim Psaros (University of Newcastle)
- Peter Roebuck, University of New South Wales)
- Philip Ross (Macquarie University)
- Stephen Rowe (Southern Cross University)
- Dan Schiewe (Queensland University of Technology)
- Nava Subramaniam (Griffith University)
- Margo Wade (University of Canberra)
- Ming Wei Zhang (Monash University)
- Brian West (University of Ballarat)

We gratefully acknowledge the permission of the International Federation of Accountants, Institute of Chartered Accountants in Australia and CPA Australia to quote from auditing and assurance standards and associated professional pronouncements. We acknowledged permission given by the Institute to use material from its Professional Year and CA Programs. In addition, we thank the American Institute of Certified Public Accountants, the Canadian Institute of Chartered Accountants, the Chartered Institute of Management Accountants and the Institute of Internal Auditors for permission to use material from their professional examinations. We especially would like to thank Richard Mifsud for his kind words in the foreword.

We are indebted to ACL Australia, who allowed us the use of ACL Software—which is used by the major accounting companies—for an auditing case study to accompany this book. Our thanks to the staff at McGraw-Hill for all their assistance, in particular Luisa Cecotti, Valerie Reed, Jo Munnelly and Megan Maniscalco. We also express our gratitude for the assistance of Bibi Moore and Lei Chen. Finally, our sincere thanks to our families and colleagues, without whose patience and understanding this book would not have been possible.

Grant Gay
Roger Simnett

PREFACE

When we wrote the previous edition of this book in 2003, we were referring to a crisis of confidence in the underlying financial system. Over the period 2001-2003 we had seen a number of corporate collapses (HIH Insurance and One.Tel in Australia, and Enron and WorldCom in the United States, just to name a couple) and the demise of the auditing firm, Arthur Andersen. As a result there was a loss of confidence by the investing community in the financial reporting processes worldwide, of which the auditing profession is an integral part.

We are now writing this new edition in 2005. Over these last two years we have actually seen the auditing profession go from strength to strength. The need of society for a strong independent auditing and assurance profession has been recognised over these two years. To aid this process, there have been a lot of reform activities that have been undertaken. This book will outline the initiatives that have been achieved up until 2005, as well as identify those which are planned over the next couple of years.

These issues provide a background to the current auditing environment. It is not possible to fully understand the environment confronting auditors without contemplating the impact of these issues. All these issues will be considered at various stages throughout this text.

The initiatives contained in the previous edition of this book have continued to be built upon in this new edition. First, it emphasises an auditing approach called the business risk approach. This approach is becoming standard in audit practice and has been incorporated into both national and international auditing standards over the last two years. It involves the auditor obtaining a greater knowledge of their clients than was required under previous audit approaches, including obtaining increased understanding of their business strategy and methods of dealing with business risks. The auditor then needs to consider the impact of this knowledge and the evaluation of these business risks on potential misstatements that may occur in the financial report.

The second major initiative is the extension of the business evaluation, evidence collection and reporting model from simply a consideration of providing assurance on financial reports to providing assurance on a whole range of other services. This initiative has been supported by developments over the last two years, such as the approved assurance framework. It is hard to argue against the premise that people need assurance on a whole range of information or services other than financial reports. This may include assurance that the party at the other end of the web address is going to deliver the product or service that you have paid for, of a quality or at the time that is agreed. Or it may be that assurance is required that the sporting memorabilia recently acquired is genuine, or the claims that the business is not hurting the environment are of substance. This book outlines the extension of the audit methodology to other services, and reflects the recent and likely future developments in this area.

The third major initiative concerns the increasing impact of globalisation on accounting and the auditing profession. There is an increasing alignment of national and international accounting and auditing standards. This book continues to reflect the convergence to international auditing standards by including references to both Australian and International Auditing Standards and examining the convergence policy of Australia with International Standards. We argue that further attention needs to be paid by the standard-setters to the increasingly complex environment confronting the auditor.

Over the next few years it is expected that auditing standard setting bodies will pay greater attention to the increase in complexity which is being confronted by the auditor. This is associated with factors such as the increasingly complex client structures that the auditor is being required to audit, and the increased complexity of accounting issues being faced, such as the move away from historical cost accounting as a basis for preparing financial reports. This book reflects on how issues such as increased globalisation and client complexity are likely to be addressed by the profession.

Grant Gay
Roger Simnett

MAJOR CHANGES TO THE THIRD EDITION

This new edition highlights the major initiatives that have been undertaken by national and international legislators and professional bodies to restore faith in the profession. We cover major changes to legislation and the auditing standards up until the end of 2004, and also look forward to changes which will impact the profession up until 2006. This has resulted in the following inclusions:

- initiatives in the auditing environment in response to the era of corporate collapse around 2002
- Australian Auditing Standards released during 2002–04
- recent changes to International and Australian auditing standards, including the revised audit risk and audit evidence standards (which take effect in 2005), and the audit reporting standards (which take effect from the end of 2006).

1

- new framework for auditing standards and assurance engagements (AUS108)
- more detail on the structure of auditing and assurance standards
- new standards for assurance engagements other than financial report audits (AUS110 / ISAE3000)
- developments in the internationalisation of auditing requirements
- discussion of fundamental principles underlying an audit, as outlined in IAASB and AUASB 2005 draft consultation paper
- introduction to new business risk standards (AUS402 / ISA315)
- IAASB and AUASB 'clarity project'

2

- emphasising restructure of the auditing standard setting process in Australia
- establishment of Auditing and Assurance Standards Board (AUASB) as an independent statutory body
- role of the Financial Reporting Council and Financial Reporting Panel
- discussion of revised standard AUS206 / ISA220 (Quality Control for Audits of Historical Financial Information)
- changes to ASIC responsibilities following CLERP 9
- exposure draft of changes in professional requirements for APS 5
- changes to the structure of audit firms as result of authorised audit companies now being permitted under the CLERP 9 amendments

3

- new corporate governance and code of ethics/conduct guidelines issued by industry and other bodies such as ASX, IFAC, AICD, IFSA
- developments in International Auditing Standards in relation to governance
- regulatory developments flowing from CLERP 9 regarding the independence of auditors and protection for whistle blowers
- revised AUS210 / ISA240 (Auditor's Responsibility to Consider Fraud and Error in an Audit of a Financial Report)
- updates in respect of Sarbanes–Oxley Act 2002

4

- limiting of auditors' liability as a result of CLERP 9
- incorporation of revised fraud responsibilities AUS210 / IAS240

CONTENTS IN BRIEF

5

- revised AUS202 / ISA200 (Objective and General Principles covering an Audit of a Financial Report), 2004
- revised AUS402 / ISA315 (Understanding the Entity and its Environment and Assessing the Risks of Misstatement), 2004
- new AUS406 / ISA330 (The Auditor's Procedures in response to Assessed Risks), 2004
- new coverage of revised AUS502 / ISA500 (Audit Evidence), 2004

6

- revised AUS206 / ISA220 (Quality Control for Audits of Historical Financial Information), 2004
- revised AUS402 / ISA315 (Understanding the Entity and its Environment and Assessing the Risks of Misstatement), 2004
- new AUS406 / ISA330 (The Auditor's Procedures in Response to Assessed Risks), 2004
- new sections on Understanding the internal control; Assessing the risks of material misstatement; Response to assessed risks; Tests of control; Substantive procedures

- changes that affect the auditing environment resulting from the Corporate Law Economic Reform Program (CLERP 9)
- revised structure of the Australian Auditing and Assurance Standards Board (and the Financial Reporting Council)
- integration of 'Stop Press' boxes from the second edition into the chapter text.
- new, additional end-of-chapter questions in most chapters.

9
- tests of controls linked through to expanded financial report assertions
- revised AUS502 / ISA500 (Audit Evidence), 2004
- revised AUS402 / ISA315 (Understanding the Entity and its Environment and Assessing the Risks of Misstatement), 2004
- new AUS406 / ISA330 (The Auditor's Procedures in Response to Assessed Risks), 2004

10
- substantive tests of transactions and balances are linked through to expanded financial report assertions
- new AUS406 / ISA330 (The Auditor's Procedures in Response to Assessed Risks), 2004
- revised AUS502 / ISA500 (Audit Evidence), 2004
- flow on changes from AASB116 / IAS16 (Property, Plant and Equipment) and AASB117 / IAS17 (Leases), AASB138 / IAS38 (Intangible Assets)

12
- revised AUS502 / ISA500 (Audit Evidence)
- revised AASB110 / IAS10 (Events After the Balance Sheet)
- Framework for the Preparation and Presentation of Financial Statements

13
- update of examples of audit qualifications
- identification of changes that need to take place to AUS702 with regards emphasis of matter reports (as a result of adopting international accounting standards)
- new audit reporting formats approved to take effect from the end of 2006
- discussion of Audit and Assurance Alert No. 11 (Communicating with Entities in Relation to Auditor Independence) and Practice Note 34 (Auditors' Obligations: Reporting to ASIC)
- AUS708 / ISA580 (Going Concern)
- updates flowing from CLERP 9

7
- revised AUS202 / ISA200 (Objective and General Principles covering an Audit of a Financial Report), 2004
- revised AUS402 / ISA315 (Understanding the Entity and its Environment and Assessing the Risks of Misstatement), 2004
- new AUS406 / ISA330 (The Auditor's Procedures in Response to Assessed Risks), 2004
- CLERP 9 amendment S.295A(2) to require a CEO/CFO declaration
- revised AUS210 / ISA240 (Auditor's Responsibility to Consider Fraud and Error in an Audit of a Financial Report)

8
- revised AUS402 / ISA315 (Understanding the Entity and its Environment and Assessing the Risks of Misstatement), 2004
- new AUS406 / ISA330 (The Auditor's Procedures in Response to Assessed Risks), 2004

14
- new developments relating to AUS108 (Framework for Assurance Engagements; International Framework for Assurance Engagements)
- new developments relating to AUS110 / ISAE3000 (Assurance Engagements Other than Audits or Reviews of Financial Information)
- increased discussion on Assurance on the effectiveness of internal controls, picking up international initiatives

17
- developments at the international level with regards environmental and sustainability assurance, and details of review of current practice in this area

MaxMark

The Auditing and Assurance Services MaxMark has been prepared by Grant Gay.

Maximise your marks with this unique, online self-assessment tool, exclusive to McGraw-Hill Australia. With MaxMark, approximately 30 multiple choice questions per chapter, covering all the key concepts, are available for self-paced revision.

Importantly, you will receive extensive 'Feedback' and 'More Information' from the text to help you in your understanding. You can randomise the questions and set yourself time limits, track your progress throughout the semester, and thoroughly test your knowledge before exams.

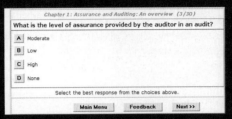

There are approximately 30 multiple-choice questions per chapter

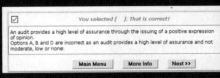

Feedback to explain each answer

More information from the text for additional explanation

Auditing News Centre

This invaluable section contains twice-yearly updates, prepared by the authors. It includes coverage of all new information in the auditing world, and references it back to individual chapters and topics covered within the book.

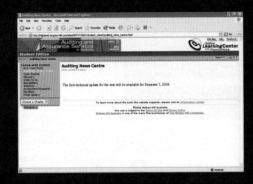

Case studies

A suite of case studies is being developed, featuring real-world situations. Current case studies include One.Tel, HIH and Qantas.

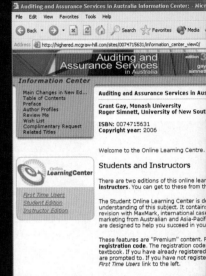

Online Learning Centre

The Online Learning Centre with PowerWeb and MaxMark that accompanies this text is an integrated online product designed to help you get the most from your course. This text provides a powerful learning experience beyond the printed page. The Premium content areas,

Wish list What do you want to see online or in future editions of this text? Email us your with your feedback.

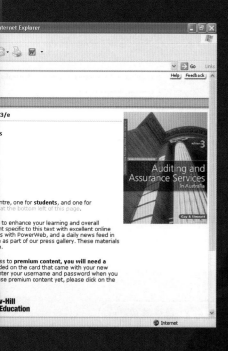

Case Study in Audit Command Language

A CD is packaged with this book, containing an auditing assignment in the ACL Software used by many practicing auditors including the Big 4 accounting companies. This gives you a great opportunity to carry out an auditing assignment within a real-world IT environment. A tutorial is included, to allow you to become familiar with the software before you undertake the assignment. The ACL software and technical help desk (available via email support@aclaust.com.au) have been made available courtesy of ACL Australia, as part of their commitment to education. The tutorial and assignment have been prepared by Poonam Bir and Grant Gay, of Monash University.

which are accessed by registering the code at the front of this text, provide you with our exclusive online resources. After registration, you will have seamless access to international PowerWeb articles and the MaxMark revision program.

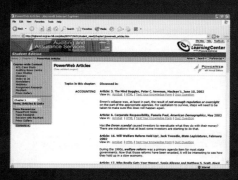

PowerWeb

Exclusive to McGraw-Hill, PowerWeb provides you with full text international articles on auditing, published in international journals and magazines. These articles are updated annually and organised to each chapter of the text.

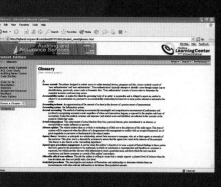

The audit trail

- Transactions traced from initial entry in system to intermediate records, where transactions become components of subtotals, and ultimately to disposition in final records, where subtotals are summarised for presentation in financial report.

- Direction of tracing can be modified: auditor can trace from point of initiation of transaction to final recording (assertion of completeness), or trace from final record back to point of initiation (assertion of existence).

PowerPoint® slides

Prepared by Roger Simnett, these slides summarise learning objectives and key points contained in the chapter. They can be downloaded as a revision aid.

Glossary

Unsure of an auditing term? The glossary contains quick reference to key terms and definitions.

-INSTRUCTOR

Instructor resource manual

Prepared by Grant Gay and Roger Simnett, the Instructor Resource Manual contains learning objectives, a listing of chapter sections, and a lecture plan linked to the PowerPoint slides. A comprehensive solutions manual is also included.

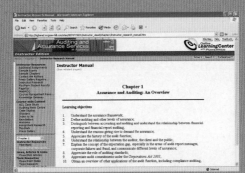

PowerPoint® Slides

Prepared by Roger Simnett, these slides summarise the key points of each chapter and can be used in conjunction with a lecture plan outlined in the Instructor Resource Manual.

The audit trail

- Transactions traced from initial entry in system to intermediate records, where transactions become components of subtotals, and ultimately to disposition in final records, where subtotals are summarised for presentation in financial report.

- Direction of tracing can be modified: auditor can trace from point of initiation of transaction to final recording (assertion of completeness), or trace from final record back to point of initiation (assertion of existence).

MaxMark student results

The integrated MaxMark to accompany this text provides you with diagnostics on the performance of your class, as your students interact online with the key concepts in each chapter of the text.

Test bank

Prepared by the authors, the test bank has been thoroughly revised. New questions relating to ethics have been included.

PowerWeb

Exclusive to McGraw-Hill, PowerWeb provides you with full text international articles on accounting and auditing, published in international journals and magazines. These articles are updated annually and are organized to each chapter of the text.

Sample exams

Two sample exams are available as an additional resource for lecturers.

Additional assignments (questions, problems and cases)

A significant number of additional questions, problems and cases are available on the web site. Solutions are also provided.

Auditing News Centre

Provided twice-yearly by the authors, the comprehensive updates link all major news and developments in auditing to topics covered in the book. Each item is referenced back to the relevant area of the text book.

Case study in Audit Command Language

A CD is packaged with this book, containing an auditing assignment in the ACL Software used by many practicing auditors including the Big 4 accounting companies. This gives students a great opportunity to carry out an auditing assignment within a real-world IT environment. A tutorial is included, to step students through the software before they undertake the assignment. The ACL software and technical help desk (available via email support@aclaust.com.au) have been made available courtesy of ACL Australia, as part of their commitment to education. The tutorial and assignment have been prepared by Poonam Bir and Grant Gay, of Monash University.

Course Management Systems (CMS) (WebCT, Blackboard, PageOut)

Course Management Systems allow you to deliver and manage your course via the internet. McGraw-Hill can provide online material to accompany this text, formatted for your chosen CMS. See your McGraw-Hill representative for details.

Web MCQ

Set up your own online assignments and exams, using our powerful and flexible on-line quizzing tool. Sophisticated tracking and reporting capabilities allow instructors to highlight topics where students are weak and target these areas in tutorials.

Case studies

A suite of case studies is being developed, linking items in the news to theoretical aspects of the text. Current case studies cover One.Tel, HIH and Qantas.

Contact the authors

The authors welcome your feedback and comments on the text. Email links are provided for instructors.

How to use this book

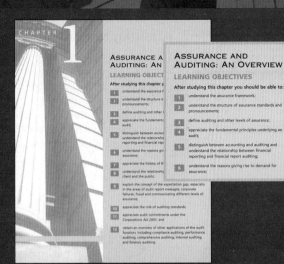

Learning objectives

Every chapter opens with a showcase of the chapter's learning objectives. These tell you what you should be able to do after you have finished reading that chapter. Make these the foundation for your exam revision by testing yourself. The end-of-chapter assignments also link back to these learning objectives (see Chapter 1, p.3).

Relevant guidance

Both Australian and International Auditing and Assurance Standards and other guidance relevant to topics covered are listed at the start of each chapter. This gives you the advantage of being not only fully conversant with the Australian Standards that govern auditing in this country now, but importantly, ensuring that you are familiar with the new international standards.

Chapter outlines

Each chapter starts with a comprehensive overview of material to be covered, placing it in context with current Australian and international practice (see Chapter 3, p.82).

Key terms

Key terms are bolded in the text where they first appear and listed at the end of the chapter. Learn the lingo as you go! Then at exam time you'll already be half-way prepared (see Chapter 3, p.120).

Glossary

The glossary defines all key terms (see p.770).

Quick reviews

These short recaps are a valuable revision aid. Key points covered in the text are summarised at appropriate junctures within chapters (see Chapter 1, p.20).

Examples

Worked and illustrative examples explain theoretical aspects and show
their relevance to actual situations (see Chapter 3, p.118).

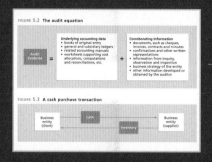

Figures

Numerous flow charts and graphical representations help you understand the stages
and sequence of accounting and auditing processes (see Chapter 5, p.193).

Exhibits

In-text exhibits provide you with examples of typical and actual
documentation — such as standard letters of appointment, ASX listing
rules and standard guidelines (see Chapter 3, p.95).

Auditing in the news

News items and snippets impacting on auditing highlight the relevance of chapter
topics to events in auditing (see Chapter 1, p.7).

Chapter summaries

The chapter in a nutshell. Use these summaries as an excellent pre-exam
revision tool (see Chapter 9, p.420).

Comprehensive end-of-chapter assignments

Linked directly to the chapters learning objectives, and grouped by topic,
problems and questions give you an opportunity to test how well you've
understood the chapter topics (see Chapter 1, p.42).

**Additional questions, problems and case studies are available at
the Online Learning Centre:** www.mbhe.com/au/gay3e

DEDICATION

This book is dedicated to Gaye, Liz, Sarah and David, and Shakila and Sharina, in appreciation of their continued love and support.

THE AUDITING AND ASSURANCE SERVICES PROFESSION

This part of the textbook introduces the concepts of auditing and assurance services and explains the relationship between them. It outlines recent developments arising from the assurance framework adopted by the International Auditing and Assurance Standards Board (IAASB) and also outlines the major influences in society that give rise to a demand for auditing and assurance services. This part also considers other influences on the environment associated with assurance service providers, including the internationalisation of auditing, the development of industry specialisations by audit firms, the roles played by the corporate governance structure within organisations and the ethical rules and ethical decision-making models associated with the auditing profession. It considers current impacts on the profession, including the Corporate Law Economic Reform Program (CLERP 9), the US *Sarbanes-Oxley Act*, the recently amended IFAC Code of Ethics and the revised structure of the Australian Auditing and Assurance Standards Board, under the Financial Reporting Council. The text considers recent changes to International and Australian Auditing Standards, including the revised audit risk and audit evidence standards, which take effect from 2005, and the audit reporting standards, which take effect from the end of 2006.

CHAPTER 1

ASSURANCE AND AUDITING: AN OVERVIEW

LEARNING OBJECTIVES

After studying this chapter you should be able to:

1 understand the assurance framework;

2 understand the structure of assurance standards and pronouncements;

3 define auditing and other levels of assurance;

4 appreciate the fundamental principles underlying an audit;

5 distinguish between accounting and auditing and understand the relationship between financial reporting and financial report auditing;

6 understand the reasons giving rise to demand for assurance;

7 appreciate the history of the audit function;

8 understand the relationship between the auditor, the client and the public;

9 explain the concept of the expectation gap, especially in the areas of audit report messages, corporate failures, fraud and communicating different levels of assurance;

10 appreciate the role of auditing standards;

11 appreciate audit commitments under the *Corporations Act 2001*; and

12 obtain an overview of other applications of the audit function, including compliance auditing, performance auditing, comprehensive auditing, internal auditing and forensic auditing.

Chapter**outline** and review of current auditing environment

When we wrote the second edition of this book in 2003, we referred to a crisis of confidence in the underlying financial system. Over the period 2001 to 2003 we saw a number of corporate collapses (HIH Insurance and One.Tel in Australia, and Enron (see Auditing in the News 1.1 on p. 7) and WorldCom in the United States to name just a few) and the demise of the auditing firm Arthur Andersen. As a result, the investing community lost confidence in the financial reporting system worldwide—a system to which the auditing profession is integral.

Our vantage point for the third edition is 2005. Over the past two years we have, in fact, seen the auditing profession go from strength to strength. Society's need for a strong independent auditing and assurance profession has been recognised over this period. A range of reform activities have been undertaken with a view to meeting this need. This book will outline the strategies that have been implemented up to 2005 and identify initiatives planned for the next couple of years.

All these developments provide the background for the current auditing environment. It is not possible to fully understand the environment within which auditors must work without contemplating the impact of these developments. All these issues will be considered at various stages throughout the text.

While recent developments are relevant to putting the audit into a current context, the main aim of this book is to inform the reader about the nature of **audits** or, from a broader perspective, **assurance services**, and about the various stages involved in providing such services. There are some points that need to be made about how the book achieves this.

Entities achieve their goals through the use of human and economic resources. Audits and assurance services exist primarily because there is a separation of those who have an interest in the activities of an entity (for example, shareholders) and those who are responsible for managing the human and economic resources of the entity (for example, management). In order to account for the use of these human and economic resources, entities must issue reports explaining the use of the resources entrusted to their control. These reports can take a number of forms, including financial reports, which are prepared in accordance with accounting standards in order to provide information on the financial position and performance of an entity, and environmental reports, which are prepared in accordance with environmental standards to provide information on the environ-

mental performance of an entity. A primary function of the public accounting profession is to render independent and expert opinions on these reports based on an examination of the evidence underlying the data reported. This examination is commonly referred to as an audit if it involves performing assurance procedures on financial information and as an assurance service if it involves performing assurance procedures on other information.

What initiatives have given rise to the increased level of confidence that is reflected in this edition? They include:

- **Development of a framework for all assurance engagements** In 2004 we saw the approval of the assurance framework. This framework covers both audits of historical financial information (including financial reports) and other assurance services. The auditing standards will be governed by this framework. This is discussed further in Chapter 1.

- **Consideration of the fundamental principles underlying an audit** In 2005 the auditing standard-setters released for discussion a draft set of fundamental principles underlying an audit. These are discussed in Chapter 1.

- **New standards for assurance engagements other than financial report audits** During 2004, we also saw the approval of a standard to cover all assurance engagements other than those on historical financial information. This provided a comprehensive standard which covers all the other assurance engagements that an auditor may be involved in, including engagements providing assurance on historical financial information. This is discussed in Chapters 1 and 14.

- **Developments in the internationalisation of auditing and the regulation of the auditing profession** During the past two years we have seen Australia commit itself to a policy of converging with International Auditing Standards, as well as to a shift in the regulatory structure of the standard-setting function towards a more independent, government-based structure with public oversight. These developments are discussed primarily in Chapters 1 to 3.

- **Corporate governance initiatives** In the second edition of the text we asked you to consider the appropriateness of the corporate governance mechanisms in place at the time. In particular, the expertise and independence of boards of directors and sub-committees of these boards, and their relationship with external auditors were called into question. There have been a number of initiatives in this area, including corporate governance guidelines issued by the Australian Stock Exchange (ASX) Corporate Governance Council and developments in International Auditing Standards with regard to auditors' communications with those charged with governance. These are outlined primarily in Chapter 3.

■ **Ethics initiatives** A number of concerns were raised about the level of ethics being practised, as well as the ethical and leadership responsibilities of both management and auditors. We have seen initiatives taken over the past two years in the International Federation of Accountants' (IFAC) Code of Ethics, which have been incorporated in the Code of Professional Conduct in Australia. These developments are outlined in Chapter 3.

■ **The independence of auditors** A number of questions have been raised regarding the independence of auditors from management, and over the past two years we have seen a number of initiatives taken in this area. For example, concerns have been raised about the high levels of other (non-audit) services being offered by auditors to their audit clients, which may compromise their independence, as well as about practices such as ex-members of auditing firms taking on management roles with audit clients. There have been a number of regulatory developments in this area, which are outlined primarily in Chapter 3.

■ **Initiatives aimed at addressing increased business complexity and globalisation** In the second edition of the text we pointed out that the fact that audit clients are increasing in complexity intensified the general confidence crisis, making the audit more difficult. However, the audit profession has tackled this issue head on, revising its audit risk standards (see the next bullet point) and exposing an auditing standard on the audit of group accounts. The pervasive effect of these new standards is evident in Chapters 5 to 11.

■ **New business risk auditing standards** In 2004 the audit profession approved a series of auditing standards which underpinned the business risk approach emphasised in this text, as it relates to financial report audits. Although the second edition was based on the audit approach that informs these new standards and was written in anticipation of these standards, this edition fully incorporates these standards. These three new standards, AUS 402 (ISA 315) 'Understanding the Entity and its Environment and Assessing the Risks of Material Misstatements', AUS 406 (ISA 330) 'The Auditor's Procedures in Response to Assessed Risks' and AUS 502 (ISA 500) 'Audit Evidence' have a pervasive effect throughout the planning, risk assessment and evidence-collection stages of the audit (Chapters 5 to 11).

■ **New audit reporting strategies** The audit profession approved in 2005 a revised standard on audit reporting for financial report audits, to take effect from the end of 2006. The proposed changes to audit reports and the reasons for these changes are outlined in Chapter 13.

■ **New assurance services initiatives** The development of the assurance framework has placed greater emphasis on the provision of assurance services on information other than historical financial information. These initiatives include developments in the area of limited assurance engagements, which used to be called review engagements, and a range of other assurance services such as reporting on internal controls and environmental and sustainability assurance. These are covered primarily in Chapters 14 and 17.

Progress with initiatives outlined in the second edition of the text is detailed in this new edition. The second edition emphasised first an auditing approach called the business risk approach. This approach is becoming more common in audit practice and has been incorporated in both national and international auditing standards over the past two years. It involves the auditor obtaining greater knowledge of their clients than was required under previous audit approaches, including an increased understanding of their business strategy and methods of dealing with business risks. The auditor then needs to consider the impact of this knowledge and evaluate the business risks on potential misstatements that may occur in the financial report.

The second major initiative of the second edition concerned the extension of the business evaluation, evidence-collection and reporting model from simply a consideration of providing assurance on financial reports to providing assurance on a whole range of other services. This initiative has been supported by developments over the past two years such as the approved assurance framework. Again it is hard to argue against the premise that people need assurance on a whole range of information or services other than financial reports. This may include assurance that the party at the other end of the web address is going to deliver the product or service that you have paid for—of the quality or at the time agreed upon. Or it may be that assurance is required that the sporting memorabilia recently acquired is genuine, or the claims that a business is not hurting the environment are of substance. This new edition outlines the extension of the audit methodology to other services, and reflects recent and likely future developments in this area.

The third major initiative of the previous edition was the growing impact of **globalisation** on the accounting and audit professions. Whereas the first two initiatives have been directly addressed over the past two years, further attention needs to be paid by the standard-setters to the increasingly complex environment confronting the auditor. There is an increasing alignment of national and international accounting and auditing standards. This edition continues to reflect convergence with International Auditing Standards by including references to both Australian and International Auditing Standards and examining the convergence policy of Australia with international standards. With regard to client complexity, over the next few years it is expected that auditing standard-setting bodies will pay greater attention to the increasing client complexity auditors are facing. This is associated with factors such as the increasingly complex client structures auditors are being required to audit, and the increasing complexity of accounting issues they face, such as the move away from historical cost accounting as a basis for preparing financial reports. Some of the guidance being considered is a standard on auditing complex group structures, and a review of guidance on auditing fair values. This text reflects on how issues such as increased globalisation and client complexity are likely to be addressed by the profession.

Relevant guidance

Australian		International	
AUS 102	Foreword to Australian Auditing Standards and Guidance Statements		Preface to International Standards on Auditing and Related Services
AUS 104	Glossary of Terms		Glossary of Terms
AUS 106	Explanatory Framework for Standards on Audit and Audit Related Services		—
AUS 108	Framework for Assurance Engagements (Revised 2004)		International Framework for Assurance Engagements
AUS 110	Assurance Engagements other than Audits or Reviews of Historical Information (Issued 2004)	ISAE 3000	Assurance Engagements other than Audits or Reviews of Historical Financial Information (Issued 2004)
AUS 202	Objectives and General Principles Governing an Audit of a Financial Report (Revised 2004)	ISA 200	Objectives and General Principles Governing an Audit of Financial Statements (Revised 2004)
AUS 402	Understanding the Entity and its Environment and Assessing the Risks of Material Misstatement (Revised 2004)	ISA 315	Understanding the Entity and its Environment and Assessing the Risks of Material Misstatement (Issued 2004)
AUS 702	The Audit Report on a General Purpose Financial Report	ISA 700	The Auditor's Report on Financial Statements
APS 1.1	Conformity with Auditing Standards		—

Enron's aftermath: negligence and slippery numbers

It was just a year ago, in the fading light of the tech wreckage, that corporate America returned to the blue chips of the bourse. Balance sheets were back in vogue.

With the ephemeral Internet stocks cleared away, the star of the show was the energy giant Enron. Its name was emblazoned on the covers of business magazines, feted as a model for the new business paradigm. Investors made fortunes and analysts cheered as Enron madness propelled the stock higher.

Today, the integrity of the whole North American financial system is faltering. Enron and other brilliants such as Global Crossing, Tyco and even the seemingly indestructible GE still cover the front pages. But the news is very different. The Enron model is in tatters as America, from the White House to Wall Street, tries to work out how it all went wrong.

Enron has collapsed and is under investigation by the Justice Department, the Securities and Exchange Commission and about a dozen congressional committees for alleged fraud and deception. Its auditor, Arthur Andersen, has been indicted on charges of obstruction of justice for allegedly shredding the records. The financial world has been treated to the spectacle of Andersen, a true global Goliath, disintegrating as it tries to sell itself piecemeal to crowing rivals. The corporate sector is struggling to sustain investor confidence in the very machinery of American capitalism as scrutiny falls on boards of directors, audit committees, the accounting industry, regulators and the law-makers themselves.

One truism remains: Enron's role as a poster child for the new paradigm. Negligence, slippery numbers, fictitious income statements, insider dealings, conflicts of interest—these are the new bywords for corporate America. As Arthur Andersen goes on trial, the honesty and reliability of corporate America is in the dock too. ...

Audit committees, responsible for reviewing the accuracy of a company's financial reports, have been steadily drawing fire. The special, internal Powers report into what went wrong on the Enron board singled out the audit committee, citing cosy ties between committee members and the company. At least one director sat on the board at the same time as being a paid consultant to the company. ...

WorldCom, which owns MCI, is under SEC investigation for accounting practices, disputed customer accounts and commissions on corporate business. ... The biotech cancer cure firm, ImClone, has been hauled before Congress as allegations mount about conflicts of interest, insider sales and dubious deals.

Wall Street heavy CSFB is barely out of hot water. The company has been accused of abuses in the way it dealt out hot IPOs during the tech boom. The firm paid $US100 million in January to settle investigations into the extortion of huge commissions from clients. A string of CSFB executives have been fined internally amounts from $US250 000 to $US500 000. Even after last year's congressional inquiries into the way analysts rated tech stocks during the Internet crash (when investors lost billions of dollars following their recommendations), Wall Street has paid only scant attention to calls to shape up. ...

Arthur Andersen now has the reputation of a repeat offender, with Enron following disasters at Sunbeam and Waste Management. In the case of Sunbeam and former chief executive Al Dunlap—another one-time Wall Street poster boy—the story of fraudulent financial statements and fabricated transactions led to slashed profits, restated earnings, bankruptcy and SEC charges that Andersen paid heavy shareholder settlements for both Sunbeam and Waste Management. ...

At the end of January a former chief accountant at the SEC told *Businessweek* that investors had lost probably $US200 billion in earnings restatements and lost market capitalisation after audit failures in the past six years alone.

The excesses of giant corporate payouts, old-boy networks and cross-directorships, insider share sales and duplicitous earnings have left investors reeling. ...

The question hanging in the air is whether anyone can be trusted with other people's money anymore.

Source: P. Williams, (2002) 'Enron's Aftermath: Negligence and Slippery Numbers', *Australian Financial Review*, 25 March, p. 1.

THE ASSURANCE FRAMEWORK

In many situations in today's society, people who are responsible for a specific task (called responsible parties or managers) need to account for their performance on that task. There may be many groups who will rely on this accounting for performance as an aid to their decision making. These groups may be either resource providers or third parties to the process (users). There are many examples of such relationships including:

- shareholders relying on financial reports produced by companies' management;
- government agencies relying on reports produced by entities to account for environmental considerations; and
- people relying on information produced by schools when deciding where to send their children.

In order for users to judge the performance of the responsible party they may ask the responsible party to provide them with a report of how resources under their care have been used in achieving the aims of the relationship. However, the report by the responsible party is seen as potentially biased, as the responsible party may have an incentive to prepare a report that reflects their performance in the best possible light. Thus, before the report is made available to the user, the credibility of the report is enhanced by having someone who is both independent and expert (called the auditor or assurance service provider) examine the subject matter in accordance with suitable criteria and report on it.

In 2004 the International Auditing and Assurance Standards Board (IAASB) released 'International Framework for Assurance Engagements' (issued in Australia as AUS 108, 'Framework for Assurance Engagements'). The assurance framework covers both audits and reviews of historical financial information and all other assurance engagements. This initiative therefore recognises the increasing demand for assurance over a wide range of subject matter.

The framework defines an **assurance engagement** as 'an engagement in which a practitioner expresses a conclusion designed to enhance the degree of confidence of the intended users other than the responsible party about the outcome of the evaluation or measurement of a subject matter against criteria' (para. 7). Five elements of an assurance engagement are identified (para. 20):

1 **Three-party relationships:**
   - *Practitioner (auditor)* In Australia this would be a member of CPA Australia or The Institute of Chartered Accountants in Australia (ICAA), and one who is bound by the profession's Code of Ethics.
   - *Responsible party* The responsible party is the person or persons responsible for the subject matter. For example, management is responsible for the preparation of the financial report or the implementation and operation of internal control.
   - *Intended user* The intended user is the person or persons expected to use the practitioner's report. Often the intended user will be the addressee of the report by the practitioner, although there will be circumstances where there will be other identified users.

2 **Subject matter** The subject matter of an assurance engagement can take many forms, such as:
   - financial performance (for example, historical or prospective financial information);
   - non-financial performance (for example, information aimed at efficiency and effectiveness);
   - physical characteristics (for example, capacity of a facility);
   - systems and processes (for example, internal controls);
   - behaviour (for example, corporate governance, compliance with regulation, human resource practices).

Thus, the definition of assurance services is very broad in its coverage and includes both existing assurance services and newly evolving assurance services. The framework also draws a distinction between the subject matter (such as the underlying financial position and performance of an entity) and the report on the subject matter, which is called subject matter information (such as the balance sheets and income statements).

3 **Suitable criteria**   Criteria are the standards or benchmarks used to measure and evaluate the subject matter of an assurance engagement. Criteria are important in the reporting of a conclusion by a practitioner as they establish and convey to the intended user the basis on which the conclusion has been formed. Without this frame of reference any conclusion is open to individual interpretation and misunderstanding.

4 **Sufficient appropriate evidence**   The engagement process for an assurance engagement is a systematic methodology requiring specialised knowledge, a skill base and techniques for evidence gathering and evaluation to support a conclusion, irrespective of the nature of the engagement subject matter. The process involves the practitioner and appointing party agreeing to the terms of the engagement. Within that context, the practitioner considers materiality and the relevant components of engagement risk when planning the engagement and collecting sufficient and appropriate evidence.

5 **A written assurance report**   The practitioner draws a written conclusion that provides a level of assurance about the subject matter.

The practitioner will seek to obtain sufficient appropriate evidence as the basis for the provision of the level of assurance. In conjunction with the nature and form of the subject matter, criteria and procedures, the reliability of the evidence itself can impact on the overall sufficiency and appropriateness of the evidence available.

Figure 1.1 is a diagrammatic summary of the interrelationship of the five components.

There are a number of characteristics that make it appropriate for the profession to provide assurance on a range of subject matter. As mentioned earlier, the profession is leveraging off its reputation as a high-quality professional provider of assurance services. In particular, it is the independence and expertise of the practitioner that are sought after.

FIGURE 1.1 Diagramatic summary of an assurance service engagement

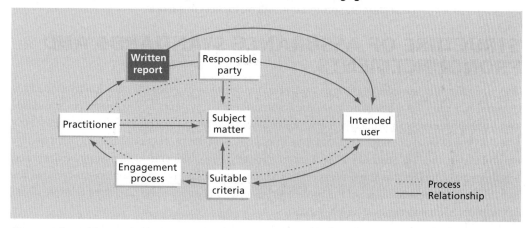

Source: Adapted from ED72, 'Assurance Engagements', para. 29; reproduced with the permission of The Institute of Chartered Accountants in Australia and CPA Australia.

Independence

Users derive value from the knowledge that a member of the profession has no interest in the information other than its usefulness. Assurance independence is an absence of interests that create an unacceptable risk of material bias with respect to the quality or content of information that is the subject of an assurance engagement. Independence remains the cornerstone on which the assurance function is based.

Expertise: quality of professional judgment

The exercise of professional judgment permeates the notion of professional service. An assurance service engagement requires the exercise of judgment. The provision of a professional service requires the practitioner to offer only those services (s)he has the competence to complete, exercise due care in the performance of the service, adequately plan and supervise the performance of the service and obtain sufficient relevant information to provide a reasonable basis for conclusions or recommendations. Consideration must also be given to the appropriateness of measurement criteria and the need to communicate the engagement results. Users can obtain assurance from the service only if they are aware of the practitioner's involvement.

It could be argued that professional reputation is the critical factor that adds value to the assurance services offered by the professional accountant. As a profession, we need to protect or even improve the profession's brand name, thus enhancing the value of the assurance services. A further advantage to having members of the accounting profession provide assurance is that accountants are subject to many professional quality controls and disciplining mechanisms, and this should provide assurance to the user about the quality of the inputs and processes to our services, and therefore the quality of the final report, the output. It is through this process that assurance services add value.

Whether the accounting profession is successful in becoming the most appropriate group for providing assurance in a wide range of areas will depend on a number of factors, including whether society sees accountants as experts in the subject matter of the assurance engagement. Financial report auditors are expert in the subject matter of accounting information, and have developed processes and a reputation as high-quality assurance providers. Whether this reputation easily transfers to other areas such as environmental reporting, and possibly as a high-cost provider given the necessity of having high-level quality controls in place associated with being a member of the accounting profession, will be the test of success.

STRUCTURE OF ASSURANCE STANDARDS AND PRONOUNCEMENTS

The structure of assurance standards and pronouncements in Australia and internationally is outlined in Figure 1.2. The figure gives the international equivalents of the Australian standards and pronouncements in brackets. A few points about Figure 1.2 warrant explanation. First, the Code of Professional Conduct (CPC), or the ethics code, and the professional standards on quality control (APS 4 and 5 in Australia; ISQC 1 internationally) are applicable to all assurance firms and engagements. The fact that the profession has a body of ethics and quality control procedures has helped to boost the reputation of the profession. These measures will be discussed in more detail in Chapters 2 (quality control) and 3 (ethics).

Second, the assurance services framework (AUS 108 'Framework for Assurance Services') applies to all assurance engagements. It provides a general framework for all assurance services, and defines

FIGURE **1.2 Structure of auditing pronouncements**

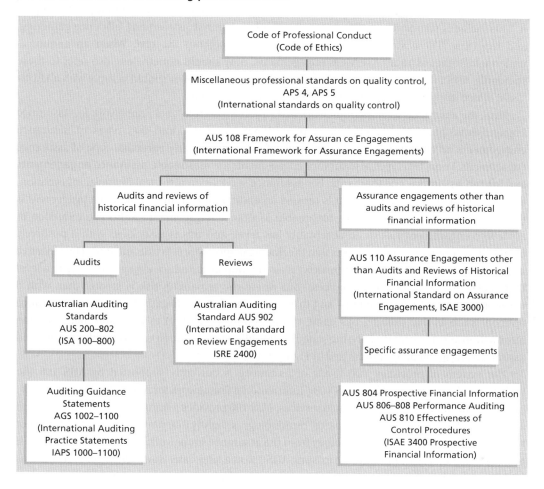

and describes the elements of an assurance engagement (as discussed under the previous learning objective). The framework also identifies engagements to which the auditing and assurance standards both do and do *not* apply, as will be discussed later under this learning objective.

Third, under the assurance framework, the standards are evidently split between audits and reviews of historical financial information, and other assurance engagements. This demonstrates that audits and reviews of financial reports (which are classed as assurance on historical financial information) are just one type of assurance engagement. However, there is no doubt that they are an important type, since they are the primary service on which the profession has developed its reputation. These assurance services are also underpinned by a detailed infrastructure of standards. With regard to other assurance engagements, fewer standards and pronouncements have been developed. There is currently AUS 110 (ISAE 3000) 'Assurance Engagements other than Audits and Reviews of Historical Financial Information', which contains requirements for all assurance engagements other than those on historical financial information. Standards have also been developed for some specific assurance engagements, these being a standard on future (prospective) financial information (AUS 804/ ISAE 3400) and standards on assurance services for which standards have been developed in Australia but which currently have no international equivalents: performance audits (AUS 806 and AUS 808) and effectiveness of control activities (AUS 810).

Fourth, as outlined above, we know that assurance on historical financial information (financial reports) has a detailed infrastructure of standards which has been developed to support it. This includes standards on client acceptance, planning, risk assessment, evidence gathering, and reporting. These standards will be discussed throughout the text. When an auditor is undertaking other assurance services engagements, they should nonetheless also refer to these standards. AUS 110.03 (ISAE 3000.03) stipulates that the practitioner should comply with all AUSs (ISAs) *which are relevant* when preforming such an engagement.

Fifth, the assurance services framework (AUS 108.11/'International Framework for Assurance Engagements' para. 11) directs that a practitioner can enter into two types of assurance engagements or, effectively, provide two levels of assurance on any particular type of assurance engagement. These two types of assurance engagements are **reasonable assurance engagements** and **limited assurance engagements**. For assurance services on historical financial information, a reasonable assurance engagement is termed an audit, and a limited assurance engagement is termed a review. The objective of a reasonable assurance engagement (audit) is a reduction in assurance engagement risk to an acceptably low level, and this is associated with a positively expressed assurance opinion (such as that the financial information is true and fair). The objective of a limited assurance engagement (review) is a reduction in assurance engagement risk to a level that is acceptable in the circumstances—but where the remaining risk is greater than with a reasonable assurance engagement—and this is associated with a negatively expressed assurance opinion (such as that nothing has come to the auditor's attention to persuade them that the information has been materially misstated). The difference between a reasonable and limited assurance engagement is summarised in Figure 1.3.

The system of providing two levels of assurance is currently supported by AUS 106 (no international equivalent). While AUS 108 ('International Framework for Assurance Engagements') provides a framework for all assurance services, AUS 106 provides a framework only for audit and audit-related services. The two standards' terminology is slightly different—a result of AUS 106 not being updated with the new terminology from the assurance framework. In June 2004, the AUASB indicated that they will withdraw the existing AUS 106 at a later date. However, because it contains additional information on matters such as agreed-upon procedures engagements, it is being retained for the present. AUS 106 identifies specific levels of audit and audit-related services, as outlined in the following definitions.

- **Audit** is defined in AUS 106.05 as the provision of a service where the auditor's objective is to provide a **high level of assurance**. This may be done by issuing a positive expression of opinion that enhances the credibility of a written assertion(s) about an accountability matter ('attest audit'); or by providing relevant and reliable information and a positive expression of opinion about an accountability matter where the party responsible for the matter does not make a written assertion(s) ('direct reporting audit'). In the glossary to the assurance standards (AUS 104-ISA 'Glossary of terms') reasonable assurance is defined as a **high but not absolute level** of assurance. Thus high assurance and reasonable assurance are commonly taken to be equivalent terms.
- **Review** is defined in AUS 106.07 as a service where the auditor's objective is to provide a **moderate level of assurance**, being a level of assurance lower than that provided by an audit. This may be done either by issuing a negatively expressed statement of assurance that enhances the credibility of a written assertion(s) about an accountability matter ('attest review'); or by providing relevant and reliable information and a negatively expressed statement of assurance about an accountability matter where the party responsible for the

FIGURE **1.3** Differences between reasonable assurance and limited assurance engagements

Type of engagement	Objective	Evidence-gathering procedures	The assurance report
Reasonable assurance engagement	A reduction in assurance engagement risk to an acceptably low level in the circumstances of the engagement, as the basis for a positive form of expression of the practitioner's conclusion. (AUS 108.11)	Sufficient appropriate evidence is obtained as part of a systematic engagement process that includes: • obtaining an understanding of the engagement circumstances; • assessing risks; • responding to assessed risks; • performing further procedures using a combination of inspection, observation, confirmation, recalculation, reperformance, analytical procedures and inquiry (such further procedures involve substantive procedures, including, where applicable, obtaining corroborating information, and tests depending on the nature of the subject matter, of the operating effectiveness of controls); and • evaluating the evidence obtained. (AUS 108.51 and .52)	Description of the engagement circumstances and a positive form of expression of the conclusion. (AUS 108.58)
Limited assurance engagement	A reduction in assurance engagement risk to a level that is acceptable in the circumstances of the engagement but where that risk is greater than for a reasonable assurance engagement, as the basis for a negative form of expression of the practitioner's conclusion. (AUS 108.11)	Sufficient appropriate evidence is obtained as part of a systematic engagement process that includes obtaining an understanding of the subject matter and other engagement circumstances, but in which procedures are deliberately limited relative to a reasonable assurance engagement. (AUS 108.53)	Description of the engagement circumstances, and a negative form of expression of the conclusion. (AUS 108.59)

Source: Appendix to AUS 108 'Framework for Assurance Engagements'

matter does not make a written assertion ('direct reporting review'). In the glossary to the assurance standards (AUS 104-ISA 'Glossary of terms') moderate assurance is equated with **negative assurance** and hence the term 'limited assurance'. Thus moderate assurance, negative assurance and limited assurance are commonly taken to be equivalent terms.

■ **Agreed-upon procedures** is defined in AUS 106.04 as where the auditor's objective is to issue a **report of factual findings** to the parties that have agreed to the procedures being performed, in which no conclusion is communicated and which therefore **expresses no assurance**. However, it provides the user with information to meet a particular need, from which the user can draw conclusions and derive their own level of assurance as a result of the auditor's procedures.

AUS 106 and AUS 108.11 ('International Framework for Assurance Engagements' para. 11) state that the framework, and therefore all assurance pronouncements, do not cover agreed-upon procedures engagements, the compilation of financial information engagements, the preparation of tax returns where there is no conclusion conveying a level of assurance or management consulting services. An auditor who undertakes such engagements is required to apply procedures and an appropriate level of professional skill and care. This may involve having due regard to auditing pronouncements insofar as they are relevant or adaptable to the work being undertaken. However, this work is not deemed to be of an assurance nature.

Appendix 1 to AUS 106, which is adapted and reproduced as Figure 1.4, distinguishes in diagrammatic form first between 'audit and audit-related services' and 'other services' and then between the different types of 'audit and audit-related services'.

As can be seen from the discussion of both 'audit' and 'review', it is necessary also to distinguish between **attest reporting** and **direct reporting**. An attest engagement requires the auditor to issue an opinion on written assertions made by others. This form of engagement is also commonly referred to as an **assertion-based engagement** (AUS 108- 'International Framework for Assurance Engagements'). The audit report on general purpose financial reports is an example of an attest audit. Throughout this text there is discussion of the assertions made by management in financial reports. These assertions are the responsibility of management, and they declare their responsibility for these assertions in a management representation letter, which is discussed in more detail in Chapter 12. The auditor provides a written report (the audit opinion) that expresses a conclusion about the reliability of the assertions.

A direct reporting engagement requires the auditor to provide assurance on an accountability matter on which the responsible party has not made a written assertion. For example, an audit report could be issued on the adequacy of internal control. Where management does not issue a report on the adequacy of internal control, and therefore the auditor is required to report directly on its adequacy, the engagement is classed as a direct engagement. If, however, management has stated an opinion on the adequacy of internal control, and the auditor is required to attest to this statement, it is an attest engagement.

Quick review

1. Audits provide a reasonable (high) level of assurance and practitioners report on this with a positive expression of opinion.
2. Reviews provide a limited (moderate) level of assurance and practitioners report on this with a negative expression of opinion.
3. Agreed-upon procedures report factual findings and no level of assurance is expressed.
4. Auditing pronouncements are applicable to audit and audit-related services, but not to 'other service' engagements, such as consulting engagements, where the auditor's objective is to assist or advise the client on any aspect of business management.
5. An audit and a review can be either an attest engagement, where an auditor issues an opinion on written assertions made by others, or a direct reporting engagement, where the auditor expresses an opinion on an accountability issue on which written assertions have not been made.

 learning objective 3

AUDITING DEFINED

In today's environment, the type of assurance engagement that is most common is an audit of historical financial information. Part of the reason for this is because the requirement for an audit is contained in many pieces of legislation, including the *Corporations Act 2001* that governs the audit of annual financial reports for reporting entities. This means that public companies listed on stock exchanges must have their annual financial reports audited, and it is for this activity that the audit and assurance profession is best known.

FIGURE **1.4** **Explanatory framework for standards on audit and audit-related services**

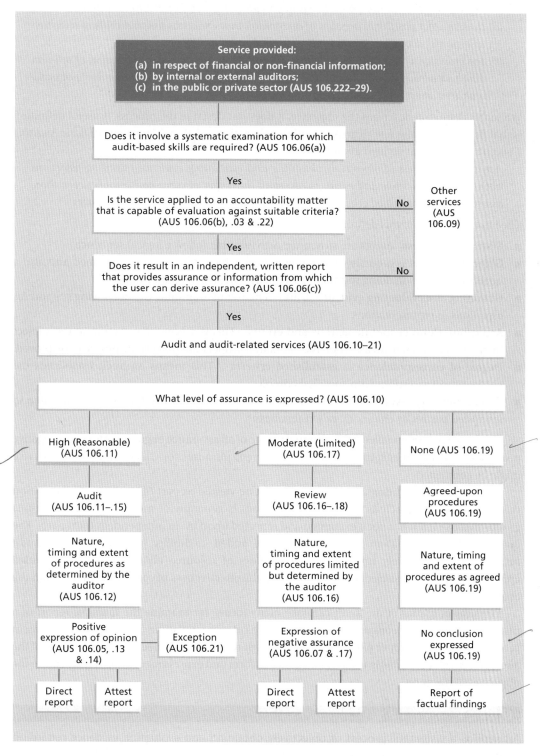

Source: Adapted from Appendix 1 to AUS 106. Reproduced with permission of The Institute of Chartered Accountants in Australia and CPA Australia.

Auditing is defined in AUS 104 as:

A service where the auditor's objective is to provide a high level of assurance through:

(a) the issue of a positive expression of an opinion that enhances the credibility of a written assertion(s) about an accountability matter ('attest audit'); or

(b) the provision of relevant and reliable information and a positive expression of opinion about an accountability matter where the party responsible for the matter does not make a written assertion(s) ('direct reporting audit').

While this definition describes the objective, it does not describe the process. A useful definition is that developed by the American Accounting Association (AAA) in *A Statement of Basic Auditing Concepts* (ASOBAC). It defined auditing as:

A systematic process of objectively obtaining and evaluating evidence regarding assertions about economic actions and events to ascertain the degree of correspondence between those assertions and established criteria and communicating the results to interested users.

The important parts of this definition are:

- **Systematic process**   Audits are structured activities that follow a logical sequence.
- **Objectivity**   This is a quality of the methods by which information is obtained and also a quality of the person doing the audit. Essentially it means freedom from bias.
- **Obtaining and evaluating evidence**   This is a matter of examining the underlying support for assertions or representations.
- **Assertions about economic actions and events**   This is a broad description of the subject matter that is audited. An assertion is essentially a proposition that can be proved or disproved.
- **Degree of correspondence ... established criteria**   This means an audit establishes the conformity of assertions with specified criteria.
- **Communicating results**   To be useful, the results of the audit need to be communicated to interested parties by either oral or written means.

This broad definition reflects the essential nature of all assurance engagements as investigative processes sufficient to encompass the many different purposes for which an assurance service might be conducted.

The function of auditing as an activity should be viewed as part of the general proposition that subject matter (such as financial information) is generally of more value to the various groups that use it if it has been examined and reported upon by an independent third party. The quality of that information is enhanced by the added credibility given through the audit function. This ultimately impacts on the process of resource allocation, with the added credibility given to the subject matter enhancing the effectiveness of communication within the economic system.

The subject matter of the audit can take many forms, for example the financial report of a private or public entity, compliance with prescribed rules or regulations, the cost of a government program or the efficiency or effectiveness with which resources have been used. The nature of the audit process and the criteria used by an auditor to form and express an opinion depend upon the objectives of the audit.

Quick review

An audit is a systematic process of objectively obtaining and evaluating evidence regarding assertions about economic actions and events to ascertain the degree of correspondence between those assertions and established criteria and communicating the results to interested users.

FUNDAMENTAL PRINCIPLES UNDERLYING AN AUDIT

Underlying the audit process is a basic framework of auditing principles that guide the development of auditing as a discipline. However, a comprehensive theory of auditing has not yet been devised. There have been several notable attempts to provide a conceptual basis from which auditing could proceed and, while each makes a contribution, no comprehensive framework has yet been formulated. In many respects, the lack of progress on this front reflects the mix of theoretical and policy issues that have influenced supporting disciplines such as accounting.

Given that auditing standards adopted internationally and in Australia are reportedly principles-based, it has always been a concern that these principles have not been properly enunciated. To address this concern, in 2005 the IAASB and AUASB released for discussion a draft consultation paper in which they outlined possible fundamental principles underlying an audit.

Fundamental principles were described as encompassing the high ideals of professional conduct and the essential qualities underpinning every ISA audit. In preparing this draft of the principles, it was ensured that the principles accorded with the assurance framework discussed earlier. Conceptually, fundamental principles should:

- underpin the objective(s) of an audit, and help drive the conduct of the auditor in using professional judgment to meet the professional requirements of the auditing standards;
- be easily understood both by auditors and other readers of auditing standards;
- be universally applicable to all audits; and
- entrench the expectations that auditors are expected to accept and abide by.

The expectation is that auditors will not depart from or override these principles. These principles comprise (a) the fundamental principles of professional ethics, and (b) the fundamental principles that underlie the objective of an audit undertaken in accordance with auditing standards and pronouncements. They are as follows:

Fundamental principles of professional ethics

- **Integrity**
  An auditor should be straightforward and honest in all professional and business relationships.
- **Objectivity**
  An auditor should not allow prejudices or bias, conflict of interest or undue influence of others to override professional or business judgment.
- **Professional competence and due care**
  An auditor has a continuing duty to maintain their professional knowledge and skill at the level required to ensure that a client or employer receives the advantage of competent professional service based on current developments in practice, legislation and techniques. An auditor should act diligently and in accordance with applicable technical and professional standards in all professional and business relationships.
- **Confidentiality**
  An auditor should respect the confidentiality of information acquired as a result of professional or business relationships and should not disclose any such information to third parties without proper and specific authority unless there is a legal or professional right or duty to disclose. Confidential information acquired as a result of professional and business relationships should not be used for the personal advantage of the practitioner or third parties.
- **Professional behaviour**
  An auditor should comply with relevant laws and regulations and should avoid any action that discredits the profession.

Fundamental principles underlying the objective of an audit

- **Knowledge**

  The auditor should possess a sufficient understanding of the entity and its environment to appropriately plan and perform the audit, interpret audit findings and report on the financial report.

- **Responsibility**

  The auditor should take responsibility for the audit opinion, maintaining an adequate level of involvement in the audit engagement, properly supervising any assistants, and evaluating the work of experts or others upon whom reliance is placed.

- **Quality control**

  The auditor should follow quality control procedures, including consultation with others as necessary, that support the issuance of an audit report that is appropriate in the circumstances.

- **Rigour and scepticism**

  The auditor should plan and perform an audit with thoroughness and with an attitude of professional scepticism, critically assessing with a questioning mind the validity and reliability of evidence, and recognising that circumstances may cause the financial report to be materially misstated.

- **Professional judgment**

  The auditor should exercise professional judgment, within the bounds of the fundamental principles and the applicable professional requirements, in discharging the auditor's responsibilities.

- **Evidence**

  The auditor should obtain sufficient appropriate evidence to constitute a reasonable basis for expressing an opinion on the financial report.

- **Documentation**

  The auditor should document matters that are important in providing evidence to support the audit opinion

- **Communication**

  The auditor should communicate significant matters affecting the entity's financial report to management, to those charged with governance and, while respecting the confidentiality of information, to others where compliance with local laws and regulations require additional communication in the broader public interest.

- **Association**

  The auditor should not be associated with or allow the use of the auditor's name or their report to be associated with information known by the auditor to be misleading, unless the auditor reports on the information and how it is misleading.

- **Reporting**

  The auditor should report to those who have appointed the auditor to the engagement. The auditor's report should contain a clear expression of opinion in writing and set out all information necessary for a proper understanding of the opinion and its basis.

Quick review

1. Current auditing standards are principles-based, although these principles have not been clearly enunciated.

2. The standard-setting bodies have released for discussion a draft set of fundamental principles. These cover both ethics and the objectives of an audit.

3 The fundamental principles of professional ethics are:
- integrity
- objectivity
- professional competence and due care
- confidentiality
- professional behaviour

4 The fundamental principles underlying the objective of an audit are:
- knowledge
- responsibility
- quality control
- rigour and scepticism
- professional judgment
- evidence
- documentation
- communication
- association
- reporting

ATTRIBUTES OF ACCOUNTING INFORMATION

To understand the audit process as it relates to accounting information, it is important to appreciate the role of accounting information and the process of communication through financial reports. The definition of auditing provided on page 16 was formulated within the context of *A Statement of Basic Accounting Theory* (ASOBAT), produced by a committee of the American Accounting Association, which defined accounting as: '... the process of identifying, measuring and communicating economic information'.

The definition of auditing, combined with this definition of accounting, clearly links the auditing function with the communication of accounting information. It is relevant, therefore, to consider some aspects of accounting information: the characteristics of that information represent a variable in the environment in which the audit function occurs.

The fundamental objective of financial reporting in its broadest sense is defined in the Australian Accounting Standards Board (AASB)/International Accounting Standards Board (IASB) 'Framework for the Preparation and Presentation of Financial Statements' issued in 2004. This Framework identifies the objective of financial reports as the provision of information useful to a wide range of users for making economic decisions. In meeting this objective, general purpose financial reports also represent the means by which management and governing bodies meet their accountability obligations to report to users by providing information about the performance, the financial position and the financing and investing activities of the entity.

The functions served by financial reporting comprise economic decision making, control and accountability. The potential users of financial reports include current and potential investors, creditors, employees and their representatives, customers, the government and the public. Some of these users do not have direct access to accounting information nor do they have the power to demand it. In those circumstances, such users rely on general purpose financial reports for information relevant to their needs. To enable the financial reporting system to meet the fundamental objectives of financial reporting, the information should possess several interrelated characteristics.

The characteristics that are identified in the Framework include:

1 **Relevance** This requires that the information provided must be useful in assisting financial report users to make and evaluate decisions about the allocation of scarce resources and to assess the accountability of the preparers of these reports. The information in a financial report is, therefore, directed to meeting the common information needs of a range of users to assist them in predicting the outcomes of past, present or future events, and/or confirming or correcting past evaluations. One of the important aspects of the definition of auditing provided above is the determination of the degree of correspondence between assertions about economic actions and events and established criteria. In terms of general purpose financial reporting, the established criteria are those directed towards the provision of relevant information. In that context, accounting standards represent a financial reporting framework directed toward providing relevant financial information. The relevance of information is also a function of its timeliness, and it should be available when it is needed.

2 **Reliability** The reliability of financial information is the extent to which the information presented to users represents, without bias or undue error, the underlying transactions and events that have occurred. This requires that the facts be impartially determined and reported, since biased information is not acceptable to financial reporting. The information should be neutral and not be designed to lead users to conclusions that serve particular needs, desires or preconceptions of report preparers. The reliability of information in a financial report also requires that such information be capable of reliable measurement before it can be recognised in the financial report as compared with disclosure in the notes to the financial report. Accounting standards also play a role in providing measurement techniques to be used in the preparation of reliable financial information.

3 **Comparability** The usefulness of information requires that its presentation in a financial report results in users being able to compare aspects of an entity at one time and over time, and between entities at one time and over time. Comparability requires that like things are measured and reported in a consistent manner within an entity and over time for that entity, and that there is consistency between entities.

4 **True and fair presentation** The application of the qualitative characteristics and of appropriate accounting standards (suitable criteria) will normally result in financial reports that convey a true and fair view. The audit will provide assurance of this result.

learning objective 6

DEMAND FOR ASSURANCE

The attributes of information (relevance, reliability, comparability and true and fair presentation) provide a basis for the assurance function. Users of assurance services require some assurance as to the quality of information in terms of those attributes. The role of auditing (and assurance) is seen as being especially important to reliability and relevance. With regard to financial report audits, the role of the auditor is to be satisfied that the general purpose financial report represents what it purports to represent without bias, and that the contents are verifiable. As an independent expert, there is also an expectation that the auditor is satisfied as to the relevance of the information for assessments of the performance, financial position, financing and investing and compliance of the reporting entity. This role arises because most financial report users are not in a position to produce financial accounting information personally or to establish the credibility of the process by which such information is prepared and presented to them. The need for the independent financial report audit arises, therefore, because of the following conditions:

- **Conflict of interest** Because the user (e.g. the owner) perceives an actual or potential conflict with the preparer (management). Management could have an incentive to present biased information in a financial report because these reports are a means to convey information about management's performance. This conflict creates uncertainty as to the objectivity of the information preparer. An independent, third-party examination will reduce the possibility of bias and enhance the credibility of the information.
- **Consequence** When a user is contemplating using information to make decisions of consequence, the quality of that information is of direct concern.
- **Complexity** The subject matter and the process by which the data (e.g. transactions) is converted into information (e.g. financial reports) is complex and, as it becomes more complex, the possibility of error is increased. The average user of that information does not possess the required level of expertise to judge the quality of information.
- **Remoteness** The separation of owner and manager, and therefore user and preparer, whether due to physical, legal or time and cost constraints, prevents the user from assessing information quality.

These four conditions have given rise to the following three hypotheses to explain the demand for auditing (Sundem et al., 1996; Wallace, 1980) and these hypotheses could equally be used to understand the demand for assurance:

1 **Agency theory** (Stewardship hypothesis) In an agency relationship, investors, as principals in the relationship, entrust their resources to managers, who act as their agents or as stewards of the resources. However, in this relationship a potential conflict of interest arises (management should be trying to maximise returns to investors but have an incentive to consume or reallocate resources for their own benefit). In an attempt to monitor their activities, managers are asked to account for the level and performance of resources under their control by producing periodic financial reports. Because of the potential conflict of interest outlined above, the complexity of the subject matter and the remoteness of the investors from the managers, the financial reports may be biased. The use of an agreed-upon reporting framework, generally accepted accounting principles (GAAP), is one attempt to reduce the bias, and getting assurance on these reports from an expert who is independent of management also increases the confidence in the information that is communicated. This is shown in Figure 1.5 overleaf.

To try to align the interests of managers with those of shareholders, maximising shareholder wealth, a common practice in today's environment is for managers to be rewarded through schemes such as bonuses based on profit and share option schemes. As rewards may be influenced by the financial information that they produce, management again may have incentives to bias the financial reports. This provides even further demand for assurance in today's society.

2 **Information hypothesis** An assurance service is a means of improving the quality of information. For example, investors require information to make an assessment of expected

FIGURE **1.5** **Simple diagram of agency relationship between managers and investors**

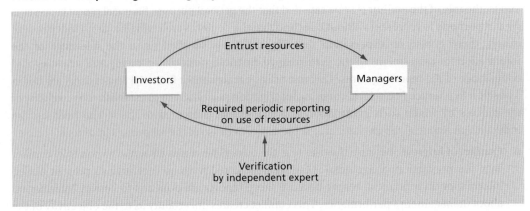

returns and risks associated with their investment. An assurance service is also valued as a means of improving financial and non-financial data for internal decision making, detecting errors and motivating employees to exercise more care in preparing records.

The information hypothesis also states that investors benefit through the increased confidence of external users of the information. For example, a study by Blackwell et al. (1998) showed that for private companies seeking funds from lending institutions, the costs incurred in audit fees were more than recompensed by the increased savings associated with lower interest rates when compared with the interest rates charged to similar companies that weren't audited.

3 **Insurance hypothesis**   The insurance hypothesis states that demand for assurance occurs from those who may suffer loss when things go wrong. For example, if an organisation goes into liquidation and has no resources to pay its debts, it may be possible to recover some of the losses from the auditor (the circumstances in which this is possible are discussed in Chapter 4). As auditors are required to have insurance against such potential losses, this has given rise to a 'deep-pockets' effect in that the auditor is seen to have a greater ability to pay. As audit firms will be very concerned with maintaining their reputation, any legal action undertaken against them that may damage this reputation will be treated very seriously.

There is overlap between the hypotheses, in particular the agency theory and information hypothesis. When providing evidence on stewardship and monitoring, the assurance provider is also providing information of a particular type to aid the decision-making process of principals to the contract. While the information hypothesis may be the major reason for many of the assurance services other than financial report auditing, the insurance hypothesis will be less likely to explain all these engagements. While this hypothesis was originally derived to explain demand for financial report audits, it may also be applied to other specific assurance services, such as expert opinions given in takeover situations. However, where the level of assurance sought is something below an audit, implying that it is acknowledging that the assurance services provider will use a reduced set of evidence-gathering procedures, it is unlikely that insurance will be a major determinant of demand.

Quick review

1 The four conditions which result in a need for financial report audits are conflicts of interest, the importance of the decision, the complexity of the subject matter and the remoteness of users from managers.

2 The following three hypotheses, which incorporate these conditions, have been used to explain the demand for financial report audits:
- agency theory (stewardship hypothesis)
- information hypothesis
- insurance hypothesis

3 The generation of information (and thus assurance) will be a major determinant of demand for many other assurance engagements, while the insurance hypothesis is unlikely to explain demand for assurance provided at something other than the audit level.

HISTORY OF THE AUDIT FUNCTION

Audits have been performed at least since the thirteenth century. The exact origin of audits of financial reports is unclear. However, it is known that in England as far back as 1298 the Chamberlain of the City of London was subject to audit. Those audits were intended to assure the absence of fraud, emphasising arithmetical correctness and compliance with the authority given to the custodian. While its origins are ancient, development of the audit function has occurred most rapidly in the last century.

The development of auditing in Australia, New Zealand and North America has its origins in the British system. Australia and New Zealand have been particularly influenced by UK development because of the derivation of their legal systems from the British system.

Independent audits prior to 1900

Prior to 1900 in the UK, public companies were formed under a law enacted in 1844. The *Joint Stock Companies Act* required registration of all new companies with 25 or more members. The *Companies Act* of 1845 included a provision that required incorporated companies to have their annual financial report audited. This development was considered necessary because of the demands for increased capital as a result of the Industrial Revolution. Capital could now be raised from shareholders who would have no part in managing the firm. Consequently, the need for managers to report periodically to those who had contributed the capital became apparent. The Act required the auditor to examine and report on the balance sheet presented by the company to its shareholders. At this stage the auditor was in most cases a non-accountant, with the main objectives being to report on the company's solvency and to detect fraud and error. While the requirement for compulsory audits was suspended under the *Joint Stock Companies Act* of 1856, with audits remaining optional until 1900, the legislation facilitated the spread of companies and the development of an accounting profession in the UK.

In Australia during the nineteenth century, the rate of industrial expansion was not as great as that in the UK. It was only toward the last quarter of the century that commercial enterprise became well established. Any statutes were based on the prevailing British legislation. For example, following legislation in Great Britain in 1879 requiring banking companies to appoint an auditor, the requirement for all publicly held companies to be audited began appearing in the Companies Acts of various Australian states. In general, the requirement was for the auditor to provide an opinion on whether the balance sheet was a 'full and fair' balance sheet, properly drawn up so as to exhibit a 'true and correct' view of the state of affairs of the company. This report had to be read before the company in a general meeting. As in the UK, the primary audit objective was the detection of fraud and error.

A similar situation existed in the USA during this period. The audit function exported from Britain to the USA adopted the British form of reporting even though there were no comparable statutes. The absence of statutory requirements for audits to be submitted to shareholders resulted in nineteenth-century audits that varied from balance sheet audits to full, detailed examinations of all accounts of companies. An auditor was engaged usually by management or by the board of directors of a company, and the report was addressed and directed to these insiders rather than to shareholders. Reports to shareholders on the representations of management were not common. Instead, company management was interested in being assured by the auditors that fraud and clerical errors had not occurred. Even today, the state laws under which US companies are formed generally do not require audits. Rather, audit requirements generally arise from requirements of stock exchanges, regulations of the Securities and Exchange Commission and general acceptance of the usefulness of an independent auditor's opinion on financial representations.

1900 onwards

Legislative influences

From these beginnings, the concept of an audit developed to the stage where by the early 1900s professional accountants became prominent as auditors, and verification of financial record accuracy and attestation to financial report credibility were added to the detection of error and fraud as audit objectives. The 1900 *Companies Act* in the UK reintroduced the requirement for every company to have an audit.

During the 1930s and 1940s the continued improvements in financial accounting and reporting in the UK and the acceptance by management of the responsibility for prevention and detection of fraud and error produced a change in emphasis. Detection of fraud and error became a secondary objective of auditing. The emergence of the verification and attest function was formalised by the 1948 *Companies Act* in the UK, and has carried through into subsequent provisions.

The development of the profession in terms of skill and status carried through into Australia. However, the absence of a strong organised profession, and the consequent lack of native sources of authority, saw standards from other countries being used to fill existing voids. Up until the end of World War II the significant professional influence came from the adoption of auditing concepts from the UK. Australian companies' legislation also followed that which was developed in Britain. The Companies Acts of the various states were, however, sufficiently different as to make it difficult to generalise, although several key requirements can be listed. These various Acts required auditors to report to shareholders on every balance sheet laid before the company in general meeting in the following terms:

1   whether or not they had obtained all the information and explanations they required; and
2   whether, in their opinion, the balance sheet was properly drawn up so as to exhibit a true and correct view of the state of the company's affairs according to the best of their information and the explanations given to them, and as shown by the books of the company.

The Victorian and Western Australian Acts of this time also required an opinion on the profit and loss account or the income and expenditure account, indicating whether they reflected a true and correct view of the results of the business of the company for the year. The Acts in New South Wales and Queensland required that auditors state whether, in their opinion, the register of members and other records required to be kept were properly kept. It became apparent during the 1950s that because of revisions and re-enactments in each state at different times, the disparity between Companies Acts did not provide adequate protection for investors. As a result, the *Uniform Companies Act* evolved in 1961. This Act formed the basis of statutory audit requirements in Australia for 20 years, until replaced by the *Companies Act 1981*, which was implemented on

1 July 1982. The 1981 Act achieved greater uniformity as it was one Act legislated initially in the Australian Capital Territory and, under the provisions of a co-operative agreement, adopted by each state (except the Northern Territory) as its Companies Code through the operation of state Companies (Applications of Laws) Acts.

In 1989, the Commonwealth Parliament introduced the *Corporations Act* as a national law governing companies; this did not require state co-operation. Due to constitutional issues, the legislation and the national scheme did not come into force until 1 January 1991. The Acts under that scheme were collectively given the name 'the *Corporations Law*'. References to the *Corporations Law* throughout this text refer to the provisions of the 1991 legislation, as amended. The specific provisions of the *Corporations Law* (and its predecessor legislation) relating to financial reporting and auditing have influenced the nature and direction of the financial report audit function in Australia. This was further amended in 2001, and is now referred to as the *Corporations Act 2001*. A more detailed discussion of audit commitments under the *Corporations Act 2001* is contained later in this chapter and also in Chapter 3.

Professional influences

A further influence on the development of the audit function in Australia has been the role of the two professional accounting organisations in Australia. The formal role of the accounting profession in the development of auditing in Australia is evidenced by the promulgation of professional statements on auditing. Pronouncements relevant to the audit function first occurred during 1956 with the establishment by the ICAA of the Australian Chartered Accountants Research and Service Foundation. During a five-year period the foundation produced six technical bulletins relating to aspects of the conduct of a professional practice. While not authoritative, these bulletins provided guidance to accountants in public practice. For example, Bulletin No. 2 dealt with the audit of stock-in-trade and Bulletin No. 5 with audit working papers. The next significant development took place in 1969 when the ICAA established a new Accounting Principles Committee that developed several statements that were included in the Members' Handbook. For example, this committee produced Technical Bulletins F2, 'Internal Control in a Computer-based Accounting System', and F3, 'The Audit of Computer-based Accounting Systems'. These documents were based on similar documents produced by the Institute of Chartered Accountants in England and Wales. In 1971 the Council of the ICAA established an Audit Practices Committee that also produced several statements on auditing. The ongoing role of the profession in this area through the activities of CPA Australia and the ICAA is dealt with later in this chapter and in Chapter 2.

Recent developments

The profession is now heavily influenced by and reflects the increasingly global nature of the business world and the international affiliations of the larger accounting firms. The globalisation of the business world, and the accounting profession, is a current issue that is discussed later in this chapter. This trend is reflected in developments such as the increasing importance of the International Federation of Accountants (IFAC), which is discussed in Chapter 2. In 2005 its member accountancy bodies total 161, representing 119 countries, including Australia. One of the standing committees of IFAC is the International Auditing and Assurance Standards Board (IAASB), whose aim is to develop standards and issue guidelines on generally accepted auditing practices. Australia is represented on that committee. The International Standards on Auditing issued by the IAASB provide the basis for the auditing standards of most member countries.

Changes in the audit objectives

The change in the traditional audit objective from fraud detection and prevention to a determination of the truth and fairness of the reported financial position and results of operations of an entity is reflected in the audit process itself.

The period prior to 1900 required the audit process to include the detailed verification of every transaction. During the period from 1900 to the 1930s the objective of auditing was modified to include a determination of the fairness of reported financial position and results of operations as well as detection of fraud and error. During this period there was some recognition that a complete transactions audit was not appropriate, and that an accounting system and organisational structure could be harnessed to assist in the orderly production of accounting records. During the 1940s the audit objective was specified by the profession as the determination of the fairness of the reported financial position and results of operations of an entity.

This objective has not changed significantly since then, as reflected in the current Australian auditing standard, AUS 202 (ISA 200). This identifies the objective of the audit as the expression of an opinion by the auditor as to whether the financial report is prepared, in all material respects, in accordance with an identified financial reporting framework.

Approaches to auditing since the 1940s

The objective of establishing whether the financial information is fairly presented (or true and fair) in all material respects resulted in a change to the audit approach of verification of all transactions. To be able to provide assurance of fairness with a materiality consideration meant that not all transactions had to be tested.

Four audit approaches have evolved over time. These approaches are outlined below.

Balance sheet approach

The **balance sheet approach** concerns itself with the accounting equation, that is:

Proprietorship = Assets – Liabilities

Given that proprietorship is made up of capital and profit, and that capital remains fairly static in most cases, then profit will equal the increase in net assets (assets minus liabilities). Therefore, the balance sheet approach is to audit the assets and liabilities, such as cash, accounts receivable, accounts payable and non-current assets and liabilities.

This traditional approach to audit involves the audit of financial report balances with little emphasis on profit and loss account items, limited planning of the audit and a limited use of analytical procedures. Because the audit examination is based on the balances outstanding as at year-end, the examination is concentrated at or around the client's year-end. This approach assesses internal control in only a limited capacity. As outlined in Chapter 9, this audit approach is currently used for many small-business audits, where internal controls may be weak, but is rarely used for large entities.

Transactions cycle approach

For large entities it was recognised that a **transactions cycle approach** was more cost effective than the balance sheet approach for the following reasons:

■ The number of items in ending balances, while still less than the number of transactions that affect the balances, was relatively large.

- The accounting system for processing major classes of transactions was generally well designed and produced more reliable accounting data because management in a larger company has to rely extensively on the accounting data to monitor and control the business.
- There were generally enough employees (needed because of the volume of transactions processed) to achieve effective separation of duties.

In these circumstances, by testing the processing of transactions, the auditor could restrict the testing of balance sheet accounts that would otherwise be necessary. This involved testing the controls operating within transactions cycles. These transactions cycles included the sales–accounts receivable–cash receipts cycle, purchases–inventory–creditors–cash payments cycle, payroll–cash payments cycle and other purchases–cash payments cycle.

Standard *internal control questionnaires* were developed for each of the business cycles, with the result that the chances of discovering fraud or potential fraud were significantly increased. This also had the advantage of generating a significant number of observations concerning conflicts in duties that could be passed on to management.

The problem with this approach in practice was that it tended to be highly structured with standard programs, allowing little judgment or original thought to be exercised by the auditor.

Financial risk analysis approach

The **financial risk analysis approach** to auditing has been used in practice since the 1980s. This approach involves:

- a systematic approach to planning where the auditor acquires an overall understanding of an entity's business;
- evaluation of internal control from a business perspective; and
- analytical procedures applied in all phases of the audit to see that the financial and operating trends and relationships make sense.

The auditor must give due consideration to the issues of *relative risk* and *materiality* in preparing the audit program and in adopting a risk analysis approach to determine the audit program for the operating cycles of a business. Only by designing the audit program to emphasise the material and high-risk components of the audit can a cost-effective audit that satisfies professional, contractual and legal standards be produced.

Business risk approach (audit risk approach)

In the late 1990s the financial risk analysis approach was modified to give greater consideration to the strategic or business risks facing the client. This approach is currently evolving in practice and is referred to in this book as the **business risk approach**. It is also commonly referred to as the 'audit risk approach.' The auditor must understand the business risks faced by the client in addition to understanding the risks that affect the traditional processing and recording of transactions.

Consideration of an entity's business risks requires that the auditor know the client's business strategy and how it plans to respond to, or control, changes in its business environment. Numerous rapid or momentous changes have significantly affected an industry or an entity within that industry. For example, the sale of books over the Internet by companies such as Amazon.com through a 'virtual' bookstore significantly affected the retail book industry. Traditional bookstores had to respond to this new form of competitor or lose sales and customers. Similarly, rapid and significant technological changes in telecommunications and in computers and peripheral equipment increase the business risks for entities that operate in those industries. A further example is that deregulation in the banking industry has significantly affected the risks for entities that operate in those industries.

This emphasis is contained in AUS 402 (ISA 315), where the auditor is required to gain an understanding of the entity and its environment, including its objectives and strategies and related business risks (AUS 402.30–.34/ISA 315.30–.34). This focus on the client's business risks leads to a more strategic and systematic approach to the audit. The auditor uses knowledge of the client's business and industry to develop a more efficient and effective audit. It is this business risk approach that is the audit approach that is outlined in more detail in Part 2 (Chapters 5 to 11).

Quick review

1. The UK *Companies Act* of 1845 included the first provision within legislation for audit.
2. The major objectives of audits prior to 1900 were to report on solvency and the detection of fraud and error.
3. From 1900 onwards, attesting to financial report credibility became a major objective.
4. Audit approaches used to attest to financial report credibility have evolved since the 1940s from a balance sheet approach, to a transactions cycle approach, to the current business risk approach.
5. Within the business risk approach, greater attention is currently given to strategic or business risks facing the client.

THE AUDITOR–CLIENT–PUBLIC RELATIONSHIP

Today many different types of entities render reports on the administration of their resources. A comprehensive but not exhaustive list would include commercial and industrial companies, banks, railways, airlines, electric and gas utilities, insurance companies, hospitals and governmental bodies such as municipal councils and the state and federal governments.

In spite of the diverse activities of these entities, they all issue some type of report concerning their fulfilment of responsibilities to outside parties. Regulated entities issue reports to regulating authorities to serve as a basis for regulation. Creditors use financial reports for assessment of repayment ability before extending credit and as evidence of compliance with the loan agreement after issuance. There are many examples of such reports, and the audit function may be applied to all of them.

The auditor–client–public relationship is, however, complicated and delicate. The reports are the representations of management about its effectiveness in administration of resources to interested third parties. Entities represented by management are clients of auditors, but auditors generally report to the public. The client entity engages an auditor and pays the fee. Professions other than auditing confine their responsibilities almost solely to clients. However, independent auditors have for many years acknowledged responsibilities to several parties other than those who directly engage them and pay their fees.

As outlined earlier in this chapter in the section 'Demand for Assurance', management may exercise discretion in preparing financial reports and in using resources entrusted to it in operating the entity. An audit provides reasonable assurance that management's conduct in both activities has been appropriate. Thus, an audit has value because management's representations on its performance and stewardship are examined and reported on by an expert outside management's control.

However, in practice auditors are selected and paid by people affected by their work. In addition, an audit of a financial report requires a close working relationship with management. The auditor needs intimate knowledge of many of management's actions, decisions and judgments because of their significant effect on the financial report. An independent auditor is subject to conflicting pressures. The auditor depends on fees from clients and necessarily has a close relationship with clients. Thus, total independence is very difficult to achieve. Nevertheless, the auditor must often persuade a client to disclose unfavourable information in fulfilling the duties imposed by the audit function. As a result, independent auditors as a group have adopted ethical rules and professional standards to guide individual auditors in resolving the conflicts that inevitably arise, and to ensure the quality of the audit process and therefore the utility of the audit function. This is discussed in Chapter 3.

Quick review

1 Auditors have entities as clients but owners or other members of the public use their reports.

2 Being selected by and paid by the clients on whom they reported makes total independence difficult to achieve.

EXPECTATION GAP

It is appropriate at this point to recognise that there are differences between the expectations of auditors and financial report users concerning the role and responsibilities of auditors. The existence and nature of this **expectation gap** was first indicated in a number of empirical studies and inquiries conducted in various countries during the 1970s and supported by further investigations in the 1980s and 1990s.

Liggio (1974, p. 27) first applied the term 'expectation gap' to auditing and defined it as the difference between levels of expected performance as envisaged by auditors and users of financial reports. Porter (1993, p. 50) argued that the definition was too narrow, as auditors may not accomplish expected performance. Therefore, she defined it as 'the gap between society's expectations of auditors and auditors' performance, as perceived by society'. As a result, two components of the expectation gap can be identified:

1 The 'reasonableness gap': a gap between what society expects auditors to achieve and what they can reasonably be expected to accomplish.

2 The 'performance gap': a gap between what society can reasonably expect auditors to accomplish and what they are perceived to achieve. This may be further subdivided into:

- 'deficient standards': a gap between the duties which can reasonably be expected of auditors and auditors' existing duties as defined by law and professional promulgations; and
- 'deficient performance': a gap between the expected standard of performance of auditors' existing duties and auditors' perceived performance, as expected and perceived by society.

This structure of the audit expectation gap is shown in Figure 1.6 (overleaf).

The potential causes of the audit expectation gap are many and varied. Humphrey et al. (1992) point out that the gap has been attributed to a number of different causes:

- the probabilistic nature of auditing;
- the ignorance, naivety, misunderstanding and unreasonable expectations of non-auditors about the audit function;
- the evaluation of audit performance based upon hindsight not available to the auditor at the time the audit was completed;
- the evolutionary development of audit responsibilities, which create response time lags to changing expectations;
- corporate crises which lead to new expectations and accountability requirements, and periods of high standard-setting activities; or

FIGURE **1.6** Structure of the gap between audit expectation and audit performance

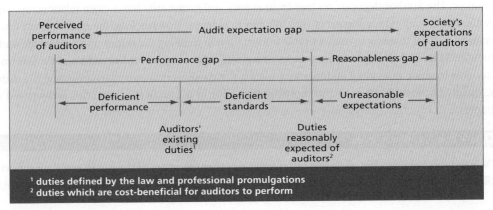

Source: Porter, 1993, p. 50.

- a self-interested profession which is a self-regulatory monopoly attempting to control the direction and outcome of the expectation gap debate to maintain the status quo, rather than risk their profitability.

While a consensus as to the cause of the audit expectation gap has not been achieved, its persistence has been acknowledged and bears testimony to the profession's inability or reluctance to narrow the gap. Humphrey et al. (1992) indicate that the accounting profession's responses to the gap may be categorised as either defensive or constructive. First, its defensive responses have included the profession emphasising the need to educate the public and reassure them about the exaggerated public outcries over isolated audit failures; codifying existing practices to legitimise them; and attempting to control the audit expectation gap debate and repeatedly propounding the views of the profession. Second, its constructive response has included emphasising an awareness and readiness to extend the scope of the audit. However, such extensions have been criticised for resulting in auditing being viewed as a package of services or a commodity for management's benefit.

The debate about the audit expectation gap consistently centres on a number of perennial issues. Four major expectation gap issues are:

1 the nature and meaning of audit report messages;
2 early warning by auditors of corporate failure;
3 the auditor's responsibility for the detection and reporting of fraud; and
4 the auditor's ability to communicate different levels of assurance.

The loss of faith in audited financial statements in the early part of this century has resulted in the auditing profession looking very closely at elements of the expectation gap again. For instance, the ICAA recently released a report entitled 'Financial Report Audit: Meeting the Market Expectations' (Trotman 2003). As outlined below and in later chapters, the auditing profession is looking at whether it can better communicate its intended message and address areas of concern, and reconsidering its responsibilities in relation to detecting and reporting fraud.

Audit report messages

Research studies have shown that many financial report users believe that an unqualified audit report indicates that the auditor is guaranteeing that the audited financial report is completely accurate. This view is quite different from that expressed by the auditing profession in AUS 202 (ISA 200), that is, that the auditor's opinion *helps establish the credibility* of the financial information.

Until approximately 10 years ago, the standard audit report consisted of a single paragraph, with very few details of the different parties' responsibilities, level of work performed or level of assurance that the auditor was intending to convey. In the early 1990s, the auditing profession attempted to overcome these problems through amendments to the contents of the auditor's standard report by adopting the expanded audit report, the most recent example contained in the guidance note issued by the AUASB in 2003 entitled 'Improving Communication between Auditors and Shareholders'. (Refer to Exhibit 1.1.) In Australia, Gay and Schelluch (1993) and Monroe and Woodliff (1994a) found that the wording of the expanded audit reports increased users' understanding of the audit process and the role and responsibilities of auditors and management. They found that the expanded audit report reduced the expectation gap but did not eliminate it and that there was still room for improvement in the wording of the audit report.

INDEPENDENT AUDIT REPORT TO MEMBERS OF [NAME OF ENTITY] LIMITED

Scope
The financial report and directors' responsibility
The financial report comprises the statement of financial position, statement of financial performance, statement of cash flows, accompanying notes to the financial statements and the directors' declaration for [name of entity] Limited (the company), for the year ended 30 June 2003.

The directors of the company are responsible for the preparation and true and fair presentation of the financial report in accordance with the *Corporations Act 2001*. This includes responsibility for the maintenance of adequate accounting records and internal controls that are designed to prevent and detect fraud and error, and for the accounting policies and accounting estimates inherent in the financial report.

Audit approach
We conducted an independent audit in order to express an opinion to the members of the company. Our audit was conducted in accordance with Australian Auditing Standards [and International Standards on Auditing] in order to provide reasonable assurance as to whether the financial report is free of material misstatement. The nature of an audit is influenced by factors such as the use of professional judgment, selective testing, the inherent limitations of internal control, and the availability of persuasive rather than conclusive evidence. Therefore, an audit cannot guarantee that all material misstatements have been detected.

We performed procedures to assess whether in all material respects the financial report presents fairly, in accordance with the *Corporations Act 2001*, including compliance with Accounting Standards and other mandatory financial reporting requirements in Australia, a view which is consistent with our understanding of the company's financial position, and of its performance as presented by the results of its operations and cash flows.

We formed our audit opinion on the basis of these procedures, which included:
- examining, on a test basis, information to provide evidence supporting the amounts and disclosures in the financial report; and
- assessing the appropriateness of the accounting policies and disclosures used and the reasonableness of significant accounting estimates made by the directors.

While we considered the effectiveness of management's internal controls over financial reporting when determining the nature and extent of our procedures, our audit was not designed to provide assurance on internal controls.

Independence
In conducting our audit, we followed applicable independence requirements of Australian professional ethical pronouncements and the *Corporations Act 2001*.

Audit opinion
In our opinion, the financial report of [name of entity] is in accordance with:
(a) the *Corporations Act 2001*, including:
  (i) giving a true and fair view of the [company/registered scheme/disclosing entity]'s financial position as at 30 June 2003 and of its performance for the year ended on that date; and

Continued . . .

EXHIBIT 1.1

Independent audit report

Source: AUASB Guidance Note 'Improving Communication between Auditors and Shareholders', 2003.

This recommended standard form audit report has been used by nearly all auditors up until the current day. There is hardly an example where the auditor has attempted to add additional information to this recommended form (except of course for qualifications, and then only within the recommended guidelines). The auditing firms are currently contemplating the inclusion of additional material to improve the information content, and reconsidering the structure of the report. With regard to information content, there are suggestions that paragraphs could be added outlining the controls in the audit firm that help ensure its overall quality, or a description of the procedures the audit firm went through to ensure that they were independent. With regard to the structure of the audit report, there are suggestions to place the audit opinion paragraph before the scope paragraph. As will be discussed in Chapter 14, the IAASB/AUASB has recently approved an expanded-scope standard audit report, which includes more wording, especially in the areas of managements' and auditors' responsibilities. This expanded-scope audit report is to be used for financial report audits signed after December 2006. These are all suggestions to decrease the expectation gap.

Corporate failures

According to a survey by the Institute of Chartered Accountants in England and Wales in 1986, the general public expects external auditors to provide them with an early warning of corporate failures. While an entity's financial report is normally prepared based on the assumption that it is a going concern, this does not necessarily mean that the entity will continue in existence. The dilemma faced by the auditors is the requirement to state any unresolved doubts about the auditee's future versus the risk that any such comments may generate a self-fulfilling prophecy by undermining the confidence of the entity's owners and creditors. Nevertheless, if facts and circumstances raise doubts about the viability of the entity, those doubts must be dispelled or disclosed. Porter (1991) argues that too often this duty is not performed. Trotman (2003) points out that the profession could do more in this area, including auditors reporting on key non-financial indicators that can evidence corporate failure and providing commentary on entities' financial health.

Earnings management and fraud

Another area where there appears to be a large 'expectation gap' is in regard to the auditor's duty to detect and report earnings management and fraud. The general public appears to have a high expectation that auditors will detect or prevent all fraud whereas the auditing profession has generally not regarded fraud detection as a primary audit objective.

A survey of shareholders in Australia by Beck (1973) indicated that 93 per cent believed that an audit provided an assurance that company officials had committed no frauds. This result was supported by a US survey by Arthur Andersen for the Cohen Commission Report, in 1974, which revealed that 66 per cent of the investing public considered that detection of fraud was the most important function of an external audit (Gwilliam, 1987, p. 6). A study by Ernst and Whinney in Britain in 1985 similarly indicated that a significant proportion of investors consider either that the auditor has an obligation to detect all fraud or that the auditor's obligations should be extended to this level (Gwilliam, 1987, p. 6). Surveys by Porter (1993) in New Zealand and Monroe and Woodliff (1994b) and Gay et al. (1997) in Australia of auditors, auditees, the financial community and the general public present findings similar to these earlier surveys.

In his now famous 'Numbers Game' speech in 1998, Arthur Levitt, then Chairman of the Securities and Exchange Commission (SEC) in the United States, charged that many companies were involved in inappropriate earnings management and fraud. He also accused auditors of directly or indirectly assisting management by not challenging management's actions. Mr Levitt cited cases where a company's stock price dropped dramatically because the company missed the financial analysts' earnings forecasts by a penny or two a share, or failed to meet revenue forecasts. His speech led the SEC to instigate a number of important events and actions.

As a result of these concerns and the recent corporate collapses, the profession has been more willing to take on an increased responsibility for identifying fraud. Recently released auditing standards indicate that the auditor accepts a greater responsibility for actively searching for material frauds. Because of the nature and sophistication of these frauds, the auditors still disclaim their responsibility, or the expectation, of finding all material frauds. A more detailed discussion of the auditor's responsibility for fraud detection is contained in Chapter 4.

Ability to communicate different levels of assurance

As outlined earlier, the assurance framework (AUS 108/'International Framework for Assurance Engagements') allows either a reasonable level of assurance to be issued (audit) or a limited level of assurance to be issued (review). An important question as we move to an environment where reports will attempt to ascribe different levels of assurance is whether the user receives the level of assurance that is intended by the assurance provider. Using subjects from different backgrounds, Gay et al. (1998) provided some insight into whether users of review and audit reports understand the messages conveyed, and whether they are able to distinguish between the two levels of assurance. They found that users of financial information had different perceptions of the degree of reliability of financial information and the levels of assurance provided by review and audit reports. Results indicated that users found financial information to be less reliable compared to auditors. While all groups recognised that an audit report with a positive assurance opinion provided greater assurance than a review report with a statement of negative assurance, auditors had significantly stronger beliefs as to the extent of assurance being provided than did user and preparer groups. The findings suggested that such reports, once observed for financial report audits, were used in the form of a 'clean bill-of-health' stamp rather than giving information to the reader about the work performed.

Roebuck et al. (2000) researched whether users responded to changes in some of the factors that determine the level of assurance by manipulating, first, the subject matter of the work undertaken (historical (internal control) versus prospective (prospective information)) and, second, the level of work undertaken (higher work level versus moderate work level). In examining the level of assurance conveyed by the assurance report, it was found that shareholders did perceive a higher level of work for historical compared with prospective information. However, they did not change their level of assurance on the report as a result of the description of the work performed by the assurance provider (for which standard wording suggested for assurance reports and already used for audit and review reports was used). This demonstrates that at this time the auditing and assurance profession has problems communicating the level of work performed and that other means of reporting the level of work should be considered in order to communicate this dimension of the assurance process accurately to report users. Whether or not recent changes in reporting requirements contained in the assurance framework have adequately addressed this issue is a research question that is as yet unanswered.

Quick review

1. Auditors have entities as clients but owners or other members of the public use their reports.
2. Auditors and financial report users have different perceptions of the role and responsibilities of auditors.
3. The expectation gap is the gap between society's expectations of auditors and auditors' performance, as perceived by society.
4. The expectation gap consists of a reasonableness gap and a performance gap.
5. The performance gap may be due to deficient standards or deficient performance.
6. Four major expectation gap issues are the nature and meaning of audit report messages, auditors giving early warning of corporate failure, the auditor's duty to detect and report fraud, and the communication of different levels of assurance.

THE ROLE OF AUDITING STANDARDS

Throughout this book reference will be made to the **auditing standards** (AUSs/ISAs) issued by auditing and assurance standard-setting bodies in Australia and internationally. The Auditing and Assurance Standards Board (AUASB), which is discussed in Chapter 2, currently develops the auditing and assurance standards in Australia. These standards prescribe the basic principles and essential procedures that govern the professional conduct of an auditor. It is important to understand the role that the standards have in the conduct of the audit function and the regulation of the auditing profession.

It is the essence of a profession that it should have standards that govern the way in which an assurance service is provided, and outline what the assurance service provider is required to do. Codified standards make it clear to third parties that the profession does have standards that its members should achieve and against which performance can be measured. Standards also assist an individual auditor by providing a benchmark against which to assess individual performance. In this regard the auditing standard-setting bodies seek to improve the quality of auditing practice, and by updating their standards these bodies can inform individual auditors about changes in the audit function. Codified standards also provide the courts with an authoritative benchmark against which to measure an auditor's performance in the event of an auditor's work being subject to litigation.

The auditing standards are applicable to all audits and will have legislative backing as a result of the recent CLERP 9 changes to auditing requirements contained in the *Corporations Act 2001*. Failure to observe these standards may expose a member to investigation and disciplinary action from the Australian Securities and Investments Commission (ASIC), as discussed in Chapter 2. There is also a series of **Auditing Guidance Statements** (AGSs) which are approved and issued by the board but do not establish new principles and do not amend existing standards. The AGS series provides guidance on procedural matters or on entity- or industry-specific issues, or clarifies and explains principles in an AUS. The AGS statements are not mandatory professional requirements but have the status of authoritative guidance. From 1998, the AUASB also started issuing **Audit and Assurance Alerts**, to bring to the attention of members of the profession matters considered to be of significant and immediate concern.

Authority of auditing standards

As indicated above, the AUSs contain the basic principles and essential procedures to be complied with by auditors in the conduct of an audit, together with related guidance. For audits undertaken under the *Corporations Act 2001*, the auditing standards have legal authority by virtue of the amendments contained in CLERP 9. For other audits there is a mandatory professional obligation for members of the accounting bodies in Australia to comply with the AUSs, which is found in Miscellaneous Professional Statement APS 1.1, issued by the national councils of the accounting bodies. APS 1.1 states that the basic principles and essential procedures in an AUS are mandatory and are to be complied with in the planning, conduct and reporting of an audit engagement. APS 1.1 indicates that the standards are to be applied to all financial report audits, and to all audits of other financial and non-financial information, adapted as necessary.

The status of the guidance in the AUSs/ISAs, and the responsibility of members of the accounting bodies to apply that guidance, is influenced by the style of the statements. The basic principles and essential procedures are identified in the AUSs/ISAs by **black lettering** (bold type) and are supported by explanatory and other material to assist an auditor in interpreting and applying the basic principles and essential procedures. The status of the guidance is explained in APS 1.1 as follows (at the international level there is equivalent guidance contained in the Preface to International Standards on Auditing and Related Services):

- AUSs apply in addition to ethical and legal requirements relevant to a particular audit.
- The basic principles and essential procedures ('black letter' requirements) are mandatory and are to be complied with in the planning, conduct and reporting of an audit.
- The mandatory basic principles and essential procedures are to be interpreted and applied in the context of the supporting explanatory information. Where in the rare and exceptional circumstance of a specific audit engagement an auditor determines that it is necessary to depart from a basic principle or essential procedure to meet effectively the objective of an audit, that departure must be explained in the audit report. This disclosure has been imposed on the basis that if the black letter mandatory requirements in the AUSs are the minimum professional basic principles and essential procedures for a quality audit, the auditor should be prepared to explain and justify how the integrity and quality of the audit has been maintained where there has been a necessary departure from any of those requirements. It is also a logical consequence of having the audit report include the statement that the 'audit has been conducted in accordance with Australian Auditing Standards ...' If it has not, this should be explained to the users of the audit report.

In 2005 the IAASB and AUASB are conducting a 'clarity project', with the aim of making the auditing standards easier to read. There have been concerns that auditors have been following only the black-lettered 'basic principles' and ignoring the grey-lettered 'guidance'. This project proposes that the black and grey lettering should have **equal authority**, with the auditor having to pay equal attention to both. There is also a proposal to change some of the language conventions. For example, all auditing black-letter requirements at present contain the word 'should' (i.e. the auditor *should* act in a certain way). This is likely to be changed to the more imperative 'shall' or 'must' (i.e. the auditor *shall/must* act in that way).

1. The Auditing and Assurance Standards Board of Australia currently develops auditing standards in Australia, based on international auditing standards.

2. These standards prescribe the basic principles and essential procedures that govern the professional conduct of the auditor.

3. Auditing standards are mandatory for audits conducted under the *Corporations Act* and have legal backing.

4. The basic principles and essential procedures are identified in the AUSs by 'black lettering', and it is these black letter requirements which are mandatory.

5. There should be no departures from basic principles, and essential procedures should be undertaken in all except the rare circumstances where it is determined that the audit objective can be achieved more effectively with alternative procedures.

6. As part of a current project, the IAASB/AUASB are expected to depart from the convention of black lettering for basic principles and essential procedures and grey lettering for guidance to adopt a system under which black and grey lettering have equal authority, in other words the auditor will have to read the black and grey lettering in conjunction and may not ignore any grey-lettered text.

AUDITS UNDER THE CORPORATIONS ACT 2001

Within the context of the general auditing process previously established, this section will outline the financial report audit function under Australian corporations legislation. As a prelude to these provisions, it is important to understand the rationale of corporations legislation in relation to the preparation and audit of financial reports. The underlying logic of the financial reports and audit divisions of the *Corporations Act 2001* can be found in the separation of ownership and control inherent in the corporate form of business entity. Within these sections of the legislation, management (directors) is required to present to the owners (shareholders) financial information concerning the activities of the company during the relevant financial period, accompanied by an audit report. The provisions of the *Corporations Act 2001* vest with the owners the powers dealing with the appointment and removal of auditors.

As a result, Part 2M.3 of the *Corporations Act 2001* establishes an accountability process whereby management is responsible for the preparation and presentation of appropriate financial reports, with those financial reports to be accompanied by a report of an independent auditor appointed by the shareholders. The provisions of the *Corporations Act 2001* dealing with the appointment and removal of an auditor are found in Part 2M.4, ss 324–31, and are discussed in Chapter 3.

The responsibilities of directors

When discussing the audit provisions of companies legislation, it is important to note the responsibilities given to the directors of a company for the preparation and presentation of the financial report. Sections 292–306 require the directors to prepare annually a financial report (which includes an income statement, balance sheet, statement of changes in equity, cash flow statement, directors' declaration and other related notes and reports) and any other information or explanation as is necessary to give a true and fair view and, unless exempted under s. 301(2), to ensure that the financial report is audited. Section 296(1) also requires the directors to ensure that the financial report is prepared in accordance with the accounting standards. The accounting standards referred to are those that have been approved by the Australian Accounting Standards Board (AASB). The principal objective of the AASB is to improve the quality of financial reporting by reporting entities under the *Corporations Act 2001*. In meeting this objective, it develops and promulgates accounting standards and statements of accounting concepts. The accounting standards issued by the AASB are legally enforceable under the Law. However, under ss 295(3)(c) and 297 if a company's financial report, when prepared in accordance with accounting standards, would not otherwise give a true and fair view, the directors are required to add such information and explanations as will give a true and fair view.

Section 295A requires the chief executive officer and chief financial officer to attach to the company's financial report a declaration that indicates whether or not, in their opinion, the financial report and notes to the financial report give a true and fair view. Section 295(4)(c) also requires the directors to state whether there are reasonable grounds to believe that the company will be able to pay its debts as and when they become due and payable. These representations by the directors are subject to audit. In addition to the preparation of the annual financial report, a company that is a disclosing entity must lodge a half-year financial report with the Australian Securities and Investments Commission (ASIC), accompanied by an audit or review report.

The auditor's responsibilities

The powers and duties of auditors to report on the annual financial report prepared by the directors are found under s. 308 of the Act. The auditor's basic obligation is to report to the members of the company on the financial report presented by the directors at the annual general meeting, and on the accounting and other records relating to that financial report. The specific responsibility of the auditor is to report an opinion as to whether the financial report is in accordance with the law, including compliance with accounting standards (s. 296), and provides a true and fair view (s. 297). These reporting responsibilities are discussed in more detail in Chapter 13.

Quick review

1. The *Corporations Act 2001* establishes an accountability process whereby directors are responsible for the preparation and presentation of appropriate financial reports, with an independent auditor appointed by the shareholders reporting on these financial reports.

2. The *Corporations Act 2001* requirements deal with the appointment and removal of auditors and their reporting responsibilities.

OTHER APPLICATIONS OF THE ASSURANCE FUNCTION

The evidence-gathering methods of auditing can be applied for diverse purposes and are not confined to an expression of opinion on financial reports. An audit may also result in one or both of the following:

1 recommendations to improve the efficiency and effectiveness of operations; and/or
2 a positive influence on the behaviour of people whose activities are audited.

Audit recommendations normally cite some deficiencies in the activities audited and suggest possible improvements in performance. Recommendations may contain both an explanation of the causes of problems and the solution to those problems, or they may merely identify problems and suggest investigation. For example, auditors typically make recommendations to their clients on internal control and insurance coverage. Recommendations on internal control normally suggest improvements in procedures to correct weaknesses, but recommendations on insurance coverage are normally confined to identifying inadequate coverage.

Auditing textbooks normally list the effect on employees audited as one of the many benefits of auditing. Only recently, however, has research been conducted to support what auditors assumed to be true from their own experience. In laboratory simulations of the audit process it was found that people whose activities were audited conformed to established procedures more readily when told that their work would be audited than did another group who had not been previously audited. This performance prevailed even though more efficient alternatives were available. Thus, an audit has a beneficial effect on control activities.

The evidence-gathering methods of auditing are employed in activities other than auditing financial reports, for example in compliance audits and performance audits. These activities can be undertaken as separate engagements or as part of a comprehensive audit, and by external auditors, government auditors or as part of an internal audit function.

Compliance audits

Compliance audits are an examination of financial information for the purpose of reporting on the legality and control of operations and the probity of those responsible for the administration of funds provided by external parties, including the expression of an opinion on an entity's compliance with statute, regulations or other directives that govern the activities of the entity. In Australia, compliance auditing is particularly relevant in government.

In our society the largest organisation of all is the federal government. Government is truly a big business. The conventions of the Constitution and parliamentary practice in Australia, supported by statute, require accountability by government departments for receipts and expenditure. These departments, as well as statutory authorities, are also responsible for the administration of complex regulations and are themselves subject to regulations.

The responsibility for the audit of federal government operations rests with the Australian Auditor-General and state government operations with an appointed State Auditor-General. Essentially, the Auditor-General is required to report to Parliament on compliance by the government departments with the appropriate financial and legal regulations. The role of the Auditor-General also involves functioning in effect as the internal auditing department of the government.

The compliance auditing function also extends to the auditing of sections of some government departments that are concerned with the compliance of private sector entities and individuals with government regulations. For example, Australian Taxation Office inspectors are in essence auditors concerned with compliance of the community at large with government policy.

Performance audits

Performance auditing is often referred to as 'management auditing', 'value for money', 'operational auditing', 'efficiency auditing' and 'program results auditing'. It is more often associated with auditing in the public sector, although it is, in various forms, becoming more popular in other areas and is an integral part of many internal audit functions.

Performance auditing is a more comprehensive activity designed to analyse organisation structure, internal systems, work flow and managerial performance. It is usually associated with issues of efficiency, effectiveness and economy. In short, performance auditing is intended to provide a measure of an organisation's achievement of its goals and objectives.

The products of performance audit can range from reports recommending improvements in efficiency and effectiveness of current operations to general suggestions about the organisation's use of resources to provide the greatest long-range benefit to the entity. Performance audit reports may contain recommendations for restructuring of departments or divisions, recommendations for training and replacement of personnel, or results of cost–value analyses of internal controls of an entity. The performance audit has a broad scope and may encompass all major functions of an entity. This type of audit is dealt with further in Chapter 16.

Comprehensive audits

The discussion of the audit function to date has covered the following audit types that may be undertaken as discrete tasks or on an interactive basis:

- financial report audit
- compliance audit
- performance audit.

Collectively, these audits can be integrated and described as a **comprehensive audit**. This term is used to describe a broad-scope audit mandate comprising a combination of elements of the above three types of audits. In Australia, this approach is currently more prevalent in public sector auditing, where auditors undertake an examination for the purpose of expressing an opinion on financial reports, reporting on the legality and control of operations (including an opinion on an entity's compliance with statute, regulations and directives), and reporting on the economy, efficiency and effectiveness with which the entity has achieved its objectives.

Internal audits

Internal audit is not a separate type of audit, as are financial report, compliance, performance or comprehensive audits, but it is, in effect, an audit undertaken by a body of audit professionals who are internal to or employees of the audited entity. Over the last 50 years internal auditing has evolved from a simple clerical function into a highly professional activity. The Institute of Internal Auditors, formed in the US in 1941, is today an international association concerned with the development of the internal auditing profession. Like the external auditing profession, the Institute of Internal Auditors has instituted a code of ethics and standards for the professional practice of internal auditing. An Australian Institute of Internal Auditors was formed in 1986 with an affiliation to the international body.

The role of an internal auditor within an entity varies. Internal audits are performed by employees of organisations functioning in a staff capacity and reporting to a high-level officer in the organisation. The scope of internal auditing is evolving. Seen traditionally as an appraisal activity within an organisation for the review of accounting, financial and other operations as a basis for service to management, many internal auditors have today found that they can be of increased value to an organisation by participating in the business risk analysis of the organisation. The role of the internal auditor is discussed further in Chapter 15.

Forensic audits

Forensic auditors are employed by companies, government agencies, accounting firms, and consulting and investigative services firms. They are trained in detecting, investigating and deterring fraud and white-collar crime. Some examples of situations where forensic auditors have been involved include:

- Analysing financial transactions involving unauthorised transfers of cash between companies.
- Reconstructing incomplete accounting records to settle an insurance claim over inventory valuation.
- Proving money-laundering activities by reconstructing cash transactions.
- Investigating and documenting embezzlement, and negotiating insurance settlements.

Quick review

1 Benefits from the audit process include recommendations to improve the efficiency and effectiveness of operations, and provision of an incentive for people to perform prescribed internal control activities more carefully.

2 The evidence-gathering methods of auditing are employed in activities other than auditing financial reports, including:
- *compliance auditing*—the examination of financial information for the purpose of reporting on the legality and control of operations;
- *performance auditing*—the analysis of organisation structure, internal systems, work flow and management performance;
- *comprehensive auditing*—which includes the aspects of financial report, compliance and performance auditing;
- *internal auditing*—an appraisal activity within an organisation for the review of financial and business risks and other operations as a basis for service to management; and
- *forensic auditing*—an investigative/assurance activity aimed at detecting, investigating and deterring fraud.

Summary

This chapter has attempted to give the reader a feel for the recent crisis of confidence in the financial systems and the ways in which the auditing profession and standard-setters have responded to this crisis over the period 2003 to 2005. It has also tried to place the audit in a broader assurance framework. While this text deals with the concept of audit generally, with emphasis on the financial audit process in the private sector, much of the material in relation to audit principles, concepts and methods is applicable to the other types of assurance services and entities. For example, guidance on auditing in the public sector would reflect differences in matters of emphasis and practice rather than in basic principles and concepts. This reflects the view that users of audit reports are entitled to a uniform quality of assurance when audit objectives are the same. The same standards should apply regardless of the nature of the entity being audited, with users of the audit report not being well served by the application of alternative standards to the same type of audit.

Key terms

References

AICPA (1987) (Treadway Commission), *Report of the National Commission on Fraudulent Financial Reporting*, October, AICPA, New York.

ASCPA and ICAA (1993) (Middleton Report), *Research Study on Financial Reporting and Auditing—Bridging the Expectation Gap*, December, Melbourne.

ASCPA and ICAA (1996) *Report of the Financial Reporting and Auditing Expectation Gap Task Force to the Joint Standing Committee*, June, Melbourne.

Beck, G.W. (1973) 'The role of the auditor in modern society: An exploratory essay', *Accounting and Business Research*, Spring, 117–22.

Bell, T.B., Marrs, F.O., Solomon, I. and Thomas, H. (1997) *Auditing Organizations through a Strategic-Systems Lens: The KPMG Business Measurement Process*, KPMG Peat Marwick LLP, New York.

Blackwell, D.W., Noland, T.R. and Winters, D.B. (1998) 'The value of auditor assurance: Evidence from loan pricing', *Journal of Accounting Research*, Spring, 57–70.

Elliott, R.K. (1994) 'Confronting the future: Choices for the attest function', *Accounting Horizons*, September, 106–24.

Epstein, M.J. and Geiger, M.A. (1994) 'Investor views of audit assurance: Recent evidence of the expectation gap', *Journal of Accountancy*, January, 60–6.

Gay, G.E. and Schelluch, P. (1993) 'The impact of the long form audit report on users' perceptions of the auditor's role', *Australian Accounting Review*, Vol. 3, No. 2, November, 1–11.

Gay, G., Schelluch, P., and Baines, A., (1998) 'Perceptions of messages conveyed by review and audit reports', *Accounting Auditing and Accountability*, Vol. 11, No. 4, 472–94.

Gay, G.E., Schelluch, P. and Reid, I. (1997) 'Users' perceptions of the auditing responsibilities for the prevention and reporting of fraud, other illegal acts and errors', *Australian Accounting Review*, Vol. 7, No. 1, May, 51–61.

Gwilliam, D. (1987) 'The auditor's responsibility for the detection of fraud', *Professional Negligence*, January/February, 6.

Houghton, K.A. and Messier, W.F. Jnr (1990) 'The wording of audit reports: Its impact on the meaning of the message communicated', in S. Moriarty (ed.), *Accounting Communication and Monitoring*, University of Oklahoma, 89–106.

Humphrey, C., Moizer, P. and Turley, S. (1992) 'The audit expectation gap—Plus ça change, plus c'est la même chose?', *Critical Perspectives in Accounting*, June, 137–61.

Humphrey, C., Moizer, P. and Turley, S. (1993) 'The audit expectations gap in Britain: An empirical investigation', *Accounting and Business Research*, Vol. 23, 395–411.

Levitt, A. (1998) 'The numbers game', NYU Centre for Law and Business, 28 September. (Also refer Loomis, C. (1999) 'Lies, damned lies, and managed earnings', *Fortune*, 2 August, 74–92).

Liggio, C.D. (1974) 'The expectation gap: The accountant's legal Waterloo', *Journal of Contemporary Business*, Vol. 3, Summer, 27–44.

Monroe, G.S. and Woodliff, D. (1994a) 'An empirical investigation of the audit expectation gap: Australian evidence', *Accounting and Finance*, May, 47–74.

Monroe, G.S. and Woodliff, D. (1994b) 'Great expectations: Public perceptions of the auditor's role', *Australian Accounting Review*, Vol. 4, No. 2, 42–53.

Porter, B.A. (1991) 'The audit expectation performance gap: A contemporary approach', *Pacific Accounting Review*, 1–36.

Porter, B.A. (1993) 'An empirical study of the audit expectation–performance gap', *Accounting and Business Research*, Vol. 24, No. 93, 49–78.

Roebuck, P., Simnett, R. and Ho, H.L. (2000) 'Understanding assurance services reports: A user perspective', *Accounting and Finance*, November, 211–32.

Schelluch, P. and Green, W. (1996) 'The expectation gap: The next step', *Australian Accounting Review*, September, 19–23.

Sundem, G.L., Dukes, R.E. and Elliott, J.A. (1996) *The Value of Information and Audit*, Coopers & Lybrand, New York.

Sutton, S. and Cullinan, C. (2002) 'Defrauding the public interest: A critical examination of reengineered audit processes and the likelihood of detecting fraud', *Critical Perspectives on Accounting*, Vol. 13, 297–310.

Trotman, K. (2003) 'Financial Report Audit: Meeting the Market Expectations', Institute of Chartered Accountants in Australia, Sydney.

Wallace, W.A. (1980) *The Economic Role of the Audit in Free and Regulated Markets*, Touche Ross & Co., New York.

Assignments

MaxMARK

MAXIMISE YOUR MARKS! There are approximately 30 interactive overview questions on assurance and auditing available online at www.mhhe. com/au/gay3e

Additional assignments for this chapter are contained in Appendix A of this book, page 763.

REVIEW QUESTIONS

1.1 The following questions deal with the relationship between audit and assurance.

(a) The highest level of assurance is provided by:

    A agreed-upon procedures

    B compiling financial reports

    C audit

    D review

(b) The relationship between audit and assurances services is best described by which of the following:

    A the audit function is a subset of assurance services

    B the relationship will depend on the terms of the contract

    C the audit function and assurance services are the same

    D assurance services are a subset of the audit function

(c) Which of the following would be suitable criteria for an assurance engagement?

    A An organisation's internal documents prescribing what constitutes satisfactory internal control, for providing assurance on internal controls.

    B An indicative list of corporate governance practices prescribed by ASIC for providing assurance on corporate governance practices.

    C Neither of A and B above.

    D Both of A and B above.

1.2 The following questions deal with the nature of the audit function. Select the *best* response.

(a) Which of the following best describes why an independent auditor is asked to express an opinion on a financial report?

    A To provide increased assurance to users as to the fairness of the financial report.

    B To relieve management of the responsibility for the financial report.

    C To satisfy legislative requirements.

    D To guarantee that there are no misstatements in the financial report.

(b) Users of financial reports demand independent audits because:

    A users expect auditors to correct management errors

    B management relies on the auditor to improve the internal control

    C users demand assurance that fraud does not exist

    D management may not be objective in reporting

(c) Independent auditing can best be described as:

    A a professional activity that measures and communicates financial and business data

    B a regulatory function that prevents the issuance of improper financial information

    C a branch of accounting

D a discipline that attests to the results of accounting and other functional operations and data

(d) The independent auditor adds credibility to the client's financial report by:
- **A** attaching an auditor's opinion to the client's financial report
- **B** testifying under oath about client financial information
- **C** stating in the auditor's communication of internal-control-related matters that the audit was made in accordance with Australian auditing standards
- **D** maintaining a clear-cut distinction between management's representations and the auditor's representations

1.3 (a) Independent auditors are referred to as 'independent' because:
- **A** they are not employees of the entity being audited
- **B** their offices are not at the entity's place of business
- **C** they report to users outside of the audited entity
- **D** they are paid by parties outside of the audited entity

(b) What is the general character of the work conducted in performing a forensic audit?
- **A** Offering an opinion on the reliability of the specific assertions made by management.
- **B** Identifying the causes of an entity's financial difficulties.
- **C** Providing assurance that the financial report is not materially misstated.
- **D** Detecting or deterring fraudulent activity related to the financial report.

(c) Which of the following *best* describes why an independent auditor is asked to express an opinion on the fair presentation of financial statements?
- **A** The opinion of an independent party is needed because a company may *not* be objective with respect to its own financial report.
- **B** It is a customary courtesy that all shareholders of a company receive an independent report on management's stewardship in managing the affairs of the business.
- **C** It is difficult to prepare financial statements that fairly present a company's financial position and changes in cash flows without the expertise of an independent auditor.
- **D** It is management's responsibility to seek available independent aid in the appraisal of the financial information shown in its financial report.

(d) The definition of auditing refers to auditing as a 'systematic process of objectively obtaining and evaluating evidence regarding assertions …' What is meant by 'systematic process'?
- **A** There should be a well-planned approach for conducting the audit.
- **B** All assertions are equally important for all audits.
- **C** All audits involve obtaining the same evidence.
- **D** All audits involve evaluating evidence in the same manner.

The assurance framework

1.4 Discuss the five elements of an assurance report for the audit of a financial report.

Structure of assurance standards and pronouncements

1.5 Explain what is meant by 'assurance' and distinguish between the various levels of assurance provided by an auditor, as described by AUS 106.

Define auditing and other levels of assurance

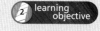

1.6 What is the objective of an independent audit?

1.7 Why do assurance providers report their findings as an expression of opinion rather than as a statement of fact?

Fundamental principles underlying an audit

1.8 Identify the fundamental principles of auditing and trace these through to the relevant auditing standards. Are all the fundamental principles supported by auditing standards?

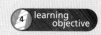

Demand for assurance

1.9 Why are independent audits necessary?

1.10 To what types of activities other than audits of financial reports are the evidence-gathering methods applied?

History of the audit function

1.11 What has been the major change in audit emphasis and methodology since the nineteenth century?

Relationship between auditor, client and public

1.12 Does society as a whole benefit from the services of independent auditors, or are the benefits restricted to individual third parties?

Expectation gap

1.13 What is meant by the term 'expectation gap'? Provide some examples of the expectation gap.

1.14 What action has the auditing profession taken to reduce the expectation gap?

Role of auditing standards

1.15 Are auditing standards mandatory? Explain.

Performance, comprehensive, internal and forensic auditing

1.16 Give one example each of compliance, operational and forensic audits.

1.17 The following are major issues confronting the profession: expanding assurance and other services, introduction of new audit methodologies and globalisation. Are these issues all related to the concept of independence? Justify your answer.

DISCUSSION PROBLEMS AND CASE STUDIES

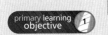

Understand the assurance framework

1.18 **Moderate** For the last two years Maree Williams has been working as a trainee accountant with a local practice that specialises in auditing. During that time she has been involved in financial report audits, compliance audits and performance audits and feels she has a good understanding of auditing. As part of her traineeship, she is required to undertake a university degree and has just commenced her study of auditing and assurance services. During the first lecture the lecturer asks the class to indicate three types of engagements an assurance provider could undertake. Maree answers: 'financial report, compliance and performance audits'. The lecturer replies that these are not types of engagements but different applications of the audit function. Further, each application she has identified can be undertaken in conjunction with any of the three types of engagements. Maree is very confused and has asked you for an explanation.

Required

(a) Identify and describe the three types of engagements an auditor can undertake by reference to the assurance framework.

(b) Discuss the relationship between the applications identified by Maree and the engagements identified in AUS 106.

Define auditing and other levels of assurance

1.19 **Moderate** 'The evidence-gathering methods of auditing can be applied for diverse purposes and are not confined to an expression of opinion on financial reports.'

Required

Provide an example of one (1) application of the audit function other than the audit of general purpose financial reports.

For the application identified indicate:

(a) whether this service meets the AAA definition of auditing provided in your text;

(b) the level of assurance usually provided by the auditor when performing this service;

(c) whether the engagement involves direct reporting or an attest engagement; and

(d) the type of auditor that usually provides this service.

1.20 **Complex** A1 Computers Ltd ('A1') is a major client of your firm. A1 has recently acquired B2 Modems Pty Ltd ('B2'). The price for the acquisition has been agreed at $5 million, providing A1 is satisfied with the financial records of B2. To allow A1 to assess these records, B2 have agreed to allow the auditors of A1 access to their books and records.

B2 is a small proprietary company and as such has not prepared statutory financial reports or undergone an audit since incorporation in 20X2 (three years ago).

A1 have approached your firm and asked that you assist. Specifically they have requested:

(a) a review of all transactions occurring from the date negotiations commenced until the settlement date to ensure all transactions were in the normal course of operations;

(b) a review of the management accounts for the years 20X3 and 20X4; and

(c) a review of the financial report prepared at the acquisition date.

In order to clarify your responsibilities, you have asked A1 to indicate the level of assurance they require for each item. The CEO has indicated that the most recent financial report is very important as is the review of transactions but he is willing to have less work done on the previous year's management accounts.

Required

Using AUS 106, identify the type of engagement that will most likely be undertaken for each of the tasks. Provide reasons for your decisions.

Demand for assurance

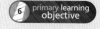

1.21 **Basic** Auditors have been engaged to assure the propriety of the balloting to determine outstanding motion picture and television programs, actors, directors and technicians. Explain why auditors have been chosen for these tasks.

1.22 **Moderate** List as many reasons as you can for each of the following types of entities to have an annual audit.

(a) church

(b) municipal government

(c) trade union

(d) national hobby organisation

(e) professional accounting organisation

What benefits would such entities receive from an independent audit?

History of audit function

1.23 **Moderate** Your text identifies three of the early approaches to auditing, namely the balance sheet, transactions cycle and financial risk analysis approach.

Required

(a) Provide a brief description of each approach.

(b) Define the term 'transactions cycle' and provide two examples of common transactions cycles, together with the account balances arising from the identified cycles.

(c) If an auditor adopts a risk-based approach to auditing, does this mean they do not consider the balance sheet or transactions cycles?

1.24 **Moderate**

The audit product has not changed fundamentally. Yeah, there are some bells and whistles but it has not changed fundamentally in a Century.

(Elliott, R. (1998) 'Audit Symposium Panel Discussion on Assurance Services', *Auditing: A Journal of Practice and Theory*, Vol. 17 Supplement, 1–9)

Required

Discuss the extent to which you agree or disagree with this statement. Your answer should consider the four main approaches to auditing employed during the twentieth century.

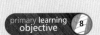

Relationship between auditor, client and public

1.25 Complex Shelly Ling has recently been employed by a small accounting practice and is working on her first audit. During Shelly's testing she has found a number of large errors that she has brought to the attention of the audit manager. Shelly believes some of the errors are so large that a qualified audit opinion will be necessary. Towards the end of the audit Shelly is told that the audit manager has scheduled a meeting with the client in order to discuss audit adjustments and the type of audit opinion that is likely to be given.

After the meeting Shelly is told an unqualified audit opinion will be issued. Shelly is quite shocked as she thought that the auditor reported the results of the audit directly to shareholders. Instead she has found that results are discussed with management before communication to external users.

Required

Assume Shelly has come to you, the senior auditor, and expressed her dismay at the audit process.

(a) Explain to Shelly why the auditor would normally meet with the client prior to releasing the audit report.

(b) Identify and describe the mechanisms in place to ensure auditors fulfil their duties to shareholders.

Expectation gap

1.26 Basic Discuss the following observation recently made by a businessman: 'Published financial reports should be designed to enable the efficiency and skill of management to be evaluated'.

1.27 Basic One of the common expectations of users of financial reports is that the audit report provides absolute assurance that there are no material misstatements in the financial report. Do you believe this is a reasonable expectation? Provide reasons for your decision.

1.28 Moderate The following statement is representative of attitudes and opinions sometimes encountered by auditors in their professional practices:

> *An audit is essentially negative and contributes to neither the gross national product nor the general wellbeing of society. Auditors do not create; they merely check what someone else has done.*

Evaluate this statement and indicate:

(a) areas of agreement with the statement, if any;

(b) areas of misconception, incompleteness or fallacious reasoning included in the statement, if any.

Describe the authority weighting of the black and grey lettering in the auditing standards. Discuss the potential concerns with these levels of authority and the proposals for dealing with these concerns.

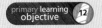

Performance, comprehensive, internal and forensic auditing

1.29 Moderate The managing director of your company (a multidivision company) has been discussing the company's internal operations with several colleagues in the business community. He has discovered that most of them have an internal audit staff. The activities of the staff at other companies include financial audits, compliance audits and sometimes performance audits. Describe for him the meaning of the terms (a) financial auditing, (b) compliance auditing and (c) performance auditing as they would relate to the internal audit function.

1.30 Moderate G. Johnson, a local real estate agent, is a member of the Board of Directors of Kelly Ltd. At a recent board meeting, called to discuss the financial plan for 2000, Mr Johnson discovered two planned expenditures for auditing. In the management department's budget he found an internal audit activity and in the accountant's budget he found an estimate for the 2000 annual audit by an external audit firm.

Mr Johnson could not understand the need for two different expenditures for auditing. Since the external audit fee for the annual audit was less than the cost of the internal audit activity, he proposed eliminating the internal audit function.

Explain to Mr Johnson the different purposes served by the two audit activities.

CHAPTER 2

THE STRUCTURE OF THE PROFESSION

LEARNING OBJECTIVES

After studying this chapter you should be able to:

1. identify the attributes of professional status and describe to what extent they exist in public accounting;

2. describe the regulation of auditing;

3. describe the regulation of the subject matter of audits;

4. explain the impact of internationalisation on auditing;

5. outline the characteristics of the professional bodies and accounting firms engaged in the auditing profession;

6. describe the internal structure of an audit firm;

7. identify the elements of quality control within audit firms and explain practice-monitoring programs; and

8. explain how auditing in the public sector fits into the Australian auditing and assurance environment.

Chapter outline

The auditor is a member of a time-honoured profession, and the status of the profession and the responsibilities that accompany this status affect the audit and assurance function and the structure of the profession. The auditor is subject to regulations imposed by the profession and society. The audit and assurance function is carried out in a complex environment composed of interrelationships between governmental and professional organisations and individual auditors and audit firms. These regular and enduring relationships form the structure of the profession. In addition, the audit environment includes the requirements of legislation, particularly the *Corporations Act*, discussed in Chapter 1; public expectations of the audit and the existence of the expectation gap, also discussed in

Chapter 1; and the legal liability of an auditor and the impact of common law, discussed in Chapter 4.

This chapter explains the role of government and professional associations in the auditing and assurance environment and the relationship between them. It recognises the impact of globalisation on business and the auditing profession and discusses how the profession has reacted to the need for internationalisation. It outlines the characteristics of the types of audit firms that make up the auditing profession and the services they provide. The internal structure of an audit firm and the influence of that structure on an auditing practice is also covered. In addition, there is discussion of the place of public sector auditing within the structure of the Australian auditing profession.

Relevant guidance

Australian		International	
AUS 206	Quality Control for Audits of Historical Financial Information (Revised 2004)	ISA 220	Quality Control for Audits of Historical Financial Information (Revised 2004)

learning objective **1**

PROFESSIONAL STATUS OF THE AUDITOR

The status of a **profession** can be determined by the extent to which the professional group exhibits certain attributes. Professional occupations possess certain common attributes which distinguish them from those that are non-professional. Greenwood (1957) indicates that all professions seem to possess five elements: systematic theory, professional authority, community sanction, regulative codes and culture.

Systematic theory

One significant difference between a professional and a non-professional occupation is the underlying body of theory which supports the work of the professional. Although non-professional work may require procedural skill, that skill does not rest on a body of systematic theory. The underlying theory of the auditing profession consists of auditing theory and accounting theory. Knowledge of systematic theory can be achieved best through formal education in an academic environment. Today, therefore, a tertiary education is considered a prerequisite for people entering the auditing profession. They are then required to complete the education program of one of the two accounting bodies (CA Program or CPA Program) and also undertake continuing professional development throughout their audit career.

Professional authority and expertise

Expertise in the systematic theory of auditing and accounting is the basis for the auditor's work in these areas. Professionals have authority within the area of their expertise because their clients lack the requisite theoretical knowledge. However, professionals only have authority if society confers that authority upon them.

Community sanction

Professionals normally attempt to formalise their authority by gaining community approval of certain powers and privileges. First and foremost among the powers for which professions strive is control over admissions to the profession. To be a registered company auditor a person must, among other things, be a member of one of the accounting bodies (discussed later in this chapter) or other prescribed bodies, each of which controls admission to their own organisation.

Another privilege which professions strive for is *relative* immunity from community judgment on technical matters. Although professions are responsible to the community for their actions, it is generally accepted that a professional's performance should be judged by standards established by the profession itself. Prior to CLERP 9, the setting of auditing and assurance standards was undertaken by the accounting bodies through the Australian Accounting Research Foundation (AARF).

Among the powers and privileges for which professions strive, privileged communication stands out as perhaps the ultimate criterion of professionalism. Professional performance is facilitated if the client feels free to volunteer information which otherwise might not be divulged. Privileged information is a right granted by the community to protect the client from legal encroachment on confidential communications with a professional. Although the professions of medicine and law have generally been granted this privilege, legal privilege between auditor and client does not exist. However, because an auditor will have access to information that a client would not normally make available to external parties, the ethical rules of the accounting bodies (discussed in Chapter 3) prohibit auditors from disclosing such information to a third party without specific authority from the client or unless there is a legal or professional duty to disclose, such as under section 311 of the *Corporations Act*.

Regulative codes

The powers and privileges granted to a profession by the community effectively constitute a monopoly. In Australia, registered company auditors have been granted a monopoly on rendering external audit opinions on the financial reports of companies. Since any monopoly is subject to abuse, a profession must take steps to assure the community that the profession will discipline its members. Professions therefore establish regulative codes. Regulation of the auditing profession is directed at two areas: technical and ethical. Auditing standards govern the technical work of the auditor while the ethical rules govern the auditor's behaviour.

A culture

Another distinguishing feature of a profession is a well-established culture which applies to the professional group. Sociologists call this a *subculture*. A subculture contains specific behavioural prescriptions and proscriptions. For example, auditors are expected to behave in a way that is in accord with the Code of Professional Conduct, including exhibiting integrity, independence, objectivity, confidentiality and public interest. New members of the profession must learn what is expected of them or they will not be accepted as colleagues by their associates.

Quick review

1. Auditing is a profession.
2. The auditing profession is regulated largely by the auditing and assurance standards and its own ethical rules.
3. Confidentiality is an important requirement for the auditing profession.

REGULATION OF AUDITING

Our society is so complex that there is a whole set of organisations whose function is to organise and supervise other organisations. They might be called second-order organisations. The organisations of this type that are of concern to the auditing profession include both **government agencies** and professional associations that regulate auditing.

Financial Reporting Council

The Financial Reporting Council (FRC) is a statutory body established under s. 225(1) of the *Australian Securities and Investments Commission Act 2001*. The FRC was established during 1999 as a peak body with responsibility for the broad oversight of the accounting standard-setting process for the private, public and not-for-profit sectors. As a result of the CLERP 9 amendments, the FRC's role has been significantly expanded to include broad oversight of the auditing standard-setting process and monitoring of auditor independence.

Specific matters for which the FRC is responsible include:

- overseeing the operations of the Australian Accounting Standards Board (AASB) and the Australian Auditing and Assurance Standards Board (AUASB), including appointing their members, other than the Chairs, who are appointed by the Treasurer;
- monitoring the development of international accounting and auditing standards and accounting and auditing standards that apply in major international financial centres;
- furthering the development of a single set of accounting and auditing standards for worldwide use with appropriate regard to international developments;
- monitoring the operation of Australian accounting and auditing standards to assess their continued relevance and effectiveness in achieving their objectives;
- monitoring auditors' independence;
- monitoring the effectiveness of the consultative arrangements used by the AASB and AUASB;
- seeking contributions towards the costs of the Australian accounting and auditing standard-setting process; and
- monitoring and periodically reviewing the level of funding, and the funding arrangements, for the AASB and AUASB.

The legislation expressly limits the FRC's ability to become involved in the technical deliberations of the AASB and AUASB. As a result, the FRC does not have the power to direct the AASB or AUASB in relation to the development, or making, of a particular standard, or to veto a standard formulated or recommended by the AASB or AUASB. This provision is designed to ensure the independence of the AASB and AUASB.

Auditing and Assurance Standards Board

As a result of the CLERP 9 amendments, the Auditing and Assurance Standards Board was reconstituted and established as an independent statutory body on 1 July 2004. The AUASB is responsible for developing and maintaining auditing and assurance standards and other publications. It consists of 10 members appointed by the FRC and a Chair appointed by the Treasurer. Membership currently includes auditing practitioners from the private and public sectors and non-auditors from academia and other stakeholder groups, plus the Australian representative on the International Auditing and Assurance Standards Board (IAASB) of the

52 **PART ONE** The auditing and assurance services profession

International Federation of Accountants (IFAC). The members are supported by the full-time technical staff of the AUASB. Responsibility for final approval of auditing and assurance standards now lies with the Parliament, as these are now disallowable legal instruments following the CLERP 9 amendments. Auditors are required to follow these standards and therefore they are an important influence on the way in which members of the profession perceive and discharge their audit responsibilities.

The AUASB has a long-standing policy of convergence and harmonisation with International Standards on Auditing (ISAs). In 2003, the AUASB issued its current policy on harmonisation and convergence of AUSs with ISAs, which states that the AUASB endeavours to ensure that the Australian Auditing and Assurance Standards:

- are issued to cover the topics addressed in ISAs; and
- comply with those standards.

The AUASB has used ISAs as the basis for its corresponding AUSs. It is the policy of the AUASB to aim to ensure that in the future compliance with AUSs will also constitute compliance with ISAs. Where it is necessary to cover specific Australian industry or regulatory requirements not addressed in an ISA, the AUASB has indicated that appropriate detailed explanation or references will be included by way of footnotes and/or appendices to the corresponding AUS. The AUASB has indicated that in certain circumstances substantive amendments may be made to the mandatory basic principles and essential procedures of an ISA to reflect additional Australian professional auditing requirements and/or in order for it to conform to Australian legislative and regulatory requirements.

In preparation for the transition to the new auditing standard-setting arrangements, the FRC established an AUASB Strategic Direction Taskforce. In a resultant AUASB Strategic Directions paper, which was issued in September 2004 for public comment, it was proposed that:

- auditing standards issued by the AUASB exhibit a clear public interest focus;
- International Standards on Auditing (ISA) issued by the International Auditing and Assurance Standards Board (IAASB) should, where appropriate, be used as the base from which the AUASB develops Australian auditing standards; and
- to ensure Australia achieves world's best practice and promotes audit quality, the AUASB should have regard to developments in other jurisdictions, such as standards issued by the US Public Company Accounting Oversight Board (PCAOB).

Irrespective of the source of a standard, the document will have been through an extensive process of development. This process is considered essential to ensure that all interested parties are given sufficient opportunity to express their views and that the standards, practices and guidelines developed are technically appropriate, relevant and logical. The following outline of the due process employed by the board in the development of an Australian auditing standard illustrates the importance attaching to these documents as mandatory requirements for members of the profession engaged in the audit function.

Research projects initiated by the board commence with the preparation of a background paper summarising the major issues to be dealt with. The paper would include information on the topic from statements, recommendations, studies or standards issued by overseas accounting organisations, and the auditing literature generally, together with preliminary comments on the topic in the Australian context. The board may then establish a project advisory panel with diverse but relevant expertise, with the functions of reviewing the progress of the project at key points and providing a resource base for the project to be accessed as necessary. Based on the issues explored in the background paper, a points outline of a draft document is prepared and reviewed by the board, and tentative decisions made on the key issues. On this basis an exposure draft is prepared. An exposure draft is a document which proposes certain auditing standards or guidance and is released for comment to determine the appropriateness of the proposed guidance. That draft document may then be distributed for selective exposure where comments are sought from various parties selected on the basis of their knowledge of, interest in and involvement with the topic. The exposure draft is reviewed and amended after consideration of the views expressed by the respondents of the selective exposure. The amended draft is again reviewed by the board, and a vote taken as to whether the document should be issued as an exposure draft for public comment. Once it is agreed that the document be issued, it is distributed to members of the profession and other interested parties for comment.

Following full consideration of the views expressed on an exposure draft, a final auditing standard is prepared and approved by the board. As a result of the CLERP 9 amendments, it is now not until the document is formally approved by the Parliament that the extensive process of development is complete (that period being one to three years) and the document achieves the status of an auditing standard and therefore an authoritative statement on the conduct of an audit, enforceable by law for audits conducted under the *Corporations Act*.

Australian Securities and Investments Commission

The Australian Securities and Investments Commission (ASIC) is an independent Commonwealth government body established by the *Australian Securities and Investments Commission Act 2001*. It operates under the direction of three full-time Commissioners, appointed by the Governor-General on the nomination of the Treasurer, and reports to the Commonwealth Parliament and to the Treasurer.

ASIC began on 1 January 1991 as the Australian Securities Commission, to administer the *Corporations Law*. It replaced the National Companies and Securities Commission (NCSC) and the Corporate Affairs offices of the states and territories.

In July 1998 it received new consumer protection responsibilities and changed its name to the Australian Securities and Investments Commission. ASIC enforces company and financial services laws to protect consumers, investors and creditors. It also regulates and informs the public about Australian companies, financial markets, financial services organisations and professionals who deal and advise in investments, superannuation, insurance, deposit taking and credit.

On 15 July 2001, the *Corporations Law* was replaced by the *Corporations Act 2001* and the *ASIC Law* was replaced by the *Australian Securities and Investments Commission Act 2001*. The new statutes are very similar to the Laws that they replaced. The changes made consist only of changes in terminology and some changes to reflect the new constitutional underpinnings of the legislation, which is now truly Commonwealth legislation, as the states have referred their powers to the Commonwealth in relation to registration and regulation of companies. Section references and numbers have remained essentially unchanged.

The *Australian Securities and Investments Commission Act 2001* requires ASIC to:

- uphold the law uniformly, effectively and quickly;
- promote confident and informed participation by investors and consumers in the financial system;

- make information about companies and other bodies available to the public; and
- improve the performance of the financial system and the entities within it.

ASIC administers the following legislation:

- *Corporations Act 2001*
- *Australian Securities and Investments Commission Act 2001*
- *Insurance (Agents and Brokers) Act 1984*
- *Insurance Contracts Act 1984*
- *Superannuation (Resolution of Complaints) Act 1993.*

ASIC exercises consumer protection-related functions under the following legislation (prudential functions under these Acts are exercised by the Australian Prudential Regulation Authority):

- *Superannuation Industry (Supervision) Act 1993*
- *Retirement Savings Accounts Act 1997*
- *Life Insurance Act 1995*
- *Insurance Act 1973.*

ASIC also has responsibility for administering various Regulations made under the legislation listed. It has the power to investigate all perceived serious breaches of the *Corporations Act*, to take action to recover property or damages and to lodge criminal prosecutions.

Following the CLERP 9 amendments, ASIC's responsibilities have been enhanced. It now has the following responsibilities concerning oversight of the audit function:

- registration of auditors;
- enforcing auditor independence;
- assessing whether auditors meet the registration requirements concerning practical experience, education and competency standards;
- post-registration supervision;
- receiving auditors' annual statements concerning the nature and complexity of audit work undertaken and compliance with any conditions of registration; and
- referring matters with respect to the conduct of auditors to the Companies Auditors and Liquidators Disciplinary Board.

Companies Auditors and Liquidators Disciplinary Board

The Companies Auditors and Liquidators Disciplinary Board (CALDB) is established under the *Australian Securities and Investments Commission Act 2001*. ASIC may make applications to the board to determine whether auditors or liquidators have breached the *Corporations Act*. The board has the power to impose penalties if it determines that a registered auditor or liquidator has failed to carry out duties properly or is not a fit and proper person to be registered. Penalties may include suspension or cancellation of the auditor's or liquidator's registration, the imposition of restrictions on conduct or an admonition.

Matters that may be referred to the CALDB include:

- failure on the part of an auditor to lodge an annual statement;
- failure to comply with the conditions of registration;
- failure to maintain sufficient practical experience, as indicated by a failure to perform any audit work during a continuous period of 5 years;

- failure to perform adequately and properly the duties of an auditor; and
- ceasing to be a fit and proper person to remain registered.

Section 324 of the *Corporations Act* provides that a person cannot be appointed as an auditor of a company unless they are a registered company auditor. Further, s. 1280 requires that a person applying for registration must:

- be ordinarily resident in Australia;
- be a member of an approved body;
- be a graduate of a prescribed university or other prescribed institution in Australia and have passed a course of study in accountancy and commercial law acceptable to ASIC;
- have sufficient auditing experience; and
- be a fit and proper person.

ASIC may approve auditing competency standards on application of any professional body or accounting firm under s. 1280A(1) of the *Corporations Act 2001*. In November 2004, ASIC approved its first auditing competency standard prepared by CPA Australia and The Institute of Chartered Accountants in Australia. The competency standard enables auditors to fill out a logbook to demonstrate on-the-job experience in their audit competency skills and have this certified by a current Registered Company Auditor. This replaces the previous requirement to meet a specified number of hours.

To meet the educational requirements, auditors will be required to have completed a specialist course in auditing, which will be prescribed under the Corporations Regulations and administered by the professional accounting bodies.

REGULATION OF SUBJECT MATTER OF AUDITS

In financial report audits, the financial information which is the subject matter of the audit has been determined within the financial reporting framework. In Australia, the key public sector agencies that directly influence the financial reporting framework are the Financial Reporting Council (FRC), which was discussed under learning objective 2, the Australian Accounting Standards Board (AASB), the Urgent Issues Group (UIG) and the Financial Reporting Panel (FRP).

Australian Accounting Standards Board

The Australian Accounting Standards Board (AASB) was reconstituted during 2000 as a body corporate with perpetual succession established under s. 226 of the *Australian Securities and Investments Commission Act 2001*. Under s. 227(1) of that Act, its functions are to:

- develop a conceptual framework, not having the force of an accounting standard, for the purpose of evaluating proposed accounting standards and international standards;
- make accounting standards under s. 334 of the *Corporations Act* for the purposes of the national scheme laws;
- formulate accounting standards for other purposes;
- participate in and contribute to the development of a single set of accounting standards for worldwide use; and
- advance and promote the facilitation of the development of accounting standards that require the provision of financial information that is relevant and reliable, facilitates comparability and is readily understandable, to allow users to make and evaluate decisions about allocating scarce resources and assess the performance and financial position of entities.

Consistent with the functions and powers conferred on it by s. 227 of the *Australian Securities and Investments Commission Act 2001*, the reconstituted AASB seeks to meet its objectives by developing and issuing Accounting Standards and Statements of Accounting Concepts.

In July 2002, the FRC released a statement supporting the adoption of international accounting standards in Australia by 1 January 2005. This decision was supported by both the Joint Committee on Public Accounts and Audit (JCPAA) and CLERP 9.

Urgent issues group

The Urgent Issues Group (UIG) was established in late 1994 to review on a timely basis accounting issues that are likely to receive divergent or unacceptable treatment in the absence of authoritative guidance, with a view to reaching a consensus as to the appropriate accounting treatment in the context of existing Accounting Standards and Statements of Accounting Concepts. The operations of the UIG are carried out in accordance with its Charter. Meetings of the UIG are held in public and issue proposals, issue summaries, minutes of meetings and draft Abstracts are available to constituents. The UIG comprises 16 members drawn from a wide range of constituent groups in the public and private sectors, and two observers.

A consensus of the UIG requires that 11 or more members vote in favour of, and no more than three members vote against, the proposed treatment for the issue in question. The AASB has a reserve power of veto over UIG consensus views. A UIG consensus view is published in an Abstract.

Under the restructured arrangements put in place during 2000, the UIG has been re-established as a committee of the AASB and revisions to its Charter and the appointment of new members have been undertaken in consultation with the FRC.

Financial Reporting Panel

The Financial Reporting Panel (FRP) was established under CLERP 9 through amendments to the *Australian Securities and Investments Commission Act 2001*. The purpose of the FRP is to provide a forum for review of disputes between ASIC and any entity that has lodged its financial report with ASIC. Either ASIC or the entity, with ASIC's approval, may refer the dispute to the FRP. The FRP considers whether in its opinion a financial report complies with the relevant reporting requirements. A report by the FRP on whether or not a financial report complies with the financial reporting requirements of the *Corporations Act 2001* is not binding. However, a Court may have regard to it in determining whether the financial report complies with the *Corporations Act*.

Disciplinary procedures

One of the most important elements in the regulation of any profession is the means of disciplining practice by imposing penalties for substandard performance. Independent auditors are subject to the **disciplinary provisions** of their professional accounting organisation, the ICAA or CPA Australia, as well as any disciplinary action that may be taken by the regulators. For example, the disciplinary provisions of the Supplemental Royal Charter of the ICAA provide for sanctions against any member who:

- violates any fundamental rule of the ICAA;
- is found to be guilty of any felony, misdemeanour or fraud;
- is held by the ICAA to have been guilty of any act, omission or default discreditable to a member of the ICAA or which involves a failure to observe a proper standard of professional care, skill or competence;
- wilfully commits any breach of the provisions of the Supplemental Charter or by-laws;

Source: Buffini, F. (2002), 'Who checks the checkers?' *Australian Financial Review*, 14 May, p. 69.

SNIPPET

2.1

AUDITING IN THE NEWS

Who checks the checkers?

No auditor has been expelled from the accounting profession for breaching auditing standards in the past 10 years, despite billions of dollars in claims against auditors of failed companies and numerous investigations by the Australian Securities and Investments Commission.

In the same period, ASIC, through the Companies Auditors and Liquidators Disciplinary Board, has brought more than 260 disciplinary cases against auditors for breaching the *Corporations Law*. That includes 25 cases of serious misconduct in which individual auditors were barred or suspended from practice for flouting standards, according to annual reports reviewed by *The Australian Financial Review*.

Furthermore, in many cases where CALDB imposed sanctions, the accounting professional bodies responsible for enforcing ethics rules and Australian auditing standards decided that no penalty was necessary.

As the auditing profession is facing calls for more independent oversight after recent high-profile company collapses, senior accountants say more should be done to enforce standards.

... any action by CALDB or professional bodies is routinely deferred until after court cases or ASIC investigations are resolved.

ICAA by-laws prohibit any action until after all appeals are exhausted, so the profession may not get to a case for years.

To be fair, the accounting profession has recently admitted it could do more. The ICAA has engaged an independent expert to review its disciplinary processes to ensure they are in the public interest.

ICAA's chief executive, Stephen Harrison, also says that the profession takes a broader view than CALDB, so it is not surprising if different conclusions are reached.

'If a person has been reprimanded for an audit by the CALDB, we have to look at what impact that should have on them as a chartered accountant. We are judging them on their service as a chartered accountant in general, but I hope that does not mean we are less determined to stamp out bad behaviour.

'For anyone to lose their company auditor registration has a devastating effect on their career. In many cases, it doesn't matter if they are still a chartered accountant. Reaching a different conclusion does not undermine the disciplinary process of the CALDB.'

In some cases, so much time has elapsed that the circumstances surrounding the original conviction have completely changed. For instance, when the ICAA heard the case of Louis Carter, the former KPMG auditor convicted of fraud in relation to Rothwells, Carter had served jail time, retired and resigned his practising certificate.

- is adjudged bankrupt or insolvent;
- is declared of unsound mind or becomes incapable of managing their own affairs; or
- fails to pay any subscription or other sum payable to the ICAA under the Supplemental Charter or by-laws, within three months of it becoming due.

The sanctions include:

- exclusion from membership;
- suspension from membership;
- disbarment from practice;
- being fined a sum not exceeding $100 000;

- being reprimanded; or
- having to pay all or any of the costs and expenses incurred by the ICAA in the investigation.

Exhibit 2.1 shows examples of the nature of allegations made against members of the ICAA and the sanctions imposed upon them.

	2000–2001	1999–2000
Cases heard		
All states	45	39
Nature of allegations		
Failure to observe proper standard of professional care and skill	10	12
Criminal conviction	2	1
Guilty of statutory offence bringing discredit on member, the ICAA or profession	4	1
Adverse finding in relation to professional or business conduct by court, statutory, regulatory or professional body	13	10
Breach of Charter, by-laws or regulations (including ethical and professional standards)	8	19
Failure to comply with direction by the ICAA (including failure to respond to correspondence)	10	14
Member's insolvency	6	4
Conduct bringing discredit on member, the ICAA or profession	9	8
Sanctions imposed		
Exclusion	3	3
Suspension	11	2
Cancellation of and/or declared ineligible to hold a Certificate of Practice	2	—
Fine	4	4
Severe reprimand	6	9
Reprimand	18	18
Practice review	5	12
Attending specified Continuing Professional Education activities	—	2
Seek advice as to conduct of practice	—	3
No sanctions imposed	4	3

EXHIBIT 2.1

Disciplinary cases against members of the ICAA

Source: The ICAA annual report, 30 June 2001.

CPA Australia has similar disciplinary provisions. Complaints against members are investigated and where there appears to be a case to answer, these are referred to the Disciplinary Committee or One Person Tribunal for a formal hearing. All penalties and findings carry the right to appeal.

As discussed earlier in this chapter, company auditors are subject indirectly to government discipline through the requirement that they be registered as a company auditor under the *Corporations Act*. Under legislation, many audit engagements can be accepted by auditors only if they are registered company auditors. Any private disciplinary action may affect that registration. In addition, the further development of 'co-regulation' may see greater government scrutiny of the disciplinary provisions of the professional accounting organisations.

However, Buffini (2002) (see Auditing in the News 2.1) points out that in the last ten years the ICAA has issued few serious sanctions against auditors, and that the most serious sanction, expulsion from membership, hasn't been used against an auditor for breaching standards.

Internationally, IFAC has set up a Compliance Committee to work with member bodies and outside agencies to encourage greater compliance with the standards, ethical code and pronouncements of IFAC and the IASB. One of the primary responsibilities of the Compliance Committee is to compare and contrast the investigative and disciplinary processes of member bodies and their adequacy and efficacy, to report on these and make recommendations to the Board and Council of IFAC.

Quick review

1. The primary government agencies that regulate auditing are the AUASB, the FRC, ASIC and the CALDB. However, auditors are also affected by the accounting regulatory framework, which includes the AASB and the UIG.
2. The auditing profession is also partly self-regulatory through the ICAA and CPA Australia, together with their involvement internationally with IFAC.
3. The ICAA and CPA Australia are able to enforce their requirements on members through their disciplinary procedures.

INTERNATIONALISATION OF AUDITING

The internationalisation of auditing commenced when multinational enterprises began preparing audited consolidated financial reports. Auditors of the parent company then needed to set rules to ensure the quality of the audits of the subsidiaries, because they had to give an opinion on the consolidated financial reports. In addition, management of the parent company wanted to be sure that the local audits were sufficient to add credibility to the information provided by the local management of the overseas subsidiaries. As a result, it soon became apparent that there was a need for the international auditing profession to harmonise the working methods of auditors in different countries and to develop international standards on auditing and assurance services, as discussed in Chapter 1.

As well as audits for multinational consolidation purposes, statutory audits of local subsidiaries are also necessary. The audit process required for statutory audit purposes is combined with that required for consolidation purposes. However, as the harmonisation of accounting has not yet reached the stage where one set of accounting principles can also be used to prepare statutory financial reports in all the countries where multinational companies operate, national accounting standards prevail.

For investors operating in international capital markets, the audit report and the quality of the audit work are important to the credibility of the financial report and other financial information used in making investment and credit decisions.

To achieve uniform quality levels of audits and to promote effective international communication through audit reports, the International Organisation of Securities Commissions (IOSCO) has supported the harmonisation of auditing standards internationally and in October 1992 IOSCO recommended that its members endorse International Standards on Auditing (ISAs) issued by IFAC. Such endorsement means that stock exchanges accept audits of financial reports and other documents from other countries that are audited in accordance with the ISAs. A number of stock exchanges have already implemented this endorsement in their listing and filing requirements. IOSCO is currently undertaking a review of all ISAs with a view to providing formal IOSCO endorsement, as part of the harmonisation and convergence process.

To a large extent, the internationalisation of auditing has taken place within international audit firms. During recent years many local audit firms around the world have merged into international groups. Some international audit firms have a centralised approach, where many of the technical and product development decisions are made centrally and there is a strong emphasis on uniform working methods and policies in the various countries where the firms have their offices. Other international audit firms follow a decentralised approach where there is a tendency for each local firm to have its own methods, for instance for reporting. However, for international work a unified approach is applied.

The international approach to auditing adopted by the international firms generally takes the form of a uniform prescriptive audit process in which different steps are narrowly defined.

According to Klaassen and Buisman (1998), the international process of auditing serves two main purposes:

1　Multinational clients are assured that, all over the world, members of the audit firm will be able to communicate easily on the outcomes of the audit and will apply one set of quality criteria to ensure the quality of the audit.

2　Uniformity of the main elements of the audit process on an international scale enables the firms to increase the efficiency and effectiveness of the audit process worldwide.

However, IFAC and the auditing profession alone cannot make all the changes necessary to achieve harmonisation of international auditing. Other stakeholders also need to be involved.

International Federation of Accountants

As indicated in Chapter 1, the ICAA and CPA Australia are members of IFAC and through the AUASB use the work of the IAASB in developing Australian auditing standards.

IFAC was formed in 1977 to harmonise the accountancy profession and auditing and assurance standards. Its mission is set out in its Constitution as: 'the development and enhancement of an accountancy profession able to provide services of consistently high quality in the public interest'.

Membership is open to accountancy bodies recognised by law or general consensus within their countries as substantial national organisations of good standing within the accountancy profession. During 2005 IFAC had 163 member bodies in 119 countries, representing more than 2 million accountants in public and private practice, industry and commerce, education and government service.

Through co-operation with member bodies, regional organisations of accountancy bodies, and other worldwide organisations, IFAC initiates, co-ordinates and guides efforts to develop international technical, ethics and education pronouncements for the accountancy profession in both the public and private sectors.

Globalisation has made it necessary to harmonise standards and guidance used by the professional accountants all around the world. IFAC sets international standards on auditing and ethical standards for global use and strongly supports the work of the International Accounting Standards Board (IASB) in the setting and promotion of international accounting standards.

The initial governance of IFAC rests with the IFAC Council, which comprises one representative from each member body. The Council meets once a year and is responsible for deciding constitutional questions and electing the Board. The Board is comprised of individuals from 15 countries. These members are elected for 3 year terms and are responsible for setting policy and overseeing IFAC operations, the implementation of programs and the work of the IFAC technical committees and task forces. The Board meets three times per year.

A Public Oversight Board (POB) will oversee the public interest activities and related governance and infrastructure of IFAC, particularly in the areas of audit standard setting, ethics, membership obligations, and quality assurance. The POB will be independent of the profession.

The standing technical committees of IFAC are:

- International Auditing and Assurance Standards Board (IAASB);
- Compliance Committee;
- Education Committee;
- Ethics Committee;
- Financial and Management Accounting Committee;
- Public Sector Committee; and
- Transnational Auditors Committee.

International Auditing and Assurance Standards Board

The International Auditing and Assurance Standards Board (IAASB) works to improve the uniformity of auditing practices and related services throughout the world by issuing pronouncements on a variety of audit and assurance functions and by promoting their acceptance worldwide. International Standards on Auditing (ISAs) contain basic principles and essential procedures together with related guidance in the form of explanatory and other material. The basic principles and essential procedures are to be interpreted in the context of the explanatory and other material that provide guidance in their application. International Auditing Practice Statements (IAPSs) provide practical assistance to auditors in implementing the standards or on related subjects and promote good practice. IAASB pronouncements are developed following a due process that includes input from the general public, IFAC member bodies and their members, and a Consultative Advisory Group that represents regulators, preparers and users of financial reports.

Membership of IAASB includes five representatives from international audit firms, proposed by the Transnational Auditors Committee of the Forum of Firms (FOF), seven from IFAC member bodies with a majority of those from countries with strong national standard-setters, and three non-auditor representatives. The Nominating Committee of IFAC is responsible for ensuring a proper balance of countries and firms, always considering the 'best person' for the role. IAASB meetings are open to the public to help promote its transparency.

Transnational Auditors Committee

The Transnational Auditors Committee (TAC) is the executive committee of the FOF. The FOF was set up in January 2001 and is an organisation of international firms that perform audits of financial reports that are or may be used across national borders. Member firms are expected, among other things, to conform to the FOF Quality Standards and subject themselves to global peer review, which will be discussed later in this chapter, to assess compliance with the standards. TAC and its subcommittees are responsible for overseeing the global peer review process and supervising the development of additional guidance regarding transnational audit work that may not currently be available through IFAC. Commitment to the obligations of membership in the Forum contributes to raising the standards of the international practice of auditing.

International Forum on Accountancy Development

The International Forum on Accountancy Development (IFAD) was created in 1999 by IFAC and the World Bank and consists of representatives of more than 30 international public and private organisations who have agreed to work in partnership to fulfil a common mission to improve financial reporting, accountability and transparency worldwide. This partnership also extends to public and private national organisations that are working to implement the IFAD Vision at country level.

IFAD partners include:

- international financial institutions;
- inter-governmental organisations;
- development assistance agencies;
- securities, banking and insurance regulators;
- standard-setters for the public and private sectors;
- capital providers;
- preparers of financial reports;
- government auditors;
- professional accounting and auditing bodies;
- professional education and training organisations; and
- large international accounting and auditing firms.

By operating as an international community of interests, their goal is to make a lasting impact and significantly improve financial reporting, within a framework of good corporate governance, effective regulation, and professional excellence in accounting and auditing. Each participating organisation retains its autonomy in management, programming and budgets. However, all are committed to more effective and efficient execution of their programs through better co-ordination, avoidance of duplication, and enhanced communication and co-operation under the IFAD umbrella.

The Asian and other financial crises in the latter part of the 1990s, and their impact on the global economy, demonstrated the importance of sound financial reporting, accountability and transparency for building a solid international financial system. High-quality financial information about corporate and other economic entities is a significant micro-economic complement to effective macro-economic policies that together contribute to national and global financial stability and sustainable growth. IFAD is dedicated to improving this aspect of international economic co-operation.

The IFAD Vision is to promote accountability and transparency by achieving a rational framework of reporting on the performance of economic entities, which serves the objectives of issuers and users across the world. This entails preparing all general purpose financial information following a single worldwide framework, with common measurement and fair and comprehensive disclosure, that provides users with a transparent representation of the underlying economics of transactions and is applied on a consistent basis.

To promote international convergence the Vision calls for:

- raising national accounting standards and practices using International Accounting Standards as the benchmark;
- raising national auditing standards and practices using International Standards on Auditing as the benchmark;
- improving corporate governance practices using the OECD Principles of Corporate Governance as a point of reference;

- assuring effective legal and regulatory structures, especially related to securities, banking and insurance supervision using principles developed by IOSCO, the Basel Committee on Banking Supervision and the International Association of Insurance Supervisors (IAIS), respectively; and
- strengthening the accounting and auditing profession through enhanced professional education and training, qualifications, and standards on independence and ethics using guidelines developed by UNCTAD (United Nations Conference on Trade and Development) and IFAC as points of reference.

The Vision also calls for improvement and greater convergence in governmental accounting and auditing standards and practices.

Quick review

1 The globalisation of business has resulted in a need for the internationalisation of auditing.

2 IOSCO has supported the harmonisation of auditing standards internationally and has recommended that its members endorse ISAs issued by IFAC through the IAASB.

3 IFAD is an international partnership between various financial reporting stakeholders who have agreed to work towards accountability and transparency in financial reporting, including raising auditing standards.

PROFILE OF THE AUDITING PROFESSION

If one considers the auditing profession to be an industry and individual accounting firms to be production units, a unique aspect of the auditing profession is revealed. As industries, most professions are composed of thousands of small units. Only recently have some professionals developed large and extended practices. The composition of the auditing profession has differed from other professions since its inception in Australia. The auditing profession as an industry may be regarded as having two major professional accounting bodies, CPA Australia and the ICAA; and three levels of audit firms, national or international, regional and local.

Professional organisations

The current structure of the **professional accounting organisations** in Australia is the result of the merger and amalgamation of a number of individual accounting organisations into two primary organisations—CPA Australia and the Institute of Chartered Accountants in Australia (ICAA). Membership of either of these two bodies by public accounting practitioners is voluntary. However, it is important because membership of CPA Australia, the ICAA or another prescribed body is necessary to satisfy the qualification element of the registration of auditors and liquidators. Membership provides for the setting of standards of competence in the profession and enables self-regulation.

The Institute of Chartered Accountants in Australia

The ICAA was established in 1928 by Royal Charter. It was formed through the merger of a number of fragmented state organisations dating back to 1885. The actual process of obtaining the charter extended over 20 years and was hindered by rivalry between state organisations.

The ICAA is now an Australia-wide body of accountants, drawn primarily from public practice and designated 'Chartered Accountants'. It operates under a Supplemental Royal Charter granted by the Governor-General in 2000. The objectives of the ICAA as stated in the Royal Charter are to:

- advance the theory and practice of all aspects of accounting;
- recruit, educate and train members skilled in these areas;
- preserve at all times the professional independence of accountants;
- maintain high standards of practice and professional conduct;
- prescribe disciplinary procedures and sanctions; and
- do all such things as may advance the profession of accounting whether in relation to public practice, industry, commerce, the public service or otherwise.

The ICAA is governed by a Board of Directors consisting of eleven Directors, ten being elected by members in each respective region and one by members on the overseas register. Directors and Regional Councillors will be elected for a 3 year term, with one-third of the positions on the Board and Regional Councils being up for election each year. The President and Deputy President are elected annually by the Board. The ICAA's administrative staff is headed nationally by a Chief Executive Officer.

The principal role of the Regional Councils is to provide advice to the Board on strategic policy and member issues, act as a link between the Board and members in their region, assist in public profiling and liaison with state and territory governments, and carry out such functions as may be delegated to them by the Board. Each Regional Council has either six or nine members elected by the members in that region.

At 30 June 2004, the membership of the ICAA was over 40 000. Of these, 40 per cent were in public practice, 41 per cent were in commerce and 19 per cent were retired or other.

Membership of the ICAA is now restricted to graduates from universities who have completed an appropriate degree with the required level of accounting and business-related subjects. In addition, graduates must complete the ICAA's CA program course and examinations, and have the prescribed period of practical experience with a chartered accountant.

The ICAA publishes a journal, *Charter*, containing technical articles, current events and official releases, maintains a library and a bookshop and undertakes a professional development program.

CPA Australia

The Australian Society of Accountants was incorporated as a company limited by guarantee in 1952. Like the ICAA it merged several individual accounting bodies whose aims and objectives were similar and which dated back to 1886. The consolidation of these individual bodies was completed in 1966 when the Australasian Institute of Cost Accountants became fully integrated with the Society. In 1990, it changed its name to the Australian Society of Certified Practising Accountants and in April 2000 it changed its name again to CPA Australia. Membership of CPA Australia as at 31 December 2004 was more than 100 000.

The mission and objectives of CPA Australia are expressed in its 2001 annual report. The mission is 'to position CPAs to be leaders in financial, accounting and business advice'. To realise this, a new 5 year strategy, CPA 2004, was adopted.

The thrust of the strategy acknowledges the impact of the current technological and information-based revolution and the need for a fast, tailored service. CPA 2004 identifies seven strategic goals: within 5 years CPA Australia will further strengthen its position as the best in the region; globally networked; recognised experts; the preferred designation; a provider of career-long learning; leading edge in service delivery; and an organisation with great staff.

CPA Australia is governed by a National Council comprising representatives of Divisional (state) Councils. Members elect the Divisional Councils. The National Council meets four times a year, with interim decisions being made by an executive committee. The elected members are supported by permanent administrative staff at the national and state levels, headed by an executive director.

The membership is more broadly based than the ICAA's, with 42 per cent in commerce, 10 per cent in government, 20 per cent in public practice, 2 per cent in academia or teaching and 26 per cent retired or other.

Like the ICAA, prospective members must have completed a recognised degree from a university. This secures provisional membership. Advancement to full membership requires completion of the CPA program and appropriate employment experience.

CPA Australia publishes a journal, *Australian CPA*, to keep members informed of latest developments in accounting theory and practice, to provide a means of communication between members and officers of CPA Australia and to provide a forum for members to express ideas and opinions. CPA Australia has 7 Centres of Excellence, including one for financial reporting and governance, which includes audit and assurance. They produce a number of documents for member information and use. CPA Australia maintains a library and undertakes a professional development program.

Integration

Several attempts have been made to integrate the two accounting bodies into one Australian accounting organisation. The most recent attempt was in December 1998. On each occasion the integration proposals did not obtain the required majority vote by members of the ICAA.

Audit firms

National and international firms

As entities have grown in size and the scope of their activities, so have some audit firms. In order to provide services to large, complex entities it is necessary to have large audit firms with the professional workforce to perform audits of their sizeable and diversified activities.

During the last decade there have been a number of mergers among public accounting firms. The largest international audit firms, previously known as the 'Big Eight', became the 'Big Five' and with the collapse of Arthur Andersen and its merger with Ernst & Young, the 'Big Four'. Similar mergers have occurred among smaller firms and between small and large firms. These mergers have been brought about by increased competition for clients, expected efficiencies resulting from economies of scale and a need to service the international activities of clients.

International firms have offices in most major cities throughout the world and dominate the practice of public accountancy. They have the resources necessary to service the multinational entities. In the US, over 90 per cent of the 'Fortune 500' companies and thousands of smaller entities are served by the 'Big Four'. In the UK, the 'Big Four' account for two-thirds of the audit market. In Australia the annual revenues of the 'Big Four' averaged $656 million for the year ended June 2003. While the figures for each firm shown in Exhibit 2.2 are not strictly comparable, they do indicate the relative size of the 'Big Four' compared to the remaining top 100 firms.

National firms have offices in the major cities in Australia and service mainly medium-sized and small clients. Many national firms have some association with similar-sized firms in other countries to handle the international needs of their clients.

Regional and local firms

While an increasing number of firms are national in scope, there are numerous regional and local firms. The size of these firms varies according to the type of services required in their area and the

	Rank	Revenue 2002–03 ($ million)	Partners	Total (ex-partners) personnel
PricewaterhouseCoopers	1	940	360	4291
Ernst & Young	2	632	256	3468
KPMG Australia	3	540	311	3612
Deloitte	4	514	242	2170
Average for Big Four		656	292	3385
Average for top 100		41.48	28	267

EXHIBIT 2.2

The top 100 audit firms in Australia

Source: Business Review Weekly, 22 July 2004, p. 69.

size of their clients. Generally, they serve small businesses and individuals in a restricted geographical area in the city or country. These firms range in size from individual practitioners with no professional staff to partnerships with five or more partners and 15 to 20 professional staff. However, some of the larger firms have established suburban and/or regional offices, thereby increasing the competition at this level.

Other services

Audit firms differ greatly in size and scope, but most offer similar basic services to clients. While the practices of many large chartered accounting firms involve a large volume of auditing and assurance services, there are other services which are an important part of current practice:

- **Tax services:** tax planning and advice, preparation of tax returns and representation of clients before government agencies.
- **Management services:** providing objective advice and consultation on various management problems, such as design and installation of information and control systems, budgeting, cost control, profit planning, capital budgeting and staff recruitment.
- **Internal audit:** providing internal audit services.
- **Accounting services:** providing special investigations and analyses, such as investigations pursuant to the purchase or sale of a business, performing bookkeeping services and preparing unaudited financial reports.
- **Insolvency services:** receivership, liquidation and voluntary administration.

Accountants are experts in the broad field of accounting and have consequently been called on to provide many services related to the measurement and communication of economic data.

In order that services be provided for all types and sizes of entities, it is necessary to have an auditing 'industry' composed of units of varying sizes that offers a range of services. While the auditing profession is different from any other profession, its structure has resulted from the unique aspects of the audit function and the complex organisations that demand it and other services.

Concerns about independence have been expressed as to whether the professional audit firms can provide both assurance and management consulting activities. The argument is that, for a range of management consulting activities, it would be hard for the firm to also provide independent assurance if they have consulted on the subject matter of the assurance. The impetus for separation of the management consulting divisions from the other divisions began in the USA when the Securities and Exchange Commission started to question whether the one professional services firm should be providing all these services to their clients. This will be discussed further in Chapter 3.

Currently, each of the Big Four audit firms has approached the issue in a different way:

1 KPMG's consulting activities are contained in the entity KPMG Consulting Australia. In the USA, KPMG Consulting has been floated on the NASDAQ exchange. KPMG Consulting Australia has not floated and currently remains part of KPMG.
2 Ernst & Young has sold its management consulting arm to Cap Gemini of France.
3 PricewaterhouseCoopers has attempted to sell its consulting business, but to date has been unsuccessful.
4 Deloitte Touche Tohmatsu's management consulting division still remains a part of its core business.

INTERNAL STRUCTURE OF AN AUDIT FIRM

Although the audit profession includes a large number of individual practitioners, most auditing and assurance services are provided by chartered accounting firms that include several professional staff members. These firms have many common features. Among them are the partnership form of organisation, internal organisation of professional staff positions and duties, fee determination, staff recruitment and remuneration, and quality control practices.

Partnership form

In spite of the size to which some audit firms have grown, they have generally practised as partnerships. Prior to CLERP 9, the functions of company auditor could not lawfully be performed by a company. Thus the liability of members was previously unlimited. The implications of this are discussed further in Chapter 4. Article 20(v) of the Supplemental Royal Charter of the ICAA states that a member must not without prior written consent of the Council be a director, shareholder or employee of an incorporated company which, in the opinion of the Council, provides or purports to provide in Australia (except as ancillary to some other business) any services ordinarily provided by a member in practice. However, the ethical rulings of the ICAA allow, subject to the consent of the National Council, members to perform certain public accounting functions through the medium of an incorporated company or trust. The specific requirements of the ICAA for establishing these companies are documented in Regulation R8, 'The Use of Incorporated Companies and Trusts'. Paragraph 1103 of R8 indicates that members may be directors of, shareholders in and employees of the following types of companies:

- **nominee companies:** act as agent, trustee or nominee, other than in respect of the conduct of an accounting practice;

- **service companies:** provide non-professional staff, premises, equipment or other facilities used by a member in the performance of any functions as a public accountant;
- **administration companies:** provide professional and non-professional staff, premises, equipment or other facilities used by a member in the performance of any functions as a public accountant; and
- **practice companies:** carry out any one or more of the functions of a public accountant which a company is permitted by law to perform.

Specific consent of the Council is not required in relation to nominee or service companies provided that the company does not use the designation 'chartered accountants' and its name does not indicate that the company provides specialised public accountancy services. Consent will only be given in the other cases where certain conditions are met. As a result of the CLERP 9 amendments, this will now include authorised audit companies.

Similar requirements for members of CPA Australia are contained in By-Law 90.

Authorised audit company

As a result of the CLERP 9 amendments to the *Corporations Act*, auditors can now apply to be an **authorised audit company** under s. 1299A However, to be eligible to be an authorised audit company, s. 1229B requires that each director of the audit company must be a registered company auditor, each share must be held and beneficially owned by an individual or their legal representative, the majority of the voting power must be in the hands of registered company auditors, and the company must have adequate professional indemnity insurance and must not be externally administered.

Positions, duties and industry specialisations

While the internal structure of firms differs, there are five basic audit staff positions in large audit firms—partners, managers, supervisors, seniors and assistants. The duties of the occupants of these positions, as well as their relative numbers, are depicted in Figure 2.1 (overleaf).

The large firms have also organised themselves into multidisciplined teams to service specific industries. Members of the teams have extensive knowledge and experience of that industry and promote their **industry specialisations** to attract potential clients. For example, in 2002 PricewaterhouseCoopers had five key business units or industry specialisations:

1. Consumer and Industrial Products
2. Energy and Mining
3. Financial Services
4. Services Industry
5. Technology, Info-Comm and Entertainment.

These industry teams combine skills and experience in assurance, business advice, taxation, management consulting and outsourcing to service their clients.

Staff recruitment and remuneration

The services provided by an audit firm can be no better than the quality of the personnel rendering the services. Most firms recruit graduates from universities to fill the position of assistant. The demand for skilled public accounting services far exceeds the supply, and advancement to higher

FIGURE 2.1 Positions and duties in an audit firm

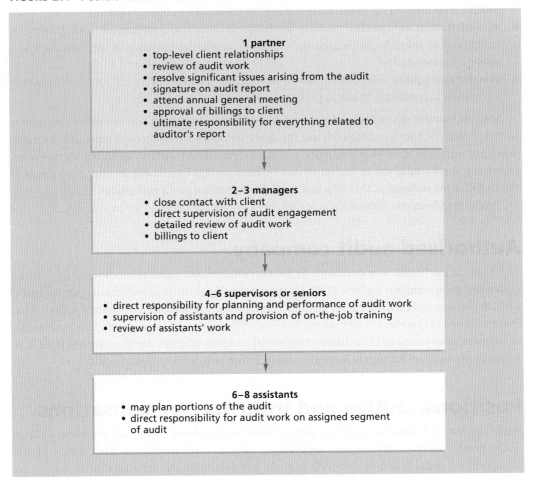

levels is rapid for competent juniors. The beginning auditor's education is expanded throughout their professional career.

Juniors and seniors are paid a salary and may receive payment for overtime. Managers are normally paid a salary package. Partners, as owners of the firm, share in the net profit earned. The capital investment required upon admission to partnership may be quite substantial in an established firm. Consequently, new partners are often allowed to accumulate their contribution by reinvesting a portion of their share of the firm's net profit.

QUALITY CONTROL

Since audits are conducted by teams and a firm must co-ordinate many separate audit engagements, methods have evolved to control the quality of audits throughout a firm. **Quality control procedures** are essential to ensure that auditors meet their responsibilities to clients, other users and regulators.

The revised AUS 206 (ISA 220) issued in June 2004 provides guidance on specific responsibilities of firm personnel regarding quality control procedures for audits of historical financial information, including financial report audits (see Example 2.1 overleaf).

AUS 206.02 (ISA 220.02) requires the audit engagement team to implement quality control procedures that are applicable to the individual engagement. Further, AUS 206.06 (ISA 220.06) requires the engagement partner to take responsibility for overall quality control on each audit engagement.

While the nature and extent of quality control procedures will vary according to circumstances, the following general policies and procedures should be adopted by auditing firms to provide reasonable assurance regarding the quality of audit work generally:

- **Ethics:** persons at all levels in the firm should adhere to the principles of integrity, objectivity, independence, confidentiality and professional behaviour.
- **Employment:** the firm should employ personnel with the necessary technical skills and professional competence to enable them to meet their responsibilities.
- **Assignment of personnel:** audit work should be assigned to personnel who have the required technical training and proficiency.
- **Supervision:** direction, supervision and review ensure that delegation policies are adhered to; that assistants understand audit directions; that the work is being carried out in accordance with the specified program; and that any questions raised have been appropriately dealt with.
- **Guidance and assistance:** consultation should occur within or outside the audit firm with those people who have the appropriate expertise.
- **Client evaluation:** prospective and ongoing clients should be evaluated in making a decision to accept or retain a client. Independence and ability to serve the client should be considered.
- **Monitoring:** the adequacy and effectiveness of quality control procedures need to be continually monitored.
- For audits of listed entities, the engagement partner should ensure that an engagement quality control reviewer has been appointed and that they discuss significant matters arising on the audit, and the conclusions reached in formulating the auditor's report, with the quality control reviewer.

In addition, there are several Miscellaneous Professional Statements which make some specific pronouncements concerning quality control standards. Of particular importance are:

- APS 1.1 'Conformity with Auditing Standards', which establishes an auditor's responsibilities in relation to compliance with Australian auditing standards;
- APS 4 'Statement of Quality Control Standard', which includes ten quality control elements that apply to a practice as a whole; and
- APS 5 'Quality Control Policies and Procedures', which provides guidance for the establishment of policies and procedures for the elements of quality control contained in APS 4.

During 2004 an exposure draft was issued of a revision to APS 5 'Quality Control for Accounting Firms'. The proposed statement will replace existing APS 4 and 5.

The proposed APS 5 restructures the approach to quality control, bringing it into line with a new international quality control standard for assurance practices, the International Standard on Quality Control 1 (ISQC 1) released in February 2004. The proposed amendments affect the quality control standard for all audit firms in Australia. Two significant proposed amendments are:

1 All firms must document their quality control policies and procedures and communicate them to the firm's personnel.
2 Assurance practices must implement more comprehensive policies and procedures for the assurance part of the practice.

In addition, APS 6 'Statement of Taxation Standards', APS 7 'Statement of Insolvency Standards', APS 8 'Management Consulting Services Standard' and APS 9 'Statement on Compilation of Financial Reports' contain the basic principles concerning the professional responsibilities imposed when an audit firm renders those services.

The firm's general quality control policies and procedures need to be explained clearly to staff members. The nature and extent of such procedures depend on such variables as the size and nature of the practice, its geographic dispersion, its organisation and relevant cost–benefit factors.

EXAMPLE 2.1 Quality controls

Facts
Tom Jones is the audit partner in a small, three-partner firm. A potential new client comes into the office and says he needs an audit done immediately and will pay the required fee upfront. Tom immediately accepts the audit.

As all the audit staff are already occupied on existing clients, Tom obtains a new graduate from the accounting division to do the work. As the graduate has no previous audit experience, Tom gives him a 2 hour briefing on basic auditing and sends him out to the new client with a copy of the audit program for another small client to use as the basis of his work. The graduate is instructed to bring the working papers back to Tom when he is finished.

Required
Indicate what quality control guidelines outlined in AUS 206 (ISA 220) have been breached.

Solution
The following quality control guidelines appear to have been breached:
1. **Assignment of Personnel to Engagements**
   The accounting graduate does not have adequate experience or training to perform an audit.
2. **Supervision**
   There does not appear to be any supervision of the graduate's work, as he has been left to complete the audit by himself.
3. **Guidance and Assistance**
   The only guidance given to the graduate was during the initial 2 hours of briefing and the provision of an audit program that may not be appropriate and will need to be tailored for the new client.
4. **Client Evaluation**
   No evaluation of this client appears to have been made before the acceptance of the engagement.

Internal review and periodical rotation of auditors

Audit firms should have in-house procedures designed to ensure that office policies are adhered to with regard to control over the quality of work and auditor independence. Under the process of **internal review**, auditors may have their engagements periodically reviewed by another auditor from within the same firm or office.

This practice of internal review may be supplemented by **periodical rotation of auditors** on engagements with other auditors from the firm. Rotating partners and staff on audit engagements is designed to bring fresh views to the audits and aid professional scepticism and promote independence. This is discussed further in Chapter 3.

Peer reviews

In addition to quality control at the firm level, there are two further developments that have gained professional support. The first development is the concept of **peer review**, which is growing in favour and which has its origins in the USA. There, public accounting firms which undertake the audits of large public companies are subject to independent periodic reviews of the quality of their audit procedures by other firms of public accountants. The purpose of a peer review is to determine and report whether the accounting firm being reviewed has developed adequate policies and procedures to cover the basic elements of quality control and is putting them into practice.

Around the world, benefits obtained from the review process include improvements in the quality controls and working methods of practitioners, an enhancement of the image of the profession and improvements in the professional development programs of accountants.

The ICAA and CPA Australia have commenced quality review programs. The reviewers consider the policies and procedures established by the member to ensure compliance with professional standards—in other words, the system of quality control. Some of the key features of the quality review programs are:

- reviews are undertaken by trained public practitioners;
- quality reviews are based on the requirements of APS 4 and APS 5 as they affect practice as a whole, as well as other applicable specific standards;
- the review takes into account any system of internal reviews conducted by the member;
- client files are reviewed (provided client permission has been obtained first due to the requirement of the Code of Professional Conduct for client confidentiality) to enable the reviewer to form an opinion on the effectiveness of, and compliance with, the quality control system used by the member;
- the reviewer does not 'second guess' the technical conclusions made by the member, but rather looks at the processes the member uses to reach and document technical conclusions;
- assessments made by the reviewers are discussed with the reviewed member;
- review findings are subject to strict confidentiality rules; and
- where the review results in unsatisfactory finding, the member is required to remedy the problems and undergo a follow-up review.

ASIC has recommended that regional offices avoid duplication between ASIC's Auditor's Surveillance Program and the Quality Review Programs conducted by the ICAA and CPA Australia. Where ASIC selects for review an auditor who has been subject to a quality review by the ICAA or CPA Australia, the member should advise ASIC of the earlier review. ASIC will discontinue its review upon confirmation of a review by the ICAA or CPA Australia unless there are significant reasons for ASIC to proceed. Examples of such reasons are: serious complaint against the auditor, existing internal ASIC intelligence or the auditor being on an ASIC watchlist.

ASIC has also implemented an Accounts Examination Program which involves the review of financial reports of Australian public companies to ensure compliance with mandatory accounting standards. The ICAA has a similar program.

Internationally, a principal element of the plan to strengthen IFAC has been to bring transnational auditing firms into association with IFAC through the creation of the FOF and its executive arm, the TAC. The goal is the creation of a global quality standard for transnational audits, which will include periodic quality assurance reviews. In addition, IFAC has established a new Compliance Committee to work with national professional bodies, is working to improve its standard-setting procedures, and is establishing a Public Oversight Board (POB) to oversee its public interest activities.

Professional development

Another important quality control requirement is the concept of **continuing professional development**. For example, paragraph 1002 of R7, 'Regulations Relating to Continuing Professional Education', requires all members of the ICAA to undertake a minimum of 20 hours continuing professional education annually and 120 hours in each 3 year period, a maximum of 30 hours of which may be technical reading. Similarly, PS 3, 'Continuing Professional Development', also requires members of CPA Australia to undertake a minimum of 120 hours of structured professional development over each 3 year period.

These activities could include, for example, attendance at courses conducted by professional organisations, discussion groups or formal studies at a university. The requirement for accountants to maintain and update their knowledge will expand as the environment within which they operate continues to change. As discussed earlier, professional development is an essential attribute of a profession.

Quick review

1. Most audit firms previously practised as partnerships, but are now allowed to be authorised audit companies.
2. Audit firms are also allowed to have companies to act as trustees or nominees, or to provide services to the practice, such as premises, equipment and staff.
3. Quality control procedures such as internal reviews, peer reviews and continuing professional development are essential to ensure auditors meet their responsibilities.

AUDITING IN THE PUBLIC SECTOR

Within the structure of the Australian auditing profession, and in addition to the private sector audit and assurance function, there is an area of audit and assurance activity concerned with the **public sector**. The public sector in Australia involves three levels of government—Commonwealth, state and territorial, and local—and includes ministries and departments, statutory authorities, local government councils and other public bodies, some of which may operate as business undertakings and companies.

Parliament and the executive government provide authority for the acquisition and use of public resources, set the overall policy direction and are responsible for overseeing management's administration of those resources. Most parliaments have standing committees to monitor the public accounts and to oversee accountability in administration of these resources. In addition, some public bodies established by Parliament operate independently and are not subject to ministerial control, while other public bodies manage financial resources of the public or operate as agents.

In Australia, many public sector entities are required to prepare financial reports and other reports to comply with government legislation, regulations, ordinances and directives of central agencies, and to demonstrate their financial accountability to the executive, Parliament and, ultimately, the community. The financial reports of such entities are prepared primarily for Parliament as the custodians of community interest, but may be used by management, government departments, central agencies or other interested parties. For local governments, however, the relationship is more complex: accountability flows through local councils, on the one hand, to departments of state, the executive and the legislature and, on the other, to ratepayers or other resource providers.

As in the private sector, one of the responsibilities of management is the preparation and presentation of reports on the use of the resources under its control. This relationship establishes a role for audit in the public sector because of the separation of those responsible for the management and reporting on the use of resources and those interested in receiving financial information from those managers.

Under the Westminster system the responsibility for external audits of financial reports prepared by executive governments rests with the Commonwealth and state Auditors-General, appointed under statute, who report directly to the Parliament. In the main, major statutory authorities are audited by Auditors-General. Other public bodies may be audited by a private sector auditor as a delegate of the Auditor-General, who retains audit responsibility for, and management of, the relevant entity.

A further involvement by private sector auditors in matters related to the public sector is in the performance of audits with respect to the provision of government grants and subsidies to private sector entities, both charitable and non-charitable. Auditors-General may also be empowered to audit such activities of their own initiative or, where the legislation provides, at the request of a minister of the Crown.

In the environment within which public sector entities operate, external audit provides information to assist the governing body in fulfilling its responsibilities for overseeing the administration of the financial affairs and resources of public sector entities. Audit mandates may prescribe a broader range of audit reporting than in many private sector audit engagements. It can be specified as one, or a combination, of a financial report audit, compliance audit and/or performance audit. Some public sector audit mandates authorise auditors to bring to the attention of the legislature any matters that in the auditor's judgment should be reported, for example cases of waste, mismanagement and fraud. This gives auditors wide discretionary powers in the interpretation and application of their mandates. Auditing in the public sector is further discussed in Chapter 16.

Quick review

1. The public sector comprises three levels of government—Commonwealth, state and local.
2. Public sector entities are accountable to Parliament and, ultimately, the community.
3. Responsibility for external audits of financial reports prepared by executive government rests with the Commonwealth and state Auditors-General.
4. Private sector auditors may also be involved in some public sector audits.
5. The audit mandate in the public sector may be a financial report audit, compliance audit and/or performance audit.

Summary

The auditing profession in Australia partly regulates itself through the efforts of CPA Australia and the ICAA. However, it also operates in a regulatory environment dominated by the *Corporations Act*, the AUASB and ASIC. It is also affected by the globalisation of business and the need for the internationalisation of auditing. IFAC and IFAD have major roles to play in the internationalisation process.

An important aspect of self-regulation is the accounting bodies' ability to enforce their requirements on members through disciplinary procedures and their quality control procedures.

The structure of the auditing profession consists of both the private sector, which is dominated by the 'Big Four' international auditing firms, and the public sector, which is dominated by the Auditors-General.

Key terms

References

Adams, K. and Fonti, A. (1995) 'Watching the watchdogs: The Auditor Surveillance Program', in *Perspectives on Contemporary Auditing*, 94–108.

Buffini, F. (2002) 'Who checks the checkers?' *Australian Financial Review*, 14 May, 69.

Burrows, G. (1996) *The Foundation*, AARF, Melbourne.

Corporate Law Economic Reform Program (2002) 'Corporate Disclosure: Strengthening the financial reporting framework', *Proposals for Reform: Paper No. 9 (CLERP 9)*, September, Canberra.

CPA Australia (2001) *Annual Report*, Melbourne.

Downes, J. (1995) 'The Quality Review Program', in *Perspectives on Contemporary Auditing*, 12–16.

Greenwood, E. (1957) 'Attributes of a Profession', *Social Work*, July, 44–55.

Klaassen, J. and Buisman, J. (1998) 'International auditing', in C. Nobes and R. Parker (eds), *Comparative International Accounting*, Prentice-Hall, UK, Ch. 19.

Institute of Chartered Accountants in Australia (2001) *Annual Report*, Sydney.

International Federation of Accountants (2001) *Enhancing Financial Reporting: New Initiatives of IFAC and the Profession*, New York.

Joint Committee of Public Accounts and Audit (2002) 'Review of Independent Auditing by Registered Company Auditors', *Report 391*, August, Canberra.

(MaxMARK) Assignments

MAXIMISE YOUR MARKS! There are approximately 30 interactive questions on the structure of the profession available online at www.mhhe.com/au/gay3e

Additional assignments for this chapter are contained in Appendix A of this book, page 763.

REVIEW QUESTIONS

2.1 Indicate whether each of the following statements is true or false.

(a) The only direct power the ICAA and CPA Australia have over their members is termination of their membership.

(b) The groups that issue registrations to practise as a company auditor in Australia are the ICAA and CPA Australia.

(c) The ICAA and CPA Australia are both members of IFAC.

(d) The role of the AUASB is to ensure that companies comply with the *Corporations Act*.

(e) The ethical principles of the accounting bodies must be adhered to and members of the ICAA and CPA Australia may be disciplined for violations of such principles.

(f) All members of the ICAA and CPA Australia engaged in auditing practice must have a peer review periodically.

(g) Peer reviews are performed within a firm, one member of the firm reviewing another in the same firm.

2.2 For each of the following questions, select the *best* response.

(a) Auditing is often referred to as a profession. A profession is a field of practice with all of the following characteristics except:

    A a specialised body of technical knowledge

    B high fees

        C public sanction

        D admission standards and self-regulation

(b) Which of the following would not be grounds for disciplinary action against an auditor?

    A Criminal conviction of the auditor

    B Insolvency of the auditor

    C Resignation by the auditor from an audit due to a dispute with the client over application of accounting standards

    D Failure by the auditor to observe a proper standard of professional care and skill

(c) An audit firm is reasonably assured of meeting its responsibility to provide services that conform with professional standards by:

    A adhering to auditing standards

    B having an appropriate system of quality control

    C joining professional organisations such as the ICAA or CPA Australia

    D maintaining an attitude of independence in its engagements

(d) Which of the following are elements of an audit firm's quality control that should be considered in establishing its quality control policies and procedures?

	Personnel management	Monitoring	Engagement performance
A	Yes	Yes	Yes
B	Yes	Yes	No
C	No	Yes	Yes
D	Yes	No	Yes

(e) Within the context of quality control, the primary purpose of continuing professional development and training activities is to enable an audit firm to provide personnel within the firm with:

    A technical training that assures proficiency as an auditor

    B knowledge required to perform a peer review

    C knowledge required to fulfil assigned responsibilities and to progress within the firm

    D professional education to ensure audit work is performed with due professional care

(f) A firm of independent auditors must establish and follow explicit quality control policies and procedures because these standards:

    A give reasonable assurance that the firm as a whole will conform to the auditing standards

    B are necessary to meet increasing requirements of auditors' liability insurers

    C are required by ASIC for auditors of all entities

    D include formal filing of records of such policies and procedures

Professional status of the auditor

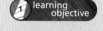

2.3 Do you believe that the auditing profession satisfies the essential attributes of a profession?

Regulation of auditing

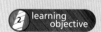

2.4 What is the role of ASIC and how does this impact on auditors?

2.5 What are the advantages and disadvantages of co-regulation of the accounting profession, as compared to either government regulation or self-regulation?

2.6 **(a)** What activities may result in a member being disciplined by the ICAA or CPA Australia?

    (b) What sanctions may be imposed by the ICAA or CPA Australia?

    (c) Do you believe that these sanctions are effective?

Regulation of the subject matter of audits

2.7 What impact do the FRC, AASB and UIG have on auditing?

Internationalisation of auditing

2.8 What is IFAC and what does it do?

2.9 What impact has globalisation had on the structure of the audit profession?

2.10 What is IOSCO and what impact has it had on the international harmonisation of auditing standards?

Profile of the auditing profession

2.11 What are the ICAA and CPA Australia and what do they do?

2.12 What types of firms make up the auditing profession?

2.13 What services other than auditing and assurance do audit firms provide?

Internal structure of an audit firm

2.14 What are the basic audit positions in an accounting firm?

Quality control

2.15 What are the elements of audit quality control for an accounting firm? Provide one policy or procedure that could be used to fulfil each element.

2.16 Explain the ICAA and CPA Australia quality review programs.

2.17 Explain why continuing professional development is important.

Auditing in the public sector

2.18 The structure of the auditing profession in Australia recognises a 'private' and 'public' sector. Discuss the two environments. Is the auditor's role different in each sector?

2.19 Explain how the concept of accountability impacts on the public sector audit environment.

DISCUSSION PROBLEMS AND CASE STUDIES

Professional status of auditor

2.20 **Basic** At present there is no legal definition of the term 'accountant'. As a result, any person or firm can describe themselves as an accountant regardless of their educational qualifications or experience. Do you believe this is appropriate? Provide reasons for your decision.

Regulation of auditing

2.21 **Basic** Both CPA Australia and the ICAA publish brief details of their disciplinary proceedings in their journals. Given the detrimental impact publication may have on the reputation of the individuals concerned, why do you think the professional bodies publish this information? Your discussion should include reasons for and against publication.

2.22 **Moderate** Auditing standards are currently developed by the Auditing and Assurance Standards Board of AARF, with most being adaptations of International Standards on Auditing. Final approval rests with the national councils of CPA Australia and the ICAA. Do you believe these groups are the appropriate groups for development and approval of auditing standards? Your answer should consider the extent to which each of the parties represents the views of financial report preparers and users.

2.23 **Complex**

'Auditors are supposed to protect investors, but they face scant discipline
from their profession when things go wrong.' (Buffini, 2002, p. 69)

Required

Comment on the above quotation. Indicate whether you believe that the profession's disciplinary procedures are effective and how you believe they could be improved.

Internationalisation of auditing

2.24 Complex

> *It is recognised, however, that IFAC and the professional alone cannot effect all the necessary changes required. Efforts to implement high quality professional standards can be impeded, or even baulked, by governments, legal requirements and cultures that are incompatible with, or even prohibit, the application of such standards. Local standards can be inadequate and result in potentially misleading financial information. In such an environment, it will be difficult, or impossible, for firms to achieve their goal of enhanced and consistent financial reporting and auditing.*

(IFAC (2001) *Enhancing Financial Reporting and Auditing: New Initiatives of IFAC and the Profession*, p. 3)

Required

Based on the above quotation, explain whether you think IFAC can achieve any progress towards the implementation of international auditing and reporting standards.

Profile of the auditing profession

2.25 Basic Beth Jones & Co. has grown from a small firm that originally included only Ms Jones and one junior accountant to a regional firm with seven partners and 21 professional staff members, occupying four offices in two states. At a recent meeting all partners were in agreement that the growth of the firm has presented some problems, but that the financial and professional rewards far outweigh those problems. The partners are unanimous in their desire to see their firm grow to the size of one of the larger national firms.

(a) Is the goal of the firm realistic?

(b) What steps can the firm take to advance toward this goal?

2.26 Complex

> *On the one hand, chartered accountants could become obsolete, their roles overtaken by technology, creeping globalisation and competitors from other disciplines ... Looking on the bright side ... accountants as we know them, could become transformed. While computers grind out the traditional work, accountants turn into business advisers—the strategic thinkers and knowledge managers of the future.*

(Blondell, J. (1999) 'Towards the Summit', *Charter*, June, p. 20)

The above quotation is taken from a report on the ICAA National Summit, held in 1999 to review the strategic direction of the ICAA subsequent to the failed merger attempt with CPA Australia, which has also undergone a similar process, with one of the most visible outcomes being a revision to the entry program.

Required

Which of the opposing views suggested by Blondell in the above quotation is likely to become reality? Provide reasons for your decision. Specifically, you should consider factors that will have a significant influence on the structure of the auditing profession over the next 10 years.

Internal structure of an audit firm

2.27 Moderate The majority of large audits are undertaken by audit teams. Each team usually comprises a partner, manager, senior and/or supervisor and a number of assistants.

(a) Why do you think this type of structure is used in auditing? Your answer should consider the advantages and disadvantages of using a team.

(b) Given the advent of computers, paperless audits and expert systems to audit practices, do you think this structure will continue in the future? Provide reasons for your decision.

Quality control

2.28 **Basic** Mary Pappas is an individual practitioner. In addition to herself, she maintains a professional staff of five auditors, and her firm is a member of a national group of accounting firms. Pappas is considering her alternatives to staff training. She is trying to decide whether to send her professional staff members to the programs offered by the professional accounting organisations, to send them to training programs offered by the national group or to attempt to offer in-house training herself. What factors should she consider in making this decision?

2.29 **Moderate** Discuss the objectives of quality control procedures in an accounting practice. Do you consider that these objectives differ between a small suburban or country practice and a large international practice? In what ways would you expect the quality control procedures adopted by a small suburban or country practice to differ from those of a large international practice? Give specific examples.

Source: This question was adapted from the Professional Year Programme of The Institute of Chartered Accountants in Australia—1994 Ethics (3) Module.

2.30 **Moderate** You are the senior partner in a medium-sized firm in the city. Two of your senior managers have decided to set up their own practice to service small audit clients in the suburbs. You wish both of them well in their new endeavour and have been speaking to them about their future plans. They already have some clients signed up (you are not concerned that they will poach your current clients) and they anticipate that the next 12 months will be exceedingly busy as they attempt to build their new practice. You raised the issue of formal policies and procedures for the practice but they have decided to put those on hold until their client base is more established. They argued it is more important to have clients before policies, otherwise there may be no one to apply them to.

Required

How would you advise the two aspiring professionals with regard to the quality control of the new practice? (*Note:* Specific policies and procedures are not required.)

Source: This question was adapted from the Professional Year Programme of The Institute of Chartered Accountants in Australia—1998 Advanced Audit.

CHAPTER 3

ETHICS, INDEPENDENCE AND CORPORATE GOVERNANCE

LEARNING OBJECTIVES

After studying this chapter you should be able to:

1 explain the nature and importance of professional ethics;

2 describe the three main categories of ethical theory;

3 outline the essence of the accounting bodies' code of ethics and describe the individual rules;

4 apply sound ethical decision-making techniques;

5 explain the concept of corporate governance;

6 explain the auditor's role as a whistleblower;

7 explain the importance of audit independence;

8 describe recent developments in auditor independence;

9 explain the major threats to auditor independence;

10 outline suggestions for improving auditor independence; and

11 explain fee determination and obtaining clients.

Chapteroutline

As discussed in Chapters 1 and 2, the auditor is a member of a time-honoured profession, and the status of the profession and the responsibilities that accompany this status affect the audit and assurance services function and the structure of the profession. The independent auditor is subject to regulations imposed by the profession and by society in general. The imposition of ethical standards on members by a profession is one aspect of this regulation.

This chapter outlines the nature and importance of ethics, and the responsibilities imposed on auditors by the profession through the code of professional ethics.

One fundamental ethical requirement for an auditor is independence. This chapter explains the concept of independence and how it is supported by legislation and the ethical rules. There have been a number of developments in auditor independence as a result of the recent corporate crises both in Australia and overseas, and these are outlined in the chapter. The major threats to auditor independence are explained and suggestions for improving auditor independence are discussed. Also discussed is the concept of corporate governance and the part played by audit committees in this function.

Relevantguidance

Australian		International	
CPC	Joint Code of Professional Conduct (Revised 2004)	IFAC	Code of Ethics for Professional Accountants
APS	Miscellaneous professional statements	—	(Revised 2004)
AUS 210	The Auditor's Responsibility to Consider Fraud and Error in an Audit of a Financial Report (Revised 2004)	ISA 240	The Auditor's Responsibility to Consider Fraud and Error in an Audit of Financial Statements (Revised 2004)
Audit and Assurance Alert No. 6: Auditors' Responsibilities in Relation to Reporting Contraventions of the *Corporations Law*		—	
Audit and Assurance Alert No. 11: Communicating with Entities in Relation to Auditor Independence		—	
Audit and Assurance Alert No. 13: The Implications of the US *Sarbanes-Oxley Act 2002* for Auditors and their Clients		—	

 learning objective 1

THE NATURE AND IMPORTANCE OF PROFESSIONAL ETHICS

Ethics is concerned with the requirements for the general wellbeing, prosperity, health and happiness of people, and with things that promote or prevent them.

Paragraph 3(f) of the Royal Charter of The Institute of Chartered Accountants in Australia (ICAA) states that one of the ICAA's principal objects is to do all things that may advance the profession of accountancy, whether in relation to the practices of public accountants or in relation to industry, commerce, education or the public service. Similarly, paragraph 3(1) of the Constitution of CPA Australia establishes one of its objects as protecting, supporting and advancing the status, character and interests of the accountancy profession generally. Community wellbeing includes the flourishing of business and industry. The objectives of the accounting bodies support an environment of personal and corporate integrity that promotes community wellbeing. This necessarily involves defining what is right and what is wrong.

The ICAA's Royal Charter and CPA Australia's Constitution give them the power to prescribe high standards of practice and professional conduct for their members, and to prescribe disciplinary procedures and sanctions.

In practice, ethics requires both knowledge of moral principles and skill in applying them to problems and decisions. In addition, sound ethical practice presupposes the development in individuals and society of the virtues or good habits that ensure the moral health of the community.

Establishing codes of ethics and disciplinary rules does not necessarily create an ethical culture in an organisation or business, nor does it ensure the moral integrity of its individual members. It is necessary to promote not only competence in ethics but also the personal qualities of responsibility and moral conscientiousness. Codes of ethics, rules, regulations and laws do not have meaning or moral legitimacy in themselves. Rather, their authority and legitimacy depend on whether they are perceived as helping to promote people's wellbeing. If rules are considered to be unjust, discriminatory or oppressive, people are likely to disregard them or demand they be changed.

A.1 of the Joint Code of Professional Conduct indicates that the ethical rules of the accounting bodies do not cover all aspects of ethical conduct and that members are expected to comply with the spirit as well as the letter of the rules. They recognise that ethics is principally an attitude of mind rather than compliance with written rules of conduct.

Society is governed by rules, regulations and laws. From an auditing viewpoint, this tends to place the focus on 'black letter' law. However, it needs to be remembered that it is always possible to question whether a rule is a good rule. Value judgments need to be made about rules as to whether they are fair, respect the rights of all parties and protect those parties who are unable to defend their rights. Sound statutory law must be based on and consistent with common law and natural justice if it is to promote human wellbeing.

ETHICAL THEORY

There are three main categories of ethical theory that will be discussed in this chapter: teleological ethics, deontological ethics and virtue ethics.

Teleological ethics

Teleological theories are also called consequential theories because they deal with the consequences or outcomes of actions. Generally, if the benefits of a proposed action outweigh the costs, then the decision is considered morally correct. The two most important teleological theories are egoism and utilitarianism.

According to Singer (1993) **egoism** states that the dominant guide to a person's behaviour should be the action that will benefit them the most. This approach has been criticised as promoting selfishness. However, it has been argued that self-interest also considers the effect on others, although only insofar as it affects the decision maker. Therefore, some proponents of ethical egoism have argued for a restricted egoism where the pursuit of self-interest should be constrained by the law and the conventions of fair play. It has been argued that this sanctions corporate self-interest, encourages competition and leads to a maximisation of utility, which is in the interests of society as a whole.

Jeremy Bentham (1784–1832) and John Stuart Mill (1806–73) are generally acknowledged as developing the theory of **utilitarianism**, which states that ethical decision making should maximise the greatest good for the greatest number. This involves an assessment of costs and benefits, not only in economic terms but also in terms of human costs and benefits. Therefore, it involves a value judgment and needs to consider all the stakeholders who are affected by a decision. The outcomes are measured in both economic terms and psychological terms, such as pain and happiness. Therefore, measuring and assigning a numeric value to the consequences of an action will often be difficult.

Deontological ethics

Deontological theories are based on duties and rights. Duties are an obligation and are actions that a person is expected to perform, while rights are an entitlement and are actions that a person expects of others. These duties and rights are set down in rules that must be followed regardless of the consequences. Hence, these theories are also sometimes called non-consequential theories. Deontological theory is particularly important to auditors in understanding their duties based on the ethical rules of the accounting bodies.

Immanuel Kant (1724–1804) placed high value on personal rights and personal moral autonomy and the basis of his ethical theory is the principle of respect for persons. This acknowledges the intrinsic value of all persons and recognises that we should not use people to achieve our own ends. Further, we should recognise a duty of care to others as expressed in the golden rule or principle of reciprocity: 'Do unto others as you would have them do unto you'.

This rule leads to the principle of beneficence, which advocates that we should do good to others rather than harm. Kant suggested the categorical imperative as a universal ethical law. This means that when considering the validity of a rule, you need to consider whether you would be happy to have this action applied in all similar circumstances regardless of the consequences. This leads to the need for the principle of justice.

John Rawls (1957) argued that the fundamental idea underlying the concept of justice is that of fairness. He argued that there are two principles which serve as the basis of justice and fairness:

> *The first principle is that each person participating in a practice, or affected by it, has an equal right to the most extensive liberty compatible with a like liberty for all; and the second is that inequalities are arbitrary unless it is reasonable to expect that they will work out for everyone's advantage and unless the offices to which they attach, or from which they may be gained, are open to all.*

Thus, Rawls argues that ethical rules should seek equality and the maximum degree of liberty that does not conflict with the liberty of others or increase inequalities or disadvantage to others.

Virtue ethics

Virtue ethics, which dates back to Aristotle, is concerned primarily with integrity, which is an essential characteristic of an auditor. Virtue ethics focuses on the person undertaking the action. Virtues are personal qualities which enable us to do what is ethically desirable and generally include traits of character such as courage, fairness, honesty, integrity, loyalty, courtesy and fidelity. Virtue ethics emphasises what makes up a morally good person, but does not necessarily make it clearer what should be done to solve an ethical conflict.

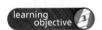

ACCOUNTING BODIES' CODE OF ETHICS

The Joint Code of Professional Conduct (CPC) sets out the main **ethical pronouncements** of the ICAA and CPA Australia and is supported by their By-Laws. AUS 202.04 (ISA 200.04) requires that auditors comply with the accounting bodies' ethical rules. The Code consists of six sections. Arguably the most important are Section B, Fundamental Principles of Professional Conduct, applicable to all members, and Section F, Professional Statements, which contain the following series of ethical statements:

- F.1 Professional Independence
- F.2 Prospectuses and Reports on Profit Forecasts
- F.3 Changes in Professional Appointments
- F.4 Referrals
- F.5 Opinion Requests
- F.6 Professional Fees
- F.7 **Incompatible Business**.

The ethical rules play an important part in an auditor's behaviour. The written code of appropriate professional conduct is designed to enable members to arrive at the proper conclusion when making ethical decisions. As a result, the ethical rules comment upon different types of relationships faced by auditors and spell out some of the auditor's responsibilities. A.2 states that compliance with the CPC is mandatory for all members, affiliates and registered graduates.

There are also 11 Miscellaneous Professional Statements, not all of which are relevant to auditors, but which are mandatory for members of both accounting bodies. In general, these statements seek to promote the fundamental principle of 'competence'. The statements consist of:

- APS 1   Conformity with Accounting Standards
- APS 1.1   Conformity with Auditing Standards
- APS 2   Engagement Letters to Clients
- APS 3   Compatibility of Australian Accounting Standards and International Accounting Standards
- APS 4   Statement of Quality Control Standard
- APS 5   Quality Control Policies and Procedures
- APS 6   Statement of Taxation Standards
- APS 7   Statement of Insolvency Standards
- APS 8   Statement of Management Consulting Services Standard
- APS 9   Statement on Compilation of Financial Reports
- APS 10   Client Money and the Maintenance and Audit of a Member's Trust Account.

The purpose of the code of ethics

A **code of ethics** is a formal and systematic statement of rules, principles, regulations or laws, developed by a community to promote its wellbeing and to exclude or punish any undermining behaviour. Therefore, a code of ethics may serve several purposes. It may:

- make explicit those values that may be implicitly required (e.g. the underlying core values or principles in CPC B, which is discussed later in this chapter);
- indicate how members should act towards one another (e.g. the responsibilities to professional colleagues exhibited through the protocol to be followed when superseding another auditor (CPC F.3), discussed in Chapter 5, and permissible forms of advertising (CPC D.5), discussed later in this chapter);
- provide an objective basis for sanctions against people who violate the rules (e.g. disciplinary action under the ICAA's Supplemental Royal Charter and CPA Australia's Constitution, discussed in Chapter 2). An individual member's behaviour can be judged, in part, by reference to the rules laid down in the CPC. An established code of ethics is one mechanism of self-regulation.

In addition, the CPCs communicate the profession's responsible attitude of accountability to the community at large.

Like many professional codes, the ethical rules of the ICAA and CPA Australia endeavour to promote standards of competence, proficiency and personal moral integrity in their members. These qualities are similar to those that Thomson et al. (1976) referred to as Aristotle's intellectual and moral virtues, discussed earlier in this chapter. Aristotle's intellectual virtues included science (knowledge), techne (practical skill and competence, intelligence, judgment, understanding, persistence and resourcefulness) and wisdom. His moral virtues included courage (loyalty and integrity), temperance (discipline, friendliness, generosity, magnanimity, communication and social skills) and justice. Thomson et al. (1976) indicated that these virtues can be depicted as an arch with intellectual values on one side and the moral virtues on the other. The keystone holding them together is the virtue of prudence or acquired practical wisdom.

However, written codes of conduct should not be viewed as the panacea for the profession's ethical problems. As mentioned previously, these codes do not by themselves make people behave 'ethically'.

The virtues of an auditor

CPC B sets out eight fundamental principles or virtues that should guide the behaviour of members of CPA Australia and the ICAA, and which underlie the remaining CPCs:

1   **The public interest** Auditors should safeguard the interests of their clients and employers provided they are not in conflict with the public interest and the duties and loyalties owed to the community, its laws and social and political institutions. This principle represents a public statement of the 'service ideal'.

2   **Integrity** Auditors should act with consistency, treating like cases in a like manner. Honesty is an integral part of this value. Integrity is supported by the fundamental ethical principle of respect for persons.

3   **Objectivity** Auditors must be fair and must not allow bias or prejudice to override their objectivity. They need to maintain an impartial attitude and not represent vested interests when auditing a financial report.

4   **Independence** Auditors should both be, and appear to be, free of any interest which might be regarded as incompatible with objectivity and integrity. Without independence, the auditor's opinion is worthless. Independence, however, can be easily compromised.

5   **Confidentiality** Auditors hold positions of trust and have access to many valuable and private pieces of information in the course of their work. They should respect the confidentiality of information obtained during the course of their work and should not disclose such information to a third party without authority or unless there is a legal or professional duty to do so. This duty to protect the interests of clients means that confidentiality reflects the fundamental ethical principle of beneficence.

6   **Technical and professional standards** Auditors should carry out their professional work in accordance with the relevant technical and professional standards. Compliance with the required standards of proficiency protects clients by ensuring that members of the accounting bodies have the level of technical expertise required to render various specialised services.

7   **Competence and due care** Auditors have a duty to maintain their level of competence and should only undertake work that they can expect to complete with professional competence and due care. Accepting work for which the auditor is incompetent could lead to damage to the client.

8   **Ethical behaviour** Auditors should display ethical behaviour and conduct themselves in a manner consistent with the good reputation of their profession and refrain from any conduct which could bring discredit to it.

Objectivity, independence and technical standards equate with Aristotle's intellectual virtues. Honesty, integrity, confidentiality and ethical behaviour equate with Aristotle's moral virtues. Professional competence equates with what Aristotle called prudence or the practical wisdom necessary to apply abstract general principles to specific situations.

Auditors are both legally and morally accountable to their clients. Therefore, competence in ethics is an important requirement of a good auditor. As discussed in Chapter 1, these fundamental principles of professional ethics are part of the draft fundamental principles underlying an audit released for discussion by the auditing standard-setters in 2005.

1. Ethics requires knowledge of moral principles and decision-making skills.
2. The ethical rules of the ICAA and CPA Australia provide important guidance to members.
3. Ethical rules cannot cover all aspects of ethical conduct.
4. Ethics is principally an attitude of mind.
5. The key ethical principles of the accounting bodies are public interest, integrity, objectivity, independence, confidentiality, technical and professional standards, competence and due care and ethical behaviour.

APPLYING ETHICS

Sound ethical practice requires responsible people with a critical understanding of sound decision making based on fundamental ethical principles. This requires:

- knowledge of the basic principles on which moral values and rules are based;
- competence in decision-making skills; and
- ability to choose appropriate policies and decision procedures in different situations.

To act ethically is to act appropriately and responsibly in different situations, providing a clear, coherent and reasoned justification for decisions and actions, based on commonly accepted values or standards.

An auditor needs to combine ethical rules with skills in making decisions and setting policies. As indicated by Leung and Cooper (1995, p. 32):

The complexity of the different ethical problems encountered by accountants requires not only a good knowledge of a set of ethical principles, but also the skills and competence to handle conflicting roles and interests relating to accountancy practice.

Ethical decision models

Because the basic steps in problem solving are the same, the various **ethical decision models** that have been developed to assist in sound ethical decision making have many common features. The features of three commonly used models are discussed below. These models should not be followed slavishly but rather used as a framework for decision making.

Ethical decision making involves consideration of the three aspects of moral theory discussed earlier in this chapter:

1. **Fundamental principles and rules or rights and duties** Deontological ethics focuses on the principles and causes, intentions and motives to be considered prior to action. Fundamental ethical principles include the principle of beneficence (duty to do good to or protect others), the principle of justice (duty to treat all people fairly) and the principle of respect for persons (duty to respect the rights of other people). In an ethical decision model this involves specifying the facts, including the stakeholders involved, and identifying the ethical principles and the rights and duties of all parties.

2. **Means, methods and the role of the agent** Virtue ethics focuses on the moral character of the agent. The integrity and competence of the agent (auditor) are vital to their capacity to act ethically. In an ethical decision model this involves identifying all the options available, considering possible outcomes and knowing the right means to achieve your goals based on intellectual and moral virtues.

3. **Ends or consequences** Teleological ethics focuses on the consequences of actions and their outcomes relative to goals. If the ultimate end of human life is happiness, this approach can

translate into the utilitarian rule of always acting so that your action brings the greatest amount of happiness to the greatest number of people. However, this has to be balanced by considering the rights of minorities. An assessment of the costs and benefits for all stakeholders is required. In an ethical decision model this involves the assessment of results in terms of achieving both short-term and long-term goals.

American Accounting Association model

The American Accounting Association (AAA) published a case book, *Ethics in the Accounting Curriculum: Cases and Readings*, in May 1990. Each case is analysed using a seven-step model, shown in Exhibit 3.1.

EXHIBIT

3.1

American
Accounting
Association
model

1. **Determine the facts**
   What? Who? Where? When? How?
   What do we know or need to know that will help define the problem?

2. **Define the ethical issue**
   List the significant stakeholders.
   Define the ethical issues.

3. **Identify the major principles, rules and values**
   (For example, integrity, quality, respect for persons, profit)

4. **Specify the alternatives**
   List the major alternative courses of action, including those that represent some form of compromise or point between simply doing or not doing something.

5. **Compare values and alternatives—see if clear decision**
   Determine if there is one principle or value, or combination, which is so compelling that the proper alternative is clear.

6. **Assess the consequences**
   Identify the short and long, positive and negative consequences for the major alternatives. The common short-run focus on gain or loss needs to be measured against the long-run considerations. This step will often reveal an unanticipated result of major importance.

7. **Make your decision**
   Balance the consequences against your primary principles or values and select the alternative that best fits.

Source: Courtesy of the American Accounting Association.

Mary Guy model

In 1990 Mary Guy listed ten core values as a checklist for reference when making ethical decisions. The values are: caring, honesty, accountability, promise keeping, pursuit of excellence, loyalty, fairness, integrity, respect for others and responsible citizenship.

Guy also suggested five rules which integrate these values and assist in ethical decision making:

- *Rule 1:* Consider the wellbeing of others, including non-participants. This rule emphasises caring and respect for others.
- *Rule 2:* Act as a member of the community, not as an isolated individual. This emphasises loyalty, integrity, respect for others and responsible citizenship.
- *Rule 3:* Obey the law, but do not depend solely on it. This emphasises integrity and responsible citizenship.
- *Rule 4:* Ask, 'What sort of person would do such a thing?' This emphasises all the values by calling each into question.
- *Rule 5:* Respect the customs of others, but not at the expense of your own ethics. This emphasises accountability, fairness, integrity and respect for others.

Laura Nash model

In 1981 Laura Nash put forward a model for ethical decision making, consisting of a checklist of questions (Exhibit 3.2). Each question is accompanied by an example or further question to challenge the decision maker's assumptions about the correctness of the decision being taken.

EXHIBIT 3.2

Laura Nash model

1. **Have you defined the problem accurately?**
   Gain precise facts and many of them.
2. **How would you define the problem if you stood on the other side of the fence?**
   Consider how others perceive it (alternative viewpoints).
3. **How did this situation occur in the first place?**
   Consider the history, problem or symptoms.
4. **To whom and what do you give your loyalties as a person and as a member of the corporation?**
   Consider private duty versus corporate policy or norms.
5. **What is your intention in making this decision?**
   Can you take pride in your action?
6. **How does this intention compare with the likely results?**
   Are the results harmful even with good intentions?
7. **Whom could your decision or action injure?**
   A good idea resulting in a bad result? Wanted A, got B.
8. **Can you engage the affected parties in a discussion of the problem before you make a decision?**
   For example, can you talk to workers before you close the plant?
9. **Are you confident that your position will be as valid over a long period of time as it seems now?**
   For example, what are the long-term consequences of your action?
10. **Could you disclose without qualm your decision or action to your boss/CEO, Board of Directors, your family or society as a whole?**
    For example, would you feel comfortable with this reported on TV?
11. **What is the symbolic potential of your action if understood? If misunderstood?**
    For example, will you be perceived to be sincere in the eyes of other people?
12. **Under what condition would you allow exceptions to your stand?**
    For example, breaking the speed limit driving a heart attack victim to hospital.

Source: Courtesy of the American Accounting Association.

Quick review

1 An auditor needs to combine knowledge of ethical rules with skills in ethical decision making.

2 There are several ethical decision models that can assist in ethical decision making by providing a framework for decision making.

3 Three ethical decision models that are commonly used are the American Accounting Association model, the Laura Nash model and the Mary Guy model.

CORPORATE GOVERNANCE

There has recently been a greater emphasis placed on proper corporate governance or management and the roles to be played by directors, accountants and auditors. **Corporate governance** is the system by which companies are directed and managed and covers the conduct of the board of directors and the relationship between the board, management and shareholders. Therefore, corporate governance is concerned primarily with management and stewardship issues such as:

- adoption of a corporate strategy;
- succession planning, including appointing, monitoring and training senior management;
- maintaining the integrity of internal control and the management information system; and
- setting a remuneration policy that is normally based on performance.

It is important to distinguish the roles played by different groups in corporate governance. The board of directors is responsible to shareholders for the formulation of overall business policies and strategies in the running of the company. Its duties generally include such matters as:

- taking responsibility for protecting the rights of shareholders;
- setting officers' salaries;
- recommending dividends;
- authorising long-term borrowing, additional share issues and major capital projects;
- reviewing internal control; and
- identifying and monitoring business risks.

The board of directors is normally composed of corporate executives, such as the chief executive officer (CEO), known as executive directors, and representatives of large shareholders. In addition, it normally includes a number of outside or part-time directors, known as non-executive directors, to ensure a more objective evaluation of management performance. The chair should in principle be separate from the CEO and be preferably a non-executive director.

Ultimately, corporate governance tries to ensure that an entity operates at the highest level of efficiency and effectiveness. Skills in ethical decision making are an important factor in good corporate governance.

Organisation for Economic Cooperation and Development

In April 1998, the OECD developed a set of corporate governance standards and guidelines. The five key areas covered by the OECD *Principles of Corporate Governance* are:

- the protection of shareholder's rights;
- the equitable treatment of shareholders;
- the role of stakeholders in corporate governance;
- disclosure and transparency; and
- the responsibilities of the board.

The OECD recommendations require that 'the corporate governance framework should ensure the strategic guidance of the company, effective monitoring of management by the board, and the board's accountability to the company and shareholders' (OECD, 1999, p. 9).

United Kingdom

In the UK, the Committee on the Financial Aspects of Corporate Governance issued its report in 1992. Known as the Cadbury Report, it advocated a code of best practice designed to achieve high standards of corporate behaviour. The code has been endorsed by the London Stock Exchange, which requires companies to publish a statement of compliance with the code in their annual report.

The Cadbury Report stresses the importance of the annual audit, describing it as one of the cornerstones of corporate governance. The report argues that audits are a reassurance to all those who have a financial interest in the company, quite apart from their value to the board of directors.

The Combined Code: Principles of Good Governance and Code of Best Practice was issued by the London Stock Exchange Committee on Corporate Governance in June 1998 and has been appended to the London Stock Exchange Listing Rules. It builds on the Cadbury and Hampel Reports, while making certain changes.

Subsequently, the Institute of Chartered Accountants in England and Wales issued a report, 'Internal Control: Guidance for Directors on the Combined Code' (Turnbull Report) (1999) to more clearly define the accountability of company directors and management.

Some key requirements of the Combined Code are:

■ Principle D.2 states that 'The board should maintain a sound system of internal control to safeguard shareholders' investment and the company's assets'.

■ Provision D.2.1 states that 'The directors should, at least annually, conduct a review of the effectiveness of the group's system of internal control and should report to shareholders that they have done so. The review should cover all controls, including financial, operational and compliance controls, and risk management'.

■ Provision D.2.2 states that 'Companies which do not have an internal audit function should from time to time review the need for one'.

■ Paragraph 12.43A of the London Stock Exchange Listing Rules states that 'in the case of a company incorporated in the United Kingdom, the following additional items must be included in its annual report and accounts:

• a narrative statement of how it has applied the principles set out in Section 1 of the Combined Code, providing explanation which enables its shareholders to evaluate how the principles have been applied; [and]

• a statement as to whether or not it has complied throughout the accounting period with the Code provisions set out in Section 1 of the Combined Code. A company that has not complied with the Code provisions, or complied with only some of the Code provisions or (in the case of provisions whose requirements are of a continuing nature) complied for only part of an accounting period, must specify the Code provisions with which it has not complied, and (where relevant) for what part of the period such non-compliance continued, and give reasons for any non-compliance'.

The Preamble to the Code, which is appended to the Listing Rules, makes it clear that there is no prescribed form or content for the statement setting out how the various principles in the Code have been applied. The intention is that companies should have a free hand to explain their governance policies in the light of the principles, including any special circumstances that have led to them adopting a particular approach.

The guidance is based on the adoption by a company's board of a risk-based approach to establishing a sound system of internal control and to reviewing its effectiveness. This should be incorporated by the company within its normal management and governance processes. It should not be treated as a separate exercise undertaken to meet regulatory requirements.

Effective monitoring on a continuous basis is an essential component of a sound system of internal control. However, the Turnbull Report points out that the board cannot rely solely on the embedded monitoring processes within the company to discharge its responsibilities. It should regularly receive and review reports on internal control. In addition, the board should undertake an annual assessment for the purposes of making its public statement on internal control to ensure that it has considered all significant aspects of internal control for the company for the year under review and up to the date of approval of the annual report and accounts.

The Turnbull Report imposes the following requirements on the board:

a) When reviewing reports during the year:
- identify the significant risks and assess how they have been identified, evaluated and managed;
- assess the effectiveness of the related system of internal control in managing the significant risks;
- consider whether necessary actions are being taken promptly to remedy any significant failings or weaknesses; and
- consider whether the findings indicate that more extensive monitoring of the system of internal control is required.

b) When reviewing the board's annual assessment:
- consider the changes since the last annual assessment in the nature and extent of significant risks, and evaluate the company's ability to respond to changes in its business and the external environment;
- consider the scope and quality of management's ongoing monitoring of risks and of the system of internal control, and, where applicable, the work of its internal audit function and other providers of assurance;
- consider the extent and frequency of the communication of the results of the monitoring to the board (or board committee(s));
- consider the incidence of significant control failings or weaknesses that have been identified during the period and the extent to which they have resulted in unforeseen outcomes or contingencies that have had, could have had, or may in the future have, a material impact on the company's financial performance or condition; and
- evaluate the effectiveness of the company's public reporting processes.

Australia

In Australia, a working group chaired by Henry Bosch (the Bosch Committee) put forward a guide, *Corporate Practices and Conduct*, in 1991 with revised versions in 1993 and 1995. This guide was the first Australian attempt to set out corporate governance standards of best practice. The guide considered the function of the public company board, its structure, the role of company accountants and auditors, the conduct of directors, the role of shareholders and codes of ethics.

While corporate governance is primarily the responsibility of the directors and senior officers of a company or other organisation, accountants have an important part to play. Accountants may hold directorships or management positions or may be involved in auditing. Therefore, they are concerned with ensuring that internal control policies and procedures are in place and working.

Auditors must inform management and directors about internal control problems. This position is supported by the *AWA* case, which is discussed in Chapter 4. However, auditors cannot force these groups to act upon their recommendations, which can create ethical dilemmas for the auditor. The problems that face an auditor in issuing a report on a client's internal control will be discussed in Chapter 14.

Lynn (1996), a former chairman of the AUASB, has argued that corporate governance is concerned with maintaining an appropriate accountability system. Management is accountable to the board of directors for its actions and the board is accountable to the owners for their supervision of management. The auditor attests to the credibility of the financial information given to the owners, to enable them to assess the quality of the stewardship being exercised on their behalf.

In Australia, several different groups have advocated the importance of corporate governance.

Business community

The Business Council of Australia, in its booklet, *Corporate Practices and Conduct*, stated that codes of conduct have a role to play in the area of corporate governance. The booklet had two objectives:

1   to guide directors, officers and professional advisers as to what is acceptable conduct and practice; and
2   to spread and reinforce high standards of corporate conduct.

It recognised that accountants and auditors must maintain their professionalism at all times and strongly endorsed the ICAA and CPA Australia principles of independence. It also recommended the adoption of a company code of ethics.

The Australian Institute of Company Directors (AICD) is Australia's professional organisation for directors. It has as one of its goals to 'be the recognised advocate for corporate governance and directors' issues'. Every member of the AICD is expected to comply with the AICD's code of conduct, which states that:

1   a director must act honestly, in good faith and in the best interests of the company as a whole;
2   a director has a duty to use care and diligence in fulfilling the functions of office and exercising the powers attached to that office;
3   a director must use the powers of office for a proper purpose, in the best interests of the company as a whole;
4   a director must recognise that their primary responsibility is to the company's shareholders as a whole but should, where appropriate, have regard to the interests of all stakeholders of the company;
5   a director must not make improper use of information acquired as a director;
6   a director must not take improper advantage of the position of director;
7   a director must properly manage any conflict with the interests of the company;
8   a director has an obligation to be independent in judgment and actions and to take all reasonable steps to be satisfied as to the soundness of all decisions taken by the board of directors;
9   confidential information received by a director in the course of the exercise of directorial duties remains the property of the company from which it was obtained and it is improper to disclose it, or allow it to be disclosed, unless that disclosure has been authorised by that company or the person by whom the information is provided, or is required by law;
10 a director should not engage in conduct likely to bring discredit upon the company; and
11 a director has an obligation, at all times, to comply with the spirit, as well as the letter, of the law and with the principles of this Code.

Both the Business Council of Australia and the AICD supported the majority of the provisions of CLERP 9 and are members of the ASX Corporate Reporting Council discussed below.

Investors

The Investment and Financial Services Association Limited (IFSA) represents the retail and wholesale funds management and life insurance industries. IFSA's hundred members manage approximately $725 billion (as at March 2004) on behalf of members of superannuation funds and retail clients. IFSA members' investment in the domestic market accounts for about 25 per cent of the capitalisation of the Australian Stock Exchange (ASX).

IFSA has published IFSA Guidance Note No. 2.00 'Corporate Governance: A Guide for Investment Managers and Corporations' (commonly known as the IFSA Blue Book). This Guidance Note is published by IFSA to assist its members to pursue an active role in monitoring the corporate governance responsibilities of the companies in which they invest. These guidelines were first developed by fund managers in 1995 to address some of the corporate excesses during the 1980s and have become widely accepted by the investment and corporate community as providing best practice guidelines for corporate governance. The fifth edition was issued in October 2004 and takes account of the CLERP 9 amendments. The first four guidelines in the Guidance Note guide IFSA members in determining their approach to corporate governance, voting and other issues proposed by public companies in which they invest. The next seventeen guidelines in the Guidance Note guide public companies in relation to a range of corporate governance issues, including disclosure, board and board committee composition, non-executive directors, board and executive remuneration policy and disclosure, and adoption of a company code of ethics.

IFSA encourages corporations to disclose in their annual report whether, and the way in which, they comply with the IFSA guidelines. Where a company does not comply with a guideline, IFSA expects it to explain clearly to shareholders the circumstances of and the reasons for its departure from that guideline.

Australian Stock Exchange

The ASX convened the ASX Corporate Governance Council in August 2002. Its membership consists of 21 business and professional groups with an interest in corporate governance and disclosure and its goals are to:

- produce best practice corporate governance principles and recommendations to guide listed entities on the standards of corporate governance expected of them;
- review and, where necessary, suggest input into published guidance recommendations for corporate governance practice in Australia, having regard where relevant to international models;
- assist ASX in building understanding of best practice on the part of listed companies, including, where appropriate, formulating suggestions as to any necessary amendments to Listing Rules and guidance notes;
- recommend to regulators and government where legislative amendment may be necessary;
- provide information on corporate governance to investors and the wider community; and
- regularly review compliance with best practice.

ASX Listing Rule 4.10.3 requires a statement disclosing the extent to which an entity has followed the best practice recommendations of the ASX Corporate Governance Council. If the entity has not followed all of the recommendations, it must identify the recommendations it has not followed and give reasons for not following them. The obligation is to explain to investors why an alternative approach is adopted; this is referred to as the 'if not, why not?' obligation. If a recommendation has been followed for only part of the period, the entity must state the period during which it was followed.

The ASX Corporate Governance Council's Principles of Good Corporate Governance and Best Practice Recommendations sets out ten principles and twenty-eight recommendations for effective corporate governance, as shown in Exhibit 3.3.

Principle 1: Lay solid foundations for management and oversight

Recognise and publish the respective roles and responsibilities of board and management.

- **Recommendation 1.1:** Formalise and disclose the functions reserved to the board and those delegated to management.

Principle 2: Structure the board to add value

Have a board of an effective composition, size and commitment to adequately discharge its responsibilities and duties.

- **Recommendation 2.1:** A majority of the board should be independent directors.
- **Recommendation 2.2:** The chairperson should be an independent director.
- **Recommendation 2.3:** The roles of chairperson and chief executive officer should not be exercised by the same individual.
- **Recommendation 2.4:** The board should establish a nomination committee.
- **Recommendation 2.5:** Provide the information indicated in *Guide to reporting on Principle 2*, including providing in the corporate governance section of the annual report the skills, experience, expertise and term of office of each director; names of the directors considered to be independent directors; procedures to take independent professional advice at the expense of the company; names of members of the nomination committee and their attendance at meetings.

Principle 3: Promote ethical and responsible decision making

Actively promote ethical and responsible decision making.

- **Recommendation 3.1:** Establish a code of conduct to guide the directors, the chief executive officer, the chief financial officer and any other key executives as to:
  3.1.1 the practices necessary to maintain confidence in the company's integrity;
  3.1.2 the responsibility and accountability of individuals for reporting and investigating reports of unethical practices.
- **Recommendation 3.2:** Disclose the policy concerning trading in company securities by directors, officers and employees.
- **Recommendation 3.3:** Provide the information indicated in *Guide to reporting on Principle 3*, including disclosing in the corporate governance section of the annual report any applicable code of conduct or a summary of its main provisions.

Principle 4. Safeguard integrity in financial reporting

Have a structure to independently verify and safeguard the integrity of the company's financial reporting.

- **Recommendation 4.1:** Require the chief executive officer and the chief financial officer to state in writing to the board that the company's financial report presents a true and fair view, in all material respects, of the company's financial condition and operational results and is in accordance with relevant accounting standards.
- **Recommendation 4.2:** The board should establish an audit committee.
- **Recommendation 4.3:** Structure the audit committee so that it consists of:
  — only non-executive directors
  — a majority of independent directors
  — an independent chairperson, who is not chairperson of the board
  — at least three members
- **Recommendation 4.4:** The audit committee should have a formal charter.
- **Recommendation 4.5:** Provide the information indicated in *Guide to reporting on Principle 4*, including providing in the corporate governance section of the annual report details of the

Continued . . .

names and qualifications of those appointed to the audit committee and the number of meetings of the audit committee and the names of the attendees. In addition, the following material should be made publicly available, ideally by posting it to the company's website in a clearly marked corporate governance section:
— the audit committee charter;
— information on procedures for the selection and appointment of the external auditor, and for the rotation of external audit engagement partners.

Principle 5. Make timely and balanced disclosure

Promote timely and balanced disclosure of all material matters concerning the company.

- **Recommendation 5.1:** Establish written policies and procedures designed to ensure compliance with ASX Listing Rule disclosure requirements and to ensure accountability at a senior management level for that compliance.
- **Recommendation 5.2:** Provide the information indicated in *Guide to reporting on Principle 5*, including making publicly available, ideally by posting it to the company's website in a clearly marked corporate governance section, a summary of the policies and procedures designed to guide compliance with Listing Rule disclosure requirements.

Principle 6. Respect the rights of shareholders

Respect the rights of shareholders and facilitate the effective exercise of those rights.

- **Recommendation 6.1:** Design and disclose a communications strategy to promote effective communication with shareholders and encourage effective participation at general meetings.
- **Recommendation 6.2:** Request the external auditor to attend the annual general meeting and be available to answer shareholder questions about the conduct of the audit and the preparation and content of the auditor's report.

Principle 7. Recognise and manage risk

Establish a sound system of risk oversight and management and internal control.

- **Recommendation 7.1:** The board or appropriate board committee should establish policies on risk oversight and management.
- **Recommendation 7.2:** The chief executive officer and the chief financial officer should state to the board in writing that:
  7.2.1 the statement given in accordance with best practice recommendation 4.1 (the integrity of the financial report) is founded on a sound system of risk management and internal compliance and control which implements the policies adopted by the board;
  7.2.2 the company's risk management and internal compliance and control system is operating efficiently and effectively in all material respects.
- **Recommendation 7.3:** Provide the information indicated in *Guide to reporting on Principle 7*, including making publicly available, ideally by posting it to the company's website in a clearly marked corporate governance section, a description of the company's risk management policy and internal compliance and control system.

Principle 8. Encourage enhanced performance

Fairly review and actively encourage enhanced board and management effectiveness.

- **Recommendation 8.1:** Disclose the process for performance evaluation of the board, its committees and individual directors, and key executives.

Principle 9. Remunerate fairly and responsibly

Ensure that the level and composition of remuneration is sufficient and reasonable and that its relationship to corporate and individual performance is defined.

- **Recommendation 9.1:** Provide disclosure in relation to the company's remuneration policies to enable investors to understand (i) the costs and benefits of those policies and (ii) the link between remuneration paid to directors and key executives and corporate performance.
- **Recommendation 9.2:** The board should establish a remuneration committee.
- **Recommendation 9.3:** Clearly distinguish the structure of non-executive directors' remuneration from that of executives.
- **Recommendation 9.4:** Ensure that payment of equity-based executive remunerations made in accordance with thresholds set in plans approved by shareholders.
- **Recommendation 9.5:** Provide the information indicated in *Guide to reporting on Principle 9*, including providing the following material in the corporate governance section of the annual report:
  — the company's remuneration policies
  — the names of the members of the remuneration committee and their attendance at meetings
  — the existence and terms of any schemes for retirement benefits, other than statutory superannuation, for non-executive directors

Principle 10. Recognise the legitimate interests of stakeholders
Recognise legal and other obligations to all legitimate stakeholders.
- **Recommendation 10.1:** Establish and disclose a code of conduct to guide compliance with legal and other obligations to legitimate stakeholders.

Australian Securities and Investments Commission

ASIC is involved primarily with enforcing the provisions of the *Corporations Act* and related legislation, including that relating to corporate governance. ASIC does not involve itself in the promulgation of codes of ethics or conduct, which it believes is the responsibility of self-regulatory organisations such as the ICAA and CPA Australia. Rather, ASIC's role is one of regulatory supervision.

Accounting bodies

The CPA Australia and ICAA report on the 'expectation gap' in Australia in 1993 saw:

> a role for new statements to exhort members 'to take all reasonable steps within their power' to ensure that various reporting initiatives relevant to corporate governance are carried through into action.

This report recommends that members of the ICAA and CPA Australia take a proactive role in corporate governance. This view is reinforced by the follow-up taskforce report issued in June 1996 and the issue of a *Best Practice Guide on Audit Committees*. In addition, the ICAA report entitled 'Financial Report Auditing: Meeting Market Expectations', issued in 2003, indicates that auditors may have a role to play in providing assurance to directors that the ASX Corporate Governance Council's Principles of Good Corporate Governance and Best Practice Recommendations have been complied with. This is discussed further in Chapter 14.

Audit committees

One result of the focus on corporate governance that has affected the auditor has been the setting up of audit committees. An audit committee is a sub-committee of the board of directors or other governing body, comprising a majority of independent/non-executive members of the governing body of an entity and represents owners rather than management. Amongst other functions, it is usually assigned the oversight of the financial reporting and auditing process, and the auditor's major dealings with the governing body will be through the audit committee, although the auditor will usually meet with the full governing body at least once per year. An audit committee is therefore an important component of corporate governance.

According to Schelluch (1991), audit committees have been established primarily to:

- assist the board of directors to fulfil its legal fiduciary responsibilities;
- add to the credibility and objectivity of financial reports;
- enhance the independence and effectiveness of auditors;
- oversee the application of appropriate accounting policies and procedures and ensure appropriate disclosure;
- establish and monitor corporate policies to prohibit unethical or illegal activities;
- establish and monitor effective internal and management controls; and
- provide a communication link between management, auditors and the board.

As we have seen, Recommendation 4.2 of the ASX Corporate Governance Council's Principles of Good Corporate Governance and Best Practice Recommendations indicates that listed public companies should have an audit committee. Further, the top 500 companies must also comply with the audit committee requirements of Listing Rule 12.7, which requires that an entity that was included in the S&P/ASX All Ordinaries Index at the beginning of its financial year is to have an audit committee during that year. The composition, operation and responsibility of the audit committee must comply with the best practice recommendations of Principle 4 of the ASX Corporate Governance Council's Principles of Good Corporate Governance and Best Practice Recommendations. As a result, the proportion of Australian listed companies with audit committees has increased from less than 50 per cent in 1990 to nearly 100 per cent today. The number of audit committees in the public sector is also growing.

Baxter and Pragasam (1999) and Arkley-Smith (1999) found that while publicly listed Australian companies disclosed the existence of audit committees in the late 1990s, in general they fell well short of the recommended best practice procedures for audit committee disclosures. However, the current ASX requirements should serve to remedy this deficiency.

An effective audit committee takes an active role in overseeing the company's accounting and financial reporting. The audit committee should maintain a direct line of communication between the board of directors and the company's auditors, permitting open discussion of sensitive matters like controversial accounting issues, disagreements with management, deficiencies in the design of internal control, failures in the operation of internal control and difficulties encountered in performing the audit. The audit committee normally discusses the general scope and timing of external audit work, although it does not review the detailed audit program. The audit committee also normally involves itself in the nomination of the external auditors, reviews the reasonableness of the audit fees and considers how the provision of non-audit services affects the auditor's independence.

The audit committee serves to strengthen the auditor's independence by providing a reference point, independent of executive management, to which problems of audit scope, contentious issues and conflicts arising during the audit can be referred on a timely basis.

The external auditor, as an independent party with a detailed knowledge of the entity's financial affairs, is able to provide substantial input to the audit committee by reporting relevant matters to it. Therefore, the external auditor is a major contributor to achieving an effective audit committee. The external auditor should also assist the audit committee by informing it of any developments such as legislative changes or new accounting standards.

The second edition of *Audit Committees: Best Practice Guide* was issued by the AUASB, Australian Institute of Company Directors (AICD) and the Institute of Internal Auditors—Australia (IIA) in September 2001. The guide states that 'the audit committee can play a key role in assisting the board of directors to fulfil its corporate governance and overseeing responsibilities in relation to an entity's financial reporting, internal control, risk management systems, and the internal and external audit functions'.

Quick review

1 There is an increasing emphasis on the importance of corporate governance, with good corporate governance procedures being advocated by many different groups.

2 While directors have the primary responsibility for corporate governance, accountants and auditors have a role to play.

3 An important aspect of corporate governance is the role of the audit and the audit committee.

WHISTLEBLOWING

If the auditor concludes that unethical behaviour has occurred, they need to consider whether it is necessary to **whistleblow** on the offender and, if so, to whom to report. A typical definition in the US *Civil Service Reform Act* of 1978 defines a whistleblower as a person

> who discloses information he (or she) reasonably believes evidences a violation of any law, rule, or regulation, or mismanagement, a gross waste of public funds, an abuse of authority, or a substantial or specific danger to public health or safety.

The main characteristics of whistleblowing are:

- a disclosure of information showing objectionable misconduct, which is not otherwise known or visible;
- a reasonable belief that disclosure of this information will allow stakeholders to determine that there has been misconduct;
- the disclosure is made in good faith, without malice;
- the disclosure is made in the public interest; and
- the disclosure is not specifically prohibited by law or contrary to considerations of national security or defence (Starke, 1991, p. 210).

It may be argued that auditors have a whistleblowing role imposed upon them by s. 311 of the *Corporations Act*. The auditor's primary responsibility is to the shareholders, and the auditor has a duty to report to ASIC as soon as practicable and in any case within 28 days any significant contravention of the *Corporations Act* which they discover in the normal course of their duties.

Audit and Assurance Alert No. 6, issued in October 1999, points out that s. 311 does not require the auditor to actively look for contraventions of the *Corporations Act*. The responsibility of the auditor under s. 311 is not to detect contraventions *per se* but rather to act upon those matters that come to the auditor's attention during the course of the audit. Section 311 requires an auditor to take action where the auditor has 'reasonable grounds' to suspect a contravention of the *Corporations Act*. This requires that there must be some facts or some evidence that would lead a reasonable auditor to hold that suspicion. The auditor's reporting responsibilities are discussed further in Chapter 13.

Accountants in business who uncover wrongdoing by corrupt management also face the problem of blowing the whistle on their employer. By virtue of the CLERP 9 amendments, Part 9.4AAA of the *Corporations Act* provides protection for officers, employees or contractors of a company who report contraventions or suspected contraventions of the Corporations legislation to ASIC, the company's external auditor, a director or another authorised person. However, in accordance with s. 1317AA, this protection is provided only where:

■ the person has reasonable grounds to suspect a contravention of the Corporations legislation;
■ the disclosure is made in good faith;
■ before making the disclosure, the person provides their name to the person to whom they are disclosing the information.

In terms of s. 1317AB, a person making a disclosure under Part 9.4AAA cannot be subject to civil or criminal liability or the enforcement of contractual rights or remedies on the basis of the disclosure. Sections 1317AC and 1317AD specifically prohibit victimisation, which carries a fine of $2750 and/or imprisonment for six months, and provide whistleblowers with a right to compensation where victimisation has occurred and damage has been suffered. If the whistleblower discloses information under Part 9.4AAA to the auditor, the auditor can disclose the information or the identity of the whistleblower only to ASIC, the Australian Prudential Regulation Authority (APRA) or the Australian Federal Police without the consent of the whistleblower.

AUS 210.102 (ISA 240.102) recognises that, in the absence of any specific mandatory reporting requirement, where an entity's governing body fails to take appropriate action in regard to a fraud, an auditor may seek legal advice as to whether to report the fraud to a third party. Further discussion of the auditor's reporting of fraud is included in Chapters 4 and 13.

The decision to blow the whistle is seldom easy, and it often involves both anguish and cost to the whistleblower. Accountants who make known their opposition to unethical practices may risk their jobs, but if they do nothing they risk action from their professional body and regulatory authorities. In the case of Enron, it was vice president Sherron Watkins who blew the whistle on the lack of disclosure of related party transactions and 'off-balance-sheet' financing and expressed her fear that the company would 'implode under a series of accounting scandals'.

An auditor who is considering going public with some information needs to resolve the conflict between the principles of independence, objectivity, integrity and public interest on the one hand, and the principle of confidentiality, on the other. Legislative requirements aside, the principle of beneficence appears to be the main force driving whistleblowers. Not only should one not participate in causing harm, but one should also act to prevent harm.

Quick review

1. Auditors have a whistleblowing role imposed on them by s. 311 of the *Corporations Act*.
2. Whistleblowing requires resolution of the conflict between the principles of independence, objectivity, integrity and public interest on the one hand, and confidentiality on the other.

THE IMPORTANCE OF AUDIT INDEPENDENCE

As mentioned earlier, for an audit or other assurance service to add credibility to a financial report or other subject matter, an auditor needs to remain independent. Independence is one of the eight fundamental ethical virtues or principles named in section B of the CPC and discussed earlier in this chapter. In Australia, the requirement of independence for auditors has been reinforced through the *Corporations Act* and the ethical rules of the accounting bodies.

Legislative requirements

The *Corporations Act* contains some provisions which give formal recognition to the need for audit independence. The CLERP 9 amendments create a general duty for the auditor to be independent and avoid conflicts of interest and to provide a written declaration to directors confirming compliance with the auditor independence requirements of the *Corporations Act*. Other key provisions introduced through CLERP 9 relate to restrictions on auditors being employed by an audit client, additional specific requirements for appointment as an auditor, auditor rotation for listed companies and disclosure of non-audit services. The existing provisions relating to auditor resignation, auditor removal, right of access to records and right to reasonable fees have been maintained.

Independence declaration

Section 307C requires an auditor to give the directors a written declaration to the effect that, to the best of the auditor's knowledge, there have been no contraventions of the auditor independence requirements of the *Corporations Act* or any applicable code of professional conduct in relation to the audit or that the only contraventions have been those set out in the declaration. The directors' report must include a copy of the auditor's independence declaration in accordance with s. 298(1)(c).

Conflicts of interest

It is a breach of the general auditor independence requirements under s. 324CA for the auditor to be aware of a conflict of interest situation in relation to the audit client and not to take reasonable steps to ensure that the conflict of interest situation ceases to exist as soon as possible. If, seven days after becoming aware of it, the conflict of interest situation still exists the auditor is required to notify ASIC. If the auditor is not aware of the conflict of interest, but would have been aware if they had in place a quality control system reasonably capable of making the auditor aware, the auditor will still be in contravention of s. 324CA.

Section 324CD indicates that a conflict of interest situation exists if:

- the auditor or a professional member of the audit team is not capable of exercising objective and impartial judgment in relation to the conduct of the audit; or
- a reasonable person, with full knowledge of all relevant facts and circumstances, would conclude that the auditor or a professional member of the audit team is not capable of exercising impartial judgment in relation to the conduct of the audit.

When considering whether an auditor is capable of exercising objective and impartial judgment, consideration needs to be given to past, current or possible relationships between:

- the auditor, audit firm, current or former audit firm member, audit company or any current or former audit company director; and
- the audited entity, its current or former directors or managers.

Former auditors

Section 300(1)(ca) requires the directors' report for disclosing entities to include the names of each officer who was formerly a partner or director of the audit firm or audit company that is the entity's current auditor and was a partner or director at a time when the audit firm or audit company conducted an audit of the entity.

Section 324 CI states that a member of an audit firm or director of an audit company who was a professional member of an audit team cannot become a director, company secretary or senior manager of an audit client or a related entity until two years after ceasing to be with the audit firm or audit company concerned. This restriction also applies to review partners under s. 324CJ. In addition, s. 324CK prohibits any more than one former partner, at any time, from being a director, company secretary or senior manager with an audit client. These restrictions on former auditors do not apply to small proprietary companies.

Rotation of audit partners

With effect from 1 July 2006, s. 324DA requires that where an individual plays a significant role (generally this would be lead or review partner) in the audit of a listed entity for five successive financial years, the individual cannot play a significant role in the audit of that entity for at least another two successive years. In addition, an individual cannot play a significant role for more than five out of seven successive financial years, where the involvement is not in consecutive years. Small or regional audit firms may apply to ASIC for an extension of the rotation period to seven years.

Non-audit services

Under s. 300(11)(B), the boards of all listed companies are required to provide a statement in the annual report identifying all non-audit services provided by the audit firm, the fee for each service and an explanation of why the provision of the service did not impair independence. The board's statement under s. 300(11)(B) must be consistent with the advice provided by the entity's audit committee.

Auditors' appointment

Section 308 of the *Corporations Act* indirectly attempts to promote audit independence by requiring auditors to report to the members of the company rather than to management, while s. 327B requires that, for a public company, members be responsible for the appointment of the auditor.

Individual auditors (s. 324CE), audit firms (s. 324CF) and audit companies (s. 324CG) are in breach of the specific independence requirements for audit appointment if the auditor is engaged in audit activity at a time that a s. 324CH(1) relationship exists and the auditor is aware of the relationship and does not take all reasonable steps to ensure that the auditor concerned does not continue to engage in audit activity in those circumstances. The relationships set out in s. 324CH(1) are quite extensive and complex. The key relationships prohibited are the following:

- An auditor, professional member of the audit team or immediate family member cannot be an officer or audit-critical employee of the audited body or have held that position within the previous 12 months, unless it is a small proprietary company. An audit-critical employee is defined under s. 9 as an employee who is able, because of his or her position, to exert significant influence over a material aspect of the contents of the financial report being audited, or the conduct or efficacy of the audit. Immediate family member is defined under s. 9 to be the person's spouse, de facto spouse or family member who is wholly or partly dependent on the person for financial support.
- An auditor or professional member of the audit team cannot be an employer, employee, or partner or employee of an employee of an officer or audit-critical employee, unless it is a small proprietary company.
- An auditor or professional member of the audit team cannot provide remuneration to an officer or audit-critical employee for acting as a consultant, unless it is a small proprietary company.

- An auditor, professional member of the audit team or immediate family member cannot have an asset that is an investment in the audited body; an asset that is a beneficial interest in an investment in the audited body and have control over that asset; or an asset that is a beneficial interest in an investment in the audited body that is a material interest. Nor can an auditor or professional member of the audit team have an investment in an entity that has a controlling interest in the audited body or a material beneficial interest in an entity that has a controlling interest in the audited body.
- An auditor cannot owe an amount of more than $5000 to the audited body, a related body corporate or an entity that the audited body controls, unless it is a housing loan in the ordinary course of the audited body's business.
- An auditor, professional member of the audit team or immediate family member cannot be owed an amount by the audited body, a related body corporate or an entity that the audited body controls under a loan, unless it is a loan to immediate family members of the audit team that is incurred in the ordinary course of business.
- An auditor, professional member of the audit team or immediate family member cannot be liable under a guarantee of a loan to the audited body, a related body corporate or an entity that the audited body controls.
- An auditor, professional member of the audit team or immediate family member cannot owe an amount to the audited body, a related body corporate or an entity that the audited body controls under a loan, unless it is made in the ordinary course of business on normal terms and conditions.
- An auditor, professional member of the audit team or immediate family member cannot be entitled to the benefit of a guarantee given by the audited body, a related body corporate or an entity that the audited body controls in relation to a loan, unless it is given in the ordinary course of business on normal terms and conditions.

Further statutory support is given to audit independence by by ss. 327B and 329, which attempt to reduce management's influence on the auditor. Under s. 327B an auditor is appointed until death, **removal**, **resignation**, ceasing to be capable of acting as auditor or ceasing to act as auditor owing to a conflict of interest, rather than being appointed annually.

Auditors' removal or resignation

Under s. 329, removal from office requires a resolution of the company at a general meeting of which special notice has been given. The auditor is entitled to make a written representation to all shareholders, at the company's expense, and to speak at the general meeting. A copy of the notice of removal must be sent to ASIC.

Further, while an auditor can resign, the auditor must have prior consent from ASIC, unless it is a proprietary company (s. 329(9)). The application for that consent must contain reasons for the auditor's request, and the auditor must notify the company of the application (s. 329(5)). If ASIC approves the resignation, it is effective from the date specified in the notice of resignation, the date the consent was given or the date fixed by ASIC, whichever occurs last (s. 329(8)).

ASIC Policy Statement 26, issued in June 1992, sets out the policies and principles which influence ASIC in the exercise of the power conferred on it by s. 329(6) to consent to the resignation of auditors. ASIC's overriding concern is to ensure that the independence and integrity of the audit function are maintained. The appointment of an auditor is primarily a matter for the members. As a result, ASIC will not consent to a resignation that does not take effect at the annual general meeting, unless there are exceptional circumstances.

Further, ASIC will consent to a resignation that takes effect at the next annual general meeting only if all of the following conditions apply:

- ASIC believes that the auditor's reasons for resignation are acceptable.
- The auditor states that all s. 311 matters have been reported to ASIC at the date of the application and that any further such matters which come to their attention before resignation will be reported.
- The auditor states that there are no disputes with company management connected with the relinquishment of office.
- The auditor states that there are no other circumstances connected with the relinquishment of office which should be brought to ASIC's attention.

Examples of such circumstances are:

- the independence of the audit function is not being preserved; or
- the outgoing auditor is aware that the resignation may be connected with opinion shopping, which is discussed later in this chapter.

ASIC will consent to a resignation that does not take effect at the next annual general meeting only if all of the following conditions apply:

- ASIC considers that there are exceptional circumstances and that a day other than the next annual general meeting is appropriate.
- The auditor states all s. 311 matters concerning significant breaches of the *Corporations Act* have been reported to ASIC at the date of the application and that any further such matters which come to their attention before resignation will be reported.
- The application includes a copy of a directors' resolution appointing a replacement auditor and a confirmation from the proposed replacement auditor stating willingness to accept the appointment, both subject to ASIC's approval of the resignation.
- The auditor states that there are no disputes with company management connected with the relinquishment of office.
- The auditor states that there are no other circumstances connected with the relinquishment of office which should be brought to ASIC's attention.

Examples of exceptional circumstances include:

- loss of independence of the auditor;
- the failing health of the auditor;
- the company is not audited by the auditor of its parent entity; or
- a relocation of the company's or auditor's principal place of business resulting in circumstances where it would be impractical for the auditor to perform the audit.

Right of access to records

Section 310 provides further protection to the auditor by giving the right of access at all reasonable times to the accounting and other records and registers, and an entitlement to require from any officer of the company such information and explanations as required for the purposes of audit.

Right to reasonable fees

Section 331 states that the auditor is entitled to receive reasonable fees and expenses for the work carried out.

Collectively, these provisions assist an auditor to maintain actual and perceived independence, and attempt to create, as far as possible, a suitable environment for an audit process that is free from undue influence and obstruction. These provisions provide some protection to the auditor in resisting management pressure. The practical effectiveness of the provisions varies with the circumstances and the extent of management control.

Ethical requirements

A number of areas related to independence are not covered in the legislation. These independence requirements have been provided for in the ethical rulings of the professional accounting bodies. The overriding principle in the ethical rules is the **reasonable person test** outlined in CPC F.1.10: would a reasonable person having access to all the facts consider that the auditor was independent?

CPC F.1.9 states that independence is a fundamental concept to the profession and requires a member to approach their work with integrity and objectivity. Further, CPC F.1.10 states that a member in public practice must both be, and be seen to be, free of any interest that is incompatible with objectivity. Therefore, the ethical rules emphasise that the auditor's **perceived independence** is as important as the auditor's **actual independence**.

Perceived independence is described in CPC F.1 as **'independence in appearance'** and is the belief of financial report users that actual independence has been achieved. It is this perception that is responsible, in part, for the credibility of the auditor's report. Users will not derive any assurance from the auditor's work unless they believe the auditor is independent.

Actual independence is described in CPC F.1 as **'independence of mind'** and is the achievement of actual freedom from bias, personal interest, prior commitment to an interest, or susceptibility to undue influence or pressure. Independence cannot be achieved simply by the application of a series of rules or regulations alone, but rather is built upon the auditor's belief in, and support for, the concept and its application during audit engagements. Three factors that contribute to an independent attitude of mind are:

1 integrity;
2 objectivity; and
3 strength of character.

Quick review

1 Actual and perceived independence is critical if an audit or other assurance engagement is to add credibility to the subject matter concerned.

2 The *Corporations Act* contains provisions that are directed toward maintaining the auditor's independence.

3 Detailed independence rules and guidance are provided in the CPCs.

RECENT DEVELOPMENTS IN AUDITOR INDEPENDENCE

learning objective 8

Ramsay Report

Interest in the issue of audit independence was increased by speculation about what role, if any, audit independence matters played in a number of high-profile corporate failures during the first half of 2001. As a result, the federal government commissioned a report by Professor Ian Ramsay on audit independence in Australia. The Ramsay Report, which was issued in October 2001, examined Australia's existing legislative and professional requirements on the independence of company auditors and compared them with equivalent overseas requirements. Where appropriate, the report proposed measures for strengthening the Australian requirements.

The recommendations covered five key issues concerned either directly with audit independence (employment relationships, financial relationships and provision of non-audit services) or with matters designed to enhance audit independence (audit committees and a board to oversee audit independence issues). These issues will be discussed later in this chapter.

The Ramsay Report recommendations envisaged the continuation of the existing co-regulatory regime under which some requirements are included in the corporations legislation and others are in the ethical rules of the professional accounting bodies. The federal government included many of the Ramsay Report recommendations in its CLERP 9 amendments to the *Corporations Act*. The accounting bodies have likewise included many of the Ramsay Report recommendations in their Code of Professional Conduct CPC F.1.

IFAC independence rules

In addition, there have been a number of developments internationally, including the release of new ethical rules by the International Federation of Accountants (IFAC). In June 2000, IFAC issued an exposure draft containing significant revisions of its rules on professional independence including the adoption of a conceptual framework approach. The exposure draft was re-exposed in April 2001 and revised ethical rules were finally issued in November 2001.

IFAC has adopted a conceptual approach to independence that uses a framework, built on principles for identifying, evaluating and responding to threats to independence. The framework establishes principles that the auditor should use to identify threats to independence, evaluate the significance of those threats, and identify and apply safeguards to eliminate the threats or reduce them to an acceptable level.

CPC F.1

CPA Australia and the ICAA approved a new professional independence standard, CPC F.1, in May 2002. The new CPC F.1 is based on the IFAC ethical rules and is tailored to reflect Australian community expectations. The new CPC F.1 became mandatory on 31 December 2003 and Audit Practice Statement AUP 32, which was issued in August 1992, was withdrawn. A revised CPC F.1 was issued in December 2004 to take account of the CLERP 9 amendments to the *Corporations Act*.

CPC F.1 requires the auditor to identify and evaluate threats to independence and to respond by applying safeguards which eliminate the identified threats or which reduce them to an acceptable level.

Threats to independence are described in CPC F.1 as:

- **Self-interest threats:** the possibility that the firm or individuals within it could benefit from a financial interest in the client.
- **Self-review threats:** the possibility that the firm or individuals within it would have to re-evaluate their own work to form a judgment.
- **Advocacy threats:** situations where the firm or individuals within it could promote the audit client's point of view in a manner which compromises objectivity.
- **Familiarity threats:** the possibility that the firm or individuals within it have become too sympathetic to the client's interests.

- **Intimidation threats:** the possibility that the firm or individuals within it may be deterred from acting objectively by actual or perceived threats from the client.

Safeguards fall into three broad categories. For an auditor, these are:

- **Safeguards created by the profession, legislation or regulation**, such as education, professional standards, monitoring and disciplinary processes, and inspections and review.
- **Safeguards within the audit client**, including competent employees and robust corporate governance structures.
- **Safeguards within the audit firm**, including policies and procedures to implement and monitor independence and quality control.

The principles and rules set out in CPC F.1 allow an auditor to evaluate any circumstance and to determine procedures and actions necessary to avoid or resolve those circumstances that pose threats or risks to objectivity.

An auditor should set up and maintain a safeguarding system that is an integral part of the firm-wide management and internal control. This safeguarding system, which encompasses all aspects of independence and quality control and not just the provision of other services to an audit client, may include:

- written independence policies that address current independence standards, threats to independence, and related safeguards;
- active and timely communication of policies;
- appropriate procedures to be applied by partners and staff in order to meet independence standards;
- documentation that summarises conclusions that have been drawn from the assessment of threats to independence and the related evaluation of the independence risk; and
- internal monitoring of compliance with safeguarding policies.

The system will apply to the engagement team and audit firm and to all other partners and staff within the audit firm. There may be differing restrictions and requirements on partners and staff within the firm depending on the nature of their work and their relationship with the audit client or engagement team. These aspects are discussed in full in F.1, Appendix 1.27–36.

Sarbanes-Oxley Act 2002

In the USA, in response to the collapse of Enron, WorldCom and other high-profile business failures the new *Sarbanes-Oxley Act* was signed into law on 30 July 2002. The *Sarbanes-Oxley Act* of 2002 dramatically affects the accounting profession and provides more stringent independence requirements and more severe penalties for breaches. Among other things, it restricts greatly the ability of auditors to provide non-audit services, mandates audit partner rotation and strengthens the role of the audit committee. These issues were outlined in *Audit and Assurance Alert No. 13*, issued in September 2002 and will be discussed in more detail in this chapter.

The *Sarbanes-Oxley Act 2002* also extends the statute of limitations for the discovery of fraud to two years from the date of discovery and five years after the act (previously one year and three, respectively). The Act establishes harsh penalties for securities law violations, corporate fraud and document shredding and requires the Chief Executive Officer (CEO) and Chief Financial Officer (CFO) to certify that the financial report fairly presents in all material respects the operations and condition of the company. It also requires management to provide a report on the effectiveness of internal control over financial reporting and the auditor to provide assurance that the report is appropriate. This is discussed further in Chapter 14.

The *Sarbanes-Oxley Act 2002* affects not only US companies and US auditors, but any audit firm actively working as an auditor of, or for, a publicly traded US company or its subsidiary. Therefore the Act covers any Australian audit firm that does the audit of a subsidiary of a US listed company or that of an Australian company that is listed on a US stock exchange. During 2004 the SEC queried whether the provision of non-audit services by KPMG to National Australia Bank was in breach of the SEC rules even though it was permitted under Australian rules.

Joint Committee of Public Accounts and Audit

Due to the major corporate collapses both within Australia and overseas, the JCPAA resolved to review independent auditing by registered company auditors. They issued their recommendations in August 2002 in Report 391. As with the *Sarbanes-Oxley Act 2002*, they recommended that the *Corporations Act 2001* be amended to require the CEO and CFO to sign a statutory declaration that the company's financial reports comply with the Act and are 'materially truthful and complete'. They also recommended that audit firms submit an annual report to ASIC on how the audit firm has managed independence issues, and that ASIC be empowered to investigate such independence issues. Many of their recommendations were consistent with the Ramsay Report and have been incorporated in the CLERP 9 amendments.

HIH Royal Commission

The major companies in the HIH Insurance Group were placed in provisional liquidation on 15 March 2001. The deficiency of the group was estimated to be between $3.6 billion and $5.3 billion. On 16 April 2003, the HIH Royal Commission issued its report 'The Failure of HIH Insurance', which contained sixty-one policy recommendations by Justice Owen covering corporate governance, financial reporting, auditing and regulation of the insurance industry. Justice Owen recommended, among other things, a broadening of the definition of independence to include situations where a reasonable person *might* believe that independence *might* be impaired. He argued that the CLERP 9 proposal that a reasonable person *would need to conclude* that the auditor is not independent imposed too high a standard of certainty of the lack of independence. He also recommended increased disclosure of the types of non-audit services and their fees, increased restrictions on employment relationships between an auditor and the audit client, and extending auditor rotation requirements to senior audit personnel.

Corporate Law Economic Reform Program

In September 2002, the federal government issued a policy paper, CLERP 9, as part of its Corporate Law Economic Reform Program, seeking stakeholder comments on proposals for legislative amendments. The paper reviewed, among other things, auditor independence. Following much discussion, stakeholder feedback, political debate and some amendments, the *Corporate Law Economic Reform Program (Audit Reform and Corporate Disclosure) Act 2004* was passed by the Senate on 25 June 2004 and received Royal Assent on 30 June 2004. The CLERP 9 legislation amends a number of Acts, including the *Corporations Act 2001*. Some of the most significant changes introduced by the CLERP 9 amendments are to auditor appointment, independence and rotation requirements. These were discussed earlier in this chapter and included:

- additional disclosures in the directors' report on the auditor and the audit
- general auditor independence requirements
- specific auditor independence requirements
- restrictions on auditors being employed by clients
- auditor rotation for public companies

Quick review

1 The Ramsay Report reviewed audit independence requirements in Australia and made recommendations concerning auditor–client employment relationships, financial relationships, provision of non-audit services, audit committees and a board to oversee audit independence issues.

2 A revised CPC F.1 has been issued based on the IFAC Ethical Code; it adopts a conceptual approach to independence based on identifying threats to independence and implementing adequate safeguards.

3 The *Sarbanes-Oxley Act 2002* in the USA introduced stringent independence requirements.

4 In Australia, the JCPAA and HIH Royal Commission made a number of recommendations for improving auditor independence.

5 The CLERP 9 legislation has introduced significant changes to auditor appointment, independence and rotation requirements.

MAJOR THREATS TO AUDITOR INDEPENDENCE

The Ramsay Report identified three major threats to auditor independence: auditor employment relationships; financial and business relationships; and provision of non-audit services.

Auditor employment relationships

The existence of employment relationships between an audit firm and an audit client can give the impression that an auditor is not independent of the client, irrespective of the actual situation. Consequently, legislators worldwide have tended to include provisions in corporate legislation that prohibit or restrict employment relationships. The professional accounting bodies have also amended their ethical codes to include prohibitions or restrictions on employment relationships.

CPC F.1 Appendix 2.52 prohibits a member of the assurance team from remaining a member of the assurance team if they are employed by the client, as it creates too great a self-interest, self-review, familiarity and intimidation threat to independence. Further, CPC F.1 Appendix 2.60 similarly prohibits any partner or employee of the audit firm serving as an officer of the client.

A particular concern recently has been retired audit partners joining the boards of their audit clients (commonly referred to as the alumni threat). The Ramsay Report noted that where this occurs, it is often seen as a particular threat to the independence of the audit firm, particularly if the former audit partner retains some financial arrangement with his or her audit firm or continues to exercise influence with the audit firm.

In the USA, the Independence Standards Board (2000) stated that the potential threats to independence when professionals leave firms to join audit clients are generally:

- *That partners or other audit team members who resign to accept positions with audit clients may not have exercised an appropriate level of scepticism during the audit process prior to their departure.*
- *That the departing partner or other professional may be familiar enough with the audit approach and testing strategy so as to be able to circumvent them once he or she begins employment with the client.*
- *That remaining members of the audit team, who may have been friendly with, or respectful of a former partner or other professional when he or she was with the firm, would be reluctant to challenge the decisions of the former partner or professional and, as a result, might accept the client's proposed accounting without exercising appropriate scepticism or maintaining objectivity.*

If the former partner or professional has retirement benefits or a capital account with the audit firm:

- *It may appear that ties between the audit firm and the partner or other professional have not been severed … and the audit firm is in effect auditing the results of its own work.*
- *If the retirement benefits of the former partner or other professional vary based on the firm's profits, then the former partner or other professional may be inclined to pay the firm higher fees to inflate his or her retirement benefits …*
- *[if the firm] is experiencing cash flow problems, the firm may be less rigorous in its audit of the client's financial statements in exchange for forbearance on the amounts owed to the former partner or other professional.*

In the USA, it was noted in the Waste Management Inc. case, which will be discussed later, that from the time it became a public company until 1997, every chief financial officer and chief accounting officer of Waste Management had previously worked as an auditor for their audit firm, Arthur Andersen. During the 1990s, 14 former Arthur Andersen employees worked for Waste Management Inc., most often in key financial and accounting positions.

Also, in Australia, in the HIH Insurance case, it was noted that the Chairman and Finance Director were former partners of HIH's audit firm, Arthur Andersen. In addition, one of the other directors, who was also a former Arthur Andersen partner, was previously the auditor of FAI Insurance in the 1980s before it became a subsidiary of HIH Insurance in 1998. The Chair of the HIH board was appointed seventeen months after retiring from Andersen, the CFO the day after he resigned from Andersen and the third partner five months after leaving Andersen.

In relation to the threat to independence when a retired audit partner joins the board of an audit client, the Ramsay Report recommended that there be a mandatory period of two years following resignation from the audit firm before a former partner of an audit firm who is directly involved in the audit of a client can become a director of the client. Although the HIH Royal Commission recommended extending this restriction to four years, the two-year restriction has been adopted in CPC F.1 Appendix 2.52, and a similar legislative restriction is now contained in s. 324CI. Justice Owen also argued in the HIH Royal Commission Report that the cumulative effect of three former partners on the HIH board affected the perception of independence to a greater extent than one former partner would have done. Therefore, he considered it appropriate to limit the number of former partners who can be appointed to the board or senior management positions to one. This recommendation was adopted in CPC F.1 Appendix 2.54 and s. 324CK.

Financial and business relationships

Investments in audit clients

The Ramsay Report recommended that an auditor will be deemed not to be independent if:

- the audit firm, any member of the audit engagement team, or any of his or her immediate family (or any entity which the firm or person controls) has any direct financial investment in the client, such as shares, notes, options, or other securities; or any material indirect financial investment in the client;
- the audit firm, any member of the audit engagement team, or any of his or her immediate family (or any entity which the firm or person controls), has a material financial interest in an entity that has a controlling interest in the client;
- any partner, principal or professional employee of the audit firm, or any of his or her immediate family (or any entity which the person controls) controls the client; or
- any other client service personnel, or any of his or her immediate family (or any entity that the person controls) has a direct financial interest or a material indirect financial interest in the client.

This recommendation has been adopted in CPC F.1 Appendix 2.5, which prohibits an auditor or their immediate family member from having a direct financial interest or a material indirect financial interest in an audit client, as it creates too great a self-interest threat. CLERP 9 has imposed similar legislative restrictions through s. 324CH(I), as discussed earlier.

Loans to and from audit clients

The Ramsay Report recommended that an auditor should not be considered to be independent if a partner of the audit firm, or an entity which the partner controls, or a body corporate in which the partner has a substantial holding, owes more than $10 000 (or such other amount as may be prescribed by regulation) to the client. In addition, independence should be considered to be breached if the audit firm, any member of the audit engagement team, or any of his or her immediate family (or an entity which the firm or person controls) accepts or makes or guarantees a loan to or from the client, except for a loan that is 'made in the ordinary course of the client's business' and the loan is made under normal lending procedures, terms and conditions. CLERP 9 has adopted this recommendation, although it has retained the existing $5000 limit by the effect of s. 324CH(I), as discussed earlier.

CPC F.1.28 prohibits loans to or from clients unless they are negotiated at arm's length in the ordinary course of the client's business. Further, CPC F.1 Appendix 2.29 prohibits loans from audit clients that are not financial institutions unless they are immaterial to the auditor and the institution, as they create too great a self-interest threat. Loans from a financial institution are allowed provided they are under normal lending procedures and, if it is material, that there are adequate safeguards.

Business relationships

The Ramsay Report recommended that an auditor should not be considered to be independent if a member of the audit engagement team has a business relationship with the client or any of its officers; or the audit firm has a business relationship with the client or any of its officers which is not clearly insignificant to both the audit firm and the client.

A business relationship for this purpose does not include professional services provided by the audit firm, or the audit firm or members of the audit engagement team being a consumer in the ordinary course of business.

CPC F.1 Appendix 2.40 points out that a close business relationship between the auditor and the client will involve a commercial or common financial interest and may create self-interest and intimidation threats.

Goods and services from clients

CPC F.1.27 states that the auditor should not accept goods or services from a client on terms more favourable than those generally available to others. Gifts or hospitality beyond normal social courtesies should not be accepted, as they would create unacceptable self-interest and familiarity threats.

AUDITING IN THE NEWS

SNIPPET

3.1

Source: Buffini, F. (2002) 'Audit Surveys Disagree on Independence Issue', *Australian Financial Review*, 5 July, p. 66.

Audit surveys disagree on independence issue

New research on whether non-audit fees compromise the performance of auditors was presented at an international symposium on audit research this week, and the findings were mixed.

The influence of non-audit fees on audit has become an important issue following recent corporate collapses, and due to the large amounts clients pay their auditors for other services.

With audit fees routinely accounting for less than half of the total fees paid by listed companies to their auditors, the perception of a conflict of interest is widespread.

However, whether independence is actually compromised is harder to prove.

A US study presented at the symposium in Sydney this week found that a high level of non-audit fees increased reliance on internal audit, potentially compromising the detection of financial statement errors and intentional misstatements.

'External auditors appear to be more affected by client pressure and less concerned about internal audit quality when making internal audit reliance decisions at clients for whom significant non-audit services are also provided', the paper, by William Felix of the University of Arizona, Audrey Gramling of Georgia State University and Mario Maletta of Northeastern University said.

'Taken together, our findings indicate that non-audit service revenues have an effect on decisions that are integral to the evidence-gathering and evaluation components of the audit process and, as a result, these revenues potentially affect the likelihood that the audit will [fail to] identify material errors and intentional misstatement.'

However, another US study, also presented at the symposium, found that non-audit fees had no impact on the willingness of auditors to issue going concern opinions.

'Our tests find no evidence of a significant association between the fee ratio and the auditors' propensity to issue a going-concern opinion', the paper from Mark DeFond, K. Raghunandan and K. Subramanyam from the University of California and Texas A&M University said.

Their findings were backed by a third study on the impact of non-audit services and earnings conservatism, which was also presented this week.

Caitlin Ruddock, Sarah Taylor and Stephen Taylor of the University of Technology, Sydney, found that clients of the big audit firms had more conservative earnings than clients of smaller audit firms.

They said their results did not support the conclusion that the provision of non-audit services by the big audit firms had resulted in less independence.

Instead, their results showed that earnings conservatism of the audit clients of the big firms increased with the extent of non-audit services.

Provision of non-audit services by auditors

The issue of whether audit firms should provide non-audit or other services to their audit clients generates a wide range of views from stakeholder groups, ranging from calls for a total prohibition on the provision of such services to claims that there is no evidence that providing the services impairs independence (see Auditing in the News 3.1). Audit independence studies examined during the course of the Ramsay Report have reached different conclusions concerning whether the provision of non-audit services impairs audit independence.

The growth of non-audit services for the largest audit firms has been substantial. In the USA, the Panel on Audit Effectiveness (2000) stated in its report that for SEC audit clients, the ratio of accounting and auditing revenues to consulting revenues dropped from approximately 6:1 in 1990 to 1.5:1 in 1999. Further, 4 per cent of Big Four firms' SEC audit clients had consulting fees that exceeded audit fees.

In a speech in the USA in June 2001, acting Securities and Exchange Commission (SEC) chief Laura Unger (2001) said conflicts of interest for auditors may be greater than regulators suspected. Unger pointed to new proxy disclosures and the SEC's recent settlement with Arthur Andersen over Waste Management Inc. as evidence of potential conflicts that can occur when large accounting firms provide non-audit services to the companies they audit.

On 19 June 2001, the SEC settled actions in connection with Andersen's audits of the annual financial reports of Waste Management Inc. for the years 1992 through 1996. Those financial reports, on which Andersen issued unqualified audit opinions, overstated Waste Management's pre-tax income by more than $1 billion. However, contrary to auditing standards, Andersen only quantified in their working papers the effect of certain of the identified misstatements. Andersen also allowed Waste Management to 'bury' certain charges by improperly netting them against unrelated, one-time gains to avoid SEC disclosure requirements.

Unger (2001) called the case 'the smoking gun that everyone was looking for' during the debate on the SEC's auditor independence rules. 'This is one very significant case that we can point to' as evidence of the pitfalls that can occur when an auditor provides other services to audit clients, Unger said in the speech. Andersen billed Waste Management about $11.8 million for non-audit services, far more than the $7.5 million it charged for its audit services over the 7 year period. In addition, a related entity, Andersen Consulting, also billed Waste Management $6 million in additional non-audit fees.

Further, the SEC's analysis of the new proxy reports have shown higher-than-expected payments for non-audit services. Based on a review of 563 proxy statements, the SEC found companies spending $2.69 for non-audit services for every $1 in audit services, with about 73 per cent of fees to auditors generated by non-audit work.

'The numbers alone don't prove that there is a conflict,' Unger acknowledged. But she said the SEC was 'very surprised' by the results. However, Unger indicated that she believes disclosure of such payments is better than prohibiting auditors from providing non-audit services.

ASIC recently conducted a survey of Australia's largest 100 listed companies to obtain evidence on the extent of non-audit services provided by the auditors of these companies. The results, which were released in January 2002, showed that the provision of non-audit services in Australia was widespread with just over half (53 per cent) of fees to audit firms being for audit services.

The Panel on Audit Effectiveness (2000) noted that there were several arguments both for and against auditors providing non-audit services to their clients. The main argument for opposing the provision of non-audit services by auditors to their clients is that when an audit firm provides non-audit services to a client it is serving two different sets of clients: management in the case of non-audit services and the audit committee, the shareholders and all those who rely on the audited financial statements in the case of the audit. As a result, the audit firm is subject to conflicts of interest. On the other hand, the main arguments supporting the provision of non-audit services by auditors to their clients are that there is no solid evidence of any specific link between audit failures and the provision of non-audit services; non-audit services have been provided by audit firms to their clients for many years; and many non-audit services are both in the public interest and beneficial to audit effectiveness. For example, a company may seek the assistance of its auditors to correct control weaknesses identified during the audit.

However, it is generally agreed that there are some services that an audit firm cannot provide to its client. For example, CPC F.1 Appendix 2.68 indicates that in all cases, engagements for an audit client that involve the following activities must be refused:

- authorising, executing or consummating a transaction, or otherwise executing authority on behalf of the assurance client, or having the authority to do so;
- determining which recommendation of the firm should be implemented;
- reporting in a management role to those charged with governance; and
- any other activity barred by legislation.

CPC F.1 also identifies a number of situations where specific safeguards may be required and identifies examples of such safeguards. Some of these situations and safeguards are summarised below. However, CPC F.1 Appendix 2 must be referred to for a full explanation of these matters. CLERP 9 supports the application of CPC F.1. The auditor's independence declaration under s. 307C must indicate whether there have been any breaches of the Code of Professional Conduct.

Preparing accounting records and financial reports

A self-review threat exists where an auditor participates in the preparation of the audit client's accounting records or financial reports. The significance of the threat depends upon the individual's involvement in the preparation process and upon the public involvement in the audit client.

Appropriate services that may be offered by the auditor include technical assistance, for example, on accounting standards or principles, disclosures, or appropriateness of controls, assisting in the preparation of consolidated financial reports and proposing adjusting journal entries. These services promote the fair presentation of the financial report and do not generally threaten independence. For other accounting and bookkeeping services, including payroll, the significance of the self-review threat is high and safeguards are required if the service is offered.

For non-listed audit clients, CPC F.1 Appendix 2.80 indicates that the self-review threat from providing accounting or bookkeeping services on financial information that forms the basis of the financial report is too high to allow the auditor to undertake the service *unless* the assistance provided is solely of a routine or mechanical nature. Examples of acceptable services include recording transactions the client has authorised, posting coded transactions to a general ledger or preparing a financial report based on the client's trial balance.

For listed audit clients, CPC F.1 Appendix 2.81 states that accounting or bookkeeping services on financial information, which forms the basis of the financial report, cannot be undertaken as there is no safeguard that reduces the threat to an acceptable level. The only exceptions to this are:

- an emergency situation where it is impractical for the audit client to make other arrangements. In this instance, the auditor must not take any managerial role or make managerial decisions, the audit client must take responsibility for the results and the personnel undertaking the work must not be members of the audit engagement teams; and
- where the services are required by statute or regulations.

In no circumstances must the auditor originate, authorise or approve transactions on behalf of an audit client.

Valuation services

A self-review threat exists whenever an auditor provides the audit client with valuation services that result in the preparation of a valuation that is to be incorporated into the client's financial report.

CPC F.1 Appendix 2.86 states that the significance of the self-review threat is considered too high to allow the provision of services where the valuation relates to amounts that are material in relation to the financial report *and* where the valuation involves a significant degree of subjectivity. In these circumstances, which include Independent Expert Reports, the valuation service should be refused, or the auditor must withdraw from the audit.

In all other cases, the auditor may undertake the service only after considering whether additional safeguards are needed to mitigate a remaining self-review threat. Such safeguards may include using an expert team with different individuals (including engagement partner) and different reporting lines to those of the audit engagement team. The auditor should also obtain the audit client's acceptance of their responsibility for the results of the work.

Taxation

Services relating to taxation include compliance and advisory services that assist entities to determine, plan and report on tax consequences related to their activities. As they are advisory services, this work should not usurp the management function of an audit client provided the client takes responsibility for decisions. Under CPC F.1, the provision of such services would not create a threat to independence.

Internal audit

Self-review threats may arise in certain circumstances where an auditor provides internal audit services to an audit client. CPC F.1 Appendix 2.93–4 indicates that where the auditor assists in the performance of an audit client's internal audit activities or undertakes outsourcing of some of these activities, the self-review threat needs to be mitigated by safeguards. These safeguards include:

- ensuring that the audit client at all times has responsibility for:
  - the overall system of internal control (i.e. the establishment and maintenance of internal controls, including the day to day controls and processes in relation to the authorisation, execution and recording of accounting transactions);
  - determining the scope, risk and frequency of the internal audit procedures to be performed and assessing their adequacy;
  - ensuring a competent employee is responsible for the internal audit activities;
  - considering and acting on findings and recommendations; and
- the auditor not accepting the outcomes of internal auditing processes for statutory audit purposes without adequate review.

Internal audit services that are appropriate with such safeguards include specialist assignments on behalf of an audit client's internal audit department and undertaking internal audit procedures determined or approved by the entity.

Providing services that involve the audit firm having responsibility for devising, undertaking and monitoring the whole of the internal audit activity or taking management decisions in respect to internal audit activity should not be undertaken by the auditor.

Design and implementation of financial information technology systems

The provision of services by the auditor to an audit client that involve the design and implementation of financial information technology systems used to generate information forming part of the audit client's financial report may give rise to a self-review threat. CPC F.1 Appendix 2.98 indicates that the significance of the self-review threat is considered too high to permit an auditor to provide such services unless:

■ the audit client acknowledges that they take responsibility for the overall system;
■ the audit client appoints a senior employee to take all management decisions with respect to the design and implementation;
■ the audit client makes management decisions and evaluates the adequacy and results of the design and implementation; and
■ the audit client is responsible for the operation of the system and information generated.

The auditor needs to consider whether additional safeguards are required to mitigate a remaining self-review threat. In particular, whether services should only be provided by an expert team with different individuals (including engagement partner) and different reporting lines to those of the audit engagement team.

Temporary staff assignments

Lending staff, or secondments, to audit clients may create a self-review threat where the individual is in a position to influence the preparation of the client's accounts or financial report. CPC F.1 Appendix 2.102 indicates that safeguards that must be in place for any temporary staff assignment are that the individual:

■ must not make management decisions;
■ must not approve or sign agreements; and
■ must not exercise discretionary authority to commit the client.

Litigation support services

CPC F.1 Appendix 2.103 acknowledges that an advocacy threat exists whenever an auditor acts for the audit client in the resolution of a dispute or litigation. A self-review threat may also arise where such a service includes the estimation of the audit client's chances in the resolution of litigation, and thereby affects the amounts to be reflected in the financial report.

The significance of both the advocacy and the self-review threat is considered too high to allow an auditor to act in the resolution of litigation that involves matters that would reasonably be expected to have a material impact on the audit client's financial report and where a significant degree of subjectivity is inherent in the case concerned. The threats are also considered too high to be capable of being reduced to an acceptable level through safeguards when the role involves the auditor making managerial decisions on behalf of the audit client.

Legal services

Legal services encompass a wide and varied range of roles. Work involving matters not expected to have a material effect on the financial report is not considered to create a threat to independence. Legal advice such as contract support, legal due diligence and restructuring may create self-review threats, but CPC F.1 Appendix 2.108 indicates that these threats may be able to be reduced to an acceptable level by implementing safeguards such as using individuals not involved with the audit and ensuring the client takes responsibility for decisions.

Advocacy work not material to the financial report may be undertaken if appropriate safeguards are in place. These would include prohibiting audit firm individuals making managerial decisions on behalf of the client and using individuals who are not involved with the audit for the legal work.

It is appropriate for the auditor to undertake dispute analysis, investigation and resolution services for an audit client. However, this work should not be undertaken in relation to matters with a material impact on the financial report.

CPC F.1 Appendix 2.111 states that the auditor should not act as General Counsel for an audit client.

Recruiting senior management

Before accepting any engagement to assist in the recruitment of senior or key staff, the auditor should assess the current and future threats to independence that may arise and consider appropriate safeguards to mitigate such threats (see Example 3.1 overleaf). Generally it is acceptable for the audit firm to advertise for and interview candidates and produce a list of potential candidates against a client's specifications. CPC F.1 Appendix 2.112 states that the decision as to who should be engaged must always be taken by the audit client.

When recruiting staff to senior financial posts, the significance of threats to independence is high. As such, the auditor should carefully consider whether there might be circumstances where even the provision of a list of potential candidates for such posts may cause an unacceptable level of independence risk.

Corporate finance and similar activities

Corporate finance encompasses a wide and varied range of services. Safeguards that are generally available to counter potential advocacy or self-review threats include:

- prohibiting the auditor making managerial decisions on behalf of the client;
- using individuals not involved in the audit to undertake the work; and
- ensuring the auditor does not commit the audit client to a transaction or the terms of a transaction.

Within these safeguards, services such as advice on corporate reorganisations or deal structures, may be appropriate services for the auditor to undertake, provided the auditor is able to reduce the risks to an acceptable level.

Promoting, dealing in, or underwriting an audit client's shares, including Initial Public Offerings, however, should not be undertaken, in accordance with CPC F.1 Appendix 2.113, as the threats to independence are too great. This does not include preparing a report as required by the *Corporations Act*, for example prospectus reporting undertaken in accordance with AUS 810. Activities that involve the auditor committing the audit client to the terms of a transaction or agreeing to a transaction are also prohibited under CPC F.1 Appendix 2.113.

Providing non-audit services consistent with the auditor's skills and expertise is an acceptable activity for an auditor and often provides additional value for an audit client. However, the provision of such services to an audit client may create real or perceived threats to independence. The auditor may provide services beyond the audit as long as any threats to independence have been reduced to an acceptable level.

Whenever an auditor provides services other than statutory audit work to an audit client, the significance of any threat must be evaluated. In some cases it may be possible to eliminate or reduce the threat by applying suitable safeguards. In other cases no safeguard will be available to reduce the threat to an acceptable level and in these situations, one of the services (the audit or non-audit service) must be refused.

The Ramsay Report (2001, p. 10) also recommended 'mandatory disclosure through the Australian accounting standards or the *Corporations Act* of non-audit services by category of service, as well as the dollar amount of fees paid for these services'. This proposal has been adopted by CLERP 9, with s. 300(II)(B) also requiring an explanation by the board of why the provision of the services does not impair independence.

For auditors of US listed companies or their subsidiaries, the *Sarbanes-Oxley Act 2002* provides a much greater restriction on the provision of non-audit services and lists eight types of services that are now 'unlawful' if provided to a publicly held company by its auditor: bookkeeping, information systems design and implementation, appraisals or valuation services, actuarial services, internal audits, management and human resources services, broker/dealer and investment banking services, and legal or expert services related to audit services. It also has one catch-all category authorising the board to determine by regulation any service it wishes to prohibit. Other non-audit services—including tax services—require pre-approval by the audit committee on a case-by-case basis. Pre-approved non-audit services must be disclosed to investors in periodic reports.

EXAMPLE 3.1 Independence

Alberto Foods Pty Ltd is a fast growing company and has now become by far your largest audit client. During the last year the services your firm has provided included completing the annual financial report audit, preparing the company's tax returns, deciding on the new computer system to be installed and preparing an independent valuation of a major investment to be included in the financial report. However, due to the need for funds for its expansion the company has not paid its audit fee for the last two years.

As a result of the expansion, the chairman has asked that you serve as a director for the current year, as he believes that your financial expertise will be invaluable in assisting the company through some very difficult times. The company's constitution requires each director to hold a minimum of 100 ordinary shares in the company.

Required
Identify any professional standards and regulatory requirements that may have been breached.

Solution
1. Although there is no information on the exact quantum of fees from Alberta Foods Pty Ltd, the fact that it is your largest client and is fast growing suggests that there may be a fee dependence issue. CPC F.1 Appendix 2.115–7 indicates that where the fees from one client constitute a large proportion of a firm's total fees, it may create a self-interest threat. Where the fees exceed 15 per cent of the firm's total fees, safeguards are necessary to reduce the proportion to an acceptable level.
2. CPC F.1 Appendix 2.119 states that where the fees for an audit client remain unpaid for a long time it creates a self-interest threat that would require adequate safeguards. Further, the auditor needs to consider whether the unpaid fees have taken on the characteristic of a loan, which if material, would be prohibited under CPC F.1 Appendix 2.29 due to self-interest threats.
3. CPC F.1 Appendix 2.90 states that taxation services are generally not seen as threats to independence. In addition, the work being done for Alberto Foods Pty Ltd is only tax compliance work and is allowed.
4. CPC F.1 Appendix 2.98 states that where the auditor is providing services involving the design and implementation of information technology systems, a necessary safeguard is that the audit client should make all the management decisions regarding the design and implementation process. In

this case the auditor is deciding on the new computer system, which is prohibited as it creates an unacceptable self-review threat.

5. CPC F.1 Appendix 2.86 states that preparing a valuation of matters that are material to the financial report creates a self-review threat that cannot be reduced to an acceptable level. Therefore, the auditor should not prepare the valuation for use in the financial report of Alberto Food Pty Ltd.

6. Unless Alberto Foods Pty Ltd is a small proprietary company you are specifically precluded from being a director under s. 324CH of the *Corporations Act*. Further, CPC F.1 Appendix 2.60 states that being a director creates self-interest and self-review threats that no safeguard could reduce to an acceptable level and so being a director of Alberto Foods Pty Ltd is prohibited.

7. Section 324CH and CPC F.1 Appendix 2.12 state that an auditor should have no direct financial interest in an audit client. The 100 ordinary shares would constitute a direct investment and therefore would also create a threat so significant that you would not be able to undertake the audit.

Quick review

1 Auditors being employed by a client, or serving as an officer of a client, creates an unacceptable independence threat.

2 Auditors having a direct financial interest or material indirect financial interest creates too great a self-interest threat to independence.

3 The provision of non-audit services by auditors to clients is now severely restricted, and the auditor is not permitted to take part in the decision-making process.

4 The entity must disclose all non-audit services, together with the fee for each service and an explanation of why the provision of the service did not impair independence.

SUGGESTIONS FOR IMPROVING AUDITOR INDEPENDENCE

 learning objective

Establishment of an Oversight Board

During August 2001, IFAC released a proposal for the establishment of a Public Oversight Board (POB) to oversee the public interest activities of IFAC, including:

- the setting of auditing, ethical, public sector and educational standards;
- the obligations of membership and compliance processes applicable to its member bodies; and
- the quality assurance, compliance and other self-regulatory processes applicable to membership of a new body called the Forum of Firms (FOF).

The FOF was established by IFAC to promote consistently high standards of financial reporting and auditing worldwide. Its membership is open to any firm that has or is interested in accepting transnational audit appointments, provided the firm:

- agrees to conform to the Forum's Global Quality Standard; and
- agrees to subject its assurance work to periodic external quality assurance reviews.

In performing its role, the POB will focus on whether the interests of users of financial reports are being appropriately reflected in the processes and outputs of IFAC and its committees, and on those activities of the FOF that impact financial reporting.

The UK is currently implementing a system of non-statutory independent regulation for its accountancy profession. The key feature of the system is its independence from control or undue influence by the accountancy profession. Its aim is to ensure that the public interest in the way the profession operates is fully met, and thus to secure public confidence in the impartiality and effectiveness of the profession's systems of regulation and discipline. The new system of regulation involves the establishment of five new bodies, including a Review Board.

In the USA, the *Sarbanes-Oxley Act 2002* has created a five-member Public Company Accounting Oversight Board (PCAOB), which has the authority to set and enforce auditing, attestation, quality control, and ethics (including independence) standards for public companies. It is also empowered to inspect the auditing operations of public accounting firms that audit public companies as well as impose disciplinary and remedial sanctions for violations of the board's rules, securities laws and professional auditing standards.

Canada has also established a new system to oversee the auditors of public companies. It will be administered and enforced by the new Canadian Public Accountability Board.

The Ramsay Report recommended that an independent supervisory board is an essential instrument in addressing the challenge of implementing new auditor independence requirements in Australia. Ramsay argued that the establishment of an Auditor Independence Supervisory Board (AISB) would play a vital role in ensuring public confidence in the independence of auditors by monitoring implementation of the new regime, compliance with it, and important international developments in the area of auditor independence.

However, as discussed in Chapter 2, through CLERP 9 the government has chosen instead to expand the responsibilities of the FRC to oversee auditor independence requirements in Australia. The AUASB has been reconstituted, with a government-appointed chairman under the auspices of the FRC, similar to the AASB.

Strengthening the role of audit committees

Communication on a number of issues with the Governance Body of an audit client is vital, as explained in the *Audit Committees: Best Practice Guide* and reaffirmed in CPC F.1 Appendix 1.33. One aspect of the audit committee role is review of the external auditor's independence based on the auditor's relationships and services with the entity and others that may impair or appear to impair the auditor's independence.

As required by the CLERP 9 amendments to the *Corporations Act*, the auditor of a listed client must provide a declaration of independence and detailed disclosure of remuneration for audit and other services that can be used for financial report disclosures. As detailed in *Auditing and Assurance Alert 11*, these items will contribute to the discussions held by the audit committee.

In the USA, the Blue Ribbon Committee sponsored by the New York Stock Exchange (NYSE) and the National Association of Securities Dealers (NASD) strongly endorsed the use of audit committees. The *Sarbanes-Oxley Act 2002* now requires all US listed companies to have an audit committee and vests the audit committee with the responsibility for the appointment, compensation and oversight of its auditor. The Act requires that audit committee members must be members of the Board of Directors, but otherwise be independent. Furthermore, the audit committee must have a financial expert on the committee or disclose the reasons for not including such an expert. In addition, the auditor is required to report to the audit committee on a timely basis:

- all critical accounting policies and practices to be used;
- all alternative accounting treatments discussed with management, together with the treatment preferred by the auditor; and
- other material written communications with management, such as any management letter or schedule of unadjusted differences.

A recent survey in the USA by Earnscliffe Research and Communications (2000) of chief executive officers of SEC registrant companies, chief financial officers of SEC registrant companies, chairs of audit committees of these companies, investment analysts, and partners of audit firms found that a strengthened oversight role for audit committees is important in ensuring the independence of auditors. According to the Blue Ribbon Committee (1999, p. 22) (cited in Psaros & Seamer, 2001, p. 47), 'several recent studies have produced a correlation between audit committee independence and two desirable outcomes: a higher degree of active oversight and a lower incidence of financial statement fraud'.

Psaros and Seamer (2001, p. 47) have concluded that the corporate governance practices of the recently collapsed Harris Scarfe 'were less than ideal. Neither the board of directors nor the audit committee possessed the recommended degree of independence to enable them to act at an optimal level'. Further, Reuters news agency reported that:

> the directors were shocked to discover critical financial management accounting irregularities, which had given the board a deliberately false and misleading view of the company's true financial position over a period of up to six years
> (Psaros & Seamer 2001, p. 44)

The board of directors and audit committee of Harris Scarfe had historically been composed of a majority of non-independent or executive directors. Further, the audit committee only met twice in 2000, 1999 and 1997, and three times in 1998. The Blue Ribbon Committee (1999) recommended that the audit committee should meet at least four times annually, or more frequently as circumstances dictate.

In the case of One.Tel, it has been claimed that the information that the executive management was providing to the non-executive board of directors was different to that being released through other sources. Thus, the issue of how much the non-executive management can rely on information provided by executives, versus how much they have to question this information, is an important issue for audit committees.

The Ramsay Report indicates that most stakeholders consulted during the preparation of the report were of the view that requiring listed companies to have an appropriately constituted audit committee would be a most effective way of enhancing the independence of auditors of such companies.

As we have noted, the ASX Listing Rules now require the top 500 companies to have an audit committee and that the composition, operation and responsibility of the audit committee should comply with the ASX Corporate Governance Council's Principles of Good Corporate Governance and Best Practice Recommendations.

Rotation of auditors

Rotation of audit partners

The Ramsay Report recommended that there be mandatory rotation of the audit partners responsible for the audit of listed companies and that the rotation is to occur after a maximum of 7 years. This leaves open the possibility that rotation may occur sooner if considered appropriate by those involved in the audit. It is also recommended that there is to be a period of at least 2 years before the partner can again be involved in the audit of the client. In the USA, the *Sarbanes-Oxley Act 2002* adopted a shorter period of rotation: every 5 years. Similarly, CLERP 9 has adopted mandatory rotation of partners every 5 years for listed companies and stipulated that this requirement should apply to both engagement and review partners under

s. 324DA. CPC F.1 Appendix 2.63 has now also adopted a 5-year rotation period for listed companies.

Rotation of audit firms

Source: Houghton, K.A. (2002) 'Audit Rotations Give Second-Rate Results', *Australian Financial Review*, 17 June, p. 52.

SNIPPET

3.2

AUDITING IN THE NEWS

Audit rotations give second-rate results

John Shanahan's proposal for five-year mandated rotation of audit firms ('Five-year rotation needed for audit firms', *AFR*, June 12) is one often-cited 'solution' for the concerns over auditor independence.

Shanahan's contribution shows some interesting insights, but in my view the potential for mandated rotation as an effective solution is limited and the likelihood of it producing damaging unintended consequences is significant.

Many in the profession acknowledge that the first year or two of an audit, even with substantial costs in additional time spent learning about the client, produce results that are significantly short of optimal.

Why would we want to institutionalise a sub-optimal audit for 20 to 40 per cent of all audits market-wide if we were to have five-year rotations? There are cases where an inappropriately 'comfortable' relationship between auditor and auditee arises with long-term engagements, but why have a 'one-size-fits-all' solution when it is probably only a problem for a small percentage of cases?

A fatal flaw of the mandated five-year rotation 'solution' is that it provides an incentive for auditors, knowing that they have a five-year tenure, to do a minimal job for the five years to maximise profitability until they lose the audit to the next profit-maximising firm.

Another concern is that rotation might provide an incentive to auditors to use the mandated changes to gain short-term access to many companies—not to do a high-quality audit but to build 'relationships' with company management so that they can sell consulting services at the end of the five years.

Threats to independence are real, economically significant and often complex, diverse and subtle in nature. I for one do not believe that a simple conventional solution, despite its apparent attractions, will be effective.

We need creative solutions that will deliver appropriate incentives for a long-term sustainable solution to the threats to auditor independence.

The Ramsay Report did not believe it appropriate to mandate rotation of audit firms. It concurred with the Audit Review Working Party, which stated that 'the anticipated cost, disruption and loss of experience to companies is considered unacceptably high, as is the unwarranted restriction on the freedom of companies to choose their own auditors'. This view has been supported by CLERP 9 (see too Auditing in the News 3.2).

Audit firm independence boards

Houghton and Jubb (2002) have recommended the establishment by each of the larger audit firms of an Auditor Independence Board as a complement to the partnership structure. They have recommended that members of the Board should be experts in fields such as auditing, commercial law, professional services, accounting or auditing standard-setting or accounting policy-making and should not be current or former partners of employees of the audit firm.

Houghton and Jubb (2002) argue that an internal independence board would be more effective than an externally imposed board as:

- independence issues and threats could be dealt with swiftly at the time of the audit;
- the board could deal with commercially sensitive issues;
- the quality-control processes of the board, and therefore of that firm, could be observed by the market;
- extremely subtle or difficult-to-measure issues could be dealt with sympathetically, yet conclusively; and
- reward structures within firms could take account of board decisions.

While the model proposed is a market-based solution, it would require an appropriate legislative or regulatory framework that required, as a minimum, compulsion for auditors of publicly traded entities to have an internal independence board.

Client auditor policies

Another market-based approach has been for some entities to designate the type of services that its auditor may supply. For example, the ANZ Banking Group Ltd issued a media release listing the type of non-audit services that its auditor may supply (reproduced in Auditing in the News 3.3). A number of other companies have done likewise.

AUDITING IN THE NEWS

Source: ANZ Media Release, 24 April 2002.

SNIPPET 3.3

ANZ enhances governance standards

The ANZ Board today announced measures to enhance ANZ's corporate governance procedures following a review of best practice by the ANZ Audit Committee.

ANZ Chairman, Mr Charles Goode, said the new measures would further strengthen ANZ's already high standard of corporate governance, disclosure and transparency.

A number of measures will be introduced to enhance governance, including plain English disclosure and expansion of discussion on critical accounting policies in ANZ's published results, disclosure of off-balance sheet structures and restrictions on the services that may be provided by its auditor.

The review established clear definitions as to which services may or may not be provided by ANZ's auditor (see below). These fall into three categories:

- The auditing firm may provide audit and audit-related services that, while outside the scope of the statutory audit, are consistent with the role of auditor.
- The auditing firm should not provide services that are perceived to be materially in conflict with the role of auditor.
- The auditing firm may be permitted to provide non-audit services that are not perceived to be materially in conflict with the role of auditor, subject to the approval of the ANZ Audit Committee.

ANZ Audit Committee Chairman, Mr John Cahlsen, commented: 'The Board wishes to ensure ANZ has the highest standards of corporate governance. This review demonstrates in a very tangible way the importance we place on open and transparent disclosure, on appropriate accounting policies, and ensuring the ANZ audit is conducted without conflict of interest.'

ANZ does not plan to put its audit out to tender at this time.

ANZ policy on auditing and non-auditing services

This policy defines the services that may or may not normally be conducted by ANZ's external auditing firm. Implicit in this policy are the principles that:

The auditing firm may provide audit and audit-related services that, while outside the scope of the statutory audit, are consistent with the role of auditor. These include audit

Continued...

related services, and regulatory and prudential reviews requested by the Bank's regulators. Examples are:

- Financial audits
- Audits of regulatory returns (e.g. APRA)
- Reviews undertaken for regulatory purposes (e.g. APRA Targeted Review)
- Other prudential audits or reviews
- Completion audits
- Audit for dealers' licences

The auditing firm should not provide services that are perceived to be materially in conflict with the role of auditor. These include investigations and consulting advice and subcontracting of operational activities normally undertaken by management, and where the auditor may ultimately be required to express an opinion on its own work. Examples are:

- Investigating accountant work on new or increased lending transactions
- Due diligence on potential acquisitions or investments
- Advice on deal structuring and assistance in deal documentation
- Tax planning and strategy
- Designing or implementing new IT systems or financial controls
- Advice on product structuring
- Book-keeping
- Valuations
- Executive recruitment and appointments
- Senior Management secondments

The auditing firm may be permitted to provide non-audit services that are not perceived to be materially in conflict with the role of auditor, subject to the approval of the ANZ Audit Committee. The ANZ Audit Committee will specifically confirm activities in this category. Examples are:

- Receiver or liquidator and related investigation work
- Junior secondments to ANZ
- Internal audit activities capped at 20 per cent of total internal audit work
- Advice on appropriate accounting standards
- Review of legislation and advice on its application to ANZ
- Compilation of accounting records to assist with queries from revenue authorities
- Tax compliance services
- Review of the adequacy of controls and recommendations for improvements

An exception can be made to the above policy where the variation is in the interests of the Group and arrangements are put in place to preserve the integrity of the audit of the Group's accounts. Any such exception requires the specific approval of the Board.

Quick review

1. Public Oversight Boards have been established overseas and that role has been given to the FRC in Australia.
2. There has been a strong push to strengthen the role of audit committees, which has been done through the ASX Listing Rules.
3. Mandatory rotation of audit partners has now been introduced in Australia and overseas.
4. Houghton and Jubb (2002) have recommended the establishment of audit firm independence boards.
5. Some companies have imposed restrictions on the non-audit services that their auditors may supply.

FEE DETERMINATION AND OBTAINING CLIENTS

Fee determination

The value of services performed by the auditor is determined by the inherent characteristics of personal integrity and professional competence. Typically, professionals are not hired primarily on the basis of the reasonableness of their fees. The client is chiefly concerned with the calibre of services to be received. Nevertheless, vigorous competition, including some fee competition, is one of the realities of practice today.

The two primary determinants of the audit fee are the time required to perform the necessary services properly and the rate to be charged for that time. Factors which significantly influence the required time are the condition of the client's records, the availability of the client's personnel for clerical assistance, the volume of the client's transactions and operations, the nature of the client's business and the effectiveness of the client's internal control. The appropriate hourly rate reflects the full cost of operating an audit firm. CPC F.6, 'Professional Fees', indicates that fees should be based on:

- the knowledge and skill required for the work involved;
- the level of training and experience of the persons necessarily engaged to complete the work;
- the time necessarily occupied by each person engaged to complete the work; and
- the degree of responsibility which the work entails.

Section 331 of the *Corporations Act* entitles the auditor to reasonable fees and expenses for the work performed. As a result, it could be argued that the fees from the practice should permit the auditor to:

- remunerate the staff adequately to attract the highest calibre of young men and women to the profession;
- maintain a respectable office with good working conditions, modern equipment and a library suitable to enable the best work to be performed; and
- undertake a fair share of public service activities for the community, profession and civic organisations.

The auditor should not enter into fee arrangements that might compromise or appear to compromise independence. Therefore, the fee for the audit must be commensurate with the service provided. Recovery of costs in one period should not be dependent upon an expectation of recovery from fees of future audits or the provision of other services to the client. Yet research such as De Angelo (1981) shows that the fees for initial audits are often lower than for continuing audits. **Low-balling** occurs in a tender situation when a bid-price for audit services by an audit firm is quoted at an unreasonably low level to win the tender, with any unrecovered audit costs recovered subsequently through other services or by other means.

The hourly rate is naturally higher for members of the staff with greater skill and experience. Rate determination, then, involves estimating the total annual cost of operating a practice and estimating the total billable time in a year for the various levels of staff.

Fees must be commensurate with the work undertaken and be sufficient to enable appropriate time to be spent by experienced staff. Fees charged for audit or assurance services must not be calculated on a predetermined basis relating to the outcome or result of the work. CPC F.1 Appendix 2.121 prohibits contingency fees for assurance engagements. Fees for other services however, may be subject to a contingent fee. The possibility of a self-interest or advocacy threat must be assessed in these circumstances and safeguards applied as appropriate. The receipt of commissions or other benefits as a result of the audit is prohibited under CFC F.1.25.

Fees from clients must be collected promptly. Overdue fees may create a self-interest threat, especially if they are not paid before the issue of a subsequent audit or review report.

When total fees generated from an audit client represent a large proportion of the auditor's total fees, the real or perceived financial dependency on that audit client creates a self-interest threat. The auditor must have policies in place to ensure that the threat is negated or reduced to an acceptable level. CFC F.1 Appendix 2.116 indicates that specific safeguards, including undertaking independent reviews of the services provided, must be in place if fees from an audit client exceed 15 per cent of the audit firm's total fees. Similar considerations must be undertaken in relation to the fees generated by individual audit engagement partners and separate offices of the audit firm.

AASB 101 requires an audit client to disclose in the financial report the amount of fees paid to the auditor, split between audit and non-audit services and disclosing separately the nature and amount of each non-audit service. *Audit and Assurance Alert No. 11*, issued in May 2002, recommends that the detailed analysis of the fees received for non-audit services should distinguish between:

- other audit-related work such as workers compensation reports;
- other assurance and assurance-related services such as due diligence and risk management;
- legal services;
- advisory services including corporate finance;
- taxation; and
- consulting.

Section 300 (II) (B) now also requires directors to include a statement identifying the fees for each non-audit service. These disclosures allow the audit client and financial report users to understand the nature of the other services provided and consider implications for the auditor's objectivity based on comprehensive information.

Obtaining clients

Since the services of public accounting firms are of a highly personal nature and involve individual character traits such as competence and integrity, the auditor's services cannot be offered in the same manner that commercial goods and services are sold. The most effective way of obtaining recommendations is to render services of a high quality. Until the accountant beginning in public practice has built a nucleus of satisfied clients, they may work for other accountants on an hourly basis. Another approach is to buy an existing practice or enter into partnership with an established practitioner. There are also many ethical and intrinsically rewarding ways that an accountant can attract favourable attention, such as participating in community activities and organisations and accepting speaking engagements before business groups.

Traditionally the profession has not supported the concept of members being able to promote their services through **advertising**. However, in 1984 the two accounting bodies agreed to allow members to advertise within the confines of rules issued by the profession. CPC D.5, 'Advertising, Publicity and Solicitation', permits advertising provided that its content and nature is not false, misleading, deceptive or otherwise reflects adversely on the profession. Potential clients may be approached personally or through direct mailing to make known the range of services that the audit firm offers. However, follow-up communications must be terminated when requested by the recipient or it will be considered harassment, which is unprofessional conduct.

The International Federation of Accountants (IFAC) provides the following as examples of false, misleading or deceptive advertising. These include advertising which:

- creates false or unjustified expectations of favourable results;
- implies the ability to influence any court, tribunal, regulatory agency or similar body or official;
- consists of self-laudatory statements that are not based on verifiable facts;
- makes comparisons with other accountants in public practice;
- contains testimonials or endorsements; and
- contains any other representation that would be likely to cause a reasonable person to misunderstand or be deceived

(IFAC, Code of Ethics, section 14)

An issue that has been around for a number of years, but continues to occur frequently in practice and has caused some concern within the audit profession, is the calling by companies for competitive tenders for audit appointments, and the active involvement by audit firms in the **tendering** process. This issue is symptomatic of the increased competition for audit work. While acknowledging the right of companies to choose their auditors in order to obtain the most cost-efficient audit, there is a major danger for the profession in the potential loss of credibility that could result from a real or perceived loss of independence of the auditor by being placed in a position where there may be an unreasonable threat of dismissal as a result of the auditor's actions. An example is the practice of **opinion shopping**. This may occur where an audit is put out to tender following the issue of a qualified opinion by the previous auditor or where a new issue arises that may involve consideration of the issuing of a qualified opinion and the client seeks the views of potential new auditors as to how they would interpret the client's action in terms of the application of a certain accounting practice. CPC F.5 indicates that when an auditor is requested by an entity to give an opinion on an actual or hypothetical accounting issue, they should consider the potential effect on the professional responsibilities of the auditor, the purpose of the request and the intended use of any response. The auditor whose opinion is requested is also required to communicate with the existing auditor and provide a copy of the opinion to them. Tendering may also subject an auditor to undue pressure because of the cost of the audit examination and the ability to conduct the necessary audit procedures and the impact of low-balling (discussed earlier). It is likely that the practice of audit tendering within the business community will continue. However, audit firms must recognise that the tender they submit needs to reflect the level of professional skill, knowledge and responsibility required for the audit work. Auditors and management should also be aware of the increased audit risk and hidden costs associated with changes of client as a result of the tendering process, for example the loss of audit continuity and the extensive knowledge of a client's business and personnel by the audit firm, which are beneficial to an effective audit process. On the other hand, the tendering process appears to have led to some increases in audit efficiency as auditors have implemented more efficient and effective audit techniques.

Evaluation of potential clients and ethical considerations in accepting an engagement are discussed in Chapter 6.

Quick review

1. Audit fees should be commensurate with the services provided.
2. Advertising, publicity and solicitation are permitted provided they are not false, misleading, deceptive or otherwise reflect adversely on the profession.

Summary

Ethics is concerned with what is good for the general wellbeing of individuals and the community. The ICAA and CPA Australia have ethical rules to help promote high ethical standards among their members. However, as ethics is an attitude of mind, these rules cannot by themselves make auditors act ethically. An auditor needs an ethical attitude, a good knowledge of ethical principles and ethical decision-making skills to handle ethical conflicts. The accounting bodies are strongly supporting the push for improved corporate governance, including the establishment of audit committees. The number of companies with audit committees is increasing steadily. Corporate governance is the set of rules or procedures that ensure that a company is managed in the best interests of the stakeholders. Ethical principles and skills in ethical decision making are important aspects of corporate governance. Auditors have an important role to play in the corporate governance process, through both the audit itself and reporting to the audit committee. At the centre of the ethical rules of the auditing profession is the need both to be, and to be seen as, independent.

Interest in audit independence has increased dramatically in recent times due to the spate of corporate failures both in Australia and overseas. As a result, we have seen the Ramsay Report into audit independence in Australia, recommendations for audit reform from the JCPAA and the HIH Royal Commission, amendments to the *Corporations Act* through CLERP 9 to strengthen auditor independence, and the issue of a revised ethical rule CPC F.1, which is based on a new code of ethics issued by IFAC. CPC F.1 adopts a conceptual approach that uses a framework based on identifying and evaluating threats to independence and introducing safeguards to eliminate the threats or reduce them to an acceptable level. As a result, the ability of auditors to provide non-audit services has been greatly reduced. This has been reduced even further by the introduction of the *Sarbanes-Oxley Act 2002* in the USA. In addition, a number of Australian companies have imposed restrictions on the non-audit services that their auditors may supply. There have also been calls for other means of improving auditor independence, such as the establishment of auditor oversight boards, strengthening the role of audit committees, rotation of auditors and the establishment of audit firm independence boards.

Key terms

References

American Accounting Association (1990) *Ethics in the Accounting Curriculum: Cases and Readings*, Florida.

Arkley-Smith, T. (1999) 'Audit committee disclosures: time to regulate?', *Australian CPA*, August, 36–9.

Ashkanasy, N.M. and Windsor, C. (1994) 'How independent are auditors? The role of personality and organisational culture', *Perspectives on Contemporary Auditing*, 105–14.

Auditing & Assurance Standards Board of the Australian Accounting Research Foundation, Australian Institute of Company Directors and Institute of Internal Auditors—Australia (2001), *Audit Committees: Best Practice Guide*, 2nd edn, AICD, Sydney.

Australian Securities Commission (1994) *How to Report Suspected Breaches of the* Corporations Law, August, Sydney.

Australian Society of CPAs and the Institute of Chartered Accountants in Australia (1993) *A Research Study on Financial Reporting and Auditing: Bridging the Expectation Gap* (Middleton Report), December, ASCPA, Melbourne, and the ICAA, Sydney.

Australian Society of CPAs and the Institute of Chartered Accountants in Australia (1996) *Beyond the Gap: Report of the Financial Reporting and Auditing Expectation Gap Task Force to the Joint Standing Committee*, June, ASCPA, Melbourne, and the ICAA, Sydney.

Baxter, P. and Pragasam, J. (1999) 'Audit committees: one size fits all?', *Australian CPA*, April, 43–4.

Beauchamp, T.L. and Bowie, N.E. (1993) *Ethical Theory and Business*, Prentice-Hall, Englewood Cliffs, New Jersey.

Blue Ribbon Committee (1999) *Report and Recommendations of the Blue Ribbon Committee on Improving the Effectiveness of Corporate Audit Committees*, New York Stock Exchange, New York.

Bosch, H. (1995) *Corporate Practices and Conduct*, 3rd edn, Pitman Publishing, Melbourne.

Business Council of Australia (1993) *Corporate Practices and Conduct*, 2nd edn, Information Australia, Melbourne.

Carson, E. (1996) 'Corporate governance disclosure in Australia: the state of play', *Australian Accounting Review*, September, 3–10.

Committee on the Financial Aspects of Corporate Governance (1992) *The Financial Aspects of Corporate Governance* (Cadbury Report), London Stock Exchange.

Corporate Law Economic Reform Program (2002) 'Corporate Disclosure: Strengthening the financial reporting framework', *Proposals for Reform: Paper No. 9 (CLERP 9)*, September, Canberra.

Culvenor, J., Stokes, D. and Taylor, S. (2002) 'A Review of the Proposals for Reform on Independence of Australian Company Auditors', *Australian Accounting Review*, July, 12–23.

De Angelo, L. (1981) 'Auditor Independence, Low Balling and Disclosure Regulation', *Journal of Accounting and Economics*, Vol. 3, 113–27.

Earnscliffe Research and Communications (2000) *Report to the United States Independence Standards Board—Research into Perceptions of Auditor Independence and Objectivity*, Earnscliffe, New York.

Gay, G.E. (2002) 'Recent Developments in Auditor Independence', *Company and Securities Law Journal*, February, 46–55.

Grace, D. and Cohen, S. (1995) *Business Ethics: Australian Problems and Cases*, Oxford University Press, Melbourne.

Guy, M. (1990) *Ethical Decision Making in Everyday Work Situations*, Quorum Books, New York, 14–19.

Hayes, C. (2002) 'The Ramsay Report and the Regulation of Auditor Independence in Australia', *Australian Accounting Review*, July, 3–11.

Houghton, K. and Jubb, C. (2002) 'An Australian Response to Recent Developments in the Market for Audit Services', *Australian Accounting Review*, July, 24–30.

ICAA (2003) *Financial Report Audit: Meeting the Market Expectations*, ICAA, Sydney.

ICAEW (1999) *Internal Control: Guidance for Directors on the Combined Code* (Turnbull Report), ICAEW, London.

Independence Standards Board (2000) *A Conceptual Framework for Auditor Independence*, Exposure Draft, November, ISB, New York.

Investment and Financial Services Association Limited (2004) *Corporate Guidance: A Guide for Investment Managers and Corporations* (IFSA Blue Book), May, IFSA, Sydney.

Joint Committee of Public Accounts and Audit (2002) 'Review of Independent Auditing by Registered Company Auditors', *Report 391*, August, Canberra.

Leung, P. and Cooper, B.J. (1995) 'Ethical dilemmas in accountancy practice', *Australian Accountant*, May, 28–33.

Lynn, R.S. (1996) 'The role of the auditor in corporate governance', *Australian Accounting Review*, September, 16–18.

Moroney, R. and Simnett, R. (1996) 'Audit committee disclosure by listed companies', *Charter*, October, 59–61.

Nash, L. (1981) 'Ethics without the sermon', *Harvard Business Review*, No. 59, 79–90.

OECD (1999) *Principles of Corporate Governance*, OECD, Paris.

Panel on Audit Effectiveness (2000) *Report and Recommendations*, Public Oversight Board, Stamford, Connecticut.

Psaros, J. and Seamer, M. (2001) 'The unravelling of the House of Scarfe', *Charter*, Vol. 72, No. 5, June, 44–7.

Ramsay, I. (2001) *Independence of Australian Company Auditors*, Department of Treasury, Canberra.

Rawls, J. (1957) 'Justice as fairness', *Journal of Philosophy*, Vol. 54, October, 653–62.

Schelluch, P. (1991) 'Audit Committees', *Accounting Communiqué No. 30*, ASCPA, Melbourne.

Singer, P. (1993) *How Are We to Live? Ethics in an Age of Self-interest*, The Text Publishing Company, Melbourne.

Slamet, D. (1993) 'Blowing the whistle: The dilemma for accountants', *Financial Forum*, November, 4–5.

Starke, J.G. (1991) 'The protection of public service "Whistleblowers"—Part 1', *The Australian Law Journal*, Vol. 65, No. 4, April, 205–19.

Thomson, J.A.K., Tredennick, H. and Barnes, J. (1976) *Aristotle's Ethics*, Penguin Classics, Harmondsworth.

Turner, J.L., Mock, T.J. and Srivastava, R.P. (2002) 'A Formal Model of Auditor Independence Risk', *Australian Accounting Review*, July, 31–8.

Unger, L. (2001) 'This year's proxy season: Sunlight shines on auditor independence and executive compensation', Speech by SEC Acting Chairman, 25 June, Centre for Professional Education, Washington.

Wade, M. (1991) 'Independence in appearance: A framework for analysis', *Accounting Research Journal*, Spring, 43–54.

MaxMARK

Assignments

MAXIMISE YOUR MARKS! There are approximately 30 interactive questions on ethics, independence and corporate governance available online at www.mhhe.com/au/gay3e

Additional assignments for this chapter are contained in Appendix A of this book, page 763.

REVIEW QUESTIONS

3.1 For each of the following questions relating to ethics, select the *best* response.

(a) Which of the following is *not* a doctrine or theory of ethics?

A virtues

B deontology

C theology

D egoism

(b) Which fundamental ethical principle provides that the auditor should safeguard the interests of their clients provided it does not conflict with their duties and loyalties to the community and its laws?

A objectivity

B confidentiality

C public interest

D whistleblowing

(c) Which of the following organisations has developed an ethical decision-making model?

A American Accounting Association

B Auditing and Assurance Standards Board

C Australian Stock Exchange

D Business Council of Australia

3.2 For each of the following questions relating to independence, select the *best* response.

(a) The ethical rules state that independence of the external audit firm is considered to be impaired if:

A the audit partner purchases the client's product at normal retail prices

B the audit firm provides management advisory services to the client

C a near relative of one of the partners is the beneficial owner of shares forming a material part of the share capital of the client

D the audit firm has served as the external auditor for many years

(b) A violation of the profession's ethical standards would be *least* likely to occur when an auditor:

A refers life insurance assignments to the auditor's spouse, who is a life insurance agent

B holds the position of company secretary with an audit client which is a public company

    C is a member of the same golf club as the managing director

    D undertakes a management advisory engagement and decides on the most appropriate computer system for a client

(c) Which of the following impairs an auditor's independence regarding the client?

    A The audit firm also prepares the client's tax return.

    B The client has not paid fees related to the previous year's audit.

    C The audit firm recommends a job description and candidate specifications for the position of financial controller of a client.

    D The audit firm trains client personnel during the implementation of a new computer system.

(d) An auditor strives to achieve independence in appearance to:

    A maintain an unbiased mental attitude

    B maintain public confidence in the auditor

    C become independent in fact

    D comply with the *Corporations Act*

(e) To emphasise auditor independence from management, many entities follow the practice of:

    A having the auditor report to an audit committee of external members of the board of directors

    B appointing a partner of the audit firm conducting the audit to the entity's audit committee

    C establishing a policy of discouraging social contact between employees of the entity and the staff of the auditor

    D requesting that a representative of the auditor be on hand at the annual general meeting

(f) Which of the following is not normally a part of an audit committee's responsibilities?

    A Nominating the independent auditors

    B Discussing the detailed audit programs of the independent auditors

    C Discussing the meaning and significance of the audited financial report

    D Discussing the problems of the independent auditors in completing the audit of the annual financial report

3.3 For each of the following questions relating to obtaining clients, select the *best* response.

(a) In determining the fees for an attestation service, an auditor may take into account each of the following, except the:

    A attainment of specific findings

    B value of the service to the client

    C degree of responsibility assumed by the auditor in undertaking the engagement

    D skills required to perform the service

(b) Inclusion of which of the following in a promotional brochure published by an audit firm would be most likely to result in a violation of the ethical rules?

    A Testimonials and endorsements by existing clients

    B Details of types of services offered

    C List of fees for services, including hourly rates and fixed fees

    D Educational and professional qualifications of partners

Professional ethics

 learning objective 1

3.4 What is ethics?

Ethical theory

learning objective 2

3.5 Explain the relevance of virtue ethics to an auditor.

learning objective 3

Accounting bodies' code of ethics

3.6 Why is it important to the accounting profession to have adopted a code of ethics?

 learning objective 4

Applying ethics

3.7 How do ethical decision models assist in resolving ethical dilemmas?

 learning objective 5

Corporate governance

3.8 Can an audit committee be used as a means of improving corporate governance?

 learning objective 6

Whistleblowing

3.9 Indicate whether you believe that auditors have a responsibility to whistleblow in their dealings with the ICAA or CPA Australia, their employing firms, their clients and each other.

 learning objective 7–10

Audit independence

3.10 Explain the difference between perceived and actual independence and indicate why both are important to the auditor.

3.11 Should auditors be allowed to provide non-audit services?

3.12 What is an audit committee and what are its functions?

 learning objective 11

Fee determination and obtaining clients

3.13 How is the fee for an audit engagement determined?

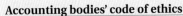

DISCUSSION PROBLEMS AND CASE STUDIES

 primary learning objective 3

Accounting bodies' code of ethics

3.14 **Moderate** After recently completing professional examinations, you have formed a partnership with an existing sole practitioner. Your partner is a registered company auditor and has decided to move into partnership as a means of offering a wider range of services. In particular he is looking to increase the amount of consultancy work the firm is undertaking. The firm's largest client is a small public company that originally joined the firm when your partner commenced practice. Over the years the services that your firm provides have grown to include taxation and financial advice.

You have just assisted this client to identify and negotiate an acquisition of a business. As the financial year-end is approaching, the managing director approaches you to undertake valuation of the brand names of the business acquired. The directors intend to include your valuation in the statement of financial position of the company as an independent valuation. They have indicated that it will save them a great deal of audit time if this matter can be resolved before the audit.

After the acquisition, the company will be an even more important client of your firm from both an audit fee and consulting perspective. There is also the prospect that they will undertake some form of capital raising in the future to fund further expansion.

Required
Outline five ethical issues relevant in assessing the relationship with the company and in deciding whether to continue offering the current range of services to this client. Cite relevant references where appropriate.

 primary learning objective 4

Applying ethics

3.15 **Complex** Fred and Barney are two audit seniors working for the same Big Four accounting firm. Both started employment with the firm around the same time. They have mutual respect for each other; however, they remain highly competitive, which has been the case since they commenced work together.

Fred is recently married and he and his wife are paying off their mortgage. Barney is single with a reputation in the firm for playing hard but working hard too. They have both been seniors for almost 18 months and are looking for promotion to audit supervisor. They are both aware that there is only one supervisor position available.

Fred recently replaced Barney on a particular job and the reason given to both Fred and Barney was that another assignment had arisen with a long-time client of Barney's. Once Fred had replaced Barney on that particular job, he realised that the client called the audit manager to say they were not impressed with Barney, as he had missed a number of issues within the audit and was arriving at work late. The audit manager had not discussed these comments with either Fred or Barney. Fred, after going through the work that Barney had done, realised that Barney had performed an excellent job, identifying a number of issues that he thought he would have possibly missed. Furthermore, Fred suspects Barney and the client had a personality conflict, and the client had misled the audit manager.

Fred realises that he can continue to finish off the audit, resolving the issues, and obtain a good review from this assignment, which would help him in the promotion stakes. He also knows that the audit manager is unlikely to bring the client's unsupported allegations to Barney's attention.

(a) Using the AAA model, work through this scenario and decide what action Fred should take.

(b) Consider the ten core values from the Mary Guy decision model to determine whether your decision would be different using this decision model.

Source: This question was adapted from the Professional Year Programme of The Institute of Chartered Accountants in Australia—1996 Ethics 1 Module.

3.16 Complex You are a senior auditor in a firm of auditors in a country town. The major client of the firm is the town's largest registered club. You are in charge of the audit and report directly to the partner.

With the rural recession and the move of certain industries from the town, your firm is dependent upon the continuance of the club as an audit client.

The secretary manager of the club has held this position for over 20 years, and is well respected in the town. He has worked hard to build the club from humble beginnings. The secretary manager has a strong personality and exerts influence on the board of directors of the club. The audit partner and the secretary manager are members of the same golf club and play regularly on Saturday mornings.

The club is currently undergoing major renovations with the work being undertaken by ABC Builders.

To get home you have to drive past the secretary manager's house. One night you notice that the secretary manager is having more renovations done to his home and that there is an ABC truck delivering materials to the house. Next day at lunchtime you drive past the house and again see an ABC truck and this time there are tradespeople working on the house.

You have just commenced the year-end audit work for the club and during your visit to the club's premises, you obtain copies of the tenders for the renovations and find that ABC was the most expensive tenderer with the directors' minutes revealing that the secretary manager convinced the board to accept ABC's tender based on their perceived quality.

You are concerned that there may be some impropriety on the part of the secretary manager. You raise your suspicions with the audit partner, who dismisses them out of hand and says that even if there was any substance to them, what could the firm do about them.

(a) What are the ethical issues?

(b) What should you do? Decide on your response by working through the Laura Nash model.

Source: This question was adapted from the Professional Year Programme of The Institute of Chartered Accountants in Australia—1995 Ethics 3 Module.

3.17 Complex Steven Brown is a promising senior manager beginning his tenth year at his firm. Steven has been a steady performer during his career and is known for his technical and personal skills.

Not all the firm's partners are enthusiastic about Steven. His track record for bringing in new clients has been marginal. This weakness has not stopped Steven moving up the ladder, but slow expansion in the client base has meant that the firm has not made a new partner for three years. Steven is well aware that his ability to bring in new clients is critical to his aspirations to become a partner.

BAC Manufacturing, a large ink manufacturer, has decided to put its audit and related accounting services out for tender. BAC's current auditor performs significant non-audit services. In fact, fees for non-audit services are well in excess of the audit fee.

Steven has been given the primary responsibility for developing and presenting the tender to BAC's board of directors. He has nearly completed preparations for the presentation and has discussed all the specifics with two partners who will have a significant involvement in servicing the audit and related service needs of BAC, should the firm be successful in its tender. As required by the board of BAC, a detailed outline of the proposal presentation and itemised preliminary budget were submitted nine weeks in advance of the presentation.

On the Monday evening before the presentation, Steven's wife receives a call from her sister, Cheryl. Cheryl's flatmate, Maria, is the secretary of BAC's managing director. Maria noticed that one of the proposal presentations was going to be done by someone named Steven Brown and asked if it was the same Steven Brown who was married to Cheryl's sister. Cheryl said it was and Maria began to tell her about some of the proposals.

Maria had said she noticed several things about the managing director's evaluation of the proposal submitted by Steven's firm. First, the bid was significantly higher than one of the other bids. Second, the managing director had mentioned two items of major importance that had been left out of the proposal. Maria could not remember these items 'off the top of her head', but she told Cheryl she would be willing to run off a copy of the memo if Cheryl wanted her to.

Steven's wife tells him about the call from Cheryl at dinner that evening.

(a) Consider the ethical issues, utilising the AAA decision model.

(b) What should Steven do?

Source: This question was adapted from the Professional Year Programme of The Institute of Chartered Accountants in Australia—1995 Ethics 1 Module.

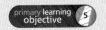

Corporate governance

3.18 Moderate 'The requirement by the Australian Stock Exchange for companies to disclose their main corporate governance practices in annual reports is capable of manipulation and distortion by unethical boards of directors.'

In light of the above comment, consider whether the nature and disclosure of corporate governance practices should be prescribed by the *Corporations Act* and form part of the financial report upon which the company's auditor expresses an opinion.

Source: This question was adapted from the Professional Year Programme of The Institute of Chartered Accountants in Australia—1996 Ethics 3 Module)

Audit independence

3.19 Moderate You are the auditor of XYZ Ltd, a company involved in gold exploration. Prior to year-end you find that the company has the following characteristics:

- a net current liability position;
- borrowings and bank overdraft facilities approaching maturity, with uncertain prospects of renewal or repayment;

- excessive reliance on short-term borrowings to finance long-term assets; and
- funding commitments in relation to mining tenements which the company cannot meet, with the result that the tenements will lapse.

Because of this information, you discuss with the directors the need to qualify the audit report on the basis that there is uncertainty whether the company can continue as a going concern. The company directors take exception to this view, because they intend to raise funds through a share issue within the next year. Rather than have a qualified audit report, the directors ask you to resign as auditor so that they can give the audit to another firm, Friendly Auditors, who will not qualify the audit report in the current year.

Required

(a) What barriers are you (the auditor) likely to encounter in attempting to resign?

(b) If you are unable to resign, what steps can the directors take to remove you as auditor?

Source: This question was adapted from the Professional Year Programme of The Institute of Chartered Accountants in Australia—1995 Accounting 2 Module.

3.20 Complex Winston Gould is the controlling shareholder of Gould Pty Ltd. He has expressed dissatisfaction with his present auditors and informs Henry Cramer, a registered company auditor and member of a professional accounting body, that he will be appointed auditor if he agrees to the following proposals:

(a) Because Gould's present dissatisfaction is related primarily to fees, which he feels are too high in relation to the time the job should take and the services rendered, Cramer is to quote a fee in advance and detail the services he would provide. This quotation must, of course, be lower than the fee presently being paid by Gould Pty Ltd.

(b) Because Gould feels quite strongly that the company's auditor should take an active part in the operation of the business, Cramer is to serve as a director of Gould Pty Ltd. While Gould appreciates that Cramer must maintain a position of financial independence, he points out that the acquisition of one qualifying common share would not interfere with his independence.

(c) Because Gould Pty Ltd has experienced financial difficulty during the past several years, Cramer is to accept redeemable preference shares in lieu of fees for the first year of the engagement. As these shares have no voting rights, Gould feels that Cramer's independence will not be affected. Moreover, if conditions improve significantly, the shares will be redeemed.

(d) Because Gould has certain personal income tax problems, Cramer is to review his affairs. As the possibility of refund is uncertain, Cramer's fee is to be 40 per cent of all recoveries.

(e) Because Gould is very impressed with a particular auditor who has been employed on the audit for the past two years by the present firm of auditors, Cramer is to hire the auditor and retain him on the audit. Gould knows that the auditor would be amenable to such a suggestion.

With respect to each of the above proposals, what answers should Cramer give to Gould? Give reasons to support these answers.

Source: CICA adapted

3.21 Complex Consider the following independent situations that arose in respect of your firm, PTL Partners. In each case Mr Adams is the audit partner, Ms Tan is the tax partner and Mr Brown is the business advisory partner.

(a) A longstanding friend and tax client, Mr Davis, recently approached Mr Adams and said: 'I'm worried about my son Leroy. He's enrolled in an accounting degree but can't find vacation work and he's getting a bit depressed about it. Do you have anything available?' In response to this request, Mr Adams organised vacation work for Leroy in the firm's audit division, even though the firm has a 'no vacation work' policy. Leroy worked on the ZX Limited engagement, a company in direct competition with Mr Davis's employer, although neither Mr Adams nor Leroy knew this at the time. A few weeks later, Mr Davis gave Mr Adams and his family free tickets to the Australian Open tennis finals in gratitude.

(b) Mega Motels is a chain of 10 motels operating on the far south coast of NSW. Your firm performs both audit and tax work for Mega Motels. The audit fees comprise around 10 per cent of total audit fee revenue, while the tax work comprises around 5 per cent of total tax-related revenue. Mega Motels has not paid any of its fees for the last three years, citing cash flow problems. However, in actual fact, Mega Motels has made impressive profits over the last few years and has significant cash reserves. The partners have been reluctant to push the issue further, as Mega Motels is a high-profile client whom they wish to retain.

Last month, your firm agreed to hold their annual staff retreat at one of Mega Motel's motels, as a partial contra against the outstanding fees. Half of the outstanding fees will be waived, even though the reasonable market value of the services to be provided is only 30 per cent of the total outstanding amount.

(c) Ms Tan has just been appointed a director of XX Co. Pty Ltd, a small proprietary company that is a travel agent. Mr Adams performs the audit of XX Co. in accordance with the relevant legislation. Mr Brown recently assisted XX Co. in selecting and installing ABC brand accounting software. ABC pay the firm a commission for every software package sold, and this fact was verbally disclosed to XX Co. In addition, Mr Brown has just performed a valuation of XX Co.'s business for the purposes of a Family Law Court dispute.

(d) Several of Mr Adams's staff recently completed a review of the internal controls at FG Pty Ltd, a large proprietary company which is also an audit client. The work was charged at 120 per cent of the usual consulting fees to partially recoup the lower audit fees brought about by a competitive tender. At the client's request, audit staff implemented all the recommended changes in procedures by updating the company's accounting manual and running a two-hour training session for the accounting staff. As audit staff have already performed significant work on FG's internal controls, the audit manager has decided to assess control risk as low and not perform any tests of control.

(e) Mr Brown prepares a compilation report for A Butchery, which supplies gourmet meats to five-star hotels. A Butchery is currently in dispute with one of Mr Adams's clients, F Feedlots. A Butchery alleges that F Feedlots supplied substandard meat to them on several occasions in the last few months. Accordingly, A Butchery have not paid their account, which is material to F Feedlots' receivables. F Feedlots are currently unable to pay your firm's audit fees, citing cash flow problems. Neither client knows your firm acts for the other.

(f) One of the firm's audit clients is JK Limited, a credit union. During the audit, the financial controller, Ms Vero, mentions to Mr Adams that she is looking for a new assistant accountant. Mr Adams mentions this to his nephew, David, who applies for and is subsequently appointed to the job. In gratitude at saving recruitment firm fees, Ms Vero arranges to have all fees on Mr Adams's home loan waived for the next 12 months. In all other respects Mr Adams's loan is on normal commercial terms. Since his appointment, David has been assisting your firm by giving verbal confirmation of audit client account balances held with JK. This has saved your firm money in bank audit certificate fees.

Required

For each of the above independent situations:

(i) Identify any professional standards and regulatory requirements which have been breached.

(ii) Recommend possible courses of action your firm could take to rectify these breaches.

Source: This question was adapted from the Professional Year Programme of The Institute of Chartered Accountants in Australia—1999 Accounting 2 Module.

3.22 Complex The following are independent situations:

(i) Chad is an audit assistant currently undertaking university studies. While auditing the books of DelTel, he comes across certain financial information that he believes will assist him in completing one of his university assignments. He copies the information and uses it in his assignment, carefully removing all reference to DelTel in order to preserve the client's confidentiality.

(ii) Ms Wang has been the engagement partner on the Plimsol Ltd audit for a number of years. Some time ago, Plimsol Ltd's longstanding company secretary retired and it took six months to find a replacement. At Plimsol Ltd's request, Ms Wang performed company secretarial duties for this period of time. Ms Wang was not company secretary at the time the annual audit report was signed.

(iii) Tim is the eldest son of the factory foreman of one of your firm's major audit clients, Enz Ltd. Enz Ltd operates in the manufacturing industry. During vacation work, Tim is assigned to the audit of Enz Ltd. Tim's work comprised testing the internal controls of the cash payments system.

(iv) Caz is an audit supervisor at Goodsell Partners. For the last two years, Goodsell Partners has been engaged by Sundew Pty Ltd to audit certain summarised financial information for submission to Sundew Pty Ltd's bankers. The summarised financial information is prepared on a quarterly basis. While filing other work papers, Caz notices that there is a typographical error in the report issued for the quarter ending 31 March 2002. This has resulted in a serious overstatement of net profit. As several months have passed since March, and neither the client nor the banker has queried the figures, Caz decides to ignore the error.

Required

For each of the independent situations (i) to (iv):

(a) List any professional standards and regulatory requirements breached.

(b) Advise as to possible alternative courses of action the auditor should have taken in order to properly discharge their professional responsibilities.

(c) In general, outline the potential consequences of breaching the Code of Professional Conduct for:

(i) an accounting practice

(ii) a member employee whose actions gave rise to breach.

Source: This question was adapted from the CA Program of The Institute of Chartered Accountants in Australia—2002 Financial Reporting and Assurance Module.

3.23 Complex You are involved in the audit of Superdrug Ltd and have been examining the documentation associated with the purchase of the expensive and troublesome Acme Filling Machine and Capper. However, the documentation is highly summarised and incomplete and it is difficult to determine whether Superdrug's capital purchasing policy has been followed.

Superdrug's General Manager—Production, Robert Boyd, would ultimately have been responsible for presenting the case for the Acme purchases to Superdrug's Board. You have a good relationship with Robert, including a common interest in the national football competition. You approach Robert, who listens carefully to your concerns and seeks to reassure you that all necessary procedures were followed. Also, he tells you not to be concerned with the teething problems that they are having with the Acme equipment as he used to work with them as an engineer prior to joining Superdrug and knows that they build top-quality machines. He suggests that you join him for lunch as his guest at an extremely expensive restaurant in the city so that you can discuss the matter further.

As you are about to leave, Robert offers you two tickets to the upcoming football Grand Final, which he says that he won in a competition and is unable to attend.

Required

(a) Identify and explain four (4) ethical issues you face.

(b) Recommend, with reasons, the most appropriate course of action that you should take. Indicate how it will overcome the issues raised in part (a).

3.24 Complex The following are independent situations:

(a) Mink and Darvis was recently awarded the audit of Hilly Farms Foods Ltd for the year ended 31 August 20X3. Bill Fox, senior-in-charge, and an assistant observed the inventory on 31 August. Upon completion of the inventory observation, Wally Warp, Hilly Farms Foods Ltd's controller, informed Fox that the shipping supervisor had a small gift for him and the assistant. Fox asked Warp what the gift was for, and Warp responded that they had always given small gifts of food items to their previous auditors upon completion of the inventory observation. Fox estimates that the value of the food is less than $200.

(b) Julia Roberto, a sole practitioner, has provided extensive advisory services for her audit client, Leather and Chains Ltd. She has interpreted financial reports, provided forecasts and other analyses, counselled on potential expansion plans, and counselled on banking relationships.

(c) Steve Rackwill has been asked by his audit client, Petry Plumbing Supply Pty Ltd, to help implement a new control system. Rackwill will arrange interviews for Petry Plumbing Supply Pty Ltd's hiring of new personnel and instruct and oversee the training of current client personnel.

(d) Bob Lanzotti is the partner-in-charge of the audit of Fleet Ltd. Over the years, he has become a golfing buddy of Fleet Ltd's CEO, Jim Harris. During the current year Lanzotti and Harris jointly purchased an exclusive vacation home on the Gold Coast. The vacation home represents more than 10 per cent of Lanzotti's personal wealth.

Required

For each situation, indicate whether the Code of Professional Conduct has been breached. Give reasons.

3.25 Complex The following are independent situations:

(a) Kraemeer and Kraemeer recently won the audit of Garvin Clothiers Ltd, a large manufacturer of women's clothing. Jock Kraemeer had a substantial investment in Garvin Clothiers Ltd prior to bidding on the engagement. In anticipation of winning the engagement, Kraemeer placed his shares in Garvin Clothiers Ltd in a trust.

(b) Zeker and Associates audits a condominium association in which the parents of a member of the firm own a unit. The unit is material to the parents' net worth, and the member participates in the engagement.

(c) Jimmy Saad, a sole practitioner, audited Dallas Conduit Pty Ltd's financial report for the year ended 30 June 20X2, and was issued shares by the client as payment of the audit fee. Saad disposed of the shares before commencing field work planning for the audit of the 30 June 20X3 financial report.

(d) Dip-It Paint Ltd requires an audit for the current year. However, Dip-It Ltd has not paid Allen and Allen the fees due for tax-related services performed two years ago. Dip-It Ltd issued Allen and Allen a note for the unpaid fees, and Allen and Allen proceeded with the audit services.

(e) Maria Harrison, sole proprietor of an audit firm, plans to establish a separate business that will provide management consulting services. She intends to operate both businesses simultaneously.

Required

For each situation, indicate whether the Code of Professional Conduct has been breached. Give reasons.

3.26 Complex 'Auditors are to blame for the recent spate of major corporate collapses. They have got too cosy with management instead of protecting shareholders and investors.'

Required

Discuss whether you agree or disagree with this statement. Your answer should consider the role that lack of independence may have played in audit failures.

Fee determination and obtaining clients

primary learning objective 11

3.27 Basic Audit tendering has become common for large audits in an attempt to reduce business costs in a competitive business environment. Discuss the advantages and disadvantages of audit tendering.

3.28 Basic Auditors budget time required to perform specific audits. Sometimes budgeted hours are exceeded in order to complete an examination.
(a) What factors might cause an auditor to exceed the time budget on an audit?
(b) Are the hours in excess of the budget charged to the client at the usual charge rate or should they be absorbed by the auditor?

3.29 Basic Read the following extract:

KPMG's Cameos

KPMG is paying up to $US17 000 a pop to have its name feature, even if only briefly, in 18 movies in the next two years. Reuters reports KPMG has signed its first deal, in which Robert De Niro will pass Dustin Hoffman a KPMG-branded coffee mug, in the movie Wag the Dog. *In Britain, the hero of a low-budget romantic comedy,* The Sea Change, *will be a KPMG accountant.*

(*Business Review Weekly*, 3 March 1997, p. 101)

Required

(a) Does this type of advertising and publicity comply with the guidelines set out in the code of professional conduct in Australia? Provide reasons for your decision.
(b) Do you believe this form of advertising may endanger the quality of audits? Provide reasons for your decision.

3.30 Moderate Vivian Lau is a sole practitioner specialising in audit and taxation services. In an attempt to attract more clients, Vivian sent out a new brochure which advertised the services she provided and followed up this mail-out with a telephone call to see if any of the potential clients were interested in using her services. However, as this approach did not attract much new business she decided to introduce a new professional service and promote it in a series of advertisements in the newspapers. The advertisements stated that she is able to provide expert advice in the franchising of a business, which she believes is a growth area. Although she has no experience in franchising, Vivian believes that this new marketing strategy will attract many new clients to her practice.

Indicate whether there are any problems arising from Vivian's two advertising strategies.

CHAPTER 4

THE LEGAL LIABILITY OF AUDITORS

LEARNING OBJECTIVES

After studying this chapter you should be able to:

1. explain the concept of reasonable care and skill;

2. define negligence and indicate the elements which need to be proved for a claim to be successful;

3. explain the auditor's legal liability to clients;

4. describe the concept of contributory negligence;

5. indicate to what extent a duty of care may be owed to third parties;

6. describe alternative proposals to limit the auditor's liability; and

7. explain the auditor's duties in regard to the prevention, detection and reporting of fraud.

This chapter will consider an auditor's legal liability to clients and third parties. The concept of reasonable care and skill will be explained and the elements necessary for a claim of negligence to be successful will be outlined with reference to legal cases. The concept of contributory negligence and proposals to limit the auditor's liability will be discussed. The auditor's responsibilities for prevention, detection and reporting of fraud will also be covered.

Relevantguidance

Australian		**International**	
AUS 210	The Auditor's Responsibility to Consider Fraud and Error in an Audit of a Financial Report (Revised 2004)	ISA 240	The Auditor's Responsibility to Consider Fraud and Error in an Audit of Financial Statements (Revised 2004)
AGS 1014	Privity Letter Requests	—	

ESTABLISHING THE AUDITOR'S DUTY

Contract, statute and common law are important in determining the nature and scope of an auditor's responsibilities. When an audit or other assurance service is carried out solely under a private contractual arrangement, the scope of the audit or other assurance service is indicated by the terms of that contract, usually set out in the engagement letter, which is discussed in Chapter 6. Audits carried out under statutory provisions also need to have regard to the requirements of the statute, and any judicial interpretations of those requirements. The relevant statutes form the basis of the contract between the auditor and the client, while the common-law decisions are important in interpreting requirements arising from the contract or giving effect to the contract. Society imposes a duty to exercise care or skill in relation to another person in two ways:

1   a duty in contract arising from an agreement between the parties; and
2   a duty imposed by law arising from a special relationship in which parties stand to one another.

REASONABLE CARE AND SKILL

The auditor must exercise the **reasonable care and skill** expected of a professional. From a professional viewpoint, this requires adherence to professional standards in all aspects of an audit. The legal position is described in the judgment by Moffit J in *Pacific Acceptance Corporation v Forsyth and Others* (1970) 90 WN (NSW) 29:

> It is beyond question that when an auditor, professing as he does to possess the requisite skills, enters into a contract to perform certain tasks as auditor, he promises to perform such tasks using that degree of skill and care as is reasonable in the circumstances as they then exist. That is the limit of his promise. That is the bare statement of the legal obligation and in the end the court must come back in any case to the legal proposition and apply it to the court's views on the facts found.

(© Council of Law Reporting for New South Wales 1970)

Similarly, Lord Bridge in the House of Lords decision in *Caparo Industries plc v Dickman & Others* (1990) 1 All ER 568 confirmed the auditor's duty to the client. He said:

> In advising the client who employs him, the professional man owes a duty to exercise that standard of skill and care appropriate to his professional status and will be liable both in contract and in tort for all losses which his client may suffer by reason of any breach of that duty.

NEGLIGENCE

Where the auditor breaches this duty of care and has been negligent in conducting the audit work or has committed fraud, the auditor may be liable for any loss suffered as a result of the auditor's actions.

Godsell (1993, p. 26) defines **negligence** as: 'Any conduct which is careless or unintentional in nature and entails a breach of any contractual duty or duty of care in tort owed to another person or persons'.

In order to succeed in a claim for negligence, the plaintiff must prove that all of the following four elements existed (Godsell, 1993, p. 29):

1 That a duty was owed to the plaintiff by the defendant—normally referred to as a duty of care—raising questions of to whom, or in what circumstances, such a duty is owed.
2 That there was a breach of the duty of care, that is, that negligent conduct actually occurred—raising questions of the standard of conduct required and what conduct would constitute a breach of this standard.
3 That a loss or damage was suffered by the plaintiff.
4 That a causal relationship existed between the breach of duty by the defendant and the harm suffered by the plaintiff. This relationship must have been reasonably foreseeable and therefore not too remote or incidental, in this sense.

Therefore, if a defendant in a negligence action can persuade the court that any one of the four elements has not been proved, the plaintiff will not be successful.

Negligence can arise from a breach of the express or implied terms of a contract, or it can arise as the specific tort of negligence, irrespective of the existence of any contract between the defendant and the plaintiff.

It is important to remember that in order to sue another person for negligence the plaintiff must first establish that a duty of care was owed to her or him. This is a complex and contentious issue which has been the focus of many recent legal cases, particularly involving claims by third parties, as will be discussed later.

Quick review

1 Contract, statute and common law are important in determining the auditor's responsibilities.
2 The auditor must exercise the reasonable care and skill expected of a professional.
3 Negligence by the auditor will result in a breach of that duty of care.
4 To succeed in a claim for negligence, a duty of care must exist, the auditor must be negligent, loss must have been suffered and the breach of duty must have caused the damage.

LIABILITY TO CLIENTS

The auditor's duty of care to a client arises both in contract and in the tort of negligence. If the auditor has been negligent, the client may sue the auditor for breach of an implicit term of the contract, and recover any consequential loss suffered. Alternatively, the client may sue the auditor in the tort of negligence to obtain damages sufficient to restore the client to its original position.

Negligence results when the auditor fails to conform to the standard of care that the law requires. Client claims of negligence against an auditor are difficult to prove. The client has the burden of proof and must prove the auditor's failure to exercise the necessary standard of care established implicitly in the contract.

A difficulty in determining whether negligence has occurred arises because the standard of 'reasonable care and skill' is determined under common law. There is no statute that specifies responsibilities. Rather, they are determined by the standards of 'the reasonable person'. It is possible that the courts may impose stricter standards in certain areas than the profession is willing to prescribe.

An understanding of the present legal interpretation of the auditor's duties and liabilities, and the concept of reasonable care and skill, is best achieved by a review of some major cases. The standard of care identified in common law is not always consistent, and comprehensive coverage of all the important cases relating to auditor's liability would require a separate book. However, the following is a selection of representative cases, accompanied by a brief explanation. Most of the cases relate to annual financial report audits.

London and General Bank Ltd

One of the most important cases relating to the liability of auditors goes back to the year 1895. In the case *Re London and General Bank Ltd (No. 2)* (1895) 2 Ch. 673 it was clearly established that the auditor's duty is to report to the shareholders, not the directors.

The facts were, briefly, that a banking company had book debts which, in the opinion of the auditors, would not realise their recorded value. Therefore the auditors recommended to the directors that no dividend be paid in that year. The auditors did not report this in their audit certificate presented to shareholders because the chairman agreed to refer to this matter in his report at the shareholders' meeting. The chairman did this, but not in a way which drew the attention of shareholders to the auditors' qualification. The company subsequently went into liquidation, and action was taken by the liquidator to recover from the auditors the dividends which had been paid out of capital. The auditors were held liable to repay the dividend because of their failure to report the true state of affairs to the shareholders. Lord Justice Lindley said:

> the auditors are to be appointed by the shareholders, and are to report to them directly, and not to or through the directors. The object of this enactment is obvious. It evidently is to secure to the shareholders independent and reliable information respecting the true financial position of the company at the time of the audit.

> ... An auditor, however, is not bound to do more than exercise reasonable care and skill in making inquiries and investigations. He is not an insurer, he does not guarantee that the books do correctly show the true position of the company's affairs;

> ... Such I take to be the duty of the auditor: he must be honest—i.e., he must not certify what he does not believe to be true, and he must take reasonable care and skill before he believes that what he certifies is true. What is reasonable care in any particular case must depend upon the circumstances of that case ... Where suspicion is aroused more care is obviously necessary; but, still, an auditor is not bound to exercise more than reasonable care and skill ...

Kingston Cotton Mill

A further case decided in the following year (*Re Kingston Cotton Mill Company (No. 2)* (1896) 2 Ch. 279) reinforced the principles established in the *London and General Bank* case concerning the responsibilities of an auditor. This case again involved a company in liquidation. The liquidator had taken action against the auditor to recover dividends allegedly paid out of capital. It was discovered, among other things, that the manager had been overstating the value of inventories in order to produce profits which did not exist. In accordance with practice at that time, the auditor had relied on certificates provided by the manager rather than verifying the quantities of stock on hand. Lord Justice Lopes commented:

> It is the duty of an auditor to bring to bear on the work he has to perform that skill, care and caution which a reasonably competent, careful and cautious auditor would use. What is reasonable skill, care and caution must depend on the particular circumstances of each case. An auditor is not bound to be a detective, or, as was said, to approach his work with suspicion or with a foregone conclusion that there is something wrong. He is a watch-dog, but not a bloodhound ... If there is anything calculated to excite suspicion he should probe it to the bottom, but in the absence of anything of that kind, he is only bound to be reasonably cautious and careful.

Thomas Gerrard & Son

It is important to note that, while the general principles established by these early cases are still useful guides to the standard of professional care and skill, the practices, procedures and standards of auditing have changed. In *Re Thomas Gerrard & Son Ltd* (1967) 2 All ER 525, Pennycuick J said:

> I am not clear that the quality of the auditor's duty has changed in any relevant respect since 1896. Basically that duty has always been to audit the company's accounts with reasonable care and skill. The real ground on which Re Kingston Cotton Mill (No. 2) is, I think, capable of being distinguished is that the standards of reasonable care and skill are, upon the expert evidence, more exacting today than those which prevailed in 1896. I see considerable force in this contention.

Therefore, for example, while the auditors were successful in defending their use of a manager's stock certificate in the *Kingston Cotton Mill* case, current auditing standards require a more objective approach to the audit of inventory.

AUS 506.07 (ISA 501.06) 'Existence and Valuation of Inventories' states that when inventory is material, the auditor should obtain sufficient appropriate audit evidence regarding its existence and condition by attending the physical stocktake, unless it is impractical to do so. It is unlikely that the courts would accept a lower standard than that set by the auditing profession. It is possible that they could require an even higher standard.

Pacific Acceptance

The most comprehensive exposition of the auditor's duties and responsibilities in recent years is found in the judgment of Moffitt J in the Australian case *Pacific Acceptance Corporation Ltd v Forsyth and Others* (1970) 90 WN (NSW) 29. In this case a finance company significantly altered the nature of some of its loans, and the auditors failed to take this into account when planning and carrying out the audit. Irregularities in making loans were undiscovered by the auditors, who not only relied heavily upon the information given by the officers of the company but also neglected to obtain sufficient and appropriate evidence as to the security which had supposedly been provided. In addition, inexperienced staff were employed on the audit and they were not properly supervised. The auditors were required to pay $1.5 million in damages. Some of the more important general issues concern whether the auditor's duty is merely to report or whether there is also a duty to audit, and a consequent duty to warn. Moffitt J said:

> auditors are appointed to safeguard the interests of the shareholders and to check on the directors and through them on management. However, this does not mean that in performing their duties the auditors deal only with the shareholders or avoid communication with management or that they can properly perform the audit without communication from and to management in appropriate cases. The shareholders are not accessible to the auditors during the course of the audit and, in any event, many matters, which call for some communication between the auditors and the company, are more appropriate to be raised and dealt with by management or the directors who are the servants of and represent the company, and through it the shareholders. The auditors perform their duty to the company and safeguard the interests of the shareholders by making communication, properly called for, to the appropriate level of management or the directors during the course of the audit, with an appropriate report to the shareholders at the annual general meeting.

Pacific Acceptance also confirmed that the standards of care and skill deemed to be appropriate will change over time and there is no guarantee that application of generally accepted professional standards automatically meets the requirements of due skill and care. They will be persuasive rather than conclusive. Moffitt J stated:

> Reasonable skill and care calls for changed standards to meet changed conditions or changed understanding of dangers and in this sense standards are more exacting today than in 1896.
>
> ... It is relevant to know if others at the relevant period adopted or did not adopt particular procedures in like circumstances. It is relevant to consider what course an experienced auditor might reasonably adopt in practice to deal with a particular aspect of an audit or as to the reasons of an expert for the framing of a procedure in some particular way or omitting some step as serving no reasonable audit purpose ... .
> However, in the end the court must make its own decision on the particular circumstances of the case, using the procedures adopted by others as but a general guide as to how others attack a particular but somewhat similar problem.

In summary, the judgment of Moffitt J in *Pacific Acceptance* confirmed, and in some areas established, the following legal principles relating to auditing:

Continued...

1 Auditors have a duty to use reasonable care and skill.

2 Auditors have a paramount duty to check and see for themselves. Reliance on independent sources or the client's personnel is an aid to, and not a substitute for, the auditor's procedures.

3 Auditors should audit the whole year.

4 Auditors should closely supervise and review the work of inexperienced audit staff.

5 Auditors should properly document procedures in a written audit program which is amended when conditions change.

6 The scope of an audit can be restricted to reliance on a satisfactory internal control for appropriate areas of audit activity.

7 Auditors have a duty to warn and inform. They are required to communicate with the appropriate level of management during the course of an audit and to the shareholders at the annual general meeting, in relation to any material matters discovered during the audit process. The discovery of fraud or suspicion of fraud must also be communicated.

8 Where the auditor's suspicion is aroused by the discovery of a large number of irregularities that indicate something is wrong or indicate the possibility of fraud, the auditor is expected to take further action.

9 The auditor's plans and procedures should be structured so that if a material error or fraud exists the auditor has a reasonable expectation of discovering it.

10 Professional standards and practice must reflect changes in the economic and business environment. Professional standards provide a guide, but the law will assess their reasonableness in specific circumstances, and therefore what is reasonable care and skill.

Following the *Pacific Acceptance* case, the Australian accounting bodies issued comprehensive and specific audit standards which dealt with a number of the issues raised in this case.

Cambridge Credit

In *Cambridge Credit Corp. Ltd & Anor v Hutcheson & Ors* (1985) 9 ACLR 545, damages of $145 million were awarded against the auditors for negligence, although the Court of Appeal subsequently upheld an appeal against the level of damages based on lack of causation. However, in 1988 the auditors agreed to an out-of-court settlement whereby they paid an estimated $19.5 million to Cambridge Credit's debenture holders, an amount approximating the level of their professional indemnity insurance cover.

In brief, the facts of the case were that Cambridge Credit was involved in the development of real estate, with large public borrowings through debenture issues. The debenture trust deed prescribed ratios between the permitted debentures on the one hand and the level of shareholders' funds and liquid assets on the other. The auditor issued an unqualified auditor's report on the financial report of the company as at 30 June 1971. Cambridge Credit had issued debentures at that time and had also made large advances to joint ventures entered into with others for the development of real estate. To finance its activities during the following two years, the company increased its borrowings. However, while the company required continued access to funds to finance its growth, the market for its stock of real estate was restricted due to a restriction on

Continued...

liquidity within the Australian economy during 1973 and 1974. In 1974, the trustee appointed receivers pursuant to the provisions of the trust deed. It was alleged that there was negligence on the part of the auditors in relation to the 1971 financial report, as they failed to form an opinion that provisions and other adjustments were required in relation to certain assets in the financial report for 1971. Also, the ratio permitted between debentures and liquid assets was breached. It was contended that had the breach been drawn to the attention of the directors in 1971, they would have been unable to remedy the breach due to its magnitude; a receiver would therefore have been appointed by the trustees at that time, thereby avoiding the collapse in 1974. The original decision by Rogers J held that the auditors were negligent, with the level of damages assessed as the difference between what might have been realised in the hypothetical 1971 receivership and the actual 1974 receivership. *Cambridge Credit* confirmed the auditor's duties established in *Pacific Acceptance*.

As indicated above, the original decision by Rogers J was appealed by the auditors and the appeal was upheld. The three appeal judges held two to one that the $145 million award was inappropriate because there was no causal connection between the auditors' breach of contract in 1971 and the loss or damages suffered by Cambridge Credit. It was held that the causes of those losses were the extensive change in the Australian economy during 1972–74 and the decisions of Cambridge Credit to expand its borrowings and real estate investments. The award of damages was set aside. However, the finding of negligence was not successfully challenged. The case was eventually settled out of court for an amount believed to approximate the auditor's professional indemnity insurance of $20 million.

Segenhoe

An Australian case clarifying the auditor's responsibility to shareholders and to the company itself was *Segenhoe Ltd v Akins & Ors* (1990) 8 ACLC 263. Segenhoe argued that it was a separate legal entity, distinct from its shareholders, and that it had suffered loss due to the negligence of its auditors, because shareholders had been paid an amount as dividends which would otherwise not have been paid. Thus, Segenhoe claimed the loss was recoverable from the auditors.

However, the auditors argued that the payment of a dividend out of capital was not recoverable, as the payment was made to shareholders and not to third parties, and therefore should not be regarded as a loss, at least in the case of a solvent company. They argued that the payment of a dividend out of capital should not be regarded as a loss to the company any more than the payment of a dividend out of profits. In both cases it was a payment to, and for the benefit of, shareholders and in that sense it was for the purposes of the company. The auditors' arguments, which really amounted to lifting the corporate veil and treating the company and the shareholders as being the same, were rejected.

Therefore, this decision supports the view that where auditors have been negligent, ultimately they are likely to be liable to their client for the full amount of any resulting dividends paid out of capital. *Segenhoe* reinforces the liability of auditors to the client company itself and indicates that the courts are unwilling to lift the corporate veil where that liability relates to dividends paid out of capital.

Galoo

The decision of the English Court of Appeal in *Galoo Ltd v Bright Graham Murray* (1994) BCC 319 reaffirmed the requirement for causation to be established between any alleged negligence and the losses incurred before an auditor is liable for damages to a client.

In 1987, Hillsdown Holdings plc purchased a controlling shareholding in Galoo Ltd. Hillsdown subsequently claimed that Galoo's audited financial reports for the years 1985 to 1989 and its draft audited financial report for 1990 were materially overstated. It was alleged that Galoo had incurred trading losses of approximately $55 million between 1986 and 1990, with a dividend payment of $1.1 million being made in 1988. It was further alleged that Galoo, relying on the negligently given audit opinions, had continued to trade when it would not otherwise have done so. Galoo sued its auditor for breach of the contractual duty to exercise appropriate care and skill, claiming that its trading losses were attributable to its continued existence, and therefore to the auditor's alleged negligence.

The Court of Appeal held that a causal connection did not exist between the alleged negligence and the losses incurred. Although the financial reports may have allowed the company to continue to exist and trade, the court held that a company's existence is not the cause of its trading losses or profits. Its trading result depends on many factors, including decisions made by the board of directors and market forces. As a result, the Court of Appeal upheld the decision of the trial judge, and struck out Galoo's claim against its auditors.

If this precedent is followed in Australia, it would mean that if, as a result of an auditor's negligence, a company's financial report overstates its financial position so that it remains in business, any trading losses incurred will not be considered to have been caused by the inaccurate financial report, and therefore the auditors will not be held liable to the company for subsequent losses.

Quick review

1. The auditor's duty of care to a client arises both in contract and in the tort of negligence.
2. The standard of reasonable care and skill required is determined under common law.
3. What is considered reasonable care and skill changes over time.
4. The courts are unwilling to lift the corporate veil and treat the company and shareholders as being the same.

CONTRIBUTORY NEGLIGENCE

An important development in the area of breach of contract by an auditor is **contributory negligence**. This is a failure by the plaintiff to meet the standard of care required for its own protection where this is a contributing cause, together with the defendant's fault, in bringing about loss.

Pacific Acceptance

In *Pacific Acceptance*, Moffitt J held that auditors may not be excused from negligence or have their damages reduced on the grounds that the client's directors or employees were also negligent:

Continued...

> *To excuse an auditor because the directors or management were also at fault, and in particular to excuse him when he failed to perform his duty with independence and to check on management and the board, would be to negate a fundamental reason for the appointment of the auditor.*
>
> (© Council of Law Reporting for New South Wales 1970. This material cannot be (i) reproduced in any form; (ii) made available to any other person other than as part of whole publication.)

AWA

In *AWA Ltd v Daniels t/a Deloitte Haskins & Sells* (1995) 16 ACSR 644, the defence of contributory negligence was upheld for the first time in Australia. In this case, AWA's foreign exchange division was managed by a person who was not qualified or experienced in the field and was not subject to the usual internal or external controls. For example, there was inadequate segregation of duties and responsibilities.

The auditor, Deloittes, performed two audits of AWA in the relevant period. The first, statutory audit did not involve any verification of the adequacy of internal controls over foreign exchange dealings. The second, non-statutory audit did review the controls on foreign exchange and the adverse conclusions were conveyed to management, but not to the board of directors.

Although the auditor advised management of some deficiencies in controls and records, no further action was taken by management nor the auditors until the board was made aware of the true position in 1987. It was argued that had the board members been aware of the situation, they would have dismissed the foreign exchange manager, sought expert advice and investigated the foreign exchange operations.

AWA suffered a $49.8 million loss from its foreign exchange transactions and sued its auditor for negligence, claiming it had failed to properly report its findings to the board. The auditor counter-claimed against the board and banks, on the grounds that the loans were entered into negligently.

Rogers CJ held that management had the obligation to put in place the relevant internal control. However, as the management had failed to do this, the auditor had a further obligation to bring the matter to the attention of the board. While the auditor discharged the initial obligation, there was an additional duty to report when management failed to act to rectify deficiencies. As a result, the court not only found that the auditor was negligent, but also held that the auditor could counter-claim against the company because of the negligence of AWA's managing director (and chairman of the board). The non-executive directors, however, were found not to be liable, because they were not in a position to exercise a level of responsibility expected of the managing director by virtue of the intermittent and periodic nature of their duties and the lack of an objective standard of a reasonably competent company director.

However, Rogers CJ also acknowledged the problem of solidary liability. This means that, although the well-insured auditor is technically able to claim contribution from other parties, the auditor is liable to pay the full amount of the loss if the other parties are unable to pay.

In May 1995, the New South Wales Court of Appeal absolved AWA's former chief executive, John Hooke, from liability for damages and reduced Deloittes's share of the damages, placing more blame on AWA management. The court upheld the notion of proportionate liability. As

Continued...

a result of the decision, the total liability was reduced from $17 million to $6 million, AWA's liability was increased from 20 per cent to 33.3 per cent and Deloittes's was reduced from 72 per cent to 66.6 per cent of the damages. Deloittes was held to be liable for $4 million and AWA for $2 million. The case ended several years of legal battles, costing $30 million.

While the decision highlights that AWA's own negligence was a major cause of the loss, Deloittes was negligent in not advising AWA's board in the appropriate manner about the foreign exchange irregularities it had discovered.

LIABILITY TO THIRD PARTIES

The situation of the auditor's liability in relation to persons other than the immediate client has been the subject of much litigation. Third parties who rely on an auditor's opinion, and suffer a loss caused by the negligence of the auditor, have no contractual claim for recovery of losses. An injured third party can, however, bring an action in tort, which is a civil wrong compensated by an award for damages. A right of action in tort depends on whether an interest protected by law has been injured. In Australia, protection from negligence is a right enforceable at law (see example 4.1 on pp. 151–2).

Until relatively recent times it was believed that, because of the lack of a contractual relationship between third parties and the auditor, recovery of losses from auditors for negligence (in the absence of fraud) was not possible. Recent legal cases have altered that position.

Donoghue v Stevenson

The analysis of liability to third parties for negligence started with the case of *Donoghue v Stevenson* (1932) AC 562. This case established the precedent in English law that negligence was redressable despite the lack of a contractual relationship between the two parties. Reasonable care must be taken in all circumstances where it can be foreseen that a failure to do so could result in damage. This case, however, established a duty of care only in acting reasonably to avoid causing physical injury.

Candler

The case of *Candler v Crane Christmas & Co.* (1951) 2 KB 164 reinforced the notion that third parties were not entitled to recover monetary losses resulting from auditors' negligence. In this case, Mr Candler, relying upon a set of negligently audited company accounts, invested money which he eventually lost when the company became insolvent. Mr Candler sued the auditor, but a majority of the Court of Appeal in England held that, provided there was no

Continued...

contractual or fiduciary relationship between the parties, the auditor did not owe a duty of care to the plaintiff. Reference was made to the American case, *Ultramares Corporation v Touche* (1931) 174 NE 441, where it was held that negligence does not make the auditors liable to third parties, unless that negligence is so gross that it is constructive fraud. In *Ultramares*, Cardozo CJ stated that auditors' liability does not extend 'to a liability in an indeterminate amount for an indeterminate time to an indeterminate class'. However, the court did suggest that an auditor would be liable to a third party for negligence if the auditor knew that the audit was being performed for the *primary benefit* of a third party and that third party was specifically identified.

The dissenting judgment of Lord Denning in the *Candler* case was an indication of the future direction of Australian law in this area. In his judgment, he said:

> Let me now … suggest the circumstances in which I say that a duty to use care in making a statement does exist apart from a contract in that behalf. First, what persons are under such duty? My answer is those persons such as accountants, surveyors, valuers and analysts, whose profession and occupation it is to examine books, accounts, and other things, and to make reports on which other people—other than their clients—rely in the ordinary course of business. Their duty is not merely a duty to use care in their work which results in their reports. Secondly, to whom do these professional people owe this duty? I will take accountants, but the same reasoning applies to the others. They owe the duty, of course, to their employer or client; and also, I think, to any third person to whom they themselves show the accounts, or to whom they know their employer is going to show the accounts so as to induce him to invest money or take some other action on them. But I do not think the duty can be extended still further so as to include strangers of whom they have heard nothing and to whom their employer without their knowledge may choose to show their accounts. Once the accountants have handed their accounts to their employer, they are not, as a rule, responsible for what he does with them without their knowledge or consent.

Hedley Byrne

The opinion of Lord Denning was effectively endorsed in 1963 in the important case of *Hedley Byrne & Co. Ltd v Heller and Partners Ltd* (1963) 2 All ER 575. The defendants in this case were merchant bankers who provided a favourable credit reference on a customer to another bank which, in turn, made the reference available to one of its customers. On the strength of the reference, Hedley Byrne & Co. Ltd extended credit to a company which subsequently went into liquidation. This caused a substantial loss to Hedley Byrne, which took legal action against the defendant bank on the grounds of negligent misrepresentation.

While the court found for the defendant, because of a disclaimer attached to the reference, the judgment included discussion of the law relating to a duty of care in the absence of contractual relationships, and the issue of financial loss. These discussions were the most significant result of the case.

While the case did not involve accountants or auditors, the principles established had implications for both groups. Some detail and brief extracts from the case will highlight the important principles.

Continued…

The defendant, Heller and Partners Ltd, argued that because it could not foresee that anyone other than the plaintiff's bank would use the information, no duty of care existed. The judgment rejected this, suggesting that a reasonable banker ought to have realised that some third party was going to rely on the information.

The judgment therefore expanded the tort of negligence to cover cases involving economic loss, but confined the duty of care to a situation where there is a '**special relationship**' between the person giving the advice and the person relying on the advice. A 'special relationship' exists where a person occupying a position of skill and care professes or offers advice to another person and the advice was given at the direct request of the recipient, or the adviser knew or ought to have known that the advice being given would be relied on by a person such as that recipient in the relevant circumstances.

MLC v Evatt

The application of that principle was, however, restricted in *Mutual Life and Citizens Assurance Co. Ltd v Evatt* (1971) AC 793. In this case Evatt approached Mutual Life and Citizens Assurance Co. Ltd (MLC) seeking advice on one of its subsidiaries. On the basis of that advice, Evatt invested and suffered a large monetary loss. Using the *Hedley Byrne* principle, the Australian High Court found for Evatt. However, on appeal to the Privy Council, the decision went in favour of MLC, as they were not experts in providing investment advice.

The Privy Council limited the application of the *Hedley Byrne* principle to situations where a statement is made, or advice given, on a matter where the person giving the advice has some degree of competence and expertise. The duty of care does not apply to advice given on a casual basis or in a primarily social setting.

On the basis of *MLC v Evatt*, a special relationship exists where persons giving advice hold themselves out to be experts. Clearly this would include auditors when making statements dealing with financial reports. As an expert having competence in such matters, the accountant or auditor owes a duty of care when giving advice in a professional capacity to parties whom the accountant or auditor knows, or ought (as a reasonable person) to know, will rely on that advice. The duty of care toward those third parties is to not cause them economic loss by careless words.

Scott Group

In a New Zealand case, *Scott Group Ltd v McFarlane* (1978) 1 NZLR 553, the auditors failed to discover an error of $38 000 in the consolidated group accounts of John Duthie Holdings Ltd. Scott Group Ltd relied on those accounts in formulating a takeover offer, which was made and accepted by all shareholders of John Duthie Holdings Ltd. Scott Group claimed that the accounts were negligently prepared, with assets overstated and, to the extent to which Scott Group suffered a loss based on that negligence, the auditor was liable. In essence, the auditor was being sued for negligence by a third party who the auditor was unaware would be relying on the audited financial report.

Continued...

In a majority judgment the New Zealand Court of Appeal found that the auditors did owe a duty of care, but did not award damages because of disagreement on the basis for awarding damages. Woodhouse J listed four reasons which suggested there was a special relationship between the parties, and thus a *prima facie* duty of care.

1   The auditors were professionals, and were in the business of providing expert advice for reward.
2   Financial reports are prepared to assist shareholders and the state to oversee company activity, and to provide information to potential investors. As a result, the judgment indicated that auditors accepted a duty of care not only to shareholders, but to other persons 'whom they can reasonably foresee will need to use and rely upon them when dealing with the company or its members in significant matters affecting the company's assets and business'.
3   There is no opportunity in the ordinary case for any intermediate examination of the underlying authenticity of the company's accounts. In any event, it would be impractical for many persons to do so. The auditor should realise this when accepting the audit function for shareholders.
4   While the auditors had no direct knowledge of the Scott Group or that a takeover from that quarter was contemplated, the accounts and the audit report, under the provisions of the *Companies Act*, were public documents on which third parties can rely.

In summary, the decision provides argument relating to the concept of **reasonable foreseeability**. In this case, the auditors owed a duty of care to a specific third party of whom they were not aware but who was part of a class of persons of whom the auditors should have been aware would rely on their audit opinion.

Shaddock and Associates

In another important decision, *L. Shaddock and Associates Pty Ltd v The Council of the City of Parramatta* (1979) 1 NSW LR 566, the High Court of Australia, being no longer bound by the precedent set by the Privy Council, reinstated its original decision in the *MLC v Evatt* case. This, in effect, reinforced in Australia the concept of foreseeability: where a person gives information or advice and realises that the other party will rely and/or act on it, there is a duty to exercise reasonable care in providing that information or advice.

JEB Fasteners

The above principles were tested in the UK case *JEB Fasteners Ltd v Marks Bloom & Co.* (1981) 3 All ER 289. The judgment in this case confirmed that auditors and accountants do have a liability to third parties, but that the circumstances are not clear cut. It also confirmed the view that the burden of proof on the injured third party is great. The facts of the case are as follows (taken from the headnote in the All England Law Reports):

In April 1975 the defendants, a firm of accountants, prepared an audited set of accounts for a manufacturing company for the year ended 31st October 1974. The company's

Continued...

*stock, which had been purchased for some £11 000, was shown as being worth £23 080,
that figure being based on the company's own valuation of the net realisable value of the
stock. The defendants nevertheless described the stock in the accounts as being 'valued
at lower of cost and net realisable value'. On the basis of the inflated stock figure the
accounts showed a net profit of £11 250, whereas if the stock had been included at cost
with a discount for possible errors the accounts would have shown a loss of over £13 000.
The defendants were aware when they prepared the accounts that the company faced
liquidity problems and was seeking outside financial support from, inter alios, the
plaintiffs, who manufactured similar products and were anxious to expand their
business.*

*The accounts prepared by the defendants were made available to the plaintiffs, who,
although they had reservations about the stock valuation, decided to take over the
company in June 1975 for a nominal amount, because they would obtain the services
of the company's two directors who had considerable experience in the type of manufacturing carried on by the plaintiffs.*

*... The plaintiffs' take-over of the company proved to be less successful than they had
anticipated and they brought an action for damages against the defendants alleging
that the defendants had been negligent in preparing the company's accounts, that they
had relied on the accounts when purchasing the company, and that they would not
have purchased the company had they been aware of its true financial position.*

The court held that the defendants were negligent in preparing the financial report. They
ought reasonably to have foreseen that a takeover was a possible means of obtaining the
financial support the company required, and that if anyone examined the accounts with a
takeover in mind they would rely on them. Therefore the auditors were in breach of their
duty to act with care and skill.

However, in relation to the causation, Woolf J found the plaintiffs had not succeeded.
He concluded that the plaintiffs would have acted the same way even if they had known
the true position as to the accounts, as their primary aim was to obtain the services of the
two directors. Therefore, they could not claim a loss because of the information in the
accounts.

The case therefore reaffirmed the basic principles of third-party liability and confirmed
the notion of reasonable foreseeability.

Twomax

In *Twomax v Dickson, McFarlane & Robinson* (1983) SLTR 98 the plaintiff and two other
investors relied on the 1973 audited financial report to acquire a controlling interest in
Kintyre Knitwear Ltd. Kintyre subsequently went into liquidation and the auditors were
sued for damages. It was held that there were errors in the financial report and the audit
was performed negligently. Following the precedent of the *JEB Fasteners* case, it was held
that the probability of a takeover was reasonably foreseeable and the investors were owed
a duty of care. The auditors did not meet that duty of care, so damages were awarded to
the plaintiff.

Caparo

A landmark decision in the UK was *Caparo Industries Pty Ltd v Dickman* (1990) 1 All ER 568, where it was held that three necessary conditions for the imposition of a duty of care to a third party are:

1. foreseeability of damage;
2. **proximity** of relationship; and
3. the reasonableness or otherwise of imposing a duty.

Of course, in order for damages to be awarded against the auditor there must also be a loss suffered by the third party, negligence by the auditor and causation. In the *Caparo* case, it was accepted that the auditor should have foreseen economic loss as a result of the negligent misstatements. However, the arguments put to the court rested on whether there was a sufficient degree of proximity between the auditor and the shareholders and potential investors to create a duty of care.

The key element of the judgment was that the Law Lords held that the auditor did not owe a duty of care to potential investors or to individual shareholders. The duty is owed to shareholders as a body and not to individual shareholders. The Law Lords held that the auditor's liability for economic loss suffered should be limited by reference to specific situations and/or transactions and relationships, rather than by reference solely to the broad concept of reasonable foreseeability. Lord Oliver pointed out that foreseeability is not synonymous with proximity.

The *Caparo* decision goes back to the era before *Hedley Byrne*, relying heavily on the narrow tests of liability espoused in the *Candler* case and the classic judgment handed down by Cardozo CJ in *Ultramares*. The Law Lords effectively dismissed a number of cases which relied to a great extent on the foreseeability precedent, such as *Scott Group*, *JEB Fasteners* and *Twomax*.

If followed in Australia, the *Caparo* decision would severely limit the avenues for redress open to individual investors and shareholders where there is negligence by the auditor. However, the narrow interpretation given to the role of statutory financial reports and, as a consequence, to the auditor's duty of care in the *Caparo* decision appears contrary to developments in Australia. In 1983, the *Companies Act* was amended to require financial reports to be prepared in accordance with accounting standards, which therefore have statutory backing.

SAC 2.26 clearly enunciates that the 'objective of general purpose financial reporting is to provide information to users that is useful for making and evaluating decisions about the allocation of scarce resources'. This is elaborated in SAC 2.16–.20, which identifies those individuals and organisations that make up the most common classes of users; that is, resource providers, recipients of goods and services, parties performing a review or oversight function as well as management and governing bodies.

While SACs are not mandatory, the accounting standards issued by the Australian Accounting Standards Board (AASB) do have legislative backing. AASB 1031 'Materiality' specifically refers to SAC 2 and users in defining materiality.

The responsibilities of the auditor, as envisaged by the AASB through its reliance on the conceptual framework in the development of legally enforceable standards, appear to be

Continued...

considerably more onerous than those delineated in the *Caparo* judgment, particularly in relation to individual shareholders and investors. It has been argued that the auditor's report could not add credibility to financial report representations if the auditor could not be subjected to individual user action in the case of negligence. However, as will be discussed shortly, while some Australian cases, such as *Columbia Coffee*, support this argument, other cases, including the High Court of Australia in *Esanda*, reject it.

AGC

An Australian case which considered the *Caparo* decision was *R. Lowe Lippmann Figdor & Franck v AGC (Advances) Ltd* (1992) 10 ACLC 1168. In this case, the company sought to increase its finance facilities from AGC, and a firm of auditors was asked to prepare and provide audited financial reports to AGC so that it could assess the company's financial position. After receiving additional finance from AGC, the borrowing company went into receivership.

The financial reports which the auditors had prepared contained a material over-statement of work-in-progress. The auditors sought to rely on the *Caparo* decision to avoid liability, by arguing that AGC had not indicated to the auditors the intended use of the financial reports.

The Appeal Division of the Supreme Court of Victoria reversed an earlier decision of the Victorian Supreme Court and endorsed the *Caparo* outcome. The court maintained that, although Franck knew that the audited financial report would be made available to AGC, and would be relied upon by it for the purpose of reviewing and extending credit facilities, this did not amount to the auditor making a statement directly to AGC.

The auditors had not made a statement to AGC in order to induce AGC, or members of a class which might include AGC, to act or refrain from acting in a particular way in reliance on this statement. Mere belief that AGC would rely on the report did not constitute making a statement to AGC with the intention of inducing it to act in a particular way on the report. It was maintained that the auditors, in issuing their audit report, were merely discharging their statutory obligations.

Columbia Coffee

A wider interpretation of liability to third parties occurred when the Supreme Court of New South Wales subsequently distinguished *Columbia Coffee and Tea Pty Limited v Churchill & Ors t/a Nelson Parkhill* and *Saunders v Donyoke Pty Ltd & Ors* (1992) 10 ACLC 1 659 from both *Caparo* and *AGC*. The auditors (Nelson Parkhill) were appointed by Columbia Coffee to audit its 1987 financial report. They issued an unqualified report on the financial report, which understated Columbia Coffee's creditors to the extent that a deficiency in shareholders' funds would have been created had they been properly accounted for. A shareholder, Donyoke, claimed that shares in Columbia Coffee were purchased on the strength of the accuracy of the 1987 financial report and unqualified audit report.

Continued...

It was argued that a potential investor had sufficient proximity to be owed a duty of care by the auditor, primarily because of statements which were made in their own *Audit Manual*, namely:

Section 2.2:

It is the policy of the firm that any audit which we undertake will be conducted in such a way as will fulfil our responsibilities properly. This will involve a competent exami-nation of the accounts and records to the extent required by the appointment, followed by a clear and forthright report as to the results of the audit. The use of the word 'responsibilities' in this statement rather than the word 'contracts' is deliberate. It acknowledges that there will be interested parties who read and rely upon our reports, and this extends beyond the persons who employ us in the first instance or those to whom the report is addressed initially.

Section 2.28:

Many readers of a company's accounts rely upon them as a basis for assessing the company's prospects. It is important, therefore, that any inherent trends in a company's profitability should be shown in the accounting statements.

Rolfe J clearly interpreted these sections of the *Audit Manual* as implying that the auditor had assumed a greater level of responsibility than just to the company and its existing share-holders. He also took into account expert evidence presented in relation to the extent of reliance that may be placed on audited accounts. Rolfe J indicated that he relied on a commonsense approach and on the prevailing community standards and perceptions in relation to audited accounts, in order to justify a departure from the *Caparo* decision. However, the decision in *Columbia Coffee* is inconsistent with earlier and later cases. As the damages involved were nominal, the decision was never appealed.

Esanda

The *Columbia Coffee* decision was rejected by the Full High Court of Australia in *Esanda Finance Corp v Peat Marwick Hungerfords* (1997) 15 ACLC 483. Esanda alleged that it had lent money to Excel Finance Corporation Ltd on the basis of negligently audited financial reports for 1988–89. Excel was subsequently placed in receivership.

The auditors, Peat Marwick Hungerfords, applied to the court to strike out the plea of negligent misstatement from the plaintiff's Statement of Claim on the grounds that it did not establish that a duty of care was owed by the defendant to the plaintiff. The auditor's appli-cation was initially unsuccessful before a single judge, but this decision was overturned on appeal by the Full Court of the Supreme Court of South Australia in 1994. The case was appealed to the High Court, which also ruled in favour of the auditors in a judgment deliv-ered on 18 March 1997.

King CJ stated in the Supreme Court of South Australia that, in the absence of some feature indicating an assumption of responsibility to the plaintiff to exercise care in relation to the preparation of the audit report, an auditor is not under a duty of care to the plaintiff unless the auditor intended to induce the plaintiff to act in reliance on the audit report.

Continued...

While it may be assumed that the defendant could reasonably foresee that persons contemplating financial transactions with the plaintiff might consult the financial report and rely upon its accuracy and the audit report, King CJ stated that this falls short of establishing the relationship of proximity needed to give rise to a duty of care.

King CJ also specifically considered whether the auditors, by way of their obligation to adhere to Australian accounting standards, which refer to the objective of financial reports as being to provide information for users of the financial reports to make evaluations or decisions, had assumed a responsibility to the plaintiff giving rise to a legal duty of care. King CJ rejected the reasoning adopted by Rolfe J in *Columbia Coffee*, stating:

> I do not think that the mere inclusion in a manual or set of standards of an acknowledgment of a professional responsibility to have the interest of users other than the client in mind in determining what is to be included in the accounts or in carrying out the audit, can have the effect of enlarging the area of legal duty by creating a legal duty of care to persons to whom it would not otherwise be owed.

Brennan CJ in the High Court of Australia stated that based on the facts it was not possible for the third party to rely on the report prepared by the auditor. He held that for a third party to succeed in such circumstances, the following would have to be established:

- The report was prepared on the basis that it would be conveyed to a third party.
- The report would be conveyed for a purpose which was likely to be relied on by that third party.
- The third party would be likely to act in reliance on that report, thus running the risk of suffering loss if the statement was negligently prepared.

Summary of cases

There are several marked differences of judicial opinions and interpretations in the judgments, both within and between individual cases. However, the decision of the High Court of Australia in the *Esanda* case indicates that the auditor's liability to third parties under the tort of negligence is very restricted. This may increase the importance of Trade Practices legislation discussed overleaf.

EXAMPLE 4.1 Determining an auditor's liability to a third party

Facts

Dairy Ltd was a large dairy products manufacturer that was considered a prime takeover target. Green & Associates completed the annual audit for 20X3 and gave an unqualified audit report. Shortly afterwards Dairy Ltd was taken over by Milk Ltd, which used the audited financial report as the basis of the takeover.

After the takeover was completed Milk Ltd found that the inventory of Dairy Ltd was materially overstated. Green & Associates had relied on management representations about the quality of the dairy products. In fact, 20 per cent of cheeses were adversely affected by a fungus that rendered them worthless. In addition, Green & Associates only attended the Melbourne stocktake, as it accounted for 60 per cent of the stock. No work was completed on interstate locations. However, subsequent investigation showed significant shortages in these locations.

Continued...

Required

Explain whether Green & Associates is liable to Milk Ltd for damages under the tort of negligence.

Solution

1. Green & Associates were negligent, as they did not comply with the auditing standards concerning verification of inventory. They did not attend the stocktakes for the 40 per cent of inventory held in other locations nor verify its existence by alternative audit procedures. They also accepted management representations concerning valuation of inventory, when other audit evidence could reasonably have been expected to exist.
2. Milk Ltd suffered a loss due to the inflated price paid for Dairy Ltd due to the overstatement of inventory.
3. Milk Ltd relied on the financial reports, which caused them to suffer the loss.
4. It was reasonably foreseeable that Dairy Ltd would be taken over, as it was considered a prime takeover target, and that the acquirer would look at and rely on the financial report.
5. However, there is no proximity between Green & Associates and Milk Ltd, as Green & Associates did not prepare their report for Milk Ltd's use nor induce them to rely on it.

Therefore, Green & Associates did not owe Milk Ltd a duty of care and consequently would not be liable to them under the tort of negligence, even though the other necessary conditions have been satisfied.

Privity letters

Since the *Caparo* judgment, some third parties have adopted the practice of requesting a privity letter from auditors in which the auditor acknowledges the third party's reliance on an audited financial report. The purpose of the privity letter is to establish a relationship with the required foreseeability and proximity and thereby establish a duty of care by the auditor to the third party. AGS 1014 was issued in 1991 and subsequently revised to take account of the *Esanda* case. It provides guidance to auditors where they receive requests for privity letters. The decision whether to provide such a letter is an individual business risk/management judgment.

AGS 1014.11 indicates that unless an auditor intends to accept responsibility to a third party, the auditor should respond unequivocally to a request for a privity letter stating that the body of shareholders is the only group entitled to rely on the audit report. However, if the third party has evidence that the auditor's conduct was misleading and deceptive and in breach of s. 52 of the *Trade Practices Act* or its equivalent state *Fair Trading Act* as discussed below, then the existence of the disclaimer will not of itself protect the auditor.

Where an auditor acknowledges a responsibility to a specific third party, the nature and scope of the duty of care will depend on the circumstances of the case. This should be viewed as a separate engagement from the statutory audit under the *Corporations Act* and the auditor must obtain the consent of the audit client to undertake the engagement.

In addition, under AGS 1014.17, the auditor should obtain a written representation from the third party stating that the third party:

■ is aware of the nature and scope of the audit as explained in the audit engagement letter;
■ acknowledges that the audit will not be specifically planned for the specific benefit of the third party and will not necessarily address the third party's needs;
■ is a sophisticated investor/lender/provider of goods/services and will diligently perform their own inquiries, with due care, in connection with the transaction; and
■ will, if it enters into the transaction, subsequently perform its own ongoing monitoring activities.

If the third party refuses to provide the required representation, the auditor should refuse to issue a privity letter and decline responsibility.

Trade Practices Act

Even if the common law rights of individual investors and shareholders are restricted by the *Caparo* and *Esanda* decisions, consideration needs to be given to the provisions of the Commonwealth *Trade Practices Act* and state *Fair Trading Acts*. Section 52 of the *Trade Practices Act* prohibits misleading and deceptive conduct, and it has been the basis for several successful actions by investors against promoters and others for misleading statements. These actions could have been taken by the investors under common law for deceit and negligence.

Similar provisions to s. 52 of the *Trade Practices Act* are to be found in state *Fair Trading Acts*. These provisions may offer a further avenue of redress to shareholders and investors.

In a preliminary judgment in September 1994, the Supreme Court of South Australia refused to strike out an alternative statement of claim filed by Esanda Finance Corp. (1994) under the *Fair Trading Act* (SA). (The initial claim under the tort of negligence was discussed above.) Esanda claimed that in providing an unqualified audit report on Excel's accounts, the auditors were guilty of conduct which was misleading or deceptive, or likely to mislead or deceive. The auditors applied to have the matter dismissed, claiming that the auditor's duty to report is statutory, is merely incidental to the provision of accounting and auditing services for reward, and does not arise in trade or commerce. They also argued that the provision of auditing services is not, in itself, an activity in trade or commerce.

Bollen J rejected these arguments and held that the words 'in trade or commerce' may be given a very wide meaning. He also held that it is not necessary for trade or commerce to be carried on between the defendant and the plaintiff, or that a misleading or deceptive misrepresentation is made directly to the plaintiff.

He concluded that:

> The words 'trade or commerce' are to be given a wide import. The lending of money is surely in trade or commerce. Accountants assist those who lend money. Auditors work for those who lend money. It may be held in the end that an auditor is right in the middle of trade or commerce.

Criminal liability

Auditors also need to be concerned with **criminal liability**, because they can be subject to criminal prosecution under various Commonwealth and state laws.

Statutory offences by auditors may arise through failure to comply with the statutory duties specified in s. 311 of the *Corporations Act*. An offence is most likely under s. 1308(2), which specifies penalties of $22 000 and/or 5 years imprisonment for knowingly making or authorising false and misleading statements. Failing to take reasonable steps to ensure that a statement is not false or misleading may also constitute an offence. An auditor may also commit an offence under s. 83(1) by failing to properly report a contravention of the *Corporations Act*, of which the auditor is aware, to the directors or ASIC. In addition, s. 1311 makes it an offence to do anything forbidden by, or fail to do anything required by, any provision of the *Corporations Act*.

There have been very few criminal actions brought against auditors. In 1969, John McBlane was sentenced to 3 years imprisonment for the knowing certification of a false prospectus. Also, the former auditor of Rothwells Ltd, Louis Carter, was charged in 1990 on four counts of concurring in publishing false written statements and one count of conspiring to falsely state the financial position of the company in 1986 and 1987. In December 1996 he was sentenced to 4 years imprisonment.

In the USA, the *Sarbanes-Oxley Act 2002*, which was discussed in Chapter 3, has widened the scope of criminal penalties for auditors of US listed companies.

AUDITING IN THE NEWS

Urgent need for government focus on professional liability

4.1

Source: Extracted from Barker, P. (2002) 'Chairman's Message', *CA Local News*, May, 1.

Professional indemnity insurance is mandatory for members of the ICAA in public practice and over recent months the ICAA has received reports from members of professional indemnity insurance premiums increasing in the order of 100–200%. One Victorian member reported his firm's premium had increased 360% from $800 000 in 2001 to just under $2.9 million in 2002.

It is inevitable these increased costs will create strong pressure to pass cost increases onto clients and the Institute has also had reports from members who have been unable to find insurance for certain activities in the market, particularly audit work.

Speaking to the media, ICAA CEO Stephen Harrison said, 'The reality is that over the past decade we have seen auditors acting as de facto underwriters of business risk. If a company collapses, the liquidators often turn to the auditors in a bid to recoup losses, as auditors have been perceived as "deep pocket" defendants,' said Mr Harrison (CEO, National Board of the Institute).

'Furthermore, under the law of joint and several liability, auditors can be held 100% liable for a loss even where other parties have been found to have contributed to the loss suffered. Against that backdrop many accountants are simply choosing not to undertake the audit function,' he said.

'It is in the public interest to have a strong, independent audit profession. However, the future viability of the profession is in question because of the risk auditors face in carrying out their jobs and because this risk is becoming increasingly difficult to insure', he stated.

Our Institute has been lobbying government on the need for liability reform for more than 10 years, both at state and federal levels. Governments have been advised that unless steps are taken to limit our profession's liability, the insurance well could run dry, an increasingly real and alarming possibility.

learning objective 6

LIMITATION OF LIABILITY

As discussed in Chapter 2, prior to CLERP 9 auditors were required to operate as sole traders or partnerships. Therefore, auditors were personally liable for their professional services. This unlimited liability put the auditor's personal assets at risk in the event of a legal claim.

An auditor should always aim to provide a high-quality, independent service. The application of high professional standards and procedures is essential and may prevent claims from eventuating. In addition, protection against claims brought by clients is provided to some extent by an engagement letter which explicitly states the scope and responsibility assumed by an auditor when undertaking an examination. Engagement letters are discussed further in Chapter 6.

However, to protect themselves against the risks inherent in the practice of public accounting, auditors are required by the accounting bodies to secure liability insurance. Through insurance, auditors try to ensure that they will be reimbursed for direct monetary loss arising from claims and the legal cost of defending themselves. Such protection does not, of course, compensate for the damage to reputation that may arise from a successful negligence claim.

Auditors have become increasingly concerned at the size and magnitude of the legal claims against them and the effect of these claims on their professional indemnity insurance. In 1994, KPMG settled a $1.1 billion claim by the Victorian Government in relation to auditing the collapsed Tricontinental merchant bank, with a record payout of $136 million. The $3.9 billion claim against KPMG over the State Bank of South Australia was settled in 1998 for an undisclosed sum. This trend is a global one, with the seventh largest US accounting firm, Laventhol & Horwath, collapsing during the 1990s under the weight of ambit liability claims made against it. It claimed that although it had a good defence it could not afford the costs of fighting the claims. In Australia, the Court of Appeal in the *AWA* case reduced the damages to $6 million, of which the auditors were liable for $4 million and the company the balance. The final result was a massive reduction from the $50 million originally claimed from the auditors, but the legal and associated costs in defending the action are reported to have totalled more than $30 million, raising the claim that the auditors would have been better off financially to have settled out of court.

Professional indemnity insurance

The increasing risk associated with claims against auditors has meant that the costs of professional indemnity insurance have risen steeply over recent years (see Auditing in the News 4.1). The Big Four audit firms, in their submissions to the JCPAA, claimed that the cost of professional liability risk for the major audit firms globally now represents at least 14 per cent of audit revenues. Apart from cost, it has also become increasingly difficult for auditors to obtain adequate professional indemnity coverage. Auditors now obtain only part of their coverage from commercial insurers, with the balance coming from either captive insurance groups, where firms pool their funds for their own insurance, or mutuals, where firms such as the Big Four in the UK have created their own insurance pool. However, these options do not offer sufficient protection from the size of the claims being made and, as a result, it has been reported that partners in audit firms have been stripping themselves of personal assets and 'running bare' with only their insurance to cover claims. This means effectively that auditors' liability is limited to their insurance threshold.

Arguments for and against limitation of liability

It has been against this background that auditors have been lobbying since the mid-1980s for the introduction of legislation to limit the magnitude of their liability. The Companies and Securities Law Review Committee (CSLRC) in its 1986 *Report to Ministerial Council on the Civil Liability of Company Auditors* identified a number of arguments for and against the limitation of auditors' liability. The arguments for limitation of liability included:

- As the legal requirement to audit satisfies a quasi-public-service role, auditors should be protected from civil liability provided they act in good faith.
- Auditors are not able to restrict the scope of their obligations and are not necessarily able to resign their appointment.
- In general, auditors are not permitted to rely on the representations of management.
- It may be argued that auditors are providing a service and as such they should be able to limit their liability as can other service providers.
- Unlimited liability may not provide better protection for investors or creditors, as court awards may exceed the auditor's capacity to pay.
- Harmful effects on reputation and the disciplinary actions of the professional bodies and ASIC may provide sufficient incentives for auditors to maintain high standards.
- Auditors carry a heavier burden than other professionals with respect to the amounts of damages (measured in fee income).

The arguments against the limitation of liability included:

- The need for auditors, like other professionals, to accept full responsibility for their work.
- Limiting the liability of auditors would set a precedent for other professionals.
- Limiting liability may result in auditors not performing their duties competently.
- Limiting auditors' liability would mean passing on to companies and the investing public a portion of the losses incurred due to the negligence of the auditor.

However, the CSLRC did not rely directly upon any one or any combination of these arguments for their decision, concluding that there was no obvious 'right' solution. Instead, they took a pragmatic approach and recommended limiting auditors' liability based on the difficulty of obtaining adequate professional indemnity insurance, the inability of auditors to pay the level of damages being awarded and the consequent undermining of the integrity of the audit system envisaged by the legislation, due to an unwillingness of some professionals to act as auditors and a divestment of assets by auditors fearful of the enormous personal liability. However, in May 1987 the Ministerial Council announced that implementation of the working party's proposals would not proceed. Since then the auditing profession has pushed for the implementation of limited liability through the Ministerial Council for Corporations (MINCO).

In its 1993 report MINCO listed a number of options for limiting the liability of auditors. The main options considered were imposition of a statutory cap on auditors' liability, incorporation of auditors and removal of **joint and several liability**.

Imposition of a statutory cap on auditors' liability

The 1986 CSLRC report favoured the introduction of a statutory limit to auditors' liability, calculated as a prescribed multiple of the fee charged for that audit and subject to compulsory professional indemnity insurance being maintained to the prescribed limit. However, in 1993 the MINCO report rejected the capping of liability.

Nevertheless, the accounting bodies have continued to advocate a capped liability based on a formula, such as 10 times the auditor's fee. It is argued that this combined with compulsory insurance would guarantee all plaintiffs would receive some compensation. Under a capping scheme, auditors would be required to have assets and insurance up to the limit of the cap. The insurance industry has also supported capping, claiming that it provides greater certainty to be able to assess risk, but also no doubt because it expects the magnitude of claims to be lower as a result.

The *Professional Standards Act 1994* (NSW) permits professional bodies to apply to a Professional Standards Committee to put in place certain standards covering their profession, including a cap on any liability incurred by its members (similar legislation has been proposed or passed in other states). The liability limit may be a set amount or a fee multiple above a threshold of at least $500 000. The legislation includes the following safeguards:

- A threshold has been set, up to which all claims will be met.
- Limitation of liability will not apply to claims for death or personal injury, or in relation to fraud, breach of trust or dishonesty.
- There must be full disclosure to clients of any limit of liability.
- Schemes for limited liability must include compulsory professional indemnity insurance.
- The introduction of risk-reduction and risk-management strategies is required.
- There must be a system to deal properly with consumer complaints.

A scheme has now been approved for members of the ICAA and CPA Australia in New South Wales. The scheme includes compulsory professional indemnity insurance, risk-management strategies and complaint and disciplinary procedures, and has a maximum liability cap of $50 million.

The Professional Standards Bill was passed by the Commonwealth in June 2004. The Bill will facilitate the introduction of a liability capping regime throughout Australia, with support for similar legislation being shown by state governments.

Incorporation of auditors

One option for limiting the liabilities of auditors, put forward by MINCO in its 1993 report, is to allow auditors to incorporate. The federal Attorney-General indicated in 1995 that the government was considering amending the *Corporations Act* to allow partners in audit firms to incorporate. However, no formal moves to implement **incorporation** occurred until the implementation of CLERP 9.

Incorporation, in the event of a claim, would protect the personal assets of partners other than the partner who conducted the audit, but would not protect the partnership assets or the personal assets of the partner being sued. Incorporation does not change the fact that an individual is responsible for his or her actions. Also, if a large claim were made against an auditing company which exceeded its professional indemnity coverage and the company assets, it could result in liquidation of the company. In addition, there are likely to be negative tax implications for individual auditors. In the UK, one of the Big Four firms has incorporated its audit practice. In the USA, Big Four firms have become limited-liability partnerships following the approval of their use in 1995. Limited-liability partnerships protect partners from personal liability for unsatisfied claims against the partnership arising from the negligence or wrongdoing of other partners. In Australia, the CLERP 9 Bill passed in June 2004 allows auditors to incorporate and form authorised audit companies, which must have adequate and appropriate professional indemnity insurance and which were discussed in Chapter 2.

Removal of joint and several liability

Under the present law, co-defendants in a lawsuit have joint and several liability for any damages awarded against them. This means that the plaintiff is able to recover 100 per cent of the damages from any one defendant, irrespective of how much that defendant was to blame vis-à-vis any other defendants. Auditing firms are perceived to be 'deep-pocket' defendants with high professional indemnity insurance coverage, and this has contributed to the extent of claims against them.

Where a company collapses or suffers a significant loss, action is usually taken against the company's directors, auditors and/or financial advisers. If the directors have limited financial resources, the bulk of the damages is usually claimed against the auditor or accounting firm, even though the auditor may be only partially responsible. To address this problem, an inquiry into joint and several liability, initiated by the federal and NSW Attorneys-General, proposed four types of **proportionate liability**:

1 **Proportionate liability in all circumstances** This system is seen as inherently fair for two reasons. First, each defendant bears only the proportion of the loss suffered by the plaintiff that can be equated to his or her level of responsibility. Second, it means the existing complicated rules as to contribution between various defendants would no longer be necessary.

2 **Proportionate liability when the plaintiff is partly at fault** Under this arrangement, which operates in British Columbia, Canada, proportionate liability is applied only when the plaintiff has been contributorily negligent. If the plaintiff is not to blame for the loss, the defendants are jointly and severally liable.

3 **Proportionate division of insolvent defendant's share** This variant is used in Ireland and has been put forward by the New Zealand Law Reform Commission. This variant is much the same as the second, except that if any defendant turns out to be insolvent or untraceable, that defendant's share of the loss or damages is divided among all the parties, including the plaintiff.

4 **Proportionate liability and defendant's degree of fault** This variation applies in some jurisdictions in the USA. Under this scheme, a defendant is proportionately liable so long as his or her share of the responsibility is less than a specified percentage. As a result, it has the advantage of limiting liability when the degree of fault is relatively minor.

The *Second Report of the Inquiry into the Law of Joint and Several Liability*, January 1995, recommended that the first alternative, proportionate liability in all circumstances, be adopted. No change was recommended to the joint and several liability of members of a partnership, as between themselves. The CLERP 9 Bill passed in June 2004 provides for apportionment between plaintiff and defendant according to blame and apportionment on the basis of proportionate liability between defendants if there are 2 or more defendants.

Quick review

1. There has been an increase in the size of legal claims and greater difficulty in obtaining sufficient professional indemnity insurance coverage.
2. Auditors have been lobbying since the mid-1980s for the introduction of legislation to limit the magnitude of their liability.
3. Ways to limit liability, which have been introduced through the CLERP 9 legislative amendments, include the imposition of a statutory cap; permitting the incorporation of auditors; and the replacement of joint and several liability with proportionate liability.

RESPONSIBILITY FOR THE PREVENTION AND DETECTION OF FRAUD

The primary objective of auditing in its early days was the detection of **fraud**. However, this emphasis has changed over the years and the detection of fraud is now considered to be only part of the auditor's responsibilities.

During the past decade quite a number of fraudulently prepared financial reports were not qualified by the auditor; this has prompted a renewed interest in the auditor's responsibility to detect and report frauds. High-profile corporate collapses have led to concerns about the role of the auditor in detecting fraud, which have culminated in allegations of negligence on the part of auditors in a number of cases.

Research conducted both in Australia and overseas has consistently shown that a significant number of people who use financial reports believe that the detection of fraud is a primary audit objective and that the auditor has a responsibility for detecting all fraud (see, for example, Monroe and Woodliff, 1994; Gay et al., 1997). The auditing profession, however, maintains that the primary objective of the audit is to provide an opinion on the truth and fairness of the financial report, and that its responsibility with respect to fraud is to exercise reasonable care and skill when planning and carrying out the audit, so that there is a reasonable expectation of detecting material misstatements which may arise as a result of the fraud. This is part of the expectation gap discussed in Chapter 1.

A review of legal cases indicates that the courts will impose a duty of reasonable care and skill on the auditor. However, what is not clear is the extent to which this duty of care and skill includes the detection of fraud.

In the 1859 UK case, *Re The Royal British Bank* (Nicol's Case) (1859) 3 De G & J 387, Lord Turner identified the detection of fraud and error as an audit objective. He stated that the auditors, having been appointed by the shareholders, 'were within the scope of their duty at least as much the agents of the shareholders as the directors were, and the false and fraudulent representations were discoverable by them'.

However, in 1896, in *Kingston Cotton Mill*, Lopes LJ made his famous statement that the role of the auditor is to be 'a watch-dog, but not a bloodhound'. He further stated that 'auditors must not be made liable for not tracking out ingenious and carefully laid schemes when there is nothing else to arouse their suspicion'. Nevertheless, he did acknowledge that 'if there is anything calcu-lated to excite suspicion he should probe it to the bottom'. In other words, where the auditor has been placed 'on inquiry', that is, something has occurred which ought to have raised the auditor's suspicions, the auditor is expected to follow those suspicions through to the end result.

In the case of *Frankston & Hastings Corporation v Cohen* (1960) 102 CLR 607, Fullagar J said that 'a regular audit is one generally accepted means for preventing and discovering fraud by employees'. However, in considering the duties of the auditor, it was also stated by both Windeyer J and Menzies J that the auditor of the municipality had a duty to the municipality to conduct the audit with reasonable care and skill. In this case, the court held that the auditor was liable for any loss sustained as a result of the breach of that duty of reasonable care and skill, rather than any specific duty in respect of fraud detection.

The duty of a statutory auditor concerning the possibility of fraud was put this way by Moffitt J in *Pacific Acceptance*:

> it is clear that in planning and carrying out his work an auditor must pay due regard to the possibility of error or fraud. Once it is accepted that the auditor's duty requires him to go behind the books and determine the true financial position of the company ... it follows that the possible causes to the contrary, namely, error, fraud or unsound accounting, are the auditor's concern.
>
> The matter cannot be dismissed by reference to the well known dicta regarding suspicion and metaphors concerning dogs and detectives, for such are rather directed to the auditor's state of mind and do not suggest that a careful auditor, without suspicion in his mind, but doing his duty, will pay no heed to the reality that there is always a material possibility that human frailty may lead to error or fraud in the financial dealings of any organisation. For a

company to plan and administer its internal system of control and for an auditor to plan his programme and perform his audit work so as to take account of the possibility of fraud in the sense that if fraud exists there are reasonable prospects of it being revealed is not to say that an auditor should start his work with suspicion in his mind.

... If fraud has taken place and is undetected by the auditor he is blameworthy in the eyes of the law only so far as he has been negligent in determining the scope and character of his examination ...

AUS 210 (ISA 240) provides detailed and extensive guidance on the auditor's present legal requirements to detect and report fraud and error. It establishes the general professional obligations of an auditor for the detection and reporting of fraud and error.

AUS 210.10 (ISA 240.06) continues to maintain the principle that the auditor is not responsible for the prevention of fraud, this being the responsibility of management. AUS 210.13 (ISA 240.13) states that an audit should be designed to provide reasonable assurance that the financial report is free from material misstatement due to fraud or error.

However, the revised AUS 210 (IAS 240) issued in June 2004, which builds on the new audit risk standards issued in February 2004, increases the auditor's responsibility for focussing specifically on areas where there is a risk of material misstatement owing to fraud, including management fraud. The revised standard emphasises the need for the auditor to maintain an attitude of professional scepticism throughout the audit and requires the engagement team to discuss how the financial report may be susceptible to material misstatement owing to fraud and what audit procedures would be more effective for its detection. It also requires the auditor to design and perform audit procedures to respond to the identified risks of material misstatement owing to fraud. Assessment of the risk of material misstatements resulting from fraud will be discussed further in Chapter 7.

Reporting fraud

The auditor has a duty to report fraud, irrespective of materiality, to an appropriate level of management when suspicions are, or should be, aroused during the course of normal, careful gathering of evidence. Auditors should obtain legal advice if there is any doubt as to the appropriate course of action to take, or if they doubt whether what has been discovered might properly be called a fraud. The effect of the fraud on the financial report and on the audit report must also be considered.

The auditor should ensure that such matters are reported to an appropriate level of management. The fraud or suspected fraud must be reported promptly. It is not sufficient to wait until the preparation of the final audit report on the financial report to draw attention to such matters.

It is also very important that the auditor reports to a suitably senior level within the organisation if it is suspected that management is involved in or is condoning the fraud. A report may be made to the board of directors or, if appropriate, to the audit committee. It is also suggested that, where the persons ultimately responsible for the overall direction of the entity are involved, the auditor should seek legal advice on the appropriate procedures.

Moffitt J in *Pacific Acceptance* stated that the auditors will not have performed their duties properly:

if, having uncovered fraud or having suspicion of fraud in the course of the audit, they fail promptly to report it to the directors and perhaps in the first instance according to the circumstances immediately to management. If it involves a senior executive or a director or implicates one of them it is difficult to imagine a case where the board should not be informed without delay.

AUS 210.68 (ISA 240.68) also acknowledges that the auditor may have a mandatory responsibility to report fraud under legislation such as the *Corporations Act* or the *Crimes Act*.

If, after taking account of any adjustments made, the fraud materially affects the view given by the financial report, the auditor needs to qualify the audit opinion accordingly.

Further, notwithstanding the fact that the fraud may not have a material impact on the financial report, the auditor may still be required to report it under other reporting responsibilities. For example, if directors are involved in the fraud, they have probably breached their fiduciary responsibilities, such as safeguarding the assets of the company, under the *Corporations Act*. Section 311 requires an auditor to report to the Australian Securities and Investments Commission (ASIC) in writing any contravention of the Act.

The penalties for breaches of the auditor's duties covered in the provisions of s. 311 are set out in the general penalty provisions of s. 1311(1). Section 1311(5) provides that the applicable penalty for a breach of s. 311 will be a fine of $500. While such a nominal fine may not appear to be a significant deterrent, application may also be made by ASIC under s. 1292 of the *Corporations Act* to the Company Auditors and Liquidators Disciplinary Board to cancel or suspend for a specified period the registration of an auditor who has failed to comply with s. 311. Further, s. 83(1) provides that an auditor who is found to be 'involved in the contravention' may be held to be in default. As a result, an auditor who becomes aware of a contravention of the *Corporations Act* by an officer or employee of a client and fails to report the matter properly to the directors or to ASIC commits an offence under s. 83(1).

The auditor may be reluctant to report fraud due to the risk of defamation if the suspicions are not substantially proved, and fraud convictions are often difficult to obtain. In addition, the auditor owes a duty of confidentiality to the client, which makes it difficult to report fraud to third parties without the client's permission. While these are not valid reasons for the auditor failing to fulfil reporting responsibilities, they are practical difficulties which need to be acknowledged.

However, in most cases the auditor is protected by qualified privilege if reporting matters in good faith and without malice to people who have a proper interest in receiving the information. For example, refer to s. 1289(1) of the *Corporations Act*. Therefore, the auditor should check whether this protection exists under the legislation governing the specific audit. Also, in certain circumstances the auditor may not be bound by the duty of confidentiality. The auditor may, for example, be legally bound to make disclosure of a criminal offence if ordered to do so by a court of law or a government officer empowered to request such information. Further, s. 6 of the *Crimes Act 1914* (Cwlth) states that:

> any person who receives or assists another person, who is to his knowledge, guilty of an offence against a law of the Commonwealth or of a Territory, in order to enable him to escape punishment or to dispose of the proceeds of the offence shall be guilty of an offence.

Therefore, if an auditor knows that an offence, in the form of fraud or other illegal acts, has been committed and fails to report it, the auditor may be held to be guilty as an accessory after the fact under the *Crimes Act*.

Legal advice should be obtained if the information sought may lead to prosecution of a client or former client. If the disclosure would entail a breach of confidence with the client, the auditor should decline unless such disclosures are required by a statutory or other legal duty or a court of law, the client's permission has been obtained or legal counsel advises such disclosure.

In the absence of a specific mandatory audit reporting requirement, and where an entity's governing body fails to take appropriate action, an auditor may need to seek legal advice on whether to report fraud or an illegal act to a third party. However, before reporting any fraud or illegal act to a third party, the auditor should perform sufficient audit procedures to verify the accuracy of the facts that are to be disclosed.

Some recent Australian cases provide some guidance concerning the application of earlier legal principles in this area and the possible legal status of the provisions of AUS 210 (ISA 240). *BGJ Holding Pty Ltd v Touche Ross & Co.* (1988) 12 ACLR 481 reinforced the view that the auditor is a watch-dog and not a bloodhound. This case emphasised some of the duties associated with the position of both auditor and director. It confirmed the view that, even where the auditor does not suspect fraud, there is a duty to report to appropriate levels of management any suspected breach of policy or irregularity that may expose the client to some risk. The directors then have a responsibility to take appropriate action and consider such information. Within the context of 'reasonable care and skill', this case appears to support the principles stated in AUS 210 (ISA 240).

The judgment in *WA Chip & Pulp Co. Pty Ltd v Arthur Young & Co.* (1987) 12 ACLR 25 acknowledged that the amount involved was immaterial and that the auditor did not believe serious fraud existed. However, it was held that further inquiries were necessary and would have alerted the auditor to the fraud to be reported to management. It could be argued that AUS 210 ignores this aspect of the common-law duties of an auditor with respect to the detection of fraud.

In the *AWA* case, Rogers CJ found that auditors becoming aware of significant deficiencies in internal controls have a duty to report them initially to management, and in the absence of appropriate action, to the board.

Quick review

1 There is an expectation gap concerning the auditor's responsibilities with respect to fraud.

2 A review of the legal cases indicates that the extent to which the auditor's duty to exercise reasonable care and skill includes the detection of fraud is unclear.

3 Auditing standards maintain that the auditor must have a reasonable expectation of detecting material misstatements arising as a result of fraud or error.

4 The auditor has a duty to report fraud, irrespective of materiality, to an appropriate level of management.

Summary

Auditors are facing an ever-increasing amount of litigation under breach of contract, the tort of negligence and the Commonwealth *Trade Practices Act* or state *Fair Trading Acts*. A review of the legal cases reveals marked differences in the judgments and, as a result, the extent of the auditor's liability is unclear. Nevertheless, to avoid litigation it is vital that the auditor exercise reasonable care and skill. However, what is still unclear is the extent to which the auditor's duty to exercise reasonable care and skill includes the detection of fraud.

The law previously required auditors to operate as individuals or in partnership; thus they had unlimited liability and pledged their personal assets for claims on the business. However, there have been moves to limit this unlimited liability through advocating the imposition of a statutory cap, permitting the incorporation of auditors or removal of the joint and several liability law regarding co-defendants. These reforms have been introduced through the CLERP 9 amendments to the *Corporations Act*.

Key terms

References

Corporate Law Economic Reform Program (2002) 'Corporate Disclosure: Strengthening the financial reporting framework', Proposals for Reform: Paper No. 9 (CLERP 9), September, Canberra.

Donaldson, I. (2000) 'The Carter case: Falling into the audit gap', *Australian Accountant*, February, 36–9.

Deegan, S., Pratt, D. and Hicks, B. (1994) 'Implications of the *AWA* decision for external auditors, internal auditors and management', *Australian Accounting Review*, May, 47–59.

Gay, G.E. and Pound G.D. (1989) 'The role of the auditor in fraud detection and reporting', *Companies & Securities Law Journal*, April, 116–29.

Gay, G.E. and Schelluch, P. (1991) 'The auditor's liability to the company, shareholders and third parties', *Companies & Securities Law Journal*, February, 59–64.

Gay, G.E. and Schelluch, P. (1993) 'The auditor's responsibility for detecting and reporting irregularities including fraud, other illegal acts, and error', *Accounting Communiqué*, No. 45, ASCPA.

Gay, G.E., Schelluch, P. and Reid, I. (1997) 'Users' perceptions of the auditing responsibilities for the prevention, detection and reporting of fraud, other illegal acts and error', *Australian Accounting Review*, May, 51–61.

Godsell, D.J. (1993) *Auditors' Legal Duties and Liabilities in Australia*, Longman Professional Publishing, Melbourne.

Godsell, D.J. and Craner, J. (1995) 'Conflicting dimensions of auditors' accountability to financial statement users', *Perspectives in Contemporary Auditing*, 67–78.

Joint Committee of Public Accounts and Audit (2002) 'Review of Independent Auditing by Registered Company Auditors', *Report 391*, August, Canberra.

Latimer, P. (2002) *Australian Business*, CCH Limited, Sydney.

Monroe, G.S. and Woodliff, D.R. (1994) 'Great expectations: Public perceptions of the auditor's role', *Australian Accounting Review*, November, 42–53.

Rogers, A. and Bryant, M. (1994) 'The auditor and litigation: A view on avoidance and management', *Perspectives in Contemporary Auditing*, 1–9.

Small, B. (1994) 'When the well runs dry', *Charter*, June, 14–19.

Assignments

MaxMARK

Additional assignments for this chapter are contained in Appendix A of this book, page 764.

MAXIMISE YOUR MARKS! There are approximately 30 interactive questions on the legal liability of auditors available online at www.mhhe.com/au/gay3e

REVIEW QUESTIONS

4.1 The following questions relate to auditors' legal liability. Select the *best* response.

(a) An auditor's duty of due care to a client most likely will be breached when the auditor:

A gives a client an oral instead of a written report

B gives a client incorrect advice based on an honest error of judgment

C fails to follow generally accepted auditing standards

D fails to detect all of a client's fraudulent activities

(b) Which of the following cases established that negligence was redressable despite the lack of a contractual relationship between the two parties?

A *Hedley Byrne*

B *Candler*

C *London and General Bank*

D *Donoghue v. Stevenson*

(c) In the *Caparo* case, the court held that the auditor owes a duty of care to:

A only those parties specified in the engagement letter

B all users of the published financial report

C all shareholders but not third parties

D the shareholders as a body but not individual shareholders or third parties

(d) The decision in the *Esanda* case established that the auditor owes a duty of care to a third party if the auditor:

A held themselves out as an expert

B knew that the third party was going to rely on the audited financial report

C ought to have been able to reasonably foresee that the third party would rely on the audited financial report

D induced the third party to rely on the audited financial report

(e) Which of the following cases established that contributory negligence was a valid defence in Australia for reducing the auditor's liability for damages?

    A *Pacific Acceptance*

    B *AWA*

    C *Cambridge Credit*

    D *Esanda*

(f) An auditor, John Jupp, failed to follow generally accepted auditing standards in auditing Ace Ltd's financial report. Ace's management had told Jupp that the audited report would be submitted to several banks to obtain financing. Relying on the report, New Bank gave Ace a loan. Ace defaulted on the loan. If New Bank sues Jupp, Jupp will most likely:

    A win because there was *insufficient* proximity between Jupp and New Bank

    B lose because Jupp knew that banks would be relying on the financial report

    C win because New Bank was contributorily negligent in granting the loan

    D lose because Jupp was negligent in performing the audit

(g) The *Second Report of the Inquiry into the Law of Joint and Several Liability* recommended the introduction of:

    A limited liability partnerships for auditors

    B a statutory cap for auditor's liability

    C proportionate liability for auditors

    D incorporation of audit firms

(h) DMO Enterprises Ltd engaged the accounting firm of Martin, Seals & Anderson to perform its annual audit. The firm performed the audit in a competent, non-negligent manner and billed DMO for $16 000, the agreed fee. Shortly after delivery of the audited financial report, Robert Hightower, the assistant controller, disappeared, taking with him $28 000 of DMO's funds. It was then discovered that Hightower had been engaged in a highly sophisticated, novel defalcation scheme during the past year. He had previously embezzled $35 000 of DMO's funds. DMO has refused to pay the auditor's fee and is seeking to recover the $63 000 that was stolen by Hightower. Which of the following is correct?

    A The auditor is entitled to collect the audit fee and is not liable for $63 000.

    B The auditor cannot recover the audit fee and is liable for $63 000.

    C DMO is entitled to rescind the audit contract and thus is not liable for the $16 000 fee, but it cannot recover damages.

    D DMO is entitled to recover the $28 000 defalcation, and is not liable for the $16 000 fee.

(i) If an audit firm is being sued by a third party for common-law fraud based upon a materially false financial report, which of the following is the best defence which the auditors could assert?

    A Contributory negligence on the part of the client

    B Lack of a contractual relationship

    C Lack of reliance

    D Disclaimer contained in the engagement letter

(j) Lewis & Clark rendered an unqualified opinion on the financial report of a company that sold shares in a public offering. Based on a false statement in the financial report, Lewis & Clark is being sued by an investor who purchased shares in this public offering. Which of the following represents a viable defence?

    A The false statement is immaterial in the overall context of the financial report.

    B The investor has not met the burden of proving fraud or negligence by Lewis & Clark.

    C The investor did not actually rely upon the false statement.

    D Detection of the false statement by Lewis & Clark occurred after the audit report date.

4.2   The following questions relate to the auditors' duty in respect to fraud. Select the *best* response.

   (a)   AUS 210 (ISA 240) provides that primary responsibility for fraudulent reporting rests with:

   A   management
   B   the board of directors
   C   the audit committee
   D   the external auditor

   (b)   AUS 210 (ISA 240) requires the auditor to plan to conduct the audit in such a way as to:

   A   detect all errors and fraud
   B   have a reasonable expectation of detecting all errors and fraud
   C   have a reasonable expectation of detecting all material errors and fraud
   D   search for all material errors and fraud

   (c)   When the auditor becomes aware of the existence of fraud, reporting this information to parties outside the entity is required:

   A   when the Directors' Report fails to disclose the irregularity
   B   when s. 311 of the *Corporations Act* applies, or in the public interest
   C   in all cases
   D   in no circumstances, due to confidentiality requirements

Reasonable care and skill

4.3   What role do professional auditing standards have in relation to the exercise of reasonable care and skill?

4.4   What is the relationship between standards developed by the auditing profession and the legal duties of auditors established in the *Pacific Acceptance* case?

Negligence

4.5   Explain the matters which must be proved before a claim for negligence can be successful.

Contributory negligence

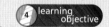

4.6   To what extent can an auditor rely on contributory negligence by the client to reduce the auditor's liability for damages?

Liabilities to third parties

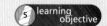

4.7   Briefly explain the applicability of the *Caparo* decision in Australia, with reference to relevant cases.

4.8   Explain what is meant by a privity letter and give three typical cases where privity letters are requested.

4.9   Explain why requests from third parties for privity letters are of concern to auditors.

4.10   What is the auditor's liability under the Commonwealth *Trade Practices Act* or the state *Fair Trading Acts*?

Limitation of liability

4.11   Outline the arguments for and against limiting an auditor's liability.

4.12   Discuss the different proposals which have been put forward to limit an auditor's liability.

4.13   What is the importance of professional indemnity insurance?

Fraud

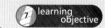

4.14   What are the auditor's duties concerning the detection of fraud?

4.15   Explain the auditor's responsibilities for reporting fraud discovered during an audit.

Reasonable care and skill

4.16 Basic 'He is a watch-dog, but not a bloodhound. He is justified in believing tried servants of the company in whom confidence is placed by the company ... the duties of auditors must not be rendered too onerous' (Lopes LJ in *Re Kingston Cotton Mills Co. (No. 2)* (1896) 2 Ch D 279).

Required

With reference to the above statement and other relevant common-law rulings, discuss the requirements for an auditor to discharge their duty to 'exercise reasonable skill and care' in an audit engagement.

Reasonable care and skill/Liability to third parties

4.17 Complex James Wong, the owner of a small company, asked Deirdre Smith, a public accountant, to conduct an audit of the company's records. Wong told Smith that an audit was to be completed in time to submit an audited financial report to a bank as part of a loan application. Smith immediately accepted the engagement and agreed to provide an auditor's report within three weeks. Wong agreed to pay Smith a fixed fee plus a bonus if the loan was granted.

Smith hired two accounting students to conduct the audit and spent several hours telling them exactly what to do. Smith told the students not to spend time reviewing the controls but instead to concentrate on proving the mathematical accuracy of the ledger accounts and summarising the data in the accounting records that supported Wong's financial report. The students followed Smith's instructions and after two weeks gave Smith the financial report, which did not include footnotes. Smith reviewed the financial report and prepared an unqualified auditor's report. The working papers, however, did not refer to the use of acceptable accounting policies or compliance with relevant regulations and statutory requirements.

Wong received the loan from the bank. Unfortunately, six months later Wong was forced into liquidation due to financial difficulties. As a result, the bank was unable to recover the amount of the loan. The bank is now attempting to recover its money from Smith on the grounds that Smith's audit report was negligently prepared.

Required

(a) Do you believe Smith has used reasonable skill and care in conducting the audit?
(b) Do you believe Smith owes the bank a duty of care?

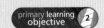

Negligence

4.18 Moderate Your firm has been the auditor of MOR Ltd, a construction company listed on the stock exchange, for several years. You have always had a good working relationship with the directors and senior management. Past audits have run smoothly and the financial reports of MOR Ltd have always been unqualified. The company has a 31 December year-end.

In 20X0, MOR Ltd decided to install a new accounting system specifically designed to accommodate all of MOR Ltd's accounting and reporting requirements. Both your firm and MOR Ltd's internal audit division reviewed the system prior to implementation and found it to be satisfactory. MOR Ltd is your largest client and has the most complex accounting system that the audit department has had to deal with. The first year in which the new system was operating you engaged an expert to assist in the development of specialised audit software that was to be significantly relied upon during the audit. This software is still used and is now maintained by your IT audit department.

In March 20X3, MOR Ltd's internal audit department discovered that, due to a programming problem, the application of the percentage of completion method of accounting for projects was inaccurate. As a result, revenue figures for each of the three preceding years' financial reports have been materially misstated.

It is now August 20X3 and the company has just commenced legal action against your firm. MOR Ltd claims that the past 3 years' audits were negligently performed given the problems with the accounting system and the undiscovered material misstatements in the financial reports.

Required

Outline relevant issues in deciding whether your firm has been negligent in the performance of their duties as the auditor of MOR Ltd.

Liability to third parties

4.19 Basic 'Auditors no longer owe a duty of care to a third party following a landmark High court ruling against Esanda Finance Corporation in the past month' (*Chartac Accountancy News*, April 1997).

Required

Do you agree with the author's contention that 'Auditors no longer owe a duty of care to a third party'? In your answer you should include reference to common-law rulings, including *Esanda*.

4.20 Basic In both the Supreme Court judgment and the High Court appeal for *Esanda*, the court left open the possibility for Esanda Finance Corporation to take action against the auditor under the *Fair Trading Act 1987* (SA).

Required

Discuss the significance of this decision for an auditor's liability to third parties.

4.21 Basic In cases involving the tort of negligent misstatement, three principles appear to have emerged over time as crucial in establishing a duty of care to a third party. The three principles are 'special relationship', 'reasonable foreseeability' and 'proximity'. Each of these principles has either extended or narrowed the range of parties to whom an auditor might owe a duty of care. The application and interpretation of these principles, however, appears to be fraught with difficulty.

Required

Compare and contrast the three principles mentioned above. Your answer should specifically consider the effect of the court's adoption of the principle on the range of parties to whom an auditor might owe a duty of care.

4.22 Moderate You are the audit partner responsible for Boulder Ltd. One week prior to signing the audit report you receive a letter from Stone Ltd stating that they are considering an investment in Boulder Ltd and will be utilising the audited accounts in formulating their investment strategy.

Required

(a) What action would you take before responding to a third party's request for a privity letter?
(b) What matters should be considered regarding the form of the response from the auditor to Stone Ltd? Why?
(c) What should the auditor do before entering into a specific engagement to meet the needs of Stone Ltd?

4.23 Complex You are the external auditor of OP Leisure Ltd, a company which promotes Japanese tours of Australia and owns a chain of duty-free shops. You have been auditing the company since it was listed on the Australian Stock Exchange in 1986. Although the financial reports have never been qualified, you are aware that the company has been making losses for the last 3 years due to short-term cash flow difficulties. The company has no long-term loans and the bank overdraft is near its limit at the end of the financial year.

During the financial year, the company has upgraded its accounting system to a computerised database. A consultant was hired to aid in the correct changeover of files for this computer information system. This system has been up and running for six months before year-end, and directors report they are happy with the way it is operating.

As you have never before audited a database system, you attend a series of courses put on by professional computing consultants to familiarise yourself with this type of system. You also ask a close friend, who is a computer audit specialist with one of the major chartered accounting firms, for a list of audit tests which were used to test a database computer system. You adopt this list of audit steps, but change it to accommodate the fact that the system changed during the year. As you do not have the expertise to review and evaluate the database management system (DBMS), you have an independent expert undertake this evaluation. This person concludes that the DBMS appears reliable and that the changeover was correctly carried out.

The internal auditor, who worked for the company since its listing, also reviewed the changeover procedures and subsequent running of the database and concluded that the system was operating satisfactorily. Reliance is placed on the work of both the expert and the internal auditor.

In your review of the minutes of the board of directors' meetings, you become aware that the Japanese parent company, which owns 35 per cent of the shares of the company, may be considering privatising the company on the basis that the company's share price is trading well below its net asset backing.

After the 30 June 20X3 financial reports were published, the takeover offer from the Japanese parent company proceeded on the basis of an offer price equivalent to the net asset backing of $1.32 per share as determined from the financial reports. This takeover offer resulted in acceptances to 96 per cent of the issued capital, and compulsory acquisition proceedings have been instituted for the other 4 per cent of share capital.

While these compulsory acquisition proceedings were being instituted, it was discovered that there were errors in the changeover of the computer system which resulted in inventory at the duty-free stores being materially misstated, and after writedown of inventory for the misstatement a new asset backing per share of $1.02 was established. The Japanese parent company is suing you for alleged negligence for their loss of 30 cents per share.

Required

(a) Outline the major questions which must be addressed in determining whether you, as the auditor, have been negligent in performing the audit. You should support your answer by reference to case law and auditing standards.

(b) Outline the major issues to be determined in deciding whether the company was guilty of contributory negligence.

(c) Assuming that you, as auditor, were negligent, do you owe a duty of care to the directors of the Japanese parent with regard to their actions in taking over the company? Support your answer by reference to case law and auditing standards.

Source: This question was adapted from the Professional Year Programme of The Institute of Chartered Accountants in Australia—1996 Advanced Audit Module.

4.24 **Complex** Factory Discount Prices Ltd is a discount chain-store which sells women's clothes. It has an excessively large inventory on hand and is in urgent need of additional cash. It is bordering on bankruptcy, especially if the inventory has to be liquidated by sale to other stores instead of to the public. Furthermore, about 15 per cent of the inventory cannot be resold except at a drastic discount below cost. Faced with this financial crisis, Factory approached several of the manufacturers from whom it purchases. Chan Apparel Ltd, one of the parties approached, indicated a willingness to lend Factory $300 000 under certain conditions. First, Factory was to submit an audited financial report for the express purpose of providing the correct financial condition of the company. The loan was to be predicated upon this financial report, and Factory's engagement letter with Dunn & Clark, its auditor, stated this.

The second condition insisted upon by Chan was that it obtain a secured position in all unsecured inventory, accounts and other related personal property. In due course, a security agreement was properly executed.

In preparing the financial report, Factory valued the inventory at cost, which was approximately $100 000 over the current fair market value. Also, Factory failed to disclose two secured creditors to whom substantial amounts were owed and who took priority over Chan's security interests.

Dunn & Clark issued an unqualified opinion on the financial reports of Factory, which they believed were fairly presented.

Six months later Factory filed a voluntary bankruptcy petition. Chan received $125 000 as its share of the bankrupt's estate. It is suing Dunn & Clark for the loss of $175 000. Dunn & Clark deny liability, based upon lack of a contractual relationship and lack of negligence.

Required

Is Chan entitled to recover its loss from Dunn & Clark? Give reasons for your conclusions.

Source: AICPA

4.25 Complex Sally Smith is the auditor for Juniper Manufacturing Pty Ltd, a privately owned company which has a 30 June fiscal year. Juniper arranged for a substantial bank loan which was dependent upon the bank receiving, by 30 September, an audited financial report which showed a current ratio of at least 2 to 1. On 25 September, just before the audit report was to be issued, Smith received an anonymous letter on Juniper's stationery indicating that a 5 year lease by Juniper, as lessee, of a factory building which was accounted for in the financial report as an operating lease was in fact a finance lease. The letter stated that there was a secret written agreement with the lessor modifying the lease and creating a finance lease.

Smith confronted the managing director of Juniper, who admitted that a secret agreement existed but said it was necessary to treat the lease as an operating lease to meet the current ratio requirement of the pending loan and that nobody would ever discover the secret agreement with the lessor. The managing director said that if Smith did not issue her report by 30 September, Juniper would sue Smith for substantial damages which would result from not getting the loan. Under this pressure, and because the working papers contained a copy of the 5 year lease agreement which supported the operating lease treatment, Smith issued her report with an unqualified opinion on 29 September.

In spite of the fact that the loan was received, Juniper went bankrupt within two years. The bank is suing Smith to recover its losses on the loan and the lessor is suing Smith to recover uncollected rents.

Required

(a) Is Smith liable to the bank? Give reasons.

(b) Is Smith liable to the lessor? Give reasons.

Source: AICPA

4.26 Complex Assume you are in public practice and that you have been the auditor of Green Limited for several years.

Your audit report for Green Limited for the year ended 30 June 20X1 was unqualified. In September 20X1 Green Limited obtained a large loan from a finance company, Amber Limited, to provide additional working capital. Subsequent to this, Green Limited experienced severe trading problems and was placed in receivership in late February 20X2.

Required

Develop a defence for your firm against the action taken by Amber Limited. Refer to relevant case law in your answer.

Source: This question was adapted from the CA Program of The Institute of Chartered Accountants in Australia—2002 Financial Reporting and Assurance Module.

4.27 Complex You have been the auditor of SHF Pty Limited (SHF) for several years. The audit report for the year ended 30 June 20X2 was unqualified. In August 20X2 SHF obtained a large loan from a finance company, LRB Limited (LRB), to provide additional working capital. The company experienced severe trading problems and was placed in receivership in May 20X3.

Your firm has been notified by legal representatives of LRB that they are taking action against your firm based on the audit of the 30 June 20X2 accounts. They claim that the cause of SHF's failure related to both the inadequate provision for doubtful debts and a fall in the value of inventories on hand, and that these problems were apparent earlier than June 20X2, but had not been adequately dealt with in the financial statements. They also claim that they would not have given the loan to SHF had those accounts been qualified.

Required

(a) Outline your defence to this action taken by LRB. Provide specific case references to support your answer.

(b) Would your answer to (a) change if LRB had written to your firm telling you that they intend to make a loan to SHF and were relying on the audited financial statements to assist them in making their decision?

Source: This question was adapted from the Professional Year Program of The Institute of Chartered Accountants in Australia—1998 Advanced Audit Module.

4.28 Complex Jake, Brown & Co. Registered Company Auditors have just completed their audit of FX Limited, a listed company which imports and manufactures electrical components. An unqualified audit report was issued.

FX operates a small treasury department which undertakes foreign currency transactions, including the use of derivative instruments in order to limit the firm's exposure to foreign currency fluctuations. The department employs two people: John Cartwright, the foreign currency dealer, and Jan Lee, an accounts clerk. Given the complexity of this area, Jake, Brown & Co. paid particular attention to the foreign currency operations of FX when planning their audit in order to ensure they would detect any material misstatements arising from any irregularities which might occur in the area.

Notes on the treasury department included the following:

1　The treasury department was initially set up to hedge FX's foreign currency exposure; however, after 2 years of operation John submitted a proposal to request authorisation for speculative investments. The proposal was approved, allowing John to engage in speculative investments, provided the total foreign currency exposure of FX did not exceed $100 million.

2　John was not required to obtain any further authorisation for individual deals, but was required to report to the board of directors quarterly on the department's position. The procedures John used for dealing were as follows:

All deals were placed over the phone and a dealer's diary maintained. The diary listed all relevant details concerning the transaction. The counterparty to the deal would then be requested to send a facsimile to confirm the arrangement. The facsimile was sent direct to John who checked the details, marked the diary to indicate it was confirmed and passed it on to Jan to update the accounting records. Jan updated the records then filed the facsimiles in date order. Once a month the accounting records were reconciled to the deal diary by John and any necessary amendments made.

3　The treasury department operates its own bank account, with John being the only signatory.

4　All mail relating to treasury transactions is sent directly to John.

As part of their audit procedures, Jake, Brown & Co. noted the following matters:

1　A number of bank confirmation certificates were returned from the bank with details of foreign currency transactions that were not recorded in the books of FX. The assistant auditor followed the matter up with John, who suggested that the banks had made an error and he would request new certificates be prepared. The assistant gave John the original certificates and a few days later new certificates were received. The additional deals had been crossed through and initialled.

2 The treasury department's bank account has not been reconciled for the last 3 months, but the difference was not considered material and no additional audit procedures were performed.

3 These problems, together with a repetition of the prior year's suggestions for improvement in internal controls, were reported to the board of directors, who indicated they would rectify the matters before the next audit. The board had also responded in this manner last year.

Six months after the audit report was signed, a major fraud was discovered in the treasury department with a trading loss of $200 million detected. As a result, the share price of FX Limited plummeted.

Mrs W is a small investor in FX. After reviewing her copy of the annual report, she decided to increase her investment in FX. Three months after her investment was made the fraud was discovered and the value of her shares dropped dramatically. Mrs W is now seeking damages from Jake, Brown & Co. for her loss.

Required

(a) Do you believe Jake, Brown & Co. owe Mrs W a duty of care? Provide reasons for your decision, citing relevant case law where appropriate.

(b) Discuss whether the shareholder is likely to be successful in a common-law action for negligence. Provide reasons for your decision, citing relevant case law and professional pronouncements where appropriate.

Limitation of liability

4.29 Moderate One of the recommendations arising from the 1996 ASCPA/ICAA report into the expectation gap was as follows:

> *to ensure equality in treatment of those parties involved in financial reporting, defined limitations to the liability levels for the directors, management and auditors should be pursued*

(ASCPA/ICAA, 1996, *Beyond the Gap*, p. 13)

Required

Do you agree or disagree with the above statement? In your answer you should include discussion on the following points:

(a) the extent of an auditor's liability to third parties in Australia at present;

(b) advantages and disadvantages of limiting an auditor's liability; and

(c) possible methods which may be used to limit an auditor's liability.

Fraud

4.30 Complex Barney & Company have been engaged to perform an audit examination of the financial report of Waldo Ltd for several years. The terms of the engagement, set out in an annual audit engagement letter signed by both parties, included the following: 'This being an ordinary examination, it is not primarily or specifically designed, and cannot be relied upon to disclose fraud, although their discovery may result'.

Three years ago, Harriet Zamp, head cashier of Waldo and an expert in computer operations, devised a previously unheard of method of embezzling funds from her employer. Zamp's thefts were small at first, but they increased as time went on. During the current year, before Barney began working on the engagement, the thefts became so large that serious variances in certain accounts came to the attention of the controller. When questioned about the variances, Zamp confessed and explained her unique embezzlement scheme. Investigation revealed that she had stolen $257 550. Zamp has no assets with which to repay the thefts.

Waldo now seeks to recover its losses from Barney. In defence, Barney asserts the following alternative defences:

(i) The claim should be dismissed because Barney's engagements with Waldo did not specifically include the discovery of fraud other than that which might arise in the process of an ordinary examination.

(ii) Even if Barney's contract had made it responsible for discoverable fraud, it could not have discovered Zamp's fraud with the exercise of reasonable care. Zamp's technique was so novel that no audit firm could have discovered the fraud in any event.

Required

Discuss the validity of each of Barney's defences.

Source: AICPA adapted

PLANNING AND RISK

Part 2 explains the importance of the concepts of planning and risk identification. This is done primarily within the structure of the financial report audit, although the concepts and processes could be extended to other assurance services. As well as providing a framework for the planning stage in Chapter 5, the various chapters take the reader into an assessment of audit and business risk (Chapter 6), specific business risks, including inherent risk (Chapter 7), and understanding and assessing internal control (Chapter 8). The important concepts of relevant financial report assertions, materiality and analytical procedures are also dealt with in detail in these chapters.

CHAPTER 5

OVERVIEW OF ELEMENTS OF THE FINANCIAL REPORT AUDIT PROCESS

LEARNING OBJECTIVES

After studying this chapter you should be able to:

1 explain the difference between accounting and auditing;

2 outline the logical process of identifying financial report assertions, developing specific audit objectives and selecting auditing procedures;

3 explain the relationships between audit procedures and evidence;

4 describe common auditing procedures used in an audit of a financial report;

5 define audit evidence and its relationship to auditing procedures;

6 outline the audit risk model;

7 define types of audit tests;

8 explain how an auditor may use the work of an expert or another auditor; and

9 describe the general requirement and contents of audit working papers.

Although a financial report audit is only one type of assurance engagement, it is the most common. Therefore, in this chapter an overview of the elements of the financial report audit process will be provided.

While a financial report audit of a complex entity is a complicated process, even the most complex audit has certain basic elements. This chapter compares financial report auditing with accounting and explains the basic elements of the audit process. These building blocks are necessary to understand how an audit is accomplished in conformity with Australian auditing standards. Most of the auditor's work in forming an opinion on the

financial report consists of obtaining and evaluating evidence about the assertions in the financial report by applying auditing procedures. It is important to understand each of the elements—audit evidence, assertions and audit procedures—in order to comprehend the audit of a financial report, which will be conducted within the framework of the audit risk model and the client's business risk.

The auditor must prepare and maintain adequate audit working papers. This chapter explains their function and content.

Relevant guidance

Australian		International	
AUS 202	Report (Revised 2004)	ISA 200	Objective and General Principles Governing an Audit of Financial Statements (Revised 2004)
AUS 208	Documentation	ISA 230	Documentation
AUS 402	Understanding the Entity and its Environment and Assessing the Risks of Misstatement (Revised 2004)	ISA 315	Understanding the Entity and its Environment and Assessing the Risks of Misstatement (Revised 2004)
AUS 406	The Auditor's Procedures in Response to Assessed Risks (Issued 2004)	ISA 330	The Auditor's Procedures in Response to Assessed Risks (Issued 2004)
AUS 502	Audit Evidence (Revised 2004)	ISA 500	Audit Evidence (Revised 2004)
AUS 520	Management Representations	ISA 580	Management Representations
AUS 526	Auditing Fair Value Measurements and Disclosures	ISA 545	Auditing Fair Value Measurements and Disclosures
AUS 602	Using the Work of Another Auditor	ISA 600	Using the Work of Another Auditor
AUS 606	Using the Work of an Expert	ISA 620	Using the Work of an Expert
AGS 1038	Access to Audit Working Papers	—	
Audit and Assurance Alert No. 3: Lessons for Auditors: Current Issues		—	

ACCOUNTING AND AUDITING CONTRASTED

As a process, financial report auditing is linked with accounting principles and procedures used by businesses and other organisations. An auditor renders an opinion on the financial report of an entity. The financial report is the product of an accounting system and judgments by directors and management.

The ultimate objective of the audit process is an opinion on the presentation of results of operations for a given period and the financial position at the end of this period. To form such a judgment about the financial report of an entity, an auditor must look behind the financial report to the data and the allocations of the data.

There is a close relationship between accounting and auditing. Auditors work primarily with accounting data. They attempt to satisfy themselves that the data which are summarised in the financial report are the data which the entity actually experienced. Further, they must make judgments about the allocations of data that have been made by directors and management and decide whether the financial report presentation is appropriate or misleading. To make these judgments, auditors cannot limit themselves to the records and accounts of the entity. They must be concerned with the total entity, because non-accounting activities, including the behaviour of the participants in the entity, influence not only the data but also, more importantly, the judgments of directors and management about accounting for and reporting the data.

The end product of an accountant's work is a financial report. The financial report may be simply the results of the work, or it may be adjusted for the desires of directors and management who wish to classify and report particular data in ways that are acceptable but perhaps unusual or unique to the accountant. It is possible to prepare different financial reports from the same data because accounting standards allow a choice between several acceptable accounting methods and judgment will be exercised in determining the amount for some accounts, such as various provisions.

The auditor analyses and reviews accounting data, accounting systems and the financial report. An auditor reviews the relevant entity activity that has taken place, including the business risks faced by the entity. In a large, complex entity where work is departmentalised, it can be difficult to comprehend the system which filters relevant data into the accounting records and the financial report. However, the auditor must understand this system.

The auditor is concerned with the validity of the data in the financial report as well as their clerical accuracy. The accounting data must reflect the actual business activity of the entity being audited. With such a formidable task, the auditor must have an overall approach which ensures that nothing which might have a bearing on the financial report is overlooked. The auditor is especially concerned with the raw accounting data, and must separate them from allocations and reclassifications made by directors, management or the accountants for the entity. The audit function focuses on accounting and the auditor must first be a competent accountant, but the audit function also extends beyond accounting (see Fig. 5.1).

FIGURE **5.1** **Relationship between accounting and auditing**

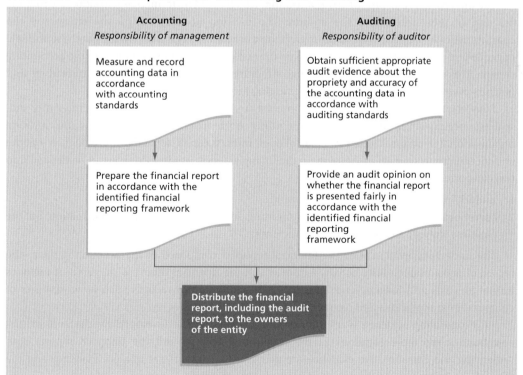

1 Accounting is concerned with measuring and recording data, while auditing is concerned with obtaining sufficient appropriate evidence as to its propriety and accuracy.

2 Accounting involves the preparation of the financial report, while auditing involves giving an opinion on the financial report.

Areas of audit interest

Separating the audit process into understandable parts requires a definition of areas of audit interest or concern. The auditor is primarily interested in the **accountable activity** of the entity. This activity is of prime concern and remains foremost until an audit is completed and an opinion given. However, there are many activities that occur in a complex entity that are never entered into the formal system of accounts. Because these activities often affect the behaviour which is reflected in the accounts, they must be considered by the auditor in rendering judgment.

The secondary audit interest is the **organisation of the entity**. 'Organisation' is used here in the broadest sense and includes both external and internal aspects with which the auditor must deal. The auditor must be familiar with the entity's organisation and also with the industry. Further, an auditor must know the differences and similarities between the entity and others in its industry and the unique aspects of the entity. Knowledge of these general external organisational relationships, which could be termed the external organisational environment, and the business strategy followed by the client give some idea of whether the data presented in the financial report are reasonable. More importantly, this knowledge is essential for the auditor to understand the accounting system and the financial report prepared from it.

The internal relationships of an organisation, which could be termed organisational structure, are also of great interest to the auditor. The division of work within the entity and the characteristics of the people who accomplish the work ultimately impact on the purchase and sale of goods and services. These transactions are the accountable events entered into the accounting system. Weaknesses in the organisational structure can produce unreliable, misleading and perhaps even fraudulent entries in the accounting records.

Thus, the two broad areas of auditing interest are, first, accountable activity of the entity and, second, organisation of the entity, including both external relationships and internal organisational structure. These two areas of audit interest can be related to the evidence that the auditor obtains to support an opinion on the financial report. Audit evidence can be divided into two categories:

1 **underlying evidence:** accounting data; and
2 **corroborating evidence:** all other supporting information, including information on the business strategy and organisation of the entity.

The underlying evidence for the financial report is composed of the accounting data—the record of accountable entity activity—from which the financial report is prepared. It includes formal journals and ledgers, and informal and memorandum records such as worksheets of computations, allocations and reconciliations.

Corroborating evidence is all information available to, or developed by, the auditor that corroborates the representations in the accounting records and the financial report. Both underlying and corroborative evidence are necessary to support an opinion. Evidence and the ways of obtaining it are further discussed later in this chapter.

Accountable entity activity

The auditor's perspective of the accounting process may appear quite different from that of the accountant, because an auditor must understand the results of accounting and report findings to interested parties. From an auditing perspective, there are three stages in the accounting process:

1 the collection of original data;
2 the allocations, reclassifications and resulting valuations of these data after admission to the process; and
3 the form, terminology and explanatory notes used to present the results of the analysis of these data in the financial report.

Most writing on accounting appears to deal with the latter two stages, while the first is rarely discussed as a subject in its own right. In fact, the first is so basic to accounting that it appears to have been taken for granted. However, the auditor cannot afford the luxury of ignoring this first and basic stage in the accounting process.

The original accounting data

The original accounting data are exchanges of consideration between an entity and other entities or individuals. Further, accountants generally assume that consideration exchanged is of equal value. Individual arm's length exchange transactions dominate our economy. All the activity that goes on in a large, complex entity is aimed at ultimately consummating an exchange transaction. These transactions take the form of sales of product, purchases of raw materials, purchases of labour, lending of money, borrowing of money, repaying money and being repaid. These are the basic data of accounting and the first and most basic area of interest to the auditor.

The basic data of accounting—transactions—are recorded in an accounting system. Thus, accounting records are the link between the economic activity of the entity—its exchange transactions—and the financial report. The auditor must understand the flow of transactions through the accounting system. Therefore, one of the important parts of the audit is a review of the accounting system, because a substantial part of the effort in an audit is concerned with the operation of that system.

The auditor's concern at this basic stage of accounting is that the exchange transactions recorded by an entity are all exchanges *actually* experienced by that entity and *only* the exchanges experienced by that entity. An attempt is also made to substantiate the money values that have been placed on the items exchanged. To make these judgments, the auditor must first define the entity which is being audited. With the advent of inter-ownership among entities and consolidated financial reports, this is not always an easy task. However, this is the only way an auditor can obtain reasonable assurance that they have the right batch of exchanges, that there are no exchanges that are the experience of some other entity, and that all the experience of the entity under audit is available.

In summary, the auditor is concerned with the three basic concepts that make up this first stage—the *exchanges* of an *entity* expressed in *money values*.

Allocations and reclassifications of accounting data

Accounting journals are often called the 'books of original entry', because the first stage of the accounting process consists of recording the exchange transactions of an entity in a journal. However, accounting journals also contain entries that do *not* represent exchange transactions. These entries are made to allocate and reclassify original exchange data to other accounts in preparation for placement in the financial report.

)cations and reclassifications are varied and difficult to delimit. They result from the
procedures that prescribe inventory methods, depreciation methods, amortisation
rofit determination in general. These manipulations of original data form the second
iccounting process: allocating original data to time segments of an entity's life.

aps unfortunate that accountants mix original data with allocations of those data, for
can be confusing to the uninformed. The auditor must separate the two different
ries in the accounting system. All the allocations and reclassifications in an entity's
e made according to procedures and practices that have been developed by
s over the years. There are both acceptable and unacceptable ways of determining
alances and the resulting amount for cost of goods sold for the period. Similarly, there
are acceptable and unacceptable ways of depreciating fixed assets, amortising other long-lived
assets and allocating labour and materials costs to time periods.

The principles and practices that guide an accountant in making the allocations and
reclassifications have not been ordered in any fashion. A series of procedures is available to the
accountant, some of which have been determined to be acceptable and others unacceptable. The
unifying concept in all of them is the well-known one of 'matching'.

This part of the audit depends on the auditor's knowledge as an accountant. As an accountant, the
auditor knows which allocation and reclassification methods are acceptable, and must observe what
the entity has done and decide whether it has followed acceptable methods and made acceptable
choices where judgment is involved. The auditor reviews the accounting principles and methods used
by the entity, and evaluates their selection and application by directors and management.

The accounts must include a summary of the accounting policies adopted by management.
Accounting standard AASB 101 (IAS 1) 'Presentation of Financial Statements' requires that a
summary of the entity's accounting policies is presented in the initial section of the notes to the
financial report. The summary should disclose any departure from the accrual and/or going-
concern basis of accounting, and detail all accounting policies which have been important in
preparing and presenting the financial report. Any changes in accounting policy should also be
disclosed, along with the reason for the change and the monetary impact of that change on the
financial report presented.

The auditor should prepare a schedule of such important accounting policies and evaluate
them at the beginning of the audit in order to be aware of departures or changes during the course
of the audit and their impact. It should be noted, however, that some allocations and
reclassifications of accounting data require estimates and judgments by directors and
management. The auditor must evaluate these and be satisfied that they are valid and proper. For
example, the allowance for doubtful accounts receivable requires an estimate of the amount that
will be uncollectible. Several proper accounting methods could be applied to record the estimated
amount, but the reasonableness of the estimate must also be evaluated.

In many cases, the financial report of an entity contains comparative figures for the prior
period as an integral component of the current period's financial report. For example, in
accordance with AASB 101.36 (IAS 1.36) a financial report is required to disclose corresponding
amounts of the preceding financial year for all items in the company's financial report. The
purpose of comparative figures is to complement the amounts relating to the period under audit,
not to re-present the complete financial report of the preceding period. The relationship of the
financial report of the preceding period to the current period's financial report is covered in
Chapter 13.

Presentation of the results of the accounting process

The final stage in the accounting process deals with reporting the results of an entity's accomplishment for a period of time and its status at the end of that period. The form of such reporting is usually an income statement, a balance sheet and a statement of cash flows.

From a professional viewpoint, the auditor is required to report on whether the financial report 'presents fairly the financial position and operating results in accordance with Australian Accounting Standards'.

There are rules that govern the placement of various items in the financial report and the terminology used to present them. Most of the accepted procedures for presenting financial reports are similar. The auditor must use accounting knowledge, at the allocation stage, to decide whether the client has properly prepared the financial report. Further, the auditor must review the accompanying notes to the financial report and judge their adequacy and completeness. Guidance on these issues is available by reference to accounting standards and other professional statements and the disclosure requirements contained in the *Corporations Act*.

In summary, the auditor must consider whether:

- *all* the *exchanges* and *only* the exchanges of an entity have been admitted to the accounts at exchange value;
- all allocations and reclassifications of exchange data have been properly made according to acceptable accounting procedures; and
- the financial report is in an acceptable form and uses acceptable terminology.

The subject of this text is auditing, not accounting, and it is assumed that the reader is familiar with accounting and reporting principles and procedures. However, the effect of dividing data into two groups, original data or exchange transactions and allocations and reclassifications of original data, is of special importance to auditing. Generally, auditing is concerned with the collection of evidence necessary to substantiate the existence, occurrence, completeness, rights and obligations, valuation, measurement and presentation and disclosure of an entity's exchange transactions. Allocations and reclassifications can then be substantiated and judged by reviewing the procedures and accounting policies adopted by accountants in the entity. The auditor is then in a position to provide an opinion on the financial report.

The fact that financial reports usually cover only a short interim period in the life of an entity creates the need for allocations and reclassifications. If the entire lifetime of a business or other entity were considered, these allocations of exchange transaction data would be unnecessary.

Organisation of the entity

The auditor also has the internal organisational structure of the entity with which to work. In auditing terminology this is referred to as **internal control**. The auditor can make inquiries of client personnel and review the system of documentation used by the entity; trace various types of transactions from initial to ultimate disposition in the system to observe its functioning; and, finally, make an evaluation of the system to identify strengths and weaknesses. These activities are part of the auditor's evaluation of the controls over the accounting system. The accuracy and reliability of the accounting system depends on how it is controlled.

The objectives of internal control are linked with the auditor's concern with the flow of transactions through the accounting system and the impact of business risk on the entity's ability to achieve its objectives. Internal control is defined in AUS 402.42 (ISA 315.42) as the process

l effected by those charged with governance and management and other personnel
asonable assurance about the achievement of the entity's objectives with regard to
y of financial reporting, effectiveness and efficiency of operations and compliance
ble laws and regulations. As a result, internal control is designed and implemented to
tified business risks that threaten the achievement of any of these objectives. Internal
scussed further in Chapter 8.

because the entity exists and is operating, the auditor has a great deal of other infor-
vidence that can be obtained to support the accounting system and the accounts
om it. There are knowledgeable people both within the entity and outside it to whom
can direct inquiries. Physical assets are available for inspection by the auditor, and the
activities of entity personnel can be observed. The validity of representations in the accounts can
be judged in part by reference to various conditions observed by the auditor, for example internal
control.

Auditing, as a discipline, works with accounting. The auditor's areas of interest include the
activity or exchange transactions of an entity, and the organisation of an entity and related,
corroborating information.

Quick review

1. The primary area of audit interest is the accountable activity of the entity, which includes
the collection of original accounting data; the allocation and reclassification of
accounting data; and presentation of the results in the financial report.
2. The second area of audit interest is the organisation of the entity, including both external
relationships and internal organisational structure.

learning
objective 2

FINANCIAL REPORT ASSERTIONS AND AUDIT OBJECTIVES

In effect, by presenting a financial report, directors and management are stating certain things
about the entity's financial position and operations. These assertions by directors and
management which are embodied in the financial report are referred to as **financial report
assertions**. The auditor uses assertions to assess risks by considering the different types of
potential misstatements that may occur and then designing audit procedures that are
appropriate. The assertions deal essentially with recognition and measurement of the various
elements of the financial report and related disclosures. AUS 502 (ISA 500) has three categories of
assertions: classes of transactions, account balances, and presentation and disclosure. These are
set out in AUS 502.17 (ISA 500.17) as follows:

1. **Assertions about classes of transactions and events for the period under audit**
    (a) **Occurrence**—transactions and events that have been recorded have occurred and pertain
    to the entity
    (b) **Completeness**—all transactions and events that should have been recorded have been
    recorded
    (c) **Accuracy**—amounts and other data relating to recorded transactions and events have been
    recorded appropriately
    (d) **Cutoff**—transactions and events have been recorded in the correct accounting period
    (e) **Classification**—transactions and events have been recorded in the proper accounts

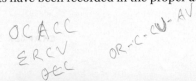

2 **Assertions about account balances at the period end**
   (a) **Existence**—assets, liabilities and equity interests exist
   (b) **Rights and obligations**—the entity holds or controls the rights to assets and liabilities are the obligations of the entity
   (c) **Completeness**—all assets, liabilities and equity interests that should have been recorded have been recorded
   (d) **Valuation and allocation**—assets, liabilities and equity interests are included in the financial report at appropriate amounts and any resulting valuation adjustments are appropriately recorded

3 **Assertions about presentation and disclosure**
   (a) **Occurrence and rights and obligations**—disclosed events, transactions and other matters have occurred and pertain to the entity
   (b) **Completeness**—all disclosures that should have been included in the financial report have been included
   (c) **Classification and understandability**—financial information is appropriately presented and described, and disclosures are clearly expressed
   (d) **Accuracy and valuation**—financial and other information is disclosed fairly and at appropriate amounts

The major distinction between this categorisation and that contained in the previous standards is the greater emphasis placed on presentation and disclosure. This is a direct result of corporate collapses such as Enron and HIH and is discussed in more detail in Chapter 12. However, AUS 502.18 (ISA 500.18) does indicate that the auditor may express the assertions differently, provided all aspects described above have been covered.

The auditor needs to obtain evidence that supports each of the assertions for every material component of the financial report. A component of the financial report may be an account balance (or group of account balances), a class of transactions or disclosures.

The categories of assertions provide a framework for developing specific audit objectives for each material account balance, class of transactions or disclosures. An audit objective is an assertion translated into terms that are specific to the particular balance or class, the entity's circumstances, the nature of its economic activity and the accounting practices of its industry. Consider Example 5.1 overleaf, which shows some specific audit objectives.

A number of accounting pronouncements now contain complex measurement and disclosure provisions based on fair value. AUS 526 (ISA 545) 'Auditing Fair Value Measurements and Disclosures' addresses audit considerations relating to the valuation and allocation, accuracy, presentation and disclosure of material financial report items presented or disclosed at fair value. These include understanding the entity's process for determining fair value, assessing its appropriateness and considering the use of an expert.

Quick review

1 Directors and management make assertions about the entity's financial position and operations and these are embodied in the financial report.

2 The auditor obtains evidence to support these assertions for material components of the financial report.

Financial report assertion	Illustrative audit objectives
Existence	• Inventories included in the balance sheet physically exist. • Inventories represent items held for sale in the normal course of business.
Completeness	• Inventory quantities as per the accounting records include all products, materials and supplies owned by the company that are on hand. • Inventory quantities include all products, materials and supplies owned by the company that are in transit or stored at outside locations.
Rights and obligations	• The company has legal title or similar rights of ownership to the inventories. • Inventories exclude items billed to customers or owned by others.
Valuation and allocation	• Inventories are properly stated at cost (except when net realisable value is lower). • Slow-moving, excess, defective and obsolete items included in inventories are properly identified and valued.

AUDIT PROCEDURES AND EVIDENCE

Audit procedures are the actions an auditor takes in acquiring evidence. The procedures are *not* evidence; they are the means of acquiring evidence. **Audit evidence** is all of the information used by the auditor in arriving at the conclusions on which the audit opinion is based. It includes all the data and information underlying the financial report and corroborating information. AUS 502.03 (ISA 500.03) indicates that audit evidence includes evidence obtained from audit procedures performed during the audit and may also include evidence obtained from other sources such as previous audits and an audit firm's quality control procedures for client acceptance and continuance. The audit equation can be expressed as:

> Audit evidence = *Underlying accounting data* + *Corroborating information*

The auditor needs to test the propriety and accuracy of the underlying accounting data to be able to express an opinion on the financial report. However, some corroborating information for material assertions within the financial report is essential. This audit equation is illustrated in Figure 5.2.

The use of audit procedures to obtain evidence to corroborate accounting data can be illustrated by focusing on one type of transaction. Consider the diagram of a cash purchase transaction in Figure 5.3. The auditor may inspect the documentary evidence in the entity's records. The item received is recorded as an increase in inventory, a copy of the purchase order is sent to the supplier and a receiving report is prepared to indicate receipt of the merchandise. The item given up is recorded as a cash reduction, and there will probably be a paid cheque indicating payment. The transaction is also recorded by the supplier, from whom information can be obtained if necessary.

FIGURE 5.2 The audit equation

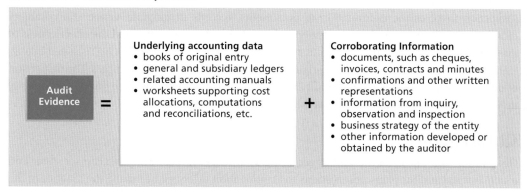

FIGURE 5.3 A cash purchase transaction

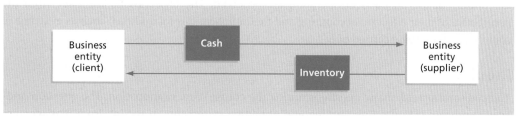

At the end of the accounting period, the entity holds a number of items in inventory as the result of many purchase transactions. Evidence may be obtained by examining the final inventory, which is the net result of exchange transactions, including both purchases and sales. The inventory balance in the balance sheet can be corroborated partially by looking in the warehouse and noting that there are a certain number of boxes of a given item. Seeing the items is evidence that they exist and therefore, provided other assertions such as ownership are satisfied, should be reflected in the client's balance sheet. However, the balance sheet does not show this item as a total number of boxes; therefore, the auditor must obtain further evidence concerning the acquisition cost of this inventory. This may be done by locating the purchase invoice. Then, by recomputing the extension of inventory quantities multiplied by prices and the addition of these extensions, the auditor corroborates the amount shown for inventory in the accounting records.

In practice, the counting of inventory is so time consuming that auditors usually observe the client's employees making the counts and only make test counts. AUS 506 (ISA 501) 'Existence and Valuation of Inventories' sets out the required procedures for the audit of inventory. These procedures are more extensive than those illustrated in this simple example and are discussed in Chapter 10.

COMMON AUDIT PROCEDURES

A list of all the audit procedures to be used in the corroboration of a particular account is called an audit program. Some common audit procedures outlined in AUS 502.26–38 (ISA 500.26–38) are: **inspection**, **observation**, **inquiry**, **confirmation**, **recalculation**, **reperformance** and **analytical procedures**. Several of these, such as inspection, observation and inquiry, are familiar methods for obtaining information. However, in auditing these methods are employed in circumstances which require additional explanation.

Inspection

Inspection involves the examination of documents, records or tangible assets. The reliability of inspection of records or documents depends on their nature or source and the effectiveness of internal control over their processing. In addition, *Audit and Assurance Alert No. 3*, issued in May 1999, emphasises the need to inspect original documents rather than photocopies. The inspection of tangible assets provides reliable audit evidence concerning their existence but not necessarily their valuation, completeness or ownership.

Observation

Observation is a universal method of acquiring knowledge. Almost everyone can see, hear and touch, but the auditor plans observations to acquire audit evidence by linking the realities of the client's business operations with accounting information. By physically observing phenomena, the auditor gains firsthand knowledge of their existence. Behaviour of operating personnel and the functioning of the business in operation are observed. The observations are made from the perspective of their effect on accounting and their implications for auditing, such as evidence of control activities being carried out.

Inquiry

The auditor must ask many questions during the course of an examination. The question-and-answer process includes interviewing and obtaining statements in writing from management and employees. Explanations of significant variations in accounting data are frequently obtained from employees. However, the auditor cannot rely on unsupported answers but must obtain support for the reasonableness of the answer given. One formal application of the procedure of inquiry is the use of an internal control questionnaire to gain information about the prescribed control activities.

Confirmation

Confirmation is a type of inquiry by which an auditor normally obtains a written statement from outside parties such as banks, solicitors or accounts receivable on information which they are qualified to give. The independent party questioned must be reliable and knowledgeable about a subject of interest to the auditor. Confirmation is often used as a substitute for observation. In some cases the object of interest may be held by outside parties. For example, the auditor typically confirms cash on deposit in banks. In other cases, the auditor may need information concerning an item that does not have a physical existence, such as an obligation owed to the client. Thus, an auditor typically confirms accounts receivable.

A feature of the procedure of confirmation is that the statement of the outside party should be communicated directly to the auditor. The possibility of influence or change of information by client employees should be avoided. Steps must therefore be taken to maintain control over confirmations. Maintaining control is further complicated by the need to have the request for confirmation come from the client. The outside parties have engaged in transactions with the client and will not disclose information about their dealings to everyone who asks. If the client makes the request, co-operation is much more likely. This necessitates the following controls over confirmation requests:

1 The letter is prepared by the client's personnel and given to the auditor for inspection and mailing.

2 The auditor inserts the confirmation request in an envelope bearing the auditor's return address and mails it personally.

3 Included in the confirmation request is a stamped return envelope addressed to the auditor.

Recalculation

The arithmetical accuracy of the many calculations required in the processing of data can be proven by recomputing the results. Examples of typical calculations include additions of ledger account balances, depreciation computations, amortisation calculations and inventory extensions and additions.

Reperformance

The auditor may independently execute procedures or controls that were originally performed as part of the entity's internal control.

Analytical procedures

These procedures are based on the dual nature of business transactions (reflected in the double-entry bookkeeping system) and the interrelationships between the variables of business operations. They involve the investigation of fluctuations in relationships to ascertain whether there are inconsistencies in relation to other relevant information or variations from predicted amounts. The different types of analytical procedures are discussed in Chapter 6.

The audit trail

An important requirement for the audit process is the existence of an **audit trail**, which consists of all accounting documents and records prepared as transactions are processed from origin to the financial report. Although it is commonly called the audit trail, it is created for the use of those operating and using the system and is really a management trail. The audit trail enables transactions to be traced from initial entry in the system to intermediate records, where the transactions become components of subtotals, and ultimately to disposition in the final records, where subtotals are summarised for presentation in the financial report. The direction of the tracing can be modified: the auditor can trace from the final record back to the point of initiation or in either direction from intermediate records.

Selecting audit procedures

The selection of particular procedures to achieve specific audit objectives is influenced by the following considerations contained in AUS 502 (ISA 500) and AUS 406 (ISA 330):

- the auditor's assessment of business risk and inherent risk;
- the nature of the internal control and the assessment of control risk;
- the materiality of the particular component of the financial report;
- experience gained from previous audits;
- the results of other audit procedures; and
- the source and reliability of information available.

Example 5.2 overleaf shows some audit procedures that may be applied to achieve specific audit objectives.

EXAMPLE 5.2 Relationship between financial report assertions, audit objectives and evidence/procedures for the account balance of inventory

Financial report assertion	Illustrative audit objective	Example of an audit procedure/evidence
Existence	Inventories included in the balance sheet physically exist	Stocktake—select from inventory records and count physical stock
Completeness	Inventory quantities as per the accounting records include all products, materials and supplies owned by the company that are on hand or in transit	Stocktake—select from physical stock, count and check to inventory records
Rights and obligations	The company has legal title or similar rights of ownership to the inventories	Check shipping documents (bills of lading) for ownership of goods in transit
Valuation and allocation	Inventories are properly stated at lower of cost and net realisable value	Compare subsequent sales prices to cost

SUFFICIENT APPROPRIATE AUDIT EVIDENCE

The basic criterion of AUS 502.02 (ISA 500.02) is that the procedures selected should provide **sufficient appropriate audit evidence** for the auditor to form conclusions concerning the validity of the individual assertions embodied in the components of the financial report and to give an audit opinion.

Sufficiency relates to the quantity of audit evidence necessary to provide the auditor with a reasonable basis for an opinion on the financial report. Appropriateness relates to the quality of the audit evidence. Therefore, appropriate evidence must be both relevant and reliable. Relevance is largely a matter of the relationship between the evidence and the financial report assertion involved. For example, if the related assertion concerns the existence of an asset, the auditor may select items included in the account balance and physically examine or confirm the items. However, these procedures are not relevant to the completeness assertion. To achieve an audit objective related to completeness, the auditor must select from evidence indicating that an item should be included in the account balance and see whether it is included.

The reliability of audit evidence is influenced by its source and nature. Although reliability depends on individual circumstances, the following generalisations adapted from AUS 502.09 (ISA 500.09) are useful:

- Evidence from sources outside an entity is more reliable than evidence obtained solely from within an entity. (For example, a written confirmation directly from a customer is more reliable than a duplicate sales invoice indicating a sale was billed.)
- Evidence generated internally is more reliable when internal control is effective than when internal control is ineffective. (For example, prenumbered documents combined with a sequence check are more reliable than unnumbered documents.)
- Evidence obtained directly by the auditor is more reliable than evidence obtained from the client. (For example, a confirmation obtained directly from the bank is more reliable than sighting a copy of the bank statement held by the client.)
- Evidence in the form of documents or written representations is more reliable than oral representations. (For example, a written confirmation from a debtor is more reliable than a telephone confirmation.)
- Evidence provided by original documents is more reliable than evidence provided by photocopies or facsimiles.

The two aspects of appropriateness have to be considered together because evidence may be highly reliable but of limited relevance to the audit objective. For example, adding up an account provides direct personal knowledge but is of limited relevance in achieving an audit objective related to existence. The converse is also true. Inquiry of management may produce highly relevant evidence but it is of limited reliability.

Audit evidence is also more reliable when the auditor obtains corroborating evidence from different sources. Conversely, if evidence obtained from one source is inconsistent with that obtained from another, the auditor will need to determine what additional audit procedures are required to resolve the conflict.

The auditor is required by AUS 406.13 (ISA 330.13) to obtain evidence about the accuracy and completeness of information produced by the entity's information system when that information is used in performing audit procedures. For example, if the auditor uses non-financial information such as production reports or budgeted data produced by the entity's information system in performing audit procedures, the auditor must obtain information about the accuracy and completeness of such information.

Examples of reliability of evidence

In the selection of audit procedures, the relative reliability of the available evidence is important. The relationship between reliability of evidence and selection of procedures is well illustrated by tests of accounts receivable. There are two methods of determining the existence of receivables—confirmation and examination of documentary evidence. Confirmation is generally more reliable than documentary examination, because evidence obtained from an independent source is more reliable than evidence routed through the client's system. Thus, a confirmation coming directly from a debtor can be relied on more than documentary evidence, which may be suppressed or manipulated in the client's system.

However, not all accounts receivable confirmation requests are answered, perhaps because the debtor is unco-operative or has a recording system that cannot determine the total amount owed to one firm at a given time. In such circumstances, an alternative procedure—examination of documentary evidence—must be employed. Alternative procedures take two forms: review of subsequent payments and examination of sales documents. Just as confirmation provides more reliable evidence than alternative procedures, review of subsequent payments provides more reliable evidence than examination of sales documents.

The auditor should examine the authenticity of subsequent payments and compare them with the accompanying remittance invoices. These amounts should be traced through to duplicate deposit slips, cash receipts records and the accounts receivable subsidiary ledger. These payments should be checked against specific invoices being paid, because some invoices may be in dispute. However, not all accounts are collected subsequent to the balance date and before completion of the audit, and so often other documentary evidence must be examined.

Examination of sales documents involves analysing outstanding balances into individual outstanding charges and examining the documentary support for these charges. Pertinent documents include duplicate sales invoices, delivery records, contracts and correspondence.

Subsequent payments are a more reliable form of documentary evidence because the cheque is sent by an independent source, the debtor, to the client, and the debtor expects it to be credited to his or her account. On the other hand, the sales documents all originate within the client's system and are, therefore, more subject to control and manipulation.

Thus, there is a chain of evidence—sales documents, subsequent payments and confirmation—whose reliability corresponds with the degree of independence from the client's system.

In examining the source documents supporting accounts payable, the reliability of evidence available is also an important consideration. A source document prepared by outsiders is preferred to one prepared by employees of the client. Therefore, in addition to examining vouchers in support of accounts payable, the auditor examines the creditor's invoice and, if applicable, the client's paid cheque in payment of the invoice. The invoice is prepared by the creditor and the cheque passes through his or her hands. Further, the act of cashing it acknowledges acceptance by the creditor. The cheque also passes through the hands of an independent third party, the bank. Note that the documentary evidence for accounts payable (creditor's invoices, creditor's statement and cancelled cheques) is more reliable than the corresponding documentary evidence for receivables (duplicate sales invoices, delivery records and subsequent payments, if the auditor cannot gain access to incoming cheques). For these reasons, the accounts payable balances are frequently proven by examination of documentary evidence, rather than by confirmation. Confirmation may be used for a few large account balances, however, or when internal accounting control is weak.

Electronic information

In many entities, some of the accounting data and corroborating information are available only in electronic form. For example, when entities use Electronic Data Interchange (EDI), the entity and its customers or suppliers use communication links to transact business electronically. Purchase, shipping, billing, cash receipt and cash payment transactions are often completed entirely by the exchange of electronic messages between the parties. Some of this electronic information may exist only at a particular point in time and may not be retrievable after a specified period of time if files are changed.

Representations by management

During the course of an audit the auditor obtains from management many representations, either verbal or written, on matters related to the information in the financial report. These representations are one form of audit evidence obtained during the audit. In evaluating the sufficiency and appropriateness of audit evidence, representations by management need to be carefully assessed. *Audit and Assurance Alert No. 3* emphasises the importance of supporting management representations by independent or other appropriate corroborating evidence. AUS 520 (ISA 580) provides guidance on the use of such representations as audit evidence and is discussed further in Chapter 12.

Quick review

1. Audit procedures are used to obtain evidence to corroborate accounting data.
2. Common audit procedures include inspection, observation, inquiry, confirmation, computation and analytical procedures.
3. The selection of audit procedures is influenced by a number of factors, including the assessment of inherent and control risk and the materiality of the component of the financial report.
4. Audit evidence needs to be sufficient and appropriate.
5. The reliability of audit evidence is influenced by its nature and source.

OVERVIEW OF THE AUDIT RISK MODEL

Auditors now adopt a business risk approach to determining what is sufficient appropriate audit evidence. AUS 202.14 (ISA 200.14) defines **audit risk** at the financial report level as the risk that the auditor will give an inappropriate audit opinion when the financial report is materially misstated.

Recent changes in the business environment, including the way entities are organised and how they conduct their businesses, the effects of globalisation and technology and significantly increased pressures have led to greater risk of fraudulent financial reporting. In view of these changes, the auditing standard-setters reviewed the core auditing standards that address various aspects of audit risk. As a result, three new or revised auditing standards were issued in March 2004: AUS 402 (ISA 315) 'Understanding the Entity and its Environment and Assessing the Risks of Material Misstatement'; AUS 406 (ISA 330) 'The Auditor's Procedures in Response to Assessed Risks'; and AUS 502 (ISA 500) 'Audit Evidence'. In addition, amendments were made to AUS 202 (ISA 200) 'Objective and General Principles Governing an Audit of a Financial Report'.

These audit risk standards deal with the auditor's assessment of the risk that the financial report could be wrong, and how the auditor designs the rest of the audit to provide an effective audit response to the identified risk. The new standards are designed to enhance the auditor's implementation of the audit risk model, which is the fundamental statement of the theoretical basis for completing an audit. It is expected that the new standards will increase audit quality as a result of better risk assessments and improved design and performance of audit procedures to respond to the risks and improve linkage of audit procedures and assessed risks, resulting in a greater concentration of effort in areas where there is greater risk of misstatement of the financial report. In some cases, this may result in a change to the audit approach, including the audit procedures performed.

Engagement risk is the auditor's exposure to loss or injury to the professional practice from litigation, adverse publicity or other events arising in connection with a financial report audit. Auditors will consider the reputation of management and the financial strength and credit rating of a prospective client in order to help assess the overall risk of association with the business. Engagement risk is increased when the client company is in a weak financial position or is greatly in need of additional capital. When an audit client goes bankrupt, the auditors often are named as defendants in lengthy and costly lawsuits, with possible damage to their professional reputation. For that reason, some audit firms choose to avoid engagements that have a relatively high business risk; others may accept such engagements, recognising the need to expand audit procedures to compensate for the unusually high levels of risk.

Engagement risk cannot be directly controlled by the auditor, although some control can be exercised through the careful acceptance and retention of clients. Audit risk, on the other hand, can be directly controlled by the scope of the auditor's procedures.

Before issuing an opinion on the financial report, the auditor needs to reduce audit risk sufficiently to make the opinion reliable. The auditor reduces audit risk by performing audit procedures until there is sufficient appropriate evidence for each assertion of each significant transaction class or balance to provide reasonable assurance that the financial reports are not materially misstated. The audit risk model focuses audit effort on those classes of transactions or balances that are likely to contain material misstatements.

The auditor carries out audit procedures until audit risk is low enough to issue an opinion. However, the nature of the procedures is important. Some are more efficient than others for specific accounts and assertions. In planning the audit procedures in each area, the auditor can choose:

- those designed to provide reasonable assurance that the inherent nature of the item and the internal control are such that the risk of a material misstatement in the financial report is low; or
- those designed to validate an item directly, so that the auditor has reasonable assurance that any material misstatement in the area will be detected.

The auditor's approach is nearly always a combination of the two.

Components of audit risk

AUS 202.20–3 (ISA 200.20–3) states that audit risk is made up of three components:

1 **Inherent risk:** the susceptibility of an assertion to material misstatement given the inherent and environmental characteristics, but without regard to related internal controls. For example, cash is more susceptible to theft than an inventory of cement. Complex calculations are more likely to be misstated than simple calculations. The methods of assessing inherent risk are explained in Chapter 7.

2 **Control risk:** the risk that a material misstatement in an assertion may not be prevented or not be promptly detected by the entity's internal control. For example, poor controls over the custody of inventory increase the possibility of theft. For each account balance the auditor identifies the transaction classes that affect the balance and considers whether there is reasonable assurance that the specific control objectives for those transaction classes have been achieved. There is an inverse relationship between the degree of assurance that control objectives have been achieved and the degree of control risk. An auditor determines a preliminary assessed level of control risk at the planning stage, based on the auditor's understanding of the internal control. A final actual assessed level of control risk is determined based on the results of tests of controls during interim testing. The methods of assessing control risk are explained in Chapter 8.

3 **Detection risk:** the risk that an auditor's substantive procedures will lead the auditor to conclude that a material misstatement does not exist when the account balance or class of transaction is actually materially misstated. In the planning phase of the audit, a planned acceptable level of detection risk is determined for each significant assertion. The planned levels of detection risk are revised, where necessary, if the auditor encounters evidence that alters the original assessments of inherent risk or control risk.

Audit risk is a combination of inherent risk, control risk and detection risk and the audit risk model can be depicted graphically as in Figure 5.4.

While the auditor cannot change inherent or control risk, the auditor can obtain evidence of a reduced *assessed* level of control risk by examining the control environment, the entity's risk assessment process, the information system, the control activities and monitoring of controls, and testing their effectiveness. If the evidence indicates that internal control is effective, the auditor can assess a lower level of control risk. If the evidence indicates that there are problems with internal control, the auditor's assessed level of control risk accordingly remains high. There is always some control risk because of the inherent limitations of any internal control.

The auditor can, however, alter the level of detection risk. For example, the auditor can reduce detection risk by means of:

- appropriate planning, direction, supervision and review;
- decisions on the nature, timing and extent of audit procedures; and
- the effective performance of the procedures and evaluation of the results.

Detection risk is inversely related to the effectiveness of auditing procedures. The less detection risk that can be accepted, the more effective auditing procedures must be. Generally, the effectiveness of auditing procedures is related to the persuasiveness of the evidence obtained by applying the procedures. Evaluating the effectiveness of auditing procedures requires experienced professional judgment.

Because the level of detection risk relates specifically to the auditor's procedures, it can be divided into two types, based on the two categories of substantive procedures (discussed later in this chapter):

1   **analytical procedures risk:** the risk that analytical procedures will fail to detect a material misstatement; and

2   **substantive tests of details risk:** the risk that detailed substantive tests of transactions and account balances will fail to detect a material misstatement.

These two components of detection risk may be treated independently because of the different nature of the procedures.

Detection risk can arise for two reasons, which need to be addressed separately by the auditor:

1   **Sampling risk:** the risk that the sample is not representative of the population. It is the risk that the auditor's conclusion based on the sample used would be different if the entire

FIGURE **5.4 Audit risk, graphically depicted**

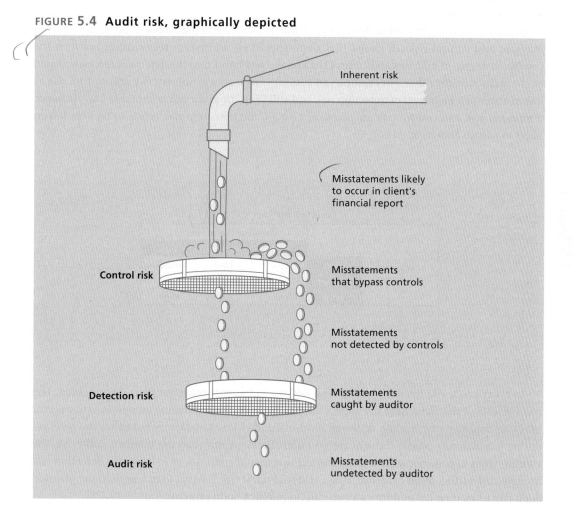

population had been subjected to the same audit procedure. Sampling risk can be reduced by increasing the sample size, but cannot be eliminated unless the entire population is tested.

2 **Non-sampling risk:** the risk of arriving at incorrect audit conclusions by failing to apply appropriate or effective audit procedures, by applying the procedures improperly or by drawing incorrect conclusions from the results. It exists even if the auditor applies the audit procedures to the entire population. Non-sampling risk can be controlled through the use of quality-control procedures and by adhering to the audit standards.

These two types of risk are discussed further in Chapter 11.

Assessment of audit risk

There are a variety of approaches to making an assessment of the various components of audit risk. AUS 202.21 (ISA 200.21) points out that although the auditing standards ordinarily describe a combined assessment of the risk of misstatement, the auditor may make separate or combined assessment of inherent and control risk, depending on preferred audit techniques or methodologies and practical considerations.

The assessment of the degree of risk is a subjective assessment by the auditor based on professional judgment. Firms tend in practice to categorise risk as high, medium or low rather than using specific percentages.

Exhibit 5.1 shows the level of detection risk that is usually acceptable based on assessments of inherent and control risks. It shows that there should be an inverse relationship between the combined degree of inherent and control risks on the one hand, and the detection risk established by the auditor on the other. For example, an auditor who assesses inherent risk and control risk as low can accept a high level of detection risk and still keep the audit risk acceptably low. However, if inherent risk and control risk are assessed as high, the detection risk needs to be kept low in order to reduce audit risk.

EXHIBIT 5.1

The interrelationships of the components of audit risk

Detection risk matrix

		Assessment of control risk		
		High	Medium	Low
Assessment of inherent risk	High	Low	Low	Medium
	Medium	Low	Medium	High
	Low	Medium	High	High

In every audit, risk needs to be assessed and the judgments made properly documented. The relative level of risk influences the audit evidence required. Before issuing an opinion the auditor needs to consider whether the achieved level of audit risk is satisfactory based on the level set during the planning phase. If the achieved audit risk is greater than the planned audit risk, the auditor needs to consider whether to reassess the required audit risk or to lower the detection risk by gathering further audit evidence. If the achieved audit risk is equal to or less than the planned audit risk level, then the auditor can issue an unqualified audit opinion.

Quantitative assessment of detection risk

The estimation of detection risk as a specific percentage is necessary only when the auditor uses statistical sampling. The only component of audit risk that can be objectively quantified is the sampling risk associated with statistical sampling, as is explained in Chapter 11. However, the quantitative audit risk model is discussed here in some detail because it is useful for visualising the interaction of the components of audit risk. Remember that in practice the auditing profession in Australia uses qualitative risk categories of high, medium or low, although specific percentages are widely used by audit firms in the USA.

Table 5.1 (overleaf) summarises the audit risk model. The underlying rationale of the model is that the combined risk of a material misstatement remaining undetected is a product of the independent component risks. This combined risk should be relatively low, for example 5 per cent or 10 per cent.

To use the quantitative model the auditor has to quantify, as a percentage, the inherent, control and analytical procedures risks. This is a subjective professional judgment. An approach often used in practice is to associate a percentage with a qualitative level of assessment. The highest level is obviously 100 per cent. Specification of the percentage associated with the minimum is a critical professional judgment because it quantifies the lowest degree of risk and, implicitly, the highest level of assurance ever attributed to the component. For example, AUS 406 (ISA 330) states that control risk cannot be assessed at so low a level that the auditor would not perform substantive tests for significant account balances or transactions classes. In practice, the percentages associated with qualitative levels may be established as a matter of audit firm policy.

The interaction of the component risks is most easily explained by an example. Assume that an auditor has assessed the component risks as follows:

$$\text{Inherent risk (IR)} = 100\% \text{ (high)}$$
$$\text{Control risk (CR)} = 70\% \text{ (medium)}$$
$$\text{Analytical procedures risk (AP)} = 40\% \text{ (low)}$$

Then the model can be solved for the detection risk for the test of details being planned as follows:

$$TD = \frac{AR}{IR \times CR \times AP}$$
$$= \frac{0.05}{1.0 \times 0.7 \times 0.4}$$
$$= 18\%$$

where AR represents audit risk and TD represents test of details.

This means that the auditor can accept a detection risk of 18 per cent in the test of details being planned and still hold the audit risk for the account balance to 5 per cent.

If the component risks are all assessed at the highest level, then the detection risk for the tests of details being planned would be estimated as follows:

$$TD = \frac{0.05}{1 \times 1 \times 1}$$
$$= 5\%$$

In this case, the test of details is the only procedure being relied on to detect material misstatement, and the acceptable risk is the same as the audit risk for the account balance.

If the component risks are all assessed at the minimum, the estimation of detection risk would be as follows:

$$TD = \frac{0.05}{0.4 \times 0.4 \times 0.4}$$
$$= 78\%$$

When the acceptable detection risk is high, the auditor will only need to perform very limited tests of details.

TABLE 5.1 Quantitative risk assessment model for estimation of detection risk for test of details

Risk component	Audit risk	= Inherent risk	x Control risk	x Analytical procedures risk	x Test of details risk
Formula symbol	AR	= IR	× CR	× AP	× TD
Concept	The combined risk of a material misstatement remaining in the account balance	The susceptibility of the account balance to material misstatement without regard to internal control policies and procedures	The risk that material misstatement may occur and not be prevented or detected by internal control policies and procedures	The risk that analytical procedures will fail to detect material misstatement in the account balance	The acceptable risk that the test of details being planned will fail to detect a material misstatement
Guidelines	Should be relatively low, for example 5% or 10%	Assessed as:* Low 40% Medium 70% High 100%	Assessed as:* Low 40% Medium 70% High 100%	Assessed as:* Low 40% Medium 70% High 100%	Calculated on the basis of specified percentages for other risks

* The number of levels and the specific percentages are subjective probabilities determined by individual judgment or audit firm policy.

Business risk

Bell et al. (1997) have defined a client's **business risk** as 'the risk that an entity's business objectives will not be attained as a result of the external and internal factors, pressures, and forces brought to bear on the entity and, ultimately, the risk associated with the entity's survival and profitability' (p. 15). The auditor must have extensive knowledge about the nature of the client's business and industry in order to determine whether financial report assertions are valid. The auditor must understand the business risks faced by the client in addition to understanding the risks that affect the traditional processing and recording of transactions (Auditing in the News 5.1).

5.1 AUDITING IN THE NEWS

5.1

Source: Bell et al. (1997)

Impact of globalisation on business risk

As the global economy, the business organisations operating within it, and organisations' business strategies become increasingly complex and interdependent, we believe more attention should be paid to the development of auditing methods and procedures that focus on assertions at the entity level—methods and procedures that promise greater power to detect material misstatements as they allow the auditor to ground key judgments in a more critical and holistic understanding of the client's systems dynamics (p. 12).

In today's world, distance is no longer a barrier to market entry, technologies are rapidly replicated by competitors, and information and communications technologies are shaping a new economic order. To manage their business risks effectively, organisations must now view their playing field as the whole global economy (p. 27).

In order to judge properly the fair presentation of the financial report, the auditor needs to understand the entity's business strategy, risks faced by the entity and its ability to respond to, or control, changes in its business environment. The auditor must then determine if those business risks affect audit risk. Figure 5.5 shows how client business risk relates to audit risk. The auditor's assessment of client business risk is part of the assessment of the risk of material misstatement in the financial report. In other words, the auditor assesses the specific business risks that the entity faces in order to determine if they might result in errors, fraud or other irregularities, and ultimately in a materially misstated financial report.

This focus on the client's business risks leads to a more strategic and systematic approach to the audit. The auditor uses knowledge of the client's business and industry to develop a more efficient and effective audit. The auditor places less emphasis on routine transactions that are likely to be well controlled through the client's internal control and focuses on identifying non-routine transactions, accounting estimates and valuation issues that are much more likely to lead to misstatements in the financial report. Focusing on client business risk in this manner should lower audit risk. The new audit risk standards discussed earlier in this chapter adopt a business risk approach and will impact on the auditor's work in four key ways:

FIGURE 5.5 The relationship of client business risk and the risk of material misstatement in the financial report to the determination of audit risk

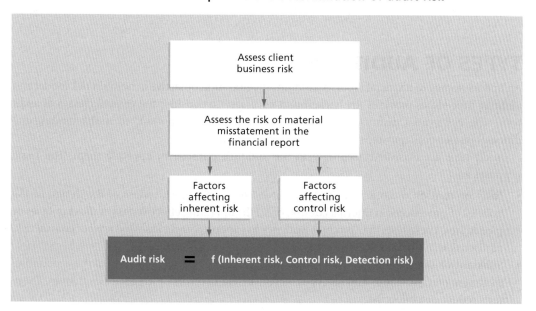

1. The auditor is required to obtain an enhanced understanding of the entity's business. The auditor is required to perform audit procedures to obtain a broader and deeper understanding of specified aspects of the entity and its environment, including its internal control.

2. The auditor is required to make risk assessments in all cases. The required understanding of the entity provides a better basis for identifying risks of material misstatement at the financial report level and in classes of transactions, account balances and disclosures. The auditor is required to perform a more rigorous assessment in relating the identified risks to what can go wrong at the assertion level. By requiring the auditor to make risk assessments in all audits, the auditor can no longer default to a high-risk assessment.

3. The auditor is required to link the identified risks to audit procedures. In designing and performing further audit procedures, the nature, timing and extent of the procedures are linked to the assessed risks.

4. The auditor is required to document specific matters. The proposed documentation requirements are more specific and recognise the importance of documentation in conducting the audit.

A detailed discussion of the auditor's understanding and evaluation of business risk is contained in Chapter 6.

Quick review

1 Auditors use a business risk approach in determining what is sufficient appropriate audit evidence.

2 Audit risk is a function of inherent risk, control risk and detection risk.

3 Detection risk may occur because of sampling risk or non-sampling risk.

4 There is an inverse relationship between the combined degree of inherent and control risks on the one hand, and the detection risk established by the auditor on the other.

TYPES OF AUDIT TESTS

An understanding of financial report assertions, specific audit objectives, the audit risk model and auditing procedures provides the background necessary to consider the general classes of audit tests. The conceptual distinction between types of tests is important to understanding the different phases or major steps in a financial report audit.

Audit tests are classified according to the auditor's purpose in applying them. The basic purposes are:

- **Tests of control**: to obtain evidence about either (1) the effectiveness of the design of the policies or procedures in internal control, or (2) the operating effectiveness of those policies or procedures. These tests may produce evidence to support a lower assessed level of control risk, as discussed in Chapter 8.

- **Substantive tests:** to obtain evidence about the validity and the propriety of the accounting treatment of transactions and balances or, conversely, of errors or irregularities therein. These tests reduce detection risk.

Tests of control

The auditor performs tests of control to see whether the control activities of the internal control system are effective.

How the auditor performs the audit test differs, depending on whether the client's procedure to be tested leaves a visible audit trail of evidence that it was performed. The use of tests of control is covered in AUS 406 (ISA 330) and will be discussed further in Chapter 9.

Substantive tests

Substantive tests are performed on the specific transactions and balances to see whether the dollar amount of the account balance is materially misstated. There are two general categories of substantive tests: analytical procedures and tests of details.

Analytical procedures

As mentioned previously, essentially these procedures involve the study and comparison of relationships between accounting data and related information. They focus on the reasonableness of relationships and also identify unusual fluctuations for investigation.

Analytical procedures are used for three purposes:

1   to assist the auditor in planning other audit procedures (Chapter 6);
2   as a substantive test to obtain evidence about an assertion (Chapter 10); and
3   as an overall review of the financial information near the end of the audit (Chapter 12).

It is important to recognise that analytical procedures are substantive tests that may achieve specific audit objectives if the evidence is considered persuasive by the auditor.

Tests of details

These involve obtaining evidence on the items (or details) included in an account balance or class of transactions. Thus, tests of details are also referred to as follows:

- **Tests of transactions**   The auditor tests the processing of individual transactions by inspecting the relevant documents and accounting records. For example, a sample of shipping documents is traced to the sales journal to see whether shipments have been recorded as sales. Tests of transactions are discussed in Chapter 10.
- **Tests of balances**   These are tests applied directly to the details of balances in general ledger accounts. For example, the balances in the accounts receivable ledger are confirmed with individual customers. Tests of balances are discussed in Chapter 10.

Tests of transactions (substantive tests) and tests of control that leave a documentary trail may both involve the inspection of documents that support transactions. For this reason, these tests are often applied together to the same group of documents. In that case, the test is referred to as a *dual-purpose test*, which is discussed in Chapter 9.

Quick review

1   The two main types of audit tests are tests of control and substantive tests.
2   The two general categories of substantive test are analytical procedures and tests of details which include transactions or balances.

USING THE WORK OF AN EXPERT OR ANOTHER AUDITOR

Using the work of an expert

The practice of auditing often requires **expert** knowledge of several highly technical and rapidly expanding subjects. These subjects require advanced training and experience. While these issues now form an integral part of the audit environment it is neither practical nor necessary for every member of the audit staff to have the detailed knowledge needed to be expert in them. Within an audit firm it is common for members and employees to be assigned as experts or specialists on an industry, functional or technical basis.

Industry specialists

Audit firms often designate members as **specialists** in particular industries that have unique organisational or operating characteristics that raise special accounting or auditing considerations. For example, banks, insurance companies, retailers and extractive industry firms all have unique operating characteristics that create special problems in the application of accounting principles or the audit of accounting estimates.

Every auditor in charge of an engagement is expected to have an in-depth understanding of the entity and its industry. The audit manager and partner will also have specialist skills and experience with the industry and the client. In the Big Four audit firms, industry specialisations discussed in Chapter 2 are supported by knowledge management systems, which contain information on industries and clients and audit and accounting issues that have arisen in that industry and how they have been dealt with. The industry knowledge database is usually under the control of a knowledge manager, who is responsible for maintaining the database and ensuring it is appropriately updated by staff. Naturally, a firm must have a number of clients in a specialised industry to make designation of a specialist worthwhile. The industries in which specialists are designated, and their duties and authority, depend on the size and philosophy of the audit firm.

Functional specialists

Functional specialists are often designated for the areas of taxation, management advisory services, computer information systems and statistics and other mathematical applications. Specialists in taxes and management advisory services provide services to clients in separate engagements, and consult on request on pertinent matters that arise in audits.

Specialisation in computers and statistics often requires two levels of expertise. First, there are specialists in data processing and mathematics. Trained professionals in their own fields, they may work in the management advisory services section of a firm. Their special skills are used from time to time in audit engagements when unique or sophisticated problems arise. They also usually participate in the development of firm-wide policies and procedures for statistical or computer applications.

Second, there are computer audit specialists and statistical audit specialists. They are normally auditors, equipped with advanced training and experience in their specialised fields. They usually work as members of the audit team, and plan and review the application of the specialised tools—use of the computer or statistical sampling—in an audit engagement. It is usually unreasonable to expect staff auditors to have enough time or expert knowledge to assure the valid use of these complex tools. However, staff auditors must recognise when the assistance of a computer audit specialist or a statistical audit specialist is required, and supervise the work. In a large firm, computer and statistical specialists may also be supervised by co-ordinators in each respective area.

Technical specialists

Some audit firms have designated technical specialists. The subjects of accounting and auditing in many ways can today be viewed as specialities. Every auditor is expected to be an expert in accounting and auditing. However, so many authoritative pronouncements exist in accounting and auditing, and so many complexities arise in the application of pronouncements, that some firms have designated specialists in this area. These specialists advise on questions that arise in particular engagements and develop policies and procedures for the firm that assure uniform implementation and compliance with new pronouncements. In addition, auditors often need to call on outside specialists for assistance or consultation during the audit process, for example to value assets such as land and buildings, and plant and machinery, or to determine quantities of assets such as stockpiled minerals or petroleum reserves. These specialists may be engaged by the client or the auditor.

AUS 606.04 (ISA 620.04) states that, while education and experience equip the auditor with knowledge about business matters in general, the auditor is not expected to have the expertise of a person trained or qualified to engage in another profession or occupation, such as an actuary or an engineer.

When planning to use the work of an expert as audit evidence, whether that expert is internal or external to the audit firm, AUS 606.02 (ISA 620.02) requires that the auditor must obtain sufficient appropriate audit evidence that such work is adequate for the purposes of the audit. In these circumstances the auditor should do the following things as required by AUS 606.09–.17 (ISA 620.08–.15):

- Assess the skills and competence of the expert by reference to any professional certification or licence, and the experience and reputation of the expert.
- Assess the objectivity of the expert. This is especially relevant where the expert is employed by the audit client. In this case the auditor should determine whether there are any professional and/or statutory obligations governing the work of the expert that mitigate any concern as to objectivity. For example, many actuaries are employed by life insurance companies, but they have professional and statutory obligations over and above their employee status which require them to maintain an objective approach to their work.
- Communicate with the expert to confirm the terms of the engagement and ensure the expert understands the objective and use of the work undertaken, and the information required by the auditor.
- Evaluate the work of the expert by discussion or review of the assumptions and methods used by the expert, the auditor's knowledge of the client and results of related audit procedures. The auditor, of course, evaluates and understands the work only as a reasonable person and not as an expert.

Using the work of another auditor

In audit engagements where the client entity comprises one or more divisions, branches or subsidiaries (components), the audit work may be undertaken by several different auditors. In these situations the principal auditor responsible for the opinion on the primary financial report (that containing the information from the various components) is responsible for the use made of the work of any other external auditor. AUS 602.02 (ISA 600.02) requires the principal auditor, when using the work of **another auditor**, to determine how that work will affect the audit.

In some situations the components of the client entity are audited by another external auditor where the component is in a separate geographical location or where the client has an existing commitment with another auditor. In these cases the audit of the component could be undertaken by another office of the principal auditor's firm (perhaps in a different country), an affiliated firm of auditors or a totally unrelated firm of auditors. In all these cases the primary auditor must be satisfied as to the work undertaken by the other auditor, as this work forms part of the audit evidence which the principal uses to form an opinion. The principal auditor's procedures are set out in AUS 602.07–.14 (ISA 600.07–.14), and can be summarised as follows:

1   Obtain information regarding the professional competence of the other auditor in terms of the specific tasks undertaken by that auditor. Such information could be obtained by reference to any professional organisations to which the auditor belongs, by inquiries of third parties and by discussions with the other auditor.
2   Advise the other auditor of the professional, accounting and auditing requirements applicable to the engagement, including independence. This is especially relevant where the other auditor is overseas. The principal should seek a representation as to the other auditor's compliance with these requirements.
3   Advise the other auditor of the use to be made of the work, the areas that the principal auditor knows require special attention and the timetable for the completion of the audit. This assists the co-ordination of the audit process and the evaluation of the audit work.

In order for the principal auditor to place reliance on the work of another auditor, some procedures may need to be applied to that work. The nature and extent of these procedures depend on the circumstances of the engagement and on the principal auditor's familiarity with the work and competence of the other auditor. The procedures applied could take the form of discussions with the other auditor; the completion of a written summary, questionnaire or checklist identifying the audit procedures applied by the other auditor; or, in extreme cases, a review of the other auditor's working papers. This process should be documented by the principal auditor, along with the conclusions reached as to the use to be made of the work of the other auditor.

Quick review

1   When using the work of an expert, internal or external, an auditor must assess the skills, competence and objectivity of the expert and obtain sufficient appropriate evidence that the work is adequate for the purposes of the audit.

2   When part of the entity or group is audited by another auditor, the principal auditor is responsible for the opinion on the primary financial report.

3   The principal auditor must be satisfied that the other external auditor is independent and competent and that their work provides satisfactory evidence to support the principal auditor's opinion.

 learning objective 9

RECORD OF AUDIT TESTS: WORKING PAPERS

As the auditor carries out the steps in the audit, collecting evidence to support an opinion on the financial report, there must be some means of recording the evidence for future study and consideration. Audit **working papers** are the specific means used to record evidence. The exact form and the detailed content of working papers must be designed to meet the circumstances and the needs of individual engagements. The form and content of working papers are influenced by the nature of the engagement, the nature and complexity of the client's business, the condition of the client's records and internal control, and the approach and staffing of each audit engagement. Many auditing firms have standardised the details of working papers, and the formats vary. For these reasons, primary attention is given here to the general aspects of working papers rather than the detailed methods of their preparation. The new audit risk standards issued in 2004 emphasise the importance of the auditor documenting the work that has been done and the decisions that have been made.

The function of working papers

The three main functions of working papers are to aid in:

1 planning and performing the audit;
2 supervising and reviewing the audit work; and
3 gathering evidence and providing essential support for the auditor's opinion, including evidence that the examination was conducted in accordance with professional auditing standards.

Working papers are an important physical aid in recording the results of audit tests. For example, when a sample is taken the items drawn must be recorded and computations must be made. Working papers, in addition, are necessary for co-ordination of the work leading to an opinion. Final decisions concerning the opinion on the financial report are made by partners and managers who perform few, if any, of the actual audit tests. There must be a means of reviewing the work performed. They use the working papers as a basis for evaluating the evidence gathered.

To be useful, the working papers need to be clear and unambiguous, and be appropriately referenced and stored. The most critical aspect of working papers is that they should stand in their own right and not require oral comments by the auditor for completeness or clarity.

After an opinion has been given, working papers are the only evidence the auditor has that an adequate examination was conducted. The auditor works with original documents and accounting records which must be left with the client when the examination has been completed. The auditor must include in the working papers a description of the work done and the results of the tests performed. There is always a possibility that the auditor will have to prove the adequacy of the examination in court, and in such circumstances the working papers will be critical to the defence.

The requirement that audit working papers be properly prepared and maintained is found in AUS 208.02 (ISA 230.02), which requires the auditor to document important evidence to support the audit opinion and show that the audit was conducted in accordance with Australian auditing standards. This basic principle is amplified in AUS 208.05–.06 (ISA 230.05–.06), which requires the auditor:

■ to prepare complete and detailed working papers to provide an understanding of the audit; and
■ to prepare working papers that show planning, the nature, timing and extent of the audit procedures performed, the results of the audit work and the conclusions reached by the auditor based on the evidence obtained.

In addition, AUS 208.08 (ISA 230.08) states that the form and content of working papers are affected by matters such as:

■ the nature of the engagement;
■ the nature and complexity of the business;
■ the nature and condition of internal control;
■ the need for direction, supervision and review of work performed by assistants; and
■ the audit methodology and technology used in the course of the audit.

The contents and requirements of working papers

While audit firms have different approaches, there are two main divisions of audit working papers for each engagement: the **permanent file** and the **current working paper file**.

Permanent file

The permanent file is used to store documents, schedules and other information that are pertinent to the current audit and of continuing significance for the audit engagement in future years. It normally contains the following items:

1 Excerpts and/or copies of the company constitution or replaceable rules which describe the regulations of the company and the basic approach to be adhered to by management. These documents identify the objectives of the company, the number and types of shares that can be issued and their par value, the rights of shareholders and the powers and duties of directors.

2 Documents relating to ongoing contracts and agreements, such as loan agreements, debenture deeds, labour agreements, trade contracts, leases and service agreements. All of these matters could significantly affect a company's operations and its financial report, and the auditor should have evidence of the provisions of these documents and the review thereof. These documents also assist the auditor in verifying such matters as loan interest payments and receipts and lease assets and liabilities.

3 Continuing analysis of accounts that have ongoing importance to the auditor, for example shareholders' funds, long-term debt and fixed assets. With this information in the permanent file, the auditor can concentrate on analysing changes in the accounts during the current year while having the results of previous years available for review.

4 The results of analytical procedures from previous years. These include ratios and percentages computed by the auditor, and trend analysis of relevant accounts, such as sales and gross profit margins by major product class. This assists the auditor in determining whether there are unusual changes in the current year which require further audit consideration.

5 Extracts from minutes of relevant shareholder and management meetings and committees. These provide the auditor with evidence for verifying various events that may be reflected in the financial report, for example details of share issues, approval of capital projects and changes in accounting policies.

6 Details relevant to audit planning, such as the locations of branch offices or subsidiaries, details of cost centres and bank accounts, inventory storage capacity and locations. This information is useful to the auditor where certain audit procedures are performed on a rotating basis or at different locations each year.

7 Copies of significant correspondence between the auditor and the client, such as any management letters sent to the company's board of directors detailing matters of concern arising from previous audits.

The permanent file also holds the chart of accounts and accounting procedure manuals, flowcharts and notes on internal control, organisation charts and excerpts from job manuals, industry information, a list of related parties and the previous year's audited financial report.

At the start of an examination, the permanent file and the previous year's current working paper file are studied and used for reference purposes.

Current working paper file

This contains all papers accumulated during the current year's examination, comprising the evidence gathered and conclusions reached in the audit for that year. While the current file contains a range of detailed information, the following items are the most important:

1 Evidence of planning, including a copy of the audit plan.
2 The details of the review of the accounting system and related internal controls, the client's activities and accounting records, and the basis upon which the nature, timing and extent of audit procedures were determined. This may include flowcharts or narratives of the client's systems and the auditor's internal control questionnaires. Some of this information may be transferred to the permanent file following completion of the audit.
3 The audit program, listing the audit procedures undertaken and the names of audit staff completing those procedures. The audit program helps to ensure that the audit is co-ordinated and integrated.
4 Details of the tests of controls and substantive tests of transactions and balances completed.
5 The working trial balance, which is the schedule of general ledger accounts used as the basis of preparation of the financial report. Many audit firms use the working trial balance as the focus of working paper preparation. Schedules are prepared supporting each item on the trial balance, and these schedules provide evidence of the work performed and conclusions reached. Where the audit work results in an adjustment to a particular account, the trial balance and supporting schedules reflect the adjustment.
6 Trial balance working paper schedules, which include documents from sources external to the entity confirming items in the accounting information supporting the financial report. Examples are confirmations from debtors and creditors, confirmations from the entity's bank detailing bank account balances held by the entity, the balances of those accounts and any securities held, and letters from the entity's solicitors. There are also reconciliations prepared by the auditor, the results of numerical and narrative analyses of accounts, tests of reasonableness, results of audit inquiries to members of the entity's staff, excerpts from minutes of the meetings of the board of directors, copies of important contracts and the conclusions drawn by the auditor on each matter considered.
7 The original draft of the financial report and auditor's report, and evidence of appropriate review and conclusions drawn to support the audit opinion.

While the preparation of certain working papers by the client's employees is desirable for an efficient audit, there is a clear distinction between preparation of working papers and accumulation of audit evidence. While the client can assist by providing information and preparing schedules, the auditor is responsible for checking the accuracy of those schedules. For example, if the auditor receives a schedule from the client listing the acquisition of fixed assets during the period, the auditor checks the numerical accuracy of the schedule, traces the information to the general ledger, and then verifies the acquisitions by examining supporting documents. The client schedule is retained as the working paper with the auditor's notations and conclusions recorded thereon.

Legal aspects of working papers

AUS 208.14 (ISA 230.14) states that working papers are the property of the auditor. The auditor should not permit general access to the audit files by clients' staff, as this would enable staff to become familiar with the procedures used by the auditor and could facilitate fraud or malpractice.

The ownership of audit working papers has also been dealt with through the courts. The decision in *Chantrey Martin & Co. v Martin* (1953) 3 WLR 459 established that ordinarily the auditor owns the working papers. It was a decision of the Court of Appeal in England. The case involved a firm of chartered accountants (the plaintiffs) and a former employee whose employment had been terminated. The employee said that he was dismissed because he refused to acquiesce in certain irregularities he had discovered while auditing the accounts of a client. So that this issue could be explored, the defendant sought access to the working papers. The plaintiffs resisted this on the basis that those papers were the property of the client, but the Court of Appeal held otherwise.

This decision has not been called into question. In fact, it can be argued that the increasing emphasis placed upon the responsibilities and liability of an auditor, along with the more onerous consequences of default, have reinforced the view that in compiling audit working papers the auditor is acting independently of the client. Because auditors are responsible for their actions, the working papers must be held independently of the client whose activities are being audited. Legal ownership of the working papers, however, does not change the auditor's ethical responsibility not to violate the confidential relationship with the client.

Whether working papers constitute 'evidence' in the legal sense is not relevant, although logically their role in a legal action is as a store of information about the purpose and accomplishment of an audit. Working papers provide the auditor's defence in terms of whether the audit was undertaken in accordance with proper standards.

Therefore, AUS 208.13 (ISA 230.13) requires that the auditor should adopt reasonable procedures for safe custody and confidentiality of working papers and retain working papers for a period sufficient to meet the needs of the audit firm and accord with legal and professional requirements. As a result of the CLERP 9 amendments, s. 307B now requires auditors to retain working papers for 7 years. Following the collapse of Harris Scarfe Ltd in Australia, in early 2001, their auditors, PricewaterhouseCoopers (PwC) were ordered by the South Australian Supreme Court to provide original files from PwC's audits and half-yearly reviews from 1997 until 2000. Ernst & Young, the company's auditors before PwC, were also required to provide original documents on audits from 1995 to 1997. In the US, Arthur Andersen had criminal proceedings brought against them after the collapse of Enron for allegedly destroying working papers concerning the audit. The *Sarbanes-Oxley Act 2002* now requires auditors of US listed companies or their subsidiaries to also maintain audit working papers for a minimum of 7 years.

Access to working papers

As indicated in Chapter 3, the auditor has a duty of confidentiality under CPC B5 and should not disclose information about a client to a third party without specific authority from the client unless there is a legal or professional duty to disclose it. This is supported by AUS 208.13 (ISA 230.13), which requires that the auditor have appropriate procedures for maintaining the confidentiality of the working papers.

AGS 1038 provides specific guidance to auditors when establishing and agreeing to conditions under which third parties are granted access to audit working papers and related documentation. AGS 1038.03 indicates that requests for access to an auditor's working papers may arise when:

- a controlling entity's auditor wishes to review the working papers of a controlled entity, in accordance with section 323B of the *Corporations Act*;
- a representative of a potential purchaser, investor or lender wishes to review the audit working papers, to assist their client in an investment decision concerning the acquisition of the audited entity;

- an accountant seeks to review the audit working papers to facilitate the preparation of an independent accountant's report for a prospectus or information memorandum; and
- an entity's newly appointed auditor seeks to review the outgoing auditor's working papers in connection with the next audit of the entity.

AGS 1038.04 states that whenever a third party seeks access to audit working papers the auditor should first obtain from the client or the third party an indemnity against any liability which arises through that access. While in most cases a company cannot indemnify its auditor in respect of a liability to the company which arises in the capacity as the company's auditor, it can indemnify its auditor against such liabilities to third parties. In addition, the third parties themselves can indemnify the auditor against liability to those or other parties.

AGS 1038.04 provides that audit working papers and other documents to which access is given should in all cases include an express disclaimer of reliance and exclusion of liability. In addition, AGS 1038.05 indicates that the auditor should consider seeking legal advice to ensure that additional obligations are not unduly imposed on the auditor.

Preparing working papers

Certain matters concerning the mechanics of working papers are so traditional in the practice of auditing that they require mention even in a general discussion. These matters are tick marks, indexing and adjusting journal entries.

Ticks are symbols used by the auditor to indicate the nature and extent of procedures applied in specific circumstances. Like all symbols, they are shorthand. For example, after the auditor has examined vouchers supporting disbursements for every item on a working paper listing the charges to an expense account, the auditor places a tick (e.g. ✓) after each item. At the bottom of the working paper the auditor explains the meaning of the mark in this manner:

> ✓ *Voucher with supporting papers examined and found satisfactory.*

Individual audit firms develop their own standardised markings and indexing.

Indexing working papers is a matter of coding the individual sheets of paper so that needed information may be found easily. The auditor prepares cross-references, creating a trail through the records for the same reasons that make an audit trail in the client's accounting records important. A variety of indexing systems are in use: sequential numbering, combinations of letters and numbers, and digit-position index numbers. A short example of the third system is sufficient to illustrate the general principle:

1000	Draft of audit report
. . .	
. . .	
2000	Cash
2001	Count of petty cash
2002	Bank reconciliation
2100	Accounts receivable
. . .	
. . .	
3000	Fixed assets
. . .	
. . .	

Sometimes the client makes errors of omission or misapplies accounting standards when preparing the financial report. Adjusting journal entries are the corrections the auditor feels are required. The auditor does not make the entries in the client's records. Proposed entries are made on the auditor's working papers, and their later recording by the client is reviewed. If the client declines to make the adjusting entries which the auditor considers necessary for the financial report to give a true and fair view, the auditor issues a qualified audit opinion.

For example, suppose an ordinary expense is incorrectly capitalised as follows:

Dr Machinery and Equipment $175
    Cr Cash $175

The adjusting journal entry necessary to correct the accounts is:

Dr Repair Expense $175
    Cr Machinery and Equipment $175
    (to record ordinary repair expense incorrectly capitalised)

Illustrative audit working papers

A typical audit program (list of procedures) for the audit of fixed assets is illustrated in Exhibit 5.2.

Exhibit 5.3, consisting of five hypothetical working papers, illustrates the accomplishment of the procedures specified in this audit program. This illustration presents one possible format for working papers. The indexing system is a combination of letters and numbers. The lead schedule is indexed 'B', while the supporting working papers are numbered 'B/1' to 'B/4'. A lead schedule is prepared for each major account classification and is used to summarise all final amounts that will appear in the financial report. Cross-referencing of individual items from one working paper to another and to the lead schedule is also illustrated.

On each working paper in the set, the procedures undertaken are indicated at the bottom. These procedures reflect the types of evidence obtained for each of the items comprising the balances of fixed assets and related accounts. By clearly showing the procedures undertaken, the auditor's working papers reflect the types of evidence used, the timing of the procedures used to gain the evidence and the extent of the procedures used. Finally, the set of working papers illustrated in Exhibit 5.3 shows the interrelationship between accounts as well as the integrated approach to the audit of such accounts.

The trial balance and lead schedules can be prepared manually or a microcomputer can be used. The client's general ledger accounts and balances can be entered into the trial balance program. When adjusting and reclassification entries are entered, the computer software posts the entries and updates the trial balance and lead sheets. The microcomputer software can also be used to consolidate financial reports and prepare the final drafts of the financial report.

The microcomputer can also be used to assist in preparing working papers, particularly when standard working paper format is applicable. Additionally, the auditor may be able to download information from the client's computer files directly into the audit working papers for further analysis and testing. For example, the auditor can use software such as Audit Command Language (ACL) or Interactive Data Extraction and Analysis (IDEA) to scan a client's cash payments file and select all items over a specified dollar amount for further analysis.

EXHIBIT 5.2

Simplified example of an audit program for property, plant and equipment

CLIENT Palmwood Ltd	Reviewed by
AUDIT PROGRAM FOR Repairs and maintenance expense	DRS
AUDIT PERIOD 30/6/X4	Date 5/8/X4

Item no.	Audit procedures	Done by	Working paper reference
1.	Obtain or prepare a schedule of property, plant, equipment, and accumulated depreciation.	RP	B
2.	Trace additions and retirement from the accounts through records to supporting vouchers and examine support.	RP	B/1, B/2
3.	Examine supporting vouchers for repairs and maintenance to ascertain whether such charges should be capitalised or expensed.	RP	B/4
4.	Recompute depreciation calculations.	RP	B/3
5.	Trace depreciation to depreciation expense accounts.	RP	B/3
6.	Ascertain that depreciation rates and depreciable lives being used appear to be reasonably adequate.	RP	B/3
7.	Ascertain that depreciation rates and depreciable lives being used are consistent with previous years.	RP	B/3
8.	Recompute gains or losses on disposals trace to gain or loss accounts.	RP	B/1, B/2

EXHIBIT 5.3

Audit working papers

Palmwood Ltd	W.P. No: B
Fixed assets and accumulated depreciation	Compiled by: RP
Audit 30/6/X4	Date 4/8/X4

	Assets				Accumulated depreciation			
	Per audit 30/6/X3	Additions	Retire-ments	Balance 30/6/X4	Per audit 30/6/X3	Retire-ments	Depreci-ation	Balance
Land	∅ 15 000	—	—	15 000	—	—	—	
Building	∅ 75 000	(B/1) 15 000	—	90 000	∅ 25 000	—	(B/1) 4125	29 125
Equipment	∅ 40 500	(B/4) 1 500 (B/2) 16 000	(B/2) 3 500	54 500	10 125	(B/2) 1 000	(B/1) 4750	13 875
	130 500	32 500	3 500	159 500	35 125	1 000	8 875	43 000
				(T/B)		(T/B)	(T/B)	

∅ Per last year's working papers

Conclusion: based on the audit work completed and the adjusting entries proposed, fixed assets are fairly stated.

Palmwood Ltd	W.P. No: B/1
Building and accumulated depreciation	Compiled by: RP
Audit 30/6/X4	Date 29/7/X4

		Cost	Accum. dep'n
Balance	30/6/X3	75 000 ↘	25 000 ↘
15/12/X3	Bolivar Construction Ltd—building addition	15 000 n	
30/6/X4	JV 19/6 Depreciation provision		4125 (B/3)
	Balance 30/6/X4 per audit	90 000 (B) (T)	29 125 (B) (T)

↘ per last year's working papers
n vouched to original contract and
invoice and examined paid cheque
(T) additions checked OK

Palmwood Ltd	W.P. No: B/2
Equipment and accumulated depreciation	Compiled by: RP
Audit 30/6/X4	Date 29/7/X4

		Cost	Accum. dep'n
Balance	30/6/X3	40 500 ↘	10 125 ↘
1/11/X3	Bolston Ltd — milling machine	72 000 ⊘	
3/3/X4	Bagley Bros Ltd — casting machine	8800 ⊘	
JV1–19	Sale of milling machine purchased 11/1/X0	(3500) n	(1000) n
30/6/X4	Depreciation provision		4750 (B/3)
	AJE no. 4	1500 (B/2)	
	Balance 30/6/X4 per audit	54 500 (B) (T)	13 875 (B) (T)

↘ per last year's working papers
⊘ traced and vouched to invoices and paid cheques
(T) additions checked OK
n traced, vouched, recomputed OK
Loss on sale $800 (E)

			Building	Equipment
Palmwood Ltd			W.P. No: B/3	
Depreciation expenses			Compiled by: RP	
Audit 30/6/X4			Date 29/7/X4	

			Building	Equipment
Computations:				
Building				
5% x 75000 (B/1)	=	3750		
⅟ ½ (5% x 15000) (B/1)	=	375	4125	
Equipment				
10% x 40500 (B/2)	=	4050		
½ (10% x 16000) (B/2)	=	800		
½ (10% x 35000) (B/2)	=	(175)		
new machine —				
½ (10% x 16000) (B/4)	=	75		4750
Balance 30/6/X4 per audit			4125 (B)	4750 (B)
Balance 30/6/X4 per books			4125	4675
AJE no. 6			0	75

Ⓨ Company consistently takes ½ year depreciation on additions

and retirements—OK

(AJE no. 6)

		Building	Equipment
Depreciation expense		75 –	
Accum. dep'n equip.			75 –
To adjust 20X4 dep'n expense			

Palmwood Ltd					W.P. No: B/4
Repairs and maintenance expense					Compiled by: RP
Audit 30/6/X4					Date 29/7/X4

25/7/X3	Alto Equip. Repair Ltd		625 ✗	
11/9/X3	Bolton Paint Ltd		775 ✗	
15/11/X3	Minot Elec. Repair Ltd		350 ✗	
17/1/X4	Beardsley Equip Ltd		1500 ⊗	B/2
13/4/X4	Manner Welding Ltd		640 ✗	
	Various items all under $200—not examined		720 ✗	
	Balance 30/6/X4 per books		4610	
	AJE no. 4		(1500)	
	Balance 30/6/X4 per audit		3110	

✗ traced and vouched to invoice OK

⊗ traced and vouched — invoice indicates this is a purchase of a new

211 casting machine

AJE no. 4

Equipment	1500 –	
Repairs & maintenance expense		1500 –

To reclassify and capitalise cost

of 211 casting machine

1 Working papers are necessary for the planning and co-ordination of the audit work.

2 Working papers enable a review to be conducted of the work completed.

3 Working papers provide evidence that the audit has been properly carried out.

4 The two main categories of working papers are the permanent file and the current working paper file.

5 Working papers are the property of the auditors.

6 The auditor needs to ensure safe custody and confidentiality of the working papers.

7 The auditor should only provide access to working papers in limited circumstances and should provide a disclaimer of reliance and try to obtain an indemnity against any liability which may arise.

Summary

The overall audit objective in a financial report audit is to give an opinion on the financial report. This is achieved by gathering and evaluating evidence regarding management assertions contained in the financial report. Management makes assertions concerning existence, occurrence, completeness, rights and obligations, valuation and allocation, accuracy, cutoff, classification and disclosure and presentation. The auditor needs to gather sufficient appropriate audit evidence to enable an audit opinion to be given. The auditing procedures to be applied and the type of evidence to be gathered to support each assertion are matters of the auditor's judgment. Where the auditor uses the work of experts or other auditors, the audit procedures will need to ensure that the work is adequate for the purposes of the audit. The working papers should provide support for the audit opinion by documenting the procedures performed, the evidence obtained and the conclusions reached.

Key terms

References

Bell, T.B., Marrs, F.O., Solomon, I. and Thomas, H. (1997) *Auditing Organisations Through a Strategic-Systems Lens: The KPMG Business Measurement Process*, KPMG, New York.

Flesher, D.L. and De Magalhaes, R. (1995) 'Electronic workpapers', *Internal Auditor*, August, 38–43.

Holstrum, G.L. and Mock, T.J. (1985) 'Audit judgment and evidence evaluation', *Auditing: A Journal of Practice and Theory*, Fall, 101–8.

Moeckel, C.L. and Plumlee, R.D. (1989) 'Auditor's confidence recognition of audit evidence', *The Accounting Review*, October, 653–66.

(MaxMARK) Assignments

MAXIMISE YOUR MARKS! There are approximately 30 interactive questions on the financial report audit process available online at www.mhhe.com/au/gay3e

Additional assignments for this chapter are contained in Appendix A of this book, page 765.

REVIEW QUESTIONS

5.1 The following questions relate to types of audit tests and financial report assertions. Select the *best* response.

(a) Which of the following is not a financial report assertion?

   A   rights and obligations

   B   inspection

   C   existence

   D   valuation and allocation

(b) Which of the following audit objectives relates primarily to the financial report assertion, valuation and allocation?

   A   Inventory quantities include all products, materials and supplies owned by the company that are in transit.

   B   Inventory listings are accurately compiled and the totals are properly included in the inventory accounts.

   C   Inventories exclude items billed to customers or owned by others.

   D   Slow-moving, excess, defective and obsolete items included in inventories are properly identified.

(c) Which of the following audit objectives relates primarily to the financial report assertion, completeness?

   A   Inventory quantities include all products, materials and supplies owned by the company that are in transit.

   B   Inventories are reduced, when appropriate, to net realisable value.

   C   Inventories exclude items billed to customers or owned by others.

   D   Slow-moving, excess, defective and obsolete items included in inventories are properly identified.

(d) Which of the following procedures would an auditor most likely rely on to verify management's assertion of completeness?

   A   Reviewing a standard bank confirmation

   B   Comparing a sample of shipping documents to related sales invoices

   C   Observing the client's distribution of payroll cheques

   D   Confirming a sample of recorded receivables by direct communication with the debtors

(e) In testing the existence assertion for an asset, an auditor ordinarily works from the:

   A   financial report to the potentially unrecorded items

   B   potentially unrecorded items to the financial report

     C   accounting records to the supporting evidence

     D   supporting evidence to the accounting records

(f) Which of the following is not an auditing procedure?

     A   disclosure

     B   physical examination

     C   confirmation

     D   vouching

(g) In a financial report audit, substantive tests are audit procedures that:

     A   may be either tests of transactions, direct tests of financial balances or analytical procedures

     B   are designed to discover significant subsequent events

     C   may be eliminated under certain conditions

     D   will decrease proportionately with the auditor's assessed level of control risk

(h) Which of the following would be *least* likely to be included in an auditor's test of controls?

     A   inquiry

     B   observation

     C   inspection

     D   confirmation

(i) Which of the following best describes the primary purpose of audit procedures?

     A   To gather corroborative evidence

     B   To comply with the accounting standards

     C   To detect errors or irregularities

     D   To verify the accuracy of the account balance

5.2 The following questions relate to audit evidence. Select the *best* response.

(a) Which of the following statements concerning evidence is correct?

     A   A client's accounting data cannot be considered sufficient audit evidence to support the financial report.

     B   Appropriate evidence supporting management's assertions must be convincing rather than merely persuasive.

     C   Effective internal control contributes little to the reliability of the evidence created within the entity.

     D   The cost of obtaining evidence is not an important consideration to an auditor in deciding what evidence should be obtained.

(b) Which of the following is the *least* persuasive type of evidence?

     A   Computations made by the auditor

     B   Bank statements obtained from the client

     C   Suppliers' invoices

     D   Prenumbered client invoices

(c) To be appropriate, evidence must be both:

     A   reliable and relevant

     B   reliable and well documented

     C   extensive and timely

     D   useful and independent

(d) Which of the following factors is most important in determining the appropriateness of audit evidence?

     A   The sampling method used by the auditor

       B   The reliability of the evidence in meeting the audit objective

       C   The objectivity of the auditor gathering the evidence

       D   The quantity of the evidence obtained

(e) Which of the following procedures would provide the most reliable audit evidence?

       A   Inspection of prenumbered client purchase orders filed in the accounts payable department

       B   Inquiries of the entity's internal audit staff held in private

       C   Inspection of bank statements obtained directly by the auditor from the entity's financial institution

       D   Analytical procedures performed by the auditor on the entity's trial balance

5.3 The following questions relate to the audit risk model. Select the *best* response:

(a) Which of the following audit risk components may be assessed in non-quantitative terms?

	Control risk	Detection risk	Inherent risk
A	Yes	No	Yes
B	Yes	Yes	Yes
C	No	Yes	Yes
D	Yes	Yes	No

(b) The risk that an auditor's procedures will lead to the conclusion that a material misstatement does not exist in an account balance when, in fact, such a misstatement does exist is:

       A   detection risk

       B   audit risk

       C   inherent risk

       D   control risk

(c) As the acceptable level of detection risk decreases, an auditor may change the:

       A   assessed level of inherent risk to a higher amount

       B   timing of substantive tests by performing them at an interim date rather than at balance date

       C   nature of substantive tests from a less effective to a more effective procedure

       D   timing of tests of controls by performing them at several dates rather than at one time

(d) The acceptable level of detection risk is inversely related to the:

       A   risk of failing to discover material misstatements

       B   preliminary judgment about materiality levels

       C   risk of misapplying auditing procedures

       D   assurance provided by substantive tests

5.4 The following questions relate to working papers. Select the *best* response.

(a) Which of the following is not a primary purpose of audit working papers?

       A   To support the financial report

       B   To assist in preparation of the audit report

       C   To co-ordinate the audit

       D   Report to provide evidence of the audit work performed

(b) The current file of an auditor's working papers is most likely to include a copy of the:

       A   constitution

       B   superannuation fund contract

    C   bank reconciliation

    D   flowcharts of the internal control activities

(c) An auditor's permanent files are most likely to include:

    A   analyses of share capital and other owners' equity accounts

    B   schedules that support the current year's adjusting entries

    C   previous years' accounts receivable confirmations that were classified as exceptions

    D   documentation indicating that the audit work was adequately planned and supervised

(d) Which of the following eliminates voluminous details from the auditor's working trial balance by classifying and summarising similar or related items?

    A   lead schedules

    B   account analyses

    C   supporting schedules

    D   control accounts

(e) Using micro-computers in auditing may affect the methods used to review the work of assistants because:

    A   working paper documentation may not contain readily observable details of calculations

    B   the audit standards for supervision may differ

    C   documenting the supervisory review may require the assistance of consulting services personnel

    D   supervisory personnel may not have an understanding of the capabilities and limitations of microcomputers

Accounting and auditing contrasted

5.5 How do accounting and auditing differ?

Financial report assertions

5.6 Identify and explain the broad categories of assertions that apply to account balances, classes of transactions and disclosures.

Audit procedures

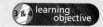

5.7 Identify some common audit procedures and give one example of each type.

5.8 What is the 'audit trail', and what combination of procedures is normally involved in the auditor's use of it?

Sufficient appropriate audit evidence

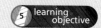

5.9 Define 'sufficient appropriate audit evidence'.

5.10 Discuss the relative reliability of different types of audit evidence.

Audit risk model

5.11 What is the audit risk model?

5.12 What is meant by business risk, and why is it important for the auditor to properly assess this risk?

Types of audit tests

5.13 Explain the difference between tests of control and substantive tests.

Using the work of an expert or another auditor

5.14 What must an auditor do before they rely on the work of:

(a) an expert?

(b) another auditor?

Audit working papers

5.15 What are the main functions served by audit working papers?

DISCUSSION PROBLEMS AND CASE STUDIES

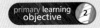

Financial report assertions

5.16 Basic Listed below are misstatements that audit procedures may detect related to inventory. For each misstatement, identify the broad category of assertion involved.

(a) Some inventory items are out on consignment and were not counted during the physical inventory.

(b) During the physical count the client's employees mistakenly counted some items twice.

(c) The basis of inventory valuation is not included in the financial report.

(d) Included in the inventory counts are some items that are held on consignment.

(e) Some inventory items are listed at cost, but realisable value is lower.

5.17 Moderate You are currently planning the audit of inventory at Healthy Bite Limited, a manufacturer and wholesaler of health foods. While planning for the audit, you have obtained the following information from client staff:

1   Year-end inventory is expected to be as follows:

	$000
Raw materials	1700
Work-in-progress	1050
Finished goods	2010
	4760

This represents 20% of total assets.

2   The company uses standard costing to value its 100 product lines. At year-end, relatively equal stock value of each of these lines will be held.

3   Goods are manufactured centrally at a Perth factory and then shipped to one of 20 warehouses nationally. The company has a policy of taking out short-term leases on unused warehouse space, in order to minimise rental costs. Hence, the number of warehouses in use varies from time to time.

4   Raw materials largely comprise bulk stocks of flour, rice, dried fruits and nuts. These are held in large storage bins at the Perth factory.

5   There are two basic storage phases for work-in-progress: sealed vats, awaiting processing, and mixing bowls attached to the ten different production lines. Work-in-progress largely comprises half-processed ingredients.

6   As in previous years, all warehouses and the Perth factory will be closed on balance date to allow a full stocktake to take place. A perpetual inventory system is used.

7   During the year Healthy Bite has experienced declining demand for a number of its products and has had to discount a number of its product lines considerably.

Required

(a) Identify the key financial report assertions for the audit of inventory at Healthy Bite.

(b) Identify and discuss specific issues to be considered in relation to the audit of the valuation and allocation assertion for inventory. Describe the audit procedures you would undertake to address these issues.

Audit procedures

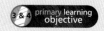

5.18 Basic Indicate the type of error that each of the following audit procedures is designed to or is likely to disclose:

(a) reconciliation of interest expense with loans payable

(b) review of the maintenance and repairs account

(c) confirmation of a portion of accounts receivable

5.19 Basic For each of the following audit procedures, indicate which type of evidence-gathering procedure is being used: (1) inspection, (2) computation, (3) confirmation, (4) analytical procedures, (5) inquiries, or (6) observation.

(a) Sending a written request to the client's customers requesting that they report the amount owed to the client.

(b) Examining large sales invoices for a period of two days before and after year-end to determine if sales are recorded in the proper period.

(c) Agreeing the total of the accounts receivable subsidiary ledger to the accounts receivable general ledger account.

(d) Discussing the adequacy of the allowance for doubtful accounts with the credit manager.

(e) Comparing the current-year gross profit percentage with the gross profit percentage for the last four years.

(f) Examining a new plastic extrusion machine to ensure that this major acquisition was received.

(g) Watching the client's warehouse personnel count the raw materials inventory.

(h) Performing test counts of the warehouse personnel's count of the raw material.

(i) Obtaining a letter from the client's solicitor indicating that there were no lawsuits in progress against the client.

(j) Tracing the prices used by the client's billing program for pricing sales invoices to the client's approved price list.

Sufficient appropriate audit evidence

5.20 Basic Evidence comes in various types and has different degrees of reliability. Following are some statements that compare various types of evidence:

(a) a bank confirmation versus observation of the segregation of duties between cash receipts and recording payment in the accounts receivable subsidiary ledger

(b) an auditor's recalculation of depreciation versus examination of raw material requisitions

(c) a bank statement included in the client's records versus shipping documents

(d) physical examination of common stock certificates versus physical examination of inventory components for a personal computer

Required

For each situation, indicate whether the first or second type of evidence is more reliable. Provide a rationale for your choice.

5.21 Moderate You are the audit senior on the audit of Harmony Pty Ltd, a large manufacturing company, for the year ended 30 June 20X0. It is now 25 August 20X0 and you are reviewing the audit working papers prepared by the audit assistant, Susan Jones. You notice the following matters:

1 Susan attended the stocktake on 30 June and observed that the client followed the stocktake instructions. She selected numerous items for test counting from the client's inventory sheets and all were found to be correct. Cut-off details were noted and subsequently checked and found to be correctly treated. Susan concluded that inventory was fairly stated.

2 Susan selected 20 invoices to test the control that the sales clerk checks that the prices agree with the authorised price list. She found 3 instances where the sales clerk had not signed the 'prices checked' box in the invoice. The sales manager explained that the sales clerk always checks the prices but sometimes forgets to sign the box. As the prices on all the invoices agreed with the authorised price list, Susan concluded that the control was operating satisfactorily.

3 As part of her work on subsequent events, Susan noted that there were a large number of returns in July of Product 75L. However, as this product was first sold in June and represented only 1% of sales for the year, Susan concluded that the amount was immaterial and no further work was necessary.

4 Advertising expenses are material, although only 50% of last year's balance. Susan selected a large sample of entries and agreed them to supporting documents. No errors were found. Susan concluded that advertising expenses was reasonable.

5 As part of the verification work on accounts payable, Susan carried out a search for unrecorded liabilities. She tested a random sample of 20 payments made after 30 June 20X0 and found 3 instances of cheques that related to services provided in June that had not been accrued. However, as the total of the 3 cheques was immaterial, she concluded that no adjustment was required for unrecorded liabilities.

Required

For each of the five scenarios presented above, indicate whether you believe that sufficient appropriate audit evidence has been obtained to support the conclusions reached. Give reasons for your decision.

5.22 Complex You are reviewing the files of DEF Ltd, a small manufacturing company. You are the audit senior on the engagement reviewing the work of a graduate. You note the following in the working papers:

1 The graduate obtained a copy of the client's fixed asset register and movements schedule and agreed them to the trial balance. He agreed the opening balance in the movement schedule to the previous year's audit file. He agreed the two largest additions to client cheque requisitions. These additions represent 27% of assets purchased during the year. The description on the cheque requisition for one of the additions examined by the graduate was 'Overhaul of motor'. The addition was material. He asked the accountant whether this should be capitalised and was told: 'The mechanic wrote the wrong description on the invoice. It was a motor for the new lathe that was purchased.' The graduate noted that the explanation appeared reasonable. (Assume the fixed asset balance is being audited substantively.)

2 The graduate explained that there was no need to ensure that the written-down value of disposed assets had been taken out of the ledger because the written-down value of all assets disposed was not material.

3 The graduate obtained the creditors' aged trial balance, agreed it to the trial balance and checked the additions. He agreed material balances to a combination of reconciled supplier statements and invoices. He concluded that creditors were fairly stated. (Assume the creditors balance is being audited substantively.)

4 LMN was a creditor with a material $20 000 balance. As there was no statement available, the graduate agreed the balance to an invoice. On reviewing the invoices that relate to LMN, the graduate noted that there were two invoices for $20 000. Both were for the same item, but one was dated 13 June 19XX and the other 20 June 19XX. The invoices were not numbered. The explanation the accountant gave the graduate was: 'We hadn't paid the invoice by the 20th so they sent us another. They are for the same item. We only owe them $20 000.' The graduate did no further work on this item.

5 A test of control for the proper authorisation of expenses was undertaken. The graduate examined 20 payments and found 2 errors. He noted that each of these errors related to immaterial amounts and concluded that the system was operating effectively.

6 In auditing the balance of deferred tax asset, the graduate noted that DEF faces a tax loss and that he has ascertained from discussion with the accountant that a new contract has been received which will return the company to a profitable situation next year.

7 A part of the accounts receivable balance consists of retention accounts. These monies were withheld by a large customer because the product was new and untested. A review of customer complaints revealed a number of complaints in relation to the quality of the new product. The graduate agreed the retention balance to signed contracts. The contracts showed that the amount was not due to be received for another two months. He concluded that the balance was fairly stated. The retention accounts receivable balance was material.

Required

Explain why sufficient and appropriate evidence has not been obtained for the steps undertaken.

Source: This question was adapted from the Professional Year Programme of The Institute of Chartered Accountants in Australia—1995 Accounting 2 Module.

5.23 **Complex** You are the audit senior on the 30 June X1 audit of QP Limited. You have just been given the audit file to review by your assistant. Materiality for this client has been set at $200 000. The client is based in Orange, NSW. The following information has been obtained from reading the audit file and talking with the assistant:

1 The balance noted for borrowings in the general ledger at 30 June 20X1 is $158 000. This compares with a balance as at 30 June 20X0 of $450 000. The audit assistant noted that 'As the borrowings balance is immaterial in the current year, only limited audit work is necessary'. The only work performed by the assistant was to select the three largest borrowings from the client's detailed listing (which had been agreed to the general ledger) and agree them to statements provided by the lenders.

2 QP holds stock at a number of different locations in New South Wales. The balances noted by the client for the various locations at balance date are as follows:

	$000
Orange	817
Dubbo	204
Parramatta	989
Total	2010

You note that the assistant has attended the stocktake at Orange and Dubbo only. He has documented all test counts and found no exceptions.

When you asked the assistant why he had not attended the stocktake at Parramatta, he replied:

> I had originally planned to go to Parramatta, but I had already exceeded the budgeted time allocated for stock. As I considered Parramatta to be too far away, I attended the stocktake at Dubbo instead. I rang the warehouse manager at Parramatta and received verbal confirmation that the stocktake had proceeded smoothly and that only minor exceptions from the perpetual records were noted.

Required

(a) For each situation, comment on whether the audit assistant has obtained sufficient appropriate audit evidence.

(b) If you conclude that sufficient appropriate audit evidence has not been obtained, what further procedures should the assistant perform?

5.24 Complex You are the audit senior on WXY Limited and have just been given the audit file to review by your assistant. The balance date of WXY is 30 June 20X0 and materiality for this client has been set at $500 000. The following information has been obtained from reading the audit file and talking with the assistant:

1 The balance of cash was tested using a lower assessed level of control risk approach. One of the key controls relied upon was the monthly bank reconciliations. The assistant had noted that all bank reconciliations for the year had been reviewed. For the last three months there was a 'net miscellaneous reconciling item' of $60 000.

   The assistant questioned the accountant about this item and was told that the client did not have time to follow up on this matter. As the reconciling item was immaterial, the assistant had performed no further work in this area.

2 When reviewing the bank confirmation, you note that it had been faxed to the client's premises. You ask the audit assistant what happened, and he replies:

> We had not received a reply from the bank and when we contacted them they asked us to resend the confirmation. The accountant could see that I was very busy so he offered to chase it up on my behalf. I gave him a blank copy of the confirmation letter and he filled in details of bank account numbers. The client contacted the bank and they sent the reply directly to him.

   The cover sheet on the fax was not on file. As the fax confirmed the bank balances to the cent, no further testing was performed.

3 The testing on payroll expense was completed using analytical procedures (comparing this year's expense with that of last year). As the current expense was within a few thousand dollars of last year's amount, the assistant concluded that the expense was reasonable and that no further testing was necessary.

Required

(a) For each situation, comment on whether the audit assistant has obtained sufficient appropriate audit evidence.

(b) For situations where you believe sufficient appropriate audit evidence has not been obtained, indicate one procedure which should have been performed by the assistant.

5.25 Complex BW Industries Ltd is a manufacturer and supplier of 'after-market' spare parts for heavy machinery such as that used in the mining and construction industries. BW has few competitors in this market due to the small number of users and numerous trade agreements which BW has negotiated with the original manufacturers of the machinery. The market is highly lucrative, with an annual turnover of $100 million.

BW distributes its product through four distributors. These distributors account for 96% of BW's turnover and outstanding credit sales at balance date. Credit terms are 30 days. The remaining 4% of sales are made direct to mining entities usually involved in offshore operations.

The number of distributors and the percentage of company sales attributed to each geographical segment are as follows:

	No. of distributors	%
New South Wales/Victoria	1	20
Queensland/Northern Territory	1	30
South Australia/Tasmania	1	6
Western Australia	1	40
Other	—	4
Total	4	100

You are about to commence your audit work on BW's debtors balance. The total debt is $1.2 million, aged as follows:

	$000
Current	600
30 days	350
60 days	150
90+ days	100
Total	1200

The company has a history of bad debt write-offs, representing approximately 0.5% to 1.0% of turnover each year. A provision for doubtful debts of $10 000 has been made.

Required

(a) Identify the areas of concern for the audit of debtors at BW, and discuss why they represent a potential audit risk.

(b) Identify the main financial report assertion(s) and risk(s), and describe in detail the substantive audit procedures that you would employ to address the risk(s) identified.

Types of audit tests

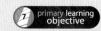
primary learning objective

5.26 Complex You are the auditor in charge of a car fleet leasing company, CF Pty Ltd. The company owns and leases cars and related equipment to government bodies.

The following table summarises the planning outcomes of CF, including the preliminary assessment of inherent risk (IR), control risk (CR) and detection risk (DR):

	Preliminary risk assessment			Planned approach: Test of controls v substantive tests
Objective	**IR**	**CR**	**DR**	
Disclosure and existence of finance leased assets	Medium	Medium	Medium	Primarily tests of controls with some components of substantive procedures at the balance date
Measurement and completeness of depreciation expense	Low	Low	High	More significant level of test of controls with minimal substantive procedures at the balance date
Rights and obligations in relation to vehicles acquired	Low	Medium	High	More significant level of test of controls with minimal substantive procedures at the balance date
Valuation of vehicles	High	High	Low	No tests of controls. 100% reliance on substantive procedures

Required

(a) What are the general issues related to deciding whether to use a test of controls approach or a substantive approach?

(b) How do the risk assessments above relate to the choice of audit approach?

(c) If you adopted the approach set out in the planning summary, what audit procedures would you use for the measurement and completeness of depreciation expense objective?

Using the work of an expert

5.27 **Moderate** You are an assurance services senior and your client is Outback Antiques Pty Ltd, a small proprietary company which specialises in buying and selling Australian-made antique bush furniture. Outback Antiques Pty Ltd purchases pieces at auction, cleans and repairs them, then sells them to the general public. This is the first year your firm has conducted the audit.

At year-end, Outback Antiques Pty Ltd expects to have around 500 pieces of furniture on hand, ranging from small items worth $150 to more expensive items worth over $10 000. No two items of furniture are the same and some items are only partially restored.

Due to the complex nature of inventory, the partner has decided to engage an expert to provide a year-end valuation report. The expert is to use the client's (unpriced) inventory list, and append their estimate of the (lower of cost or net realisable) value of each item. The partner intends to place full reliance on the expert's report in order to reach an opinion on Outback Antiques Pty Ltd's inventory balance and has informed you that year-end stocktake attendance by audit staff is not planned.

Required

(a) Compile a list of arguments for and against relying on the expert's report in lieu of attendance at Outback Antiques Pty Ltd's stocktake.

(b) What reliance would you place on the expert's report if:

(i) your firm set the scope of the expert's work *and* paid the expert's fee?

(ii) your firm set the scope of the expert's work and the client paid the expert's fee?

Source: This question was adapted from the CA Program of The Institute of Chartered Accountants in Australia—2002 Financial Reporting and Assurance Module.

5.28 Moderate To comply with auditing standards an auditor includes certain evidence in the working papers, for example evidence that the engagement was planned and that the work of assistants was supervised and reviewed. What other evidence should an auditor include in audit working papers to comply with auditing standards?

Source: AICPA adapted

5.29 Moderate Goldstein and Weinstock, accountants, were employed for several years by Retrograde Co. Ltd to make annual audits. As a result of a change in control, the company discontinued the engagement of Goldstein and Weinstock and retained another firm of accountants. Retrograde Co. Ltd thereupon demanded that Goldstein and Weinstock surrender all working papers they had prepared in undertaking audits for the company. Goldstein and Weinstock refused on the grounds that the working papers were their property. The company brought legal action to recover the working papers. Should it succeed? State briefly what the law is, in general, as to ownership of accountants' working papers.

Source: AICPA

5.30 Moderate Sandra Day, an accountant who has been practising alone, decides to 'sell her practice' to Bill Knight. As a part of the transaction, Knight asks Day to turn over to him all her files and working papers. One client, John Dostine, does not want Knight as his accountant and objects to the transfer of the files and working papers relating to his affairs. Would such transfer be valid or desirable? Discuss.

Source: AICPA adapted

CHAPTER 6

PLANNING, KNOWLEDGE OF THE BUSINESS AND EVALUATING BUSINESS RISK

LEARNING OBJECTIVES

After studying this chapter you should be able to:

1 explain why the decision to accept a client is important and describe the primary features of client acceptance and continuance;

2 indicate the purpose and content of an engagement letter;

3 describe the decisions made by an auditor in preparing an audit plan, the knowledge on which the decisions are based and the procedures used to obtain that knowledge;

4 describe how an auditor develops an overall audit strategy and prepares an audit program;

5 describe the process of assigning and scheduling audit staff;

6 identify the important aspects of the auditor's knowledge of a client's business;

7 assess client business risk; and

8 outline the types and uses of analytical procedures and distinguish those that are useful in obtaining an understanding of the client.

Chapter outline

A financial report audit is a systematic process made up of a number of logical steps.

Before commencing an audit, the auditor must determine whether to accept the client and undertake the audit. This requires an understanding of the client's business. After the audit commences, the planning and conduct of the audit are influenced by the auditor's understanding of the client's operations, trends within its industry and the effect on the client of economic and political influences. The auditor uses this knowledge to identify existing or potential accounting and auditing problems and to develop an overall strategy for the conduct and scope of the audit.

The major topics covered in this chapter are the nature of audit planning, including an outline of the major steps in the audit process; acceptance and continuance of audit clients, including evaluation of potential clients, communications with a previous auditor, engagement letters and preliminary conferences with the client; obtaining knowledge of the entity's organisational structure, its operations and its industry; assessing client business risk; and using analytical procedures for identifying and investigating unusual changes in account balances or transaction totals for planning purposes.

Relevant guidance

Australian		International	
AUS 204	Terms of Audit Engagements	ISA 210	Terms of Audit Engagements
AUS 206	Quality Control for Audits of Historical Financial Information (Revised 2004)	ISA 220	Quality Control for Audits of Historical Financial Information (Revised 2004)
AUS 302	Planning	ISA 300	Planning
AUS 402	Understanding the Entity and its Environment and Assessing the Risks of Misstatement (Revised 2004)	ISA 315	Understanding the Entity and its Environment and Assessing the Risks of Misstatement (Revised 2004)
AUS 406	The Auditor's Procedures in Response to Assessed Risks (Issued 2004)	ISA 330	The Auditor's Procedures in Response to Assessed Risks (Issued 2004)
AUS 510	Initial Engagements—Opening Balances	ISA 510	Initial Engagements—Opening Balances
AUS 512	Analytical Procedures	ISA 520	Analytical Procedures
AUS 518	Related Parties	ISA 550	Related Parties
CPC F3	Changes in Professional Appointments	IFAC	Code of Ethics
Audit and Assurance Alert No. 12: The Implications for Auditors of the Private Sector Amendments to the Privacy Act		—	

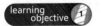

CLIENT ACCEPTANCE AND CONTINUANCE

The auditor's need to understand the client starts when considering **acceptance of an engagement** and continues throughout association with the client. The steps in accepting an audit client are shown in Figure 6.1.

Quality control policies and client evaluation procedures

As part of its quality control, an audit firm needs to establish policies and procedures for investigating potential clients and acceptance of an engagement and for periodically reviewing **continuance of clients**. Policies and procedures for client acceptance and continuance are important because an audit firm needs to take precautions to avoid association with a client whose management lacks integrity. As discussed in Chapter 3, care should be exercised to avoid also situations where the auditor–client relationship lacks independence and where there are

FIGURE 6.1 Steps in accepting an audit

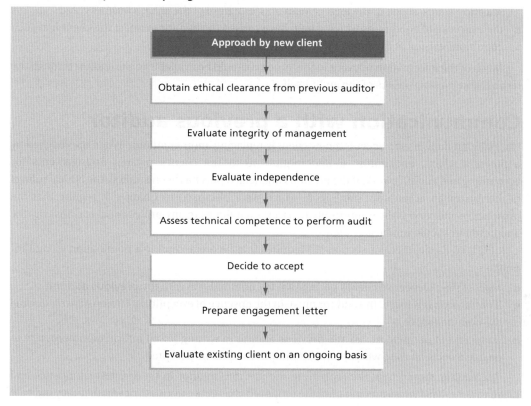

other impediments to undertaking the audit function, such as inability to serve the client properly. In addition, an auditor needs to consider the effect of a client's reputation on its image in the financial community and the increased risk of litigation, which was discussed in Chapter 4.

AUS 206.14 (ISA 220.14) requires that the engagement partner should be satisfied that appropriate procedures regarding the acceptance and continuance of clients have been followed. Procedures that may be used to establish the appropriateness or otherwise of accepting clients include:

- obtain and review available financial information concerning the prospective client, for example annual reports, interim financial reports and income tax returns;
- make inquiries of third parties, such as the client's bankers, legal advisers or investment banker, concerning the integrity of the prospective client and its management;
- communicate with the previous auditor;
- consider circumstances in which the engagement would require special attention or present unusual risks;
- evaluate the firm's independence and ability to serve the client, including technical skills, knowledge of the industry and personnel; and
- determine that acceptance of the client would not violate the professional bodies' code of professional conduct.

AUS 206.17–18 (ISA 220.17–18) also states that the auditor should evaluate existing clients where significant matters have arisen to determine whether the relationship should be continued. Examples of significant matters include:

- a major change in ownership, directors, management, legal advisers, financial condition, litigation status, scope of the engagement and/or nature of the client's business; and
- the existence of conditions which would have caused the auditor to reject the client had such conditions existed at the time of the initial acceptance.

Much of the information relevant to this process should be available to the auditor through the records and working papers of the audit itself.

Communication with a previous auditor

Normally, an auditor who accepts a new client is replacing another auditor. When approached by a potential client, an auditor should inquire about the client's present arrangements for accounting and auditing work. If the previous financial report has been audited, the ethical rulings of the Australian accounting profession, which were discussed in Chapter 3, require that the prospective auditor has the opportunity to ascertain if there are any professional reasons why the appointment should not be accepted.

CPC F.3.6 (Code of Ethics section 13) requires that before accepting a nomination an auditor must:

- request the prospective client's permission to communicate with the **previous auditor**;
- if permission is refused, the auditor must, in the absence of exceptional circumstances, decline the nomination; or
- on receipt of permission, ask the previous auditor in writing for all information necessary to enable a decision as to whether the nomination should be accepted.

The auditor should treat the reply from the previous auditor in the strictest confidence and judge whether the factors precipitating the proposed change are unusual, or whether they indicate that the previous auditor is being treated unfairly.

CPC F.3.7 requires the previous auditor to:

- request permission from the client to discuss the client's affairs freely with the proposed auditor;
- if permission is refused, this fact should be reported to the proposed auditor, who in the absence of exceptional circumstances, should not accept the nomination; or
- on receipt of permission, disclose fully all information needed by the proposed auditor to enable a decision to be made whether to accept the nomination and discuss freely with the proposed auditor all matters relevant to the appointment of which they should be aware.

CPC F.3.9 requires that if the auditor does not receive, within a reasonable time, a reply to the communication to the previous auditor, they must endeavour to communicate with them by some other means. If this is not successful, a further letter must be sent, stating that the auditor assumes there is no professional reason why the appointment should not be accepted and that they intend to do so.

As a result of this process of communication, the interests of three groups are protected:

- an auditor does not accept an appointment in circumstances of which they are not fully aware;
- shareholders are fully informed of the circumstances in which the change is proposed;
- the existing auditor cannot be easily removed or interfered with in the conscientious exercise of duty as an independent professional.

While inquiries of the previous auditor about matters that bear on acceptance of the client are required prior to acceptance, the auditor may also make inquiries of the previous auditor after acceptance. For example, the auditor needs to consider the relationship of the financial report of the previous period to the financial report of the current period on which the auditor will express an opinion. AUS 510.02 (ISA 510.02) requires that for initial audit engagements, the auditor obtains sufficient appropriate audit evidence that:

- the opening balances do not contain material misstatements affecting the current period's financial report;
- the previous period's closing balances have been correctly brought forward to the current period, or have been restated when appropriate; and
- appropriate accounting policies are consistently applied or changes have been properly accounted for and adequately disclosed.

This process could be facilitated by reviewing the working papers of the previous auditor. AUS 510.06 (ISA 510.06) points out that in these circumstances the auditor also needs to consider the independence and professional competence of the previous auditor.

CPC F.3.11 states that the previous auditor is not obliged to provide information and advice to enable the auditor to substantiate the existence and value of assets and liabilities as at the end of the previous financial year. However, the previous auditor is encouraged to do so as a professional courtesy, with the knowledge and consent of the client. The audit working papers of the previous auditor are their property and there is no obligation to make available any information contained therein.

Where the working papers of the previous audit are not available, the auditor applies other audit procedures in order to form an opinion about the opening balances, accounting policies and comparative figures. These could include:

- further consultation with management;
- review of the records and working papers of the client and the accounting and internal control activities that relate to the previous period;
- analysis of the audit work of the current period to the extent that it relates to the opening balances;
- review of the minutes of the board of directors and other important committees; and
- review of policy manuals.

If the previous financial report was not audited, the first examination needs to be even more extensive.

AUS 510.11–.13 (ISA 510.11–.13) states that the auditor needs to qualify the audit report if:

- the auditor is unable to obtain sufficient appropriate audit evidence concerning opening balances;
- the opening balances contain misstatements which materially affect the current period's financial report and these are not properly accounted for and adequately disclosed; or
- the current period's accounting policies have not been consistently applied in relation to opening balances and the change has not been properly accounted for and adequately disclosed.

ENGAGEMENT LETTERS

After accepting an appointment, AUS 204.02 (ISA 210.02) requires the auditor and the entity to agree on the terms of engagement. The auditor should document the arrangements made with the client and clarify matters that may be misunderstood. This should help protect the audit firm and ensure that the client fully understands the position. In July 2000 the AUASB amended AUS 204 to require that the terms of engagements that are agreed with clients are to be recorded in writing. The AUASB indicated that this proposal is in line with the expectations expressed by the courts and should help reduce disputes and misunderstandings between auditors and clients.

Most audit firms already meet this requirement by means of an **engagement letter**. This letter to the client documents and confirms the auditor's acceptance of the appointment, the objective and scope of the audit, the extent of the responsibilities to the client and the form of any reports.

The form and content of the audit engagement letter vary for each client. It should generally include reference to the following matters set out in AUS 204.05 (ISA 210.06):

- the objective of the financial report audit;
- responsibility of management for the financial report;
- the scope of the audit;
- the form of any reports;
- an explanation of the extent to which an audit can be relied upon to detect material misstatements; and
- the auditor's right to unrestricted access to whatever records, documents and other information are necessary to complete the audit.

An example of an engagement letter is contained in the Appendix to AUS 204 (ISA 210). A sample of an engagement letter prepared on this basis is presented in Exhibit 6.1. The letter may need to be modified in accordance with the circumstances. Other matters which could be included are: specification of the schedules to be prepared by the client; arrangements concerning the involvement of other auditors, experts or internal auditors; and the method and frequency of billing fees.

In addition, *Audit and Assurance Alert No. 12*, issued in August 2002, points out that entities need to be satisfied that they meet the obligations of the *Privacy Act 1988*, as amended by the *Privacy (Private Sector) Amendment Act 2000*, before providing auditors with access to records of personal information. As a result, the auditor may need to clarify in the engagement letter issues in relation to access, collection, use and disclosure of personal information under this privacy legislation.

EXHIBIT

6.1

Sample auditor's engagement letter

Jan Smith & Associates

Chartered Accountants
30 Banks St
Newtown

The Managing Director
ABC Ltd
15 Queen Street
Newtown

Dear Mr Spencer

Scope
You have requested that we audit the financial report of ABC Ltd as of and for the year ending 30 June 20X5. We are pleased to confirm our acceptance and our understanding of this engagement by means of this letter. Our audit will be conducted pursuant to the *Corporations Act* with the objective of expressing an opinion on the financial report.

We will conduct our audit in accordance with Australian auditing standards to provide reasonable assurance as to whether the financial report is free of material misstatement. Our procedures will include examination, on a test basis, of evidence supporting the amounts and other disclosures in the financial report, and the evaluation of accounting policies and significant accounting estimates. These procedures will be undertaken to form an opinion whether, in all material respects, the financial report is presented fairly in accordance with Australian accounting standards, Urgent Issues Group Consensus Views and the *Corporations Act* so as to present a view which is consistent with our understanding of ABC Ltd's financial position, the results of its operation and its cash flows.

The work undertaken by us to form an opinion is permeated by judgment, in particular regarding the nature, timing and extent of the audit procedures for gathering of audit evidence and the drawing of conclusions based on the audit evidence gathered. In addition, there are inherent limitations in any audit, and these include the use of testing, the inherent limitations of any internal control, the possibility of collusion and the fact that most evidence is persuasive rather than conclusive. As a result, our audit can only provide reasonable not absolute assurance that the financial report is free of material misstatement.

In addition to our report on the financial report, we expect to provide you with a separate letter concerning any material weaknesses in internal control that come to our notice.

We remind you that the responsibility for the preparation of the financial report, including adequate disclosure, is that of the Board of Directors of ABC Ltd. This includes the maintenance of adequate accounting records and internal control, the selection and application of accounting policies, and the safeguarding of the assets of ABC Ltd. As part of our audit process, we will request from management written confirmation concerning representations made to us in connection with the audit.

Quality control

The conduct of our audit in accordance with Australian auditing standards means that information acquired by us in the course of our audit is subject to strict confidentiality requirements. Our audit files may, however, be subject to review as part of the quality control review program of The Institute of Chartered Accountants in Australia, which monitors compliance with professional standards by its members. We advise you that by signing this letter you acknowledge that, if requested, our audit files relating to this audit will be made available under this program. Should this occur, we will advise you. The same strict confidentiality requirements apply under this program as apply to us as your auditor.

Fees

We look forward to full co-operation with your staff and we trust that they will make available to us whatever records, documentation and other information are requested in connection with our audit. Our fees, which will be billed as work progresses, are based on the time required by the individuals assigned to the engagement plus out-of-pocket expenses. Individual hourly rates vary according to the degree of responsibility involved and the experience and skill required.

Privacy

In undertaking this engagement it is acknowledged that we will have access to and collect personal and sensitive information concerning the shareholders/employees. Disclosure by you of personal information to us in the course of our engagement is subject to the *Privacy Act 1988*. Personal Information means information or an opinion (including information or an opinion forming part of a database), whether true or not, and whether recorded in a material form or not, about an individual whose identify is apparent, or can be reasonably ascertained, from the information or opinion. Accordingly, the services are provided on the basis that:

(a) you acknowledge that you are bound by the *Privacy Act 1988*;
(b) you will only disclose Personal Information to us where that disclosure is necessary for our performance of the services and is permitted by Privacy Law (Privacy Law means all legislation, principles, industry codes and policies relating to the collection, use, disclosure, storage or granting of access rights to the Personal Information, and includes the *Privacy Act 1988*);
(c) you have made all disclosures required under Privacy Law;
(d) you have obtained any consents required under the Privacy Law;
(e) you will not do anything with the Personal Information that will cause us to breach any Privacy Law;
(f) you will notify us immediately if you become aware that a disclosure of Personal Information:
   (i)   has been made in breach of this clause or any Privacy Law; or
   (ii) may be required by law; and
(g) you comply with our instructions to do anything required for us to comply with Privacy Law.

Clauses (a) to (g):
• apply notwithstanding any other clause in the agreement and prevail to the extent of any inconsistency; and
• survive the termination of the agreement.

You agree to indemnify and keep us and our partners and staff indemnified against, and must pay us on demand the amount of all losses, liabilities, costs (including any legal costs) expenses and

Continued...

damages incurred or arising in connection with any breach of your obligations under clauses (a) to (g) by you or any of your officers, employees, agents, advisers, auditors, consultants or third parties.

This indemnity is a continuing obligation, independent from your other obligations under the agreement and continues after the agreement ends. It is not necessary for us to incur expense or make payment before enforcing this indemnity.

If the performance of the services requires a third party to supply personal information to us on your request, it is your obligation to ensure that the third party complies with clauses (a) to (g) above and you indemnify us against any claim, loss or expense resulting from that party's failure to do so, or to otherwise comply with Privacy Law.

Other

This letter will be effective for future years unless it is terminated, amended or superseded.

Please sign and return the attached copy of this letter to indicate that it is in accordance with your understanding of the arrangements for our audit of the financial report.

Yours faithfully

Jan Smith
Partner
15 September 20X5

Acknowledged on behalf of ABC Ltd by

Jim Spencer
Managing Director
30 September 20X5

Conferences with the client's personnel

Soon after acceptance of an engagement, the auditor should confer with key client personnel. The auditor meets principal administrative, financial and operating officers, and the chief internal auditor and IT (Information Technology) manager if applicable, to discuss matters expected to have a significant effect on the financial statements or on the conduct of the audit.

Good relations with client personnel are important. An audit usually causes considerable inconvenience and disruption to some personnel, and their assistance is often needed to obtain documents, records and explanations of various matters. Effective early conferences establish a foundation for a good working relationship with all client personnel.

Effective communications with top management are particularly important. The auditor should have an opportunity to consider the accounting implications of important planned transactions, such as merger negotiations or lease or purchase decisions. The chief executive officer should be informed on a regular basis of new accounting and disclosure requirements that may affect company plans. A good working relationship throughout the engagement helps to avoid a crisis conference at year-end over a potential qualification of the audit report.

Quick review

Important steps in relation to accepting and continuing an audit engagement are:

1 Obtain ethical clearance from previous auditor.

2 Evaluate management's integrity, unusual risks and the auditor's independence, skills and competence to complete the audit.

3 Issue an engagement letter to confirm the terms of the engagement.

4 Arrange a conference with key client personnel soon after accepting the engagement.

AUDIT PLANNING

The conduct of an efficient and effective audit requires adequate **planning**. AUS 302.02 (ISA 300.02) requires the auditor to plan the work to enable the audit to be performed in an effective manner. The concept of adequate planning involves obtaining an understanding of the client's business operations and developing an overall strategy to organise, co-ordinate and schedule the activities of the audit staff. The timing of the audit can be viewed as three stages—planning, interim and final. **Interim work** is done before the date of the financial report and **final work** is done at or after that date.

The nature of audit planning

The audit planning process has two aspects: an overall **audit plan** for the expected scope and conduct of the audit; and an **audit program** directing the nature, timing and extent of audit procedures. The plan and the program often need to be revised due to changes in conditions or the unexpected results of audit procedures. The reasons for such changes need to be documented in the audit working papers.

The audit plan helps to ensure that important and potential risk areas of the audit are given appropriate attention, and that problems are identified and dealt with. Adequate planning also helps to make the audit efficient and effective by allocating the appropriate quality and quantity of audit staff to the engagement, and co-ordinating resources and work done by other auditors or experts.

The extent of planning for an engagement depends on the size and complexity of the client and whether the auditor has had previous experience with the client. The responsibility for the overall audit plan is the auditor's. However, discussion of elements of the plan and proposed audit procedures with the client's management and staff enables the auditor to co-ordinate the work of the client's staff and the auditor's staff.

As indicated in AUS 402.57–63 (ISA 315.57–63), in planning the audit the auditor also needs to consider the methods the entity uses to process accounting information because such methods influence the design of the accounting system and the nature of control activities. The extent to which the computer is used in significant accounting applications, as well as the complexity of that processing, also influences the nature, timing and extent of audit procedures.

Because most audit clients have accounting systems with both manual and IT portions, all auditors need to be proficient at understanding the accounting system and internal control (both IT and manual) and planning the audit to address both portions of the accounting systems. As explained in Chapter 5, computer audit specialists may still be used, but the determination of the need for their skills and the evaluation of their results and conclusions are the responsibility of the auditor who issues the opinion on the financial report.

Major steps in the audit process

The elements which make up the audit process are drawn together through a strategy which is a matter of deciding between alternatives for audit emphasis and timing. Every audit of a financial report has certain identifiable steps that remain constant. However, the timing of these steps and the emphasis given to each vary, depending on the auditor's judgment of the priorities in the circumstances and the size and complexity of the client's operations. A knowledge of these steps and their general purpose provides a framework for the study of auditing.

The initial phase of every financial report audit is the decision whether to accept a new client or continue with an existing client. Once this decision has been made the following major steps can be identified. Sometimes some of these steps are performed at the same time or are given a different emphasis.

Knowledge of the business

The auditor must obtain or update an understanding of the client's operations and circumstances, including management policies, the company's position in its industry and the economy, and its legal obligations. The objective is to understand the client's business risk and the events, transactions and practices that may have a significant effect on the client's financial report. Typical audit procedures for this step are inquiry of company personnel, observation of operations and facilities, undertaking preliminary analytical procedures and review of documentation such as company manuals and legal documents. Much of the detailed planning for the audit, including preliminary risk assessment, can be done only after the auditor has obtained a knowledge of the business.

Understanding internal control

The next step in the audit is to obtain an understanding of internal control to identify types of potential misstatements, consider factors that affect the risk of material misstatement, and design the nature, extent and timing of further audit procedures. Obtaining an understanding of internal control involves evaluating the design of controls to consider whether they are capable of effectively preventing or detecting and correcting material misstatements. It also involves determining whether the control has been implemented—that is the control exists and the entity is using it. Typical audit procedures to obtain evidence about the design and implementation of controls are inquiry of entity personnel, observing the application of specific controls, inspecting documents and reports, and tracing transactions through the information system relevant to financial reporting. However, inquiry alone is not sufficient.

Assessing the risks of material misstatement

The auditor should identify and assess the risks of material misstatement at the financial report level and at the assertion level. The auditor identifies risks throughout the process of obtaining an understanding of the entity and its environment, including relevant controls that relate to the risks. The auditor needs to consider whether the risks identified are of a magnitude that could result in a material misstatement of the financial report. As part of the risk assessment process, the auditor should determine which risks are significant risks as these require special audit consideration.

Response to assessed risks

The next step requires the auditor to determine overall responses to address risks of material misstatement at the financial report level and the assertion level. The auditor's response at the overall financial report level may include emphasising to the audit team the need to maintain professional scepticism, assigning more experienced staff, using experts or making general changes to the nature, timing and extent of audit procedures such as performing substantive procedures at balance date instead of at an interim date. At the assertion level, the auditor's assessment of identified risks provides a basis for designing and performing further audit procedures. There should be a clear link between the nature, timing and extent of the auditor's further audit procedures and the assessed risks. These further procedures may be either tests of control or substantive tests or both, depending on the circumstances.

Tests of control

The auditor is required to perform tests of control when the risk assessment includes an expectation of the operating effectiveness of controls or when substantive procedures alone will not provide sufficient appropriate audit evidence at the assertion level. Tests of the operating effectiveness of controls are performed only on those controls that the auditor has determined are suitably designed to prevent or detect and correct a material misstatement at the assertion level.

Substantive procedures

Substantive procedures are performed in order to detect material misstatements at the assertion level and include tests of classes of transactions, balances and disclosures. They may be tests of details or analytical procedures. The auditor plans and performs substantive procedures to be responsive to the related assessment of risk of material misstatement.

Completion and review

The final step in the audit consists of: following up issues raised in earlier steps; performing certain procedures, such as the subsequent events review, a final analytical procedures review and a final review of working papers, which can be completed only at the end of field work; and evaluating all the evidence obtained to form an opinion on the financial report.

Each of the seven steps is covered in one or more chapters in this book, as follows:

- knowledge of the business (Chapter 6);
- understanding internal control (Chapter 8);
- assessing the risks of material misstatement (Chapters 6, 7 and 8);
- response to assessed risks (Chapters 6, 9 and 10);
- tests of controls (Chapter 9);
- substantive tests of transactions and balances (Chapter 10); and
- completion of the audit (Chapter 12).

When all seven steps have been completed, the auditor issues the audit report that accompanies the client's financial report (Chapter 13).

Overall timing of engagement

The three phases of the audit—planning, interim and final—are normally related to the major steps in the audit in defined ways. Obtaining an understanding of the client is part of planning. The study and evaluation of internal control and assessment of control risk span both the planning and interim phases. The review of the accounting system is a necessary part of planning.

Tests of controls must be undertaken on an interim basis. In contrast, tests of transactions undertaken for substantive purposes may be either interim or final work. In an extreme case, a small entity with few controls and a relatively small volume of transactions might permit all audit tests to be undertaken as final work with no tests of controls.

Some substantive tests, such as observation of the client's physical inventory taking and the sending out of confirmations, require preparation and follow-up. An inventory observation must begin with a review of the client's planned counting procedures well before the physical inventory is taken. The timing of confirmation procedures must allow time to receive replies, investigate discrepancies disclosed and satisfactorily verify non-responding accounts by alternative procedures. For both tests, the auditor must co-ordinate with the client's operations. For example, accounts receivable confirmation is best done soon after the client mails debtor statements.

An auditor's opinion as it relates to balance sheet accounts is on the account balances at the year-end. If substantive tests are moved back from year-end, there is a risk that changes in the nature and composition of accounts may invalidate the conclusions from the tests. To evaluate the need for additional substantive tests at year-end, the auditor reviews transactions from the date of any interim substantive tests to year-end and considers the effectiveness of relevant internal control activities.

Interim work permits the audit firm to allocate its staff efficiently among clients, and enables the auditor to identify potential accounting or auditing problems early so that they can be resolved with the client on a timely basis. In addition, reporting deadlines may not allow the auditor to perform extensive audit procedures after the balance date.

Some substantive tests can conveniently be performed at or near the balance date and there is no particular advantage in doing them on an interim basis. For example, counts of assets such as cash and marketable securities are usually performed at or near the balance date. Similarly, the auditor is concerned with obtaining evidence that transactions are recorded in the proper accounting period. These so-called cut-off tests must be performed around the balance date.

Other substantive tests are done as close to the completion of the engagement as possible, because they depend on evidence collected in the earlier steps in the audit. These so-called completion and review procedures are always done as final work. Exhibit 6.2 shows the overall timing of an audit engagement. The example indicates the approximate date when certain typical procedures might be performed. However, there is substantial variation in practice on the timing of audit tests and the time between the date of the financial report and the delivery of the audit report.

DEVELOPING AN OVERALL AUDIT STRATEGY

The planning process and the documentation produced during this process are important to the efficiency and effectiveness of an audit. The auditor must balance the potential conflict between the need for sufficient appropriate evidence and the cost and time needed to obtain that evidence to allow the drawing of conclusions and the issue of an audit opinion.

One of the most important aspects of the audit planning process is obtaining knowledge of the

EXHIBIT 6.2

Example of the overall timing of an audit engagement

Financial report period	1 July 20X4	Beginning of financial year
	10 September 20X4	Planning
	25 November 20X4	First interim visit to conduct transactions tests
	29 May 20X5	Second interim visit to conduct transaction tests
	30 June 20X5	Confirmation of receivables, observation of inventory stocktake and completion of cut-off tests
Subsequent period	27 August 20X5	Completion of fieldwork
	9 September 20X5	Delivery of draft audit report for consideration by directors
	14 September 20X5	Signing of the directors' declaration and directors' report
	15 September 20X5	Signing of audit report*
	10 October 20X5	Distribution of annual report
	30 October 20X5	Annual general meeting

* Many auditors sign their report on the date the directors sign their report and declaration. The statutory requirement is that the directors' declaration be signed prior to the audit report.

client's business and its business risk and, through that understanding, making judgments in relation to areas of audit risk and materiality to assist in the development of a detailed audit program. The determination of the initial **audit strategy** and plan requires the auditor to make decisions in relation to the scope of the audit, the general evidence requirements for the forming of an opinion, and the initial choice as to the nature, timing and extent of audit procedures to make efficient use of resources. The auditor also considers the terms of the engagement and any statutory responsibilities, the effect of new accounting or auditing standards and the work of internal auditors. Examples of the specific decisions coming from the determination of the audit strategy are: whether and where to use statistical sampling or computer-assisted audit techniques; the appropriate levels of audit staff to assign to particular parts of the audit; the involvement of experts; and whether another firm of auditors might be engaged to audit a branch location to save travel by audit staff.

The interrelationship between materiality, audit risk and what constitutes sufficient appropriate audit evidence impacts on the auditor's choice of strategy. Two alternative audit strategies, representing opposite ends of a continuum of possible strategies, are a lower assessed level of control risk and a predominantly substantive approach.

Lower assessed level of control risk approach

If the internal control is well designed and expected to be highly effective, the auditor may adopt a lower assessed level of control risk approach. However, this approach will only be adopted where it is expected that the cost of the more extensive procedures necessary to obtain the required understanding of the internal control and test controls will be more than offset by reduced costs from performing less extensive substantive procedures.

The audit strategy will be as follows:

- use a planned assessed level of control risk of low or medium;
- obtain an extensive understanding of relevant parts of the internal control;
- plan extensive tests of control; and
- plan restricted substantive audit procedures based on the planned acceptable level of detection risk being high or medium.

Predominantly substantive approach

If the auditor believes that adequate controls do not exist or are likely to be ineffective, the auditor will adopt a predominantly substantive approach. This approach might also be adopted when an auditor expects that the cost of the procedures necessary to obtain an extensive understanding of the internal control and test controls so as to enable a lower level of control risk will be more than the cost of performing extensive substantive procedures.

The audit strategy will be as follows:

- use a planned assessed level of control risk of high;
- plan to obtain a minimum understanding of the internal control;
- plan no tests of control; and
- plan extensive substantive audit procedures based on a planned acceptable level of detection risk of low or medium.

These audit strategy determinations and the resultant broad audit plan should be documented in accordance with AUS 302 (ISA 300), and are then reflected in a more detailed audit program.

Impact of business risk assessment on audit strategy

The business risk approach, which will be discussed in more detail later in this chapter, means that more time is spent at the planning stage gaining an understanding of the competitive strategy of management and the risks associated with this strategy, and developing an expectation of what the entity's financial report should look like. The auditor will develop an understanding of the critical success factors and identify the key performance indicators. For example, a critical success factor in an airline's performance to maximise shareholder value may be to attract more business-class travellers. A key performance indicator may be the average yield per passenger kilometre. The auditor will also identify the risks associated with this strategy, for example the costs of servicing these customers may increase or insufficient attention may be given to economy-class passengers. The controls in place to offset these risks will then be considered by the auditor.

As a result, the audit strategy may be to:

- increase the use of sophisticated analytical procedures;
- undertake tests of controls for routine transactions (such as sales and purchases);
- increase substantive testing of non-routine transactions (such as management's estimates); and
- decrease the emphasis on detailed substantive audit procedures if the financial report is in accordance with the auditor's expectations developed from the business risk analysis.

Preparing a detailed program

An audit program is a detailed list of the audit procedures to be applied to a particular account or class of transactions needed to implement the audit plan. AUS 302.10 (ISA 300.10) requires the auditor to develop and document an audit program, setting out the nature, timing and extent of planned audit procedures required to implement the audit plan. Thus, the audit program provides a set of instructions to assistants involved in the audit and provides a means to control and record the proper execution of the work.

A well-prepared audit program provides:

- **Evidence of proper planning of the work**   It allows a review of the proposed scope of the audit before the work is performed, when there is still time to modify the proposed audit procedures.
- **Guidance to inexperienced staff**   It lays down the specific audit procedures to be performed by each staff member.
- **Evidence of the work performed**   Each staff member signs or initials each step in the program on completing the required work.
- **A means of controlling the time spent on the engagement**   The program may show the estimated time required to complete each audit step and have provision for recording the actual time taken.
- **Evidence of the consideration of internal control in relation to the proposed audit procedures**   Many programs include a brief summary of the important internal control activities relevant to the area to be tested so the auditor can evaluate the work undertaken in terms of the strengths and weaknesses of internal control.

It must be remembered that the audit program is only tentative, based on assumptions about the client's accounting procedures and internal control. When the audit work commences, if the conditions are not as anticipated the auditor may revise the program on the basis of the conditions actually found. For example, if the auditor's preliminary review and evaluation of internal control for accounts receivable shows strong internal control, the program may be designed to confirm only a limited number of accounts receivable. If, however, as a result of the work undertaken the anticipated strengths are not found, the program should be changed to meet these circumstances.

The audit program is generally prepared by the audit senior (in charge) in conjunction with the manager, and is reviewed and approved by the audit partner. The audit program for a particular engagement is influenced by the nature and size of the client's business, the strategy of management and its associated risks, the internal control and the client's accounting procedures. The factors that define audit procedures in preparing a detailed program are:

1 **nature:** the particular audit procedures to use and the particular items to which a procedure will be applied;
2 **extent:** the number of items to which the procedure will be applied (the sample sizes) and the number of different tests to be performed; and
3 **timing:** the appropriate time to perform the procedure.

Thus, the questions the auditor must ask can be summarised as what, how many and when. In answering these questions, the auditor considers, for a particular account or class of transactions:

1 the risk of undetected errors or other irregularities getting through in the audit;
2 the practical availability of evidence that would indicate the presence or absence of a material error or irregularity of that type; and
3 the maximum dollar amount of errors or irregularities acceptable (the materiality decision).

Client-specific audit programs

The types of errors and other irregularities that can occur and the reliability of evidence produced by particular procedures bear some similarity from client to client. Thus, it is possible to produce a standardised list of audit tests for particular accounts and classes of transactions that can be adapted to the circumstances of a specific engagement. Exhibit 6.3 overleaf illustrates a simplified audit program for accounts payable.

Caution is required in using a standardised list of audit tests because circumstances differ between clients. The auditor must consider the evaluation of audit risk and the likelihood of errors and irregularities for the particular account in order to determine the need for additional or unusual procedures. Also, each audit program must be adapted by deciding the extent and timing of procedures. In that sense, every audit program should be tailor-made. Many of the audit firms have computer software available to them that takes the assessment of inherent risk and control risk (by prompting audit staff's responses to specific questions) and combines it with knowledge of the client to produce tailor-made audit programs for the account balances and classes of transactions for that client. The decisions made in last year's audit about the nature, timing and extent of procedures should not be followed routinely.

The timing of audit procedures was considered earlier in this chapter. The extent of audit procedures is probably the most difficult decision in detailed program planning. The auditor must constantly decide how much evidence is enough. In most cases, this question is answered by reference to accumulated experience, supported by decision support systems maintained within the audit firm. Such judgments are not intuitive. They are based on a consideration of the effectiveness of controls, the knowledge of and experience with the client, an understanding of what has worked in similar circumstances and the composition of the account being tested. For example, some

EXHIBIT

6.3

Example of a
simplified audit
program for
accounts
payable

		Prepared by: Date:
		Approved by: Date:

Accounts Payable
[CLIENT'S NAME]
AUDIT PROGRAM FOR ACCOUNTS PAYABLE
[AUDIT PERIOD]

Item no.	Audit procedures	Done by	Remarks as to extent covered, etc.	W.P. ref.
1	Obtain or prepare a schedule of accounts payable.			
2	Examine creditors' invoices and monthly statements on a test basis for support of individual balances.			
3	Investigate large, irregular, old or disputed balances and obtain an explanation for old and disputed items.			
4	Consider confirming accounts with unusual balances (3) and with principal suppliers (2).			

5	Search for unrecorded liabilities by
	(a) referring to minutes;
	(b) examining unentered invoices;
	(c) examining invoices entered for
	    period after balance date;
	(d) examining cash disbursements
	    after balance date.			

accounts contain only a few large items that represent most of the balance. This makes it easy to verify the majority of the accounts balance by substantively verifying a few large items.

Quick review

1 An audit plan covers the overall scope and conduct of the audit.

2 The seven major steps in a financial report audit are: knowledge of the business and business strategy, understanding the internal control, assessing the risks of material misstatement, response to assessed risks, tests of control, substantive tests and completion and review.

3 The three phases of the overall timing of the engagement are planning, interim and final.

4 The auditor will normally choose an audit strategy of either a lower assessed level of control risk or a predominantly substantive approach, depending on the interrelationship between materiality, audit risk and sufficient appropriate audit evidence. The choice will take account of the cost effectiveness of each approach.

5 An audit program will be prepared to reflect the detailed procedures for the strategy chosen and will be approved by the audit partner.

6 Many audit firms use computer software to produce audit programs which are adapted or tailored to the particular audit.

ASSIGNING AND SCHEDULING AUDIT STAFF

A number of planning activities relate to arranging and **scheduling audit work**. Pertinent activities are:

- co-ordinating the assistance of entity personnel in data preparation;
- determining the extent of involvement, if any, of consultants, specialists and internal auditors; and
- establishing and co-ordinating staffing requirements.

Savings in time and cost can often be achieved by having client personnel prepare various schedules and analyses of accounts for the auditor's use. Also, client personnel must be available to provide access to facilities, records and documents. Discussing arrangements for this assistance with the client's officers is an important part of planning, and the amount of this work done by client personnel affects the number and competence of the audit staff that are needed.

Similarly, the auditor needs to consider the extent to which it is possible to make use of the work of an internal auditor in the audit process. This will be discussed in Chapter 8.

In the audit of a complex entity the auditor may require the assistance of:

- specialists within the auditor's own firm, such as experts in computers, mathematical techniques, government regulations or taxes;
- specialists within or serving the client's organisation, such as internal auditors, engineers or legal counsel; and
- independent specialists, such as consulting actuaries.

Arranging to use specialists is part of the planning stage.

Establishing and co-ordinating the staff involves selection of competent people, preparing a time budget and work schedule and supervising audit staff. These activities are interdependent. For example, the amount and kind of supervision depends on the experience and competence of staff.

Staff capabilities

The number and quality of audit staff needed on an engagement depends on the complexity and extent of audit work anticipated. Most audit firms rely on quality control practices related to hiring, development and advancement to ensure that staff have the necessary competence. In assigning staff to audit engagements, the matching of the competence and experience of staff with the requirements of the various audit engagements under way is a difficult task, involving both human resource personnel and senior professional staff.

Supervision of staff

AUS 206.21 (ISA 220.21) states that an auditor who delegates work to assistants should carefully direct, supervise and review the delegated work. The instruction and review provided by a supervisor on an engagement are important, both for assuring satisfactory completion of audit work and for educating audit staff. A great deal about auditing can be learned only in the field, and the quality of this experience depends on the effort and ability of the supervisor.

Supervisors observe staff, review the results of audit work in working papers and hold conferences with staff. To achieve an organised approach to supervision and assure the control of field work, most audit firms use checklists and specially-designed memoranda for such things as appraising staff performance and identifying and resolving significant matters raised during the engagement. For example, some firms use a memorandum of matters for the attention of the partner. The memorandum identifies significant accounting or auditing problems encountered and is updated throughout the engagement.

Most of the field supervision in an audit is the responsibility of the accountant-in-charge or senior. An overriding review of this person's work is made by the manager and partner.

Time budgets and work schedules

A **time budget** is an estimate of the total hours it is expected to take to complete an audit. It is based on the information obtained in the first major step in the audit—obtaining an understanding of the client. A time budget takes into consideration such things as the entity's size, as indicated by its gross assets, sales, number of employees, etc.; the locations of its facilities; the anticipated accounting and auditing problems; and the competence and experience of staff available.

The total time must be allocated by the preparation of work schedules showing who is to do what work and how long it should take. Thus, total hours are budgeted by major categories of audit procedures and may be scheduled on a weekly basis.

Time budgets are used to control the work on an engagement, and variances from budget serve to highlight matters requiring supervisory attention. Variances may indicate unanticipated accounting or auditing problems, inadequate instruction by supervisors or misunderstanding by staff.

An example of a time budget for an audit is illustrated in Exhibit 6.4. The extent of detail shown in a budget and the categories of audit work may vary substantially.

Quick review

1. The auditor should have the client prepare as many schedules as possible to save time and costs.
2. The number and capabilities of audit staff required on an audit depend on the complexity and extent of audit work required.
3. An auditor who delegates work to an assistant must direct, supervise and review the work delegated.
4. Audit firms use time budgets to control work on an audit.

KNOWLEDGE OF THE CLIENT'S BUSINESS

As previously stated, the audit must be adequately planned. The steps in planning the audit are shown in Figure 6.2 overleaf.

In accordance with AUS 402.02 (ISA 315.02), planning requires that an auditor gain **knowledge of the client's business**. This knowledge assists the auditor to identify the events, transactions, practices and risks that may have a significant effect on the financial report, particularly the appropriateness of the accounting policies adopted and the reasonableness of assumptions and estimates incorporated into the client's financial report. The auditor's knowledge of the client's business should include an understanding of such factors as its organisational structure, objectives and strategies, accounting policies and procedures, capital structure, product lines and methods of production and distribution. The auditor should also be familiar with matters affecting the industry within which the client operates, including economic conditions, financial trends, business risk, technological developments and government regulation. Extensive guidance on matters the auditor may consider when

	Staff at $100/h (hours)	Senior at $150/h (hours)	Manager at $250/h (hours)	Partner at $350/h (hours)	Budgeted hours	Budgeted cost ($)
Audit areas						
Planning 20X3 audit	–	8	20	–	28	6 200
Preliminary discussions with management	–	1	2	–	5	650
Review internal control	–	8	2	–	10	1 700
Tests of control	–	5	–	–	5	750
Year-end procedures	20	3	1	–	24	2 700
Field work						
General audit procedures	7	–	–	8	15	3 500
Audit cash	31	7	–	3	41	5 200
Audit receivables	10	8	2	–	20	2 700
Observation of inventory	16	12	8	2	88	6 100
Inventory pricing	154	33	12	6	205	25 450
Audit other current assets	27	4	–	–	31	3 300
Audit fixed assets	29	9	–	4	42	5 650
Audit liabilities	102	28	15	8	153	20 950
Audit share capital reserves and retained profits	–	–	–	1	1	350
Audit sales	10	5	1	–	16	2 000
Audit COGS	42	7	4	2	55	6 950
Audit other revenues and expenses	17	7	1	–	25	3 000
Solicitor's letter	–	–	1	–	1	250
Management letter	–	–	1	–	1	250
Subsequent review	12	8	6	4	30	5 300
Financial report	–	12	3	–	15	2 550
Prepare tax returns	–	–	12	–	12	3 000
Partner/manager review	–	–	4	4	8	2 400
Total hours	477	165	95	42	779	110 900

EXHIBIT 6.4

Example of time budget scheduled by area and staff member

obtaining an understanding of the entity and its environment is contained in Appendix 1 to AUS 402 (ISA 315).

Knowledge of the client's organisational structure, its operations and legal structure and relevant industry and economic conditions can help the auditor to:

- assess risks and identify problems;
- plan and perform the audit efficiently and effectively;
- evaluate audit evidence; and
- provide better service to the client.

Steps in planning the audit

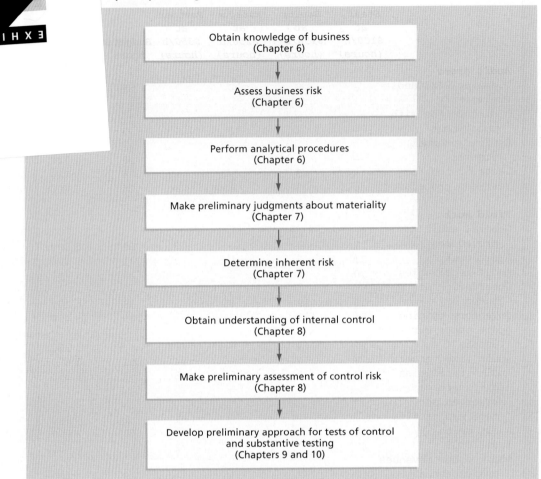

AUS 402.06–13 (ISA 315.06–13) identifies a number of methods for obtaining knowledge of the client's business, which are called risk assessment procedures, including:

■ previous experience with the entity and the industry;

■ discussion with senior people within the entity;

■ discussion with internal auditors and review of their reports;

■ discussion with other auditors, legal advisers and other advisers who have provided services to the entity or within the industry;

■ discussion with knowledgeable people such as industry economists, industry regulators, suppliers, customers and competitors;

■ industry publications such as government statistics, surveys, texts, trade journals, bank reports and financial newspapers;

■ significant legislation and regulations affecting the entity;

■ visits to the entity's premises;

■ documents produced by the entity, such as minutes of meetings, promotional literature, previous periods' annual reports, budgets, internal management reports, interim financial reports, management policy manuals, accounting manuals, chart of accounts, job descriptions and marketing and sales plans; and

- analytical procedures.

Organisational structure

A plan of organisation is essential to specify the responsibilities and tasks of the various components of any entity. The **organisational structure** of an entity divides tasks between individual employees, groups or departments and locations. To control the work of an entity, procedural methods and measures are adopted which provide evidence that the tasks specified by the organisational structure have been carried out.

Organisational structure may be formal or informal. In a large, complex entity there are formal determinants of behaviour, or formal norms (see below). They take the form of organisation charts, charts of accounts, rules, office memos, manuals, contracts and, in general, all specifications developed and supported by most or all of the top personnel. The auditor reads the manuals and other specifications of formal structure, makes inquiries about policies and procedures in effect and observes the actions of employees and top management. There are also informal determinants which influence the behaviour of the employee or member of an entity.

Structure is also a behavioural concept. In behavioural science, human relationships that exist and remain stable over a period of time, regardless of the individuals involved, are called **social structures**. In any social situation there are things one ought to do and things one ought not do. Sometimes individuals violate these rules, but the rules themselves are generally known to everyone. Thus, we can say that buying and selling, receiving and giving or teaching and learning are each carried on in a similar fashion regardless of the individual people involved.

Social scientists identify the guides to interaction as norms. A **norm** is simply a prescription or proscription—something one should or should not do in a given situation. These norms can be formal and explicit or informal and only implicit. Laws are examples of formal norms, as are written rules of any club, organisation or company. However, norms can be informal and may simply be generally known but unwritten. Patterns of dress and manners of speech fall into this category.

The auditor needs to understand the business purpose served by the various components of the organisational structure in order to understand the business purpose of material transactions.

Operational and legal structure

The auditor needs to understand the client's **operational structure**, its **legal structure**, and related management policies and procedures. Operating characteristics include types of products and services, locations, and methods of production, distribution and compensation. Some of this information is obtained by reading manuals and other specifications of formal structure together with related inquiries and observations. In a continuing engagement the auditor can also review correspondence files, permanent files and the working papers of last year. Once the auditor has a basic understanding of operating characteristics, efforts are directed to examining important changes in operations and current business and accounting developments.

Knowledge of operations

An auditor must commence an audit with a sound knowledge of the operations and circumstances of the entity being audited. The auditor prepares a brief description of the nature of the business activities, including all significant factors which have a bearing on operations. To interpret the evidence gathered throughout the audit intelligently, the auditor must be familiar both with the client's strategy and business and with the many factors which can influence the client's operations.

A sound knowledge of the business will assist the auditor in assessing the areas of importance and risk for purposes of gathering audit evidence, and also increase the opportunity to be of service to the client by suggesting improvements in operations. For example, if the auditor determines that the client has a much lower profitability than other entities in the same industry, inventory valuation may deserve extra attention. A comparison of the production schedule with sales forecasts may reveal overproduction of some product lines and the corresponding need to give greater consideration to questions of inventory obsolescence. These same observations can form the basis for recommendations of corrective action to be taken by management. In any case, proper inventory valuation requires a sound knowledge of pricing methods and the marketing and distribution system.

A good understanding of the business has implications for the entire examination. Even in the examination of documentary evidence, the auditor's background knowledge can serve as the basis for important observations and useful recommendations to the client. In tests of sales invoices, examination may reveal excessive back ordering, indicative of poor inventory planning. By determining the lapse of time from receipt of an order to dispatch, delays in the dispatch department may be disclosed. Tests of purchase vouchers can determine whether the entity is buying in economic order quantities.

Tour of plant

Important knowledge about the client can also be obtained by a tour of the client's physical facilities. A visit to the offices and plant provides background knowledge on such things as materials handling methods, the physical layout of facilities and the general condition of fixed assets and inventory. During the tour the auditor is also able to meet key personnel.

Legal documents

A review of the entity's legal documents is essential to enable intelligent interpretation of the accounting records and financial report. The auditor generally takes excerpts from the company constitution or partnership agreement, the minute book, tax returns of previous years, major contracts and important correspondence for inclusion in the audit working papers. This information contributes to an understanding of the business and contains information about specific items that should be compared with data in the accounting records.

The constitution of the company shows the name of the company, the objects for which it has been formed and its rules or by-laws. This document details the rights and duties of shareholders and provisions relating to the holding of meetings and election of directors. A partnership agreement contains similar information about the operating rules of a business organised as a partnership.

Minutes, contracts and correspondence

The minutes of the meetings of an entity's board of directors officially record the important strategic decisions, transactions and agreements of the entity. By examining the minutes, the auditor obtains information to be substantiated during the remainder of the audit. The declaration of dividends, authorisation of fixed asset expenditures, purchases and sales of investments and opening and closing of bank accounts are examples of the important information contained in the board's minutes.

Correspondence and contracts with customers, suppliers, personnel, trade unions and various government agencies contain information that enables the auditor to understand the business practices and problems of the client, as well as providing information for audit tests.

Related parties

The auditor needs to have a level of knowledge of a client's business and industry sufficient to identify events, transactions and practices that may have a material effect on the financial report. It is important, therefore, that the auditor's understanding of the client's business covers the existence and identity of related parties and the extent of the client's involvement with those parties.

Related parties are defined in AASB 124 (IAS 24), 'Related Party Disclosures'. Entities are related if one entity can significantly influence or control the operating, financing or investing decisions of another, or if several entities are subject to significant influence or control from the same entity. For example, directors are entities separate from the business, but they are related parties because they can significantly influence the operating, financing and investing decisions of the business. A parent company and a subsidiary are related parties, as are a significant investor and an associated company. The subsidiaries of the same parent are also related parties.

After related parties have been identified during this planning phase, their names are provided to the personnel involved in the audit of the entity and its components so that they will recognise transactions with such parties encountered during the audit.

Importance of information

This information about the entity is useful to the auditor in determining the propriety and reasonableness of the transactions recorded in the accounting records. Knowledge of the client's activities is a source of independent evidence. Many errors of omission can be disclosed only by acquiring independent evidence outside the accounting records. For example, an unrecorded liability for dividends payable cannot be discovered by a 100 per cent examination of the accounting records. However, by reading the minutes the auditor can gain the knowledge that such a liability should have been recorded. Similarly, knowledge that the manufacturing process employed by a client normally results in large quantities of scrap creates an expectation of revenue from scrap sales in proportion to the level of production activity. In this manner, the auditor may detect unrecorded revenue.

This phase of the audit examination is so important that a restriction on the scope of the examination in this area, such as a client's refusal to allow the auditor to review the directors' minute book, may result in an inability to give an audit opinion. Much of the independent evidence gained in this manner cannot be acquired in any other way.

Industry and economic conditions

As outlined earlier and identified through techniques discussed later, such as PEST analysis, the auditor should have a basic understanding of **industry and economic conditions**, government regulations, changes in technology and competitive conditions that affect a client's operations. Of particular importance is knowledge about accounting practices common to the client's industry.

Some sources of such information are trade journals, books of industry statistics and, in some cases, professional statements. If government regulations are an important factor in recognition of revenues or expenses, the auditor may need to investigate the administration of those regulations and inspect contracts, noting pertinent conditions and terms.

In general, the auditor should be aware of developments pertinent to clients as identified through their knowledge management database (most large audit firms have knowledge management databases that, among other things, identify any news releases about their clients) or from normal reading of financial and business magazines and newspapers.

BUSINESS RISK
Risk assessment procedures

In Chapter 5, client **business risk** was defined as the risk that an entity's business objectives will not be attained as a result of the external and internal factors, pressures and forces brought to bear on the entity and, ultimately, the risk associated with the entity's profitability and survival. In order to assess whether the financial report is fairly presented, the auditor must undertake risk assessment procedures to understand the entity's business strategy and risks and its ability to respond to changing environmental conditions. The entity's business strategy is usually spelt out by top management and may be broad, such as 'to maximise shareholder value'. This is then supported by a number of operational strategies such as 'expand our sales by selling into Asia' or 'reduce costs by selling on the Internet'. The auditor assesses the specific business risks that the entity faces in achieving these strategies to determine if they could result in a materially misstated financial report. Bell et al. (1997) argue that by taking a top-down view of the entity, rather than the traditional bottom-up transaction-based approach, where inferences about information contained in the financial report are made based on tests of transactions and balances, the auditor can use strategic analysis to plan the audit in a more efficient manner. Figure 6.3 shows some factors that affect the client's internal, local and global environments.

FIGURE 6.3 **The relationship between client business risk and the global, local and internal environments**

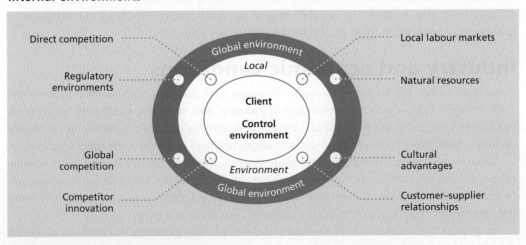

Source: Adapted from Bell et al. (1997), Exhibit 3, p. 27.

To assess client business risk properly the auditor must understand the entity's business and industry at two levels. First, the auditor must obtain a thorough understanding of the industry in which the entity operates. This includes knowledge concerning:

- the profitability and structure of the industry;
- the relationship between the industry and the broad economic and business environment;
- the critical issues facing the industry; and
- the significant industry business risks.

Second, the auditor must understand how the entity fits within the industry by obtaining knowledge concerning:

- the entity's position within the industry in terms of factors such as profitability and market share;
- opportunities and plans the entity has for increasing or maintaining profitability and market share;
- threats to the entity's position in the industry;
- the way the entity deals with its customers and competitors; and
- the methods the entity uses to measure and monitor its performance.

The auditor uses the industry and entity information to identify business risks that may have an impact on the audit. Once the risks have been identified, the auditor should ascertain whether the entity has controls in place to monitor those risks and determine whether the auditor should test those controls. The assessment of client business risk is an input into the auditor's assessment of the risk of material misstatement in the financial report. Client business risk affects inherent risk and control risk and therefore the nature, timing and extent of the auditor's work through the required level of detection risk.

The members of the audit engagement team should discuss the susceptibility of the entity's financial report to material misstatement (AUS 402.14/ISA 315.14). This discussion will allow all members of the audit management team to obtain a better understanding of the potential for material misstatement and how the results of audit procedures that they perform may affect other aspects of the audit. This discussion should be documented.

As discussed in Chapter 5, the new audit risk standards were issued in March 2004 to incorporate the business risk approach into the audit risk model contained in the auditing standards. The aim was to achieve better risk assessments and improved design and performance of audit procedures to respond to the risks and improve linkage of audit procedures and assessed risks, resulting in a greater concentration of effort in areas where there is greater risk of misstatement of the financial report. The auditor is required to make a risk assessment for all audits and can no longer simply default to a high risk assessment. An overview of the new standards is contained in Figure 6.4 overleaf.

SWOT analysis

Assessing client business risk requires analysis of both the entity's capabilities and external environment. External and internal critical environmental factors can be organised into the entity's internal strengths and weaknesses and its external opportunities and threats. **SWOT analysis** is a method of analysing an entity's competitive situation by assessing its strengths (S), weaknesses (W), environmental opportunities (O) and threats (T). This identification of opportunities and detection of threats requires assessment of all relevant environmental factors.

A *strength* is an internal aspect that can improve the entity's competitive situation. A strength is something an entity is good at doing or a characteristic that gives it enhanced competitiveness.

FIGURE **6.4** **Overview of the audit risk standards**

Perform risk assessment procedures
Perform audit procedures to understand the entity and its environment:
- Industry regulatory and other external factors, including applicable financial reporting framework
- Nature of the entity
- Objectives and strategies and related business risks
- Measurement and review of the entitys finan cial performance
- Internal control

See AUS 402.06–99
(ISA 315.06–99)

Assess the risks of material misstatement
Assess the risks of material misstatement at the financial report level and at assertion level by:
- Identifying risks through considering:
  1. the entity and its environment, including its internal control
  2. classes of transactions, account balances and disclosures
- Relating the identified risks to what can go wrong at the assertion level
- Considering the significance and likelihood of the risks

See AUS 402.100–119
(ISA 315.100–119)

Respond to assessed risks
Respond to the risks at the financial report level and assertion level by:
- Developing overall responses to the assessed risks at the financial report level
- Determining the nature, timing and extent of further audit procedures at the assertion level

See AUS 406.04–21
(ISA 330.04–21)

Perform further audit procedures
Perform further audit procedures that are clearly linked to risks at the assertion level by:
- Performing tests of the operating effectiveness of controls
- Performing substantive procedures

See AUS 406.22–65
(ISA 330.22–65)

Evaluate audit evidence obtained
Evaluate whether sufficient and appropriate audit evidence has been obtained

See AUS 406.66–72
(ISA 330.66–72)
and AUS 502 (ISA 500)

An entity's strengths include its skills and expertise, its collection of assets, its competitive capabilities and its market achievements. Sometimes entity strengths may relate to fairly specific skills and expertise and sometimes they may result from different resources combining to create a competitive capability. These resources, in conjunction with industry and competitive conditions, help determine how well the entity will be able to perform. Obviously, some strengths are more competitively important than others because they play a larger role in contributing to a strong market position and in determining profitability.

A *weakness* is an internal aspect where the entity is potentially vulnerable to competitors' strategic moves. Therefore it is something an entity lacks or does poorly in comparison to its competitors or a condition that puts it at a disadvantage. An entity's internal weaknesses can relate to deficiencies in competitively important skills or expertise; a lack of competitively important physical, human organisational or intangible assets; or missing or weak competitive capabilities in key areas. Whether a weakness will make an entity competitively vulnerable depends on how much the weakness matters in the marketplace and whether it can be overcome by the entity's resources and strengths. Some weaknesses can prove fatal if not overcome, while others are inconsequential, easily remedied or offset by entity strengths.

An *opportunity* is an environmental condition that can significantly improve an entity's situation relative to that of its competitors. Not every industry opportunity is an entity opportunity, as not every entity in an industry is equipped with the resources to pursue each opportunity that exists. The market opportunities most relevant to an entity are those that offer profitable growth, the most potential for competitive advantage and match up well with the financial and organisational resource capabilities which the entity already possesses or can easily acquire.

A *threat* is an environmental condition that can significantly undermine an entity's competitive situation. Some examples of factors in an entity's external environment that may pose threats to its profitability and market standing include the introduction of new or better products by rivals, the entry of lower-cost foreign competitors into the entity's market stronghold or new regulations that are more burdensome to the entity than to its competitors (Example 6.1). External threats may pose only a moderate degree of adversity or they may make an entity's situation and outlook quite tenuous. Most entities are aware of what their competitors are doing and actively plan strategies for coping with these threats. Auditors should be aware of both the threats and management's strategies for dealing with them.

EXAMPLE 6.1 Audit impact of a threat

Motor Limited is facing severe competition from existing competitors, new entrants and substitute products. These threats are likely to affect sales, creating a downward pressure on prices and introducing the possibility of obsolete inventory. This will increase the audit risk associated with the valuation of inventory. It may also affect the valuation of manufacturing plant used to produce those goods and ultimately the ability of the entity to continue as a going concern.

Some issues that may be considered in SWOT analyses are shown in Table 6.1 (overleaf). SWOT takes into account the interactions between the entity and its environment with respect to what the entity does or plans to do to achieve its goals and objectives and provides a starting point for the auditor to assess the client's business risk.

PEST analysis

PEST analysis involves identifying the political, economic, social and technological influences on an entity. This involves consideration of the external environmental influences that have been particularly important in the past, and the extent to which there are changes occurring which may make any of these more or less significant in the future for the entity and its competitors.

Political risks arise from legal or regulatory constraints on an entity. Laws on employment, equal opportunity, occupational health and safety, and consumer and environmental protection have a significant effect on an entity. Compliance with these laws may be complex and expensive, but non-compliance may be even more costly. Many laws and regulations are industry-specific and need to be considered when auditing an entity.

Economic risks relate to general or regional trends in economic conditions that can have an adverse effect on an entity. Risks can arise from a change in interest rates, inflation, economic

TABLE 6.1 Major issues to consider in SWOT analysis

Potential internal strengths	Potential internal weaknesses
A powerful strategy	No clear strategic direction
Adequate financial resources	Obsolete facilities
Good competitive skill	Too much debt
Strong brand name	Sub-par profitability
An acknowledged market leader	Higher overall unit costs relative to key competitors
Access to economies of scale	Lack of managerial depth and talent
Proprietary technology	Missing some key skills or competence
Superior technological skills	Poor track record in implementing strategy
Cost advantages	Plagued with internal operating problems
Better advertising campaigns	Falling behind in R & D
Product innovation skills	Too narrow a product line
Proven management	Weak market image
Better manufacturing capability	Weak distribution network
Better product quality	Below-average marketing skills
Wide geographic coverage	Unable to finance needed changes in strategy
Alliances/joint ventures with other entities	Underutilisation of plant
	Behind on product quality

Potential external opportunities	Potential external threats
Serve additional customer groups	Entry of lower-cost competitors
Enter new markets or segments	Rising sales of substitute products
Expand product line to meet broader range of customer needs	Slowdowns in market growth
Diversify into related products	Adverse shifts in foreign exchange rates and trade policies of foreign governments
Vertical integration	Costly regulatory requirements
Falling trade barriers in attractive foreign markets	Vulnerability to recession and business cycle
Complacency among rival firms	Growing bargaining power of customers or suppliers
Faster market growth	Changing buyer needs and tastes
Acquisition of rival firms	Adverse demographic changes
	Vulnerability to industry-driving forces

Source: Adapted from Thompson and Strickland, 1998, p. 107.

growth, foreign exchange rates or unemployment. For example, industries such as construction and real estate are sensitive to small increases in interest rates. See Example 6.2.

Social risks are affected by cultural attitudes, lifestyles and social pressures. For example, in many countries, employees expect a level of benefits and management consideration, such as in-house childcare, that is unheard of in other countries. Some products, such as furs or ivory, are acceptable in some countries and unacceptable in others. A business that opens a branch or subsidiary in another country needs to carefully consider local employment practices, customs and social attitudes in the planning of the facility.

Technological risks typically relate to the rate of innovation in an industry. Technology can affect many facets of an entity, including the manner in which it conducts its basic operations, processes information, markets its products, designs its manufacturing process and develops new products. A manufacturer lacking new technology may be at a competitive disadvantage.

Table 6.2 provides a summary of some of the questions to ask about key forces at work in the macroenvironment.

PEST analysis may involve identifying a number of key drivers of change, that is, forces likely to affect the structure of an industry or market. A good example is the forces that are increasing the globalisation of some markets. PEST analysis may also help the auditor to examine the differential impact of external influences on entities, both historically and in the future. It looks at the extent to which key drivers will affect industries differently.

EXAMPLE 6.2 Audit impact of an economic factor

Ace Concrete Ltd's major customers are in the construction industry, which is in economic recession. As a result, receivables may not be able to be collected at the normal historic rate. This will increase the audit risk associated with the valuation of receivables, as the allowance for doubtful debts may have to be increased. It may also have going concern implications due to a shrinking customer base and its impact on cash flow.

TABLE 6.2 **A PEST analysis of environmental influences**

1. What environmental factors are affecting the organisation?
2. Which of these are the most important at the present time? In the next few years?

Political/legal factors	Economic factors
Monopolies legislation	Business cycles
Environmental protection laws	GNP trends
Taxation policy	Interest rates
Foreign trade regulations	Money supply
Employment law	Inflation
Government stability	Unemployment
	Disposable income
	Energy availability and cost

Sociocultural factors	Technological factors
Population demographics	Government spending on research
Income distribution	Government and industry focus on
Social mobility	technological effort
Lifestyle changes	New discoveries/development
Attitudes to work and leisure	Speed of technology transfer
Consumerism	Rates of obsolescence
Level of education	

Source: Johnson and Scholes, 1999, p. 105.

Value-chain approach

To effectively assess the entity's ability to generate cash flows and create value the auditor should develop a comprehensive understanding of the client's positioning within its value chain and its ability to create and sustain competitive advantage within that environment. According to Porter (1985), the **value-chain approach** is a way of systematically viewing the series of activities an entity performs to provide its customers with a product. The value chain disaggregates an entity into its strategically important activities to provide an understanding of the behaviour of the entity's costs and the entity's existing or potential sources of differentiation. An entity gains competitive advantage by performing these strategically important activities or key internal factors at a lower cost or better than its competitors.

Every entity can be viewed as a collection of value activities that are performed to design, produce, market, deliver and support its product. A firm typically performs a number of discrete activities that may represent key strengths or weaknesses. Service activities, for example, may include such discrete activities as installation, repair, and parts of distribution and upgrading, any of which could be a major source of competitive advantage or disadvantage. Through the systematic identification of these activities, auditors using the value-chain approach can target potential strengths and weaknesses for further evaluation.

A framework proposed by Bell et al. (1997) for obtaining that comprehensive understanding of the value chain is:

- understand the client's strategic advantage;
- understand the risks that threaten attainment of the client's business objectives;
- understand the key processes and related competencies needed to realise strategic advantage;
- measure and benchmark process performance;
- document the understanding of the client's ability to create value and generate future cash flows by using a client business model, process analyses, key performance indicators and a business risk profile;
- use the comprehensive business knowledge decision frame to develop expectations about key assertions embodied in the overall financial report; and
- compare reported financial results to expectations and design additional audit test work to address any gaps between expectations and reported results.

Nonfinancial performance measurement

Many risks, especially within processes, are more effectively measured using nonfinancial measures. Common nonfinancial measures include:

- *Market share:* This is the percentage of total market consumption that is filled by a specific entity or product. A successful company will have a larger market share.
- *Customer satisfaction:* Long-term success for most entities depends on providing satisfying experiences to their customers. A drop in customer satisfaction generally leads to reduced revenue and profits (Example 6.3).
- *New product success rates:* Companies introduce many new products and multiple product introductions maximise the chance that some of the products will prove successful and profitable.
- *Time-to-market for new products:* This is the length of time it takes a company to conceive a new product and begin to sell it. The longer it takes to get a new idea to market, the more risk there is that a competitor will get there first, or external developments will cause early obsolescence. The computer industry, for example, is particularly sensitive to time-to-market issues.
- *Warranty rates:* Warranty rates are an indicator of the quality of the product.

The use of nonfinancial measures is of course dependent on the availability of systematic and reliable data. Nonfinancial performance measures can be extremely useful for assessing the significance of strategic and process risks and for evaluating the effectiveness of management responses to these risks. Nonfinancial measures are particularly important to process analysis because accounting measures are often not available nor feasible for many risks at the process level.

The auditor will generally choose a mix of financial and nonfinancial performance measures to monitor and measure the entity's performance over time using a **balanced scorecard** approach. A balanced scorecard identifies and reports on performance measures for each key strategic area of the business. The objective is to provide a balance of financial and non-financial measures that focus on both short-term and long-term performance and support the entity's competitive strategy. While there are a number of approaches to developing balanced scorecards, they all tend to be based on similar principles. For example, Kaplan and Norton

(1992) identified the following four perspectives: financial perspective; customer perspective; internal perspective; and innovation and learning.

Within each perspective the auditor will choose a mix of financial and nonfinancial measures to monitor and measure performance over time. For example, financial measures might include items such as cash, profit or earnings per share; while customer satisfaction measures might include items such as warranty rate, volume of customer complaints, or customer satisfaction index.

EXAMPLE 6.3 Audit impact of a nonfinancial performance measure

Diamond Engineering Limited has experienced an increase in the volume of customer complaints. This could be due to a drop in the quality of their product and may necessitate more rework or warranty claims. Audit risk would increase in relation to possible understatement of warranty expenses and accruals. It may also affect the valuation of inventory and the overall viability of the entity. For an entity that has adopted a strategy of high quality, loss of reputation is likely to significantly reduce its chances of success.

Response to assessed risks

In order to reduce audit risk to an acceptably low level, AUS 406.03 (ISA 330.03) requires that the auditor should determine overall responses to assessed risks at the financial report level and perform further audit procedures to respond to assessed risk at the assertion level. Responses at the financial report level may include:

- emphasising to the audit team the need to maintain professional scepticism in gathering and evaluating audit evidence;
- assigning more experienced staff or staff with special skills;
- using experts;
- providing more supervision;
- incorporating additional elements of unpredictability in the selection of further audit procedures to be performed;
- making general changes to the nature, timing and extent of audit procedures such as performing substantive procedures at balance date instead of at an interim date.

At the assertion level, AUS 406.07 (ISA 330.07) requires that the auditor's assessment of identified risks provide a basis for designing and performing further audit procedures. There should be a clear link between the nature, timing and extent of the auditor's further audit procedures and the assessed risks. These further procedures may be either tests of control or substantive tests or both, depending on the circumstances. In designing further audit procedures the auditor must consider:

- the significance of the risk;
- the likelihood that a misstatement will occur;
- the characteristics of the class of transactions, account balance, or disclosure involved;
- the nature of the specific controls used by the entity, including whether they are manual or IT;
- whether the auditor expects to obtain evidence to determine if the entity's controls are effective in preventing, or detecting and correcting, material misstatements.

1 An auditor must understand an entity's strategy and associated business risks in order to assess whether the financial report is fairly presented.

2 To assist in assessing business risk, the auditor will use various strategic management techniques including SWOT analysis, PEST analysis, the value-chain approach and a balanced scorecard.

3 In order to reduce audit risk to an acceptably low level, the auditor should determine overall responses to assessed risks at the financial report level and the assertion level.

learning objective **8**

ANALYTICAL PROCEDURES

AUS 512.08 (ISA 520.08) requires the auditor to apply **analytical procedures** at the planning stage to assist in understanding the business and identifying areas of potential risk. Analytical procedures may reveal aspects of the business about which the auditor was unaware, and assist in determining the nature, timing and extent of other audit procedures.

Analytical procedures are also discussed in Chapters 5, 10 and 12, and involve the use of ratios, trend analysis and operating statistics for comparison with internal and external data. The different types of analytical procedures are discussed below. The use of these techniques in preliminary planning allows the auditor to identify areas requiring audit attention, thereby assisting in the determination of the nature, timing and extent of audit procedures. It also gives the auditor some knowledge of the business and a base against which to compare subsequent evaluations of the reasonableness of the financial report. The early isolation of errors, omissions, changes in accounting policy or practice and the identification of unusual trends allow these matters to be dealt with on a timely basis. This prevents last-minute adjustments or reporting problems, and therefore improves the efficiency and effectiveness of the audit.

Analytical procedures applied during the planning stage assist the auditor to obtain knowledge of the business and industry, via the information produced from the data analysis and investigation of the results. Also, the process of implementing the analytical procedures requires the auditor to obtain information about the client and its industry. For example, the auditor needs to determine the relevant industry data and what statistics are appropriate for analysis and review. Also, it is necessary to consider the relationship between financial report items and any relevant nonfinancial data. Examples are the relationship between payroll costs and number of employees or revenue disclosed by an airline compared with the number of flights and the average number of paying customers per flight.

Most of the computer software used for trial balance preparation can also be used to perform analytical procedures on the financial report data. The software allows the auditor to (1) maintain previous years' financial report data so that absolute and percentage comparisons can be made and (2) calculate financial report ratios for current and previous years. Spreadsheets can also be used to perform this type of analysis.

Types of analytical procedures

Details of the different types of analytical procedures are contained in the appendix to AUS 512 (ISA 520). It classifies analytical procedures as either simple or complex. Simple procedures are:

- simple comparisons;
- ratio analysis (see Example 6.6 on p. 275);

- common-size statements;
- trend statements; and
- time series analysis.

Complex procedures are:

- time series modelling;
- regression analysis; and
- financial modelling.

While these procedures may be used at various stages of the audit, the most useful in preliminary planning include:

- comparison of current balances in the financial report with balances of previous periods and budgeted amounts (simple comparisons); and
- computation of ratios and percentage relationships for comparison with previous years' budgets and industry averages (ratio analysis). Significant variations indicate areas requiring investigation, and reasonable explanations should be obtained for these variations.

Biggs et al. (1999) state that a review of research studies of audit practice indicates that simple judgmental approaches such as comparisons and ratio analysis are used more frequently than complex statistical approaches such as time series modelling or regression analysis. This conclusion is supported by a survey of Australian practice by Smith et al. (1999), which found that the five most commonly used analytical procedures consisted of:

- three simple comparisons: current year with previous year's financial report, financial with budgeted information, and relationship of individual items with yearly totals; and
- two ratios: gross profit ratio and accounts receivable turnover.

Other analytical procedures commonly used included activity ratios, such as inventory turnover, and solvency ratios, such as current ratio, quick asset ratio and debt to equity ratio.

Simple comparisons

Simple comparisons are probably the most commonly used analytical procedure. The auditor can identify account balances that have changed significantly simply by comparing the amounts for the current and previous year on the working trial balance in the working papers. Similar comparisons can be made to budgeted amounts, or the client's internal reports comparing and analysing budgeted and actual amounts can be reviewed.

An auditor may also compute percentage relationships between balances that are expected to be related (receivables and bad debts, equipment and depreciation, interest expense and borrowings) and compare them to previous experience and budget data.

Ratio analysis

To gain a better understanding of the client, the auditor may use **ratio analysis**, calculating common liquidity, activity, profitability and solvency ratios. It must be remembered that at the planning stage the auditor is undertaking this ratio analysis on unaudited financial information. Thus any ratios not in accordance with the auditor's expectations will indicate areas requiring significant audit attention. These ratios may be compared to the following:

1 **Industry data** Information on average ratios in industries may be obtained from sources such as the Australian Stock Exchange, trade publications and computer database services.
2 **Internal data** Internal information useful for comparison of ratios includes:

- *Previous years* Comparable ratios are computed for the client for previous years, and trends are analysed.
- *Budgets* If the client has effective budgeting procedures, significant variations from the budget indicate activity that the client did not expect at the time the budget was prepared.
- *Segment or division data* If a client can disaggregate its financial information into geographic or operating segments or divisions, unusual figures or trends may help to isolate specific areas that should receive audit attention.

Comparisons of internal data (with previous periods, budgets or segment or division data) is most common. Initially, comparison with industry data may seem appealing and may, in fact, be useful. However, the industry information may not be comparable if the client differs from industry norms in regard to its lines of business, accounting methods and geographical influences.

However, care needs to be taken, as audit research by Kinney (1987) has shown that material misstatements may not significantly affect certain ratios. This is particularly true for activity ratios. Also, the auditor needs to be careful not to evaluate a financial ratio in isolation. A ratio may be favourable because its components are unfavourable. If related ratios are not examined, the auditor may draw an incorrect conclusion. For example, suppose that a client's accounts receivable turnover ratio and inventory turnover ratio are getting smaller. The negative trend in these ratios may indicate that accounts receivable are getting older and that some inventory may be obsolete. However, both of these factors positively affect the current ratio. If the auditors calculate only the current ratio, they may reach an incorrect conclusion about the entity's ability to meet current obligations.

There are many different financial ratios available to the auditor. The principal ratios are contained in Table 1 to AUS 512 (ISA 520). We will discuss below some of the ratios used most commonly by the auditor.

Short-term liquidity ratios

Short-term liquidity ratios indicate the entity's ability to meet its current obligations. Three ratios commonly used for this purpose are the **current ratio**, **quick asset ratio** and the **operating cash flow ratio**.

Current ratio
The current ratio is calculated as follows:

$$\text{Current ratio} = \frac{\text{Current assets}}{\text{Current liabilities}}$$

It includes all current assets and current liabilities and a commonly used benchmark is 2 to 1 or better, although what is an acceptable ratio may vary for different companies and industries. For example, a company that turns over its debtors and inventory quickly, such as a grocery store, will require smaller levels of assets on a balance sheet to generate a given level of cash to meet repayments and so can exist with a lower current ratio. Generally, a high current ratio indicates an entity's ability to pay current obligations. However, if current assets include old accounts receivable or obsolete inventory, this ratio can be distorted. It is also important to look at the trend in the ratio as well as the absolute amount. A declining trend in this ratio indicates prima facie that the entity is becoming short of working capital and may have difficulty in meeting its current obligations.

Quick asset ratio
The quick asset ratio includes only those assets that are most readily convertible to cash and is calculated as follows:

$$\text{Quick asset ratio} = \frac{\text{Liquid assets}}{\text{Current liabilities}}$$

Liquid assets include cash, marketable securities and net accounts receivable. Thus, inventories and prepaid items are not included in the numerator of the quick asset ratio. The quick asset ratio may provide a better picture of the entity's liquidity position if inventory contains obsolete or slow-moving items. A ratio greater than 1 is a commonly used benchmark indicating that the entity's liquid assets are sufficient to meet the cash requirements for paying current liabilities.

Operating cash flow ratio

The operating cash flow ratio measures the entity's ability to cover its current liabilities with cash generated from operations and is calculated as follows:

$$\text{Operating cash flow ratio} = \frac{\text{Cash flow from operations}}{\text{Current liabilities}}$$

The operating cash flow ratio uses the cash flows, as opposed to assets, to measure short-term liquidity. It provides a longer-term measure of the entity's ability to meet its current liabilities. If cash flow from operations is small or negative, the entity is likely to need alternative sources of cash, such as additional borrowings or sales of assets, to meet its obligations.

Activity ratios

Activity ratios indicate how effectively the entity's assets are managed. Only ratios related to accounts receivable and inventory are discussed here because for most wholesale, retail or manufacturing companies these two accounts represent the assets that have high activity. Activity ratios may also be effective in helping the auditor determine if these accounts contain material misstatements.

Receivables turnover and days in receivables

These two ratios provide information on the activity and age of accounts receivable. The receivables turnover ratio and days in accounts receivable are calculated as follows:

$$\text{Receivables turnover ratios} = \frac{\text{Net credit sales}}{\text{Average receivables}}$$

$$\text{Days in receivables} = \frac{365 \text{ days}}{\text{Receivables turnover}}$$

The **receivables turnover ratio** indicates how many times accounts receivable are turned over during a year. However, the **days in receivables** may be easier to interpret because this ratio can be compared to the client's terms of trade. For example, if an entity's terms of trade are net 30 days, the auditor would expect that if management was doing a good job of managing receivables, the value for this ratio would be 30 days or less. If the auditor calculates the days outstanding to be 60 days, the auditor might suspect that the account balance contains a material amount of bad debts. Any declining trend in the actual collection period would raise doubts about the system of credit control and the adequacy of the provision for doubtful debts, and hence the valuation of accounts receivable. Comparing the days outstanding to industry data may be helpful in detecting a slowdown in payments by customers that is affecting the entire industry.

Inventory turnover and days in inventory

These activity ratios provide information on the inventory and are calculated as follows:

$$\text{Inventory turnover ratio} = \frac{\text{Cost of goods sold}}{\text{Average inventory}}$$

$$\text{Days in inventory} = \frac{365 \text{ days}}{\text{Inventory turnover}}$$

The **inventory turnover ratio** indicates the frequency with which inventory is consumed in a year. The higher the ratio, the better the entity is at liquidating inventory. This ratio can be easily compared to industry standards or previous years. If the inventory turnover is below the industry average or is declining over time, the auditor might suspect that inventory contains obsolete or slow-moving goods; this raises doubts about the valuation of inventory. In addition, it may indicate that working capital is being tied up and liquidity reduced. Also, there is a risk that unnecessary costs are being incurred for storage space and that the buying, inventory control and production planning functions are inadequate.

Although a high inventory turnover is generally considered to be desirable, in some cases it may be a cause for concern. The auditor needs to check that inventory levels have not been reduced to such dangerously low levels that it is not possible to meet delivery dates or increase sales turnover.

The **days in inventory** measures the average number of days it takes to sell the inventory, and when added to the days in receivables shows how long it takes to convert inventory to cash.

Profitability ratios

Profitability ratios indicate the entity's success or failure at generating a profit for a given period. A number of ratios measure the profitability of an entity, and each ratio should be interpreted by comparison to industry data.

Gross profit ratio

The **gross profit ratio** is generally a good indicator of potential misstatements and is calculated as follows:

$$\text{Gross profit ratio} = \frac{\text{Gross profit}}{\text{Net sales}}$$

If this ratio varies significantly from previous years or differs significantly from industry data, the entity's financial data may contain errors. Numerous errors can affect this ratio. For example, if the client has failed to record sales the gross profit ratio will be less than in previous years. Similarly, any errors that affect the inventory account can distort this ratio. For example, if the client has omitted goods from the ending inventory, this ratio will be smaller than in previous years.

Net profit ratio

The **net profit ratio** is calculated as follows:

$$\text{Net profit ratio} = \frac{\text{Net profit}}{\text{Net sales}}$$

While the gross profit ratio measures profitability after cost of goods sold is deducted, the net profit ratio (usually measured after interest and taxes) measures the entity's profitability after all expenses are considered. Significant fluctuations in this ratio may indicate that misstatements exist in the selling, general or administrative expense accounts.

Return on total assets

The **return on total assets ratio** is calculated as follows:

$$\text{Return on total assets} = \frac{\text{Net profit}}{\text{Total assets}}$$

This ratio indicates the return earned on the resources invested by both the shareholders and the creditors. In practice, this ratio is usually calculated before interest and taxes. It indicates how well management has used the assets available to it. In using this ratio, the auditor needs to examine the underlying factors to explain the level of the rate of return compared to other entities and movements in the rate from previous periods.

Return on shareholders' equity

The **return on shareholders' equity ratio** is calculated as follows:

$$\text{Return on shareholders' equity} = \frac{\text{Net profit}}{\text{Ordinary shareholders' equity}}$$

This ratio is similar to the return on total assets ratio except that it shows only the return on the resources contributed by the shareholders. Thus, it is calculated after interest and taxes.

Solvency ratios

Solvency ratios provide information on the long-term solvency of the entity. These ratios give the auditor important information on the ability of the entity to continue as a going concern.

Debt to equity

The **debt to equity ratio** is calculated as follows:

$$\text{Debt to equity} = \frac{\text{Short-term} + \text{Long-term debt}}{\text{Shareholders' equity}}$$

This ratio indicates what portion of the entity's capital comes from debt. The lower the ratio, the less debt pressure on the entity. If the entity's debt to equity ratio is large relative to the industry's, it may indicate that the entity is too highly leveraged and may not be able to meet its debt obligations, including debt servicing costs, on a long-term basis.

Times interest earned

The **times interest earned ratio** is calculated as follows:

$$\text{Times interest earned} = \frac{\text{Net profit}}{\text{Interest expense}}$$

The times interest earned ratio indicates the ability of current operations to pay the interest that is due on the entity's debt obligations. The more times that interest is earned, the better the entity's ability to service the interest on long-term debt.

Common-size statements

Common-size statements express balance sheet components as a percentage of total assets and income statement items as a percentage of total revenue. An example of a common-size income statement is shown in Example 6.4 overleaf. This technique can either be undertaken on a cross-sectional basis (for example, comparing the entity to competitors or the industry) or on a time series basis allowing the auditor to concentrate on changes in percentages over time. It is a technique which is particularly relevant for the evaluation of profit and loss accounts where variable expenses will have some relationship to total sales.

EXAMPLE 6.4 A common-size statement

Common-size Income Statement for Ace Manufacturers Ltd for the 3 years 20X1 to 20X3

	20X1	20X2	20X3
Sales	100	100	100
Less Cost of Goods Sold	60	58	60
Gross Profit	40	42	40
Less Expenses			
Operating	10	10	16
Administration	5	5	8
Net Profit	25	27	16

This common-size statement shows the increase in operating and administration expenses that may not be so obvious from the raw figures.

Trend statements

Trends may be disclosed by comparison of account balances by month, within the year and between years, and by year with those of previous years. **Trend statements** are similar to common-size statements in that all numbers are expressed as a percentage of a base. However, each number in a trend statement is expressed as a percentage of its own level calculated from some base year. The focus is on the trend rather than the absolute magnitude of dollar changes. The trend statements would be evaluated by the auditor based on their knowledge of the business as to whether past trends are expected to continue or change. An example of a trend statement is shown in Example 6.5.

EXAMPLE 6.5 A trend statement

Income Statement Trend Statement for Ace Manufacturers Ltd for the 3 year period 20X1 to 20X3

	20X1	20X2	20X3
Sales	100	120	250
Less Cost of Goods Sold	100	116	250
Gross Profit	100	125	250
Less Expenses			
Operating	100	120	400
Administration	100	100	400
Net Profit	100	128	160

This trend statement shows that net profit is up 28% in 20X2 and 60% for 2 years to 20X3. It also shows that operating and administration expenses are increasing at a much faster rate than sales or cost of goods sold. This may not have been as easy to observe with other analytical procedures.

Time series analysis and modelling

Simple **time series analysis** is a predictive technique involving the extrapolation of past values of an item of financial information into the current audit period. For example, the past values of sales are examined to identify some trend which can be used to predict the level of the current audit balances. This prediction is compared with the client's records and unexpected fluctuations are further examined. Simple time series analysis can be accomplished through a graphical approach. The aim of more complex **time series models** is to forecast what the current level of various financial report items should be, based on the pattern of past amounts of different variables. In their simplest or univariate form, these models provide forecasts based solely on the past history of the variable of interest. When additional independent variables are added to the model (multivariate form), the methodology generates forecasts based on past observations of both the variable of interest and the related independent variables. This technique is facilitated by the use of computer programs and can consider a wide range of models while searching for an appropriate model for a particular set of data.

Regression analysis

Regression analysis estimates the relationship between a dependent variable (for example, sales) and one or more independent variables (for example, cost of sales or shipping costs). Values of the independent variable(s) are used to predict the dependent variable value. Regression analysis can be applied on a time series or a cross-sectional basis and provides a line of best fit for the data points.

The advantages of regression analysis are that it provides an objective quantification in statistical terms of the probability that an account is misstated by a material amount, it provides more precise evidence than simpler techniques because it incorporates more factors and builds more complex relationships, and, as a result, it allows the auditor to reduce the level of tests of details work. The major limitations of regression analysis are the high training costs, the unavailability of sufficient data over a short time to establish a stable plausible relationship and the fact that if the assumptions of regression analysis are violated the model cannot be relied upon to produce statistically valid inferences about the entity's recorded values.

Financial modelling

Financial modelling involves the identification of a key input variable from which values of other accounts can be calculated. For example, using sales as the key variable, other accounts such as cost of goods sold, inventory, accounts receivable, selling costs and administration costs can be determined. On the basis of these values, an estimate of funds and profit from operations can be obtained, and along with the provision of other financial and investment information a pro-forma financial report can be calculated. Significant deviations of this report from management's financial report can be highlighted to provide the basis for further investigations, while if the two sets of reports generally agree the auditor will have increased confidence in the overall reasonableness of the financial report.

The main advantage of financial models is that they provide a complete financial report, while other analytical procedures focus on one relationship at a time and rely on auditor judgment to aggregate across tests to arrive at a conclusion on the overall reasonableness of the financial report. However, this technique can be very costly and does not have the advantages of regression analysis of providing statistical measures of reliability.

Data used in analytical procedures

In planning analytical procedures, the auditor must consider whether the data needed are easily available and thus the time needed to gather the particular information. Other audit procedures may be more effective for the same effort.

The auditor must also consider the reliability of the data used in the analytical procedures. More reliable primary data results in analytical procedures providing more effective audit evidence. Factors influencing the reliability of data used in analytical procedures include the following:

- Data from an independent source outside the entity are generally more reliable than internal data.
- Data from a system with effective internal controls are more reliable than data from a poorly controlled system.
- Data audited in the previous year or in the current audit are more reliable than unaudited data. (Remember that unaudited data are used at the planning stage, while audited data are used at the completion stage, to achieve the different objectives of those stages.)
- Data from a variety of sources that corroborate each other are more reliable than data from only one source.
- Data from the department within the entity that is responsible for the amount being audited are generally less reliable than data from another department.

The auditor also considers the plausibility, predictability and precision of the analytical relationship. For example:

- Relationships in a stable environment are more predictable than relationships in a dynamic, changing environment.
- Direct relationships are more predictable than indirect relationships. For example, the auditor's prediction of annual rental income (12 times the monthly rent per lease) is more predictable than selling and administrative expenses as a ratio of sales volume.
- Disaggregated relationships are more precise and show clearer relationships than combined or aggregated relationships. For example, comparisons by line of business are generally more effective than company-wide comparisons, and monthly comparisons are generally more effective than annual comparisons.
- Relationships involving income statement amounts (transactions over a period of time) tend to be more predictable than relationships involving only balance sheet accounts (amounts at a point in time).
- Relationships involving transactions that are subject to management discretion are less predictable than transitions independent of management discretion.

Examination of significant fluctuations

The auditor must decide which fluctuations are significant and thus warrant investigation. The auditor must also be alert to the possibility that the absence of expected fluctuations may also need to be investigated. Each significant fluctuation (or the lack of an expected fluctuation) must be investigated to determine the reason for it.

The auditor's first step in investigating significant fluctuations should be to discuss them with the client's management. Management may already be aware of the fluctuations and have determined their causes or be able to provide an explanation for them. However, the auditor needs to consider whether the explanations received are reasonable in light of the auditor's knowledge of the business and industry and the information obtained through other audit procedures. Explanations provided by management should not be accepted at face value. While the explanations may corroborate what the auditor already expects, they cannot be relied on without further checking unless they are supported by conclusions already arrived at as a result of other audit procedures.

Thus, the audit working papers must show:

- identification of significant fluctuations;
- explanations provided by management; and
- the results of work done to corroborate explanations received.

EXAMPLE 6.6   Analytical procedures

You are the auditor of Charles Company, a large hardware retailer operating with stores throughout the country. As part of the planning stage of the audit you have performed analytical procedures with the following results:

	Actual results	Budgeted results	Previous year	Industry average
Inventory turnover ratio	4.35	5.00	4.70	4.66
Current ratio	1.80	1.70	1.51	1.66
Quick asset ratio	1.10	1.10	1.10	1.20
Debt to equity ratio	0.60	0.55	0.62	0.58
Number of times interest earned ratio	8.50	7.20	6.80	5.00

Analysis of ratios and audit implications
- The decrease in the inventory turnover ratio indicates an increased audit risk that inventory is overstated due to the presence of obsolete stock. Suggests additional audit testing should be undertaken for the inventory valuation and allocation assertion.
- The increase in the current ratio is likely to be due to the increase in inventory, as indicated by the inventory turnover ratio.
- This is further supported by the fact that the quick asset ratio has not changed, also indicating that the increase in current ratio could be due to an increase in inventory levels.
- The liquidity position of a company is important in ensuring that the going concern basis of accounting is appropriate. Charles Company's ratios do not indicate any problem in this area, as the quick asset ratio is above the normal benchmark of 1:1.
- The debt to equity ratio indicates that the gearing level of Charles Company, although relatively high, is consistent with that of the industry average and thus does not significantly increase audit risk.
- The number of times interest earned considers the ability of the company to meet its interest commitments as they fall due. This rise in the ratio indicates reduced audit risk concerning the ability of the company to meet its interest commitments. This may be due to falling interest rates, good profitability or understatement of interest expense. This ratio needs to be investigated further to determine what has actually caused the change.

Cash flow analysis

Most analytical procedures such as ratio analysis are based on accrual accounting numbers. However, an entity must also generate positive cash flow over a reasonable period of time or it will not be able to pay its debts or satisfy its investors. The importance of cash flows is indicated by the fact that the *Corporations Act* requires companies to prepare a statement of cash flows as part of their annual financial report. There are three components of cash flow: cash from operations, cash from investing activities and cash from financing activities. Cash from operations refers to the net cash flows generated from the day-to-day activities of the company such as producing and selling inventory. Cash from investing activities reflects the purchase (and sale) of long-lived assets such as plant assets and market investments. Cash from financing reflects the sources of financing (debt, equity) and payments to investors and lenders.

Over an extended period, an entity needs to generate a positive cash flow if it is to survive. The cash flow profile of an entity will generally follow a predictable pattern based on its life cycle. In the early growth stages, most entities will have a negative cash flow from operations, significant cash inflows from financing, and outflows for investments. In a mature, stable period, the entity should have a relatively balanced cash flow from all three sources, with any new financing activity being used mainly to fund replacement of productive assets. In the decline stage, cash flow from operations may still be positive (but reduced), investing activity will slow down and possibly create a positive cash flow as productive assets are sold, and cash will flow out to investors and creditors as the entity winds down its operations.

Quick review

1. Analytical procedures are required at the planning stage of the audit to assist in understanding the business and identifying area of potential risk.

2. Simple analytical procedures include simple comparisons, ratio analysis, common-size statements, trend statements and time series analysis.

3. Complex analytical procedures include time series modelling, regression analysis and financial modelling.

4. When planning the use of analytical procedures the auditor considers the availability and reliability of data, and the plausibility, predictability and precision of the analytical relationship.

5. Significant fluctuations must be investigated.

Summary

Before accepting an engagement, an auditor needs to determine that it can be completed in accordance with Australian auditing standards and professional ethics. Important steps in accepting the audit engagement include gaining ethical clearance from any previous auditor, evaluating management's integrity, identifying unusual risks or circumstances, evaluating the auditor's independence and determining whether the auditor has the required skills and competence. An engagement letter should be issued to confirm the terms of the engagement.

Appropriate planning is essential for the audit to be completed in an efficient and effective manner. Proper planning includes obtaining an understanding of the entity; assessing client business risk; completing analytical procedures to identify potential audit risk areas; determining responses to assessed risks; and developing audit strategies to obtain sufficient appropriate audit evidence for significant financial report assertions. An audit program will then be developed to reflect that strategy and audit staff will be scheduled accordingly.

Key terms

References

Bell, T.B., Marrs, F.O., Solomon, I. and Thomas, H. (1997) *Auditing Organisations Through a Strategic-Lens: The KPMG Business Measurement Process*, KPMG, New York.

Biggs, S.F., Mock, T.J. and Simnett, R. (1999) 'Analytical procedures: Promise, problems and implications for practice', *Australian Accounting Review*, Vol. 9, No. 1, 42–52.

Booth, P. and Simnett, R. (1991) 'Auditors' perceptions of analytical review procedures', *Accounting Research Journal*, Spring, 5–12.

Carey, P., Clarke, B. and Smyrnios, K.X. (1996) 'The audit engagement letter: Use, content and effectiveness', *Australian Accounting Review*, September, 64–71.

Harper, R.M., Strawser, J.R. and Tang, K. (1990) 'Establishing investigation thresholds for preliminary analytical procedures', *Auditing: A Journal of Practice and Theory*, Fall, 115–33.

IFAC (2001) 'IAASB Addresses Audit Risk and the Future of Auditing' IFAC, New York.

Johnson, G. and Scholes, K. (1999) *Exploring Corporate Strategy*, 5th edn, Prentice-Hall, London.

Kaplan, R.S. and Norton, D.P. (1992) 'The balanced scorecard: Measures that drive performance', *Harvard Business Review*, January–February, 71–9.

Kinney, W.R. Jr (1987) 'Attention-directing analytical review using accounting ratios: A case study', *Auditing: A Journal of Practice and Theory*, Spring, 59–73.

Lemon, W.M., Tatum, K.W. and Turley, W.S. (2000) *Developments in the Audit Methodologies of Large Accounting Firms*, ABG Professional Information, London.

Porter, M.E. (1985) *Competitive Advantage: Creating and Sustaining Superior Performance*, The Free Press, New York.

Schultz, A.K.-D. and Booth, P. (1995) 'The effects of presentation format on the effectiveness and efficiency of auditors' analytical review judgments', *Accounting and Finance*, May, 107–31.

Smith, G., Psaros, J. and Holmes, S. (1999) 'A research note on the use and perceived usefulness of analytical procedures by Australian auditors', *Australian Accounting Review*, Vol. 9, No. 2, 64–72.

Thompson, A.A. Jr and Strickland, A.J. III (1998) *Strategic Management: Concepts and Cases*, 10th edn, Irwin/McGraw-Hill, Boston.

Trotman, K. (1990) Analytical Review, Audit Monograph 1, AARF.

Assignments

Additional assignments for this chapter are contained in Appendix A of this book, page 766.

REVIEW QUESTIONS

6.1 The following questions relate to client acceptance and communication with a predecessor auditor. Select the *best* response.
   (a) What is the responsibility of an auditor with respect to communicating with the previous auditor in connection with a prospective new audit client?
      A The auditor should contact the previous auditor regardless of whether the prospective client authorises contact.
      B The auditor has no responsibility to contact the previous auditor.
      C The auditor should obtain permission from the prospective client to contact the previous auditor.

MaxMARK

MAXIMISE YOUR MARKS! There are approximately 30 interactive questions on planning, knowledge of the business and evaluating strategic business risk available online at www.mhhe.com/au/gay3e

D The auditor need not contact the previous auditor if the successor is aware of all available facts.

(b) A prospective client's refusal to give permission to communicate with the previous auditor and review certain portions of the previous auditor's working papers will bear directly on the auditor's decision concerning the:

    A apparent scope limitation

    B ability to establish consistency in application of accounting principles between years

    C adequacy of the planned audit program

    ✓**D** integrity of management

(c) An auditor's inquiries of the previous auditor prior to acceptance should cover the previous auditor's:

    A opinion of any events occurring since the previous audit report was issued

    B evaluation of all matters of continuing accounting significance

    C awareness of the consistency in the application of accounting principles between periods

    D understanding as to the reasons for the change of auditors

(d) The understanding between the client and the auditor as to the responsibilities to be assumed by each are normally set forth in:

    A a management letter

    ✓**B** an engagement letter

    C a representation letter

    D a comfort letter

6.2 The following questions concern knowledge of the business. Select the *best* response.

(a) An auditor obtains knowledge about a new client's business and its industry to:

    A understand the events and transactions that may have an effect on the client's financial report

    B make constructive suggestions concerning improvements in the client's internal control

    C develop an attitude of professional scepticism concerning management's financial report assertions

    D evaluate whether the aggregation of known misstatements causes the financial report taken as whole to be materially misstated

(b) Prior to beginning the work on a new audit engagement when the auditor does not possess expertise in the industry in which the client operates, the auditor should:

    A obtain a knowledge of matters that relate to the nature of the entity's business

    B reduce audit risk by lowering the preliminary levels of materiality

    C design special substantive tests to compensate for the lack of industry expertise

    D engage financial experts familiar with the industry

(c) Which of the following events most likely indicates the existence of related parties?

    A Making a loan without scheduled terms for repayment of the funds

    B Selling real estate at a price that differs significantly from its book value

    C Borrowing a large sum of money at a variable rate of interest

    D Discussing merger terms with a company that is a major competitor

(d) An auditor searching for related-party transactions should obtain an understanding of each subsidiary's relationship to the total entity because:

    A this might reveal whether particular transactions would have taken place if the parties had not been related

    B intercompany transactions may have been consummated on terms equivalent to arm's length transactions

    C   this might permit the audit of intercompany account balances to be performed as of concurrent dates

    D   the business structure may be deliberately designed to obscure related-party transactions

6.3   The following questions relate to the use of analytical procedures in general planning. Select the *best* response.

    (a)   Analytical procedures may be classified as being primarily:

        A   detailed tests of balances

        B   tests of control

        C   substantive tests

        D   tests of ratios

    (b)   Analytical procedures used in planning an audit should focus on identifying:

        A   the various assertions that are embodied in the financial report

        B   the predictability of financial data from individual transactions

        C   material weaknesses in internal control

        D   areas that may represent specific risk relevant to the audit

    (c)   Which of the following is not a typical analytical procedure?

        A   Comparison of recorded amounts of major disbursements with budgeted amounts

        B   Study of relationships between financial and relevant nonfinancial information

        C   Comparison of financial information with similar information regarding the industry in which the entity operates

        D   Comparison of recorded amounts of major disbursements with appropriate invoices

    (d)   An example of an analytical procedure is the comparison of:

        A   results of a statistical sample with the expected characteristics of the actual population

        B   recorded amounts of major disbursements with appropriate invoices

        C   financial information with similar information regarding the industry in which the entity operates

        D   computer-generated data with similar data generated by a manual accounting system

    (e)   Which result of an analytical procedure suggests the existence of obsolete inventory?

        A   Decrease in the ratio of inventory to accounts receivable

        B   Decrease in the inventory turnover rate

        C   Decrease in the ratio of gross profit to sales

        D   Decrease in the ratio of inventory to accounts payable

    (f)   Auditors sometimes use comparison of ratios as audit evidence. For example, an unexplained decrease in the ratio of gross profit to sales may suggest which of the following possibilities?

        A   Merchandise purchases charged to selling and general expense

        B   Unrecorded sales

        C   Unrecorded purchases

        D   Fictitious sales

    (g)   Significant unexpected differences identified by analytical procedures will usually necessitate:

        A   an explanation in the representation letter

        B   a review of internal control

        C   addition of an 'emphasis of matter' paragraph to the audit report

        D   investigation by the auditor

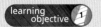

Client acceptance

6.4 Why should an audit firm adopt policies and procedures for client acceptance and continuance?

Engagement letters

6.5 Why are engagement letters used, and what subjects do they usually cover?

Planning

6.6 What are the important planning decisions made near the start of an audit engagement?

Audit program

6.7 Why is it important to develop an audit program?

Scheduling audit staff

6.8 What are three important aspects of establishing and co-ordinating the staffing requirements for an audit?

Knowledge of the client's business

6.9 What audit procedures does an auditor use to obtain knowledge of a client's business?

6.10 Why does an auditor need to understand the client's business?

Assessing business risk

6.11 Why is an assessment of client business risk important to obtaining an understanding of the business?

6.12 What are SWOT analysis, the value-chain approach and PEST analysis? How are they useful in assessing business risk?

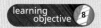

Analytical procedures

6.13 State three uses of analytical procedures in an audit and indicate which are required on all audits.

DISCUSSION PROBLEMS AND CASE STUDIES

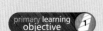

Client acceptance

6.14 **Basic** You have been successful in a recent tender for a publicly listed cement manufacturing company. The tendering process was very aggressive and the previous auditors have so far not allowed you access to their working papers for last year. The previous year's audit report gave an unqualified opinion.

Required
(a) Outline the legal and other considerations that need to be considered by the new auditor and the previous auditor.
(b) What impact, if any, will the refusal of the previous auditor to allow access to their working papers for last year have on the planning and completion of the current year's audit?

6.15 **Basic** When an auditor has accepted an engagement from a new client who is a manufacturer, it is customary for the auditor to tour the client's plant. Discuss the ways in which the auditor's observations made during the course of the plant tour would be of help in planning and conducting the audit.

Source: AICPA adapted

6.16 **Moderate** The audit firm of Glitsos & Co. has been approached by the following potential clients:

    1 Columbus Entertainment Pty Ltd, which recently made news in the financial press when its board of directors reinstated the chief executive officer who had misappropriated cheques totalling $15 000 (an amount that was immaterial to Columbus and the CEO's annual salary). The board said the CEO was essential to operations and that his theft was the result of mental problems rather than a sign of dishonesty.

2   Harridan Press Enterprises Pty Ltd, which publishes a magazine for women that features explicit male nudes and operates clubs around the country that feature male go-go dancers.

3   Lansker Ltd, which operates vending machines in several states and has a part interest in a casino.

Required

(a)   What procedures would Glitsos & Co. use to investigate these three potential clients? Would any unusual procedures be applicable to any of the three?

(b)   Explain the considerations of Glitsos & Co. in deciding whether to accept any of the three companies.

Engagement letters

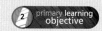

6.17 **Basic** At the planning meeting for the audit of X Ltd, the audit partner presented the managing director with an engagement letter and asked that she sign the letter as acknowledgment of the terms of the engagement. The managing director had not seen an engagement letter before and indicated that there was no need for such a letter, as she understood the auditor's duties perfectly.

Required

Should the audit partner insist that the engagement letter be signed? Why or why not?

Audit planning and audit strategy

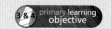

6.18 **Basic** Sue Yang has been assigned to the audit of a new client: C Pty Ltd. C is a small company operating in the consumer electronics industry. As part of her responsibilities Sue has been asked to prepare an overall plan for the audit. Having only participated in the planning process before, Sue is unsure exactly what this will involve and has asked you to explain to her the steps she will need to undertake in order to develop the audit plan.

Required

Provide Sue with a brief description of each of the steps she should undertake in order to plan for the audit.

6.19 **Complex** Your client is Noysee Limited, a listed company that manufactures a wide range of products used in the building industry. One range of products is manufactured in Indonesia for sale in South-East Asian markets, while another range is manufactured in Australia for Australian and New Zealand markets.

You are completing the planning phase of the audit for the year ending 30 June 20X2 and have the following information (consider each situation independently).

1   In the past few months, there has been increasing civil unrest in Indonesia. At present, the accounting records at the Indonesian branch office appear to be intact. However, your Indonesian branch office has received reliable advice that at least half the stock has been burnt in a fire. The fire was caused by rioting and therefore is not covered by insurance.

2   Rainaway roof tiles, sold mostly to large Australian building companies, comprise around 2% of total revenues. Over the last couple of months, several reports have been received that the tiles are disintegrating in heavy rain, causing leakage and property damage.

3   In accordance with current business practice, the board has approved a new management compensation scheme. In future, the entire senior management team

(comprising 40 people and including the Finance Director) will receive a bonus based on the increase in Noysee Limited's net profit from year to year.

4. Noysee Limited is having difficulty keeping track of payables invoices received by the Indonesian branch. Some go missing, while others have been paid twice. The problems appear to have stemmed from the loss of two of Noysee Limited's most experienced accounts payable staff, who have not yet been replaced.

5. Management has recently introduced a new, state-of-the-art fixed assets register. Fixed assets are now bar coded, scanned and classified, with depreciation calculated automatically based on asset class. A big advantage of the new register is the variety of detailed reports it can produce, for example: depreciation by asset class, additions for the year, and profit on disposal.

6. Your audit approach for payroll expense places substantial reliance on internal controls and analytical procedures. Preliminary walkthrough tests indicate that internal controls over payroll have broken down over the last few months, coinciding with changes in the payroll system.

7. Last year, Noysee Limited received negative comments from debtors regarding the confirmation letters they were sent. As a result, Noysee Limited's credit controller has asked that you do not send confirmation letters to debtors this year. She has offered you every possible assistance in verifying debtors by other means. You note that last year 70% of debtors who received a confirmation letter responded.

8. An IT manager was appointed this year. She mentions in passing that one of her priorities is drafting and implementing Noysee Limited's first disaster recovery plan. She also notes that regular backups have only been made since she was appointed a couple of months ago.

Required

Draft a work paper for review by the audit manager, explaining how each of your allocated situations will affect the audit plan.

Source: This question was adapted from the CA Program of The Institute of Chartered Accountants in Australia—2002 Financial Reporting and Assurance Module.

6.20 Complex Forestcrest Limited is a closely held company that has existed since 1920. The company manufactures high-quality woollen cloth for men's and women's outerwear. Your firm has audited Forestcrest Limited for 15 years.

Five years ago, Forestcrest Limited signed a settlement with the Environmental Protection Agency. The company had been convicted of dumping pollutants (such as bleaching and dyeing chemicals) into the local river. The agreement provided that Forestcrest Limited construct a water treatment facility within eight years.

You are conducting the current-year audit, and you notice that there has been virtually no activity in the water treatment facility construction account. Your discussion with the financial controller produces the following comment: 'Because of increased competition and lower sales volume, our cash flow has decreased below normal levels. You had better talk to the CEO about the treatment facility.'

The CEO (and majority shareholder) tells you the following: 'Given the current cash flow levels, we had two choices: lay off people or stop work on the facility. This is a poor rural area with few other job opportunities for our people. I decided to stop work on the water treatment facility. I don't think that the state will fine us or close us down.' When you ask the CEO if the company will be able to comply with the agreement, he informs you that he is uncertain.

Required

(a) Discuss the implications of this situation for the audit.

(b) Would your answer change if these events occurred in the seventh year after the signing of the agreement?

6.21 Complex Consider the following independent situations, all of which apply to audits of entities for the year ending 31 December 20X2:

1   Domane Limited, a listed company, has been experiencing declining sales over the last two years. Cost cutting has proved difficult due to the high level of imported machinery used in Domane Limited's operations and, consequently, margins have been falling. While the bankers are presently happy to continue providing Domane Limited with loan facilities, they do expect to see improved results in the next financial report. Articles about Domane Limited's expected financial results appearing in recent press reports all had quite a pessimistic tone.

2   Cheepa Limited is a large supermarket chain with offices in all capital cities around Australia. Until 31 December 20X1, data processing relating to payroll was performed at Cheepa Limited's centralised processing bureau in Adelaide. However, as from 1 January 20X2, processing of payroll transactions has been carried out centrally by an independent computer service bureau based in Melbourne.

3   Salt Pty Limited is an established firm which has been operating a boutique hotel in the Blue Mountains for over 20 years. During this time, it has adopted a conservative business strategy that has seen it produce adequate, though slightly unimpressive, results. A new CEO has been appointed to run the firm from 1 June 20X2. He has already released his plans for renovating the hotel, despite not officially serving as CEO yet. You have also heard him discuss the implementation of a new marketing strategy to boost occupancy rates.

4   Barbar Pty Limited is a small primary producer specialising in the production of angora wool. Barbar Pty Limited's recent display at a trade show has seen orders flood in from overseas buyers. The accountant, Mike, has done his best to satisfy the orders as quickly as possible while maintaining the appropriate (foreign currency) accounting records. He has just hired Val, a CA with several years' relevant experience, to take over the responsibility for foreign currency.

Required

For each of the independent situations 1) to 4):

(a)   Describe the overall impact on audit risk.

(b)   Predict the impact on your overall audit plan.

Source: This question was adapted from the CA Program of The Institute of Chartered Accountants in Australia—2002 Financial Reporting and Assurance Module.

Scheduling audit staff

6.22 Basic You are meeting with executives of Coral Cosmetics Pty Ltd to arrange your firm's engagement to examine the financial report for the year ended 31 December 20X0. In order to minimise audit time, avoid duplication of staff effort and curtail interference with company operations, one executive has suggested that the audit work be divided among three audit staff members. One person would examine asset accounts, a second would examine liability accounts and the third would examine revenue and expense accounts.

Required

(a)   To what extent should an auditor follow a client's suggestions for the conduct of an audit? Discuss.

(b)   List and discuss the reasons why audit work should not be assigned solely according to asset, liability and revenue and expense categories.

Source: AICPA adapted

Knowledge of the client's business

6.23 Complex You are the audit manager responsible for the audit of ABC Limited. ABC operates in the mining industry and was first listed in 20X0. Your firm has performed the audit since listing.

You have the following additional information:

1 Since listing, the company has changed the focus of its business activities from underground mining to open-cut mining, which it believes is a cheaper option. It also has a side interest in property investment.

2 The company finances most of its developments by borrowing against the value of its existing assets and mining infrastructure, which include a large holding of investment properties.

3 The company currently has four major projects in progress (P1, P2, P3 and P4).

4 P1 involves the development of a resort-style hotel on the north coast of New South Wales. Although council approval for the project was granted, the company is unable to proceed with the work owing to pressures from environmental lobbyists. Apart from the negative publicity involved, the company has also borne additional financing costs, as loan repayments must be made regardless of the delay in development.

5 P2 is a joint venture between ABC and an overseas company. It involves a mining operation in the far west of New South Wales. ABC owns the land and has contributed this to the joint venture project. The overseas company is providing the funding for the development. The joint venture was proceeding smoothly until last month, when the discovery of previously unknown Aboriginal sacred sites put the whole development into doubt. In addition, solicitors have advised that the foreign company's interest in the project may exceed that permitted under foreign ownership laws.

6 P3 and P4 involve exploration of new coal seams in Western Australia. The market for black coal has been quite volatile, but ABC feels that both projects are commercially viable.

7 ABC's major competitors are DEF Limited and GHI Limited. In addition, an aggressive new foreign competitor has emerged. In some cases the foreign competitor has undercut the price of black coal in ABC's Japanese market by 25%. In order to maintain good relationships with customers ABC has been forced to offer extended credit terms and some discounts for timely payment.

8 As in previous years, your firm has been engaged to perform the annual statutory audit, with the audit report due to be signed by 30 April 20X4. The audit fee is $105 000. Last year, the firm's computer audit division was engaged by ABC to oversee installation of the new inventory work-in-progress system. They are still performing routine monthly checks of the system's output.

Required

Assume that for planning purposes you need to investigate further the following:

• the company's competitors;
• the company's credit policy;
• the legal position surrounding developments involving Aboriginal sacred sites;
• the viability of the coal mining operations in Western Australia.

Identify the type of information you need and potential sources of that information in order to conduct your investigations.

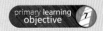

Assessing business risk

6.24 Complex Julie and her husband Darren founded WS Pty Limited a little over 12 months ago and have watched their company grow nearly exponentially since its humble beginnings. WS produces a home page authoring tool for use by children on the worldwide web (the Internet), titled W4K.

W4K is a highly graphical, easy to use, drag-and-drop style program that allows children between five and ten years of age to design their own worldwide web home pages. It was the result of a rainy Saturday afternoon when the couple's five-year-old son wandered up to his parents' computer, looked at the pretty graphics of someone else's home page, and screamed 'I want'. Julie and Darren, who met while studying computer science at university, began programming that afternoon. On 5 August 20X0 the first version of W4K was released for sale on the Internet.

Since that date W4K has sold nearly 250 000 copies at a retail price of $25. The program is marketed, distributed, sold and supported over the Internet. The original version has been subsequently updated over several releases and now contains a sophisticated 'waterpainting' and drawing section (which has proved highly popular according to parental feedback) as well as an inventory of nearly 1000 images which were scanned into computer-readable format from the family's slide collection.

Within the computing industry the software is known as 'shareware'. This means that anybody using the Internet can download a copy of the software from WS's home page and can evaluate it for 14 days. After the evaluation period expires, the software must be registered in order to continue using the program. To register, buyers simply fill in a secure form on the WS Internet site, leaving their personal and credit card details. WS processes these forms daily and sends an electronic mail message back to purchasers with their registration number once the credit card details have been verified.

From the electronic mailing list compiled from their database of customers and inquiries, WS has discovered that almost 45 per cent of customers are located in North America, 20 per cent in the UK and 15 per cent in the Pacific (including Australia and New Zealand). The remainder are spread throughout the rest of the English-speaking world (the software is available only as an English-language version).

The product has received glowing reviews in computer magazines worldwide and is recognised in the Internet community as being the best product in its category. WS's home page even boasts that some of the world's largest software companies have bought copies of the program from their Internet site.

WS has grown in 12 months from a two-person company to one that now employs nearly 30 people in its Sydney offices. These comprise mostly computer programmers, but also include a number of accounts staff to process the flood of purchases received daily. By employing additional programmers, Julie and Darren have been able to take a break from the operational issues of the business and are contemplating launching a new product to try to capitalise on WS's good reputation. Specifically, they plan to develop and release an adult version of the authoring tool titled W4BK which, at this point, they anticipate will also sell for $25.

Required

Conduct a SWOT analysis on WS to evaluate business risk.

Source: This question was adapted from the Professional Year Programme of The Institute of Chartered Accountants in Australia—1996 Accounting 2 Module.

6.25 Complex The following is based on an article from *The Sydney Morning Herald* which relates to the value chain of printers.

Printers team up to press home digital advantage

A group of eight small companies has set up a digital printing network which enables each member to do business around the country via the Internet. The eight have all adopted the same digital technology so that one member can bid for a national printing contract and then print the documents using the other members' facilities.

For example, rather than printing in Sydney and then physically transporting the hard copies of documents to Melbourne and Brisbane, a member of the Electric Printer Network

(EPN) can send electronic files around the country via the Internet and then print where they are needed, saving time and money.

Mr G, founder of EPN, says that lead times can be reduced from one or two weeks to as little as a day. 'With digital printing, instead of printing 100 000 documents and then distributing from one location to another, you distribute electronically and print where and when you want,' he says.

'Digital printing on demand also means there is no need for costly document warehousing or the risk of thousands of prospectuses becoming redundant because small changes need to be made to the information.' Mr G says the network gives the small companies the opportunity to compete against major new players, such as KK's which opened its first Australian store in Sydney 6 months ago. The big US-based printing and office support firm is planning to open up to 100 stores around Australia in the next 5 years. 'Fifteen years ago owning a printing company was a license to print money but now you've got to be very adept to stay in business. There is a lot of technological change happening in the industry and you have to invest huge amounts of money to keep up,' Mr G says.

EPN is also linked to the International Printers Network, so Australian member firms can have jobs printed overseas. The international network was set up $2\frac{1}{2}$ years ago, and now has members with compatible digital printing technology in Europe, Asia and North America.

'Printing has gone from being a craft to becoming part of the information technology industry,' Mr G says. 'Print runs are becoming shorter and people are personalising documents more—and you need digital technology to do that sort of target marketing.'

EPN came together after $2\frac{1}{2}$ years of negotiations. Mr G says it was difficult convincing each of the companies to buy the necessary $500 000 digital printing machines. The biggest problem was getting an understanding and acceptance of the concept among the members. 'It was not easy to convince everyone to get the compatibility in equipment and in mindset, but eventually everyone realised we could beat each other up or get together.'

The eight printers in the network all use the same digital printing technology. That means a client of one firm can be guaranteed the same quality when members in other cities print its documents. 'It makes both environmental and economic sense to distribute electronic files and print where needed, rather than print and then distribute. We also save on export costs by electronic distribution to overseas counterparts who then print locally as required.'

Digital printing accounts for about 20 per cent of printing in Australia but is growing faster than traditional offset printing. 'All printing will be digital within 5 years,' Mr G says. 'A lot of printers are very frightened of the technology because it's so new, so expensive, and because it's changing the way the industry works.'

Required

(a) Outline how the value chain has changed for the members of the EPN network. In particular, what activities are different?

(b) How is value provided to the customer using the EPN network?

(c) How might the strategy of a member of the EPN network change as a result of the network, what new management issues will each member need to address as a result and what will be the impact on the audit?

Source: This question was adapted from the Professional Year Programme of The Institute of Chartered Accountants in Australia—1999 Accounting 2 Module.

6.26 **Complex** Undertake a PEST analysis for a major international airline. In order to facilitate this analysis you may wish to review the most recent financial report on the web site of Qantas <http://www.qantas.com.au>.

Analytical procedures

6.27 Moderate You are the auditor of DSX Company, a large retailer operating stores throughout the country. DSX Company appointed you as auditor in the current year after an analysis you performed for it. As part of the planning stage of the audit, your analytical review procedures have found the following information:

	Actual results	Budgeted results	Previous year	Industry average
Net profit ratio	0.031	0.0271	0.0266	0.0253
Number of times interest earned ratio	5.50	5.20	4.80	5.00
Return on total assets	0.075	0.07	0.066	0.061
Days in inventory	83.89	75.00	76.50	78.40
Gross margin	0.52	0.47	0.49	0.49
Current ratio	1.61	1.70	1.51	1.66
Quick asset ratio	1.10	1.10	1.10	1.20
Equity ratio (debt to equity)	0.47	0.55	0.52	0.48
Inventory turnover	4.35	5.00	4.78	4.66

Required
(a) Why are analytical procedures performed at the planning stage of the audit?
(b) What are the implications to your audit of the ratios calculated above?
(c) What are the limitations of comparing current data to:
   (i)   budgeted data?
   (ii) industry averages?
   (iii) prior periods?

Source: This question was adapted from the Professional Year Programme of The Institute of Chartered Accountants in Australia—1995 Accounting 2 Module.

6.28 Moderate You are the audit senior on the audit of EasyFit Pty Ltd, a large manufacturer of shoes, whose main market lies in the 18–24 age group.

This is the first year your firm has performed the audit. As part of the planning work, you have performed analytical procedures on an annualised basis and compared the results to industry averages and last year's audited financial information. The results are given below:

Ratio	Industry Average 2001	Industry Average 2000	EasyFit Pty Ltd 2001	EasyFit Pty Ltd 2000
1 Current ratio	2.84	3.27	1.89	2.24
2 Receivables turnover ratio	4.9	4.6	6.3	7.0
3 Inventory turnover ratio	3.7	3.8	5.0	5.5
4 Return on total assets	7%	5%	13%	11%
5 Net profit ratio	0.06	0.06	0.04	0.04
6 Gross margin	0.20	0.26	0.20	0.18

Required
Explain the general meaning of each of the above ratios, discuss the conclusions that you can draw about EasyFit Pty Ltd's financial position and identify potential audit risks to be investigated further.

6.29 Complex Read the following case.

'We had a fairly good year,' said the managing director of Mitchell Pty Ltd. 'Sales exceeded $2 000 000 for the first time in our history, though net profit didn't keep pace with the sales increase because of higher labour costs.'

Mitchell Pty Ltd is a manufacturing company; its factory and most of its sales branches are located in Western Australia, but it also has sales branches and warehouse facilities in Melbourne, Sydney and Brisbane.

The company products are specialised industrial chemicals divided into 'Product Line A' and 'Product Line B'. Due to the technical developments and competitive industry the products are subject to a substantial obsolescence risk. If a product becomes obsolete, the company is often able to offload the chemicals to other manufacturers for reprocessing; however, they will generally only receive 40c in the dollar for the product.

The company's accounting functions are concentrated at the factory; the sales branches and warehouses maintain only payroll, petty cash and inventory records, which are subject to review by the head office. The company's four principal officers (the managing director, the sales manager, the product development manager and the factory manager) own substantially all its shares and manage the company in a highly individualistic manner.

Assume that you are the partner of the Mitchell Pty Ltd audit. Following is financial information for the years ended 30 June X3, X2 and X1. (The X2 and X1 figures were those reported in the audited financial report, but the X3 figures were as prepared by the chief accountant prior to the audit.)

Mitchell Pty Ltd
Income Statements for years ended 30 June

	X3 $	X2 $	X1 $
Sales	2 100 000	1 800 000	1 700 000
Cost of sales	1 690 000	1 380 000	1 320 000
Gross profit	410 000	420 000	380 000
Selling and administrative expenses:			
Advertising and promotion	117 000	77 000	51 000
Bad debts	10 000	7 000	6 000
Depreciation	10 000	15 000	15 000
Insurance	7 000	7 000	7 000
Salaries	182 000	160 000	150 000
Sundry	28 000	12 000	11 000
Utilities and telephone	26 000	22 000	20 000
	380 000	300 000	260 000
Operating income	30 000	120 000	120 000
Other expense (income):			
Interest and bank charges	63 000	41 000	38 000
Profit on sale of land	(80 000)		
Cash discounts and sundry	(1 000)	(3 000)	(4 000)
	(18 000)	38 000	34 000
Income before tax	48 000	82 000	86 000

	X3 $	X2 $	X1 $
Income taxes:			
Current	(10 000)	21 000	20 000
Deferred	3 000	5 000	8 000
	(7 000)	26 000	28 000
Net profit for the year	55 000	56 000	58 000
Dividends paid	25 000	25 000	25 000

Mitchell Pty Ltd
Schedules of Gross Profit for years ended 30 June

	X3 $	X2 $	X1 $
Product line A			
Sales	850 000	825 000	800 000
Cost of sales:			
Materials (standard)	417 000	386 000	378 000
Labour (standard)	231 000	160 000	156 000
Overhead (standard)	84 000	56 000	50 000
Standard cost variances	(22 000)	(2 000)	1 000
Depreciation	20 000	35 000	35 000
	730 000	635 000	620 000
Gross profit	120 000	190 000	180 000
Product line B			
Sales	1 250 000	975 000	900 000
Cost of sales:			
Materials (standard)	482 000	347 000	323 000
Labour (standard)	297 000	223 000	207 000
Overhead (standard)	173 000	113 000	103 000
Standard cost variances	(32 000)	(3 000)	2 000
Depreciation	40 000	65 000	65 000
	960 000	745 000	700 000
Gross profit	290 000	230 000	200 000
Total gross profit	410 000	420 000	380 000

Note: The overhead standards shown above do not include depreciation. However, when the finished goods are transferred to inventory, a factor for depreciation is added to the materials–labour–overhead standard to get the inventory carrying cost.

Mitchell Pty Ltd

Balance Sheets as at 30 June

	X3 $	X2 $	X1 $
Cash	148 000	234 000	210 000
Accounts receivable:			
Trade	387 000	263 000	219 000
Employees	8 000	6 000	5 000
Income taxes recoverable	10 000	—	—
Land sale	130 000	—	—
Provision for doubtful accounts	(15 000)	(15 000)	(15 000)
Inventories:			
Raw materials (cost)	69 000	72 000	78 000
Finished goods (standard cost):			
Product line A	204 000	124 000	84 000
Product line B	166 000	156 000	149 000
Shop supplies (cost)	23 000	—	—
	1 130 000	840 000	730 000
Land (cost)	150 000	200 000	200 000
Plant and equipment (cost)	1 600 000	1 600 000	1 600 000
Provision for depreciation	(870 000)	(800 000)	(685 000)
	880 000	1 000 000	1 115 000
	2 010 000	1 840 000	1 845 000
Bank loan	170 000	110 000	80 000
Accounts payable	374 000	304 000	241 000
Trade notes payable	97 000	34 000	21 000
Provision for income tax	—	9 000	8 000
Shareholder loan	—	12 000	100 000
Current portion of mortgage	75 000	60 000	60 000
	716 000	529 000	510 000
Mortgage (6%)—less current portion	440 000	500 000	560 000
Provision for deferred income tax	71 000	68 000	63 000
	1 227 000	1 097 000	1 133 000
Ordinary share capital	210 000	200 000	200 000
General reserve	50 000	50 000	50 000
Retained profits	523 000	493 000	462 000
	783 000	743 000	712 000
	2 010 000	1 840 000	1 845 000

Required

Prepare a detailed note to file indicating those areas on which you believe additional emphasis should be placed during the audit. Support your answer by calculation of appropriate ratios and/or comparisons.

6.30 **Complex** You are currently carrying out the planning for the 31 December 20X1 audit of HomeChef Pty Ltd. HomeChef manufacture, supply and retail quality ingredients for use in the home kitchen or small restaurant market. Recently, they have extended their product range and services to include 'pre-packaged' meals suitable for a dinner party, with customers ordering off a set menu. In addition, they have opened a number of small cafes where customers can sample the company's product range. Your firm has acted as the auditor of HomeChef for a number of years.

The company currently has 30 outlets of varying sizes and has been the market leader in the boutique food and beverage industry for the last 2 years after a focused marketing and promotion strategy and the acquisition of a number of smaller competitors.

The management team at HomeChef is experienced, all managers having been with the company for over 5 years, with the exception of the new finance director who joined the company last month.

The company installed a new computer system in February 20X1. The system was installed by a professional computer company and the old and new systems were run parallel for 3 months. The new system allows each outlet to process its own stocktake results, accounts payable invoices and payments. Management has experienced no major problems with the new system to date.

HomeChef has an internal audit group that may be able to assist you in this year's audit for the first time. The client has provided you with draft financial information in respect of the year ended 31 December 20X1. No taxation figures are included, as the client has engaged your firm to provide these figures.

HomeChef Pty Ltd
Income Statement for the year ended 31 December 20X1

	20X1 $000	20X0 $000
Revenue		
Cafe revenue		
Food	75 440	76 518
Beverage	23 608	21 422
Other	9 000	—
Store revenue		
Food and beverages	203 366	189 612
Ready to Cook range	11 562	15 930
Other revenue	6 560	3 098
Total revenue	329 536	306 580
Total cost of sales	177 056	159 132
Gross profit		
Cafe		
Food	46 772	53 268
Beverages	23 608	21 422
Other	8 730	—
Store		
Food and Beverage	68 636	66 778
Ready to Cook	4 734	5 980
Total gross profit	152 480	147 448
Direct wages	18 312	22 198
Direct expenses cafe	12 914	15 082
Direct expenses stores	4 858	7 072
Total direct expenses	36 084	44 352
Indirect expenses		
Wages	13 424	14 610

Continued...

	20X1 $000	20X0 $000
On costs	9 010	7 830
Advertising	266	370
Cleaning	2 748	2 560
Security contractors	1 092	986
Fees and permits	586	578
Depreciation	4 210	4 196
Repairs and maintenance	4 960	5 304
Interest	16 538	10 422
Total indirect expenses	52 834	46 856
Total expenses	88 918	91 208
Profit from ordinary activities before tax and extraordinary item	63 562	56 240
Extraordinary item	(231 004)	—
Net profit (loss) before tax	(167 442)	56,240

HomeChef Pty Ltd
Draft Balance Sheet as at 31 December 20X1

	Note	20X1 $000	20X0 $000
Current assets			
Cash		110	64
Receivables	(a)	34 858	24 690
Inventories		37 262	44 640
Other	(b)	17 908	—
Total current assets		90 138	69 394
Non-current assets			
Receivables	(a)	52	90
Property, plant and equipment	(c)	392 954	461 314
Other	(d)	135 710	51 296
Total non-current assets		528 716	512 700
Total assets		618 854	582 094
Current liabilities			
Creditors and borrowings	(e)	491 680	300 008
Provisions		52 000	56 000
Total current liabilities		543 680	356 008
Non-current liabilities			
Creditors and borrowings	(e)	44 000	44 000
Provisions		19 654	40 786
Total non-current liabilities		63 654	84 786
Total liabilities		607 334	440 794
Net assets		11 520	141 300
Shareholders' equity			
Share capital		100 000	100 000
Reserves		157 662	120 000
Accumulated losses		(246 142)	(78 700)
Total shareholders' equity		11 520	141 300

HomeChef Pty Ltd
Notes to the Draft Financial Report

	20X1 $000	20X0 $000
(a) Receivables—Current		
Trade debtors	37 220	26 510
less: Provision for doubtful debts	(2 400)	(1 820)
	34 820	24 690
Amounts owing from related parties	38	—
Receivables—Non-current		
Amounts owing from related parties	52	90

Amounts owing from related parties represents a 4 year loan made to the finance director. The current portion receivable on this loan is $19 000.

(b) Other—Current

This amount is represented by the land and buildings of one of the company's retail outlets in Mosman NSW, held subject to contract of sale.

(c) Property, plant and equipment

	20X1 $000	20X0 $000
Freehold land at valuation 20X0	275 694	299 082
Buildings at valuation 20X0	105 950	148 380
less: Accumulated depreciation	(8 210)	(7 560)
Total buildings	97 740	140 820
Plant and equipment at cost	27 280	25 612
less: Accumulated depreciation	(7 760)	(4 200)
Total plant and equipment	19 520	21 412
Total property, plant and equipment	392 954	461 314

(d) Other—Non-current

	20X1 $000	20X0 $000
Investment project		
Capital works in progress at cost	24 448	—
Site lease, liquor and entertainment		
Development expenditure at cost	13 314	—
	43 962	—
Future income tax benefit	51 748	11 296
Goodwill at cost	40 000	40 000
	135 710	51 296

On 19 July 20X1 the company entered into a number of agreements for the construction and development of a restaurant and entertainment complex, and its leasing upon completion. This is HomeChef's first venture into the hospitality industry.

The future income tax benefit includes both tax losses and timing differences. Future income tax benefits of $580 000 in respect of previous years' tax losses have not been brought to account.

Continued...

(e) Creditors and borrowings—Current

	20X1 $000	20X0 $000
Bank overdraft (secured)	380 000	192 768
Trade creditors	111 680	107 240
	491 680	300 008
Creditors and borrowings—Non-current		
Secured loan	44 000	44 000

The loans and other bank accommodation are secured against the remaining property, plant and equipment. These loans are subject to a covenant agreement which specified that the company maintain the following ratios:
- net tangible asset ratio which is positive
- a positive current ratio

(f) Capital expenditure commitments

Aggregate capital expenditure contracted for 31 December 20X1 for the construction and development of the restaurant and entertainment complex not provided for in the financial information.

	$000
Payable no later than one year	57 728
Payable later than one year, not later than two years	33 432
	91 160

Required

Carry out a preliminary analytical review based on the draft financial information and discuss briefly the effect of your findings on your audit plan.

CHAPTER 7

ASSESSING SPECIFIC BUSINESS RISKS AND MATERIALITY

LEARNING OBJECTIVES

After studying this chapter you should be able to:

1 explain the factors that influence the assessment of inherent risk;

2 explain the auditor's consideration of the special risk area of fraud;

3 explain the auditor's consideration of the special risk area of related parties;

4 explain the auditor's consideration of the special risk area of the appropriateness of the going concern basis; and

5 explain the concept of materiality.

Chapter outline

Specific business risks and materiality impact significantly on the auditor's decisions concerning audit evidence. The auditor considers both concepts in developing an overall audit strategy and planning the nature, extent and timing of audit procedures.

The major topics of this chapter are the specific business risks associated with inherent risk; the special risk areas of fraud, related parties and the appropriateness of the going concern basis; and materiality.

Relevant guidance

Australian		International	
AUS 202	Objective and General Principles Governing an Audit of a Financial Report (Revised 2004)	ISA 200	Objective and General Principles Governing an Audit of Financial Statements (Revised 2004)
AUS 210	The Auditor's Responsibility to Consider Fraud and Error in an Audit of a Financial Report (Revised 2004)	ISA 240	The Auditor's Responsibility to Consider Fraud and Error in an Audit of Financial Statements (Revised 2004)
AUS 218	Consideration of Laws and Regulations in the Audit of a Financial Report	ISA 250	Consideration of Laws and Regulations in the Audit of Financial Statements
AUS 302	Planning	ISA 300	Planning
AUS 306	Materiality	ISA 320	Audit Materiality
AUS 402	Understanding the Entity and its Environment and Assessing the Risk of Material Misstatement (Revised 2004)	ISA 400	Understanding the Entity and its Environment and Assessing the Risks of Material Misstatement (Revised 2004)
AUS 406	The Auditor's Procedures in Response to Assessed Risks (Issued 2004)	ISA 330	The Auditor's Procedures in Response to Assessed Risks (Issued 2004)
AUS 708	Going Concern	ISA 570	Going Concern
Audit Guide No. 5 Auditing in an IT Systems Environment		—	
Audit and Assurance Alert No. 3: Lessons for Auditors: Current Issues		—	
Audit and Assurance Alert No. 8: Electronic Commerce and its Impact on Audits		—	
Audit and Assurance Alert No. 10: Earnings Management by Entities: Audit Considerations and Issues		—	

INHERENT RISK

AUS 406.12 (ISA 330.12) points out that when considering the reasons for the assessment of the risk of material misstatement at the assertion level, the auditor needs to consider both the particular characteristics of each class of transactions, account balance or disclosure (i.e. the inherent risks) and whether the auditor's assessment takes account of the entity's controls (i.e. control risk).

Inherent risk is the susceptibility of an account balance or class of transactions to material misstatement given inherent and environmental characteristics, but without regard to internal control. Inherent risk at the financial report level is considered in general planning because it specifically affects other decisions made at this time, such as staffing requirements, and other aspects of the audit plan. For example, some of the possible responses to high inherent risk are to assign more experienced audit personnel, to increase the extent of supervision and to conduct the audit with a heightened degree of professional scepticism (AUS 406.04/ISA 330.04).

AUS 202.21 (ISA 200.21) points out that the AUSs no longer ordinarily refer to inherent and control risk separately, but rather to a combined assessment of risk of material misstatement.

However, the auditor may make separate or combined assessments of inherent and control risk depending on preferred audit techniques or methodologies and practical considerations. Regardless of the approach adopted, the auditor needs to assess inherent risk at the financial report level when developing the audit plan. This assessment must then be related to the assertions at the account balances, classes of transactions and disclosures level when developing the audit program. (See Example 7.1 on p. 300.)

Inherent risk at the financial report level and relationship with business risk

The entity's business strategy and associated risks, as discussed in Chapter 6, will affect the auditor's assessment of inherent risk at the financial report level. The auditor will trace business risks to the areas of the financial report which are most likely to be misstated. In addition, there are a number of factors which affect inherent risk at the financial report level, including:

1 **Integrity of management** If management lacks integrity they are more likely to be prepared to produce materially misleading financial reports. Lack of integrity may be indicated by a poor reputation in the business community, prior disputes with auditors, unreasonable demands on the auditor, attempts to limit the auditor's access to people or information, a history of litigation or a reluctance to correct internal control weaknesses.

2 **Management experience, knowledge and changes during the period** Inexperience of management and its lack of knowledge may affect the preparation of the financial report. In addition, if poor business decisions are made, as identified by the business risk analysis outlined in Chapter 6, this may introduce pressure to bias the results. If a single person dominates the entity's operating and financing decisions, there is a higher risk that a material misstatement could occur because these important decisions may not be reviewed, and actions that are not in the best interests of the entity may be taken. When important operating and financing decisions are reviewed and approved by the entity's board of directors or audit committee, there is less risk that the financial report will be materially misstated. This is part of the corporate governance structure discussed in Chapter 3. When the auditor observes frequent personnel turnover in important management positions, inherent risk increases because honest individuals are likely to resign their management positions rather than perpetuate some type of fraud.

3 **Unusual pressure on management** This may provide incentives for management to misstate the financial report. If the entity is facing cash flow problems, poor liquidity, poor operating results or insufficient capital to continue operations, there may be an incentive to make the financial position look better than the true situation. If the industry is experiencing a large number of business failures and declining customer demand, there may be pressure on management to report higher sales even if revenues are declining. Significant issues may also arise in relation to valuation of items such as inventory and accounts receivable in the financial report. In addition, the financial or operating problems currently being faced by competitors are also likely to affect the entity being audited. If management compensation schemes are tied to earnings or share prices, there is an incentive for management to misstate the result in order to obtain a bonus. (Refer to demand for audit services, discussed in Chapter 1.) Similarly, if management has significant shareholdings, they have a vested interest in reporting a good result. Pressure may also be placed on management by head office, major investors or lenders to meet budgets or forecasts. Similarly, new management may be under pressure to outperform previous

results. Management is also likely to be under pressure to show good results where a takeover or public float of the entity appears likely.

4 **Nature of the entity's business** Many of the inherent risk factors associated with the nature of the entity's business will be identified during the business risk assessment (discussed in Chapter 6) and will have a flow-through effect on the inherent risk at the financial report level. Some types of businesses are inherently risky. For example, while Internet companies have potential advantages, until they establish a reputation and a reliable revenue source they will be inherently risky. Other companies will be inherently risky because their products are subject to a high inherent risk of obsolescence. For example, high-technology products, such as computers; or fashion products, such as designer clothes, may become obsolete due to changes in technology or consumer tastes. The auditor considers both the supply chain and the value chain (discussed in Chapter 6) in assessing business risk, which also impacts on inherent risk. If an entity deals with many vendors and prices tend to be relatively stable, there is less risk that the entity's operations will be affected by raw material shortages or that production costs will be difficult to control. However, if an entity is dependent on a single vendor to supply a critical component, such as a specialised computer chip, there is a risk that the vendor may be unable to provide the component, causing the entity to suffer production shortages and shipping delays that may significantly affect financial performance. Industries that produce basic commodities such as oil, coal and precious metals can have their financial results significantly affected by swings in the prices of their products, while industries that use commodities such as oil as raw materials may be subject to both shortages and price instability. There are also a number of other factors associated with the nature of the entity's business. If the entity has a complex capital structure this will increase inherent risk. The existence of related-party transactions would also increase inherent risk as the transactions are not with an independent party and the required related-party disclosures are complex. If the entity buys or sells goods in a foreign currency, inherent risk will increase as there is a risk of incurring foreign exchange losses. If hedges are taken out, the hedging contracts may be complex. The complexity of the accounting standard also increases the chance of an error. Operating in a number of geographic locations would increase inherent risk as it becomes more difficult to keep control of the operations.

5 **Factors affecting the industry in which the entity operates** While many of these factors will be identified through the business risk analysis stage (e.g. through SWOT or PEST analysis) changes in economic and competitive conditions would be expected to have a major impact on the inherent risk of an entity. The possibility of breaches of restrictive covenants in loan agreements increases during economic downturns. Failure to maintain working capital and certain ratios at the level stated in the debt agreements is a common violation. An entity which breaches a debt covenant is considered to be in default and may be required to repay the loan and any accrued interest on demand. This increases the risk of misstatements to avoid breach of the debt covenants. Economic downturns also often produce uncertainty concerning the ability of an entity to continue as a going concern. If an entity is reporting a significant increase in earnings while the industry is experiencing a decline, the inherent risk concerning the truth and fairness of reported earnings would increase. Generally, industries that are subject to rapid changes are more likely to have a materially misstated financial report. For example, in the high-technology sector, frequent changes may affect obsolescence and therefore the fair market value of products sold. As a result, there is increased inherent risk of inventory overstatement due to the lower of cost or net realisable value rule in accounting standard AASB 102. Also, the amount of capital investment necessary may be

increased as a result of technological change and replacement of equipment. Intense competition may affect inventory valuation due to the lower of cost and net realisable value rule. Foreign competition, in particular, often adopts a price-cutting strategy to gain market share, which may affect inventory valuation. Technological, marketing or manufacturing advancements by competitors may also affect inventory valuation. Competition within the industry can affect the entity's pricing policies, credit terms and product warranties. Where accounting practices are common to the industry the auditor needs to determine whether the practice is in accordance with generally accepted accounting principles and to be aware of the acceptable alternatives. In addition, some reporting obligations may be unique to the industry, such as special reporting requirements for insurance companies, thus increasing the risk of non-compliance.

As information technology (IT) risks can be pervasive throughout the entity, factors affecting overall inherent risk associated with IT are outlined here. Audit Guide No. 5 identifies the following six red flag areas that will increase inherent risk in relation to IT:

1   **Significant change in IT** Errors may occur through incorrect conversion of a new system or because information in the previous system is unacceptable to the new system. The new system may not be able to be delivered. New technology may not work as expected, may never work or may be unreliable.

2   **Insufficient IT skills and resources** The skills of staff should be relevant and current so that they can operate and understand the system. Sufficient staff resources need to be available to operate the system. Excessive use of contractors can create risk of errors, and disruption due to their unavailability. High turnover of computer staff will also increase risk of errors.

3   **Lack of entity support and focus** Senior management needs to demonstrate their accountability for IT by appropriate commitment and involvement. Otherwise fragmentation and lack of direction can occur. Positive management focus and support directly affects the attitude of other staff members and is likely to result in IT issues being given the appropriate degree of importance.

4   **High dependence on IT** An entity that requires IT to support its core business from an operational perspective has a higher level of inherent risk than an entity that depends on IT only to produce their financial information. Although the extent to which an entity relies on IT can be influenced largely by the industry in which it operates, entities in every industry are increasingly becoming more reliant on IT to transact their financial dealings, automate their factories, link them to suppliers and produce information to make faster and better decisions about their future. Where the survival time without IT is very short, there may be a risk that the entity could go out of business in the event of a disaster or disruption.

5   **Reliance on external IT** Outsourcing IT operations may mean that changes to response time, service and capacity affect the user's ability to meet customer needs. The entity also needs to consider the long-term viability of the service provider. A likely reduction in the number of people within the entity with computer knowledge will increase its dependence on the service provider.

6   **Reliability and complexity of IT** The reliability of IT will directly affect the risk of errors in processing. The more complex the system the greater the risk of errors or misinterpretation.

In addition, *Audit and Assurance Alert No. 8* highlights the potential impact of e-commerce (discussed in Chapter 17) on business risk and its effect on inherent risk. It identifies three major categories of risk that could increase inherent risk:

1 risks arising through the nature of the relationships with e-commerce trading partners, such as the authenticity and integrity of trading partners;

2 risk related to the recording and processing of transactions initiated through e-commerce, for example the integration of the entity's internal reporting system with the e-commerce system may mean that trade initiated by an unknown person using the Internet may generate accounting entries in the entity's financial records;

3 pervasive e-commerce business risks, such as the technical competency required by staff, computer crime, computer viruses and legislation in different jurisdictions.

Monroe et al. (1993) conducted an empirical study of auditors and found that auditors perceived the following inherent risk factors at the financial report level to be the most important:

- management bonus schemes are tied to reported earnings;
- there has been a high turnover of top management in the past few years;
- top management have a reputation for taking unusual business risks;
- this is the first year that your audit firm has conducted an audit of the company; and
- in the past, top management has been reluctant to accept audit adjustments.

EXAMPLE 7.1 Inherent risk assessment

G Ltd is a construction company. Control of the company is in the hands of the G family, who have been majority shareholders for over 20 years. Mr G is chairman and managing director. The other three directors, one of whom is a member of the G family, all hold senior positions within the organisation. Seventy per cent of the company's construction contracts are government contracts, with the remaining contracts being small shopping centres or business centres.

Mr G has informed you of the following facts concerning the past year and future trends:

1. During the year the company won a major contract to construct a number of buildings on a university campus. The project is particularly interesting as all the facilities must be capable of transmitting and receiving videoconference broadcasts. G have not been involved in this type of work before but feel it will lead to a lot of similar work in the private sector.

2. Reconciliation of debtors' statements to the debtors' ledger were performed incorrectly for a 3 month period while a clerk was on leave. These reconciliations were approved by the accountant. The errors were detected by the debtors clerk on his return and all errors were corrected.

3. G Ltd keeps a small store of building materials in its main warehouse. The warehouse manager is responsible for ordering goods, receipting goods and payments to creditors.

4. A bonus incentive scheme was introduced for the 'leading hands' (supervisors) at the construction sites to ensure buildings were completed on time.

Impact on inherent risk

Effects on inherent risk (IR) are as follows:

1. Being a construction company increases IR, because of the complexity of valuation of work in progress.

2. The extensive involvement of the family and the board of directors in company management increases IR, as the board may not always act in the interests of all shareholders.

3. Economic dependence on the government may increase the risk of going concern problems should a change of government occur. The new government may restrict construction or open the market to other players.

4. Entry into a new market in which the company has little expertise increases inherent risk as they may underestimate the cost and difficulty of this work, thus reducing the accuracy of any estimates of the value of work in progress.

5. Bonus scheme increases IR as the scheme may encourage poor construction work or premature recording of stages of completion. This increases the possibility of error in the valuation of work in progress and raises the possibility of future warranty claims on work performed.

The incorrect reconciliation of debtors' statements and the lack of segregation of duties for the warehouse manager affect control risk only.

Inherent risk at assertion level

AUS 202.20 (ISA 200.20) points out that inherent risk is greater for some assertions and related classes of transactions, account balances and disclosures than for others. In assessing inherent risk at the account balance or class of transactions level, the auditor makes a focused consideration of the implications of the auditor's understanding of the client, its industry, its business and the nature of the account and the transactions for the likelihood of a material misstatement existing in a particular account balance, class of transactions or disclosure. Normally, the auditor will focus on the following six factors:

1. **Accounts likely to require adjustment** Accounts that were found to be misstated in previous audits are likely to contain similar misstatements in the current years. Thus, when an auditor has encountered material misstatements in previous audits the auditor should assess inherent risk as being higher in the accounts where the past misstatements have occurred.

2. **Complexity of underlying transactions** Transactions characterised by difficult calculations or a complex accounting standard are more prone to error than simple repetitive transactions. For example, complex calculations, such as lease capitalisation, are more likely to be misstated than simple calculations such as straight-line depreciation.

3. **Judgment involved in determining account balances** The greater the degree of judgment involved in determining account balances, the greater the chance of an error. Accounting estimates, such as provision for doubtful debts, obsolescence and warranty, are more likely to be misstated than routine factual data. Items or events which require using the work of an expert for verification, such as the value of properties, are more susceptible to misstatement than those which can be verified by a non-expert. Decisions involving subjective judgments, such as whether to capitalise mining exploration expenditure, the amount of percentage of completion on a construction contract and whether an entity is subject to control or significant influence, have a high inherent risk.

4. **Susceptibility of assets to loss or misappropriation** If an entity processes large amounts of cash, such as a supermarket, susceptibility to misappropriation is increased. Similarly, if the entity produces small, highly valuable products such as computer chips or gemstones, such assets are more likely to be stolen than an inventory of steel pellets or coal.

5. **Occurrence of unusual and complex transactions, particularly at or near year-end** Material and/or unusual transactions occurring near the end of the year have a higher inherent risk as they may have been undertaken with the objective of manipulating profits or covering a poor liquidity position.

6. **Transactions not subject to ordinary processing** Transactions that are not subject to ordinary processing are more susceptible to errors or misappropriation. Similarly, accounts with a highly visible audit trail are less risky than those with no audit trail.

The more that any one or a combination of the above factors influences an account, the higher the value that should be placed on inherent risk, thus increasing the auditor's assessment of the likelihood of a material misstatement in that account.

Monroe et al. (1993) found that auditors perceived that the five most important inherent risk factors at the account balance, class of transactions and disclosure level were:

- the results from previous audits indicate that many errors are made in the recording of accounts receivable;
- there is a substantial number of accounts receivable that are significantly overdue;
- the company has a history of inventory pricing errors;

- management estimates for the provision for doubtful debts have not been accurate in the past; and
- the company has a history of inventory cut-off problems.

As outlined earlier, the auditor is required to relate the assessment of the risks to the assertions underlying the account balances, classes of transactions or disclosures. AUS 406.07 (ISA 330.07) requires auditors to perform further audit procedures whose nature, timing and extent are responsive to the assessed risks of material misstatement at the assertion level. For example, the risk of inventory obsolescence due to technological development mentioned earlier affects the assertion of valuation in relation to the account balance of inventory. This will help direct the auditor's evidence-gathering procedures when carrying out tests of control or substantive testing, which are broken down to the assertion level, discussed further in Chapters 9 and 10.

For an example of the flow of inherent risk through an account balance see Figure 7.1.

FIGURE **7.1 Effect of inherent risk on an account balance assertion**

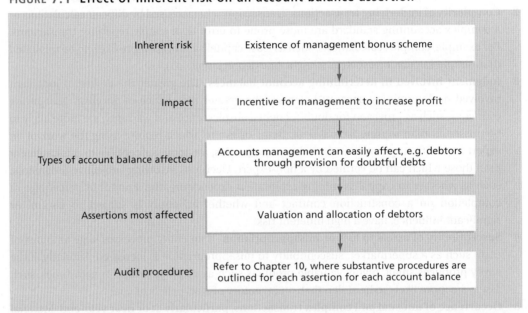

Q u i c k   r e v i e w

1 Inherent risk is the risk of misstatement arising from the characteristics of the entity and the environment and industry in which it operates.

2 Inherent risk needs to be considered as part of the planning process because it affects other decisions made at this time.

3 Inherent risk must be assessed at both the financial report level and at the assertion level.

SPECIAL AREAS OF AUDIT RISK

Fraud

At the planning stage of the audit the auditor should consider the **risk of fraud or error**, that is, that material misstatements resulting from fraud or error will not be detected. The auditor is responsible for controlling detection risk by determining the nature, timing and extent of audit procedures. It is easier to miss a material misstatement resulting from fraud than a material misstatement resulting from error, because fraud usually involves acts designed to conceal it, such as collusion, forgery or intentional misrepresentation to the auditor.

Fraud may involve:

- manipulation, falsification or alteration of records or documents;
- suppression or omission of the effects of transactions from records or documents;
- recording of transactions without substance; or
- intentional misapplication of accounting policies.

Errors are unintentional mistakes in or omissions of amounts or disclosures from financial reports. Errors may involve:

- mathematical or clerical mistakes in the underlying records and accounting data;
- oversight or misinterpretation of facts; or
- misapplication of accounting policies.

The nature of fraud makes its detection intrinsically difficult and, as an element of audit risk, it needs to be carefully considered. This is compounded by the nature of the audit process itself (for example, the judgment necessary as to the nature and extent of testing, evidence which is persuasive rather than conclusive). The profession's position, as expressed in AUS 210 (ISA 240), is that the audit should be planned to obtain reasonable assurance that fraud which may be material has not occurred or, if it has, that the effect of the fraud is properly reflected in the financial report. The auditor's responsibility for the detection of fraud was discussed in Chapter 4.

The elements of audit risk due to the possibility of fraud are reduced where effective internal control is in place. However, there is always a risk that the internal control will fail to operate as designed. Moreover, internal control may be ineffective against fraud because certain personnel within an entity are in a position to override controls designed to prevent frauds.

In planning and conducting the audit the auditor must exercise reasonable care and skill and maintain an attitude of professional scepticism (AUS 202.06/ISA 200.06 and AUS 210.24/IAS 240.24). Throughout the audit the auditor needs to consider the risk of any fraud occurring that may result in a material misstatement in the financial report, notwithstanding the auditor's previous experience with the entity concerning the honesty and integrity of management and those charged with governance (AUS 210.24/ISA 240.24). The auditor needs to be aware of the possibility of fraud, particularly in times of economic recession. Audit staff must have the knowledge, experience and training to identify danger signs of fraud, or 'red flags', and initiate appropriate actions.

If there is a particular risk of fraud because of the nature of an item, it should receive more attention. For example, cash is subject to greater inherent risk of misstatement through fraud than are fixed assets. Accordingly, even where fixed assets have a larger balance than cash, the tests of cash transactions may be more extensive.

The auditor needs to have a thorough knowledge of the client's business in order to be able to identify opportunities for the perpetration of fraud. The auditor must be open-minded and aware of the management's practices and conduct.

AUS 210 was revised in January 2002 and again in June 2004 to require auditors to pay greater attention to fraud. In planning the audit, the auditor now needs to specifically consider the risks of material misstatements in the financial report owing to fraud (AUS 210.03/ISA 240.03); discuss with other members of the audit team the susceptibility of the entity to material misstatements in the financial report resulting from fraud (AUS 210.27/IAS 240.27); and make more extensive inquiries of management with respect to fraud (AUS 210.34/IAS 240.34). In the assessment of inherent and control risk the auditor needs to consider and assess how the financial report might be materially misstated because of fraud; and the presence of fraud risk factors. AUS 210 (ISA 240) now specifically requires the auditor to consider risks of fraud in revenue recognition and the possibility of management override of controls. Identified fraud risk factors and the auditor's response to them should be documented and should be addressed specifically in the design of audit procedures. Examples of possible audit procedures to address the assessed risks of material misstatement owing to fraud are contained in Appendix 2 to AUS 210 (ISA 240). The auditor needs to consider whether an identified misstatement may be indicative of fraud and the implications of this on other aspects of the audit, including the reliability of management representations. The auditor should obtain written representations from management about the disclosure of all facts relating to any fraud or possible fraud; and management's belief that the effects of the uncorrected financial report misstatement aggregated by the auditor are immaterial to the financial report taken as a whole.

Appendix 1 of AUS 210 (ISA 240) provides guidance to the auditor in planning and conducting the audit by outlining factors that should be considered in assessing the risk of material misstatement resulting from fraud.

Conditions or events that indicate an increased risk of fraud are often referred to as 'red flags' (refer to Table 7.1). The existence of these danger signs or 'red flags' does not mean necessarily that fraud is being perpetrated. However, it does indicate that the inherent risk of fraud has increased, and this may cause the auditor to modify the nature, timing or extent of audit procedures with a view to detecting it.

TABLE **7.1 Examples of 'red flags' that indicate an increased risk of fraud**

Management
- a motivation exists for management to engage in fraudulent reporting due to factors such as management bonuses for achieving specific results;
- management is dominated by one person (or a small group) and there is no effective oversight board or audit committee;
- evidence of management override;
- the corporate structure is complex and appears unwarranted;
- a lack of board members who are independent of management;
- failure by management to display and communicate an appropriate attitude regarding internal control;
- a high turnover of key accounting and financial personnel;
- understaffing of the accounting department;
- frequent changes of legal advisers;
- frequent disputes with current or previous auditors; and
- the internal audit function is not properly constituted or staffed.

Unusual pressures within an entity
- inadequate working capital due to declining profits or rapid expansion;
- the quality of earnings is deteriorating: for example, there is increased risk-taking with respect to credit sales or changes in business practice;
- the entity needs a rising profit trend to support the market price of its shares due to a contemplated public offering, a takeover or for another reason;
- the entity has a significant investment in an industry or product line noted for rapid change;
- the entity is heavily dependent on one or a few products or customers; and
- pressure is exerted on accounting personnel to complete the financial report in an unusually short period.

Market pressures
- the industry is declining and failures are increasing;
- the industry is subject to specific or complex legislation; and
- the industry is volatile, with numerous corporate takeovers or mergers.

Unusual transactions

- unusual transactions, especially near the balance date, that have a significant effect on profit;
- transactions with related parties;
- payments for services (for example, to solicitors, consultants or agents) that appear excessive in relation to the services provided;
- payments for goods that appear to be significantly above or below market price;
- evidence of falsified documents;
- large payments in cash or by bankers' draft to, or via, overseas 'shell' companies or numbered bank accounts;
- payments made to officials of domestic or overseas authorities or governments;
- correspondence between the entity and its regulatory authority concerning problems;
- correspondence between the entity and its legal adviser, the substance of which is to advise against a particular course of action, which the entity has ignored;
- investigation by a government regulatory body or the police; and
- evidence of unduly lavish lifestyles of officers or employees.

Unsatisfactory records

- inadequate accounting records: for example, incomplete files, excessive adjustments to accounts, transactions not recorded in accordance with normal procedures and out of balance control accounts;
- inadequate documentation of transactions, such as lack of proper authorisation, supporting documents not available, and alteration to documents (these documentation problems assume greater significance when they relate to large or unusual transactions);
- an excessive number of differences between accounting records and third-party confirmations, conflicting audit evidence and inexplicable changes in operating ratios; evasive, unreasonable or unsatisfactory responses by management to audit inquiries (for instance, any failure to adequately explain trends or results which do not accord with expectations, unusual items in the reconciliation of suspense accounts, or the unusual investment of funds held in a fiduciary capacity); and
- significantly fewer responses to confirmation requests than expected.

IT environment

- minimal planning for the installation of new hardware and software technology;
- inadequate computer skills among relevant entity staff and/or the concentration of CIS knowledge in a particular individual or individuals;
- the use of inappropriate hardware or software to perform important functions;
- poor physical or logical access controls;
- inadequate or inappropriate file access hierarchy;
- the lack of a clear audit trail and transaction log;
- shared or non-specific ownership of data;
- hardware failures, including excessive amounts of downtime and resultant input backlogs;
- software failures;
- failure to restrict access to software and documentation to authorised personnel;
- program changes that are not documented, approved and tested;
- inadequate overall balancing of computer transactions and databases to the financial accounts;
- inappropriate data and program storage media; and
- inadequate detection procedures for system viruses.

Although this list of danger signs of fraud is extremely useful, it is not all-inclusive. Given the nature of fraud—its great variability in design, execution and underlying motive—it is not possible to reduce the auditor's consideration of the possibility of fraud to a checklist. An analysis of the danger signs of fraud highlights the need to put into place effective monitoring mechanisms as part of internal control. However, employees may circumvent even effective internal controls through collusion, either among themselves or with outsiders.

7.1 AUDITING IN THE NEWS

Fraud survey

It is clear from the survey results that fraud is, and continues to be, a major problem for business in Australia and New Zealand. The following is a summary of the major findings:

- the 361 respondents lost a total of $273 million to fraudulent conduct in the survey period from October 1999 to September 2001;
- 44 654 instances of fraud were reported (approximately 50% of these were credit card fraud against banks, involving the use of stolen credit cards or fraudulently manufactured credit card numbers);
- $1.4 million was the average loss for organisations experiencing fraud;
- 55% of respondents experienced at least one fraud incident in the survey period;
- 73% of organisations with more than 1000 employees experienced at least one fraud incident;
- more than $30 million was lost to fraud in off-shore operations, an increase of more than 100% over the loss reported in the 1999 survey;
- the overriding of internal controls was the most important contributing factor allowing major fraud to occur;
- respondents acknowledge that in more than one third of the reported cases of major fraud, early warning signs were either ignored or not acted upon quickly enough;
- senior management is seen as having primary responsibility for fraud prevention; and
- more than 60% of respondents have neither planned, nor implemented, appropriate fraud control strategies.

In a survey of fraud in Australia, KPMG (2002) (Auditing in the News 7.1) identified override of controls, collusion between employees and third parties, poor internal controls and collusion between employees and management as the main reasons for fraud. The survey revealed that the majority of frauds were perpetrated internally. The main types of frauds perpetrated by employees included theft of inventory or plant, manipulation of petty cash, purchases for personal use, payroll fraud, kickbacks, manipulation of expense accounts and cheque forgery. The main types of fraud perpetrated by management included theft of inventory or plant, theft of information, purchases for personal use, conflict of interest, manipulation of expense accounts, unnecessary purchases, false financial reports, credit card fraud and diversion of sales.

Earnings management

Audit & Assurance Alert No. 10 (AAA 10), 'Earnings Management by Entities: Audit Considerations and Issues', was issued by the AUASB in November 2001. AAA 10 points out that **earnings management** occurs when judgment in financial reporting and in structuring transactions is used to alter financial reports to influence the perceptions of stakeholders about the underlying economic performance of the company and/or to influence outcomes that depend on reported accounting numbers. Earnings management affects the transparency of underlying economic reality and stakeholder decisions in the allocation of scarce resources. Incentives for earnings management may be classified as either behavioural or market-based. Behavioural incentives include:

- political considerations to avoid regulation or enhance eligibility for concessions;
- executive remuneration based on financial or share price performance;

- discretionary transactions over which there is ambiguity or flexibility within Accounting Standards or where no accounting standard exists;
- financial distress and closeness to debt covenant constraints;
- restructuring;
- complex ownership and financial structures;
- related-party transactions; and
- limitations to corporate governance mechanisms.

Capital market-based incentives include:

- pressure to maintain excessive dividend payout rates;
- extreme positive or negative performance;
- (top) management transition creating 'clean up';
- equity offerings takeovers;
- management buyouts or privatisation;
- significant following by analysts and media;
- declaration of growth of high-growth company; and
- material insider shareholdings.

AAA 3, issued in May 1999, identified four broad categories into which earnings management by clients may fall:

- intentional violations of accounting standards and other reporting requirements which are individually immaterial;
- inappropriate revenue recognition;
- 'big bath' charges under the guise of restructuring; and
- improper accruals and estimation of liabilities in good times.

In the USA, the recent financial scandals involving companies such as WorldCom and Xerox have revealed numerous examples of inappropriate earnings management over several years. Levitt (1998) accused auditors of directly or indirectly assisting management by not challenging management's actions. This has resulted in a number of Securities and Exchange Commission investigations. It also led to the introduction of the *Sarbanes-Oxley Act 2002*, which requires management to certify the financial report and has severe penalties for misleading statements. A similar requirement was introduced in Australia through the CLERP 9 amendments whereby s. 295A(2) now requires a CEO/CFO declaration regarding the truth and fairness of the financial report, compliance with accounting standards and proper maintenance of financial records.

In Australia, ASIC has directed its accounting surveillance program at areas of accounting abuse such as those uncovered in the USA. ASIC's recent reviews have concentrated on areas such as capitalised and deferred expenses, recognition of revenue and recognition of controlled entities and assets.

A sound knowledge of the client and its industry, coupled with professional scepticism, is crucial to the auditor's judgment of what are acceptable and unacceptable levels of earnings management. Many earnings management techniques involve accruals, particularly those of a discretionary nature. Abnormal levels of, or unexplained changes in discretionary accruals may be indicative of earnings management.

Illegal acts

Certain categories of **illegal acts** have a greater potential than others to affect the financial report directly and to result in material misstatements. If the client entity operates under a particularly complex legal framework, the auditor may need to seek expert advice when planning the audit to help identify such laws and regulations. The AUASB issued AUS 218 in January 2002 to establish standards and provide guidance regarding the auditor's consideration of non-compliance with laws and regulations in the audit of a financial report.

AUS 218 (ISA 250) includes specific guidance on understanding the legal and regulatory framework applicable to the entity and industry, and on reporting of non-compliance to management, users of financial reports and third parties.

AUS 218.02 (ISA 250.02) emphasises that when planning and performing an audit, the auditor needs to consider the risk of non-compliance with laws and regulations that results in material misstatements in the financial report.

An audit provides only a reasonable assurance that illegal acts will be detected: the audit normally does not include procedures designed specifically to detect illegal acts, although they may be identified by other procedures. Also, the auditor may not be in a position to determine the legality of an act, as this may involve the exercise of professional legal judgment.

The auditor must recognise circumstances which require special attention. For example, a debenture deed may require that a specific current ratio be maintained, which would require increased attention to items classified as current. Transactions which are not consummated at arm's length are commonly considered of special significance, and transactions with officers and employees receive more attention than similar transactions with outsiders. (Consideration of related-party transactions was discussed in Chapter 6 and will be discussed further later in this chapter.) Errors that arouse suspicion of fraud are given greater attention than other errors of an equal amount.

When preparing audit programs the auditor should consider whether fraud, earnings management or illegal acts are likely to cause an overstatement or an understatement in an account balance or transaction total or an inadequate or misleading disclosure. For example, a management that wants to improve the appearance of liquidity in its financial position may do so either by overstating current assets or by understating current liabilities.

In considering the possibilities that an account may be misstated, the auditor should bear in mind that a test of one account simultaneously tests one or more other accounts. An overstatement or understatement of one account affects one or more other accounts by an equivalent amount. The direction of an error (understatement or overstatement) depends on whether the account being tested is an asset, liability, revenue or expense. For example, a test of an asset account for overstatement simultaneously tests one or more of the following:

1 other assets for understatement;
2 liability accounts for overstatement;
3 revenue accounts for overstatement; and
4 expense accounts for understatement.

This characteristic of the original data of accounting allows the auditor to use tests which, when taken together, test most of the accounts for both understatement and overstatement.

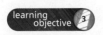

RELATED PARTIES

As discussed in Chapter 6, it is an important part of the planning process that when obtaining knowledge of the business the auditor identifies any **related parties**. The identification of the existence of related parties has been given greater attention because of the growing recognition that transactions with related parties can have a significant impact on a client's financial report. For example, Rogers J in *Cambridge Credit Corporation Limited & Anor v Hutcheson & Ors* (1985) 9 ACLR

545 made several references in his judgment to the auditor's apparent failure in regard to transactions with related parties, and the consequent unreality or lack of 'substance over form' concerning certain transactions. AUS 518 (ISA 550) was revised in February 2000 to require auditors to specifically assess the risk that related parties and related-party transactions will not be identified, or appropriately disclosed and/or measured. AUS 518.02 (ISA 550.02) requires the auditor to perform audit procedures designed to obtain sufficient appropriate audit evidence concerning the identification of related parties and the effect that related-party transactions have on the financial report.

Therefore, the auditor needs to be aware of the identity of related parties for the following reasons:

- The existence of related parties or related-party transactions can affect the financial information. For example, the accounting standards require the disclosure of information relating to related parties, and the tax laws may require special consideration of related-party transactions, thereby affecting the client's tax expense and liability.
- The reliability of audit evidence is a function of the source of that evidence. Because related parties are associated with the client, evidence from such parties and transactions with those parties need to be more carefully evaluated.
- The initiation of a related-party transaction may be motivated by other than ordinary business conditions, such as fraud; because such a transaction may be more readily accepted than others, there is greater potential for error.

It is also relevant for the auditor to understand the means by which management fulfils its responsibility for the control and recording of related-party transactions. AUS 518.07 (ISA 550.07) identifies the following procedures for identifying related parties:

- review the previous period's working papers for known related parties;
- make inquiries of management concerning the names of all related parties;
- review the entity's procedures for identifying related parties;
- inquire about management's and directors' affiliations with other entities;
- review shareholder records for principal shareholders;
- review minutes of the meetings of shareholders, the governing body and other important committees, and statutory records such as the register of directors' interests;
- inquire of other auditors involved in the audit, including previous auditors, as to their knowledge of additional related parties;
- review the income tax return and other information supplied to regulatory agencies; and
- inquire as to the names of pension and other trusts established for the benefit of employees, and the names of their management and trustees.

Related-party transactions played a major role in the collapse of Enron, which used a complex web of Special Purpose Entities, such as limited partnerships with outside parties, to undertake off-balance sheet financing. The substance of these related-party transactions was not disclosed and was hidden from the auditors.

PRELIMINARY ASSESSMENT OF GOING CONCERN BASIS

There have been a number of high-profile corporate collapses recently in Australia: for example, Harris Scarfe, HIH Insurance, One.Tel and Ansett Airlines. HIH Insurance, which collapsed with potential losses of $4 billion, was the subject of a Royal Commission. Rodney Adler, a non-executive director of HIH, wrote a letter to Ray Williams, the Chief Executive Officer, on 6 September 1999, 20 months before the collapse of HIH Insurance. Adler was formerly the chief executive of FAI Insurance, which was taken over by HIH in 1998. In his letter Adler criticised the company's corporate structure and direction and expressed concerns about its financial strength.

He stated: 'My own assessment of the insurance reserves of the company is that you are grossly under-provided, probably to the tune of $400-plus million. If this is true it makes HIH hopelessly insolvent.' Concerns had also been raised about the risks in the insurance industry in general. In a paper entitled 'Lack of Industry Profitability and Other Stories' presented at the Institute of Actuaries in Australia's annual seminar on general insurance 18 months before the HIH collapse, two actuaries named McCarthy and Trahair attacked the under-pricing of policies, the pressure on actuaries to reduce the projected level of outstanding claims liabilities and the poor quality of staff and senior management in the insurance industry.

Such corporate collapses naturally raise the question of what are the auditors' responsibilities in relation to assessment of the going concern basis.

For reasons similar to those discussed in relation to fraud, auditors at the planning stage of the audit consider the likelihood of a client becoming insolvent after the audit. An imminent business failure may have an effect on the appropriateness of the presentation of the financial report or may motivate management misrepresentation. In addition, a liquidation increases the chance that the auditor will have to defend the quality of the audit in court. AUS 708.02 (ISA 570.02) requires that when planning and performing audit procedures and evaluating the results, the auditor must consider the appropriateness of the **going concern basis** which underlies the financial report. AUS 708.03 (ISA 570.03) defines 'going concern' to mean that the entity is expected to be able to pay its debts as and when they fall due, and continue to operate without any intention or necessity to liquidate or otherwise wind up its operations.

Also, for audits undertaken in accordance with the provisions of the *Corporations Act*, s. 295(4) requires the directors to state their opinion as to whether at the date of the directors' declaration there are reasonable grounds to believe that the entity will be able to pay its debts as and when they fall due. The auditor's duty to report on the financial report under ss 307–8 includes examining the directors' declaration.

The auditor's general interest in the going concern assumption and the specific statutory provision require that the nature, timing and extent of the audit procedures be planned to meet these requirements.

Certain circumstances may indicate that the going concern basis requires audit attention. The auditor should be aware of these matters when assessing risk at the beginning of the audit and throughout the audit process. AUS 708.17 (ISA 570.17) requires the auditor to specifically assess the risk of going concern problems as part of the planning process. Early identification of such a problem helps focus audit effort on the appropriate assertions in the financial report, for example the valuation of assets, and permits early communication with management and preparation and examination of any additional information which may be necessary.

Typical indications of going concern problems are contained in Appendix 2 of AUS 708 (ISA 570) and illustrated in Table 7.2. The listing is not all-inclusive: the existence of one or more of these indications does not necessarily signify that the going concern basis needs to be questioned.

TABLE 7.2 Examples of indications of going concern problems

Operating indications
- lack of strategic direction, including well-documented policies, plans and forecasts;
- deficiencies in the governing body, such as lack of independent members, or little involvement in key decisions;
- lack of management expertise or loss of key management personnel;
- concentration of risk in a few products or projects;
- loss of major market, licence or franchise;
- prolonged industrial action;
- shortages of important supplies or loss of a major supplier;
- deficiencies in management information systems;
- rapid or unplanned development of business without commensurate developments in support areas;
- uninsured or underinsured disasters such as drought, fire, flood, fraud or sabotage.

Financial indications
- high gearing or a net liability position;
- fixed-term borrowings nearing maturity without realistic prospects of renewal or repayment;
- reliance on short-term borrowings to finance long-term assets;
- adverse key financial ratios;
- lack of sustainable operating profits or cash flows from core business activities;
- dividend arrears or discontinuance;
- inability to pay creditors on time;
- excessive reliance on transactions with related parties;
- potential losses on long-term contracts or uneconomic long-term commitments;
- difficulty in complying with the terms of loan agreements or the need to restructure debt;
- denial of trade credit by suppliers;
- inability to obtain necessary financing;
- need to seek new sources or methods of financing or to dispose of substantial assets;
- reduction in government funding.

Other indications
- non-compliance with capital or statutory requirements;
- undue influence of a market-dominant competitor;
- legal proceedings against the entity that may result in judgments that could not be met or in restrictions on trading opportunities;
- technical developments which render a key product obsolete;
- adverse changes in legislation or government policy;
- failure of other entities in the same industry;
- lack of adequate back-up and recovery capabilities for key information systems.

Source: AUS 708 (ISA 570), Appendix 2. Reproduced with the permission of The Institute of Chartered Accountants in Australia and CPA Australia.

The significance of these matters may, of course, be mitigated by other factors. Examples of mitigating factors are given in Appendix 3 of AUS 708 (ISA 570) and illustrated in Table 7.3 overleaf.

TABLE 7.3 Examples of mitigating factors

The significance of those going concern indications which are related to cash flow or solvency can often be mitigated by the existence of, and management plans with respect to, factors such as:

Asset factors
- disposability of assets that are not operationally interdependent;
- capability to delay the replacement of assets consumed in operation or to lease rather than purchase certain assets;
- possibility of using assets for factoring or sale and leaseback.

Debt factors
- availability of unused lines of credit or similar borrowing capacity;
- capability to renew or extend the due dates of existing loans;
- possibility of entering into debt restructuring agreements.

Cost factors
- separability of operations producing negative cash flows;
- capability of postponing expenditures such as maintenance or research and development;
- possibility of reducing expenditures on overheads and administration.

Equity factors
- variability of dividend requirements;
- capability to obtain additional contributions by owners;
- possibility of increasing cash distributions from subsidiaries or associates.

Source: AUS 708 (ISA 570), Appendix 3. Reproduced with the permission of The Institute of Chartered Accountants in Australia and CPA Australia.

The audit consideration of whether an entity is a going concern is an important factor both in assessing audit risk and in audit planning. If at any time, either during the planning phase or during the course of the audit, the auditor has reason to believe that the client entity may not be a going concern, special consideration should be given to the planning and performance of audit procedures. The auditor's responsibility with respect to the going concern basis is stated in AUS 708.10 (ISA 570.10): the auditor must be satisfied that it is appropriate, based on all reasonably foreseeable circumstances facing the entity, for the financial report to be prepared on the going concern basis. As possible events become more distant, there is less likely to be reliable evidence available about them. Therefore, although the auditor must be alert to the possibility that a going concern problem might arise at any time in the future, AUS 708.11 (ISA 570.11) indicates that the auditor's work will ordinarily be focused primarily on anticipated events during the relevant period, which is the period of approximately 12 months from the date of the current audit report to the expected date of the audit report on the succeeding financial period.

When a question arises concerning the appropriateness of the going concern basis, it may be necessary to employ additional procedures, to modify or extend existing procedures or to update earlier information. AUS 708.13 (ISA 570.13) also requires the auditor to perform such modified procedures as are appropriate should the auditor become aware that a going concern issue may exist beyond the relevant period. Details of significant documents examined and discussions held should be recorded and retained by the auditor, together with copies of cash flow, profit and other forecasts and notes of special audit procedures. If it is not clear whether the going concern basis is appropriate, most of the additional audit procedures necessary to establish the position will be performed during the completion stage of the audit; these are discussed in Chapter 12.

If the going concern basis is not appropriate, the auditor assesses the impact that a forced sale of assets would have on the book values and the classification of assets. The auditor also assesses the amount and classification of liabilities, including any provision for staff termination payments and other closing-down expenses.

Some audit firms have introduced, as part of their going concern evaluation, audit tests using models that attempt to predict firm failure. For example, the statistical techniques of discriminant analysis or regression can be used in auditing for the prediction of bankruptcy. However, Simnett and Trotman (1992) indicate that traditional financial distress models have not been widely used in practice for three reasons:

1   they have not been part of the formal training of most auditors;
2   the models have been criticised for both their data sets and statistical assumptions; and
3   the models have not been developed sufficiently to take account of factors which are accepted as affecting an entity's financial profile, such as size, industry, geographic location and age.

Dean and Clarke (2001) point out that the 'functionality of both the quantitative and qualitative distress prediction models currently in use is contestable'. The empirical evidence indicates that no unique bracket of financial ratios will outperform all others in distress prediction. Dean and Clarke (2001, pp. 182–3) argue that 'debate and uncertainty over when HIH Insurance and One.Tel became insolvent serves to reinforce the difficulties of identifying the onset of financial distress from financial data produced in compliance with the accepted Accounting Standards. It suggests that a "wild card" in this type of analysis is the extent to which adjustments for "creative accounting" need to be made'. The use of such models is, of course, only one part of the evidence gathered to make a judgment as to whether a client is likely to remain a going concern.

Analytical procedures, particularly ratio analysis, are commonly used to address the appropriateness of the going concern basis for an entity. Simnett and Trotman (1992) found that the cash flow ratios were the most significant class of ratios for predicting financial distress, while earnings ratios were also significant and followed a similar trend to the cash flow ratios. Some other ratios which are not widely used, such as market value of equity to book value of debt, also proved to be reliable and significant predictors.

Quick review

1   The auditor needs to pay attention to the possibility of fraud at the planning stage and make enquiries of management concerning the existence of fraud.
2   Earnings management has been involved in a number of the recent corporate scandals.
3   Related-party transactions contributed to the collapse of Enron.
4   Recent corporate collapses highlight the need to assess an entity's risk of suffering going concern problems.

MATERIALITY

learning objective 5

In addition to evaluating audit risk, the auditor must make a preliminary estimate of materiality when planning the audit. According to AUS 306.03 (ISA 320.03), **materiality** means information which if misstated, omitted or not disclosed separately in a financial report may adversely affect decisions about the allocation of scarce resources made by users of the financial report or the discharge of accountability by management, including the entity's governing body.

The auditor uses materiality in two ways:

1   in evaluating the presentation of financial data (materiality in accounting); and

2 in deciding questions involving the planning and execution of the audit program (materiality in auditing).

The audit should be planned to ensure that the auditor has a reasonable expectation of detecting material misstatements. The assessment of what is material is a matter of the auditor's professional judgment, which is influenced by their perception as to who are or are likely to be the prime users of the financial information and what their information needs are. This involves consideration of both the amount and the nature of the misstatement. The auditor's assessment of materiality levels is influenced by overall considerations of the financial report as well as matters relating to invalid account balances and relationships and legal and statutory requirements. It is possible to use different levels of materiality during the audit, depending on the matters being dealt with. The IAASB will be issuing an exposure draft during 2005 of a proposed new materiality standard, which may have a bearing on some of the issues discussed in this section.

Bases for evaluating materiality

Materiality in accounting is covered in accounting standard AASB 1031, 'Materiality in Financial Statements', which has a similar definition to that contained in AUS 306 (ISA 320) outlined above and requires that the nature and amount of an item should be considered when deciding upon materiality. Materiality is a matter of relative significance. It depends upon the relationship between the amount of the item of interest and the amount of some relevant basis of comparison. Some common bases are net profit, sales, total assets, current assets, liabilities and total share capital and reserves. The criteria for choice of a basis for comparison are relevance and stability. The materiality of an understatement of a liability is determined by the relevance criterion rather than the absolute amount. Even where the amount of misstatement is the same, an understatement of accounts payable may be more material than an understatement of non-current liabilities. The accounts payable figure affects the current ratio, and hence is related to the entity's short-term liquidity position.

Any quantitative guideline for determining materiality must necessarily be arbitrary. However, AASB 1031 states that in the absence of evidence or convincing argument to the contrary:

- an amount which is equal to or greater than 10 per cent of an appropriate base amount is presumed to be material;
- an amount which is equal to or less than 5 per cent of an appropriate base amount may be presumed not to be material;
- to determine whether an amount between 5 per cent and 10 per cent is material is a matter of judgment.

In determining whether an amount or aggregate of an item is material, the item should be compared with one of the following base amounts:

- **balance sheet items:** equity or the appropriate asset or liability class total;
- **income statement items:** (1) net profit or loss and the appropriate revenue or expense amount for the current financial year, or (2) average net profit or loss and the average of the appropriate revenue or expense amounts for a number of years (including the current financial year) if net profit varies greatly from year to year, or (3) an amount determined after allowing for any income tax effect where the base amount has itself been determined after allowing for any income tax effect. Materiality judgments relating to the income statement should ordinarily exclude the effect of unusual items or fluctuations, exceptional events or transactions, and discontinued operations.

cash flow items: (1) net cash provided or used in the operating, investing, financing or other activities as appropriate for the current financial year, or (2) average net cash flows provided by or used in the operating, investing, financing or other activities, as appropriate for a number of years (including the current financial year).

Setting the preliminary materiality judgment

When planning the audit, the auditor should make a preliminary estimate of the amount that is to be considered material for audit purposes, as this determines the items that are to receive more attention, in terms of either the conclusiveness of evidence gathered or the extent of items examined.

The auditor's preliminary judgment about the amount to be considered material conceptually encompasses the total of known, likely and potential undetected misstatements for the financial report taken as a whole. These terms have the following meaning in auditing:

- **Known misstatements** The amount of misstatement specifically identified by the auditor as a result of applying audit procedures to items examined. For example, an auditor vouches all additions to plant and equipment that exceed $10 000 and detects monetary misstatements totalling $5000. The $5000 misstatement actually detected is known misstatement.
- **Likely misstatements** The auditor's best estimate of the total misstatement in an account balance based on an extrapolation or projection of the misstatements actually detected. For example, assume that there are five additions to plant and equipment that exceed $10 000 (and were tested above) and 70 below that amount, and an auditor vouches 25 of those 70 and detects monetary misstatements totalling $1000. The auditor might extrapolate misstatement for that portion of the account balance as $2800 ($1000 ÷ 25 × 70). In this case the auditor's best estimate of the likely misstatement is $2800 which includes $1000 of known misstatements in the 25 items selected from the 70.
- **Potential undetected misstatements** The auditor's allowance for misstatements that remain undetected after applying audit procedures. For example, in the illustration of known misstatements and likely misstatements presented above, the auditor estimates total known and likely misstatements for additions to plant and equipment to be $7800 ($5000 + $2800). However, the auditor has only vouched 30 of 75 additions so there are potential undetected misstatements in total additions.

Procedures for estimating these potential undetected misstatements arising from sampling are discussed further in Chapter 11.

A single dollar amount is normally estimated for materiality because misstatements usually affect both the balance sheet and the income statement. For example, an overstatement of ending inventory overstates both assets and net profit. The only practical approach is to use the smallest aggregate amount that would affect one of the financial statements.

In all of its uses, materiality is a concept of relative significance. It depends on the amount of the item of interest and some relevant basis of comparison. Absolute dollar amounts are unworkable. An error of $10 000 might materially misstate the financial report of a small business, but an error of $100 000 might not materially misstate the financial report of a large business.

To estimate an amount for planning materiality, the auditor selects a base and a suitable percentage to apply to that base. This requires professional judgment, and not all auditors do it the same way. Some audit firms use a rule of thumb to estimate materiality for planning purposes. Table 7.4 (overleaf) summarises possible percentage methods. Most auditors use the most appropriate base for the entity being audited, while some auditors use a blend of these, making several calculations on a variety of bases and then taking the average. Others use a sliding scale, such as a declining percentage of total assets.

The choice of a rule of thumb depends on value judgments about relevance, stability and predictability. Net profit may be the most relevant base for a company with publicly traded securities. However, because net profit can fluctuate significantly from year to year it lacks stability, and it is not relevant to entities such as non-profit organisations. Generally, size-related bases such as total assets or total revenue are preferred because of their relative stability. Also, the information in Table 7.4 is often combined in the rule of thumb. For example, another approach is to use the larger of 1 per cent of total assets or total revenue.

TABLE **7.4** **Rules of thumb for planning materiality**

Common bases	Range of percentages applied to base	Relative advantages
Net profit	5–10	Relevance
Total revenue	0.5–1	Stability
Total assets	0.5–1	Predictability and stability
Equity	1–2	Stability

A rule of thumb as a decision aid in general planning is not universal in auditing practice. An audit firm may adopt a specific rule of thumb or the judgment may be left to the individual auditor in the circumstances.

The financial information used as a base may be taken from:

1 the financial report to be audited (if available and not likely to be adjusted significantly as a result of the audit);
2 interim financial information (adjusted for expected seasonal or cyclical fluctuation and annualised); or
3 the previous period's financial reports (adjusted for unusual matters and known significant changes, such as a new wage contract or a merger).

The preliminary judgment about the amount to be considered material to the financial report taken as a whole is an important general planning decision. The auditor may use this judgment to identify components of the financial report to be emphasised, the locations to visit in a multilocation company, and, naturally, in planning the nature, timing and extent of specific auditing procedures. A smaller materiality amount results in more extensive testing and larger sample sizes for tests. Since different approaches to calculating materiality can lead to substantially different amounts, the auditor's judgment in the circumstances is a key factor.

In June 2001, the AUASB revised AUS 306 in order to further clarify existing practice regarding the auditor's consideration of materiality in planning an audit and evaluating audit evidence.

AUS 306 now provides guidance on how the auditor should establish a preliminary assessment of materiality to plan audit procedures. It discusses quantitative and qualitative factors that may affect the assessment of materiality and highlights the importance of qualitative factors when assessing the impact of individual misstatements and the appropriateness of aggregating misstatements.

AUS 306.10 requires that when establishing a preliminary assessment of materiality, the auditor should have regard to:

- the reliability of management information;
- any factors that may indicate deviations from normal activities; and
- qualitative factors.

The auditor should select benchmark(s) appropriate to the entity's circumstances for a quantitative evaluation of materiality at the financial report level and in relation to individual account balances, classes of transactions and disclosures. A quantitative materiality level, represented by a percentage or dollar threshold, provides a basis or initial step for the preliminary assumption that without considering all relevant circumstances, a deviation of less than the specified amount is unlikely to be material. The auditor applies this materiality level to audit procedures where appropriate and uses it to evaluate the outcome of those procedures. The auditor uses professional judgment to record misstatements below the materiality level, having regard to the qualitative factors which may cause misstatements of quantitatively small amounts to be material.

However, the magnitude of a misstatement alone is only one factor used to assess materiality. The auditor reviews each misstatement in the context of information relevant to users of the financial report, by considering qualitative factors and the circumstances in which the misstatement or judgment has been made.

AUS 306.17 requires that the auditor should consider qualitative factors that impact on the materiality of individual misstatements to assess:

- the significance of the item to the particular entity;
- the pervasiveness of the misstatement (for example the misstatement might affect the presentation of numerous items in the financial report); and
- the effect of misstatement on the financial report as a whole.

Examples of qualitative material misstatements given in AUS 306.19 include:

- the inadequate or improper description of an accounting policy when it is likely that a user of the financial report would be misled by the description;
- failure to disclose the breach of regulatory requirements when it is likely that the consequent imposition of regulatory restrictions will significantly impair operating capability;
- matters that affect the integrity of the financial records;
- matters that indicate weaknesses in the entity's system of internal control that may have further impact on various aspects of the financial reporting process; and
- matters that suggest fraudulent financial reporting practice or that management is attempting to 'manage' or manipulate the entity's reported earnings.

AUS 306 also considers the potential impacts of misstatements in relation to internal control, financial records and fraud. It advises auditors to adopt an attitude of professional scepticism when assessing whether immaterial misstatements are being used as a method of earnings management and provides further guidance on reporting responsibilities when misstatements (whether material or not) are identified.

An empirical study by Martinov and Roebuck (1998) of the guidelines used in determining the materiality assessment for the large audit firms in Australia showed that only one firm did not use judgment for materiality levels in the planning stage of the audit. This firm used a specific formula based on the size of the entity. The other firms reported that a considerable amount of judgment is involved in determining materiality, although some general guidance on the appropriate base to use is provided.

As indicated in AUS 306.11 (ISA 320.11), the amount considered material does not remain fixed after its initial calculation. The auditor may revise this judgment as a result of audit tests' findings and new information as the audit progresses, and the approach used in evaluation at the completion of the audit may be considerably different. This means the amount estimated for planning materiality should not be confused with the amount used in the evaluation of the materiality of individual misstatements.

The auditor's use of materiality in evaluation is influenced by qualitative considerations, additional information and the nature of the decisions to be made. Qualitative considerations, for example, may include the nature of the transaction, such as related-party transactions or possible illegal acts. The use of materiality in evaluation is explained in Chapter 12, Completion and Review.

The auditor documents the basis of the materiality decision and the factors considered in making it.

Allocation of materiality to account balances and classes of transactions

In determining the nature, timing and extent of procedures to be applied to a specific account balance the auditor needs to obtain a reasonable assurance of detecting misstatements which, based on the preliminary materiality judgment, could be material to the financial report as a whole when aggregated with misstatements in other balances. AUS 306.07 (ISA 320.07) states that the auditor must consider materiality at both the financial report level and in relation to individual account balances, classes of transactions and disclosures. However, AUS 306 (ISA 320) does not mandate the specific steps an auditor should take to achieve that goal. In practice, some auditors use rules of thumb to explicitly relate materiality to substantive tests at the account balance or class of transactions level. Other auditors establish materiality for this purpose judgmentally.

The purpose of allocating a portion of the preliminary judgment about materiality to account balances or classes of transactions is to plan the scope of audit procedures for the individual account balance or class of transactions. For example, if a small amount of materiality were allocated to a specific account more evidence would be gathered than if a larger amount of materiality were allocated.

Due to the many factors involved there is no required or optimal method for allocating materiality to an account balance or class of transactions. The process can be done judgmentally or by using some formal quantitative approach. In allocating materiality the auditor needs to consider:

- The magnitude of the account relative to the financial report. For example, the larger an account balance, the greater the amount of materiality that can be allocated to it. It is assumed that a $30 million account balance can contain a larger misstatement than a $3 million account balance.
- The expectation of error. If the auditor expects little or no misstatement in an account, a larger materiality threshold can be allocated to the account. As the auditor's expectation of error is low, the scope for auditing the account can be reduced.

Relationship between materiality and audit risk

AUS 306.10 (ISA 320.10) points out that the relationship between audit risk and materiality is inverse. This means that the auditor sets a lower materiality threshold for accounts which have a higher audit risk. Thus, if the auditor determines that a particular account is important, even a low level of error cannot be tolerated. The auditor allows for this by increasing the extent of audit procedures, selecting a more effective audit procedure and/or performing audit procedures closer to balance date.

The audit should be planned so that audit risk is kept at an acceptably low level. The audit risk the auditor seeks to restrict is the risk of a *material* misstatement remaining undetected after applying audit procedures. This requires the auditor to plan the nature, timing and extent of audit procedures by taking into account the level of materiality.

Thus, the auditor's consideration of materiality and audit risk are really inseparable. Materiality relates to how precise auditing procedures need to be, and audit risk relates to the degree of certainty achieved by the procedures.

It is important, therefore, that during the planning of the audit the auditor knows the business sufficiently to understand what is material in the circumstances of that client, and takes into account the audit risk in formulating the nature, timing and extent of the audit procedures.

Quick review

1. Materiality needs to be considered at the financial report level and at the account balances or transaction classes level.
2. Planning materiality determines the items that will receive more attention in terms of conclusiveness of evidence required or extent of items examined.
3. Planning materiality needs to consider qualitative as well as quantitative factors.
4. Assessment of what is material is a matter of auditor judgment.
5. There is an inverse relationship between audit risk and materiality.

Summary

A major component of audit risk is inherent risk, which is the risk of errors occurring due to the characteristics of the entity and the environment in which it operates. Special risk areas that need to be considered are fraud, including earnings management; related party transactions; and the appropriateness of the going concern basis for preparing the financial report. Materiality is a matter of judgment and is considered at both the overall and account balance levels.

Key terms

Earnings management	306	Inherent risk	296
Error	303	Materiality	313
Fraud	303	Related parties	308
Going concern basis	310	Risk of fraud or error	302
Illegal acts	307		

References

Alderman, C.W. and Tabor, R.H. (1989) 'The case for risk-driven audits', *Journal of Accountancy*, March, 55–61.

Dean, G. and Clarke, F. (2001) 'Distressed businesses—predicting failure' in *Collapse Incorporated: Tales, Safeguards and Responsibilities of Corporate Australia*, CCH, Sydney, 147–84.

Holstrum, L.G. and Messier, F.W. (1982) 'A review and integration of empirical research on materiality', *Auditing: A Journal of Practice and Theory*, Vol. 2, No. 1, Fall, 45–62.

KPMG (2002) *Fraud Survey*, KPMG, Sydney.

Leslie, D.A. (1985) *Materiality: The Concept and its Application to Auditing*, CICA, Toronto.

Levitt, A. (1998) 'The numbers game', *NYU Centre for Law and Business*, 28 September.

Martinov, M. and Roebuck, P. (1998) 'The assessment and integration of materiality and inherent risk: An analysis of major firms' audit practices', *International Journal of Auditing*, Vol. 2, No. 2, 103–26.

Monroe, G.S., Ng, J.K.L. and Woodliff, D.R. (1993) 'The importance of inherent risk factors: Auditors' perceptions', *Australian Accounting Review*, Vol. 3, No. 2, 34–45.

Pany, K. and Wheeler, S. (1989) 'A comparison of various materiality rules of thumb', *The CPA Journal*, Vol. 59, No. 6, 62–3.

Simnett, R. and Trotman, K. (1992) 'Identification of key financial ratios for going concern decisions', *Charter*, April, 39–41.

Yardley, J. (1989) 'Explaining the conditional nature of the audit risk model', *Journal of Accounting Education*, Vol. 7, 107–14.

Assignments

(MaxMARK)

MAXIMISE YOUR MARKS! There are approximately 30 interactive questions on inherent risk assessment and materiality available online at www.mhhe.com/au/gay3e

Additional assignments for this chapter are contained in Appendix A of this book, page 768.

REVIEW QUESTIONS

7.1 The following questions relate to the factors that affect the auditor's risk and materiality planning decisions. Select the *best* response.

(a) Which of the following does *not* increase inherent risk for the revenue transaction cycle?

   A Sales are made on a sale or return basis.

   B Sales commissions are paid to sales staff.

   C Sales are made in $US to a large US listed company.

   D The accounts receivable clerk opens the daily mail.

(b) Which of the following will increase inherent risk?

   A Sales invoices were not authorised while the sales manager was on annual leave.

   B The management is well respected in the industry.

   C The industry is mature and stable.

   D The entity's primary product is software for the expanding Internet market.

(c) With respect to errors and irregularities, which of the following should be part of an auditor's planning of the audit engagement?

   A Plan to search for fraud or errors that would have a material effect on the financial report

   B Plan to search for fraud or errors that would have a material or immaterial effect on the financial report

   C Plan to discover fraud or errors that are either material or immaterial

   D Plan to discover fraud or errors that are material

(d) An audit performed in accordance with Australian auditing standards generally should:

   A encompass a plan to actively search for illegalities which relate to operating aspects

   B disclose all violations in lending laws

   C provide assurance that illegal acts will be detected where control risk is minimal

   D not be relied upon to provide assurance that illegal acts will be detected

(e) An auditor believes that there is substantial doubt about the ability of Expo Australia Ltd to continue as a going concern for a reasonable period of time. In evaluating Expo Australia Ltd's plans for dealing with the adverse effects of future conditions and events, the auditor would most likely consider, as a mitigating factor, Expo Australia Ltd's plans to

   A negotiate reductions in interest rates on outstanding debt

   B accelerate research and development projects related to future products

    C enhance the quality of existing product lines by investing in new manufacturing technology

    D purchase equipment and production facilities currently being leased

(f) Which of the following statements is correct concerning related-party transactions?

    A In the absence of evidence to the contrary, related-party transactions should be assumed to be outside the ordinary course of business.

    B An auditor should determine whether a particular transaction would have occurred if the parties had *not* been related.

    C An auditor should substantiate that related-party transactions were consummated on terms equivalent to those that prevail in arm's-length transactions.

    D The audit procedures directed toward identifying related-party transactions should include considering whether transactions are occurring but are not being given proper accounting recognition.

(g) The concept of materiality with respect to the attest function

    A requires the auditor to make judgments as to whether misstatements affect the fairness of the financial report

    B applies only to publicly held entities

    C has greater application to the standards of reporting than the other generally accepted auditing standards

    D requires that relatively more effort be directed to those assertions that are more susceptible to misstatement

(h) Which of the following would an auditor be most likely to use in determining the preliminary judgment about materiality?

    A The contents of the management representation letter

    B The anticipated sample size of the planned substantive tests

    C The entity's annualised interim financial statements

    D The results of the internal control questionnaire

7.2 The following questions relate to the overall audit strategy and other general planning decisions. Select the *best* response.

(a) An audit program should be designed for each individual audit and should include audit steps and procedures to:

    A ensure that only material items are audited

    B detect and eliminate all fraud

    C increase the amount of management information available

    D provide assurances that the objectives of the audit are met

(b) Which of the following statements concerning the auditor's use of the work of a specialist is correct?

    A If the auditor believes that the determinations made by the specialist are unreasonable, only an adverse opinion may be issued.

    B If the specialist is related to the client, the auditor is not permitted to use the specialist's findings as corroborative evidence.

    C The specialist should be identified in the audit report if the auditor has relied on the specialist in issuing an unqualified audit opinion.

    D The specialist should have an understanding of the auditor's corroborative use of the specialist's findings.

Inherent risk

7.3 What is inherent risk and why is it important to evaluate inherent risk as a part of planning?

Risk of fraud

7.4 Why are risks concerning fraud important to the audit planning process?

Related parties

7.5 List three audit procedures that may be used to identify transactions with related parties.

Going concern risk

7.6 Why are risks concerning irregularities and the going concern basis important to the audit planning process?

Materiality

7.7 Identify the matters an auditor is particularly concerned about when evaluating materiality as part of planning.

DISCUSSION PROBLEMS AND CASE STUDIES

primary learning objective 1

Inherent risk

7.8 **Basic** Jack Splat has been assigned to the audit of the inventory section of two companies. The first company, Massive Trucks Pty Ltd, sells trucks used on construction sites and makes goods to order. Inventory comprises spare parts for trucks plus a number of 'add-ons' such as backhoes and buckets for its existing product range. The second client, Gems Jewellery Pty Ltd, is a jewellery retailer which has a number of showrooms located in major metropolitan hotels.

Required

Which client do you believe Jack will assess as having the higher inherent risk? Provide reasons for your decision.

7.9 **Moderate** You are currently involved in planning for the audit of 123 Limited. 123 produces educational books and toys for children. The market is highly competitive and the company has been experiencing declining sales over the last two years. Cost cutting has proven quite difficult, as the cost of paper and other resources used in 123's operations has continued to increase each year. While the bankers are presently happy to continue providing 123 with loan facilities, they do expect to see improved results in the next financial report and have placed a number of quite restrictive covenants in their lending agreements. Articles about 123's expected financial results appearing in recent press reports have all had quite a pessimistic tone.

Required

For the situation outlined above:
(a) describe the overall impact on audit risk;
(b) identify the specific component(s) of audit risk affected;
(c) describe the impact on your overall audit plan.

7.10 **Moderate** You are about to begin the year-end audit of P Ltd, a large multinational company. Consider each of the following independent situations.

1 Inventories of iron ore are kept at a central mine site. Mr V, an independent valuer, has surveyed the ore and issued a valuation certificate for the last 10 years. Mr V has recently

retired and Mr X has taken his place. Mr X has reviewed several of Mr V's past valuations and has described them as being 'absolute rubbish'. In past years you have placed full reliance on Mr V's valuations.

2   One of P Ltd's divisions was sold just prior to year-end. Although the division contributed about 10 per cent of revenues and operating profits it was not considered part of P Ltd's core business. The purchaser paid a deposit of 20 per cent of the purchase price. The remainder will be paid in 12 months' time, providing the division maintains certain key operating ratios.

3   During the year, one of the divisions established an overseas branch in Country Z. The product was so successful that the division's warehousing facilities were moved to Country Z. While overseas sales are booming, Australian customers now have to wait several weeks for their orders to be filled. Currency fluctuations since year-end in Country Z have doubled the price the consumer in Z pays for the product.

4   P Ltd's internal auditors have informed you of a payroll fraud discovered in an overseas branch. A senior officer of the company breached internal controls by entering temporary staff on the payroll register and later collecting their wages (which were made out in cash). This is believed to have taken place on a weekly basis over the last two years. In past years you have not visited the branch because it is immaterial to the operations of P Ltd.

Required

For each situation:

(a)   explain the impact on inherent risk, and

(b)   list the major balance sheet and income statement accounts affected. Outline your audit approach for each account.

Source: This question was adapted from the Professional Year Programme of The Institute of Chartered Accountants in Australia—1995 Advanced Audit Module.

7.11   Moderate   Electro Ltd distributes and supplies electrical appliances. The company is an ongoing client of your audit firm. From a telephone call to the General Manager prior to the commencement of the audit you have ascertained the following:

1   During the year several members of the board of directors retired and were replaced by prominent businesspeople previously associated, but not directly connected, with the company.

2   The company has experienced considerable staff turnover in the accounts payable department, including the resignation of the manager early in the year. This has created some delays in the processing of payments.

3   The company plans to upgrade its general ledger reporting with a new software package. The conversion is planned for three months before financial year-end.

4   One of the advantages of the new computer system is that it provides detailed information on sales, inventory levels and gross margins, by both product line and geographical area.

5   During the year the company received a visit from the Australian Tax Office for a desk audit. As a result of this a number of issues were raised, but to date no assessment has been issued. The company's tax advisers are presently following up these matters.

6   During the year a new management incentive scheme was introduced. The bonus is calculated on the basis of the increase in net profit over the previous year.

7   The company decided to retrench its internal audit department two months before year-end as part of its cost-cutting program.

8   You have been informed that some internal controls over the accounts payable cycle are not operating correctly due to the cut in staff numbers.

Required

How will the above matters affect your overall plan for the expected scope and conduct of the audit?

Source: This question was adapted from the Professional Year Programme of The Institute of Chartered Accountants in Australia—1995 Advanced Audit Module.

7.12 Moderate You are the audit senior responsible for the audit of Sampson Limited. You are currently planning the audit for the year ended 31 December 2001, and during your initial planning meeting with the financial controller he told you of the following changes in the company's operations.

1   Due to the financial controller's workload, the company has employed a treasurer. The financial controller is excited about the appointment, because in the two months the treasurer has been with the company he has realised a small profit for the company through foreign-exchange transactions in yen.

2   Sampson Limited has planned to close an inefficient factory in country New South Wales before the end of 2001. It is expected that the redeployment and disposal of the factory assets will not be completed until the end of the following year. However, the financial controller is confident that he will be able to determine reasonably accurate closure provisions.

3   To help achieve budgeted sales for the year, Sampson Limited is about to introduce bonuses for sales staff. The bonuses will be an increasing percentage of the gross sales made by each salesperson above certain monthly targets.

4   The managing director has just returned from the USA, where he signed a contract to import a line of clothing that has become the latest fashion fad there. The company has not previously been engaged in the clothing industry.

Required

Explain how each of the scenarios above affect inherent risk.

7.13 Complex You are auditing JJ Ltd, a large clothing manufacturer that sells clothing whole-sale to large department stores. The industry is highly competitive and fast-moving due to continual changes in fashion. JJ Ltd has been established for 20 years but for the last three years has been making only small profits. JJ Ltd has a bank loan that is contingent on JJ Ltd producing at least break-even results.

You have noted the following independent events in relation to the 30 December 20X3 audit:

1   Due to increased competitive pressures, JJ Ltd has recently moved the manufacture of some of its clothing lines to China. The fabric is made in Australia, sent to China to be cut and stitched, then returned to Australia in finished form. JJ Ltd saves around 20% in costs compared to the equivalent Australian-made item. However, the manufacturing process takes longer and on a few occasions late delivery from China has resulted in lost sales.

2   Sales staff are currently paid a salary based on years of experience, plus a flat $5000 bonus each per quarter if quarterly sales targets are met or exceeded. This system will end on 30 September 20X3 and a new scheme will be implemented. Under this new scheme, sales staff will be paid a lower salary and sales will be tracked by the individual staff member. If an individual's target is met or exceeded, the salesperson will receive a commission of 5% of their sales.

3 At present JJ Ltd maintains warehouses in each state to ensure goods can be delivered to customers with minimal delay. Unfortunately this has resulted in high warehousing costs due to the duplication of premises and staff. On 1 November 20X3, the lease agreements for the state warehouses will be terminated and the warehouses closed. All inventory will be transferred to a new, leased warehouse in an industrial estate on the outskirts of Melbourne.

4 In the past 18 months, JJ Ltd has experienced staff shortages in the accounts payable area. Clerical work in this area is highly specialised and JJ Ltd has been unable to recruit the appropriate personnel. This has resulted in errors in the accounts payable ledger, particularly double-counted invoices. However, last month JJ Ltd secured the services of two experienced accounts payable clerks, both on 2 year contracts. They are slowly clearing the backlog of entries and intend to fully reconcile each creditor's account prior to year-end.

5 With the move of some manufacturing offshore, JJ Ltd has found itself with some excess factory machinery. A proposed sale to a small firm in Brisbane has recently fallen through, and JJ Ltd is having difficulty finding other buyers. The accountant has told you that JJ Ltd is considering consigning the machinery to an auction house to sell it for the best possible price.

6 Recent reports have appeared in the financial press regarding PM Pty Ltd, a chain of 100 retail clothing shops operating in all parts of Australia. PM Pty Ltd's owners are seeking to exit the business and JJ Ltd has entered into a contract to purchase the store leases and stock as at 31 December 20X3. JJ Ltd's move into retail is driven by a desire to improve its trading results; retail margins are on average 10% higher than wholesale. JJ Ltd intends holding a 'closing down' sale in January to clear old stock; it will then close and refurbish the stores, re-stock them with its own lines, and re-open in early February.

7 In order to reduce its wages expense and gain a more flexible workforce, JJ Ltd has recently signed enterprise bargaining agreements with its factory workers. Under these agreements, the workers will be contractors instead of employees from 1 January 20X4. Although JJ Ltd will pay a 20% higher hourly rate, it will no longer incur sick, annual or long service leave.

8 In order to secure its key customers as long-term clients, JJ Ltd now offers some of its clothing lines on a 'sale or return' basis. The accountant estimates that around 30% of sales are now made on these terms. Sales staff estimate around 10% of 'sale or return' items are returned to JJ Ltd for a refund. At present, manual records are kept of 'sale or return' items, which for accounting purposes are recorded as sales at the time the goods are delivered. As 'sale or return' sales are expected to increase, the accountant is considering having the computer system modified to automatically track these goods.

Required

Identify the financial report areas/accounts affected by each of the above independent events. Would audit risk for each area increase or decrease and why? Where appropriate, include discussion of the key audit assertions affected.

Source: This question was adapted from the PY Program of The Institute of Chartered Accountants in Australia—2000 Accounting 2 Module.

7.14 Complex You have been assigned to the financial report audit of Richfast Pty Limited, a large firm that provides financial planning services and investment advice to the general public. This is the first year your firm has performed the audit. You and the assurance services manager have just returned from a briefing with the finance director, Ms Nomer. Your notes from the meeting are reproduced below.

1   Ms Nomer expects us to get 'up to speed' with Richfast Pty Limited's operations ASAP. She has instructed her staff to co-operate fully with us and to answer any queries we may have.

2   Ms Nomer was quite impressed with the prior audit firm although she felt they were a bit too keen to sell her additional services.

3   Richfast Pty Limited has branches in each capital city. These branches report to head office monthly via a standard set of management reports submitted by secure email.

4   In the past, the branches largely 'did their own thing' as regards accounting and accounting records. However, this resulted in many problems at year-end. Software consultants were engaged at the beginning of the year and have installed a networked accounting package that all branches now use. The system appears to be functioning well.

5   Richfast Pty Limited is privately owned by around 60 principals. Shareholdings (and therefore profit shares) vary according to seniority. Some principals have salary and drawings paid directly to their private companies; Ms Nomer doesn't get involved in this. Another firm of accountants, BSD & Co., handles this aspect of the business, including the maintenance of statutory registers.

6   Richfast Pty Limited is generally seen as lagging behind the market leaders in the industry; the firm tends to be seen as a bit old-fashioned and conservative.

7   Richfast Pty Limited's general purpose financial report is quite complex, but an unqualified audit report has been issued every year an audit has been carried out.

Required

(a)   Contrast inherent risk and control risk. Explain, using examples, how one event or factor relating to a client may affect both inherent and control risks.

(b)   Identify factors in the above information that affect your inherent risk assessment for Richfast Pty Limited. For each factor, state whether inherent risk will increase or decrease and justify your answer.

Source: This question was adapted from the CA Program of The Institute of Chartered Accountants in Australia—2002 Financial Reporting and Assurance Module.

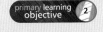

Risk of fraud

7.15   Basic   Dean Williams has been assigned to the audit of a new client operating in the finance and banking sector. The audit plan indicates that the client has an extensive computer information system and as such all auditors should consider the possibility of fraud. Dean is confused by this comment as he thought auditors did not concern themselves with fraud and has asked the manager to explain the comment.

Required

(a)   Explain to Dean why the audit plan requires the audit team to consider the possibility of fraud.

(b)   Identify six (6) factors that may increase the susceptibility of computer information systems to fraud.

7.16   Moderate   At the beginning of the annual audit of Hinson Pty Ltd, a wholesale distributor, Lynn Magnum, the shareholders' auditor, was given a copy of the company's financial report as prepared by the company's accountant. On reviewing the report, Magnum noted the following abnormal conditions:

1   The accounts receivable outstanding at the year-end represents an unusually high number of average days' credit sales.

2   The inventories on hand at the year-end represent an unusually high proportion of the current assets.

3   The working capital ratio of the company is almost twice that of the previous year.

4   The percentage of gross profit on net sales is considerably in excess of that of previous years.

5   The rate of turnover of inventory is unusually low in comparison with previous years.

Required

Taking all the above conditions together, what irregularities might Magnum suspect regarding sales and inventories?

Source: CICA adapted

Related parties

7.17 Basic Having read the entire strategy, Dean Williams has found a paragraph requiring the team to consider related parties when conducting the audit. Dean knows that the company must disclose information to comply with AASB 1017 (IAS 24) but does not understand why the audit strategy has referred to related parties as a 'special risk area' and approaches his manager for an explanation.

Required

Assuming you are the manager, explain to Dean why it is necessary to consider related parties as part of the audit planning process.

Going concern risk

7.18 Basic Dean Williams has not noticed that the audit strategy includes a paragraph specifically requiring the firm to consider going concern. Dean quickly looks at the interim financial report attached and notes that the entity does not appear to have any going concern problems. He is unsure why specific comment has been made and asks his manager.

Required

Assuming you are the manager, explain to Dean why it is necessary to assess the risk of going concern problems as part of the audit planning process.

7.19 Complex You are the engagement manager assigned to the audit of V Limited, a listed Australian company that manufactures and installs videoconferencing equipment. V usually has two or three large contracts (ranging from $100 million to $150 million each) in progress at any one time. The contracts usually take up to six months to complete, although unexpected on-site communications difficulties usually result in lengthy delays in completion (up to 12 months). V finances its operations with a mixture of equity, long-term debt (secured by fixed assets) and short-term bank loans.

It is now November 20X0 and your planning of the audit of V for the year ended 31 December 20X0 is nearing completion. Your discussions with the management of V and review of the preliminary information provided by V have revealed a number of issues that may have implications for the company's ability to continue as a going concern. The relevant issues are:

1   The review of work-in-progress indicates that all the contracts in progress at year-end are due for completion within 6 months of balance date. There are no new contracts in place for the coming year, although management have indicated that there are orders currently being negotiated. The nature of the business is such that sales will

fluctuate considerably from year to year depending on the timing of one or two large contracts.

2 Included in provisions is a large provision for warranty for one of V's jobs completed at a university site 2 years ago. It appears that the system is still not working and the university is now requesting a substantial refund of the contract price.

3 Competition in the industry is becoming more intense, with many customers now installing their own equipment.

4 Included within V's assets are benefits expected to arise from tax losses incurred in previous years. This benefit will only be obtained if the company returns to a profitable situation in the future.

5 The company's bank has requested cash flow forecasts for the coming year to support the short-term loans. It has indicated that it may need to withdraw funding or restructure debt if the forecasts are not adequate.

6 Assets consist chiefly of plant and equipment, some of which is specialised to the industry. Debtors are significant, but recoverability is not considered an issue as the ongoing projects are with reputable customers and management is not aware of any problems. Creditor balances are at normal levels, and the company is in a positive working capital position.

Required

Do you believe the area of going concern should be assessed as high risk for V? Provide reasons for your decision.

Materiality

7.20 Moderate The concept of materiality is important to an auditor in an examination of a financial report and expression of opinion upon it.

(a) How are materiality (and immateriality) related to the proper presentation of a financial report?

(b) In what ways will considerations of materiality affect the auditor in:
   (i) developing an audit program?
   (ii) the performance of auditing procedures?

(c) What factors and measures should the auditor consider in assessing the materiality of an exception to required financial report presentation?

Source: AICPA adapted

7.21 Moderate Bitchoomen Limited is a listed company with a wide spread of shareholders. The company is mainly involved in the manufacture and retail of civil engineering products. Your firm has completed the financial report audit for the past five years and has not encountered any significant problems or misstatements during this period.

Bitchoomen Limited has been operating with its present company structure and its basic product range for the past $3\frac{1}{2}$ years. The company has built a strong reputation in the marketplace based on its astute, conservative management style and quality produce range.

The 'geotextile' products are targeted mainly at the road construction market, which represents 40% of Bitchoomen Limited's revenue. These products have come under heavy competition in the last 6 months, eroding Bitchoomen Limited's profit margins significantly.

The following is a summary of Bitchoomen Limited's key financial data:

Year	Turnover $	Operating profit before tax $	Operating profit after tax and extraordinaries $	Total assets $	Net assets $
20X4	1986	84	9	2333	1133
20X3	1899	108	108	2241	1028
20X2	1913	135	135	2426	923
20X1	2268	117	93	2081	870
20X0	2609	101	35	2444	908

Required

(a) From the information provided, identify and discuss the factors you need to consider when setting the preliminary materiality for Bitchoomen Limited for the 20X4 financial year. Explain the impact each of the factors would have on your materiality calculation.

(b) Calculate the preliminary materiality figure to be adopted in the planning of the 20X4 financial report audit of Bitchoomen Limited. Justify your selection of the key financial data used as a base for the materiality calculation and the percentage applied to this base.

Source: This question was adapted from the CA Program of The Institute of Chartered Accountants in Australia—2002 Financial Reporting and Assurance Module.

7.22 Complex You have just completed audit testing on the 31 December 20X3 financial report of Maykit Pty Ltd, a manufacturing firm. Extracts from the final draft financial report are given below.

	$000
Current assets	15 724
Non-current assets	10 786
Current liabilities	7 319
Non-current liabilities	5 850
Shareholders' equity	13 341
Operating profit before tax	3 714
Operating profit after tax	3 033

The audit manager has asked you to review the summary of audit differences work paper to determine if there are any material misstatements in the financial report. This work paper is set out below.

Details of misstatement found	Actual misstatement $	Projected misstatement (if applicable) $	Total misstatement $
i) Non tax-deductible fine imposed as a result of court case; not taken up as at 31 December 20X3.	350 000	—	350 000
ii) Incorrect prices on sales invoices issued in June (customers overcharged).	45 000	123 000	168 000

iii) Unrecorded payables due to 31 December 20X3 stock purchases not being taken up (cut-off misstatement).	91 000	—	91 000
iv) Interest payable on bank overdraft not taken up.	225 000	—	225 000

The projected misstatement for Item (ii) was calculated using your firm's monetary unit sampling software, which has been independently tested and found to give statistically accurate and reliable results.

Required

(a) Under what circumstances might a misstatement be judged to be material because of its nature rather than its amount? Give examples.

(b) Are any of the misstatements in items (i) to (iv) material? In each case, explain, showing calculations, how you reached your conclusion.

Source: This question was adapted from the CA Program of The Institute of Chartered Accountants in Australia—2002 Financial Reporting and Assurance Module.

7.23 Complex

PART A

You are planning the 30 June 20X3 audit of ABC Ltd and have obtained the following projected summary financial information from the financial controller:

	Projected to 30/6/X3 $000
Current assets	
Cash	200
Receivables	1 500
Inventory	1 040
Total current assets	2 740
Non-current assets	
Property, plant and equipment	3 040
Goodwill	400
Total non-current assets	3 440
Total assets	6 180
Current liabilities	
Creditors and borrowings	1 820
Provisions	500
Total current liabilities	2 320
Non-current liabilities	
Creditors and borrowings	1 400
Provisions	620
Total non-current liabilities	2 020
Total liabilities	4 340
Net assets	1 840
Shareholders' equity	
Share capital	1 000
Retained profits	840
Total shareholders' equity	1 840
Profit before tax	1 000

You have the following additional information:

1 Under the terms of their contracts, senior management will be paid a significant bonus if actual profit before tax reaches $1m.

2 A significant portion of both current and non-current borrowings consist of a loan from XYZ Bank. Under the terms of the contract, the loan is due for immediate repayment if the ratio of current assets to current liabilities drops below 1.15.

3 In prior years, you have placed reliance on the company's internal control and you plan to place reliance on controls again this year.

4 ABC is expecting a slight increase in final quarter sales figures over those projected due to the expected positive impact of the GST on the industry.

Required

(a) Why do auditors set a materiality level at the planning stage of the audit?

(b) What relevance does planning materiality have when evaluating the actual errors remaining in the financial report at the end of the audit?

(c) For each of the points under additional information, discuss whether materiality is likely to increase, decrease or remain unaffected.

PART B

The audit partner has now approved the planning materiality level to be used on the audit. The audit manager has instructed the audit team to:

- perform detailed substantive procedures on all Balance Sheet and Income Statement items > materiality level.
- perform analytical procedures on all Balance Sheet and Income Statement items < materiality level.

Required

Discuss, using examples, whether or not you agree with the manager's instructions.

Source: This question was adapted from the Professional Year Programme of The Institute of Chartered Accountants in Australia—2000 Accounting 2 Module.

7.24 Complex

PART A

You are currently planning the audit of GC Pty Ltd. You have calculated the following ratios in order to assist you in identifying potential audit risk areas:

Ratio	Unaudited 30/6/X3	Audited 30/6/X3	Industry Average
Cost of goods sold/sales (%)	73.27	79.34	69.24
Operating expenses/sales (%)	12.96	16.25	14.81
Selling and administrative expenses/sales (%)	4.00	4.51	4.90
Interest expense/sales (%)	3.31	3.44	5.23
Total costs/sales (%)	92.99	97.40	93.25
Profit/sales (%)	4.47	3.91	5.15
Inventory turnover (times per year)	1.44	1.95	2.15
Accounts receivable turnover (days)	80.00	95.00	75.00
Current assets/current liabilities	1.37	1.20	1.45
Receivables/current liabilities	0.25	0.25	0.40
Profit/capital (% per year)	13.89	15.81	18.19
Times dividend earned	1.60	2.00	1.80

In addition, you have the following information:

- GC Pty Ltd is a large proprietary company involved in property development and residential construction in the Melbourne region. It experienced losses a few years ago but in recent years has improved its performance and returned to profitability.
- Current year operating profit has increased by nearly 50% while sales have fallen slightly from last year's levels.
- Eight months ago, GC Pty Ltd became involved in a consortium building a large residential project on the outskirts of Melbourne. The project is expected to take 7 years to finish, with completed dwellings being sold in stages 'off-the-plan'. Off-the-plan sales have become increasingly popular with consumers as only a small deposit is required to secure the property, with the balance not payable until completion (often up to 12 months later).
- In order to finance participation in the residential project, GC Pty Ltd doubled its bank loan.
- Industry average data was obtained from the Australian Bureau of Statistics, and is calculated using figures from all listed property development companies in Australia.

Required

(a) Outline the circumstances under which basing analytical procedures on:
  (i) unaudited figures; and
  (ii) prior year comparisons
  would be inappropriate.

(b) In the case of GC Pty Ltd, discuss the problems that might arise when comparing GC Pty Ltd's results to industry averages.

PART B

Your assistant has reviewed the data in Part A and has made the following notes:

1 Cost of goods/sales, operating expenses/sales, and selling and admin expenses/sales have all fallen, indicating an improvement in management efficiency. In addition, these ratios are all lower than industry averages, indicating GC Pty Ltd has good cost control measures in place.

2 The inventory turnover ratio has fallen, indicating that inventory is held for less time than prior years. This should lessen our concerns regarding obsolescence.

3 Debtors are now being collected 15 days (or 16%) faster than the prior year, reducing cash flow concerns and lessening pressure on the provision for doubtful debts.

4 Current assets to current liabilities has increased, indicating an improvement in GC Pty Ltd's liquidity position. In addition, this ratio is above the industry average.

Required

Discuss the validity of your assistant's comments, and where appropriate, provide an alternative interpretation. Briefly discuss the implications for year-end audit testing.

Source: This question was adapted from the Professional Year Programme of The Institute of Chartered Accountants in Australia—2000 Accounting 2 Module.

CONTINUOUS CASE STUDY

7.25 Complex This is a continuation of question 6.30. Please also refer to the information contained in that question.

Required

(a) Outline the factors that would affect your assessment of inherent risk associated with the audit of HomeChef Pty Ltd.

(b) For each of the inherent risk factors you outlined in (a), indicate:

    (i) whether it increases or decreases audit risk; and

    (ii) its effect on your audit procedures.

(c) Your partner had originally set a preliminary materiality level for the audit of HomeChef Pty Ltd at $3 000 000. After your review of inherent risk your partner has lowered this materiality level to $1 600 000. Outline how the new lower materiality level will affect the nature and extent of audit procedures planned.

CHAPTER 8

UNDERSTANDING AND ASSESSING INTERNAL CONTROL

LEARNING OBJECTIVES

After studying this chapter you should be able to:

1 explain the audit logic of assessing control risk;

2 understand the concepts of reasonable assurance and inherent limitations with regard to internal control;

3 describe the general objectives of internal control and how the auditor uses them to develop specific control objectives;

4 define internal control and each of its components;

5 identify the steps by which the auditor obtains an understanding of internal control and assesses control risk, and the methods and procedures used by the auditor in each step;

6 distinguish between user controls and information technology (IT) controls, general controls and application controls, manual controls and programmed controls, and identify the application controls and general controls that affect the auditor's assessment of control risk in a computerised system; and

7 explain the role of the internal audit function in internal control and how it may affect the audit.

Chapter outline

As part of understanding the entity and its environment, the auditor needs to obtain an understanding of internal control. This is the basis for a preliminary assessment of control risk and an evaluation of the extent to which controls may be relied on to assure the accuracy and reliability of accounting records.

The auditor needs to obtain a sufficient understanding of internal control to plan the audit and develop an effective audit approach. The auditor must use professional judgment to assess audit risk and design audit procedures to reduce it to an acceptably low level. As a result of the adoption of the business risk approach, auditors now place more importance on controls related to risk monitoring and decision making. The auditor needs to develop a thorough understanding of the way management uses internal control to respond to business risks.

The auditor also studies and evaluates the internal control because of interest in the reliability of accounting data. In the past, the auditor has tended to focus mainly on those transaction controls that relate to the prevention or detection of errors in recording accounting data.

The auditor's understanding of internal control makes it possible to assess control risk in order to determine the nature, timing and extent of other audit tests. Control risk is one of the elements of audit risk in the model introduced in Chapter 5.

The objective of the review of internal control is not to determine the adequacy of the internal control for management purposes. This would go beyond the normal scope of a financial report audit, and evidence on which to base an opinion on internal control would require the application of additional audit procedures beyond those specified in AUS 402 (ISA 400). This is discussed in Chapter 14.

This chapter discusses the relationship of the internal control to the audit strategy; the elements of internal control; and the auditor's consideration of internal control in a financial report audit. From the external auditor's viewpoint, internal audit forms part of internal control. This chapter discusses the effects of internal audit on the external audit function.

Relevant guidance

Australian		International	
AUS 402	Understanding the Entity and its Environment and Assessing the Risks of Material Misstatement (Revised 2004)	ISA 315	Understanding the Entity and its Environment and Assessing the Risks of Material Misstatement (Revised 2004)
AUS 404	Audit Implications Relating to Entities Using a Service Entity	ISA 402	Audit Implications Relating to Entities Using Service Organisations
AUS 604	Considering the Work of Internal Auditing	ISA 610	Considering the Work of Internal Auditing
AGS 1018	IT Environments—Stand-Alone Personal Computers	IAPS 1001	IT Environments—Stand-Alone Personal Computers
AGS 1020	IT Environments—On-Line Computer Systems	IAPS 1002	IT Environments—On-Line Computer Systems
AGS 1022	IT Environments—Database Systems	IAPS 1003	IT Environments—Database Systems

 learning objective 1

AUDIT STRATEGY AND INTERNAL CONTROL

According to AUS 402.42 (ISA 315.42) **internal control** is the process designed and implemented by those charged with governance, management and other personnel to provide reasonable assurance regarding the achievement of the entity's objectives concerning financial reporting, the effectiveness and efficiency of operations, and compliance with laws and regulations. Therefore, it is designed and implemented to address business risks that threaten any of these objectives. The importance of internal control has developed as business entities have become larger and more complex. Both management and auditors see the benefits of a framework within which business activity is directed and co-ordinated.

Management recognises that the internal control is an effective means of controlling a business (e.g. asset protection, efficient use of resources) where size prevents direct involvement at all levels, and of meeting statutory responsibilities for the maintenance of accounting and other records. The directors of a company are responsible for the overall control of that company and effective internal control is central to efficient risk management (Auditing in the News 8.1 overleaf) and therefore is an important part of the corporate governance process discussed in Chapter 3.

AUS 402.41 (ISA 315.41) requires that the auditor obtain an understanding of internal control relevant to the audit. The risk of material misstatement at the financial report level is affected by the auditor's understanding of the control environment (AUS 406.05/ISA 330.05). At the assertion level, the auditor needs to consider whether their assessment of the risk of material misstatement takes account of the entity's controls, that is control risk (AUS 406.12/ISA 330.12).

Audit strategy

Auditors recognise that sound internal control, by enhancing the credibility of accounting records, reduces the need for routine checking of large volumes of transactions. Evidence obtained from sound internal control is generally more reliable. This view is supported by common law, such as the *Pacific Acceptance* case, which was discussed in Chapter 4.

The evidence supporting the financial report consists of the underlying accounting data and the corroborating information available to the auditor. Thus, confidence in the propriety and accuracy of underlying accounting data contributes to the auditor's opinion on the financial report. The internal control affects the propriety and accuracy of accounting data and thus the value of those data as audit evidence.

The auditor may reach a conclusion on the accuracy and reliability of underlying accounting data by testing the accounting data itself (reducing detection risk) or performing procedures to understand and evaluate the internal control to see whether the accounting data were developed under conditions likely to ensure accuracy and reliability (assessing control risk).

As discussed in Chapter 5, in order to issue an opinion on the financial report, the auditor must consider audit risk for each assertion for each significant account balance and transaction class, and reduce it to an acceptable level. Control risk is one of the three elements of audit risk and is the risk that a material misstatement could occur in an assertion and not be prevented or detected on a timely basis by the entity's internal control. The auditor can assess the control risk as high, or alternatively assess control risk as less than high and then test the controls to obtain evidence to support this assessment. The tests will need to show that specific control activities have been consistently applied throughout the period under audit.

Figure 8.1 (overleaf) illustrates alternatives available to the auditor when considering the accounting flow of transactions for credit sales and collections. To substantiate the accuracy and reliability of the accounting for credit sales and collections, the auditor has the following alternatives:

- test the sales and cash receipts transactions to establish the occurrence, completeness, cutoff and accuracy of recording of the recurring debit and credit entries to accounts receivable;
- identify and test the policies and procedures that ensure the occurrence, completeness, cutoff and accuracy of recording these transactions; or
- some combination of the above.

The substantiation of the underlying accounting data is interrelated with the corroborating information the auditor needs to obtain for balances. For example, the number of confirmations

FIGURE **8.1** **Overview of flow of transactions for credit sales**

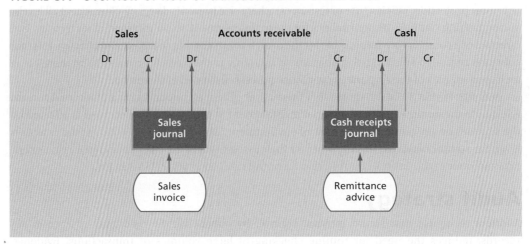

sent to debtors on the amount owed at balance date is influenced by the auditor's confidence in the propriety and accuracy of the debits and credits to accounts receivable. Also, confirmations of the accounts receivable balance provide some assurance of the accuracy and reliability of the debits and credits recorded. Obtaining evidence that the control risk is low for specific assertions for specific accounting data is an alternative to substantiating the data directly. The choice of the mix of auditing procedures necessary to test the accounting data and obtain corroborating information is discussed in Chapter 9.

INTERNAL CONTROL CONCEPTS

Several aspects of the definition of internal control should be recognised. Some aspects are implicit; others are explicit but require elaboration. Whether a manual system or a computer system is used to process transactions, the objectives of internal control remain the same.

Responsibility for internal control

Achieving satisfactory internal control is initially a management responsibility, although ultimate responsibility rests with the directors. Every entity needs to keep track of its assets and know whom it owes to and who owes it. Thus, to maintain control over operations and accounting data, management needs to adopt, maintain and supervise an appropriate internal control system.

Inherent limitations of internal control

As indicated by AUS 402.64 (ISA 315.64), internal control cannot *assure* a reliable financial report because it has **inherent limitations**. Therefore, the auditor can never rely completely on the internal control.

Internal control usually depends both on the quality and integrity of people working within the entity and on those people following prescribed policies and procedures. Thus, it is subject to breakdowns caused by carelessness and fatigue, and it can be circumvented intentionally through collusion. Management may also override the controls, since someone must supervise the system. Internal control is designed to prevent fraud or errors by people operating within the system. Someone in a supervisory position may perpetrate fraud or errors by acting outside the system.

Undue reliance on management to automatically 'do the right thing' may create opportunities for managers who lack integrity to behave inappropriately. Also, most control activities are directed at routine transactions rather than non-routine transactions, and they may become inadequate due to changes in conditions.

In addition, internal control recognises the concept of *reasonable assurance,* because the cost of controls must bear a reasonable relationship to the benefits expected. Management needs to evaluate this cost–benefit trade-off and adopt control methods and measures that are prudent for the assets at risk. This evaluation is usually subjective, but it should be based on a careful consideration of the risks and the alternatives for achieving control.

Management also makes accounting estimates, such as allowance for doubtful accounts receivable, and selects accounting principles, such as the method of accounting for inventory (e.g. FIFO or average cost), that are subject to judgment. Thus, the reliability of the financial report is not assured even if accounting records are reliable.

AUDITING IN THE NEWS

S
N
I
P
P
E
T

8.1

Source: Extract from *Internal Control: Guidance for Directors on the Combined Code* (Turnbull Report), ICAEW, September 1999.

The importance of internal control and risk management

A company's system of internal control has a key role in the management of risks that are significant to the fulfilment of its business objectives. A sound system of internal control contributes to safeguarding the shareholders' investment and the company's assets.

Internal control facilitates the effectiveness and efficiency of operations, helps ensure the reliability of internal and external reporting and assists compliance with laws and regulations.

Effective financial controls, including the maintenance of proper accounting records, are an important element of internal control. They help ensure that the company is not unnecessarily exposed to avoidable financial risks and that financial information used within the business and for publication is reliable. They also contribute to the safeguarding of assets, including the prevention and detection of fraud.

A company's objectives, its internal organisation and the environment in which it operates are continually evolving and, as a result, the risks it faces are continually changing. A sound system of internal control therefore depends on a thorough and regular evaluation of the nature and extent of the risks to which the company is exposed. Since profits are, in part, the reward for successful risk-taking in business, the purpose of internal control is to help manage and control risk appropriately rather than to eliminate it.

INTERNAL CONTROL OBJECTIVES

Internal controls are concerned with ensuring that:

- risks are identified and minimised;
- management decision making is effective and business processes are efficient;
- transactions are carried out in accordance with management's general or specific authorisation;
- laws, rules and regulations are complied with;

- transactions are promptly recorded in the correct amount, in the appropriate accounts and in the correct accounting period so as to allow the preparation of the financial report within a framework of recognised accounting policies and to maintain accountability for assets;
- access to assets is permitted only in accordance with management's authorisation; and
- the record of accountability for assets is compared with the existing assets at reasonable intervals and appropriate action is taken with respect to any differences.

The quality of an entity's internal control affects not only the reliability of financial data, but also the ability of the entity to make good decisions and remain in business. The internal control should be designed to parallel the risks present in the entity, industry and global environment. In the UK, the Turnbull Report (ICAEW, 1999), which was discussed in Chapter 3 in relation to corporate governance, stressed the importance of the internal control in managing risks to achieve an entity's business objectives.

Management controls

Management controls are the activities undertaken by senior management to mitigate strategic risks to the entity and to promote the effectiveness of decision making and the efficiency of business activities. Management controls tend to focus on overall effectiveness and efficiency within an entity rather than on details of individual transactions or activities. Generally, they are designed to provide an overall indication that processes and activities are functioning properly, and to provide an effective response to risk in a timely manner. Management controls include activities such as:

- communicating business objectives and goals throughout the entity;
- establishing lines of authority and accountability;
- establishing and enforcing appropriate codes of corporate conduct;
- monitoring both the external and internal environment for risks;
- defining policies and procedures for dealing with these risks; and
- monitoring performance of key segments of the entity through performance indicators and benchmarking.

For example, establishing and enforcing a corporate governance policy on dealing with conflicts of interest for managerial personnel is a management control that reduces the risk of self-serving behaviour by people in positions of authority within the entity.

To be able to assess the effectiveness of management controls for reducing strategic risks, the auditor will first have to develop an understanding of what procedures and policies management has implemented. To do this, the auditor may review procedures manuals, periodic reports and internal audit testing in order to evaluate how effective management is in monitoring and controlling risk. However, in most situations, a complete understanding of management control is best obtained by interviewing the key personnel who are assigned the responsibility of managing critical risks.

For each of the significant business risks identified, the auditor should give consideration to any existing management controls that may mitigate the risk. If a business risk has significant implications for the audit, then the related controls are also relevant. The relationship between management controls and auditing planning is shown in Example 8.1.

Management control

Retro Ltd continually monitors its main competition to estimate their time-to-market for new products. The market data may be a leading indicator of potential competitive problems and evidence of new products.

Audit implications

Monitoring competitors' actions is an important management control for managing the risk that competitors will introduce new products, reduce prices or improve service to obtain a competitive advantage. This risk is important to an auditor because of its effect on revenue levels, profit margins and inventory valuation.

Transaction controls

As well as management controls, there are many other control activities that are performed by staff employees and lower-level management as part of the various processes within the entity. These controls are generally focused on internal risks within systems and processes and reflect the formal policies and procedures defined by senior management. Such controls deal primarily with the reliability of accounting information and compliance with rules and regulations. For example, assigning responsibility for authorising transactions to specific individuals is a form of process control.

The objectives of these accounting controls are to control the flow of transactions through the accounting system and to safeguard the related assets by authorising transactions, recording transactions, restricting access to assets and checking for existence of recorded assets.

Every transaction goes through the identifiable steps of authorisation, execution and recording. The accuracy and reliability of transaction records depends on making reasonably sure that there are controls over the financial report assertions discussed in Chapter 5.

Characteristics of satisfactory internal control

The objectives and concepts outlined above are reflected in the following general characteristics of satisfactory internal control:

1 There should be controls to monitor and minimise business risks.
2 There should be proper segregation of responsibilities (Example 8.2 overleaf). There should be no incompatible functions, so that no person is in a position to perpetrate and conceal fraud in the normal course of duties. For example, as far as possible, different individuals should perform the following functions: authorising a transaction; recording a transaction; maintaining custody of the assets that result from a transaction; comparing assets with the related amounts recorded in the accounting records.
3 The internal control should have a system of authorisation, recording and other procedures adequate to provide accounting control of assets, liabilities, revenues and expenses.
4 There should be sound business practices in performance of duties and functions by each department, including the prenumbering of documents originating within the entity, completing a sequence check of documents used and maintaining control over unused documents.
5 Internal procedures should ensure that persons have capabilities commensurate with their responsibilities.

Facts

Machinery Ltd's storeroom clerk, Bob Johnson, authorises inventory acquisitions and also keeps the accounting records related to inventory.

Audit implications

Johnson could authorise the acquisition of unneeded inventory, remove the material from the premises, or even have it delivered to another location, and alter the accounting records to make it look like the inventory never existed, or had been sold. Provided the accounting records agreed with the amount of inventory on hand, the theft would be difficult to detect without a special investigation, which is outside the scope of a normal audit.

Quick review

1. Internal control affects the propriety and accuracy of accounting data and therefore their reliability as audit evidence.
2. The auditor needs to obtain an understanding of the internal control as a basis for assessing control risk.
3. Achieving satisfactory internal control is management's responsibility.
4. Internal control cannot assure a reliable financial report because of its inherent limitations.

ELEMENTS OF INTERNAL CONTROL

AUS 402.43 (ISA 315.43) states that a company's internal control consists of five elements:

1 control environment;
2 entity's risk assessment process;
3 information system;
4 control activities; and
5 monitoring of controls.

Control environment

AUS 402.67 (ISA 315.67) states that the **control environment** includes management's overall attitude, awareness and actions regarding internal control and its importance in the entity. The control environment sets the tone of an entity. It influences the control consciousness of all personnel and is the foundation for the other components.

The auditor needs to obtain an understanding of the control environment because it influences the consistency of procedures and the general effectiveness of the accounting system and control activities. The auditor needs to obtain an understanding of the control environment sufficient to assess its effectiveness. When conducting this assessment, the auditor must concentrate on the substance of management's policies, procedures and actions rather than their form. It is important to remember that management may establish appropriate policies and procedures but not act on them.

The auditor's understanding of the control environment includes consideration of the following factors set out in AUS 402.69 (ISA 315.69):

- communication and enforcement of integrity and ethical values;
- commitment to competence;
- participation by those charged with governance;
- management philosophy and operating style;
- organisational structure;

- assignment of authority and responsibility; and
- human resource policies and practices.

Communication and enforcement of integrity and ethical values

Integrity and ethical values are essential elements of the control environment and will influence the effectiveness of the design, administration and monitoring of other components of internal control. Integrity and ethical behaviour are a product of the entity's ethical standards and how they are communicated and reinforced in practice. Management should remove or reduce incentives and temptations that result in personnel engaging in dishonest, illegal or unethical acts. Entity values and behavioural standards should be communicated to personnel through policy statements, codes of conduct and by management example.

Commitment to competence

Management needs to consider the competence levels for specific jobs and take action to ensure that individuals have the necessary skills and knowledge to perform their jobs.

Participation by those charged with governance

An entity's attitude to internal control is influenced significantly by those charged with governance. Factors to be considered include: their independence from management; their experience and stature; their scrutiny of activities; the appropriateness of their actions; the information they receive; the extent to which they raise and pursue difficult questions with management; and their interaction with internal and external auditors. The auditor will also consider whether there is an audit committee that understands the entity's business transactions and evaluates whether or not the financial report gives a true and fair view.

Management's philosophy and operating style

Management's philosophy and operating style includes its overall control consciousness. Management's attitude toward control sets the stage for the entire entity. If management emphasises the importance of maintaining reliable accounting records and adhering to established policies and procedures then the entity's personnel are more likely to have a high regard for these matters in performing their duties. Therefore, this is a subjective, but critical, aspect of the auditor's consideration of whether the environment is conducive to good control.

Other characteristics the auditor may consider are: management's approach to taking and monitoring business risks; management's attitudes and actions vis-à-vis financial reporting; and management's attitude to information processing and accounting functions and personnel.

Organisational structure

An entity's organisational structure is the overall framework for planning, directing and controlling operations to achieve the entity's objectives. It includes the form and nature of the entity's organisational units, and related management functions and reporting relationships. An effective control environment requires clear definitions of responsibilities and lines of authority.

Assignment of authority and responsibilities

Methods of assigning authority and responsibility influence how well responsibilities are communicated, how well they are understood and how much responsibility personnel feel in performing their duties. There should be appropriate delegation of authority and all personnel should understand that they are accountable for activities for which they are responsible.

Human resources policies and practices

Human resources policies and practices cover recruitment, orientation, training, evaluating, counselling, promoting, compensating and taking remedial action for personnel. For example, high recruitment standards demonstrate an entity's commitment to competent and trustworthy people.

Entity's risk assessment process

An entity's risk assessment process is its way of identifying and responding to business risks. Once risks are identified management needs to consider their significance and how they should be managed. Management may introduce plans, programs or actions to address specific risks or it may accept a risk on a cost–benefit basis.

Information system

Information must be identified, captured and exchanged in a form and timeframe that enables entity personnel to carry out their responsibilities. An entity's **information system** includes its accounting system and consists of the methods and records established to identify, assemble, analyse, classify, record and report exchange transactions and relevant events and conditions, and to maintain accountability for the related assets, liabilities, revenues and expenditures. An information system includes infrastructure such as hardware and other physical components, software, people, procedures and data. Many information systems make extensive use of IT, while some remain largely manual.

An effective information system duly considers establishing records and methods that:

- identify and record all valid transactions;
- describe on a timely basis the transactions in sufficient detail to permit proper classification for financial reporting;
- measure the value of transactions in a manner that permits recording of their proper monetary value in the financial report;
- determine the period in which transactions occurred, to permit recording of transactions in the proper accounting period; and
- present the transactions and related disclosures properly in the financial report.

An important feature of an information system is the audit trail, which was discussed in Chapter 5. This term implies that individual transactions can be traced through each step of the accounts to their inclusion in the financial report and, similarly, from the financial report the amounts can be vouched or traced back to original source documentation. The audit trail consists of all the accounting documents and records that are prepared as transactions are processed from origin to final posting. Source documents, journals and ledgers are the main elements in the audit trail. Source documents are the initial record of transactions in the system. Processing usually creates a source document when a transaction is executed. For example, goods received are usually entered on a receiving report and goods shipped on a shipping report. Source documents are evidence of the authenticity of a transaction.

The most important and frequent user of the audit trail is the entity's management. A clear audit trail is needed to track down the specific sources of errors. For example, when a customer complains that a bill is too high, management must be able to determine whether an error has been made and identify specifically the cause and amount of the error (or explain in detail what goods or services were included in the bill that resulted in the 'high' amount).

Nearly all businesses use a computer for at least part of their accounting. Computerisation ranges from personal computers that summarise transactions to extremely complex systems. The methods an entity uses to process significant accounting applications may influence the control activities designed to achieve the internal control objectives. The characteristics that distinguish computer processing from manual processing include the following:

- **Transaction trails:** some computer systems are designed so that a complete transaction audit trail exists for only a short period or only in computer-readable form.
- **Uniform processing of transactions:** computer processing uniformly processes transactions with similar characteristics through the same branch of the program.
- **Segregation of functions reduced:** many control activities once performed by separate individuals in manual systems may be concentrated.
- **Potential for misstatements:** there may be greater potential for individuals to gain unauthorised access to data or alter data without visible evidence, as well as to gain access (direct or indirect) to assets.
- **Potential for increased management supervision:** computer systems offer management a wide variety of analytical tools to review and supervise operations.

Control activities

Control activities encompass both policies and procedures established by management to ensure its directives are carried out. Control activities should be distinguished from the accounting system discussed earlier. An entity needs an accounting system, for example, for billing shipments to customers, recording these individual transactions and summarising them for recording in the general ledger. Control activities are added to ensure that the accounting system produces accurate and reliable data. For example, control activities are added to a billing system to ensure that all shipments are billed and that all billings are for the correct amount.

Appendix 2 to AUS 402 indicates that control activities may be categorised as policies and procedures that pertain to:

- performance reviews;
- information processing;
- physical controls; and
- segregation of duties.

A strong internal control will include management controls such as **performance review** control activities that independently check the performance of individuals or processes. An example of a performance review activity would be comparing actual performance with budget and investigating any unexpected differences. As discussed earlier, management controls are concerned primarily with monitoring and controlling business risk. Performance indicators may be useful for highlighting a problem or risk at an early stage.

A number of different controls are performed to check the accuracy, completeness and authorisation of transactions. The two broad groupings of **information processing** control activities are application controls and general IT controls. Application controls apply to processing of individual applications while general controls are policies and procedures that apply to many applications. These will be discussed in more detail later in this chapter.

Physical control activities include measures such as locked storerooms for inventory and fireproof safes for cash and securities on hand. Accounting records and source documents must also be protected. The nature of the item usually dictates the physical precautions that are necessary. For example, an inventory of gemstones would be treated differently from an inventory of cement.

Segregation of duties is an integral part of the plan of organisation. A person should not be in a position to both perpetrate and conceal errors or fraud in the normal course of duties. Different people are assigned the responsibilities of authorising transactions, recording transactions and maintaining custody of assets.

In order for an entity to operate, some personnel must have access to assets. Restricting access limits the opportunities for irregularities but cannot prevent them. Control is achieved through segregation of duties by limiting the opportunities both to perpetrate and conceal the act.

Thus, the most basic segregation of duties is to have different individuals or departments responsible for custody of assets and the keeping of records of those assets. A transaction may be considered to pass through four phases:

1. **authorisation:** the initial authorisation or approval for an exchange transaction;
2. **execution:** the act commits the entity to the exchange, such as placing an order;
3. **custody:** the physical act of accepting, delivering or maintaining the asset; and
4. **recording:** the entry of the transaction data into the accounting system.

Ideally, all four phases should be kept separate. However, in practice, for convenience and efficiency phases 1 and 2 may be combined without significant risk. Clearly, phases 2, 3 and 4 should not be combined, and normally direct physical access (phase 3) and record keeping (phase 4) are incompatible. However, the risk of incompatible combinations should be evaluated by considering specific circumstances in conjunction with the following general guideline: no one person should be in a position to misappropriate an asset or improperly record a transaction without detection.

The following discussion of control activities is organised by assertions under the headings of: occurrence; completeness; accuracy; cutoff; and classification.

Occurrence

Control activities for authorisation and approval help to ensure that only transactions that occurred are processed and that invalid transactions are rejected. Effective control activities for processing transactions usually start with clear policies for **authorisation** and **approval**. An entity's board of directors has the ultimate authority, but its approval is usually reserved for important financing and investing activities, such as major acquisitions and dispositions involving real estate, debt and share capital. The day to day authority of running a business is the responsibility of senior management, who delegate that authority to operating personnel.

Management's authorisation of transactions may be general or specific. General authorisation applies to transactions that are recurrent and have a high volume. Examples include the use of price lists and credit limits for credit sales transactions. Specific authorisation is applied when management has decided that individual transactions must be approved, such as all purchases in excess of an established dollar amount. *Approval* is the actual step of checking that the conditions established for authorisation have been met. Examples of authorisation and approval procedures include requiring a second signature on cheques over a specified limit and limiting certain error-correction functions to persons who sign on to the computer with a manager's ID and password.

Related control activities that provide assurance of **occurrence** concern the proper use of documents that serve as the original record of transaction execution. These source documents should be designed to reduce the risk that a transaction will be recorded incorrectly, recorded more than once or not recorded at all. Desirable features of source documents include:

- **Prenumbering:** allows for physical control of the documents.
- **Preprinted instructions:** show the steps to fill out the document and route it through the system.
- **Approval blocks:** provide a designated space for necessary approval signatures, stamps and initials.
- **Simplicity:** the document is easy to use and the number of copies is minimised.

In some systems, source documents are recorded on a computer screen. The four features of information are little changed:

- **Numbering:** generally assigned automatically by the software.
- **Instructions:** appear on the screen or are available through a help function.
- **Approval:** the operator signs on with a password or other unique key, which is recorded for each transaction.
- **Simplicity:** the screen is user-friendly.

Control activities that help ensure occurrence are concerned with the proper handling of such source documents, whether in a computer or a manual system. For example, control activities include comparing details on a receiving report, such as description and quantity, with details on the supplier's invoice. Another example of a control activity is cancellation of supporting documents for a purchase when payment is approved. This prevents inadvertent or fraudulent re-use of the source documents to support a duplicate payment or fictitious purchase.

Control activities can be designed as part of the data-entry system to help ensure **validity**. The computer may reject invalid dates by requiring a month between 1 and 12 and a day between 1 and 31. Any entry in an amount field that is not numeric may be rejected. These are called computer *editing* controls.

Completeness

Proper handling of documents also helps ensure **completeness**. One control activity is to inspect prenumbered documents to see that they have all been processed. This procedure is often called *accounting for the sequence of prenumbered documents*. If documents are not prenumbered they should be numbered when a transaction originates, but that is less effective in controlling completeness. Another control activity to check completeness is the use of *control totals*. If ten documents totalling $500 in cash receipt transactions were supposed to be entered into the computer system, the system should report that it processed ten entries totalling $500.

A third control activity involves *matching related source documents* to see if related processing steps have been completed. For example, purchase orders or receiving reports can be matched with vendors' invoices to see that goods ordered or received have subsequently been recorded as accounts payable.

Accuracy

An organised set of accounting records is an essential starting point for achieving recording **accuracy**. In all but the smallest entities a double-entry accounting system is essential. The requirement that debits equal credits is a built-in error-detecting feature. Also, the debits and credits to ledger balances provide an effective record of accountability. The use of ledgers also contributes to recording accuracy in two ways: a trial balance prepared from the ledger proves the balancing of debits and credits; and the ledger contains control accounts for use in balancing subsidiary ledgers.

The use of control totals, discussed above under completeness, also contributes to the accuracy of records. If a cash receipt of $23 is mistakenly entered as $32, the system will report that it processed $509 for the ten receipts, instead of the $500 control total.

All the features of accounting systems described above provide the foundation for controls to help ensure recording accuracy. However, the actual control activities are usually in the form of independent checks, reviews and approvals established at the points in the processing of transactions and handling of related assets where errors or irregularities could occur. For example, the financial controller may review supporting documents for a disbursement before payment.

Cutoff

The **cutoff** period is generally the few days either side of the reporting date. Cutoff controls are to ensure that transactions during the cut-off period are recorded in the correct period. In the absence of appropriate controls, such as review of transactions during the cutoff period by someone independent of the relevant function, cutoff errors may occur because year end is a hectic time and staff may make errors under stress or because of fraudulent misstatement of the accounting records to manipulate the results for the period.

Classification

Classification is concerned with transactions being recorded in the proper account. An example of a classification control activity would be to have someone check that the account coding on source documents was in accordance with the entity's chart of accounts.

Monitoring of controls

Monitoring of controls is a process to assess the effectiveness of the performance of internal control. It involves evaluating the design and operation of controls and taking corrective action where necessary. Management may monitor controls through ongoing activities such as supervisory activities and/or separate evaluations. In addition, communications from external parties such as customer complaints may indicate problems. In many entities, internal auditors also contribute to the monitoring process.

An internal audit function is an individual, group or department within an entity that acts as a separate, higher level of control to determine that the internal control is functioning effectively. Internal auditors may make special inquiries at management's direction or generally review operating practices to promote increased efficiency. However, the external auditor is concerned with internal auditors who act as a higher level of control—an additional layer, in effect—to ensure that the accounting system and control activities are operating. An effective internal audit function can significantly strengthen the monitoring of control.

Internal audit may affect the external audit in three ways:

1 **The internal audit function is part of the internal control.** If an entity has an internal audit function that acts as a higher level of control, it will influence the external auditor's assessment of control risk and as a result affect the scope of audit procedures.
2 **The internal auditors may have descriptions and other documentation of the internal control.** These documents may help the external auditor obtain an understanding of the internal control.
3 **The internal auditors may provide direct assistance to the independent auditor** by making substantive tests or tests of controls.

Many internal audit departments have also become involved in assessing the business strategy of the entity and identifying the associated risks. This work will be useful to the external auditor when undertaking a business risk approach to the audit. The involvement of internal audit in assessing business strategy will be discussed further in Chapter 15.

To be effective, the internal auditor needs to possess adequate skills, knowledge, experience, integrity and objectivity and to communicate directly with the external auditor, governing body and audit committee.

The extent to which the external auditor may utilise the work of internal auditing will be discussed later in this chapter.

Quick review

1. Internal control consists of the control environment, the entity's risk assessment process, information system, control activities and monitoring of controls.
2. The control environment includes consideration of communication and enforcement of integrity and ethical values; commitment to competence; participation by those charged with governance; management's philosophy and operating style; the organisational structure; assignment of authority and responsibilities; and policies and practices.
3. Control activities include policy and procedures that pertain to performance reviews, information processing, physical controls and segregation of duties.
4. Control activities relate to the risk of material misstatement at the assertion level.

CONSIDERING INTERNAL CONTROL IN A FINANCIAL REPORT AUDIT

In every audit the auditor obtains a sufficient understanding of each of the five components of internal control to plan the audit and determine the tests to be performed. The nature and extent of the auditor's consideration of internal control varies considerably from audit to audit. In all audits, the auditor must understand the internal control, particularly those controls associated with the accounting system. No matter what audit strategy is followed, substantiating the underlying data is important. The auditor's understanding must be sufficient to identify types of potential misstatements, to consider factors that affect the risk of material misstatement and to design effective audit tests. On the other hand, for some assertions for some balances or transaction classes, an understanding of the control activities element of internal control may be minimal, depending on the audit strategy followed.

An overview of the auditor's consideration of internal control

Figure 8.2 (overleaf) presents the steps in the auditor's consideration of internal control in the audit of a financial report. The process presented in the figure is discussed in this section. The following is an outline of the steps to be taken.

1 Obtain an understanding of the internal control.
  • Obtain an understanding of the company's *control environment.*
  • Obtain an understanding of the entity's process for identifying risks relevant to financial reporting objectives and deciding upon actions to address these risks.
  • Obtain an understanding of the *information system* for significant classes of transactions, account balances and disclosures.
  • Obtain an understanding of the *control activities* to assess the risk of misstatement at the assertion level.

FIGURE **8.2** **Steps in the auditor's consideration of internal control**

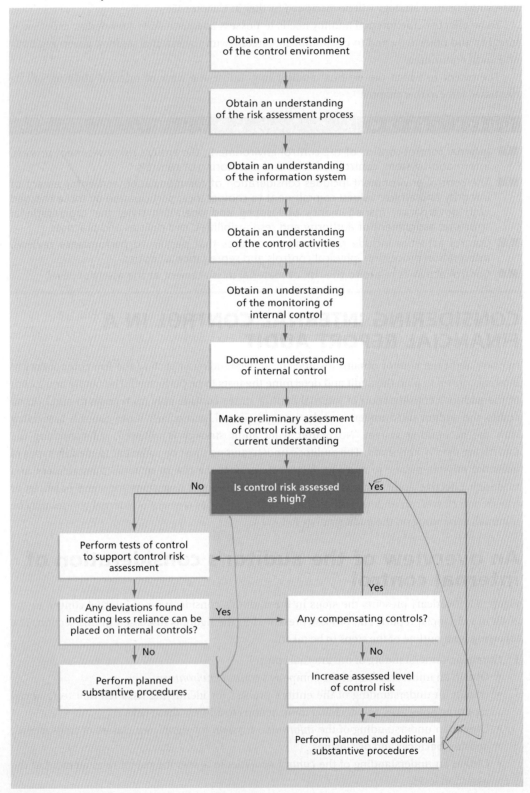

- Obtain an understanding of the major types of activities that the entity uses to monitor internal control over financial reporting.
- Document the understanding.

2   Assess the level of control risk based on the understanding obtained.
- The auditor may assess control risk at high for any one of the following three conditions:
  — Internal control policies and procedures are unlikely to relate to the specific assertion (that is, the client does not have controls for this assertion).
  — The evidence that would be obtained by additional testing would probably not support a reduced level of control risk (testing would probably prove control for the assertion is weak).
  — Obtaining additional evidence to support the control risk level would not be the most efficient audit approach for the assertion (substantive tests are easier to perform than tests of controls).
- Consider whether further reduction in control risk would be an efficient audit approach and whether further evidence would be likely to support the reduced level.

3   For each assertion within each significant transaction class, account balance or disclosure for which the auditor plans to assess control risk at a level less than high, consider whether sufficient evidence has been obtained to support the desired control risk level.
- Perform tests of controls to evaluate the design or operation of the internal control policy or procedure to obtain needed evidence. (This step will be covered in Chapter 9.)
- Document the basis for conclusions about the assessed level of control risk.

4   Design substantive tests to detect potential material misstatements. This step will be covered in Chapter 10.

Understanding internal control

The auditor generally performs the procedures to obtain an understanding of the internal control during the general planning phase of the audit, as described in Chapter 5. The auditor obtains an understanding of the internal control to:

- identify the types of potential misstatements that could occur and the factors that contribute to the risk that they will occur;
- understand the accounting system sufficiently to identify the client documents, reports and other information that may be available and ascertain what data will be used in audit tests; and
- determine an efficient and effective approach to the audit.

Operating effectiveness is the manner in which entity personnel apply the policies that are in place. Have the policies and procedures been used consistently throughout the year? Are they used by all the employees performing the function? When the employee ordinarily responsible for a procedure is ill or on leave, is the procedure still effective? Does the employee take the appropriate action when an exception is noted, or are overrides common?

AUS 402.56 (ISA 315.56) indicates that obtaining an understanding of an entity's controls is not a sufficient test of operating effectiveness, unless there is some automation that provides for the consistent application of the operation of the control. However, an auditor who decides to reduce the assessed level of control risk to less than high must consider operating effectiveness and gather evidence to support this assessment. The auditor then needs evidence that the internal control exists and has operated effectively throughout the relevant period. Evidence will be obtained through tests of control, which will be discussed in Chapter 9.

Understanding the control environment

AUS 402.67 (ISA 315.67) requires the auditor to obtain an understanding of the control environment sufficient to assess its effectiveness. The methods and audit procedures used to understand the control environment include:

- making inquiries of key management personnel;
- inspecting entity documents, to the extent the entity has documented relevant policies and procedures;
- observing entity activities and operations; and
- considering past experience with the client.

Audit evidence for some elements of the control environment may not be available in documentary form, particularly in smaller entities where communication between management and other personnel may be informal. Therefore, management's attitudes, awareness and actions are important in the design of a smaller entities control environment.

The nature of the control environment means that it has a pervasive effect on assessing the risk of material misstatement. For example, an active and independent board of directors may influence the philosophy and operating style of senior management. The control environment influences the nature, timing and extent of the auditor's further procedures.

Understanding the risk assessment process

AUS 402.76 (ISA 315.76) requires that the auditor obtain an understanding of the entity's business risk assessment process and to decide about actions to address those risks and their results. Therefore, the auditor needs to determine how management identifies business risks relevant to the financial report, estimate the significance of the risks, assess their likelihood of occurring, and decides upon actions to manage them. The auditor will inquire of management about business risks that management has identified and consider whether they may result in a material misstatement. If the auditor identifies a risk of material misstatement during the audit that management failed to identify, the auditor needs to consider whether management should have identified it and, if so, why the process failed.

Understanding the information system

The audit procedures necessary to obtain an understanding of the information system include inquiry of management, supervisory and staff personnel; inspection of records, documents and reports; reading the client's descriptions of the system or similar client documentation such as a chart of accounts or a procedures manual; observation of company activities and operations; previous experience with the client; and review of the previous year's working papers.

The auditor is required by AUS 402.81 (ISA 315.81) to obtain sufficient knowledge of the information system to understand:

- significant classes of transactions;
- initiation of transactions;
- records, documents and accounts used in processing and recording transactions;
- accounting processing; and
- financial reporting procedures.

The auditor needs first to obtain an understanding of the path that transactions take through both the manual and computerised portions of the information system. The auditor then considers the anticipated computer-related controls that may contribute to a control risk assessment at less than high, and documents and tests controls in order to assess the control risk.

One approach to understanding the information system is to start at the end, rather than the beginning. The auditor identifies significant amounts in the financial reports being audited. The transactions that affect those amounts are traced back from the financial reports to their sources—the original source document prepared or data screen used when the data are captured by the accounting system. The auditor then identifies the processing points in that flow. These are the points at which transactions are initiated, recorded, calculated, summarised or reported. Misstatements can occur at any of these processing points, and these are the points at which control activities are necessary.

During general planning the auditor generally obtains the following information on the client's computer installation:

- type of computer equipment and its configuration, including input and processing modes used;
- types of systems software;
- organisational structure of computer processing activities, including the organisational location of the IT department, number of personnel and internal organisation plan; and
- number and nature of computerised accounting applications.

As part of understanding the information system, the auditor identifies the extent to which the computer is used in each significant accounting application and obtains the following information:

- the purpose of the application, particularly the documents, reports and updated master files generated by the application and the general ledger account balances affected by the application;
- the source, volume and form of input to the application, particularly the user departments in which transactions originate and other computerised accounting applications that generate input for the application;
- the master files affected by the application, including particularly the storage media, file maintenance process and the size and organisation of files;
- the mode and frequency of processing; and
- the form of output of the application and the distribution of output.

This information enables the auditor to understand the relationship between the manual and computerised portions of the information system and to assess the size and complexity of the computerised portion of the information system and how much assistance will be required from computer audit specialists.

AUS 402.89 (ISA 315.89) requires the auditor to obtain an understanding of how the entity communicates financial reporting roles and responsibilities and significant matters relating to financial reporting. It includes the extent to which personnel understand how their activities in the information system relate to others and the means of reporting exceptions to a higher level within the entity. The auditor's understanding of communication also includes communication between management and those charged with governance, particularly the audit committee, as well as communication to regulators.

Understanding the control activities

The auditor is required by AUS 402.90 (ISA 315.90) to obtain an understanding of the control activities sufficient to develop the audit plan. The audit procedures normally used to obtain an understanding of control activities involve:

- making inquiries of appropriate client personnel;
- inspecting documentation; and
- observing the processing of transactions and handling of related assets.

Many auditors use a technique called a **walk-through** to clarify their understanding of information obtained. A walk-through involves the auditor tracing one or a few transactions of each type through the related documents and accounting records and observing the related processing and control activities in operation. For example, the auditor might select a few transactions recorded in the sales journal and trace them back to the related source documents (invoice, customer order, shipping and control account). In doing this the auditor actually walks the selected transactions through the system by visiting the relevant departments and talking to the personnel responsible for the various processing and control activities.

The walk-through clarifies the auditor's understanding of how the system and the control activities work. The audit procedures applied for a walk-through are substantially the same as those that would be applied to a larger number of transactions in doing tests of controls. The distinction between a walk-through and tests of controls is based on the auditor's purpose in applying the procedures.

The auditor must obtain a sufficient enough understanding of the control activities to consider how a specific control activity, individually or in combination with others, prevents or detects and corrects material misstatements in classes of transactions, account balances or disclosures. Control activities relevant to the audit are those that the auditor considers necessary to obtain an understanding in order to assess the risk of material misstatement at the assertion level and design and perform further audit activities responsive to the assessed risks. An understanding of all of the client's control activities is not needed for audit planning.

The nature and extent of audit procedures necessary to obtain an understanding of the control activities varies considerably from entity to entity. A key issue is the level of complexity and sophistication of the accounting system and operations. In a small business, for example, the auditor may find a control environment in which there are too few employees to achieve an adequate separation of duties, thus resulting in the auditor adopting a substantive approach. In that case, sufficient knowledge of the control activities to plan the audit may have been achieved as part of the understanding of the control environment, the risk assessment process and the information system and additional work on specific control activities will not be needed.

Most computerised accounting applications include both manual and computer portions. The auditor needs to understand the path that transactions take through both portions of the information system. Some aspects of the computerised portion of the system are obviously different from a manual system. They are unique to computer processing and not difficult to identify. For example, some control activities may be included in a computer program and leave no visible evidence of their execution. If the auditor intends to assess control risk at less than high based on such control activities it may be necessary to test the computer program. However, it is often possible to substantiate computer-generated information directly or to test manual controls maintained by computer users, instead of testing programmed control activities. The most common forms of reliance on the computer occur when a manual control activity or an audit procedure is dependent on computer-generated information.

In some cases, a manual control activity that is necessary to achieve a specific control objective is dependent on the results of computer processing. For example, in a computerised billing application the auditor wants to know whether control activities provide reasonable assurance that products shipped are billed. If the control activity that achieves this objective is a review by a billing clerk of a computer-generated report of missing shipping documents based on a numerical sequence test in a computer program, then the auditor must rely on the computer in order to use the manual control activity in assessing the control risk.

If there are significant computerised accounting applications, the auditor may need to obtain an understanding of the general controls, which will be discussed later in this chapter. Auditors may review general controls even when they do not plan to assess control risk at less than high, as a service to clients. Usually the review is done by a computer audit specialist or an auditor with additional training in computerised systems. The review is conducted by inquiry and observation of client IT personnel and review of existing documentation, such as client manuals, previous years' work papers and other information on the computer installation and computerised accounting applications. The auditor's objective is to decide whether there is reasonable assurance that:

- there is an adequate separation of duties between IT and users and also within the IT department;
- the development or acquisition of programs and changes to programs are authorised, tested and approved before implementation; and
- access to data files is restricted to authorised users and programs.

After obtaining an understanding of general controls, the auditor comes to a conclusion as to whether they appear to be effective. Whether it is necessary or desirable to include such controls as part of the basis to reduce the control risk assessment depends on the auditor's consideration of application controls. If the general controls are part of the basis for reducing the control risk assessment, it is necessary to test the control activities.

Understanding monitoring of controls

AUS 402.96 (ISA 315.96) requires that the auditor obtain an understanding of the major activities that the entity uses to monitor internal control over financial reporting and how the entity initiates corrective actions to its controls. In many entities internal auditors contribute to the monitoring of an entity's activities. The auditor needs to obtain an understanding of the sources of the information related to the entity's monitoring activities and the basis upon which management considers the information to be sufficiently reliable.

Documenting the understanding

Documentation of the understanding of the internal control system commonly includes:

- internal control questionnaires and checklists;
- narrative memoranda; and
- flowcharts.

Unless the auditor believes that understanding of particular activities is needed for audit planning, the internal control activities need not be documented.

The auditor's objective is to identify and document the *minimum number* of specific control activities that provide reasonable assurance of achieving specific control objectives. As a result, the documentation prepared by the auditor may be much less detailed than would be prepared by a systems analyst. For example, if an entity's cash payments system provides for the financial controller's review and approval and cancellation of supporting documents before payment, the auditor may not be concerned with prior processing steps for individual supporting documents such as purchase orders. The auditor documents and tests those specific control activities that provide reasonable assurance of achieving specific control objectives for specific assertions.

Internal control questionnaires and checklists

Auditors generally use decision aids such as **internal control questionnaires** and checklists in obtaining an understanding of the internal control. These act as both a memory aid and a convenient way to document the understanding obtained.

Generalised forms relating to the control environment vary from detailed checklists that present all the potential features of a control environment to simple forms that list broad categories of features, such as personnel policies and procedures and organisational structure, leaving space to describe the particular client's methods.

Questionnaires and checklists to document the understanding of the information system tend to be less detailed than the generalised forms for the control environment and the control activities. They usually have a separate section for each transaction class or cycle. The questions (requiring a written answer rather than a 'yes' or 'no') require listing of each transaction type, the source document to initiate the transaction and the party responsible for the initiation, the approximate volume of each transaction type, the accounts and computer files in which the transaction is recorded, what processing occurs and where the transaction is summarised in the financial report.

Questionnaires and checklists are also used to document control activities. Exhibit 8.1 presents a segment of an internal control questionnaire. Some questions require a 'yes' or 'no' answer about whether specific control methods and features are in place. Others are organised by detailed control objective and the auditor writes in the client's procedures that achieve the listed objective.

EXHIBIT

8.1

Example of part of an internal control questionnaire

(Each question must be answered 'Yes' or 'No' or 'N/A'. If the answer is 'No', attach an explanation.)

Sales

☐ 1 Are sales orders approved by the credit department before they are accepted?

☐ 2 Is the credit function separated from other functions, particularly cash sales and accounting functions?

3 Are shipping documents

☐   (a) used?

☐   (b) used on all items leaving plant?

☐   (c) prenumbered?

☐ 4 Are shipping documents checked to customers' orders for quantity and descriptions to determine that items shipped are those ordered?

5 Are invoices

☐   (a) prepared on all sales?

☐   (b) prenumbered?

☐ 6 Is a check made to determine that there are notices of shipment for all invoices and invoices for all notices of shipments?

☐ 7 Are invoices checked to notices of shipment for quantity and descriptions to determine that items shipped are being billed?

☐ 8 Is a check made to determine that all invoices are recorded and all invoice numbers accounted for?

9 Are invoices checked for

☐   (a) extensions?

☐   (b) footings?

☐   (c) terms?

☐   (d) prices?

☐ 10 Are partial shipments subject to the same procedures as regular sales?

☐ 11 Do miscellaneous sales follow the same procedures as regular sales, e.g. sales of equipment, sales of scrap and sales to employees, etc.?

☐ 12 Are sales summaries prepared, independent of the accounting department, which may be used as a check on recorded sales?

Source: Adapted from AICPA, *Case Studies in Internal Control Number 2.*

Narrative memoranda

A **narrative memorandum** is a written description of internal control policies and procedures. Narratives may be used to document all three components of internal control. Exhibit 8.2 presents a narrative description of a segment of a sales accounting system. An auditor does not require exhaustive documentation of every step in all information systems or enumeration of all control activities. The narrative provides the flexibility to write only what is significant to the specific audit. However, this form of document has nothing to jog the memory to ensure that all important aspects are adequately documented, and narratives are more dependent than questionnaires on the ability of the auditor to write well. Narratives are more suited to documenting relatively simple systems.

The shipping department, based on an approved sales order, prepares a three-copy shipping document when a shipment is made. The distribution of the document is as follows:

1. Sent to customer with goods as a packing slip.
2. Forwarded to accounts receivable record-keeping. The sales order is filed numerically.
3. Forwarded to billing department.

The billing department uses the shipping document to prepare a two-copy sales invoice with the following distribution:

1. Sent to customer.
2. Forwarded to accounts receivable record-keeping. The shipping document is filed numerically.

The accounts receivable record-keeping function periodically matches sales invoices with shipping documents received.

1. Matched sales invoices are posted to accounts receivable ledger.
2. Matched sales invoices and shipping documents are filed alphabetically by customer name.

EXHIBIT 8.2

Example of a narrative description of part of a sales accounting system

---

Flowcharts

Flowcharts use symbols to make a diagram of an information system and control activities. Preparing a flowchart is particularly useful for systems that mix manual and computer processing in significant accounting applications.

Figure 8.3 (overleaf) presents some common flowchart symbols. Several audit firms have devised unique approaches when preparing flowcharts that use non-standard symbols. These approaches are too diverse to illustrate, but they all emphasise exclusion of document or information flows that are not relevant to the understanding of internal control for the purposes of audit planning. The standardised symbols in Figure 8.3 are used in the computer industry and by many audit firms and their clients.

Figure 8.4 (overleaf) presents a flowchart for a portion of a simple information system. Figure 8.5 (overleaf) presents a system flowchart for a portion of a batch computerised accounting application. One of the advantages of making flowcharts is that a graphic presentation of a series of related processing steps is easier to understand and comprehend than a long narrative description. However, if a flowchart includes all the document and information flows in the system, it also may become too complex to be understood easily and the significant control activities can be difficult to identify. As a result, the emphasis in practice is on simplifying flowcharts.

FIGURE 8.3 Standard flowchart symbols

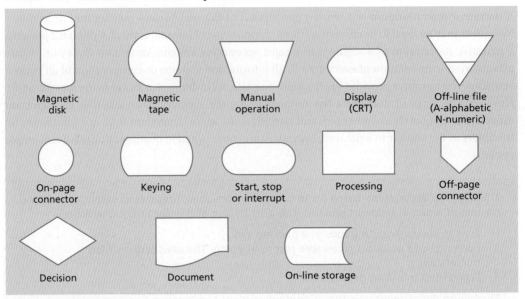

FIGURE 8.4 A flowchart of the first part of the sales accounting system described in Exhibit 8.2

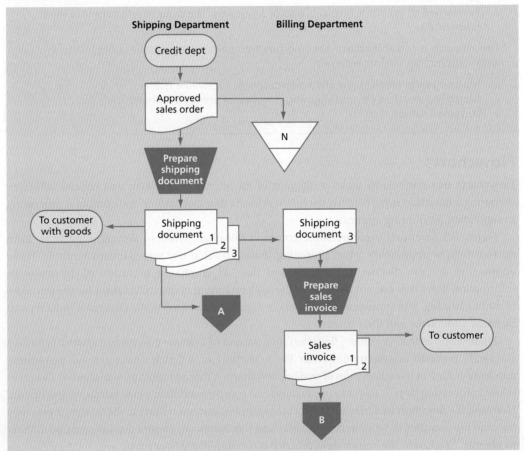

FIGURE 8.5 Segment of a flowchart on the billing function in a batch computerised sales accounting system

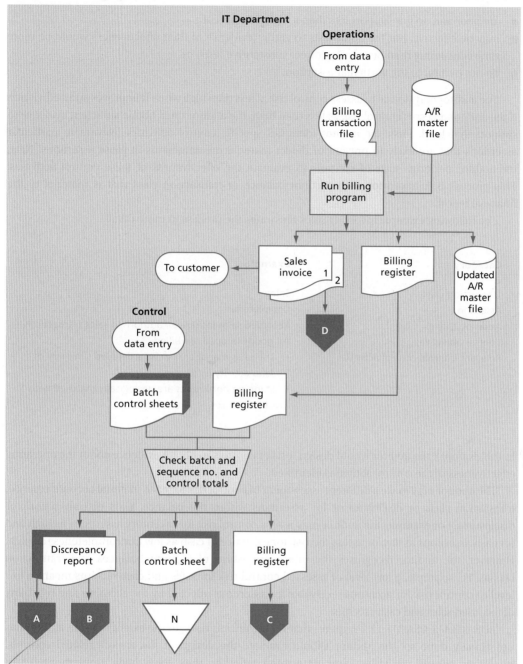

Assessing control risk

After obtaining an understanding of the components of internal control, the auditor **assesses control risk** for the assertions embodied in the account balance, transaction class and disclosure components of the financial report. The auditor must decide whether to assess control risk for a particular assertion at high or at less than high.

The auditor may assess control risk at high because the entity's internal control policies and procedures in the area:

- are poor and do not support less than a high assessment;
- may be effective, but the audit tests to gather evidence of their effectiveness would be more time consuming than performing direct substantive tests; or
- do not pertain to the particular assertion.

The auditor may decide to assess control risk at less than high when it improves audit efficiency. If the auditor assesses control risk as less than high, the auditor must obtain sufficient evidence to support that level. First, the auditor identifies specific control activities relevant to particular assertions that are likely to prevent or detect material misstatements in those assertions. Next, the auditor performs tests of controls to evaluate the effectiveness of these control activities. This process is followed for each account balance or transaction class that is material to the financial report.

The following example involving sales illustrates the process in more detail.

Category	Example
Transaction class	Sales
Assertion	Completeness
Audit objective	Recorded sales include all authorised sales transactions
Control objective	All goods shipped are billed
Relevant internal control activities	• The sales manager reviews a detailed summary of sales activity by location
	• Shipping documents are periodically matched with sales invoices

In this example, the auditor would design tests of controls to obtain evidence about the operating effectiveness of the control activities identified.

The auditor may make a different assessment of control risk for each material account balance, transaction class or disclosure or for assertions within the balance, class of transactions or disclosures. For example, the auditor may assess control risk for inventory assertions as high and for cash assertions as low, or assess the risk for existence of cash as low but completeness as high. However, the auditor recognises the interrelationships of account balances and transaction classes. For example, a low level of assessed control risk for sales and cash receipts means a low level of control risk for accounts receivable for assertions affected by the accuracy and reliability of recorded sales and cash receipts.

AUS 402.113 (ISA 315.113) requires that for significant risks, to the extent that the auditor has not already done so, the auditor should evaluate the design of the entity's related controls, including control activities, and determine whether they have been implemented. An understanding of the entity's controls relating to significant risks is considered necessary to provide the auditor with adequate information to develop an effective audit approach, even if the auditor does not intend to rely on those controls.

AUS 402.115 (ISA 315.115) also requires the auditor to evaluate the design and determine the implementation of the entity's controls, including relevant control activities, over those risks for which, in the auditor's judgment, it is not possible or practicable to reduce the risk of misstatements at the assertion level to an acceptably low level with evidence obtained solely from substantive procedures. Therefore, the auditor cannot simply default to a high assessment of control risk, without first evaluating the controls in these two areas.

Tests of controls

If control risk is assessed at less than high, the auditor has identified specific policies and procedures that are likely to prevent or detect misstatements. Evidence is needed to support the conclusion that those policies and procedures are effective. The evidence should demonstrate both:

- the effectiveness of the design of the policies and procedures; and
- the operating effectiveness of the policies and procedures, that is, their consistent and proper application.

The evidence necessary to support a specific level of control risk is a matter of audit judgment. However, the auditor requires stronger evidence of the effectiveness of a procedure if the assessed level of control risk is low than if it is only medium.

Tests of controls will be discussed in Chapter 9.

Documentation of the assessment of control risk

The auditor must document the assessment of control risk for the various assertions for significant transaction classes, account balances and disclosures. AUS 402.122 (ISA 315.122) requires the auditor to document their understanding of each of the components of internal control, the sources of the information from which the understanding was obtained, the risk assessment procedures, the identified and assessed risks of material misstatement, including control risk. The manner in which these items are documented is for the auditor to determine, using professional judgment.

Effect on design of substantive tests

The result of the auditor's consideration of the internal control is the assessment of control risk, which is then used in planning substantive tests for the various assertions within the transaction classes or account balances. Using the audit risk model discussed in Chapter 5, if the auditor assesses control risk at high, detection risk must be minimised. Detection risk is reduced by performing substantive tests. The higher the level of assessed control risk, the lower the level of reliance placed on the internal control and the more assurance the auditor must obtain from substantive tests.

Ineffective internal control causes the auditor to increase the quantity and effectiveness of the substantive tests because there is a general relationship between control objectives and audit objectives. Because it is not consistent, the relationship must be considered for each transaction class separately. For example, *approval* of credit sales (goods shipped to customers do not exceed established credit limits) is related to the specific audit objective of *valuation* of accounts receivable. On the other hand, approval of disbursements is related to specific audit objectives concerning *existence* or *occurrence*.

However, the following generalisations can be made about the impact of an effective internal control on the nature, timing and extent of substantive tests:

- **Substantive tests related to existence** Effective internal control may allow the auditor to modify the nature or reduce the extent of substantive tests of the existence of recorded assets or liabilities. For example, the number of confirmations sent to customers may be reduced when control activities over the occurrence and measurement of debits and credits to accounts receivable are effective.

- **Substantive tests related to completeness** Effective internal control may allow the auditor to modify the nature or reduce the extent of substantive tests of the completeness of recorded assets or liabilities. For example, if processing and control activities relating to the completeness of sales transactions are effective (all goods shipped have been billed), the auditor's tests related to the completeness of receivables may be limited to analytical procedures. There is a direct relation between control and audit objectives related to completeness for all transaction classes.

- **Substantive tests related to all audit objectives for income statement accounts** Because of the relationship between income statement and balance sheet accounts, substantive tests of opening and closing balance sheet accounts substantiate the amount of net profit for the period. When processing and control activities for the major transaction classes that affect income statement amounts are effective, the substantive tests of these accounts can often be limited to analytical procedures.

- **Timing of substantive tests** Effective internal control in regard to safeguarding assets may permit the auditor to conduct principal substantive tests of recorded assets at an interim date rather than at year-end, for example confirming accounts receivable at May for a June year-end. The auditor will then need to review transactions during the roll-forward period and investigate significant fluctuations.

The relationship between specific control objectives and specific audit objectives for major classes of transactions is considered further in Chapter 9.

Quick review

1. The auditor needs to obtain an understanding of internal control; assess the level of control risk based on the understanding obtained; perform tests of control to gain evidence that the controls exist and operate effectively throughout the period; and design substantive tests.
2. The auditor will document the internal control using internal control questionnaires and checklists, narrative memoranda and flowcharts.
3. The auditor may assess control risk along a range from high to low depending on the effectiveness of internal control.
4. The auditor must obtain evidence to support the assessed level of control risk.
5. The higher the level of assessed control risk, the more assurance the auditor must obtain from substantive tests.

COMPUTERISED SYSTEMS

It is expected that many students will have an understanding of the basic concepts of IT. Students who wish to revise these concepts should refer to the material on the basic concepts of IT on the web site associated with this book.

In considering internal control that involves a computerised system, it is useful to distinguish between various categories of controls.

Levels of control in computerised systems

There are two major categories of controls in computerised systems: user controls and IT controls. **User controls** are those controls established and maintained by departments whose processing is performed by computer. User departments are responsible for the validity, completeness, authorisation and accuracy of information outside the IT department. This means that users are responsible for any errors that originate outside the IT department. User departments are also responsible for establishing and maintaining controls over the information from their department which is processed by computer. For example, a payroll department may determine gross payroll and the number of payroll cheques to be prepared before processing, and then compare the computer output received from the IT department with those totals.

The distinction between user controls and **IT controls** is therefore based on location. IT controls are maintained in the location of the computer. IT controls are discussed below and can be sub-divided into general controls and application controls. User controls are always application controls.

General controls versus application controls

General controls are those controls that relate to all or many computerised accounting applications. For example, controls over the development of and changes to application software affect all accounting applications and they are included in the auditor's consideration of the control environment. **Application controls** relate to specific individual computerised accounting applications. For example, a programmed control for validating customers' account numbers and credit limits affects only the sales accounting application and is considered in assessing control risk for assertions in that area. This example leads to another important distinction—that between programmed and manual controls.

Programmed versus manual controls

An IT control may be either a programmed or a manual control activity. A manual activity is performed by people, and a programmed activity is performed by computer software. The rejection of an invalid account number by the computer is a programmed control, while a data-entry operator checking for the authorised signature on a document before keying in data is a manual control. When the computer generates a report of unusual transactions or conditions (e.g. payroll hours exceeding 50 for one week) for management review, that review is a manual control that depends on a programmed control.

General controls

General controls are defined in AUS 104 (ISA 110) as those manual and computer controls that relate to all or many computerised accounting applications to provide a reasonable level of assurance that the overall objectives of internal control are achieved. A variety of controls fall into this category, but the general controls that are usually important to the planning and conduct of an audit of financial reports are:

- **Segregation of duties**   This involves reviewing the plan of organisation and operation of IT for appropriate separation of incompatible functions.
- **Control over programs**   This involves reviewing control activities to ensure that development, acquisition and changes to applications and systems programs are authorised,

tested and approved before being used for processing. Access to programs should also be restricted to authorised personnel.

- **Control over data** This involves reviewing control activities to ensure that access to the system and data files is restricted to authorised users and programs. Transactions entering the system should be appropriately authorised.

Segregation of duties

In a computerised accounting system the segregation of duties related to IT comprises:

- separation between IT and user department functions; and
- separation of incompatible functions within the IT department.

The IT department must be separate from user department functions if the user controls are to be effective. Ideally, of the functions of authorisation, execution, recording and accountability, the IT department should be responsible for recording. However, in some systems, initiation or execution of transactions is an automatic step in an application program.

Normally there is an adequate segregation of duties if user departments independently exercise review and reconciliation controls over original input and resubmissions. User departments should independently reconcile manual documentation of input with computer output. Also, errors should be returned for correction to the originating user department and the user department should maintain an independent record (log) of corrections and resubmissions.

Within a large IT department the following positions or functions may exist:

- IT manager, the senior management position within the department responsible for supervising the data-processing staff;
- systems analyst, responsible for designing accounting systems, developing data processing projects in conjunction with user departments and developing specifications for applications programmers;
- applications programmer, responsible for developing and testing new applications programs and changes to existing programs that meet the specifications established by the systems analyst;
- systems programmer, responsible for maintaining and adapting the operating system and other systems software;
- computer operator, responsible for the human intervention required to run application programs and for the distribution of output;
- data-entry clerk, responsible for keying information from manual source documents to computer-readable form;
- data-control clerk, responsible for the handling and control of data within the IT department, including comparing computer-calculated control totals to manually established or data preparation totals and correcting errors that originate in the IT department; and
- librarian, responsible for maintaining and releasing for authorised use computer files maintained offline and written documentation of production programs.

Ideally, all these computer-related functions should be kept separate. However, the critical separation of duties is that between operations and systems development. These functions are incompatible and should not be combined: those who have knowledge of the operation of the accounting systems and applications programs, including how to modify programs, should not be permitted to access data files and production programs that accompany operations. Table 8.1 presents the common IT department functions, showing those positions with knowledge of and those positions with access to data files or production programs.

TABLE 8.1 Segregation of duties within IT

Separate	Positions within IT department
Knowledge: those with an understanding of systems and programs	• IT manager • Systems analysts • Applications programmers
Access: those with access to the computer, production programs and data files	• Computer operators • Data-entry clerks (no access to computer console, data control records or programs) • Data-control clerks (no access to computer console) • Librarian (no access to computer console) • Systems programmers*

* The position of systems programmer must have access to perform the function. Systems programmers should have no detailed knowledge of the company's accounting systems or application programs.

In a small computer system (minicomputer or microcomputer), there are often not enough people to achieve an adequate segregation of duties within the IT department or between the IT department and the user. In such circumstances the auditor will usually conclude that general controls are seriously deficient and that the control risk must be assessed as high on the basis of IT controls. However, in some circumstances the auditor might still assess control risk below high on the basis of user controls.

Control over programs

Usually, controls over programs apply to all computerised accounting applications. One of the major risks for the business and therefore for the auditor is at the acquisition, development or change stages of the program. Development of new programs, acquisition of programs from software vendors and changes to existing programs must be adequately controlled. Adequate control includes authorisation, testing and approval before new or changed programs are used in processing applications.

Control activities for development, acquisition or changes to programs are conceptually similar to other control activities that leave a documentary trail and they may be tested by inspection of documents for approval signatures. The essential features of control are written procedures and documentation for the following steps:

1 **Initiation** Authorisation for the IT department to develop or acquire new programs or change existing programs. There should be documentation, such as a program request form, that is formally approved by the relevant user department and IT management.
2 **Testing** Formal testing procedures that include the involvement of users, IT management and internal auditors. There should be an approved testing plan and the test data and results, indicating approval, should be retained.
3 **Implementation** Formal approval by users and IT management before a program is placed into production by IT personnel independent of programming. Programmers should not have access to production programs so there should be separate test programs and production programs should be protected from unauthorised access.

Outside these steps, the major concerns of the business and the auditor are about unauthorised access and/or changes to the programs.

In many computerised systems, access to programs is protected by specialised systems software. For example, **program library management software** protects application programs that are stored online. This systems software also logs changes to programs and any attempts to obtain unauthorised access to programs. When this type of systems software is used the auditor may be able to use management reports produced by the software to determine the date of the last change to each program. Where this software is modified, such modifications should be properly authorised, approved, tested and documented. Only authorised personnel should have access to systems software and its documentation.

Control over data

Control activities in user departments and IT application controls over input and processing help to ensure that processed data are authorised, valid, complete and accurate. Control over access to data maintained on computer-readable files ensures that the data *remain* authorised, valid, complete and accurate.

The control activities that restrict access to data files to authorised users and programs are a mixture of physical devices, manual control activities and programmed control activities. Physical security measures are necessary to ensure that only authorised personnel have access to the computer room. These measures include locks, badges and passes to obtain admittance. In an online system, physical security measures for terminals, such as locks and a supervised location, are also important. In a system where there is remote transmission from terminals to the central processing unit (CPU), physical security is more difficult to achieve and programmed procedures assume even greater importance.

Where data files are maintained offline, a librarian function separate from programming and operations is important. The librarian should release files only in accordance with established procedures for authorised use. Authorisation should include both the individuals to whom files may be released and an authorised processing schedule. Proper labelling of files (both internal and external) also helps to ensure protection of data files from incorrect and unauthorised use.

In an online system, files are accessed through terminals. Thus a variety of programmed procedures is necessary, particularly procedures accomplished by systems software. When terminals are located in user departments, only appropriate terminals should have access to master files. For example, terminals in the billing department should not have access to the accounts payable master file. This can be achieved by online storage of a list of authorised terminals for each function, so that when a terminal requests access its identity is compared with a list of authorised terminals for the requested file. It is also necessary to restrict use of terminals to authorised users. This can be achieved by systems software that requires users to enter an ID and a password in order to obtain access to particular data files and programs.

Measures should also be taken in an online system to restrict the access to data files of those involved in the programming function. Application programmers need to use files in testing programs and these files should be copies, or files of fictitious data, rather than live data files. Also, **systems software** may be used to bypass programmed control activities that restrict the access of application programs to data files. Therefore, use of systems software should be controlled and systems programmers' use of systems software should be monitored.

Systems security software packages are available that monitor access to data files and control unauthorised access. This software either prevents or detects unauthorised access to data files. However, some systems software of this type may be operated in different modes at the client's choosing, and only some modes prevent unauthorised access. Other modes detect and produce a management report of unauthorised access to data files and their effectiveness is dependent on manual investigation and follow-up of the reports.

Where control over access to data files is dependent on systems software, the assistance of a computer audit specialist is usually required. The computer audit specialist assists in obtaining an understanding of the systems-software-dependent controls and evaluates whether they are effective in restricting access to data files to authorised users and programs.

Other general controls

There are other general controls but usually they do not have an effect on the auditor's assessment of control risk. For example, some general controls are concerned with the ability to recover computer operations if various problems arise. These **back-up and recovery controls** relate to measures taken to back up hardware, software and files and to ensure recovery when the computer installation or particular files or programs are damaged or destroyed. For example, the client should have a contingency plan to follow if computer processing is disrupted by a disaster such as a fire or a flood.

Back-up procedures relate to the ability to reconstruct data files if the current version of the file is damaged by hardware or software error. For example, in a system with batch input and batch processing, files should be retained to allow the reconstruction of master files. A retention policy often used is called the **grandfather–father–son concept**. As the name implies, it involves retaining three generations of a particular master file and the related transaction files. The current version of the master file is the son file and the two previous versions are the father and grandfather. In an online entry system, data file retention requires dumping the entire contents of master files onto magnetic tape or disk on a daily basis and creating a transactions log of processed transactions.

Application controls

Application controls often depend on general controls. For example, a programmed IT control or a manual control activity that depends on computer-generated information may not be effective if control over development and changes to application software are ineffective. However, application controls contribute to achievement of specific control objectives that the auditor considers in tests of controls. The auditor assesses the effect of application controls on control risk in order to restrict the scope of direct tests of balances. As explained earlier, application controls may be user controls or IT controls.

User controls

User controls are performed by personnel in user departments and therefore are manual control activities and so these controls may be tested in the same manner as control activities in a manual processing system. The auditor may test the functioning of user controls by inquiry, observation and inspection of documents.

The user controls relevant to providing reasonable assurance of the occurrence, completeness and accuracy of data processed by the computer may be classified as: control totals; review and reconciliation of data; error correction and resubmission; and authorisation controls.

Control totals are used to detect errors in input or processing when information is batched before entry. Generally, there are three types:

1 **Financial totals:** the totals of field amounts for all the records in a batch that are normally computed as a result of processing. For example, in a sales accounting system, financial totals are total dollars received or total dollars billed.

2 **Record totals:** the totals of the number of logical or physical records in a batch. For example, the total number of sales invoices and the total number of inventory items on invoices in a batch are record totals.

3 **Hash totals:** the totals of field amounts for all the records in a batch that are computed for control purposes only. For example, the total of customer numbers is a hash total.

If a user department establishes control totals before data entry and reconciles those totals to output returned from the IT department, loss of data or changes in data that occur outside the user department can be detected. For this control activity to be effective, the user department must maintain detailed documentation, reconcile output to input and investigate discrepancies. The procedures are as follows: a batch number is assigned; the number of items in a batch is limited to facilitate reconciliation; control totals are recorded manually in a log maintained by the user and on a transmittal ticket (batch header) that accompanies the batch; the control totals on output reports are reconciled to the input control totals; differences and their resolution are also documented.

For a computerised system, review and reconciliation of data by users is an important control activity. Users should make a manual review of the data before its transmittal or entry, to help ensure the accuracy and completeness of data submitted for processing. Also, users should carefully review computer output received and reconcile it to input. As transactions may be automatically initiated or executed by application programs, users should review a list of all computer-generated transactions for their applications. Review of file maintenance changes to master files is also important. For example, there may be changes to customer credit limits or addresses on the accounts receivable master file. Changes not authorised by user control activities should be investigated. User review of changes helps to ensure that they are authorised and accurate. Since users are knowledgeable about the file data for their applications, user reviews of output for reasonableness are important.

There are generally formal error correction and resubmission procedures in computerised systems. Users are responsible for correcting errors that originate outside the IT department. Procedures in user departments generally should include a user's procedure manual with written procedures for correcting errors, maintenance of a log for errors and resubmissions, and careful review and approval of resubmitted source documents before transmittal.

Authorisation controls are important to ensure that only valid transactions are processed. During batching, individual transactions should be appropriately authorised. There should also be an authorisation procedure for each of the batches from the user department to the IT department for input.

IT controls

Every time data are transferred from one medium to another or are changed by processing, such as summarisation or calculation, there is potential for error. Therefore, IT application controls are usually classified as input, file, processing and output controls. Errors may be introduced at each of these stages in a computerised system.

Input controls naturally differ for batch input and online entry. Batch input goes through a data preparation step for conversion of manual source documents to computer-readable form. Batch data preparation generally includes the following control activities:

■ **Control totals:** computed as a by-product of data preparation and compared to the total manually established by the user department. Also, as part of data preparation, a batch header record (computer readable) including control totals is often created and added to the input.

- **Key verification:** a duplicate keying of data to detect errors of entry. A second operator rekeys the same source documents and differences from the first keying are identified and corrected. As key verification is expensive, it is usually confined to critical data fields on source documents.
- **Key entry validation:** data validation is a general term for tests to detect inaccurate or incomplete data. Key-to-tape or key-to-disk equipment has logic capabilities that permit data validation.

Online entry controls include (a) batch controls in online entry with batch processing and (b) general controls, which were discussed earlier, to ensure that only authorised and valid transactions are entered into terminals.

After data preparation in batch input systems, the batch input is read online from tape or disk into primary storage. This step takes place under control of the CPU and a variety of edit and data validation tests can be made using the logic capability of the CPU. The following edit and data validation tests are examples of programmed control activities:

- **Check digit** Used to validate record identification fields. For example, a check digit may be used for customer numbers or employee numbers. The check digit is calculated from the identification number and attached to it when the number is originally assigned. The calculation is a numeric operation on the identification number. A simple check digit algorithm might operate in the following way:
  — Assume an inventory item code was 6595 1. Once entered, the computer might divide the number 6595 by 7 (referred to as the modulus), and the result of this division would be 942 with a remainder of 1. The computer would then compare the remainder with the final digit in the code (in this case, 1). Since the remainder agrees with the 'check digit', the code is valid. If the remainder is not the same as the check digit, then the code is invalid and should be rejected.
- **Limit or reasonableness test** A logic test used to determine whether a data amount falls within previously established limits. An amount that is outside the limit is identified for investigation. For example, in a weekly payroll application, employee time records with greater than 48 hours or less than 0 hours might be rejected or printed out for investigation. In a cash payments system all disbursements over a specified amount, such as $10 000, might be printed out for investigation. This type of programmed control activity helps compensate for the lack of human involvement in computer processing. Humans notice when data do not make sense or are out of line; computers do not, unless specifically programmed to apply predefined criteria.
- **Field test** A logic test based on the characteristics that data in particular fields should exhibit. For example, characters should be alphabetic or numeric (alphanumeric test); the field should have a specified size (for example, a field contains 5 characters, not 4 or 6); the field should have a specified sign (sign test) or in some cases a specified value.
- **Valid code test** A logic test in which a code field in a record is compared to a table of valid codes stored online. For example, a transaction code can be used in accounts receivable processing so that only transactions with certain codes, such as credit sales or cash collections, are accepted to update the debtors' master file.

These programmed control activities are examples rather than an exhaustive list of the possible procedures.

File controls ensure that the proper versions of files are used in processing. For example, the current period's transaction file and the latest version of the master file should generally be used in processing. Control activities in this area include file label controls. **Internal file labels** are computer-readable data that are actually part of the file and they identify the data and content of the file. **External file labels** are printed or handwritten adhesive labels on a diskette or magnetic tape reel.

Processing controls detect errors in data and errors that occur in processing as a result of logic errors in application programs or systems software errors. Controls for data errors include programmed control activities, such as transaction code tests, checking the numerical sequence of records on a file and comparing related fields in files. Controls to prevent or detect processing errors include programmed control activities such as reasonableness or limit tests and use of redundant program calculations (double arithmetic). Also, control totals accumulated during processing are compared to input totals and previous computer-run totals. This is commonly known as a **run-to-run control total reconciliation**.

Output controls include manual control activities in which IT personnel and users review output to ensure propriety and reasonableness; and proper output handling to ensure that output is distributed only to authorised users. Output controls also include programmed controls restricting access to display specified information (for example, payroll data) on a terminal or PC. Other programmed output control activities include automatic dating of reports, page numbering and end-of-report messages. These ensure that no pages can easily be inserted, added or removed.

Relationship between the review of general and application controls

In an IT environment the auditor should start the internal control evaluation by looking at the general controls. If these controls are found to be unreliable, then the auditor can have little confidence in programmed application controls and confidence in manual application controls may be reduced. In this situation there is limited benefit in continuing to review, document and perform tests of programmed controls; the auditor must take a more substantive approach to the audit.

If the general controls are reliable the auditor makes a preliminary evaluation of application controls and, if appropriate, a more detailed evaluation of application controls. Thus, the auditor determines the degree of tests of controls and substantive testing which will result in the most efficient and effective audit.

Control systems in different environments

Database systems

A database is a computer-readable file of records that is used by several accounting applications. For example, a file of suppliers or vendors might be used by purchases, accounts payable, and inventory applications. In a file-based system, there is usually a separate file for each application even though essentially similar information is maintained on each file. In a database system, such a file is shared by the applications.

The database approach requires a file index with primary and secondary identifying key fields because different applications require different identifying keys. Because of the complexity of the file structure, special systems software called a **database management system (DBMS)** is necessary to handle programming and related tasks for managing the database. The person with overall responsibility for the data is the database administrator.

The key risk that exists in a database is the risk that general controls are inadequate to properly control the operations of the database. This risk arises largely because a database is a collection of data that is shared and used by a number of different users for different purposes. Therefore, an error in one piece of data can potentially affect a number of different applications across the entity.

Guidance for the audit of database systems is provided in AGS 1022 (IAPS 1003) 'IT Environments—Database Systems'. AGS 1022 (IAPS 1003) identifies four categories of general controls of particular importance in a database environment:

- a standard approach for development and maintenance of application programs;
- data ownership;
- access to the database; and
- segregation of duties.

As data is shared among all applications, the need to control its completeness and accuracy is critical. Inadequate general controls may lead to problems such as:

- inappropriate authorisation of changes to database information. For example, inadequate access controls may result in many users being able to change database information. This will reduce the integrity of database information;
- inadequate segregation of duties. For example, users who change data may also check those changes, removing the automatic checking function normally provided by appropriate segregation of duties; and
- inaccurate data, which would lead to pervasive errors in the client's processing. For example, an error in say a customer's address can affect many functions, such as invoicing, ordering and dispatch.

The effect on internal control depends on the extent to which the database system is used by the entity. Generally, if controls over the database are good, then the risk of error is reduced as each piece of data is recorded only once, thus reducing the possibility of mistakes. However, if controls over the database are poor, then the risk of error increases substantially as incorrect data could be used by several different applications.

Stand-alone PC systems

A PC can be used in various configurations. These include:

- a stand-alone workstation operated by a single user or a number of users at different times;
- a workstation which is part of a local area network (LAN) of micro-computers; and
- a workstation connected to a central computer.

When the PC is used as a stand-alone workstation, guidance is contained in AGS 1018 (IAPS 1001) 'IT Environments—Stand-Alone Personal Computers'. Control considerations and characteristics of the hardware and software are different when a PC is linked to other computers; AGS 1020 (IAPS 1002) 'IT Environment—On-line Computer Systems' provides guidance in such cases.

With PCs, the distinction between general IT controls and application controls may be blurred. Generally, the IT environment in which PCs are used is less structured than a centrally-controlled IT environment. In the former, application programs can be developed relatively quickly by users who have only basic data-processing skills. In such cases, the controls over the system development process (for example, adequate documentation) and operations (for example, access control activities), which are essential to the effective control of a larger computer environment, may not be viewed by the developer, the user or management as being as important or cost-effective. However, because the data are processed on a computer, users of such data may tend to place unwarranted reliance on the financial information that is stored or generated.

Where PCs are used, it may not be practicable or cost-effective for management to implement sufficient controls to reduce the risks of undetected errors to a minimum level. Thus, the auditor often assumes that control risk is high in such systems.

In this situation, the auditor may find it more cost-effective, after obtaining an understanding of the control environment and flow of transactions, not to make a review of general or application controls, but to concentrate the audit efforts on substantive tests of transactions and balances at or near the end of the year.

LANs and other networks

In the past few years, many companies have moved accounting applications from mainframes to PCs on **local area networks (LANs)**. In most cases, internal control risk has risen significantly. Over the years, companies with critical mainframe applications developed effective security and control activities. Because the processing is distributed to PCs at many locations, the security and control activities and techniques designed for the mainframe no longer apply, and often little has been put in place to replace them. Viruses (unauthorised programs causing mischief or significant damage) can spread quickly from one PC to another in a LAN environment. Complicating the design of the controls is the increasing trend to connect LANs with other LANs, or even with nationwide networks.

The operating system software that runs the LANs does not have the built-in control features that were developed for mainframe and mid-range computers. Software to add onto the LAN operating system to provide security and control features is being developed, but it has significant weaknesses. Encryption software slows processing, and some encryption packages have a tendency to cause networks to crash. Utility software designed to troubleshoot LAN problems often permits users to discover others' IDs and passwords.

Security and control features for LANs and other networks will continue to improve. Originally, mainframe computers had few control features, but the industry responded to the demand for internal control over the applications processed. A similar process will result in improved control in LANs.

Computer service bureaux

A client may have some or all computerised accounting applications processed at an outside service bureau, or centre, rather than using its own computer. Even companies with large computer installations prefer to have applications such as payroll processed externally.

Guidance for the auditor when confronted by a **computer service bureau** is provided in AUS 404 (ISA 402), 'Audit Implications Relating to Entities Using a Service Entity'. When an audit client (user) employs a service entity, audit evidence that is ordinarily located at the user's premises may be located at the service entity. The auditor needs to understand the nature and extent of the services provided by the service entity because they affect the nature, timing and extent of audit procedures, and it may not be effective to obtain audit evidence from the service entity.

When a service entity is used, transactions that affect the financial report of the user flow through an internal control system which is, at least in part, separate from the user; thus some or all of the evidence which the auditor needs may be under the control of the service entity. For the auditor to draw reasonable conclusions about the transactions, and in some cases the resultant balances, which flow through the service entity's internal control, it may be necessary to obtain audit evidence from the service entity or to have access to its records. In such circumstances, the auditor may find it necessary to consider the internal control of the service entity.

Where an entity uses a service entity there must be adequate planning at an early stage in the audit process. To determine the significance of the service entity's activities to the user and their relevance to the audit, the auditor needs to consider the nature of the services, and the terms of the contract and relationship with the user.

The auditor needs to consider the division of internal control between the user and the service entity. The user may have implemented controls that provide reasonable assurance that irregularities at the service entity would be detected. In some circumstances, the auditor may be able to plan to rely on the internal control of the user without obtaining an understanding of the internal control of the service entity.

An auditor who plans to obtain audit evidence through the use of a report prepared by the service entity's auditor may communicate with the user, the service entity, and the service entity's auditor to establish the form of report to be provided by the service entity's auditor, the purpose for which the report is to be used, the date at which the report is required, the period it is to cover, and the responsibility for the cost of the services provided.

The user's auditor obtains an understanding of internal control at the user business and, where appropriate, the service entity, and makes a preliminary assessment of control risk. Guidance is provided in AUS 402 (ISA 400) 'Risk Assessments and Internal Controls'. The auditor obtains audit evidence by testing controls to support any assessment of control risk that is less than high.

This evidence, as it relates to the service entity, is obtained by one or a combination of the following: obtaining from the service entity's auditor a report on the tests performed on its internal control and the results thereof; requesting the service entity's auditor to conduct agreed-upon procedures; or conducting audit procedures at the service entity.

Where a service entity maintains internal control that does not interact with the user's internal control system—for example, where the user permits the service entity to execute transactions without specific authorisation—the user may not have independent records of the occurrence and measurement of these transactions or of the existence of assets and liabilities. Accordingly, a written description of the internal control and the tests of control conducted by the service entity's auditor do not constitute sufficient appropriate audit evidence on transactions and balances, without substantive procedures being performed by either the service entity's auditor or the user's auditor.

If audited financial information from the service entity on the transactions and balances of the user is unavailable, the user's auditor can obtain sufficient appropriate evidence by asking the service entity's auditor to perform agreed procedures; or the user's auditor can make arrangements to perform audit procedures at the service entity.

In considering reports issued by the service entity's auditor, attention must be paid to the black letter requirement of AUS 404.27 (ISA 402.13), which states:

> When using a report issued by the service entity auditor, the user auditor should consider the scope of the work performed and assess whether the report is sufficient and appropriate for its intended use by the user auditor.

Ideally, reports provided by the service entity's auditor to assist the user's auditor in forming an opinion on the financial report of the user should cover the same reporting period as the financial report of the user. In circumstances where the reporting period is not identical, the auditor considers the audit implications and the need for additional procedures.

1 The distinction between controls established and maintained by the user department (user controls) and those maintained by the IT department (IT controls) is important.

2 Controls are usually classified in two broad categories: general controls and application controls.

3 General controls are controls that relate to all or many computerised accounting applications. They include:
- the plan of organisation and operation of IT;
- control activities over development, acquisition and changes to programs; and
- control activities to ensure that access to data files is restricted to authorised users and programs.

4 Application controls are controls relating to individual computerised accounting applications. They include:
- user controls:
  - —control totals;
  - —review and reconciliation of data; and
  - —error correction and resubmission procedures,

and
- IT controls:
  - —input controls;
  - —file controls;
  - —processing controls; and
  - —output controls.

5 An IT control can either be a programmed control or a manual control.

6 Advanced computer-related considerations include:
- database management systems;
- stand-alone PC systems;
- LANs and other networks; and
- computer service bureaux.

CONSIDERING THE WORK OF AN INTERNAL AUDITOR

In many large entities the organisational structure includes an internal audit function. The role of internal audit was discussed briefly in Chapter 1 and earlier in this chapter, and the changing role of internal audit will be discussed further in Chapter 15. The extent to which the external auditor can use the **work of the internal auditor** when forming an opinion on the financial report depends on an evaluation of the internal audit function by the external auditor.

The internal audit function within an entity is determined by management, and differs from the external audit function. Nevertheless, some of the means of achieving their objectives are similar. Therefore, it is possible that the external auditor can use the work of the internal auditor, thereby influencing the nature, timing and extent of the external audit procedures.

While recognising the similarities between the external and internal audit functions, it is important to bear in mind the fundamental differences between them. In the case of a company, the following major differences can be identified:

1 **Objectives** The external auditor has a statutory responsibility to report on the truth and fairness of the financial report and whether proper accounting records and registers have been

kept. These responsibilities cannot be delegated to others. The objectives of internal audit are determined by management to assist them in their decision making.

2 **Independence** The external auditor is appointed by and is responsible to the shareholders of the company in accordance with the provisions of the *Corporations Act*. The internal auditor may be appointed by and be responsible to management, the board or the audit committee.

3 **Qualifications** The qualifications of persons permitted to accept appointment as external auditors are stipulated in the *Corporations Act*. There are no statutory qualification requirements in the case of persons appointed to act as internal auditors. The type of qualification and/or experience are determined by management.

Despite these comments, AUS 604.04 (ISA 610.04) recognises that internal auditing may affect audit risk and therefore the nature, timing and extent of audit procedures. As a result, AUS 604.02 (ISA 610.02) requires that an external auditor, in obtaining an understanding of the entity's internal control, must assess the effect of internal auditing on control risk for planning the audit and developing an effective audit approach.

The work of an internal auditor may be used in an external audit where it is viewed as part of an audit client's internal control. The external auditor evaluates the internal audit function and determines the extent to which it can be used in the audit process.

AUS 604.12 (ISA 610.13) states that when obtaining an understanding and performing a preliminary assessment of internal auditing, the external auditor should consider:

- **Organisational status** Internal auditing's status in the entity and the effect this may have on its ability to be objective. In particular, internal auditing must be free to communicate fully with the highest level of management and the external auditor, and must be free of any other operating responsibility.
- **Scope of internal auditing** The nature and extent of assignments performed by internal auditing.
- **Technical competence** Whether internal auditing personnel have adequate technical training and proficiency, including professional qualifications and experience.
- **Due professional care** Whether internal auditing is properly planned, documented, supervised and reviewed. Evidence of this would be adequate audit manuals, audit programs and working papers.

The appendix to AUS 604 (ISA 610) provides a sample questionnaire that the external auditor may use to gain information and to evaluate the degree of reliance to be placed on internal auditing. The audit program of the external auditor should include a section to cover the review and assessment of the information gathered through the use of the questionnaire and the overall evaluation of the internal auditing as it affects the external auditor. For example, the following audit steps may be appropriate:

1 Ensure that the letter to the client confirming the reliance to be placed by the external auditor on the internal audit is current and correctly sets out the position. This may be embodied in the engagement letter.

2 Obtain details of the qualifications and experience of the members of the internal audit team for the client's permanent file. Determine whether the ratio of qualified to unqualified staff is satisfactory.

3 Review the client's organisation chart and ascertain whether the chief internal auditor reports to (or has direct access to) the chair of the governing body, the chief executive officer or the audit committee.

4   Arrange a meeting early in the year with the chief internal auditor to ascertain the planned internal audit program, including functions to be covered and locations to be visited.

5   At appropriate intervals during the year arrange for the internal audit work to be reviewed (preferably by the external audit manager). The review should include:
- *Audit program*: whether all sections have been signed off and dated and no unauthorised alterations have been made.
- *Audit working papers*: whether they are properly prepared so as to record evidence of work done, items selected for test, conclusions reached and internal audit manager review.
- *Internal audit reports*: whether these are addressed to the chair of the governing body, the chief executive officer or the audit committee and contain all material points arising from the audit. Where working papers include evidence of internal control weaknesses which are not reflected in the report, the reasons should be followed up with the chief internal auditor.

Meet with the chief internal auditor to discuss the audit and points arising from the review.

6   Review evidence of follow-up by management of matters raised in the internal audit report.

7   On the basis of this review, the external audit manager prepares a brief report, setting out:
- details of areas not covered by internal audit which should be covered by external audit;
- details of material problems revealed by the internal audit requiring external audit follow-up;
- conclusions as to the quality of performance of the internal audit.

8   The audit partner responsible for the client discusses this report with the external audit manager and, if necessary, makes further inquiries in order to form an opinion on the reliability of the internal audit work and the extent to which the external audit work may be varied or reduced.

9   Where necessary, prepare additional paragraphs for the external audit program, to cover:
- follow-up work on internal control breakdowns or deficiencies revealed by the internal audit to determine whether corrective action has been taken;
- areas where internal audit is not appropriate for the purpose of the external audit.

The external auditor is required to undertake a *general* evaluation of the internal audit function as part of the review of the client's internal control, but where the auditor intends to use specific internal audit work as a basis for modifying the nature, timing and extent of audit procedures, the external auditor must specifically review the internal audit working papers. AUS 604.16 (ISA 610.16) requires that an external auditor who relies on specific internal audit work to support a preliminary assessment of control risk must evaluate and test that work to ensure that it is adequate for external audit purposes.

The purpose of this review is primarily to determine that the work of internal audit is appropriate and to ascertain whether adequate standards have been applied in relation to such matters as planning, audit scope, supervision, review, documentation and evidence. The external auditor should also test that work; the nature, timing and extent of that testing will depend on the materiality of the area concerned and the results of the previously mentioned general and specific evaluations. This testing may encompass items already examined by internal audit, testing of similar items and observation of internal audit procedures.

Quick review

1 The extent to which the external auditor can use the work of internal auditing depends on the evaluation of the internal audit function.

2 Internal auditing may reduce audit risk and therefore the extent of the external auditor's work.

3 The evaluation of internal auditing will consider its organisational status; the scope of internal auditing; the technical competence of internal auditing personnel; and whether internal auditing exercises due professional care.

4 Where the external auditor intends to use specific internal audit work, the external auditor will review the internal auditor's working papers and test the internal auditor's work.

Summary

The study and evaluation of internal control is an important aspect of a financial report audit. The auditor must obtain a sufficient understanding of an entity's internal control, including the internal auditing function if applicable. The auditor's understanding of the internal control must be documented in the working papers through completed flowcharts, questionnaires and/or narrative descriptions. The auditor then needs to perform tests of controls, assess control risk for each significant financial report assertion and document the assessment. Making the correct assessment is crucial to completing an efficient and effective audit.

Key terms

Accuracy	347	Inherent limitations	338
Application controls	363	Input controls	368
Approval	346	Internal control questionnaires	355
Assessing control risk	359	Internal control	336
Authorisation	346	Internal file labels	369
Back-up and recovery controls	367	IT controls	363
Check digit	369	Key entry validation	369
Classification	348	Key verification	369
Completeness	347	Limit or reasonableness test	369
Computer service bureau	372	Local area networks (LANs)	372
Control environment	342	Management controls	340
Control activities	345	Narrative memorandum	357
Control totals	367	Occurrence	346
Cutoff	348	Output controls	370
Database management system (DBMS)	370	Performance review	345
External file labels	370	Processing controls	370
Field test	369	Program library management software	366
File controls	369	Record totals	368
Financial totals	367	Run-to-run control total reconciliation	370
Flowcharts	357	Systems software	366
General controls	363	User controls	363
Grandfather–father–son concept	367	Valid code test	369
Hash totals	368	Validity	347
Information processing	345	Walk-through	354
Information system	344	Work of internal auditor	374

References

Best, P. (2000) 'Auditing SAP R/3—Control Risk Assessment', *Australian Accounting Review*, November, Vol. 10, No. 3, 31–42.

Canadian Institute of Chartered Accountants (1984) *Audit Strategy and Reliance on Internal Control*, Audit Technique Study, CICA, Toronto.

Committee of Sponsoring Organisations of the Treadway Commission (1992) *Internal Control: Integrated Framework*, September, AICPA, New York.

ICAEW (1999) *Internal Control: Guidance for Directors on the Combined Code* (Turnbull Report), ICAEW, London.

Mock, T.J. and Willingham, J.J. (1983) 'An improved method of documenting and evaluating a system of internal accounting controls', *Auditing: A Journal of Practice and Theory*, Vol. 2, No. 2, Spring, 91–9.

Schelluch, P. (1995) 'Internal control—a new focus', *Accounting Communiqué No. 60*, ASCPA, Melbourne.

Spires, E. (1991) 'Auditors' evaluation of test-of-control strength', *Accounting Review*, April, 259–76.

Assignments

MaxMARK

MAXIMISE YOUR MARKS! There are approximately 30 interactive questions on understanding the internal control and assessing control risk available online at www.mhhe.com/au/gay3e

Additional assignments for this chapter are contained in Appendix A of this book, page 768.

REVIEW QUESTIONS

8.1 The following questions relate to the auditor's consideration of internal control. Select the *best* response.

(a) The primary purpose of the auditor's consideration of internal control is to provide a basis for:

A determining the nature, extent and timing of audit tests to be applied

B constructive suggestions to clients concerning improvements in internal control

C determining whether procedures and records that are concerned with the safeguarding of assets are reliable

D the expression of an opinion on internal control

(b) An auditor's primary consideration regarding an entity's internal controls is whether they:

A prevent management override

B relate to the control environment

C reflect management's philosophy and operating style

D affect the financial report assertions

(c) Which of the following statements about internal control is correct?

A Properly maintained internal control reasonably ensures that collusion among employees cannot occur.

B The establishment and maintenance of internal control is an important responsibility of the internal auditor.

C Exceptionally strong internal control is enough for the auditor to eliminate substantive tests on a significant account balance.

D The cost–benefit relationship is a primary criterion that should be considered in designing internal control.

(d) After obtaining an understanding of internal control in an audit engagement, the auditor should perform tests of controls on:

A a random sample of the control activities that were identified

B those control activities for which reportable conditions were identified

C those control activities that the auditor identified to reduce the assessed level of control risk

D those control activities that have a material effect upon the financial report balances

(e) A procedure that would most likely be used by an auditor in performing tests of control activities that involve segregation of functions and that leave no transaction trail is:

A reperformance

B observation

C inspection

D reconciliation

(f) Which of the following is *not* a factor considered in assessing the control environment?

    A Management's philosophy and operating style

    B Personnel policies and procedures

    C Proper authorisation of sales transactions and activities

    D The entity's organisational structure

(g) When the auditor assesses control risk as high for a specific assertion:

    A the extent of documentation is not related to the level of assessed risk, but rather to the complexity and sophistication of the entity's operations and systems

    B the auditor must document the assessment but need not document the basis for that assessment

    C the auditor need not document the assessment

    D the auditor must document both the assessment and the basis for it

(h) Which of the following is not a reason to assess control risk as high?

    A Evaluating the effectiveness of the internal control policies or procedures would be more time consuming than another audit approach.

    B Internal control policies or procedures are unlikely to be effective.

    C Internal control policies or procedures are unlikely to pertain to an assertion.

    D The auditor has assessed detection risk as high.

8.2 The following questions relate to internal control in computerised systems. Select the *best* response.

(a) Which of the following computer documentation would an auditor most likely utilise in obtaining an understanding of internal control?

    A record layouts

    B systems flowcharts

    C record counts

    D program listings

(b) In which of the following situations would an auditor most likely use a strategy of reliance on internal control?

    A The client has been slow to update its IT system to reflect changes in billing practices.

    B The auditor hired an IT specialist whose report to the auditor reveals that the specialist did not perform sufficient procedures to allow the auditor to properly assess the effect of IT on control risk.

    C A client receives sales orders, bills customers, and receives payment based only on information generated from IT—no paper trail is generated.

    D The auditor has been unable to ascertain whether all changes to a client's IT were properly authorised.

(c) Which of the following situations most likely represents a weakness in IT internal control?

    A The systems analyst reviews output and controls the distribution of output from the IT department.

    B The accounts payable clerk prepares data for computer processing and enters the data into the computer.

    C The systems programmer designs the operating and control functions of programs and participates in testing operating systems.

    D The control clerk establishes control over data received by the IT department and reconciles control totals after processing.

(d) An auditor anticipates assessing control risk at a low level in an IT environment. Under these circumstances, on which of the following procedures would the auditor initially focus?

      A data capture controls

      B application controls

      C output controls

      D general controls

(e) The completeness of IT-generated sales figures can be tested by comparing the number of items listed on the daily sales report with the number of items billed on the actual invoices. This process uses:

      A validity tests

      B control totals

      C check digits

      D process tracing data

(f) After obtaining an understanding of a client's IT control, an auditor may decide not to perform tests of controls within the IT portion of the client's system. Which of the following would not be a valid reason for choosing to omit tests of controls?

      A The time and dollar costs of testing controls exceed the savings in substantive testing if the tests show the controls to be operative.

      B There appear to be major deficiencies that preclude reliance on the stated procedure.

      C The controls duplicate controls existing elsewhere in the system.

      D The controls appear to be adequate and thus can be relied upon in assessing the level of control risk.

(g) If a control total were to be computed on each of the following data items, which would best be identified as a hash total for a payroll IT application?

      A employee's identification number

      B hours worked

      C gross pay

      D number of employees

(h) The completeness of IT-generated sales figures can be tested by comparing the number of sales transactions recorded on the batch header with the computer-generated number of transactions on the transactions file. This process uses:

      A control totals

      B validity tests

      C check digits

      D process tracing data

Audit strategy

8.3 Why does the auditor assess control risk?

Internal control concepts

8.4 What are the explicit and implicit concepts that underlie the definition of accounting control?

Internal control objectives

8.5 What are incompatible functions and how is an appropriate segregation of functions achieved?

Elements of internal control

8.6 What are the principal features of a satisfactory internal control?

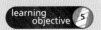

Considering internal control in a financial report audit

8.7 What procedures does the auditor use to obtain an understanding of the flow of transactions and the related controls?

8.8 What is the purpose of tests of control?

Computerised systems

8.9 Distinguish between general controls and application controls in a computerised system. Give three examples of each.

Internal audit

8.10 Explain how the external auditor is able to use the work of an internal auditor.

DISCUSSION PROBLEMS AND CASE STUDIES

Internal control objectives

8.11 Basic In conducting an examination in accordance with auditing standards, the auditor studies and evaluates the existing internal control of the client.

Required
(a) List and discuss the characteristics of satisfactory internal control.
(b) List the purposes for which the auditor reviews the client's internal control.

Source: AICPA adapted

Elements of internal control

8.12 Moderate The size of an entity can affect the components of internal control. Segregation of duties is a control activity that is important for adequate control. The following example presents a scenario where the auditor can provide assistance to the entity in establishing proper segregation of duties. TameBird Industries Ltd produces meals for airlines and nursing homes. For the prior two audit engagements, your firm has written a management letter recommending that TameBird Ltd establish better segregation of duties in the accounts receivable and accounts payable functions. Tom Tuffnut, controller for TameBird Ltd, has received authorisation to hire an additional clerk to work in the accounting area. Tom now has three accounting clerks available, and he has asked you to provide advice on how to best assign the following functions:

1 Responsibility for petty cash fund
2 Opening of mail and listing of cash receipts
3 Depositing cash receipts in bank
4 Maintaining accounts receivable subsidiary records
5 Determining which accounts receivable are uncollectible
6 Maintaining cash disbursements journal
7 Preparing cheques for signature
8 Reconciling bank statements

Required
Prepare a recommendation to Tom Tuffnut on how best to distribute the various functions among the three accounting clerks.

8.13 Complex Preview Ltd, a diversified manufacturer, has five divisions that operate throughout Australia. Preview Ltd has historically allowed its divisions to operate autonomously. Corporate intervention occurred only when planned results were not obtained. Corporate management has high integrity, but the board of directors and audit committee are not very active. Preview Ltd has a policy of hiring competent people. The company has a code of conduct, but there is little monitoring of compliance by employees. Management is fairly conservative in terms of accounting principles and practices, but employee compensation packages depend highly on performance. Preview Ltd does not have an internal audit department, and it relies on your firm to review the controls in each division.

Ted Harris is the general manager of the Fabricator Division. The Fabricator Division produces a variety of standardised parts for small appliances. Harris has been the general manager for the last seven years, and each year he has been able to improve the profitability of the division. He is compensated based largely on the division's profitability. Much of the improvement in profitability has come through aggressive cost cutting, including a substantial reduction in control activities over inventory.

During the last year a new competitor has entered Fabricator's markets and has offered substantial price reductions in order to grab market share. Harris has responded to the competitor's actions by matching the price cuts in the hope of maintaining market share. Harris is very concerned because he cannot see any other areas where costs can be reduced so that the division's growth and profitability can be maintained. If profitability is not maintained, his salary and bonus will be reduced.

Harris has decided that one way to make the division more profitable is to manipulate inventory, because it represents a large amount of the division's statement of financial position. He also knows that controls over inventory are weak. He views this inventory manipulation as a short-run solution to the profit decline due to the competitor's price cutting. Harris is certain that once the competitor stops cutting prices or goes bankrupt, the misstatements in inventory can be corrected with little impact on the bottom line.

Required

(a)   Evaluate the strengths and weaknesses of Preview Ltd's control environment.
(b)   What factors in Preview Ltd's control environment have led to and facilitated Harris's manipulation of inventory?

Considering internal control in a financial report audit

8.14 Basic For each of the following cases, outline internal control features which should be present with respect to the revenue.

(a)   Mail receipts from donations pledged during the annual fundraising campaign of a charitable organisation.
(b)   Management fees received by a parent company from its numerous subsidiaries.

Source: CICA adapted

8.15 Basic Having just completed the annual financial audit of A Ltd, the audit partner and supervisor are holding a final debriefing meeting with the client. As part of this meeting the managing director of A Ltd indicates: 'I'm glad we got a clean bill of health on that audit report. I had some concerns about controls at the warehouse but I see there is nothing to worry about.'

The audit partner replied: 'Our audit procedures did not involve a full review of controls, so I don't know whether your specific concerns would be addressed or not.'

The managing director retorted, 'Well, what are we paying you for then?'

Required

Advise the partner on an appropriate reply to the managing director.

8.16 Basic Phil King has recently been assigned to the audit of Q Pty Ltd. Q is a recurring audit for Phil's firm. Specifically, Phil has been asked to identify and document the internal control of Q. This information will then be used to plan the annual financial statement audit of Q. Phil has not undertaken this type of work before and has asked you for assistance.

Required

Advise Phil on the procedures that he could use to identify and document internal controls at Q.

8.17 Moderate You have been engaged by the management of Alden Ltd to review its internal control over the purchase, receipt, storage and issue of raw materials. You have prepared the following comments, which describe Alden's procedures.

1   Raw materials, which consist mainly of high-cost electronic components, are kept in a locked storeroom. Storeroom personnel include a supervisor and four clerks. All are

well trained and competent. Raw materials are removed from the storeroom only upon written or oral authorisation of one of the production supervisors.

2   There are no perpetual inventory records; hence the storeroom clerks do not keep records of goods received or issued. To compensate for the lack of perpetual records, a physical inventory count is taken monthly by the clerks, who are well supervised. Appropriate procedures are followed in making the inventory count.

3   After the physical count, the storeroom supervisor matches quantities counted against a predetermined reorder level. If the count for a given part is below the reorder level, the supervisor enters the part number on a materials requisition list and sends this list to the accounts payable clerk. The accounts payable clerk prepares a purchase order for a predetermined reorder quantity for each part and mails the purchase order to the vendor from whom the part was last purchased.

4   When ordered materials arrive at Alden they are received by the storeroom clerks. The clerks count the merchandise and check the counts against the supplier's bill of lading. All suppliers' bills of lading are initialled, dated and filed in the storeroom to serve as receiving reports.

Required

Describe the weaknesses in internal control and recommend improvements of Alden's procedures for the purchase, receipt, storage and issue of raw materials.

8.18 **Moderate** Scented Pty Ltd is a small company manufacturing toiletries. There are 25 people working in the factory and the office staff includes the owner, Mr Bath, the accountant, a secretary, a debtors clerk and an accounts clerk, Ms Foam. Ms Foam has been employed by the company for over 12 years and is well regarded by Mr Bath for her efficiency and reliability. The owner has been thinking of employing a part-time person to assist Ms Foam, who is overworked at the moment.

The following information relates to the cash disbursements of the company:

1   Mail is opened by the secretary, who passes all invoices on to Ms Foam.

2   All invoices are given an account classification and entered the same day by Ms Foam onto the company's computer system. Each invoice is then marked as 'entered'.

3   The invoices are then filed into order of the dates due for payment. This was the idea of Mr Bath, who is concerned about cash flows and wishes to take advantage of any interest-free credit days.

4   Orders for stocks are placed by the factory foreman. All purchases for stock are checked against a delivery docket from the factory. The foreman is required to initial these dockets to indicate that he has checked that the description of goods is what was ordered and the amount per the docket has actually been received. As instructed by Mr Bath, Ms Foam will not pay for any stock that does not have a matching delivery docket.

5   All orders of items for the office are placed by Ms Foam. The company uses only a small number of suppliers. If an invoice is received for items that Ms Foam does not recall ordering, she brings it to the attention of the accountant.

6   Cheques for payments that are due are drawn manually by Ms Foam. All cheques require two signatories, one of which must be the owner. All invoices are then marked as 'paid', with the date and cheque number also recorded. The invoices are then filed in alphabetical order.

7   Payments are recorded in a standard cash payments journal and entered onto the computer by Ms Foam. The journal is marked as 'entered'.

8   Ms Foam leaves the cheques with Mr Bath who signs them and returns them to Ms Foam. She then attaches the remittance advice and gives them to the secretary, who arranges for the mailing.

9 At each month-end Ms Foam obtains an accounts payable listing and prepares a bank reconciliation for Mr Bath.

Required

Identify the strengths and weaknesses in Scented Pty Ltd's internal control over the cash disbursements function. For the weaknesses identified, recommend ways in which the system could be improved.

Source: This question was adapted from the CA Program of The Institute of Chartered Accountants in Australia—2002 Financial Reporting and Assurance Module.

8.19 Moderate You are the auditor of Blackwattle Pty Ltd, which is involved in the manufacture of quality wooden furniture. One of the directors of Blackwattle Pty Ltd has requested that you perform a review of the internal controls within the purchases and payments cycle of the company's operations. From your discussions with management and staff you ascertain that the company is a small operation and only has the following staff:

- warehouse manager
- assistant to the warehouse manager
- four machinery operators who are involved in the manufacturing process
- accounts payable clerk
- accounts receivable clerk
- banking clerk
- secretary/receptionist
- four directors (one of whom is responsible for the day to day operations of the company—the 'executive director').

All operations are contained at one location.

The warehouse manager is able to order from any supplier and will usually telephone a number of suppliers to obtain quotes. The warehouse manager will then order from one of these suppliers by telephone and confirm the order by facsimile. The only documentation kept is the facsimile confirmation of order, which is kept by the warehouse manager.

Once an order is confirmed, the warehouse manager will complete a purchase order ('PO'). The warehouse manager keeps one copy of the PO and the other is forwarded to the accounts payable clerk where the clerk files the POs in date order.

When goods are received at the warehouse, the warehouse manager checks the goods received to the delivery note attached to the goods and signs the delivery note as evidence of this check. The delivery note comprises two copies, one of which is retained by the persons delivering the goods and the other by the warehouse manager.

The warehouse manager forwards a copy of the signed delivery note to the accounts payable clerk who posts a journal entry to the creditors' ledger for the amount shown on the delivery note. The clerk then stamps the delivery note 'entered' and files the delivery notes by supplier.

Required

(a) Identify the strengths and weaknesses in Blackwattle Pty Ltd's internal control for the purchasing area.

(b) What impact will your assessment of internal controls have on your audit approach?

8.20 Moderate B Ltd is a large retailer with approximately 400 stores located throughout Australia. Each employee is assigned an encoded identification badge that is only to be used by the individual. When an employee arrives for work, he or she runs the badge through an electronic reader that records the time of arrival. The employee repeats the procedure when he or she leaves work for the day. Employees are required to remain on duty at all times during their shifts.

Information gathered by the badge reader is transmitted electronically to B's central office computer on a weekly basis. This computer updates the payroll files and computes and prepares weekly payroll that is subject to review and authorisation electronically by B's payroll section manager. After authorisation, the payroll is transmitted to each employee's bank account by direct deposit using electronic funds transfer. A printout showing the payroll computation and year-to-date information is prepared and mailed to each employee by the payroll department. Employees are requested to report all suspected errors to the payroll department. Store managers can access payroll information for their location using their computer terminal. Payroll is also reflected in the monthly store profit and loss report received by each manager and regional supervisor.

Required

(a) Identify the major audit risk areas in the payroll system.

(b) Identify three areas in the payroll system where you would expect to find an internal control. For each area identified provide an example of a control you would expect to find.

8.21 Complex Assume that you are the auditor of X Ltd, which has annual sales of $5 million. One of the members of your audit staff has provided the following list of internal control descriptions and has noted what she believes to be the related weaknesses.

Staff member's internal control descriptions

Because the company has no purchasing department, many employees make purchases. In general, employees make purchases applicable to their area of the company's operations, but it is not uncommon for employees to make purchases of personal items through the company. A three-part purchase order form is supposed to be used whenever merchandise is ordered, one copy to be sent to the supplier, one to be sent to the dispatch receiving clerk and one to be kept by the individual doing the ordering. When the merchandise arrives, the dispatch/receiving clerk checks the merchandise and sends the packing slips and purchase order copies to the accounts payable clerk. If there is no purchase order for the merchandise, the dispatch/receiving clerk ascertains by telephone who ordered the merchandise and attaches a copy of a mimeographed form with this information on it to the packing slips.

Inventories are stored at various locations in the plant, usually handy to where they will be used. Because the company's sales and production activities have increased so much since last year, it has occasionally used public warehouses for its overflow inventory. A material requisition form is supposed to be completed whenever material is withdrawn from the raw materials inventory and put into production, but the nightshift people often neglect to follow this rule. The company does not have much money invested in shop supplies so there is no necessity to use requisition forms when supplies are consumed. Also, the company often has leftover supplies (purchased for special jobs but not used) that can be used to some extent on other jobs. The dispatch/receiving clerk keeps perpetual inventory records (quantities) for most inventory items, but 30 per cent of the items are not included in the records. The clerk does physical inventory counts to check the records whenever time allows.

When the supplier's invoice arrives, the accounts payable clerk checks the additions and extensions on it, initials it and staples the packing slip and purchase order or mimeographed form to it. The invoice is then entered in the accounts payable subsidiary account for the supplier and sent to the manager of the department for which the employee ordering the goods works; the manager writes on the invoice the account number to which it is to be charged and then sends it to the cash disbursements department.

The accounts payable clerk balances the accounts payable subsidiary ledger to the general ledger control account every month and keeps track of credits due to the company for purchases returned to suppliers. Occasionally the company pays some larger suppliers round amounts of money rather than paying according to specific invoices as is its usual policy. When there is time, the suppliers' accounts payable clerk attempts to reconcile suppliers' monthly statements to the subsidiary ledger accounts.

Staff member's notes as to believed weaknesses

1   No control over company's commitment to purchase goods.
2   No control over employees' personal purchasing.
3   Mimeographed forms are not prenumbered.
4   Little physical control over raw materials inventories.
5   No control over inventory of leftover supplies.
6   Dispatch/receiving clerk keeps perpetual records and has access to inventories.
7   Incomplete perpetual records.
8   Casual checking of perpetual records.
9   No control over manager's coding of invoices.
10   Apparent lack of price checking.
11   Managers do not specifically approve invoices for payment.
12   Accounts payable clerk balances ledger and reconciles suppliers' statements.
13   Irregular reconciliation of suppliers' statements.

Required

For each point considered by the audit staff member to be a weakness:

(a)   Explain briefly the significance of the weakness, in terms of the materiality of errors that could result from it.
(b)   Describe the effect, if any, of the weakness on your normal audit procedures required to form an opinion on the financial report, in terms of any additional or extended procedures required because of it.

Source: CICA

Computerised systems

8.22 Basic Bob Johnson was engaged to examine the financial report of Horizon Ltd, which has its own computer installation. During the preliminary review, Johnson found that Horizon Ltd lacked proper segregation of the programming and operating functions. As a result, Johnson intensified the study and evaluation of internal control and concluded that the existing compensating general controls provided reasonable assurance that the objectives of internal control were being met.

Required

(a)   In a properly functioning IT environment, how is the separation of the programming and operating functions achieved?
(b)   What are the compensating general controls that Johnson most likely found? Do *not* discuss hardware and application controls.

Source: AICPA adapted

8.23 Basic A number of controls exist in an entity's IT system. Select the type of control from the following list and enter it in the appropriate place on the grid.

Control policy or procedures:

1   Echo check
2   Limit test
3   Existence test
4   Parity check
5   Hash total
6   Control total
7   Check-digit verification
8   Sequence check
9   Financial total

Description of Control	Control
a. A check bit used to verify the transmission of data	
b. A test of an ID number or code by comparing it to a file that contains valid ID numbers or codes	
c. A total of some nonfinancial field in a batch of transactions	
d. Verification of the transmission of data to and from the components of the system	
e. A test to ensure that a numeric value does not exceed some predetermined value	
f. Totals that ensure the accuracy and completeness of processing	
g. A numeric value computed to provide assurance that the original value was not altered	

8.24 Moderate You are the audit manager for your firm's client, BeesWax Pty Ltd. You are now in the planning phase of your audit engagement for BeesWax Pty Ltd and you have been advised by the client that, since the end of the last financial year (30 June 20X1), BeesWax Pty Ltd has replaced their software to support their fixed assets business processes.

It is now 15 January 20X2 and you have been advised of the following facts about the software replacement:

- The former software, called 'AssetBee', was developed in-house by the programmers employed at BeesWax Pty Ltd. It has been operating for over 10 years with ongoing modifications to reflect changes to the fixed asset business processes of the company.
- AssetBee was used by two employees who had the responsibility for performing all the tasks associated with the recording of all additions, disposals, changes to depreciation rates, asset life details and other information regarding the description and location of the fixed assets.
- The replacement software is an off-the-shelf package called EasyAssets. No modifications have been made to the package. The software was implemented into production on 1 October 20X1. Both fixed assets personnel were trained in the new software and the changes to the business procedures surrounding the fixed asset operations.
- In the month of November 20X1, both fixed assets personnel left the company. To date only one person has been recruited and has been in the role since 4 January 20X2.

Required
For each of the elements of the IT environment (technology, people and procedures) identify an accounting outcome implication that would need to be addressed during the planning phase of the audit.

Source: This question was adapted from the CA Program of The Institute of Chartered Accountants in Australia—2002 Financial Reporting and Assurance Module.

8.25 Complex East & Company is a small, specialised firm that provides gravel and other road-building materials to mining companies operating in the Kimberley region of Western Australia. East & Company has been established for 35 years. East & Company operates two depots, No. 1 and No. 2; No. 1 acts as head office.

The founder of the firm, Easton Senior, passed away some 6 months ago and his eldest daughter, Eastleigh, took over the running of the business. Eastleigh plans to capitalise on the firm's niche market by radically updating management practices and increasing efficiency. She also intends to approach a lender within the next 6 months to borrow funds to enable her to open two more depots in the region.

One of Eastleigh's pet projects over the last 3 months has been the installation of the company's first computer system. The system is a local area network (LAN). The file server and one micro-computer are located at No. 1, with two other micro-computers located at No. 2.

You have the following information about the general controls:

- Eastleigh and two other clerical staff are the only ones having logical access privileges to the computer. Their access privileges are as follows:
  —Eastleigh: access to all software and all files
  —Molly: access to payroll, payments, payables and stock
  —Mark: access to receipts, sales and debtors.
- Eastleigh generally works at No. 1; Molly and Mark are based at No. 2.
- All software was purchased off-the-shelf with the exception of the stock program. Due to the specialised nature of East's stock, a contractor was engaged to design, develop, test and install their program. Eastleigh decided this was the best approach as she believes in 'leaving specialised computer matters to the experts'.
- The contractor fully documented the workings of the stock system, however, neither Eastleigh or the clerical staff understand the documentation.
- Molly and Mark, both long-serving employees, have been a little overwhelmed by their new IT environment. Mark does not trust the computer and has maintained the old manual records as a check against the computer's performance. So far, he has not found any discrepancies between the manual and computer records.
- Molly was a little offended that the contractor did not draw on her experience when designing the stock program, although she concedes it is working well.
- The computer hardware at both No. 1 and No. 2 is kept in a locked shed that also serves as a general office.
- Eastleigh backs up all data kept on the file server on a daily basis. She takes the back-up disks home every evening.
- Molly and Mark print summary reports of sales, cash receipts, cash payments, debtors, payables and payroll on a weekly basis. Any apparent errors or problems are referred to Eastleigh for resolution.

Required

As part of your contribution to audit planning, the audit manager has asked you to:

(a) Identify the strengths and weaknesses in East & Company's general controls.

(b) Outline how each of these strengths and weaknesses affect the audit overall.

Source: This question was adapted from the CA Program of The Institute of Chartered Accountants in Australia—2002 Financial Reporting and Assurance Module.

8.26 Complex You have been assigned to conduct an audit of your client's database system. Through previous work you know that their system includes a centralised database shared by all users. Access to the database is direct by the users through remote terminals and is controlled by the database software system. The IT department includes a manager of operations and a manager of computer programming, both of whom report to the IT director.

Your preliminary understanding of the database system includes the following points:

1 There are no restrictions regarding the type of transaction or access to the online terminals.

2 All users and IT personnel have access to the extensive system documentation.

3 Before being entered into the user authorisation table, user passwords and access codes are established by user management and approved by the manager of computer programming.

4 The manager of computer programming established the database directory and controls it. Users approve any changes in data definition.

5 User requests for data are validated by the system against a transactions-conflict matrix to ensure that data is transmitted only to authorised users.

6 System access requires the users to input their passwords, and terminal activity logs are maintained.

7 Input data are edited for reasonableness and completeness, transaction control totals are generated, and transaction logs are maintained.

8 Processing control totals are generated and reconciled to changes in the database.

9 Output is reconciled to transaction and input control totals. The resulting reports are printed and placed in a bin outside the IT room for pickup by the users at their convenience.

10 Back-up copies of the database are generated daily and stored in the file library area, access to which is restricted to IT personnel.

Required

(a) From the results of your preliminary review, describe five controls in the system.

(b) List five specific audit steps you would include in your audit program to determine whether transaction input is properly authorised.

(c) Evaluate the relative strengths of the general and application controls for the database system.

Source: CIA adapted

Internal audit

8.27 Basic Katie Jackson has been assigned to the audit of D Ltd, a large manufacturing company. One of the duties she has been allocated is an evaluation of the internal audit department of D. Katie is unsure as to the reason for undertaking this task as she cannot understand how the abilities of the internal audit department will impact on the financial report. In order to ensure she understands her task, she approaches her manager and asks the following: 'Why do we have to review internal audit? They don't prepare the financial report, so if they get it wrong it won't affect our audit opinion, will it?'

Required

Assume you are Katie's manager and explain to her why it is necessary to evaluate the internal audit department.

8.28 Moderate As part of the audit of Bank Limited, the auditors rely heavily on the work of the internal audit function in testing the systems of internal control. The internal audit function is attached to the accounting and finance division, and reports directly to the finance director in his capacity as chair of the audit committee.

The work that the internal auditors do on behalf of the external auditors is planned and programmed by the external audit manager. As the audit senior, you have been assigned to review the work of the internal auditors prior to the commencement of the year-end audit. During your review, the following issues came under consideration:

1 During the year the staff of the internal audit function changed significantly. The division employed three new staff to undertake the external auditor's testing, while the more senior personnel who had previously done these tests concentrated on the performance auditing schedule of the internal audit function. The new staff have no previous audit or accounting experience.

2 For many of the audit tests prescribed, the staff have no detailed documentation of the work that has been completed. They have simply initialled the audit program and noted that the test has been satisfactorily performed.

3 The work which has been documented appears to be quite thorough and competent.

In three circumstances where compliance errors were detected in the loan approvals area, they were not followed up. The working papers showed that the internal auditors did not believe that three compliance errors in 250 selections constituted a significant compliance problem.

4   The audit plan and program requires dual items to be selected from each of the expense accounts in the general ledger. It became clear from the review that no wages selections were made. When you discussed this with the internal auditors, they revealed that the financial controller had altered their instructions because he felt there was little risk of compliance error in the wages area.

Required

Outline how your findings will affect the reliance which can be placed on the work of the internal audit function.

Source: This question was adapted from the Professional Year Programme of The Institute of Chartered Accountants in Australia—1994 Advanced Audit Module.

CONTINUOUS CASE STUDIES

8.29   **Complex**   This is a continuation of question 6.29. It may be completed independently of that question.

You have just been involved in the audit of Mitchell Pty Ltd, a manufacturer of industrial chemicals. As part of your interim review you have completed a 'walk-through' of the procedures involved in the purchases and payments cycle. The following is a summary of the procedures you have documented on your file:

1   The warehouse manager is responsible for placing orders for chemical 'ingredients'. Because of the bulk quantity discounts, he will usually place an order for three months' ingredients when there is one month of ingredients left. He is able to determine how much the company uses in manufacture each month by reviewing the inventory records held at the warehouse.

2   To order, the warehouse manager contacts any of the approved suppliers and places an order over the phone. No record is kept of the conversation, nor does the warehouse manager require any approval. To make sure he doesn't reorder in error he 'ticks' the inventory ledger and writes the date of order next to the product number.

3   When goods are received the warehouse assistants check the delivery note against the ingredient coming in and then let the deliverer pump the ingredient into the company's storage tank. At no point do they check the actual quantity received. The warehouse assistant then gives the delivery note to the warehouse manager. The warehouse manager will then post a journal entry to the inventory system by keying the entry to the terminal.

4   When the journal is accepted, the computer will generate a journal number. (Note: the journal posted by the system is Dr Raw materials inventory; Cr Creditor.) The warehouse manager writes the journal number onto the delivery note and sends it to the accounts payable clerk at head office. The accounts payable clerk files the note by supplier.

5   The accounts payable clerk at head office receives all supplier invoices. On receipt of the invoice the clerk checks the details to the delivery note received from the warehouse. If there are no discrepancies she will prepare a cheque requisition for the amount of the invoice and forward the cheque requisition, with the invoice and delivery note attached, to the financial controller for authorisation. If the payment is over $20 000 the financial controller must forward the requisition to the MD for authorisation.

6   The financial controller and/or MD signs the cheque requisition to indicate authorisation and forwards the documentation to the banking clerk who keys the payment into

the general ledger (the journal posted by the system is Dr Creditor; Cr Bank). Once the journal is accepted by the system, the system generates a journal number which the banking clerk writes on the cheque requisition. She then files the cheque requisition together with supporting documentation by cheque requisition number.

7 All cheques are printed and signed (counter stamped) by the computer. When they have been printed they are returned to the banking clerk who checks the details and then sends them to the supplier.

Required

Discuss the strengths and weaknesses of the purchases and payments system. For each strength, indicate one test to be performed to test the controls. For each weakness, indicate the likely impact of this weakness on the audit risk and a test which can be used to minimise this risk.

8.30 Complex This is a continuation of questions 6.30 and 7.25. It may be completed independently of those questions.

You are currently planning the audit of HomeChef Pty Ltd, a large private company specialising in the supply of boutique food and beverages. The company has a balance date of 31 December. To maximise audit efficiency the audit partner has requested you investigate the possibility of using the work of the internal audit group (IAG). The IAG was established five years ago and now comprises the following staff:

- The manager, M, a CPA with 10 years experience, including 5 years in internal audit.
- The supervisor, S, currently undertaking the CA in Commerce program, under the direction of the financial controller. The supervisor has 6 years experience, including 2 years in internal audit.
- Two assistant auditors: A, who is halfway through a part-time commerce degree, and B, a university graduate. A joined the division 6 months ago, having worked in a small chartered accountancy firm for the previous 2 years. B has 12 months experience, having commenced employment with HomeChef upon completion of her full-time university degree.

The IAG functions as follows:

- Annual workplans are prepared in conjunction with the audit committee. These workplans set out the objectives and scope of the tasks to be carried out.
- Each task is performed, appropriate workpaper files prepared and reviewed, and a summary report of findings presented to the committee.
- The committee reviews the summary report, comments in writing on the findings and implements changes where considered necessary.

The audit committee and the IAG have a good working relationship. The committee usually accepts the recommendations of the IAG and requires a follow-up report annually on implementation of recommendations.

You have obtained an extract from the IAG's 20X1 workplan relating to trade creditors. This extract is reproduced below.

IAG Workplan for the year ended 31 December 20X1, Trade Creditors

Objectives:

1 To examine the payment terms requested by creditors, and determine whether all discounts offered are being taken.
2 To examine existing relationships with creditors and ensure supply arrangements are consistent with the company's objectives of providing high-quality goods at a competitive price.

3   To ensure supplier lists are reviewed annually to ensure all supply agreements have been adhered to. If not, ensure procedures have been followed to negotiate new supply agreements.

4   To examine the payments made to creditors and determine whether longer payment terms could be taken without adversely affecting the customer–supplier relationship.

5   To examine payments made to creditors throughout the year, and determine whether the procedures laid down in the accounting manual have been properly followed.

6   To examine all material year-end creditors' balances, and determine whether these are complete.

Required

(a)   Explain the overall objectives and scope of the work of both internal and external auditors.

(b)   What information can external auditors share with internal auditors which may be of benefit to the client?

(c)   Assume that you could independently set the objectives and scope of the IAG's work. Would it be possible for you to rely on their testing? Why or why not?

(d)   Which of the objectives set out in the IAG Trade Creditors Workplan are relevant to you as the external auditor? Why?

PART three

TESTS OF CONTROLS AND TESTS OF DETAILS

Part 3 covers the major evidence-gathering procedures of the assurance services engagements. Chapter 9 covers tests of controls for the control risk assessment and Chapter 10 covers substantive tests of transactions and balances for the detection risk assessment. Chapter 11 explains the specialised considerations associated with the use of sampling as a form of evidence gathering.

CHAPTER 9

TESTS OF CONTROLS

LEARNING OBJECTIVES

After studying this chapter you should be able to:

1 appreciate that tests of controls are part of a co-ordinated approach to the audit in order to gain the most efficient and effective audit approach;

2 identify the types of tests of controls undertaken;

3 identify factors impacting the auditor's assessment of the sufficiency and appropriateness of evidence of tests of controls;

4 describe the audit procedures for testing controls in the revenues, receivables and receipts system;

5 describe the audit procedures for testing controls in the expenditures, payables and disbursements system;

6 describe the audit procedures for testing controls relating to contractual transactions; and

7 understand the auditing approaches used to test the controls contained in the client's program, including test data and integrated test facilities.

Chapter outline

Until this stage of the audit, the auditor has not undertaken any testing of details. As part of the planning process the auditor has undertaken an assessment of business risk and a preliminary evaluation of inherent and control risk. From these assessments and evaluations the auditor has determined the risks and accounts that require attention, and also determined the required detection risk. The auditor then prepares an audit program, which outlines the audit tests they intend to undertake.

There are two major types of audit tests, tests of controls and substantive tests. The purpose of tests of controls (to support an assessed level of control risk) is very different from that of substantive tests of transactions and balances (used to reduce the auditor's detection risk). If control risk is assessed at any level less than high (reliance is to be placed on controls) then tests of control must be undertaken to provide evidence of the existence, effectiveness and continuity of these key controls. In this chapter, tests of controls for the major systems of revenue, receivables and receipts, and expenditures, payables and disbursements are covered. Variations in testing for other types of expenditure transactions, including payroll, are also considered.

Relevant guidance

Australian		International	
AUS 402	Understanding the Entity and its Environment and Assessing the Risks of Material Misstatements (Revised 2004)	ISA 315	Understanding the Entity and its Environment and Assessing the Risks of Material Misstatements (Revised 2004)
AUS 404	Audit Implications Relating to Entities Using a Service Entity	ISA 402	Audit Considerations Relating to Entities Using Service Organizations
AUS 406	The Auditor's Procedures in Response to Assessed Risks (Issued 2004)	ISA 330	The Auditor's Procedures in Response to Assessed Risks (Issued 2004)
AUS 502	Audit Evidence (Revised 2004)	ISA 500	Audit Evidence (Revised 2004)
AGS 1060	Computer Assisted Audit Techniques	IAPS 1009	Computer Assisted Audit Techniques (Withdrawn 2005)

TESTS OF CONTROLS

The auditor must obtain evidence sufficient to support the assessed level of control risk. As outlined in Chapter 8, if at the planning stage the auditor assesses control risk as high for an account balance or assertion there will be no **tests of controls** for that account balance or assertion. This is because the auditor does not plan to place any reliance on the related controls. Control risk will be assessed as high if the auditor has determined that (i) controls do not exist, (ii) the controls that do exist will not provide reliable evidence, or (iii) it is more efficient or effective to gather the required evidence by undertaking substantive testing.

In addition, to assess control risk as high the auditor must expect that substantive procedures alone will provide sufficient appropriate audit evidence (AUS 406.22/ISA 330.22). If substantive procedures alone do not provide sufficient appropriate evidence, under the revised audit risk standards (2004) the auditor is required to perform tests of controls to obtain audit evidence about the operating effectiveness of these controls (AUS 502.21/ISA 500.21). Areas where substantive procedures alone may not provide sufficient appropriate evidence include the routine recording of significant classes of transactions, such as an entity's revenue, purchases, cash receipts and cash payments. The characteristics of these routine transactions often permit highly automated processing with little or no manual intervention. In such circumstances it might not be possible to perform only substantive procedures in relation to risk (AUS 402.115–118/ISA 315.115–118).

An example of a routine system where it may not be possible to perform only substantive procedures would be airline ticket sales by Qantas. These sales transactions would be subject to routine control procedures. With numerous sales transactions within an accounting period, the auditor would be able to verify only a very small proportion of these transactions by using substantive tests of transactions. It would be expected in such systems that the auditor would evaluate control risk at less than high and undertake tests of controls in such systems. In addition, any control deficiencies in such automated systems would be expected to lead to systematic errors, which would be better identified by evaluating and testing internal control rather than substantively verifying a small proportion of transactions or account balances. In assessing the control risk at less than high, the auditor has identified specific internal control policies and procedures that they believe will prevent or detect misstatements for the assertion. Evidence is needed to support the appropriateness of this assessment (AUS 406.23/ISA 330.23).

Tests of controls are usually concerned with gathering evidence concerning the controls associated with the processing of particular classes of transactions through the accounting system. Transactions can also be substantively tested to provide evidence to support the assessment of detection risk. The best way of distinguishing between tests of controls and substantive tests of transactions is that tests of controls relate only to the assessment of controls and do not directly measure monetary error in accounting records. Substantive tests, whether of transactions or balances, are concerned with whether monetary errors have occurred.

The co-ordinated program of tests of controls and substantive tests of transactions and balances (which will be discussed further in Chapter 10) is commonly referred to as the **audit program**. The audit program sets out the combination of evidence-gathering procedures that the auditor believes will result in the most efficient and effective audit. If at any stage during this testing phase the auditor determines that controls are not working as they expected and that they have placed too much reliance on these controls they can reduce the extent of tests of controls and increase the extent of substantive testing.

Planning the scope of tests of controls

The auditor's underlying objective in undertaking tests of controls is to gain reasonable assurance that the controls associated with the processing of a particular class of transactions are working as expected. This will enable the auditor to reduce substantive tests. The considerations that affect the nature, timing and extent of tests of controls are explained in the following discussion.

Nature

Based on the understanding of the internal control system gained in assessing control risk (discussed in Chapter 8), the auditor identifies whether there are internal control policies or activities to provide reasonable assurance of achieving control objectives. If such policies or activities are prescribed, the auditor designs tests of their operating effectiveness (tests of controls). As the planned level of assurance increases, the auditor seeks more reliable evidence (AUS 406.28/ISA 330.28). If there are no internal control procedures prescribed that provide reasonable assurance of achieving specific control objectives, the auditor designs substantive tests of transactions or balances. This planning process is best understood by considering Example 9.1 overleaf

A specific control objective for sales transactions is that goods shipped (or services rendered) have been recorded. A test of controls is to see that shipping documents are prenumbered, the numbers are accounted for and the shipping documents are matched to sales invoices and approved sales orders. The auditor would need to conduct a test of the numerical sequence of shipping documents issued and select a sample of shipping documents and trace them to the related sales invoices and sales orders.

Timing

To aid the auditor's ability to meet deadlines and the scheduling of staff, the auditor sometimes schedules tests of controls to provide audit evidence for an interim period (this testing is usually undertaken one to three months before balance date). The auditor would not normally undertake this testing at an early stage unless they believed that there were adequate controls in place to allow 'roll-forward of testing' (extending tests until year-end). When obtaining evidence about the design or operation of internal control policies and procedures during this interim period, the auditor determines what additional evidence should be obtained for the remaining period.

The factors that influence whether tests of control are necessary for the remaining period (the period between the interim date and the balance date) are as follows:

- **Results of the tests of the interim period**   If results indicate that internal control policies and procedures lack operating effectiveness, control risk should be assessed at a high level and substantive tests of transactions and balances should be made for the remainder of the period. If expanded tests show that the accounting data are not reliable, tests of controls should not be relied on in determining the extent of substantive tests of transactions and balances.
- **Inquiries concerning the remaining period**   Inquiries should be directed at determining whether there were any significant changes in control or accounting procedures during the remaining period.
- **Nature and amount of the transactions and balances involved** If the transactions occurring between the completion of tests of controls and the end of the year are atypical of the transactions for the year, this implies the need to test further. That is the case with a highly seasonal business and with an entity that has several large or unusual transactions near the end of the year.
- **Evidence of compliance within the remaining period obtained from substantive tests**   Evidence obtained through tests such as the pricing of inventory or confirmation of accounts receivable at balance date (covered in Chapter 10) shows both the accuracy of total debits and credits to those accounts and the propriety of the ending balances. If these tests indicate satisfactory results, there is less need to test controls for the remaining period.
- **Other matters the auditor considers relevant in the circumstances**   These include the auditor's assessment of business risk and inherent risk and the results of analytical procedures applied as an aid in planning the audit program.

Extent

The more the auditor relies on the operating effectiveness of controls, the greater will be the extent of the auditor's tests of controls (AUS 406.46/ISA 330.46).

The extent of tests of controls that consist of inspecting documents for indication of the performance of a checking routine or approval by stamps, initials or signatures that involve inspection of documents are determined using audit sampling techniques. Determination of the extent of tests of controls using audit sampling is explained in Chapter 11.

The extent of tests of controls that consist of reperformance of completed accounting routines is not, however, determined by reference to audit sampling. Many reconciling and balancing routines (for example, bank reconciliations) are performed monthly by the client. A common audit approach is to recompute one or a few such reconciliations or balancings and evaluate controls associated with these accounting routines (such as review or authorisation) and then see that the routine and related control procedures were performed in the other months. If the routine is performed much more frequently, the common approach is still to recompute only one or a few of the routines. However, a sample of routines is selected, rather than all of them, to see whether the routine was performed throughout the period. The rationale for this approach is that inspecting a reconciliation or trial balance provides reasonable evidence that the routine and related control procedures were properly performed, and if not, sloppy or improper performance will be apparent.

The only exception to an increase in extent with increasing reliance is in the area of automated IT processing. Because of the inherent consistency of IT processing, an automated control should function consistently unless the program is changed. Therefore, audit tests may be to ensure changes have not been made to the program (AUS 406.47/ISA 330.47).

Quick review

1 Tests of controls are required to be undertaken if reliance is to be placed on controls (i.e. control risk is assessed at a level less than high).

2 Tests of controls will normally only be undertaken if the increased effort is more than offset by a reduced level of substantive testing. The auditor chooses the most efficient and effective combination of tests of controls and substantive tests of transactions and balances. The new audit risk standards also require tests of controls to be undertaken when substantive procedures alone do not provide sufficient appropriate evidence.

3 The auditor does not normally have to undertake tests of controls if there is no reliance to be placed on controls, or if a substantive approach will result in a more efficient or effective audit. In either of these circumstances control risk should be assessed as high.

4 When planning the scope of tests of controls, the auditor considers the:
- *nature:* the specific control objectives for a transaction class provide a framework for designing tests of controls;
- *timing:* many tests of control are undertaken at an interim period and the auditor should determine what additional evidential matter should be obtained for the remaining period; and
- *extent:* usually determined by reference to audit sampling techniques.

EXISTENCE, EFFECTIVENESS AND CONTINUITY OF CONTROLS

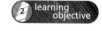

For internal controls to provide audit evidence about the risk of material misstatements at the assertion level, the auditor must collect audit evidence about the existence, effectiveness and continuity of controls. Evidence of the existence of controls is usually gained when the auditor is evaluating control risk. Tests of controls are aimed at establishing their effectiveness and continuity. As required by AUS 406.23 (ISA 330.23) 'the auditor should perform tests of controls to obtain sufficient appropriate audit evidence that controls were operating effectively at relevant times during the period . . .'. As, for most controls, the relevant time is the entire period, this is referred to as continuity. These three aspects of internal control are summarised in Table 9.1 (see also Example 9.2, both overleaf).

TABLE 9.1 Aspects of internal control for which evidence is gathered

Aspects	Definitions	How tested
Existence	Whether prescribed internal control procedures actually exist. For example, if a clerk is supposed to verify the mathematical accuracy of an invoice, does he/she actually perform the verification?	Existence normally identified when considering the design of the internal control policy and activities, using the audit procedures outlined in Chapter 8 under control risk assessment.
Effectiveness	Whether the control is operating effectively. That is, does the control prevent or detect the misstatements that it is designed to prevent or detect?	Effectiveness usually evaluated as part of the tests of controls. Procedures include re-performing the control (e.g. checking the price, quantities and maths on invoices). Sighting documents to see that controls were complied with (e.g. checking that a voucher contains supporting documentation). If the control is programmed, such as checking authorisation codes, run unauthorised transactions through the program to make sure they are correctly identified and excluded.
Continuity	Whether the control operated through-out the period of intended reliance. For example, if the control was - operational for only part of the year, then no reliance can be placed on the control when it was not operating.	Continuity usually evaluated as part of the tests of control. Usually achieved by ensuring that the sample of transactions to be tested is selected from throughout the year.

Note: The new audit risk standards refer to effectiveness and continuity as 'operating effectiveness'.

EXAMPLE 9.2 Existence, effectiveness and continuity of controls

Assume there is a control where, before cash payments are authorised, a manager must ensure that there is appropriate supporting documentation (such as a supplier's invoice, and evidence that goods were received) to support the payment. Existence will involve ensuring that authorisation for the payment is signed and this is usually established when assessing control risk (refer to Chapter 8). Effectiveness will involve ensuring that the control is doing what it is supposed to do, which is stopping unauthorised payments with insufficient supporting documentation. Continuity involves ensuring that the control has been in existence and effective over the period of intended reliance, and would involve sampling from all the cash payments in the period of audit. Tests of controls are undertaken to establish the effectiveness and continuity of the controls.

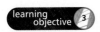
learning objective 3

SUFFICIENCY AND APPROPRIATENESS OF EVIDENCE

AUS 502.07–14 (ISA 500.07–14) requires the auditor to consider the sufficiency (quantity) and appropriateness (quality) of the audit evidence to support the assessed level of control risk. The quantity of evidence necessary to support a specific level of control risk is a matter of audit judgment. The auditor requires stronger evidence as to the adequate design and operation of a procedure if the assessed level of control risk is low rather than medium. This is because a low assessment of control risk indicates that the auditor is going to place greater reliance on this procedure as an appropriate form of audit evidence: the greater the reliance, the greater the evidence required. Other factors that the auditor considers in determining whether the tests of controls have yielded sufficient appropriate evidence include: type and source of evidence; timeliness of evidence; and interrelationship with other evidence.

Type and source of evidence

As for audit evidence in general (refer to Chapter 5), the auditor recognises that some audit tests of controls provide stronger evidence than others. For example, inquiry and observation that the accounts payable manager reviews invoices and supporting documents before cheques are written provide some evidence, but inspection of written approvals for a sample of cheques throughout the period provides more assurance of the existence of this control.

Timeliness

Timeliness enhances the amount of assurance provided by the evidence. The two factors in *timeliness* are:

1 *When the evidence was obtained* For example, the auditor may look at evidence obtained from interim testing. The auditor must then consider whether the procedure in place has changed, and whether the assurance provided decreases as the amount of time since the test of controls was performed lengthens.
2 *Whether it applies to the entire audit period or only a portion of it* To evaluate continuity of controls, tests of controls should demonstrate the effectiveness of the policy or procedure for the entire audit period.

Interrelationship of evidence

The auditor considers the combined effect of all the evidence that the auditor collects. Included in the consideration is the interaction of the internal control components and how this affects overall risk of material misstatement. Individual pieces of evidence that, taken alone, are not sufficient may be sufficient when taken together. Conversely, evidence that is persuasive taken by itself may be relied upon less if, for example, there is evidence that the control environment is weak.

Effect of documentation of controls along the audit trail

The methods and procedures the auditor uses for tests of controls depend on whether the control activities leave a documentary trail of their performance. If there is:

- **no documentation of controls along the audit trail**, this involves inquiries and observation of accounting personnel and routines to determine how control activities are performed and, especially, who performs them. For example, this approach is used to evaluate the control that cash is handled by someone who does not record cash transactions.
- **a documentary trail**, this involves inspection of documents supporting a particular type of transaction to see whether a control procedure, such as approval or checking, was performed (by noting signatures or initials) and whether the procedure was performed effectively.

The auditor usually observes the client's personnel and processing routines and makes corroborative inquiries of appropriate personnel when on the client's premises for other purposes. The inquiries and observations are done at this time, but the auditor is concerned with operations for the entire period covered by the financial report. Thus, the auditor's inquiries extend beyond the immediate duties of the personnel being interviewed. The auditor inquires about the employee's understanding of the duties of others; what happens when review and reconciliation procedures detect errors; who handles the investigation and resolution of errors; and what happens when employees with key assigned duties are on vacation.

When documentary support of consistent application of a control procedure exists, the auditor inspects a sample of the documents to see whether they were approved or checked as prescribed and to see who performed the control activities.

Relationship between tests of controls and financial report assertions

As outlined earlier, the auditor is required to identify and assess the risks of material misstatement at the financial report level and at the assertion level for classes of transactions, account balances and disclosures. When the auditor's assessment of material misstatement at the assertion level includes an expectation that controls are operating effectively, the auditor should perform tests of controls to obtain sufficient appropriate audit evidence that the controls were operating effectively at relevant times during the audit (AUS 406.23/ISA 330.23).

However, some controls relate directly to assertions, while others do not. As a general rule controls that relate to the control environment element of a company's internal control system relate less directly to specific financial report assertions. Also, many of the controls associated with the entity's risk assessment process will concern future strategic decisions and relate less to historical financial information.

However, the other three elements of internal control: information systems, control activities and monitoring of controls are usually built around major classes of transactions and events. Therefore tests of controls for these areas can relate to the category of assertions concerning the classes of transactions or events to which they relate.

Assertions and testing the control environment and the entity's risk assessment process

For many of the environmental controls and risk assessment processes (discussed in Chapter 8) that are emphasised in organisations today (e.g. an ethical approach by management), the auditor may find it difficult to relate these controls directly to financial report assertions. Evidence of a satisfactory control environment may include the observation that there is a code of ethics, and the fact that this code of ethics is followed may be evidenced by the impression that the control environment has an 'ethical feel' about it. However, these controls are not necessarily aimed directly at particular account balances or transactions or related assertions. Nonetheless, they are important.

As outlined in AUS 402.107 (ISA 315.107), 'concerns about the integrity of the entity's management may be so serious as to cause the auditor to conclude that the risk of management misrepresentation in the financial report is such that an audit cannot be conducted'. It may, of course, not be this serious, but a lack of integrity can cause the auditor to carefully consider whether or not reliance can be placed on any tests of controls and how management might misrepresent in the financial report (such as areas requiring judgment) and may lead the auditor to assign these areas a high risk of material misstatement. Because of concerns about the control environment and the risk assessment processes, the auditor would have to evaluate these areas as having a high control risk and would therefore undertake a substantive approach to the audit.

Assertions and testing the information system, control activities and monitoring of controls

As three of the elements of internal control, the information system, control activities and monitoring of controls, are built around major flows of transactions and events, it is possible to relate most of the tests of controls for these elements to the assertions about classes of transactions and events. As outlined in AUS 502 (ISA 500) these assertions are:

(i) *Occurrence*— transactions and events that have been recorded, have occurred and pertain to the entity.

(ii) *Completeness*—all transactions and events that should have been recorded have been recorded.

(iii) *Accuracy*—amounts and other data relating to recorded transactions and events have been recorded appropriately.

(iv) *Cutoff*—transactions and events have been recorded in the correct accounting period.

(v) *Classification*—transactions and events have been recorded in the proper accounts.

In the next section, we relate the tests of controls in these areas to the major transaction flows and events of most businesses; the buying of goods or services from vendors or suppliers and the selling of goods or services to customers.

Quick review

1 The auditor must undertake tests of controls to support an assessed level of control risk at any level less than high. If control risk is assessed as high, no reliance is to be placed on the particular internal control. If control risk is assessed at some level less than high, then some evidence is required to support this assessment. The more reliance that is placed on the particular internal control (the lower the assessment of control risk), the greater the quantity of evidence through tests of controls that is required.

2 Other factors affecting sufficiency of evidence include:
- type and source of evidence;
- timeliness of evidence; and
- interrelationship with other evidence.

3 The evidence should support both:
- *existence:* the internal control exists and is suitably designed to prevent and/or detect and correct material misstatements; and
- *effectiveness and continuity:* the internal control has operated effectively throughout the relevant period.

4 Evaluation of controls directed toward existence generally include inquiries of entity personnel, inspection of documents and reports and observation of the application of specific internal control policies and procedures, including walk-throughs. These tests often require the preparation of flowcharts or questionnaires if the internal control system is complex, as discussed in Chapter 8.

5 Tests of the effectiveness and continuity of controls include inquiries of entity personnel, inspection of documents and reports indicating performance of the policy or procedure, observation of the application of the policy or procedure and reperformance of the policy or procedure by the auditor.

6 The auditor's tests of controls relating to the control environment and risk assessment processes are not necessarily aimed directly at related assertions. If tests of environmental controls show that there is not a sound control environment, the auditor would question whether any reliance could be placed on any controls. Auditors' tests of controls concerning the information system, control activities and monitoring of controls will normally be related to evidence collection for specific assertions about classes of transactions and events, as a means of collecting sufficient appropriate evidence to reduce the risk of material misstatement to an acceptable level.

AUDITING CONTROLS OF MAJOR ACTIVITIES

The next two sections of this chapter explain tests of controls of the information systems and control activities for the central activities of most businesses—buying and selling. Although some of the descriptive terms differ, most businesses are engaged in acquiring goods or services from vendors or suppliers and providing goods or services to customers. These activities are usually characterised by a large volume (many relatively small transactions) and are repetitive and recurrent in nature (transactions of a particular type are very similar and continuing). For these reasons, the audit approach in these areas often emphasises tests of controls. When tests of controls are not feasible or efficient, the scope of substantive tests of transactions or balances for the related account balance has to be expanded.

REVENUES, RECEIVABLES AND RECEIPTS

This section is primarily concerned with the controls relating to transactions of merchandise to customers on credit. The sales accounting system of such an entity is relatively unaffected by whether the merchandise is acquired from others (retailing or wholesale merchandising) or produced by converting raw materials to a finished product (manufacturing). Thus, the discussion applies to most manufacturing and retail entities. Some special considerations that apply to other industries or other types of revenue-generating transactions are discussed briefly at the end of the section.

One characteristic of this type of revenue accounting system is that the audit problems tend to be those related to high-volume clerical processing rather than complex accounting principles. For example, revenue is typically recognised when merchandise is shipped and recording of sales and receivables is routine and does not involve complicated issues of revenue recognition. A relatively large number of clerical staff work in the accounting and operating departments and there is a fairly standard document flow among operating and accounting departments which can be confusing to junior auditors.

An overview of functions, documents, inputs and accounting systems

A narrative of a typical credit sales cycle is outlined below, while a corresponding flowchart is shown in Figure 9.1. An *order entry function* is the starting point in the credit sales cycle. In this function, orders are received, accepted and then translated into shipping and billing instructions. Order entry may or may not be integrated with the accounting system. The original order may be a written purchase order mailed in by a customer, or be taken over the phone or through electronic lodgment by mechanisms such as the Internet. The first document or input by the audit client is usually a *sales order*. At this point, a decision needs to be made concerning whether to accept the

FIGURE 9.1 **Typical credit sales flowchart**

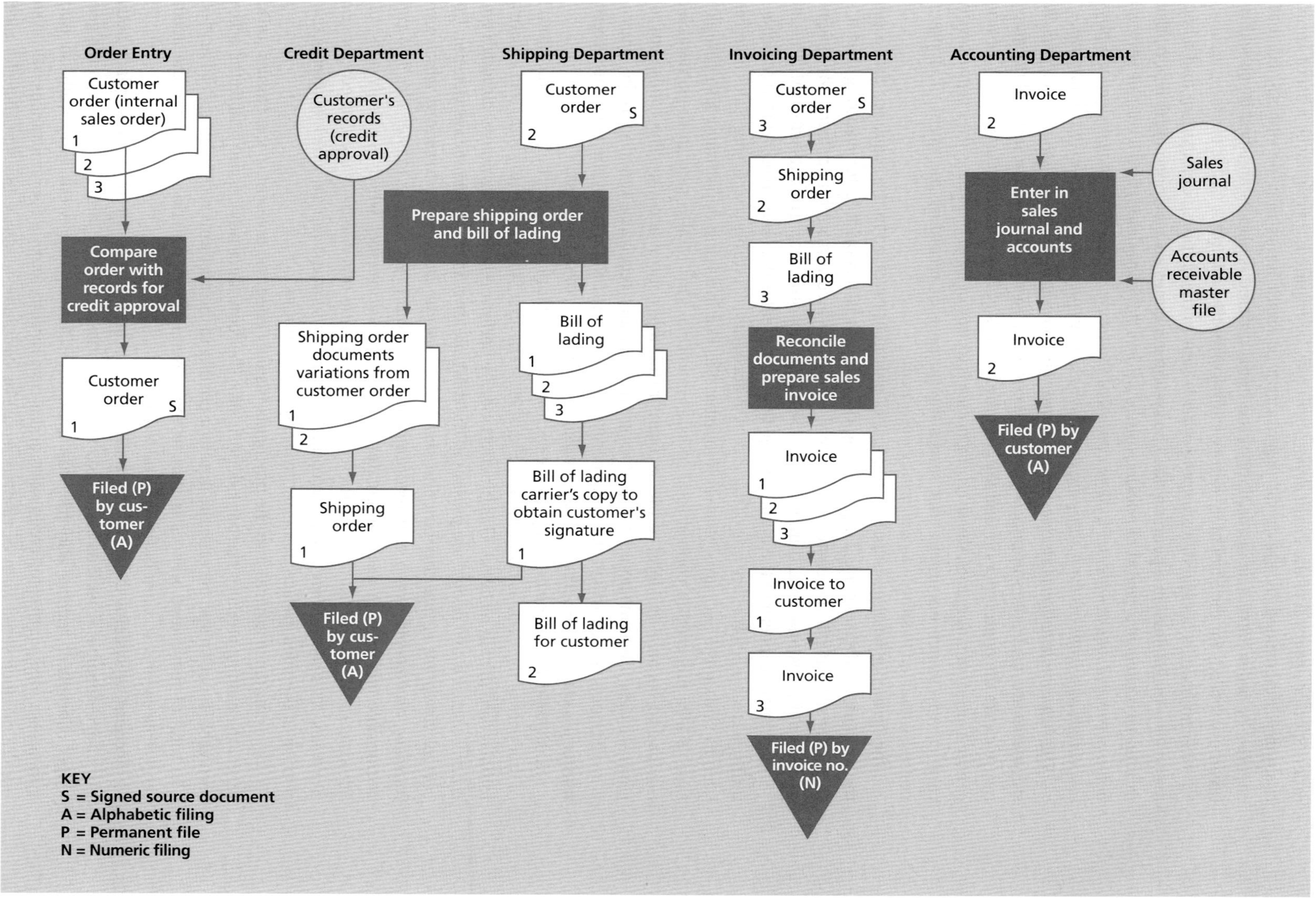

Order Entry

Customer order (internal sales order) 1, 2, 3 → Compare order with records for credit approval → Customer order S 1 → Filed (P) by customer (A)

Credit Department

Customer's records (credit approval)

Shipping order documents variations from customer order 1, 2 → Shipping order 1 → Filed (P) by customer (A)

Prepare shipping order and bill of lading

Shipping Department

Customer order S 2 → Prepare shipping order and bill of lading → Bill of lading 1, 2, 3 → Bill of lading carrier's copy to obtain customer's signature 1 → Bill of lading for customer 2

Invoicing Department

Customer order S 3 → Shipping order 2 → Bill of lading 3 → Reconcile documents and prepare sales invoice → Invoice 1, 2, 3 → Invoice to customer 1 → Invoice 3 → Filed (P) by invoice no. (N)

Accounting Department

Sales journal

Accounts receivable master file

Invoice 2 → Enter in sales journal and accounts → Invoice 2 → Filed (P) by customer (A)

KEY
S = Signed source document
A = Alphabetic filing
P = Permanent file
N = Numeric filing

order. Specific approval of the *credit department* may be required; there may be a list of approved customers determined by the credit department; or credit limits may be established that are checked by order entry. The availability of the items ordered is also established by checking the inventory records for the level of inventory items currently on hand.

After an order is accepted, a *shipping order* is sent to the shipping department and a copy of the order is maintained in a pending file. The system generates an aged open order report. Usually this report is used as a record of backlog orders (orders not completed) and a routine review of it helps to prevent loss of orders. Physical control of the forms used as shipping orders and physical inspection of shipments for a shipping document help to prevent unauthorised shipments.

The *shipping function* is an operating department that sends merchandise to customers. When shipments are made, the shipping department completes a *shipping notice*. Input of the shipping notice clears the open order file and initiates the process of invoicing the customer. If a common carrier is used for shipments, the shipping notice is a copy of a *bill of lading* (the contract with the carrier). Any source document that serves the purpose of recording the event of shipment is normally referred to simply as a *shipping document*.

The *invoicing function* is usually the first department involved in the sequence that is part of the accounting department. The invoicing department is responsible for ensuring that a *sales invoice* is sent to bill the customer. Usually, a sales invoice is a multipart form: the original is mailed to the customer and duplicates are used to notify other departments within the business.

Of primary concern to the auditor is the flow that creates the *debit to accounts receivable*. The individual sales invoices are one of the inputs to accounts receivable processing. Sales invoices are used to update the accounts receivable master file. The invoicing department also compares a total of bills prepared (a control total of sales invoices). This total is sent to the general ledger function to become the debit to the accounts receivable control account. The totals sent to the general ledger function should not go through the accounts receivable function. If this separation is maintained, a reconciliation of the control account with the total of the accounts receivable master file can be a key control in the auditor's assessment of control risk.

Cash collection is the next step in the cycle and several functions may be involved. A flowchart of this part of the cycle is contained in Figure 9.2. The first step is *opening mail* and creating an initial record of cash received. This function may be performed by a receptionist, although greater control occurs if two people are present at the mail opening. The important consideration from a control viewpoint is that this function should be separate from other functions which involve handling and keeping cash and recording in the accounts receivable master file. The person responsible for opening the mail creates a *prelist of cash receipts*, which is simply a list of the amounts received and from whom they were received, and this is usually used strictly for control purposes. Mail receipts are usually accompanied by a *remittance advice*, which is often a tear-off portion of the sales invoice that is returned by the customer.

The remittance advices and the payments (usually cheques) are sent to the cashier function, where the cashier prepares the bank deposit slip. The remittance advices are sent to the accounts receivable function and become the input for posting to the accounts receivable subsidiary ledger. The total of remittance advices is sent to the general ledger function to update the accounts receivable control account in the general ledger.

Accounting systems differ substantially in the summarisation steps that take place between the source document, such as a sales invoice or remittance advice, and the entries to the general ledger. Computer reports and files are generally titled as they were historically in manual systems—a *sales journal* for credit sales and a *cash receipts journal* for remittances. The systems usually produce some form of printed report or computer-readable file that includes all daily

FIGURE **9.2 Typical cash collection flowchart**

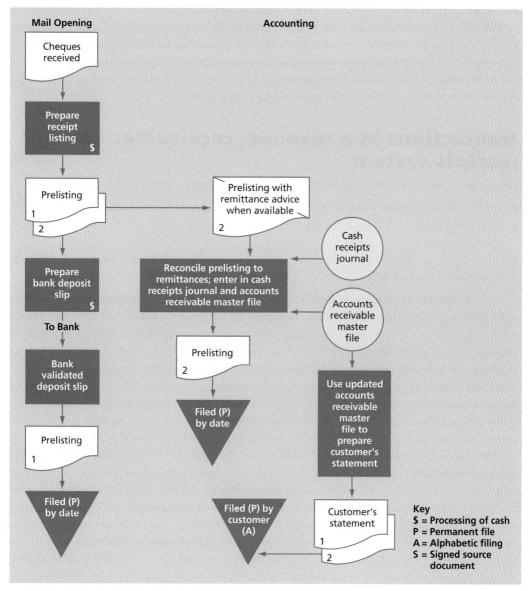

activity. That is, all the transactions entered that day are recorded and retained for back-up and recovery purposes. The auditor can generally use these *daily activity reports* or sales journals. However, in some systems only summary information is retained for more than a short time and advance arrangements must be made if more detail is required by the auditor.

Adjustments and cost of sales

From a control standpoint, these adjustments are of concern because they are less routine than sales and collections and require the exercise of some discretion in deciding whether that adjustment should be allowed. The usual approach is to use a specialised source document, a *credit memorandum* or *debit memorandum*, and to require the approval of responsible supervisors before processing.

The other complication is the relation between sales and cost of sales. Ideally, there should be a direct correlation between the items of merchandise recorded as sales and the items recorded as cost of sales. In some accounting systems the recording of sales and cost of sales are simultaneous, and copies of the shipping document are used as notification both for billing the customer and for relieving the inventory of the quantity and cost of merchandise sold. Although this chapter will not discuss in detail the integration of the recording of cost of sales with the recording of sales, the correlation between sales and cost of sales should always exist.

Transactions in a revenue, receivables and receipts system

Usually, the transactions recorded in a revenue, receivables and receipts accounting system are:

- credit sales to customers (recognition of revenue, recording of receivable owing);
- cash collections from customers (recording that receivable owing is now paid and the cash received); and
- adjustments for return of merchandise, allowances for defective merchandise, and write-offs or allowances of bad debts.

In addition, the revenue, receivables and receipts cycle includes accounting estimates that are not exchange transactions but more in the nature of allocations of recorded amounts among accounting periods that require the judgment of management. Invariably, an estimate is necessary of customer accounts that will become uncollectable (doubtful debts expense and provision for doubtful debts). In some cases liability under warranty arrangements has to be estimated (warranty expense and provision for warranty expense). While, on the basis of materiality, sales returns and allowances are normally recorded in the period in which they occur, if the auditor believes that such items are becoming material, an adjusting entry for expected returns and allowances should be suggested so that they are recorded in the period of sale.

One of the areas that the business risk audit approach emphasises is that control systems around **routine transactions** (such as sales and cash collections) are usually very well controlled, and well suited to tests of controls. As outlined earlier in this chapter, the new audit risk standards require that for such systems, where substantive procedures alone do not provide sufficient appropriate evidence, the auditor should evaluate control risk as less than high, and undertake tests of controls (AUS 402.115–118/ISA 315.115–118). Control systems for **non-routine transactions**, such as the return of goods or the estimates of the doubtful debts provisions, are not usually well developed. Because these non-routine transactions involve managerial discretion rather than rules (and thus can be more easily manipulated) they will usually receive increased emphasis from the auditor, although this will be more likely of a substantive testing nature (discussed in Chapter 10).

Primary control-related features

Specific control activities are considered later in relation to specific control objectives. However, at this point it is worthwhile to summarise the primary control-related features of a sales accounting system.

Segregation of duties

As explained in the overview of sales accounting, the departments or functions in Table 9.2 are involved in processing transactions and handling assets.

TABLE 9.2 Operating departments and accounting functions involved in transaction processing

Operating departments	Accounting functions
Sales and order entry	Invoicing
Credit approval	Accounts receivable master file update
Opening mail	General ledger update
Cashier	

Ideally, all these functions should be independent. Combining them makes it easier to perpetrate and conceal errors or irregularities. However, separation of these functions is usually an integral part of the plan of organisation. In other words, separation can usually be achieved as a by-product of efficient specialisation of tasks rather than as an overlay on existing processing and handling of assets. A small business, however, may have too few people in the accounting department to achieve an adequate separation of accounting functions. The most important functions to keep separate are those that involve the handling of assets and those that involve the recording of transactions. This will allow the recording function to act as a check or control and, via inspection and reconciliation with accounting records, allow for a comparison of the assets that should be there (as recorded) with the assets that are there. The authorisation of adjustments to records, such as the issuing of credit notes or the writing off of bad debts, should also be kept separate from the handling of assets and the recording function. This is done so that the accounting records cannot be adjusted for items that are misappropriated or lost, and also to aid the reconciliation process.

Control over source documents and inputs

The source documents created during processing, such as shipping documents, invoices and credit notes, should be printed on prenumbered forms. Thus, personnel can account for the sequence independent of processing to help ensure the **completeness** of processing. Missing or out-of-sequence numbers may indicate lost or improper transactions. Adequate physical safeguards are necessary for unused forms and files of forms used in processing.

Often copies of originals of prepared forms are maintained in the originating department. These files usually serve both control and operating purposes. Table 9.3 provides examples.

TABLE 9.3 Examples of source documents and their maintenance

Department or function	Source document	File
Sales and order entry	Customer order	Customer order file
	Accepted sales order or shipping order	Open order file (for orders accepted but not yet shipped)
Shipping	Bill of lading or shipping document	Bill of lading file
Invoicing	Sales invoice	Sales invoice file
Opening mail	Prelist of cash receipts	Prelist file
Cashier	Bank pay-in slip	Bank records file

These files, which are usually maintained in the departments responsible for organisation, are technically not part of the accounting system. Even though invoicing is usually an accounting department function, the initial entry in the accounting records is the debit to accounts receivable. However, the files are used for implementation of control procedures and are part of the internal control system, hence they are inspected when applying audit procedures for tests of controls.

Checks, approvals and reconciliations

The checks, approvals and reconciliations that are added to processing are overlays for control purposes. For instance, independent approval could be required before each processing step, each step could be checked for completeness and accuracy by a second person, and many reconciliations between separate but related records and files could be made. Review and approval by supervisors at various points are also possible. In general, the more independent checks, reviews, approvals and reconciliations there are, the greater the control.

Additional cost is associated with such controls and a balance must be achieved. The checks, reviews, approvals and reconciliations that are commonly used to achieve specific control objectives are discussed later in relation to specific tests of controls.

Tests of controls for sales

The exact nature and extent of tests of controls for sales are influenced by the specific control activities and the auditor's consideration of the most efficient audit strategy. The auditor may, on the basis of the understanding of the internal control system, decide that it is more efficient to apply more extensive substantive tests. In that case, tests of controls for a particular class of transactions, such as sales, may be omitted. Substantive tests for related balances such as accounts receivable and the relationship of those tests to tests of controls are discussed in Chapter 10. An auditor who plans to assess control risk at less than high for a particular transaction class needs to identify specific control procedures that provide a basis for the risk assessment, and perform tests of controls for those control activities.

Identifying specific control objectives and procedures

Table 9.4 presents specific control objectives for sales transactions for the type of entity described in the overview of functions, documents and accounting systems for the sales cycle. Because of the correlation between sales and cost of sales, it is important to separate the functions of shipping, invoicing and merchandise (inventory) storekeeping. It can be seen that the list of policies and procedures outlined in this table covers the procedures outlined in Chapter 8 for determining the accuracy and reliability of transactions. For example, the first control objective of bona fide transactions includes policies and procedures for authorisation and approval, occurrence and reconciliation. The second control objective of all sales shipped being invoiced and properly recorded includes policies and procedures related to completeness. The third control objective, relating to invoices having been recorded correctly as to amount and period, includes policies and procedures related to measurement.

Common control procedures to achieve these specific control objectives are also presented in Table 9.4. Not all the listed procedures are necessary in every circumstance to achieve the objective, and other control activities may achieve the objective.

Specific control objectives and assertions	Common control policies and procedures	Tests of controls
• *Occurrence* All sales recorded are bona fide transactions for merchandise actually shipped to customers	• Policy of authorisation of credit and terms • Evidence of quantities shipped reconciled to quantities invoiced • Monthly statements mailed to customers and queries followed up	• Select a sample of sales transactions from sales journal (daily activity report), check for appropriate authorisation and trace to shipping document file • Inspect reconciliation of shipments to invoices • Observe mailing of monthly statements, and enquire about follow up of queries
• *Completeness* All sales shipped are invoiced and recorded in accounting records	• Shipping documents and sales invoices prenumbered and sequence accounted for • Quantities shipped periodically reconciled to quantities invoiced independently of shipping and invoicing • Shipments checked for shipping documents	• Review the evidence of control of accounting for numerical sequence of shipping documents and sales invoices, or test numerical sequence • Inspect reconciliations of shipments to invoices • Observe checking of shipments or inspect selected shipments
• *Accuracy* Invoices have been recorded correctly as to amount and summarised correctly	• Recomputation and comparison of details (quantity, price, terms) to supporting documents • Monthly statements mailed to customers • Authorisation and independent follow-up of correspondence with customers • Supervisory review and approval of summarisation and posting • Approval of write-offs of uncollectable accounts • Programmed controls in processing sales to identify unusual sales amounts	• Select a sample of transactions from the sales journal (daily activity report) and review evidence that comparison with supporting documentation undertaken and that prices traced to approved list and extensions and footings recomputed • Observe mailing of monthly statements • Review evidence of follow-up of correspondence with customers • Inspect indication of supervisory review and approval of summarisation and posting • Inspect approval of write-offs of uncollectable amounts • Test data techniques to test specific programmed controls

Continued...

Specific control objectives and assertions	Common control policies and procedures	Tests of controls
• *Cutoff* Invoices have been recorded in correct period	• Written procedures detailing the last sales (and related COGS) recorded before balance date, and first sale (and related COGS) of next period recorded in next period • Independent check that written procedures followed	• Observe or ascertain that written procedures followed and independent check carried out. (Because of the nature of this assertion, it is likely that the auditor will undertake substantive tests of transactions by selecting the last sales transactions before balance date and the first after balance date and ensuring they are recorded in the correct period—outlined in Chapter 10).
• *Classification* Sales classified in accordance with written policies	• Appropriate account codings on sales documents	• Review approval of and account codings for related-party sales

The auditor needs to consider whether the specific control and monitoring activities the client has adopted provide *reasonable assurance* of achieving the objective. Reasonable assurance is influenced by the extent of supervision and the auditor's assessment of the control environment. For example, consider the objective that 'all merchandise shipped is invoiced' (completeness). In an entity with a strong control environment and good supervision of separate shipping and invoicing functions, an independent reconciliation of quantities shipped to quantities invoiced may be unnecessary for reasonable assurance of achieving the objective. However, some testing, be it a different control or a substantive test, is necessary. In another entity, this independent reconciliation may be essential for reasonable assurance.

Tests of controls for cash receipts

The specific control objectives for cash receipts and examples of common control policies and procedures and tests of controls are summarised in Table 9.5. In general, the concepts discussed for sales transactions—identifying control policies and procedures that achieve specific control objectives and selecting audit procedures for tests of controls and substantive tests—also apply to cash receipts transactions. This discussion concentrates on matters that might be misunderstood without further explanation.

Notice that some control activities for sales transactions, such as sending monthly statements to customers, contribute to the achievement of specific control objectives for cash receipts. Tests of these control activities are performed either in testing sales transactions or in testing cash receipts; they are not duplicated.

Potential misstatements

Generally, the types of misstatements that may occur in an accounting system are classified as:

■ clerical mistakes (omissions, misclassifications or miscalculations);
■ employee fraud;

TABLE 9.5 Control policies and procedures and tests of control for cash receipts transactions

Specific control objectives	Common control policies and procedures	Tests of controls
• *Occurrence* Recorded cash receipts are for collection of receivables resulting from sales to customers of the entity	• Cash receipts matched to specific sales invoices in posting to accounts receivable master file (for verification that sale occurred, refer to Table 9.4)	• Select a sample of entries in cash receipts journal and review evidence that matched to specific sales invoices
• *Completeness* All cash receipts are recorded and deposited	• Opening of mail and prelisting of cash receipts independently of cashier, accounts receivable master file and general ledger • Policy of depositing cash receipts each day • Comparison of deposit slips, prelists and posting from cash receipts journal (daily activity report) • Prelist forms prenumbered and sequence accounted for	• Observe opening of mail and preparation of deposits • Enquire about policy of depositing cash receipts each day • Select a sample of remittance advices or items on prelist and trace deposits on bank statement and recorded cash receipts • Review the prelist forms for evidence that numerical sequence accounted for
• *Accuracy* Cash receipts have been recorded correctly as to amount	• Cash handling (receipt and deposit) independent of accounting functions and authorised cheque signing • Authorisation of remittance invoices for discounts • Supervisory review and approval of posting to general ledger • Monthly statements mailed to customers • All bank accounts are reconciled promptly with cash records and general ledger • Review reconciling items and bank approved programmed controls to identify unusual cash receipts	• Observe that cash handling is independent of accounting (recording functions) • Select a sample of remittance advices, ensure discounts are appropriately authorised and trace to accounts receivable subsidiary ledger • Inspect posting for indication of supervisory review and approval • Observe mailing of monthly statements • Inspect client bank reconciliations for evidence of approval and reperform one or a few reconciliations • Test data techniques to evaluate programmed controls
• *Cutoff* Cash receipts have been recorded in correct period	• Review by person independent of bank to ensure all cash receipts for period recorded and associated sales recognised (cash sales) or debtors balance reduced (prior credit sales) and cash receipts for next period not included in current period	• Because of the nature of this assertion, it is likely that auditor will undertake substantive tests of transactions, by selecting the last cash receipt transactions before balance date, and the first after balance date, and ensuring they are recorded in the correct period (refer to Chapter 10)
• *Classification* Cash receipts are classified in accordance with company policy	• Independent check that cash receipts are classified correctly	• Examine evidence that independent check of cash receipt classification carried out

- misapplied accounting principles; and
- management fraud.

Clerical mistakes

At each step in processing it is possible for transactions to be lost or for unauthorised or duplicate transactions to be inadvertently added. If computations, such as extensions or summarisations, are made in processing they can be done incorrectly.

Employee fraud

Many clerical mistakes can be made intentionally to conceal employee fraud. For employee fraud to occur, the employee must have access to cash or other negotiable assets: either by handling the asset, for instance having access to cash receipts (including cheques); by being an authorised cheque signatory; or by being in a position to intercept signed cheques. However, misappropriating the asset is only part of the problem. If the misappropriation is to be concealed to avoid detection, the accounting records must be brought into agreement with the physical asset. Concealment may take place before or after the misappropriation, as long as it occurs before the accounting records are reconciled with the asset count.

One of the difficulties of concealing misappropriation of assets in a double-entry accounting system is that credits achieve the concealment, but the problem is where to put the related debits. For example, if cash is misappropriated, a fraudulent credit entry to cash can be made to bring the cash account into agreement with cash in the bank. However, the debit half of the fraudulent entry needs to be concealed in the accounting records. Accounts receivable is a possible storehouse for concealing debits because it has a normal debit balance and often there are many individual customer accounts. This is one of the reasons that audit procedures and control activities emphasise ensuring the existence of recorded accounts receivable.

A type of employee fraud associated with accounts receivable is called **lapping**. An employee misappropriates cash received from a customer and covers the shortage the next day by using receipts from another customer. Continued concealment requires continually delaying the recording of credits to different customers' accounts so that the receipts may be credited to accounts affected by the initial misappropriation. To perpetrate this fraud, an employee must have access to cash receipts *and* be able to make entries to the accounting records for both cash and accounts receivable.

Misapplied accounting principles

As mentioned previously, when sale, delivery and collection occur within a relatively short period, complex revenue recognition issues do not arise. When an extended period is required for sale (real estate), delivery (construction contracting) or collection (instalment sales), the accounting principles for revenue recognition are more often misapplied.

On the other hand, accounting estimates almost invariably create a risk of misapplication of accounting principles. Accounts receivable should be stated at net realisable value. Failure to identify promptly and provide an adequate allowance for uncollectible accounts may arise from extending credit without control, poorly controlled billing practices or insufficient management monitoring of the ageing and collection follow-up. Even if these areas are well controlled, unanticipated changes in economic conditions or customer mix may cause a misstatement of doubtful debts expense and the allowance. Other accounting estimates that may be misstated for similar reasons include unissued credits for sales returns and allowances for warranty expenses.

Management fraud

A management motivated to inflate net profit may engage in fictitious sales transactions. This risk is more likely to be an audit problem in industries where revenue results from a relatively few large transactions, such as real estate. The possibility of this type of fraud is the primary reason that auditors assess inherent risk to identify circumstances that might predispose management to make material misrepresentations. The audit procedures applied include:

■ scanning the accounting records for large or unusual transactions, particularly those recorded late in the period;

■ identifying related parties and considering whether material transactions may involve parties with an undisclosed relationship; and

■ making analytical tests to identify revenue or gross profit changes that are seriously disproportionate to changes in the level or volume of activity.

Accounting estimates are also susceptible to management bias, which may range from exaggerated optimism to outright misrepresentation. Generally, accounting estimates affect the presentation of sales and receivables at net realisable amounts, but in industries using long-term contracts, accounting estimates, such as percentage of completion, may affect revenue recognition.

In industries with a relatively large number of small-revenue transactions, the inherent risk of recording fictitious sales and receivables is reduced but not eliminated. If management engages in this type of deception to achieve an increase in earnings, it is usually necessary to reduce the receivables in the next period by non-cash credits, such as sales returns and allowances, or by writing off accounts as uncollectible.

Quick review

1 The revenue, receivables and receipts section is usually characterised by a large volume repetitive transactions. For these reasons the audit approach often emphasises tests of controls, with anticipated testing of control and monitoring activities providing the evidence to support the earlier assessment of control risk at less than high.

2 The revised audit risk standards now require tests of controls in cases of large volume and repetitive transactions, as substantive procedures alone do not provide sufficient appropriate evidence. In such cases control risk for revenue receivables and receipts is assessed at less than high and tests of controls are undertaken.

3 The auditor undertakes tests of controls for revenue receivables and cash receipts as part of a co-ordinated audit approach to reduce the risk of material misstatement in the following assertions:
   • occurrence—all revenues, receivables and cash receipts that have been recorded have occurred and pertain to the entity
   • completeness—all revenues, receivables and cash receipts that should have been recorded have been recorded
   • accuracy—amounts and other data relating to revenue, receivables and cash receipts have been recorded appropriately
   • cutoff—revenues, receivables and cash receipts have been recorded in the correct accounting period
   • classification—revenues, receivables and cash receipts have been recorded in the proper accounts

4 The common evidence-gathering procedures for tests of controls can be categorised under:
   • inquiry and observation of segregation of duties and restricted access to assets;
   • inspection of evidence that control activities undertaken and reperformance of routines to test not only existence of controls but effectiveness of controls;
   • inspection of a sample of shipping documents and sales transactions.

EXPENDITURES, PAYABLES AND DISBURSEMENTS

Conceptually, the expenditures cycle includes all exchange transactions in which assets or services used in operating the business are acquired for cash or on credit. However, because of the diversity of the 'buying' activities of most entities, auditors often organise the audit approach by transaction type (e.g. purchases from trade creditors, other purchases, payroll) within the expenditures transaction class. This is one of several differences from the sales cycle, and is discussed in more detail in the next section.

Differences from the sales cycle

The differences between the normal audit approach to the expenditures cycle and the approach to the sales cycle are influenced by differences between the transaction types within each cycle and matters related to audit efficiency.

Focus on type of transaction

The acquisition of assets and services, and the payments for them, encompass many types of transactions. For example, auditors often distinguish the following categories:

- payroll costs, including salaries, wages and related benefits for production, service, selling or administration;
- property and equipment;
- purchase of goods and services for inventory (production or merchandising);
- income taxes;
- selling and administrative expenses; and
- miscellaneous expenses paid from petty cash.

Control risk assessments for specific control activities are made separately for each type of transaction. The central focus of the discussion of the expenditures cycle in this chapter is on purchases of goods and services for inventory. The acquisition and payment of selling and administrative expenses are similar to purchases of goods and services for inventory, and the minor variations in controls and audit tests for these expenditure transactions are explained later in this section. Payroll is largely a stand-alone accounting application, and some of the basic features of controls tests for payroll are explained later in this section, along with controls tests for petty cash disbursements (an inconsequential area in most audits).

The acquisition of property and equipment and payments for income taxes are discussed in Chapter 10 because a substantive audit approach aimed at verifying the related account balances is normally used for these items.

Concurrent testing of disbursements and acquisitions

Primarily for reasons of audit efficiency, the normal audit approach is to test concurrently the items acquired and the related cash disbursement. For example, the auditor selects a sample of cash disbursements for selling or administrative expense items and applies audit procedures to the documents supporting acquisition of the goods or services. In contrast, the audit tests in the sales cycle are normally applied separately to sales and cash receipts.

Increased concern with classification of debits

Another distinguishing feature of transactions in the expenditures cycle compared to the sales cycle is the significantly greater number of account balances. For example, *administrative expenses* include office supplies, rent, legal and audit fees, property taxes and insurance. *Selling expenses* include advertising, commissions, travel and entertainment and freight out. For a manufacturing entity, *purchases of goods or services for inventory* include raw materials purchases and overhead expenses, such as supplies, electricity, repairs and maintenance and freight in.

The greater number of account balances causes an increased concern with the proper classification of the debit when a liability is incurred or a cash disbursement made. The auditor is concerned with proper classification in testing sales transactions also, but the relative risk of misclassification is much greater for the expenditures cycle. Sales accounting systems are generally designed to process credit sales to customers. The risk of another type of transaction, such as disposition of manufacturing equipment or marketable securities, being recorded as a sale in the ordinary course of business is usually relatively low. In contrast, the account classification of an expenditure is far more susceptible to error.

Differences between accounts payable and accounts receivable

In the sales cycle the account of primary concern in the balance sheet is accounts receivable. In the expenditures cycle it is accounts payable. Except for the obvious point that one is an asset and the other a liability, the account balances are in some respects similar. Accounts receivable represents uncollected sales invoices; accounts payable represents unpaid suppliers' invoices. However, important differences between the perspective of the client's management and that of the auditor have auditing implications.

Generally, processing of accounts payable is influenced more by cash management concerns than is processing of accounts receivable. An entity can only encourage prompt collections, but, within limits, it can control precisely the timing of disbursements. Often, the system for processing accounts payable is designed primarily to facilitate the timing of the payment of individual supplier invoices on the most advantageous basis, such as realising discounts, and there is less concern with the accuracy and completeness of recording the obligation to each supplier or in total.

From the auditor's perspective, the primary difference from accounts receivable is the focus on detecting understatement of accounts payable. Many auditors emphasise detection of understatement because of risk considerations. They argue that an overstatement of net assets caused by understating liabilities is far more likely to result in litigation than an understatement of net assets. Also, the inherent risk for accounts payable is one of understatement because of the emphasis on timing of the payment of individual invoices, explained earlier, and the apparent improvement in financial performance and position that can be achieved by omitting liabilities.

Functions, documents, inputs and accounting systems

This section explains the functions, documents, inputs and accounting systems for purchases of inventory items. In a manufacturing entity this includes raw materials and overhead expenses. In a merchandising entity it includes goods acquired for resale and related acquisition costs.

An overview of functions, documents, inputs and accounting systems

A narrative of a purchases and cash payments system is contained below, while a corresponding flowchart is contained in Figure 9.3 (overleaf). A purchase requisition is the starting point for this category of transactions in the expenditure cycle. It is a formal request from an operating department for raw materials or merchandise, or goods or services used in production. For example, automatic reorder points may be established for various inventory items that trigger a computerised request.

The purchase requisition is sent to the purchasing department. As far as possible, it is desirable for acquisition of goods and services to be handled by a centralised purchasing function. This permits centralised review of requisitions for compliance with established policy and sound practices such as obtaining competitive bids. The purchasing department prepares a purchase order and sends it to the supplier of the goods or services. The order is processed through the supplier's sales accounting system and the result is shipment and billing or delivery of service and billing.

Goods received are accepted by a *receiving department*. The receiving department inspects and counts the goods before determining whether to accept them. To evaluate whether the goods conform to the specifications ordered, the receiving department is sent a copy of the purchase order. The receiving department prepares a *receiving report* and forwards notification copies to the purchasing department and the accounting department. The accepting of the goods is a very important stage because at this point the entity incurs a liability for payment.

Within the accounting department, the *accounts payable function* receives *suppliers' invoices*. Services, such as electricity or insurance, are received directly by operating departments rather than through the receiving department. The usual approach is to send invoices for such services to supervisors in operating departments or to company officers, who approve the invoices and acknowledge receipt of the service. They are one of the inputs that enable the processing of accounts payable. Suppliers' invoices are used to update the accounts payable master file. The system records and summarises the day's invoices in a *purchases journal*, which is a daily activity report.

To help ensure that disbursements are made only for goods or services that are authorised and received, a specialised source document designed for control purposes is often used. This source document, called a *voucher*, is simply a cover sheet or large envelope for collecting the source documents that support disbursements. A type of expenditures accounting system, explained in the next section, is called a **voucher system**. However, vouchers may be used in several types of expenditures accounting systems. The account distribution (classification of debits) is normally indicated on the voucher.

The *cash disbursements function* assembles the supporting documents for disbursements (suppliers' invoices, receiving reports and purchase orders). This is called 'putting together the voucher package'.

Most entities take all reasonable precautions possible to prevent unauthorised disbursements. It is important to use *prenumbered cheques*, to protect unissued cheques and to account for the numerical sequence of issued and unissued cheques. This includes defacing and retaining voided cheques. Segregation of duties is also extremely important. In this respect, a distinction should be made between preparing cheques for signature and actually signing cheques.

Personnel responsible for preparing cheques for signature should not be in a position to initiate purchase requisitions or other requests for disbursement, or to prepare receiving reports. Individuals with authority to sign cheques should be separated from the accounting function of recording accounts payable and the general ledger. Usually a manager or another responsible supervisor is responsible for signing cheques. For disbursements above a specified amount, a co-signature may be required. Many entities use a cheque-signing machine because of the large volume of cheques. The machine or its removable signature plates should be protected and kept under the control of authorised cheque signers.

The scheduling of payments to suppliers and other creditors is an important part of cash management. The computer may generate a report for manual identification of items to be paid, or items may be selected for payment by computer. The output of computer selection may be a report of the details necessary for manual review and approval, or may be cheques ready for signature.

FIGURE **9.3** **Typical purchases and cash payments flowchart (voucher system)**

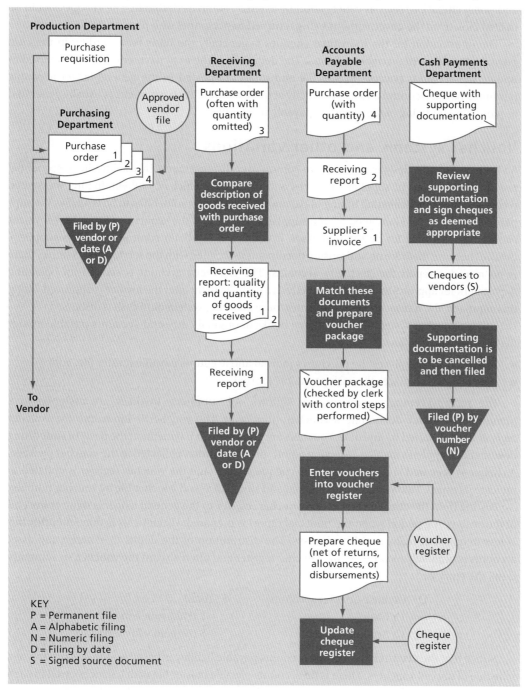

Production Department

Purchase requisition

Purchasing Department

Approved vendor file

Purchase order 1 2 3 4

Filed by (P) vendor or date (A or D)

To Vendor

Receiving Department

Purchase order (often with quantity omitted) 3

Compare description of goods received with purchase order

Receiving report: quality and quantity of goods received 1 2

Receiving report 1

Filed by (P) vendor or date (A or D)

Accounts Payable Department

Purchase order (with quantity) 4

Receiving report 2

Supplier's invoice 1

Match these documents and prepare voucher package

Voucher package (checked by clerk with control steps performed)

Enter vouchers into voucher register

Prepare cheque (net of returns, allowances, or disbursements)

Update cheque register

Voucher register

Cheque register

Cash Payments Department

Cheque with supporting documentation

Review supporting documentation and sign cheques as deemed appropriate

Cheques to vendors (S)

Supporting documentation is to be cancelled and then filed

Filed (P) by voucher number (N)

KEY
P = Permanent file
A = Alphabetic filing
N = Numeric filing
D = Filing by date
S = Signed source document

Authorised cheque signatories should have evidence at the time of signing the cheque that disbursement is appropriate. The cheque signatory should review the supporting documents (supplier's invoice, receiving report and purchase order), inspect indication of prior checking and assembly of supporting documents and indicate supervisory approval. Supporting documents should be cancelled so they cannot be re-used to support another disbursement. Often, the cheque number and date are written on the supporting documents for this purpose, but additional alteration, such as cancellation by a 'PAID' stamp, is desirable. The cheque should be mailed directly to the payee without being returned to personnel who process disbursements.

The information for the individual cheques is generally the basis for recording in the *cash payments* or *cash disbursements journal*. The details from the cash payments journal are used to update the accounts payable master file and totals are posted to the general ledger accounts (accounts payable control and cash). A daily activity report of cash payments is usually generated as part of the updating of the accounts payable master file.

Voucher systems and other variations

A voucher system is designed to improve control over disbursements by establishing a sequential prenumbered record of suppliers' invoices and to improve efficiency by eliminating inessential record keeping and facilitating timing of payments. A voucher number has to be issued as the supplier's invoices are prenumbered for the supplier's system, and the sequence of supplier's invoices cannot be accounted for by the purchaser. It is difficult to obtain control over some suppliers' invoices because there are no authorising documents associated with the service. For example, there is no receiving report for electricity accounts. The electricity account is sent to an operating department for approval and entered directly as a cash payment after the invoice is approved. Using this approach, the transaction does not enter the accounting system until cash is disbursed.

Using a voucher system, the traditional books of original entry and accounts payable master file are changed as follows:

- *voucher register* replaces the purchases journal and accounts payable master file; and
- *cheque register* replaces the cash payments journal.

The record-keeping sequence is as follows. All suppliers' invoices are assigned to a prenumbered source document, a voucher, on receipt. The voucher is input into the voucher register file and sorted by due date. Vouchers are approved for payment on the basis of supporting documents (supplier's invoice, receiving report, purchase order) collected in the voucher package. A cheque is prepared and recorded in the cheque register and the voucher register is updated to indicate payment. Paid vouchers are marked and stored in a paid voucher file by voucher number.

Posting from the cheque register and voucher register to the general ledger is done at the end of the accounting period when the financial report is prepared. Usually this is done monthly but is less frequent in many small businesses. The distribution of the debits to expense and asset accounts is originally recorded in the voucher register and often also on the voucher. In summary form, the entry is:

Dr (Expense or asset accounts)	$ (Total)
Cr Cash	$ (Paid vouchers)
Cr Accounts payable	$ (Unpaid vouchers)

Notice that the determination of the accounts payable liability is based on the preparation of a schedule of unpaid vouchers. There is no accounts payable master file with balances owed to each supplier. This makes it difficult to reconcile suppliers' statements (monthly statements mailed to customers by suppliers, showing the balance owed) with the entity's records. However, within the entity's accounting system there should be an independent reconciliation of the following:

1 total of the schedule of unpaid vouchers;
2 the accounts payable balance of the general ledger; and
3 total of vouchers in the unpaid vouchers file.

Adjustments and inventory

The processing of accounts payable has additional complicating factors that are similar to those for the processing of accounts receivable. In addition to the credits to accounts payable for purchases and debits for cash disbursements, there are adjustments for such things as returns to suppliers of goods that do not meet purchase order specifications. Controls and processing for those adjustments are similar to those for sales accounting. Prenumbered debit memoranda are used and supervisory approval is required before processing. Also, memoranda issued can be matched with shipping reports for goods returned and the corresponding credit memoranda (credit notes) received from suppliers.

In an expenditures system, the receiving reports for raw materials or merchandise are the input for updating inventory records. Perpetual inventory records are a running total of inventory items on hand and they may be maintained in quantities only or in both quantities and dollars. Perpetual records in dollars are integrated with sales accounting systems. However, personnel responsible for inventory storekeeping should be separated from purchasing, receiving and accounting. Audit considerations for inventory are further discussed in Chapter 10.

Primary control-related features

The primary control-related features of the expenditures cycle are concerned with: segregation of duties; control over source documents; and checks, approvals and reconciliations.

- **Segregation of duties** The basic separations that should be incorporated in the plan of organisation are the purchasing, receiving, storekeeping, access to cash (cheque-signing) and accounting functions. Within the accounting department, responsibility for the accounts payable master file should be separated from the general ledger function. In a voucher system, voucher preparation should be separated from voucher approval. Finally, any reconciliations should be made independently of the other functions.
- **Control over source documents** The source documents used in accounts payable processing —purchase orders, receiving reports, vouchers and cheques—should be prenumbered and the sequence should be accounted for. The periodic accounting for cheques should include both used and unused cheques, and they should be compared with recorded cash disbursements. Unused documents should be maintained in a secure location such as a safe.
- **Checks, approvals and reconciliations** In general, the more checks and approvals at each processing step, the more effective the control. In an expenditures system, two very important controls are the comparison of supporting documents (purchase order, receiving report, supplier's invoice) and recomputation of the supplier's invoice, both of which should be made before approval for payment. Reconciliations of physical holdings of assets to accounting records, or between differing accounting records, are also important but vary with the type of accounting system.

Tests of controls for purchases for inventory

Conceptually, the approach to tests of controls for purchases of goods or services for inventory is similar to that for testing controls in the sales system. The auditor needs to consider whether the specific control and monitoring activities that the client follows provide reasonable assurance of achieving the specific control objectives.

The specific control objectives for purchases of goods or services for inventory and examples of common control activities and tests of controls are summarised in Table 9.6 overleaf. The arrangement and approach to listing audit procedures is, as explained earlier, referred to as an audit program. The auditor needs to eliminate duplications and reorder the procedures into a logical and efficient sequence. It can be seen that the list of policies and procedures outlined in this table covers the procedures for determining the accuracy and reliability of transactions. For example, the first control objective of occurrence (bona fide transactions) includes policies and procedures related to authorisation and approval. The second control objective of completeness relates to policies and procedures to help ensure all purchases received are being properly recorded. The third control objective relating to accuracy relates to policies and procedures to help ensure purchases are being recorded in the correct amount.

TABLE 9.6 Control policies and procedures and audit tests for purchases of inventory transactions

Specific control objectives	Common control policies and procedures	Tests of controls
• *Occurrence* All recorded purchases are bona fide transactions in that they relate to goods or services authorised or received	• Approval of purchase order • Goods received are counted, inspected and compared to purchase order before acceptance • Services received are acknowledged in writing • Comparison of purchase order, receiving report and supplier's invoice before recording liability	• Examine evidence of approved purchase and service orders • Select a sample of order entries in purchases journal, trace back to vouchers and inspect supporting documentation including receiving report, ensuring agreement of details, indication of approval
• *Completeness* All purchases for the period of inventory received are recorded	• Suppliers' invoices numbered using an invoice register or prenumbered vouchers and the sequence accounted for • Suppliers' invoices matched to receiving reports and unmatched items investigated • Receiving reports prenumbered and the sequence accounted for	• Review the evidence of the accounting for numerical sequence of invoices • Review reports of unmatched items for evidence of investigation and inquire about disposition • Review the accounting for numerical sequence of receiving reports
• *Accuracy* Purchases of goods or services for inventory are recorded correctly as to amount and summarised correctly	• Established procedures for review of purchase amount and verification to supporting documentation • Programmed controls (e.g. reasonableness check) to identify any unusual purchase transactions	• For the sample of vouchers selected, examine for evidence that review of purchase amount and verification to supporting documentation undertaken • Test data techniques to verify that programmed controls are working
• *Cutoff* Purchase invoices have been recorded in correct period	• Review by person independent of purchasing to ensure all purchases for period (and related cash payments/creditors) included, and purchases for next accounting period not included	• Because of the nature of this assertion, it is likely that auditors will undertake substantive tests of transactions, selecting the last purchase transaction before balance date, and the first after balance date, and ensuring they are recorded in the correct period (refer to Chapter 10)

Specific control objectives	Common control policies and procedures	Tests of controls
• *Classification* Purchases are classified in accordance with classification policies	• Procedures to ensure appropriate account coding on purchases documents • Separate accounts in Chart of Accounts for purchases from related parties, and possibly additional authorisation for related-party transactions	• Check that procedure aimed at establishing appropriate account and appropriate authorisation for related-party transactions undertaken

Tests of controls for cash disbursements

The specific control objectives for cash disbursements and examples of common control policies and procedures and tests of controls are summarised in Table 9.7. For tests that involve inspection of documents, audit sampling is used. The appropriate sample size of the number of documents to inspect can be determined in accordance with the procedures outlined in Chapter 11.

TABLE **9.7** **Control policies and procedures and audit tests for cash disbursements transactions**

Specific control objectives	Common control policies and procedures	Tests of controls
• *Occurence* Recorded cash disbursements are for goods or services authorised and received (for verification that purchase occurred, refer to Table 9.6)	• Cheques printed or prepared only when receipt of goods or services and approval are documented (e.g. supporting documents compared, recomputed and voucher approved) • Cheques signed only after viewing supporting documentation and prior approval • Supporting documentation cancelled and reference to cheque number • Signed cheques mailed directly to payees	• Select a sample of cash disbursement transactions from cash payments journal and inspect supporting documentation for indication of checking, review and approval • Observe and inquire about cheque preparation and signing and protection of unissued cheques • For the sample of cash disbursement transactions inspect supporting documents for cancellation, cheque number and endorsement • Observe and inquire about cheque signing and mailing
• *Completeness* All cash disbursements are recorded	• Voucher packets and cheques prenumbered and sequence accounted for • Unissued cheques protected and the sequence accounted for • Voided cheques defaced and retained • Presented cheques listed on bank statement compared to cash payment records (The above control activities are usually done as part of the bank reconciliation)	• Review evidence that sequence check of voucher packets and cheques is properly undertaken • Observe and inquire about cheque signing, including protective measures for unissued cheques and cheque-signing devices • For sample of voided cheques, ensure retained and defaced • Observe and inquire about preparation of bank

Continued...

Specific control objectives	Common control policies and procedures	Tests of controls
		reconciliation and reperform one or a few
• *Accuracy* Cash disbursements are recorded correctly as to amount	• Summarisation and posting of cash disbursement records reviewed and approved • Programmed controls (e.g. reasonableness check) to identify any unusual cash disbursement transactions	• For the sample of cash disbursements transactions selected to test occurrence assertion, compare amount, payee and date with cash payment record and identify approval and review of summarisation and posting carried out • Test data techniques to verify that programmed controls are working
Cutoff Cash disbursements recorded in correct period	• Bank transfers and cheques written independently reviewed for recording in correct period	• Because of the nature of this assertion, it is likely that auditors will undertake substantive tests of transactions, selecting the last cheques issued before balance date and first cheque issued after balance date, and ensuring they were recorded in the correct period. They will carefully review all bank transfers around balance date to ensure they are recorded in the correct period (refer to Chapter 10)
Classification Cash disbursements are recorded correctly as to account	• Cheque signatory reviews and authorised expense classification	• Review sample of cash disbursement transactions for evidence of authorisation of expense classification

Potential misstatements

One goal of developing specific control objectives as a basis for designing tests of controls is to avoid the need for memorisation of long lists of control activities or misstatements that can occur. However, auditors should be aware of the following types of irregularities that may occur in the expenditures cycle:

■ **Classic disbursements fraud** The classic pattern for employee fraud in the disbursements area involves the preparation of fraudulent supporting documents that are used to obtain an authorised cheque. Because this fraud requires careful planning the deception is often elaborate. Some frauds of this type have included the opening of post office boxes and bank accounts in the names of fictitious entities. Clever frauds may be difficult for internal auditors or independent auditors to detect as long as the perpetrator is not too greedy. Appropriate procedures for approving suppliers, and checking that transactions are with approved suppliers becomes an important

control. If the discrepancy between goods or services received and goods or s҉
becomes too great, accountability tests may disclose the fraud. This fraud is one of t҉
auditors investigate unusual or unfamiliar names of suppliers.

- **Kickbacks** Personnel responsible for purchasing may enter into arrangements w҉
  to receive kickbacks on goods or services purchased from them. Since collusion ҉
  it could be argued that auditors have little chance of detecting kickbacks. Howe҉
  competitive bidding practices are not followed, many auditors compare unit prices o҉
  the same type acquired from different suppliers in order to consider the possibi҉
  kickback scheme.

- **Illegal acts** The auditor's responsibility with respect to illegal acts is explained in Cha҉
  Questionable transactions that may indicate bribery or other illegal payments are most lik҉ ҉
  come to the auditor's attention in the examination of disbursement transactions. The most likely
  transaction type is selling or administrative expense. For example, a sales commission may be a
  bribe to obtain business. As explained in Chapter 4, the auditor does not undertake audit
  procedures specifically to detect illegal acts but remains aware of the possibility of such acts.

- **Unauthorised executive perks** The personal use of business assets is inappropriate unless
  the use is authorised and appropriately considered as part of executive compensation. For
  public companies, the Australian Stock Exchange requires disclosure of management
  remuneration. For private companies and other entities, the auditor may still be concerned
  with such practices because they affect the tax return preparation responsibilities and liability
  for fringe benefits tax.

- **Kiting** The term 'kiting' is used to describe the practice of inflating the cash balance by using the
  fact that cash which is recorded as a deposit on one day may not be considered withdrawn from
  another bank account until the next banking day. Cash is transferred from one bank account to
  another and the cash receipt (deposit) is recorded in the period under audit, but the
  disbursement (withdrawal) is not recorded until the following period. During this period, the
  money transferred appears to be in both bank balances. This device may be used by an employee
  to conceal a cash shortage or by management to improve the entity's financial position.

Quick review

1. The expenditures, payables and disbursements section is usually characterised by large-volume and repetitive transactions. For these reasons the audit approach often emphasises tests of controls.

2. The revised audit risk standards now require tests of controls in cases such as large volume and repetitive transactions, since substantive procedures alone do not provide sufficient appropriate evidence. In such cases control risk for expenditures, payables and disbursements is assessed at less than high and tests of controls are undertaken.

3. From the auditor's perspective, the primary difference between accounts receivable (and associated cash receipts) and accounts payable (and associated cash payments) is generally that the auditor is more concerned with detecting overstatement of accounts receivable and understatement of accounts payable.

4. As completeness of accounts payable and cash payments is a concern, a voucher system is commonly implemented to establish a sequential prenumbered record for payments and payables.

5. The numerical sequencing and accounting for receiving reports are also an important control for completeness because on the acceptance of the goods a liability is established for the entity.

VARIATIONS FOR OTHER TYPES OF EXPENDITURE TRANSACTIONS, INCLUDING CONTRACTUAL TRANSACTIONS

The following discussion explains the primary variations in the nature of control policies and procedures and audit tests for some other categories of types of expenditure transactions.

Selling and administrative expenses

The processing and related control policies and procedures for selling and administrative expenses are similar to those for purchases for inventory. The primary difference is a greater emphasis on budgetary control of selling and administrative expenses. Review and approval of budgets and obtaining satisfactory explanation of variances are important. For some expenses, such as travel and entertainment, a well-defined expense reimbursement policy is important. The auditor needs to understand the business purpose of selling and administrative expense transactions examined, and should review supporting documentation, such as expense reports for appropriate approval.

Petty cash disbursements

The expenses paid out of petty cash are usually so insignificant (immaterial) to the business as a whole that the auditor applies no tests. However, the primary control activity is an **imprest fund**. The total of cash on hand and the documentation of expenses paid out of the fund should always equal a pre-established control total. When the fund is reimbursed, someone other than the custodian counts the cash and documents. If audit procedures are applied, the auditor counts the fund *in the custodian's presence* and examines the supporting documents for disbursements out of the fund for propriety and reasonableness.

Payroll

Effective analytical procedures are often possible for payroll, due to the fact that periodic payrolls (weekly, fortnightly or monthly) can be compared and analysed for explanation of fluctuations. In undertaking such comparisons the auditor would have to establish that the base payroll to which other payrolls are compared is appropriate. This may be achieved by undertaking tests of controls. Important control activities for payroll include segregation of the following duties:

- approval of hiring and firing and determination of pay rates (personnel or senior management);
- approval of time worked (supervisor);
- payroll preparation;
- payroll distribution; and
- where cheques are not paid into a nominated bank account, custody of unclaimed pay cheques.

Instead of maintaining a separate large payroll department, many organisations engage a service entity to perform their payroll function. The audit implications arising from the use of such a service entity are contained in AUS 404 (ISA 402) 'Audit Implications (Considerations) Relating to Entities Using a Service Entity (Organization)', and are discussed in Chapter 8.

The primary misstatements that may occur are a padded payroll (fictitious employees), overpayment for work performed and misappropriation of unclaimed pay cheques. Generally, employees can be relied on to detect errors of understatement. Audit procedures for payrolls are similar to those for other expenditures, but the terms for source documents differ. For example, time cards may be used instead of vendors' invoices. The auditor is concerned with assessing the accuracy of pay rates and occurrence of time worked. The personnel department should be separated from other payroll-related functions, and payroll data can be compared to personnel records. On the disbursement side, an important control is comparison of net payroll with payroll cheques issued. Identification of employees on the payroll, once a common audit procedure, is now used only when there is a serious risk of fictitious employees on the payroll. Also, many employers, rather than distributing pay cheques, pay directly into an employee's nominated bank account.

Payroll is characterised by enterprise and industrial agreements and various state and federal awards. These contracts and agreements often specify the kinds of service to be performed by the employee and the compensation to be paid, as well as the pay period. The compensation may be in the form of set payments each payday; it may, in addition, include bonuses at year-end and contributions toward superannuation. Generally, all these specifications are spelled out in the award or contract, which should be known by the auditor.

Tests of controls for payroll

If the auditor finds that tests of controls are necessary, the following may be undertaken.

The main controls for which the auditor is seeking evidence are the authorisation of time worked (by supervisors) and the approval of pay rates (by personnel department). The documents to be examined relative to payroll are time cards for those employees who must use them, as well as personnel department records to establish wage or salary rates and to make sure that the employees' names and rates correspond to those on time cards. Main sources of information are the applicable industrial awards for correctness of rates of pay, and the board of directors' minutes authorising executive salary rates and/or bonuses and commissions.

Under the provisions of the Australian taxation system, employees may claim the general exemption from tax on the first portion of their taxable income, and have any dependant or other rebates reflected in the tax instalments deducted from their earnings. To do so, they must lodge an Income Tax Instalment Declaration with their employer. These forms should be examined, as should employee authorisations for deductions such as medical fund contributions, superannuation contributions and union fees.

Other tests for payroll

Data found in original personnel records, industrial awards and minutes of the board of directors' meetings are traced to time cards and time reports. In addition, the proper percentages for required deductions from payroll amounts are traced to journal entries and ledger accounts. The total amounts of payrolls are traced through the journals to the appropriate ledger accounts. The auditor also traces amounts under superannuation plans to the appropriate journals and ledger accounts.

There are many deductions from an employee's wage or salary for such things as medical funds and union fees. Normally awards or laws that ought to be known to the auditor can substantiate these items. Therefore, the audit of these items usually consists of recomputation, using the appropriate percentages or amounts and tracing to the appropriate ledger accounts.

Interest expense

The audit of interest is generally easy. The auditor identifies the contracts, the interest rate and the time the particular instrument has been outstanding during the fiscal period under audit and determines the total interest expense. A comparison is then made with the entries, both payment and accrual, made by the client and any discrepancy is reconciled. Thus, interest is almost totally determined by the contract under which this transaction exists. The control that the auditor is most concerned about is evidence of authorisation, the authorisation of any contractual obligations and evidence of the checking of mathematical accuracy in accordance with the terms of the loan.

Rent, lease and insurance payments

Lease transactions are becoming common, and the auditor can find such transactions in the audit of almost any client. Many businesses also rent some kind of property or asset, even if it is not leased, and most carry insurance against fire, theft and loss of profits. The details of these transactions are set out in contracts: rental agreements, lease agreements and insurance contracts. The auditor's primary concern with lease contracts is to determine that the entity is in fact receiving the services for which it is paying and that these services are being used in a manner that was intended under the contract. The auditor also is interested in whether or not the client is performing all the tasks required under the contract, for example keeping the item in good repair. Finally, the auditor is concerned that the accounting treatment for leases is in accordance with AASB 117 (IAS 17), 'Leases'. Again the auditor is most concerned with obtaining evidence that the controls of authorisation and checking of mathematical accuracy in accordance with the term of the contract are working.

Quick review

1. Procedures for the audit of selling and administrative expenses are similar to those for purchases for inventory, with the primary difference being the greater emphasis on budgetary control of selling and administrative expenses. The analytical procedure of comparing actual expenses with both budgeted and previous year's expenses is an important audit procedure.
2. Petty cash disbursements are usually immaterial, so the auditor applies no direct tests.
3. Effective analytical procedures are often possible for payroll. Tests of control include segregation of duties, vouching to agreements and awards, recomputation and retracing data processing.
4. The audit of interest expense is relatively easy, being determined by the terms of the contract under which the transaction exists.
5. Rent, lease and insurance payments should also be made in accordance with a contract. The auditor examines the contract, recomputes the rates specified and retraces the data processing to the supporting documentation.

TESTING CONTROLS IN CLIENT COMPUTER PROGRAMS

As explained in Chapter 8, client application programs include programmed accounting procedures for calculating and summarising data, and programmed control and monitoring activities for providing reasonable assurance that data are authorised, valid, complete and accurate. If the auditor tests the client's programs, both aspects are usually tested.

Auditing through the computer techniques are predominantly tests of controls and will be used where control risk is less than high and the auditor wishes to place reliance on controls in the programs. The need for computer-assisted audit techniques that test controls is greater in complex systems with real-time processing. Auditing firms that have relatively large numbers of computer audit specialists also use such computer-assisted techniques more frequently.

This section explains some common computer-assisted audit techniques for testing controls contained in client programs. One of the categories of computer-assisted audit techniques as outlined in AGS 1060 (IAPS 1009) is test data techniques, which covers the concepts of test data and integrated test facility.

Test data

The **test data** approach is explained first not because it is the most widely used, but because it demonstrates what the auditor is trying to accomplish by testing client programs.

When using this approach, the auditor prepares simulated transaction data. These test transactions include both correct data to test processing and incorrect data to test control activities in the client's application program. The auditor manually calculates what the processing results should be and compares them to the results produced when the test data are processed by the client's application program (see Figure 9.4 overleaf).

The auditor needs to ensure that the program tested is the production program used in actual processing, and that the same program was used throughout the period covered by the control risk assessment. Generally, it is necessary to identify general controls and consider their effectiveness for that assurance.

The test data approach may be used in a system with online entry capability if the auditor obtains client permission to use a terminal to enter transactions. In most circumstances the program is tested in a non-live environment (on a copy of the client's files) to ensure that there is no risk of corrupting the client's files. The use of test data is illustrated in Example 9.3.

Integrated test facility

An **integrated test facility (ITF)** is an adaptation of the test data approach. Dummy records are included in the client's files. For example, dummy customers might be included for an accounts receivable application. The auditor's simulated transactions are processed with the production program against the live files during regular processing. This approach overcomes several of the drawbacks of the test data approach, but the auditor must still assess general controls for reasonable assurance that the program tested is not changed during the period. It is essential to prevent dummy records from being summarised with live data when financial reports or other reports are prepared.

A diagrammatic representation of the integrated test facility is contained in Figure 9.5 (overleaf). The method outlined for excluding the ITF transactions in this figure is to produce one report without the ITF data for the client, and one containing the ITF data for the auditor.

EXAMPLE 9.3 Using test data

The auditor is undertaking testing of the client's payroll system. They undertake an evaluation of the general control environment and conclude that this is strong. They then start to test the application controls, and in particular want to collect audit evidence on some of the limit and reasonable tests that are contained in the program. One of these programmed controls is that the number of payroll hours per week cannot exceed 50. To test this control the auditor designs test transactions, such as employee A having payroll hours per week equalling 50 and employee B having payroll hours equalling 51. (The auditor tends to work around the parameters set in the program.) The expectation is that if the programmed control is working as the auditor believes, employee A's transaction will be accepted and employee B's transaction will be rejected and written to an error or exception report.

FIGURE **9.4** **Processing of test data**

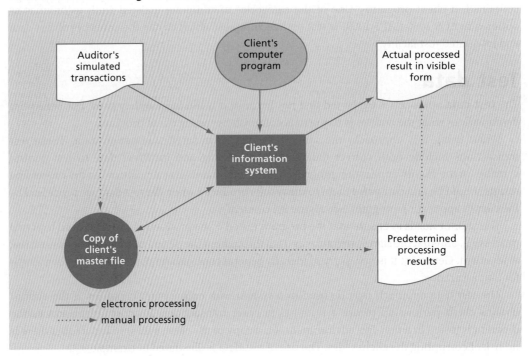

Both test data and ITF, which use simulated data, are tests of controls only (they are not dual-purpose tests because they do not substantiate real transactions). The use of the integrated test facility is illustrated in Example 9.4.

FIGURE **9.5** **Integrated test facility for a payroll system**

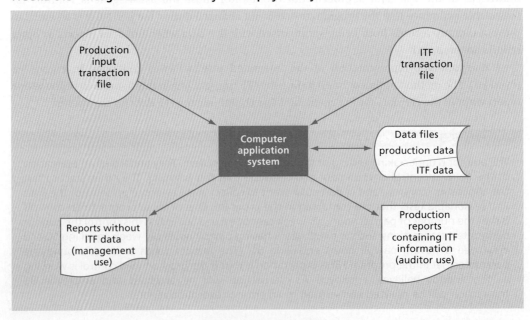

Following on from Example 9.3, the auditor can test the programmed control of maximum weekly hours by including a dummy record (employee) in the payroll master file. They can then feed through test transactions designed to test this control at any stage during the year. Thus in a payroll file they may have a dummy employee working 51 hours in the week, and they would expect this dummy employee's hours not to be processed, but to be written to some exception report for follow-up.

Processing client data

Both the test data approach and the ITF use simulated transactions. Another group of techniques for testing client programs uses actual client data to test processing, and simulated data to test controls. These techniques are presented together below because of this similarity, but the auditor might use only one of the techniques for a particular computerised accounting application:

- **Controlled processing**   The auditor establishes control over client input and independently calculates key processing results, such as the ending balance of a control account. The auditor maintains control over the computer processing and output, and compares the computer output to the calculated results.
- **Controlled reprocessing**   The auditor maintains control over the reprocessing of previously processed results, having tested the appropriate version of the program, and compares the computer output of the original processing and reprocessing.
- **Parallel processing (parallel simulation)**   The auditor compares the results of the client's processing with results obtained by using the client's input and files and the auditor's own program. The program used for this purpose may be custom-designed or generalised audit software (see the next section of this chapter). Generally, the auditor's program calculates key processing results rather than duplicating all the client's processing.

These techniques are generally more useful for testing the processing accuracy of the client's programs than for testing programmed control activities.

Reviewing client's program code or results of job processing

Program code review involves the auditor reviewing the client's program documentation, and the source code. The auditor goes over the relevant code line by line and considers whether the processing steps and control activities are properly coded and logically correct. This approach is widely used as a prelude to the use of test data, and is one of the main ways in which the auditor identifies key programmed controls that they may wish to test through the use of test data. Software that aids this approach includes programs that can be used to map or flowchart systems. This will help the auditor understand the logic flow of the program being evaluated.

Review of job (batch) accounting data involves the auditor reviewing the printed log produced as jobs (or batches of transactions) are run, and considers any excessive processing time, error conditions or abnormal halts. (While this technique does not test the client's program, it has similar objectives.) This helps the auditor identify potential batches of transactions on which they should concentrate their audit attention.

Advanced computer-assisted audit techniques

There are a number of advanced computer-assisted audit techniques that are very useful in helping the auditor establish reliance on controls in the computer programs. These techniques use live data, files or programs and are especially useful when computer reliance is necessary and there is no visible audit trail, as in some real-time processing systems. These techniques produce evidence on current system performance and require extensive on-site audit supervision. For these reasons, they are currently used more frequently by internal auditors than by external auditors. However, there is increased advocation for their use associated with the greater prevalance of e-commerce applications and the move towards providing continuous assurance (discussed in Chapter 17).

Some examples of these advanced computer-assisted audit techniques are:

- **Systems control audit review file (SCARF)** Audit modules embedded in application programs monitor transaction activity at designated points and select transactions for the auditor's review. The auditor provides criteria when the application program is developed so that the auditor's program module can be inserted at the point in processing logic where errors are most likely to occur, and so that transactions selected meet the auditor's specifications. The auditor will then apply normal evidence-gathering techniques to these high-risk transactions.
- **Snapshot** Transactions are tagged (an indicator is added to the data) at input, and at selected points in the system the tagged transactions are recorded. Tags may be assigned randomly or in accordance with specified criteria. An application program which encounters a tagged transaction writes the details—the transaction data, date and time of occurrence, the application program involved and the point in the program at which generated—to an audit log. This provides the auditor with a picture, hence the term snapshot, of the data at particular points in processing. It gives more detailed information than is provided by a technique such as SCARF and permits review of intermediate results during processing.
- **Audit hooks** Exit points are provided in application programs that allow the auditor to insert commands for special processing. For example, a database system might contain an audit hook that allows the auditor to insert additional coding to obtain independent control totals as a result of normal processing.

It should be noted that two of these techniques, SCARF and snapshots, outlined as CAATs in AGS 1060 (IAPS 1009), are under the common heading **embedded audit modules**. These techniques all permit the auditor to conduct testing during normal computer processing. However, they require advanced computer knowledge and training, and can cause modification of transaction data; thus they should only be undertaken by computer audit specialists.

Quick review

1. Using the test data approach the auditor prepares simulated transaction data to test program control activities. The auditor manually calculates what the processing results should be and compares them to the results obtained by processing the test data with the client's application program.
2. The integrated test facility is an adaptation of the test data approach using simulated transactions. Dummy records are included on the client's files, and simulated transactions are processed against the live files during regular processing.
3. It is possible that actual client data may be used to test the processing of the IT systems. These techniques include controlled processing, controlled reprocessing and parallel simulation.

4 Non-processing approaches may also be used to provide confidence concerning the client's programs. These are usually used in conjunction with computer-assisted techniques, and include program code review and review of job accounting data.

5 Systems control audit review, snapshot and audit hooks are advanced computer-assisted audit techniques which permit the auditor to conduct testing during normal computer processing. They are still rarely used in practice, although there is greater advocacy of their use.

Summary

Tests of controls are an important source of audit evidence. If the auditor assesses control risk at any level below high, the auditor has identified specific internal control policies and procedures that are capable of being relied upon. Evidence gathered to determine the appropriateness of this intended reliance is known as tests of controls.

The auditor undertakes that combination of tests of controls and substantive tests that results in the most efficient and effective combination of audit procedures.

In some areas, where substantive procedures alone may not provide sufficient appropriate audit evidence (for example for organisations that process a large number of routine transactions through a control system), control risk is required to be assessed at less than high, and tests of controls are required to be undertaken.

Key terms

Audit hooks	432	Non-routine transactions	408
Audit program	397	Program code review	431
Classic disbursements fraud	424	Review of job (batch) accounting data	431
Completeness	409	Routine transactions	408
Embedded audit modules	432	Snapshot	432
Imprest fund	426	Systems control audit review file (SCARF)	432
Integrated test facility (ITF)	429	Test data	429
Kickbacks	425	Tests of controls	396
Kiting	425	Unauthorised executive perks	425
Lapping	414	Voucher system	418

References

Armour, M. (2000) 'Internal control: Governance framework and business risk assessment', *Auditing: A Journal of Practice and Theory*, Supplement, 75–82.

Basu, P. and Wright, A. (1997) 'An exploratory study of control environment risk factors: Client contingency considerations and audit testing strategy', *International Journal of Auditing*, June, 77–96.

Brown, C.E. and Solomon, I. (1990) 'Auditor configural information processing in control risk assessment', *Auditing: A Journal of Practice and Theory*, Fall, 17–38.

Daniel, S.J. (1988) 'Some empirical evidence about the assessment of audit risk in practice', *Auditing: A Journal of Practice and Theory*, Spring, 174–81.

Kinney, W.R. (2000) 'Research opportunities in internal control quality and quality assurance', *Auditing: A Journal of Practice and Theory*, Supplement, 83–90.

Messier, W.F. Jr (2003) *Auditing and Assurance Services: A Systematic Approach*, 3rd edn, McGraw-Hill/Irwin, New York.

Reimers, J., Wheeler, S. and Dunsenbury, R. (1993) 'The effect of response mode on auditors' control risk assessments', *Auditing: A Journal of Practice and Theory*, Fall, 62–78.

Simpson, B. (1993) 'Using flowcharts as an information systems audit tool', *EDPACS*, February, 15–19.

Waller, W.S. (1993) 'Auditors' assessments of inherent and control risk in field settings', *The Accounting Review*, October, 783–802.

MAXIMISE
YOUR MARKS!
There are
approximately
30 interactive
questions on
tests of controls
available online
at www.mhhe.
com/au/gay3e

Assignments

Additional assignments for this chapter are contained in Appendix A of this book, page 770.

REVIEW QUESTIONS

9.1 The following questions relate to aspects of interest in general when undertaking tests of controls.

  (a) Test of controls must be performed:
  - **A** when inherent risk is high
  - **B** to ensure that for controls that are to be relied upon they are operating effectively throughout the entire year
  - **C** when control risk is high
  - **D** in areas of business risk

  (b) When control risk is evaluated at less than high, tests of control should be undertaken of:
  - **A** both design and operation of the internal control system
  - **B** effectiveness and continuity of controls that have been determined to exist
  - **C** design of the internal control system
  - **D** both the control environment and the entity's risk assessment process

  (c) Tests of controls:
  - **A** allow the auditor to increase the level of acceptable detection risk
  - **B** should focus on transactions with high dollar value
  - **C** should not be used in areas where inherent risk is evaluated as high
  - **D** allow the auditor to reduce the level of inherent risk

  (d) Which of the following audit tests would be regarded as a test of controls?
  - **A** Test of the signatures on purchase documents for appropriate authorisations
  - **B** Tests of additions to property, plant and equipment by physical inspections
  - **C** Tests of the specific items making up the balance in a given general ledger account
  - **D** Tests of the inventory pricing to vendors' invoices

  (e) After obtaining an understanding of an entity's internal control system, an auditor may assess control risk at the maximum level for some account balances because he or she:
  - **A** performs tests of controls to restrict detection risk to an acceptable level
  - **B** identifies internal controls that are likely to prevent material misstatements
  - **C** believes the internal controls are unlikely to be operating effectively
  - **D** determines that the pertinent internal control components are *not* well documented

9.2 The following questions relate to the revenue, receivables and receipts cycle. Select the *best* response.

  (a) Which of the following tests of control would provide audit evidence for the management assertion of completeness of revenue?
  - **A** For each sales invoice, verify that there is an appropriately authorised dispatch.
  - **B** Ensure customer's credit limit is checked prior to each sale.
  - **C** Observe separation of duties between filling and dispatching orders.
  - **D** Check to ensure that all dispatch orders have been properly matched to a sales invoice.

  (b) At which point in an ordinary sales transaction of a wholesaling business would a lack of specific authorisation be of *least* concern to the auditor in the conduct of an audit?
  - **A** Determination of discounts
  - **B** Selling of goods for cash

    C Granting of credit

    D Shipment of goods

(c) Tracing copies of sales invoices to shipping documents will provide evidence that all:

    A debits to the accounts receivable master file are for sales shipped

    B shipments to customers were billed

    C shipments to customers were recorded as receivables

    D billed sales were shipped

(d) Tracing bills of lading to sales invoices provides evidence that:

    A recorded sales were shipped

    B invoiced sales were shipped

    C shipments to customers were invoiced

    D shipments to customers were recorded as sales

(e) For the internal control activities to be effective, employees maintaining the accounts receivable subsidiary ledger should *not* also approve:

    A write-offs of customer accounts

    B cash disbursements

    C employee overtime wages

    D credit granted to customers

(f) Which of the following controls is most likely to help ensure that all credit revenue transactions of an entity are recorded?

    A The accounting department supervisor controls the mailing of monthly statements to customers and investigates any differences reported by customers.

    B The billing department supervisor matches prenumbered shipping documents with entries in the sales journal.

    C The billing department supervisor sends a copy of each approved sales order to the credit department for comparison to the customer's authorised credit limit and current account balance.

    D The accounting department supervisor independently reconciles the accounts receivable subsidiary ledger to the accounts receivable control account monthly.

(g) Which of the following internal controls would be most likely to deter the lapping of collections from customers?

    A Segregation of duties between receiving cash and posting the accounts receivable ledger

    B Supervisory comparison of the daily cash summary with the sum of the cash receipts journal entries

    C Independent internal verification of dates of entry in the cash receipts journal with dates of daily cash summaries

    D Authorisation of write-offs of uncollectible accounts by a supervisor independent of the credit approval function

9.3 The following questions relate to the expenditures, payables and disbursements cycle. Select the *best* response.

    (a) To ensure the completeness of purchases made during the year, the auditor should:

        A select a sample of invoices received before the year-end and ensure that they are appropriately recorded in the accounts payable master file

        B select a sample of transactions from the accounts payable master file and vouch to related invoices

        C select a sample of receiving reports before and after the year-end and ensure they have been appropriately recorded

        D perform a bank reconciliation

(b) Which of the following is a primary function of the purchasing department?
  A Verifying the propriety of goods acquired
  B Reducing expenditures for goods acquired
  C Authorising the acquisition of goods
  D Ensuring the acquisition of goods of a specified quality

(c) Which of the following procedures would prevent a paid disbursement voucher from being presented for payment a second time?
  A The date on a disbursement voucher is within a few days of the date the voucher is presented for payment.
  B The official who is signing the cheques compares the cheque with the voucher and cancels the voucher documents.
  C Vouchers are prepared by individuals who are responsible for signing disbursement cheques.
  D Disbursement vouchers are approved by at least two responsible managers.

(d) Which of the following control activities is not usually performed in the vouchers payable department?
  A Controlling the mailing of the cheque and remittance advice
  B Matching the receiving report with the purchase order
  C Determining the mathematical accuracy of the vendor's invoice
  D Having an authorised person approve the voucher

(e) Which of the following is the most effective control activity to detect vouchers that were prepared for the payment of goods that were not received?
  A Compare goods received with goods requisitioned in receiving department.
  B Verify vouchers for accuracy and approval in internal audit department.
  C Count goods upon receipt in storeroom.
  D Match purchase order, receiving report and vendor's invoice for each voucher in accounts payable department.

9.4 (a) In a properly-designed accounts payable system, a voucher is prepared after the invoice, purchase order, requisition and receiving report are verified. The next step in the system is:
  A entering of the voucher into the voucher register
  B approval of the voucher for payment
  C cancellation of the supporting documents
  D entry of the cheque amount in the cheque register

(b) When goods are received, the receiving clerk should match the goods with:
  A the vendor shipping document and the purchase order
  B the receiving report and the vendor shipping document
  C the purchase order and the requisition form
  D the vendor invoice and the receiving report

(c) Internal control is strengthened when the quantity of merchandise ordered is omitted from the copy of the purchase order sent to the:
  A purchasing agent
  B accounts payable department
  C department that initiated the requisition
  D receiving department

(d) Which of the following internal control activities is *not* usually performed in the accounts payable department?
  A Indicating the asset and expense accounts to be debited
  B Accounting for unused prenumbered purchase orders and receiving reports
  C Matching the vendor's invoice with the related receiving report
  D Approving vouchers for payment by having an authorised employee sign the vouchers

(e) In a properly-designed purchasing process, the same employee most likely would match vendors' invoices with receiving reports and also:

  A   reconcile the accounts payroll ledger
  B   cancel vendors' invoices after payment
  C   post the detailed accounts payable records
  D   recompute the calculations on vendors' invoices

9.5 The following questions relate to the business processes cycle including payroll.

(a) Which of the following procedures would be most likely to be considered a weakness in an entity's internal controls over payroll?

  A   The employee who distributes payroll cheques returns unclaimed payroll cheques to the payroll department.
  B   The personnel department sends employees' termination notices to the payroll department.
  C   A voucher for the amount of the payroll is prepared in the general accounting department based on the payroll department's payroll summary.
  D   Payroll cheques are prepared by the payroll department and signed by the treasurer.

(b) The purpose of segregating the duties of hiring personnel and distributing payroll cheques is to separate the:

  A   authorisation of transactions from the custody-related assets
  B   operational responsibility from the custody-related assets
  C   human resources function from the controllership function
  D   administrative controls from the internal accounting controls

9.6 The following question relates to the use of test data techniques. Select the best response.

(a) An auditor will use test data in order to gain certain assurances with respect to the:

  A   controls contained within the program
  B   degree of keying accuracy
  C   input data
  D   machine capacity

(b) Which of the following statements is not true of the test data approach when testing a computerised accounting system?

  A   The test data must consist of all possible valid and invalid conditions.
  B   Test data are processed by the client's computer programs under the auditor's control.
  C   The test data need only consist of those valid and invalid conditions which interest the auditor.
  D   Only one transaction of each type need be tested.

(c) An approach to testing real-time processing of a computer-based information system is known as the integrated test facility (ITF) technique. This approach involves:

  A   validating as well as editing of all input transactions entering the real-time system
  B   testing the computer hardware at the same time as test transactions enter the real-time system
  C   setting up a small set of records for a fictitious entity in the master files, and then processing dummy transactions against the fictitious entity
  D   running monthly activities simultaneously with current transactions so that the two are integrated in the result of the test

(d) An auditor who is testing IT controls in a payroll system would most likely use test data that contain conditions such as:

A time cards with invalid job numbers
B payroll cheques with unauthorised signatures
C deductions *not* authorised by employees
D overtime *not* approved by supervisors

Test of controls overview

9.7 How are tests of controls related to the evaluation of control risk?

9.8 Distinguish between the types of testing that the auditor would undertake in testing the existence of internal control versus the effectiveness and continuity of internal control.

9.9 Identify the three internal control aspects for which the auditor has to gather audit evidence for the verification of the operation of internal control.

Sufficient appropriate evidence

9.10 Identify the factors that will determine whether the auditor has obtained sufficient appropriate audit evidence to support their assessed level of control risk.

Testing controls in the revenues, receivables and receipts system

9.11 What are the two major controls for sales returns and allowances transactions?

9.12 Define lapping and kiting and explain the audit procedures used to detect these irregularities.

Testing controls in the expenditures, payables and disbursements system

9.13 Briefly describe each of the following documents or records: purchase requisition, purchase order, receiving report, vendor invoice, and voucher. Why would an entity combine all documents related to a purchase transaction into a 'voucher packet'?

9.14 List the key segregation of duties in the purchasing process. What errors or fraud can occur if such duties are not segregated?

9.15 List two inherent risk factors that directly affect the purchasing process. Why should auditors be concerned about issues such as the supply of raw materials and the volatility of prices?

Testing controls relating to contractual transactions

9.16 How do contractual transactions differ from other major classes of transactions?

Testing controls contained in the client's computer program

9.17 What are the fundamental differences between test data and an integrated test facility?

DISCUSSION PROBLEMS AND CASE STUDIES

Testing controls in the revenues, receivables and receipts system

9.18 **Basic** You have been assigned to the audit of Moroney Ltd, a large manufacturing company. The audit strategy indicates that a 'lower assessed level of control risk' strategy has been adopted. Key controls on which the team intends to rely for the revenue cycle are as follows:

1 All sales orders are taken over the phone. At the time the sale is taken the customer service officer checks that the customer is an approved customer and that the sale will not result in the customer exceeding their credit limit.

2 All sales must be followed up by a written sales order (in triplicate) before goods are shipped from the warehouse.

3 On receipt of the sales order, one copy is matched to the computer records and the customer order is flagged as 'OK to proceed' within the system. A second copy is sent to the debtors clerk and a third copy is forwarded to the warehouse.

Required

For each of the controls identified above:

(a) indicate the purpose of the control (i.e. what is the control designed to prevent or detect?);

(b) indicate the balance and assertion which this control will have an effect on in the financial report; and

(c) provide an example of one procedure which could be used to test the control.

9.19 Complex You are engaged in your first audit of Pesky Pest Control Pty Ltd for the year ended 30 June. The company began doing business in July of the previous year and provides pest control services for industrial enterprises. Additional information is as follows:

1 The office staff consists of a bookkeeper, a typist and the president, V. Tran. In addition, the company employs 20 service representatives on an hourly basis who are assigned to individual territories to make both monthly and emergency visits to customers' premises. The service representatives submit weekly time reports, which include the customer's name and the time devoted to each customer. Time charges for emergency visits are shown separately from regular monthly visits on the reports.

2 Customers are required to sign annual contracts which are prenumbered and prepared in duplicate. The original is filed in numerical order by contract anniversary date and the copy is given to the customer. The contract entitles the customer to pest control services once each month. Emergency visits are billed separately.

3 Fees for monthly services are payable in advance—quarterly, semi-annually or annually—and recorded on the books as 'income from services' when the cash is received. All payments are by cheques received by mail.

4 Prenumbered invoices for contract renewals are prepared in triplicate from information in the contract file. The original invoice is sent to the customer 20 days prior to the due date of payment, the duplicate copy is filed chronologically by due date and the triplicate copy is filed alphabetically by customer name. If payment is not received by 15 days after the due date, a cancellation notice is sent to the customer, and a copy of the notice is attached to the customer's contract. The bookkeeper notifies the service representatives of all contract cancellations and reinstatements, and requires written acknowledgment of receipt of such notices. Tran approves all cancellations and reinstatements of contracts.

5 Prenumbered invoices for emergency services are prepared weekly from information shown on the service representative's time reports. The customer is billed at 200 per cent of the service representative's hourly rate. These invoices, prepared in triplicate and distributed as shown above, are recorded on the books as 'income from services' at the billing date. Payment is due 30 days after the invoice date.

6 All remittances are received by the typist, who prepares a daily list of collections and stamps a restrictive endorsement on the cheques. A copy of the list is forwarded with the cheques to the bookkeeper, who posts the date and amount of each cheque received on the copies of the invoice in both the alphabetical and the chronological files. After posting, the copy of the invoice is transferred from the chronological file to the daily cash receipts binder, which serves as a subsidiary record for the cash receipts book. The bookkeeper totals the amounts of all remittances received, posts this total to the cash receipts book and attaches the daily remittance tapes to the paid invoices in the daily cash receipts binder.

7   The bookkeeper prepares a daily bank deposit slip and compares the total with the total amount shown on the daily remittance tapes. All remittances are deposited in the bank the day they are received. (Cash receipts from sources other than services need not be considered.)

8   The financial report is prepared on an accrual basis.

Required

List the audit procedures you would employ in the examination of the revenue from services account for the year ended 30 June.

9.20 Complex The following flowchart depicts activities relating to the sales, shipping, billing, and collection processes used by Newton Hardware, Inc.

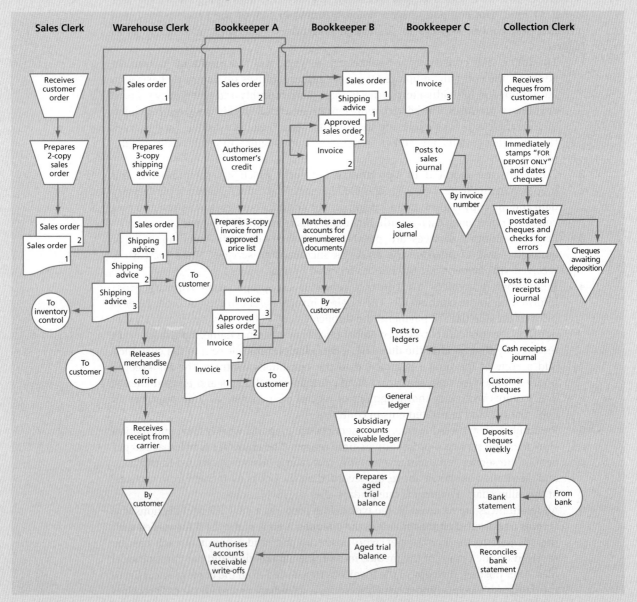

Source: Messier, 2003, p. 417.

Required

Identify the weaknesses in internal control relating to the activities of:

(a) the warehouse clerk;

(b) bookkeeper A; and

(c) the collections clerk.

Do not identify weaknesses relating to the sales clerk or bookkeepers B and C. Do not discuss recommendations concerning the correction of these weaknesses.

Testing controls in the expenditures, payables and disbursements system

9.21 Moderate You have been assigned to the audit of Carey Ltd and are currently involved in a review of control activities in the cash disbursement area. As part of your review you have noted the following procedures:

1   A prenumbered cheque requisition is prepared by the clerk for all payments.

2   The cheque requisition requires the clerk to indicate that he has performed the following procedures for each payment:

  • Checked the additions on the invoice

  • Ensured that the details on the invoice have been matched to a delivery note by the warehousing department

  • Ensured a valid purchase order exists for the goods

3   The cheque requisition together with supporting documentation (invoice and any other relevant correspondence) is forwarded to the financial controller for approval.

Required

For each of the controls identified above:

(a) indicate the purpose of the control (i.e. what is the control designed to prevent or detect?);

(b) indicate the balance and assertion which this control will have an effect on in the financial report; and

(c) provide an example of one procedure which could be used to test the control.

9.22 Complex The flowchart opposite depicts the activities relating to the purchase, receiving and account payable departments of Georgie Girl Ltd Inc.

Required

Based only on the flowchart, describe the internal control activities that most likely would provide reasonable assurance that specific internal control objectives with regards purchases and accounts payable will be achieved. Do *not* describe weaknesses in internal control. Outline how you would test these identified internal controls.

9.23 Complex In 2003 Pearson Company purchased more than $10 million worth of office equipment under its 'special' ordering system, with individual orders ranging from $5000 to $430 000. 'Special' orders entail low-volume items that have been included in an authorised user's budget. Department heads include in their annual budget requests the types of equipment and their estimated cost. The budget, which limits the types and dollar amounts of office equipment a department head can requisition, is approved at the beginning of the year by the board of directors. Department heads prepare purchase requisition forms for equipment and forward them to the purchasing department. Pearson's 'special' ordering system functions as follows:

• *Purchasing:* Upon receiving a purchase requisition, one of five buyers verifies that the person requesting the equipment is a department head. The buyer selects the appropriate vendor by searching the various vendor catalogues on file. The buyer then phones the vendor, requests a price quotation, and gives the vendor a verbal order. A prenumbered purchase order is processed with the original sent to the vendor, a copy

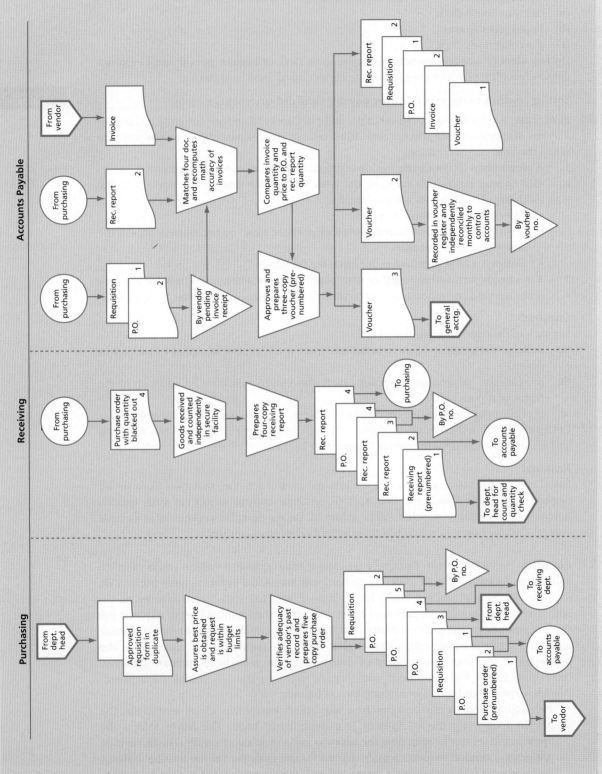

Accounts Payable

From vendor → Invoice

From purchasing → Rec. report 2

From purchasing → Requisition 1 / P.O. 2

Matches four doc. and recomputes math accuracy of invoices

By vendor pending invoice receipt

Compares invoice quantity and price to P.O. and rec. report quantity

Approves and prepares three-copy voucher (pre-numbered)

Rec. report 2 / Requisition 1 / P.O. 2 / Invoice 1 / Voucher

Voucher 2 → Recorded in voucher register and independently reconciled monthly to control accounts → By voucher no.

Voucher 3 → To general acctg.

Receiving

From purchasing → Purchase order with quantity blacked out 4 → Goods received and counted independently in secure facility → Prepares four-copy receiving report

Rec. report 4 / P.O. → To purchasing / By P.O. no.
Rec. report 4
Rec. report 3 → To accounts payable
Receiving report (prenumbered) 1 → To dept. head for count and quantity check
Receiving report 2

Purchasing

From dept. head → Approved requisition form in duplicate → Assures best price is obtained and request is within budget limits → Verifies adequacy of vendor's past record and prepares five-copy purchase order

Requisition 2 / P.O. 5 → By P.O. no.
P.O. 4 → From dept. head → To receiving dept.
P.O. 3 → To accounts payable
Requisition 1 / P.O.
Purchase order (prenumbered) 1 / Requisition 2 → To vendor

Source: Messier, 2003, p. 457.

to the department head, a copy to receiving, a copy to accounts payable and a copy filed in the open requisition file. When the buyer is orally informed by the receiving department that the item has been received, the buyer transfers the purchase order from the unfilled file to the filled file. Once a month the buyer reviews the unfilled file to follow up on and expedite open orders.

- *Receiving:* The receiving department receives a copy of the purchase order. When equipment is received, the receiving clerk stamps the purchase order with the date received and, if applicable, in red pen prints any differences between the quantity shown on the purchase order and the quantity received. The receiving clerk forwards the stamped purchase order and equipment to the requisitioning department head and orally notifies the purchasing department.
- *Accounts payable:* Upon receiving a purchase order, the accounts payable clerk files it in the open purchase order file. When a vendor invoice is received, the invoice is matched with the applicable purchase order, and a payable is set up by debiting the equipment account of the department requesting the items. Unpaid invoices are filed by due date, and at the due date a cheque is prepared. The invoice and purchase order are filed by purchase order number in a paid invoice file, and the cheque is then forwarded to the treasurer for signature.
- *Treasurer:* Cheques received daily from the accounts payable department are sorted into two groups: those over $10 000 and those $10 000 and less. Cheques for $10 000 and less are machine signed. The cashier keeps the key and signature plate to the cheque-signing machine and records all use of the cheque-signing machine. All cheques over $10 000 are signed by the treasurer or the controller.

Required
(a) Prepare a flowchart of Pearson Company's purchasing and cash disbursements system.
(b) Outline the tests of controls that may be undertaken for Pearson Company's purchasing and cash disbursement system. Consider the use of test data techniques.
(c) Describe the internal control weaknesses relating to purchase of and payments for 'special' orders of Pearson Company for the purchasing, receiving, accounts payable, and treasurer functions.

9.24 **Complex** Pearce, CPA, prepared the flowchart opposite, which portrays the raw materials purchasing function of one of Pearce's clients, a medium-sized manufacturing company, from the preparation of initial documents through the vouching of invoices for payment. The flowchart represents a portion of the work performed on the audit engagement to evaluate internal control.

Required
Identify and explain the control strengths and weaknesses evident from the flowchart. Include the internal control strengths and weaknesses resulting from activities performed or not performed. What tests of controls will be undertaken? (Consider the use of test data techniques.) All documents are prenumbered.

Testing controls relating to contractual transactions

6 primary learning objective

9.25 **Moderate** We Build Pty Ltd (WB) is a small company that builds duplex units for the rental market. The usual arrangement is that WB retains ownership of the units and leases the buildings to a wholly owned subsidiary, We Rent Pty Ltd (WR), for the expected life of the building. WR then rents to occupiers for periods of between 12 months and five years, with an option to renew. The usual length of time a tenant occupies the buildings is three years.

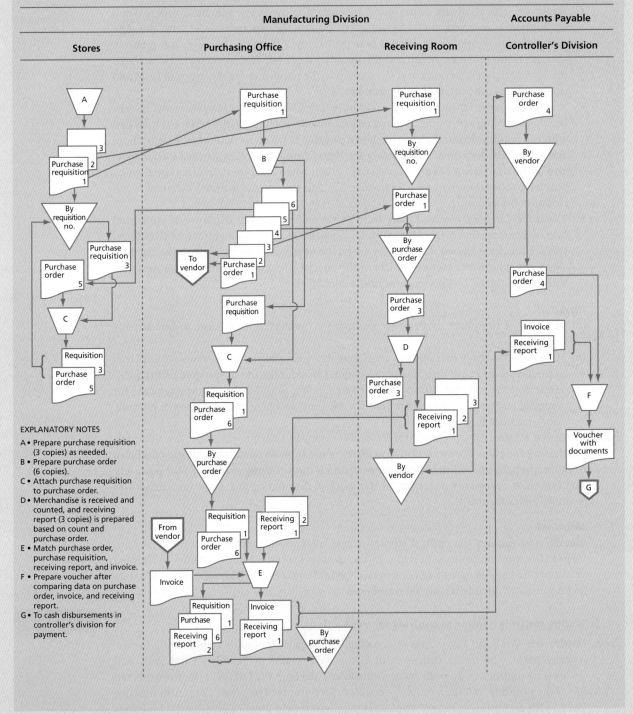

Medium-sized Manufacturing Company
Flowchart of Raw Materials Purchasing Function

Date _____

Prepared by _____

Approved by _____

Manufacturing Division			Accounts Payable
Stores	Purchasing Office	Receiving Room	Controller's Division

EXPLANATORY NOTES

A • Prepare purchase requisition (3 copies) as needed.
B • Prepare purchase order (6 copies).
C • Attach purchase requisition to purchase order.
D • Merchandise is received and counted, and receiving report (3 copies) is prepared based on count and purchase order.
E • Match purchase order, purchase requisition, receiving report, and invoice.
F • Prepare voucher after comparing data on purchase order, invoice, and receiving report.
G • To cash disbursements in controller's division for payment.

Source: Messier, 2003, p. 512

You have been assigned to the audit of the WB group and are currently preparing a program for the audit of the leasing transactions.

Required

For each of WB and WR, indicate three procedures which could be used to audit the leasing transactions.

9.26 Complex An auditor's audit work papers contain a narrative description of a segment of the Croyden Factory payroll system and an accompanying flowchart, on page 446.

The control activities of the internal control system with respect to the personnel department function well and are *not* included in the accompanying flowchart.

At the beginning of each work week, Payroll Clerk No. 1 reviews the payroll department files to determine the employment status of factory employees, and then prepares time cards and distributes them as each individual arrives at work. This payroll clerk, who is also responsible for custody of the signature stamp machine, verifies the identity of each payee before delivering signed cheques to the supervisor.

At the end of each week, the supervisor distributes payroll cheques for the preceding week. At the same time, the supervisor reviews the current week's employee time cards, notes the regular and overtime hours worked on a summary form and initials the time cards. The supervisor then delivers all time cards and unclaimed payroll cheques to Payroll Clerk No. 2.

Required

(a) Using the description above and the flowchart opposite, list the deficiencies in internal control.

(b) What inquiries should be made with respect to clarifying the existence of *possible additional deficiencies* in internal control?

(c) Outline the tests of controls that could be undertaken in verifying payroll.

Note: Do not discuss the control activities of the personnel department.

Testing controls contained in the client's computer program

9.27 Complex You have been assigned to conduct an audit of your client's database system. Through previous work you know that the system includes a centralised database shared by all users. Access to the database is direct by the users through remote terminals and is controlled by the database software system. The IT department includes a manager of operations and a manager of computer programming, both of whom report to the IT director.

Your preliminary understanding of the database system includes the following points:

1 There are no restrictions regarding the type of transactions or access to the online terminals.

2 All users and IT personnel have access to the extensive system documentation.

3 Before being entered into the user authorisation table, user passwords and access codes are established by user management and approved by the manager of computer programming.

4 The manager of computer programming established the database directory and controls it. Users approve any changes in data definition.

5 User requests for data are validated by the system against a transactions-conflict matrix to ensure that data is transmitted only to authorised users.

6 System access requires the users to input their passwords, and terminal activity logs are maintained.

7 Input data are edited for reasonableness and completeness, transaction control totals are generated, and transactions logs are maintained.

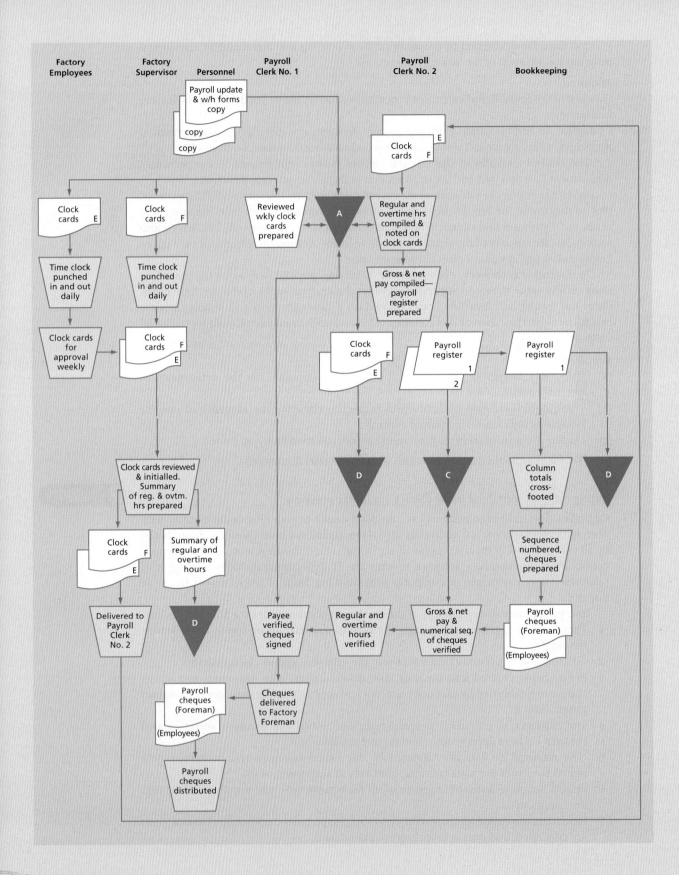

Factory Employees	Factory Supervisor	Personnel	Payroll Clerk No. 1	Payroll Clerk No. 2	Bookkeeping

Payroll update & w/h forms copy
copy
copy

Clock cards E
F

Clock cards E

Clock cards F

Reviewed wkly clock cards prepared

A

Regular and overtime hrs compiled & noted on clock cards

Time clock punched in and out daily

Time clock punched in and out daily

Gross & net pay compiled—payroll register prepared

Clock cards for approval weekly

Clock cards F
E

Clock cards F
E

Payroll register 1
2

Payroll register 1

Clock cards reviewed & initialled. Summary of reg. & ovtm. hrs prepared

D

C

Column totals cross-footed

D

Clock cards F
E

Summary of regular and overtime hours

Sequence numbered, cheques prepared

Delivered to Payroll Clerk No. 2

D

Payee verified, cheques signed

Regular and overtime hours verified

Gross & net pay & numerical seq. of cheques verified

Payroll cheques (Foreman)
(Employees)

Payroll cheques (Foreman)
(Employees)

Cheques delivered to Factory Foreman

Payroll cheques distributed

8 Processing control totals are generated and reconciled to changes in the database.

9 Output is reconciled to transaction and input control totals. The resulting reports are printed and placed in a bin outside the IT room for pickup by the users at their convenience.

10 Back-up copies of the database are generated daily and stored in the file library area, access to which is restricted to IT personnel.

Required

(a) From the results of your preliminary review, describe five controls in the system.

(b) List five specific audit steps you would include in your audit program to determine whether transaction input is properly authorised.

(c) Explain how you may use test data to gather audit evidence in this system.

(d) Evaluate the relative strengths of the general and application controls for the database system.

CONTINUOUS CASE STUDY

9.28 Complex This is a continuation of question 8.30. It may be completed independently of that question.

You are currently involved in the audit of HomeChef Pty Ltd (HC), a large private company operating in the boutique food and beverages market. The company has a balance date of 31 December. To maximise audit efficiency, the audit partner has decided to use the work of the internal audit group (IAG).

The manager of IAG has now given you a copy of the work performed to ensure payments made to creditors throughout the year were in accordance with procedures laid down in the Accounting Manual.

The relevant work papers are reproduced below:

Work paper IA 4   *Prepared by: A*
       Reviewed by: M
       Date: 3.2.02

Objective:

To examine payments made to creditors throughout the year and determine whether the procedures laid down in the Accounting Manual have been properly followed.

Work performed:

Payments were selected from the cheque register of creditors for the year ended 31 December. A sample size of 60 was determined and cheques were selected randomly.

A copy of the latest Accounting Manual was obtained. Evidence of control activities carried out on the payments was compared to the control activities laid down in the Accounting Manual and any exceptions noted.

Results:

A summary of the results obtained is given below:

Payments which showed evidence that all control activities had been followed	40
Payments which were not matched to an approved purchase order; however, all other documentation was attached[3]	5
Payments which were not made to an approved supplier[3]	5
Payments which were authorised by a second party, although this was not required[1]	2
Payments which had no supporting documents attached[2]	5
Payments which did not bear evidence that computation on creditors' invoices had been checked[3]	3
Total sample size	60

1   Breach due to new financial accountant being unaware of firm policy—now remedied.
2   Payments relate to rental on the firm's leased printer and photocopier. The cheque requisition referred to a cheque requisition number that contained a copy of the original lease agreements. No change in the amount has occurred.
3   No explanation given.

Required
(a) Discuss the implications of the errors noted by the internal auditor.
(b) What additional work do you believe should now be performed?

CHAPTER 10

SUBSTANTIVE TESTS TRANSACTIONS AND BALANCES

LEARNING OBJECTIVES

After studying this chapter you should be able to:

1 identify and distinguish between tests of controls and substantive tests of transactions, and also between substantive tests of transactions and substantive tests of balances;

2 identify the financial report assertions associated with both tests of transactions and tests of balances and how these relate to substantive audit procedures;

explain the specific audit objectives and the common audit procedures traditionally used to achieve those objectives for:

3 cash, cash receipts and cash payments;

4 accounts receivable;

5 purchases and sales, and inventories;

6 accounts payable and cash payments;

7 non-current assets;

8 liabilities and owners' equity;

9 identify the different substantive test approaches that may be used for account balances included in the income statement; and

10 describe and understand the use of computer-assisted audit techniques in substantive testing.

...lances are used
...esired level of
...ntive tests of
...ely verify the
...tive tests of
...e the ending
...substantive
...nce of the
...balance or
...monetary
..., of factors,
... the financial report is
... or to understate the balance. In
...ng audit programs for account balances, the
auditor is concerned with whether the balance is
overstated or understated by a material amount.

Tests of controls and substantive tests of transactions

and balances are two of the main evidence-gathering procedures, and the auditor needs to co-ordinate the audit approach detailed in the audit program to ensure that the most efficient and effective combination of audit procedures is used.

No matter what audit strategy is adopted, the auditor must undertake substantive tests. In audits of the financial reports of small businesses, many auditors rely almost exclusively on them. The following discussion of substantive tests considers their objectives. For each major financial report component, the specific objectives are explained and the common procedures used to achieve them are discussed. The components are considered in the following order: cash; accounts receivable; inventories; accounts payable; non-current assets and liabilities and owners' equity; and the income statement.

Relevantguidance

RELATIONSHIP BETWEEN EVIDENCE-GATHERING PROCEDURES

The auditor has to obtain sufficient appropriate evidence to be able to draw reasonable conclusions on which to base the audit opinion (AUS 502/ISA 500). Tests of controls (discussed in Chapter 9) and substantive tests of transactions and balances (discussed in this chapter) are two of the main evidence-gathering procedures, and the auditor selects the most efficient and effective combination of audit procedures that allows them to achieve the audit objective.

As outlined in Chapter 5, the auditor uses assertions for classes of transactions and events, account balances, and presentation and disclosures to help them in their risk assessment of material misstatement, and to direct their audit procedures to the assessment of these risks.

The management assertions about classes of transactions and events (that are therefore relevant to the income statement) that serve as a structure for risk assessment and evidence-collection procedures are:

(i) *Occurrence*—transactions and events that have been recorded have occurred and pertain to the entity

(ii) *Completeness*—all transactions and events that should have been recorded hav[e been] recorded

(iii) *Accuracy*—amounts and other data relating to recorded transactions and events have be[en] recorded appropriately

(iv) *Cutoff*—transactions and events have been recorded in the correct accounting period

(v) *Classification*—transactions and events have been recorded in the proper accounts

As outlined in Chapter 9, as most internal controls are structured around transaction or event flows, the auditor uses the most efficient and effective combination of tests of controls and substantive tests of transactions. Tests of controls were discussed in Chapter 9, and the relationship between substantive tests of transactions and balances is discussed in what follows.

The management assertions about account balances at period end (and therefore relevant to the balance sheet) that serve as a structure for risk assessment and evidence-collection procedures are:

(i) *Existence*—assets, liabilities, and equity interests exist

(ii) *Rights and obligations*—the entity holds or controls the rights to assets, and liabilities are the obligations of the entity

(iii) *Completeness*—all assets, liabilities and equity interests that should have been recorded have been recorded

(iv) *Valuation and allocation*—assets, liabilities and equity interests are included in the financial report at appropriate amounts and any resulting valuation or allocation adjustments are appropriately recorded

The amount of substantive testing of balances that needs to be undertaken is directly affected by the testing of controls that has been undertaken, as is the basis of the audit risk model described in detail in Chapter 5. There are two types of substantive testing: substantive testing of transactions and substantive testing of balances. Substantive testing of balances is where the auditor tests amounts resulting from the summation of a number of transactions (for example, amounts receivable is increased by credit sales and decreased by associated receipts of cash—the summation of these transactions can be either at the total amounts receivable balance or at the individual debtor balance). As account balances are the sum of related transactions, the extent of one type of substantive testing will reduce the extent of testing required for the other type of substantive testing. The relationship between substantive tests of transactions and substantive tests of balances is discussed later in this learning objective.

The third and final category of management assertions is presentation and disclosure. The four assertions are:

(i) *Occurrence and rights and obligations*—disclosed events, transactions, and other matters have occurred and pertain to the entity

(ii) *Completeness*—all disclosures that should have been included in the financial report have been included

(iii) *Classification and understandability*—financial information is appropriately presented and described, and disclosures are clearly expressed

(iv) *Accuracy and valuation*—financial and other information is disclosed fairly and at appropriate amounts

As these assertions require the auditor to consider the disclosures in the draft financial report, the auditor's consideration of these assertions is discussed in Chapter 12 under the section 'Review of the finanical report and other information contained in the annual report'.

scussed in Chapter 9, evaluate the reliance to be placed on the internal control
of controls do not directly measure monetary error in accounting records.
be performed to detect material misstatements in the financial report
substantive tests of transactions and balances, and analytical procedures
auditor's judgment of the likelihood of monetary errors, based on risk
nd tests of controls, determines the extent of substantive tests considered

provide the underlying evidence for financial reports. The auditor's
making **substantive tests of transactions** is to obtain reasonable assurance that the
accounting records are accurate and reliable. The auditor's approach in substantive tests of
transactions is to inspect underlying documents, to trace the flow of transactions through the
system and to recompute for clerical accuracy.

The direction of the trace determines the objective to be satisfied. For example, **tracing** from a
source document to the accounting record provides evidence of completeness of the recording of
transactions, that is, it detects errors of understatement. Tracing from the accounting record to the
source document (commonly called **vouching** to the source document) provides evidence of
occurrence of the transactions, that is, it detects errors of overstatement. Usually some tests are made
in both directions. The extent of testing in a particular direction depends on the auditor's judgment
of the likelihood of error. When an error is detected the auditor needs to consider the cause of the
error and determine whether any change is called for in the planned nature and extent of testing.

Dual-purpose tests

Since both tests of controls and substantive tests of transactions can involve inspection of the
same documents for individual transactions, they are usually performed simultaneously on
the sample of documents chosen. Although several tests can be performed simultaneously on the
same transaction documents, it is important to be specific about the purpose of particular
procedures. **Dual-purpose tests** should be narrowly defined to include only those tests that are
specifically planned to provide direct evidence of both controls and substantive matters.

In a broad sense, all audit tests are dual-purpose tests. Whenever an error is discovered when
undertaking substantive tests of transactions, there is some evidence of a breakdown in controls.
Whenever no errors are discovered, there is indirect evidence that controls are operating. This is
the reason that some auditors say the evaluation of controls is not final until the audit is
completed. Substantive audit tests can always provide some additional evidence of the
functioning of controls.

In a true dual-purpose test, different procedures are performed to satisfy different objectives,
but they are performed using the same documents at approximately the same time. For example,
controls in the processing of purchase invoices may require a clerk to compare the data with
supporting documents, check the classification in the purchases journal, recompute amounts and
initial the invoice to indicate performance of the procedures. The auditor inspects documents for
the clerk's initials—the test of controls—and recomputes and retraces the clerk's other procedures,
which satisfies several substantive objectives.

On the other hand, if controls are absent or not functioning, there will be no testing of controls,
and more extensive substantive testing (of either transactions or balances) will be necessary. Thus,

in practice, a sample of transactions selected to test controls will virtually always be a dual-purpose test, or the sample of transactions may be selected for substantive tests only.

Relationship between substantive tests of transactions and substantive tests of balances

Substantive tests of transactions can also be distinguished from substantive tests of balances. If the account balance is affected by many relatively small transactions, the auditor designs substantive tests of balances directed to selected items (e.g. individual customers, inventory items) which are an aggregate of a number of transactions and which aggregate to create the ending account balance. This commonly occurs for the accounts receivable and inventory balances. Consider the following extract of the accounts receivable subsidiary ledger:

Customer	Year-end balance	Transactions for Able	
Able	5000	Sale	2000
		Receipt	(1000)
		Sale	4000
Baker	500		
Chan	1000		

The balance of accounts receivable would be composed of the balances of many customers. Consider customer Able, whose ending year balance of $5000 is composed of three transactions. If the auditor verifies the $5000 ending balance (such as through confirmation procedures discussed later in this chapter) this is a substantive test of balances. If the auditor verifies the dollar value of the individual transactions comprising the $5000 (such as by verifying sales invoices and remittance advices associated with cash receipts transactions) this is a substantive test of transactions.

Tests of transactions (both tests of controls and substantive tests of transactions) are usually performed for major classes of transactions that are repetitive and large in volume. The major classes of transactions—sales, purchases, cash receipts and cash disbursements—affect balance sheet accounts in the following manner:

Accounts receivable	Cash	Accounts payable
Beginning balance	Beginning balance	Beginning balance
Additions (sales DR)		Additions (purchases CR)
Reductions (cash receipts CR) ⟷	Additions (cash receipts DR)	
	Reductions (cash disbursements CR) ⟷	Reductions (cash disbursements DR)
Ending balance	Ending balance	Ending balance

In the abstract, if beginning balances were tested in the previous year, it would be possible to indirectly test the major transactions by substantive tests of balances of these balance sheet accounts. There might be other sources of cash receipts and cash disbursements, but they would be substantiated by direct tests of balances of the balance sheet accounts affected. Substantive tests of balances of balance sheet accounts are generally preferred because there are fewer items in the ending balance than there are transactions that affect the balance, and there is generally more persuasive evidence available to support the ending balance.

Note also that the substantive tests of balances of balance sheet accounts indirectly test the income statement account balances (sales and expenditure). For example, the testing of accounts receivable will verify the sales that gave rise to this asset. Taking one step back from this abstraction, it is obvious that even in a highly condensed income statement there is normally more than one category of expenditures. This means some tests of recording accuracy as to account classification would be necessary. However, it is still possible to plan an audit that consists primarily of substantive tests of balances of balance sheet accounts, with selected tests of transactions for particular specific audit assertions.

This kind of audit—with emphasis on substantive tests of balances of balance sheet accounts—is, in fact, the approach typically used for small businesses. It is also used when a large entity has material deficiencies in the processing of particular classes of transactions. This approach is called the substantive approach to an audit. Generally, it is the most efficient and effective means of auditing the financial report of a small business. It is especially efficient if the auditor designs effective analytical tests for those specific audit objectives, such as income statement, account classification and those related to the completeness assertion, that are not achieved by substantive tests of balances. For a large business, however, the substantive approach is often not cost effective for the following reasons:

- The number of items in ending balances, while still fewer than the number of transactions that affect the balances, is relatively large.
- The accounting system for processing major classes of transactions is generally well designed and produces more reliable accounting data because management in a large entity has to rely extensively on the accounting data to monitor and control the business.
- There are generally enough employees to achieve effective separation of duties.

In these circumstances, by testing the processing of transactions the auditor can restrict the substantive tests of balances that would otherwise have been undertaken.

Quick review

1. Dual-purpose tests are specifically planned to provide direct evidence concerning both controls and substantive matters in order to satisfy different audit objectives. They are performed using the same documents at approximately the same time.
2. In practice, if documents are selected to test controls they will virtually always be examined to achieve substantive testing objectives and the tests are classed as dual-purpose tests. Documents may also be selected with no intention of testing controls (for substantive purposes only) and these are classed as substantive tests of transactions.
3. Account balances are composed of a series of transactions. It is possible to substantively verify either the transactions comprising the account balance or the account balance itself.

FINANCIAL REPORT ASSERTIONS AND SUBSTANTIVE AUDIT PROCEDURES

The auditor develops specific audit procedures to evaluate the risk of material misstatement for classes of transactions and events and account balances of financial report assertions introduced in Chapter 5 and earlier in this chapter.

Assertions about transactions and events (income statement accounts) and audit procedures

- **Occurrence** is concerned with whether transactions that generated financial report accounts actually occurred. The focus is on whether all transactions recorded during a period are *bona fide* transactions and that no fictitious transactions have been recorded. This assertion is concerned with overstatement—making sure that nothing has been recorded and reported to inflate any account balance. Verification of transaction occurrence includes two subordinate objectives. First, the transactions should be supported by proper internal control and the auditor should evaluate the existing internal control underlying each of the various types of transactions recorded during the period. Second, the auditor must ascertain that proper documentary support exists to validate the transactions creating the various account balances. The extent of documentary support required varies with the nature of the client and the transaction, but some documentary support should exist for all transactions.

- **Completeness** In designing audit tests for the assertion of completeness, the auditor identifies evidence indicating items that should be included in the class of transactions and investigates whether they are, in fact, included. A logical procedure is to trace from documentation created when transactions originate, or other evidence of origination, to the recording of the transactions in the accounting records. In other words, the direction of the test is the opposite of that for objectives relating to the occurrence assertion. Note that these are tests for understatement of transactions and events.

- **Accuracy** Accuracy relates to determining the appropriate recording of the dollar value and other information of transactions. This means tracing the specific details of the transactions, or recalculating the amount associated with events such as a depreciation expense, and ensuring these details are correctly recorded in the accounting records.

- **Cutoff** Cutoff involves checking that transactions are recorded in the correct period. It involves selecting transactions around the end of the accounting period and tracing their details to the accounting record to verify that the last transactions for the accounting period are recorded in the accounting period's accounting records, and that the first transactions for the next accounting period are correctly excluded.

- **Classification** In designing substantive tests for the assertion of classification, the auditor considers the appropriate classification of the item in the financial report. Thus the auditor will include in the audit program specific procedures to examine whether transactions (such as cost of goods sold or repairs and maintenance) have been appropriately classified.

Assertions about account balances at period end (balance sheet accounts) and audit procedures

- **Existence** In designing substantive tests for the assertion of existence, the auditor selects from items contained in the accounting records and obtains evidence that supports them. The logical procedures to accomplish such objectives include physical examination, confirmation and vouching. Note that these are tests for overstatement of the balance.

As shown in Example 10.1, procedures to achieve the objective relating to existence for accounts receivable should also aid in achieving the objective relating to occurrence for sales. Directly testing the accounts receivable balance for overstatement (existence) simultaneously indirectly tests the occurrence of sales.

EXAMPLE 10.1 Relationship between existence and occurrence

The relationship between specific audit objectives for related account balances can be demonstrated by an example from the sales cycle. The financial report assertion of 'existence or occurrence' is translated into specific audit objectives as follows:

Financial report assertion	Specific audit objectives	
	Balance Sheet (Existence)	Income Statement (Occurrence)
Existence or occurrence	Accounts receivable are authentic obligations owed by customers at the balance date	Reported sales to customers actually occurred during the period covered by the profit and loss statement

---

■ **Rights and obligations** In designing substantive tests for the assertion of rights and obligations, the auditor must ascertain that the assets are owned/controlled by the client and that the liabilities are those of the client. Although possession may be accepted as evidence for ownership of some assets, the auditor must take further steps in ascertaining that many of the recorded assets are in fact owned/controlled by the client (Example 10.2).

The auditor may also need to obtain information on the terms of the agreement between the parties to the exchange transaction that created the right or obligation. Common procedures used to accomplish such objectives are inquiry and inspection of contracts, agreements, minutes and similar documentation. Many of these are called general procedures because they are not directed to a specific account balance. For example, reading the minutes of meetings of the board of directors is a general procedure used to obtain evidence relevant to many account balances that specific transactions pertain to the entity.

EXAMPLE 10.2 Difficult areas associated with rights and obligations

Inventories held by the client under consignment arrangements exist, but may not be owned by the client. The auditor must therefore determine that inventories as represented on the balance sheet do not contain significant amounts of consigned inventories owned by others. It is also possible that inventories out on consignment at distributors at the time of counting stock may still be owned by the audit client at the time of the audit, as identified by the terms of the consignment. The auditor will have to carefully consider rightful ownership of the inventory in these circumstances.

■ **Completeness** In designing substantive tests for the assertion of completeness, the auditor identifies evidence indicating items that should be included in the account balance and investigates whether they are in fact included. A logical procedure is to trace from documentary evidence of origination, to the account balance. In other words, the direction of the test is the opposite of that for objectives related to the existence assertion. Note that these are tests for understatement of the balance.

- **Valuation and allocation** In designing substantive tests for the assertion of valuation and allocation, the auditor needs to consider the basis of valuation of the asset or liability in terms of approved accounting standards and the basis of any allocation of this valuation across accounting periods. If the basis is historical cost less accumulated depreciation or amortisation, the likely procedure to accomplish the audit objective of valuation is vouching the cost to historical records and the likely procedure for allocation is inquiries to determine the basis and recomputation of the depreciable amount. If the basis is net realisable value, or something similar, the likely procedures are inquiry and analytical procedures to assess the reasonableness of management's estimation, or inspection of external information on market prices. Naturally, omission of items (completeness) or inclusion of improper items (existence) will also affect valuation. However, because the cause of these types of misstatements is usually different, they are considered separately under those specific assertions.

Nature of the item and available evidence

The nature of the item has an important influence on the auditor's selection of audit procedures. For example, the preceding discussion indicates that, for audit objectives related to the existence assertion, likely audit procedures are physical examination, confirmation and vouching. For the procedure of physical examination to be useful, the item must have a physical existence and be present. An auditor can count cash or securities on hand, but must confirm an accounts receivable balance with a customer or cash in a bank account with the client's bank.

Another aspect of the nature of the item is the size and volume of transactions during the period covered by the financial report. If an account balance is affected by only a few large transactions, the auditor may design substantive tests directed to the individual transactions that increase or decrease the balance (assuming the beginning balance was substantiated last year) in order to substantiate the ending balance. For example, account balances for property and equipment, long-term debt and shareholders' equity are often of this nature. This is referred to as, and understood by auditors to be, a substantive test of balances utilising a transactions approach. Thus substantive tests of balances by the transactions approach can be distinguished from tests of transactions (as outlined earlier in this chapter) by identifying whether the concern is with specific isolated transactions or with an entire class of transactions.

The available evidence also influences the selection of procedures to achieve audit objectives. For example, to confirm accounts receivable with individual customers, the auditor needs a detailed listing of the amount owed by each customer. The availability of evidence may influence the auditor's selection of procedures to achieve specific audit objectives. If a common audit procedure cannot be applied because the evidence is unavailable, an alternative procedure may be selected. Thus, for example, if the auditor was unable to confirm the existence of an outstanding balance with a debtor, the existence of this balance may be confirmed by a subsequent payment and by inspecting accompanying documentation for the amount of that balance.

Quick review

1 Tests of transactions and events consist of tests of controls and substantive tests of transactions and are aimed at gathering audit evidence for the following assertions by management:
- occurrence, which means that transactions and events that have been recorded have occurred and pertain to the entity;

- completeness, which means that all transactions and events that should have been recorded have been recorded;
- accuracy, which means that amounts and other data relating to recorded transactions and events have been recorded appropriately;
- cutoff, which means that transactions and events have been recorded in the correct accounting period;
- classification, which means that transactions and events have been recorded in the proper accounts.

2 Substantive tests of balances are audit tests that substantiate account balances at period end. They will be affected by the amount of tests of controls and substantive tests of transactions that are undertaken. They are aimed at gathering audit evidence for the following assertions:
- existence, which means that assets, liabilities, and equity interests exist;
- rights and obligations, which means the entity holds or controls the rights to assets, and liabilities are the obligations of the entity;
- completeness, which means that all assets, liabilities and equity interests that should have been recorded have been recorded;
- valuation and allocation, which means that assets, liabilities and equity interests are included in the financial report at appropriate amounts and any resulting valuation or allocation adjustments are appropriately recorded.

CASH, CASH RECEIPTS AND CASH PAYMENTS

The account balance cash is directly affected by both the cash receipts and cash payments systems. As these are both routine and major transaction systems the auditor may have to undertake tests of controls of both these systems (discussed in Chapter 9). The auditor would be most worried about the assertions of *occurrence* and *completeness* of transactions when undertaking substantive testing of these transactions systems. *Accuracy* of the dollar value will become an assertion of concern if transactions involve foreign currencies.

The essential feature of substantive tests of the cash balance is substantiation of the client's bank reconciliations to achieve specific audit objectives related to *existence* and *completeness*. Most cash receipts and cash payments pass through the client's bank accounts, and thus the cash balance at year-end should reflect what has flowed through those bank accounts. *Valuation and allocation* may become an assertion of concern if the cash balance at year-end includes amounts converted from foreign currencies. Thus, most of the direct tests of the cash balance make use of information obtained directly from banks. Usually, cash on hand is clearly immaterial and not counted. However, in industries that require substantial amounts of cash on hand, such as banks or casinos, a cash count may be an important and time-consuming procedure.

It may be necessary to undertake both tests of transactions and tests of balances. Some errors that ultimately affect cash may be better assessed by tests of controls and substantive tests of transactions. For example, not invoicing a customer, invoicing the wrong amount, paying a supplier's invoice twice or paying for goods or services not received are not detected by substantive tests of cash balances. However, errors confined to cash receipts and cash payments may be detected in tests of cash transactions or by cash balance procedures. For example, omission of a cheque from recorded cash payments or inclusion of cash received after year-end in cash receipts of the current period might be detected by examining cash transactions or testing bank reconciliations.

Assertions, objectives and procedures

The financial report assertions, specific audit objectives and common audit procedures traditionally used to achieve the objectives for auditing cash are summarised in Table 10.1 overleaf. The primary procedures are:

■ confirmation of balances and related information for all general bank accounts; and
■ tests of the client's bank reconciliations.

General procedures and scanning aim to identify restrictions on cash or cash commitments arising from such things as escrow accounts (monies kept in the custody of a third party until some condition has been fulfilled) or compensating balance arrangements. Generally, valuation of cash is not a significant concern unless the company engages in foreign currency transactions. Rights and obligations to cash are generally established by the procedures used to achieve objectives related to existence, completeness and valuation and allocation.

Confirmation of bank balances

The auditor commonly confirms the year-end cash balance by direct correspondence with all banks with which the client has had accounts during the period. Confirmation procedures provide evidence that the cash in the balance sheet exists at the balance date and that it is owned by the entity and is not restricted or committed. Audit guidance on bank confirmation procedures is provided by AGS 1002, 'Bank Confirmation Requests' (no equivalent international guidance). **Bank confirmation requests** ask a bank to provide independent confirmation of the audit client's account balances and other information held by the bank on behalf of the client, including securities, treasury management instruments and documents. Two standard bank confirmation request forms have been developed in conjunction with the Australian Bankers' Association and are recommended for use by auditors:

1 **Bank Confirmation—Audit Request (General)**   The information contained on this confirmation relates to the normal banking activities and is used to confirm cash. A standard form is contained in Appendix 1 to AGS 1002 (IAPS 1000).
2 **Bank Confirmation—Audit Request (Treasury Operations)** The information to be confirmed or requested in this confirmation relates to the entity's treasury operations and use of treasury management instruments. A standard form is contained in Appendix 2 to AGS 1002.

The standard Bank Confirmation—Audit Request (General) requests the following:

■ Details of all account balances in favour of the client at a certain date (usually balance date). This includes details of any current accounts, interest-bearing deposits, foreign currency accounts, convertible certificates of deposit and money market accounts.
■ Details of all account balances owed by the client to the bank at a certain date (usually balance date) in respect of overdraft accounts, bank loans and term loans, and details of repayment terms.
■ Promissory notes and bills of exchange held for collection on behalf of the audit client.
■ The audit client's other liabilities to the bank.
■ Items held as security for the audit client's liabilities to the bank.
■ Accounts opened or closed during the 12 months prior to confirmation date.
■ Any sealed packets, locked boxes or security packets held on behalf of the audit client.
■ All available unused limits and facilities as at confirmation date.
■ Any other details relating to any financial relationships not dealt with under the above points.

TABLE 10.1 Assertions, objectives and substantive procedures for cash balances

Financial report assertion	Specific audit objective	Common substantive audit procedures to achieve objectives
Assertions about classes of transactions and events (cash receipts and cash payments)		
Occurrence	The transactions giving rise to cash receipts and cash payments occurred during the period.	• Sight supporting documentation. For cash receipts, sight remittance advice; for cash payments, sight documents supporting payment
Completeness	All transactions and events giving rise to cash receipts and cash payments that should have been recorded have been recorded	• Sequence check of transaction details, remittance advices and cheques
Accuracy	Cash receipts and payments are recorded in the correct amount.	• Sight supporting document to verify dollar amount of transactions
Cutoff	Cash receipts and payments are recorded in the correct period	• Check last cash receipts and cash payment recorded before balance date and first cash receipts and cash payments recorded after balance date are recorded in the correct period
Classification	Cash receipts and payments are recorded in the correct accounts	• Check that cash receipts and cash payments recorded correctly in accordance with the chart of accounts
Assertions about account balances (cash)		
Existence	Cash in the balance sheet exists at the balance date	• Bank confirmation • Tests of bank reconciliations
Rights and obligations	Cash in the balance sheet is owned by the entity and not restricted or committed	• Bank confirmation • General procedures
Completeness	Cash in the balance sheet includes all cash items at the balance date	• Tests of bank reconciliations
Valuation and allocation	Cash in the balance sheet is stated at the correct amount	• Tests of bank reconciliations • Test conversion rates for any foreign currency balances

The auditor should complete all known details on the confirmation request before forwarding three copies to the bank. The bank is required to ensure that all details supplied are as at the confirmation date, to list all relevant information from details contained in its records and to confirm the details provided by the auditor as to correctness. Any variation is marked in red on all copies, and any information not included on the confirmation request by the auditor is in[...] in red. All three copies of the confirmation are to be signed: the original is returned directly to [...] auditor, the duplicate forwarded to the client and the triplicate copy retained by the bank.

The standard form contains a disclaimer that the certificate has been completed from records held at the branch level. The bank is therefore unable to warrant the correctness of that information and thus disclaims all liability. The effect of the disclaimer is discussed in AGS 1002.09–.10. While the disclaimer may limit the liability of the bank to the auditor, the legal advisers of the Auditing and Assurance Standards Board at the time of issuance provided an opinion that the disclaimer does not affect the information obtained from a bank confirmation request in terms of its reliability as appropriate audit evidence. The auditor can reasonably rely upon information given by the bank provided it is not clearly wrong, suspicious, internally inconsistent, ambiguous or in conflict with other evidence gathered during the course of the audit. When there is evidence to suggest that the information provided by the bank is inaccurate or incomplete, the auditor contacts the bank and requests clarification in writing.

In view of this disclaimer and notification by the Australian Bankers' Association that the present recording systems of banks do not necessarily maintain together all information for different entities that form part of an economic entity or all accounts of a customer, an auditor cannot rely solely on the standard form to satisfy the completeness assertion. An auditor who believes that there is a 'risk that material accounts, agreements or transactions exist of which the auditor is unaware' should contact the bank and request further information.

Tests of a client's bank reconciliations

The essential objective of testing a client's **bank reconciliations** is to substantiate that the balance confirmed with the bank agrees with the client's cash accounting records. Differences are caused by deposits in transit, outstanding cheques and other reconciling items. The auditor's objective is to obtain reasonable assurance that reconciling items are authentic, complete and treated accurately.

The extent of testing of the client's reconciliations varies depending on the assessed level of control risk. Recall that the auditor plans for three assessment levels: low, medium or high. Possible procedures for a client's reconciliation are as follows:

1 Compare amounts on the reconciliation with totals in the bank statement, general ledger and cash receipts and cash payments records, including a comparison of the balance per bank with the amount confirmed by the bank.
2 Test the clerical accuracy of the reconciliation.
3 Compare deposits in transit on the reconciliation with deposits appearing in the subsequent period's bank statement and consider whether the time lag between the end of the period and recording by the bank is reasonable.
4 Vouch other reconciling items in the reconciliation to supporting documents.
5 Consider the need to investigate outstanding cheques or other reconciling items that have not been cleared.
   (Large or unusual items are always investigated.)

When the level of control risk is assessed as low, substantive procedures might be confined to scanning the client reconciliations and comparing balances per bank to bank confirmations. A medium assessed level might result in applying the procedures listed above at year-end, together with some additional procedures described below.

If the level of control risk is assessed as high, the auditor extends the substantive procedures in testing the client's reconciliation by examining the individual details of reconciling items. The rting documents are examined and traced to the cash accounting records. ques that did not clear are traced to cash payment records, and old or unusual ghly investigated and resolved.

d cash procedures

is assessed as high because of deficiencies in internal control, there is usually a ud. A high control risk is unusual because most clients tend to maintain at least tive controls over cash. In cases of high control risk, a common audit procedure n and review of a **bank transfer schedule**. One of the more common frauds kiting (described in Chapter 9). Such a schedule is used when there is a serious risk of kiting because cash controls are deficient and there are many bank accounts and many bank transfers. When there are few bank accounts and few transfers, the auditor scans the bank statements and cash records to determine whether deposits and withdrawals between bank accounts are recorded in the same and the correct period. A bank transfer schedule lists all transfers and the dates of recording on the books and bank statements.

Quick review

1. The major assertions of interest to the auditor in testing the account balance of cash are existence and completeness, and valuation if foreign currencies are included.
2. The major assertions of interest to the auditor in testing the associated transactions of cash receipts and cash payments are occurrence and completeness, and accuracy if transactions involve foreign currencies.
3. The essential feature of substantive tests of the cash balance is substantiation of the client's bank reconciliations.
4. The standard bank confirmation requests are used to help confirm information from the client's banks.
5. Cash on hand is usually immaterial and not counted.

SALES, CASH RECEIPTS AND ACCOUNTS RECEIVABLE

The essential feature of substantive tests of balances for accounts receivable is emphasis on specific audit objectives related to *existence* and *valuation and allocation*. For the related transactions of sales and cash receipts the major assertions are *occurrence* and *accuracy*. In practice there is commonly an emphasis on substantive tests of balances, primarily for reasons of audit efficiency. These are achieved primarily by confirmation directly with customers (although recently there has been an increased emphasis on reviewing subsequent receipts rather than direct confirmations) and audit work based on a review of the aged trial balance of accounts receivable. As explained in more detail later, the aged trial balance is the basic work paper schedule in the receivables area because of audit efficiency considerations.

Assertions, objectives and procedures

Table 10.2 (overleaf) summarises the financial report assertions, specific audit objectives and common audit procedures traditionally used to achieve the objectives for accounts receivable and the related class of transaction account, sales (credit sales increasing accounts receivable). Cash receipts, which increase cash and decrease accounts receivable, were discussed in the previous learning objective. The common audit procedures listed are the primary procedures traditionally used to achieve the related specific audit objective. As applied in the accounts receivable area, the procedures have the following features:

- **Confirmation** Requests are mailed directly to selected customers, asking them to 'confirm' an amount owed at a date specified in the request. This procedure has lost prominence in recent years, because of its failure to adequately address the important assertion of valuation and allocation. However, because it is still relatively important in many audits, and demonstrates the evidence-gathering technique of external confirmations in general, it is explained further (later in this learning objective).
- **Subsequent receipts review** The auditor verifies whether the amount in outstanding receivables is subsequently received. This provides the auditor with evidence that the debt existed, and evidence of the amount that was collectible (valuation and allocation assertion). As it covers both of the major assertions for accounts receivable, in many cases it is preferred to confirmation procedures. Because of the growing importance of this technique, it is also discussed later in this learning objective, as an alternative procedure to confirmation.
- **Cutoff** Audit procedures addressing the cutoff assertion are designed to determine that all significant transactions of the current period are recorded and no significant transactions of the next period are recorded, as of a specified date. For accounts receivable, cutoff tests are concerned with *shipments* and *cash collections*. The auditor identifies the numbers of the last prenumbered shipping document and the last prenumbered sales invoice for the period and determines that lower numbers are recorded in the current period and higher numbers in the next period. If documents are not prenumbered or the sequence is not accounted for, the auditor examines all sales transactions above a specified amount within a few days before and after the end of the period, to test proper cutoff. Cash collection cutoff is tested by identifying the last cash receipt recorded in the period and comparing the date to the date of deposit in the bank. The 'as of' date for cutoff tests for receivables should be the same as that used for debtor's confirmation. A review of credit notes issued after the end of the period is also undertaken in order to identify transactions from the previous period that may require adjustment.
- **Analytical procedures** In the accounts receivable area, these include comparison of amounts and ratios for relationships between sales and receivables, allowance accounts and sales, and sales and cost of sales. Comparisons are made to previous periods, budgets and information on unit quantities (units shipped to units billed).
- **Tests of sales transactions** Tests of sales transactions are usually dual-purpose tests, having both control and substantive elements. With regard to substantive testing, they can be especially useful for testing assertions that aren't well tested by other audit procedures, in particular the completeness assertion. This is because the primary evidence-gathering procedures in this area—confirmation and subsequent receipts review—are directed to other assertions, especially existence and valuation and accuracy. The auditor may rely on controls to ensure that all transactions that should be included are actually included. If the audit approach does not include tests of controls related to completeness of sales transactions (which may be required under the revised audit risk standards—refer to Chapter 9) the auditor has to consider the need for transaction testing as part of direct tests of the receivable balance. The transactions test that is relevant to completeness of receivables is tracing from shipping documents to sales invoices. In practice, analytical tests of sales and receivables, combined with consideration of the results

of audit procedures applied to inventory, are often considered sufficient for the assertion of completeness. (Note that unrecorded sales should also result in inventory shrinkage.)

- **General procedures** These procedures, such as reading minutes and contracts, are usually applied separately to the audit, rather than in relation to specific balances. However, the results of general procedures are considered in relation to the balances affected. For receivables, the relevant information would concern the existence of pledging, factoring or other liens on receivables (addressing the rights and obligations assertion).

- **Inquiry and scanning** Inquiries relevant to accounts receivable include the existence of non-standard sales terms (consignment sales or other rights of return) and related-party transactions. Scanning includes visually reviewing accounting records and financial reports in relation to the knowledge obtained from applying other audit procedures, including reviewing for items about which inquiries were made.

- **Review of aged trial balance** An aged trial balance of receivables lists all customer balances as of a specified date, and shows the total balance for each customer and the components of the overall balance by age category, such as 30 days or below, 31 to 60 days, 61 to 90 days, and over 90 days. A periodic ageing is used by an entity's financial management to monitor collectibility and for cash management. The auditor reviews the aged trial balance as of the balance date with the credit manager as part of the evaluation of the reasonableness of the allowance for doubtful debts related to the valuation and allocation assertion. The older the debt, the greater the risk of the debt not being paid, thus the greater the likelihood that an allowance has to be made for non-payment. Since the aged trial balance is usually prepared by the client, the auditor needs to test the accuracy of the ageing by footing and tracing. The extent of the testing depends on the controls over completeness and accuracy of processing sales and cash receipts.

Confirmation procedures

Up until the year 2000, AUS 504/ISA 505 required that the auditor should plan to obtain direct confirmation of accounts receivable or individual entries in an accounts balance, in all but exceptional circumstances. However, in 2000 the AUASB/IAASB extended AUS 504/ISA 505 from confirmations of receivables to cover all external confirmations undertaken by the auditor. The standard was adjusted with the expectation of allowing the auditor the opportunity to choose auditing procedures most suitable for the client, rather than effectively mandating procedures. In the revised standard the auditor is required to determine whether the use of external confirmations is necessary to obtain sufficient appropriate audit evidence to support certain financial report assertions. In making this determination, the auditor should consider materiality, the assessed level of inherent and control risk, and how the evidence from other planned audit procedures will reduce audit risk to an acceptably low level for the applicable financial report assertions. These changes reflect the fact that accounts receivable confirmations are used much less in practice than they were 10 years ago, and are commonly seen as a less appropriate form of audit procedure for assertions requiring audit attention when compared with other audit procedures. In particular, confirmations do not provide evidence of intention of the client to pay (valuation and allocation assertion), while procedures such as review of subsequent receipts show clearly the amount paid attributable to amounts outstanding at balance date.

If it is decided that an accounts receivable confirmation is an appropriate procedure there are two alternatives in the method of requesting a direct confirmation—positive and negative:

TABLE 10.2 Assertions, objectives and substantive procedures for sales and accounts receivable

Financial report assertion	Specific audit objective	Common substantive audit procedures to achieve objectives
Assertions about classes of transactions and events (sales)		
Occurrence	The transactions giving rise to sales occurred during the period.	• Vouch entries in sales journal to supporting documentation of sale (invoice, delivery note)
Completeness	All sales transactions and events that should have been recorded have been recorded	• Test from supporting documentation (invoice, delivery note) to sales journal or subsidiary ledger
Accuracy	Sales amount and other data are recorded appropriately	• Verify prices, quantity and computation on sales invoices, prices verified to master price list, quantity verified to shipping documentation
Cutoff	Sales are recorded in the correct period	• Check last sales invoices recorded before balance date and first sales invoices recorded after balance date are recorded in the correct period, consider when delivered by evidence of shipping documents
Classification	Sales are recorded in the correct accounts	• Check that sales recorded correctly in accordance with the chart of accounts
Assertions about account balances (accounts receivable)		
Existence	Accounts receivable in the balance sheet exist at balance date	• Debtors' confirmation procedures • Subsequent receipts review
Rights and obligations	Accounts receivable in the balance sheet is owned by the entity and not restricted or committed	• Debtors' confirmation procedures • General procedures • Inquiry and scanning about any restrictions or commitments
Completeness	Accounts receivable in the balance sheet includes all accounts receivable at the balance date	• Subsequent receipts review • Sequence check of all sales invoices
Valuation and allocation	Accounts receivable in the balance sheet is stated at the correct amount	• Review of aged trial balance and follow-up procedures for amounts overdue, such as review of subsequent receipts, discussions about the debtor's ability to pay • Test conversion rates for any foreign currency accounts receivable

1 **Positive form of debtors' confirmation** (most commonly used) Once a debtor has been selected for positive confirmation, the auditor must obtain evidence on the account balance, either through a response to the confirmation or alternative procedures. The positive form asks the debtor to respond, whether or not the debtor agrees with the information on the amount owed in the request. The receipt of a response from the debtor provides evidence of the authenticity of the receivable and, if the debtor agrees, evidence of the accuracy of the amount. It provides no positive evidence of collectibility but may detect a disputed amount which indicates doubtful collectibility. Some auditors provide all details of the transaction except the amount and request recipients of the confirmation to provide the balance or invoice amounts owed.

2 **Negative form of debtors' confirmation** The negative form of request asks the debtor to respond only if there is disagreement with the information given. Generally, the negative form is considered to provide less reliable evidence, as a non-response may be for reasons other than the client agreeing with the balance, such as difficulty of reconciling. For this reason the number of negative confirmation requests sent should be greater than the number of positive requests that would be sent in similar circumstances. If the number of confirmations returned as undeliverable is more than expected, the auditor may suspect the possibility of fictitious receivables.

A combination of positive and negative forms may be used. For example, where the total accounts receivable balance comprises a small number of large balances and a large number of small balances, the auditor may decide to confirm all or a sample of the large balances with positive confirmation requests, and a sample of the small balances or the remaining other balances using negative confirmation requests.

AUS 504/ISA 505 states that negative confirmations may be used to reduce audit risk to an acceptable level when:

1 the assessed levels of inherent and control risk are low;
2 a large number of small balances is involved;
3 a substantial number of errors is not expected; and
4 the auditor has no reason to believe that the confirmation recipients will not seriously consider the requests.

Exhibit 10.1 shows a positive form. Generally, auditors have found that the response rate is improved when the request accompanies a regular monthly statement to the customer. Note that the request comes from the client, and the auditor should ensure that adequate control over confirmations is maintained.

The confirmation process has to be started early enough during the audit to allow adequate time to mail initial requests, send second and third requests if necessary, and analyse responses.

When planning the accounts receivable confirmations, the auditor considers the following:

- **Prior experience** Experience with the client or similar clients may have shown poor response rates or other indications that confirmations are ineffective. Is enough information provided to help the recipient respond? Is the confirmation being directed to the wrong person?
- **The nature of the information being confirmed** Should invoices or balances be confirmed? For example, if most of the debtors' accounting systems track individual invoices rather than balances, it is ineffective to send a balance confirmation.
- **Have there been unusual transactions, such as large sales at or near year-end?** The auditor might design the confirmation to identify inflated sales for the period, such as through invoice-and-hold transactions, where merchandise is invoiced to customers before delivery in order to inflate sales for a particular accounting period.

EXHIBIT 10.1

[Client's Letterhead]

[Date]
[Debtor's Name and Address]

Dear ....,
Our auditors, [Name] ...., are making an annual audit of
our financial report. Please confirm the balance due at [Date] ...., which
is shown on our records and the enclosed statement as $ ....

Please indicate in the space below whether this is in agreement with your records. If
there are differences, please provide any information that will assist our auditors in
reconciling the difference.

Please sign and date your response and mail your reply directly to [Auditor's Name
and Address] .... in the enclosed return envelope.
PLEASE DO NOT MAIL PAYMENTS ON YOUR ACCOUNT TO THE AUDITORS.

Yours sincerely,

....
[Officer's Signature and Title]

....
[Client's Name]

To: [Auditor's Name] ....
The balance due [Client's Name] .... of $...........................
as of [Date] .... is correct with the following exceptions (if any):

....
....
Signature ....
Title: ....
Date: ....

- **Is there a medium or high risk of oral agreements, such as lenient rights of return of merchandise?** If so, the confirmation should request information on the terms of agreements.
- **Respondent** Care should be taken to direct the confirmations to the individuals knowledgeable about the transactions or arrangements.

In evaluating responses the auditor considers whether disagreements noted by debtors merely indicate discrepancies caused by timing, such as those caused by mailing time for cash receipts or shipping time for shipments, or are a result of actual clerical errors or disputed amounts. The auditor does not want to project monetary misstatement for timing discrepancies or isolated errors, so the qualitative analysis of confirmation responses is extremely important.

Further requests may be sent if an initial positive request does not result in a response. The reasons for this are: the lack of response may be an indication of fictitious receivables or a bad debt and these possibilities must be pursued; and the alternative procedures to confirmation are more costly and time-consuming.

If management requests that the auditor not confirm certain accounts receivable balances, the auditor should consider whether there are valid grounds for such a request. Such a request might be justified if, for example, the particular account is in dispute and communication on behalf of the auditor might jeopardise sensitive negotiations between the entity and the debtor. Before accepting a refusal as justified, the auditor should examine any available evidence to support management's explanations, such as correspondence between management and the debtor. In such cases, alternative procedures should be applied to the accounts receivable not subjected to confirmation.

Alternative procedures to confirmation

As outlined earlier, use of direct confirmations has reduced in practice as auditors have determined that other procedures are a more appropriate form of audit evidence (in particular as regards the assertion of valuation and allocation). These alternative procedures may include examination of evidence of subsequent cash receipts, examination of sales and shipping documents and/or oral confirmation of the balance with the debtor. Generally, subsequent cash receipts are considered to be a superior form of evidence because sales and dispatch documents originate in the client's system, and substantiating subsequent collection simultaneously achieves the audit objectives related to existence and valuation and allocation. The alternative procedures are essentially the same: vouching, tracing and recomputing of source documents as are used in tests of transactions. However, instead of a representative sample of source documents, the auditor applies procedures to the specific documents for selected account balances (and a cash receipt may cover more than one transaction).

These alternative procedures can also be applied to non-respondents to a confirmation procedure in order to gain sufficient appropriate audit evidence. The auditor also needs to consider the qualitative characteristics of the non-responses. Is there a systematic characteristic, such as a tendency to be the year-end transactions?

Materiality

Materiality is used primarily to identify individually significant customer accounts for testing, either through confirmation or alternative procedures. Examples of customer accounts that might be identified as individually significant are:

■ large dollar balances;
■ significant balances past their due dates;
■ significant balances as a result of sales near the end of the accounting period;
■ accounts with unusual names;
■ related-party balances; and
■ credit balances.

Often the recorded amount that remains after identifying individually significant items is in total a very large dollar amount, and audit sampling is necessary (audit sampling procedures are discussed in Chapter 11). In fact, confirmation of accounts receivable is one of the most frequent audit sampling applications among substantive tests of balances.

Audit risk

The timing and extent of audit procedures is influenced significantly by consideration of audit risk. The inherent risk factors considered include the nature of products, the nature of distribution methods, the complexity of the invoicing system and economic developments. The control risk evaluation focuses on specific control objectives. The extensiveness of procedures to test collectibility is influenced by environmental considerations, such as changes in national or an industry's economic conditions, and whether controls directed towards authorisation, approval of credit limits and establishing terms for sales transactions were operating effectively.

Audit efficiency

Efficiencies in testing in the accounts receivable area can be achieved by organising the documentation of audit procedures around the schedule for the *aged trial balance of accounts receivable*. Debtors' accounts can be selected from the aged trial balance for further testing. By footing (adding up) the trial balance and comparing the total to the general ledger and financial report, the auditor simultaneously establishes the population being sampled and the clerical accuracy of the trial balance.

Quick review

1. The major assertions of interest to the auditor in substantive tests of balances for accounts receivable are existence and valuation and allocation.
2. The major assertions of interest to the auditor in substantive tests for the related transactions of sales and cash receipts are occurrence and accuracy.
3. The main audit procedures are confirming balances directly with the customers, review of subsequent receipts and reviewing the aged trial balance of accounts receivable.
4. There are two types of accounts receivable confirmation: the positive form, where the debtor is asked to respond, whether or not the debtor agrees with the information on the amount owed in the request; and the negative form, where the debtor is asked to respond only if there is disagreement with the information given.

PURCHASES AND INVENTORIES

learning objective 5

Inventories consist of goods to be sold, or used in production of saleable goods, in the ordinary course of business. The transactions involving inventory are an increase when goods are purchased, and a decrease when goods are sold. Usually, especially for retail and manufacturing entities (but not for service entities), inventory is very material and one of the most complex areas of the audit. The form of inventory varies depending on the nature of the business. A manufacturer has inventories of raw materials, work-in-process and finished goods. A retailer or wholesaler has goods acquired for resale. The related transactions cycles are purchases of raw materials (manufacturer) or finished goods (retailer), and cash payments. This discussion is generalised to apply to both types of inventory, identifying significant differences at relevant points. Some types of service industries, such as hospitals or repair services, also have supplies that can be inventoried, and while in these situations inventories are usually less material, if considered material the audit approach is generally similar.

Differences from the sales and expenditures cycles

The inventory area of the audit is sometimes referred to as the production or conversion function, and there is a relationship between inventory and the sales and expenditures cycles. For example, for a manufacturer the sales cycle includes the shipment of finished goods and the expenditures cycle includes the acquisition of raw materials, direct labour (payroll) and overhead expenses. However, the inventory area is different in nature for reasons explained in the following discussion.

Nature and frequency of accountability tests

Recall that for the sales and expenditures cycles, accountability tests are usually important control activities used as a basis for the auditor's assessment of control risk. For example, the accounts receivable subsidiary ledger is reconciled to the general ledger control account, prelists of cash receipts are reconciled to deposits and accounting postings, and cash in bank accounts is reconciled to cash accounting records. Also, outside parties may provide information that acts as a type of accountability test. Monthly statements are mailed to customers and complaints are independently resolved. Suppliers' statements may be reconciled with accounts payable balances.

The accountability tests in the sales and expenditures cycles are usually performed at least monthly, and some are more frequent. Almost invariably, these tests are control activities that are important for achieving specific control objectives that permit the auditor to reduce the assessed level of control risk.

For inventories, an accountability test is also made, and it is probably the single most important control activity in that area. It is the undertaking of a **physical inventory count**, or **stocktake**, by the client. Inventory items are counted and listed, and the results are compared to accounting records. However, this accountability test commonly occurs only once a year, and it is essentially a stand-alone procedure—its effectiveness depends on procedures that are applied only when the inventory is counted. In practice, there are usually two ways of counting inventory: in a **complete inventory count**, operating activity largely stops and all inventory is counted at one time; in a **cycle count**, periodic counts of selected inventory items are made during the year, with all items counted at least once each year. Auditors' procedures regarding inventory counts are dual-purpose tests (see beginning of this chapter), because the auditor is concerned with both the accuracy of the physical count and the effectiveness of the control activities over the client's counting and pricing.

Importance of accounting principles

As discussed earlier, audit problems associated with the sales and expenditures cycles tend to be those related to high-volume clerical processing rather than complex accounting principles. Accounting principles cannot be totally ignored: for example, the auditor has to be concerned with classification and recording in the proper period. However, in the inventory area there may be both a large number of items and complex matters of accounting principle.

Generally, the auditor is concerned with application of accounting principles in the following respects:

- assignment of costs to inventory in accordance with an acceptable accounting method, such as first-in, first-out (FIFO) or average cost, and the consistency of the accounting method and the methods of application;
- identification and proper accounting treatment of obsolete, slow-moving, excess or defective inventory items; and
- reduction of inventory items to replacement cost or net realisable value (lower of cost or net realisable value).

It can be very difficult to assign costs to inventory. A manufacturer may use a **standard cost system**, and the auditor must be concerned with whether the adjustments to standard cost result in a reasonable approximation of actual cost. A retailer may use the **retail inventory method**, and the auditor must be concerned with whether the adjustment of inventory at selling price approximates actual cost (or net realisable value if this is lower). For a manufacturer, the allocation of overhead expenses involves several considerations. No matter what accounting method is used for allocation by a manufacturer, the auditor must be concerned with conformity with regulations on the proper inclusion of expenses in overhead. For example, if a *direct costing* method is used, only variable overhead expenses are assigned to inventory; this method is not in accordance with approved accounting standards. These standards require the use of absorption costing, where both fixed and variable production overhead related to bringing inventories to their present location and condition are allocated to inventory.

The client's costing or pricing of the quantities determined by counting inventory usually occurs some time after the inventory count to allow for investigation of differences identified between quantities counted and those recorded. Under both the complete and cycle count methods, the physical count is reconciled to perpetual inventory records if they are maintained, with the pricing and summarisation being based on the reconciled amount.

Materiality and method of allocation

In accounting, the process of apportioning costs incurred between expenses of the current period and assets that benefit future periods is broadly referred to as *allocation*. The general accounting records accumulate the totals of costs incurred for inventory, such as purchases and payrolls. Source documents provide a record of units purchased (receiving reports) and units sold (shipping reports), or, as in a perpetual inventory system, a separate record of units may be maintained.

At the end of the accounting period the costs incurred for inventory during the period must be allocated between units sold and units on hand. This is the function of the cost accounting system. The term 'cost accounting system' is usually applied to manufacturers. However, even a merchandiser who acquires goods for resale often needs a system for assigning costs of acquiring and storing goods, such as freight and warehousing, to inventory. Inventory costs are seldom confined to the supplier's invoice price.

Cost accounting systems vary greatly in complexity and sophistication. A job order or a process cost system may concurrently track the internal use and movement of inventory units and costs and be integrated with the general accounting system. On the other hand, the system may consist simply of spreadsheets based on general accounting records and unit records that are prepared periodically or only annually.

Whether the costing approach is sophisticated or rudimentary, the resulting allocation between the current period and future periods usually has a material effect on profit. Cost of sales is often 60 per cent or more of sales, the largest expense in the income statement. Also, inventory is usually material to the balance sheet and a very material component of current assets. Thus, the misstatement of the allocation between cost of sales and inventory can cause a material misstatement of the operating results and financial position.

The substantiation of both cost of sales and ending inventory is usually dependent on direct tests of the ending inventory balance, combined with tests of transactions for the expenditures cycle or direct tests of balances of accounts related to that cycle. In a continuing engagement, beginning inventory has been substantiated in the previous period. The amount of cost of sales is, in effect, a residual of the following activity analysis:

	Beginning inventory
Plus	Expenditures for goods and services for inventory
Less	Ending inventory
	Cost of sales

It is usually tested indirectly by tests of inventory and expenditures.

The significance of ending inventory to the determination of net profit, combined with the high volume of activity and accounting complexities, often creates a *high risk of material misstatement*. The inventory area is particularly susceptible to intentional misstatements designed to manipulate profit, and it is important for the auditor to maintain professional scepticism. If the auditor's procedures detect discrepancies between accounting records and supporting documentation or other corroborating information, the auditor should consider the possibility of material misrepresentations by management.

Assertions, objectives and procedures

The essential feature of direct tests of balances for inventories is emphasis on specific audit objectives related to the assertions *existence* and *valuation and allocation*, achieved primarily by *observation of physical inventory* and *tests of pricing* and *summarisation*. AUS 506 'Existence and Valuation of Inventory' (ISA 501 'Audit Evidence—Additional Considerations for Specific Items: Part A: Attendance at Physical Inventory Counting') establishes standards and provides guidance on obtaining sufficient appropriate audit evidence regarding these two assertions. The financial report assertions, specific audit objectives and common audit procedures to achieve these objectives are summarised in Table 10.3. As applied in the inventory area, these procedures have the following features:

TABLE 10.3 **Assertions, objectives and substantive procedures for purchases and inventory**

Financial report assertion	Specific audit objective	Common substantive audit procedures to achieve objectives
Assertions about classes of transactions and events (purchases)		
Occurrence	The transactions giving rise to purchases occurred during the period	• Select transactions from purchases journal and agree to supporting documentation (e.g. goods received note)
Completeness	All purchases transactions and events that should have been recorded have been recorded	• Test from supporting documentation (purchase invoice, good received note) to purchases journal or subsidiary ledger
Accuracy	Purchases amount and other data are recorded appropriately	• Check dollar value of purchases to supporting documentation (purchase invoice), and that other data such as supplier's name recorded accurately
Cutoff	Purchases are recorded in the correct period	• Check last purchases recorded before balance date and first purchases recorded after balance date are recorded in the correct period, consider when received by evidence of goods received note
Classification	Purchases are recorded in the correct accounts	• Inquire and scan that purchases recorded correctly in accordance with the chart of accounts • General procedures

Assertions about account balances (inventory)		
Existence	Inventories included in the balance sheet physically exist and represent items held for sale in the ordinary course of business	• Inspection of physical inventory (checking from inventory records to physical stock) • Analytical procedures • Confirm stock held at other locations
Rights and obligations	Inventory in the balance sheet is owned by the entity and excludes items billed to customers or owned by others	• Inquire about legal ownership of goods being shipped to entity and any goods on consignment and inspect supporting documentation
Completeness	Inventory in the balance sheet includes all inventories on hand at balance date, or in transit or at other locations that is the property of the entity	• Inspection of physical inventory (checking from physical stock to inventory records) • Analytical procedures • Inquire about stock held at other locations, and review purchase documents for shipping terms for inventory in transit
Valuation and allocation	Inventory in the balance sheet is stated at the correct amount with respect to: • cost determined by an acceptable method consistently applied • slow-moving, excess, defective, and obsolete items identified • reduced to net realisable value if lower than cost	• Tests of pricing and summarisation • Analytical procedures • Observation of physical inventory (look for obsolete or damaged items) • Inquiry and scanning • Check subsequent sales prices and compare with cost

■ **Observation of physical inventory** This term is used to describe the combination of observation, inquiry and physical examination (test counts) that provides the basis for achieving several specific audit objectives for inventory. It is explained further in a separate section.

■ **Analytical procedures** In the inventory area these include computation of ratios for inventory turnover and detailed gross margin (by product type or code and location) and comparison to previous periods. For a manufacturer, computation of the ratio of overhead to materials and labour and comparison to previous periods may be an important substantive test. If a standard cost system is used, it is usually important to study variance reports and consider the reasonableness of explanations for variances. Sales forecasts and marketing plans may provide information relevant to the net realisable value of inventory. In general, analytical tests usually receive more emphasis in the inventory area than in many other audit areas.

■ **Cutoff** Procedures relating to this assertion are directed to the control over shipping and receiving activities around the end of the accounting period. Usually, the auditor identifies the numbers of the last prenumbered shipping and receiving documents at the time of the observation of physical inventory. These numbers are used for cutoff tests for accounts receivable and accounts payable recording. The document numbers are also used to determine whether the related inventory items were properly included or excluded from the physical inventory count and, if perpetual records are maintained, the inventory records. The inclusion or exclusion of inventory items in transit should ideally be based on passage of title as determined by the shipping terms Free on Board (FOB), where title passes at the shipping point, and Cost, Insurance and Freight (CIF), where title passes at destination. However, unless the difference would be material, purchases are often recorded when received and sales when shipped.

■ **Tests of pricing and summarisation** This term is used to describe the combination of vouching, tracing and recomputation procedures used to test the client's pricing and summarisation of inventory counts. It is explained further in a separate section.

■ **General procedures** The general procedures relevant to inventory include reading minutes, debt instruments and agreements to find indications of liens or pledging of inventory, unrealised losses on purchase commitments or inventories held on consignment.

■ **Inquiry and scanning** The important inquiries for inventory include discussion with management concerning obsolete, excess or slow-moving inventory, and the same matters as described above for general procedures. Scanning includes reviewing perpetual records or other records or reports of inventory usage and movement in order to identify any such obsolete, excess or slow-moving items.

Observation of the physical inventory

The following list highlights points that are often misunderstood about observation of physical inventory:

1   The client's taking of the physical inventory is a control activity, but it is a stand-alone activity and its effectiveness is not dependent on control over processing transactions. Thus it is one of the very few areas where controls are directed towards account balances, rather than being associated with transaction or event flows.

2   The procedures the auditor uses are a combination of observation, inquiry and physical examination (making test counts of client's counts).

3   The auditor's goal is to obtain reasonable assurance that the client's methods of counting inventory result in an accurate count, which is a test of controls. The auditor undertakes test counts as an aid in making this assessment, rather than attempting to directly substantiate inventory quantities by counting.

4   In most circumstances there are no satisfactory alternative procedures to making or observing some counts of items in inventory for verifying the ending inventory.

When inventory is material, the auditor is required to obtain sufficient appropriate audit evidence regarding its existence and condition by attendance at a physical inventory count unless it is impractical (AUS 506/ISA 501). In exceptional circumstances, the auditor may judge it necessary to depart from this procedure in order to achieve the same objective more effectively; the justification for this departure should be documented in the audit working papers.

In planning attendance at the physical inventory count, the auditor considers the following matters:

■ inherent, control and detection risks and materiality related to inventory;

■ whether adequate procedures are expected to be established and proper instructions issued for physical inventory counting;

■ the timing of the count;

- the locations at which inventory is held; and
- whether an expert's assistance is needed.

In determining the need to use an expert, the auditor would consider the materiality of the inventory, the nature and complexity of the items and other evidence that is available. Situations in which experts are normally required include where minerals are stored in stockpiles or where the client is in the business of selling items such as gems or paintings that require expert valuation. If an expert is required, the auditor follows the standards and guidance outlined in AUS 606/ISA 620 'Using the Work of an Expert', as discussed in Chapter 5.

The desirable features of client procedures for taking a physical inventory include the following:

- a written plan of instructions for inventory counting which is communicated to all relevant staff;
- proper arrangement of inventory items to facilitate counting;
- procedures for the identification and recording of obsolete or excess inventory;
- numerical control of inventory tags or count sheets and accounting for all used and unused tags or sheets;
- personnel on inventory count teams who are independent of inventory storekeeping; and
- supervision of counting by internal auditors or supervisory personnel who re-count on a test basis.

To obtain assurance that management's procedures are adequately implemented, the auditor observes employees' procedures and performs test counts. When performing counts the auditor may test both the completeness and the existence of inventory by tracing items selected from the records to the physical inventory (existence), and items selected from the physical inventory to the count records (completeness). The auditor considers the extent to which copies of such count records need to be retained for subsequent testing and comparison. The auditor also considers cutoff procedures, including details of the movement of inventory just before, during and after the count, so that the accounting for such movements can be checked at a later date.

A physical inventory count conducted at a date other than period end is usually adequate for audit purposes only when control risk is assessed as less than high. The auditor assesses whether, through the performance of appropriate procedures, changes in inventory between the count date and period end are correctly recorded. When the entity operates a perpetual inventory system which is used to determine the period-end balance, the auditor would assess, through the performance of additional procedures, whether the reasons for any significant differences between the physical count and the perpetual inventory records are understood, and whether the records are properly adjusted.

Sometimes the inventory balance may be material, but attendance at an inventory count is impractical because of the nature or location of the inventory, or in exceptional circumstances the auditor is able to justify not attending the physical inventory counting (e.g. counting cattle that are roaming around a Northern Territory cattle ranch). In these circumstances the auditor should consider whether alternative procedures provide sufficient appropriate audit evidence of existence and condition to conclude that they need not make reference to a scope limitation in the audit report (refer to Chapter 13). For example, the auditor may not be engaged until after the client's physical inventory. A satisfactory alternative procedure is for the auditor to make test counts at a later date and, by examining the documentation of inventory receipts, issues, movements and shipments, to work back to the quantities on hand at the count date and make comparisons to the client's counts. This means the client must maintain either good perpetual records or other sufficient documentation of inventory movements to permit the equivalent of perpetual records to be prepared for the period between the count date and the auditor's test counts. The auditor reviews client documentation of counts and counting methods.

In order to test the completeness assertion for inventory, the auditor needs to make inquiries about stock held at locations other than the client's. Incomplete inventory may also be detected using analytical procedures such as the ratio of sales to cost of sales to discover irregularities.

If inventory is under the custody and control of a third party, the auditor ordinarily obtains direct confirmation from the third party as to the quantities and condition of inventory held on behalf of the entity. Depending on the materiality of this inventory the auditor would also:

- consider any apparent lack of integrity and independence of the third party;
- observe, or arrange for another auditor to observe, the physical inventory count;
- obtain another auditor's report on the adequacy of the third party's internal control for ensuring that inventory is correctly counted and adequately safeguarded; and
- inspect documentation regarding inventory held by third parties, for example warehouse receipts, or obtain confirmation from other parties when such inventory has been pledged as collateral.

Tests of pricing and summarisation

The auditor's tests of **pricing and summarisation** are a combination of vouching, tracing and recomputation to test the following aspects of the client's procedures:

- summarisation of quantities from the count tags or sheets to the inventory list;
- application of prices to the quantities in the list;
- computation of the extensions and footings of the list; and
- identification of obsolete, excess or slow-moving items and reduction of their prices to net realisable value where this is lower than cost.

The auditor's procedures for testing the summarisation of quantities are designed to provide reasonable assurance that all items counted are included in the listing (giving evidence that the listing is complete), and that no items have been inappropriately added (giving evidence that all inventory items on the list exist). Therefore, the auditor is concerned with both existence and completeness. The auditor reviews the listing to see that only tags or count sheets used for the client's counts are included, and compares selected items on the list to the record of the auditor's test counts and to the client's tags or count sheets.

The auditor is required to evaluate the bases used by management in the valuation of inventory and to perform audit procedures designed to obtain sufficient appropriate audit evidence regarding these bases. Audit sampling may be used, and the extent of testing may be restricted when the control risk for the purchases subsystem is evaluated as less than high.

The extent of testing for obsolete, excess or slow-moving items depends on the care and thoroughness of the client's own review for such items. If the entity has adopted specific criteria, such as a reduction in cost for all items for which they have over a year's supply on hand and all items that have not been sold or used within six months, the auditor evaluates the reasonableness of the criteria and tests the client's application. The auditor may also vouch unit prices to suppliers' invoices, open purchase orders, current supplier price lists or published prices and review records of internal usage and movement of inventory.

Materiality

The auditor uses materiality in the inventory area primarily as a means of ide[ntifying]
significant inventory items and regards items as individually significant be[cause of their]
size. The auditor usually includes these items among the items test counte[d. The]
number of test counts to make on the basis of risk and materiality consid[erations. These]
materiality considerations will be influenced by whether the physical [layout]
facilitates observation and accurate counting, and the extent of the client[s' counts]
and testing of the counts.

Audit risk

The extent of the auditor's coverage of the client's physical inventory is based largely on the re[view]
of the client's plans and arrangements and past experience. Many clients will have their inventory
stocktake on or near to balance date. However, there will be others who will undertake the
stocktake at an interim date.

Consideration of audit risk is a very important factor in deciding whether the observation of
physical inventory can be made at the earlier date. The specific control risk assessments that are
relevant to this consideration include those for controls associated with sales and purchases
(discussed in Chapter 9) and safeguarding controls over inventory. Important safeguarding
controls for inventory are:

- for storage areas to be secured against unauthorised admission by protective measures such as
  guards, alarm systems, fences or locked areas, and admission by an identification badge or
  pass;
- inspection of all materials leaving the premises for authorised shipping documents; and
- use of prenumbered documents, with the sequence accounted for independently, for
  receiving, materials requisitions, production orders and shipping.

The auditor needs reasonable assurance that the relevant control activities continue to
function in the period between the date of the observation and the balance date. This means the
auditor has to test the control activities related to safeguarding around the balance date. If
controls over purchases and sales are functioning satisfactorily at an interim date, the auditor's
understanding of these control activities may also be updated by inquiry and observation. If there
are deficiencies in these controls but safeguarding procedures are adequate, the auditor may be
able to test transactions during the intervening period so as to enable the auditor to extend the
conclusion based on the interim observation to the balance date. If there are serious deficiencies
in safeguarding controls, or if the auditor believes there is a serious risk of management
misrepresentations, then the observation of the physical inventory must be performed at or near
the balance date.

Quick review

1. Due to the significance of inventory to the determination of net profit, and the
   associated high levels of activity and accounting complexities, inventory is often one of
   the most complex and high-risk areas to audit.
2. The main assertions of interest to the auditor in undertaking tests of balances for
   inventory are existence and valuation and allocation.
3. The main audit procedures are observation of physical inventory and tests of pricing and
   summarisation.

When inventory is material the auditor is required to attend a physical inventory count unless impractical. To obtain assurance that management's procedures for the inventory count are adequately implemented the auditor observes employees' procedures and performs test counts.

5   The auditor tests the summarisation of quantities from the inventory count to obtain reasonable assurance that all items counted are included in the inventory list, and that no items have been inappropriately added.

6   The auditor tests valuation and allocation by vouching items to suppliers' invoices and cost accounting records, and examines the client's review of obsolete, excess and slow-moving items.

ACCOUNTS PAYABLE AND PAYMENTS

A major part of accounts payable is trade creditors, which is related to the purchases/inventory/cash payments cycle. When shipments of raw materials and finished goods are received and placed in inventory, this gives rise to an equivalent liability, trade creditors, until payment is made. Accounts payable is also comprised of other suppliers (such as suppliers of electricity or other items not used in production or resale), also sometimes termed 'other creditors'. An essential feature of substantive tests of balances for accounts payable is emphasis on the specific audit objective related to *completeness*. This is a reflection of the fact that the auditor's major risk is in understatement of this account. For example, a major risk is that inventory is received and included as an asset, but the equivalent liability is not immediately taken up. The completeness objective is achieved primarily by a search for unrecorded payables, a review for any goods received but not taken up as a liability, and analytical tests of related expense account balances.

Assertions, objectives and procedures

The financial report assertions, specific audit objectives and the common audit procedures traditionally used to achieve the objectives for accounts payable and related accounts are summarised in Table 10.4. As applied in the accounts payable area, these procedures have the following features:

■ **Confirmation** Confirmation procedures for accounts payable balances are less common in practice compared with confirmation of accounts receivable. Confirmation is generally considered relevant to achieving specific audit objectives related to existence, rights and obligations and to some extent valuation and allocation, and can be an efficient and effective procedure for achieving these specific audit objectives. However, some auditors use confirmation procedures for accounts payable balances when control objectives related to occurrence and accuracy of associated transactions have serious deficiencies. Confirmation requests are sent to suppliers with whom the entity has done a relatively large volume of business during the period. The auditor is concerned with what should be recorded rather than what is recorded, so the emphasis is placed on selecting suppliers who are *likely* to have large balances. The accounts payable balances selected may therefore include zero and small recorded balances. The normal form of confirmation request for payables is positive and asks the supplier to state the balance due from the client. The auditor's analysis of responses is similar to that for confirmation of receivables. A distinction must be made between discrepancies caused by payments and shipments in transit, such as a cheque drawn before year-end which the supplier doesn't receive until after year-end, and those caused by clerical errors, disputes and unrecorded invoices.

TABLE 10.4 Assertions, objectives and substantive procedures for accounts payable and related accounts

Financial report assertion	Specific audit objective	Common substantive audit procedures to achieve objectives
Assertions about classes of transactions and events (purchases)		
Occurrence	Transactions giving rise to accounts payable occurred during period	• Select transactions from accounts payable listing and agree to supporting documentation (e.g. suppliers' invoices)
Completeness	All purchase transactions and events that should have been recorded have been recorded	• Test from supporting documentation (suppliers' invoice, goods received note) to purchases journal or subsidiary ledger • Review for any unmatched receiving reports and suppliers' invoices
Accuracy	Purchase amounts and other data are recorded appropriately	• Verify prices, quantity and computation on suppliers' invoices, quantity purchased verified to goods received notes
Cutoff	Purchases and expenses are recorded in the correct period	• Check last suppliers' invoices recorded before balance date and first suppliers' invoices recorded after balance date are recorded in the correct period (consider when goods received/services provided by reviewing goods received/services provided documentation)
Classification	Purchases and expenses are recorded in the correct accounts	• Inquiry and scanning • General procedures
Assertions about account balances (accounts payable)		
Existence	Accounts payable and accrued liabilities are valid obligations to suppliers at the balance date	• Confirmation with suppliers • Vouching to supporting documentation (e.g. suppliers' invoices)
Rights and obligations	Accounts payable and accrued liabilities are obligations owed by the entity	• Confirmation with suppliers • Vouching to supporting documentation (e.g. suppliers' invoices) • General procedures
Completeness	Accounts payable and accrued liabilities include all obligations owed at the balance date	• Out-of-period liability search • Review for any unmatched receiving reports and suppliers' invoices • Analytical procedures • General procedures

Continued...

TABLE 10.4 Assertions, objectives and substantive procedures for accounts payable and related accounts (cont.)

Financial report assertion	Specific audit objective	Common substantive audit procedures to achieve objectives
Valuation and allocation	Accounts payable in the balance sheet is stated at the correct amount	• Agree dollar value of accounts payable to supporting documents (e.g. suppliers' invoices) • Recomputation • Analytical procedures

■ **Vouching** Some auditors regard vouching recorded payables balances to suppliers' statements as equivalent in reliability to confirmation because the evidence, the suppliers' statement, originates outside the client's accounting system. Vouching is effective when recorded accounts payable are reconciled to monthly statements received from suppliers. However, if the client's system does not include an accounts payable subsidiary ledger or suppliers' master file, such a reconciliation can be time-consuming and difficult.

■ **Search for unrecorded liabilities** The emphasis with this procedure is on identifying obligations that should have been recorded at the balance date. It directly tests the accounts payable balance for understatement and because it is the central procedure in the accounts payable area it is explained further in a separate section (below).

■ **General procedures** The search for unrecorded liabilities focuses on detecting unrecorded accounts payable or accrued liabilities for goods or services received at the balance date. However, other unrecorded liabilities may arise from matters such as commitments under contracts, legal claims against the entity or other loss contingencies. The auditor normally relies on general procedures, such as reading minutes, contracts, loan agreements, leases and correspondence from government agencies, to detect unrecorded liabilities for which no indication exists in the accounting records or source documents. For example, the minutes of meetings of the board of directors may reveal a potential legal liability.

■ **Cutoff** The auditor determines the last receiving report, last voucher and last payment of the current period by reference to the prenumbered sequence for those documents, and then checks that the transactions immediately before and after cutoff are recorded in the correct period.

■ **Analytical procedures** Comparison of expenses, budgets and level of activity in the current period with similar information from previous periods can provide evidence for recorded expense and liability balances. In some cases an analytical test can substantiate the total expense and related accrued liability. For example, sales commission expense and accrued commissions payable can usually be reliably estimated based on recorded sales and knowledge of the terms for commissions.

■ **Recomputation** Some accrued liabilities, such as electricity and telephone accounts, can be substantiated by examining payments in the subsequent period and calculating the portion attributable to the previous period under audit. In general, recomputation is used for accruals and deferrals that are recurring adjustments in closing the accounting records.

■ **Inquiry and scanning** The auditor uses inquiry and scanning in conjunction with other general procedures to identify matters relevant to the description, classification and related disclosure of liabilities in the balance sheet. For example, inquiry and scanning may identify related-party payables or losses under sales or purchase commitments.

Search for unrecorded liabilities

This procedure is also sometimes called 'the out-of-period liability search' or 'the review of subsequent payments'. This audit procedure is invariably included in audit programs for substantive tests of the accounts payable balance.

The potential for unrecorded liabilities arises from both errors and irregularities. Errors result because of practical problems in closing the accounting records. Invariably some goods or services received before the end of the period do not become known and recorded until the next period. Controls over suppliers' invoices and receiving reports, matching of these source documents and investigation of unmatched items can minimise this problem. The auditor's objective is to obtain reasonable assurance that material liabilities have not been omitted.

Intentional omission of liabilities that exist at balance date does not change the auditor's objective. In fact, the same audit procedures should detect material omissions whether they are inadvertent or intentional. Goods or services received will ultimately have to be paid for in the next period to avoid disputes with suppliers, loss of credit lines or litigation with creditors.

The auditor selects from cash payments recorded in the subsequent period and traces them to the schedule of accounts payable outstanding at balance date, identifying those payments that pertain to the period under audit. Those identified payments not included in the schedule are unrecorded liabilities. The auditor also reviews and selects from unmatched receiving reports and suppliers' invoices received by balance date and suppliers' invoices received in the subsequent period in order to detect liabilities that should have been recognised at balance date.

Any suppliers' invoices representing unrecorded liabilities at balance date that are not received or paid before the auditor applies these procedures would not be detected. Thus, effectiveness is improved by doing the search for unrecorded liabilities relatively late in the audit. Confirmation of accounts payable balances is not subject to this disadvantage. It can therefore be an important complement to the search for unrecorded liabilities, particularly when the audit is scheduled for completion relatively close to balance date.

Materiality

In the search for unrecorded liabilities, materiality is used primarily to identify the items to be selected. In other words the auditor selects all cash payments, suppliers' invoices or receiving reports from the relevant period that exceed a cutoff amount. Since all items above a threshold amount are selected, audit sampling is not being used (refer to Chapter 11).

Audit risk

The inherent risk factors the auditor considers include the number of principal suppliers, supplier billing practices, the clients' purchasing methods and the principal types of goods or services purchased. Also, organisational considerations such as management's attitude to control and factors that predispose management to make material misrepresentations are particularly important.

Control risk generally focuses on specific control objectives related to completeness and reconciliation. Considerations that are particularly important in determining the extent of the out-of-period liability search are the effectiveness of:

- the client's review and investigation of unmatched prenumbered purchase orders and receiving reports at the end of the period;
- the client's reconciliation of suppliers' statements with accounts payable balances; and

- the client's monthly reconciliation of the schedule of accounts payable with the general ledger accounts payable balance.

Audit efficiency

Some audit efficiencies are possible in the accounts payable area. For example, because selection of suppliers for confirmation is based on the expected volume of purchases rather than the amount of the recorded balance, the confirmation requests can be sent before the accounts payable trial balance is prepared or tested. Also, sending the confirmation requests on or around the balance date allows the supplier to respond directly to the auditor with information they have gathered through their normal billing process. However, the primary efficiency consideration is co-ordination of the out-of-period liability search and confirmation of payable balances in order to avoid duplication of audit procedures to achieve specific audit objectives related to completeness and valuation and allocation.

Quick review

1. The main assertion of interest to the auditor when undertaking substantive tests of accounts payable is completeness.
2. The main audit procedures are a search for unrecorded accounts payable, confirmations and analytical procedures on related expense account balances.

NON-CURRENT ASSETS

The audit approaches for each of the account balances in this broad category are generally similar. The account balances are usually affected by a few large transactions, and amounts from previous periods have continuing significance; that is, the account does not turn over frequently. Thus, the approach to substantive tests for account balances in this category is to directly test the transactions that affected the account during the period; this indirectly substantiates the ending balance. The related revenue and expense accounts are normally examined in conjunction with the balance sheet accounts. For example, depreciation expense is tested in conjunction with the testing for property, plant and equipment.

Property, plant and equipment

The asset category of property, plant and equipment generally includes land, buildings and manufacturing equipment. It may also include office equipment, furniture and fixtures and even when these assets are classified separately the audit approach is generally the same as for property, plant and equipment.

The essential feature of substantive tests of balances for property, plant and equipment is emphasis on specific audit objectives related to *existence, rights and obligations* and *valuation and allocation*, achieved primarily by *substantiating additions* and *identifying retirements* during the period, considering any revaluations undertaken during the year and analytically testing or recomputing related expense and allowance accounts. The *occurrence* of the transactions associated with purchases of property, plant and equipment is covered by verifying the *existence* of the additions to property, plant and equipment as listed at balance date. *Cutoff* is not an issue because there is no continuous flow of transactions relating to this account. Testing whether the recording takes place in the correct period is usually achieved when testing for *existence* or *completeness*.

Assertions, objectives and procedures

Table 10.5 (overleaf) summarises the financial report assertions, the specific audit objectives and the common audit procedures traditionally used to achieve the objectives for property, plant and equipment and related account balances. As applied in the property, plant and equipment area, these procedures have the following features (Note that in Table 10.5, the assertions about classes of transactions and events are not included. This is because, as discussed above, the account balances are usually affected by a few large transactions, and therefore addressing the accounts balance assets will effectively address the assertions about transactions and events.):

- **Vouching** This procedure consists of inspecting the supporting documentation for additions, retirements and changes in valuation or allocation methods during the period. For example, the auditor examines the supplier's invoice and the receiving report for new equipment, and considers the appropriateness of capitalisation in light of entity policy and accounting principles. If assets are revalued, the new values may need to be sourced back to supporting evidence such as an independent expert's opinion.

- **Physical examination** The auditor obtains knowledge of additions and retirements through inquiries to client personnel, reviewing accounting records and touring the plant. The auditor notes whether any identified new equipment is entered in the accounting records and whether items in the accounting records can be located in the plant.

- **Analytical procedures** Several analytical procedures are useful for detecting misclassified additions, unrecorded retirements and miscalculation of depreciation expense. The auditor compares property, plant and equipment balances and depreciation expense with amounts of previous years and budgets, and current additions to the capital budget. Also, the auditor computes the ratio of depreciation expense and accumulated depreciation to equipment balances in the current and previous periods. The auditor also relates changes in property, plant and equipment balances to expected related changes in insurance expense, land taxes and repairs and maintenance expense.

- **Inquiry and scanning** The auditor asks operating management and personnel about actual additions and retirements. Inquiries to executive management may reveal where revaluations have taken place. The auditor also asks about decisions, such as adding or discontinuing a product or a line of business or revaluing a class of assets, that affect additions and retirements or an asset valuation. A scan of the accounting records for proceeds resulting from the sale of retired equipment may be undertaken in circumstances where the auditor considers that this amount may be potentially material.

- **Recomputation** The auditor recomputes depreciation expense and considers whether depreciation is calculated in accordance with an acceptable accounting method consistently applied. Usually, the auditor does not need to make a detailed recomputation when depreciable assets are voluminous. Depreciable assets may be grouped in categories with similar lives and the same depreciation method, and the calculation made on an overall basis. Technically, this is an analytical procedure.

- **General procedures** The general procedures relevant to property, plant and equipment include reading minutes, inspecting debt agreements and making inquiries to management in order to identify significant changes in the composition or valuation of property, plant and equipment and related liens and mortgages requiring disclosure.

TABLE 10.5 Assertions, objectives and substantive procedures for property, plant and equipment

Financial report assertion	Specific audit objective	Common substantive audit procedures to achieve objectives
Assertions about classes of transactions and events	Because transactions comprise the movements in account balances, these assertions will be addressed by addressing the assertions about account balances	
Assertions about account balances		
Existence	Property, plant and equipment included in the balance sheet physically exists. Retirements are removed	• Vouching to invoices • Physical examination of additions • Analytical procedures
Rights and obligations	The entity has legal title or equivalent ownership rights to property, plant and equipment included in the balance sheet and the related lease obligation of capitalised leased assets is recognised	• General procedures • Inquiry and scanning
Completeness	Property, plant and equipment includes all capitalisable costs (capitalisable costs are not expensed)	• Inquiry • Scanning repairs and maintenance for items that were expensed rather than capitalised
Valuation and allocation	Property, plant and equipment are appropriately valued and allowances for depreciation or depletion are computed on the basis of acceptable and consistent methods. Additions include only the capitalisable cost of assets purchased, constructed or leased	• Recomputation of depreciation or depletion calculations • Analytical procedures • Vouching costs to invoices • Inquiries about revaluations • Test clerical accuracy of property, plant and equipment listing

Substantiation of additions

The auditor uses a combination of vouching (inspecting supporting documentation), physical examination (touring the plant) and analytical procedures to substantiate additions to property, plant and equipment. The vouching includes both additions recorded in property, plant and equipment accounts and items recorded in the repairs and maintenance expense account. In reviewing the charges to repairs and maintenance expense, the auditor is concerned with the specific audit objective related to *completeness* for property, plant and equipment. Repairs and maintenance expense may contain costs that should be capitalised rather than expensed. Whether the item is capitalised or expensed depends on conformity with approved accounting standards and adherence to entity policy.

Identifying retirements

In achieving the specific audit objective related to existence for property, plant and equipment, the auditor is concerned with detecting significant unrecorded retirements. Generally, the auditor uses a combination of vouching, physical examination and analytical procedures to identify them.

When vouching additions the auditor notes whether the item is new or a replacement, and traces the replacements to the recording of a retirement. The auditor observes whether or not significant recorded items are in the plant. A study of relationships between related accounts, such as property insurance, land taxes and miscellaneous revenue, may also disclose unrecorded retirements. For example, sale of retired equipment as scrap may be recorded as miscellaneous income. Also, the auditor's knowledge of the business can be an important factor in identifying unrecorded retirements. For example, the auditor's knowledge of the discontinuance of a particular product, combined with knowledge that certain equipment is used exclusively for making that product, lead the auditor to expect to see a recorded retirement or reclassification for that equipment.

Valuation of property, plant and equipment

The auditor must be satisfied that the property, plant and equipment is valued in accordance with the accounting standards. AASB 116 (IAS 16) 'Property, Plant and Equipment' permits either the cost model or the revaluation model to be used for valuing assets. Under both methods of valuation, the auditor must consider whether there is any impairment of the carrying value of the asset. There are three principal ways of finding evidence of impairment: observing obsolete or damaged units during a tour of the plant; identifying assets associated with discontinued activities but not yet disposed of; and inquiry of management as to budgets and forecasts in relation to the carrying value of assets.

When the revaluation model is used, property, plant and equipment items are required to be valued at their fair value (less any subsequent accumulated depreciation and subsequent accumulated impairment losses). Revaluations to fair value are required with sufficient regularity to ensure that the carrying value does not differ materially from fair value. AUS 526/ISA 545 'Auditing Fair Value Measurements and Disclosures' outlines that substantive tests may involve:

- testing management's significant assumptions, the value model, and the underlying data (paragraphs .39–.49) and
- developing independent fair estimates to corroborate the appropriateness of the fair value measurement.

If the valuation is undertaken by an independent expert the auditor needs to be satisfied as to their skill, competence and objectivity. The auditor vouches the valuer's report, paying regard to the basis of valuation, and considers its appropriateness as a basis for determining the carrying amount of that class of assets in the financial report. Major revaluations should be discussed by the board of directors or audit committee, and the auditor should review minutes of such discussions. If classes of assets are revalued, the auditor must ensure that there is adequate disclosure, including the basis of revaluation and, if an independent valuer was used, the name and qualifications of this person.

If, after considering the available evidence, there is still a risk of a material misstatement, the auditor may consider getting an independent expert valuation. In such a situation the auditor needs to follow the standards and guidance outlined in AUS 606/ISA 620 'Using the Work of an Expert', discussed in Chapter 5.

Materiality and audit risk

The usual approach to substantiating additions is to vouch all those above a specified cut-off dollar amount. In the property, plant and equipment area, account balances are relatively more susceptible to misstatement caused by misapplication of accounting principles. The accounting principles for determining the proper costs to include in acquisition cost and the proper accounting treatment of significant repairs, improvements and similar matters are relatively complex. Also, the accounting standard related to capitalisation of leased assets (AASB 117/ IAS 17 'Leases') is relatively complex, increasing the associated risk.

The auditor's assessment of control risk over purchases of property, plant and equipment may result in a planned adjustment to substantive tests of balances for property, plant and equipment by adjusting the cutoff amount for additions to be vouched. Other factors the auditor considers in assessing the likelihood of material misstatement in property, plant and equipment include whether the client's procedures contain the following measures to reduce control risk:

- use of capital budgeting for acquisition of property, plant and equipment, with careful monitoring and follow up;
- detailed property, plant and equipment ledgers maintained and periodically reconciled to general ledger control accounts;
- identification tags fixed to new property, plant and equipment and issued tags reconciled to a property, plant and equipment ledger; and
- formal policy for capitalisation/expense decisions, partial depreciation and procedures for reporting of retirements established and incorporated in procedures manuals.

Normally, entities do not make an annual physical inspection of property, plant and equipment comparable to a physical inventory count. Such inspections may be made every three to five years. The auditor normally does not insist on observing a physical inspection of property, plant and equipment unless there are very serious deficiencies in controls.

Quick review

1. The main assertions of interest to the auditor when undertaking tests of balances for property, plant and equipment are existence/occurrence, rights and obligations, and valuation and allocation.
2. The main audit procedures for property, plant and equipment are substantiating additions and identifying retirements during the period, checking supporting documentation for changes in valuation and allocation and establishing analytical procedures for related expense and allowance accounts.

Investments and intangible assets

The audit approach and the audit problems for investments and intangibles are similar to those for property, plant and equipment. The auditor tests the account balances, directly testing the transactions that affect the balances during the period, and conformity with approved accounting standards is very important. However, investments at balance date are normally substantiated directly.

Investments

The form of investments can vary considerably. Investments may be in debt or equity securities; the securities may be marketable or non-marketable; the entities whose securities are held may be associated or non-associated. Also, an investment may be a loan or advance rather than a security. This discussion focuses on long-term investments. However, the primary distinction between long-term investments and investments classified as current assets is management's intention and ability to hold the investment for longer than one year. Thus, the discussion generally applies to most investments.

The financial report assertions, specific audit objectives and common audit procedures traditionally used to achieve the objectives for investments are summarised in Table 10.6. The essential features of direct tests of balances for long-term investments are emphasis on specific audit objectives related to *existence* and *rights and obligations*, achieved primarily by physical examination or confirmation and vouching; and emphasis on specific audit objectives related to *valuation and allocation*, achieved by a combination of recomputation, vouching and tracing or other specialised procedures. The *occurrence* of the transactions associated with investments is covered by verifying the *existence* of the investments at balance date.

If the investment has a physical existence and is in the client's possession, such as debt instruments that were purchased, physical examination is appropriate. If the investment has no physical existence, such as a loan or advance, or is held in safekeeping by an independent custodian, then the auditor should examine any documentary evidence such as a loan agreement and also consider sending a confirmation request to the investment custodian.

The difficult accounting and auditing issues in the long-term investment area usually relate to specific audit objectives concerned with valuation and allocation. Generally, the relevant auditing procedures are determined largely by the method of valuation and allocation that is most appropriate under the accounting standards.

TABLE 10.6 **Assertions, objectives and substantive procedures for investments**

Financial report assertion	Specific audit objective	Common substantive audit procedures to achieve objectives
Assertions about classes of transactions and events	Because transactions comprise the movements in account balances, these assertions will be addressed by addressing the assertions about account balances	
Assertions about account balances		
Existence	Investments in securities (shares, bonds, notes) exist and loans and advances exist	• Physical examination • Confirmation
Rights and obligations	The entity owns or has ownership rights to all investments included in the balance sheet	• Vouching • Physical examination • Confirmation
Completeness	All investments are included in the balance sheet	• General procedures
Valuation and allocation	Investments are valued properly with respect to the accounting standards	• Recomputation, vouching and tracing • Inspection of market quotations or reviewing investee's financial statements • Test clerical accuracy of listing of investments

Whether investments in securities are carried at cost or at market value depends on their nature and classification. Cost is substantiated by vouching the acquisition price in the accounting records, and market price is substantiated by comparing with published market quotations.

The substantive tests of balances for investments also include tests of the related investment income and of gains or losses in investment transactions. By reference to the financial press, the auditor can substantiate dividend and interest income on investments and the trading price at the time of purchase or sale of securities.

Intangible assets

A variety of items fall into this asset category: patents, copyrights, intellectual property, organisational costs, franchise fees and goodwill acquired in a business combination. The essential feature of direct tests of balances for intangibles is emphasis on specific audit objectives related to *existence* and *valuation and allocation*, achieved primarily by vouching, inspection of legal documents and recomputation or analytical procedures. The primary risk of misstatement arises from misapplication of principles set out in approved accounting standards.

The accounting issues generally relate to whether or not a cost may properly be deferred and the appropriate amortisation period. For example, research and development costs must be accounted for in accordance with AASB 138 (IAS 38) 'Intangible Assets', and the cost cannot be deferred, with expenditure on research being recognised as an expense when it is incurred. However, the standard does allow other types of internally developed intangible assets to be recognised as such if they meet specific criteria.

Quick review

1. The main assertions of interest to the auditor when undertaking substantive tests of balances for investments are existence, rights and obligations and valuation and allocation.
2. The main audit procedures for the verification of existence and rights and obligations of investments are physical examination or confirmation and vouching. Evidence for valuation and allocation may be gained by recomputation, vouching and tracing or other specialised procedures.
3. The main assertions of interest to the auditor when undertaking tests of balances for intangibles are existence and valuation and allocation.
4. The main audit procedures for intangible assets are vouching, inspection of legal documents and recomputation or analytical procedures.

learning objective 8

NON-CURRENT LIABILITIES AND OWNERS' EQUITY

Non-current liabilities

Generally, non-current liabilities include loans, bonds, and notes payable that are due after one year from the balance date. The current portions of otherwise long-term obligations are classified as current liabilities, but are examined in conjunction with non-current liabilities. Also, interest expense and other related account balances are examined in conjunction with non-current liabilities.

The essential feature of direct tests of balances for non-current liabilities is the emphasis on the specific audit assertion of *completeness*, achieved primarily by confirmations, general procedures and analytical procedures.

Assertions, objectives and procedures

The financial report assertions, specific audit objectives and common audit procedures that are traditionally used to achieve those objectives for non-current liabilities are summarised in Table 10.7 overleaf. As applied to non-current liabilities, these procedures have the following features:

- **Confirmation** Normally, the auditor confirms the balance and related details, such as security held, interest rate and terms and interest paid and accrued, directly with all significant debt holders. The form of confirmation is similar to that which is used for accounts payable. Where a trustee keeps the detailed records of debt holders and makes interest payments to them, the confirmation request is sent to the trustee. The standard bank confirmation form can be used for banks that are holders of debt. Details of compensating balances, lines of credit and contingent liabilities are also separately confirmed with the bank. Care should be taken to achieve the specific audit objectives related to completeness as well as those related to existence.

- **General procedures** For non-current liabilities, general procedures contribute more directly to the achievement of audit objectives than is often the case in other areas. The most important general procedures are reading minutes of meetings of the board of directors and reviewing debt agreements. The auditor is concerned with ascertaining that all obligations are authorised by the board of directors. Debt agreements are extremely important because violation of the terms may result in automatic acceleration of the due date on which the debt has to be repaid. When the debt is reclassified as current, this may materially affect the entity's financial position and its ability to meet its obligations on a timely basis. Debt agreements often contain provisions requiring maintenance of specified working capital and debt to equity ratios and restricting the payment of dividends or other financing activities. Also, the debt may be secured by either specific or floating charges over assets of the entity. The auditor must also consider the possibility of the entity being placed in liquidation through violation of debt covenants.

- **Analytical procedures** Analytical procedures for non-current liabilities include comparison of balances with the previous period, and comparison of new debt proceeds and principal repayments with cash flow projections. Also, the auditor considers the reasonableness of the entity's average interest rate incurred (interest expense divided by the average of the beginning and ending debt balances). An unreasonably high average interest rate incurred might indicate unrecorded debt, and therefore concerns about the completeness assertion for non-current liabilities.

- **Inquiry** The classification of debt as current or non-current may depend on the intent and ability of management to refinance obligations. The auditor substantiates this ability by examining evidence of actual refinancing in the subsequent period or the non-cancellability of financing agreements. The auditor also makes inquiries of management to corroborate intent. Some obligations, such as obligations that arise when a decision is made to dispose of a segment of a business, are recognised before a liability is legally incurred, and it is important to ask management about such obligations.

- **Recomputation, vouching and tracing** The auditor tests interest expense by recomputing the amount based on the outstanding balance, interest rate and fraction of the year outstanding, with these details being agreed to loan documentation. Interest payments are vouched to cash payments records, and the proceeds of new issues are traced to cash receipts records. The volume of debt transactions is generally low and all items are tested. If volume is high, analytical procedures may be used.

Financial report assertion	Specific audit objective	Common substantive audit procedures to achieve objectives
Assertions about classes of transactions and events	Because transactions comprise the movements in account balances, these assertions will normally be addressed by addressing the assertions about account balances	
Assertions about account balances		
Existence	Debt and similar obligations in the balance sheet exist at the balance date	• Confirmation of identified liabilities with debt-holders • General procedures, read minutes of meetings and review debt agreements
Rights and obligations	Debt and similar obligations are legal or specific and definite obligations of the entity	• General procedures, read minutes of meetings and review debt agreements • Inquiry
Completeness	The balance sheet includes all debt and similar obligations incurred at the balance date	• General procedures, read minutes of meetings and review debt agreements • Analytical procedures
Valuation and allocation	Debt and similar obligations are presented at the proper amounts	• Recomputation, vouching and tracing • Test clerical accuracy of listing of non-current liabilities

Materiality and audit risk

For non-current liabilities, consideration of materiality is not usually a significant factor in the nature, timing and extent of tests. There are usually a few large transactions or items and all of them are material.

Considerations of importance for audit risk include adherence to a stated policy that all non-current liabilities must be authorised by the board of directors, and formal assignment of responsibility for monitoring compliance with the requirements and restrictions of debt agreements.

Owners' equity

Equity accounts differ depending on the form of organisation. This discussion focuses on shareholders' equity in a company.

The specific audit objectives and common audit procedures for shareholders' equity are substantially the same as for non-current liabilities, so a separate table summarising them is not presented. The primary differences for particular procedures are as follows:

■ **Confirmation** Many companies use the services of independent share registry offices to maintain detailed records of shareholders. In that case, confirmation requests are sent to those agents. If a company keeps its own share records, the auditor examines the records rather than sending confirmations to shareholders. The auditor's chief concern when the company keeps shareholder records is with the specific objective related to completeness. The auditor examines the shareholder register and observes company procedures to ensure that all issued shares are recorded and that all unissued shares are safeguarded.

- **General procedures** In addition to reading the minutes of meetings of the board of directors, the auditor would read the company's constitution. The description of shares as presented in the financial report should correspond to the information in the company's constitution. Authorisation of dividends should be in the minutes of board meetings.
- **Recomputation, vouching and tracing** The auditor's procedures for cash dividends are similar to those for interest payments.

Quick review

1. The main assertions of interest to the auditor when undertaking tests of balances for non-current liabilities are completeness and valuation and allocation.
2. The main audit procedures are confirmations, reading minutes of meetings of the board and examining debt agreements.
3. The main assertions of interest to the auditor when undertaking tests of balances for owners' equity are completeness and valuation and allocation.
4. The main audit procedures are inspection of shareholders' registers or confirmation with an independent share registrar, and reviewing the minutes of the meetings of the board of directors.

INCOME STATEMENT

This section explains the relationship between specific audit objectives for income statement account balances and those for balance sheet accounts. This is also an area where controls, such as budgets and variance analyses, are very important in undertaking tests of balances.

In a double-entry accounting system, testing one side of a transaction automatically tests the other side. Thus a procedure that achieves an audit objective for one side of a transaction should achieve a comparable audit objective for the other side. Thus, for example, if the auditor verifies the existence of an accounts receivable balance, this will verify the occurrence of the sales transactions that comprise the accounts receivable balance. For this reason the extent of substantive tests of transactions is negatively related to the amount of substantive testing of balances that is undertaken.

Audit procedures for income statement accounts

The account balances in the income statement are generally tested by one of the following procedures:

- **Substantiation by simultaneous tests** This category includes those income statement account balances that are tested indirectly as a result of substantive tests of balances of related balance sheet accounts. As outlined in this chapter, the auditor therefore realises that, for example, audit tests of sales transactions also provide evidence for the verification of the accounts receivable balance. It is for these reasons that the related transactions and balances have been discussed together within this chapter. The primary income statement account balances that usually fall in this category are sales, cost of sales and many of the expense accounts.

- **Substantiation directly in conjunction with balance sheet accounts** Some income statement account balances are verified when undertaking substantive tests of related balance sheet balances. Examples of these account balances, with the related balance sheet accounts shown parenthetically, are as follows:
  - depreciation expense (property, plant and equipment)
  - amortisation expense (intangible assets)
  - investment income (investments)
  - interest expense (loans or notes payable).
- **Substantiation directly by analytical procedures** The auditor usually applies several analytical tests to income statement account balances as additional overall tests of reasonableness, or to provide necessary assurances on appropriate classification or completeness. Income statement account balances are compared with amounts of previous periods and budgets. Also, the relationships of amounts that are expected to follow a predictable pattern are considered. For example, a relationship should exist between the amount of sales, cost of sales, accounts receivable and doubtful debt expense. When there are significant variances from logical or historical relationships, the auditor should obtain explanations, consider whether they are reasonable and follow up on information gained through these explanations, as required by AUS 512/ISA 520 and by law (refer to the Pacific Acceptance Corporation case in Chapter 4). Analytical procedures may be particularly important for considering the appropriate classification of expenses.
- **Substantiation directly by separate direct tests** Some income statement account balances are usually substantiated by separate direct tests of balances. Generally, these fall into two broad categories—individually significant transactions or events and account balances of intrinsic interest.

Individually significant transactions or events

Some income statement items that enter into the determination of net profit are individually significant, and the auditor applies separate substantive tests to these items. Examples of items that are individually significant include:

- **Discontinued operations** The results of discontinued operations and any related gain or loss are reported separately from continuing operations. Usually, the amount is very material and complex accounting issues are involved in the recognition of gain or loss.
- **Accounting principle changes** The cumulative effect of changing to a new accounting principle also needs to be considered. The auditor needs to obtain evidence to evaluate management's justification for the change, the accounting effect and treatment of the change, the acceptability of the new accounting principle and the adequacy of the disclosures associated with the change.

These items generally involve complex accounting issues. The auditor uses recomputation to test the proper application of accounting principles, but audit procedures are also usually necessary to substantiate the underlying transactions or event. In specific circumstances, other transactions or events, such as a sale of land and buildings, may be individually significant and would be tested directly.

Account balances of intrinsic interest

Some account balances are analysed and the details of items in the balance are vouched to supporting documents because there is some interest in the account balance that is out of

proportion to the effect of the balance on net profit. For example, *travel and*
expenses and *officers' salaries* often fall into this category because of the income
and specific disclosure requirements associated with these items. Another cc
legal fees. The auditor is concerned with identifying all solicitors consulted by
the period. An analysis of the legal fees account is a good way to identify th
and why they have been consulted. Because separate disclosures of all *au*
fees are required, transactions underlying these accounts may also be se

Quick review

1 Some income statement accounts are substantiated when undertaking tests ᴜ. balance sheet accounts. These include sales, cost of sales and many expenses.

2 Some income statement accounts are substantiated directly in conjunction with tests of balances of related balance sheet accounts. These include investment income, depreciation, amortisation and interest expenses.

3 Necessary assurances on many income statement accounts are provided by analytical procedures. These are account balances where the relationship of amounts is expected to follow a predictable pattern, or account balances which individually are not of sufficient risk or materiality.

4 Some income statement account balances are individually significant because of their nature or size. These include discontinued operations, specific significant revenues and expenses from ordinary activities, and items of intrinsic interest such as travel and entertainment expenses and legal, auditors' and directors' fees. Details of items in these accounts are usually vouched to supporting documents.

AUDITING WITH THE COMPUTER: TESTING CLIENT FILES

 learning objective

If client files are voluminous, it is usually efficient to apply audit procedures to records in their computer-readable form. For example, a very large entity may have master files with over 100 000 individual records in applications such as inventory and accounts receivable. In these circumstances it may be more efficient for the auditor to use a computer program to automate the auditing procedures. An auditor's program may be used with master files or transaction files, so the audit procedures may be tests of details of transactions or balances. However, it is more common to use an auditor's program to test a client's master files. One of the main ways is to use a program that is designed to read the data existing on a client's file, and undertake auditing tasks on this data, including identifying items deemed to be of risk or material. How this is done will be described in more detail below.

AGS 1060/IAPS 1009 'Computer Assisted Audit Techniques' (CAATs) identifies a number of categories of CAATs (Example 10.3 overleaf). These include a number of evidence-gathering techniques involving the use of computer programs.

Generalised audit software (GAS)

The most widely used form of CAAT is generalised audit software, which is also referred to in AGS 1060/IAPS 1009 as **package programs**. A software package is used to perform specific audit tasks, such as footing and comparing items, on a computer-readable file. A generalised program that can perform several audit tasks for many clients is more efficient than programs specially written for particular clients and tasks. However, a generalised package is not an purpose device. The auditor's software must interact with the operating system of the client's computer. Particular packages are designed for families of hardware that use particular operating systems. Large auditing firms have developed their own packages, and some software vendors offer audit packages. In some cases, versions have been developed for different hardware and operating systems.

Since there are many audit software packages, this discussion describes the general features of this type of software. When generalised software is run, the first programmed step is to read the client's file. The processing is usually performed on a copy of the client's file, ensuring that the client's data are not changed. The other two aspects of generalised audit software are:

1 **File formats** Client file formats vary considerably. For example, the number, type and size of fields in a record on an accounts receivable master file differ widely from client to client. One of the advantages of generalised audit software is its ability to deal with different file formats. The file format is defined by the auditor as part of the input specification. Some packages reformat the data in a standardised manner. The auditor specifies the file layout and the fields and their location in the file.

2 **Processing instructions** Generalised audit software is designed to perform several types of processing tasks. The package provides some means for the auditor to determine the particular tasks to be performed. Several approaches are used. In many cases, the auditor fills out coding or specification sheets to identify the tasks. In others, the auditor writes a simplified program in a specially designed command language.

Generalised audit software programs that are currently available perform an extensive range of functions and can:

- select sample items (e.g. select customer balances for positive and negative confirmation);
- identify records meeting specified criteria (exception reporting) (e.g. identify customer balances over credit limit);
- test and make calculations (e.g. recalculate interest charges);
- compare data in separate fields or on separate files (e.g. compare change in balance of an account with details on transactions files);
- summarise data (e.g. summarise accounts receivable by age (one month, two months, etc.)); and
- write reports (e.g. an accounts receivable confirmation letter or work paper account analysis).

Note that in general, audit software is used to test computer file data. It is difficult to test system logic, except implicitly by the results that appear in the data files. These programs contain no explicit testing of programmed controls. The existence of controls may be inferred. For example, take a programmed control which does not allow the account balance to exceed the credit limit. By undertaking an exception report, and observing no records where the account balance is greater than the credit limit, the existence of this control may be inferred. However, the control has not been directly tested—this would require the use of one of the auditing through the computer techniques outlined in Chapter 9.

To make effective use of generalised software the auditor needs to plan carefully. Specific audit objectives remain the same whether audit procedures are applied manually or with generalised software. The starting point in both cases is to develop specific audit objectives from financial report assertions. However, in using generalised software, it is extremely important to specify objectives and criteria in advance of testing. The auditor who manually selects specified items from the accounting records may notice other unusual items. When generalised software is used, an item cannot be selected unless the auditor has completely specified the criteria for its selection in advance.

EXAMPLE 10.3 Use of CAATs

You are auditing the accounts receivable of your client. The accounts receivable master file contains the following fields:

Field	Field Title
1	Debtor Number
2	Debtor Name
3	Debtor Address
4	Credit Limit
5	Outstanding Balance
6	Balance < 30 days
7	Balance 30–60 days
8	Balance > 60 days
9	Total dollar value of transactions this year
10	Date of last transaction

Required

Describe how the auditor may use audit software to aid in verifying the existence and valuation and allocation assertions of the debtors' master file.

Solution

The main way in which the auditor verifies existence is to undertake a debtors' confirmation procedure or verify subsequent receipts from the debtors. Both of these techniques will involve the auditor selecting a group of auditors' outstanding balances to be tested. Thus the auditor would use the sampling function of the audit software.

In testing for the valuation and allocation assertion, the auditor needs to identify accounts where there may be a difficulty of payment. This will involve the auditor using the exception reporting function of the audit software. Some of the exception reports may include:

- Accounts with Outstanding Balance (field 5) greater than Credit Limit (field 4)
- Accounts with amounts outstanding > 60 days (field 8 > 0)
- Accounts where total dollar value of transactions (field 9) is less than outstanding balance (field 5).

If these accounts are identified, they too may be included in the debtors' confirmation procedure or review of subsequent receipts.

Specialised audit software (SAS)

If generalised audit software cannot be used on a particular client's computer, the auditor might consider having a program written to accomplish specific audit tasks. SAS is also commonly referred to as **purpose-written programs**.

Alternatively, there is currently available a wide range of SAS for specific industries, and it is more efficient for major routines in these industries. For example, in the insurance industry there are purpose-written programs for the calculation of premium income and reinsurance premiums, which are major issues in the insurance industry. Another example of an application for purpose-written programs is municipal council audits, where the calculation of rates is a major issue.

Specialised software can be written by auditors, outside programmers, software vendors or client programmers. In deciding how to develop it, there is a trade-off between cost and independence. Use of client programs or programmers, while normally cheaper, is less independent.

Utility programs

Software and hardware vendors have developed software designed to accomplish common tasks and routines, such as sorting records or merging files. These types of routines are commonly available in most major applications. The auditor can use a utility program to print the entire contents of a file, merge files or sort records in a file into a sequence useful for an audit task (such as size or location).

Systems management programs

Systems management programs are defined in AGS 1060/IAPS 1006 as enhanced productivity tools that are typically part of a sophisticated operating systems environment, for example data retrieval software or code comparison software. These programs are sometimes suitable to assist with the auditor's objectives, performing functions such as retrieving data which meets specific criteria. Management also has an interest in identifying and following up on records that are large or unusual, for example debtors that haven't paid for over 60 days, and this can be aided by such programs.

EXAMPLE 10.4 Using audit software: your chance to use ACL

The development of audit software, such as ACL, has resolved a persistent problem plaguing auditors—the difficulty of directly accessing client computer information. Recent innovations have allowed auditors with little or no computer background to perform tasks that used to be reserved for information system auditors. With the increased usage of personal computers (PCs) in the business community and other advances in technology, auditors now enjoy greater access to client data, directly from their PCs. Today's auditors are able to quickly access data to perform such tasks as sorting files, sampling, exception reporting and analytical procedures.

In summary, Computer Assisted Audit Techniques (CAATs) are changing the way auditors perform their responsibilities, allowing them to complete their audits more efficiently *and* more effectively. Audit software is being used to analyse large data files, identify anomalies, compare fields, perform queries, develop reports and document audit steps. More importantly, tests performed with the aid of audit software can be performed on entire populations, rather than just samples. Internal auditors can report to management on the basis of '100 per cent' tests, thus giving management a complete picture of the area in question.

For example, audit software may assist an auditor in comparing an Accounts Payable file, a Payroll file and a Contractor file, to determine whether any current employees are being paid as contractors. Similarly, lists of vendor addresses can be compared to employee address files to see whether employees are paying invoices to companies that they own or operate. Finally, auditors can play a consultative role by instructing clients on how to use CAATs for their own benefit.

For the most part, the widely used audit software packages are very similar. Most have been developed from standard spreadsheet applications with which students are already familiar. These specialised spreadsheet applications, however, have been modified such that common audit tasks can be performed through accessing redeveloped macros at the touch of a button. In addition, the audit software packages can handle much larger data sets than most spreadsheet packages.

The CD with this book contains a tutorial on using ACL audit software. It will allow you to become familiar with the audit tests that can be applied using ACL. The CD also contains a case study using ACL. If you wish to explore ACL further, there is also a web site demo <http://www.acl.com> that is free for students. ACL asks you to indicate that you are a student, so that a salesperson will not follow up on the contact.

Quick review

1. The major technique for testing the client's files involves a program under the auditor's control. The program can be used to read the client's files and identify areas where the auditor may wish to concentrate audit testing, and also to automate many time-consuming processes.

2. Auditing with computer techniques includes the use of:
   - generalised audit software—used with many clients;
   - specialised audit software—programs especially written for a client, task or industry;
   - utility programs—routines designed to accomplish common tasks for many clients;
   - systems management programs—enhanced productivity tools that are typically associated with sophisticated systems environments.

3. The functions that can be performed by such software include selecting sample items, exception reporting, testing and making calculations, summarising data and report writing.

Summary

The auditor undertakes the most efficient and effective combination of tests of controls and substantive tests of transactions and balances to achieve a required level of audit risk. For each of the major account balances or classes of transactions, this chapter has identified the relative importance of the assertions and the substantive audit procedures that would be used to gather audit evidence for those assertions. The chapter has also outlined the computer-assisted audit techniques that would be used in the gathering of audit evidence.

Key terms

Accuracy	455	Package programs	493
Bank confirmation requests	459	Physical inventory count	470
Bank reconciliations	461	Positive form of debtors' confirmation	466
Bank transfer schedule	462	Pricing and summarisation	476
Classification	455	Purpose-written programs	495
Complete inventory count	470	Retail inventory method	470
Completeness	455	Rights and obligations	456
Confirmation	463	Standard cost system	470
Cutoff	455	Stocktake	470
Cycle count	470	Substantive tests of transactions	452
Dual-purpose tests	452	Systems management programs	496
Existence	455	Tracing	452
Negative form of debtors' confirmation	466	Valuation and allocation	457
Occurrence	455	Vouching	452

References

Bailey, C.D. and Bellard, G. (1986) 'Improving response rates to accounts receivable confirmations: An experiment using four techniques', *Auditing: A Journal of Practice and Theory*, Spring, 77–85.

Carleton, J. and Compton, C. (1988) 'Bank confirmations: A new look', *The CPA Journal*, January, 93–6.

Caster, P. (1992) 'The role of confirmations as audit evidence', *Journal of Accountancy*, February, 73–6.

Coderre, D. (1993) 'Computer assisted audit tools and techniques', *Internal Auditor*, February, 24–7.

Edge, W.R., Farley, A.A. and Simnett, R. (1988) 'A review of the capabilities and availability of generalised audit software', *The Chartered Accountant in Australia*, November, 63–7.

Fensome, M. (1993) 'Statement of Auditing Practice AUP 1 "Bank Confirmation Requests"', *Charter*, September, 32–3.

File, R.G. and Ward, B.H. (1995) 'Improving the results of second request confirmation procedures', *Auditing: A Journal of Practice and Theory*, Spring, 87–93.

Locke, C. (1998) 'Auditing issues—Bank confirmation requests', *Charter*, March, 76–7.

O'Leary, C. (1993) 'Debtors confirmations—handle with care', *Australian Accountant*, May, 35–7.

Pasewark, W.R. and Strawser, J.R. (1992) 'An investigation of auditor judgements of the effect of preliminary analytical procedures on the extent of substantive testing', *Accounting and Finance*, November, 91–108.

Schwerseriz, J. (1987) 'Accounts payable confirmations: why and how used', *The CPA Journal*, May, 101–93.

Windsor, S. (1991) 'The use of audit sampling techniques to test inventory', *Journal of Accountancy*, January, 107–11.

Winograd, B. and Herz, R.H. (1995) 'Derivatives: What's an auditor to do?', *Journal of Accountancy*, June, 75–80.

Assignments

MAXIMISE YOUR MARKS! There are approximately 30 interactive questions on substantive tests of transactions and balances available online at www.mhhe. com/au/gay3e

Additional assignments for this chapter are contained in Appendix A of this book, page 771.

REVIEW QUESTIONS

10.1 The following questions relate to audit procedures for inventories. Select the *best* response.

   (a) During a client's stocktake you select a sample of items from the floor, count them and trace the quantities to the inventory summary sheet. Which financial report assertion is this audit procedure related to?

     A rights and obligations
     B valuation and allocation
     C existence
     D completeness

   (b) Your client sells a high-technology product which is subject to frequent technological improvements and design changes in order to keep current with the market. Based on this information, for the inventory account, the assertion upon which you should concentrate your audit procedures is:

     A existence
     B valuation and allocation
     C rights and obligations
     D completeness

   (c) An auditor, having accounted for a sequence of inventory tags, traces information on a representative number of tags to the physical inventory sheets. The purpose of this procedure is to obtain assurance that:

     A the final inventory is valued at cost
     B inventory sheets do not include untagged inventory items
     C all inventory represented by an inventory tag is bona fide
     D all inventory represented by an inventory tag is listed on the inventory sheets

   (d) A client maintains perpetual inventory records in both quantities and dollars. If the assessed level of control risk is high, an auditor would probably:

     A apply gross profit tests to ascertain the reasonableness of the physical accounts
     B insist that the client perform physical counts of inventory items several times during the year
     C request the client to schedule the physical inventory count at the end of the year
     D increase the extent of tests of controls of the inventory cycle

   (e) Your client's inventory turnover has decreased from 8.2 times to 5.6 times during the year. Based on this decrease, which financial report assertion would you be least concerned with?

     A rights and obligations
     B existence
     C completeness
     D valuation and allocation

10.2 The following questions relate to audit procedures for accounts receivable. Select the *best* response.

   (a) During the process of confirming receivables as of 30 June, a positive confirmation was returned indicating the 'balance owed as of 30 June was paid on 9 July'. The auditor would most likely:

     A reconfirm the zero balance as of 9 July
     B verify that the amount was received

    C determine whether there were any changes in the account between 1 July and 9 July

    D determine whether a customary trade discount was taken by the customer

(b) An auditor reconciles the total of the accounts receivable subsidiary ledger to the general ledger control account, as of 31 October. By this procedure, the auditor would be most likely to learn which of the following?

    A An opening balance in a subsidiary ledger account was improperly carried forward from the previous accounting period.

    B An account balance is past due and should be written off.

    C An October invoice was improperly computed.

    D An October cheque from a customer was posted in error to the account of another customer with a similar name.

(c) Which of the following is not a primary objective of the auditor in undertaking substantive testing of accounts receivable?

    A Establish existence of the receivables

    B Determine the completeness of the recorded receivables

    C Determine the approximate amount that can be expected to be received

    D Determine the adequacy of the internal control

(d) An auditor should perform alternative procedures to substantiate the existence of accounts receivable when:

    A collectibility of the receivables is in doubt

    B pledging of the receivables is probable

    C no reply to a positive confirmation request is received

    D no reply to a negative confirmation request is received

(e) Once an auditor has determined that accounts receivable have increased due to slow collections in a 'tight money' environment, the auditor would be likely to:

    A review the credit and collection policy

    B expand tests of collectibility

    C increase the balance in the allowance for bad debts account

    D review the going-concern ramifications

10.3 The following questions relate to audit procedures for investments. Select the *best* response.

(a) Which of the following is not one of the auditor's primary objectives in an examination of marketable securities?

    A To determine whether securities are the property of the client

    B To determine whether securities are properly classified on the balance sheet

    C To determine whether securities are authentic

    D To determine whether securities actually exist

(b) Which of the following is the most effective audit procedure for verification of dividends earned on investments in marketable equity securities?

    A Comparing the amounts received with dividends received in the preceding year

    B Tracing deposit of dividend cheques to the cash receipts book

    C Recomputing selected extensions and footings of dividend schedules and comparing totals to the general ledger

    D Reconciling amounts received with published dividend records

(c) To establish the existence and ownership of a long-term investment in the shares of a publicly traded company, an auditor ordinarily performs a security count or:

    A determines the market price per share at the balance sheet date from published quotations

    B confirms the number of shares owned with the issuing company

C relies on the client's internal control if the auditor has reasonable assurance that the control activities are being applied as prescribed

D confirms the number of shares owned that are held by an independent custodian

10.4 The following questions relate to audit procedures for property, plant and equipment. Select the *best* response.

(a) In the examination of property, plant and equipment, which of the following does the auditor not try to determine?

A The capital nature of items included in repairs and maintenance

B The reasonableness of the depreciation

C The adequacy of future replacement funds

D The extent of property disposed of during the year

(b) In violation of company policy, Warren Ltd erroneously capitalised the cost of painting its warehouse. The auditor examining Warren's financial report would most likely detect this when:

A observing during the physical inventory observation that the warehouse had been painted

B examining maintenance expense accounts

C discussing the capitalisation policies with Warren's financial controller

D examining the construction work orders supporting items capitalised during the year

(c) An auditor analyses repairs and maintenance accounts primarily to obtain evidence that:

A non-capitalisable expenditures for repairs and maintenance have been recorded in the proper period

B expenditures for property, plant and equipment have been recorded in the proper period

C non-capitalisable expenditures for repairs and maintenance have been properly charged to expenses

D expenditures for property, plant and equipment have not been charged to expenses

10.5 The following questions relate to audit procedures for non-current liabilities and shareholders' equity.

(a) When a client company does not maintain its own share records, the auditor should obtain written confirmation from the transfer agent and registrar concerning:

A guarantees of preferred share liquidation value

B the number of shares subject to agreements to repurchase

C the number of shares issued and outstanding

D restrictions on the payment of dividends

(b) The primary reason for preparing a reconciliation between interest-bearing obligations outstanding during the year and interest expense presented in the financial report is to:

A detect unrecorded liabilities

B ascertain the reasonableness of accrued interest

C assess control risk for securities

D determine the validity of prepaid interest expense

(c) An auditor would be least likely to use confirmations in connection with the examination of:

A property, plant and equipment

B long-term debt

C shareholders' equity

D inventories

10.6 The following questions relate to the use of computer-assisted audit techniques. Select the *best* response.

    (a) Which of the following is true of generalised audit software packages?

       A They each have their own characteristics which the auditor must carefully consider before using in a given audit situation.

       B They enable the auditor to perform all manual test procedures less expensively.

       C They can be used only in auditing online computer systems.

       D They can be used on any computer without modification.

    (b) Auditors often make use of computer programs that perform routine processing functions such as sorting and merging. These programs are made available by CIS companies and others and are specifically referred to as:

       A utility programs

       B user programs

       C compiler programs

       D supervisory programs

    (c) A primary advantage of using generalised audit software in the audit of an advanced CIS system is that it enables the auditor to:

       A verify the performance of machine operations which leave visible evidence of occurrence

       B gather and store large quantities of supportive evidential matter in machine-readable form

       C substantiate the accuracy of data through self-checking digits and hash totals

       D utilise the speed and accuracy of the computer

    (d) An auditor using audit software would probably be *least* interested in which of the following fields in a computerised perpetual inventory file?

       A date of last purchase

       B quantity sold

       C economic order quantity

       D warehouse location

    (e) While undertaking the audit of the debtors' balance, you use your audit software to extract from the accounts receivable master file a report which shows those debtors with a positive balance owing and which is overdue by greater than 30 days. At which of the following account balance assertions is this report aimed?

       A valuation and allocation

       B completeness

       C existence

       D occurrence

Nature of substantive tests

10.7 What are the major differences between tests of controls and substantive tests of transactions?

Assertions associated with substantive tests

10.8 Cutoff tests relate to testing transactions around balance date. What is its purpose and for which transactions is cutoff usually tested?

Testing of specific accounts

10.9 What factors influence the auditor in determining whether to use the negative or positive confirmation method for accounts receivable?

10.10 What alternative audit procedures are acceptable in obtaining satisfaction about inventory quantities?

10.11 What assertion is the auditor's primary concern in tests of balances for liabilities? Why?

10.12 What are the auditor's major concerns when auditing accounting estimates?

Use of computer-assisted audit techniques

10.13 Identify and explain the types of computer programs that are available for testing the client's files.

10.14 What functions of generalised audit software are useful for audit tests?

DISCUSSION PROBLEMS AND CASE STUDIES

Tests of transactions and balances

10.15 **Basic** You are carrying out the 30 June year-end audit of Riverina Limited, a large listed company. As part of year-end testing, your audit manager has obtained a report of all transactions processed by the client in the month of June. The objective of the report was to obtain information on all large and unusual transactions processed during the month, so that follow-up testing could be performed. The manager has selected the following transactions for follow-up:

		Dr $000	Cr $000
1	Provision for obsolescence	400	
	Inventory		400
2	Cash	100	
	Investments—shares in XYZ Pty Ltd		80
	Gain on disposal of shares		20
3	Lease liability	84	
	Interest expense	6	
	Cash		90

Required
(a) Explain the likely transaction underlying each of the above journal entries.
(b) Describe the audit evidence you would gather in relation to each of the above journal entries. Include discussion of the implications for other areas of the audit where applicable.

10.16 **Moderate** John's Jobs (JJ) is a small business providing home maintenance services in the Blue Mountains area of New South Wales. John is interested in purchasing some new machinery for his business and has approached a bank for funding. In order to be given a loan the bank has requested an audited financial report. John has approached your firm for this service and you have been allocated the task of auditing JJ. Your preliminary review of the business indicates that a substantive testing approach would be appropriate and you are now preparing audit programs. In particular you are working on the testing for the revenue cycle.

The information you have obtained from your review is as follows:
• John usually works 50 hours a week. Part of this time is spent travelling between clients and is not charged to the clients. The remaining time is charged at $40 per hour, regardless of the task undertaken.
• John is usually paid in cash, except for a small number of regular small-business customers who John allows to pay on account on a monthly basis by cheque.
• In all cases John provides the customer with a written receipt. Receipts are prepared manually from a receipt book purchased at the newsagency. The book contains prenumbered blank receipts, which are completed in duplicate.

Required
Provide one procedure you could use to audit each of the assertions of accuracy, completeness and occurrence for JJ's revenue balance.

10.17 Moderate Consider each of the following material independent situations:

(i) You are auditing the sales and trade debtors of Eastern Block Limited (EB). All of EB's customers are in Eastern Europe. Due to language differences, and the current political situation in many countries, direct confirmation of debtors' balances is unlikely to give satisfactory results.

(ii) You are auditing the purchases and trade creditors at FE Pty Limited (FE). One of FE's major creditors is very slow in sending invoices for goods delivered. Also, owing to a quality control problem a large number of goods supplied by FE have been deemed faulty and have had to be returned with a request for credit.

Required

(a) Identify the key audit assertion(s) at risk in relation to the balances described in each of the situations above.

(b) Describe the audit procedures you would perform in order to gather sufficient, appropriate audit evidence on each of these assertions.

10.18 Complex You have been assigned to the audit of LMN Limited (LMN), a large listed company with diverse operations. During the audit you become aware of the following:

(i) LMN has a $5 million investment in RBT Pty Limited (RBT), a controlled entity based in Russia. This company imports and sells Australian wheat, flour, yeast and other bakery products to Russian manufacturers. With the devaluation of the rouble, sales have plummeted and many customers are unable to settle their accounts. By year-end, RBT expects to have incurred losses of over $3 million.

(ii) LMN's trade creditors are recorded in a ledger that is produced monthly. Lately accounting staff have been having difficulties with the ledger as it has reached the maximum permissible number of creditor accounts. Management have approved an upgrade of the system, but in the meantime staff are having to keep extensive manual records in order to derive accurate creditor figures.

(iii) One of LMN's controlled entities, ICE Pty Limited (ICE), is an ice-cream manufacturer. Part of ICE's agreement with its distributors is that ICE will supply a freezer complete with advertising signs for the distributor's use. These freezers are rented out to the distributors and recorded as fixed assets in the books of ICE. Most distributors are either service stations or corner shops.

(iv) As with many other businesses, LMN is finding it extremely difficult to recruit and retain skilled factory staff. Accordingly it has been decided that staff in the most difficult to retain award categories will be rewarded with annual bonuses. These are calculated using a relatively complex formula that takes into account employee's length of service, award rate, seniority and estimated contribution to profit.

Required

For each independent item (i) to (iv) above:

(a) Identify up to two key audit assertion(s).

(b) Outline the audit procedures you would perform to gather sufficient appropriate audit evidence on each assertion.

Source: This question was adapted from the Professional Year Programme of The Institute of Chartered Accountants in Australia—1999 Accounting 2 Module.

Substantive tests of cash, cash receipts and payments

10.19 Moderate C Pty Ltd (C) is a large company operating in the tourism industry. C has a number of subsidiaries formed to concentrate on specific aspects of C's activities (e.g. ecotourism, harbour cruises, holidays, etc.). C and each of its subsidiaries have a bank account, but the main banking activities of the group are undertaken through the bank account of C. All of the accounts are maintained and monitored by Ms X, the senior banking clerk of C. Your preliminary discussions with Ms X indicate the following:

- Subsidiary bank accounts are used for depositing the proceeds of the tourism operations.
- All expenses of the group are paid by C. These expenses include the costs of tourism operations.
- Each of the subsidiaries then reimburses C for costs associated with its activities together with a management fee. Reimbursement occurs on a monthly basis and is completed via a direct transfer between the bank accounts authorised by the financial controller of C and the CEO of the relevant subsidiary.
- Ms X is responsible for preparing a schedule of transfers each month and reconciling each of the bank accounts.

Required

(a) Identify the assertions that are most likely to be assessed as high risk for the cash balances of C and its subsidiaries. Provide reasons for your decision.

(b) Provide three procedures which could be used to minimise this risk. For each procedure indicate the assertion addressed.

primary learning objective **4**

Testing of accounts receivable

10.20 Moderate You are the audit senior assigned to the audit of Chocorama Pty Ltd (C), a manufacturer and wholesaler of chocolate products. Your assistant has performed a positive debtors' circularisation of 50 of C's debtors, with the following results:

1 No reply has been received for eight confirmations.

2 Four debtors' confirmation letters have been returned unopened marked 'No longer at this address'.

3 One confirmation letter was returned signed but with no indication on the confirmation letter whether the account balance was correct or incorrect.

4 Four confirmations were received indicating that the balance was incorrect. The assistant followed this matter up with the debtors clerk and found that C had issued credit notes after year-end and the balance confirmed by the debtors reflected the details of the credit notes.

Required

Indicate the effect of the above findings on the audit approach, specifically identifying the risk that has been highlighted as a result of the audit testing performed, and any additional procedures which you consider that your assistant should perform.

10.21 Moderate R Inc. is an 'Aussie Rules' club operating in the suburbs of Melbourne. You have been assigned to the audit of unearned revenue and accounts receivable for the club. Unearned revenue comprises membership fees paid in advance and accounts receivable comprises late membership fees. Your discussion with the club's manager has indicated the following:

- The club was formed for the purpose of supporting a local Aussie Rules competition. It provides sporting and social facilities for its 15 000 members.
- Membership fees are $30 per person payable annually. Membership is usually paid in advance in December of the previous year. If members do not pay by 31 December the club allows non-financial members to use the club's facilities for a period of three months. After this time they must pay their membership or they will not be allowed to use the facilities. The club accounts for the 'past-due' members' fees as accounts receivable. Where membership is not renewed after the three months the debt is written off.

- Past experience indicates that approximately 60 per cent of members will pay in advance. Of the remaining 40 per cent, 20 per cent of total members will pay in January and 15 per cent will pay in February. Only 5 per cent of members do not renew membership.

Required
(a) Indicate two procedures you could use to audit unearned revenue for the 31 December review of R Inc.'s financial report.
(b) Indicate two procedures you could use to audit accounts receivable for the 31 December audit of R Inc.'s financial report.

Testing of purchases and inventories

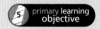

10.22 Basic In auditing a company engaged in wholesaling goods, you find that a very substantial part of the inventory of merchandise is on consignment to customers in other cities and at independent warehouses in other cities. State the procedures you would follow in your tests of the inventory on consignment and in warehouses.

10.23 Complex Your client, Sharina Ltd, manufactures baby carriages as its only product. The corporation maintains perpetual inventory records in quantities and values, and also takes a complete physical inventory each 30 April. You observed the physical inventory on 30 April 20X0 and were satisfied with the procedures followed. From your test counts, you are satisfied that the client's counts were substantially accurate. There were differences between the client's count and the perpetual records for about 75 per cent of the items. Before adjusting the inventory records for the larger differences, of which there were about 25, the records were checked and the items were recounted. Typical examples of adjustments for the larger differences are as follows:

	Perpetual record before adjustment	Perpetual record after adjustment
Black paint (in litres)	662	647
Cotter pins (in dozens)	2260	2160
Hub caps	8592	8703
Assembled wheels	6901	6883

Sharina Ltd made no further physical tests of inventories during 20X0. For its year-end closing at 30 June 20X0, the company used inventory quantities shown by perpetual inventory records.

Required
Prepare in outline form an audit program setting out the essential procedures to be followed in your audit of inventories as of 30 June 20X0. Do not include procedures unless you believe them to be essential under the conditions as stated.
Source: AICPA adapted

Substantive tests of accounts payable and cash payments

10.24 Moderate In auditing trade creditors, the audit assistant has:
- selected a sample of creditors from the year-end creditors' ledger;
- vouched each creditor's balance to selected invoices and subsequent cash payments; and
- agreed the total of the creditors' ledger to the trial balance and general ledger.

Required
(a) Which audit assertion is each of the procedures performed by the assistant directed towards?

(b) Identify the assertions you believe the assistant should perform further testing on. Ignore disclosure issues.

(c) In relation to the assertions identified in (b), what additional procedures would you advise the assistant to perform in order to gather sufficient appropriate audit evidence?

Source: This question was adapted from the Professional Year Programme of The Institute of Chartered Accountants in Australia—1999 Accounting 2 Module.

Substantive tests of non-current assets

10.25 Basic You have been assigned to the audit of Investments for P Ltd (P) and its subsidiaries. The treasury department of P undertakes investments on behalf of P and its subsidiaries. P has an 'active' investment strategy, involving the purchase and sale of all types of investments, including listed and unlisted shares and fixed interest securities. Investments are currently valued at $5 million.

Required

(a) Which assertion(s) are likely to be considered the highest risk for the audit of investments at P?

(b) Provide three procedures that could be used to test the valuation and allocation assertion for investments at P.

10.26 Complex You are the audit senior on the audit of ABC Limited, a chemicals manufacturer. A significant asset in the balance sheet of ABC Limited is the property, plant and equipment balance, which is made up as follows:

	Estimated balance at year-end $000s
Freehold land and buildings (at cost)	25 000
Provision for depreciation	(4 000)
	21 000
Chemical plant and equipment	140 000
Provision for depreciation	(37 000)
	103 000
Office furniture and equipment	750
Provision for depreciation	(280)
	470
Capital works-in-progress	12 000

ABC Limited has other assets of $95 million and other liabilities of $170 million. From discussions with management you are aware of the following:

- The directors have decided to revalue the freehold land and buildings as land values have risen and they consider that the 'balance sheet will look better' with a higher asset value. The revaluation of freehold land and buildings is to be performed by Mr X, an independent valuer.
- The ammonia plant (with a carrying value of $10 million) is currently shut down. Due to low market prices it has been cheaper for ABC Limited to import ammonia for use in the production of other chemical compounds than to produce it themselves.
- The capital works-in-progress relates to a new hydrochloric acid plant which is expected to be completed five months after year-end. This will replace the existing hydrochloric acid plant, which will be dismantled once the new plant is commissioned.

Required

(a) Identify the audit objectives for the property, plant and equipment balance of ABC Limited.

(b) Identify the main areas of inherent risk in the property, plant and equipment balance.

(c) Outline specific procedures you would include in the audit program for the property, plant and equipment at ABC Limited.

Source: This question was adapted from the Professional Year Programme of The Institute of Chartered Accountants in Australia—1995 Accounting 2 Module.

Substantive tests of liabilities and owners' equity

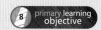

10.27 Moderate You have been assigned to the audit of shareholders' equity of AB Ltd (AB), a large publicly listed company. AB uses the services of ShareReg Pty Ltd, an independent share registry office, to maintain detailed records of their shareholders. Your preliminary review of this area has revealed the following information:

• One month prior to year-end AB had a large share issue. The share issue was 90 per cent subscribed.

• Prior to the share issue, AB declared a dividend to its existing shareholders. The dividend remains unpaid at year-end.

Required

Outline the audit procedures you would undertake in order to obtain sufficient appropriate audit evidence in respect of the share issue and dividend payment.

Substantive testing of income statement

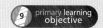

10.28 Moderate In auditing payroll expense, the audit assistant has:

• selected a sample of individual pays from the monthly payroll listings of May and June;

• vouched the pay rates used to the related industrial awards;

• checked the calculations of each pay;

• traced any annual, sick and other leave to authorised forms; and

• agreed the balance of the payroll listings for May and June to the general ledger.

Required

(a) Which audit assertion is each of the procedures performed by the assistant directed towards?

(b) Identify the assertions you believe the assistant should perform further testing on. Ignore disclosure issues.

(c) In relation to the assertions identified in (b), what additional procedures would you advise the assistant to perform in order to gather sufficient appropriate audit evidence?

Source: This question was adapted from the Professional Year Programme of The Institute of Chartered Accountants in Australia—1999 Accounting 2 Module.

Use of computer-assisted audit techniques

10.29 Basic F Financing Pty Ltd (FF) is a subsidiary of F Ltd, a large motoring company established to provide finance to purchasers of F Ltd's products. One of the largest balances in FF's accounts is interest income. Interest income is calculated using software specifically designed for FF. You are currently designing a testing strategy for this balance and believe that the use of computer-assisted auditing techniques (CAATs) may be appropriate, but you are unsure of the type of CAAT which should be used. You have approached a colleague in the information systems audit area who has suggested that you use either generalised audit software or test data.

Required

(a) Indicate how each of generalised audit software and test data could be used to assist with the audit of interest income at FF.

(b) Identify and describe the key factors that should be considered when choosing between the two types of CAATs identified.

10.30 Moderate KJA Pty Limited is a manufacturer of fishing equipment and has recently installed a computer system to maintain its inventory records.

An inventory listing can be obtained from the computer system, which provides data in the following format:

- item code—a six-digit number, the first two digits indicating the physical location of the item
- item description
- quantity on hand
- unit cost
- total value on hand
- date of last sale
- quantity sold during the year and the sales value of the stock sold
- supplier's code number (the company has a list of preferred suppliers).

Required

Prepare a list of reports that could be obtained from the stock ledger of KJA Pty Ltd by the use of GAS and indicate ways in which those reports could be used to achieve audit objectives.

Source: This question was adapted from the Professional Year Programme of The Institute of Chartered Accountants in Australia—1994 Accounting 2 Module.

10.31 Complex Simbuck Ltd is a medium-sized printing company. As part of its management incentive policy, top management are given a bonus equivalent to 50 per cent of their salary if they increase the return on total assets ratio (operating profit to total assets) above that of last year, which was 2 per cent. An interim financial report has been prepared by the client which shows a return on total assets of 2.1 per cent.

Your assessment of inherent risk suggests that a major audit exposure lies in the area of non-current assets. It was noted during the planning phase that the majority of this year's additions to non-current assets are building improvements. Practically all of the work was done by Simbuck Ltd employees, and the cost of materials and overheads was paid by Simbuck Ltd. Because of the immaterial nature of these additions last year, no follow-up audit work was undertaken.

It is also noted that the company had revised its depreciation rates at the beginning of the year.

The non-current assets master file contains the following information:

Field no.	Field title	
1	Asset number	
2	Description	
3	Asset category	01—land
		02—buildings
		03—equipment
		04—fixtures and fittings
4	Invoice costs	
5	Additions/improvements during year	
6	Date of purchase	
7	Last date of improvement	
8	Depreciation rate	

9	Accumulated depreciation (beginning-of-year)
10	Depreciation expense for year
11	Accumulated depreciation (end-of-year)
12	Written-down value (end-of-year)
13	Estimated residual value
14	Date sold
15	Proceeds from sale
16	Profit/loss on sale

This master file is updated monthly for additions, improvements and deletions.
The additions transactions file contains the following fields: field nos 1, 3, 4, 5, 6, 8.
The improvements transactions file contains the following fields: field nos 1, 5, 7.
The deletions transactions file contains the following fields: field nos 1, 14, 15.

Required

(a) After a review of the general control environment you have concluded that tests of control of application controls are appropriate. Identify programmed controls that you may expect to see in the program which creates the additions transactions file. Using as an example one of these controls identified, describe the procedures by which the auditor would gain confidence that the control is working.

(b) A batch-input batch-processing system is used for updating the non-current assets master file. Give examples of application controls, other than programmed application controls, that the auditor may expect to see associated with such a system and which would provide evidence of the completeness and accuracy of input and processing.

(c) (i) Given the return on total assets identified in the interim financial report of 2.1 per cent, would the auditor be more concerned with upward or downward movements in depreciation rates from last year? Why?

(ii) Outline an exception report that may be useful to the auditor in identifying depreciation rates on which the auditor should concentrate audit attention, and in identifying which audit steps should be undertaken with regard to this report.

10.32 Complex You are auditing the superannuation fund of your audit client. This client maintains its own superannuation fund for its employees. The employees are paid fortnightly, and at every pay period 7 per cent of their gross wage (not including any overtime) is deducted from each and every employee's account and transferred to an equivalent account for that employee which is maintained on the superannuation fund master file. Thus every employee who is included on the payroll master file should be included on the superannuation fund master file. The employees can be identified on both master files by their unique employee number. The company then contributes an equivalent amount to the superannuation fund for every employee.

This total amount is invested in government bonds at a rate of 10 per cent per annum. After a 2 per cent management fee is taken out, these earnings are added to a field on the superannuation fund master file called 'interest earned on invested funds (during the year)'.

Your evaluation of the general controls indicates that they are reliable.

You have access to the superannuation fund master file, the payroll master file and the 26 payroll transaction files. The superannuation fund master file contains the following fields:

Field no.	Field title
1	Employee number
2	Employee name
3	Employee address
4	Superannuation contributions by employee (beginning-of-year balance)
5	Superannuation contributions by employee (during the year)

6	Superannuation contributions by employee (end-of-year balance)
7	Superannuation contributions by employer (beginning-of-year balance)
8	Superannuation contributions by employer (during the year)
9	Superannuation contributions by employer (end-of-year balance)
10	Interest earned on invested funds (beginning-of-year balance)
11	Interest earned on invested funds (during the year)
12	Interest earned on invested funds (end-of-year balance)
13	Total employee entitlement (end-of-year balance)

The arithmetic checks (field 4 + field 5 = field 6, field 7 + field 8 = field 9, field 10 + field 11 = field 12, field 6 + field 9 + field 12 = field 13) have already been carried out by the auditor.

Required

(a) Detail where and how the auditor may use analytical procedures in verifying the valuation and allocation assertion contained in field 13 for the superannuation fund. Detail also how analytical procedures can aid in auditing payroll expense, a field on the payroll master file of the audit client.

(b) Detail how the auditor would use computer-assisted audit techniques (CAATs) to aid in the assessment of control risk.

(c) Describe how the auditor would use CAATs to aid in verifying the completeness of the superannuation master file.

(d) Compare and contrast the major differences between audit software approaches and test data approaches.

(e) Describe how an integrated test facility could be used in the superannuation fund system and whether it would provide evidence of a compliance and/or a substantive nature.

10.33 **Complex** You are currently auditing S Credit Union (S), a small state-based organisation with branches in regional locations. S holds a portfolio of around 2000 mortgages over residential owner-occupied properties. The mortgage ledger is maintained on a computer file which includes the following fields:

Field	Description
1	Mortgage registration number
2	Date of commencement
3	Original principal
4	Mortgage term
5	Interest rate
6	Balance outstanding: due within 12 months
7	Balance outstanding: due after 12 months
8	Provision amount (if applicable)
9	Credit rating (A to D)

Your manager has decided that generalised audit software should be used to perform as many of the tasks involved in auditing mortgages as possible.

Required

(a) Describe the reports you would have the generalised audit software produce. Include details of the report title, fields used, the use you would make of the report and the audit objectives each report would help achieve.

(b) Assume S Credit Union's internal audit department has offered to lend you the software program they use to verify mortgages outstanding. In comparison to using your generalised audit software, what are the advantages and disadvantages of accepting their offer?

Source: This question was adapted from the Professional Year Programme of The Institute of Chartered Accountants in Australia—1999 Accounting 2 Module.

10.34 Complex This is a continuation of question 9.28. It may be completed independently of that question.

You are currently involved in the audit of HomeChef Pty Ltd (HC), a large private company operating in the boutique food and beverages market. The company has a balance date of 31 December. To maximise audit efficiency, the audit partner has decided to use the work of the internal audit group (IAG) to assist with the testing of controls.

The manager of IAG has given you a copy of the work performed to ensure payments made to creditors throughout the year were in accordance with procedures laid down in the Accounting Manual. After assessing the adequacy and competency of the work performed by IAG and the results of their testing you believe it will not be possible to rely on controls in the creditors area and have decided to use a substantive approach to audit this area.

The balance of trade creditors at 31 December 20X1 is $111 680 000. The net assets and net loss of HC at the same date are $11 520 000 and $167 442 000. Total liabilities are approximately $607 million. This balance includes secured loans of $424 million of which $380 million is current. The loans are secured by a charge over the company's property and are subject to a covenant agreement which requires that the company maintain a net tangible asset ratio which is positive. Current assets are $90 138 000.

Required
(a) Identify the financial report assertions that carry the greatest risk in the audit of HC's creditors.
(b) For each of the risk areas identified indicate two procedures which could be used to provide audit evidence.

CHAPTER 11

AUDIT SAMPLING

LEARNING OBJECTIVES

Note: For ease of understanding we have divided this chapter into two sections, the first being the theory of sampling (learning objectives 1–6), the second a more detailed consideration of current sampling techniques (learning objectives 7–9). Because there are some concerns that, when evaluating sample results using statistically-based techniques, current sampling techniques do not adequately consider elements such as sampling risk and characteristics of the errors found, we have included two appendices that outline techniques that take into account these elements.

After studying this chapter you should be able to:

Sampling theory

1 define audit sampling and describe the requirements that apply to all audit samples—statistical and non-statistical;

2 identify the various means of gathering audit evidence;

3 identify planning and design considerations for sampling, including defining audit objectives and the appropriate population, the potential use of stratification and potential alternative definitions of the sampling unit, including dollar-unit sampling;

4 identify factors influencing the determination of sample size;

5 understand the appropriate methods of selecting sample items; and

6 appreciate the application of audit procedures to a selected sample, and the evaluation of sample results.

Sampling techniques

7 consider sampling approaches to tests of controls, in particular attribute sampling;

8 consider sampling approaches to substantive tests, in particular dollar-unit sampling; and

9 consider other statistical sampling approaches to substantive tests.

Chapter outline

While prior chapters have discussed the types of audit testing (tests of controls and substantive testing) that the auditor may undertake, to this stage it is still unclear how many transactions or account balances an auditor may test, which transactions or account balances, and how the auditor will know that they have collected sufficient appropriate evidence to support their conclusion. These issues will be addressed in this chapter. Audit sampling is the application of an audit procedure to less than 100 per cent of the items within a population to obtain audit evidence about a particular characteristic of the population. This chapter discusses determining the extent of audit tests, selection of sample items and evaluation of sample results, for both statistical and non-statistical sampling.

Relevant guidance

Australian		International	
AUS 502	Audit Evidence (Revised 2004)	ISA 500	Audit Evidence (Revised 2004)
AUS 514	Audit Sampling and Other Selective Testing Procedures	ISA 530	Audit Sampling and Other Selective Testing Procedures

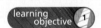

DEFINITION AND FEATURES

Audit sampling is the application of an audit procedure to less than 100 per cent of the items within a **population** to obtain audit evidence about particular characteristics of the population. By undertaking audit tests on items selected or included in the sample, the auditor will be able to draw inferences about the account balances or transactions that comprise the population.

Some auditing procedures can be applied by sampling, but many auditing procedures do not involve sampling. For example, inquiry, observation, analytical procedures and general procedures, such as reading minutes and contracts, do not involve sampling. Also, sampling is not involved when the auditor applies a procedure only to the significant items in an account balance or reviews a client's completed accounting routines.

While the earlier chapters have provided a distinction between different types of audit evidence and the circumstances in which each type will be sought, audit sampling is important because it provides information on:

- how many items to examine;
- which items to select; and
- how sample results are evaluated and extrapolated to the population.

Two features of particular importance to understanding audit sampling are sampling risk and characteristic of interest.

Sampling risk

Sampling risk is the probability that the auditor has reached an incorrect conclusion because audit sampling was used rather than 100 per cent examination. While sampling risk can be reduced to an acceptably low level by using an appropriate sample size and selection method, it can never be eliminated. In other words, the only way to eliminate sampling risk is to apply the audit procedure to every item instead of to a sample. There are two types of sampling risk:

1 The risk the auditor will conclude, in the case of a test of controls, that control risk is higher than it actually is, or, in the case of a substantive test, that a material error exists when in fact

it does not. Audit efficiency is affected by this type of risk, because it would usu[...] additional work to establish that initial conclusions were incorrect.

2   The risk the auditor will conclude, in the case of a test of controls, that control risk i[...] it actually is, or, in the case of a substantive test, that a material error does not e[...] fact it does. Audit effectiveness is affected by this type of risk, as it is more likely t[...] erroneous audit opinion.

Sampling risk can be compared with **non-sampling risk**, which arises from factors [...] sample size that cause the auditor to reach an incorrect conclusion. Such factors i[...] possibility that the auditor will fail to recognise misstatements contained in examine[...] that the auditor applies a procedure that is not effective in achieving a specific objective. Generally, auditors try to hold this non-sampling risk to a negligible level through adequate planning and supervision and appropriate quality control.

Characteristic of interest

The second feature of the definition of audit sampling distinguishes sampling from other approaches to audit tests. The auditor examines a sample of items 'to obtain evidence about a particular characteristic(s) of the population'.

When the auditor uses sampling in tests of controls, the **characteristic of interest** is usually a *deviation rate* from an internal control policy or procedure. In other words, the auditor is concerned with the rate of deviation from a prescribed policy or procedure, such as the matching of a supplier's invoice with a goods received note before payment is authorised, and specifically with whether the deviation rate exceeds a rate the auditor has specified as acceptable.

When the auditor uses sampling in substantive tests, the characteristic of interest is *monetary misstatement* in the balance. In other words, the auditor is concerned with the dollar amount of misstatement and specifically with whether monetary misstatement exceeds a material amount.

Auditors using sampling sometimes refer to both monetary misstatements and deviations as errors. However, there is an important distinction between these two types of error. A monetary misstatement indicates the misstatement of an account balance. A deviation does not necessarily indicate the presence of monetary misstatement. As the deviation rate increases, the risk of monetary misstatement increases. However, deviations from a prescribed internal control policy or procedure do not automatically result in monetary misstatement. For example, if the procedure is recomputation of a sales invoice by a second clerk, that clerk's failure to perform the procedure does not mean the invoice amount is wrong: the first clerk may have computed the invoice correctly. Normally, the auditor considers the increased risk of monetary misstatement associated with a particular deviation rate in assessing the control risk component of audit risk.

VARIOUS MEANS OF GATHERING AUDIT EVIDENCE

learning objective 2

AUS 502 (ISA 500) discusses the need to collect and evaluate sufficient and appropriate audit evidence. The means available to the auditor for selecting items for testing are (AUS 514/ISA 530):

1   **100 per cent examination** Examination of every item is *not* a sampling method. It means examining the entire population (100 per cent) of items that make up an account balance or class of transactions (or a sub-group within that population). Such examination is unlikely in the case of tests of controls, but it is not uncommon for substantive procedures. It is commonly used when the population constitutes a small number of large-value items. It is also used when

both inherent and control risks are evaluated as high and other means do not provide sufficient appropriate audit evidence, or when the repetitive nature of a calculation or other processes performed by a computer makes a 100 per cent examination cost effective.

2 **Selecting specific items** Similarly, selecting specific items in a population is *not* a sampling method. The auditor may decide to select specific items within a population because they are of high value or exhibit some other characteristic of interest, for example if they are suspicious, unusual, particularly risk-prone or have a history of error. A common technique in practice is to select all items over a specific dollar value in order that the auditor concentrates on the more material items. The results of procedures applied to items selected in this way cannot be projected to the entire population because not all items in the population had a chance of being selected.

3 **Audit sampling** This means that all sampling units in the population should have an opportunity (preferably an equal opportunity) of being selected. If this is achieved, it gives the best chance for the sample to be representative of the population. Audit sampling is a common evidence-gathering technique, and can involve either a statistical or a non-statistical approach.

Non-statistical versus statistical audit sampling

When an auditor uses audit sampling, the same basic requirements apply whether the approach is statistical or non-statistical. Non-statistical sampling was once called judgment sampling, but as both approaches require judgment, the imprecise term of judgment sampling has been removed from the literature. The basic principles and essential procedures identified in AUS 514/ISA 530 apply equally to statistical and non-statistical approaches to audit sampling.

Statistical sampling is defined in AUS 514.10 (ISA 530.10) as:

any approach to sampling that has the following characteristics:
(a) random selection of a sample; and
(b) use of probability theory to evaluate sample results, including measurement of sampling risk.

Non-statistical sampling is therefore any sampling approach that does not have both of the characteristics of statistical sampling.

Both the two essential characteristics contained in the definition of statistical sampling (random sample selection and probability theory) must be met for the sample to qualify as statistical. For example, use of a random number table to select sample items does not mean that statistical sampling is being used unless the sample results are evaluated mathematically. Mathematical evaluation based on a non-random sample is not valid.

The mathematical evaluation that is the distinguishing feature of statistical sampling leads to quantification of sampling risk. One of the advantages of statistical sampling is that sampling risk can be objectively calculated as a percentage and controlled precisely by adjusting sample size. An auditor using non-statistical sampling has to consider sampling risk and hold it to an acceptable level, but cannot quantify sampling risk precisely. It is argued that the quantification of sampling risk allows the auditor to explain and defend the decisions undertaken in the audit.

Distinction between statistical and non-statistical sampling

There is clearly a similarity between the basic requirements applicable to all audit samples (see below), including non-statistical samples, and the essential features of statistical sampling. The requirement for opportunity of selection that applies to all audit samples is achieved by random selection. In practical application, however, some selection methods are considered to produce a representative sample although they do not qualify as random selection, and should not be used for statistical sampling. The requirement for projection of sample results that applies to all audit samples is a form of mathematical evaluation. Therefore, the chief conceptual difference between the two types of sampling is that the mathematical evaluation of a statistical sample includes quantification of sampling risk, as outlined earlier.

In the implementation of audit sampling the conceptual similarity of statistical and non-statistical sampling may not be readily apparent. Statistical sampling has an inevitable degree of formality. For example, a formula is normally used to compute a sample size intended to restrict sampling risk to an acceptable level. Non-statistical sampling is less formal and can take a variety of forms. For example, some non-statistical plans have been designed to approximate the results of certain statistical plans and include use of a similar formula and steps. For both statistical and non-statistical sampling, sample size may be determined by the auditor's judgment.

The choice of statistical or non-statistical sampling

The decision whether to use a statistical or non-statistical approach is a matter for the auditor's judgment about the most efficient means of obtaining sufficient appropriate audit evidence in the particular circumstances. For example, when performing tests of controls, the auditor's analysis of the qualitative characteristics of errors (for example, considering the reasons why they occur, and whether similar errors are likely to occur) is often more important than the mere presence or absence of error. The best ways of incorporating the impact of qualitative characteristics of errors are through utilising the auditor's professional judgment and experience.

Another reason some audit firms prefer non-statistical to statistical sampling is that errors or irregularities in a population are not random. For example, computer environments lead to repetitive errors; many fraud schemes are systematic; and management may override only some controls. However, in these situations, unless auditors know something about the expected pattern of errors or irregularities, and can use this knowledge in developing their sampling plan, there is no reason why non-statistical sampling approaches should be preferred to statistical sampling approaches.

Current practice in Australia and the impact of the business risk approach

In Australia, there are significant disparities with regard to the practice of sampling within the large audit firms. Firms will usually use an unbiased approach such as random sampling to select their sample items, but the size of the sample they select will be determined judgmentally or with the help of decision aids within the firm. One large audit firm routinely selects sample sizes of five items for specific tests, while another firm routinely selects sample sizes of 20 or 30 items. A sample size of five does not lend itself to a meaningful calculation of sampling risk, which can be (but is not necessarily) meaningfully calculated for a sample size of 20 or 30.

Most large audit firms in Australia would class themselves as primarily undertaking non-statistical sampling approaches, although this may differ for specific engagements, applications or even personnel. A reduction in emphasis on undertaking large samples is supported by the business risk approach, which emphasises a 'top-down' approach to the audit, where an understanding is gained of the entity's business, strategy and associated risks. Large sampling applications are more consistent with a 'bottom-up' approach, where characteristics of a population are inferred from examining specific transactions or account balances.

Basic requirements of all audit samples

Whenever an auditor uses audit sampling (statistical or non-statistical) the following requirements apply:

- **Planning and design** In planning and designing an audit sample the auditor considers the relationship of the sample to the relevant specific audit objective or control objective and considers certain other factors that should influence sample size.
- **Selection** Sample items are selected in such a way that the sample can be expected to be representative of the population. Thus, all items in the population have an opportunity of being selected. (The methods that meet this requirement for representative selection are explained later.)
- **Performing the procedure and evaluating the results** The auditor projects the results of the sample to the population from which the sample was selected and considers sampling risk. (The methods for projecting sample results are explained later. The sample results would be a monetary misstatement for a substantive test and deviation rate for tests of controls.)

These requirements are necessarily an integral part of statistical sampling. Their application to non-statistical sampling is relatively new in auditing practice. The rationale of AUS 514/ISA 530 for imposing these requirements on all audit samples is that there is an underlying logic for sampling that holds true whether the sampling approach is statistical or non-statistical.

Quick review

1. Audit sampling is the application of an audit procedure to less than 100 per cent of the items in a population to obtain audit evidence about a particular characteristic of the population.
2. Audit sampling can be either statistical or non-statistical. Statistical sampling involves the use of (a) random sample selection and (b) probability theory to evaluate sample results, including measuring sampling risk. Non-statistical sampling is any sampling approach that does not have all the characteristics of statistical sampling.
3. Sampling risk is the probability that the auditor reached an incorrect conclusion because audit sampling was used rather than 100 per cent examination.
4. When sampling, the major characteristics of interest are monetary misstatement of an account balance or transaction class (substantive tests), or deviation rates for internal control (tests of controls).
5. The business risk approach has de-emphasised the practice of large sampling applications.

PLANNING AND DESIGNING THE SAMPLE

The auditor should design a sample carefully to ensure that it achieves the required audit objective. The auditor needs to consider:

- the *objectives* of the audit test;
- the *population* from which to sample;
- the possible use of *stratification*; and
- the definition of the *sampling unit.*

Audit objectives

The auditor first considers the specific audit **objectives** and the combination of audit procedures which is likely to best achieve them. Consideration of the nature of the audit evidence sought and possible error conditions or other characteristics relating to that evidence assist the auditor in defining what constitutes an error and what population to use for sampling.

The auditor considers what conditions would constitute an error. For example, in testing the control of approval of purchase requisitions, the auditor needs to know who may approve such requisitions and how this approval would be evidenced. Thus missing signatures or approvals by persons not duly authorised constitute an error. A clear understanding of what constitutes an error is important to ensure that all, and only, those conditions that are relevant to the audit objectives are included in the projection of errors. For example, in a substantive procedure aimed at verifying the existence of accounts receivable, an error of posting to an incorrect customer account does not affect the total accounts receivable balance. Therefore it is not appropriate to consider this an error in evaluating the sample results relating to the existence assertion, even though it may have an effect on other areas of the audit, such as the valuation and allocation assertion through assessment of doubtful debts for specific debtors.

Population

The population is the entire set of data from which a sample is selected and about which the auditor wishes to draw conclusions. It is therefore essential for the auditor to ensure that the population identified is both complete and appropriate to the objective of the sampling procedure.

- **Completeness** For example, if the auditor intends to select payment vouchers from a file, conclusions cannot be drawn about all vouchers for the period unless the auditor has reasonable assurance that all vouchers have in fact been filed. Similarly, if the auditor intends to use the sample to draw conclusions about the operation of an internal control during the financial reporting period, the population must include all instances when this control should be initiated.
- **Appropriateness** This includes consideration of the direction of testing. For example, if the auditor's objective is to test for existence of accounts payable, the population could be defined as the accounts payable listing. On the other hand, when testing for completeness of accounts payable, the population is not the accounts payable listing but rather subsequent dis- bursements, unpaid invoices, suppliers' statements, unmatched receiving reports or other populations that provide audit evidence of understatement of accounts payable.

Stratification

Audit efficiency may be improved if the auditor stratifies a population. This means dividing it into discrete sub-populations which have an identifying characteristic, such as dollar value.

When performing substantive procedures, an account balance or class of transactions is often stratified by dollar value, allowing greater audit effort to be directed to the large-value items which contain the greatest potential for monetary error in terms of overstatement. An example of this is contained in Example 11.1. Similarly, a population may be stratified by risk of error: for example, when testing the valuation of accounts receivable, debtors may be stratified by age.

It needs to be noted, however, that the results of procedures applied to a sample of items within a stratum can be projected only to the items that make up that stratum. To conclude on the entire population, the auditor needs to consider the impact of potential misstatement in other strata. For example, 20 per cent of the items in a population may comprise 90 per cent of the value of an account balance. The auditor may decide to examine a sample of these items. The auditor would evaluate the results of this sample and conclude on the 90 per cent of the value separately from the remaining 10 per cent (on which a further sample or other means of gathering evidence would be used, or which may be considered immaterial).

Defining the sampling unit

The **sampling unit** is commonly each of the transactions (especially for tests of controls where controls, such as authorisations, are related to transactions) or balances making up the account balance (for example, if sampling from accounts receivable, each individual debtor is a sampling unit).

A sampling technique specific to auditing is a technique called **probability proportionate to size (PPS) sampling**. It is also commonly referred to as **monetary-unit sampling** (MUS), **dollar-unit sampling** (DUS) or **value-weighted selection**. Under this technique the sampling unit is individual dollars rather than physical units. It is commonly used in auditing because it is often efficient in substantive testing for the auditor to identify the sampling unit as the individual dollars that make up an account balance or class of transactions. This approach to defining the sampling unit ensures that audit effort is directed to the large-value items because they have a greater chance of selection, and has the advantages of resulting in smaller sample sizes than would result under traditional sampling approaches where the individual transactions or components of account balances (such as individual debtors or inventory items) would comprise the sampling units. Thus, a balance containing $10 000 will be 10 times more likely to be selected than an account containing $1000. Having selected individual dollars from within the population of, for example the accounts receivable balance, the auditor then examines the particular items, for example individual debtors, that contain those dollars. DUS will be further discussed later in this chapter.

Quick review

1 In planning and designing the sample, the auditor carefully considers the objectives of the audit procedure. This will determine the attributes of the population from which the sample is to be drawn. The auditor should ensure that the population is complete and appropriate for the objectives of the sampling procedure.

2 Audit efficiency may be improved if the auditor stratifies a population, which involves dividing the population into discrete sub-populations which have an identifying characteristic such as dollar value. Because of reduced variability within each stratum, sample size can be reduced without an increase in sampling risk.

3 Sampling units in auditing are usually each transaction, component of account balance or each individual dollar making up an account balance or class of transactions.

DETERMINING SAMPLE SIZE

The auditor's major consideration in determining the sample size is whethe[r sampling risk can be] reduced to an acceptably low level. Sample size is affected by the degree of [sampling risk the] auditor is willing to accept. As outlined earlier, sampling risk is the probabil[ity that the auditor has] reached an incorrect conclusion because sampling, rather than 100 per[cent examination, was] used. While sampling risk can be reduced to an acceptably low level b[y appropriate choice of] sample size and selection method, it can never be eliminated. The lower [the sampling risk they] accept, the greater the sample size needs to be.

The sample size can be determined by the application of a statist[ical formula or through] professional judgment applied to the circumstances. When a formula is [used, the auditor docu-] ments the reasons for selecting the various values used in the formula. S[imilarly, when judgment] alone is used the auditor documents the factors considered and their impact on the sample size [being] determined.

Appendix 1 to AUS 514/ISA 530 outlines the factors that influence sample size for tests of controls (see Table 11.1):

1. **The auditor's intended reliance on internal control** The more assurance the auditor intends to obtain from internal control, the lower the assessment of control risk and the larger that sample size needs to be. For example, a preliminary assessment of control risk as low indicates that the auditor plans to place considerable reliance on the effective operation of particular internal controls. The auditor therefore needs to gather more audit evidence to support this assessment than would be the case if control risk were assessed at a higher level (that is, if less reliance were planned).

2. **The rate of deviation from the prescribed control activity the auditor is willing to accept (tolerable error)** The lower the rate of deviation that the auditor will accept, the larger the sample size needs to be.

3. **The rate of deviation from the prescribed control activity that the auditor expects to find in the population (expected error)** The higher the expected rate of deviation, the larger the sample size needs to be, so the auditor is in a position to make a reasonable estimate of the actual rate of deviation. Factors relevant to consideration of the expected error rate include the auditor's

TABLE **11.1** Factors that influence sample size for tests of controls

Factor	Effect on sample size
1 An increase in the auditor's intended reliance on the accounting and internal control system	Increase
2 An increase in the rate of deviation from the prescribed control procedure that the auditor is willing to accept (tolerable error)	Decrease
3 An increase in the rate of deviation from the prescribed control procedure that the auditor expects to find in the population (expected error)	Increase
4 An increase in the auditor's required confidence level (or, conversely, decrease in the risk that the auditor will conclude that the control risk is lower than the actual control risk in the population; commonly referred to as allowable risk of over-reliance)	Increase
5 An increase in the number of sampling units in the population	Negligible effect

Source: Reproduced with the permission of The Institute of Chartered Accountants in Australia and CPA Australia.

...standing of the business (in particular, procedures undertaken to obtain an understanding ...he internal control), changes in personnel or in internal control, the results of audit procedures applied in previous periods and the results of other audit procedures. High expected error rates ordinarily warrant little, if any, reduction of control risk, and therefore in such circumstances tests of controls are usually omitted.

4   **The auditor's required confidence level** (or, conversely, the risk that the auditor will conclude that the control risk is lower than the actual control risk in the population; commonly referred to as **allowable risk of over-reliance**). The greater the level of confidence that the auditor requires that the results of the sample are in fact indicative of the actual incidence of error in the population, the larger the sample size needs to be.

5   **The number of sampling units in the population** For larger populations, sometimes specified as greater than 3000 items, the actual size of the population has little effect on sample size.

Appendix 2 to AUS 514/ISA 530 outlines the factors that influence sample size for substantive testing (see Table 11.2):

1   **The auditor's assessment of inherent risk** The higher the auditor's assessment of inherent risk, the larger the sample size needs to be. A higher inherent risk means that auditors will have to collect more audit evidence in order to lower detection risk and reduce audit risk to an acceptable level. If further audit evidence involves sampling, then this will be achieved by an increase in sample size.

2   **The auditor's assessment of control risk** The higher the auditor's assessment of control risk, the larger the sample size needs to be. For example, an assessment of control risk as high indicates that the auditor cannot place any reliance on the effective operation of internal controls with respect to the particular financial report assertion. Therefore in order to reduce audit risk to an acceptably low level, the auditor needs to rely more on substantive tests. The more reliance that is placed on substantive tests, the larger the sample size will need to be.

3   **The use of other substantive procedures directed at the same financial report assertion** The more the auditor relies on other substantive procedures (tests of detail or analytical procedures) to reduce the detection risk regarding a particular account balance or class of transactions, the less assurance required from sampling from the proposed test and, therefore, the smaller the sample size can be.

4   **The auditor's required confidence level** The greater the confidence the auditor needs that the results of the sample are indicative of the actual dollar error in the population, the larger the sample size needs to be. For example, the auditor may require greater confidence in areas where management has greater discretion, such as the expense versus capitalise decision for repairs and maintenance, thus the auditor may have to look at a larger sample for these items.

5   **The total error the auditor is willing to accept (tolerable error)** The lower the total acceptable error, the larger the sample size needs to be. For substantive procedures, the auditor's tolerable error will equate to (be less than or equal to) the auditor's preliminary estimate of materiality used for the individual account balances being audited (AUS 514.51/ISA 530.51).

6   **The errors the auditor expects to find in the population (expected error)** The higher the expected errors, the larger the sample size needs to be so that the auditor is in a position to make a reasonable estimate of the actual errors. Factors relevant to the auditor's consideration of the expected error rate include the extent to which items are determined subjectively or by the application of complex formulae, the results of tests of controls, changes in personnel or in the internal control, the results of audit procedures applied in previous periods and the results of other substantive procedures.

7 **Stratification** When the population has been stratified, each subpopulation is more homogeneous, and therefore the aggregate of the sample sizes from the sub-populations is less than the sample size that would have been required had one sample been drawn from the whole population.

8 **The number of sampling units in the population** For larger populations, sometimes specified as greater than 3000 items, the actual size of the population has little effect on sample size.

TABLE **11.2** **Factors that influence sample size for substantive testing**

Factor	Effect on sample size
1 An increase in the auditor's assessment of inherent risk	Increase
2 An increase in the auditor's assessment of control risk	Increase
3 An increase in the use of other substantive procedures directed at the same financial report assertion	Decrease
4 An increase in the auditor's required confidence level (or, conversely, a decrease in the risk that the auditor will conclude that a material error does not exist when in fact it does)	Increase
5 An increase in the total error that the auditor is willing to accept (tolerable error)	Decrease
6 An increase in the errors the auditor expects to find in the population (expected error)	Increase
7 Stratification of the population when appropriate	Decrease
8 The number of the sampling units in the population	Negligible effect

Source: Reproduced with the permission of The Institute of Chartered Accountants in Australia and CPA Australia.

Quick review

1 In determining sample size the auditor should consider whether sampling risk will be reduced to an acceptably low level.

2 Factors which will have a significant effect on sample size for tests of controls are:
- the auditor's intended reliance on internal control
- tolerable error
- expected error
- required confidence level that the results of the sample reflect population characteristics.

3 Factors which will influence sample size for substantive testing are:
- the auditor's assessment of inherent risk
- the auditor's assessment of control risk
- other substantive procedures directed at the same financial report assertion
- required confidence level
- tolerable error
- expected error
- stratification.

SELECTING THE SAMPLE

Since the purpose of sampling is to draw conclusions about the entire population or stratum from which the sample has been drawn, the sample needs to be typical of the characteristics of that

population or stratum. To achieve this, the sample needs to be selected without bias so that all sampling units in the population or stratum have a chance of selection.

Appendix 3 of AUS 514/ISA 530 outlines selection procedures. Sample items should be selected in such a way that the sample is expected to be representative of the population. Three sampling methods are believed to achieve this: **random selection**, **systematic selection** and **haphazard selection**.

Random selection

In this procedure, each sampling unit making up the account balance or class of transactions has a known chance of selection. This often results in each item having an equal chance of selection. The concept requires that the person selecting the sample will not influence or bias the selection either consciously or unconsciously, so some form of impartial selection process is used to make the sample truly random. Auditors use computerised random number generators or random number tables to generate numbers which correspond with the pre-numbered sample items selected for further testing. If selecting from pre-numbered transactions the auditor can identify the first and last transaction numbers for the period under audit, between which the random numbers are generated. If sampling from components of account balances, such as individual debtors or inventory items, the software can randomly select from the population of valid debtors' numbers or inventory item numbers.

This approach is appropriate for both non-statistical and statistical sampling, since the sample is selected on a basis that allows the auditor to measure the probability of selecting the combination of sampling units actually chosen.

Systematic selection

This method is useful for non-statistical sampling and, if the starting point is a random number, it is also useful for statistical sampling. Technically, this method is not a random sampling process but is a practical approach that closely approximates random sampling. The technique involves selecting every *n*th item in the population, the sample interval being determined by dividing the number of items in the population by the sample size and selecting a random starting point. For example, if the auditor wants a sample of 20 from a population of 20 000 items, the sample interval is every 1000th item. The auditor randomly selects a starting point (falling between the first item in the population and the sample interval) and selects every 1000th item from that starting point.

This method produces a random sample only if the population is randomly arranged. For example, if large-value sales invoices are always assigned a number in a particular group, a systematic sampling process may result in a biased sample of primarily large or small invoices. This technique is useful where the population comprises a series of unnumbered transactions, such as those on magnetic tape or computer listings. There is no need to number the items because the sample can be chosen by counting off the sample interval. Again, software can be used to select systematic audit samples from computer-based files. This method is illustrated by Example 11.2.

Random selection and systematic selection are the most common techniques. In comparing these techniques, systematic selection may be advantageous in ensuring an even distribution of selection throughout the population (e.g. in testing the continuity objective of internal control). However, if there are potential patterns in the population (e.g. control fails for every 100th transaction), care must be taken in using systematic sampling: if the pattern corresponds to the sample interval an unrepresentative sample will result.

EXAMPLE **11.2** Sampling by systematic selection

Assume the sample size has been determined as 20 and the number of items in the population is 10 000:

- **Step 1:** Calculate the sample interval:

$$\frac{\text{No. of items in population}}{\text{Sample size}} = \frac{10\ 000}{20} = 500$$

- **Step 2:** Give every item in the population an equal chance of selection by choosing a random number (random start) within the range of 1 and the sampling interval (in this example, 500), for example 217.
- **Step 3:** Continue to add the sampling interval to the random start to identify sample items, e.g. 217, 717, 1217, 1717 ... 9217, 9717.

This gives an even spread of items throughout the population.

Haphazard selection

This method is permitted by the standards although it cannot normally be used for statistical sampling applications because it does not allow the auditor to measure the probability of selecting the combination of sampling units and cannot guarantee that the auditor will select without bias. In this method the auditor selects sampling units without any conscious bias, and in a manner that can be expected to be representative of the population. This technique may be useful when selecting a sample from a population which is physically stored in an unsystematic manner. For example, where all sales invoices are filed in a filing cabinet drawer, the auditor selects invoices from the drawer irrespective of any distinctive feature of any of the individual documents. Humans are however subject to sub-conscious biases which may affect the randomness of this approach. These include an affinity with the number seven, and also a bias to select towards the middle of a sequence rather than at the extremes. Both of these biases have been demonstrated a number of times by research, with the affinity for the number seven again illustrated in Auditing in the News 11.1 overleaf.

Unacceptable sample selection methods

In the past, auditors have used some selection methods that cannot be expected to produce representative samples. Such methods are not acceptable for audit sampling, whether statistical or non-statistical. Examples are:

- **Block selection** With this method the auditor selects all items of a specified type processed on a particular day, week or month. For example, the auditor might examine all cash disbursement transactions in the first week of June and the last week of December. The problem with this selection method is that the sampling unit is a period of time rather than an individual transaction. In the example given the auditor has selected two units in a population of 52 units. If the blocks or periods were selected randomly the sample might be representative, but a valid sample size would normally be impractically large. For example, to have reasonable assurance the auditor might need to select 30 out of 52 weeks.
- **Judgmental selection (based on sample item characteristics)** With this method the auditor selects large or unusual items from the population or uses some other judgmental criterion for selection, with the result that there is bias towards high-value or key items. This method is an example of 'selecting specific items' which was discussed earlier in this chapter under learning objective 2, and is not a sampling technique. Obviously, this method has a conscious bias and

AUDITING IN THE NEWS

Biases from haphazard sampling

*T*his note describes a technique that we have used for several years to illustrate the problems inherent in judgment sampling techniques.

The question (asked)...select a number from 1 to 10 and write it in the space below...The results reported below are from a group of approximately 140 students

A truly random selection would have led to each number being selected by approximately one-tenth of the class. This question is, however, intended to highlight the human affinity for the number seven (our weeks are seven days long, we split our oceans into seven seas, we are tempted to indulge in seven deadly sins, Snow White had seven dwarfs, we drink 7-Up and so on). Whether the students were aware of this or not, their selection of a 'random' number was hopelessly biased by this innate affinity.

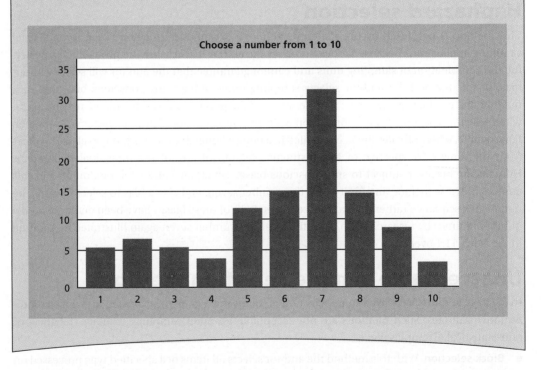

Choose a number from 1 to 10

cannot be considered representative. Because these judgmental selection methods have traditionally been used extensively in practice as a method of selecting sample items, it is important to recognise that they are unacceptable today even for non-statistical sampling.

Judgmental selection for non-sampling applications

The fact that judgmental selection with bias towards high-value or key items is not appropriate for audit sampling does not mean that auditors should stop using judgment in selecting items to examine. The point is that the items selected using judgmental criteria are not necessarily representative of the population, and conclusions based on items selected judgmentally should not be extended to the rest of the population.

In establishing the *extent* of an audit test, an auditor normally first identifies the large and/or unusual items and plans to examine all of them. If the remaining items are sampled, this approach usually allows smaller sample sizes and is effectively equivalent to stratification, which was discussed under learning objective 3. However, while the large and unusual items are being tested, they are not being sampled. Audit sampling is being used only for the remaining items. AUS 514.26/ISA 530.26 explains the point as follows:

> While selective examination of specific items from an account balance or class of transactions will often be an efficient means of gathering audit evidence, it does not constitute audit sampling. The results of procedures applied to items selected in this way cannot be projected to the entire population. The auditor considers the need to obtain appropriate evidence regarding the remainder of the population when that remainder is material.

Quick review

1. The auditor should select sample items so as to have a reasonable expectation that all sampling units in the population have a chance of selection.
2. Three selection methods commonly used are:
   - random selection;
   - systematic selection; and
   - haphazard selection.
3. Unacceptable sample selection methods include:
   - block selection; and
   - judgmental selection, where the auditor uses judgmental criteria, such as large or unusual items, for selection.
4. While judgmental selection will often be an efficient means of gathering audit evidence, it does not constitute audit sampling.

PERFORMING THE AUDIT PROCEDURES AND EVALUATING SAMPLING RESULTS

The auditor should apply audit procedures that are appropriate for the particular audit objective to each item selected. If the application of the procedure is not appropriate for a selected item, the procedure is ordinarily performed on a replacement item. For example, a cancelled cheque may be selected when testing for evidence of payment authorisation, in which case it would be appropriate for the auditor, once satisfied that the cheque had been properly cancelled and did not constitute an error, to examine a replacement.

Sometimes, however, the auditor is unable to apply the planned audit procedures to a selected item because, for instance, documents relating to that item have been lost. If suitable alternative procedures cannot be performed on that item, the auditor usually considers that item to be in error. An example of a suitable alternative procedure might be the examination of subsequent receipts when no reply has been received in response to a positive confirmation request.

The auditor evaluates the sample results to determine whether the preliminary assessment of the relevant characteristic of the population ought to be accepted or rejected. This will be determined on the basis as to whether tolerable error, or materiality level, has been exceeded. Rejection would lead the auditor to conclude that, unless further audit evidence is obtained:

- the preliminary assessment of control risk cannot be accepted (in the case of tests of controls); or
- the relevant account balance or class of transactions is materially misstated (in the case of substantive procedures).

The auditor should consider the nature and cause of any errors identified and their possible effect on the particular audit objective and on other areas of the audit. In analysing the errors discovered, the auditor may observe that many have a common feature, for example type of transaction, location, product line or period of time. In such circumstances, the auditor may decide to identify all items in the population that possess the common feature and extend audit procedures in that stratum.

Errors found in the sample should be projected to the population. The auditor estimates the total error for the population in order to obtain a broad view of the scale of possible errors, and compares this to the total error considered tolerable (tolerable error) given the objectives of the audit procedure. The auditor can project errors in a number of ways. A simple way, (which does not take into account sample size or other elements affecting sampling risk) is to directly project an error rate from a sample to a population. For example, if the auditor finds a total of $10 000 misstatement when sampling 20 per cent of a population, this projects to a total error of $50 000 for 100 per cent of the sample (the population). For tests of controls, no explicit projection of deviations (errors) is necessary since a sample deviation rate expressed as a percentage (e.g. 2% of items deviate from the control condition) is the projected deviation rate of the population as a whole (AUS 514.53/ISA 530.53).

The closer the total projected error is to the auditor's tolerable error, the more closely the auditor needs to consider the persuasiveness of the sample results as audit evidence in light of the objectives of the particular audit procedure and the results of other audit procedures.

If the evaluation of the sample results indicates that the preliminary assessment of the relevant characteristic of the population ought to be rejected (total projected error > tolerable error), the auditor takes one or more of the following actions:

- Requests that management investigate identified errors and the potential for further errors and make any necessary adjustments.
- Modifies planned audit procedures. For example, in the case of a test of controls, the auditor might test an alternative control or reduce reliance on controls and increase related substantive procedures.
- Considers the effect on the audit report.

Quick review

1. The auditor applies audit procedures that are appropriate for the particular objective to each item selected.
2. The auditor considers the nature and cause of any errors identified.
3. The auditor projects errors found in the sample to the population, compares this to tolerable error (materiality), and considers the effect of the projected error on the particular audit objective and on other areas of the audit.

SAMPLING FOR TESTS OF CONTROLS: IN PARTICULAR, ATTRIBUTE SAMPLING

In this section of the chapter we run through the stages of applying sampling to tests of controls. A sampling technique that is suitable for tests of controls is **attribute sampling**. This involves examining documents for particular attributes and providing a given level of confidence on these attributes. Controls for which there is documentary evidence—such as requirements to match documents, or evidence of authorisation—are attributes or characteristics of a transaction. Using attribute sampling, the auditor then examines these characteristics and is able to estimate the rate of deviations from the prescribed controls in a population, and the results can be used to support or refute an initial assessment of control risk.

Audit objectives

Use of audit sampling forces the auditor to be specific, before testing, about certain relationships. For example, the following steps are necessary in considering the relationship between the sample and the objective of the test.

- **Identify relevant control objectives, policies and procedures** The auditor needs to specify the control objectives, and the internal control policies and procedures that achieve them, that are relevant to restricting substantive tests of the related account balances. For each trans-action class, the auditor identifies the control objectives that, if achieved, permit an assessed level of control risk at less than high. For example, for both credit sales and cash receipts, relevant control objectives include those related to the occurrence, completeness and meas-urement of transaction processing. Controls that may be tested by attribute sampling are those which are applied to individual transactions, such as authorisation and the requirement to match documents. Other higher-level controls which are at an organisational level (rather than a transaction level), such as segregation of duties or codes of ethics, are tested by non-sampling techniques such as observation and inquiry.
- **Identify population and sample unit** In tests of controls, identifying the population includes specifying the period covered by the test. In tests of credit sales, for example, the auditor might identify the population as all credit sales transactions for a financial year. A sample unit is any of the individual items included in the population. In this example, a sample unit would be an individual sales invoice. The auditor also needs to establish that the population is physically complete. Usually this is accomplished by footing (adding the totals of all the individual records in a computer file). For example, the auditor might establish that the dollar total of invoices in a sales journal agrees with the dollar total of sales posted to the general ledger. This step is important because the auditor must establish correspondence between the sample frame and the population to validly project conclusions from the sample to the population. Naturally, the appropriate population and sample unit are influenced by the objective of the test. For example, if the auditor is concerned with a control objective related to completeness of sales transactions, the auditor would not sample from the sales invoices but rather from the shipping documents to ensure that there is a sales invoice for each shipping document.
- **Define the characteristic of interest** Tests of controls use a characteristic of interest that is a condition or an attribute. An attribute either exists or does not exist, which means that a control activity has either been complied with or not complied with. For example, if the control is authorisation, the attribute is evidence of the authorisation by a person who is approved to authorise. In many situations, samples for testing controls are used for dual-purpose tests (both a test of controls and a substantive test are applied to the same sample items). For example, the auditor selects a sample of sales invoices, inspects them to see whether they are initialled to indicate recomputation (test of controls) and reperforms the computation (substantive test).

Control risk assessment and tolerable error

The maximum rate of deviation that would support the auditor's planned assessed level of control risk is the tolerable error. In general, as the tolerable error increases, sample size decreases. In practice, auditors usually assess control risk across three levels: high, medium and low. For 'high', the auditor would omit tests of controls.

The next decision the auditor has to make is what tolerable error to associate with the levels of control risk. Tolerable error decreases as the level of control risk is reduced. Auditors sometimes use tolerable error rates of 1 to 5 per cent for a low level of control risk and 5 to 20 per cent for medium level, and assess control risk at the high level when the rate exceeds 20 per cent (no reliance on the control).

Such large errors for a low level of control risk may at first seem relatively high. However, it must be remembered that a deviation does not necessarily mean that a monetary misstatement has resulted. Where lack of compliance with a prescribed internal control policy or procedure is certain to result in monetary misstatement, tolerable errors need to be lower. When both control deviations and monetary misstatements are evaluated as a rate, the auditor should switch to a monetary misstatement evaluation if sample results are predominantly monetary misstatements.

Table 11.3 relates tolerable errors and planned assessed level of control risk to the risk model outlined in Chapter 5. Control risk is expressed as a specific percentage only when statistical sampling is being used. However, the quantitative model makes the relationships easier to visualise.

TABLE 11.3 **Relationship between tolerable error and planned level of control risk**

Qualitative level of control risk	Tolerable error for deviations (approximately) %
Low	1 to 5
Medium	5 to 20
High	Omit test

Determining sample size

As outlined in AUS 514.41 (ISA 530.41), sample size can be determined by the application of a statistically based formula or through the exercise of professional judgment objectively applied to the circumstances.

Using statistically-based formula allows the computation of a maximum rate of error/ deviation at a specified confidence level, given a rate of occurrence in a sample of size n. In tests of controls, an occurrence is a deviation from prescribed policies or procedures. Rather than introduce the traditional symbols for the statistical model and then equate them with the audit sampling terms, the formula for the maximum deviation (error) rate is presented using audit sampling terms and simple letter symbols.

$$\text{Maximum deviation rate (MDR)} = \frac{R}{n}$$

where R = **reliability factor** for required confidence level

n = sample size

The reliability factor (R) that corresponds to a required confidence level for an expected number of errors is found in Table 11.4. For example, the reliability factor for a required confidence level of 95% with no expected errors is 3.00.

The related formula for minimum sample size to achieve a tolerable error is as follows:

$$\text{Sample size (n)} = \frac{R}{TE}$$

where TE = tolerable error

TABLE **11.4** **Reliability factors for assessing required confidence level**

Number of errors	Required confidence level				
	99%	95%	90%	85%	80%
0	4.61	3.00	2.31	1.90	1.61
1	6.64	4.75	3.89	3.38	3.00
2	8.41	6.30	5.33	4.72	4.28
3	10.05	7.76	6.69	6.02	5.52
4	11.61	9.16	8.00	7.27	6.73
5	13.11	10.52	9.28	8.50	7.91

Source: Adapted from AARF, 1983, p. 99.

To use the model to estimate sample size in planning tests of controls, the auditor needs to specify the following:

- the tolerable error;
- the required confidence level; and
- the expected number of deviations.

Use of the statistical model to estimate sample size can best be explained by an example (refer to Example 11.3).

EXAMPLE 11.3 **Determining sample size for attribute sampling**

Assume an auditor has specified a tolerable error of 7 per cent (0.07) and a required confidence level of 90 per cent and expects to find at most one error. Using the formula, a minimum sample size of 56 could be computed as follows:

$$n = \frac{R}{TE} = \frac{\text{Reliability factor}}{\text{Tolerable error}}$$

$$= \frac{3.89}{0.07}$$

$$= 56$$

Notice that 3.89 is the reliability factor for one expected error at a 90 per cent required confidence level, from Table 11.4.

Sample size can also be determined using Tables 11.5 and 11.6 (overleaf), which assess the expected error rate in percentage terms. If the auditor expects to find at most 1 per cent error in the population, then by referring to Table 11.5, using the above example of a tolerable error of 7 per cent and a required confidence level of 90 per cent, a minimum sample size of 56 (the 55 in the table is due to rounding) is required (as calculated above) and one error (the figure in parentheses) is expected.

Table 11.5 provides sample sizes where the required confidence level is 90 per cent (which, as outlined in Table 11.3 can equate to an initial assessment of control risk as medium) while Table 11.6 provides sample sizes where the required confidence level is 95 per cent (which, as outlined in Table 11.3 can equate to an initial assessment of control risk as low).

TABLE 11.5 Statistical sample sizes for tests of controls. Required confidence level is 90 per cent (with number of expected errors in parentheses)

Expected error (%)	Tolerable error										
	2%	3%	4%	5%	6%	7%	8%	9%	10%	15%	20%
0.00	114(0)	76(0)	57(0)	45(0)	38(0)	32(0)	28(0)	25(0)	22(0)	15(0)	11(0)
0.25	194(1)	129(1)	96(1)	77(1)	64(1)	55(1)	48(1)	42(1)	38(1)	25(1)	18(1)
0.50	194(1)	129(1)	96(1)	77(1)	64(1)	55(1)	48(1)	42(1)	38(1)	25(1)	18(1)
0.75	265(2)	129(1)	96(1)	77(1)	64(1)	55(1)	48(1)	42(1)	38(1)	25(1)	18(1)
1.00	*	176(2)	96(1)	77(1)	64(1)	55(1)	48(1)	42(1)	38(1)	25(1)	18(1)
1.25	*	221(3)	132(2)	77(1)	64(1)	55(1)	48(1)	42(1)	38(1)	25(1)	18(1)
1.50	*	*	132(2)	105(2)	64(1)	55(1)	48(1)	42(1)	38(1)	25(1)	18(1)
1.75	*	*	166(3)	105(2)	88(2)	55(1)	48(1)	42(1)	38(1)	25(1)	18(1)
2.00	*	*	198(4)	132(3)	88(2)	75(2)	48(1)	42(1)	38(1)	25(1)	18(1)
2.25	*	*	*	132(3)	88(2)	75(2)	65(2)	42(1)	38(1)	25(1)	18(1)
2.50	*	*	*	158(4)	110(3)	75(2)	65(2)	58(2)	38(1)	25(1)	18(1)
2.75	*	*	*	209(6)	132(4)	94(3)	65(2)	58(2)	52(2)	25(1)	18(1)
3.00	*	*	*	*	132(4)	94(3)	65(2)	58(2)	52(2)	25(1)	18(1)
3.25	*	*	*	*	153(5)	113(4)	82(3)	58(2)	52(2)	25(1)	18(1)
3.50	*	*	*	*	194(7)	113(4)	82(3)	73(3)	52(2)	25(1)	18(1)
3.75	*	*	*	*	*	131(4)	98(4)	73(3)	52(2)	25(1)	18(1)
4.00	*	*	*	*	*	149(6)	98(4)	73(3)	65(3)	25(1)	18(1)
5.00	*	*	*	*	*	*	160(8)	115(6)	78(4)	34(2)	18(1)
6.00	*	*	*	*	*	*	*	182(11)	116(7)	43(3)	25(2)
7.00	*	*	*	*	*	*	*	*	199(14)	52(4)	25(2)

* Sample size is too large to be cost effective for most audit applications.
Note: This table assumes a large population (> 500 items).
Source: Adapted from AARF, 1983, p. 91.

TABLE 11.6 Statistical sample sizes for tests of controls. Required confidence level is 95 per cent (with number of expected errors in parentheses)

Expected error (%)	Tolerable error										
	2%	3%	4%	5%	6%	7%	8%	9%	10%	15%	20%
0.00	149(0)	99(0)	74(0)	59(0)	49(0)	42(0)	36(0)	32(0)	29(0)	19(0)	14(0)
0.25	236(1)	157(1)	117(1)	93(1)	78(1)	66(1)	58(1)	51(1)	46(1)	30(1)	22(1)
0.50	*	157(1)	117(1)	93(1)	78(1)	66(1)	58(1)	51(1)	46(1)	30(1)	22(1)
0.75	*	208(2)	117(1)	93(1)	78(1)	66(1)	58(1)	51(1)	46(1)	30(1)	22(1)
1.00	*	*	156(2)	93(1)	78(1)	66(1)	58(1)	51(1)	46(1)	30(1)	22(1)
1.25	*	*	156(2)	124(2)	78(1)	66(1)	58(1)	51(1)	46(1)	30(1)	22(1)
1.50	*	*	192(3)	124(2)	103(2)	66(1)	58(1)	51(1)	46(1)	30(1)	22(1)
1.75	*	*	227(4)	153(3)	103(2)	88(2)	77(2)	51(1)	46(1)	30(1)	22(1)
2.00	*	*	*	181(4)	127(3)	88(2)	77(2)	68(2)	46(1)	30(1)	22(1)
2.25	*	*	*	208(5)	127(3)	88(2)	77(2)	68(2)	61(2)	30(1)	22(1)
2.50	*	*	*	*	150(4)	109(3)	77(2)	68(2)	61(2)	30(1)	22(1)
2.75	*	*	*	*	173(5)	109(3)	95(3)	68(2)	61(2)	30(1)	22(1)
3.00	*	*	*	*	195(6)	129(4)	95(3)	84(3)	61(2)	30(1)	22(1)
3.25	*	*	*	*	*	148(5)	112(4)	84(3)	61(2)	30(1)	22(1)
3.50	*	*	*	*	*	167(6)	112(4)	84(3)	76(3)	40(2)	22(1)
3.75	*	*	*	*	*	185(7)	129(5)	100(4)	76(3)	40(2)	22(1)
4.00	*	*	*	*	*	*	146(6)	100(4)	89(4)	40(2)	22(1)
5.00	*	*	*	*	*	*	*	158(8)	116(6)	40(2)	30(2)
6.00	*	*	*	*	*	*	*	*	179(11)	50(3)	30(2)
7.00	*	*	*	*	*	*	*	*	*	68(5)	37(3)

* Sample size is too large to be cost effective for most audit applications.
Note: This table assumes a large population (> 500 items).
Source: Adapted from AARF, 1983, p. 90.

Selection of sample items for tests of controls

Having determined the appropriate sample size, it is then a matter of determining which sample items to select. The representative selection methods of random selection and systematic selection discussed earlier generally apply to both tests of controls and substantive tests. However, stratification is not usually applicable to tests of controls. In auditing, stratification is normally based on the recorded amount of items included in an account balance. Usually, the same control and processing activities apply to transactions in a class regardless of the dollar amount of the transactions. If a particular type of transaction in a class is subject to different processing or different control activities, tests of these transaction types should be planned and evaluated separately. For example, if a company makes both retail and wholesale sales, and retail sales are subject to different processing steps and control activities, samples for testing controls associated with retail sales and wholesale sales should be designed separately.

Systematic selection (defined earlier in this chapter) is often useful for tests of controls because it helps to ensure the auditor's internal control objective of testing continuity of controls is achieved, by ensuring sampling is continuous throughout the year.

Evaluation of sample results

The auditor applies audit procedures to the selected items and determines the deviation rate of the sample. If the auditor cannot apply the planned procedure (or an effective alternative) to the item, it should be counted as a deviation in evaluating the sample. For example, suppose the control activity being tested is approval of a voucher based on examination of supporting documents. The auditor selects a voucher and sees that it is initialled indicating approval, but cannot locate the supporting documents. This item should be counted as a deviation (error). However, legitimately voided or unused documents are not deviations. The auditor then estimates the total error for the population to obtain a broad view of the scale of possible errors and compares this to the tolerable error.

The sample deviation rate is the auditor's best estimate of the population deviation rate. For example, the auditor selects a sample of 25 items, applies the planned audit procedure and finds one error. The sample deviation rate is therefore 4 per cent ($1 \div 25$), and the best estimate of the population deviation rate is also 4 per cent. If the tolerable error was established as say 5 per cent (something greater than 4 per cent) for the planned assessed level of control risk, the sample result supports the auditors' reliance on the internal control. This simple approach is currently advocated in the auditing standards (AUS 514.53/ISA 530.53) but may be criticised, in that it does not take into account sampling risk (or the auditor's required confidence level). This is even more of a concern with the small sample sizes that are currently used in practice. For example, if the auditor had sampled 20 transactions and found one error (5% sample error), rather than 60 transactions with three errors found (still 5% sample error), the risk that the sample was not representative of the population (sampling risk) would have been higher with the smaller sample size. A method of taking into account sampling risk when evaluating sample results for tests of controls is considered in Appendix 1 to this chapter.

Occasionally the auditor can establish that an error arises from an isolated event that has occurred only on identifiable occasions and is therefore not representative of similar errors in the population (an anomalous error). An example is an error caused by a computer breakdown that is known to have occurred only once during the period. In that case, the auditor assesses the effect of the breakdown, for example by examining specific transactions processed on that day, and considers the effect of the cause of the breakdown on audit procedures and conclusions. In specific instances an auditor can exclude such anomalies when extrapolating a sample deviation rate to a population deviation rate.

In analysing errors, the auditor may observe that many have a common feature, for example type of transaction, location, product line or period of time. In such circumstances the auditor may decide to identify all items in the population that possess the common feature and extend audit procedures in that stratum.

The auditor's evaluation of sample results is not limited to quantitative analysis. A projection of sample results and consideration of sampling risk are required for all audit samples (quantitative aspects), but the auditor also needs to consider the nature and cause of the deviations. If the analysis of deviations indicates that prescribed internal control policies or procedures have been intentionally circumvented, the auditor should consider the possibility of material fraud.

Quick review

1 The types of tests of controls for which audit sampling is especially useful are those which involve the inspection or matching of source documents.

2 In determining sample size, the auditor can either use professional judgment or the application of statistically-based formula. If using statistically-based formula, the auditor needs to specify the tolerable error, required confidence level and expected number of deviations.

3 Samples for tests of controls are commonly selected using systematic selection techniques, which helps ensure that controls are tested throughout the entire period.

4 The sample error rate is the auditor's best estimate of the population error rate. If the sample error rate is greater than the tolerable error rate, the auditor cannot rely on the internal control being assessed. It should be recognised that this method does not explicitly consider sampling risk.

learning objective **8**

SAMPLING FOR SUBSTANTIVE TESTS: IN PARTICULAR, DOLLAR-UNIT SAMPLING

Audit sampling applies to substantive tests, where the auditor intends to extend a conclusion reached by testing a portion of the items to the balance of the account. The sampling approach which weights individual transactions or account balances evenly is known as the traditional sampling approach to substantive testing. Another approach which is commonly used in practice is the dollar-unit sampling approach (DUS). The difference between these two approaches is in the definition of the sampling unit. Under traditional sampling, the sampling unit is, for example, each inventory item on the inventory or each debtor contained in the accounts receivable master file.

Thus, rather than giving each debtor an equal chance of being selected, the DUS approach gives each dollar an equal chance of being selected. Under traditional sampling debtor A and debtor B have an equal chance of selection, whereas under DUS, if debtor A owes $1000, and debtor B owes $100, and dollars are the sampling unit, debtor A is 10 times more likely to be selected. Thus, DUS directs the auditor's attention to the more significant accounts or line items. As the auditor then tests the debtor (e.g. through confirmation) or inventory item (e.g. through sighting) that the selected dollar belongs to, rather than the individual dollar, it increases the auditor's dollar coverage, which is an important advantage in substantive tests.

DUS is beneficial in testing specific assertions, such as existence, which is related to overstatement. Under DUS, an overstatement will increase the likelihood of an account being selected. Thus, if the true value of a debtor's balance is $10 000, but it is in the accounts at $50 000, this overstatement will increase the likelihood of the account being selected. However, DUS will direct the auditor's attention away from understatements, related to the completeness assertion. If the true debtor's balance of $10 000 is understated so that it is in the accounts at $2000, the number of sampling units has been decreased. Thus, DUS is seen as an appropriate sampling approach for testing relating to the existence assertion, but another testing procedure not reliant on sampling would need to be taken in relation to testing the completeness assertion.

Planning for substantive tests

The following matters should be considered in planning the sample:

- the relationship of the sample to the relevant audit objective;
- preliminary judgments about materiality levels (tolerable error);
- the auditor's allowable risk of incorrect acceptance;
- characteristics of the population, that is, the items comprising the account balance; and
- the use of other substantive procedures directed at the same financial report assertion.

The relationship of the sample to the relevant audit objective

The objectives that are relevant to substantive tests are the specific audit objectives for an account balance derived from the broad categories of assertions: existence, rights or obligations, completeness, accuracy, valuation and allocation and disclosure. Because of the characteristics of misstatements that can be detected by sampling, the relevant assertions are usually those related to existence or valuation. For example, by selecting from a list of items included in an account balance and applying audit procedures to them, the auditor could detect fictitious items or items incorrectly included in the balance (existence), or incorrectly valued items. However, the auditor could not detect items that should be there but are omitted from the balance (completeness).

Generally, the other decisions in this step are similar to those for the comparable step in planning tests of controls. The auditor should identify the population and sample unit; specify the population from which sample items will be selected; and establish that the population is complete (usually by footing (adding) the list or master file). Naturally, the characteristic of interest is a monetary misstatement of the account balance.

An aspect of identifying the population that is unique to substantive tests is the undertaking of a preliminary analysis of the account balance to identify individually significant items. An item could be significant because of its size or its nature. Essentially, anything that causes the auditor to believe that particular items in the account balance are subject to a greater risk of material misstatement could cause those items to be considered significant. For example, a gross profit analysis by product and location may indicate that certain inventory items are more likely to be misstated. The portion of the account balance remaining after identification and testing of individually significant items then becomes the population subject to sampling.

Preliminary judgments about materiality levels (tolerable error)

The tolerable error for an account balance is, in effect, the materiality assessment at the account balance level. It is the maximum amount of monetary misstatement that can exist in an account balance that, when combined with monetary misstatement in other account balances, would not cause the financial report taken as a whole to be materially misstated. As tolerable error increases, the necessary sample size decreases.

Risk of incorrect acceptance

The allowable risk of incorrect acceptance is the risk the auditor is willing to accept that the sample supports the conclusion that the recorded account balance is not materially misstated, when it is in fact materially misstated.

In planning the sample for a substantive test of a balance, the risk of incorrect acceptance is the *detection risk* for the test. The auditor assesses inherent risk and control risk and establishes detection risk at the level appropriate to keep the audit risk for the account balance relatively low. Notice that it is audit risk and not detection risk that needs to be held to this relatively low level. If the auditor concludes that the likelihood of material misstatement in the account balance is low, the detection risk for the direct test of a balance, using audit sampling, can be relatively high. As the allowable risk of incorrect acceptance increases, the necessary sample size decreases.

When the auditor uses statistical sampling for a direct test of an account balance, the detection risk for the audit procedure using sampling (the risk of incorrect acceptance) is usually specified as a percentage. The model for quantitative estimation of detection risk explained in Chapter 5 can be used for this purpose. For non-statistical samples the evaluation can be entirely qualitative.

There is another aspect of sampling risk for substantive tests—the *risk of incorrect rejection*. It is possible that the sample supports the conclusion that the account balance is materially misstated when it is not. This aspect of sampling risk is not specified as a consideration in planning samples because it relates to audit efficiency rather than effectiveness. An auditor who incorrectly concludes that an account balance is materially misstated usually expands substantive tests and ultimately reaches the appropriate conclusion.

Population characteristics: expected error, variability and population size

The characteristics of the population that are relevant to a substantive test of balances are expected error, variability and population size. Generally, as the size and frequency of expected error increase, or as the variability or population size increase, larger sample sizes are necessary. However, expected error and variability have a much more significant influence on sample size than the size of the population. The auditor can reduce the effects of variability in the population by stratifying the population.

The use of other substantive procedures directed at the same financial report assertion

The more the auditor relies on other substantive procedures (either tests of detail or analytical procedures) to reduce to an acceptable level the detection risk regarding a particular account balance or class of transactions, the less assurance is required from sampling and, therefore, the smaller the sample size can be.

Determination of sample size for substantive tests

As was outlined for tests of controls, sample size can be determined by the application of a statistically based formula or through the exercise of professional judgment objectively applied to the circumstances.

If using a statistically-based formula, recall that the underlying statistical model estimates sample size by dividing the appropriate reliability factor by the tolerable error (*TE*). The same method can be used for a substantive test of a balance by converting tolerable error to a rate. If the population subject to sampling is designated as book value (*BV*), then the ratio of tolerable error to book value is the tolerable error rate. The formula presented earlier then becomes:

$$n = \frac{R}{TE \div BV} = \frac{\text{Reliability factor}}{\text{Tolerable error} \div \text{Book value}}$$

For convenience, this is usually presented as:

$$n = \frac{BV \times R}{TE}$$

Assume the portion of the balance subject to sampling is $1 000 000 (*BV*), the tolerable error is $50 000 (*TE*), there is zero expected error, and the risk of incorrect acceptance is 5 per cent. An appropriate reliability factor (*R*) of 3.00 can be identified from Table 11.4. The sample size (*n*) can then be estimated as follows:

$$n = \frac{\$1\ 000\ 000 \times 3.00}{\$50\ 000} = 60$$

Selecting the reliability factor

The reliability factors are the same for both tests of controls and substantive tests. However, it is usually more efficient to construct a specialised table for substantive tests, for several reasons.

One reason is that there are more complex considerations for establishing the risk of incorrect acceptance. The risk of assessing control risk too low needs to be relatively low because there are few relevant sources of information other than the results of the tests of controls. However, the allowable risk of incorrect acceptance (detection risk for the audit procedure using sampling) is established by considering audit risk at the account balance level, as explained in Chapter 5. Audit risk has to be relatively low, but the risk of incorrect acceptance may be higher if other components of audit risk, such as control risk, have been assessed as relatively low.

The method for making a quantitative estimate of detection risk, explained in Chapter 5, may be used to establish a specific percentage for the risk of incorrect acceptance. The relationship between reliability factors and specific percentages of the risk of incorrect acceptance is as follows (this is a variation of Table 11.4 for zero expected errors):

Risk of incorrect acceptance (%)	Reliability factor
1.0	4.6
5.0	3.0
7.5	2.6
10.0	2.3
12.5	2.1
15.0	1.9
20.0	1.6

The reliability factors outlined above for the specified risk levels are for zero expected misstatement. The consideration of expected misstatement is another reason for the additional complexity of selecting the appropriate reliability factor. The statistical model incorporates the frequency of sampling units in error, but a direct test of a balance is concerned with the dollar amount of misstatement. In the approach presented here, expected misstatement is considered in establishing tolerable error, as explained later, and the reliability factors used to estimate sample size are those presented above for specified percentages of the risk of incorrect acceptance.

Selection of sample items for substantive tests

The representative selection methods of random, systematic and haphazard selection are all appropriate for selecting samples items for substantive tests. However, as mentioned earlier, some form of stratification may increase efficiency. Stratification reduces the variability of items within each stratum and therefore allows sample size to be reduced without a proportional increase in sampling risk. When performing substantive procedures, an account balance or class of transactions will often be stratified by dollar value, allowing greater audit effort to be directed to the large-value items which contain the greatest potential monetary error in terms of overstatement.

Using the DUS approach, the sample unit is individual dollar units rather than physical units. A population of $1 000 000 that contains 1000 physical units is viewed as a population with 1 000 000 sample units—the individual dollars. When an individual dollar is selected, however, it is naturally attached to the other dollars associated with the physical unit (e.g. individual debtor or inventory item), and the selected dollar drags the dollar amount of the item with it. In other words, the dollar unit identifies which physical unit the audit procedure is used to test.

In practice, the most commonly applied sampling technique is systematic sampling. This method of sample selection was outlined earlier in this chapter. To use systematic selection the auditor needs to establish the cumulative dollar total of items in the population. A random start is established within the first sampling interval to determine the first item selected, and the dollar interval is added to determine the next item. The random start plus two times the sampling interval determines the third item, and so on through the population. Example 11.4 demonstrates the use of this DUS selection method.

Evaluation of sample results for substantive tests

After the planned audit procedures have been applied to selected items, the auditor may have detected a level of monetary misstatement. This misstatement has to be projected to the population from which the sample was selected.

There are simple and complex approaches to evaluating sample results. The guidance in the auditing standards suggests that, for substantive testing, an unexpectedly high error amount (level of monetary misstatement) in a sample may cause the auditor to believe that an account balance or class of transactions is materially misstated (AUS 514.54/ISA 530.54). The standard requires the auditor to project monetary errors found in a sample to a population. This projection is then compared to tolerable error.

There are several ways to do this. One way is outlined in Example 11.5 (overleaf).

The method of evaluating sample results outlined in Example 11.5 is in accordance with auditing standards and is widely used in practice. However, it does not take account of sampling risk, the risk that this result might be obtained from a sample of $100 000 from a population of $1 000 000, although the true monetary misstatement may exceed tolerable error (except to the extent that the auditor is asked to consider sampling risk after undertaking this calculation). This is even more of a concern with the small sample sizes that are currently widely used in practice. For example, if we had sampled $50 000 out of $1 000 000, rather than $100 000 as above, there would have been an even greater possibility that the sample did not accurately reflect the

Invoice no.	Amount of item	Cumulative total
A1001	$ 6 000	$ 6 000
A1002	1 000	7 000
A1003	15 000	22 000
A1004	5 000	27 000
A1005	12 000	39 000
A1006	10 000	49 000
A1007	9 000	58 000
A1008	17 000	75 000
A1009	11 000	86 000
A1010	8 000	94 000
A1011	7 000	101 000
•	•	•
•	•	•
•	•	•

Population size (*BV*)	$1 000 000
Sample size (*n*)	60
Sampling interval (*SI*)	
($1 000 000 ÷ 60)	$16 667
Random start (*RS*)	$14 068

Items selected	$	Invoice no.	Amount $
RS	$14 068	A1003	$15 000
RS + *SI*	30 735	A1005	12 000
RS + 2*SI*	47 402	A1006	10 000
RS + 3*SI*	64 069	A1008	17 000
RS + 4*SI*	80 736	A1009	11 000
RS + 5*SI*	97 403	A1011	7 000
•	•	•	•
•	•	•	•
•	•	•	•

The invoice numbers and dollar amounts of the items are listed in the client's accounting records. The cumulative total is computed by the auditor.

Assume the random start is the 14 068th dollar. This dollar is contained in item A1003, so that is the first item selected and the audit procedure is applied to this invoice. The calculated sampling interval (16 667) is added to the random start to determine the next item to be selected. The 30 735th dollar is contained in item A1005, so that is the next item selected. The selection process continues in this manner through the population. Notice that all items larger than the sampling interval will always be selected. This process is usually automated using audit software, such as ACL (described in Chapter 10).

Assume that an auditor has examined the supporting documentation for additions to property, plant and equipment and found a net monetary overstatement in the sample. The relevant information is as follows:

Amount of additions	$1 000 000
Number of additions	1 000
Sample size	60
Dollar value of sample	$100 000
Tolerable error	$50 000
Error found in sample	$2 000

For simplicity, it is assumed that the auditor did not identify individually significant items or stratify the items, so that the total dollar amount of additions and the population subject to sampling are the same. Using dollar-unit sampling, where each dollar is weighted evenly, the projected error is $20 000 ($2000 $\div$ 100 000 $\times$ 1 000 000).

The auditor next compares projected error to tolerable error and considers the sampling risk. In the example given, projected error of $20 000 is less than tolerable error of $50 000, and the auditor would accept that the additions to plant and equipment are not materially misstated.

population. A method of taking into account sampling risk when evaluating sample results, as well as other considerations such as the potential offsetting influences of over and understatements, is considered in Appendix 2 to this chapter.

The auditor also needs to consider the qualitative aspects of sample error: the nature and cause of the misstatement and the implications for other phases of the audit. This analysis may allow the auditor to focus on a particular cause of misstatement and thus to modify the projected error. For example, if the auditor finds that all misstatements in additions to property, plant and equipment occurred in only one division out of four in the company, the misstatement would be projected only for the portion of the population attributable to that division. If further audit testing was required, the auditor might decide to extend testing only in the particular division where errors were identified.

Finally, the auditor needs to relate the sample evaluation to the results of other audit procedures relevant to the account balance and combine the results of all audit tests. The auditor then evaluates the effect on the financial report taken as a whole.

Quick review

1. Sampling for substantive tests is usually aimed at the assertions of existence and valuation.
2. The characteristic of interest is monetary misstatement of the account balance.
3. Dollar-unit sampling directs the auditor's attention toward items that are overstated, but away from items that are understated.
4. Systematic sampling with a dollar interval is the most commonly applied method for sample selection when undertaking DUS.
5. Stratification is widely used to allow greater audit effort to be directed to the large-value items.
6. The auditor is required to project the errors found in the sample to the population. The auditor accepts an account balance as not materially misstated if projected total error is less than tolerable error.

OTHER STATISTICAL SAMPLING APPROACHES

The other statistical models that can be used in substantive tests differ in many respects from the DUS model. Generally, these models are referred to as classical statistical sampling methods because they all use the normal distribution and related mathematics. They are also called **variables sampling** methods because the characteristic of interest is a variable rather than an attribute, and **estimation sampling** methods because they are used to estimate the characteristic that is of interest. In auditing, the characteristic of interest is monetary misstatement, and the estimation sampling methods are used in a hypothesis-testing format—does monetary misstatement in a recorded balance exceed a material amount? In using the audit-hypothesis-testing approach, the auditor needs to be concerned about both the *risk of incorrect rejection* and the *risk of incorrect acceptance*. Further details on estimation sampling using an audit-hypothesis-testing approach are on the web site associated with this book.

The auditor uses sampling to create an estimate of the amount, and compares it to the amount recorded by the client. If the estimate is reasonably close to the recorded amount, the sampling procedure has provided audit evidence supporting the balance. The primary classical statistical sampling methods used in auditing are mean-per-unit estimation, difference estimation and ratio estimation.

Mean-per-unit estimation

In the **mean-per-unit estimation** technique, the auditor selects sample items from the population and determines the audited value of each item selected. The auditor calculates the average value (the mean) of the items and multiplies the average value by the number of items in the population. This type of estimate is called a *simple extension*. If the average value of the items is $1375 and there are 1000 items in the population, the estimated value is $1 375 000. The mean times the number of items is called the *point estimate*. The audit sample assures the auditor that the point estimate plus or minus the precision limit at a specified reliability percentage includes the true value of the population. For example, using this technique the auditor can say, 'I am 95 per cent confident that the range of $1 375 000 plus or minus $38 450 (the precision limit, which would be determined by reference to the standard deviation of the sample) includes the actual value of the inventory'. Mean-per-unit estimation can be applied to individual strata or to populations.

Difference estimation

In **difference estimation**, the auditor calculates the difference between the audited value and the book value of each item in the sample. The average of the differences is calculated and then multiplied by the number of items in the population to obtain an *estimated total projected difference*. The population value is then estimated as the total book value plus the total projected difference. The sample sizes when using this method tend to be much smaller than those using mean-per-unit estimation.

Ratio estimation

Ratio estimation is similar to difference estimation. For each item selected, the auditor determines an audited value and a book value. In ratio estimation, the sum of all of the book values of the sampled items is calculated, and the sum of all of the audited values of the sampled items is calculated. The auditor calculates a ratio by dividing the sum of the audited values by the sum of the sample book values. The ratio is multiplied by the recorded total book value for the account balance to create the estimated audited value.

As in difference estimation, achieved precision is calculated (using the standard deviation of the individual ratios in the sample). The auditor calculates a range—the estimated audited value plus or minus the achieved precision—and determines whether the recorded book value falls within the range.

Comparison of estimation techniques with DUS

Some of the essential differences of the above three sampling methods from the DUS model are as follows:

- Sample size is influenced by the standard deviation of the population (a measure of population variability). The standard deviation needs to be estimated to determine sample size. (Thus, sample size can be reduced by stratification to reduce the standard deviation within each sub-group.)
- Both the risk of incorrect acceptance and the risk of incorrect rejection are specified to estimate sample size.
- The tolerable error for a sampling application is not equal to an overall financial report materiality level. The overall materiality needs to be allocated to sampling applications, but the relationship is still not additive. The sum of tolerable errors for sampling applications can exceed the overall materiality level for the financial report.

No matter what statistical model is used for substantive tests, the basic requirements are those established by AUS 514/ISA 530. The relationships between tolerable error, risk of incorrect acceptance, expected error and sample size remain the same. The auditor should consider these relationships in planning and evaluating the sample for all audit sampling applications.

Summary

Audit sampling is a very important part of the evidence-gathering procedures of the audit process. It is through sampling techniques that the auditor can determine the number of items in a population that need to be tested, which particular items in the population will be selected for audit testing and how, after audit testing has been carried out, the auditor can extrapolate sample results so that a conclusion can be formed on the population.

Key terms

Allowable risk of over-reliance	522	Objectives	518
Attribute sampling	528	Population	514
Audit sampling	514	Probability proportionate to size sampling (PPS)	520
Block selection	525	Random selection	524
Characteristic of interest	515	Ratio estimation	541
Difference estimation	541	Reliability factor	530
Dollar-unit sampling (DUS)	520	Required confidence level	522
Estimation sampling	541	Sampling risk	514
Expected error	522	Sampling unit	520
Haphazard selection	525	Statistical sampling	516
Judgmental selection	525	Stratification	523
Mean-per-unit estimation	541	Systematic selection	524
Monetary-unit sampling (MUS)	520	Tolerable error	521
Non-sampling risk	515	Value-weighted selection	520
Non-statistical sampling	516	Variables sampling	541

References

Australian Accounting Research Foundation (1983) *Audit Sampling*, Audit Guide No. 1, Melbourne.

Elder, R.J. and Allen, R.D. (1998) 'An empirical investigation of the auditor's decision to project errors', *Auditing: A Journal of Practice and Theory*, Fall, 71–87.

Dworin, L.D. and Grimlund, R.A. (1984) 'Dollar unit sampling for accounts receivable and inventory', *The Accounting Review*, April, 218–41.

Gillett, P.R. and Srivastava, R.P. (2000) 'Attribute sampling: A belief-function approach to statistical audit evidence', *Auditing: A Journal of Practice and Theory*, Spring, 145–55.

Grimlund, R.A. (1988) 'Sampling size planning for the moment method of MUS: Incorporating audit judgments', *Auditing: A Journal of Practice and Theory*, Spring, 77–104.

Grimlund, R.A. and Felix, W.L., Jr (1987) 'Simulation evidence and analysis of alternative methods of evaluating dollar unit samples', *The Accounting Review*, July, 455–79.

Grimlund, R.A. and Schroeder, M.S. (1988) 'On the current use of the Stringer method of MUS: Some new directions', *Auditing: A Journal of Practice and Theory*, Fall, 53–62.

Leslie, D.A., Teitlebaum, A.D. and Anderson, R.J. (1979) *Dollar unit sampling: A practical guide for auditors*, Copp, Clark and Pitman, Toronto.

Levine, N. (1985) 'Probability-proportional-to-size sampling and its application to audit testing', *The Chartered Accountant in Australia*, August, 53–7.

Messier, W.F., Jr (2001) 'An experimental assessment of recent professional developments in nonstatistical audit sampling guidance', *Auditing*, March, Vol. 20, No. 1, 81–97.

Rogers, D. (1985) 'Sampling to confirm the operation of internal control', *The Chartered Accountant in Australia*, April, 58–60.

Robertson, J.C. and Rouse, R. (1994) 'Substantive audit sampling—The challenge of achieving efficiency along with effectiveness', *Accounting Horizons*, March, 35–44.

Stewart, M. and Dunn, J. (2000) 'Introducing audit sampling', *The Auditor's Report*, Summer, 15–16.

Assignments

MaxMARK

Additional assignments for this chapter are contained in Appendix A of this book, page 772.

MAXIMISE YOUR MARKS! There are approximately 30 interactive questions on audit sampling available online at www.mhhe.com/au/gay3e

REVIEW QUESTIONS

11.1 The following questions relate to general aspects of audit sampling. Select the *best* response.

(a) Which of the following is an element of sampling risk?

A Failing to detect a deviation on a document that has not been inspected by the auditor.

B Failing to perform audit procedures that are required by the sampling plan.

C Choosing an audit procedure that is inconsistent with the audit objective.

D Choosing a sample size that is too small to achieve the sampling objective.

(b) Which of the following best illustrates the concept of sampling risk?

A An auditor may fail to recognise deviations in the documents examined for the chosen sample.

B The documents related to the chosen sample may *not* be available for inspection.

C A randomly chosen sample may *not* be representative of the population as a whole on the characteristic of interest.

D An auditor may select audit procedures that are *not* appropriate to achieve the specific objective.

(c) In which of the following cases would the auditor be most likely to conclude that all of the items in an account under consideration should be examined rather than tested on a sample basis?

	The measure of tolerable error is:	Misstatement frequency is expected to be:
A	Large	Low
B	Small	High
C	Large	High
D	Small	Low

(d) An advantage of using statistical sampling techniques is that such techniques:

    A define the values of precision and reliability required to provide audit satisfaction

    B have been established in the courts to be superior to judgmental sampling

    C mathematically measure risk

    D eliminate the need for judgmental decisions

(e) The risk of incorrect acceptance and the required confidence level relate to:

    A the preliminary estimates of materiality levels

    B the allowable risk of tolerable error

    C the effectiveness of the audit

    D the efficiency of the audit

11.2 The following questions relate to the selection of audit samples and sampling approaches.

(a) Which of the following statistical selection techniques is least desirable for use by an auditor?

    A block selection

    B random selection

    C systematic selection

    D haphazard selection

(b) If certain forms are not consecutively numbered:

    A stratified sampling should be used

    B haphazard selection will result in a superior sample

    C selection of a random sample probably is not possible

    D systematic sampling may be appropriate

(c) Which of the following sampling approaches is most useful to auditors when performing a test of controls?

    A variables sampling

    B unrestricted random sampling with replacement

    C stratified random sampling

    D attribute sampling

(d) When performing a test of controls with respect to control over cash disbursements, an auditor may use a systematic sampling technique with a start at any randomly selected item. The biggest disadvantage of this type of sampling is that the items in the population:

    A may systematically occur more than once in the sample

    B must be systematically replaced in the population after sampling

    C must be recorded in a systematic pattern before the sample can be drawn

    D may occur in a systematic pattern, thus destroying the sample randomness

(e) Stratified sampling is a statistical technique that may be more efficient than unstratified sampling because it usually:

    A increases the variability among items in a stratum by grouping sampling units with similar characteristics

    B yields a weighted sum of the strata standard deviations that is greater than the standard deviation of the population

    C is applied to populations where many monetary errors are expected to occur

    D produces an estimate having a desired level of precision with a smaller sample size

11.3 The following questions relate to the use of audit sampling for tests of controls.

(a) Which of the following would have the effect of decreasing the sample size for a test of control?

    A Decrease in the required confidence level on internal control

    B Higher expected rate of deviation for planned reliance on internal control

    C Higher level of reliance being placed on internal control

    D A decrease in the size of a large population

(b) The tolerable error for a test of controls is generally:

    A identical to the expected deviation rate in the related accounting records

    B unrelated to the expected deviation rate in the related accounting records

    C lower than the expected deviation rate in the related accounting records

    D higher than the expected deviation rate in the related accounting records

(c) A sample selection procedure that is beneficial for helping ensure that items are continuously sampled over the period of interest is:

    A random sampling

    B haphazard sampling

    C systematic sampling

    D block sampling

11.4 The following questions relate to use of audit sampling for substantive tests. Select the *best* response.

(a) A number of factors influence the sample size for a substantive test of details of an account balance. All other factors being equal, which of the following would lead to a larger sample size?

    A Smaller expected frequency of misstatements

    B Smaller measure of tolerable error

    C Greater reliance on internal control

    D Greater reliance on analytical procedures

(b) When planning a sample for a substantive test of balances, an auditor should consider tolerable error for the sample. This consideration should:

    A be related to preliminary judgments about materiality levels

    B not be changed during the audit process

    C be related to the auditor's business risk assessment

    D not be adjusted for qualitative factors

(c) Which of the following would be designed to estimate a numerical measurement of a population, such as a dollar value?

    A block sampling

    B numerical sampling

    C sampling for variables

    D sampling for attributes

Defining terms and basic requirements

11.5 What factors have led to the basic concept of sampling becoming well established in auditing practice?

11.6 Define and differentiate between non-statistical and statistical sampling.

11.7 Describe the difference between sampling and non-sampling risk.

Various means of collecting audit evidence

11.8 Selecting from a list of accounts receivable, the auditor uses their judgment to bias their selection towards the larger dollar value items. Is this an example of audit sampling? Explain why or why not.

Planning and designing the sample

11.9 Explain what is meant by stratification. Why do auditors stratify audit populations?

Determining sample size

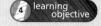

11.10 What relationships exist between risk, precision, expected error in population and sample size?

11.11 Will an increase in the auditor's intended reliance on an internal control increase or decrease a sample size for tests of controls?

Methods of selecting sample items

11.12 Describe the circumstances in which the auditor may have a preference for random sampling techniques over systematic selection, and vice versa.

Evaluation of sample results

11.13 What courses of action are available to the auditor if the evaluation of sample results suggests that there is material misstatement in the population?

Sampling approaches to tests of controls

11.14 What is attribute sampling?

11.15 Assume that the auditor's sample result shows an unacceptable error rate in a test of control. What are the actions the auditor may take as a result of this finding?

Sampling approaches to substantive testing

11.16 For which account balances is it beneficial to use dollar-unit sampling? Why?

DISCUSSION PROBLEMS AND CASE STUDIES

Various means of collecting audit evidence

11.17 Basic The following is a list of audit procedures that might be applied to sales transactions. Identify those procedures that would be applied using audit sampling.
- **(a)** Scan the accounting records to identify large and unusual transactions.
- **(b)** Observe the mailing of monthly statements to customers.
- **(c)** Inspect sales invoices for indication of checking and recompute extensions and footings.
- **(d)** Trace shipping documents to sales invoices and compare details (customer, description, quantity and amount).
- **(e)** Foot sales journals and trace to the general ledger.

11.18 Basic An auditor has analysed additions to property, plant and equipment for the year as follows:

Number of additions	Range	Amount ($)
5	Above $10 000	90 000
20	1 000 to 9 999	60 000
25		150 000

The auditor plans to substantiate all the additions above $10 000 and rely on analytical procedures for the remaining amount.
- **(a)** Is this audit approach acceptable?
- **(b)** Is there any detection risk associated with this approach?
- **(c)** Is there any sampling risk associated with this approach?

Planning and designing the sample

11.19 Basic An auditor is selecting shipping documents as part of testing sales transactions. There were 3000 shipping documents issued during the period being tested and the auditor has judgmentally decided to select 60 documents. The auditor counts through the documents, selecting every 50th one. The auditor uses a random start and during the selection process makes several additional random starts.
- **(a)** Is audit sampling being used?
- **(b)** Is the selection method a random-based method?

(c) Is statistical sampling being used to date?

(d) Why did the auditor use more than one random start?

11.20 Complex MOP Motors (MOP) sells car accessories such as seat covers, headlight protectors and towbars from six retail outlets spread across Sydney, Melbourne and Brisbane. MOP also has a main warehouse located at head office in Sydney.

MOP has about 250 stock lines active at any one time. The value of individual items ranges from 10c to $2500. Around 25% of year-end stock is expected to be held at the warehouse, with the remainder spread relatively evenly across the six retail outlets. A full stocktake will be carried out at all locations at year-end.

The inventory system produces the following reports at year-end:

1   Complete stock listing, showing:
- stock code
- total quantity held
- cost per unit
- total cost per stock item.

The report also gives a breakdown of where the stock items are held by location, and the total value of items held at each location.

2   Ageing report of all stocklines, showing:
- stock code
- total quantity held
- sales quantity over each of the last three months
- month by month purchase details.

In addition, the system produces a stocksheet report for each location. It lists the description and stock code of each item held at that location per the perpetual records. Quantities are omitted as these are completed by the count team.

Required

(a) Performing test counts at the stocktake helps the auditor gather evidence about the existence and completeness assertions. In general, identify the populations from which samples must be selected to satisfy each of these assertions.

(b) In the case of MOP, describe how you would select samples to test the existence and completeness assertions at each location. Which assertion would you pay more attention to, and why?

(c) How would your test count sample sizes for a retail outlet be affected if the following independent events occurred:

(i)   a higher value of stock was held at that outlet compared to other outlets

(ii)   stock thefts had occurred at the outlet over the last few months

(iii)   your preliminary assessment of internal controls was that they were very good, however the audit manager decided no tests of controls would be performed

(iv)   the outlet had a history of only minor differences between the perpetual records and actual stock held compared to other outlets

(v)   the branch auditors assigned to the stocktake were new to the job

(vi)   three out of five outlet staff, including the manager, had commenced work in the last three months

(vii)   the number of stock lines held was 500, not 250.

Briefly explain your answer in each case.

Source: This question was adapted from the Professional Year Programme of The Institute of Chartered Accountants in Australia—1999 Accounting 2 Module.

Determining sample size

11.21 Moderate You are examining additions to property, plant and equipment for the year using the DUS. The remaining population recorded amount is $1 000 000. You believe a tolerable error of $25 000 is appropriate and you expect to find no errors. You have concluded that a 10% risk of incorrect acceptance is appropriate.

(a) What sample size should you use?

(b) What dollar sampling interval should you use in sample selection?

(c) In determining the remaining population recorded amount, what dollar cut-off would have been a reasonable amount for identifying individually significant additions?

11.22 Moderate The questions below relate to estimating the sample size necessary for tests of controls, given the specified decisions for the considerations that affect sample size.

Situation	Required confidence level (%)	Tolerable error (%)	Expected number of errors
(i)	90	7	0
(ii)	95	7	0
(iii)	90	12	0
(iv)	90	12	2
(v)	95	25	1
(vi)	90	10	3

(a) For each of the situations (i)–(vi) above, what is the initial sample size for the test of controls?

(b) Based on your understanding of the relationships between the factors above and sample size, explain the effect of changing each of the following while the others remain unchanged.

(i) Required confidence level is decreased

(ii) Tolerable error is decreased

(iii) Number of deviations expected increases

(iv) Population size increases.

Evaluation of sample results

11.23 Moderate An auditor is testing investments and finds the following monetary errors:

Recorded amount ($)	Correct value ($)	Difference
134 000	136 799	2 799
25 456	26 539	1 083
45 900	49 500	3 600
526 000	572 568	46 568
Total		54 050

The total sample size was 50 items with a total dollar value of $1 000 000. The recorded value of investments is $2 100 000. Each of the errors is a result of a transposition error in recording the investment, or when calculating the effect of discounts or accrued interest, or failure to adjust for interest or discounts.

The auditor compares the total misstatement to the population total and concludes 'Given total error is less than 5% of the balance, investments are not materially misstated.'

Required

Do you agree with the auditor's conclusion? Provide reasons for your decision.

11.24 Moderate For the sample sizes calculated in question 11.22 above, assume that application of the planned audit test to the items selected produced the following results:

Situation	Number of deviations found
(i)	0
(ii)	1
(iii)	1
(iv)	2
(v)	3
(vi)	1

(a) What is the maximum deviation rate for situations (i)–(vi) at the specified allowable confidence level in question 11.22?

(b) For which situations does the maximum deviation rate not exceed the tolerable error?

(c) Was it necessary to answer part (a) to be able to answer part (b) above?

Sampling approaches to tests of controls

 primary learning objective 7

11.25 Moderate Dennis, a chartered accountant, has selected a sample of 50 sales transactions. The sample size was based on Dennis's judgment rather than being statistically estimated, but it was selected using a random number generator. However, Dennis, since planning the audit, has taken a continuing education course on audit sampling and has decided to evaluate all audit samples statistically. The first selected sales transaction examined disclosed a deviation.

Required

(a) Is it acceptable for Dennis to evaluate statistically the results of a sample whose size was determined judgmentally?

(b) Without regard to your answer to part (a), make a statistical evaluation of finding one deviation in a sample of 50 assuming that Dennis believes a 90% required confidence level and a tolerable error of 5% are appropriate for assessing control risk at a low level.

(c) If the first transaction in a sample of 50 discloses a deviation, is it necessary to apply the planned procedures to the remaining items, assuming the same evaluation criteria as stated in part (b)?

(d) Based on the evaluation criteria stated in part (b), what alternatives or options does Dennis have if the first transaction in a sample of 50 disclosed a deviation?

Sampling approaches to substantive testing

 primary learning objective 8

11.26 Moderate Listed below are the initial ten items from the accounts receivable population of Leong Ltd.

Population item	Recorded amount ($)	Cumulative value ($)
1	5 430	5 430
2	7 857	13 287
3	821	14 108
4	1 894	16 002
5	3 500	19 502
6	10 000	29 502
7	2 740	32 242
8	4 716	36 958
9	2 669	39 627
10	1 427	41 054

The total of the accounts receivable listing is $400 000, with over 150 customers.

Required

(a) For an account such as accounts receivable, is the audit more likely to be concerned with testing for overstatement or understatement? Justify your answer.

(b) Assume that DUS with selection by a systematic sampling technique is to be used. The sample size has been determined to be 25 and a random start of 14 320 has been chosen. Which will be the second item to be selected?

(c) You have undertaken your sampling plan of 25 items and your evaluation of errors reveals that the upper error limit exceeds the tolerable error. List what courses of action you have available.

11.27 Moderate Below are the initial 20 items from the population of inventory items for Ramsay Ltd.

Population item	Recorded amount ($)	Cumulative value ($)	Population item	Recorded amount ($)	Cumulative value ($)
1	1 890	1 890	11	425	72 105
2	6 250	8 140	12	11 895	84 000
3	825	8 965	13	3 270	87 270
4	32 110	41 075	14	1 150	88 420
5	6 225	47 300	15	975	89 395
6	1 000	48 300	16	910	90 305
7	770	49 070	17	2 465	92 770
8	5 725	54 795	18	4 220	96 990
9	9 130	63 925	19	735	97 725
10	7 755	71 680	20	1 760	99 485

The total for the inventory account is $2 000 000, consisting of 500 items. The value 8365 is randomly selected to start the sample selection procedure and a sample of 80 items is to be selected. Which items listed will be the first four included in the sample? Show all calculations.

11.28 Moderate You are the assurance services senior reviewing your assistant Tamara's work on trade payables testing in XYZ Pty Ltd. You note her conclusion to a substantive test on the valuation of trade payables:

In order to test the trade payables year-end balance, I selected all balances over $20 000 and vouched these to supporting invoices. The sample selected comprised $455 850 of total trade payables of $1 572 995. One invoice for $18 274 was incorrectly recorded on the trade payables listing as the goods were not actually received until later year-end.

Given that the error relates to only 4.0% of the trade payables tested, which would be a total error of $63 058 of the overall trade payables balance, it is still below the materiality level and, therefore, no further work has been performed. I am satisfied that the trade payables balance is fairly stated.

Required

Review the work performed by Tamara and prepare an email to her commenting on the appropriateness of the conclusion reached.

11.29 Complex You are currently auditing FMP Limited (FMP), a wholesaler and manufacturer of gardening tools sold in hardware stores. FMP has branch offices in Sydney, Melbourne and Adelaide and its head office is located in Sydney. The company's only factory is also located in Sydney. The audit is administered out of your Sydney office, with some work performed by your firm's branch offices.

Your manager has asked you to complete the audit programs for various audit file sections by inserting detailed instructions on sample selection. In order to maintain tight control over costs, the audit manager wants all samples to be selected by the Sydney head office auditors. Branch offices will then simply be given details of the items they are to test.

You have the following information about various account balances of FMP:

(i) FMP's fixed assets consist of office furniture and equipment (held at all branches) and factory machinery (held in Sydney). Factory machinery comprises around 50 items, totalling 80% of the value of fixed assets. Each branch maintains it own fixed asset register on an off-the-shelf software package.

You need to select a sample of fixed assets for existence testing.

(ii) Trade creditors are handled centrally in Sydney. Branches send in authorised invoices with related supporting documents for processing on a weekly basis. Each month, an alphabetical list of creditors is produced showing the invoices outstanding and the total balance owing. FMP uses a wide range of suppliers and accordingly there are no individually significant creditors.

You need to select a sample of creditors for valuation testing.

(iii) Each branch processes its own sales invoices using a unique series of invoice numbers (i.e. each branch has a different sequence). A sales listing is produced monthly by each branch, and gives a sequential listing of the invoices used, the customer name and code, date and amount.

You need to select a sample of sales invoices on which to perform tests of controls to ensure credit limits are complied with.

(iv) Debtor collections are handled centrally at head office. A consolidated monthly alphabetical debtors listing is produced showing the invoices making up each debtor's balance, the amounts paid that month and the amount outstanding. Ageing details are also provided (current, > 30 days, > 60 days and > 90 days).

You need to select a sample of debtors for existence testing.

(v) To meet reporting deadlines at year-end, each branch handles its own accruals. Once the creditors ledger is closed off, branches track year-end related invoices using a listing showing creditor name and cost, invoice amount and accrual amount.

You need to select a sample of accruals for valuation testing.

(vi) About 200 of FMP's stock lines carry 12 month 'free replacement' warranties. When a customer in a particular state makes a warranty claim, the item is returned to that branch office. Each branch keeps a list of items returned in product number order, so that trends in warranty claims can be identified by product. At year-end, the warranty provision is calculated by determining the return percentages of major sales items, plus a general allowance for other items.

You need to select a sample of items to test valuation of the warranty provision.

Required

(a) For each independent situation (i)–(vi) above:

  (i) Describe the steps you would follow to select a sample for testing. Include details of any information you might require from the client's branch offices and assume only annual selection techniques will be used.

  (ii) Briefly describe the analytical procedures that could help corroborate the evidence gained from detailed testing of the sampled items.

(b) What action would you take if:

  (i) a sales invoice you selected was subsequently found to be cancelled;

  (ii) your sampling plan for debtors resulted in no debtors from the Melbourne branch being selected.

(c) Give examples of situations where sampling from the recorded population might not be appropriate.

Source: This question was adapted from the Professional Year Programme of The Institute of Chartered Accountants in Australia—2000 Accounting 2 Module.

11.30 Complex In using dollar-unit sampling for the audit of the accounts receivable of Simbuck Ltd for the year ended 30 June 20X0, the auditor set the following requirements:

Tolerable error:	$50 000
Allowable risk of incorrect acceptance:	5%
Dollar-unit sample:	50
Expected misstatement rate for zero errors:	100%

Other information includes:

Recorded account balance:	473 000
Number of open account balances:	760

Positive confirmation procedures revealed the following differences:

Accounts receivable per records	Accounts receivable per confirmation	Follow-up comments of auditor
1. 1530	1683	Goods shipped 23/6 Sale recorded 1/7
2. 3975	1975	Customer mailed cheque for $2000 on 27/6, received 4/7
3. 3390	2712	Goods returned 28/6 and included in inventory, credit not issued
4. 220	352	Addition error on invoice
5. 1780	—	Goods shipped and sale recorded 29/6, customer received goods 1/7
6. 280	490	Pricing error
7. 2350	1175	Invoice incorrectly billed twice
8. 200	80	Goods returned 29/6 and counted in inventory, credit issued 15/7

Required

(a) Calculate the upper and lower error limits (net maximum overstatement and understatement) on the basis of the client errors in the sample.

(b) Is the total book value of accounts receivable materially misstated? What options would be available to the auditor in the case of material misstatement?

Appendix 1

Evaluation of sample results for tests of controls using statistically-based techniques

As outlined earlier under learning objective 7, the sample deviation rate is the auditor's best estimate of the population deviation rate; simply extrapolating sample results to a population is the technique outlined in AUS 514/ISA 530. However, this technique does not take into account sampling risk. Thus, for example, there is greater risk that a sample of 20 items from which there was one identified deviation is not representative of population compared with a sample of 60 items from which there were three identified deviations.

The following technique is used to consider sampling risk. It involves comparing a calculated maximum deviation rate (MDR) to tolerable error, rather than comparing the sample deviation rate (SDR) to tolerable error.

Assume the details outlined in Example 11.3 and that the auditor applies the planned procedures to the 56 items and finds no deviations. The maximum deviation rate (MDR) that could exist in the population at the specified risk level, given these sample results, can be determined as follows:

$$MDR = \frac{R}{n} = \frac{\text{Reliability factor}}{\text{Sample size}}$$

$$= \frac{2.31}{56}$$

$$= 4\%$$

This means that there is 90 per cent assurance that the true deviation rate is no greater than 4 per cent, given a sample of 56 with no deviations (SDR = 0.0). Since the tolerable error was specified as 7 per cent, the sample results indicate that the planned assessed level of control risk is appropriate. Notice that the appropriate reliability factor is 2.31 for a 90 per cent confidence level with zero deviations (from Table 11.4 on p. 517).

If the auditor found two deviations in the sample of 56 (SDR = 3.6%), the evaluation computation would be as follows:

$$MDR = \frac{R}{n} = \frac{\text{Reliability factor}}{\text{Sample size}}$$

$$= \frac{5.33}{56}$$

$$= 9.5\%$$

Since the true deviation rate could be as high as 9.5% (given a sample of 56 with two deviations with a 90 per cent required confidence level) and a tolerable error of 7 per cent was originally assessed, the auditor would conclude that the planned assessed level of control risk was not appropriate.

The maximum deviation rate can also be determined through use of Tables 11.7 and 11.8 (overleaf). The values in these tables are the calculated maximum deviation rate, for a given sample size and number of deviations found, for 90 per cent (Table 11.7) and 95 per cent (Table 11.8) confidence levels.

TABLE **11.7** **Statistical sample results evaluation: table for tests of controls, upper limits at 90 per cent confidence**

Sample size	Actual number of deviations found										
	0	1	2	3	4	5	6	7	8	9	10
20	10.9	18.1	*	*	*	*	*	*	*	*	*
25	8.8	14.7	19.9	*	*	*	*	*	*	*	*
30	7.4	12.4	16.8	*	*	*	*	*	*	*	*
35	6.4	10.7	14.5	18.1	*	*	*	*	*	*	*
40	5.6	9.4	12.8	16.0	19.0	*	*	*	*	*	*
45	5.0	8.4	11.4	14.3	17.0	19.7	*	*	*	*	*
50	4.6	7.6	10.3	12.9	15.4	17.8	*	*	*	*	*
55	4.1	6.9	9.4	11.8	14.1	16.3	18.4	*	*	*	*
60	3.8	6.4	8.7	10.8	12.9	15.0	16.9	18.9	*	*	*
70	3.3	5.5	7.5	9.3	11.1	12.9	14.6	16.3	17.9	19.6	*
80	2.9	4.8	6.6	8.2	9.8	11.3	12.8	14.3	15.8	17.2	18.6
90	2.6	4.3	5.9	7.3	8.7	10.1	11.5	12.8	14.1	15.4	16.6
100	2.3	3.9	5.3	6.6	7.9	9.1	10.3	11.5	12.7	13.9	15.0
120	2.0	3.3	4.4	5.5	6.6	7.6	8.7	9.7	10.7	11.6	12.6
160	1.5	2.5	3.3	4.2	5.0	5.8	6.5	7.3	8.0	8.8	9.5
200	1.2	2.0	2.7	3.4	4.0	4.6	5.3	5.9	6.5	7.1	7.6

* Over 20 per cent

Note: This table presents upper limits as percentages. This table assumes a large population (> 500 items).
Source: Adapted from AARF, 1983, p. 92.

TABLE **11.8** **Statistical sample results evaluation: table for tests of controls, upper limits at 95 per cent confidence**

Sample size	Actual number of deviations found										
	0	1	2	3	4	5	6	7	8	9	10
25	11.3	17.6	*	*	*	*	*	*	*	*	*
30	9.5	14.9	19.6	*	*	*	*	*	*	*	*
35	8.3	12.9	17.0	*	*	*	*	*	*	*	*
40	7.3	11.4	15.0	18.3	*	*	*	*	*	*	*
45	6.5	10.2	13.4	16.4	19.2	*	*	*	*	*	*
50	5.9	9.2	12.1	14.8	17.4	19.9	*	*	*	*	*
55	5.4	8.4	11.1	13.5	15.9	18.2	*	*	*	*	*
60	4.9	7.7	10.2	12.5	14.7	16.8	18.8	*	*	*	*
65	4.6	7.1	9.4	11.5	13.6	15.5	17.4	19.3	*	*	*
70	4.2	6.6	8.8	10.8	12.6	14.5	16.3	18.0	19.7	*	*
75	4.0	6.2	8.2	10.1	11.8	13.6	15.2	16.9	18.5	20.0	*
80	3.7	5.8	7.7	9.5	11.1	12.7	14.3	15.9	17.4	18.9	*
90	3.3	5.2	6.9	8.4	9.9	11.4	12.8	14.2	15.5	16.8	18.2
100	3.0	4.7	6.2	7.6	9.0	10.3	11.5	12.8	14.0	15.2	16.4
125	2.4	3.8	5.0	6.1	7.2	8.3	9.3	10.3	11.3	12.3	13.2
150	2.0	3.2	4.2	5.1	6.0	6.9	7.8	8.6	9.5	10.3	11.1
200	1.5	2.4	3.2	3.9	4.6	5.2	5.9	6.5	7.2	7.8	8.4

* Over 20 per cent

Note: This table presents upper limits as percentages. This table assumes a large population (> 500 items).
Source: Adapted from AARF, 1983, p. 92.

ADDITIONAL FEATURES OF THIS APPROACH

This particular statistical model can be flexibly implemented. As a review of the illustrations for planning and evaluation indicates, whenever the number of errors found exceeds the number expected, the maximum error rate exceeds the specified tolerable error.

This means that the auditor may stop applying the planned procedures to selected items as soon as the expected number of errors is exceeded. For example, if the first two items of the 56 selected are found to have errors, there is no need to continue. However, this statistical model makes continuation convenient. For example, if after finding two errors the auditor believes it is reasonable to expect no more errors in additional items selected, a new sample size could be calculated as follows:

$$n = \frac{R}{TE} = \frac{\text{Reliability factor}}{\text{Tolerable error}}$$

$$= \frac{5.33^*}{0.07}$$

$$= 77$$

* from Table 11.4, 90% required confidence level, two errors expected.

The auditor could expand the sample size to 77 and, if no more errors were found, conclude that the maximum error rate did not exceed the tolerable error.

Because of this feature of the statistical model, it is sometimes called *stop-or-go sampling*. In other statistical models it is not possible to incrementally expand the sample size and continue testing.

Appendix 2

Evaluation of sample results for substantive testing using statistically-based techniques

The evaluation of sample results can be one of the most complex aspects of statistical sampling for substantive tests. As outlined earlier, the simple evaluation method of extrapolating a sample error rate to a population does not take into account sample risk, nor does it consider other characteristics of identified errors, such as the offsetting influences of over and understatement.

The following method allows for a consideration of sample error, as well as these other characteristics. The first important concept to understand is the so-called **basic bound** of monetary misstatement. The 'basic bound' is the maximum monetary misstatement that could exist in the population when no monetary misstatements are found in the sample. The ability to compute an upper limit on monetary misstatement when no misstatements are found in the sample is one of the advantages of this method.

The computations used are similar to those explained in Appendix 1 for tests of controls. Recall that the maximum deviation rate is computed by dividing the appropriate reliability factor (R) by sample size (n). To compute the basic bound, the ratio of R to n is multiplied by the dollar amount of the population (BV). The formula is:

$$\frac{R_0}{n} \times BV$$

The designation R_0 indicates the reliability factor for zero misstatement at the specified risk percentage. For example, if the auditor took a sample of 60 from a population of $1 000 000 and found no monetary misstatements, the basic bound at a 5 per cent risk of incorrect acceptance would be computed as follows:

$$\frac{3.0}{60} \times \$1\,000\,000 = \$50\,000$$

The reliability factor for zero error, 3.0, and other reliability factors used in the following discussion are sourced from Table 11.4 (p. 517).

Notice that if other matters remain the same the basic bound equals the tolerable error used to estimate sample size. As explained earlier, the sample size formula is:

$$n = \frac{BV \times R_0}{TE}$$

At a specified risk of incorrect acceptance of 5 per cent:

$$n = \frac{\$1\,000\,000 \times 3.0}{\$50\,000}$$

$$= 60$$

The tolerable error and sample size are established in planning, but as demonstrated above, the basic bound computed in evaluation equals the tolerable error used to estimate sample size. Of course, if monetary misstatements are found and the initial sample size is expanded, the basic bound may also be changed.

The computation of the basic bound explained above is a conservative allowance for undetected error in the population. It combines the upper limit on frequency of error ($R_0 \div n$) with an assumption that each item in error is completely misstated. In accounting populations that is seldom the case, but this conservative approach is generally suggested because of the inability to determine a reasonable basis for a less than complete misstatement.

When monetary misstatements are found in the sample there is a reasonable basis for evaluating partial rather than complete misstatements. For example, if a $100 item (book value or recorded value) is misstated by $10 (audited value or true value is $90), the **misstatement proportion** (the misstatement amount expressed as a percentage of the recorded amount) is 10 per cent.

Assume that in testing property and equipment additions, the auditor detects the following errors and computes the sum of misstatement proportions as shown in Table 11.9.

TABLE **11.9** **Sample items that contain misstatements**

Recorded amount ($)	Audited amount ($)	Misstatement amount ($)	Misstatement proportion
10 530	10 310	220	0.02
5 740	4 018	1722	0.30
3 114	3 425	(311)	(0.10)

The misstatement proportion of each misstatement is used to compute **additions to the basic bound** for the effect of finding each misstatement. The incremental effect of each misstatement is computed by the difference between reliability factors. For example, $(R_1 - R_0) \div n$ is the incremental effect of finding one monetary misstatement, and $(R_2 - R_1) \div n$ is the incremental effect of a second monetary misstatement. This incremental effect is then weighted by the misstatement proportion and multiplied by the book value to compute the addition to the basic bound. An addition to the basic bound is made for each misstatement, and overstatements and understatements are usually computed separately. Also, misstatements need to be ranked in descending order. Ranking in descending order allows for the most conservative estimate of maximum overstatement or understatement.

The result of these computations is a maximum monetary overstatement and a maximum monetary understatement that include quantification of sampling risk. Example 11.6

presents these computations for the three monetary misstatements contained in the example outlined in Table 11.9.

EXAMPLE 11.6 Computation for evaluation of sample error using DUS statistical methods

Overstatements
1st addition to basic bound:

$$\frac{4.75 - 3.00}{60} \times \$1\,000\,000 \times 0.30 = \$8750$$

2nd addition to basic bound:

$$\frac{6.30 - 4.75}{60} \times \$1\,000\,000 \times 0.02 = \underline{\$517}$$
$$= \underline{\underline{9267}}$$

Understatements

$$\frac{4.75 - 3.00}{60} \times \$1\,000\,000 \times 0.10 = \underline{\underline{\$2916}}$$

Maximum overstatement
$50\,000 + \$9267 = \$59\,267$

Maximum understatement
$50\,000 + \$2916 = \$52\,916$

Projected overstatement
$$\frac{0.32}{60} \times \$1\,000\,000 = \$5333$$

Projected understatement
$$\frac{0.10}{60} \times \$1\,000\,000 = \$1667$$

Net maximum overstatement = Maximum overstatement – Projected understatement:
$59\,267 - \$1667 = \$57\,600$

Net maximum understatement = Maximum understatement – Projected overstatement:
$52\,916 - \$5333 = \$47\,583$

Also illustrated in Example 11.6 are computations for projected overstatement and projected understatement. These projected errors represent the auditor's best estimate of misstatement. They are computed for both overstatements and understatements, using the sum of misstatement proportions for misstatement of each type. The projected overstatement is deducted from the maximum understatement to determine net maximum understatement. Conversely, the projected understatement is deducted from the maximum overstatement to determine net maximum overstatement. As a result of this calculation, the auditor can say that they are 95 per cent confident that the account balance is not understated by more than $47 583 or overstated by more than $57 600.

The purpose of these adjustments is to control the risk of incorrect rejection. The auditor's evaluation of sample results is based on these net maximum amounts. The auditor has to decide whether to accept the account balance as not materially misstated or to reject it. However, the projected error for the account balance needs to be combined with uncorrected known misstatements and projected errors from other account balances to consider the effect on the financial report taken as a whole.

The auditor's basic criterion in deciding whether to accept or reject an account balance is whether the projected error exceeds the tolerable error considered in planning the sample. If the auditor rejects the account balance, the most effective approach is usually to expand the portion of the account balance that is 100 per cent examined. The auditor identifies individually significant items and examines all of them. The remaining population is sampled. Any monetary misstatement in items examined 100 per cent is known misstatement, and the known misstatement can readily be corrected by the client.

In DUS, all items larger than the sampling interval are considered to be individually significant and are all examined. Monetary misstatement in these items is known misstatement and is not projected. It is also possible that items larger than the sampling interval may be selected more than once if systematic sampling is used, or any items with more than one dollar may be selected more than once using random numbers. Thus by testing the one transaction or account balance, more than one sampling item can be tested. For this reason the actual sample size, in terms of transactions or account balances, may be smaller than the planned sample size.

Key terms

Additions to the basic bound	556	Misstatement proportion	556
Basic bound	555		

COMPLETION AND COMMUNICATION

PART four

Part 4 covers the completion and communication stages of the assurance services engagement. Chapter 12 deals with the general procedures and related matters dealt with near the completion of the engagement. Chapter 13 covers the standard financial report audit report and the various ways in which it can be modified or qualified, as well as the reporting mechanisms for other assurance services, and other mechanisms for communicating with report users.

CHAPTER 12

COMPLETION AND REVIEW

LEARNING OBJECTIVES

After studying this chapter you should be able to:

1 explain the significance of the date of the auditor's report and the audit engagement;

2 define subsequent events of audit interest and describe the audit procedures applied specifically to identify such events;

3 describe the nature and purpose of written representations obtained from the entity's management and solicitors;

4 explain the purpose and steps involved in reviewing working papers and the financial report, including the summarisation and evaluation of audit results and performance of analytical procedures in an overall review; and

5 understand the auditor's responsibilities in consideration of the entity's ability to continue as a going concern.

A number of audit tests are completed after balance date. Most substantive tests of balances may be carried out in the last quarter of the financial year, provided internal control is strong. However, some audit procedures must wait until after the accounting records are closed. Procedures are necessary after year-end to complete and evaluate the results of audit tests, and review the financial report and working papers. This chapter covers the nature of completion and

review procedures and their relationship to: the date of the auditor's report; the review of subsequent events, including the characteristics of events of audit interest and the procedures used to identify them; and documentation of representations from the entity's solicitors and management. The chapter also covers the final review and evaluation of working papers and the financial report, and activities after the audit, including maintaining the quality of audit practice.

Relevantguidance

Australian		International	
AUS 212	Other Information in Documents Containing Audited Financial Reports	ISA 720	Other Information in Documents Containing Audited Financial Statements
AUS 306	Materiality	ISA 320	Audit Materiality
AUS 502	Audit Evidence (Revised 2004)	ISA 500	Audit Evidence (Revised 2004)
AUS 508	Inquiry Regarding Litigation and Claims	ISA 501	Audit Evidence—Additional Considerations for Specific Items
AUS 512	Analytical Procedures	ISA 520	Analytical Procedures
AUS 516	Audit of Accounting Estimates	ISA 540	Audit of Accounting Estimates
AUS 518	Related Parties	ISA 550	Related Parties
AUS 520	Management Representations	ISA 580	Management Representations
AUS 706	Subsequent Events	ISA 560	Subsequent Events
AUS 708	Going Concern	ISA 570	Going Concern
AASB 110	Events After the Balance Sheet Date (Issued 2004)	IAS 10	Events After the Balance Sheet Date (Issued 2004)
—	Framework for the Preparation and Presentation of Financial Statements (Issued 2004)	—	Framework for the Preparation and Presentation of Financial Statements (Issued 2004)

THE NATURE OF COMPLETION AND REVIEW PROCEDURES

Almost every audit engagement has a deadline for the audit report. Many engagements have a deadline for release of the audited financial report. Other engagements have a self-imposed deadline based on the audit plan, but there is usually some pressure for release of audited data.

An example of a timeline that reflects the relationship between the financial report period and the subsequent events period is contained in Exhibit 12.1. In the case of a disclosing entity or regulated scheme, the *Corporations Act* requires it to lodge an audited financial report with the Australian Securities and Investment Commission (ASIC) within three months of its balance date. For other entities required to lodge an audited financial report with ASIC, the time limit is within four months of balance date. Small companies have had the requirement to hold annual general meetings removed and are not required to prepare a financial report unless 5 per cent of shareholders make a request, the company is foreign controlled or ASIC makes a requisition. The financial report must be distributed 21 days before the annual general meeting.

Thus, audit procedures need to be completed in time to allow for adequate review and evaluation of working papers and the financial report before the audit opinion is signed.

EXHIBIT 12.1

Financial report period	1 July 20X4	Beginning of financial year
	30 June 20X5	Balance date
Subsequent events period	14 September 20X5	Signing of directors' declaration and report $(2\frac{1}{2})$
	15 September 20X5	Signing of audit report* $\}$ 15 day
	30 September 20X5	Distribution of annual report $\}$
	30 October 20X5	Annual general meeting 30 day

* Many auditors sign their report on the date the directors sign their report and declaration. The statutory requirement is that the directors' declaration be signed prior to the audit report.

Examples of the timing of the financial report period, subsequent events period and annual general meeting

THE DATE OF THE AUDIT REPORT

learning objective 1

The **date of the audit report** is important because it establishes the date of the auditor's responsibility for knowledge of important events that should be reflected in the financial report. The auditor cannot provide an audit opinion based upon events that occur after the audit report is signed. The audit report must, therefore, be dated with the actual date upon which it is physically signed.

When the auditor completes all audit tests and leaves the entity's premises, the field work is completed. Usually, this is the date of the final conference with management to agree on the form and content of the financial report. Before this conference, the auditor must decide whether any material adjustments need to be made to the draft financial report, and whether the results of audit tests support the type of opinion to be given on the financial report.

In addition, the date of the auditor's report is determined by the date of the directors' declaration. Sections 295(4) and (5) of the *Corporations Act* require a declaration by a director, in accordance with a resolution of the directors of a company, stating that the financial report complies with the accounting standards and *Corporations Act*; the financial report gives a true and fair view of the company's financial position and performance; there are reasonable grounds to believe that the company is able to pay its debts as and when they become due and payable; and directors have been given a CEO/CFO declaration about the entity's financial records and financial statements required by s. 295A. The date of the audit report should therefore be no earlier than the date on the directors' declaration. This establishes that the report was completed and formally accepted by the officers of the company prior to the expression of an opinion by the auditor.

Audit procedures after balance date

Some audit procedures are performed after balance date as a normal part of tests of balances. Examples of such procedures are tests of subsequent transactions to determine that proper cut-offs have been applied and tests of valuation of assets. For example, the collectibility of receivables may be evaluated by reviewing cash collections after balance date. The search for unrecorded liabilities, explained in Chapter 10, is another example of audit procedures applied to subsequent transactions.

If substantive tests of balances, such as observation of physical inventory-taking, are made at an interim date, audit procedures must be applied to transactions in the period from that interim date to the balance date. The auditor will perform roll-forward procedures including scanning the activity in the account for large or unusual transactions, investigating significant intervening transactions, inquiring about other changes that might affect the balance and applying analytical procedures.

Working papers are reviewed to assure completion of the audit program, disposal of remaining exceptions and unusual matters, summarisation of the results of audit tests for evaluation and, in general, preparation of the working papers for the inspection of audit managers and partners.

A review is made of the period after balance date to identify events that may need to be reflected in the financial report. This review, called the subsequent events review, is explained in the next section. As part of the review, documentation is obtained of the representations of the entity's solicitors and management.

A final review and evaluation of the financial report and audit working papers is made and a closing conference is held with management before the auditor's report is issued.

Analytical procedures

AUS 512.13 (ISA 520.13) states that the auditor should apply analytical procedures at or near completion of the audit in order to assist in the overall review of the reasonableness of the financial report; to corroborate conclusions formed during the audit; and to ensure that the financial report as a whole is consistent with the auditor's knowledge of the business. The different types of analytical procedures undertaken on unaudited figures in the planning stage were discussed in Chapter 6. Similar procedures will be undertaken on the audited financial report at or near the completion of the audit.

If significant unexpected balances or relationships are discovered by analytical procedures at the completion stage of the audit, it means that the auditor has not collected sufficient appropriate evidence and is not in a position to issue an audit report. The identification of these unexpected balances or relationships should indicate to the auditor where to concentrate the additional audit testing which is required.

Analytical procedures also corroborate or strengthen the conclusions formed by the auditor during the audit. If the movements in other financial items are consistent with the conclusions formed on individual items, it increases the auditor's confidence that the view presented by the financial information as a whole is consistent with the auditor's knowledge of the entity.

Quick review

1. The date of the audit report establishes the date up to which the auditor has responsibility for knowledge of events that should be included in the financial report.
2. The audit report must be dated when it is actually signed and it must not be signed earlier than the date of the directors' declaration.
3. Year-end procedures include substantive tests of balances, analytical procedures, subsequent events procedures and review of working papers.

SUBSEQUENT EVENTS AND RELATED REVIEW PROCEDURES

Some specific audit procedures are necessary to provide reasonable assurance that the auditor is aware of significant **subsequent events** that occur after the balance date but before the date of the audit report. The length of the period reviewed depends on the practical requirements of each engagement. It might be a few weeks if there is a tight deadline for the audited report, or a few months if there are problems in closing the accounting records or the entity does not have a tight reporting deadline.

The subsequent events review

The auditor is reporting on a balance sheet for a given date and the associated profit and loss account for a period ending on the balance date. However, AASB 110 (IAS 10) 'Events Occurring After Balance Date' indicates that the financial report should be prepared on the basis of conditions existing at balance date; this may entail recognition of the financial effects of certain events that have occurred after balance date, and up to the time of completion. Under the provisions of AUS 706 (ISA 560), the auditor has a responsibility for ascertaining that management adequately discloses events occurring after balance date but prior to **time of completion** (for companies, the date of the directors' declaration on the financial report; for other entities, the date of the final approval of the financial report by the owners or controlling management) which have a material impact on the financial report. In fact, AUS 706 (ISA 560) extends the 'subsequent period' to the date on which the auditor signs the audit report.

Two types of events may materially affect the financial reports and thus require consideration by management and evaluation by the auditor. One requires adjustment of the financial report, while the other requires disclosure only (see Example 12.1 overleaf). The distinction between the two events rests on both their nature and timing.

Type 1 or adjusting events

Type 1 events require **adjustment** to the figures contained in the balance sheet and/or income statement and are those events, both favourable and unfavourable, that provide evidence of, or further elucidate, conditions that existed at balance date. To be consistent with the objective of preparing the financial report on the basis of conditions existing at balance date, the financial effect of such events needs to be brought to account in finalising the financial report for the period ended on the balance date in accordance with AASB 110.08 (IAS 10.08). Events of this type, in particular, may have a bearing upon the estimates made in the preparation of the financial report and appropriate adjustments may be needed.

Thus, the auditor may need to investigate the circumstances of an event to determine whether it relates to a condition that existed at balance date. For example, the provision for doubtful debts is an inherent estimate. The subsequent collection of a material account receivable which has been treated as uncollectible at balance date requires adjustment. Further examples of this first type of event are:

- a commercial assessment or legal determination, subsequent to balance date, which establishes definitively a claim that was in existence, but of uncertain amount, at balance date;
- legislation after balance date which retrospectively changes the company income tax rate applying to the fiscal period ended on or prior to balance date; and
- ascertainment of selling prices for inventory items, subsequent to balance date, where those prices were previously uncertain and thereby affected the determination of net realisable values.

The auditor should have audit procedures designed to reveal such events.

Type 2 or disclosing events

If a subsequent event does not relate to a condition that existed at balance date, adjustment of the figures in the balance sheet and/or income statement is not appropriate but disclosure by way of footnote may be required in accordance with AASB 110.10 (IAS 10.10). **Type 2 events** or **disclosing events** are those events, both favourable and unfavourable, that create new conditions, as distinct from any that may have existed at balance date. It is inappropriate to bring to account the financial effect of such events in finalising the financial report for the period ended on the balance date, because this conflicts with the objective of a proper demarcation between accounting periods. The financial effect of events of the second type will be reflected in the financial report of the next period. However, non-disclosure would affect the ability of users to make proper evaluations and decisions on the basis of the financial report.

For example, events that require disclosure but that do not result in adjustment include:

- a fire or flood loss after balance date not fully covered by insurance;
- a major currency realignment subsequent to balance date;
- raising of additional share or loan capital after balance date;
- mergers and acquisitions after balance date;
- cessation of significant trading activities where such cessation was not contemplated at balance date; and
- expropriation, after balance date, of a significant overseas investment or asset.

EXAMPLE 12.1 Adjusting and disclosing subsequent events

Consider each of the following separate situations for Global Enterprises Ltd. In each case:

- the balance date is 30 June 20X5;
- the field work was completed on 20 August 20X5; and
- the financial report and audit report were signed on 3 September 20X5.

(a) On 22 August 20X5, you discovered that a debtor at 30 June 20X5, had gone bankrupt on 3 August 20X5. The cause of the bankruptcy was an unexpected loss of a major lawsuit issued by the debtor on 15 June 20X5.

(b) On 22 August 20X5, you discovered that the company's major debtor had gone bankrupt on 3 August 20X5. The cause of the bankruptcy was a major uninsured fire at one of the debtor's premises on 15 July 20X5.

Required
Indicate the appropriate action for each situation and justify your response.

Solution
(a) This is an adjusting event as it further elucidates conditions that existed at balance date. Accordingly, as the financial report has not been signed, the effect should be adjusted in the 30 June 20X5 financial report.

(b) This is an example of an event that creates new conditions, as distinct from any that may have existed at balance date. Therefore, the standard does not require the financial effects of such events to be brought to account in finalising the financial report for the current financial year. However, a note disclosure will be required if it is likely to affect the company's solvency or would be a major factor in evaluating the company's future prospects. As the bankrupt debtor is Global Enterprises Ltd's major debtor, it is likely to have an impact on both solvency and future prospects and therefore should be disclosed.

Events between balance date and date of audit report

The auditor should date and sign the audit report at the date the examination is completed. However, this should not be before the time of completion, since it is the auditor's responsibility to report on the financial report presented by management. This imposes an obligation on the auditor to apply audit procedures relating to subsequent events up to the date of the audit report.

The auditor need not conduct an ongoing review of all matters to which audit procedures have already been applied and conclusions reached; rather, procedures should be designed to ensure that relevant subsequent events are identified.

If the auditor discovers events between balance date and the date of the audit report which require disclosure, and management fails to disclose such events, this should be reflected in the auditor's report.

The following are examples of procedures that can be performed as near as practicable to the date of the audit report to achieve the audit objective, including those procedures discussed in AUS 706.05 (ISA 560.05):

1   Review procedures established by management to ensure that subsequent events are identified.
2   Review the minutes of meetings of directors and/or management and/or other committees, and inquire into any matters disclosed therein which may have a bearing on events occurring after balance date.
3   In the case of companies, review the directors' report for any matters that may provide information to the auditor of any significant events occurring after balance date.
4   Review the latest available management interim financial report and inquire into any matters noted. For such a comparison to be effective, inquiry should be made to ensure that the management interim financial report is prepared on a similar basis to the financial report being audited.
5   Obtain legal advice as to the current status of any material litigation or claims involving the entity.
6   Consider the activities of the entity in the subsequent period and whether they have been affected by such matters as marked changes in legislation, tariff restrictions, variations in foreign exchange rates and financial considerations which may indicate an inability to continue as a going concern.
7   Inquire of the directors and/or management whether, during the subsequent period:
    (a) there have been any material changes in major balance sheet items;
    (b) sales of assets have occurred or are planned;
    (c) the issue of new debentures or shares or an agreement to liquidate or merge has been made or is planned;
    (d) assets have been expropriated by government or destroyed by fire or flood;
    (e) any contingent liabilities or commitments have arisen which may reflect on the financial report;
    (f) estimated amounts included in the financial report have been substantiated since balance date;
    (g) there have been any developments regarding risk areas and contingencies;
    (h) any unusual adjustments have been made or are contemplated;
    (i) any events have occurred or are likely to occur which will bring into question the appropriateness of accounting policies such as the going concern assumption; and
    (j) proper accounting records have been maintained.
8   Make additional inquiries or perform audit procedures necessary and appropriate to dispose of any matters which have arisen out of the foregoing procedures, inquiries and discussions.
9   Where a group financial report is prepared, ensure that audit procedures discussed above are updated for subsidiaries and the parent entity to the time of completion of the group financial report.

If these procedures identify subsequent events, the auditor should apply further audit procedures to these events to assess whether they have been appropriately reflected in the financial report.

AUS 706 (ISA 560) also identifies the auditor's responsibilities in relation to two further areas:

1 the period subsequent to the date of the audit report but prior to the financial report being issued (forwarded to shareholders); and

2 facts discovered after the financial report has been issued.

Events subsequent to the date of the audit report

AUS 706.08–.12 (ISA 560.08–.12) states that the auditor has no responsibility to undertake audit procedures to identify events subsequent to the date of the audit report. Management has a responsibility to monitor events during that time and to inform the auditor of any events that affect the financial report. An auditor who becomes aware of events occurring after the date of the audit report but before the financial report is issued, and who believes the financial report should be amended, should discuss this with management. If the financial report is amended, the auditor should perform procedures that will enable the preparation of an audit report on the amended financial report. As indicated above, the dating of the audit report on the amended financial report should not precede the date the financial report is approved. If the auditor believes the financial report should be amended to reflect the impact of the subsequent events, and management has not made these amendments, the action taken by the auditor depends on whether the original audit report has been released to the client. If that report has not been released, the auditor should issue a qualified audit report on the financial report. If the audit report has been released, the auditor should advise the client that action will be taken to prevent reliance on that report. The action taken depends on the circumstances and the legal rights available to the auditor. In the case of an audit undertaken under the provisions of the *Corporations Act*, the auditor has the right to be heard at any general meeting on matters that concern the auditor. Further, s. 311 requires the auditor to report to ASIC any significant failure to comply with the provisions of the law. Management's failure to amend or reflect in the financial report a relevant subsequent event appears to fall within that category.

Events subsequent to issue of financial report

The second category of subsequent events relates to matters that the auditor becomes aware of after the financial report has been issued that materially affect the financial report previously reported upon, and which existed but were not known to the auditor at the date of the auditor's report. AUS 706.13–.18 (ISA 560.13–.18) states that while the auditor has no obligation to conduct a continuing inquiry of the financial report, knowledge of such events should result in discussions with management. If as a result of the knowledge of the relevant event management decides to revise the original financial report, the auditor needs to apply procedures necessary to issue a new audit report on the revised financial report. This requires the auditor to review subsequent events for the period from the date of the previous audit report to the date of the new report, in order to determine that there are no further material events that need to be reflected in the financial report.

The auditor's report on the revised financial report has a new date, refers to the previous report issued by the auditor and includes an emphasis of matter paragraph (discussed further in Chapter 13) which refers to the explanatory note in the financial report that explains the reason for the revised financial report. If management does not issue a revised financial report where the auditor believes such a report is required, the auditor should advise those persons ultimately responsible for the overall direction of the entity that steps will be taken to prevent future reliance on the original audit report.

The need for a revised financial report must be evaluated in the context of the period to elapse before the issue of the financial report for the next period. The shorter that period, the less necessary it is to issue a revised financial report, provided appropriate disclosures are to be made in the financial report for the next period.

REPRESENTATION LETTERS

As part of the subsequent events review, the auditor normally obtains two types of formal representation letters—one from the entity's solicitors and one from management. Since the inquiries documented in the letters may result in new information that requires investigation, the usual practice is to prepare the letters in draft form for review and discussion before the completion of field work.

Solicitors' representation letters

Litigation, claims and assessments are contingencies that may require recognition of a loss or a gain, or disclosure in the financial report. The auditor is concerned with obtaining evidence of the existence, completeness, valuation and presentation of legal contingencies. Such matters may be disclosed by several audit procedures usually performed during the examination, such as reading the minutes of meetings of shareholders or directors and reading contracts and correspondence. However, the most direct search for legal contingencies is inquiries of management and the entity's solicitor that are documented in a **solicitor's representation letter** and in related written representations by management.

In general, the auditor obtains information on the existence of litigation, claims and assessments from management, and attempts to substantiate the completeness of this information through representations. Not being qualified to make legal judgments, the auditor also attempts to obtain evidence of the valuation of legal matters by obtaining the solicitor's opinion on their potential outcome.

However, in responding to this request for information most solicitors are concerned with maintaining solicitor–client privilege and avoiding any admissions that might prejudice an entity's position in litigation. The effect of disclosures to the auditor on the privileged status of solicitor–client communications is unclear. Auditors maintain that the client, to meet financial reporting obligations, has a duty to make adequate disclosure of contingencies, including litigation, claims and assessments, and needs sound advice on such matters from legal counsel. Further, the auditor, in meeting the obligation to obtain sufficient appropriate evidence to support an opinion on the entity's financial report, needs reliable evidence of the entity's litigation and related matters.

AUS 508 (ISA 501) provides the guidelines for auditors in ascertaining and confirming contingent liabilities arising from pending legal matters and other actions against an entity. The process suggested is to review the entity's system of recording claims and the manner in which such matters are communicated to management. This is supported by reading the minutes of directors' meetings, reviewing fee accounts rendered by solicitors and correspondence with them, reviewing unusual agreements to which the entity is a party, and making inquiries of appropriate officers of the entity.

An important step in this process is to ask management to send a letter of inquiry to those solicitors whom it has consulted during the period. AUS 508 provides a standard letter which seeks solicitors' comments on a list of pending or threatened litigation provided by management. This letter is illustrated in Exhibit 12.2.

EXHIBIT 12.2

A sample solicitor's representation letter

Any Client Company Ltd

15 Smith Street Melbourne, Vic. 3000

Tan, Lau and Leong
Solicitors
25 Elizabeth Street
Melbourne, Vic. 3000

15 August 20X5

Dear Mr Tan,

In connection with the preparation and audit of the financial report of the company and the following subsidiaries:

Newtown Pty Ltd
Oldtown Pty Ltd

for the reporting period ended 30 June 20X5 we request that you provide to this company, at our cost, the following information:

1. Confirmation that you are acting for the company in relation to the matters mentioned below and that the directors' description and estimates of the amounts of the financial settlement (including costs and disbursements) which might arise in relation to those matters are in your opinion reasonable.

Name of company	Directors' description of matter (including current status)	Directors' estimate of the financial settlement (including costs and disbursements)
Any Client Company Ltd	Claim for damages resulting from chemical accident. Initial judgment against client.	$500 000
Newtown Pty Ltd	Prosecution for breach of copyright. Case pending.	$100 000
Oldtown Pty Ltd	Claim for compensation for breach of terms of contract. Still in negotiations with other party.	$50 000

2. Should you disagree with any of the information included in 1 above, please comment on the nature of your disagreement.
3. In addition to the above, please provide a list of open files that you maintain in relation to the company (and the above-mentioned subsidiaries and/or divisions).
4. In relation to the matters identified under 2 and 3 above, we authorise you to discuss these matters with our auditor—Johnson and Hinsey, 1217 Blynwood Avenue, Melbourne—if requested, and at our cost.

It is understood that:

(a) the company and subsidiaries may have used other solicitors in certain matters;
(b) the information sought relates only to legal matters referred to your firm which were current at any time during the above-mentioned reporting period and up to the date of your response;
(c) unless separately requested in writing, you are not responsible for keeping the auditors advised of any changes after the date of your reply;
(d) you are required to respond only on matters referred to you as solicitors for the company or subsidiaries, not on those within your knowledge solely because of the holding of any office as Director, Secretary or otherwise of the company or subsidiaries by a consultant, partner or employee of your firm; and
(e) your reply is sought solely for the information of, and assistance to, this company in connection with the audit of, and report with respect to, the financial report of the company and subsidiaries, and will not be quoted or otherwise referred to in any financial report or related documents of the company and subsidiaries, nor will it be furnished to any governmental agency or other person, subject to specific legislative requirements, without the prior written consent of your firm.

Your prompt assistance in this matter will be appreciated.

Would you please forward a signed copy of your reply directly to our auditors, Johnson and Hinsey, 1217 Blynwood Avenue, Melbourne 3000, by 5 September 20X5.

Yours faithfully,

Any Client Company Limited

per: S. J. Argent
Secretary

The auditor requires sufficient appropriate evidence to enable reasonable conclusions about: whether all legal matters have been identified; the likelihood of any loss or gain; and the estimated amount thereof. Since it is the responsibility of management to adopt policies and procedures to identify, evaluate and account for all liabilities, including contingent liabilities, and the conditions that should be considered in the accounting for and reporting of legal matters that are within management's direct knowledge and control, management is the primary source of information. However, because the reliability of audit evidence is influenced by its source—internal or external—and by its nature, the auditor needs to seek evidence from different sources to support management assertions. The legal representation letter fulfils this role.

The audit procedures required prior to the preparation and distribution of a solicitor's representation letter are:

1 Review and discuss with management the entity's internal control for bringing claims to the attention of management and the arrangement for instructing solicitors, as well as the system for recording legal expenses for control and identification.

2   Obtain from management a list of legal matters referred to solicitors, including a description of the matter and an estimate of possible liabilities.

3   Read the minutes of management meetings for reference to legal matters.

4   Review documents in management's possession concerning legal matters, correspondence with solicitors and accounts rendered by third-party solicitors.

5   Obtain an assurance from management that the information is complete.

The auditor may also detect reference to legal matters from audit procedures undertaken earlier during the audit and applied for different purposes. For example, while examining contracts, loan agreements or leases, or inquiring of officers of the entity, legal matters may have been identified. The procedures discussed above assist the auditor in identifying outstanding legal matters and solicitors consulted by the entity. These procedures do not necessarily provide an auditor with sufficient appropriate evidence concerning the likely amounts for which an entity may ultimately be responsible, nor do they show whether the information is complete. Thus, a legal representation letter is required. As indicated earlier, the auditor ordinarily does not possess the skills necessary to make legal judgments concerning the outcome and possible obligations that may arise from legal matters, however the legal representation letter assists in this regard.

Sometimes solicitors who are employees of the client entity have the primary responsibility for legal matters, and are in the best position to corroborate management's representations. In this situation, a written representation similar to that sought from a third-party solicitor should be obtained from these employees.

If both employee and third-party solicitors are involved in advising on the same matter, the auditor seeks confirmation or representation from the solicitor with the primary responsibility for that matter. However, there may be circumstances where the employee solicitor has primary responsibility, but the matter is of such significance, and has involved substantial participation by a third-party solicitor, that the auditor should consider obtaining a confirmation from the third-party solicitor that their opinion does not differ materially from that of the employee solicitor.

Legal representation letters, prepared by management, should be sent by the auditor to each solicitor identified as handling outstanding legal matters, instructing the solicitor to respond on a timely basis, preferably as close as possible to the expected date of the audit report, and also requesting that a signed copy of the reply be sent direct to the auditor.

An auditor may request that management send a letter of inquiry to solicitors not identified as currently handling client legal matters, for example when an auditor becomes aware that the entity has changed solicitors on a particular matter or that a solicitor engaged by the entity has resigned. In this case the auditor should consider the need for inquiries concerning the reasons the solicitor is no longer associated with the client. Further, an auditor who becomes aware of a matter that appears to have been resolved may wish to confirm the resolution of that matter or confirm that there are no outstanding claims.

The solicitor's response to a letter of inquiry may require the auditor to undertake additional work. If the solicitor disagrees with management's original evaluation of a particular matter, the auditor should seek discussions with the client and solicitor to try to resolve the matter. In conjunction with evidence from other audit procedures, the auditor considers the effect of such disagreement on the audit opinion.

When a solicitor does not respond or provides an incomplete response, the auditor asks management to contact the solicitor requesting that a complete answer to the original letter or an explanation for the lack of response be sent directly to the auditor. If the solicitor provides a valid and acceptable reason for the lack of response, the auditor seeks discussions with the client and solicitor. Information obtained from such discussions is documented, and the solicitor is asked to advise of any inaccuracies. If the auditor considers the solicitor's reasons for not responding are unacceptable, the auditor determines whether alternative procedures can provide sufficient appropriate evidence. Otherwise, the lack of response is considered to be a limitation on the scope of the auditor's examination.

Because of inherent uncertainties a solicitor often cannot give an opinion concerning the likelihood of an unfavourable outcome of a legal matter or the amount or range of potential loss. The auditor, after pursuing all effective alternative means of obtaining sufficient appropriate audit evidence, usually concludes that the financial report is affected by an uncertainty and issues a modified opinion, as discussed in Chapter 13.

When reviewing subsequent events, an auditor should be aware that new matters may be referred to a solicitor by the client subsequent to the date of the solicitor's letter. The auditor should inquire of management as to such new matters. If any such matter indicates litigation, the auditor asks management to prepare a further solicitor's letter with respect to the matter. When audit procedures lead to the discovery of significant matters not previously identified, the auditor extends the audit procedures and requests the client to address further inquiries to, or arrange a meeting with, the solicitors or other relevant experts, at which the auditor should be present.

The solicitor's representation letter is, therefore, a significant element of the audit process. It has the primary role of providing evidence on the completeness of management's assertions relating to liabilities arising from legal matters, and providing the opinion of an expert on matters which are beyond the auditor's skills.

Management representation letters

AUS 520.02 (ISA 580.02) requires the auditor to obtain appropriate representations from management. AUS 520.03 (ISA 580.03) acknowledges that where the directors or management make representation required by statute or regulation concerning the financial report, as in the directors' report or directors' declaration, the auditor does not need to obtain further representations on those matters. However, AUS 520.11 (ISA 580.11) points out that the auditor usually includes in the working papers evidence of management representations in the form of a summary of oral discussions with management or written representations from management. Written evidence, such as a **management representation letter**, is better than oral representations.

Obtaining a representation letter from management serves two primary purposes:

1   The inquiry procedure is formalised by putting in writing management's replies to inquiries made by the auditor during the examination. For example, in the examination of inventory, the auditor asks many questions concerning such things as pricing methods and the existence of consigned merchandise. The management representation letter is a record that is placed in the working papers to indicate that such questions have been answered.
2   Management responsibility for the financial report is clarified and the client is reminded that it bears the primary responsibility for the truth and fairness of the financial report. In some cases, management is aware of important matters such as contingent liabilities, but does not realise the importance of disclosing them in the financial report. The management representation letter draws attention to such items in an effort to avoid misunderstandings.

These written representations do not relieve the auditor from gathering adequate evidence about the items covered. They complement other audit procedures but are not a substitute for them.

Although representation letters are signed by management, they are normally prepared by the auditor and submitted for signing. The letters may cover specific subjects such as inventories and liabilities, or they may be comprehensive, covering nearly all items in the financial report.

A comprehensive letter is normally signed by a senior executive officer of the client and the principal accounting officer. When separate letters are obtained for specific items, the company official responsible for the particular item is asked to sign. An example of a management representation letter is shown in Exhibit 12.3.

Any Client Company Ltd

15 Smith Street Melbourne, Vic. 3000

Johnson and Hinsey   15 September 20X5
Chartered Accountants
1217 Blynwood Avenue
Melbourne, Vic. 3000

Dear Sirs,

In connection with your examination of the financial report for the year ended
30 June 20X5 we confirm, to the best of our knowledge and belief, the following representations made to you during your examination:

1. We are responsible for the presentation in the financial report in conformity with Australian accounting standards.
2. We have made available to you all:
   (a) accounting records and related data;
   (b) minutes of the meetings of shareholders, directors and committees of directors, or summaries of actions of recent meetings for which minutes have not yet been prepared.
3. There have been no:
   (a) irregularities involving management or employees who have significant roles in internal control;
   (b) irregularities involving other employees that could have a material effect on the financial report;
   (c) communications from regulatory agencies concerning non-compliance with, or deficiencies in, financial reporting practices that could have a material effect on the financial report.
4. The stocks of raw materials, work in progress, finished goods and supplies are based on physical quantities determined as at 30 June 20X5, and the accounts were adjusted to agree with the physical inventory.
5. The inventories do not include any items invoiced to customers but not dispatched or any items returned by customers for which credits have not been recorded.
6. All inventories were priced at the lower of cost or net realisable value, and adequate provision has been made for obsolete, damaged or unusable items. Inventories are recorded generally in the same manner as for the preceding financial year.
7. Accounts receivable represent valid claims against customers and other debtors, and adequate provision has been made for uncollectible and doubtful amounts.
8. All units of property which have been retired, abandoned, replaced or otherwise disposed of up to balance date have been removed from the accounts.
9. Adequate depreciation has been provided to write off depreciable assets over their useful lives. Depreciation has been determined in a manner consistent with the preceding year, and no circumstances have arisen which render that basis inappropriate.
10. The company has good title to all assets shown in the financial report, with all encumbrances over assets disclosed in the financial report.

11. All known assets of the company at balance date were recorded in the books of account.
12. All known liabilities of the company at balance date were recorded in the books of account.
13. There were no material contingent liabilities at balance date which are not shown in the financial report.
14. Contractual commitments amounting to $2 million had been entered into by the company at balance date.
15. We have complied with all aspects of contractual agreements that would have a material effect on the financial report in the event of non-compliance.
16. No events have occurred subsequent to the balance date that would require adjustment to, or disclosure in, the financial report.
17. All assets and insurable risks of the company are adequately covered by insurance.
18. The results of operations for the period ended 30 June 20X5 have not been materially affected by transactions of an unusual nature, other than as disclosed in the financial report.

E. M. Silver

Managing Director

T. Aranoff

Principal Accounting Officer

AUS 502 (ISA 500) states that the validity of evidence is a matter of professional judgment. An auditor, in exercising that judgment, should consider a number of interrelated variables, including quality, consistency, independence, sufficiency and cost. Evaluated in the context of these variables, client representation letters appear to be limited as primary audit evidence. At best, the evidence is usually corroborative: the letter supports propositions on which the auditor has already formed a judgment based on stronger forms of evidence. However, it may be the only evidence available of management's intentions.

The quality of evidence is determined by the process which creates or generates the evidence. Management representations have a high degree of susceptibility to manipulation. In terms of balance and consistency, it is generally accepted that evidence created by processes under the control of the auditor is preferable to other types of audit evidence. However, to rely entirely on such evidence would be inefficient and costly, and to place too great a reliance on external evidence may be unwise because of the inability in many cases to determine the quality of third-party evidence. Equally, too great a reliance on internally generated evidence, even under strong internal control, exposes the auditor to the risk of a mistaken assessment of evidence quality.

An auditor must therefore seek a balance of evidence and look for consistency between sources when making a judgment on a financial report or an individual account. Consistent pieces of evidence reduce audit risk through reinforcement. Viewed in this context, the management representation letter has some value as evidence. This proposition, however, requires further analysis. While generalisations from specific examples are not always valid, the case of inventory provides a useful illustration.

Suppose an auditor has verified the inventory figure for a client, using evidence from the following accepted auditing procedures:

1 review and evaluation of internal control;
2 attendance at physical stocktakes;

3 reference to third-party documentation for valuation; and

4 audit review to ensure consistent application of Australian accounting standards.

If the evidence from each source is consistent, the addition of a fifth procedure, a representation from management on inventory, does not provide any greater audit assurance. The auditor should have made a judgment on inventory prior to a letter of representation. Reviewed in terms of evidence quality, the representation of management has the lowest ranking of all five sources.

If the evidence from sources 1 and 2 is inconsistent, the client may have sound internal control over inventory, but there is evidence of material stocktaking errors. In this case support from management confirming the inventory figure in the accounts is not a sufficient basis on which to formulate an audit judgment. This is supported by reference to the case law on stock certificates, and reliance on client representations generally. The decision in *re Thomas Gerrard & Son Ltd* (1967) All ER 525, which was discussed in Chapter 4, modified the proposition established in the *Kingston Cotton Mill* case of 1896 that stock certificates from management were acceptable evidence in their own right. Pennycuick J, in the *Thomas Gerrard* decision, established that changed economic and business conditions require auditors to satisfy themselves through direct investigation about the existence and value of inventories. Clearly, this implies that management representations are unacceptable as a primary source of evidence; it has been more directly stated in the case of *Dominion Freeholders Ltd v Aird* (1967) SR (NSW) 150. Jacobs JA stated:

> They [the auditors] must not rely or depend on company officers for information or representations in respect of matters upon which they are required in the course of their duties to reach an independent conclusion and, if they so rely, they cannot shed their responsibility by casting the liability on to the company or officers concerned.

Those views were reinforced in the *Pacific Acceptance* case, although Moffitt J warned:

> Nothing I have said is intended to suggest that in the course of an audit, where appropriate, it may not be proper or necessary for an auditor to seek explanations from management, or that an auditor cannot in appropriate circumstances reasonably rely on such explanations. Such a course provides an adjunct to checking and is an essential element of an audit.

In terms of the audit evidence principle of balance and consistency, management representation letters play, at best, a supporting role.

Statutory requirements

The view that management should acknowledge responsibility for the preparation and presentation of the financial report is sound. However, in the context of a statutory audit in Australia, the utility of a representation letter is more uncertain than in other audit situations. The CEO and CFO are required by s. 295A to sign a declaration that the financial records have been properly maintained and the financial report complies with accounting standards and gives a true and fair view. The responsibility of directors for the financial report is acknowledged under company legislation through the provisions of the *Corporations Act*, with s. 295(4) imposing a positive obligation on the directors to prepare and sign a declaration as to the appropriateness of the financial report and confirming that they have received a s. 295A declaration from the CEO and CFO. Further, s. 298 requires a directors' report on various matters concerning the entity's operations and activities. These published statements are signed by the directors prior to the signing of the audit report, and they acknowledge management's responsibility for the representations supporting the financial report. While the directors have a statutory obligation to provide this information (much of which overlaps with the suggested content of a representation letter), the auditor cannot legally demand that company directors sign a letter of representation.

In relation to other entities, such as partnerships and trusts, different circumstances may apply. In the case of a partnership, the scope of the audit may be limited by agreement. Therefore, it is desirable that an auditor should obtain written representations from the management in respect of all matters, including those covered by the audit.

Quick review

1 The auditor should obtain a legal representation letter from the entity's solicitor in order to obtain evidence of possible legal contingencies.

2 The auditor must obtain appropriate representations from management. A written representation letter formalises management responses to inquiries made during the audit and clarifies management's responsibilities.

3 Representations by management are of limited reliability as audit evidence and are usually used to corroborate other evidence. However, they may be the only evidence available to support management's intentions.

REVIEW OF WORKING PAPERS AND FINANCIAL REPORT

The auditor continuously reviews the working papers and evaluates the results of audit tests as the audit progresses. Planning and supervision continue throughout the engagement. Each major step in the audit increases the auditor's understanding of the support for the financial report, and audit procedures are modified as the results of audit tests either confirm or call into question the auditor's earlier understanding. The reviews of working papers and the financial report made at the end of the engagement are a final check to ensure that all significant matters and problems have been identified, considered and satisfactorily resolved. Although one phase of the final review blends into the next, for purposes of discussion it can be divided into summarisation and evaluation of audit results to enable a final assessment of materiality and audit risk, financial report review and administrative completion of working papers.

Final assessment of materiality and audit risk

An essential part of completing the audit and coming to an audit opinion is the final assessment of materiality and audit risk. As the audit tests for each item in the financial report are completed, the auditor doing the work signs off completion of the steps in the audit program, identifies material errors in the financial report and proposes adjustments to the financial report. This work is reviewed by a more senior audit staff member.

Material errors are errors that cause a distortion of the financial report. The distortion may be a misstatement of net profit or net assets, an error in classification or a non-disclosure of required information such as related-party transactions. Classification errors are misstatements of components of the financial report, such as current assets or net profit before extraordinary items, with no misstatement of net amounts. Errors may result from mistakes in processing transactions, such as mistakes in quantities, prices or computations, mistakes in the selection or application of accounting principles, and mistakes in facts or judgments about accounting estimates. Errors may be accidental, a matter of opinion or deliberate misrepresentations.

The cause of errors must be considered and the implications determined for earlier decisions about the reliability of accounting records and controls and the extent of audit tests. An important part of the review is to evaluate whether audit procedures were adequate in the light of the results of audit tests and the acceptable level of audit risk specified in the planning stage. This evaluation is usually made jointly by the audit senior and the audit manager.

The other part of the review is disposition of monetary errors. Individual material known errors are usually corrected routinely. Adjustments are proposed and the entity's recording of them reviewed. Other errors are summarised for the attention of the manager and partner and evaluated by them. These include material items on which there are differences of opinion with the client, errors that are individually immaterial and potential errors that are not known but are possible because of conditions or inconclusive audit tests.

The summarisation of errors is considered to re-evaluate whether the items are 'hard' errors or a qualitative judgment, and to determine whether the total of the errors exceeds an amount considered material to the financial report taken as a whole. If the auditor concludes that the misstatements may be material, the level of audit risk may be reduced either by extending audit procedures or by requesting management to make adjustments to the financial report.

The usual approach to individually immaterial errors is to compute the net effect on significant components of the financial report, such as net profit, net assets and working capital. Individual errors can have a cumulative effect on the financial report that is material. The auditor must also make some allowance for undetected errors. If the cumulative effect of immaterial and undetected errors is material, adjustments must be discussed with the client. At this stage, the auditor considers performing additional procedures to reduce the risk of undetected errors and/or requesting management to adjust the financial report for identified misstatements.

Material errors on which there is a difference of opinion must always be discussed individually in a conference with the client and the differences resolved. The auditor attempts to persuade the entity's management of the need for adjustment, and management usually attempts to have adjustments waived as immaterial. Management may be able to supply information or raise points that the auditor has not considered. However, AUS 306.05 (ISA 320.15) states that if management will not adjust the financial report and the results of the extended audit procedure do not enable the auditor to conclude that the aggregate of uncorrected misstatements is not material, an unqualified opinion cannot be issued. Such modifications of the audit report are considered in Chapter 13.

Accounting estimates

An **accounting estimate** is an approximation of the amount of a financial report item in the absence of a precise measurement. Examples include provision for doubtful debts, provision for warranty expenses and useful lives of assets for depreciation purposes. Management is responsible for making these estimates, which involve considerable judgment. As these estimates are often made in conditions of uncertainty concerning the outcome of events, the risk of misstatement is high.

AUS 516.10 (ISA 540.10) requires an auditor to adopt one of the following approaches in the audit of an accounting estimate:

■ Review and test the process management has used to develop the estimate. This will involve evaluation of the data, consideration of assumptions used, testing of calculations, comparison with previous periods and consideration of management's approval procedures.

■ Use an independent estimate for comparison with that used by management. Auditors may obtain an independent estimate or make one themselves.

- Review subsequent events that confirm the estimate made. Transactions and events that occur after period end, but prior to the completion of the audit, may provide evidence to support the reasonableness of the estimate.

Review of the financial report and other information contained in the annual report

Review of the financial report

The final review of the financial report and the final review of the working papers are closely related, and some parts are completed simultaneously. For example, when the working paper for an item in the financial report is completed, the related financial report presentation and disclosure are usually considered. Information to be included in the notes to the financial report is usually tested along with related amounts in the financial report. For example, the note disclosing inventory details is considered as part of audit tests of inventory.

In considering these presentations and disclosures for each account balance, related note disclosure and other required note disclosures, the auditor must gather evidence to support the following assertions concerning presentation and disclosure (AUS 502/ISA 5002), as outlined earlier in Chapters 5 and 10:

  (i) *Occurrence and rights and obligations* disclosed events, transactions and other matters have occurred and pertain to the entity
 (ii) *Completeness* all disclosures that should have been included in the financial report have been included
(iii) *Classification and understandability* financial information is appropriately presented and described and disclosures are clearly expressed
(iv) *Accuracy and valuation* financial and other information is disclosed fairly and at appropriate amounts

Having collected evidence on the assertions of occurrence and rights and obligations, completeness, and accuracy and valuation, the auditor will proceed to ensure that the disclosures are fairly represented. The auditor will further ensure that the financial information is classified in accordance with the requirements of the financial reporting framework (for example, as current or non-current assets, or as liabilities or equity), and is understandable.

The auditor should also ensure that their name is not associated with misleading information. Thus, after all presentation and disclosure assertions have been evaluated, the auditor should 'step back' and ensure that the view presented by the financial report and all associated information is consistent with the underlying state of affairs. For example, if the auditor believes that an entity is not performing well, yet the underlying financial information suggests that the organisation is performing very well, the auditor would have to consider whether additional information needs to be added to reflect the true financial performance (i.e. the auditor is effectively questioning the completeness assertion relating to presentation and disclosure). This is consistent with what is called a 'true and fair override', part of a true and fair view, which is discussed in Chapter 13.

Review of other information contained in the annual report

AUS 212.02 (ISA 720.02) requires that the auditor read **other information**, on which there is no obligation to report, if it is included in documents containing audited financial reports, in order to identify material inconsistencies with the audited financial report or misstatements of fact. This requirement applies for an annual report and it may also apply to other documents. An example of other information included in the annual report is the directors' report, which in accordance with s. 299(1) must include matters such as a review of operations for the current year and the likely developments in the entity's operations in future years. An auditor who identifies a material inconsistency or misstatement of fact needs to determine whether the audited financial report or the other information needs to be amended. This is discussed further in Chapter 13.

The final review of the financial report also includes a review of a draft of the audit report that accompanies the financial report.

Examining related-party transactions

As explained in Chapter 6, when planning the audit, the auditor identifies **related parties** so that transactions with them may be noted during the audit examination. Towards the completion of the audit, the auditor examines all identified related-party transactions and, where necessary, performs additional procedures in accordance with AUS 518 (ISA 550) to determine their nature and type. The auditor also obtains written representation from management as to the completeness and accuracy of the related-party disclosures.

The auditor needs to verify compliance with the disclosure requirements of AASB 124 (IAS 24) 'Related Party Disclosures'. The auditor should observe the requirements of the 'Framework for the Preparation and Presentation of Financial Statements', which requires due consideration to reporting the substance of transactions where this differs from the apparent legal form.

Administrative completion of working papers

The primary purpose of the review of working papers is to ensure that the audit of the financial report is complete and adequately documented and that there is sufficient appropriate audit evidence to support the audit opinion given. Documentation is important because the quality of the audit may be challenged in litigation and the working papers will be used in planning future audits. The preparation and ownership of working papers was discussed in Chapter 5.

A review is complex and difficult, and audit firms attempt to assist reviewers by preparing review forms and checklists to assure completeness and to document the review procedures.

As the working papers on the engagement are reviewed, the reviewers systematically file and index them and determine if any may be discarded, so that the file will be as integrated and concise as possible. A separate, permanent file containing material of continuing interest, such as excerpts of important contracts is maintained and it is updated each year.

The manager on the engagement usually has supervisory responsibility for the review. The partner makes an independent review and may consult specialists for particularly complex or sensitive problems.

As was discussed in Chapter 2, most audit firms have some form of additional independent review by someone not associated with the engagement, but its nature and extent vary. A second partner may make the review, or there may be a separate review department with no direct client responsibilities. The review may be confined to the financial report and the audit report, or it may be a 'cold look' at the entire audit. AUS 206.17 (ISA 220.17) suggests augmentation of review procedures, particularly for large complex audits, by requesting personnel who are not involved in the audit to perform additional procedures before the auditor's report is issued.

After the audit

After the completion of the audit and review of working papers, several administrative and technical details remain. The auditor will prepare a management letter covering internal control weaknesses discovered during the audit and will have meetings with management and the audit committee or board of directors. Communications with management are discussed in Chapter 13. There may be special reports to be prepared or tax returns to be filed. Also, the time spent on the audit must be summarised, variances from budget analysed and bills for fees prepared. Then planning begins for the next year's audit.

An additional activity that may take place after the audit relates to maintaining the quality of the audit practice. The policies and procedures that audit firms may adopt to maintain the quality of practice were discussed in Chapter 2. One of the elements of quality control is inspection to assure that other quality controls are being observed in practice. An important aspect of inspection is a form of internal audit or internal review. Teams of auditors are organised to inspect practices in other offices of multi-office firms. These teams review the working papers, financial reports and audit reports in selected engagements.

Quick review

1. The causes of any errors need to be considered to determine if they affect any earlier decisions concerning risk assessment.
2. The auditor needs to summarise errors to determine whether individually or in total they are material and require adjustment.
3. The audit working papers are reviewed to ensure that the audit is complete and properly documented and the working papers contain sufficient appropriate audit evidence to support the audit opinion given.

APPROPRIATENESS OF THE GOING CONCERN BASIS

The 'Framework for the Preparation and Presentation of Financial Statements' recognises that the **going concern basis** is generally adopted in the preparation of financial reports. Where financial reports are prepared on a going concern basis, the auditor must consider whether this basis is appropriate for the valuation and measurement of items appearing in the financial report and for the directors' assertion as to solvency in the directors' statement. AUS 708 (ISA 570) requires the auditor to assess the risk of going concern problems at the planning stage and again during the final review. Consideration of this basis at the planning stage is discussed in Chapter 7. The period to be considered by such an assessment extends to the expected date of the auditor's report for the succeeding financial reporting period, which is defined as the relevant period.

The definition of going concern basis includes the expectation that an entity is able to pay its debts as and when they fall due. The inclusion of this condition in the definition formally recognises solvency as a going concern issue. It also means that debt repayment needs to be considered for the time period over which the debt is to be repaid, which may be several years. As a result, AUS 708 (ISA 570) requires the auditor to take a proactive role to assess the appropriateness of the going concern basis during the relevant period and, in addition, to take a reactive role if the auditor becomes aware of any circumstances that may raise doubt about the going concern basis after the relevant period.

If it is not clear that the going concern basis is appropriate, additional audit procedures may be necessary. Most are performed during the period of completion of the audit, and may require the auditor to:

- review after-balance-date events;
- analyse the latest interim financial report, cash flow and profit forecasts;
- read the minutes of directors' meetings for references to financial difficulties;
- review the terms of debenture and loan agreements;
- request information from the entity's solicitors; and
- consider the effect of unfilled customer orders.

When a going concern problem is identified, the auditor discusses with management its plans for overcoming the problem, for example by raising additional finance, or the presence of mitigating factors. The auditor needs to obtain a written representation about such plans and consider their feasibility. Where appropriate, written confirmation should be obtained from third parties, such as banks, as to the existence of their commitment to additional lending and their willingness to be identified in the financial report as having entered into such arrangements.

AASB 110.14 (IAS 10.14), which applies to accounting periods beginning on or after 1 January 2005, states that an entity is not to prepare its financial report on a going concern basis if management determines after the reporting date that it intends to liquidate the entity or cease trading or has no realistic alternative but to do so. The former AASB 1002 took the view that non-adjusting events cannot affect the basis of the financial report and therefore required disclosure only of the expected amounts on realisation and settlement in such cases.

Confirmation and evaluation of financial support

The auditor should obtain a confirmation of the existence, legality and enforceability of arrangements made with third parties to maintain or provide additional financial support to the entity. The auditor will also need to be satisfied as to capacity and intention of the third party to provide the necessary level of support. In practice, many entities would be unable to continue operations without the aid of such support, and the auditor will need to identify and assess any instances where doubts are raised as to the continuity of the support.

When the provider of the financial support is a state or the Commonwealth government, a bank or a major financial institution, the auditor should not normally encounter any major problems in carrying out the above procedures. The situation might, however, be entirely different where the entity is supported financially by proprietors/shareholders and/or related entities. Formal agreements may not exist or may be legally unenforceable and there may be insufficient evidence available to the auditor to assess the financial standing of the provider.

Comfort letters

Often a parent entity will support a subsidiary which is in financial difficulty. The support of parent entities is usually evidenced by the provision to their subsidiaries of **comfort letters**, which can be categorised as letters of support or letters of subordination.

The basic characteristics of a **letter of support** are:

- that the parent entity agrees to provide financial assistance to a subsidiary for a fixed period (usually 12 months);

- that this arrangement is an appropriate mechanism where the subsidiary *cannot* afford to pay its debts (either to the parent entity or external creditors) as and when they fall due;
- that this arrangement is active in nature (as the parent entity promises to *take action* by providing financial assistance).

The basic characteristics of a **letter of subordination** are:

- that the parent entity agrees not to demand repayment of debts the subsidiary owes (for a fixed period, usually 12 months);
- that this type of arrangement is appropriate where the subsidiary *can* afford to pay all its debts *except* those to the parent entity;
- that this arrangement is passive in nature (as the parent entity promises *not* to *take action* to recover its debts).

In the UK in *Kleinwort Benson Ltd v Malaysia Mining Corporation Berhad* [1988] 1 WLR 799, Hirst J held that the provisions of a letter of comfort constituted a contractual term binding on the defendants. However, the Court of Appeal in [1989] 1 WLR 379 allowed an appeal from that decision. The Court of Appeal accepted that a promise made for consideration in a commercial transaction will be taken to have been intended to have contractual effect in law unless the contrary is clearly shown. The Court of Appeal affirmed that a promise or an undertaking contained in a letter of comfort, which is ancillary to the principal contractual document or which one of the contracting parties requires as a condition to it entering into the contract, may be just as contractually binding as the contract itself.

Whether the contractual document is so binding depends upon the intention of the parties and the words actually used. In this case, the parent entity provided a comfort letter to a merchant bank in support of its subsidiary's application for a loan. The letter of comfort read in part: 'It is our policy to ensure that the business of [our subsidiary] is at all times in a position to meet its liabilities to you under the above arrangements'.

With a decline in the market following the collapse of the International Tin Council, the subsidiary ceased trading and sustained heavy losses, owing the merchant bank some £12 million plus interest. The merchant bank claimed immediate repayment from the parent entity who denied liability, contending that no contract existed between it and the merchant bank.

At first instance in the Commercial Court, the above statement in the comfort letter was held to be contractual because it was prepared as part of a commercial banking transaction and its wording was unequivocal in expressing a legal obligation by the parent entity. Damages were, therefore, awarded for breach of contract. However, the English Court of Appeal reversed this decision and rejected the contractual status of the statement on the basis that it was only a statement of the parent entity's policy, and not a promise that this policy would be continued in future. In its letter it did not expressly promise to accept liability for its subsidiary's losses. The statement was, therefore, in marked contrast to the promise analysed as contractual in the preceding paragraph of the letter, which read: 'We confirm that we will not reduce our current financial interest in [the subsidiary] ...'.

Therefore, in order to determine the effect of a letter of comfort, it is necessary to take into account the following matters:

- whether the letter of comfort is given in circumstances where the party giving the letter has refused to assume legal liability;
- whether the letter of comfort contains a promise as to future conduct rather than a representation of existing fact;
- whether there is evidence that the parties had specifically agreed that the words of the comfort letter should not have legal effect;

- whether there is a 'promise made for consideration in a commercial transaction' in the background to the giving of the letter, in the actual agreement (if any) made between the parties as to the effect of the comfort letter and in the actual words used in the comfort letter; and
- if yes to the preceding point, whether it has been clearly shown that the promise is not intended to have contractual effect in law.

Where auditors wish to place any reliance on either a letter of support or a letter of subordination, they should consider the following points:

- The agreement needs to be carefully drafted to ensure that its objectives are achieved. Agreements of this kind are often drawn up on an informal basis without their implications having been properly considered. Consequently, some informal agreements are ineffective. For example, for agreements to be legally enforceable the documents often need to be under seal. Therefore, the auditors should check that any agreement that is intended to be legally binding has been approved by the parent entity's and subsidiary's solicitors. If the auditors have any doubts on the matter, they will need to obtain separate legal advice concerning the effectiveness of the agreement.
- The directors who sign the agreement on behalf of the parent entity must have sufficient authority to bind the parent entity, otherwise the agreement may not be binding on the parent entity. It will, however, become binding on that entity if it is subsequently ratified by its board. This is a complex area of law and therefore the auditors should ascertain that the agreement has been approved by a resolution of a quorum of the parent entity's board, and minuted in the parent entity's books.
- The auditor should also recommend that the subsidiary entity's board should minute the details of the agreement. If it is later alleged that the subsidiary traded while it was insolvent, these minutes would provide evidence of the basis for the action of the subsidiary entity's directors.
- The agreement may have been drafted in a way that permits termination either unilaterally by the parent entity or, more usually, by the agreement of the parent entity and its subsidiary. Therefore, the auditor should check that no termination has occurred and to the extent that it is possible for them to do so, assess whether termination is likely to occur in the near future.
- If it appears that the subsidiary is unable to pay its external creditors (quite apart from the inter-entity debt), the auditors cannot rely on a letter of subordination.
- Irrespective of whether the auditors of the subsidiary are also the parent entity's auditors, they must satisfy themselves both that the parent entity is capable of offering the support it purports to offer in its agreement and that the amount of that support is adequate.

The effect of going concern problems on the audit report will be discussed in Chapter 13.

Quick review

1. The auditor must consider whether the going concern basis is appropriate for the valuation and measurement of items appearing in the financial report.
2. Where there are doubts about the appropriateness of the going concern basis additional audit procedures may be necessary during the final review stage of the audit.
3. The auditor needs to obtain confirmation of arrangements made with third parties to provide additional finance to support the entity and assess the capacity of the third party to provide the promised support.
4. Parent entities may provide support to their subsidiaries through a letter of comfort, which may be in the form of a letter of support or a letter of subordination.

Summary

The date of the auditor's report is important as it establishes the date up to which the auditor is required to carry out audit procedures to have a reasonable assurance that all appropriate information is included in the financial report. Audit procedures for subsequent events are necessary to identify significant events that occur after balance date but before the date that the audit report is signed. Two types of subsequent events may materially affect the financial report. Type 1 events require adjustment as they provide additional information about events that existed at balance date. Type 2 events require disclosure only, as they relate to a condition that did not exist at balance date.

Steps involved in completing the audit include obtaining a management representation letter and a solicitor's letter; completing analytical procedures; considering the effect of transactions with related parties; assessing the applicability of the going concern basis; making a final assessment of materiality and audit risk; making a technical review of the financial report; and making a final review of the working papers.

Key terms

References

Davey, J. (1980) 'Are letters of representation a waste of time?', *Accountancy*, February, 59–60.

Greenwood, P.M. (1978) 'A consideration of the accounting principles for post-balance-date events', *The Chartered Accountant in Australia*, April, 17–32.

Pound, G. and Besley, R. (1982) 'Are representation letters needed?', *The Chartered Accountant in Australia*, March, 11–13.

Tucker, R.R. and Matsumera, E.M. (1997) 'Second-partner review: An experimental economics investigation', *Auditing: A Journal of Practice and Theory*, Spring, 78–98.

Wright, A. and Ashton, R.H. (1989) 'Identifying audit adjustments with attention-directing procedures', *The Accounting Review*, October, 710–28.

Assignments

Additional assignments for this chapter are contained in Appendix A of this book, page 773.

MAXIMISE YOUR MARKS! There are approximately 30 interactive questions on completion and review available online at www.mhhe. com/au/gay3e

REVIEW QUESTIONS

12.1 The following questions relate to the auditor's responsibility with respect to subsequent events. Select the *best* response.

    (a) 'Subsequent events' for reporting purposes are defined as events which occur subsequent to:

        A the date of the audit report

        B the balance date

        C the balance date but prior to the date of the audit report

        D the date of the audit report, and concern contingencies which are not reflected in the financial report

(b) An auditor is concerned with completing various phases of the examination after the balance date. This 'subsequent period' for audit testing extends to the date of the:

    A auditor's report

    B final review of the audit working papers

    C public issuance of the financial statements

    D delivery of the auditor's report to the client

(c) Which of the following material events that occurred after the 30 June balance date would not ordinarily require adjustment of the amounts in the financial report before it is issued on 5 September?

    A Write-off of a receivable from a debtor who filed for bankruptcy on 3 July

    B Acquisition of a subsidiary on 23 July, after negotiations commenced on 15 June

    C Settlement of extended litigation on 15 August in excess of the recorded liability

    D Finalisation of a loss of profits insurance claim on 1 September for a fire which destroyed the factory on 10 June

(d) Which event that occurred after the end of the fiscal year under audit, but prior to issuance of the audit report, would not require disclosure in the financial report?

    A A large debenture or share issue

    B Large loss of plant or inventories as a result of fire or flood

    C A drop in the quoted market price of the shares of the company

    D Settlement of major litigation when the event giving rise to the claim took place after the balance sheet date

(e) Which of the following procedures would an auditor most likely perform to obtain evidence about the occurrence of subsequent events?

    A Confirming a sample of material accounts receivable established after year-end

    B Comparing the financial report being reported on with those of previous periods

    C Investigating personnel changes in the accounting department occurring after year-end

    D Inquiring as to whether any unusual adjustments were made after year-end

(f) Which of the following procedures would an auditor most likely perform to obtain evidence about the occurrence of subsequent events?

    A Recompute a sample of large-dollar transactions occurring after year-end for arithmetic accuracy.

    B Investigate changes in shareholders' equity occurring after year-end.

    C Inquire of the entity's solicitor concerning litigation, claims, and assessments arising after year-end.

    D Confirm bank accounts established after year-end.

(g) Analytical procedures used in the overall review stage of an audit generally include:

    A considering unusual or unexpected amount balances that were *not* previously identified

    B testing transactions to corroborate management's financial statement assertions

    C gathering evidence concerning account balances that have *not* changed from the prior year

    D retesting control procedures that appeared to be ineffective during the assessment of control risk

12.2 The following questions relate to the auditor's responsibility with respect to litigation, claims and assessments. Select the *best* response.

    (a) When auditing contingent liabilities, which of the following procedures would be *least* effective?

        A Reviewing the bank confirmation letter

        B Reading the minutes of the board of directors

       C Examining the solicitor's letter

       D Examining customer confirmation replies

(b) The letter of audit inquiry addressed to the entity's solicitor will not ordinarily be:

       A a source of corroboration of the information originally obtained from management concerning litigation, claims and assessments

       B sent to a solicitor who was engaged by the audit client during the year and soon thereafter resigned the engagement

       C needed during the audit of clients whose securities are not listed on the Australian Stock Exchange

       D limited to references concerning only pending or threatened litigation with respect to which the solicitor has been engaged

(c) When obtaining evidence regarding litigation against a client, the auditor would be *least* interested in determining:

       A the period in which the underlying cause of the litigation occurred

       B an estimate of when the matter will be resolved

       C an estimate of the potential loss

       D the probability of an unfavourable outcome

(d) An auditor should request that an audit client send a letter of inquiry to those solicitors who have been consulted concerning litigation, claims or assessments. The primary reason for this request is to provide:

       A the opinion of a specialist as to whether loss contingencies are possible, probable or remote

       B a description of litigation, claims and assessments that have a reasonable possibility of unfavourable outcome

       C an objective appraisal of management's policies and procedures adopted for identifying and evaluating legal matters

       D corroboration of the information furnished by management concerning litigation, claims and assessments

(e) If a solicitor refuses to furnish corroborating information regarding litigation, claims and assessments, the auditor should:

       A honor the confidentiality of the client–solicitor relationship

       B consider the refusal to be tantamount to a scope limitation

       C seek to obtain the corroborating information from management

       D disclose this fact in a footnote to the financial report

12.3 The following questions relate to the auditor's responsibility for obtaining written representations from the entity's management. Select the *best* response.

(a) A representation letter issued by a client:

       A is a substitute for testing

       B is essential for the preparation of the audit program

       C reduces the auditor's responsibility only to the extent that it is relied upon

       D does not reduce the auditor's responsibility

(b) If management refuses to furnish certain written representations that the auditor believes are essential, which of the following is appropriate?

       A The entity's refusal does not constitute a scope limitation that may lead to a modification of the opinion.

       B The auditor can rely on oral evidence relating to the matter as a basis for an unqualified opinion.

       C The auditor should issue an adverse opinion because of management's refusal.

       D This may have an effect on the auditor's ability to rely on other representations of management.

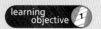

Date of audit report

12.4 How is the date of the audit report established?

Subsequent events

12.5 Define the two types of subsequent events of audit interest and explain how each type is accounted for in the financial report. Give two examples of each type.

Solicitors' representation letter

12.6 How does the inquiry of the entity's solicitor about pending or threatened litigation differ from the inquiry about unasserted claims?

Management representation letter

12.7 What is the purpose of a management representation letter and what categories of subjects does it cover?

Review of working papers and financial report

12.8 What is the primary purpose of the review of audit working papers?

12.9 Why are analytical procedures required as part of the final overall review of the financial report?

Going concern basis

12.10 What procedures should the auditor use to confirm the appropriateness of the going concern basis when an entity is dependent on its parent entity for financial support?

DISCUSSION PROBLEMS AND CASE STUDIES

Subsequent events

12.11 **Basic** You are making an annual examination for the purpose of rendering an opinion regarding the financial report for use in an annual report to shareholders. Answer the following questions concerning events subsequent to the date of the financial report.
  (a) What auditing procedures should normally be followed in order to obtain knowledge of subsequent happenings?
  (b) What is the period with which the auditor is normally concerned with regard to post-balance-date events?
  (c) Give five different examples of events or transactions that might occur in the subsequent period.
  (d) What is the auditor's general responsibility, if any, for reporting such events or transactions?
  (e) In your report, how would you deal with each of the examples you listed in (c) above?
  Source: AICPA

12.12 **Moderate** Susan Pitt is the engagement partner for the financial report audit of Compressor Ltd for the year ended 30 June 20X3. The following material events or transactions have come to Pitt's attention before she is scheduled to issue her report on 31 August 20X3.
  (a) On 3 July 20X3, Compressor Ltd received a shipment of raw materials from Bangkok. The materials had been ordered in March 20X3, and shipped FOB shipping point in May 20X3.
  (b) On 15 July 20X3, the company settled and paid a personal injury claim of a former employee as the result of an accident that occurred in March 20X0. The company had not previously recorded a liability for the claim.
  (c) On 25 July 20X3, the company agreed to purchase for cash the outstanding shares of Electrical Ltd. The acquisition is likely to double the sales volume of Compressor Ltd.
  (d) On 1 August 20X3, a plant owned by Compressor Ltd was damaged by a flood, resulting in an uninsured loss of inventory.

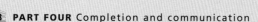

Required

For each of the above events or transactions, discuss audit procedures that should have brought the item to the auditor's attention, and indicate the treatment required in the financial report. Give reasons for your decision.

12.13 Complex Your firm is the external auditor of ABC Limited, a large and diversified entity, and the following timelines apply:

- balance date: 30 June 20X0
- directors' declaration and audit report signed: 20 July 20X0
- financial report and audit report mailed to shareholders: 27 July 20X0.

Consider each of the following independent and material situations which have occurred in relation to ABC:

(i)   On 20 June 20X0, ABC entered into a contract to purchase ore from XYZ Pty Ltd. The ore was shipped on 21 June 20X0. At the time of entering into the contract, the mineral content of the ore was estimated to be 60%, and the liability calculated accordingly. However, when the shipment was received on 13 July 20X0, the mineral content was found to be 80%, resulting in the liability being understated.

(ii)   On 10 July 20X0, the state government announced it had approved plans for the construction of a new freeway. The plans will result in the resumption of some vacant land owned by ABC. As at 20 July 20X0, the amount of compensation payable had not been determined. ABC management was unaware of the construction of the proposed freeway until the government announcement was made.

(iii) Assume the same facts as for (ii), except that ABC management had been informed of the freeway construction on 25 June 20X0, but the public announcement was not made until 10 July 20X0.

(iv)   On 22 July 20X0, ABC received notice that one of its customers was taking legal action in relation to a disputed warranty claim. The customer purchased the goods in May 20X0, and first informed ABC of problems with the goods on 26 June 20X0.

(v)   On 30 July 20X0, ABC management informed you that, after 12 months of financial difficulty, one of its debtors was declared bankrupt on 23 July 20X0. Preliminary indications are that none of the debt is likely to be recovered. As at 30 June 20X0, ABC had raised a specific provision against this debtor's balance amounting to 50% of the balance owed.

(vi)   Assume the same facts as (v), except that the debtor had been declared bankrupt on 18 July 20X0.

(vii) ABC owns a mining lease in Western Australia. As at balance date, this lease was valued by an independent expert at $6 million. On 2 August 20X0 management informed you that on 21 July 20X0 the board signed an agreement to sell the lease for $5 million. The sale will take place on 1 September 20X0.

(viii) Assume the same facts as for (vii), except that management informed you on 19 July 20X0 that the contract had been signed that day.

(ix)   On 12 August 20X0, management informed you that the internal auditors had uncovered a major fraud at one of ABC's branches. The fraud was perpetrated by three senior staff, apparently acting in collusion over a number of years. The internal auditors released their report to management on 30 July 20X0, after a highly confidential investigation spanning several months. They had not previously informed you that they were undertaking this investigation.

(x)   On 5 July 20X0, several hundred people suffered serious food poisoning as a result of eating one of ABC's tinned fish products. All stock of the product held by retailers was recalled and destroyed on 19 July 20X0, along with all stock of the product held in ABC's warehouse.

(xi)   Assume the same facts as for (x), except that the stock was not destroyed until 30 July 20X0.

(xii) On 10 July 20X0, ABC announced that it would be offering a rights issue to its share-holders. The offer will open on 1 August 20X0 and close on 31 October 20X0.

Required

(a) Outline the two types of subsequent events as per AASB 1002 'Events Occurring After Reporting Date'.

(b) For each of the events (i) to (xii), select the appropriate action A to D from the list below and justify your response:

    A Adjust the 30 June 20X0 financial report.

    B Disclose the information in a note to the 30 June 20X0 financial report.

    C Request the client to recall the 30 June 20X0 financial report for revision.

    D No action is required.

(c) What additional information would you obtain in relation to each of the events (i) to (xii) to ensure that the information you had obtained was correct?

Source: This question was adapted from the Professional Year Programme of The Institute of Chartered Accountants in Australia—1998 Accounting 2 Module.

12.14 Complex Assume that an auditor is expressing an opinion on Azalea Ltd's financial report for the year ended 30 September 20X3, that field work was completed on 21 October 20X3, and that the audit opinion to accompany the financial report is now being prepared. In each item a 'subsequent event' is described. This event was disclosed to the auditor either in connection with the review of subsequent events or after the completion of field work. You are to indicate in each case the required disclosure of this event in the financial report. Each of the five cases is independent and is to be considered separately.

(a) A large account receivable from Lau Industries (material to financial report presentation) was considered fully collectible at 30 September 20X3. Lau suffered a plant explosion on 25 October 20X3. Since Lau was uninsured, it is unlikely that the account will be paid.

(b) The court ruled in favour of the company on 25 October 20X3 concerning deductions claimed on the 20X1 and 20X2 tax returns. Azalea had provided in accrued taxes payable for the full amount of the potential disallowances. The Commissioner of Taxation will not appeal the court's ruling.

(c) Azalea's manufacturing division, whose assets constituted 75% of Azalea's total assets at 30 September 20X3, was sold on 1 November 20X3. The new owner assumed the indebtedness associated with this property.

(d) On 15 October 20X3, a major investment adviser issued a pessimistic report on Azalea's long-term prospects. The market price for Azalea's ordinary shares subsequently declined by 50%.

(e) At its 5 October 20X3 meeting Azalea's board of directors voted to double the advertising budget for the coming year and authorised a change in advertising agencies.

12.15 Complex Your firm is the external auditor of Pyne Limited, a large and diversified entity, and the following timelines apply:

- balance date: 30 June 20X3
- directors' declaration and audit report signed: 20 July 20X3
- financial report and audit report mailed to shareholders: 27 July 20X3.

Consider each of the following independent and material situations which have occurred in relation to Pyne:

(i) On 15 June 20X3, Pyne entered into a contract to purchase ore from Appel Pty Ltd. The ore was shipped on 25 June 20X3. At the time of entering into the contract, the mineral content of the ore was estimated to be 50%, and the liability calculated accordingly. However, when the shipment was received on 15 July 20X3, the mineral content was found to be 80%, resulting in the liability being understated.

(ii) On 22 July 20X3, Pyne received notice that one of its customers was taking legal action in relation to a disputed warranty claim. The customer purchased the goods in April 20X3, and first informed Pyne of problems with the goods on 21 June 20X3.

(iii) On 2 August 20X3, Pyne's management informed you that, after 12 months of financial difficulty, one of its debtors was declared bankrupt on 25 July 20X3. Preliminary indications are that none of the debt is likely to be recovered. As at 30 June 20X3, Pyne had raised a specific provision against this debtor's balance amounting to 50% of the balance owed.

(iv) On 10 July 20X3, Pyne announced that it would be offering a rights issue to its shareholders. The offer will open on 1 August 20X3 and close on 31 October 20X3.

Required

(a) For each of the events (i) to (iv) choose a response from the list below, and justify your choice:
   (i) Adjust the 30 June 20X3 financial report.
   (ii) Disclose the information in a note to the 30 June 20X3 financial report.
   (iii) Request the client to recall the 30 June 20X3 financial report for revision.

(b) What additional information would you obtain in relation to each of the events (i) to (iv) to ensure that the information you had obtained was correct?

Source: This question was adapted from the CA Program of The Institute of Chartered Accounts in Australia—2002 FRA Module.

12.16 Complex Your client is MPD Ltd, a diversified business operating in all parts of Australia. Balance date was 30 June 20X3, the audit report was signed on 31 July 20X3 and the financial report mailed to shareholders on 14 August 20X3.

During your subsequent events review you noted the following independent and material items:

(i) MPD Ltd has been involved in a legal dispute with a competitor for a number of years. The dispute relates to alleged breaches of copyright by MPD Ltd. On 27 July you discovered that MPD Ltd had settled the legal action out of court on terms more favourable than expected.

(ii) As for (i) above, except that the legal action was settled on 5 August.

(iii) On 10 July one of MPD Ltd's major product lines developed a fault that rendered the product unusable. MPD Ltd became aware of the fault on 30 July. Although the fault posed no safety risks to consumers, MPD Ltd decided to launch a full product recall on the following day.

(iv) On 30 July 20X3 the Bureau of Meteorology issued a cyclone warning for parts of far North Queensland. MPD Ltd has a large sugar cane plantation in this area. On 2 August the cyclone hit, wiping out about 90% of the crop.

(v) MPD Ltd has invested significant funds in developing a new type of cholesterol-reducing margarine. On 7 July, MPD Ltd applied for a patent for the margarine, only to discover that a competitor had lodged a similar application on 28 June. The granting of MPD Ltd's application is now in doubt.

(vi) MPD Ltd's bank loan is conditional upon certain ratios being maintained at all times. On 20 August you discovered that one of the ratios was breached for a 24-hour period on 16 August.

(vii) MPD Ltd has large landholdings on the outskirts of Sydney. On 20 July, MPD Ltd received preliminary notice from the Federal Government informing them that, should the new Sydney airport proceed, about 30% of this land will be forcibly acquired. MPD Ltd has no legal right to challenge the acquisition.

(viii) In early June, one of MPD Ltd's largest debtors informed MPD Ltd that it was experiencing serious financial difficulties. On 5 July, MPD Ltd was informed that the debtor had gone into receivership. Preliminary reports suggest MPD Ltd will recover only 10 cents in the dollar of the outstanding debt.

Required

(a) Create a timeline showing balance date, the date of the audit report and the date of distribution of the financial report. Indicate the following on the timeline:
   (i) The time period/s during which the auditor is responsible for discovering subsequent events.
   (ii) The time period/s during which management is responsible for informing the auditor of subsequent events.
   (iii) Would the auditor ever be concerned about events discovered after the financial report is distributed?

(b) Outline the key additional audit procedures you should have performed in relation to each of the above events.

(c) What action should you have recommended to management in relation to each of the above events?

Source: This question was adapted from the Professional Year Programme of The Institute of Chartered Accountants in Australia—2000 Accounting 2 Module.

12.17 Complex Consider each of the following situations separately. In all cases:
- the balance date of the companies are 30 June 20X3;
- the financial report and audit report were signed on 3 September 20X3;
- the financial report and audit report were mailed to the members on 9 September 20X3; and
- the annual general meeting of the companies are scheduled for or were held on 30 September 20X3.

All the following events are highly material.

Consider the following situations:

(i) A draft investigative report commissioned by a government enquiry was leaked to the media on 24 August 20X3. The report has questioned the continued need for a segment of your client's business. Accordingly, there is significant uncertainty regarding the future necessity for one of the services offered by the company and its industry colleagues. There has been significant media attention and speculation on this issue.

(ii) Your client, Explorer Mining NL, owns a large oil and gas permit in central Australia. The directors revalued their interest in the permit at 30 June 20X3 to $6 million, based on an independent expert's assessment of its net worth. The company signed Heads of Agreement on 30 June 20X3 to sell their interest in the permit for $8 million. The sale is conditional on the ratification of the sale by the company's shareholders. The ratification will be put to the shareholders at the company's annual general meeting.

(iii) The same situation as in (ii) above except that the company had signed the Heads of Agreement on 31 August 20X3.

(iv) On 8 September 20X3, you discovered an uninsured legal action against the client that had originated on 31 March 20X0.

(v) On 20 August 20X3, the company settled a legal action out of court that had originated in 20X0 and was listed as a contingent liability at 30 June 20X3.

(vi) On 18 September 20X3, the company lost a court case that had originated in 20X0 for an amount equal to the legal action. The notes to the 30 June 20X3 financial report state that in the opinion of legal counsel there will be a favourable settlement.

Required

For each of the above events (i)–(vi), state the appropriate action from (a)–(d) for the situation and justify your response. The alternative actions are as follows:

(a) Adjust the 30 June 20X3 financial report.

(b) Disclose the information in the notes to the 30 June 20X3 financial report.

(c) Request the client to recall the 30 June 20X3 financial report for revision.

(d) No action is required.

Solicitor's representation letter

12.18 Basic In the course of auditing the financial report of Lowe Ltd for the year ended 31 December 20X0, you request that your client ask her solicitor to furnish a legal representation letter. The solicitor's letter includes information on unbilled legal fees and comments on specific litigation identified in the entity's request. However, with respect to 'an outline of the general nature of any litigation threatened' of which he has knowledge, the solicitor has responded: 'The firm does not disclose information privileged under the solicitor–client privilege, but if such information were disclosed, it would be material.'

Explain the impact that this response will have on your audit approach.

12.19 Complex Your client is DD Ltd, a property developer whose year end is 31 March 20X3. The audit report will be signed on 28 April 20X3. It is now 25 April 20X3 and you are in the process of performing the final review of the audit workpapers.

DD Ltd is suing a local council for interest costs and loss of profits in relation to a proposed waterfront hotel development. DD Ltd claims the council:

- took excessive time to consider the development application; and
- illegally refused consent for the application as the proposal met all relevant planning laws.

The council claims the delay was due to DD Ltd not providing all relevant documents at the time of lodgement. It also claims that the proposed development breaches foreshore height restrictions.

Both DD Ltd's internal solicitor (Ms Y) and external solicitors (SM Partners) are working on the case. The solicitor's representation letter received from SM Partners is opposite:

On your behalf, DD Ltd has also requested Ms Y to sign a letter similar to the above. However, on reviewing the files, you note no reply has yet been received. Instead, the audit senior has made the following file note:

> *As discussed with Ms Y on 23 April 20X3, she refuses to sign the solicitor's representation letter. She says that as an employee of DD Ltd, it is inappropriate for her to sign a letter in which she accepts personal responsibility for carrying out work performed in accordance with instructions from her employer. In addition, she believes her opinion has been given indirectly anyway, as she prepared the solicitor's letter sent to DD Ltd on our behalf.*

You also note that on the file copy of the letter sent to SM Partners, the amount claimed by DD Ltd is $2.2 million.

Required

(a) List the auditors' duties and responsibilities in relation to solicitors' representation letters.

(b) Does the letter from SM Partners constitute sufficient, appropriate audit evidence? Why or why not?

(c) What procedures do you need to perform in relation to the matter prior to signing the audit report?

Source: This question was adapted from the Professional Year Programme of The Institute of Chartered Accountants in Australia—1997 Advanced Audit Module.

𝒮ℳ 𝒫artners

123 Law Street, Courtsville VIC 3171

A Partner
PP Chartered Accountants
456 Report Avenue
Gainsborough VIC 3815

23 April 20X3

Dear Sir

In response to the letter from DD Ltd, dated 31 March 20X3, we make the following statements:

1. This letter covers the entity known as DD Ltd, a public company listed on the Australian Stock Exchange.

2. In response to DD Ltd's request, we can confirm that:
    - SM Partners are acting on behalf of DD Ltd in the matter of *DD Ltd v Local Council*. The matter relates to a development application refused by Local Council on 1 February 20X3 under Section 778(b) of the *Local Planning Act*.
    - Management's estimate of likely costs of $300 000 and probability of success of 60% is reasonable at this point in time (based on the evidence we have to date). We can also confirm that management's statement as to the amount claimed ($1.2 million) is correct.
    - The open files we have in relation to the above matter are:
      —*DD Ltd v Local Council*: preliminary hearing;
      —*DD Ltd v Local Council*: evidence and time reports.

3. The confirmation is based on our review of the matter as described by management. We cannot comment on any evidence that DD Ltd may be holding and of which we, as yet, are unaware. Please note that Ms Y of DD Ltd has also received instructions from DD Ltd regarding this case.

4. This review has been performed by Ms P, senior partner, as Mr X, the instructing solicitor is currently on leave.

Yours sincerely

Ms P
Senior Partner

Management representation letter

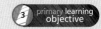

12.20 Basic As is customary in completing your examination, you request the client to furnish you with a management representation letter. Your client reads the representations you are requesting him to make and refuses to furnish the letter. The client states his position as follows: 'You are asking me to tell you all kinds of things that I hired you to figure out. For example, you are asking me to say that "all known assets of the company at balance date were recorded in the books of account". I paid you to carry out an audit and you should know whether or not that's true yourself.'

Required

(a) What explanation would you give the client of the need for a client representation letter?

(b) What would be the impact on your audit report if the client did not accept your explanation and continued to refuse to furnish the letter?

12.21 Moderate You are currently reviewing the audit files of Ace Holdings Ltd, a large Australia-wide group. Year end was 30 June 20X3. The following work was performed by your audit assistant:

A management representation letter was requested from the client, to be signed by both the financial controller and the company secretary. The letter was duly signed and returned, however, the following paragraph had been crossed out:

We confirm that all contingent liabilities likely to have a material effect on the financial report have been brought to your attention.

The company secretary attached a note to the representation letter stating that he believed this paragraph was unnecessary.

The audit assistant has made the following comment:

As all correspondence files were made available for our review, and as the solicitors' representation letter confirms the amounts recorded in the financial report, no further action is necessary.

Required

(a) Outline any queries that you would raise with your audit assistant.

(b) Describe the additional audit procedures you believe need to be performed to ensure that sufficient appropriate audit evidence is obtained.

12.22 Complex Under the terms of a major loan contract, DD Ltd is required to maintain certain financial ratios. If the ratios are breached, the loan is immediately due for repayment. This would create significant short-term cash flow problems.

In order to comply with the loan covenant and maintain the ratios, DD Ltd must continue to hold its 100% shareholding in AA Ltd as a long-term investment.

You have obtained a representation letter from the client that says in part:

DD Ltd warrants that for the period 1 April 20X3 to 31 March 20X4, it intends to retain ownership of its entire parcel of ordinary shares in AA Ltd. DD Ltd has not entered into any discussions with any party, directly or indirectly, regarding the sale of these shares.

On 24 April 20X3 you noted an article in the financial press that described the rumoured sale of the business assets of AA Ltd to a foreign investor.

Required

(a) Does the management representation letter from DD Ltd regarding its shareholding in AA Ltd constitute sufficient appropriate audit evidence? Why or why not?

(b) What procedures do you need to perform in relation to the situation prior to signing the audit report?

Source: This question was adapted from the Professional Year Programme of The Institute of Chartered Accountants in Australia—1997 Advanced Audit Module.

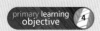
Review of working papers and financial report

12.23 Moderate You are now completing the audit of AX Ltd and have noted the following errors:

Balances affected		Amount $	Over or Under	Description 1
1	Expense and provision for warranty	95 000	Under	One inventory line has shown faults. Client believes they are one-off problems and no adjustment is necessary.
2	Fixed assets and creditors	100 000	Over	Purchase of fixed asset at year-end incorrectly recorded.
3	Expense and provision for obsolescence	50 000	Under	Provision for inventory line for which repairs have been required. Client believes adverse publicity has affected sales and written back 25% of inventory. Audit estimate is 50% based on level of sales.

Materiality for the audit has been set at $100 000 (before tax).

Required

Which of the above items should be adjusted? Provide reasons for your decisions.

12.24 Complex Henry Chan has been assigned to the audit of related parties for G Ltd and its controlled entities. The company structure for the group is as follows:

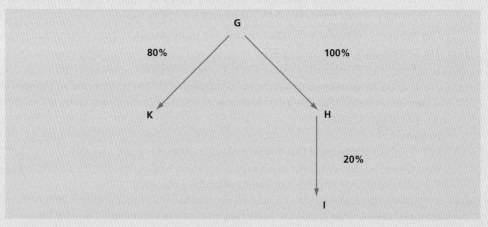

Each of the companies, G, H and I, have common directors while I has two additional directors. Henry's firm is responsible for the audit of G, H and K, while I is audited by another large audit firm.

To date, Henry has reviewed all intercompany transactions and sent out questionnaires to all known related parties requesting details of any related-party transactions. The questionnaires have now been received and Henry is reviewing the disclosure in the financial report for accuracy and completeness.

Required

(a) Does Henry have adequate evidence to complete his task? If not, identify other sources of evidence Henry could use.

(b) What other sources of guidance are available to Henry to assist with his task?

Appropriateness of going concern

12.25 Moderate You are the audit manager assigned to the audit of Oceana Pharmaceuticals Pty Ltd, a wholly owned subsidiary of Global Pharmaceuticals Inc., a company listed on the New York Stock Exchange. Oceana was established in 1996 to provide Global with access to the Australian and South-East Asian markets. Since establishment, Oceana have found trading conditions difficult.

The audit evidence obtained and final review of this evidence suggests that unless Oceana receives a significant cash flow injection or trading conditions improve, it will be bankrupt within three months.

You have approached the CEO of Oceana with your concerns and he has indicated there is nothing for you to worry about. The company's owners have guaranteed financial support of the company for as long as it takes to establish a market presence.

Required

(a) Discuss the impact of the parent company's support on your assessment of going concern at Oceana.

(b) What further evidence will you require to assess the appropriateness of going concern at Oceana?

(c) Assuming the company is considered a going concern, what impact will the company's financial situation have on the financial report?

12.26 Complex You are currently auditing MP Pty Ltd, a subsidiary of DP Ltd. MP Pty Ltd is an Internet service provider that provides free Internet access to its subscribers. In return, subscribers agree to provide their name, address and other details to MP Pty Ltd, who on-sells the information to various mail-order and telemarketing companies.

When MP Pty Ltd was established two years ago, the business plan stated it would need 20 000 subscribers in order to break even. MP Pty Ltd has experienced demand far in excess of this but unfortunately, due to software problems, can only provide services to 17 000 subscribers at the present time. This has reduced the price third parties are prepared to pay for subscriber information as they need a certain volume of each type of 'consumer' (e.g. male > 30 years old earning > $35 000 per annum) to make direct sales and telemarketing worthwhile.

MP Pty Ltd is the third largest of eight 'free access' providers in the industry. The two largest providers are around 30% larger than MP Pty Ltd and both are seeking to rapidly expand their customer base. Over the last few months, MP Pty Ltd has been negotiating to buy the business of one of its smaller rivals, IP Pty Ltd. This would give MP Pty Ltd access to more subscribers, but more critically, give it access to IP Pty Ltd's software, which has the capacity to support another 50 000 users.

In response to MP Pty Ltd's directors' concerns regarding MP Pty Ltd's financial position, DP Ltd has agreed to become a 'lender of last resort' should MP Pty Ltd need urgent financial assistance. However, DP Ltd's management have made it clear that the assistance will only be provided if MP Pty Ltd is in serious danger of going into receivership.

MP Pty Ltd's six directors are all young whiz-kids with backgrounds in the computer and technology industries. All have an equity share in the business. Recently the board has split into two distinct factions and relationships among the board members are less than harmonious. The financial controller has expressed concern that some key business decisions are being delayed because the board are not focused on the business. The unresolved issues include a proposed additional capital injection from each director to see MP Pty Ltd through its current difficulties.

Required

(a) Which of the above factors indicate MP Pty Ltd may have a going concern problem?

(b) What key additional information would you obtain prior to reaching a conclusion on going concern?

(c) Assume all eight entities in the industry were experiencing software problems and were unable to satisfy demand for their services. Discuss whether this would change the way you assessed going concern for MP Pty Ltd.

Source: This question was adapted from the Professional Year Programme of The Institute of Chartered Accountants in Australia—2000 Accounting 2 Module.

12.27 Complex You are the manager on the audit of Z Pty Ltd for the financial year ended 30 June 20X1. Initially, Z made substantial profits but over the past two years its market share has declined, resulting in Z reporting an operating loss for the year ended 30 June 20X0.

In April 20X1, while you were planning this year's audit, you noticed that Z's liquidity ratios had weakened considerably since last year and that a substantial loss was projected for the current year. You also noticed that Z has taken out a new 180 day bill which will be due for repayment in September 20X1. The accountant told you that the bill was used to finance the acquisition of a new manufacturing machine. Analysis of the minutes confirmed that Z's existing long-term bank note is due for repayment by or on 30 June 20X1. A quick calculation of the company's ability to meet this obligation showed that it will be unable to repay the note unless it raises significant funds through either debt or asset sales. Z has minimal cash at the bank but has significant current assets, being trade receivables. Z's accountant assured you that the company would be able to repay the note when it was due.

On 25 May 20X1 you asked the accountant how the note was going to be repaid. He replied that an intercompany loan was to be established with Z's holding company, X Ltd (you do not act as auditors for X), for the value of the note.

You commenced the year-end audit in early September. The note had been repaid and replaced by an interest-bearing loan from X which had been classified as non-current. You asked for documentation supporting this classification. The accountant explained that the arrangement was that X would not call on the debt until Z was able to repay it, which would not be within the next year. You were also concerned about Z's ability to repay the bill due in September. He explained that he expected that Z would be able to repay it, but in the event of problems X had agreed to meet any shortfall. He drafted a letter requesting the board of X to confirm this arrangement with you. You subsequently received a letter from the board which set out an arrangement identical to the one outlined by Z.

The accountant also showed you Z's strategic plan and cash flow forecasts which showed that Z would become cash flow positive within the 20X2 financial year and would produce a small operating profit in 20X3 and a larger operating profit in the following year. The cash flow forecast included outflows for servicing and repayment of the bill and servicing the intercompany loan. Results and cash flows for the two months to August 20X1 are in line with forecasts and budgets.

Audit field work was completed on 25 September 20X1. There were no unadjusted errors. Z reported a substantial operating loss. The balance sheet showed a net liability situation; however, the position was positive when the intercompany loan was excluded.

The partner has scheduled a meeting with Z's managing director to discuss the audit. He asked you to prepare a memorandum in relation to Z's ability to continue as a going concern and areas where further evidence is required (if any).

Source: This question was adapted from the Professional Year Programme of The Institute of Chartered Accountants in Australia—1995 Accounting 2 Module.

12.28 Complex Runway Pty Ltd is a large private company that manufactures special reinforced concrete and other products used in the construction of airport runways and heavy use motor vehicle freeways. During the course of the audit for the year ended 30 June 20X3, the government announces it intends to scrap its proposed third runway project. You know that Runway Pty Ltd's projections include a major share of the work expected to flow from this project.

The company has been experiencing some cash flow difficulties, although this is not unusual in the industry. Management has recently fully extended their overdraft facility in order to pay day to day expenses such as wages and salaries. The audit partner is concerned that the company may be facing going concern problems, but the managing director maintains that future capital expenditure can be cut back to alleviate the going concern issue. In addition, surplus assets can be sold to the growing Asian market, and long-term debt rescheduled if necessary.

Required

(a) Give examples of three other possible mitigating factors that have not yet been mentioned.

(b) What evidence should you obtain with respect to management's representation about the various mitigating factors presented in the problem and identified in part (a) above?

(c) Assume that the engagement partner has decided to qualify the financial report on the basis of uncertainty as to going concern. However, the managing director argues that, as the company is privately held and all the shareholders are involved in the business, going concern problems should not be viewed as seriously as if it were a publicly listed company and therefore an unqualified report should be signed. How would you respond to the managing director's comments?

(d) What would be the impact on the audit if there was a letter of comfort from a related company promising to provide financial support in the event that Runway Pty Ltd was unable to meet its debt commitments.

CONTINUOUS CASE STUDIES

12.29 Complex This is a continuation of question 8.29. It may, however, be completed independently.

The 30 June X3 audit of Mitchell Pty Ltd, a manufacturer and supplier of chemical products, is nearing completion. The audit team has completed testing of year-end balances and is now reviewing events subsequent to year-end. The audit assistant has reviewed the minutes of directors' meetings and has noted the following:

(i) On 5 July X3 Mitchell entered into a new contract to supply bulk petrochemicals to Valley Petroleum, a small retailer of petrochemical products. The contract was similar in nature to other contracts previously negotiated.

(ii) On 20 June X3 a chemical leak occurred in the company's main storage facility. The leak was brought under control quickly, but a number of employees complained of nausea and were treated on the spot for problems associated with the inhalation of fumes. Two of the employees treated have been on sick leave since the incident and have now lodged a claim for workers' compensation. The claim was lodged on 2 August X3 alleging permanent incapacity for work. The company does not believe its employees have a valid claim.

(iii) On 20 July X3 goods being supplied to Mitchell by sea ran aground, resulting in a large chemical spill off the coast of southeastern Victoria. The Victorian government has filed a lawsuit against both Mitchell and the shipping company, alleging negligence.

Required

For each of the items noted above:

(a) discuss the impact on the financial report; and

(b) discuss what further evidence the auditor should obtain.

12.30 Complex This is a continuation of question 10.34. It may, however, be completed independently.

You are the audit manager in charge of the 31 December audit of HomeChef Pty Ltd, a large private company operating in the boutique food and beverages market. The audit is now nearing completion and you are preparing a schedule of adjustments to discuss with the client. The schedule of adjustments includes the following:

| Balances affected | Adjustment required | | Explanation |
	Dr $000	Cr $000	
1 Obsolescence expense	500		Store of dried goods in Darwin ware-
Inventory		500	house destroyed by vermin.
2 Interest expense	600		Interest not recorded on borrowings.
Borrowings		600	
3 Income tax expense	400		Underprovision for tax for year ending
Provision for tax		400	30/6/X1. Client disagrees with treatment of claimed deductions for tax year ended 20X1.
4 Depreciation expense	1000		Record additional depreciation expense
Accumulated depreciation		1000	on catering equipment. Discussions indicate it will be scrapped next year. Client believes it has high scrap value; review of publications in this area suggests this is unlikely.

Materiality for the audit has been set at $1 600 000.

Required

Which of the above items, if any, do you believe require adjustment?

THE AUDITOR'S REPORTING OBLIGATIONS

LEARNING OBJECTIVES

After studying this chapter you should be able to:

1 understand the nature and significance of the auditor's reporting obligations;

2 appreciate the concepts of 'true and fair' and 'presents fairly in accordance with ...';

3 understand the structure and qualitative characteristics of the audit report;

4 identify the different types of opinions—unqualified opinion, except for opinion, adverse opinion, and inability to form an opinion—and describe the circumstances in which the auditor would issue each type of report; explain the circumstances in which an auditor might add explanatory language to the standard report without expressing a qualified opinion—an emphasis of matter;

5 identify the possible reasons for departure from a standard report and describe the types of audit reports other than a standard report;

6 describe the auditor's responsibility for reporting on comparative financial reports and understand the auditor's responsibility with respect to other information in an annual report;

7 describe communications other than an audit report between the auditor and shareholders, boards of directors, audit committees and management; and

8 describe future changes to the standard form audit report that will take place from December 2006.

Chapter outline

The entire audit process is geared toward the expression of an opinion on the financial report. All of the auditor's planning decisions and evidence collection procedures are aimed at placing the auditor in the position where they can issue their audit report. As such, it is important that the audit report be an effective means of communication. This chapter explains how the auditor decides upon the type of report that is appropriate and the various modifications of the standard unqualified opinion that may be appropriate in particular circumstances. This chapter also describes the auditor's communications with corporate clients, including communications with shareholders, boards of directors, audit committees and senior management.

Relevant guidance

Australian		International	
AUS 212	Other Information in Documents Containing Audited Financial Reports	ISA 720	Other Information in Documents Containing Audited Financial Statements
AUS 702	The Audit Report on a General Purpose Financial Report	ISA 700	The Auditor's Report on Financial Statements (includes reference to revised version 2004)
AUS 704	Comparatives	ISA 710	Comparatives
AUS 708	Going Concern	ISA 580	Going Concern
AUS 710	Communication with Management on Matters Arising from an Audit	ISA 260	Communications of Audit Matters with those Charged with Governance
AGS 1028	Uncertainty	—	
AGS 1046	Responding to Questions at an Annual General Meeting	—	
AGS 1050	Audit Issues Relating to the Electronic Presentation of Financial Reports	—	
Audit and Assurance Alert No. 2: Auditors' Responsibilities in Relation to the Adequacy of Financial Records and Internal Controls throughout the Year		—	
Audit and Assurance Alert No. 4: Auditor Association with Electronic Financial Reporting		—	
Audit and Assurance Alert No. 6: Auditors' Responsibilities in Relation to Reporting Contraventions of the Corporations Law		—	
Audit and Assurance Alert No. 11: Communicating with Entities in Relation to Auditor Independence		—	
Practice Note 34 Auditors' Obligations: Reporting to ASIC (Reissued 2004)		—	

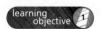

OBLIGATIONS TO REPORT

AUS 202.02 (ISA 200.02) states that the objective of an audit of the financial report is to enable the auditor to *express an opinion* whether the financial report is prepared, in all material respects, in accordance with an applicable financial reporting framework. Auditors are required to conduct an audit in accordance with Australian auditing standards (AUS 202.05, APS 1.1 (para .05)). The standards numbered 700–799 cover what may be regarded as the final stage of the financial report audit process, the audit conclusions and reporting stages concerning general purpose financial reports. In Australia there are currently five audit conclusions and reporting standards (some of the equivalent international standards are noted at the beginning of this chapter):

1 AUS 702 The Audit Report on a General Purpose Financial Report
2 AUS 704 Comparatives
3 AUS 706 Subsequent Events

4 AUS 708 Going Concern

5 AUS 710 Communication with Management on Matters Arising from an Audit.

Two of these standards, AUS 706 (ISA 560) on subsequent events and AUS 708 (ISA 570) on going concern, are covered in Chapter 12, as these are areas on which an auditor must make a decision before the audit report can be issued.

As well as meeting the requirement to conduct an audit in accordance with Australian auditing standards, the auditor also has an obligation to form a conclusion as to whether the financial reports have been prepared using Australian accounting standards issued by the AASB. There is also a professional requirement contained in miscellaneous professional statement APS 1, para. 13, which states that, where an entity is either a reporting entity or is not a reporting entity but prepares a general purpose financial report, a member can express an unqualified opinion only when general purpose financial reports are prepared in accordance with accounting standards and the Urgent Issues Group (UIG) Abstracts. It should be remembered that the auditor's professional obligations under these accounting standards should be exercised for all types of entities, not just companies. This distinguishes them from the statutory responsibilities that occur as a result of the Australian Accounting Standards Board (AASB) standards, which apply only to companies, registered schemes and disclosing entities covered by the *Corporations Act 2001*.

In many engagements the auditor's reporting responsibilities are governed by the statute under which the auditor is appointed. Often, compliance with statutory reporting responsibilities also satisfies the professional reporting requirements outlined above. However, some engagements undertaken under statute require a different form of reporting and/or additional information in the audit report (e.g. engagements to audit banks and superannuation funds, which will be discussed in more detail in Chapter 14).

One of the significant areas of reporting which is governed by statute is an audit undertaken in accordance with the requirements of the *Corporations Act 2001*. This section will deal with those requirements and the specific reporting obligations of the auditor. These obligations are found in s. 307 of the *Corporations Act 2001* and require the auditor to form an opinion as to:

> *(a) whether the financial report is in accordance with the Act, including:*
> > *(i) section 296 or 304 (compliance with accounting standards); and*
> > *(ii) section 297 or 305 (true and fair view); and*
> *(aa) if the financial report includes additional information . . . (to give a true and fair view of the financial position and performance)—whether the inclusion of that information was necessary to give the true and fair view required by section 297 or 305; and*
> *(b) whether the auditor has been given all information, explanation and assistance necessary for the conduct of the audit; and*
> *(c) whether the company, registered scheme or disclosing entity has kept financial records sufficient to enable a financial report to be prepared and audited; and*
> *(d) whether the company, registered scheme or disclosing entity has kept other records and registers as required by this Act.*

The *Corporations Act 2001* also clearly specifies that the audit report shall state the auditor's opinion in relation to point (a) (i) and (ii) above (s. 308(1)). If for any reason the auditor is not satisfied about any of these matters, the audit report must state why not. If in the auditor's opinion the financial report is not drawn up in accordance with a particular applicable accounting standard, the audit report must show the quantified financial effect on the financial report of failing to draw them up in accordance with that accounting standard (s. 308(2)).

While the auditor is required to form an opinion on the matters noted in points (b) to (d) above, under the exception basis of reporting the auditor need only report particulars of any deficiency, failure or shortcoming in respect of any of those matters (s. 308(3)(b)). The exception reporting basis was introduced as a response to concerns about the expectation gap, and has resulted in a simplified and more concise form of audit report that it is believed is more effective in communicating its primary message. The advantage of reporting on these items only when the requirements have not been met is that it draws the attention of the reader of an audit report more directly to inadequacies in the financial report. This enhances the effectiveness of the reporting process by highlighting and explaining exceptions when they occur. With regard to (c) and (d) just quoted, *Audit and Assurance Alert No. 2* points out that the auditor is required to form an opinion as to whether the financial records have been kept satisfactorily *throughout* the relevant period, not only at the end of the period.

The audit report must also describe any defect or irregularity in the financial report (s. 308(3)(a)). Further professional considerations for the reporting of fraud are contained in AUS 210 (ISA 240), which is discussed in Chapter 4.

There is also a responsibility for the entity to comply with applicable accounting standards under s. 296 of the *Corporations Act 2001*. Applicable accounting standards are those prepared by the AASB. It is possible that particular accounting standards may not be appropriate, and relief may be granted by the Australian Securities and Investments Commission (ASIC) from compliance with such standards under s. 340 of the *Corporations Act 2001*. Essentially, the auditor is required to consider two sets of accounting standards:

1 AASB standards which must be complied with in the preparation of accounting reports of companies unless relief is provided under s. 340 of the *Corporations Act 2001*; and
2 AAS standards which must be complied with in preparing general purpose financial reports for all entities, in both the private and public sectors.

Under s. 308(3A) the auditor's report must include any statements or disclosures required by the auditing standards. If the financial report includes additional information to give a true and fair view of financial position and performance, the auditor's report must also include a statement of the auditor's opinion on whether the inclusion of that additional information was necessary to give the true and fair view required by s. 297 (s. 308(3B)). The auditor's report must also specify the date on which the statement is made (s. 308(4)).

Who the auditor has an obligation to report to

The governing body and members

The engagement letter (discussed in Chapter 6) should clearly spell out who the auditor has an obligation to report to. As outlined in AUS 702.16 (ISA 700.07), the audit report should be addressed as required by the terms of the engagement, normally to either the governing body or the members of the entity.

Under the *Corporations Act 2001*, the auditor's primary reporting responsibility is a report to the company's members (see s. 308(1)). This has been supported by common law. For example, in the *Pacific Acceptance Corporation* case, Moffit J stated that one of the primary duties of the auditor was to report to the members (refer to Chapter 4).

Management and the board of directors

Justice Moffit also said that the auditor's reporting responsibilities extended beyond the audit report. The auditor also had a responsibility to report to management anything that was prejudicial to the interests of shareholders (for further discussion, refer to Chapter 4). What constitutes adequate reporting to management was discussed in the *AWA* case. In this case it was stated that the auditor had a responsibility to bring a material weakness in internal control to the attention of the full board of directors, and that reporting the weakness only to the managing director was insufficient. This will be considered in more detail under learning objective 7 of this chapter.

Australian Securities and Investments Commission (ASIC)

Section 311 of the *Corporations Act 2001* states that if the auditor of a company has reasonable grounds to suspect that there has been a contravention of, or failure to comply with, any of the provisions of the *Corporations Act 2001* and believes that the matter will not be adequately dealt with by comment in the audit report or notifying the directors, then the auditor must immediately inform ASIC in writing. Failure to report such a breach is a criminal offence, subject to strict liability (meaning that intention is not relevant).

As a result of initial concerns about the breadth of auditors' obligations, ASIC issued Practice Note 34 'Auditors' Obligations' (reissued 2004). The auditor's reporting obligations with regard to infringements of corporations legislation have been increased as a result of ASIC's interpretation, contained in Practice Note 34, of the requirements of the CLERP 9 Act. Under the amended provisions an auditor is obliged to report a 'significant' contravention of the Act directly to ASIC. Types of suspected contraventions that could be considered to be significant by an auditor include:

■ insolvent trading by a company;
■ a breach of accounting standards or the true and fair view requirement; and
■ suspected dishonest or misleading and deceptive conduct.

An auditor is required to notify ASIC if the auditor has 'reasonable grounds to suspect' there has been a significant contravention of the Act. This test is satisfied by circumstances that would create in the mind of a reasonable auditor an actual apprehension or fear that a contravention has occurred. The suspicion has to be honest and reasonable, and based upon facts that would create suspicion in the mind of a reasonable auditor (refer George v. Rockett (2003) 93 ALR 483).

Quick review

1. The auditor is required to express an opinion as to whether the financial report is prepared, in all material respects, in accordance with an applicable financial reporting framework.
2. Legislative reporting obligations are contained in the statutes that govern the audit. Audits undertaken in accordance with the requirements of the *Corporations Act 2001* should form a conclusion that accounting standards prepared by the AASB (AASB standards) were followed.
3. Compliance with statutory reporting responsibilities usually satisfies professional reporting requirements.

4 The auditor's primary reporting responsibility is normally to the governing body or members of the entity as outlined in the engagement letter. For audits of companies under the *Corporations Act 2001*, the primary responsibility is to the company's shareholders.

5 The auditor has a duty to report to management and the board of directors certain issues which may be judged as being prejudicial to the interests of shareholders.

6 The auditor has a duty to report to ASIC when they have reasonable grounds to suspect a contravention of the *Corporations Act 2001* that could not be adequately dealt with in the audit report or by notifying the board of directors.

TRUE AND FAIR VIEW

One of the major differences between the form of audit opinion recommended by AUS 702 (ISA 700) and that required by legislation such as the *Corporations Act 2001* is the terminology used in expressing that opinion. AUS 702.02 (ISA 700.02–.04) requires the auditor to express an opinion as to whether the financial report '**presents fairly** in accordance with applicable accounting standards and other mandatory professional reporting requirements [and, when appropriate, relevant statutory and other requirements]'. However, s. 297 of the *Corporations Act 2001* requires the auditor to give an opinion as to whether the accounts are drawn up so as to give a *true and fair view*. The **'true and fair'** form of opinion has been used in companies legislation in Australia since 1955 and is taken from UK statutes. It has been formalised as a legal obligation for both directors and auditors. However, it is not defined in the initiating legislation or by court cases in which this reporting requirement has been called into question. The interpretation and application of the term by auditors over time has generated much debate.

Two major interpretations have been given to the words 'true and fair': a technical interpretation and a literal interpretation. The technical interpretation is that a true and fair view will be provided if the financial report is prepared in accordance with generally accepted accounting principles (accounting standards, other authoritative pronouncements of the AASB, and UIG abstracts). While there are a number of definitions of the literal interpretation, a commonly accepted one is that the view presented by the financial information as a whole is consistent with the auditor's knowledge of the business and situation of the entity. Thus a distinction may arise between the technical and literal approach where, if the generally accepted accounting principles are followed, the view presented by the financial information is not consistent with the auditor's knowledge.

Section 297 of the *Corporations Act 2001*, the section requiring a true and fair view, states that this section does not affect the obligation under s. 296 for a financial report to comply with accounting standards. Therefore, it can be argued that the standard setters have currently adopted a technical interpretation of a true and fair view. The arguments are that, in all but rare and exceptional cases, following accounting standards should lead to a view of the company that is consistent with its financial position and performance. Emphasising a literal interpretation would have given management much more discretion in selecting 'appropriate' accounting policies. Corporate accounting must now comply with accounting standards without exception. While under the *Corporations Act 2001* directors must add such information as is necessary to give a true and fair view (s. 297), this additional information is de-emphasised by being disclosed only in the notes to the financial report.

In accordance with AUS 702.23, as mentioned above, the preferred wording contained in the standard to express the auditor's opinion is: '*presents fairly* in accordance with applicable accounting standards and other mandatory professional reporting requirements'. When a statutory mandate makes this wording inappropriate, the auditor should ensure that the wording required by the mandate, supplemented as necessary, is adequate to convey the opinion required to be expressed. For example, 'giving a true and fair view of ... and complying with Accounting Standards and the Corporations Regulations' is appropriate in the case of audits under the *Corporations Act 2001*.

STRUCTURE AND QUALITATIVE CHARACTERISTICS OF THE AUDIT REPORT

Structure

An example of an unqualified audit report from the 2004 audit report for the Commonwealth Bank is contained in Exhibit 13.1 (overleaf). This standard form audit report is prepared in accordance with a guidance note issued by the AUASB in 2003. It contains wording additional to that contained in the standard form audit reports in the Appendices to AUS 702, with regard to the director's responsibilities and the audit approach. It also contains an additional section on the independence of the auditor. This additional wording aims to improve the communication between auditors and shareholders and narrow the expectations gap (discussed in Chapter 1).

The expanded standard audit report is in conformity with the requirements of AUS 702 and has a number of basic elements and key words and phrases that concisely express the responsibility assumed by the auditor in issuing the report.

AUS 702.15 (ISA 700.06) requires that the title of the audit report should include the word 'independent'. This is to assist users in identifying the audit report and to clearly distinguish it from other reports. An audit report is normally addressed to the person or group who engaged the auditor. In the case of a company, the auditor is engaged to report to the shareholders (members), and they therefore become the addressees (AUS 702.16/ISA 700.06).

The **scope section** (AUS 702.17/ ISA 700.12–.16) contains two sub-sections, the first being the financial report and the directors' responsibility and the second being the audit approach. These elements are explained below (refer to Exhibit 13.1).

- 'The financial report comprises ...' The auditor clearly identifies the components that comprise the financial report, which will be covered by the audit. These are the statement of financial position (balance sheet), the statement of financial performance (income statement), the statement of cash flows, the accompanying notes to the financial statements and the

EXHIBIT

13.1

Example of an
unqualified
audit report

Independent audit report to the members of Commonwealth Bank of Australia—2004

Scope

The financial report and directors' responsibility

The financial report comprises the statement of financial position, statement of financial performance, statement of cash flows, accompanying notes to the financial statements, and the directors' declaration for Commonwealth Bank of Australia and the consolidated Group, for the year ended 30 June 2004. The consolidated Group comprises both the Bank and the entities it controlled during that year.

The directors of the Bank are responsible for preparing a financial report that gives a true and fair view of the financial position and performance of the Bank and the consolidated Group, and that complies with Accounting Standards in Australia, in accordance with the *Corporations Act 2001*. This includes responsibility for the maintenance of adequate accounting records and internal controls that are designed to prevent and detect fraud and error, and for the accounting policies and accounting estimates inherent in the financial report.

Audit approach

We conducted an independent audit of the financial report in order to express an opinion on it to the members of the Bank. Our audit was conducted in accordance with Australian Auditing Standards in order to provide reasonable assurance as to whether the financial report is free of material misstatement. The nature of an audit is influenced by factors such as the use of professional judgment, selective testing, the inherent limitations of internal control, and the availability of persuasive rather than conclusive evidence. Therefore an audit cannot guarantee that all material misstatements have been detected.

We performed procedures to assess whether in all material respects the financial report presents fairly, in accordance with the *Corporations Act 2001*, including compliance with Accounting Standards in Australia, and other mandatory financial reporting requirements in Australia, a view which is consistent with our understanding of the Bank's and the Group's financial position, and of their performance as represented by the results of their operations and cash flows.

We formed our audit opinion on the basis of these procedures, which included:

- examining, on a test basis, information to provide evidence supporting the amounts and disclosures in the financial report; and
- assessing the appropriateness of the accounting policies and disclosures used and the reasonableness of significant accounting estimates made by the directors.

While we considered the effectiveness of management's internal controls over financial reporting when determining the nature and extent of our procedures, our audit was not designed to provide assurance on internal controls.

We performed procedures to assess whether the substance of business transactions was accurately reflected in the financial report. These and our other procedures did not include consideration or judgment of the appropriateness or reasonableness of the business plans or strategies adopted by the directors and management of the Bank.

Independence

We are independent of the Bank, and have met the independence requirements of Australian professional ethical pronouncements and the *Corporations Act 2001*. In addition to our audit of the financial report, we were engaged to undertake the services disclosed in the notes to the financial statements. The provision of these services has not impaired our independence.

Audit opinion

In our opinion, the financial report of Commonwealth Bank of Australia is in accordance with:

(a) the *Corporations Act 2001*, including:
   (i) giving a true and fair view of the financial position of Commonwealth Bank of Australia and the Group at 30 June 2004 and of their performance for the year ended on that date; and
   (ii) complying with Accounting Standards in Australia and the Corporations Regulations 2001; and

(b) other mandatory financial reporting requirements in Australia.

Ernst & Young   S.J. Ferguson
Sydney   Partner

11 August 2004

directors' declaration. This is important in an annual report, which contains other information that has not been subject to audit (although it is considered by the auditor, as outlined under learning objective 6 of this chapter).

■ 'The directors of the Bank are responsible for preparing a financial report that gives a true and fair view ...' This directs attention to the fact that the financial report is the representation of the governing body of the entity being audited, not the auditor. Management and the governing body are responsible for the adequacy and accuracy of the financial report.

■ 'We conducted an independent audit ... in order to express an opinion ... to [addressee].' This explains the role and objective of the audit and, in conjunction with the preceding reference, distinguishes the responsibilities of the governing body and the auditor. The auditor is conducting the audit to add credibility to the representations in the financial report prepared by the governing body by expressing the auditor's independent opinion on the financial report to the report addressee.

■ 'Our audit was conducted in accordance with Australian Auditing Standards ...' The audit report indicates the auditing standards followed in conducting the audit. The auditor indicates that an audit adequate to support an opinion on the financial report was performed with professional competence by properly trained persons. This provides the report user with an assurance that the audit has been carried out in accordance with established standards.

- 'to provide reasonable assurance as to whether the financial report is free of material misstatement ...' This sentence attempts to correct any misperception that the auditor's opinion is a guarantee of the accuracy of the financial report. It points out that the audit opinion provides only reasonable—not absolute—assurance that the financial report, within the context of materiality, does not contain misstatements.

- 'We performed procedures to assess whether in all material respects the financial report presents fairly, in accordance with ...' This information is included to indicate that the audit has been undertaken to form an opinion within the context of an identified financial reporting framework. It therefore informs the user of the basis upon which the audit opinion has been formed, by identifying the benchmark for assessing whether the financial report has met with the objectives of providing relevant and reliable information to meet the needs of such users.

- We formed our opinion on the basis of these procedures, which included:
    - examining, on a test basis ...
    - assessing the appropriateness of the accounting policies and disclosures used and the reasonableness of significant accounting estimates made by directors'

This emphasises the fact that an audit involves tests of selected underlying data rather than a complete review of all such data, and therefore does not involve an examination of 100 per cent of the accounting records. In addition, the fact that the auditor assesses the appropriateness of the accounting policies and disclosures used and significant accounting estimates made by management indicates that the financial report includes a number of estimates and approximations, for example provisions for depreciation and doubtful debts. Overall, it attempts to indicate that the precision of an audit, and the financial report being audited, cannot be absolute.

- 'While we considered the effectiveness of management's internal controls over financial reporting ... our audit was not designed to provide assurance on internal controls,' is aimed specifically at addressing the expectation that the auditor is providing assurance on the Bank's internal controls.

- 'These and other procedures did not include consideration or judgment of the appropriateness or reasonableness of the business plans or strategies adopted by the directors ...' This signifies that although the auditors considered these strategies in developing their audit approach, their opinion does not cover the reasonableness or appropriateness of such strategies.

The scope section of the audit report establishes why it would be illogical for the auditor to issue something stronger than an opinion. As the financial report includes estimates and approximations, and the audit process is based on test checks tailored to the circumstances of a particular engagement, the audit report cannot be more than a statement of belief. This belief is based on a series of judgments made after an expert examination of available evidence.

The independence paragraph is newly added and allows the auditor to be assessed not only on their expertise but on their independence. It conveys that the auditors have met the independence requirements of Australian professional ethical pronouncements and the *Corporations Act 2001* (discussed in Chapter 3) and while they have provided other services to the Bank as disclosed, the provision of these services has not impaired their independence.

The **opinion paragraph** of the audit report presents the auditor's conclusions. Again, refer to Exhibit 13.1.

- 'In our opinion …' An auditor's opinion is an expression of informed judgment. Auditors are experts in the fields of accounting and auditing and therefore their opinions carry substantial weight. Nevertheless, they cannot ensure or warrant the accuracy of the financial report.
- 'the financial report … is in accordance with: (a) the *Corporations Act 2001*, including (i) giving a true and fair view … (ii) complying with Accounting Standards in Australia and the Corporations Regulations 2001; and (b) other mandatory professional reporting requirements.' This presents the auditor's overall opinion.

The audit report is signed in the name of the appointed auditor. If this is an audit firm, the signing partner signs their own name as well as the name of the partnership. The report also shows their location, usually the city in which the auditor's office is located. This advises the report user of the person and firm responsible for the report, and their location if contact is necessary.

The audit report is dated as of the date the auditor signs that report. This informs the reader that the auditor considered the effect on the financial report of events and transactions which had occurred up to that date and about which the auditor had become aware. Auditors' responsibilities for events before and after this date are discussed in Chapter 12 under subsequent events.

Qualitative criteria

As well as the elements of scope and opinion, the audit report is required to possess a number of qualitative criteria, which are discussed in AUS 702 (ISA 700). These are that:

- the information in the audit report should be relevant to the needs of those to whom it is addressed;
- the report's reliability depends upon the sufficiency and appropriateness of the audit evidence and the degree of correspondence between that evidence and the type of audit opinion expressed;
- any explanatory information included in a qualification section or an **'emphasis of matter' section** (see p. 616) should satisfy the test of materiality;
- the report should be timely, in that the auditor should not unreasonably defer issuing a report in the hope of obtaining further evidence to resolve a possible situation that may result in a modified audit report; and
- the report should be comparable with other audit reports. A measure of uniformity in the form and content of the audit report is desirable so that the message is communicated by different auditors in a comparable manner, to promote understandability and to highlight unusual circumstances when they are reported.

AUS 702 (ISA 700) promotes comparability by describing the elements of the audit report and including as appendixes examples of audit reports containing unqualified and modified audit reports. In practice, these examples provide standard forms of audit reports that are very rarely departed from.

Q u i c k   r e v i e w

1 Australia has recently revised its standard form unqualified audit report to include additional information on the directors' responsibilities, the audit approach and a description of the auditors' independence. These are attempts to improve communication between auditors and shareholders.

2 The standard form unqualified audit report is a very standardised form of reporting, consisting of a scope section and an opinion section. Standardised wording is used in the report to convey the different parties' responsibilities and the work that has been undertaken by the auditor in preparing the report. Even though the wordings contained in the auditing standards or other guidance material are only suggestions, they are very rarely departed from in practice.

3 Standard form audit reports are encouraged to produce comparability, to promote understandability and to highlight unusual circumstances when they are reported.

4 The audit report should have the following qualitative characteristics:

- relevance;
- reliability;
- additional explanatory information if material;
- timeliness;
- comparability; and
- understandability.

TYPES OF AUDIT OPINIONS

The opinion expressed in the audit report should be either unqualified or qualified. In Australia there are three types of **qualified opinion** (in ISA 700 a qualified opinion refers only to the category of 'except for' opinion, the three categories being qualified, adverse and disclaimer of opinion):

1 an 'except for' opinion;

2 an adverse opinion; and

3 an inability to form an opinion (disclaimer of opinion).

Furthermore, the category 'modified audit opinion' is also referred to in AUS 702 (ISA 700). **Modified audit opinions** refer to all qualified opinions, plus unqualified opinions to which additional information has been added to emphasise specific matters. These 'emphasis of matter' opinions are discussed later in this section.

The use of standard form opinions helps to highlight that a qualification or modification has occurred. In the audit report the qualification is described in a separate paragraph under the heading 'Qualification', and the usual heading for the next section, 'Audit Opinion', is replaced by 'Qualified Audit Opinion'. Real-life examples of these circumstances are contained in Exhibits 13.2–13.4. However, these qualified opinions have become rare in recent times, as discussed in Auditing in the News 13.1.

Unqualified opinion

An **unqualified opinion** is expressed when the auditor is satisfied in all material respects that the financial report is presented fairly in accordance with:

1 accounting standards and UIG Abstracts, and

2 relevant statutory and other requirements

so as to present a view which is consistent with the auditor's understanding of the entity's financial position, the results of its operations and its cash flows (AUS 702.26/ISA 700.27).

AUDITING IN THE NEWS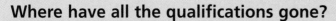

Where have all the qualifications gone?

In a review of the audit reports of listed companies, Aitken & Simnett (1991), and Craswell (1986–1996) found that, up until the end of 1996, approximately 15 per cent of such companies received audit qualifications. Less than 3 per cent of companies received the more serious adverse or inability to form an opinion qualifications. There were in fact very few adverse opinions issued. The qualification rate for the larger (top 500) companies was slightly lower, about 10 per cent.

In 1997 there was a change to AUS 702 which eliminated the ability to issue 'subject to' opinions (subject to the reservation of some uncertainty, the rest of the financial report was true and fair) and permitted the use of 'emphasis of matter' opinions (which are unqualified). A review of the audit reports for companies listed on the Australian Stock Exchange shows that since the beginning of 1997 the rate of qualification has fallen to below 10 per cent, with a qualification rate for the top 500 companies of about 5 per cent.

A review of the top 500 listed companies in Australia 2000–2001 shows that the qualification rate has continued to fall, and that the rate of qualification is currently about 3 per cent.

What would explain this fall?

There are a number of possible causes. Certainly the change in the audit reporting standard explained part of this fall, with 'subject to' qualifications comprising about 6 per cent of audit reports. But it doesn't explain all of the fall. Other possible reasons are the potential improvements to the internal control systems of clients that have taken place over recent years, or the fact that clients are less likely to depart from accounting standards since they now have legislative backing. It is also possible that the auditor's bargaining power with regard to the negotiation of any disagreements with management has increased. Or it may be that auditors are less willing to qualify and risk losing clients. Can you think of any other reasons?

'Except for' opinion

An **'except for' opinion** is expressed when the auditor concludes that an unqualified opinion is inappropriate. This may be because of a disagreement with management, a conflict between applicable financial reporting frameworks or a scope limitation, the effects or possible effects of which are not of such a magnitude or so pervasive or fundamental as to require the expression of an adverse opinion or an inability to form an opinion (AUS 702.27). In International standards the except for opinion is referred to as a 'qualified opinion' (ISA 700.39). An example of a qualification paragraph and a qualified audit opinion paragraph (which are included as an additional paragraph after the scope paragraph) is contained in Exhibit 13.2 (overleaf). By far the most common types of 'except for' opinions today are for material departures from a specific AASB or other Australian accounting standard, or material disagreements over the carrying value of a specific asset or liability and its potential effect on profit.

In issuing this type of opinion the auditor is communicating that, in their opinion, except for the reservations outlined, the remainder of the financial report can be relied upon. The auditor attempts to quantify their reservations so that the user can appropriately adjust the information contained in the financial report if desired.

EXHIBIT

13.2

Example of the
qualification
and qualified
audit opinion
paragraphs for
an except
for opinion

Intermoco Ltd—Independent Audit Report—2004

Qualification

As a result of the acquisition of Intermoco Solutions Pty Ltd (formerly Australon Enterprises Australia Pty Ltd), intangible assets representing intellectual property of $18 000 000 and goodwill of $48 330 204 were recognised. The valuation of the intellectual property is based on an independent valuation. The valuation takes into account the estimated future value of cash flows from the sale of products utilising the intellectual property. As at 30 June 2004, the written-down values of the intellectual property and goodwill were $5 503 562 and $26 720 645 respectively.

The ability of Intermoco Limited to recover the carrying amounts of the intellectual property and goodwill is dependent on the generation of sufficient future cash flows from the sale of products utilising the intellectual property. We have been unable to obtain sufficient reliable audit evidence to support the expected future profits and other cash flows associated with the intellectual property and goodwill, and therefore we are unable to conclude whether these assets are carried at amounts above their recoverable amounts in accordance with AASB 1010 'Recoverable Amount of Non-Current Assets'.

Qualified audit opinion

In our opinion, except for the effects on the financial report of such adjustments, if any, as might have been determined to be necessary had the limitation of scope referred to in the qualification paragraphs not existed, the financial report of Intermoco Limited is in accordance with:

(a) the *Corporations Act 2001*, including:
   (i) giving a true and fair view of the financial position of Intermoco Limited and the consolidated entity at 30 June 2004 and of their performance for the year ended on that date; and
   (ii) complying with Accounting Standards in Australia and the Corporations Regulations 2001; and

(b) other mandatory financial reporting requirements in Australia...

Ernst & Young
R.C. Piltz
Partner

Melbourne
30 September 2004

Source: Intermoco Ltd Annual Report 2004.

Adverse opinion

An **adverse opinion** should be expressed when the effect of disagreement with management or a conflict between applicable financial reporting frameworks is extreme and therefore is of such a magnitude or is so pervasive or fundamental that the financial report taken as a

Qualification

Note 1 discusses a number of matters that may affect the ability of the entity to continue as a going concern. In that Note, the directors state their opinion that the going concern basis used in the preparation of the financial report is appropriate. In our opinion however, it is highly improbable that the company will be able to continue as a going concern and therefore, we believe the going concern basis should not be used.

Had the going concern basis not been used, adjustments would need to be made relating to the recoverability and classification of recorded asset amounts, or to the amounts and classification of liabilities, to reflect the fact that the company may be required to realise its assets and extinguish its liabilities other than in the normal course of business, and at amounts different from those stated in the financial report.

Qualified audit opinion

In our opinion, because of the matter referred to in the qualification paragraph, the financial report of Bestway Pacific Limited is not in accordance with:

(a) the *Corporations Law*, including:

(i) giving a true and fair view of the Company's and consolidated entity's financial position as at 30 June 1999 and of their performance for the year ended on that date; and

(ii) complying with Accounting Standards and the Corporations Regulations; and

(b) other mandatory professional reporting requirements.

KPMG
Chartered Accountants

P G Steer
Partner

Gold Coast
30 September 1999

EXHIBIT 13.3

Example of the qualification and qualified audit opinion paragraphs for an adverse opinion

Source: Bestway Pacific Limited Annual Report, 30 June 1999.

whole is, in the auditor's opinion, misleading or of little use to the addressee of the audit report (AUS 702.28–.29/ISA 700.39–.40). An example of the qualification and qualified audit opinion paragraphs for an adverse opinion, which follow the standard scope paragraph, is contained in Exhibit 13.3. These types of opinions are very rare in practice. The most common use is where there are going concern considerations—where the accounts are prepared on a going concern basis and the auditor concludes that it is highly improbable that the entity will continue as a going concern (refer AUS 708, Appendix 1). The most recent one that we can identify for listed companies in Australia is reproduced in Exhibit 13.3.

Inability to form an opinion

An **inability to form an opinion**, which is also referred to as a **disclaimer**, is expressed when a scope limitation (an unacceptable restriction to the extent of the auditor's investigations) exists and:

- sufficient appropriate audit evidence to resolve the uncertainty resulting from the limitation cannot reasonably be obtained; and

- the possible effects of the adjustments that might have been required had the uncertainty been resolved are extreme, and therefore of such a magnitude or so pervasive or fundamental that the auditor is unable to express an opinion on the financial report taken as a whole (AUS 702.30/ISA 700.38).

However, it should be recognised that the auditor has a duty to form an opinion. Where there is significant uncertainty the auditor should first exhaust all effective alternative means of obtaining sufficient appropriate audit evidence before issuing an inability to form an opinion. An example of the qualification and qualified audit paragraphs for an inability to form an opinion is contained in Exhibit 13.4. These audit qualifications are very rare in practice, with only 1–2 per cent of listed companies receiving such qualifications (Humphries et al., 1999).

EXHIBIT

13.4

Example of qualified audit opinion paragraph for a statement of inability to form an opinion

---

Bougainville Copper Limited—Independent Audit Report—2003

Qualified Audit Opinion

Because of the existence of the limitation in the scope of our work and the fundamental uncertainties, including the matters described in the qualification paragraphs below, and the effects of such adjustments, if any, as might have been determined to be necessary had the uncertainties not existed:

(a) we have not obtained all the information and explanations that we have required, and

(b) we are unable to, and do not express, an opinion as to whether the financial report of Bougainville Copper Limited:

    (i) gives a true and fair view of the financial position of Bougainville Copper Limited as at 31 December 2003 and its performance for the year then ended; and

    (ii) is presented in accordance with the Companies Act 1997, International Financial Reporting Standards and other generally accepted accounting practice in Papua New Guinea.

In our opinion proper accounting records have been kept by the company as far as appears from our examination of those records.

This opinion must be read in conjunction with the qualification paragraphs below and the rest of our audit report.

PricewaterhouseCoopers
by J.C. Seeto
26 February 2004

Source: Bougainville Copper Limited, Independent Audit Report, 31 December 2003.

Thus, the auditor is communicating that there has been such a limitation on the evidence-gathering procedures that they are unsure whether the financial report is reliable or not. The adverse opinion and the disclaimer of opinion can be distinguished as follows: for the adverse opinion, the auditor knows that the financial report, taken as a whole, is of little use, whereas for the disclaimer of opinion, the auditor has been unable to collect sufficient appropriate audit evidence and is thus unable to form an opinion regarding the financial report. Again, these reports are rarely observed in practice.

'Emphasis of matter' section

In certain limited circumstances it is appropriate for the auditor to draw attention to or emphasise a matter that is relevant to the users of the audit report, but which, because of its nature, does not affect the audit opinion. The auditor has to be careful that use of an 'emphasis of matter' does not make the audit report too difficult to understand. Except for the very specific exceptions for which an emphasis of matter is appropriate and allowed, the audit report should not draw attention to or emphasise any matter which the auditor is satisfied has been adequately dealt with in the financial report (AUS 702.31/ISA 700.30).

An 'emphasis of matter' section can accompany either an unqualified or a qualified audit opinion. It should be suitably headed and should be placed immediately after the audit opinion section (AUS 702.32/ISA 700.30). An 'emphasis of matter' is not a qualification, and care needs to be taken to make this clear to the user of the audit report when describing the matter. It can be introduced by use of words such as 'Without qualification to the opinion expressed above, attention is drawn to ...' or, when the audit opinion has been qualified, 'Without further qualification to the opinion expressed above, attention is drawn to ...'.

The 'emphasis of matter' section included after the audit opinion should be used to draw the users' attention to the following circumstances as outlined by AUS 702.39 (in ISA 700.31–.32 the circumstances are limited to highlighting matters regarding a going concern problem, and issues of significant uncertainty, the resolution of which is dependent upon future events and which may affect the financial statements):

1 **Additional disclosures** When a general purpose financial report contains additional disclosures which are contrary to the requirement of accounting standards and/or UIG Abstracts, and the auditor agrees with these disclosures, the 'emphasis of matter' section draws the users' attention to these disclosures (AUS 702.58). It states that in the auditor's opinion application of the particular accounting standard and/or UIG Abstract has, in this instance, resulted in the financial report being potentially misleading. The auditor states specifically why the additional disclosures are necessary to ensure the financial report as a whole is not misleading, and these reasons are stated in the audit report itself rather than only by reference to the reasons included in the financial report. The auditor also states that the additional disclosures are relevant and reliable in meeting the objectives of a general purpose financial report. (Where an 'emphasis of matter' section is included for this reason the auditor's professional reporting obligation is extended: AUS 702.59 requires that a copy of the audit report must be sent to the Executive Director of the Australian Accounting Research Foundation within seven days of signing.) This type of emphasis of matter opinion is very rare in practice.

2 **Inherent uncertainties** Although it is recognised that accounting estimates are often necessary in connection with the financial reports, in most cases auditors can satisfy themselves as to the reasonableness of such estimates. AGS 1028 points out that in certain instances, however, the outcome of a matter is contingent upon future events, and its effect cannot be reasonably measured at the date of the audit report by virtue of the nature of the matter, the facts of the particular situation or the lack of objective evidence. When its potential to affect the financial report is not so remote as to make its disclosure irrelevant, such a matter should be disclosed in a note to the financial report and be included in an 'emphasis of matter' in the audit report. An inherent uncertainty is likely to be resolved at a future date and may arise, for example, regarding the continued appropriateness of the going concern assumption (AUS 702.60–.62).

From 1997 to 1999 about 5 per cent of listed companies received 'emphasis of matter' opinions (Humphries et al., 1999). The majority of these were for inherent uncertainties. When such an inherent uncertainty exists, the audit report includes an 'emphasis of matter' section headed 'Inherent Uncertainty Regarding ...' and the auditor carefully considers the adequacy of the disclosure of the uncertainty and the reliability of all amounts and other disclosures affected by it. The adequate disclosure of an inherent uncertainty by the client requires the expression of an unqualified opinion. The auditor, however, needs to add an 'emphasis of matter' to draw users' attention to the uncertainty. An emphasis of matter paragraph relating to inherent uncertainties is contained in Exhibit 13.5.

The auditor issues a qualified opinion only when an uncertainty has not been adequately disclosed in the financial report. In such a case an 'except for' or adverse opinion is issued. So if in the auditor's opinion the disclosure of the uncertainty is inadequate, or amounts and other disclosures are unreliable, the qualified opinion is expressed on the basis of a disagreement with management and the 'emphasis of matter' section is not included.

3   **Inconsistent other information** When other information in the annual report is inconsistent with information contained in the audited financial report, the audit report includes an 'emphasis of matter' section describing the material inconsistency (AUS 702.63). In order to deal with the auditor's responsibility for identifying material inconsistencies, the auditor should refer to AUS 212 (ISA 720), discussed later in this chapter. This type of emphasis of matter opinion is rarely observed in practice.

4   **Revised financial report** When discovery of a subsequent event results in a revised financial report, the accompanying new audit report should include an 'emphasis of matter' section referring to a more extensive note that explains why the previously issued financial report was revised (AUS 702.65) (see Exhibit 13.6). In practice in Australia, the revision of a previously issued report is rare, and hence the issuing of such 'emphasis of matter' opinions will also be a rare occurrence.

At the time of writing (January 2005), a fifth issue contained in AUS 702 on which an 'emphasis of matter' section could be added to the audit report regarded where the going concern basis became inappropriate as a result of new conditions occurring after balance date (AUS 702.64). As a result of the adoption of IFRSs, in particular the Events Subsequent to Balance Date standard, AASB 110.14, which states that an entity shall not prepare its financial report on a going concern basis if management determines after the reporting date either that it intends to liquidate the entity or cease trading or that it has no realistic alternative but to do so, it is no longer appropriate to give an emphasis of matter for these circumstances. As a result, it is expected that AUS 702 will soon be amended to reflect this change, making it inappropriate to issue this particular 'emphasis of matter'.

EXHIBIT

13.5

'Emphasis of matter' paragraph relating to inherent uncertainties

(The following appears after the audit opinion paragraph.)

Inherent uncertainty regarding valuation of mining tenements

Without qualification to the opinion expressed above, attention is drawn to the following matter:

As disclosed in Note 12 of the financial report, exploration and evaluation expenditure on mining tenements is included in the Consolidated Entity and Company at $1 941 693 in respect of areas of interest in exploration and evaluation phases. The ultimate recovery of the Consolidated Entity's and Company's capitalised exploration expenditure is dependent upon the discovery, exploitation and development of commercially viable mineral deposits, the generation of sufficient future income therefrom and/or sale of the interests at an amount at least equal to the carrying values of the interests in mining tenements.

PKF
D.J. Garvey
Partner

29 September 2004

Source: Yamarna Goldfields Limited Annual Report 2004—Independent Audit Report.

(The following appears after the audit opinion paragraph.)

Emphasis of Matter

Without qualification to the opinion expressed above, attention is draw
matters.

As stated in Note 1 to the financial statements, the consolidate
comparative figures, being the figures for the year ended 31 Decemb
restated by the directors due to the discovery of material error
previously issued figures for that year.

The financial report has been revised subsequent to the issue of
5 April 2001. Note 1(p) to the financial statements sets out the reaso
revised financial report.

In our opinion, the additional disclosures are relevant for a pro
the financial report.

SOMES & COOKE
Chartered Accountants

Source: United Overseas Australia Annual Report, 31 December 2000.

Quick review

1 The audit report will provide either an unqualified opinion or a qualified opinion.

2 An unqualified opinion should be expressed when the auditor is satisfied in all material respects that the financial report is presented fairly in accordance with the appropriate auditing standards and regulations.

3 There are three types of qualified audit opinion:
- 'except for' opinion, where the auditor has a reservation that is not so material as to preclude an expression of opinion on the financial report taken as a whole (i.e. with the exception of the stated reservation, the rest of the financial report is fairly presented);
- adverse opinion, where the financial report taken as a whole is misleading; and
- inability to form an opinion, where due to some limitation on scope the auditor was not able to form an opinion on the financial report.

4 An 'emphasis of matter' section may be included in the audit report to draw attention to certain matters which are considered relevant but do not affect the audit opinion and have been adequately disclosed in the financial report.

5 A modified audit opinion means that the standard-form unqualified opinion is not issued and refers to both qualified audit opinions and audit opinions containing an 'emphasis of matter' section.

AUDITING IN THE NEWS

HIH qualification, 2000 accounts

A point that seems to have been missed by many commentators is that the audit report on the HIH accounts for 2000 does not contain a clean opinion.

The auditors draw attention to Notes 1 and 13 of the accounts and the uncertainty surrounding 'whole of account reinsurance', which totals $1 819.9million.

This reporting of uncertainties is unlikely to have been welcomed by the managers and, consequently, is an expression of the independence of the auditor.

Of course, if investors fail to react to this and other warnings about HIH, it is hardly the fault of the auditors ...

Continued...

SNIPPET 13.2

Source: A. Craswell, (2001), 'US Audit Rules Debated', *Australian Financial Review*, 14 June, p. 60.

The 2000 accounts of HIH contain the following emphasis of matter section in the audit report:

> **Whole of Account Reinsurance**
> *Without qualification to the opinion expressed above, attention is drawn to the following matter. As indicated in Note 7(t) to the financial statements, the consolidated entity enters into whole of account reinsurance contracts to protect its underwriting portfolio. The realisation of benefits arising from a contract entered into during the financial year are dependent on factors described in Note 13.*

Do you think the emphasis of matter was sufficient to alert the investors to the situation in HIH?

Is this an issue that the judiciary should have paid attention to in determining the liability of the auditors in the HIH case?

CIRCUMSTANCES GIVING RISE TO A QUALIFICATION

A qualified opinion should be expressed when any of the following are likely, in the auditor's opinion, to result in material effects:

- a disagreement with management regarding the financial report;
- a conflict between applicable financial reporting frameworks; and
- a limitation on the scope of the audit (AUS 702.42).

However, the auditor should take all reasonable steps to express an unqualified opinion before expressing a qualified one. These will include attempts to overcome the limitations on the scope or discussions with management to attempt to resolve the disagreement satisfactorily.

Disagreement with management

In practice, disagreements with management are the most common cause of qualification. Management and the auditor may disagree over the appropriateness of accounting policies selected, the method of their application, including the appropriateness of accounting estimates, and the adequacy of disclosures in the financial report. Accounting policies and disclosures are determined by accounting standards, UIG Abstracts and other statutory and regulatory requirements. A qualified opinion is expressed when there is a material departure from an accounting standard and/or a UIG Abstract. The audit report cites the specific standard and/or UIG Abstract subject to departure or disagreement (AUS 702.44–.50/ISA 700.45–.46).

As outlined earlier in this chapter when discussing the 'emphasis of matter' section, when accounting standards and UIG Abstracts have been adhered to but are subject to additional disclosures which imply that the application of an accounting standard and/or Abstract could be misleading, a qualified opinion is expressed in relation to such additional disclosures, unless, in rare circumstances, the auditor is of the opinion that:

- it is likely, in the absence of the additional disclosures, that users would be misled when using the information; and

- the additional disclosures contain all, and only, relevant and reliable information, and are presented in such a manner as to ensure the financial report as a whole is comparable and understandable in meeting the objectives of a general purpose financial report.

The auditor must form an opinion on compliance with statutory and other requirements that affect the form and content of the financial report. Compliance with these requirements may be imposed by an Act of Parliament, including regulations, rules and directives. Most frequently such requirements are aimed at separate disclosures, for example the separate disclosure of directors' and audit fees. These items are usually considered material because of their nature, rather than their amount, and a failure to meet such requirements will normally result in a qualified audit opinion (almost invariably an 'except for' opinion).

Conflict between applicable financial reporting frameworks

Sometimes the accounting policies adopted by management, although required or allowed by statute or other requirements, do not result in fair presentation in accordance with accounting standards and/or UIG Abstracts. In such cases an unqualified opinion is expressed on the presentation in accordance with the statute or other requirements and a qualified opinion is expressed with respect to the presentation in accordance with accounting standards and UIG Abstracts. If, however, the accounting policies adopted are contrary to those required by statute or other requirements, the auditor qualifies with respect to presentation in accordance with those other requirements (AUS 702.51–.52; no equivalent ISA). Qualifications on this basis are rarely seen in practice.

Scope limitation

A limitation on the scope of the auditor's work exists when sufficient appropriate audit evidence on which to base an unqualified opinion does or did exist, or could reasonably be expected to have existed, but is not available to the auditor (AUS 702.53/ISA 700.41).

When a limitation in the terms of an engagement is such that the auditor is unable to form an opinion, the limited engagement should not be accepted or continued past the current period as an audit engagement. An auditor should not accept an audit engagement when a known limitation infringes on the auditor's legal duties or ethical or other professional responsibilities (AUS 702.54/ISA 700.41).

When a scope limitation exists, the wording of the auditor's opinion should indicate that it is qualified as to the effects on the financial report of such adjustments, if any, as might have been required had the limitation not existed (AUS 702.56/ISA 700.43).

The effect of materiality on the audit qualification

As is evident from Exhibit 13.7 (overleaf), the primary factor when considering whether to qualify an audit opinion, or attempting to determine what sort of qualification to apply, is the degree of materiality of the subject matter giving rise to the qualification. One critical aspect is the dollar magnitude of the effects, or potential effects, of the matter on the financial report. However, as discussed in Chapters 7 and 12, materiality does not depend entirely on dollar magnitude. The auditor also needs to consider the nature of the matter when making judgments regarding materiality. A departure from an accounting standard need not be noted in the audit report where it relates to an item of financial information that is not material. However, qualifications may arise if there is a legal requirement to disclose specific items irrespective of their dollar magnitude. As outlined earlier, these include the requirement to disclose specified directors' and executive fees, and audit fees through AASB 1046 and AASB 101 respectively. If not disclosed, such items will normally give rise to an except for opinion. For a matter to be considered extreme, it must be of such a magnitude, or be so pervasive or fundamental, as to affect the overall usefulness of the financial report taken as a whole.

Every modified report should contain a clear description of all material matters about which the auditor has reservations. Each and every material reservation should be reported by the auditor, even if it leads to more than one qualification in the audit report. The auditor needs to consider the requirements of law and the audit mandate in relation to the reported reservation to ensure that reporting of the reservation complies with all necessary requirements.

EXAMPLE 13.1 Consideration of materiality in issuing opinion

Facts
During the attendance at the annual stocktake and while undertaking follow-up procedures, the auditor identifies a range of obsolete stock. Subsequent work by the client reveals that under the lower of cost and net realisable value rule inventory is overstated by $10 million, but the client decides not to adjust the value because the reports are close to being issued. Testing of the subsequent work of the client shows that the auditor is 95 per cent confident that the overstatement is in the range of $5–15 million. The inventory balance is $380 million and profit after tax but before extraordinary items is $693 million.

Required
Assuming that the auditor is satisfied in all other respects, what type of audit opinion would the auditor issue?

Solution
The adjusting entry required would be to debit the expense account 'inventory write-down' and to credit the asset account inventory, for $10 million. As the required adjustment is less than 5 per cent of the inventory balance as well as the appropriate profit balance, the auditor would conclude that the concern over inventory valuation is immaterial and they would issue an unqualified opinion.

Quick review

1. Qualifications may arise due to:
   - disagreements with management;
   - conflict between applicable financial reporting frameworks; and/or
   - scope limitations.

2. Materiality is an important consideration in determining whether a qualification is necessary, and, if so, the type of qualification. Consideration has to be given to both quantitative and qualitative factors in this regard.

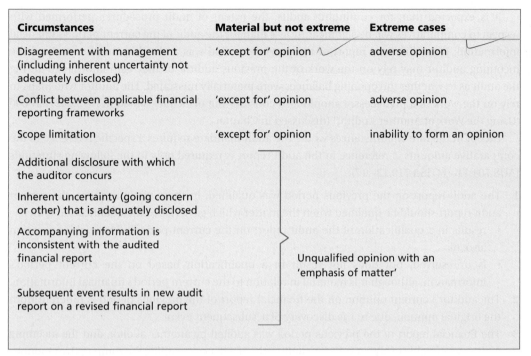

Circumstances	Material but not extreme	Extreme cases
Disagreement with management (including inherent uncertainty not adequately disclosed)	'except for' opinion	adverse opinion
Conflict between applicable financial reporting frameworks	'except for' opinion	adverse opinion
Scope limitation	'except for' opinion	inability to form an opinion
Additional disclosure with which the auditor concurs		
Inherent uncertainty (going concern or other) that is adequately disclosed		
Accompanying information is inconsistent with the audited financial report	Unqualified opinion with an 'emphasis of matter'	
Subsequent event results in new audit report on a revised financial report		

EXHIBIT 13.7

AUS 702.39 'Circumstances that result in a modified audit report'

Source: Adapted and reproduced with the permission of The Institute of Chartered Accountants in Australia and CPA Australia.

COMPARATIVE AMOUNTS AND OTHER INFORMATION IN THE ANNUAL REPORT

6 learning objective

The audit of comparative amounts

Most entities disclose information from previous periods for comparison purposes. Such **comparative amounts** are an integral part of the current period's financial report, but they are intended to be read only in relation to the amounts and other disclosures relating to the current period. Unless otherwise stated, the financial report users are entitled to expect the comparative amounts to have the same level of audit assurance as the disclosures relating to the current period. The auditor's responsibilities in the audit of comparative amounts are contained in AUS 704 (ISA 710), which requires that the auditor obtain sufficient appropriate audit evidence that the comparative amounts are not materially misstated. The assessment of risk of material misstatement includes these considerations:

- The accounting policies used for the comparative amounts should be in accordance with the financial reporting framework and consistent with those of the current period. If they are not, the auditor must consider whether appropriate adjustments and disclosures have been made.
- The comparative amounts and other disclosures required should agree with those presented in the previous period's financial report. If they do not, the auditor must consider the need for appropriate adjustments and/or disclosures to explain the variations that have been made.
- The comparative amounts should be free of material misstatement.

It is expected that, for continuing audits, the extent of audit procedures performed with respect to comparatives will be significantly less than for the audit of the current period's financial information. If the financial report of the previous period was audited by another auditor, the incoming auditor may rely on the work of the previous auditor or may gain knowledge during the audit as to whether the opening balances were materially misstated. The auditor who plans to rely on the work of a predecessor should also consider the principles stated in AUS 602/ISA 600 'Using the Work of Another Auditor' (discussed in Chapter 5).

Except in the rare circumstances where the audit mandate requires a specific reference to the comparative amounts, a reference in the audit report is required only in the following situations (AUS 704.11–.14/ISA 710.12–.17):

1 The audit report on the previous period was qualified. In these circumstances, the current audit report should be qualified when the matter which gave rise to the qualification either:
   • results in a qualification of the audit report on the current period's financial information also, or
   • is unresolved, but does not result in a qualification based on the current period's information, although it is material in relation to the current period's financial information.
2 The auditor's current opinion on the financial report of the previous period is different from the original opinion, due to the discovery of a 'subsequent event'.
3 The financial report of the previous period was audited by another auditor, and the incoming auditor was unable to obtain sufficient appropriate evidence regarding the comparative amounts.

If the previous period's financial report has not been audited, and the auditor is unable to obtain sufficient appropriate audit evidence regarding the comparative amounts, the auditor qualifies the audit report on the basis that the comparative amounts are unaudited and that no opinion on them is expressed, and encourages clear disclosure in the financial report that the comparative amounts are unaudited.

Auditor's responsibilities for other information in an annual report

Most annual reports include financial data that are not part of the basic comparative financial report. For example, there may be summaries of five or 10 years' operating results, highlights of key figures from the financial report, as well as analyses of financial data in the chairperson's or directors' reports. For companies listed on the Australian Stock Exchange, other disclosures, such as the top 20 shareholders, are required. In many cases this **other information in an annual report** is based on or related to material contained in the audited financial report.

Thus the auditor should read the entire annual report and consider whether the other information is consistent with the audited financial report. The auditor has no responsibility to apply additional audit procedures to the other information to corroborate it unless this has been specified as part of the engagement. However, where it is not so specified, it is prudent for the auditor to read it and compare it with audited data. This is important since the credibility of the audited financial report may be undermined by inconsistencies between it and accompanying other information. The auditor's responsibilities in relation to such information presented with audited financial reports are dealt with in AUS 212 (ISA 720).

Since much of the other information is derived from the financial report, the auditor has a basis for recognising material inconsistencies and material misstatements of fact. For example, the directors' report might mention an increase in net profit but omit the fact that it occurs because of a material profit from discontinued operations, thus misleading investors. An inconsistency is material when it contradicts information contained in the financial report and may therefore raise doubts about the material in the financial report and the auditor's conclusion and report. An auditor who concludes that the other information causes a material inconsistency should ask the client to revise it. If the client will not, the auditor has the following options:

1 revise the audit report in accordance with AUS 702 (ISA 700), and consider including in the audit report an 'emphasis of matter' section describing the material inconsistency;

2 withhold the use of the audit report in the annual report; or

3 withdraw from the engagement.

The appropriate action depends on the significance of the inconsistency, and why the inconsistency has arisen. In practice, management is usually happy to correct any material inconsistencies or misstatements of fact brought to their attention. If they do not, option 1 above is the most likely course of action, with options 2 and 3 being quite extreme. Note that the inclusion of an 'emphasis of matter' section in the audit report is not an audit qualification, because the deficiency is not in the audited financial report. If the other information is correct and it is the financial report which requires revision, and the client refuses, the auditor issues an 'except for' or adverse opinion, depending on the circumstances.

For audits conducted under the provisions of the *Corporations Act 2001*, a material inconsistency is most likely to be a breach of the Act by the directors. Thus, it is likely that on being brought to the attention of directors, the inconsistency will be rectified. If it is not rectified, the auditor should consider bringing the matter to the attention of ASIC.

Quick review

1. The auditor should obtain sufficient appropriate audit evidence that comparative financial information is not materially misstated.

2. The auditor should review the other information in documents containing audited financial reports for any material inconsistencies or material misstatements of fact.

3. The auditor should encourage management to correct any material inconsistencies or material misstatements of fact. If management does not, the auditor's most likely course of action is to issue an 'emphasis of matter' opinion.

COMMUNICATIONS BETWEEN AUDITOR AND OTHER PARTIES

The relationship between an auditor and client has many dimensions. One factor that has a significant effect on the relationship is the form in which the client is organised—company, partnership or sole trader. This section focuses on the corporate client whose shares are traded on the stock exchange.

Communicating with shareholders through the annual report

The primary communication between a company and its shareholders is the annual report. The financial report included in the annual report should contain a balance sheet, income statement, statement of changes in equity and cash flow statement, with accompanying explanatory notes. Beyond the inclusion of the financial report, the form and content of annual reports vary substantially. Some companies issue elaborate reports with pictures of physical facilities and personnel, graphs and charts of operating data and supplementary financial information. Other companies send shareholders only the basic financial report and statutory reports with a covering letter. Regardless of the form or content of the annual report, the auditor's opinion on the financial report included in the annual report is the principal means of communication between the auditor and shareholders. Thus, it is important that the audit report, discussed in this chapter in detail, be an effective communication device.

Communicating with shareholders at annual general meetings

A second major method of communicating with shareholders is at the company's annual general meeting (AGM). However, only a small minority of shareholders normally attend these meetings. Over the last five years in Australia, **attendance at AGMs** has been increasing. However, many of the companies listed on the Australian Stock Exchange will have attendances of less than 50, with over 200 usually only occurring for the largest public companies, or if there are contentious issues on the agenda. It is now more common that there be shareholder representatives in attendance, through associations such as the Australian Shareholders' Association. Section 250T of the *Corporations Act 2001* states that members must be allowed a reasonable opportunity to ask the auditor questions relevant to the conduct of the audit, the preparation and content of the audit report, the accounting policies adopted by the company and the independence of the auditor. Auditors have a legal obligation to attend the company's annual general meeting at which the audit report is considered (*Corporations Act*, s. 250RA).

AGS 1046 'Responding to Questions at an Annual General Meeting' provides auditors with guidance on this issue. It emphasises the educational opportunity of putting specific issues raised by shareholders into the broader context of the audit. Responses to questions relating to specific issues or procedures should be addressed by reference to the fact that the audit report relates to the financial report as a whole, after taking into account the auditor's assessment of risk and materiality. Questions about the issuing of modified or qualified opinions should be answered by reference to the audit report. If the report is an effective communication device it should contain sufficient explanation to ensure it answers all reasonable questions.

Communicating with management, directors and audit committees

AUS 710 (ISA 260) provides guidance for the auditor in communicating with all groups of management. The standard distinguishes between 'management', being the governing body (the board of directors for a listed company), the **audit committee** and other persons having responsibility for planning and directing the activities of an entity, and 'operational management', being those with responsibility for supervision of the day to day activities of the entity. It does require the auditor to report significant matters identified as a result of audit procedures performed to an appropriate level of management on a timely basis. In assessing the significance of each matter identified, the auditor should consider the nature of the matter, the relevant characteristics of the entity and the potential for the matter to materially affect the financial report. All such matters should be reported on a timely basis, and oral reports to management regarding significant matters should be documented. The auditor should also review matters raised in previous reports to management and the subsequent actions taken by management.

A specific requirement is that if the auditor is concerned that a report to management intended for the audit committee or governing body may not be distributed to all members of that committee or body, the auditor should take steps to inform all these members of the contents of the report. The consequences of not fulfilling such reporting responsibilities were demonstrated in the *AWA* appeal decision (refer to Chapter 4), where the auditors were found not to have fulfilled their reporting responsibility when they informed the managing director of material weaknesses in internal control, but did not bring it to the attention of other board members.

The auditor uses different means to communicate with various groups. The discussion below reviews communication first with executive (or operational) management, then with the audit committee and finally with the board of directors. The roles of these various groups were discussed in the corporate governance section of Chapter 3.

Communicating with executive management

Most of the communication between the auditor and the client is with the company's executive management. Contacts between the auditor and executive management are more extensive, more frequent and more informal than those with shareholders, audit committees and boards of directors. At the planning stage, executive management provides much of the information that is needed to plan the audit, including news of major changes in the entity, both strategic and operational. During the audit, executive management provides the auditor with information and explanations as required. This includes the organisation and preparation of many schedules. It is executive management that undertakes the preparation of the financial report, and it is with executive management that the auditor negotiates appropriate adjustments to the financial report as detected by the audit.

The management letter, or report to management

The principal written communication between the auditor and management is the **management letter** that normally is issued at the conclusion of every audit engagement. This letter summarises the auditor's recommendations resulting from their assessment of the entity's business risk and inherent risk, and any recommended improvements in internal control.

In Australia there is no recommended standard form for the management letter. As the auditor attempts to add value with the business risk audit methodology, they may wish to communicate to management, for each key business process:

- the risks identified which would threaten the organisation's objectives;
- the critical success factors identified;
- the key performance indicators linked to the critical success factors; and
- performance improvement opportunities.

With regard to internal control, the report should include the following main points:

- The purpose of the study and evaluation of internal control is to establish a basis for reliance on controls in determining the nature, timing and extent of other audit procedures.
- The objective of internal control is to provide reasonable, but not absolute, assurance, and costs must be balanced against benefits by management.
- Any internal control has inherent limitations and an evaluation cannot be projected to future periods.
- The auditor's study and evaluation does not necessarily disclose all weaknesses.
- The study and evaluation disclosed certain material weaknesses, which are enumerated, and other audit tests were modified accordingly.

Although the management letter will be reviewed by executive management, which is expected to respond to items contained in it, the audit committee and the full board of directors are required to be informed of the contents of this letter and review the response (refer to the *AWA* decision in Chapter 4).

Discussions with management

The most critical communication between the auditor and management concerns the form and content of the financial report. The financial report contains management's representations. If the accounting policies or disclosures proposed by management differ materially from those which the auditor believes are appropriate, either an alternative presentation must be agreed on or the auditor must express a qualified opinion.

If the auditor can convince management that a particular presentation is superior, management may be persuaded to change the financial report. The auditor attempts to demonstrate that the proposed presentation might be misleading or that it clearly departs from authoritative pronouncements or substantially favoured practice. In some cases management is unfamiliar with accounting or auditing requirements of the accounting profession and the stock exchanges, or with statutory disclosure requirements.

Sometimes questions concerning the appropriate application of generally accepted accounting principles or the adequacy of informative disclosures fall in a grey area. In this case, extensive discussion with management is usually necessary. Resolution of differences depends on the attitudes and personalities of management and the auditor and the working relationship that has developed between them. The outcome may be a change in the financial report, qualification of the auditor's opinion or loss of the client.

Communicating with the audit committee or boards of directors

There is an increased emphasis on a company having an effective audit committee. The broad objectives of an audit committee are discussed in Chapter 3. The AUASB, in conjunction with the Institute of Company Directors and Institute of Internal Auditors, recently revised their best practice guide for audit committees. AUS 710 (ISA 260) includes Appendix 1, entitled 'Communication with Audit Committees' (ISA 260 does not contain this appendix). If best practices are adopted, it can reasonably be expected that the following communications between the external auditor and the audit committee will occur:

1 The auditor is able to contact the chair of the audit committee at any time to arrange meetings or to discuss issues.
2 The auditor is informed of the proposed meeting dates of the audit committee.
3 The auditor meets with the audit committee at least twice: at the planning stage and at the completion of the audit. Other meetings while the audit is being undertaken may also be required to help resolve difficulties that may have arisen during the evidence collection stage.

Effective audit committees could also be expected to inquire of their auditor the extent to which executive management has been aggressive in their choice of accounting policies, and the auditor is independent of management. For example, they may ask the auditor to inform them of any circumstances that may affect their independence, such as the provision by the audit firm of non-audit services for that client. AAA 11 outlines suggested wording for a 'declaration of independence' by the auditor to the audit committee and/or board of directors, which helps ensure that issues that may affect auditor independence are brought to their attention. In the United States, certain stock exchanges require the auditor to communicate such issues with the audit committee. There are also a number of advocates for the requirement of such practices in Australia. However, if such a requirement was mandated it would need to be preceded by a requirement that listed companies in Australia had an audit committee. Audit committees are currently voluntary in Australia (although they are suggested best practice under the ASX Corporate Governance guidelines for the Top 500 companies in Australia), and if there is no audit committee or an ineffective audit committee, then the auditor deals directly with the board of directors.

At the planning stage the audit committee should acquaint the auditor with the company's general disclosure policies and directions, including disclosure of the company's corporate governance practices. It should also review and consider the scope of the external audit, particularly in the identified risk areas.

At the conclusion of the audit the committee should ask the auditor about any significant disagreements with management and whether or not they have been satisfactorily resolved. The auditor may also provide an independent judgment about the appropriateness, not just the acceptability, of the accounting principles and the clarity of the financial disclosure practices used or proposed to be adopted by the company, as put forward by management. The audit committee should also review the management letter which the auditor has provided and management's response to it.

As the audit committee is a subcommittee of the full board of directors, its meetings are minuted for the consideration of the full board. The auditor should review these minutes.

At present in Australia, auditors do not have the right to attend meetings of the board of directors, but they may be invited to attend to discuss accounting or auditing matters. Sometimes the auditor asks to be present at a meeting of the board, with attendance of the auditor at at least one full board meeting becoming more and more common.

One of the results of the implementation of the business risk audit methodology is that boards generally now see auditors as more relevant with regard to their deliberations. Also, matters that cannot be satisfactorily resolved with the executive management must be discussed with the board. In addition, certain other matters, such as material weaknesses in internal control, should be brought to the board's attention because of its responsibility to the shareholders. Unnecessary conflict with the executive management can usually be avoided by allowing it to make a preliminary review of matters to be presented to the board, but the auditor cannot subordinate professional judgment concerning which matters should be reported directly to the board.

Communicating through electronic presentation of financial reports

Audit and Assurance Alert No. 4 and the follow-up, AGS 1050, alert the auditor and provide guidance for the circumstances where the entity decides to publish its audited financial report on its web site. The major risks are whether the financial report on the web site is in accordance with the published financial report, and whether it is possible that the audit report may be construed as providing assurance on other information on the web site that was unaudited. For most entities which place their financial report on the web site, there is a separate link in the web site to the financial report and it is clear that the audit report is attached to and intended to be read with the financial report. The auditor should review the web site to make sure the audit report cannot be attached to or be seen as covering any information for which this was not the intention.

If in the auditor's opinion the audit report may be construed to cover information that was unaudited, they should bring this to management's attention. In certain circumstances the auditor may provide a separate audit report for electronic dissemination. This audit report may be expanded to include specific references to the audited statements by name, advice to readers that the audit report refers only to statements named in the report, and advice to readers that they consider reference to the hard copy of the entity's financial report.

1. The auditor's principal means of communication with shareholders is through the audit report on the financial report. A secondary means of communication is through their attendance at the annual general meeting.

2. Auditors have a responsibility to communicate to management matters which they believe are prejudicial to the interests of shareholders. These include significant business risks and material weaknesses in internal control. Usually the auditor lists the weaknesses and recommendations for improvement in the management letter.

3. Auditors should ensure that the full board of directors is informed of the contents of the management letter.

4. There is an increased emphasis in the current environment on the auditor's communication with the audit committee. Communications may include such items as a discussion of an assessment of aggressiveness of executive management's accounting policy choice, as well as ensuring that the auditor is independent of management.

5. Auditors should ensure that electronic presentations of the audit report provide assurance on the statements for which it was intended.

learning objective 8

FUTURE CHANGES TO THE AUDIT REPORT

At the end of 2004, the IAASB approved for issue a revised ISA 700 on audit reports on complete sets of general purpose financial statements designed to provide a true and fair view. This revised ISA 700 contained a suggested standard form audit report, designed to improve audit report comparability around the world. In keeping with its stated convergence policy (see Chapter 2) the AUASB will have to consider changes to its audit reporting standard AUS 702 in 2005. The IAASB report is reproduced in Exhibit 13.8. This audit report is suggested for use for all international audits that are signed by the auditor after December 2006. Some features of this standard form audit report are the following:

- Fuller description of management's responsibilities. This approximates the recent extension to the recently revised Australian standard form audit report.
- Fuller description of auditors' responsibilities.
- A two-part audit opinion, where the first part is standardised and meets international requirements. The second part, if needed, is used to meet a specific country's requirements. For example, if an auditor in Australia is required to comment on additional information provided in order to give a true and fair view (see learning objective 1 of this chapter), such comments would fall within the second part.

EXHIBIT 13.8

Proposed format of independent audit report for international audits signed after December 2006.

INDEPENDENT AUDITOR'S REPORT

[Appropriate addressee]

Report on the financial statements
We have audited the accompanying financial statements of ABC Company, which comprise the balance sheet as at December 31, 20X1, and the income statement, statement of changes in equity and cash flow statement for the year then ended, and a summary of significant accounting policies and other explanatory notes.

Management's responsibility for the financial statements
Management is responsible for the preparation and the fair presentation of these financial statements in accordance with International Financial Reporting Standards. This

Continued...

responsibility includes: designing, implementing and maintaining internal control relevant to the preparation and fair presentation of financial statements that are free from material misstatement, whether due to fraud or error; selecting and applying appropriate accounting policies; and making accounting estimates that are reasonable in the circumstances.

Auditor's responsibility
Our responsibility is to express an opinion on these financial statements based on our audit. We conducted our audit in accordance with International Standards on Auditing. Those standards require that we comply with ethical requirements and plan and perform the audit to obtain reasonable assurance whether the financial statements are free from material misstatement.

An audit involves performing procedures to obtain audit evidence about the amounts and disclosures in the financial statements. The procedures selected depend on the auditor's judgment, including the assessment of the risks of material misstatement in the financial statements, whether due to fraud or error. In making those risk assessments, the auditor considers internal control relevant to the entity's preparation and fair presentation of the financial statements as a basis for designing audit procedures that are appropriate in the circumstances, but not for the purpose of expressing an opinion on the effectiveness of the entity's internal control. An audit also includes evaluating the appropriateness of accounting policies used and the reasonableness of significant accounting estimates made by management, as well as evaluating the overall presentation of the financial statements.

We believe that the audit evidence we have obtained is sufficient and appropriate to provide a basis for our audit opinion.

Opinion
In our opinion, the financial statements give a true and fair view of (*or 'present fairly, in all material respects'*) the financial position of ABC Company as of December 31, 20X1, and of its financial performance and its cash flows for the year then ended in accordance with International Financial Reporting Standards.

Report on other legal and regulatory requirements
[Form and content of this section of the auditor's report will vary depending on the nature of the auditor's other reporting responsibilities.]

[Auditor's signature]

[Date of the auditor's report]

[Auditor's address]

Quick review

The IAASB has recently revised ISA 700 to include a suggested standard form audit report that is designed to promote comparability in international audit reporting.

Summary

An audit report formally communicates the auditor's conclusion on the presentation of the financial report and concisely states the basis for that conclusion. It is important that this audit report is an effective communication device, as it is the principal means of communication between the auditor and the financial report user. This chapter has considered how auditors' reporting obligations for general purpose financial reports arise and how auditors determine the type of report that is appropriate. The auditors' reporting obligations to other parties have also been considered.

Key terms

Adverse opinion	614	Modified audit opinion	612
Attendance at annual general meeting (AGM)	626	Opinion paragraph	610
Audit committee	626	Other information in an annual report	624
Comparative amounts	623	'Presents fairly'	606
Disclaimer	615	Qualified opinion	612
'Emphasis of matter' section	611	Scope section	607
'Except for' opinion	613	'True and fair'	606
Inability to form an opinion	615	Unqualified opinion	612
Management letter	627		

References

Aitken, M. and Simnett, R. (1991) 'Australian audit reports: 1980–89', *Australian Accounting Review*, Vol. 1, No. 1, 12–19.

Australian Accounting Research Foundation, Institute of Internal Auditors—Australia, Australian Institute of Company Directors (2001) *Audit committees: Best practice guide*, revised, Australian Accounting Research Foundation, Melbourne.

Carson, E. (1996) 'Corporate governance disclosure in Australia: The state of play', *Australian Accounting Review*, Vol. 6, No. 2, 3–11.

Craswell, A. (1986–1996) *Who Audits Australia*, University of Sydney.

Deegan, C., Kent, P. and Lin, C.-J. (1994) 'The true and fair view: A study of Australian auditors' application of the concept', *Australian Accounting Review*, Vol. 4, No. 1, 2–12.

DeZoort, F.T. and Salterio, S. (2001) 'The effects of corporate governance experience and financial-reporting and audit knowledge on audit committee members' judgments', *Auditing: A Journal of Practice & Theory*, Vol. 20, No. 2, 31–48.

Gay, G., and Schelluch, P. (1993) 'The effect of the longform audit report on users' perceptions of the auditor's role', *Australian Accounting Review*, Vol. 3, No. 2, 2–11.

Green, W. (1994) 'Going concern qualifications and audit switching', *Accounting Research Journal*, Vol. 7, No. 2, 4–10.

Humphries, K., Craswell, A. and Simnett, R. (1999) 'Assessing auditors' uncertainty resolution strategies', University of New South Wales Working Paper, Sydney.

Monroe, G.S. and Teh, S.T. (1993) 'Predicting uncertainty: Audit qualifications in Australia using publicly available information', *Accounting and Finance*, Vol. 33, No. 2, November, 79–106.

National Companies and Securities Commission (1984) *A True and Fair View and the Reporting Obligations of Directors and Auditors*, National Companies and Securities Commission, Sydney.

Nugent, M. (1997) 'Uncertain about what type of audit report to issue?', *Charter*, August, 84–5.

Psaros, J. and Wei, Z.M. (1994) 'The going concern audit opinion: Australian evidence', *Perspectives on Contemporary Auditing*, Vol. 1, 39–46.

Assignments

Additional assignments for this chapter are contained in Appendix A of this book, page 774.

There are approximately 30 interactive questions on the auditor's reporting obligations available online at www.mhhe.com/au/gay3e

REVIEW QUESTIONS

13.1 Select the best response to the following questions.

(a) Kelly Insurance Ltd is trading profitably at 30 June 20X0 as reflected in its financial report. On 24 July 20X0 there is a hailstorm in Sydney which creates unprecedented damage. Although Kelly had undertaken all the normal reinsurance processes, it is unlikely that they will be able to pay all claims and there is a high probability that the company will have to be wound up. The auditor believes that the financial report as at 30 June 20X0 is *true and fair, and that this natural disaster is adequately disclosed.* The auditor should issue:

    A an 'except for' or disclaimer of opinion
    B an unqualified opinion with an 'emphasis of matter'
    C an unqualified opinion
    D an 'except for' or adverse opinion

(b) Kelly Insurance Ltd is trading profitably at 30 June 20X0 as reflected in its financial report. On 24 July 20X0 there is a hailstorm in Sydney, which creates unprecedented damage. Although Kelly had undertaken all the normal reinsurance processes, it is unlikely that they will be able to pay all claims and there is a high probability that the company will have to be wound up. The auditor believes that the financial report, as at 30 June 20X0, *does not adequately disclose the financial consequences of the natural disaster.* The auditor should issue:

    A an 'except for' or disclaimer of opinion
    B an unqualified opinion with an emphasis of matter
    C an unqualified opinion
    D an 'except for' or adverse opinion

(c) ABC Ltd has reported losses two years in a row and has a debt to total assets ratio of 0.90. In addition, a $5 000 000 debenture is maturing next year and the company has not set aside a sinking fund to repay the debt. The parent entity of ABC Ltd has decided to repay the debenture when it matures and provide sufficient funding to cover any additional losses that ABC Ltd might incur. ABC Ltd has not disclosed these arrangements in its financial report and the auditor is adamant that it should be brought to the shareholders' attention. What type of opinion should the auditor express on the financial report of ABC Ltd?

    A unqualified opinion with an 'emphasis of matter'
    B disclaimer of opinion
    C 'except for' or adverse opinion
    D unqualified opinion

(d) Your client, XYZ Ltd, is being sued by one of its competitors for $20 000 000 for an alleged patent infringement. Your client has assets of $40 000 000 and a reported profit of $10 000 000. The client has disclosed the lawsuit in a note to the accounts along with a statement indicating that they intend to vigorously defend the suit and are confident of winning the suit. Your independent legal advice supports this view. What type of opinion should you express on the financial report of XYZ Ltd?

    A a disclaimer of opinion
    B an unqualified opinion with an 'emphasis of matter'
    C an 'except for' or adverse opinion
    D an unqualified opinion

CHAPTER 13 The auditor's reporting obligations **633**

(e) ABC Ltd has disclosed the fact that they are being sued for $1 000 000. ABC Ltd reported a profit for the year of $10 000 000 and has total assets of $15 000 000. You conclude that disclosure of the litigation is adequate. What type of opinion should you express on the financial report of ABC Ltd?

    A unqualified opinion with an 'emphasis of matter'

    B disclaimer of opinion

    C 'except for' or adverse opinion

    D unqualified opinion

(f) Your client has followed approved accounting standards but a note to the financial report indicates that the application of certain standards results in the financial report being materially misstated. The note details the reasons for this view. You do not concur with this view. What type of opinion should you issue?

    A a disclaimer of opinion

    B an unqualified opinion with an 'emphasis of matter'

    C an 'except for' or adverse opinion

    D an unqualified opinion

(g) Your client has followed approved accounting standards but a note to the financial report indicates that the application of certain standards results in the financial report being materially misstated. The note details the reasons for this view. You, as the auditor, concur that this additional note disclosure is necessary to give a true and fair value. What type of opinion should you issue?

    A a disclaimer of opinion

    B an unqualified opinion with an 'emphasis of matter'

    C an 'except for' or adverse opinion

    D an unqualified opinion

(h) Jodie Ltd refuses to separately disclose directors' fees of $2.5 million on the basis that they are immaterial. Profit for the last year was $980 million. The auditor should issue an:

    A 'except for' opinion

    B adverse opinion

    C unqualified opinion

    D unqualified opinion with an 'emphasis of matter'

13.2 Select the best response to the following independent situations.

(a) An entity changed from the straight-line method to the declining balance method of depreciation for all newly acquired assets. This change has no material effect on the current year's financial statements but is reasonably certain to have a substantial effect in later years. If the change is disclosed in the notes to the financial statements, the auditor should issue a report with a(n):

    A unqualified opinion

    B consistency modification

    C 'except for' qualified opinion

    D explanatory paragraph

(b) Tech Company has disclosed an uncertainty due to pending litigation. The auditor's decision to issue a qualified opinion would most likely be determined by the:

    A entity's lack of experience with such litigation

    B lack of insurance coverage for possible losses from such litigation

    C lack of sufficient evidence

    D inability to estimate the amount of loss

(c) King, CPA, was engaged to audit the financial statements of Newton Company after its fiscal year had ended. King neither observed the inventory count nor confirmed the receivables by direct communication with debtors but was satisfied concerning both after applying alternative procedures. King's auditor's report most likely contained a(n):

A unqualified opinion

B unqualified opinion with an explanatory paragraph

C qualified opinion

D disclaimer of opinion

(d) Which of the following best describes the auditor's responsibility for 'other information' included in the annual report to stockholders that contains financial statements and the auditor's report?

A The auditor should extend the examination to the extent necessary to verify the 'other information'

B The auditor must modify the auditor's report to state that the other information 'is unaudited' or 'is not covered by the auditor's report'

C The auditor has *no* obligation to read the 'other information'

D The auditor has *no* obligation to corroborate the 'other information' but should read the 'other information' to determine whether it is materially inconsistent with the financial statements

(e) Higgins Ltd is required to but does not wish to prepare and issue a statement of cash flows as part of its financial report. In these circumstances, the audit report should include:

A an unqualified opinion with a statement of cash flows prepared by the auditor included as part of the audit report

B an adverse opinion stating that the financial report, taken as whole, is not fairly presented because of the omission of the required statement

C a disclaimer of opinion with a separate explanatory paragraph stating why the company declined to present the required statement

D an unqualified opinion with an 'emphasis of matter' section explaining that the company declined to present the required statement

(f) An auditor concludes that there is a material inconsistency in the 'other information' in an annual report to shareholders containing an audited financial report. If the auditor concludes that the financial report does not require revision, and the client refuses to revise or eliminate the material inconsistency in the 'other information', the auditor may do the following:

A revise the audit report to include an 'emphasis of matter' section describing the material inconsistency

B disclaim an opinion on the financial report after explaining the material inconsistency in a separate explanatory paragraph

C issue an 'except for' opinion after discussing the matter with the client's board of directors

D consider the matter closed since the other information is not in the audited financial report

(g) Which of the following will *not* result in modification of the audit report due to a scope limitation?

A Restrictions imposed by the client

B Inability to obtain sufficient appropriate evidence

C Inadequacy in the accounting records

D Reliance placed on the report of another auditor

(h) When restrictions are imposed by the client which significantly limit the scope of the audit, the auditor generally should issue which of the following opinions?

A 'except for'

B unqualified

C adverse

D disclaimer

(i) An auditor is confronted with an exception considered sufficiently material so as to warrant some deviation from the standard unqualified audit report. If the exception relates to a departure from generally accepted accounting principles, the auditor must decide between expressing:

    A an adverse opinion and a disclaimer of opinion

    B an adverse opinion and an 'except for' opinion

    C an 'except for' opinion and an unqualified opinion

    D a disclaimer of opinion and an 'except for' opinion

(j) A solicitor limits a response concerning a litigation claim because the solicitor is unable to determine the likelihood of an unfavourable outcome. Which type of opinion should the auditor express if the litigation is adequately disclosed and the range of potential loss is material in relation to the client's financial report considered as a whole?

    A adverse

    B 'except for'

    C unqualified

    D unqualified with an 'emphasis of matter'

13.3 Select the best response to the following independent situations.

(a) Under which of the following set of circumstances might an auditor disclaim an opinion?

    A There has been a material change between periods in the method of the application of accounting principles.

    B There are significant uncertainties affecting the financial report.

    C The financial report contains a departure from generally accepted accounting principles, the effect of which is material.

    D The principal auditor decides to make reference to the report of another auditor who disclaimed an opinion on the audit of a subsidiary. The subsidiary contributed 6% of operating revenue and profit but very little in other aspects.

(b) An auditor concludes that there is substantial doubt about an entity's ability to continue as a going concern for a reasonable period of time. If the entity's disclosures concerning this matter are adequate, the audit report may include:

	Disclaimer of opinion	'Except for' opinion
A	No	Yes
B	Yes	No
C	Yes	Yes
D	No	No

(c) An auditor should disclose the substantive reasons for expressing an adverse opinion in an explanatory paragraph:

    A following the opinion paragraph

    B within the notes to the financial report

    C preceding the scope paragraph

    D preceding the opinion paragraph

(d) An auditor was unable to obtain an audited financial report or other evidence supporting an entity's investment in a foreign subsidiary considered material to the financial report. Between which of the following opinions should the entity's auditor choose?

    A 'Except for' and adverse

    B 'Except for' and disclaimer

C   Adverse and unqualified with an 'emphasis of matter'

   D   Disclaimer and unqualified with an 'emphasis of matter'

(e)   The auditor of Asia Business Opportunities Ltd determines that the accounting treatment for a certain material item is not in conformity with accounting standards, although the departure is prominently disclosed in a footnote to the financial report. The auditor should:

   A   qualify the opinion (except for) because of the departure from accounting standards

   B   express an unqualified opinion because the departure from accounting standards was disclosed

   C   express an unqualified opinion but insert a separate paragraph emphasising the matter by reference to the footnote

   D   express an inability to form an opinion

(f)   An 'emphasis of matter' is:

   A   information relating to the entity which requires emphasis in an audit opinion paragraph but which is dealt with elsewhere in the financial report

   B   information relating to the entity which requires a separate emphasis paragraph but which is dealt with elsewhere in the financial report

   C   additional information in an audit opinion paragraph

   D   information relating to the entity which requires emphasis in an audit opinion paragraph as it is not dealt with elsewhere in the financial report

(g)   On 2 July 20X0 Pretty Paint Ltd received a notice from its primary suppliers that all wholesale prices would be increased by 10%, to be effective immediately. On the basis of the notice Pretty Paint Ltd revalued its 30 June 20X0 inventory to reflect the higher costs. The details of the adjustment were disclosed in the notes to the financial report. The inventory adjustment was material. The auditor of the 30 June 20X0 financial report would:

   A   express an inability to form an opinion

   B   express an unqualified opinion with an 'emphasis of matter' of disclosure

   C   express an unqualified opinion

   D   express an 'except for' opinion

(h)   Before providing an opinion on the financial report for the year ended 30 June 20X0, the auditor must consider:

   A   all matters relating to the client up to the date of the directors' report

   B   all matters relating to the client up to a point in time determined by the auditor as reasonable

   C   all matters relating to the client up to 30 June 20X0

   D   all matters relating to the client up to the date of the audit report

(i)   Due to time and staff restrictions the auditor was unable to attend the inventory stocktake at a remote branch location for Outback Ltd. The inventory at this site accounted for 30% of total assets. Alternative procedures were applied satisfactorily. The auditor should issue:

   A   an unqualified opinion with an 'emphasis of matter'

   B   an unqualified opinion

   C   an 'except for' opinion

   D   an inability to form an opinion

(j)   An audit report on comparative financial reports should be dated as of the date of the:

   A   latest financial report being reported on

   B   last subsequent event disclosed in the financial report

   C   issuance of the report

   D   completion of the auditor's recent evidence collection procedures

Concept of 'true and fair'

13.4 What is the underlying difference between the reporting terminology of 'true and fair' and 'present fairly in accordance with Australian accounting standards'?

Structure and qualitative characteristics of audit report

13.5 Compare and contrast the advantages of standard form audit reports with a less structured form of reporting by the auditor.

Different types of opinions

13.6 Identify the three basic types of audit reports other than an unqualified opinion and explain the circumstances in which each might be issued.

13.7 What are the five circumstances in which an unqualified opinion with an 'emphasis of matter' can be issued? How commonly are these circumstances observed to give rise to such an opinion in practice?

Types of audit and standards reports

13.8 What are the basic reasons why the auditor may be unable to express an unqualified opinion?

Auditor's responsibility with 'other information' and reports

13.9 What are the auditor's responsibilities for 'other information' in an annual report?

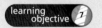

Communications other than audit report

13.10 What reporting communications could be expected between the auditor and the audit committee? To what extent would an auditor communicate with the board of directors when there is an effective audit committee?

13.11 What are the auditor's responsibilities for reporting business risk factors and material weaknesses in internal control?

Future changes to standard form audit report

13.12 Identify the major differences between the ISA 700 standard form audit report due to come into effect in 2006 and the standard form audit report currently used in Australia. Do you believe these changes will be successful in achieving their objectives?

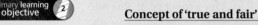

DISCUSSION PROBLEMS AND CASE STUDIES

Concept of 'true and fair'

13.13 Basic You are the audit manager of a new client. Management of the new client has prepared its accounts in accordance with generally accepted accounting principles but you believe that the overall view presented by this financial report is not true and fair.

Required
Outline in a report to your partner the approach that should be taken in these circumstances.

Structure and qualitative characteristics of audit report

13.14 Moderate An audit report prepared for Buddy Plumbing the year ended 30 June 2003 is as follows:

Audit Report

We have audited the financial report of Buddy Plumbing for the year ended 30 June 2003 as set out on pages 35 to 55. We have conducted an independent audit of the financial report in order to express an opinion on it.

Our audit has been conducted to provide high assurance whether the financial report is free of material misstatement. Our procedures included examination, on a test basis, of evidence supporting the amounts and other disclosures in the financial report, and the evaluation of accounting policies and significant accounting estimates. These procedures have been undertaken to form an opinion whether, in all material respects, the financial report is presented fairly in accordance with Accounting Standards and other mandatory professional reporting requirements in Australia so as to present a view which is consistent with our understanding of Buddy Plumbing's financial position, the results of its operations# and its cash flows.

The audit opinion expressed in this report has been formed on the above basis.

The financial report presents fairly in accordance with applicable Accounting Standards and other mandatory professional reporting requirements in Australia the financial position of Buddy Plumbing as at 30 June 2003 and the results of its operations and its cash flows for the year then ended.

Date	Firm
Address	Partner

Required

Identify five deficiencies in the audit report presented above.

13.15 Moderate You have now completed the 30 June 20X0 audit of John's Jobs (JJ), a sole trader providing home maintenance services in regional New South Wales. JJ required an audit report and general purpose financial report in order to satisfy the requirements of a bank lending agreement. During the audit you noted a number of control weaknesses typical of small businesses, some of which had the potential for fraud. You discussed the problems with the manager of JJ, John Smith, who agreed to rectify many of the problems. Fortunately, substantive testing of JJ's records provided sufficient appropriate evidence to support the balances and disclosures contained in the financial report. You are now preparing the audit report for JJ and are unsure whether mention should be made of the control weaknesses identified.

Required

(a) Should mention be made of the control weaknesses identified at JJ in the audit report? Provide reasons for your answer.

(b) Draft an appropriate audit report for JJ. Note the audit report is a report on a general purpose financial report requested by the owner of JJ and not a report prepared specifically at the request of the bank.

Different types of opinions

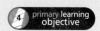

13.16 Basic Lerna Corporation (whose financial year will end on 30 June 20X0) informs you on 18 June 20X0 that it has a serious shortage of working capital because of heavy operating losses incurred since 1 April 20X0. Application has been made to a bank for a loan, and the bank's loan officer has requested a financial report.

Indicate the type of report you would render under each of the following independent sets of circumstances. Give the reasons for your decision.

(a) Lerna asks that you save time by auditing the financial report prepared by Lerna's chief accountant as of 31 March 20X0. The scope of your audit would not be limited by Lerna in any way.

(b) Lerna asks that you conduct an audit as of 15 June 20X0. The scope of your audit would not be limited by Lerna in any way.

(c) Lerna asks that you conduct an audit as of 15 June 20X0 and render a report by 16 July. To save time and reduce the cost of the audit, it is requested that your audit not include confirmation of accounts receivable or observation of the taking of inventory.

(d) Lerna asks that you prepare a financial report as of 15 June 20X0 from the books and records of the company without audit. The report is to be submitted on plain paper without your name being associated in any way with it. The reason Lerna asks you to prepare the report is that you are familiar with the proper form for financial reports.

Source: AICPA adapted

13.17 Moderate You have been the auditor of Resources Ltd and of its subsidiary companies for several years. Early in the current financial year, Resources Ltd purchased a 70% interest in each of three companies. The management of each of these newly acquired companies requested that they continue to be audited by their existing auditors. The management of Resources Ltd agreed. At the end of the year, you ask the auditors of the subsidiaries to complete a questionnaire providing details of the audit work carried out, and also requesting that you be able to review the audit working papers for these companies. Two of the three replies indicate that the subsidiary company auditors will not meet these requests, as they believe there is no need for you to make such inquiries.

(a) What reasons could there be for the managements of the newly acquired companies wishing to retain their existing auditors?

(b) What matters would you bring to the attention of the auditors of the new subsidiaries to persuade them to meet your requests concerning the questionnaire and the review of working papers?

(c) What difference would it make if you believed the figures for one of the two subsidiaries was immaterial to the group financial report?

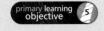

Reasons giving rise to qualifications

13.18 Basic During the audit of F Pty Ltd (F), a number of issues have arisen concerning the application of accounting standards. Many of these issues are small and may not result in material misstatement, but when considered together the audit manager of F believes the financial report will be materially misstated unless some adjustments are made. All of the issues have been discussed with the financial controller, but the audit manager is unsure whether the financial controller has discussed the issues with the board of directors. The audit manager is reluctant to issue a qualified audit opinion, and is unsure how to resolve a number of the issues as this is the first engagement in which he has been assigned full responsibility; he has asked the audit partner for guidance.

Required

Assume you are the audit partner. Advise the audit manager as to strategies he could use to assist in resolving the issues he has identified.

13.19 Moderate XYZ Limited is a listed public company that manufactures highly sophisticated navigation equipment for submarines, large ships and aircraft. The company has a 31 March 20X0 year-end and the statutory financial report is due to be signed one week after the directors' meeting on 5 June 20X0.

During the course of the audit you become aware that the government has reviewed its budget in an effort to reduce the growing deficit and as a result defence expenditure has suffered major cuts.

One of the major projects to be scrapped as a result of these cuts is the planned 20X0 upgrading of the navigation equipment for the current navy fleet. You are aware that the company's 20X0 budget and projection of sales included a major subcontract to the Defence Department and RAN for this project.

The company has been experiencing cash flow difficulties and has recently applied for a significant increase to a borrowing facility that is already fully drawn. Management is adamant that the company will continue to be viable, and if necessary can resort to cutbacks in its future capital expenditure program and can seek additional off-balance-sheet financing and/or reschedule existing debt arrangements.

Required

(a) Outline the reporting options open to an auditor when going concern issues arise. Discuss the relevant circumstances under which each of these reporting options becomes appropriate.

(b) Discuss the steps that you need to take to form a conclusion as to whether the going concern basis is appropriate in relation to XYZ. Your discussion should cover details of audit evidence to be obtained, where appropriate.

(c) Discuss the potential audit report options in relation to XYZ.

Source: This question was adapted from the Professional Year Programme of The Institute of Chartered Accountants—1996 Advanced Audit Module.

13.20 Moderate The 31 December 20X0 audit of the G Ltd group, a manufacturer and retailer of plumbing fittings, is now complete. As in the past the group have accounted for inventory using a last-in-first-out (LIFO) basis. In previous years the effect has not been material given the group usage of a 'just in time' inventory management system. In the current year, however, the company has a large stockpile of inventory at year-end due to an unexpected cancellation of a major order en route to its destination. In order to cut freight costs, the group temporarily stored the goods in Indonesia, hoping for an order from another South-East Asian customer.

Unfortunately you were not told of this problem until after balance date and did not conduct a stocktake of the inventory. You have also been told some of the inventory has since been shipped to a number of different customers to fill outstanding orders. The available audit procedures have been unable to validate the existence of this inventory. The relevant inventory is currently recorded at $2 000 000. Audit procedures have indicated that had inventory been accounted for on a first-in-first-out (FIFO) basis it would have been recorded at $3 000 000. Materiality for the audit has been set at $1 000 000.

Required

Indicate the most appropriate audit opinion for the G Ltd group. Provide reasons for your decision.

13.21 Moderate You are currently involved in the 30 June 20X0 audit of Eastern Europe Imports Pty Ltd (E), a company incorporated in Australia to import products from Eastern European countries. A large portion (67%) of E's assets, including warehouses and inventory, is located in Yugoslavia. In previous years an accountant in Yugoslavia has inspected foreign warehouses and inventory on your behalf. Unfortunately, due to the current economic and social problems resulting from the NATO campaign, you have been unable to obtain assistance from accountants in Eastern Europe. In addition, you are unsure whether the company's assets exist. Imports for the company were frozen from the commencement of the NATO campaign and E has been unable to establish regular contact with its Yugoslavian office. The total assets of E are $3 000 000, of which $2 000 000 is located in Yugoslavia; net assets are $1 000 000.

During discussions with the CEO of E you have been assured the company will be able to continue as a going concern as the company is currently obtaining new suppliers, and the company's existing customers and creditors have expressed a desire to continue trading with E. Your audit procedures, however, have not revealed any firm commitments from suppliers, customers, creditors or financiers. Faced with this information, you believe that either the financial statements should be prepared on a liquidation basis or significant disclosures of E's financial position should be made. The directors of E have agreed to make disclosures indicating the extent of the problems they are facing. After reviewing the information you are satisfied the disclosures are adequate.

Required

Indicate the most appropriate audit opinion for E. Provide reasons for your decision.

13.22 Moderate Consider each of the following independent and material situations. In each case, assume the client is a reporting entity and that a general purpose financial report has been prepared and audited:

(i) Flintstone Pty Ltd (Flintstone) is a large proprietary company that your firm has audited for the last five years. The directors refuse to include a cash flow statement in the financial report, stating that it is far too time consuming to obtain the necessary information, and that they do not believe a cash flow statement is necessary for a true and fair view.

(ii) Part of Granite Limited's operations are in South America. Recent changes of government have made it impossible for you to verify the key accounts of inventory, fixed assets and cash and the related income statement balances.

(iii) The management of Shale Limited has refused to disclose a few director-related transactions on the grounds of commercial confidentiality. The Financial Controller reminds you that no other errors have been found in the financial report and states that the transactions are immaterial and therefore irrelevant to the users of the financial report.

(iv) Pumice Limited's annual report includes a detailed graph showing sales and profit figures for the last 10 years. However, there are some inconsistencies between the graph and the figures in the audited financial report. Management does not want to change the graph because it would involve increased printing costs.

Required

Determine the type of audit report to be issued in each of the above situations, and give reasons for your answer.

Source: This question was adapted from the Professional Year Programme of The Institute of Chartered Accountants in Australia—1995 Accounting 2 Module.

13.23 Moderate For each of the following independent situations, indicate the reason for and the type of audit report that you would issue. Assume that each item is significant.

(a) HiTech Computers is suing your client, Super Software, for royalties over patent infringement. Super Software's outside legal counsel assures you that HiTech's case is without merit.

(b) In previous years, your client, Merc Ltd, has consolidated its Zimbabwean subsidiary. Because of restrictions on repatriation of earnings placed on all foreign-owned corporations in Zimbabwe, Merc Ltd has decided to account for the subsidiary on the equity basis in the current year.

(c) Upon review of the recent history of the lives of their specialised automobiles, Gas Leak Technology changed the service lives for depreciation purposes on their autos from five years to three years. This change resulted in a material amount of additional depreciation expense.

(d) During the 2003 audit of Brannon Bakery Equipment, you found that a material amount of inventory had been excluded from the inventory amount shown in the 2002 financial statements. After discussing this problem with management, you become convinced that it was an unintentional oversight.

(e) Jay Johnson, CA, holds 10% of the stock in Keonig Construction Company. The board of directors of Koenig asks Johnson to conduct their audit. Johnson completes the audit and determines that the financial statements present fairly in accordance with generally accepted accounting principles.

(f) Pavlova Bank and Loan's financial condition has been deteriorating for the last five years. Most of their problems result from loans made to real estate developers in the Sydney area. Your review of the loan portfolio indicates that there should be a major increase in the loan-loss reserve. Based on your calculations, the proposed write-down of the loans will put Pavlova into violation of the state's capital requirements.

13.24 Complex Consider each of the following independent and material circumstances:

(a) You are in the final stages of the audit of XY Ltd for the year ended 31 March 20X1. During the review of the final copy of XY's annual report prior to signing the audit report you identify the following information in the non-statutory Chairman's Report:

> *The large increase in the profits of the company is attributable to increased market share based on our successful marketing strategy, expansion of operations and product range. The increased profitability is expected to continue with the signing of a $5 million contract on 31 March, for the purchase of a new plant facility in Brisbane.*

Information in the statutory financial report is as follows:
Net profit before tax: 2000, $3 500 000; 2001, $2 400 000
Capital commitment for plant and equipment of $150 000 as at 31 March 20X1.

(b) ABC Ltd is a holding company with a number of wholly owned subsidiaries. One of these subsidiaries is a self-sustaining foreign subsidiary, FX Ltd, with manufacturing and distribution facilities throughout South-East Asia. The group financial report of ABC and its subsidiaries consists of the consolidated financial report of ABC and its subsidiaries, excluding the financial report of FX, which is attached separately. The consolidated financial report includes a note stating that the directors believe that it is misleading to consolidate FX as its operations are very diverse from the rest of the group and carried out under substantially different conditions. The note includes details of intercompany balances and transactions.

(c) XYZ Pty Ltd is a small proprietary company involved in importing and exporting equipment. XYZ produces special purpose financial reports. These financial reports do not comply with the following accounting standards:
    AASB 1012 Foreign Currency Translation
    AASB 1017 Related Party Disclosure
    AASB 1020 Tax Effect Accounting
    AASB 1026 Statement of Cash Flows

The notes to XYZ's financial report clearly specify that the financial report has been prepared as a special purpose financial report and that compliance with the above accounting standards is not deemed necessary by directors in order for the financial report to show a true and fair view.

The audit partner agrees that ABC is a non-reporting entity, but he also believes that compliance with AASB 1012 and AASB 1020 is required to show a true and fair view. The financial effect of the departure from the accounting standards is material.

(d) The audit of the statutory records of KL Ltd, a reporting entity, revealed the following problems:
- failure to update members' register for changes in shareholders
- failure to obtain written consent from directors to act
- directors' minutes not prepared in respect of current year
- failure to hold the AGM in respect of the previous financial year.

The company made no comment in respect of the failure to keep properly updated statutory registers or to hold the AGM.

(e) JJ Ltd, a reporting entity, uses the LIFO basis in respect of valuation of closing inventories, which is one of the most significant balance sheet accounts. The difference between FIFO and LIFO valuation has a material effect on the closing inventory balance.

Required

Discuss in relation to each of these circumstances the audit issues to be considered and their likely impact on the audit opinion to be issued. Justify your answer with references to the Australian auditing standards and the *Corporations Act 2001*, as appropriate.

Source: This question was adapted from the Professional Year Programme of The Institute of Chartered Accountants in Australia—1996 Advanced Audit Module.

13.25 Complex The following are independent situations relating to the year ended 30 June 20X0. Assume all entities are reporting entities and that all situations are material.

(i) You are finalising the audit of GF Limited (GF), a large proprietary company which exports grains and cereals to most regions of the world. Subsequent to balance date, regional tensions in the Middle East saw orders plummet by over 40 per cent. The fall in profit placed GF in breach of the conditions of its bank loan. Not wishing to risk losing its money, the bank placed a freeze on GF's bank account and other assets, rendering GF unable to trade. These circumstances are adequately disclosed in a note to the accounts.

(ii) The audit of CE Limited was extremely difficult this year as the client did not keep appropriate books and records. The accounting department was chronically understaffed, so transactions were not promptly entered and reconciliations not performed. A temporary accountant was employed to help sort out the mess but was unable even to reconcile the bank account at year-end. You are not satisfied that all transactions that occurred during the year are reflected in the financial report.

(iii) You have received the draft annual report from AB Club Limited. On reading the 'Year in Review' you note the club chairman states that revenues increased by 150%. On checking the accuracy of this information you note that revenues have actually fallen by 10%. The club refuses to change anything in the annual report for fear of missing printing deadlines.

(iv) The depreciation rates used by BPL Pty Limited (BPL) have not changed for the past three years. Given recent technological changes in the industry in which BPL operates, you are convinced the useful lives of BPL's assets need to be adjusted downwards. The directors refuse to make this change despite the fact that you have explained this places them in breach of AASB 1021 'Depreciation'.

(v) The original financial report of RI Limited was released to shareholders in early August. A few days later management informed you that, prior to the time of completion, they received notice of legal action being taken against them. Unfortunately, this fact was omitted from the financial report and was not detected by your audit procedures. Despite the costs involved, management insists on recalling the original financial report, including appropriate disclosures of the legal action and issuing a new financial report.

(vi) RS Limited has extensive overseas operations and accordingly has many overseas bank accounts. You were unable to obtain bank confirmations for two of these accounts, and the latest bank statements available to you are over 3 months old.

Required

(a) For each situation (i) to (vi) above, describe the additional audit procedures you would perform prior to issuing your audit report.

(b) Assuming the matters remain unresolved, discuss the audit opinion you intend to issue for each of the above entities for the year ended 30 June 20X0.

Source: This question was adapted from the Professional Year Programme of The Institute of Chartered Accountants in Australia—1999 Accounting 2 Module.

13.26 Complex You are an audit manager for REW Chartered Accountants and are currently finalising your 30 June 20X0 audits.

Company M

Company M is an Australian subsidiary of Company N, a company located and registered in Somalia. Since the beginning of the civil war in Somalia, the Somalian offices have been closed and will be relocated to the USA. Due to the relocation, you have been unable to verify intercompany account balances with Company N. You have not been able to verify the completeness of the intercompany credit account balance of $2 574 000 by alternative auditing procedures. The company made a profit of $152 780 during the year. Company M has other (Australian) assets of $30 000 000 and other (Australian) liabilities of $10 000 000.

Company S

The audit of Company S was extremely difficult as the client did not maintain appropriate books and records during the year. Although the statutory registers were maintained, the accounting records were not updated for the first 9 months of the year as the company was without an accountant during this period. An accountant was employed in April 20X0 and she tried to reconstruct records from the details of receipts and payments available. The accountant has been unable to reconcile the bank account and you are not satisfied that all transactions which occurred during the year are reflected in the financial report. The operating loss recorded by Company S in the current year is $22 190.

Company A

Company A is a listed company with three subsidiaries, Company B, Company C and Company D. Another firm (RST Chartered Accountants) act as the auditors of Company D and have qualified their audit report on the basis that continued financial support from Company A is required for Company D to continue as a going concern.

In auditing Company A and the economic entity, you are satisfied that the going concern basis of preparing the financial report is appropriate. In addition, you are satisfied that the carrying value in Company A's financial report of the investment in Company D of $200 is not stated above its recoverable amount. The company and the economic entity made profits for the year.

Company X

Company X, a property developer, holds freehold property purchased for development and resale which is classified as inventories. This property, as disclosed in the financial report at Note 10, has been valued at cost, which is $5 000 000. In your audit you found that in the current market the net realisable value of the property is $3 500 000. Although material, the client does not consider that the value of the property should be written down as future development will result in the property being worth more than the current book value. The write-down would have no tax effect. The financial report audited, including the Directors' Declaration, spans pages 5 to 38. The company made a profit for the year. Company X has other assets of $25 000 000 and liabilities of $7 000 000.

Required

(a) Discuss the type of audit opinion that you intend to issue for each of the above companies for the year ending 30 June 20X0.

(b) Draft the audit report for Company X for the year ending 30 June 20X0.

Source: This question was adapted from the Professional Year Programme of The Institute of Chartered Accountants in Australia—1995 Accounting 2 Module.

Auditor's responsibility with regard to other information and reports

13.27 Moderate The audit of the financial report of Neot Limited has now been completed and the client is preparing the annual report. You have been given a first draft of the annual report for review and have reviewed the financial report and are satisfied they are consistent with the audited information. You are now reviewing the preliminary information contained in the audit report. Within the chairperson's address you note the following statement:

> *The directors are of the opinion that the economic conditions currently facing Neot Limited will soon abate, and closure of additional manufacturing facilities will be unnecessary.*

You are quite surprised, as your discussions with management have indicated that closure of two further factories is imminent. In addition, the financial report includes a large provision for redundancies together with disclosure of the nature of the item. You approach the CEO with your concerns. The CEO replies: 'Don't worry, it's only a first draft, and anyway the auditors don't report on that.'

Required
(a) Discuss the auditor's responsibility for information accompanying a financial report.
(b) Assuming the chairperson's address is not amended, identify the most appropriate course of action for the auditor.

Communications other than audit report

13.28 Moderate You are the audit manager assigned to the 31 December 20X0 audit of a new client, Q Pty Ltd (Q), an importer of pharmaceutical products. In order to hedge its foreign currency transactions, Q entered into a number of forward rate agreements in March 20X0. Prior to this time Q had had little exposure to derivative instruments, but a series of bad experiences resulting from the Asian economic crisis has convinced the company that a hedging strategy was necessary. During planning for the audit of Q, the company's hedging arrangements were identified as inherently risky and a thorough review of controls was requested.

The audit of Q has now been completed. A number of small errors were noted in accounting for hedge transactions, but there did not appear to be any material errors and as such no adjustments were made. A review of the audit file suggests that the errors noted were a result of inexperience and poor controls in the area. While all of the errors were brought to the attention of the treasurer, who is responsible for the company's hedging strategy, no further action has been taken to date.

Required
Identify and discuss any further action which the audit manager and/or partner should take in response to the errors and control weaknesses identified.

CONTINUOUS CASE STUDIES

13.29 Complex This is a continuation of question 12.29. It may, however, be completed independently.

Mitchell Pty Ltd (Mitchell) is a small manufacturer of chemical products. During the review of subsequent events at Mitchell the auditors noted a large chemical spill which occurred at the company's Victorian shipping point. To date, the client has been unable to estimate the total financial effect on the company or determine whether Mitchell will be considered the responsible party. Previous experiences with chemical spills suggest the financial effect can be significant and it may take some months to determine the total impact, given the possibility of fines and action by other parties occupying the harbour.

Discussions with the directors of Mitchell regarding disclosure of the spill in the financial report have been productive; however, the directors have refused to specifically indicate that the spill may have the potential to bankrupt the company. The disclosure which has been agreed to date is as follows:

Note 20.

During the financial year a vessel carrying chemicals used to supply Mitchell Pty Ltd was involved in a spillage incident in southeastern Victoria while unloading chemicals. The directors are unable to estimate the financial effect of this spillage on the company at this time; however, we are of the opinion it is likely to be significant.

While the audit partner is satisfied this adequately discloses the nature of the incident, she believes the disclosure is not sufficient to alert users to the possibility of liquidation and has suggested the following amendment:

In the event the financial effect of the spillage exceeds the net assets of the company the company will be unable to continue as a going concern.

The directors have refused to make this amendment and the audit partner is considering qualifying the audit opinion.

Required

Do you believe a qualification is necessary? If so, indicate the type of opinion which should be included in the audit report of Mitchell Pty Ltd. Provide reasons for your decision.

13.30 Complex This is a continuation of question 12.30. It may, however, be completed independently of that question.

The audit of HomeChef Pty Ltd is now complete and the audit report is being prepared. As part of completion procedures the audit manager has performed a final review of the file to ensure all matters arising during the audit are noted for communication to the client. During this review the manager has noted the following matters:

(i)   A number of control deficiencies were noted in the purchases and payments area. Internal audit is aware of these deficiencies and has recommended appropriate procedures.

(ii) There were a number of immaterial errors made in recording fixed asset additions and disposals. This appears to be a result of inexperience and a lack of supervision of a new fixed asset clerk.

(iii) The company's stocktaking procedures were not followed in all stores. This appeared to be a result of a lack of understanding of procedures on the part of store managers and inappropriate planning and correspondence from head office.

In each of the above cases the audit team was able to obtain sufficient appropriate audit evidence to ensure the financial report was not materially misstated.

Required

For each of the above matters, indicate the most appropriate means of communication with the client. Where you believe communication should be documented, draft one or two paragraphs appropriate for inclusion in your correspondence with management.

OTHER ASSURANCE SERVICES

PART five

Part 5 covers assurance services other than those directly associated with a financial report audit. Chapter 14 outlines assurance services that are currently being undertaken or are being considered by the assurance services profession. Chapter 15 deals with internal audit, including the comparison of the new internal audit approach (incorporating more of a business risk approach) with more traditional internal audit approaches. Chapter 16 covers assurance services in the public sector, explaining the concepts of account-ability, audit mandates and the phases of a performance audit. Chapter 17 covers some advanced topics in assurance services, auditing in an e-commerce environment, environmental and sustainability assurance, and forensic auditing. It is important to understand how these 'other assurance services' fit into the assurance services framework, outlined in Chapter 1.

CHAPTER 14

OTHER ASSURANCE SERVICES

LEARNING OBJECTIVES

After studying this chapter you should be able to:

1 appreciate the umbrella standards under which assurance services are offered, and how specific standards relate to different types of assurance services;

2 appreciate the procedures undertaken in a limited assurance (review) engagement and the level of assurance offered;

3 understand the assurance provider's obligations in undertaking agreed-upon procedures engagements and appreciate the level of assurance offered by these engagements;

4 understand the assurance provider's obligations in relation to assurance services on financial information other than general purpose reports, including special purpose reports and summarised financial reports;

5 understand assurance services required by specific legislation or regulations, including prospective financial information and reports on the effectiveness of internal controls; and

6 appreciate the types of assurance services that the assurance profession is currently developing or may be developing in the near future, including WebTrust™, SysTrust™, ElderCare, business performance measurement and risk assessment.

Chapter outline

The recent initiatives by the profession, and more recently by the International Auditing and Assurance Standards Board (IAASB), have recognised the increased demand for assurance and the ability of the assurance profession to leverage their skills and reputation over a wide range of subject matter. The subject matter, other than historical financial information, on which assurance could be provided includes such things as prospective financial information, key performance indicators, internal controls and corporate governance practices.

This chapter will first examine audits and reviews on historical financial information and then outline other assurance services in areas that the AUASB and the IAASB have issued guidance. These relate to specific subject matter such as special purpose financial reports, summarised financial reports, due diligence engagements, reports on prospective financial information and reports on internal control. The chapter will then evaluate current or prospective assurance services that are being developed by the profession, including WebTrust™ and SysTrust™. Other assurance services believed by the authors to have potential, including reports on information provided to boards of directors, will also be presented.

Relevant guidance

Australian		International	
AUS 106	Explanatory Framework for Standards on Audit and Audit-Related Services	—	
AUS 108	Framework for Assurance Engagements (Revised 2004)	—	International Framework for Assurance Engagements (Revised 2004)
AUS 110	Assurance Engagements other than Audits or Reviews of Historical Financial Information (Issued 2004)	ISAE 3000	Assurance Engagements Other than Audits or Reviews of Financial Information (Issued 2004)
AUS 522	Audit Evidence Implications of Externally Managed Assets of Superannuation, Provident or Similar Funds	—	
AUS 802	The Audit Report on Financial Information Other than a General Purpose Financial Report	ISA 800	The Independant Auditor's Report on Special Purpose Audit Engagements
AUS 804	The Audit of Prospective Financial Information	ISRE 3400	The Examination of Prospective Financial Information (previously ISA 810)
AUS 810	Special Purpose Reports on the Effectiveness of Control Procedures	—	
AUS 902	Review of Financial Reports	ISRE 2400	Engagements to Review Financial Statements (previously ISA 910)
AUS 904	Engagements to Perform Agreed-Upon Procedures	ISRS 4400	Engagements to Perform Agreed-Upon Procedures Regarding Financial Information (previously ISA 920)
AGS 1006	Expression of an Opinion on Internal Control	—	
AGS 1008	Audit Implications of Prudential Reporting Requirements for Authorised Deposit-Taking Institutions (ADIs)	—	
AGS 1016	Audit and Review Reports on Half-Year Financial Reports of Disclosing Entities Under the *Corporations Act 2001*	—	
AGS 1042	Reporting on Control Procedures at Outsourcing Entities	—	

THE CURRENT FRAMEWORK FOR ASSURANCE SERVICES

In Chapter 1 the assurance services framework was described. Within the framework an assurance engagement is defined as 'an engagement in which a practitioner expresses a conclusion designed to enhance the degree of confidence of the intended users other than the responsible party about the outcome of the evaluation or measurement of a subject matter against criteria'. This definition recognises that the aim of these assurance engagements is to increase the credibility of information provided on a very broad, potentially limitless, range of **subject matter**.

The framework under which **assurance services** are being developed recognises that, for any particular type of assurance service, assurance can be provided at two levels, **reasonable assurance** and **limited assurance**. For the assurance service on a financial report, reasonable assurance involves undertaking an audit, which provides high assurance. This has been the focus of attention in the previous three parts (Chapters 5–13) of this text. A limited assurance engagement for a financial report is known as a review engagement, and this provides moderate assurance.

Figure 1.2 on page 11 of Chapter 1 outlined how auditing pronouncements impact on assurance services. This figure is repeated in part here in the interests of providing a structure to guide the reader through the assurance services covered in this chapter.

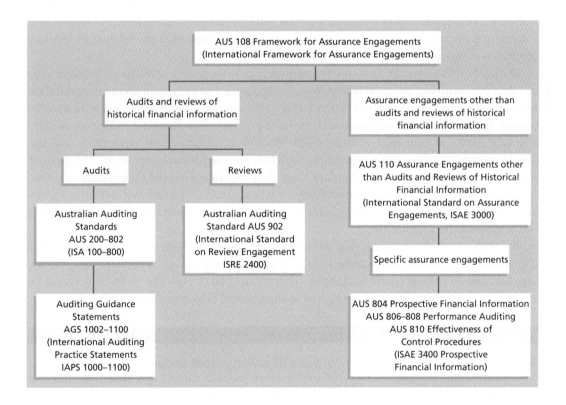

AUS 108 'Framework for Assurance Engagements' provides an overall framework for all assurance services irrespective of the subject matter. Within this framework fall the standards and these standards are divided between audits and reviews of historical financial information and assurance engagements other than audits and reviews of historical financial information. Until now the focus has been on the audit of a complete set of historical financial information, which is known in Australia as the audit of the financial report. This is the core service on which the audit profession has developed its reputation as providers of quality assurance services. As is evident from the figure just reproduced, the standards for audits of financial reports are contained in the

AUS 200–802 (ISA 100–800) series, which has been the focus of attention of Parts 2 to 4 (Chapters 5 to 13) of the text. In reality, AUS 802 (ISA 800) does not relate to the audit of a financial report but to assurance engagements on historical financial information comprising other than a complete set, as discussed in what follows.

Where a limited assurance engagement is undertaken on a complete set of historical financial information, this is called a review engagement and it is governed by the review standard AUS 902 (ISRE 2400). These types of limited assurance engagements will be further discussed under learning objective 2 of this chapter.

As outlined under AUS 106 (no international equivalent) and discussed in Chapter 1, audit and audit-related services are associated with three types of engagements: **audit**, **review** and **agreed-upon procedures**. Where the auditor undertakes specific procedures and does not have the ability to vary the audit procedures to be undertaken as agreed upon with the client, this is known as an agreed-upon procedures engagement and is discussed in greater detail under learning objective 3.

Where the assurance engagement is on other than a complete set of historical financial information, standards and guidance governing such an engagement are contained in AUS 802 (ISA 800). Such engagements would include the audit of special purpose financial reports and summarised financial reports. These types of assurance engagements are covered in learning objective 4 of this chapter.

Moving further across the figure on the previous page to the branch of assurance engagements on other than historical financial information, it is apparent that there is an overarching standard to cover such engagements (AUS 110/ISAE 3000). There are also standards in place for specific subject matter assurance engagements, including prospective financial information (AUS 804/ISAE 3400), performance auditing (AUS 806/808, no international equivalent) and the effectiveness of internal control procedures (AUS 810, no international equivalent). The types of assurance engagements on subject matter other than historical financial information that have been undertaken or evaluated by the profession will be outlined under learning objectives 5 and 6 of this chapter (performance auditing, which relates primarily to assurance in the public sector, will be discussed in Chapter 16).

It is evident that the standards that are the most developed are those that relate to the audit of a financial report. While these standards do not necessarily apply to all assurance engagements, they are seen to provide useful guidance to practitioners (AUS 110/ISAE 3000). This would be especially true in areas such as planning, risk evaluation and evidence collection.

Quick review

1. Assurance can be provided on all types of subject matter, including historical financial information, prospective financial information, internal control and environmental and sustainability issues. The framework for assurance engagements relates to all assurance engagements.

2. For any particular subject matter, assurance can be provided at two levels, reasonable assurance and limited assurance. Where the assurance engagement is on historical financial information, the reasonable assurance engagement is called an audit and the limited assurance engagement is called a review.

3. Auditing standards (AUS 200–802/ISA 100–800) provide standards for audits and reviews where the subject matter is historical financial information. For other assurance services, standards are either contained in the general assurance standard (ISA 110/ISAE 3000) or in assurance standards specific to a subject matter. The auditing standards also provide guidance to a practitioner undertaking assurance services on any subject matter.

LIMITED ASSURANCE (REVIEW) ENGAGEMENTS

Many people are confused by the distinction between the assurance provider undertaking a reasonable assurance engagement (where the subject matter is historical financial information this is called an audit) and the assurance provider undertaking a limited assurance engagement (where the subject matter is historical financial information this is called a review). The major distinguishing feature is the level of assurance provided by such engagements. With an audit the assurance provider provides **positive assurance** that the financial reports (or other subject matter) are presented fairly in accordance with an appropriate framework. Thus the assurance provider actively seeks sufficient appropriate evidence to support the assertions contained in the subject matter. The assurance provider then communicates that, in their opinion, the subject matter is fairly presented in accordance with the appropriate framework. The audit thus provides the user with a high level of assurance.

There are other times when assurance from an independent expert is needed, but a limited (moderate) rather than a reasonable (high) level of assurance is deemed appropriate, given the subject matter and the cost. This moderate level of assurance is provided by a **review engagement**. The assurance provider undertakes a limited set of evidence-gathering procedures to provide moderate assurance that the subject matter is free of material misstatement. The report provides **negative assurance** that nothing has come to the attention of the assurance provider that causes them to believe that the subject matter is not presented in accordance with the appropriate framework.

An example of the difference between an audit and a review is the requirement for attesting to half-yearly financial reports for disclosing entities. Section 302B of the *Corporations Act 2001* states that, instead of an audit engagement, a review engagement may be undertaken. The report must state whether any matter has come up that causes the assurance provider to believe that the half-yearly general purpose financial report was not prepared so as to give a true and fair view. If such a matter has arisen, the matter must be described and the assurance provider's reasons for that belief clearly stated.

Discussions with audit partners of each of the Big Four auditing firms indicate that in practice the assurances provided on half-yearly financial reports are mostly reviews rather than audits. This view is supported by Baines et al. (2000) who found that for a sample of 252 of the top 1000 companies, 234 had reviews and only 18 had audits of their half-yearly financial reports. Thus it appears that, on the basis of cost–benefit analysis, management of reporting entities believes that for half-yearly financial reports sufficient assurance is gained through the review process.

Reviews of financial reports

To aid the review of financial reports, the standard-setting bodies have released AUS 902 (ISRE 2400), with further guidance on half-yearly engagements in Australia being contained in AGS 1016 'Audit and Review Reports on Half-Year Financial Reports of Disclosing Entities under the *Corporations Act 2001*)'. This standard provides guidance on the assurance provider's professional responsibilities in a review engagement and outlines the major differences in approach between a review and an audit. These include ensuring that the entity understands the difference between a review and an audit. The engagement letter outlines that a review is being undertaken, and explicitly states that it is not an audit. A standard engagement letter is presented as Appendix 1 to AUS 902 (ISRE 2400).

In planning the review, knowledge of the entity is vital. The assurance provider who does the end-of-year audit has this knowledge and generally is the person appointed to undertake the review. Where a review engagement is undertaken by an assurance provider who does not have the knowledge acquired from recent previous engagements, there is a need to ensure sufficient understanding is acquired.

While the same materiality considerations apply for a review and an audit, the procedures that are applied to a review are a subset of those applied to an audit. The procedures commonly undertaken for reviews are outlined in AUS 902.27 (ISRE 2400.20), and consist primarily of inquiry of management and analytical procedures. They include:

- inquiries concerning the entity's accounting principles and practices;
- inquiries concerning the entity's procedures for recording, classifying and summarising transactions, accumulating information for disclosure in the financial report and preparing the financial report;
- inquiries concerning all material assertions in the financial report;
- analytical procedures, including comparison of the financial report with reports for previous periods and with budgets, and a study of predictable relationships of the elements of the financial report (e.g. gross margin);
- inquiries concerning actions taken at meetings of shareholders, the board of directors and committees of the board of directors and other meetings that may affect the financial report;
- reading the financial report to consider, on the basis of information coming to the assurance provider's attention, whether it appears to conform with the chosen basis of accounting;
- inquiries of persons having responsibility for financial and accounting matters concerning the recording of transactions and the preparation of the financial report regarding whether they know of any matters affecting the financial report; and
- obtaining written representations from management when considered appropriate.

An illustrative list of procedures which are often used for the review of a financial report is contained in AUS 902, Appendix 2 (ISRE 2400).

Reporting procedures

The reporting considerations are important because the review report must clearly show that it provides a lower level of assurance than an audit. Its format resembles that of an audit report on a general purpose financial report. Exhibit 14.1 contains the Commonwealth Bank of Australia's half-yearly (31 December 2003) unqualified review report.

In comparing the review report with an unqualified audit report, the following points are noted:

1   The title distinguishes it as a review report.
2   Under the review approach in the 'Scope' section the reader is informed:
    - that a review has been undertaken;
    - that the purpose of the review is for the assurance provider to state whether anything has come to their attention that would indicate that the reviewed matter is not presented fairly in accordance with the applicable framework;
    - that a review is limited primarily to inquiries of company personnel and analytical procedures; and
    - that these procedures do not provide all the evidence that would be provided in an audit, and thus the level of assurance is less than that given in an audit.
        The scope section concludes that an audit has not been performed, and thus an audit opinion is not expressed.
3   Under the heading 'Statement' it can be seen that the form of assurance offered is negative rather than positive (the words 'not become aware of any matter' are used).

EXHIBIT 14.1

Independent Review Report

To the Members of Commonwealth Bank of Australia

Scope

The financial report and directors' responsibility

The financial report comprises the statement of financial position, statement of financial performance, statement of cash flows, accompanying notes to the financial statements, and the directors' declaration for the consolidated entity, for the period ended 31 December 2003. The consolidated entity comprises both the Commonwealth Bank of Australia and the entities it controlled during that period.

The directors of the company are responsible for preparing a financial report that gives a true and fair view of the financial position and performance of the consolidated entity, and that complies with Accounting Standard AASB 1029 'Interim Financial Reporting', in accordance with the *Corporations Act 2001*. This includes responsibility for the maintenance of adequate accounting records and internal controls that are designed to prevent and detect fraud and error, and for the accounting policies and accounting estimates inherent in the financial report.

Review approach

We conducted an independent review of the financial report in order to make a statement about it to the members of the company, and in order for the company to lodge the financial report with the Australian Stock Exchange and the Australian Securities and Investments Commission.

Our review was conducted in accordance with Australian Auditing Standards applicable to review engagements in order to state whether, on the basis of the procedures described, anything has come to our attention that would indicate that the financial report is not presented fairly in accordance with the *Corporations Act 2001*, Accounting Standard AASB 1029 'Interim Financial Reporting' and other mandatory professional reporting requirements in Australia, so as to present a view which is consistent with our understanding of the consolidated entity's financial position, and of their performance as represented by the results of their operations and cash flows.

A review is limited primarily to inquiries of company personnel and analytical procedures applied to the financial data. These procedures do not provide all the evidence that would be required in an audit, thus the level of assurance is less than given in an audit. We have not performed an audit and, accordingly, we do not express an audit opinion.

Independence

We are independent of the company, and have met the independence requirements of Australian professional ethical pronouncements and the *Corporations Act 2001*. In addition to our review of the financial report, we were engaged to undertake other non-audit services. The provision of these services has not impaired our independence.

Statement

Based on our review, which is not an audit, we have not become aware of any matter that makes us believe that the financial report of the Commonwealth Bank of Australia is not in accordance with:

(a) the *Corporations Act 2001*, including:

    (i) giving a true and fair view of the financial position of the consolidated entity at 31 December 2003 and of its performance for the period ended on that date; and

Continued . . .

The Commonwealth Bank of Australia's half-yearly review report

Source: Commonwealth Bank of Australia, Profit Announcement for the Half-Year Ended 31 December 2003.

If there is a limitation in the scope of the engagement that in the assurance provider's opinion prevents the provision of moderate assurance, the assurance provider includes in the report a section headed 'Qualification' describing the limitation, and under the heading 'Qualified Review Statement' a statement of negative assurance that is qualified as to the effects of such adjustments had the limitation not existed.

The 'Qualified Review Statement' can take the form of either:

- an 'except for' statement of negative assurance; or
- an adverse statement that the financial report is not presented fairly in accordance with the identified financial report framework.

The adverse statement is used when the effect of the matter is of such a magnitude, or is so pervasive or fundamental, that the financial report taken as a whole is, in the assurance provider's opinion, misleading or of little use to the addressee of the review report.

The assurance provider can also include an 'emphasis of matter' section, suitably headed and placed immediately after the statement section, for the same circumstances as those described in Chapter 13.

Limited assurance engagements for other areas

It is possible to undertake limited assurance engagements for areas other than financial reports. For example, in reporting on internal controls the assurance provider can either provide a reasonable level of assurance and express the opinion in a positive form, or undertake less extensive procedures, provide limited assurance and express the opinion in a negative form, as outlined in AUS 810 'Special Purpose Reports on the Effectiveness of Control Procedures'. In fact, for most of the assurance services outlined in section 6 of this chapter, it is possible to provide either reasonable or limited assurance.

Quick review

1. Review engagements differ from audits with regard to the level of assurance they provide. Reviews provide a limited level of assurance, while audits provide a reasonable level of assurance.
2. It is important to set out in the engagement letter that a review, rather than an audit, is being undertaken and to state the level of assurance that can be gained from such an engagement.
3. The primary means of gathering evidence for review engagements are inquiries of management and analytical procedures.

4 In the review report it is important to communicate to the user the limited level of assurance that can be gained from this type of engagement, compared with the level of assurance provided by an audit.

AGREED-UPON PROCEDURES

3 learning objective

An assurance provider can undertake procedures of an audit nature that are agreed upon with the entity being audited and the user of the report. Such procedures are potentially broad-ranging and can be in any area where the client and user perceive it to be beneficial to have a report on a matter using audit-related skills. Some examples include specific tests to provide confidence that the accounts payable listing is complete and accurate, or that the Academy Awards votes are confidentially maintained and properly counted. Guidance on such testing is provided in AUS 904 (ISRS 4400). It is outlined in the standards that for such engagements no opinion is expressed and consequently no assurance is provided. Rather, the assurance provider just reports their procedures and findings, from which the user can draw their own conclusions and derive their own level of assurance.

In accepting such engagements it is essential that there is a clear understanding as to which procedures are agreed and the terms of the engagement. These matters are detailed in the engagement letter, which clearly sets out:

- the nature of the engagement, including the fact that the procedures performed do not constitute an audit or a review and that accordingly no assurance is expressed;
- a list of the procedures to be performed as agreed between the parties;
- the anticipated form of the report of factual findings; and
- a statement that the distribution of the report will be restricted to the specified parties who have agreed to the procedures to be performed.

Reporting considerations

The reports that are issued for agreed-upon procedures engagements are different from those issued for audits or reviews. As outlined above, they are factual, thus providing no opinion, and they are not aimed at providing a level of assurance. As outlined earlier, it is up to the user to draw conclusions from the information provided and to determine the level of assurance to attach to this information. An agreed-upon procedures report of factual findings in connection with accounts payable is contained in Exhibit 14.2 (overleaf).

The report clearly communicates to the user that agreed-upon procedures were undertaken, not an audit or review. Thus it:

- identifies the specific financial or nonfinancial information to which the agreed-upon procedures have been applied;
- states that the procedures performed were those agreed with the recipient;
- states that the engagement was performed in accordance with auditing standards applicable to such engagements;
- identifies the purpose for which the agreed-upon procedures were performed;
- states that the recipient is responsible for determining the adequacy or otherwise of the procedures agreed to be performed by the assurance provider;
- lists the specific procedures performed, or refers to another document, such as an engagement letter, which contains these details;
- describes the assurance provider's factual findings, including sufficient details of errors and exceptions found;

EXHIBIT

14.2

Example of a
report of factual
findings in
connection with
accounts payable

REPORT OF FACTUAL FINDINGS

To addressee

Scope

We have performed the procedures agreed with you as detailed in the written instructions of [date] and described below with respect to the accounts payable of XYZ as of [date], set forth in the attached schedules [describe and reference the schedules (not shown in this Illustration)]. Our engagement was undertaken in accordance with Australian Auditing Standards applicable to agreed-upon procedures engagements. The responsibility for determining the adequacy or otherwise of the procedures agreed to be performed is that of [those who engaged the auditor]. The procedures were performed solely to assist you in evaluating the validity of the accounts payable and are summarised as follows:

1. We obtained and checked the addition of the trial balance of accounts payable as at [date] prepared by XYZ, and we compared the total to the balance in the related general ledger account.
2. We compared the attached schedule [not shown in this example] provided by XYZ of major suppliers and the amounts owing at [date] to the related names and amounts in the trial balance.
3. We obtained suppliers' statements or requested suppliers to confirm the balances owing at [date].

Because the above procedures do not constitute either an audit in accordance with Australian Auditing Standards or a review in accordance with Australian Auditing Standards applicable to review engagements, we do not express any assurance on the accounts payable as of [date].

Had we performed additional procedures or had we performed an audit in accordance with Australian Auditing Standards or a review in accordance with Australian Auditing Standards applicable to review engagements, other matters might have come to our attention that would have been reported to you.

Findings

We report as follows:

(a) With respect to 1 above we found the addition to be correct and the total amount to be in agreement.
(b) With respect to 2 above we found the amounts compared to be in agreement.
(c) With respect to 3 above we found there were suppliers' statements for all such suppliers.

Our report is solely for the purpose set forth in the first paragraph of this report and for your information, and is not to be used for any other purpose or distributed to any other party. This report relates only to the accounts and items specified above and does not extend to any financial report of XYZ, taken as a whole.

Date   Firm

Address   Partner

Source: Adapted from AUS 904, Appendix 2. Reproduced with the permission of The Institute of Chartered Accountants in Australia and CPA Australia.

- states that the procedures performed do not constitute either an audit or a review and that, as such, no assurance is expressed;
- states that, had the assurance provider performed additional procedures, an audit or review, other matters might have come to their attention that would have been reported;
- states that the report is restricted to those parties that have agreed to the procedures to be performed; and
- states (when applicable) that the report relates only to the elements, accounts, items or financial and nonfinancial information specified and does not extend to the entity's financial report taken as a whole.

Quick review

1 Procedures of an assurance nature that are agreed between the assurance provider, the entity being audited and the user of the report are called agreed-upon procedures. These types of engagements are currently very common in practice.

2 In accepting such engagements it is essential that there is clear understanding as to which procedures are agreed and the terms of the engagement.

3 The report on agreed-upon procedures is a factual report of findings and thus does not provide an opinion or a level of assurance. Rather, information is provided from which the user can draw conclusions and derive their own assurance as a result of the assurance provider's procedures.

ASSURANCE SERVICES ON FINANCIAL INFORMATION OTHER THAN GENERAL PURPOSE REPORTS

There are a number of assurance services that have developed in practice which relate to financial information other than general purpose financial reports. These are:

- special purpose financial reports;
- components of a financial report, rather than the full financial report;
- summarised financial reports; and
- due diligence engagements.

AUS 802 offers guidance on the first three of these engagements. (The equivalent international standard, ISA 800, offers guidance only on special purpose financial reports.) Although this standard is directed towards audit engagements, the assurance provider can be engaged to perform a review or agreed-upon procedures regarding such financial information (AUS 802.04).

As its title states, AUS 802 (ISA 800) does not apply when the financial information upon which the assurance provider is to report is a general purpose financial report. Thus the first consideration is whether the financial information is intended to meet the needs of users who cannot command reports which are prepared specifically for their needs. If it is intended to meet the needs of this group, then it is a general purpose financial report; otherwise it is a special purpose report. In practice it is usually easy to determine whether the financial information is directed towards a specific sub-population or whether it is intended for a wide range of users. This consideration needs to be documented in the assurance provider's working papers.

Special purpose financial reports

Special purpose reports are reports prepared in accordance with a reporting framework other than accounting standards and UIG Abstracts. Other reporting frameworks include the cash basis of accounting, the modified cash basis of accounting or a framework set out in specific legislation. The assurance provider considers whether the financial reporting framework adopted is likely to mislead users of the financial report.

In these engagements, evidence is collected by procedures that are similar to those discussed in the earlier chapters of this book, but there is much more emphasis on agreeing on the engagement details and reporting the findings. These steps assume greater importance because this type of engagement is less standardised than the audit of general purpose financial reports. There are two reasons for this variability: the various reporting frameworks used to prepare the financial reports, and the various levels of assurance that can be offered by the assurance provider. Before undertaking the engagement, the assurance provider ensures that there is a clear understanding with the client as to the exact terms of the engagement, including the form and content of the report to be issued. This understanding is documented in the engagement letter.

The major differences in reporting obligations are contained in the scope section. An example of a scope section of an audit report (high level assurance) for a non-reporting entity using the cash basis of accounting is contained in Exhibit 14.3. This scope section:

■ identifies the financial report being audited and indicates that it is a special purpose financial report;

EXHIBIT

14.3

Scope section of a special purpose report for an entity using a modified accrual basis of accounting

Scope

We have audited the attached special purpose financial report, comprising the Balance Sheet, Income Statement, Cash Flow Statement and Notes to the financial statements of XYZ for the year ended 30 June 2005. XYZ's Committee of Management is responsible for the financial report and have determined that the accounting policies used are consistent with the financial reporting requirements of XYZ's constitution and are appropriate to meet the needs of the members. We have conducted an independent audit of the financial report in order to express an opinion on it to the members of XYZ. No opinion is expressed as to whether the accounting policies used are appropriate to the needs of members.

The financial report has been prepared for distribution to members for the purpose of fulfilling the Committee of Management's financial reporting requirements under XYZ's constitution. We disclaim any assumption of responsibility for any reliance on this report or on the financial report to which it relates to any person other than the members, or for any purpose other than that for which it was prepared.

Our audit has been conducted in accordance with Australian Auditing Standards. Our procedures included examination, on a test basis, of evidence supporting the amounts and other disclosures in the financial report and the evaluation of significant accounting estimates. These procedures have been undertaken to form an opinion whether, in all material respects, the financial report is presented fairly in accordance with the accounting policies described in Note 1 to the financial statements.

The audit opinion expressed in this report has been formed on the above basis.

Source: Adapted from AUS 802, Appendix 1, Example 1. Reproduced with the permission of The Institute of Chartered Accountants in Australia and CPA Australia.

- identifies the party responsible for the financial report;
- when appropriate, identifies the party responsible for determining that the reporting framework used is appropriate to the needs of the addressee of the audit report;
- when appropriate, states that the assurance provider expresses no opinion as to whether that framework is appropriate to the needs of the addressee of the audit report;
- identifies the purpose for which the financial report has been prepared, and any express restriction on the distribution of the audit report or on those entitled to rely on it; and
- states that the audit has been conducted in accordance with Australian auditing standards.

If a review or agreed-upon procedure is undertaken, it must be clearly stated that such an engagement has been undertaken and that the engagement has been undertaken in accordance with the Australian auditing standards applicable to such engagements, and the level of assurance offered by the engagement must be clearly stated.

'Other' financial information

The assurance provider may be requested to undertake 'procedures' on financial information which does not constitute a financial report, that is, does not contain an income statement and a balance sheet. Such procedures are classified as engagements concerning 'other' financial information. This type of engagement may be undertaken as a separate engagement or in conjunction with the audit of an entity's financial report. Examples of 'other' financial information are:

- components of a financial report, such as specified accounts (e.g. a schedule of accounts receivable, inventory or provision for doubtful debts);
- a schedule of externally managed assets and income of a superannuation fund; or
- a schedule of profit participation or employee bonus calculation.

Guidance for such engagements is contained in AUS 802.22–.27. When determining whether to accept such an engagement, the assurance provider considers whether the scope is sufficient to allow adequate consideration of the interrelationships that exist in a financial report. For example, in examining the completeness of inventory, it may be necessary to consider the internal controls on purchases and sales. Thus it is often more appropriate for the engagement to be performed on the basis of agreed-upon procedures.

Also, materiality must be considered. For example, by examining a particular account balance rather than the financial report as a whole, a smaller materiality base will be determined. Consequently, the examination will be more extensive on this account balance than if the same information were examined as part of a financial report audit.

In reporting on such information, the assurance provider clearly explains the extent and nature of procedures applied and the basis on which the report has been prepared. The degree of assurance that can be gained from the reporting, in accordance with the reporting requirements for audit, review and agreed-upon procedures, is also clearly outlined.

Summarised financial reports

Sometimes an entity prepares a **summarised financial report** (a summary of a general purpose report) in order to highlight the entity's performance and financial position. In Australia, the majority of listed entities elect, under section 314 of the *Corporations Act 2001*, to send to their shareholders a concise report, which includes a concise financial report, instead of an annual report, which includes the financial report for the year. Guidance for the assurance provider undertaking an engagement concerning such summaries is contained in AUS 802.28–.33 (ISA 800.21–.25). The assurance provider gives an opinion as to whether the information in the summary is consistent with the full financial report, and in accordance with applicable accounting standards. Unless the financial report as a whole has been audited, the assurance provider is not in a position to report on any summarised form. The assurance provider ensures that the summary is clearly described, for example with a title such as 'Summarised Financial Report—extracted from the annual statutory financial report'. In reviewing these reports in practice the standard terminology used in the opinion paragraph is one line: 'In our opinion, the concise financial report of XYZ complies with Accounting Standard AASB 1039 "Concise Financial Reports".' If the audit report on concise financial reports is signed on a date after the audit report on the unabridged financial report, then the assurance provider will have to consider the effect of any intervening after-balance-date events.

Due diligence engagements

The term '**due diligence**' is not defined anywhere in the *Corporations Act 2001*. It originated in the USA, where due diligence is used as a defence for claims that there was an untrue statement of a material fact in, or omission of a material fact from, a prospectus.

US court cases have laid down three principles: that the extent of investigation required is that of a prudent person in the particular circumstances; that the investigation must find those facts which a reasonable person would consider important; and that information provided by the issuer should be independently verified if reasonably possible.

Due diligence appears in the Australian *Trade Practices Act* as a defence against actions for breaches of the Act. To establish the due diligence defence, the assurance provider would need to prove that they took reasonable precautions and exercised due diligence specifically to avoid the contravention. If no precautions were taken, they would need to prove that there were none that could reasonably be taken.

Given the broad scope of what must be included in a prospectus and the need to identify the risks in collecting and disseminating the required information, assurance providers are increasingly being asked to carry out due diligence engagements. The aim is to ensure that statements made in a prospectus are independently verified as having the required degree of accuracy and that there is evidence that directors have taken adequate precautions.

Due diligence engagements also often involve the acquisition of a business or major shareholding. In the context of an acquisition, the objective of the due diligence engagement is to identify issues concerned with valuing the business and determining the purchase price together with contract terms and warranties. Prospective purchasers are increasingly adopting the view that it is better to discover issues concerning the value of the business before the deal is completed. A key issue in the HIH Insurance collapse was the lack of a due diligence review when it made its acquisition of its subsidiary FAI Insurance.

An assurance provider who is involved in a due diligence engagement determines whether the engagement is for an audit, a review or agreed-upon procedures, depending on the specific requirements and circumstances of the mandate. Where an engagement requires a combination of these services to be provided, each component is undertaken and reported upon in accordance with the professional guidance that applies to it. The assurance provider needs to ensure that there is a clear understanding of the nature of the service to be provided and that the engagement is consistent with any legal requirements.

1 General purpose financial reports are intended for a wide range of users, whereas special purpose reports are intended for use by a specific sub-population.

2 Assurance on special purpose engagement reports, components of financial information, summarised financial reports and due diligence engagements differ from assurance on general purpose financial reports in that the level of assurance required can, in many instances, be agreed as part of the terms of the engagement.

3 It is important when undertaking these specific engagements to have a proper understanding of the terms of the engagements, and these must be clearly spelt out in the engagement letter.

4 Reports for these specific engagements must clearly communicate the procedures that have been undertaken and the level of assurance that is provided by the engagement.

ASSURANCE SERVICES REQUIRED BY SPECIFIC LEGISLATION OR REGULATIONS

learning objective 5

Guidance is provided by the AUASB on a number of assurance services required to be provided under specific legislation or regulations. These can be fairly innovative in design and may lead to more general assurance services in these areas. Examples include:

■ assurance on future-oriented (prospective) financial information;

■ assurance on internal controls, with the specific example of reporting obligations under superannuation legislation; and

■ assurance on statistical or highlight-style information, with the specific example of the reporting between authorised deposit-taking institutions (ADIs) and the Australian Prudential Regulation Authority (APRA).

In a recent IFAC report (2002), which conducted a worldwide survey of assurance service providers on areas in which assurance is currently being provided, it was found that assurance on prospective financial information was the most common area outside financial reports on which assurance was being provided. The second most common was assurance on internal control systems, followed by assurance on environmental issues. Assurance on key performance measures was identified as a small but growing assurance service. The services identified in the IFAC report are summarised in Exhibit 14.4.

Type of service	Number of respondents offering service	Percentage of respondents offering service
Prospective financial information	36	64.29%
Internal control system	32	57.14%
Environmental performance	27	48.21%
Individual components of financial statements	19	33.93%
IT systems	12	21.43%
Performance measures	6	10.71%
Corporate governance	6	10.71%
Risk management system	5	8.92%
WebTrust™	3	5.36%

EXHIBIT 14.4

Assurance services other than financial report assurance currently being provided

Source: International Federation of Accountants (IFAC), 2002 'The Determination and Communication of Levels of Assurance Other Than High', http://www.ifac.org

Auditing pronouncements have been prepared to guide the assurance provider who is employed to undertake these engagements. Although these engagements can potentially be in the form of an audit, a review or agreed-upon procedures, their form may be prescribed under specific legislation or regulations. The next section reviews the types of engagements that can be undertaken and the reporting obligations that arise.

While on some occasions these engagements arise as a result of a statutory or regulatory requirement, on many occasions they will be voluntarily requested by the client in order to meet a specific demand or provide additional information. For example, although special purpose assurance reports on internal controls are required by statute in some circumstances, it may be that there is sufficient demand for an assurance service on a general report to shareholders on the internal controls. This will occur in situations where the benefits of an assurance report on internal controls are perceived to outweigh the costs. The relevant auditing pronouncements specifically help the auditor meet their statutory and regulatory requirements, but the basic principles and essential procedures contained in these pronouncements apply equally to all engagements.

Prospective financial information

Guidance for engagements providing assurance on reports on **prospective financial information**, such as those containing financial forecasts or projections, is contained in AUS 804 (ISA 810).

- **Forecasts** are prospective financial information prepared on the basis of *assumptions of future events expected to take place*. Thus they reflect the *expected* future financial position, financial performance and cash flows for the entity.
- **Projections** are prospective financial information prepared on the basis of *assumptions that are not necessarily expected to take place*. Thus they sometimes present a hypothetical course of action for evaluation, in response to the question 'What could happen if ... ?'

Thus a forecast is an entity's best estimate of what will actually occur. A projection is the entity's estimate of what will occur if a specified hypothetical course of action is taken.

Procedures

Before accepting the engagement the assurance provider considers a number of factors. These include the intended use of the information; the nature of the assumptions; the reputation of management responsible for the assumptions and its past record in the preparation of prospective financial information; and the assurance provider's experience both with the entity and its industry, and with such engagements. The assurance provider should refuse an engagement when the assumptions are clearly unrealistic or when the prospective information seems inappropriate for its intended use. The assurance provider also considers the period covered by the prospective information, ensuring that it does not extend beyond the time for which management has a reasonable basis for the assumptions.

The assurance provider assesses the source and reliability of the evidence supporting management's best estimates. They also consider whether the assumptions are realistic according to the entity's and management's record. The assurance provider pays attention to those areas that are particularly sensitive to variation (have a greater degree of uncertainty) and have a material effect on forecasts or projections. Although there is no need to obtain evidence supporting hypothetical assumptions, the assurance provider must be satisfied that the assumptions are realistic and consistent with the purpose of the forecast or projection. The assurance provider then undertakes recomputations and reviews internal consistency so as to be satisfied that the prospective financial information is properly prepared from management's assumptions.

Reporting

These engagements differ from the normal examinations of historical financial information. They relate to events and actions that have not yet occurred and may not occur. While evidence generated through the procedures may be available to support the underlying assumptions, the evidence itself is generally future oriented and therefore speculative in nature. The assurance provider is therefore usually not in a position to express an opinion as to whether the results shown in the prospective financial information will be achieved.

Further, given the nature of the evidence available in assessing the reasonableness of assumptions (e.g. projected sales growth) on which prospective financial information is based, the auditor may find it difficult to obtain the necessary evidence to provide them with a level of satisfaction where they can issue a positive opinion that the assumptions are free of material misstatement. Consequently it is suggested that the auditor would ordinarily provide a moderate level of assurance on best-estimate assumptions and not express an opinion on hypothetical assumptions. They would also add a sentence in the audit opinion paragraph stating that the actual results are likely to be different from the forecasts since anticipated events frequently do not occur as expected and the variation may be material. This additional disclosure would further state that no opinion would be expressed on whether the forecast would be achieved. If you wish to refer to an example of this, please refer to Example 1 in the Appendix to AUS 804.

Reporting on the effectiveness of internal controls

There is little doubt that from 2005 assurance on **reports on the effectiveness of internal controls** is going to be a growth assurance service and will receive much attention from the assurance profession. The increased attention given to reporting on the effectiveness of internal controls and providing assurance on these reports is worldwide. The increased emphasis given to internal controls is demonstrated by the recent changes in the USA as a result of the introduction of the *Sarbanes–Oxley Act* of 2002. In the future, annual reports for major listed companies in the USA are to:

1 *state the responsibility of management for establishing and maintaining an adequate internal control structure and procedures for financial reporting; and*
2 *contain an assessment of the effectiveness of the internal control structure and procedures...*

There is a report required by management as to the effectiveness of internal controls over financial reporting and the auditor, in an annual report, is required to provide an assurance report that management's assessment of the effectiveness is appropriate. This assurance engagement is part of the financial report audit, which therefore not only provides assurance that the financial statements are fairly presented, but that the internal controls are effective. The assurance report issued in these engagements covers both of these areas.

With reference to the assurance framework discussed in Chapter 1, one of the difficulties in undertaking such engagements is arriving at appropriate criteria for evaluating the effectiveness of internal control. In the USA, much effort has been applied to developing such criteria, culminating in an update of the COSO Framework, which is regarded as providing suitable criteria for such assurance engagements.

In Australia, providing assurance on internal control is not generally part of the audit, although over 50 Australian companies have to provide assurance on internal control effectiveness because they are dual-listed on US stock exchanges. There are also some specific regulatory requirements to report on internal controls. Guidance on this issue is provided in AUS 810 'Special Purpose Reports on the Effectiveness of Control Procedures'. It should be noted that the standard applies only to special purpose reports, where the report is intended for a sub-population such as the board of directors or a group to which the assurance provider may be required to report under legislation. At the moment there is no guidance in Australia on assurance engagements regarding general purpose reports on internal control, such as reporting to shareholders on the internal controls for an organisation as is required in the USA.

Reports on internal control in Australia are therefore normally separate engagements, or require the undertaking of additional procedures, to audits of a financial report undertaken with the objective of expressing an opinion on that financial report. AGS 1006 'Expression of an Opinion on Internal Control' states that financial report audits are not designed to, and therefore do not, provide sufficient appropriate evidence on which to base an opinion on the adequacy of the internal controls. AUS 402/ISA 315 recognises that the objective of the audit work done on internal controls in financial report audits is to enable the assurance provider to make a preliminary assessment of control risk in determining the nature, timing and extent of audit procedures. If control risk is assessed as high—either because the entity's internal control is not effective or because it is more efficient to collect substantive evidence—no testing of the structure will normally be undertaken. Thus reports undertaken for the specific purpose of reporting on internal controls must be distinguished from references to internal control in the management letter (see Chapter 13), which are restricted to those matters which come to the assurance provider's attention during the course of an audit on the financial reports.

Identification of suitable criteria is a key aspect for engagement acceptance. As outlined above, for the purposes of the internal control reports in the USA the revised COSO Framework is generally regarded as providing suitable criteria. Suitable criteria may be developed by the management or the assurance provider, regulatory bodies or other recognised authorities, or by users for a specific purpose. An assurance provider who believes that the identified criteria are unsuitable has two possible courses of action:

1 Where the mandate is contractual, the assurance provider agrees on suitable criteria with management before continuing with the engagement. If agreement cannot be reached the assurance provider should terminate the engagement; or
2 Where the engagement is compulsory under a legislative mandate, the assurance provider issues a qualified report.

Assessing both design and operating effectiveness

In undertaking an assurance report on internal control effectiveness the assurance provider considers both the design of the internal controls and their operating effectiveness. The design is effective when internal controls reduce to an acceptably low level the risks that threaten the achievement of the objectives of internal control. The nature and extent of audit procedures for design effectiveness is the same for both an audit and a review.

The assurance provider also considers operating effectiveness: how the controls were applied and the period of time during which they were applied. These tests ordinarily include procedures such as inquiry of appropriate personnel, inspection of relevant documentation and observation of the entity's operations.

An audit requires detailed procedures, including reperformance or other examination and follow-up of the application of significant internal controls, to substantiate the effective operation of controls. A review requires inspection of the system in operation for deviations from the specified design. This may include limited testing of the operation of the internal controls for a small number of transactions or events (for example, walk-through testing).

While the IAASB is yet to issue guidance for assurance of reports on internal control it is one of two assurance services (the other being environmental and sustainability assurance, discussed in Chapter 17) on its work program for 2005–2006.

Two examples where reports on internal control are required by regulations and the AUASB has issued guidance are for superannuation funds and authorised deposit-taking institutions (ADIs). The requirements for superannuation funds are outlined next, while the requirements for ADIs form part of a broader assurance report and are covered in the following section, Reporting on statistical or highlight information.

Superannuation funds

Reports on internal controls for systems maintained by fund managers in the superannuation industry are demanded both by the regulator of the superannuation industry and by the assurance providers of superannuation funds whose assets are externally managed by the fund managers. Specific reports on internal control for superannuation funds are required to ensure compliance with the *Superannuation Industry (Supervision) Act 1993*.

Where the assets of a superannuation fund are externally managed there is also a demand for the external manager's assurance provider to attest to the adequacy of internal control. An attestation that the manager's internal controls, as they relate to the fund's assets and transactions, are properly designed and operating effectively could be used by the fund's assurance providers to lower the assessment of control risk and thus reduce the required level of substantive testing. This is similar to the demand for reports on internal control, which may be requested from service entities. The requirements for sufficiency and appropriateness of audit evidence for externally managed funds are contained in AUS 522.

Reporting on statistical or highlight information

One of the prospective growth areas for assurance services is the reporting on statistical or highlight style information, such as key performance information. We are currently seeing this style of information being frequently disclosed, either as part of or separate to a financial report, and it is possible that specific assurance may be sought on the reliability of this information.

The Australian Prudential Regulation Authority (APRA) has requested that banks and other authorised deposit-taking institutions (ADIs) ask their assurance providers to express an opinion and report to the ADI's audit committees and APRA on certain matters. There are effectively four opinions being requested from the external auditor:

1 Whether prudential standards set for the ADI are being met, such as whether sufficient liquidity is being maintained and impaired assets are being recognised.
2 Whether certain statistical and financial information, specified by APRA on its web site <http://www.apra.gov.au>, is reliable. This is interesting because it is an example of an increasing trend to get auditors to provide assurance on this type of statistical information (such as key performance indicators) before it is distributed or relied upon by regulators.
3 Whether the relevant statutory and regulatory requirements have been met.

4   Whether there are any matters which, in the auditor's opinion, have the potential to prejudice materially the interests of depositors. Guidance in these areas is contained in AGS 1008 'Audit Implications of Prudential Reporting Requirements for Authorised Deposit-Taking Institutions (ADIs)'.

Quick review

1 In engagements covering forecasts and projections, the assurance provider examines the appropriateness of assumptions about the future. The procedures involve gathering sufficient appropriate evidence concerning whether management's assumptions are realistic and consistent with the purpose of the forecast or projection, and whether the prospective financial information is properly prepared from management's assumptions.

2 For reports issued on engagements covering prospective financial information, the assurance is usually on two levels—negative assurance is provided on the assumptions and no assurance is provided on whether the forecast will be achieved.

3 Reports on internal controls by assurance providers are becoming more common in practice as greater emphasis is being given to corporate governance. As a result of recent legislative changes in the USA assurance on a report on internal control effectiveness has become part of a financial report audit in that country.

4 In Australia, reports on internal control are not normally undertaken as part of the audit of financial reports; thus specific procedures or a specific engagement are required. Suitable criteria should be agreed before the assurance provider accepts the engagement. The procedures should assess both design and operating effectiveness.

5 Assurance on nonfinancial key performance indicators is still not very common but is recognised as a potential future assurance service.

ASSURANCE SERVICES BEING PROMOTED BY THE ASSURANCE PROFESSION

The last decade has seen the assurance profession worldwide devote considerable resources to the development of a broad range of assurance services. There was recognition that auditing of financial reports was a low-growth mature industry, and that the assurance provider would have to expand the subject matter on which they provide assurance and the levels at which they provide assurance. Initiatives such as the AICPA's Special Committee on Assurance Services (SCAS), the Canadian Institute of Chartered Accountants' (CICA) Assurance Services Development Board (ASDB), and the Joint Assurance Services Task Force of the Australian profession have contributed to the development of assurance services by the assurance profession.

A great deal of the impetus in the development of a number of new assurance services and their associated assurance levels originally came from the American Institute of Certified Public Accountants' Special Committee on Assurance Services (SCAS), who have recently been working closely with the CICA. SCAS maintains, updates and distributes their material and knowledge on a web site. For a current view, we refer you to the SCAS web site at <http://www.aicpa.org/assurance/index.htm>.

SCAS was originally set up to:

1   develop a new concept of assurance services that will be the foundation for new opportunities;
2   identify and define some specific services for practitioners to deliver; and
3   create ongoing mechanisms to develop opportunities in the future.

To realise its charges, the Assurance Services Executive Committee (ASEC) of SCAS undertook some information-gathering exercises. Research was conducted to understand the changing environment; to identify decision-makers' information and assurance needs; to identify the threats that practitioners face in the new assurance services market; and to identify the competencies that the profession needs in order to provide the new services.

The definition of assurance services that was finally settled on by ASEC covered the relevance of information as well as its reliability:

> *Assurance services are independent professional services that improve the quality of information, or its context, for decision makers.*

ASEC attempted to distinguish this concept of assurance services from attest services (audit and audit related services). The goal of assurance services is 'information improvement, not the issuance of a report on it (though there might be a report). ... It is the service itself that provides value, not the report, although a report is one way to demonstrate value. ... Assurance services help people make better decisions by improving information available to them'. (Refer to 'Assurance Services—Definition and Interpretive Commentary', <http://www.aicpa.org/assurance/index.htm>.) This can be compared to the view of the IAASB as contained in AUS 108/International Framework for Assurance Engagements (outlined in Chapter 1 and earlier in this chapter). This states in its discussion of assurance services that an assurance engagement is an engagement 'in which a practitioner expresses a conclusion designed to enhance the degree of confidence of the intended users other than the responsible party about the outcome of the evaluation or measurement of a subject matter against criteria'. Clearly the IAASB has a concept of assurance that is narrower and more audit-related than the SCAS concept.

The survey also suggested possible assurance service areas that practitioners could venture into. Specifically, the committee originally developed six main product areas (these have recently been reduced to five), which were expected to present the profession with vast revenue and growth opportunities. These main product areas are briefly outlined below (for more information, refer to http://www.aicpa.org/assurance/index.htm).

For each of the assurance services outlined, the major initiatives of the profession are to try to develop tools that can aid their members, to develop a service that can be provided at a high level of assurance and will reflect well on the reputation of the profession, and to increase the demand for the service by providing promotional material about the benefits that flow from the assurance provided.

Risk assessment

Operating in today's more dynamic and changing environment means that businesses are subjected to greater risks than ever before. If utilising a business risk methodology, auditors should be in a position to identify the business risks that an organisation faces and the risk management policies that an organisation has. Parties such as investors and management are believed to require information about the risks an entity is facing. The purpose of the **risk assessment** assurance services that are being developed by the profession is to meet the demand for such information; that is, to identify a client's profile of business risks and assess whether the entity has appropriate systems in place to effectively manage those risks. There is, of course, an argument that the auditor should be providing assurance on these risks as part of their audit. However, to date that has not been widely discussed.

Risk advisory is a product being developed by a task force that has been set up by SCAS. The goal of the Risk Advisory Services Task Force (the Task Force) is to expand risk advisory services across the profession by developing:

- a common language and framework for understanding and communicating this important issue; and
- a series of practice guides describing tools, techniques and training that support the risk management process.

As identified on the SCAS web site, these tools are under active development.

Business performance measurement

It is widely recognised that financial reports are deficient in a number of ways in determining or evaluating the performance of an organisation. While the financial report is generally regarded as capturing and reporting fairly the 'hard' assets of an organisation such as inventory and property, plant and equipment, it is not as well designed to capture the 'soft' assets such as quality of staff, systems, products and the level of innovation. These are obviously very important assets for all organisations but are extremely important in growing sectors of our economy such as the service or information technology sectors. As a result, decision-makers may require a range of information that extends beyond traditional financial reports in order to evaluate and measure business performance. One of the ways in which this has been addressed is by the use of a greater range of performance indicators than in the past. For example, many organisations are using and reporting balanced scorecard approaches to try to increase the range of criteria that they are being assessed on. Balanced scorecard approaches capture and report information on a number of dimensions, both financial and nonfinancial, such as product/service quality and customer satisfaction. Assurance services in **business performance measurement** attempt to meet this need by evaluating whether a client's performance measurement system contains relevant and reliable measures for assessing the degree to which the client's goals and objectives are achieved or how its performance compares to its competitors.

Generally, this service can be broken down into three categories:

1 For a *client with performance measurement systems*, the reliability of information being reported from the client's performance measurement system and the relevance of the performance measures are assessed;
2 For a *client without performance measurement systems*, relevant performance measures are identified and a performance measurement system is designed and implemented; and
3 For *all other clients*, advice on how the organisation can improve its performance measurement system is offered.

The example that was used earlier in this chapter (under learning objective 5) of APRA requiring assurance on particular statistical data is an example of this type of assurance. While still not large in practice, this assurance service is expected by the authors to be one of the growth assurance services of the future.

Business to consumer e-commerce: WebTrust™

Despite its rapid growth, one of the impediments to the growth of business to consumer e-commerce is consumer concerns associated with the security of transactions.

WebTrust™ is a product developed and promoted by the global accounting profession to provide assurance to consumers undertaking Internet transactions. WebTrust™ provides a framework and methodology for assurance as to the integrity and security, as well as adherence to the disclosed business practices, of an e-commerce business. Companies who pass the standardised criteria required by a WebTrust™ audit will receive the WebTrust™ seal, which they can display on their web site.

Originally designed by the AICPA and the Canadian Institute of Chartered Accountants (CICA), WebTrust™ has now been licensed to the accounting profession in the UK and Australia. WebTrust™ was launched in mid-1999 in Australia. This assurance service continues to evolve, and it now considers the following principles and criteria: availability, business practices and transaction integrity, online privacy, security, non-repudiation, customised disclosures and confidentiality.

Consumers click on a WebTrust™ seal on the client's web site in order to access the assurance report, issued by the assessor, as well as to receive background information on WebTrust™ and related criteria. Only firms which are licensed are able to issue WebTrust™ seals. A close relationship has been developed between WebTrust™ and VeriSign, a world-renowned provider of digital authentication services. VeriSign encryption and authentication technology assure the customer that the seal on a web site is authentic and that the site is entitled to display it. A VeriSign 'spider' also searches the Internet looking for unauthorised copies of the seal.

In critically assessing the success of this assurance product, it cannot be claimed that WebTrust™ has been successful. The take-up rate for this product has been slow, while there has been considerable growth in less costly competitor products. In particular, critics of this product say that the profession misread the demand for a comprehensive high level assurance product, which is quite expensive to provide if fully costed. WebTrust™ is in one of the areas where there is a big first-mover advantage. If WebTrust™ had become the product of general acceptance, then there could have been a snowballing effect where competitors would also have to provide this level of assurance. This does not seem to have been the case with WebTrust™ and therefore we believe the growth potential of this product is very limited.

Information systems reliability: SysTrust™

SysTrust™ is a product recently developed by the AICPA and CICA to provide assurance on the reliability of systems. It entails the assurance provider issuing a report on whether management maintained effective controls over its system to enable the system to function reliably. In a SysTrust™ engagement, a reliable system is one that has the characteristics of availability, security, integrity and maintainability. The assurance provider determines whether controls over the system exist and performs tests to determine whether those controls were operating effectively during the period covered by the attestation/assurance report.

If the system meets the requirements of the SysTrust™ Principles and Criteria (refer to http://www.aicpa.org/assurance/risk/index.htm), an unqualified report is issued. The SysTrust™ report addresses whether management has maintained effective controls over its system. In addition to the unqualified report, a SysTrust™ engagement will include a description of the system examined and in many cases management's assertion about the effectiveness of its controls over the system that enable it to meet the SysTrust™ criteria.

On the SysTrust™ web site it is outlined that this service should be provided at only the high level of assurance, although not all of the principles for this type of engagement need to be covered. A client may request a report that covers only selected SysTrust™ principles, and the assurance provider may report on one principle or any combination of principles. A client may also request that the assurance provider perform an agreed-upon procedures engagement related to the SysTrust™ Principles and Criteria. In such an engagement, the assurance provider performs specified procedures, agreed to by the specified parties, and reports their findings. The report is in the form of an agreed-upon procedures report. The use of such a report is restricted to the specified parties who agreed to the procedures. In the SysTrust™ principles, under 'other reporting guidance', there is a statement that a practitioner may not issue a review-level SysTrust™ attestation report. No justification for this one level of assurance approach is provided. A justification for not issuing a moderate level of assurance report would be based primarily on the fact that the assurance provider works with the client until the assurance provider is satisfied in all material aspects. The possible justifications for not permitting a lower level of assurance are less clear.

This engagement differs from WebTrust™, which is aimed at providing assurance to consumers. SysTrust™ is designed to increase the comfort of management and business partners about the continued availability, integrity, security and maintainability of a system. As such, an expected major benefit is that it would be used to promote confidence of management and major suppliers and customers in dealing with the organisation via electronic means.

ElderCare assurance

The population of many countries is ageing significantly, due in part to reduced mortality rates. Many members of the ageing group of individuals have accumulated unprecedented wealth during their lifetime and have the resources to maintain their independence. They are increasingly looking for private institutions to assist them when they can no longer completely care for themselves.

Members of the accounting profession can assist the elderly, and concerned family members, by providing assurance that care goals are achieved by various care givers, including the provision of medical, household and financial services. The purpose of the service is to provide assurance in a professional, independent and objective manner to third parties that the needs of the elderly are being met. This can include the provision of accounting services, the supervision of investments, providing information for the handling of home care and medical emergencies and assuring families that the elderly are receiving services and property maintenance at agreed-upon levels.

A number of ancillary services can be merged with the assurance services. These can encompass consulting/facilitating services and direct service provision. Consulting and facilitating services can include establishing standards of care expected. This may entail providing details of community services available and establishing goals for assistance, delivery plans and performance expectation from service providers. It may also involve assisting clients or families in the selection of care providers for each type of assistance required, including the communication of expectations and performance measurement requirements. Members of the profession may also be able to provide services directly to the elderly, including accounting and financial services, as well as making arrangements for appropriate care and transportation.

These services involve several levels of assurance—from independent objective assurance services to the direct provision of consulting services. It is identified that these services may be offered as an agreed-upon procedures, consulting, or assurance services engagement. At the moment very little guidance is offered with regard to reporting for these services.

While this particular service has proved to be relatively popular in the USA, it is yet to take off in Australia. This may be due to this country's approach of expecting the government to provide an adequate level of support and effective monitoring of this support for the elderly. Demand is expected to increase in Australia as our population ages, but the service may have to evolve in order to become more relevant to this environment.

A further assurance service: assurance on information provided to boards of directors by management

One of the assurance services with growth potential is ensuring that the information considered by directors at their regular meetings is appropriate and reliable. We continue to highlight **directors' assurance** as one of the assurance services that has major potential, but at the moment there are very few cases where we know that this is occurring. The potential and importance however has been confirmed by the recent examples of the Harris Scarfe and One.Tel cases in Australia where the independent directors claimed they were misled by executive management. This was discussed in Chapter 3 with regard to corporate governance. Excerpts from an article on One.Tel are contained in Auditing in the News 14.1 (overleaf).

Directors are concerned that the annual financial information they receive from management may be biased or incomplete, and they seek an assurance on this in the form of an annual audit. Why shouldn't they also seek assurance that the financial and nonfinancial information that is supplied to them by management for each directors' meeting is free from such bias? This would seem to be especially relevant in relation to major decisions of strategic importance to the organisation. It may be that this form of assurance is even more important than the assurance that is currently provided by the annual audit.

One of the theoretical reasons why audits of financial information occur is to reduce agency costs (refer to Chapter 1). Management acts as an agent for the resources of the organisation that are entrusted to their use by resource providers (shareholders, creditors, etc.). Management is also accountable for their use and is expected to produce reports which show its stewardship of these resources. The controls that we can use to reduce bias and manipulation of the reports are that they are prepared using generally accepted accounting concepts and are audited by independent experts. The role of the boards of directors in overseeing the operations of the company and in regulating and assessing the behaviour of management has also become much clearer recently. But boards of directors rely on the reports provided to them by management in their assessment of the performance of management, even though they realise that there is an incentive for management to selectively not reveal information, or to reveal information with a potential bias. Directors have traditionally not sought assurance on this information, and would rely on internal control in the production of this information. This suggests the opportunity for a new assurance service which would involve providing assurance to the board by independently assessing the reliability of internal control, or providing assurance directly on the papers that are discussed at the board meetings as to their completeness and accuracy. It appears that directors have been slow to appreciate how important it may be for them to be in a position to rely on the quality and relevance of management-sponsored information.

In a recent publication entitled 'Financial Report Auditing: Meeting Market Expectations', the ICAA (2003) points out that some of the areas in which directors could demand assurance are:

- the quality of accounting policies used by management in preparing the financial report
- whether the company complies with the ASX Corporate Governance Council's Guidelines and Best Practice Recommendations
- whether the company has complied with the continuous disclosure requirements of the ASX Listing Rules.

S N I P P E T

14.1

Source: Paul Barry
(2002) Sydney
Morning Herald,
4 May, p. 6.

AUDITING IN THE NEWS

One.Tel board misled over serious shortfall

One.Tel's management accounts for January and February 2001 indicated it was $30 million behind budget, Sydney's Federal Court heard yesterday. But the company's non-executive directors, including James Packer and Lachlan Murdoch, were not told.

At a crucial board meeting on March 30, the last before One.Tel's cash crisis took hold, directors were assured that the company was still on track. Five days later, the company's co-founders, Jodee Rich and Brad Keeling, repeated this promise to the public.

On March 30, One.Tel's directors were given briefing papers that showed the Australian fixed-wire business (selling local and long-distance calls) attracted revenue of $50 million to $55 million a month during the first quarter.

But management accounts for January and February showed revenue in the first two months to be $39 million and $35 million. A similar figure was later recorded for March.

One.Tel's board was told at the March 30 meeting that $40 million in 'unbilled' revenue still had to go through the system, Mr Rich said. But he could not recall directors being expressly told that this $40 million had already been included in the monthly revenue figures they were shown.

Michael Slattery, QC, for One.Tel's liquidators, put it to Mr Rich that: 'Directors were left with the belief that they were looking at actual revenue figures [which showed the company to be on track] at least for January and February.' Mr Rich disputed this ...

Quick review

1. The auditing profession is currently attempting to market itself as the high-quality provider of assurance services, by promoting a framework for assurance services, as well as developing specific assurance services.

2. Newer assurance services which are currently being marketed and developed by the profession include:
   - risk assessment
   - business performance measurement
   - business to consumer e-commerce security: WebTrust™
   - information systems reliability: SysTrust™
   - assurance for care of the elderly: ElderCare.

3. Another assurance service which has significant potential is assurance on information provided to boards of directors by management.

Summary

This chapter has reviewed the range of other assurance services that could be offered by the auditing profession. Guidance is offered by the AUASB on a range of assurance services engagements that are currently being undertaken by members of the profession, including:
- special purpose reports;
- components of financial reports;
- summarised financial reports;
- half-yearly financial reports;
- prospective financial information;
- reports on internal control; and
- reports on statistical or highlight information.

Under the framework for assurance services two levels of assurance can be given for each of these engagements. A reasonable assurance can be provided (for assurance engagements where the subject matter is historical financial information these are called audits) or, using a subset of procedures required for a reasonable assurance engagement, limited assurance can be provided (for assurance engagements where the subject matter is historical financial information, these are called reviews). Alternatively, agreed-upon procedures may be undertaken, where the assurance provider reports on factual findings and does not offer an opinion.

The chapter also evaluated current assurance services being developed by the assurance profession, including WebTrust™, SysTrust™, business performance measurement, risk assessment and ElderCare. We identified a prospective assurance services engagement on which no guidance is currently provided, being reports on information provided to boards of directors.

Key terms

References

Alford, S. (1999) 'A critical appraisal of assurance services development in Australia', *Australian Accounting Review*, July, 11–16.

Alles, M., Kogan A. and Vasarhelyi, M.A. (2002) 'Feasibility and Economics of Continuous Assurance', *Auditing: A Journal of Practice and Theory*, Vol. 21, 125–38.

American Institute of Certified Public Accountants (AICPA) (2002) *Report of the Special Committee on Assurance Services*, http://www.aicpa.org/assurance/index.htm

Baines, A., Tanewski, G. and Gay, G.E. (2000) 'Characteristics of organisations using an audit for interim financial statements', *Australian Accounting Review*, Vol. 10, 52–61.

Canadian Institute of Chartered Accountants and AICPA (1999) *Continuous Auditing*, Research Report, 3.

Canadian Institute of Chartered Accountants (CICA) (2001) Assurance Services web site http://www.cica.ca/cica/cicawebsite.nsf/public/SPAssuranceServices

Carson, E. (1999) 'Caught in the net', *Charter*, September, 24–8.

Elliott, R.K. (2002) 'Twenty-first century assurance', *Auditing: A Journal of Practice and Theory*, Vol. 21, 139–46.

Gay, G.E., Pound, G.D. and Simnett, R. (1997) 'Reporting on internal control', *Perspectives on Contemporary Auditing*, 8–16.

Hughes, D.A. (1999a) 'Assurance services issues', *Australian CPA*, October, 36–7.

Hughes, D.A. (1999b) 'Adding value through continuous assurance', *Charter*, November, 70–1.

Institute of Chartered Accountants in Australia (2003) *Financial Report Audit: Meeting the Market Expectations*, ICAA, Sydney.

International Federation of Accountants (IFAC) (2002) *The Determination and Communication of Levels of Assurance Other Than High*, IFAC, New York.

Nugent, M.N. (1999) 'The Australian accounting profession's role in developing assurance services', *Australian Accounting Review*, July, 3–10.

Simnett, R. and Trotman, K. (1999) 'Research opportunities in assurance services', *Australian Accounting Review*, July, 17–21.

Assignments

Additional assignments for this chapter are contained in Appendix A of this book, page 775.

MaxMARK

MAXIMISE YOUR MARKS! There are approximately 30 interactive questions on other assurance services available online at www.mhhe.com/au/gay3e

REVIEW QUESTIONS

14.1 **(a)** Assurance services are best described as:

    A the preparation of a financial report based on the assumptions of a responsible party

    B the expression of an opinion on the truth and fairness of a general purpose financial report

    C services designed for the improvement of operations, resulting in better outcomes

    D independent professional services that improve the quality of information, or its context, for decision makers

(b) The objective of assurance services is best described as:

    A comparing internal information and policies with those of other firms

    B improving the firm's outcomes

    C providing reliable information

    D enhancing decision making

(c) Which one of the following is generally more important in a review than in a compilation?

    A Obtaining a signed engagement letter

    B Obtaining a signed representation letter

    C Determining the accounting bases on which the financial report is to be presented

    D Gaining familiarity with industry accounting principles

(d) Which of the following assurance service products can be used to provide assurance for e-commerce applications?

    A both WebTrust™ and SysTrust™

    B neither WebTrust™ nor SysTrust™

    C WebTrust™

    D SysTrust™

(e) Which of the following professional services would be considered an assurance engagement?

    A An income tax engagement to prepare company tax and GST returns.

    B Compilation of a financial report from a client's accounting records.

    C A management consulting engagement to provide IT advice to a client.

    D An engagement to report on compliance with statutory requirements.

14.2 The following questions relate to the assurance provider's responsibilities for engagements other than audits.

(a) Which of the following procedures is *not* included in a review engagement?

    A Any procedures designed to identify relationships between data that appear to be unusual

    B Inquiries of management

    C An assessment of control risk

    D Inquiries regarding events subsequent to the balance date

(b) Which of the following would *not* be included in a report based upon a review of the financial report?

    A A statement that all information included in the financial report is the representations of management

    B An expression of positive assurance that the financial report is fairly presented

    C A statement that the review was in accordance with Australian auditing standards

    D A statement describing the principal procedures performed

(c) Inquiry and analytical procedures ordinarily performed during a review of a non-reporting entity's financial report include:

    A inquiries concerning actions taken at meetings of the shareholders and the board of directors

    B analytical procedures designed to test management's assertions regarding continued existence

    C inquiries designed to identify reportable conditions in internal control

    D analytical procedures designed to test the accounting records by obtaining corroborating evidence

(d) An assurance provider who reviews the financial report of a non-reporting entity should issue a report stating that a review:

    A provides a level of assurance that is less than that given in an audit

    B provides negative assurance that internal control is functioning as designed

    C provides a high level of assurance based on inquiry and analytical procedures

    D is substantially more in scope than a compilation

(e) During a review of the financial report of a non-reporting entity, an assurance provider becomes aware of a lack of adequate disclosure that is material to the financial report and results in it being misleading. If management refuses to correct the financial report presentations, the assurance provider should:

    A disclose this departure from accounting standards in a separate paragraph of the report

    B express only limited assurance on the financial report presentations

    C issue an 'except for' opinion

    D issue an adverse opinion

14.3 The following questions relate to specialised reporting circumstances. Select the *best* response.

(a) When reporting on a financial report prepared on a comprehensive basis of accounting other than generally accepted accounting principles, the assurance provider should include in the report a paragraph that:

    A states the financial report is *not* intended to have been audited in accordance with Australian auditing standards

    B refers to the authoritative pronouncements that explain the comprehensive basis of accounting being used

    C states that the financial report is not intended to be in conformity with Australian accounting standards

    D justifies the comprehensive basis of accounting being used

(b) A financial forecast is an estimate of financial position, results of operations and cash flows that, to the best of management's knowledge, is:

    A at the midpoint of a given precision range

    B most probable

    C conservative

    D at the low point of a given precision range

(c) An assurance provider's understanding of internal control in a financial report audit:

A is generally more extensive than that made in connection with an engagement to express an opinion on internal control

B generally results in the assurance provider expressing an opinion on internal control

C is generally more limited than that made in connection with an engagement to express an opinion on internal control

D is generally identical to that made in connection with an engagement to express an opinion on internal control

(d) An assurance provider who is requested to express an opinion on the rental and royalty income of an entity may:

A accept the engagement only if distribution of the assurance provider's report is limited to the entity's management

B accept the engagement provided the assurance provider's opinion is expressed in a special report

C not accept the engagement because to do so would be tantamount to agreeing to issue a piecemeal opinion

D not accept the engagement unless also engaged to audit the full financial report of the entity

(e) The assurance provider's special purpose report on an entity's internal control should state that:

A the examination was conducted in accordance with Australian accounting standards

B the client's management has provided assurance that the expected benefits of the internal accounting control activities exceed the related costs

C the projections of any evaluation of internal control to future periods are subject to the risk that internal control may become inadequate

D the establishment and maintenance of the system of internal control are the responsibilities of management

 learning objective 1

Assurance services other than audit on general purpose financial reports

14.4 Identify the differences in the levels of assurance offered by audit, review and agreed-upon procedures engagements.

14.5 Critically evaluate the approach undertaken by the profession of recognising that assurance can be provided over a continuum, but the engagements can only be undertaken and reported on at two levels, high and moderate. What is the rationale for reporting at only two levels?

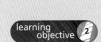 learning objective 2

Review engagement and level of assurance offered

14.6 What are the major differences and similarities between an audit engagement and a review engagement?

14.7 What are the major differences between the audit report and the review report?

 learning objective 3

Agreed-upon procedures and level of assurance offered

14.8 Do you agree with the statement that the assurance provider provides no assurance in an agreed-upon procedures engagement?

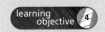 learning objective 4

Obligations and special purpose and summarised financial reports

14.9 What precautions should an assurance provider take in reporting on a financial report in a document containing supplemental financial data and schedules?

14.10 Find a copy of an audit report on a concise financial report. In what ways is it similar and dissimilar to the audit report provided on an unabridged financial report.

Legislation or regulation on financial information and internal controls

14.11 What are an assurance provider's reporting obligations in connection with a financial forecast?

14.12 How does a separate special purpose report on internal control aid corporate governance?

14.13 Does the testing of internal control for a financial report audit necessarily provide adequate evidence for a separate report on internal controls? Discuss.

New assurance services

14.14 What are the major distinguishing features between WebTrust™ and SysTrust™?

14.15 What new assurance services could have helped overcome the problems encountered at One.Tel as described in Auditing in the News 14.1 on page 658?

DISCUSSION PROBLEMS AND CASE STUDIES

Assurance services other than audit on general purpose financial reports

14.16 **Basic** May and Day, auditors, are engaged by XYZ Company Ltd to examine the records of gross sales of ABC Stores Ltd. ABC Stores leases space in a shopping centre owned by XYZ Company that is located on Island Boulevard in Surfers Paradise. The annual rental, according to the lease agreement, is based on a percentage of gross sales as defined in the agreement dated 5 March 2005.

Prepare the report that May and Day should issue on the gross sales for the year ended 30 June 2005, to be used in computing the rental. The extent of audit procedures to be applied is not restricted in any way and the lease agreement guarantees XYZ Company full access to the accounting records of ABC Stores.

14.17 **Moderate** You have been assigned to two engagements over the next few months:

1 The audit of Alpha Ltd (Alpha), a listed company. Your firm is required to give an opinion on Alpha's general purpose financial report.

2 The review of cash flow projections of Beta Pty Ltd (Beta). Beta is required to provide a five-year cash flow projection as part of a loan application to be lodged with its bankers. Your firm is required to give an opinion on Beta's five-year cash flow projections.

Required

(a) The assurance services partner has asked you to draft the engagement letter for both engagements. Compile a list of the matters to be included in each of these engagement letters.

(*Hint:* you should present your answer in the form of a table, as indicated below.)

Matters to include in Alpha's engagement letter	Matters to include in Beta's engagement letter

(b) Compare your lists. Why do they differ?

Source: This question was adapted from the CA Programme of The Institute of Chartered Accountants in Australia—2002 Financial Reporting and Assurance Module.

Review engagements

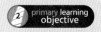

14.18 **Moderate** The audit senior assigned to the review of Q Ltd's half-yearly financial report is reviewing the audit program and notes that the program essentially requires reliance on internal controls, analytical procedures and inquiries of management. The audit senior has not performed a review before and is concerned that the procedures are inadequate. He has asked the audit manager, 'Shouldn't I at least test some of these controls or do some vouching?'

Required

Assuming you are the manager, provide an appropriate response to the audit senior.

14.19 Complex You are the audit manager responsible for the review of the half-yearly financial report of R Ltd (R), an importer and wholesaler of electrical appliances from Asia. During the course of your inquiries you discover that immediately prior to the half-year-end a major shipment of goods to Australia was affected by severe flooding in Asia, and it is possible that all goods may have been destroyed. The terms of the shipping arrangements indicated that R was the legal owner of the goods at the time of the flood. You have also reviewed the insurance agreement and have found that 'acts of God' such as severe flooding are not covered. Thus if the goods have been destroyed the company has no recourse to insurers or suppliers.

You have indicated to the management of R that they will need to adjust the financial report to write back the stock. Management has refused to make any adjustment, saying that the stock is delayed but will arrive. You have requested that management provide you with evidence to support this claim. In response, management has indicated that its evidence is verbal, that it does not believe it is necessary for you to contact the supplier and that it will not authorise the supplier to discuss this matter with you. It has, however, offered to document the claim in a management representation letter, indicating this should be sufficient given the nature of your engagement.

Required

If the client continues to refuse to make any adjustment to the half-yearly financial report or allow the auditor to contact the supplier, what should the auditor do?

14.20 Complex Your client is Sweeties Pty Ltd (Sweeties), a not-for-profit growers' association established on 1 April 2001 for North Queensland pineapple growers. Its objectives are to act as a wholesaling and marketing agent for its pineapple-grower members. An outline of Sweetie's operations is given below.

Growers grade and pack their own pineapples into boxes, which state the grower's name and address. There are four generally accepted grades of pineapple used by the industry:

A Gourmet (sold to five-star restaurants)
B Deluxe (sold to exclusive fruit and vegetable retailers)
C Standard (sold to supermarkets and other retailers)
D Cannery (sold to factories for processing into various canned pineapple products).

Growers arrange for association-owned trucks to collect the pineapples and take them to the central warehouse, where the pineapples are sorted and stored according to their grade.

Sweeties distributes the pineapples as they are ordered by customers; an invoice is included with each order, stating the quantity, price and grower details. When payment is received, Sweeties forwards the sale proceeds to the grower, deducting a percentage of the sales value as a levy to cover administrative costs. All pineapples are sold within Australia.

Sweeties is the first grower association to adopt this method of operation. Other associations only provide warehouse space to their members at reduced rates; they do not sell the produce or collect payments on the growers' behalf.

Part of the articles of association of Sweeties Pty Ltd states that three performance measures must be provided annually to members, in addition to the statutory financial report.

The measures are:
- monies spent collecting and distributing produce compared to tonnage of produce sold
- average price per grade achieved by the association compared to average market price per grade
- average number of days from harvest to cash collection.

Your firm has been requested to perform a review engagement on these performance measures as at 31 March 2002.

Required

(a) Detail the procedures you would apply in relation to each of the three performance measures in order to gain sufficient appropriate evidence to enable you to design your review report.

(b) Discuss the criteria that you would use to determine whether an error found during your review was material.

(c) You are reviewing the assistant's work and see the following note on one of his workpapers:

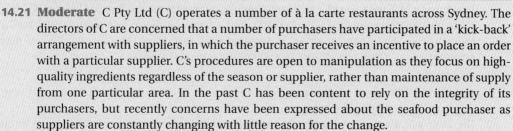

	Number of days from harvest to cash collection
per client	47
per audit procedures	52

Determine whether this is a material error or not, and explain your conclusion to your assistant.

Source: This question was adapted from the CA Programme of The Institute of Chartered Accountants in Australia—2002 Financial Reporting and Assurance Module.

Agreed-upon procedures

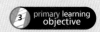

14.21 Moderate C Pty Ltd (C) operates a number of à la carte restaurants across Sydney. The directors of C are concerned that a number of purchasers have participated in a 'kick-back' arrangement with suppliers, in which the purchaser receives an incentive to place an order with a particular supplier. C's procedures are open to manipulation as they focus on high-quality ingredients regardless of the season or supplier, rather than maintenance of supply from one particular area. In the past C has been content to rely on the integrity of its purchasers, but recently concerns have been expressed about the seafood purchaser as suppliers are constantly changing with little reason for the change.

In order to ensure independence of the inquiry, the directors have contacted your firm, A & Co Auditors, to investigate the purchasing procedures. Specifically they have requested that you:

- Review all purchase orders for a 3 month period and ensure terms and conditions are within guidelines specified in the policy and procedures manual.
- Circularise all suppliers found in the period to confirm terms of trade and quantity of goods delivered.
- Agree purchase orders with delivery notes and supplier invoices.
- Observe delivery procedures and ensure they are in line with procedures documented in the firm's policy and procedures manual.

Required

(a) Identify the type of engagement being performed by the auditor.

(b) Assuming no errors were found, draft a report which could be used to communicate the auditor's findings in relation to the above engagement.

Special purpose and summarised financial reports

14.22 Basic A. Peacock, an assurance provider, has prepared the following report on the cash-basis financial report of ABC Ltd.

I have examined the balance sheet and income statement of ABC Ltd as at 30 June 20X0, and for the year then ended.

In my opinion, the above-mentioned financial report presents fairly ABC Ltd's financial position and results of operations consistent with the cash basis of accounting.

Required

Explain the deficiencies in this special report.

14.23 **Moderate** Trevor Tom has now completed the audit of Green Thumbs (GT), a small landscaping business owned and operated by Ms Jan Green. GT required an audit of a special purpose financial report (SPFR) in order to apply for a bank loan to fund business expansion. The SPFR was prepared using a cash basis for accounting and comprised a statement of cash receipts and payments and a statement of cash balances. The audit was uneventful and Trevor is satisfied the SPFR reflects the operations of the business. He is now preparing a draft audit report. Trevor is unsure of the requirements of an audit opinion for a small business and has obtained a copy of a report on a general purpose financial report for a similar-sized company, G Pty Ltd, to assist in drafting the report.

Required

Can Trevor use the audit report of G Pty Ltd to assist with drafting the report? Provide reasons for your decision.

14.24 **Complex** Green Thumbs (GT) is a small landscaping business operating in regional New South Wales. Business has been very good lately and GT is considering expansion of its services. However, in order to expand GT will require additional equipment costing approximately $100 000. GT has approached its local bank and been told that in order for the bank to consider the loan it will need to provide an audited financial report. The bank has provided GT with a leaflet indicating the requirements for the financial report. GT has taken this to its accountant who has prepared a financial report adequate for the bank's requirements. The financial report is prepared on a cash basis. The accountant has now approached your firm to perform an audit of the financial report.

Required

(a) Identify the nature of the engagement and sources of guidance that may assist your firm in completing the engagement.

(b) How will the financial report assertions, which are normally considered in an audit engagement, be applied to this engagement?

(c) Describe three procedures that could be used to perform the audit of GT's financial report.

Assurance services on prospective financial information and internal controls

14.25 **Moderate** Value Add Pty Ltd (VA) is a subsidiary of a large bauxite mining company established to exploit value-adding activities for the mining company's major products. VA is currently investigating the possibility of forming a joint venture with a finance company, F Pty Ltd (F). Under the terms of the arrangement, F will provide funds for the operations and VA will provide bauxite, personnel and facilities for processing. In order to proceed with the joint venture negotiations, F has requested that VA provide an audited cash flow forecast for the first 12 months of operations. VA has contacted your firm, requesting you to undertake the audit.

Required

(a) Identify five factors your firm should consider before accepting this engagement.

(b) Assume you have accepted the engagement and are now planning the audit. Describe three procedures which could be used to assist with the audit of the forecast.

14.26 **Moderate** You are an assurance services senior and up until now have only been assigned to general purpose financial report audits. However, next week you start on a special assignment, the audit of the internal controls of Bits Etc Pty Ltd (Bits) in accordance with AUS 810 'Special Purpose Reports on the Effectiveness of Control Procedures'.

You are a little unsure as to how basic audit principles apply to the Bits audit and so have decided to compare the Bits engagement to the audit of a general purpose financial report.

Required

As preparation for the Bits Etc Ltd audit, read and complete the following table:

	Engagement to audit a general purpose financial report	Engagement to audit internal controls
Definition of audit risk	The risk of giving an inappropriate opinion on a materially misstated financial report.	
Effect of internal control weaknesses on the audit	Depending on the nature and extent of the weakness and its impact on control risk, may affect the audit approach (i.e. whether a substantive or test of controls approach is used).	
Effect of internal control weakness on the audit report	Unlikely to have an effect, unless the weakness is of such a magnitude so as to prevent sufficient, appropriate audit evidence from being obtained.	
Effect of deteriorating economic conditions on inherent risk	Likely to increase inherent risk at the financial report level, as worsening economic conditions place pressure on the entity's results. This may increase the level of audit evidence needed in relation to specific accounts affected.	
Effect of increased inventory obsolescence on inherent risk	Likely to increase inherent risk at the account balance level (i.e. the provision for inventory obsolescence), as judgment is required to arrive at a materially correct provision balance. This will result in an increased level of substantive testing for valuation of inventory.	

Source: This question was adapted from the CA Programme of The Institute of Chartered Accountants in Australia—2002 Financial Reporting and Assurance Module.

Assurance services being developed by the profession

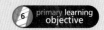

14.27 Basic The assurance profession is currently trying to develop a large range of new assurance services.

Required

(a) Discuss the advantages and disadvantages to the profession and society of the assurance services profession extending the types of assurance services on which it currently provides assurance.

(b) Discuss which of the assurance services you believe are more likely to prove successful in Australia. Justify your answer.

14.28 Moderate Your client, Gray Ltd, a local sporting goods company, has asked your firm for assistance in setting up its web site. Mike Gray, the CEO, is concerned that potential customers will be reluctant to place orders over the Internet to a relatively unknown entity. He recently heard about companies finding ways to provide assurance to customers about secure web sites, and has asked to meet with you about this issue.

Required

Prepare answers to each of the following questions that may be asked by Mike.

   (a) What type of assurance can an assurance firm provide to Mike's customers concerning the company's web site?

   (b) What process would your firm follow in providing a WebTrust™ assurance service for Mike's web site? (You could refer to WebTrust™ documentation available at <http://www.aicpa.org>.)

14.29 Moderate Cerqueira Ltd, a supplier of apparel to retail stores, has recently implemented a new information system. However, during systems development and implementation, the company experienced a great deal of turnover in personnel involved with designing and implementing the system. Consequently, the company's board of directors is concerned about whether the system is reliable. They have heard of an assurance service called SysTrust™, but would like to know more about it before discussing it with their assurance provider.

Required

   (a) What types of assurance does a SysTrust™ examination provide? What are the main principles underlying a reliable system that a SysTrust™ examination considers?

   (b) What special skills does an assurance provider undertaking a SysTrust™ examination require?

   (c) Cerqueira Ltd's Board of Directors is wondering whether any of its constituents would be interested in the SysTrust™ report. For example, the company is interested in renewing its business interruption insurance, winning business from new retailers, and making itself attractive as a takeover target. Describe how an unqualified SysTrust™ report could benefit Cerqueira Ltd from the point of view of the insurance company, potential customers, and potential buyers of the company. (*Hint:* One approach to this would be to examine the SysTrust™ principles and underlying criteria, perhaps by obtaining SysTrust™ documentation available at <http://www.aicpa.org>. You should especially consider which principles and criteria would be of interest to each of the three constituents.)

CONTINUOUS CASE STUDY

14.30 Complex This is a continuation of question 13.29. It may be completed independently of that question.

Your firm is responsible for the audit of Mitchell Pty Ltd (M), a small company operating in the chemical industry. Recent changes to legislation in the industry have had a detrimental impact on the ability of small firms to survive, and the directors of M have decided that the only way to continue operations is to undertake a significant program of expansion. Given the funds required for the expansion, the directors have decided to float the company and have approached your firm to perform a due diligence investigation for the float.

Required

   (a) Discuss the nature and purpose of the due diligence engagement.

   (b) Assuming the directors of M have indicated that they require a review of the prospectus and associated documents, indicate five procedures which the assurance provider could use to assist with the review.

CHAPTER 15

INTERNAL AUDITING

LEARNING OBJECTIVES

After studying this chapter you should be able to:

1 understand the evolving nature of internal auditing;

2 appreciate the professional standards developed for internal auditing;

3 understand what internal auditors currently do in practice;

4 gain an appreciation of the issues that may face the internal audit profession in the future; and

5 appreciate the approaches to assessing risk management, control and governance processes.

Chapter outline

As external auditing has evolved towards a business risk approach, so too there has been a recent evolution in the role of internal auditing. Once seen as an independent appraisal function evaluating the adequacy and effectiveness of other controls in an organisation, internal auditing is now seen in many organisations as a service that promotes understanding and provides assurance about risk exposures and control strategies. As such, the movement in the internal audit profession complements the movements that we are seeing in the external audit profession. This chapter will first examine the traditional view of internal auditing and then examine the evolution and current status of the new internal auditing approach.

Relevant guidance

Australian		International	
AUS 106	Explanatory Framework for Standards on Audit and Audit-Related Services	—	
AUS 604	Considering the Work of Internal Auditing	ISA 610	Considering the Work of Internal Auditing
IIA Standards	Standards for the Professional Practice of Internal Auditing	IIA Standards	Standards for the Professional Practice of Internal Auditing
Code of Ethics	Institute of Internal Auditors Code of Ethics	Code of Ethics	Institute of Internal Auditors Code of Ethics

THE EVOLVING NATURE OF INTERNAL AUDITING

The traditional view of internal auditing is that it is an independent appraisal function evaluating the adequacy and effectiveness of other controls in an organisation. This is evolving in many organisations so that internal audit is now seen as an assurance and consulting service that promotes understanding and provides assurance about risk exposures and control strategies. However, in practice a number of organisations still have what could best be described as a traditional internal audit function. The auditing standards prepared by the AUASB/IAASB reflect a more traditional view, while the Institute of Internal Auditing (IIA) standards reflect the 'new' internal auditing. This can be seen from the following discussion.

Definition and scope of internal audit

The definition of internal auditing, contained in AUS 104 (ISA, Glossary of Terms), reflects a traditional view of this function. **Internal audit** is defined as an independent appraisal activity established within an entity as a service to the entity. Its functions include examining, evaluating and monitoring the adequacy and effectiveness of internal control. AUS 104 (ISA, Glossary of Terms) points out that, from the perspective of the external auditor, internal auditing therefore is a component of the control environment. This is supported by Appendix 2 of AUS 106 (there is no equivalent ISA), which sees the role of internal audit as being directed towards the examination and evaluation of:

- internal control and information systems;
- financial and operating information;
- the economy, efficiency and effectiveness of operations; and
- whether or not the entity has complied with relevant legislation.

The definition of internal auditing contained on the Institute of Internal Auditors web site <http//:www.theiia.org>, however, reflects the more current view. This is:

> *Internal auditing is an independent, objective assurance and consulting activity designed to add value and improve an organisation's operations. It helps an organisation accomplish its objectives by bringing a systematic, disciplined approach to evaluate and improve the effectiveness of risk management, control, and governance processes.*

As will be discussed in this chapter, some reasons for the difference in the two definitions are that external audit still views internal audit as part of the control system that should be evaluated, and that the standards in this area have not been recently revisited to reflect the new internal auditing.

While the external auditor's relationship with internal audit, as reflected in the AUS 104 definition, has been discussed earlier in this book (Chapter 8), aspects of the new definition do deserve discussion:

- **'internal'** indicates that the activities are undertaken within the entity either by employees or contract personnel (outsourcing of the internal audit function is quite common, and will be discussed later in this chapter).
- **'independent, objective'** are the same tests that are generally used for external auditors, although they are harder to achieve for internal auditors because of the 'employee' nature of the relationship. For internal audit it means that the work will be carried out with unrestricted access to people and explanations, records and facilities. It is important that the internal auditor not be under the direction or control of those whose responsibilities may be audited, which would include the accounting area under the control of the Chief Financial Officer. Best practice with regard to organisational structure will be considered later in this chapter.
- **'assurance and consulting activity'** assurance activity shows that for some aspects of the internal auditor's work, the intention is to improve the credibility of the subject matter. There are also other activities undertaken that may be more consultative (providing advice) in nature.
- **'add value and improve an organisation's operations'** emphasises the changing nature of internal auditing—adding value rather than being control-oriented.
- **'a systematic, disciplined approach'** is an application of the auditing approach outlined in the early chapters of this book.
- **'to evaluate and improve the effectiveness of risk management, control and governance processes'** again emphasises the much broader role of internal audit, rather than just control. Involvement in risk management and governance processes is consistent with the themes of risk management and corporate governance which are now an intregal part of auditing as outlined in this book.

The Institute of Internal Auditors

The **Institute of Internal Auditors (IIA)** was incorporated in New York in 1941, and in 2005 had over 95 000 members in various chapters or national institutes in over 120 countries. There are also many non-members who work within internal audit, with estimates of over 150 000 in the USA and 220 000 in China (Birkett et al., 1999a). The first Australian chapter was established in Sydney in 1952, and there are now branches in every state and in the Australian Capital Territory, with membership from both the private and public sectors. It is estimated that approximately 5000 people work in internal audit in Australia, with about 60 per cent in the public sector and 40 per cent in the private sector. The vision statement of the IIA in Australia is that it be the primary professional association in Australia, dedicated to the promotion and development of the practice of internal auditing

(IIA—Australia, 2004). The Australian chapter conducts a number of technical sessions for its members, with the most recent presentations being maintained on their web site <http://iia.asn.au>. It also publishes a quarterly magazine called *The Australian Internal Auditor*, which contains articles of technical interest.

The IIA provides professional recognition for internal auditors with its **Certified Internal Auditor (CIA)** qualification. The CIA examination covers four areas in which a candidate must achieve a 75 per cent pass:

1 internal audit process;
2 internal audit skills;
3 management control and information technology; and
4 the audit environment.

In addition, candidates must have a minimum of 2 years experience as an internal auditor or the equivalent. Auditing experience in public accounting qualifies as experience in internal auditing. To retain the CIA certificate, the individual must comply with the IIA's standards and code of ethics and meet continuing professional education requirements.

The IIA auditing standards state the need for internal auditors to have the necessary knowledge, skills and disciplines to carry out the tasks assigned. Where this involves financial records and reports, proficiency in accounting principles and practice is required. For other tasks, appropriate skills such as engineering, statistics, information technology or law are necessary. An understanding of the interaction of various aspects, such as accounting, commercial law, taxation, economics, finance, quantitative methods and information technology, is necessary so that the auditor can recognise potential problems and determine whether further research should be undertaken or assistance be obtained.

In recognition of the broad nature of the investigations carried out, graduates from any discipline may sit the CIA exam. CIAs include engineers, chemists, system analysts, computer programmers and humanities graduates, as well as accountants.

Quick review

1 The objective of internal auditing is to add value to an entity and improve its operations.
2 Internal audit services are traditionally directed towards examining and evaluating internal control; financial and operating information; economy, efficiency and effectiveness; and compliance with legislation and regulations.
3 Internal audit services have more recently focused on adding value to the risk management and corporate governance areas.
4 Internal auditing is viewed by external auditors as part of the internal control environment.
5 The Institute of Internal Auditors is a professional organisation which represents, promotes and develops internal auditing.

learning objective 2

CURRENT STANDARDS FOR INTERNAL AUDITORS

The IIA has issued **Standards for the Professional Practice of Internal Auditing (IIA Standards)**, which must be followed by members. The purposes of the IIA Standards are to:

1 Delineate basic principles that represent the practice of internal auditing as it should be.
2 Provide a framework for performing and promoting a broad range of value-added internal audit activities.

3 Establish the basis for the measurement of internal audit performance

4 Foster improved organisational processes and operations.

The IIA Standards consist of **Attribute Standards** (the 1000 Series), and **Performance Standards** (the 2000 Series). These are outlined in Exhibit 15.1. The Attribute Standards address the characteristics expected of organisations and individuals performing internal audit activities. The Performance Standards describe the nature of internal audit activities and provide quality criteria against which the performance of these services can be measured. Attribute and Performance Standards apply to all internal audit services. These are supported by Implementation Standards, which apply the Attribute and Performance Standards to specific types of engagements (for example, a compliance audit, a fraud investigation, or a control self-assessment project).

Initially, the Implementation Standards are being established for assurance activities (noted by an 'A' following the Standard number) and consulting activities (noted by a 'C'). Thus for Attribute Standard 1000 on Purpose Authority and Responsibility (refer to Exhibit 15.1), there is an assurance attribute standard 1000.A1, which states that the nature of assurance services should be defined in the audit charter, and a consulting attribute standard 1000.C1 which has a similar requirement for consulting services.

Attribute Standards		Performance Standards	
1000	**Purpose, Authority, and Responsibility**	**2000**	**Managing the Internal Audit Activity**
		2010	*Planning*
1100	**Independence and Objectivity**	*2020*	*Communication and Approval*
1110	*Organisational Independence*	*2030*	*Resource Management*
1120	*Individual Objectivity*	*2040*	*Policies and Procedures*
1130	*Impairments to Independence or*	*2050*	*Coordination*
	Objectivity	*2060*	*Reporting to the Board and Senior*
			Management
1200	**Proficiency and Due Professional Care**		
1210	*Proficiency*	**2100**	**Nature of Work**
1220	*Due Professional Care*	*2110*	*Risk Management*
1230	*Continuing Professional Development*	*2120*	*Control*
		2130	*Governance*
1300	**Quality Assurance and Improvement**		
	Program	**2200**	**Engagement Planning**
1310	*Quality Program Assessments*	*2201*	*Planning Considerations*
1320	*Reporting on the Quality Program*	*2210*	*Engagement Objectives*
1330	*Use of 'Conducted in Accordance with*	*2220*	*Engagement Scope*
	the Standards'	*2230*	*Engagement Resource Allocation*
1340	*Disclosure of Noncompliance*	*2240*	*Engagement Work Program*
		2300	**Performing the Engagement**
		2310	*Identifying Information*
		2320	*Analysis and Evaluation*
		2330	*Recording Information*
		2340	*Engagement Supervision*
		2400	**Communicating Results**
		2410	*Criteria for Communicating*
		2420	*Quality of Communications*
		2430	*Engagement Disclosure of Non-*
			compliance with the Standards
		2440	*Disseminating Results*
		2500	**Monitoring Progress**
		2600	**Management's Acceptance of Risks**

EXHIBIT **15.1**

Attribute and Performance Standards of the Institute of Internal Auditors

Attribute standards

The four categories of attribute standards are outlined in bold in Exhibit 15.1. These categories will now be examined in greater detail.

Purpose, authority and responsibility

This standard outlines that the purpose, authority and responsibility of the internal audit activity should be formally defined and set out in an internal audit charter. This charter should be approved by the board of directors.

Independence

It is essential that the internal auditor is, and is seen to be, **independent** of the area being audited, as per IIA Standard 1100. Whereas an external auditor is provided with a certain amount of independence by legislative and ethical pronouncements, by definition an internal auditor is part of the entity and is employed by the entity. In principle, this relationship indicates that full independence is more difficult to achieve for internal auditors. Therefore, management must structure the entity to maximise the perceived independence of the internal auditor.

The IIA standards distinguish two ways in which auditors can be independent of the activities they audit. The first is to have sufficient organisational status (IIA Standard 1110) to permit the accomplishment of audit responsibilities. The second is individual objectivity (IIA Standard 1120), which is in part a mental attitude, and is compromised if a staff member assumes any direct operating responsibilities or audits an area for which they were responsible immediately before joining the internal audit department.

The following aspects help to ensure organisational independence:

- The internal audit department should report to a level within the organisation that allows the internal audit activity to fulfil its responsibilities. If best practice is followed this will be the board of directors or the audit committee.
- The head of internal audit should have direct access to the board to help ensure independence as well as keep the board informed.
- The board should concur with the appointment or removal of the head of internal audit.
- Management and the board should be kept informed of work schedules, staffing requirements, budgets and **scope of work**, as well as receiving regular reports about internal audit activity.

If the internal audit department answers directly to the highest levels of management, line and divisional managers cannot influence the results of audits and the audit team can carry out their work without interference. If recommendations are made and accepted by the board, changes will be directed from that level.

The following aspects help maintain individual objectivity:

- audit staff assignments should be made to prevent possible bias or conflicts of interest;
- internal auditors should immediately report any conflicts of interest to the head of the internal audit department;
- staff assignments should be periodically rotated;
- internal auditors should not assume operating responsibilities; and
- persons transferred into the internal audit department should not audit those activities they previously carried out until a reasonable period of time has elapsed.

It is not appropriate for internal auditors to design, install or operate systems or draft procedures for systems because their objectivity may be impaired.

The IIA Code of Ethics requires members to exercise honesty, objectivity and diligence in the performance of their duties. Internal auditors are prohibited from accepting anything of value from an employee, client, customer, supplier or business associate of their entity that would impair, or be presumed to impair, their professional judgment. They must also refrain from entering into any activity that could result in a conflict of interest.

Proficiency and due professional care

IIA Standard 1200 requires internal audits to be performed with **professional proficiency** and **due professional care**. IIA Standard 1220 outlines that it is the internal audit department's responsibility to assign staff to each audit who collectively possess the knowledge, skills and other competencies needed to conduct the audit. The work should be properly supervised and internal auditors should comply with professional standards of conduct, which include the Code of Ethics of the IIA. Internal auditors need to maintain their professional competence through continuing education.

IIA Standard 1220 requires internal auditors to exercise due professional care in performing internal audits. They must apply the care and skill expected of a reasonably prudent and competent internal auditor in similar circumstances. They should consider the probability of significant errors, irregularities or non-compliance, and should be alert to significant risks that might affect objectives, operations or resources. The IIA Code of Ethics requires members to maintain high standards of professional competence and states that they should not knowingly be party to any illegal or improper activity.

Quality assurance

IIA Standard 1300 requires the head of the internal audit department, referred to as the chief audit executive, to develop and maintain a **quality assurance** program to evaluate the operations of the department. The quality program assessments should include both internal and external assessments. Members of the internal auditing staff perform internal assessments periodically in order to appraise the quality of audit work. External assessments provide independent assurance of audit quality to senior management, the audit committee and others, such as external auditors. Qualified independent individuals should conduct external reviews at least once every five years, and the results should be reported to the board of directors.

Performance standards

The performance standards require internal auditors to plan each audit; to collect, analyse, interpret and document information to support audit results; to report the results of their audit work; and to follow up to ensure that appropriate action is taken on reported audit findings. The standards relating to performance of the work are similar in many respects to those that apply to external auditors.

Management of the internal audit department

IIA Standard 2000 requires the head of the internal audit department to manage the department to ensure that it adds value to the organisation. The head should establish risk-based plans to determine the priorities of the internal audit activity consistent with the organisation's goals. These plans and resource requirements should be communicated to the board for review and approval. There should also be a periodic report to the board on internal audit activity's purpose, authority, responsibility and performance relative to its plan.

Nature of work

The requirements under IIA Standard 2100 'Nature of Work' clearly show the evolving nature of internal audit work. The requirement specifies that internal audit activity evaluates and contributes to the risk management, control and governance systems. The internal audit activity should:

- assist the organisation by identifying and evaluating significant exposures to risk and contributing to the improvement of risk management and control systems;
- assist the organisation in maintaining effective controls by evaluating their effectiveness and efficiency and by promoting continuous improvement; and
- contribute to the organisation's governance process by evaluating and improving the process through which:
  - values and goals are established and communicated;
  - the accomplishment of goals is monitored;
  - accountability is ensured; and
  - values are preserved.

Engagement planning

As with external audit, it is important to develop and document a plan for each engagement (IIA Standard 2200). In planning, the auditor should consider the significant risks to an entity and its objectives, and the means by which the potential impact of these risks are kept to an acceptable level. It is also important that internal auditors determine the appropriate resources required to achieve engagement objectives. Staffing should be based on an evaluation of the nature and complexity of each engagement, time constraints and available resources.

Performing the engagement

IIA Standard 2300 states that internal audits should identify, analyse, evaluate and record sufficient information to achieve the engagement's objectives. Engagements should be properly supervised to ensure objectives are achieved, quality is assured, and appropriate staff development takes place.

Communicating results

IIA Standard 2400 states that internal auditors should promptly communicate the engagement results. The communications are not necessarily of a standard form, as was outlined in Chapter 13 for external audit, but should include the engagement's objectives and scope as well as applicable conclusions, recommendations and action plans. Where non-compliance with an IIA Standard impacts on a specific engagement, communication of results should disclose the:

- IIA Standards(s) with which full compliance was not achieved;
- reasons for non-compliance; and
- impact of non-compliance on the engagement.

Monitoring progress and management's acceptance of risks

The head of internal audit should establish and maintain a system to monitor the results communicated to management, and the resulting follow-up actions. When the head of internal audit believes that senior management has accepted a level of residual risk that is unacceptable to the organisation, the matter should be discussed with senior management. If the matter remains unresolved, the head of internal audit and senior management should take the matter to the board of directors for discussion and resolution.

THE CURRENT PRACTICE OF INTERNAL AUDIT

In 1999 the Institute of Internal Auditors Research Foundation published a global Competency Framework for Internal Auditing (CFIA). The CFIA is presented in a number of publications (Birkett et al., 1999a–e). As part of the CFIA project, a survey was undertaken in 1998 of the current status of internal auditing in Australia (Birkett et al. 1999a). This is the most recent comprehensive survey of current practice that is available. The major findings are presented below:

1   **The scope of internal auditing work in Australia** Survey responses indicated that the most important areas of work undertaken by internal auditors in Australia are computer and financial audit, internal control reviews, fraud detection and operational audits. An involvement in quality systems also rated highly. It is interesting that these survey responses in 1998 reflect a fairly traditional role for internal auditing at this time.

   The list of internal auditing work areas nominated by respondents in this demographic survey differs to some degree from that contained in a study published in 1995 titled *A Profile of Internal Audit in Australia* undertaken by Deloitte Touche Tohmatsu and the Royal Melbourne Institute of Technology (Matthews et al., 1995). The study found that the major areas of internal auditing work were financial audit, independent appraisal of internal control, audit of operations, assisting external auditors, auditing management effectiveness and information technology audit. The 1998 study differs from the earlier study in that assisting the external auditors was excluded as a work area while fraud detection was included.

2   **Profile of internal auditors** In 1998, an estimated 4000 people were employed in internal auditing work in Australia, approximately 60 per cent in the public sector and 40 per cent in the private sector. Of the estimated 4000 internal auditors practising in Australia, approximately 50 per cent are members of IIA-Australia.

3   **Qualifications of internal auditors** Internal auditors are expected to have varied experience, including managerial, accounting, internal auditing and other types of experience relating to their particular organisation. In most cases, they are also expected to have an understanding of systems and internal control.

   In many instances employers required a degree from a tertiary institution, although the discipline in which it was undertaken was regarded as having limited importance. Alternatively, sufficient work experience may be seen as equivalent to a degree. IIA-Australia supports the international CIA program, which involves the provision of tutorials (some on video) and self-study materials. It conducts the formal sitting of the CIA multiple-choice examination. The CIA qualification is in its infancy in Australia, with approximately 200 CIA certified practitioners as at 2004.

Operational auditing

In the review of current internal audit practice in Australia, Birkett et al. (1999a, c) found that operational audit was one of the areas of significant growth for internal audit. An **operational audit** is a systematic review of an entity's activities, or of a stipulated segment of them, in relation to specified objectives for the purpose of:

- assessing performance;
- identifying opportunities for improvement; or
- developing recommendations for improvement or further action.

Operational audits of non-government entities are generally conducted by internal auditors. In the public sector these audits are commonly referred to as performance audits and are completed by the Auditor-General, as discussed in Chapter 16. As there is considerable overlap between performance audit and operational audit, a detailed discussion of these audits is contained in Chapter 16.

Quick review

1. The major areas of internal auditing work in Australia are computer and financial audit, internal control reviews, fraud detection and operational audits.
2. Internal auditors may come from a range of backgrounds and disciplines, and may have a variety of qualifications and/or experience.
3. An operational audit is a systematic review of activities to assess performance, identify opportunities for improvement and develop recommendations for further action.

THE FUTURE OF INTERNAL AUDIT

The Competency Framework for Internal Auditing (CFIA) survey also requested information relating to the future directions of internal audit. This has been combined with recent research and publications to identify issues facing the internal audit profession. These are:

1 **Major issues confronting internal audit**
   - The recent tendency of companies to outsource internal auditing services is seen as a major issue confronting the profession. In their survey of publicly listed companies in Australia, Carey et al. (2004) found that about 50 per cent of respondents outsourced some or all of their internal audit. There are a number of elements to this issue. At the extreme there are concerns of independence when it comes to the external auditor being able to provide a particular client with internal audit services too (discussed in Chapter 3), although it is possible for the large accounting firms to provide internal audit services to clients other than those whose financial reports they audit. Concerns about the effect of outsourced internal audit on independence and competence have been raised in the research of Swanger and Chewning (2001) and Carey et al. (2004). A benefit of outsourcing is the greater availability of internal auditing expertise that can come from 'contracting-in' the required areas of expertise.
   - The difficulty in changing the profile of the IIA and its members, especially in relation to the perception, image and status of internal auditing. There is a perceived need to 'market' internal auditing services, especially to recruit new people to the profession.
   - The different perceptions of internal auditing by chief executive officers and heads of internal audit. Some CEOs do not yet see benefit in changing internal audit from the traditional control function. There appears to be an 'expectations gap' which needs to be addressed.
   - The advent of specialised audit groups (e.g. quality, occupational health and safety, environmental and probity auditors). There are concerns as to whether the IIA can adequately cater for the needs of these more specialised groups.

2 Factors driving change

- The ability of internal auditing to show that it adds value to an organisation and contributes to more than control activities.
- The increasing ability to benchmark against best practice to assess organisational performance and as a means of assessing the quality of the internal auditing function's performance.
- Increased emphasis on corporate governance and risk management, and the ability to help management fulfil their duties in these areas. As outlined earlier, and illustrated by the new definition of internal audit, these are seen to be major areas in which internal auditors are expected to contribute.

The change in emphasis on risk management and corporate governance that is now reflected in the IIA Standards is also illustrated by the results from the CFIA survey, where internal audit respondents all around the world were asked to identify the key tasks facing internal audit. The key tasks related to risk exposures faced by organisations; the management or control of such exposures; and the effects of change on risk exposures and related controls. The risk-related tasks that received a high score of importance in the survey are summarised in Exhibit 15.2.

- Providing expert advice about risk exposures and their management
- Raising awareness about risk exposures
- Contributing to the improvement of risk management systems
- Providing ongoing assurance about the efficiency and effectiveness of risk management systems
- Internal auditing will focus ... on the risk exposures associated with the achievement of an organisation's objectives
- The services provided by internal auditing towards the achievement of an organisation's objectives will be distinctly related to the management of risk exposures ...

EXHIBIT 15.2

Risk-related tasks identified as being of importance to internal auditors

Source: Birkett et al., 1999c, p. 29.
Copyright 1999 by the Institute of Internal Auditors Research Foundation, Altamonte Springs, Florida, USA. Reprinted with permission.

The changing role of internal auditing is also shown by how internal auditors see their role in the future with regard to the control environment. The internal auditor's role in this area seems to be changing to a more value-added approach for the organisation, as identified by responses to the issues in Exhibit 15.3.

- Providing expert advice about control strategies, structures and systems
- Raising awareness about risk exposures and related controls
- Contributing to the improvement of control systems
- Providing ongoing assurance about the efficiency and effectiveness of control strategies, structures and systems
- Internal auditing will contribute enhanced understandings of the different types of control that can be used in organisations
- Internal auditing will focus on control as a facet of risk management
- The services provided by internal auditing towards the achievement of an organisation's objectives will be more distinctly related to the management of risk exposures through appropriate forms of control

EXHIBIT 15.3

Control-related tasks identified as being of importance to internal auditors

Source: Birkett et al., 1999c, pp. 24–5.
Copyright 1999 by the Institute of Internal Auditors Research Foundation, Altamonte Springs, Florida, USA. Reprinted with permission.

Expected future relationship with external auditors

There is normally a close relationship between an entity's internal auditors and its external auditors. Sometimes the work of internal auditors can be used by the external auditor, although it is not a substitute for the external auditor's work in a financial report audit. As explained in Chapter 8, AUS 604 (ISA 610) guides external auditors on obtaining an understanding of the activities of internal auditing and its effect on audit risk. IIA Standard 2050 states that one of the responsibilities of the head of internal audit is to co-ordinate the work of internal auditors with the work of the external auditor.

As both internal and external auditors move towards a business risk analysis approach it appears to make sense that there be a greater co-ordination of their work. This co-ordination is aided by the recent improvements in corporate governance, with the second edition of the *Audit Committees: Best Practice Guide* (AASB, AICD and IIA 2001), discussed in Chapter 3, recommending that one of the major roles of the audit committee is to co-ordinate the work of internal and external audit.

In a study of family companies (Carey et al. 2000), where both external and internal audit were voluntary, it was found that internal and external audit were generally viewed as complementary products. This meant that generally there were perceived advantages in having both forms of audit in the entity. However, there were a number of companies that used only one form of audit (i.e. there was a trend towards viewing the two forms of audit as substitutes rather than complements). Where historically it would have been expected that the one form of audit selected would be external audit, it was becoming more and more likely that in a voluntary audit environment this would be internal audit. There appeared to be two principal reasons for this trend. The first was that family companies found internal audit more relevant to their needs with its move towards a more business risk-based approach. The second was that the ability to outsource the internal audit function, in particular to the larger audit firms, meant that access to high levels of expertise had become more cost effective.

Quick review

1. One of the major trends of the profession is the increasing tendency in practice to outsource internal audit.
2. Internal auditors are increasingly shifting and are expected to continue to shift from a controls-based audit to a business risk analysis approach combined with value-adding in the control environment.
3. There appears to be a greater ability of internal and external auditors to co-ordinate their work based upon their complementary business risk approaches.

APPROACHES TO ASSESSING RISK MANAGEMENT, CONTROL AND GOVERNANCE PROCESSES

The internal audit is expected to use approaches to assessing **risk management**, control and governance processes similar to the approaches used by the external auditor in evaluating business risk. A business risk model is expected to guide this assessment, and tools used in this analysis may include SWOT analysis, PEST analysis and value-chain analysis. These tools were outlined in Chapter 6.

In Australia a number of internal auditors are utilising the Australian Risk Management Standard AS/NZS 4360. This standard was developed by a diverse group of people including internal auditors, engineers and risk management consultants. The emphasis in AS/NZS 4360 is on business risk management.

The main elements of the risk management process, described in this standard and as shown in Figure 15.1, are the following:

1 **Establish the context** Establish the strategic, organisational and risk management context in which the rest of the process will take place. Criteria against which risk will be evaluated should be established and the structure of the analysis defined.
2 **Identify risks** Identify what, why and how risks can arise as the basis for further analysis.
3 **Analyse risks** Determine the existing controls and analyse risks in terms of consequence and likelihood in the context of those controls. The analysis should consider the range of potential consequences and how likely those consequences are to occur. Consequence and likelihood may be combined to produce an estimated level of risk.
4 **Evaluate risks** Compare estimated levels of risk against the pre-established criteria. This enables risks to be ranked so as to identify management priorities. If the levels of risk established are low, then risks may fall into an acceptable category and treatment may not be required.
5 **Treat risks** Accept and monitor low-priority risks. For other risks, develop and implement a specific management plan which includes consideration of funding.
6 **Monitor and review** Monitor and review the performance of the risk management system and changes which might affect it.
7 **Communicate and consult** Communicate and consult with internal and external stakeholders as appropriate at each stage of the risk management process and concerning the process as a whole (Standards Australia, 1999, pp. 7–8).

For each stage of the process adequate records should be kept, sufficient to satisfy independent audit.

FIGURE **15.1 Risk management overview**

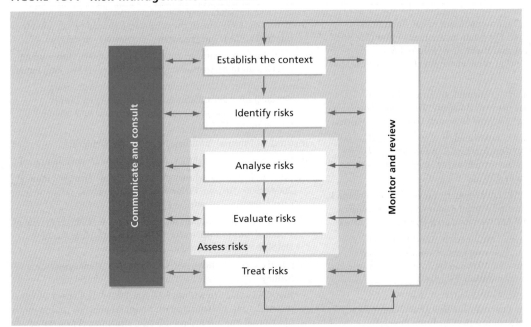

Source: Standards Australia, 1999, AS/NZS 4360, 'Risk Management' pp. 7–8.

Quick review

Strategic business risk standards to guide internal auditors in assessing risk management, control and governance processes have been developed and are being used by a number of internal auditors in practice.

Summary

Internal auditing is a significant part of the auditing profession and the IIA has an important role to play in promoting and developing it. As with financial report audits, there are standards to be met in performing internal audits. These include the auditing standards of CPA Australia and the ICAA (for members of these bodies), as well as the Standards of the IIA.

Internal audit has traditionally been seen as an important part of the monitoring mechanism of an entity's internal control. However, internal auditing also provides other valuable services to the entity, as a basis for improving managerial performance. Today internal audit is evolving, with much greater emphasis given to its role in evaluating and improving the effectiveness of risk management, control and governance processes.

Key terms

References

Auditing & Assurance Standards Board of the Australian Accounting Research Foundation, Australian Institute of Company Directors and Institute of Internal Auditors—Australia (2001), *Audit Committees: Best Practice Guide*, 2nd edn, AICD, Sydney.

Birkett, W.P., Barbera, M., Leithhead, B., Lower, M. and Roebuck, P. (1999a) *Internal Auditing: The Global Landscape*, Institute of Internal Auditors Research Foundation, Florida.

Birkett, W.P., Barbera, M., Leithhead, B., Lower, M. and Roebuck, P. (1999b) *Competency: Best Practices and Competent Practitioners*, Institute of Internal Auditors Research Foundation, Florida.

Birkett, W.P., Barbera, M., Leithhead, B., Lower, M. and Roebuck, P. (1999c) *The Future of Internal Auditing: A Delphi Study*, Institute of Internal Auditors Research Foundation, Florida.

Birkett, W.P., Barbera, M., Leithhead, B., Lower, M. and Roebuck, P. (1999d) *Assessing Competency in Internal Auditing: Structures and Methodologies*, Institute of Internal Auditors Research Foundation, Florida.

Birkett, W.P., Barbera, M., Leithhead, B., Lower, M. and Roebuck, P. (1999e) *Internal Auditing Knowledge: Global Perspectives*, Institute of Internal Auditors Research Foundation, Florida.

Brilliant, D. (1995) 'The audit committee should be satisfied that internal audit is independent', *The Banker*, November, 27.

Carey, P., Subramaniam, N. and Chua, W.C. (2004) 'Outsourcing internal audit in Australia', Monash University Working Paper.

Carey, P., Simnett, R. and Tanewski, G. (2000) 'Voluntary demand for internal and external auditing by family businesses', *Auditing: A Journal of Practice and Theory*, Supplement, 37–51.

Institute of Internal Auditors, http://www.theiia.org

Institute of Internal Auditors, Australia, http://www.iia.asn.au

Institute of Internal Auditors, Australia (2004) *Strategic Plan 2004–2006: Mission, Vision and Key Objectives*, http://www.iia.asn.au

Matthews, C.M.H., Cooper, B.J. and Leung, P. (1995) *A Profile of Internal Audit in Australia 1995—The Complete Study*, Deloitte Touche Tohmatsu, Melbourne.

Standards Australia (1999) AS/NZS 4360, Risk Management, Sydney.

Swanger, S.L. and Chewning, E.G. Jnr (2001) 'The effect of internal audit outsourcing on financial analysts' perceptions of external auditor independence', *Auditing: A Journal of Practice and Theory*, September, 115–29.

Assignments

REVIEW QUESTIONS

MAXIMISE YOUR MARKS! There are approximately 30 interactive questions on internal auditing available online at www.mhhe.com/au/gay3e

15.1 The following questions relate to aspects of internal auditing. Select the *best* response.

(a) Wendy Jones, CIA, works for a large department store. She is performing an audit of her company's cash function. Which of the following is an action in which due professional care is lacking?

    A Jones was extremely pleased with the internal controls and the operation of the cash function and in her report she states that she is sure no irregularities are currently present.

    B Jones flowcharts the work of the cash function but tests only a sample of the transactions.

    C Jones knows that the work of the cash function can be done effectively with one less employee. She includes this finding in her report even though she knows it will adversely affect employee morale in the cash function.

    D Jones reviews company records to ascertain that all employees who handle cash receipts and disbursements are covered by workers compensation.

(b) According to the IIA, the primary purpose of internal auditing is to:

    A review operations to ascertain whether results are consistent with established goals and objectives

    B reduce the costs of the annual external audit

    C provide a control over other controls

    D add value and improve an organisation's operations

(c) Of the following, which is the major objective of the IIA?

    A To investigate accusations that CIAs have violated the IIA Code of Ethics

    B To oversee the activities of internal auditors

    C To cultivate, promote and disseminate information concerning internal auditing and related subjects

    D To promulgate standards that must be followed by all corporations

(d) An internal auditor who had been supervisor of the accounts payable section should not audit that section:

    A because there is no way to measure a reasonable period of time in which to establish independence

    B until enough time has elapsed to allow the new supervisor to influence the system of controls over accounts payable

    C until after the next annual review of the external auditors

    D until it is clear that the new supervisor has assumed the responsibilities

(e) A company has outgrown its current computer system and the capabilities of its computer personnel. Management has asked the internal audit department to use its expertise to design and install a new computer system and help in hiring a new computer centre director. The internal audit department should:

    A accept the assignment because this would be very efficient and economical for the company

    B reject the assignment because making decisions concerning the design and installation of the system would impair the internal audit department's independence

    C reject the assignment because it would interfere with the completion of other internal audit work

    D accept the assignment, but not participate in the hiring of the director because this would cause a loss of independence

15.2 **(a)** Which of the following tasks receives increased attention under the new internal audit approach?

    A Evaluation of financial report details

    B Attendance at stocktakes

    C Identification and evaluation of control risk

    D Identification and evaluation of business risks

(b) Which of the evidence techniques below is the internal auditor likely to use in evaluating business risk?

    A Substantive tests of transactions

    B Substantive tests of balances

    C SWOT analysis

    D Tests of control

Understand evolving nature of internal auditing and its history

15.3 Explain the objective of internal auditing.

15.4 Explain how the role of the internal auditor has evolved over time.

Standards for internal auditing

15.5 Describe the requirements for becoming a Certified Internal Auditor.

15.6 Explain the concept of independence for an internal auditor.

Understand current internal audit practice

15.7 Does the Birkett et al. 1999 survey suggest that internal auditors are undertaking different internal audit practices compared with the Matthews et al. 1995 study?

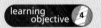

Consider future issues facing internal audit

15.8 With the external auditor increasing their undertaking of business risk analysis, are they likely to place more or less reliance on the work of internal audit? Why?

15.9 Do you believe that the trend to outsource internal audit departments is a concern? Discuss.

Appreciate approaches to assessing risk management, control and governance

15.10 What standards of the Institute of Internal Audits (IIA Standards) does the risk management process described under AS/NZS 4360 help fulfil?

DISCUSSION PROBLEMS AND CASE STUDIES

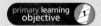

Understand the evolving nature of internal auditing and its history

15.11 **Basic** Emily Falkingham (CIA) states: 'I view strategic risk assessment as a natural extension of my traditional responsibilities. My risk assessment work is built on and integrated with my financial auditing. In a given area, say, purchasing or data processing, if I believe more attention is necessary for assessing risks, I'll expand that work and reduce the financial auditing emphasis.'

Compare this view of the internal auditor with the likely view of an independent external auditor.

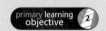

Internal auditing standards

15.12 **Basic** In June 2001 the internal audit department (IAD) of A Ltd (A) was involved in the implementation of a new information technology system. Specifically, they were required to design and implement appropriate controls for the implementation of the new system and changeover period. It is now June 2004 and A is undertaking its triennial review of the adequacy of the information technology. As usual the IAD is a main part of the team involved in this review; however, this time the head of the IAD has some concerns over the appropriateness of the department for the task. Specifically, she is concerned that the IAD will be required to report on the implementation of the new system, and she feels that this is inappropriate given the IAD's involvement in the implementation.

Required

Do you believe the IAD should participate in the triennial review? Provide reasons for your decision.

15.13 Moderate A rapidly growing manufacturing company is about to establish an internal audit department at the suggestion of their external auditor. The financial controller has proposed a charter for the internal audit department which contains, among other things, the following provisions:

(i)   The internal audit department is a staff function that is headed by a director of internal auditing who reports to the financial controller.

(ii) The internal audit department has the primary responsibility for the adequacy of internal control.

(iii) Internal audit department personnel have full access only to accounting records.

(iv) The internal audit department supports the work of the external auditor as directed by the financial controller.

(v)   Activities to be performed by the department include:

   1 participating in the design and implementation of financial internal control;

   2 ascertaining the extent to which company assets are accounted for and safe-guarded from losses of all kinds;

   3 ascertaining the extent of compliance with established accounting and financial policies;

   4 reviewing and appraising the soundness, adequacy and application of accounting internal control;

   5 ascertaining the reliability of accounting data developed within the entity; and

   6 recommending improvements in accounting internal control.

A candidate being considered for the position of director of internal auditing has reviewed the proposed charter and noted some problems with it. The candidate has pointed out that the proposed charter greatly restricts the scope of internal auditing and thus reduces its potential benefits.

Required

For each of the provisions (i) to (v), discuss any inhibiting restriction on the internal audit department's scope of work.

Source: CIA adapted

15.14 Moderate Certified Internal Auditors are often faced with situations which may involve ethical considerations. Consider the following cases:

(a) Auditor A has not participated in any type of professional development activity since the company stopped paying his institute dues three years ago.

(b) Auditor B participates in the activities of a religious organisation which provides sanctuary to undocumented political refugees. The refugees are then hired, with auditor B's assistance, to work for substandard wages by the company which also employs auditor B.

(c) Auditor C is assigned to supervise the audit of a cost-type sub-contract. The auditor's spouse is a silent partner in the company to be audited.

(d) Auditor D uses vacation time to prepare and present an in-house training session for the audit staff of the company's major customer. The agreed-upon gratuity is a video cassette recorder.

(e) Auditor E discovers evidence that the company has been disposing of toxic waste in a manner contrary to contractual provisions and public policy. The responsible department manager insists that what they are doing is in the company's best interest and requests that the auditor not mention this matter in the report.

(f) Auditor F has been assigned to work with the company's acquisition team. The auditor's father has been dealing speculatively in the securities of a firm with which the company is negotiating for an acquisition merger.

(g) Auditor G receives the following message from the company's chief executive officer, to whom the auditor reports administratively: 'The controller informs me that you have discovered a number of questionable account classifications involving the capitalisation of research and development expense. You are directed to discontinue any further investigation of this matter until informed by me to proceed. Under no circumstances is this matter to be discussed with the outside auditors.'

Required

For each of the cases listed above, state whether the condition is a violation of the IIA Code of Ethics. Justify your answer. If appropriate, suggest a course of action for the auditor that would avoid any personal violation of the Code.

Source: CIA adapted

15.15 Complex The board of directors of a diversified multinational enterprise realises that a stronger internal audit department would assist management with many operational problems that have surfaced as additional subsidiaries have been acquired. The board members are unsure how to proceed with improvements in the department, so they create a review group to conduct an evaluation in accordance with the IIA Standards. The review group notes the following:

1 The internal auditing department has a formal, written charter establishing its position within the entity. The charter authorises access to records, personnel and physical properties relevant to the performance of audits only through a chain of written approvals involving the operating personnel of the group being audited.

2 The director of internal auditing must clear all reports and presentations through the chief executive officer and chief financial officer prior to any contact with the audit committee or any member of the board. Staff members have no access to the board. The annual audit schedule, staffing plans and financial budget must go through normal operational channels for approval. The chief executive officer forwards audit activity reports and audit recommendations to the board if the information appears to be important.

3 Because of the rapid company growth, internal auditing staff members are frequently assigned to draft procedures for control systems as well as to design and install these systems. Subsidiary operating responsibilities are often assigned to a staff member who is then transferred to the subsidiary for a period of 9 to 15 months. Upon completion of the assignment the auditor returns to the audit staff at headquarters.

4 Each year the director of internal auditing prepares the audit schedule after reading staff reports and discussing critical operational areas with the audit managers. Management reviews the proposed audit schedule and changes it if the timing of the audit is in conflict with an operational activity. Several of the subsidiary operations have not been audited since acquisition. The director believes that audit coverage of the subsidiary operations is crucial to the company but is overruled by operating personnel.

5 Each of the subsidiaries has a satellite internal audit group headed by an audit manager. The position of audit manager is filled by an individual knowledgeable about the subsidiary's operations, but lacking audit knowledge and experience. Although

uniform audit policies and procedures are needed, no one is sure what should be contained in the manual. Subsidiaries hire new audit staff.

Required

As a member of the review group, prepare a draft report to the board of directors describing the deficiencies in the internal auditing department and recommending appropriate corrective action.

Source: CIA adapted

Understand current internal audit practice

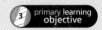

15.16 Basic In Australia, although internal auditors are not required to be members of any professional organisation the Birkett et al. (1999c) and Matthews et al. (1995) surveys indicated that the majority of internal audit managers were members of CPA Australia or the ICAA. This is despite the existence of the IIA in Australia.

Required

Do you think internal auditors should be members of a professional accounting body? If so, which body/ies do you think is/are the most appropriate?

Consider future issues facing internal audit

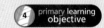

15.17 Moderate A current trend is the outsourcing of the internal audit function. In many situations this is being outsourced to either the external auditor or (another) Big Four assurance provider.

Required

What are the advantages and disadvantages for an organisation of outsourcing to:

(a) their external auditor?

(b) another Big Four assurance provider?

15.18 Moderate Consider settings where auditing is not necessarily compulsory, such as the audit of some family companies. In these settings, is the relationship between internal and external audit likely to be one of complementary services or substitute services? Why?

CONTINUOUS CASE STUDIES

15.19 Complex This is a continuation of question 14.30. It may be completed independently of that question.

Mitchell Pty Ltd is a small manufacturer of chemical products. The directors of Mitchell have recently attended a presentation on the benefits of internal audit and are considering employing an internal auditor in order to access these benefits. At the presentation they were told that in order to gain the full benefits of internal audit it is very important that the role and activities are clearly specified and the personnel are appropriate to the position. They are unsure as to how they should specify the role or the type of person they would be looking for and have approached their external auditor for some advice.

Required

Assuming you are the partner of the external audit firm, provide the directors with advice on establishing an internal audit presence within Mitchell Pty Ltd.

15.20 Complex This is a continuation of question 13.30. It may be completed independently of that question.

As a result of concerns expressed by the external auditor with regard to adequacy of stocktaking procedures, the internal audit department (IAD) of HomeChef Pty Ltd were asked to assist with the firm's stocktaking procedures. The stocktake involved assisting the manager of each of the company's stores and warehouses to perform a stocktake on a specified date. Specifically, members of the IAD were told that they should spend time explaining the importance of the procedures and training managers in the use of the procedures due to a perception that managers did not understand the importance of the stocktake to the company.

It is now 4 months after the stocktake and the head of the IAD has been asked to undertake an audit of the company's stocktaking procedures with a view to making improvements in the area. The head of the department is unsure whether they should become involved in this engagement given the assistance that they have previously provided.

Required

(a) Should the internal audit department undertake the operational audit? Provide reasons for your decision.

(b) Identify criteria which could be used to assess the economy, efficiency and effectiveness of the stocktaking activity.

(c) For each criterion identified in (b), indicate a possible source of evidence which could be used to assess the stocktaking activity.

CHAPTER 16

AUDIT AND ASSURANCE SERVICES IN THE PUBLIC SECTOR

LEARNING OBJECTIVES

After studying this chapter you should be able to:

1 explain the different levels of government in Australia and their main responsibilities;

2 explain the concept of accountability;

3 outline the different bases of accounting used in the public sector;

4 explain public sector audit requirements;

5 describe the nature of performance auditing; and

6 describe the nature of regularity audits.

Chapter outline

Some characteristics of audit and assurance services in the public sector in Australia were outlined in Chapter 2. This chapter will outline the different levels of government in Australia and discuss the nature of government accounting. The role of the public sector auditor and the nature of performance and compliance audits will also be discussed.

Relevant guidance

Australian		International	
AUS 106	Explanatory Framework for Standards on Audit and Audit-Related Services	ISA 120	Explanatory Framework for Standards on Audit and Audit-Related Services
AUS 806	Performance Auditing	—	
AUS 808	Planning Performance Audits	—	

AUSTRALIAN SYSTEM OF GOVERNMENT

In a federal system such as Australia's, the various functions of government are shared between the Commonwealth, the states and local government bodies. Section 51 of the Constitution sets out the Commonwealth government's powers, which cover matters of national importance such as defence and immigration. State governments, on the other hand, deal with social services such as education and public health; economic development; public utilities and business undertakings, such as metropolitan transport and water supply; and the administration of local government through state legislation. Local government authorities (municipal councils) are concerned primarily with civic services such as road construction and garbage disposal; and social services such as community centres and public libraries.

Responsibility for the administration of the laws and the implementation of government policies is assigned to various departments and instrumentalities. At the central government level, the conventional administrative unit is the ministerial department. However, in recent years statutory authorities, both Commonwealth and state, have become increasingly important as an instrument of government. Many of these statutory authorities conduct business undertakings, while others have regulatory or advisory functions. In some instances, government departments and statutory authorities have also established other entities including companies, joint ventures or trusts. Ultimately, it is to Parliament that all units of government must account for use of the finances provided to carry out their functions.

ACCOUNTABILITY

An important aspect of the Westminster system of government which operates in Australia is the concept of **accountability**. SAC 2.5 defines accountability in terms of financial reporting as the responsibility to provide information to users to enable them to make informed judgments about the performance, financial position, financing and investing and compliance of a reporting entity. Further, SAC 2.44 states that management and governing bodies must present general purpose financial reports in a manner which assists in discharging their accountability.

The Management Advisory Board and the Management Improvement Advisory Board of the Commonwealth Public Service take a broader view of accountability, defining it as:

existing where there is a direct authority relationship within which one party accounts to a person or body for the performance of tasks or functions conferred, or able to be conferred, by that person or body. The consequences of the application of rewards and sanctions are seen as having a logical connection with the activation of the accountability mechanism.

The cycle of accountability shown in Figure 16.1 begins with Parliament approving the use of various resources in a particular program and specifying the expected outcomes, and ends with reporting back to Parliament on the utilisation of the resources and the results achieved. The management of the public sector entities are entrusted with public resources on a stewardship basis and have a responsibility to use them economically, efficiently and effectively. They discharge their accountability role by preparing reports, including financial reports, to show the results of their administration of public funds and use of resources. Public sector auditors assist in the accountability process by providing assurance as to the credibility of management's reports and making assessments of management's performance.

FIGURE 16.1 Cycle of accountability

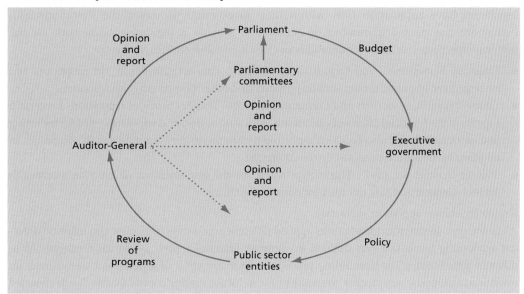

Source: Auditor-General, 1990.

Sources of government revenue and expenditure

Governments derive their revenue from taxation, charging for goods and services, fines, sale of non-current assets and borrowing. The Commonwealth also provides grants to the states and local government bodies. Public expenditure involves the amount of public moneys to be spent on providing goods and services and includes wages, salaries and other employee entitlements, rental charges and the cost of assets consumed (for example, supplies and depreciation).

The control of public expenditure is one of the most important responsibilities of Parliament. The expenditure of the funds allocated each year through the government's budget, which must be approved by Parliament, is subject to well-defined procedures to ensure that only legally permissible transactions are entered into by government departments and agencies. The system of authorising expenditure and the related accounting records are designed to ensure that disbursements by departments conform with the annual appropriations.

In the past it was thought that effective control of public funds was achieved by the limitation of expenditure and careful custody of government assets. However, it is now recognised that it is equally important that wise expenditure decisions are made at the outset, and that government departments and agencies conduct their affairs effectively and with economy and efficiency.

GOVERNMENT ACCOUNTING

There is no Australia-wide legal reporting code for all public sector entities. Individual pieces of legislation have application only within their jurisdiction. However, the Commonwealth Parliament has passed a number of Acts which provide a legislative framework for the performance, propriety and accountability of Commonwealth entities. These are:

■ *Financial Management and Accountability Act 1997* This Act provides for the proper use and management of public money, public property and other Commonwealth resources.

■ *Commonwealth Authorities and Companies Act 1997* This Act provides regulations for certain aspects of the financial affairs of Commonwealth authorities, and stipulates rules for reporting and accountability. It also contains reporting requirements for Commonwealth companies in addition to the requirements of *Corporations Act.*

■ *Auditor-General Act 1997* This Act provides for the appointment of the Commonwealth Auditor-General and sets out the functions of the Office.

Similar legislation applies in each state.

In the past, as different jurisdictions applied different accounting principles and followed different accounting formats, it was difficult to compare financial reports of similar organisations in different jurisdictions. The accounting procedures of many areas of government were simply an extension of the budgetary process, to ensure by means of accounting control that the funds allocated to departments and agencies were spent only within the constraints of the budget. As a result, these departments used 'fund accounting' and therefore their financial reports were special purpose reports. In contrast, some other government departments prepared general purpose financial reports.

However, since 31 December 1996, AAS 29 'Financial Reporting by Government Departments' has required government departments that are reporting entities to prepare general purpose financial reports using **accrual accounting**. AAS 29 states that, where legal or other authoritative requirements require government departments to comply with financial reporting requirements which differ from the standard, such requirements apply in addition to, and not instead of, the standard. The standard does not apply to government departments that are required to comply with accounting standards operative under the *Corporations Act* or the equivalent Australian accounting standards.

Preparing financial reports on an accrual rather than a cash basis of accounting is thought to provide more useful information to users of general purpose financial reports. In addition to the benefits expected of accrual accounting in the private sector, the benefits of accrual accounting in the public sector include:

- enhancing and extending public and parliamentary accountability by disclosing the full cost of services provided by the public sector and the resources used to provide those services;
- assisting decision making by promoting a management culture focused on the effective and efficient deployment of resources and the achievement of outputs, and not just the inputs consumed in delivering services;
- improving performance monitoring;
- enabling intergenerational comparisons by allowing judgments as to whether the current generation has added to or reduced the net worth of the state for future generations; and
- assisting understanding of public sector assets and liabilities.

Government businesses such as transport and postal services have accounting objectives of measuring the financial self-sufficiency or profitability of the undertaking. Thus, the form and content of their published financial reports are similar to those of companies, consisting of an income statement, balance sheet and a statement of cash flows.

AAS 31 'Financial Reporting by Government', issued in November 1996, applies to reporting periods ending on or after 30 June 1999, although earlier adoption was permitted. AAS 31 states that the Commonwealth, state and territory governments are reporting entities and should prepare general purpose financial reports on an accrual basis. In addition, a consolidated financial report for governments should be prepared in accordance with AASB 1024. This represents the introduction of 'whole of government' financial reporting.

Local government accounting procedures are prescribed by the state local government Acts and ordinances. A common feature of local government accounting used to be the use of various 'special purpose' funds. Local government authorities usually had a general fund, capital fund, trust fund and, for their business undertakings, a working fund. However, AAS 27 'Financial Reporting by Local Governments', which was issued in December 1990, deems each local government to be a reporting entity and requires general purpose financial reports to be prepared on an accrual basis. It states that where legal and other authoritative requirements cover the financial reporting of local government entities, such requirements apply in addition to and not instead of the requirements of the standard.

Quick review

1. There is no single legal reporting code covering all public sector entities.
2. Australian accounting standards apply to public sector entities in addition to the requirements of local legislation.
3. AAS 27, AAS 29 and AAS 31 require local governments, government departments and Commonwealth, state and territory governments that are reporting entities to prepare general purpose financial reports on an accrual basis.
4. Government business undertakings follow normal accrual accounting processes and prepare general purpose financial reports.

PUBLIC SECTOR AUDIT REQUIREMENTS

learning objective 4

Audit mandate

Public sector auditors carry out their duties in accordance with an **audit mandate**, which specifies the type of audit to be conducted, the entity or activity to be audited and the powers and responsibilities of the auditor. Audit mandates are usually specified in legislation.

AUDITING IN THE NEWS

SNIPPET

16.1

Source: Address by
Pat Barrett AM,
Auditor-General
for Australia,
Macquarie University,
23 August 2002.

Public sector auditing: ANAO approaches and practices

The Australian National Audit Office (ANAO) is pivotal to the system of checks and balances that support democracy in Australia. Public reports from an independent Auditor-General ensure that the Parliament, and beyond it the Australian citizenry, have a degree of assurance in relation to the proper administration of Commonwealth resources. The ANAO has a dual role in terms of reporting on both the financial management and overall performance of the public sector. Our first aim is to provide independent assurance. This is the more traditional 'watchdog' audit role. Our second role is to suggest improvements to public administration. Increasingly, it is this second, advisory, role that is most important for a public sector, which, in the proper pursuit of greater efficiency and effectiveness is challenged by diverse governance issues that are growing in complexity.

Recent corporate collapses in the private sector are again leading to calls for strengthened internal and external control and scrutiny. Although not driven by the same imperatives, the public sector governance environment is also changing. Citizens have higher expectations of government and the public service and demand more effective, efficient and economical levels of service. Public sector managers are responding to the demands of their particular operating environments by developing tailored approaches; streamlining and adapting traditional ways of providing services, particularly though technological advances; and by taking advantage of partnerships and similar alliances that blend the public and private sectors. In this latter respect, the increasing involvement of the private sector in the delivery of public services is challenging traditional notions of accountability, an issue that is central to good governance. While diverse governance approaches may now be required by the dynamic nature of the contemporary public service environment, one lesson remains constant: sound process will lead in most cases to good outcomes. Results count, but it is also important *how* these results are achieved. The latter is constantly being reinforced in the Federal Parliament.

For the ANAO, a key issue is getting the balance right between control and innovation in order to provide the guidance and the leadership demanded by a rapidly changing world virtually shrunk by modern communications and transport. The aim is to get the right mix of products and services by recruiting and retaining highly achieving staff to anticipate and plan for the challenges of the future. In setting its agenda for the future, the ANAO relies on intelligence garnered through the review and analysis of over 200 Commonwealth entities as well as ongoing feedback and guidance from the Parliament and other audit clients as to the areas they see as adding most value to public administration.

International developments

The movement toward a broad audit mandate is evident in international developments in public sector auditing. Early evidence of this were the standards set by the General Accounting Office in the USA. This office was established in 1921 by the Congress to obtain better control over the appropriation of funds. In 1972 it issued *Standards for Audits of Governmental Organisations, Programs, Activities and Functions*, which set out guidelines for increasing the scope of governmental audit. This publication defined three elements of a governmental audit:

1 **Financial and compliance**—determines (a) whether financial operations are properly conducted, (b) whether the financial reports of an audited entity are presented fairly and (c) whether the entity has complied with applicable laws and regulations.

2   **Economy and efficiency**—determines whether the entity is managing or utilising its resources (personnel, property, space and so forth) in an economical and efficient manner and identifies the causes of any inefficiencies or uneconomical practices, including inadequacies in management information systems, administrative procedures or organisational structure.

3   **Program results**—determines whether the desired results or benefits are being achieved, whether the objectives established by the legislature or other authorising body are being met, and whether the agency has considered alternatives which might yield desired results at a lower cost.

The purpose of audits of governmental organisations and programs is similar to the purpose of audits of financial reports. An audit of a government body provides an independent judgment of the credibility of public officials' statements about the manner in which they have carried out their responsibilities. The standards of the General Audit Office, which are typical of the developments in governmental auditing, follow the same pattern as the generally accepted auditing standards of the American Institute of Certified Public Accountants. The audit function is extended by considering performance auditing, which will be discussed in more detail later and includes some consideration of efficiency and economy of operatives and the effectiveness of programs.

Performance auditing has been also emphasised by the International Organisation of Supreme Audit Institutions (INTOSAI). Australia belongs to this body, which comprises auditors-general or their equivalent from member countries. INTOSAI has defined the role of Supreme Audit Institutions (SAIs), a function performed in Australia by auditors-general. INTOSAI's definition helps in understanding the development of the broad audit mandate in the public sector.

Role of the SAI

30. *The growth in government activity carried out in the form of public enterprises underlines the importance of effective audit of these entities. The definition, nature and scope of public enterprises vary widely between countries, reflecting their different constitutions, economic systems and circumstances. But each country should have its own clear and consistent definition of a public enterprise, covering in particular the enterprise's relationships with government and its responsibilities for public accountability. It is desirable that the definition be embodied in legislation.*

31. *The substantial involvement of public funds, capital investment and other resources in public enterprises requires full public accountability, which can be guaranteed only through audit by SAI. SAIs should seek to ensure that the scope of their responsibilities extends to the audit of all public enterprises, including subsidiary bodies created by the enterprises themselves. Change in the constitution or status of the bodies concerned should not be used to reduce or remove audit by the SAI. It is desirable that the SAI's responsibilities and the necessary powers to exercise them be embodied in legislation.*

32. *In order to undertake effective audit of public enterprises SAIs should be independent of government, especially in the provision of necessary resources (including staffing, finance and training). They should also have complete access to obtain all necessary information for the purposes of their audit.*

33. *In some countries the audit of public enterprises may include direct audits and supervisory audits by the SAI or other methods. Whether or not the SAI is responsible for the financial audit of public enterprises, it should have the power to conduct performance audits.*

34. *SAIs should take a leading role in the development of auditing and reporting standards relevant to public enterprises and should ensure that the audit is conducted to the highest professional standards and with full regard to the public interest.*

35. *Public accountability requires that public enterprises themselves demonstrate that they have used resources with due regard to economy, efficiency and effectiveness. This includes setting predetermined objectives and performance targets, measuring achievement and publishing relevant information on performance. SAIs should encourage the management of public enterprises to measure their own performance against clear objectives and performance targets. Enterprises should be required to provide fully informative financial statements and publish sufficient additional information on performance and results to ensure proper public accountability.*

36. *Independent reports by the SAIs are an essential element in providing information, assurance and advice. In order to meet the requirements of public accountability and to ensure that effective action can be taken to remedy weaknesses in control, improve systems for securing value for money and ensure provision of independent, relevant and timely information on the performance of public enterprises, SAIs should be empowered to report the results and recommendations of their audit of public enterprises, as appropriate, to management, the government and, in particular, the highest political bodies in each country.*

37. *SAIs should establish arrangements to preserve confidentiality where necessary.*

38. *SAIs should follow up the action taken by the management of public enterprises and government to remedy weaknesses and improve systems, and should report again if sufficient progress is not made.*

(Twelfth International Congress of Supreme Audit Institutions, 1986, pp. 4–5)

The Australian National Audit Office (ANAO) (see Auditing in the News 16.1 on p. 696) is also a member of the Asian Organisation of Supreme Audit Institutions (ASOSAI) and the International Consortium on Government Financial Management.

Australian developments

In Australia the audit of Commonwealth government departments and statutory authorities and instrumentalities is primarily the responsibility of the Commonwealth Auditor-General, through the ANAO. The Auditor-General also acts as auditor for government corporations by arrangement with the responsible minister. Each state and territory also has an auditor-general whose duties are governed by state legislation and are similar to those of the Commonwealth Auditor-General. For convenience, this chapter will refer to the specific requirements applicable to the Commonwealth Auditor-General. Some statutory authorities are audited by private firms, depending on the specific legislation under which they operate.

The origins of the Office of Commonwealth Auditor-General are found in the *Audit Act 1901*. This Act was influenced by the audit Acts of several states and New Zealand, which in turn were influenced by the *Exchequer and Audit Departments Act 1866* of Great Britain. The initial perception of the role of the Auditor-General was limited. It was restricted to the conduct of detailed examinations of government financial transactions, essentially an audit of the cash transactions of the Commonwealth.

Subsequent amendments to the Act have clarified, strengthened and expanded the role of the Auditor-General to encompass the broad audit mandate and the objectives of performance auditing reflected in the INTOSAI definition. For example, as a result of the recommendations of the Royal Commission on Australian Government Administration, the Minister of Finance introduced a Bill in 1979 to amend the *Audit Act 1901* to give the Auditor-General discretion to carry out efficiency audits. This legislation, combined with s. 54 of the Act, which allows the Auditor-General to carry out project audits, provides a mandate for performance auditing. The mandate extends to all of the departments and entities of the Commonwealth public sector of which the Auditor-General is external auditor. This mandate was confirmed in the *Auditor-General Act 1997*, mentioned earlier in this chapter. Thus, the Auditor-General's **comprehensive audit** mandate encompasses the functions of performance auditing and regularity auditing (the latter encompasses both financial report and compliance auditing). These different types of audit will be discussed in more detail later in the chapter.

In addition, the ANAO also provides other assurance services such as **protective security audits**, which are across-the-board studies that examine control frameworks and use established better practice criteria to evaluate agency performance. The three key aspects of security that are examined in these audits are information security, personnel security and physical security.

The ANAO has established an Outcome–Output Framework to assess the ANAO's performance. Its two desired outcomes, as set out in its 2001 annual report, are:

1 independent assessment of the performance of selected Commonwealth public sector activities including the scope for improving efficiency and administrative effectiveness; and

2 independent assurance of Commonwealth public sector financial reporting, administration control and accountability.

Auditing standards in the public sector

AUS 106 (ISA 120), discussed in Chapter 1, describes the framework within which the audit profession issues audit standards and audit guidance statements for services provided by external and internal auditors in the private and public sectors. The public sector auditor performs audits in accordance with Australian auditing standards. The Australian accounting bodies have endorsed these statements as applying to members working in the public sector, to the extent that they are not inconsistent with or unnecessary to the audit mandate of the public sector engagement.

The Commonwealth Auditor-General is required by s. 24 of the *Auditor-General Act 1997* to publish audit standards covering audits in the Commonwealth public sector. Prior to the implementation of this legislation, the Auditor-General had already recognised the commonality of standards expected of auditors in both the public and private sectors. This is reflected in the following statements which were included in the *Commonwealth of Australia Gazette* No. GN22 on 5 June 1996:

> *The Auditor-General recognises there is commonality in the auditing standards expected of the private and public sector auditing professions and wishes to conform to the greatest extent possible with the Auditing Standards promulgated by the ASCPA and ICAA. The Auditing Standards and Auditing Guidance Statements are equally applicable as an expression of the minimum standard of audit work expected of auditors in the public sector as they are in the private sector ...*
>
> *The ANAO adopts, as the ANAO Auditing Standards, the codified auditing pronouncements issued by the Australian Accounting Research Foundation on behalf of the ASCPA and the ICAA, known as the Auditing Standards (AUSs) and Auditing Guidance Statements (AGSs) ...*

This has since been reconfirmed by notification in the *Commonwealth of Australia Gazette* No. GN6 on 11 February 1998.

Reporting duties

Section 58 of the *Financial Management and Accountability Act 1997* requires the Auditor-General to state in the audit report whether the financial report:

- has been prepared in accordance with the Finance Minister's orders; and
- gives a true and fair view of the matters required by those orders.

If the financial report is not in accordance with the Finance Minister's orders, the audit report must quantify the financial effect of that departure.

A report on an exception basis is issued when:

- proper accounting records were not kept (stating the particulars of the contravention); or
- the Auditor-General was not able to obtain all the necessary information and explanations.

These reporting requirements are virtually identical to the requirements of the *Corporations Act*.

The Explanatory Memorandum to the *Auditor-General Act 1997* states that the audit report may contain significant matters which, in the opinion of the Auditor-General, should be brought to the attention of Parliament. Examples are:

- Matters concerning the administrative operations of the public sector to which Parliament has attached an audit priority.
- Significant breaches of legislation.
- Accounting and other records not maintained in accordance with generally accepted practice.
- Public money, or money of a Commonwealth authority or company, not accounted for correctly.
- Accounting and other records not maintained, or practices and procedures insufficient to:
  — safeguard and control public property or property of a Commonwealth authority or company;
  — ensure effective controls over the collection and allocation of receipts and payments of money;
  — ensure the proper use of Commonwealth resources;
  — ensure satisfactory monitoring, measuring and reporting of the effectiveness of operations programs; and
  — ensure that accepted standards of accountability are maintained.
- Matters relating to the propriety and probity of the transactions of the Commonwealth or the actions of its officials.
- Recommendations for change in an administrative process, a system or an operation within the Commonwealth public sector which in the opinion of the Auditor-General will lead to improved performance, better resource control and compliance with the law, or to greater efficiency or economy.
- The economy, efficiency and effectiveness of the operations of the administration of the Commonwealth public sector.

The Auditor-General must provide a copy of any report to the Finance Minister. Annual reports are then tabled in Parliament. It is important to remember that the ANAO's primary client is the Parliament.

ANAO reports are debated when they are tabled in Parliament, and they are also discussed in various parliamentary committees. Either House of Parliament may refer the audit report, once tabled, for further investigation and report by a standing or select committee. In addition, the Joint Committee of Public Accounts and Audit maintains the statutory responsibility to examine all reports of the Auditor-General under s. 8(1)(a, b) of the *Public Accounts Committee Act 1951*.

Independence

The independence of an auditor is critical to the audit function. This requirement of independence applies in the public sector as it does in the private sector. The report of the WA Inc. Royal Commission stated:

> The office of Auditor-General provides a critical link in the accountability chain between the public sector, and the Parliament and the community. It alone subjects the practical conduct and operations of the public sector as a whole to regular, independent investigation and review. This first function must be fully guaranteed and its discharge facilitated. The Auditor-General is the Parliament's principal informant on the performance of the administration system. The Parliament, therefore, has a special responsibility to ensure both that the independence and the effective resourcing of the Auditor-General are secured, and that its own investigative procedures (particularly through committees) are such that it utilises the information about government supplied to it in the Auditor-General's reports ...

(WA Royal Commission, 1992, 3.10.1)

To perform such a function, the Auditor-General must be, and be seen to be, independent.

Appointment and removal of the Auditor-General

The *Auditor-General Act 1997* defines the powers, duties and responsibilities of the Office. The Commonwealth Auditor-General is appointed by the Governor-General on the recommendation of the responsible minister for a period of 5 to 7 years. The responsible minister makes the recommendation after consultation with the Finance Minister, a nominee of the Leader of the Opposition in the House of Representatives, the Chair of the Joint Committee of Public Accounts and Audit and the Chair of the Audit Committee of the Parliament (if established). This consultative process and the appointment by the Governor-General help to ensure the Auditor-General's independence. A similar process is followed for the appointment of state auditors-general.

The independence of the position is further protected by the requirement that the Auditor-General can be removed from office only if a request for removal is presented to the Governor-General by both Houses of Parliament in the same session, or if the Auditor-General becomes bankrupt.

This level of independence, combined with the statutory powers of the auditor-general, provides the basis for an effective audit of the financial reports of Commonwealth government departments and authorities.

Quick review

1. International developments have led to the audit mandate of SAIs being expanded to include performance audits.
2. In Australia the audit mandate for public sector auditors includes financial report audits, compliance audits and performance audits.
3. Audits are carried out at Commonwealth, state and local government levels.
4. Australian auditing standards apply to members operating in the public sector.
5. The Commonwealth Auditor-General has issued auditing standards, based on the professional standards, for audits within the Commonwealth public sector.
6. The Auditor-General's primary client is Parliament.
7. It is important that the Auditor-General's independence is maintained.
8. The Auditor-General is appointed by the Governor-General and can be removed by a recommendation of both Houses of Parliament in the same session.

PERFORMANCE AUDITS

Performance auditing is also referred to as **value-for-money auditing** or **operational auditing**. The term 'performance audit' is usually applied in the public sector, with some application in the private sector. It has evolved with the broad objectives of reporting on economy, efficiency and effectiveness. The ANAO, in its Statement of Auditing Standards (1998), states that a performance audit is an independent, expert and systematic examination of the management of an organisation, program or function for the purposes of:

- forming an opinion about:
  - the extent to which the organisation, program or function is being managed in an economical, efficient or effective manner;
  - the adequacy of internal procedures for promoting and monitoring economy, efficiency and effectiveness; and
- suggesting ways by which management practices, including procedures for monitoring performance, might be improved.

The objectives of performance auditing in the public sector are thus twofold:

1 to provide Parliament with assurance about the quality of management of public resources; and
2 to assist public sector managers by identifying, promoting and protecting better management practices.

A performance audit may include a review of:

- use of human, financial and other resources;
- information systems, performance measures and monitoring arrangements; and
- procedures followed by audited bodies for remedying identified deficiencies.

Performance audits are usually directed to a combination of the following three purposes:

1 **Assess performance** The manner in which the entity is conducting activities is compared (a) to objectives established by management or the engaging party, such as organisational policies, standards and goals, and (b) to other appropriate measurement criteria.
2 **Identify opportunities for improvement** The auditor may identify specific opportunities for improvements in economy, efficiency or effectiveness by analysing interviews with individuals (within or outside the entity), observing operations, reviewing past and current reports, studying transactions, making comparisons with industry standards, exercising professional judgment based on experience, or other appropriate means.
3 **Develop recommendations for improvement or further action** The nature and extent of recommendations developed in the course of performance audits vary considerably. In many cases the auditor makes specific recommendations. In other cases further study beyond the scope of the engagement is required, and the auditor simply explains why.

In a particular performance audit engagement, one of these purposes may take precedence over the others.

It can be seen from this that the purpose of a performance audit contrasts starkly with the purpose of an audit of a financial report: the latter expresses an opinion on whether the report fairly presents the entity's financial position, results of operations and cash flows in conformity with accounting standards.

The criteria for judging the representations in a financial report are codified in authoritative accounting pronouncements. Performance auditing is very different in this respect. The performance auditor needs 'specified objectives' that perform essentially the same role as generally accepted accounting principles. These specified objectives are often unique to the program or activity being reviewed, and the detailed development of them is often part of the auditor's assignment.

Often a performance audit requires knowledge and skills outside the fields of accounting and auditing. In these cases, an expert in the relevant field has to be included in the audit team.

Like financial report auditing, where management prepares a financial report and the auditor adds credibility through an independent opinion, performance auditing expects management responsibility to ensure economy and efficiency in the use of resources, with the auditor providing a report on the extent to which predetermined goals have been achieved economically and efficiently.

Economy

AUS 806.03 defines **economy** as the acquisition of financial, human, physical and information resources of appropriate quality and quantity at the lowest reasonable cost. It is essentially a resource acquisition concept. Examples of economy audits involve determining whether the entity has:

- followed sound procurement practices; and
- acquired the appropriate type, quality and amount of resources at the right time and for the lowest cost.

An example of improved economy is a reduction in costs through bulk buying or better contracting.

Efficiency

AUS 806.04 defines **efficiency** as the use of a given set of resource inputs to maximise outputs, or the use of minimum input resources for a predetermined level of output. It is essentially a resource usage concept. Examples of efficiency audits involve determining whether the entity has:

- prevented idleness and overstaffing; and
- prevented duplication of effort by employees.

An example of improved efficiency is greater outputs from the same inputs, for example more electricity from the same amount of coal.

Effectiveness

AUS 806.05 defines **effectiveness** as the achievement of the objectives or other intended effects of activities. It focuses upon the results or outcomes of resource usage and organisational operations. Therefore effectiveness is ends oriented rather than means oriented. Examples of effectiveness audits are:

- an audit of a program to determine whether it has achieved its objective; and
- an analysis of the relevance of the entity's activities to its objectives.

An example of improved effectiveness is a reduction in the incidence of disease through a preventive health program.

Outcomes are affected by external factors and may require long-term assessment. Therefore outcomes are more difficult to measure and assess than inputs or outputs. Often, there are no objective measures by which to measure an entity's effectiveness. For example, it is much more difficult to assess whether a fire brigade is adequately meeting the public's needs (effectiveness), than it is to assess whether new fire engines of appropriate quality are being purchased at the lowest reasonable cost (economy), and are being properly maintained at the lowest reasonable cost to meet fire-fighting requirements (efficiency). Nevertheless, effectiveness is arguably the most important aspect of performance auditing: irrespective of whether the goods or services have been economically and efficiently provided, if they do not achieve their intended outcomes value for money has not been achieved.

The greater emphasis on the development of key performance indicators and the use of performance information to assess the extent to which program objectives are being achieved is a major issue in the public sector. Walker (2001) points out that AAS 29 encourages the publication of performance information on major programs, without actually prescribing that treatment. Walker (2002) asks how anyone can ensure that performance indicators are relevant and reliable and queries whether performance indicators are auditable.

Effectiveness often brings in issues of policy. However, government policy is generally outside the auditor's scope. Rather, policy is the domain of government, and the merits of policy objectives are considered a matter for political debate. However, the means by which the objectives are determined and pursued—whether policy decisions have been taken with appropriate authority and have been properly implemented—are legitimate areas of review.

The ANAO *Performance Audit Guide* (1996, para. 1.8) states that:

Performance audits do not comment on Government policy. They may examine and report on:
- *the quality of information and policy advice given to Government by officials;*
- *the existence and effectiveness of administrative machinery in place to inform the Government whether policies are meeting their objectives;*
- *whether, and to what extent, stated program objectives have been met;*
- *the economy, efficiency and performance of the means chosen to implement a program; and*
- *the intended and unintended direct and indirect program impacts.*

In simple terms, efficiency means 'doing the thing right', while effectiveness means 'doing the right thing'. The relationship between economy, efficiency and effectiveness is shown in Figure 16.2.

FIGURE **16.2 Relationship between economy, efficiency and effectiveness**

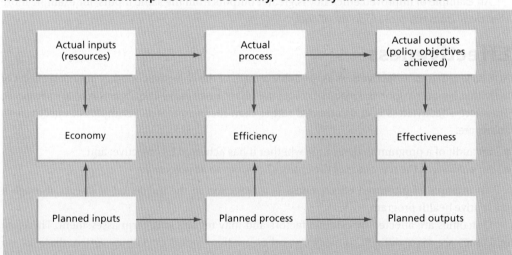

As practised by the ANAO, therefore, performance auditing is concerned with the assessment of the management and operational performance of departments and agencies in using financial and other resources. The mandate for performance auditing does not specify an obligation to report annually as is the case with financial report audits. The ANAO has an annual target of 50 performance audit reports and during 2002 produced 57 such reports.

Given the availability of resources, and the obligation to apply those resources to meeting statutory financial report audit requirements, the ANAO uses strategic planning to identify areas of the public sector exposed to risk and those areas where public administration can be improved to maximise the efficient use of resources and provide the highest rate of return on the audit investment. In 2001, 247 of the 258 recommendations made in performance audit reports were accepted by the audited entities. This represents an agreement rate of 96 per cent. The ANAO potential financial benefit of performance audit statistics is shown in Exhibit 16.1.

Description	1997–98	1998–99	1999-00	2000-01
Estimated potential annual recurring benefit	$37m[a]	$502m	$2.2m[b]	$85.5m[c]

(a) Plus a potential once-only saving of $197 million.
(b) Plus a potential once-only saving of $121.4 million.
(c) Plus one-off savings of $90.4 million.

EXHIBIT 16.1
Potential financial benefit of performance audits conducted by ANAO, 1998–2001

Source: Auditor-General, 2001, Table 4.

Stages of a performance audit

The stages in an ANAO performance audit are planning, preliminary study, implementation, reporting and follow-up. The conceptual framework for stages in a performance audit is shown in Figure 16.3 (overleaf).

Planning stage

The first stage of a performance audit, planning, requires a continuing watch on the entity to develop and maintain information which is useful in identifying potential areas for audit. AUS 806.18 and AUS 808.02 require the auditor to plan the audit work so that the performance audit is conducted effectively.

Potential audit topics are analysed and ranked to form an annual audit strategy. This ensures that the resources of the ANAO are used in the most efficient and effective manner and it therefore produces a work program that can be achieved with the expected available resources. In particular, there needs to be a good understanding of the entities and their risks, with emphasis on identifying the value that is potentially added by an audit, including financial benefits, increased accountability and better service to the public. AUS 808.06 requires the performance auditor to obtain a sufficient knowledge of the business.

Preliminary study stage

Once an audit topic has been selected, the audit team usually conducts a preliminary study to determine whether to continue. If the performance audit is to proceed, the preliminary study identifies the fundamental issues, structures the audit approach, defines the scope and focus of coverage and proposes a timetable.

FIGURE 16.3 Conceptual framework for stages in a performance audit

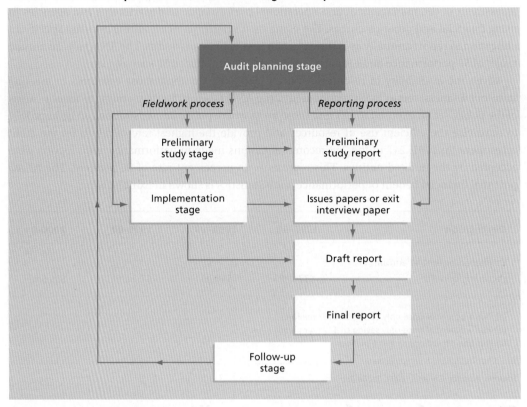

Source: Auditor-General, 1996, Fig 4.1.

During the preliminary study, information is obtained on how an activity is supposed to function and on how control activities are supposed to work. Key points are identified that appear to be difficult to control or susceptible to abuse. In a purchasing function, for example, the key points may be:

- decisions made about quantities and materials to be purchased;
- steps followed in obtaining best prices; and
- methods for determining whether correct quantities and quality are received.

If the auditor concludes that these points are critical to good performance, the auditor concentrates the testing on them.

Procedures used in the preliminary study include inquiry (interviewing), observation and inspection of internal reports.

Interviewing

The auditor usually obtains valuable information on problem areas warranting attention by talking to responsible officials and employees concerned with the operations being reviewed. The success of this process depends on the auditor's reputation for independent and constructive inquiry and the auditor's interviewing skill. Open-ended and uncritical questioning is the most productive approach. For example, it is more constructive for the auditor to ask, 'How do you know whether you have received the quantities and quality that were ordered?' than 'Why don't you use prenumbered receiving reports?'.

Observation

Physical observation of an entity's activities and facilities is a useful way of identifying possible inefficiencies or problems. Examples are excess accumulations of equipment or material, idle or little-used equipment, employee idleness, rejections of product by inspectors, extensive rework operations, or disposal of useful materials or equipment.

Inspection of internal reports

Internal reports that management regularly uses to obtain information on the progress or status of operations can be valuable sources of information on possible problems. Internal audit reports can also be valuable. Of particular interest are those reports with specific findings that management has not acted on. The auditor inquires into the reasons for inaction, which could highlight weaknesses in the management system and related administrative controls.

Walk-through

Another technique used in financial audits that is useful in a performance audit is the so-called walk-through of transactions. This is a way to obtain working knowledge of the efficiency of procedures by following several transactions pertaining to the operations under review completely from beginning to end. A walk-through provides the auditor with valuable information about the way the entity's activities are conducted, the usefulness of prescribed procedures, the capabilities of personnel and weaknesses in procedures or practices.

At the end of the preliminary study a report is prepared for presentation to senior management. The report focuses on the material findings and issues of the preliminary study, and documents evidence to support a recommendation to proceed or to terminate the audit. The recommendation takes into account the costs and benefits of the proposed audit.

Implementation stage

During the implementation stage, the auditor:

- develops an audit program which links objectives to audit procedures;
- obtains sufficient appropriate audit evidence; and
- forms audit findings, conclusions and recommendations.

AUS 808.09–.10 requires the auditor to assess the audit objectives and audit scope. This ensures that the fieldwork is clearly bounded and assists in producing an audit of reasonable extent and cost. The operational auditor needs to identify the stated purposes or objectives of the activity under review. This is usually accomplished by inspecting policy statements, procedure manuals, established performance standards, applicable laws and regulations and similar data.

The auditor is interested in any controls that have a bearing on the achievement of the goals of the activity under review, particularly administrative controls. The auditor considers whether:

- the policies of the entity comply with its charter, grant of authority or assignment of responsibility;
- the administrative controls designed to carry out those policies and activities are conducted as planned by management and in an efficient and economical manner; and
- the administrative and accounting controls adequately safeguard the entity's resources, and provide adequate internal control over revenues and expenditures.

In assessing the administrative and other relevant controls, the auditor needs to be alert to the following conditions or circumstances:

- failure by management to establish criteria for judging accomplishment, productivity or efficiency;
- lack of clarity in written instructions that may result in misunderstandings, inconsistent applications or deviations;

- lack of capability of personnel to perform their assignments;
- failure to accept responsibility;
- duplication of effort;
- improper or wasteful use of financial resources;
- cumbersome organisational arrangements;
- ineffective or wasteful use of employee and physical resources; and
- work backlogs.

These conditions or circumstances indicate problem areas to be investigated further.

Consideration needs to be given to factors such as the criteria against which the auditor will be assessing economy, efficiency or effectiveness. The matters subject to audit need to be evaluated against reasonable criteria in accordance with AUS 806.23 and AUS 808.29. The criteria represent good practice or a reasonable expectation of 'what should be'. Failure to meet the criteria indicates that improvements can be made, while exceeding the criteria shows good practice. Criteria for evaluating performance are developed from legislation, policy statements, standards developed by professional bodies or by the auditee or other similar entities. The development of these criteria may not be easy and the usual criterion of profit will often not be appropriate. Instead of trying to measure performance against precise criteria, it may be more productive to focus on whether waste is occurring or whether there is a less costly or more effective way to conduct the operations.

Evidence gathered during a performance audit is largely qualitative in nature and therefore requires considerable use of audit judgment. The audit findings are developed and evaluated throughout the various phases of a performance audit (see Figure 16.4).

FIGURE **16.4 Analysing evidence, developing findings and recommendations**

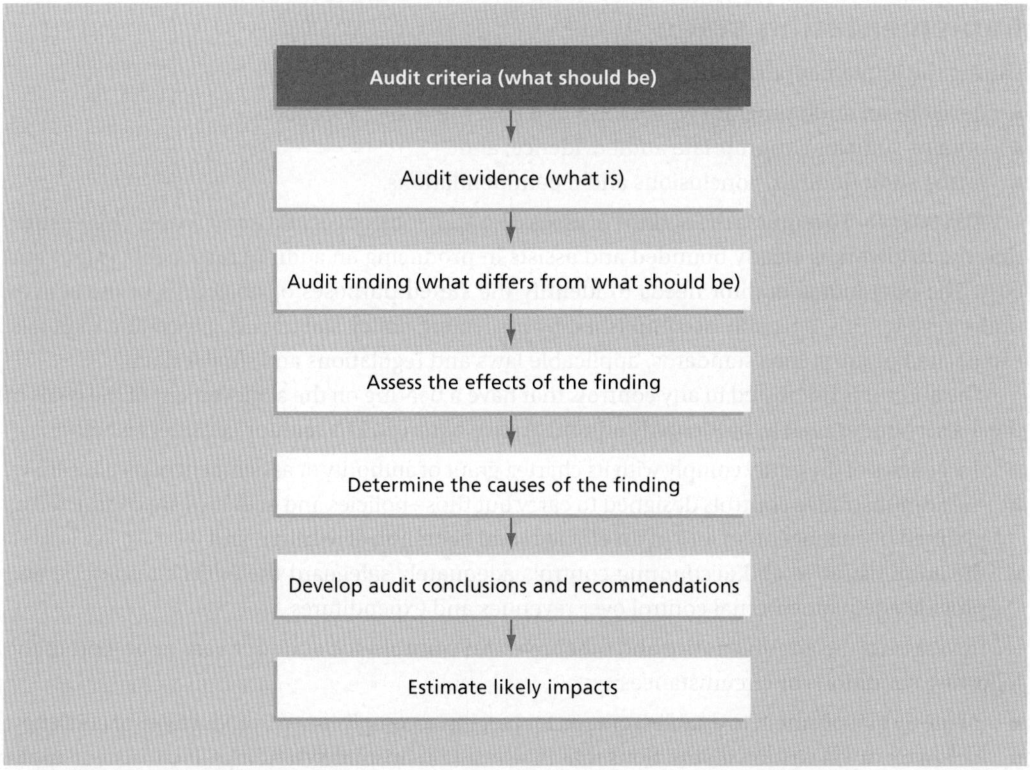

Source: Auditor-General, 1996, Fig. 8.3.

A performance audit is a process of fact finding and analysis that uses many of the procedures of the audit of a financial report: inquiry, observation, inspection of documents and analytical procedures.

Inquiry is used extensively as a means of gathering information; good interviewing skills are therefore essential to an operational auditor. The comments, impressions and suggestions of organisational personnel provide important clues to inefficiencies and opportunities for improvement.

Observation of operations is a matter of seeing what is actually being done in the activity under review. The auditor considers whether it is being done efficiently and effectively or whether some other approach would achieve the same objectives at less cost or more effectively.

An important difference between a performance audit and a financial audit is the amount of evidence that is necessary to corroborate the information obtained from interviews and observations. In the audit of a financial report by an external auditor, the auditor's judgments on the sufficiency and appropriateness of evidence are guided by Australian auditing standards and the criterion of reasonable assurance necessary to express an opinion on the financial report. In contrast, a performance audit is very different in this respect. A performance auditor may need to place more reliance on internal and oral evidence than would a financial report auditor. However, the auditor must have sufficient support for the specific findings and recommendations made. These findings and recommendations can vary widely from engagement to engagement.

Reporting stage

At the end of the field work the ANAO must hold a formal exit interview with the management of the entity to discuss the findings and recommendations. The proposed performance audit report is sent to the audited entity under s. 17(4) of the *Auditor-General Act 1997*. The legislation gives the entity 28 days to provide comments for inclusion in the report before the Auditor-General tables it.

The purpose of a performance audit report is to convey an understanding of the facts and the rationale for the auditor's conclusions. Generally, a performance audit report describes the objectives, scope and approach of the engagement, and the specific findings and recommendations.

- *Objectives, scope, and approach: A summary of the agreed objectives and scope provides the reader of the report with a framework for considering the findings and recommendations. Any limitations on the engagement imposed by the engaging party are described. A general description of the procedures (interviewing, flow-charting, and so on) is useful. This section might explain the rationale for selecting particular procedures and describe the origin and application of the measurement criteria. It may be appropriate to mention that a performance audit generally focuses on weaknesses and areas for improvement, rather than on the many strengths of the entity.*

- *Specific findings: The nature, number, and detail of recommendations are the result of the exercise of professional judgment, based on the purpose and scope of the engagement, the information gathered, and the conclusions reached during the course of the review. Recommendations are not always limited to matters that can be determined objectively. The report may recommend further study of areas that were not reviewed in sufficient detail, or of areas where recommendations were not developed due to the constraints of the engagement. Generally, a recommendation for further study is supported by an explanation of why it is needed. It may be appropriate to state that the report's findings and conclusions are based on the entity's operations during a specified period.*

(AICPA, 1982, pp. 14–15)

Follow-up stage

After a report is tabled in Parliament the auditee is expected to implement the recommendations. The ANAO follows up audit reports to ensure that the recommendations are implemented promptly and effectively.

Quick review

1. The elements of a performance audit are economy, efficiency and effectiveness.
2. The stages in an ANAO performance audit are audit planning, preliminary study, implementation, reporting and follow-up.

REGULARITY AUDITS

The ANAO has indicated that **regularity audits** involve attestation of financial accountability of the Commonwealth administration, Department of State and other Commonwealth entities involving examination and evaluation of accounting records and expression of opinions on financial reports. Therefore, these audits involve to varying degrees:

- examination of financial systems and transactions, including an evaluation of compliance with applicable statutes, regulations and administrative requirements;
- review of internal control and internal audit arrangements; and
- examination of the probity and propriety of decisions taken with respect to all aspects from or relating to the Auditor-General's activities that the Auditor-General considers should be brought to attention.

Financial report audits

Public sector auditors conduct financial report audits for all government departments, departmental commercial activities, statutory authorities and government-owned or government-controlled companies. Therefore, it is a major part of the public sector auditor's activities.

The financial reports of these entities are the principal means of reporting information on their financial position and performance to Parliament and the public. Section 58 of the *Financial Management and Accountability Act 1997*, discussed earlier in this chapter, sets out the Commonwealth Auditor-General's financial reporting responsibilities. The overall objective is to express an opinion on the financial report of the government entity being audited. The public sector auditor, just like the private sector auditor, uses a risk-based audit approach similar to that discussed in this book.

Compliance audits

Compliance auditing is another form of audit obligation that has received most attention in the public sector, although there are instances of this type of engagement in the private sector. Compliance auditing has two primary forms, which are distinguished by whether the auditing mandate requires the auditor:

1. to express an opinion on whether an entity has complied with relevant requirements or a specific requirement, such as legislation, regulations, directives or municipal by-laws; or
2. to report instances of non-compliance with relevant requirements observed during the course of discharging other audit responsibilities.

Both types of engagements can be found in the public and private sectors. However, they are mostly discussed in the context of public sector auditing because governments and other public sector entities generally carry out their operations under various enabling and incorporating legislation. This legislation sets out directions, conditions and limitations for both administration and transactions. Such a structure of authorities provides a basis for legislative control over the source, allocation and use of public resources. It has a pervasive impact on government activities and on other entities accountable for operating in accordance with the authority provided to them. As a result, compliance auditing is an important part of the accountability process of government activities.

As a general principle, where the objective of an audit is to express an opinion on financial information to reinforce the credibility of that information, the audit should be governed by the auditing standards issued by the professional accounting bodies and discussed throughout this text. Users of an auditor's opinion resulting from a compliance audit are entitled to the same quality of assurance as provided by an opinion on a financial report, so the same standards apply. As was noted under the discussion of performance auditing, an opinion on regularity may not relate specifically to representations made and reported by management. A report on compliance may provide both the representation and the added credibility in its own right, rather than adding credibility to reported information or representations.

In the first form of compliance audit, an engagement where the audit is conducted to express an opinion on compliance with specified requirements, the auditor must clearly determine the scope of the audit by identifying the entity, or part thereof, being reported on, and specifying the requirements against which compliance is being reported. Where instances of non-compliance with the requirements are discovered, a qualified report may be issued.

Where the audit mandate requires that the auditor report instances of non-compliance with the requirements that are observed during the course of discharging other audit responsibilities, it is appropriate to adopt the exception basis of reporting. In that situation, the auditor need not report on the compliance aspect of the engagement unless instances of non-compliance have been detected. The auditor's report shows the context in which the non-compliance was observed, and again describes the audit mandate, identifies the entity or part thereof being reported on, and expresses an opinion that the observed instances were departures from the relevant authorities. As with all qualified audit reports, it is desirable to identify the requirements not observed and, if relevant and practicable, to quantify the possible effect on the financial report.

Materiality in compliance audits

One significant audit issue confronted by auditors working on these engagements is the concept of materiality and its application. There is a view that any non-compliance with a specified authority should be reported by the auditor, since a breach of statute, regulation or directive is significant to the accountability process and the nature of a compliance audit requires such reporting. In this view, when an auditor is considering whether to issue a qualified audit report, all instances of non-compliance are material. This could significantly affect the audit process and reporting. For an audit undertaken for the expression of an opinion on compliance, such a view implies an audit scope well beyond the risk-based approach. At its extreme, such a view implies the need to undertake a full transactions audit, which is likely to be unmanageable and uneconomic.

The alternative view is that materiality applies to auditing for compliance as much as to any other audit examination, and therefore the auditor should exercise professional judgment as to the materiality of non-compliance. Materiality in this context requires the identification of the users of the auditor's report and their information needs, including the degree of public interest, the nature of the relevant requirements and the extent and nature of non-compliance. This assessment is made up of both quantitative and qualitative considerations. The exercise of a materiality judgment for reporting purposes requires an auditor to inform management and/or the appropriate regulatory agency promptly of any instances of both material and immaterial non-compliance discovered as a result of the audit.

Quick review

1. Regularity audits include financial report audits and compliance audits.
2. Financial report audits, as in the private sector, are undertaken to express an opinion on the financial report.
3. Compliance audits are concerned with the entity's compliance with applicable legislative and other requirements.

Summary

In Australia there are three tiers of government: Commonwealth, state and local. Within those tiers of government there are different types of government entity, with different accounting practices.

Within the public sector accountability framework, the auditor acts and reports in accordance with the audit mandate. That mandate varies from entity to entity; it is generally embodied in legislation but is occasionally established by contract. Audit mandates specify what is required and authorise the auditor to carry out the work and to report. As in all audit and assurance environments, the audit and reporting requirements specified in audit mandates establish the audit objectives.

Auditing in the public sector originally emphasised the financial operations of governmental organisations. Today, due to social, political and economic changes, there has been a worldwide move to broaden the base of governmental auditing. Auditors have increasingly

been asked to audit government organisations, programs, activities and functions. The audits may be performed by government auditors or by independent auditors.

Performance auditing considers economy, efficiency and effectiveness. While the audit process and methodology resemble those applied in the audit of a financial report, performance audits have unique requirements. The nature, timing and extent of audit procedures appropriate to a given audit engagement are always a matter of judgment in the circumstances. This is also the case with performance audits.

In the general accountability of the public sector, compliance audits are an important component. These audits are also used in the private sector. In either sector, the auditor should be clear as to the nature and extent of the audit mandate in order to apply appropriate standards and procedures.

Key terms

Accountability	708	Efficiency	719
Accrual accounting	710	Operational auditing	718
Audit mandate	711	Performance auditing	718
Compliance auditing	726	Protective security audits	715
Comprehensive audit	715	Regularity audits	726
Economy	719	Value-for-money auditing	718
Effectiveness	719		

References

American Institute of Certified Public Accountants (1982) *Operational Audit Engagements*, AICPA, New York.

Auditor-General (1990) *General Audit Manual*, Part One, ANAO, Canberra.

Auditor-General (1996) *Performance Audit Guide*, ANAO, Canberra.

Auditor-General (1998a) *Australian National Auditing Office Auditing Standards*, ANAO, Canberra.

Auditor-General (1998b) *General Guidance on the Conduct of Performance Audits*, ANAO, Canberra.

Auditor-General (2001) *Annual Report of the Australian National Audit Office*, ANAO, Canberra.

Australian Society of Certified Practising Accountants (1994) *The Importance of the Role of Independent Auditors-General*, Discussion Paper 8, ASCPA, Melbourne.

Canadian Comprehensive Auditing Foundation (1987) *Effectiveness: Reporting and Auditing in the Public Sector—Summary Report*, Ottawa.

Guthrie, J. (1992) 'Critical issues in public sector auditing', *Managerial Auditing Journal*, Vol. 7, No. 4, 27–31.

Guthrie, J., Parker, L. and Shand, D. (1990) *The Public Sector: Contemporary Readings in Accounting and Auditing*, Harcourt Brace Jovanovich, Sydney.

Hardman, D.J. (1991) 'Towards a conceptual framework for government auditing', *Accounting and Finance*, Vol. 31, No. 1, May, 23–38.

Harris, A. (1999) 'Revisiting the Review of the Victorian Audit Act', *Australian Accounting Review*, July, 32–5.

Martin, T., Rigby, E. and Shailer, G. (1994) 'The performance of Commonwealth public sector efficiency audits', in *Perspectives on Contemporary Auditing*, ASCPA, Melbourne, 57–68.

Nelson, B. (1994) 'The role of audit in improving financial reporting in the public sector', *Annual Research Lecture in Government Accounting*, ASCPA, Melbourne.

Parker, L.D. (1986) *Value-for-Money Auditing: Conceptual Developments and Operational Issues*, AARF, Melbourne.

Paul-Emile, R.J. (1986) 'Auditing compliance with legislative authorities', *CA Magazine*, September, 62–5.

Twelfth International Congress of Supreme Audit Institutions (1986) *General Statement on Performance Audit, Audit of Public Enterprises, and Audit Quality*, Sydney.

Walker, R. (2001) 'Reporting on service efforts and accomplishments on a "whole of government" basis', *Australian Accounting Review*, November, 4–16.

Walker, R. (2002) 'Are annual reports of government agencies really "general purpose" if they do not include performance indicators?', *Australian Accounting Review*, March, 43–54.

Assignments

MaxMARK

REVIEW QUESTIONS

16.1 For each of the following questions, select the *best* response.

(a) An Auditor-General is ultimately responsible to:

    A the Parliament

    B a minister

    C the Public Accounts Committee

    D the Public Service Board

(b) The Auditor-General is appointed by:

    A the Parliament

    B the Governor-General

    C the Minister of Finance

    D the Public Service Board

(c) The proposed annual expenditures of the Commonwealth government are authorised by:

    A the Treasurer

    B the Auditor-General

    C the Parliament

    D the Department of Finance

(d) A determination of cost savings is most likely to be an objective of a:

    A compliance audit

    B regularity audit

    C financial audit

    D performance audit

(e) Which of the following procedures would be most valuable in the performance audit of a government transport department?

    A Obtain written confirmation from the regulatory agency that all carriers are properly licensed.

MAXIMISE YOUR MARKS! There are approximately 30 interactive questions on audit and assurance services in the public sector available online at www.mhhe.com/au/gay3e

B Review procedures for selection of the most appropriate routes.

C Trace selected items from the transport payments register to supporting documentation.

D Verify that dispatch dockets are prenumbered.

(f) Which of the following statement best describes the term 'efficiency'?

A Introduction of charges where none previously existed.

B Greater outputs from the same inputs.

C Clarifying objectives and policies.

D A reduction in costs through better contracting.

(g) Which of the following can be considered an example of a performance indicator for effectiveness?

A The number of patients treated in a health clinic.

B A reduction in the number and severity of injuries, resulting from a road safety program.

C The costs of a job training program for long-term unemployed, per person placed in permanent employment.

D A decline in caseloads for social workers.

(h) Which of the following example is a compliance audit in relation to Bigger University?

A Reporting on its financial report to be presented to Parliament.

B Reporting to University Council on the tendering process for the construction of its new computer installation.

C Reporting to University Council on whether faculties have followed the University travel guidelines.

D Reporting to University Council as to whether the various faculties have met their objectives set out in their mission statements.

Levels of government

16.2 Name the three tiers of government in Australia and describe their functions.

Accountability

16.3 How does the notion of accountability apply to public sector auditing in Australia?

Accounting in the public sector

16.4 What basis of accounting is used in the public sector?

Public sector audit requirements

16.5 What are the procedures stipulated in legislation for the appointment and removal of the Auditor-General?

16.6 Why is independence an important characteristic of a public sector auditor?

16.7 How is the independence of public sector auditors maintained?

16.8 What role does the Auditor-General perform in governmental operations?

Performance audits

16.9 Describe the stages of a performance audit.

16.10 Discuss the difference between economy, efficiency and effectiveness in a performance audit.

16.11 What are the sources of audit criteria in a performance audit?

Regularity audits

16.12 Describe the elements of a regularity audit.

16.13 Explain how the concept of materiality applies for a compliance audit.

16.14 What is the impact of AAS 27, AAS 29 and AAS 31 on financial report audits in the public sector?

Accountability

16.15 **Basic** 'Public accountability of the executive government is the basic reason for an audit in the public sector.'

Critically discuss this statement and indicate the relative contribution of regularity and performance audits to this process.

Performance auditing

16.16 **Basic** Independent auditors are now being engaged to report on the effectiveness of social programs funded by the government. Explain why auditors have been given this task rather than professionals with expertise in social programs.

16.17 **Basic** During the performance audit of a leading government research institution, a number of problems were experienced in obtaining the active co-operation of the research institution's management. To appease management, the audit manager spent some time explaining to management the importance of the performance audit and it is now happy to co-operate with the audit team. In voicing its approval the following comment was made: 'All this time we thought you people were just checking we had complied with regulations and reporting on us; we didn't realise you were trying to improve things.'

Anxious to ensure the next auditors also receive a welcome, the audit manager replied: 'The last auditors you had may have focused on that aspect as they were performing a compliance audit but we are undertaking a performance audit.'

Management is puzzled and has asked the audit manager what the difference is.

Required

Explain the difference between compliance and performance audits.

16.18 **Moderate** Ultra Energy, a large government instrumentality, has requested an efficiency and economy audit of the company's Purchasing Department. The department is responsible for the procurement of goods and services, but not for the processing of receiving records and suppliers' invoices.

The auditor has developed for this examination an audit program with the following objectives:

1   to protect the interests of the entity; and
2   to improve operating methods and profits.

The audit program includes a questionnaire for the review of the Purchasing Department's organisation and general procedures. Prepare the questionnaire.

Source: CICA adapted

16.19 **Moderate** The NSW Audit Office was asked to undertake a performance audit of the Sydney Olympic Committee's (SOCOG) activities. Specifically, they were asked to report on whether SOCOG fulfilled their stated aim of ensuring the Sydney Olympic Games were the 'green games'.

Required

(a)   Discuss the purpose of a performance audit.
(b)   Discuss how the criteria of economy, efficiency and effectiveness might be assessed in the SOCOG engagement identified above.

16.20 **Moderate** You are an audit manager in the Office of the Victorian Auditor-General. The Auditor-General has been requested by the Premier of Victoria to undertake a performance audit of the project to construct a new tollway link in Melbourne and you have been assigned to the preliminary survey for this task.

Required

(a)   What is the purpose of the preliminary survey?

(b) Identify and discuss three matters which should be considered as part of the preliminary survey for the audit.

16.21 **Moderate** The NSW Audit Office is currently planning for a performance audit of the Department of Health's current immunisation program. The program has been in operation for 10 years in its current format; however, the minister responsible for health has indicated he will be undertaking a review of the program in the near future.

You are an audit manager employed by the Audit Office and have been asked to determine appropriate performance criteria which could be used to assess the economy, efficiency and effectiveness of the program.

Required

Determine appropriate performance criteria for the engagement.

16.22 **Moderate** You are the audit senior assigned to the performance audit of the sales function for a publicly owned power station. Since deregulation of the power industry, intermediaries in the industry have commenced direct purchase of power from stations. The government has argued that such an arrangement is conducive to efficiency, as stations will be encouraged to operate at the lowest cost in order to maximise the profit margin from the sales they have negotiated. You are currently considering the effectiveness of the sales function and have been given a benchmark price at which power is sold both in Australia and internationally with which to compare your results.

Required

Identify three procedures you could use to obtain evidence regarding the effectiveness of the sales function.

16.23 **Moderate** You are the audit manager assigned to the performance audit of the power-generating function of a publicly owned power station. Your preliminary survey of the area has suggested a number of possible criteria which might be used to assess the efficiency of the operation and you are now trying to decide which would be the most appropriate. The main inputs to the process are coal, water and personnel to operate and maintain the plant. Possible criteria include:

1 Power production per head of staff.
2 Power production per tonne of coal.
3 Power produced per dollar of input to the process.
4 The amount of 'down-time' for the station, that is, periods when the generator is being serviced or repair is required.
5 The amount of maintenance work by employees that was logged on the centralised computer during the period.

Required

Which of the above criteria should be used for the audit? Provide reasons for your decision.

16.24 **Moderate** You are an audit senior employed by the Audit Office of South Australia and are currently involved in a performance audit of the State Treasury. As part of your questioning you have asked the manager of the department to explain how she monitors the efficiency and effectiveness of the department. The manager has explained that her key method is to review financial information and ensure it is within budget. You have replied: 'Isn't that how you measure economy? How do you use this to measure effectiveness and efficiency?'

The manager is confused and says 'What do you mean? In this environment there is only one real measure that counts, and that's the numbers of dollars I spend. If I spend too little, it means trouble for next year, too much and I have trouble from above. So I think this is a measure of all three.'

Required

Explain to the manager the difference between the three concepts and into which category the current review can be put.

16.25 Moderate An audit senior with the Audit Office of Western Australia has been asked to design an audit program that could be used to assess the effectiveness of the public school system.

Required

Identify and describe issues which you believe should be considered in each of the key stages of the performance audit. Stages in the performance audit are detailed in Figures 16.3 and 16.4 of the text.

16.26 Moderate Billabong Bakery is a government-owned regional bread manufacturer. The business has expanded rapidly over the last 2 years and the CEO of Billabong Bakery, James Bolt, now finds that many of the business processes are inefficient. He is particularly concerned about the purchasing system. Purchasing decisions are made in an unplanned way by any one of five staff, and often too much or too little of various ingredients is ordered. This is having a negative impact on Billabong Bakery's sales and quality of produce.

Required

(a) How could a performance audit assist James Bolt in improving the purchasing system?
(b) What key information about Billabong Bakeries would be relevant to you when planning your performance audit?
(c) How would you arrive at suitable criteria to use during this performance audit?

16.27 Complex Northern Valley Hospital is affiliated with a leading university. Its Research Department operates on a project basis and consists of a pool of highly respected scientists and technicians who can be called upon for particular projects. Assignments are made for the duration of the project, and a project manager is given responsibility for the work.

All major projects undertaken by the Research Department must be approved by the hospital's board. Each project requires a proposal outlining the scope, cost, expected amount of time required to complete the work and expected benefits. The board must also be informed of any major projects that are terminated before completion. The status of all open projects is reviewed by the board each quarter.

The Research Department performs preliminary research work on potential major projects before requesting the board to approve the project and commit large amounts of time and money. The Research Department also assesses the potential for grants and estimates future revenues from the project. Expenditures on preliminary research must not exceed $5000 for any one project or $25 000 for any given quarter. Financial reports for the department and each project are prepared quarterly and reviewed by the board.

Over 75 per cent of the Research Department's operating cost is labour; the remaining costs are for materials used in research. Materials are purchased by the hospital's central Purchasing Department. Once they are delivered, the Research Department is accountable for storage, use and assignment of cost to the project.

In order to protect the hospital's rights to discoveries, staff members are required to sign waiver agreements at the time of hire. These agreements relinquish the employees' rights to patent and royalty fees relating to hospital work.

The Auditor-General has decided to conduct a performance audit of the Research Department. The objectives that have been set for the audit are to provide assurances that:

1   the Research Department has properly assessed revenues and costs for each project. Revenue potential should be equal to or greater than estimated costs;
2   appropriate controls provide a measure of how projects are progressing and identify, on a timely basis, the necessity for corrective actions;
3   financial reports prepared by the Research Department for presentation to the board properly reflect all revenues and all costs.

Required

(a) Evaluate the objectives of the performance audit in terms of their appropriateness. Include in your discussion the strengths of the objectives and modifications and/or additions needed to improve them.

(b) Outline, in general terms, the procedures that are suitable for conducting the performance audit of the Research Department.

(c) Identify three documents that members of the performance audit staff would be expected to review during the audit of the Research Department, and describe the purpose that the review of each document serves in carrying out the audit.

Source: CMA adapted

16.28 Complex You are an assurance services supervisor at Mackay Partners. The Department of Health has just appointed Mackay Partners to carry out a performance audit on all public, private and repatriation hospitals in New South Wales. The broad objective of the audit is to obtain detailed information on the types of patients using hospitals, by age and sex. This audit will eventually form part of a larger Commonwealth study on hospital use and costs. Its immediate purpose is to help the State Government in planning and funding hospital systems, by comparing the data collected to international benchmark standards. The State Government plans to place a high level of reliance on Mackay's report.

Your key contact is Mr Bishop, the Director-General of the Department of Health. He has arranged for you to get full co-operation from the head of each hospital to be included in the audit.

As agreed in your terms of engagement, Mackay Partners will audit the data and prepare a report on its findings. The report is to be addressed to the Director-General and be completed by 31 May 20X3. It will cover the period 1 January 20X2 to 31 December 20X2.

Required

(a) Prepare a summary of the similarities and differences between a performance audit and an attest audit carried out on a financial report under the *Corporations Act 2001*. Your summary should be in a form suitable for presentation to the Director-General.

(b) The audit partner has asked you to consider the following issues in relation to the planning of the audit:
    (i) the engagement letter
    (ii) materiality
    Briefly describe how the relevant standards might apply to the planning of its audit.

(c) What level of assurance will be expressed in your report to the Director-General? Give reasons for your answer.

(d) Discuss the type of report to be issued to the Director-General.

Source: This question was adapted from the CA Program of The Institute of Chartered Accountants in Australia—2002 Financial Reporting and Assurance Module.

primary learning objective 6

Regularity audits

16.29 Moderate Max Browning has recently taken a job with the NSW Audit Office and has been assigned to the regularity audit of a major government instrumentality. All Max's previous experience has been in auditing private companies and he has been quite surprised with the extra work involved in the regularity audit. While conducting the audit, an employee of the department has asked Max why he needs to know all this and how the information will be used. Max is unsure how to respond as he is not sure who the audit team will be reporting to and has asked you (his senior) to explain.

Required

Assuming you are the senior, indicate to Max who the audit report will be provided to and the reasons for undertaking the audit.

CHAPTER 17

ADVANCED TOPICS IN ASSURANCE SERVICES

LEARNING OBJECTIVES

After studying this chapter you should be able to:

1 understand the basis of e-commerce environments and consider current practice;

2 understand the effect of electronic commerce on the client's business risk assessment and inherent and control risk evaluations;

3 consider substantive evidence-gathering procedures in an e-commerce environment;

4 consider the concept of continuous assurance;

5 understand the basic concepts of forensic auditing; and

6 gain an understanding of environmental and sustainability assurance services.

In this chapter we look at some advanced topics in the audit and assurances services area that are currently attracting considerable interest. These include auditing in an e-commerce environment, forensic auditing and environmental assurance. We provide an introduction to e-commerce environments and consider their effects on risk assessment and evidence-gathering techniques. The related issue of continuous assurance is also considered. The chapter concludes with an overview of forensic auditing and environmental and sustainability assurance.

Relevant**guidance**

Australian		International	
AUS 110	Assurance Engagements other than Audits or Reviews of Historical Financial Information (Issued 2004)	ISAE 3000	Assurance Engagements other than Audits or Reviews of Historical Financial Information (Issued 2004)
AGS 1036	The Consideration of Environmental Matters in the Audit of a Financial Report	IAPS 1010	The Consideration of Environmental Matters in the Audit of Financial Statements
AGS 1056	Electronic Commerce—Effect on the Audit of a Financial Report	IAPS 1013	Electronic Commerce—Effect on the Audit of Financial Statements
Audit and Assurance Alert No. 5: Electronic Reporting and Continuous Assurance Engagements		—	
Audit and Assurance Alert No. 8: Electronic Commerce and its Impact on Audits		—	

ELECTRONIC COMMERCE ENVIRONMENTS

The term electronic commerce, or **e-commerce**, is heard frequently in corporate boardrooms, in management meetings, on the news and by anyone dealing with shareholders.

Definitions of e-commerce vary, but a broad definition is:

the use of electronic transmission mediums (telecommunications) to engage in the exchange, including buying and selling, of products and services requiring transportation, either physically or digitally, from location to location.

E-commerce is at the forefront of changing the ways in which organisations currently undertake business. One only has to pick up virtually any newspaper or business-related magazine to see a story about some facet of electronic commerce. Businesses are incorporating e-commerce into strategic plans, business schools are incorporating it into their curriculum and consulting and software firms are marketing e-commerce 'solutions'. The World Wide Web and the Internet have increased the speed with which e-commerce has been embraced.

Early e-commerce systems: electronic data interchange

Perhaps the first form of e-commerce to emerge, in the 1980s, was **electronic data interchange (EDI)**. In EDI systems, many problems surrounding the authenticity and privacy of transactions are mitigated because the parties to the transactions are defined and known to each other from the outset. For example, a large car manufacturer requires its many suppliers to accept orders for parts through electronically transmitted purchase orders. When the parts are shipped, the supplier transmits an invoice. This reduces data entry, mailing costs and time to complete transactions.

EDI is simply a different medium for input and output of business transactions. For example, the objectives of control over payment of invoices remain the same, as was discussed in Chapter 8, but the timing and method of performing the control activities may change when the supplier inputs the invoice onto the entity's computer. A list of the goods actually received by the entity, as recorded on receiving reports, should be input and matched to the invoice data before payment is released; the system should compare the payment terms and amounts with the originally transmitted purchase orders and any changes (back-ordered items, substitutions) should be authorised.

Those readers familiar with traditional EDI systems may be asking what makes e-commerce different from the EDI systems that have been in place for the past 20 years. EDI is a subset of e-commerce. A primary difference between the two is that e-commerce encompasses a broader commerce environment than EDI. Traditional EDI systems allow pre-established trading partners to exchange business data electronically. The vast majority of traditional EDI systems are centred around the purchasing function. These EDI systems are generally costly to implement; this high entry cost has in the past precluded many small and middle-sized businesses from engaging in EDI. Nowadays e-commerce allows a virtual marketplace to exist, where buyers and sellers can 'meet' and transact with one another.

Business-to-business and business-to-consumer e-commerce

Business-to-business (B2B) e-commerce is usually defined as companies buying from and selling to each other online. EDI was the early form for undertaking B2B e-commerce. However, other data exchange methods may today be more flexible. EDI has limitations, including an inflexible format that makes it difficult to use for any but the most straightforward transactions. Many small companies never adopted it because it was expensive. Much of the newer e-commerce software today uses XML (**eXtensible Markup Language**)—grammatical rules for describing data on the web—as a standard for data exchange. Though this software may also handle EDI transactions, XML allows for more variety in the information companies exchange and was designed for open networks.

B2C stands for **business-to-consumer e-commerce** and applies to any business or organisation that sells its products or services to consumers over the Internet. When most people think of B2C e-commerce, they think of companies such as Amazon.com, the online bookseller in the USA that launched its site in 1995 and is one of the e-commerce sites that many people around the world have visited. However, in addition to online retailers, B2C has grown to include services such as online banking, travel, online auctions, health information and real estate.

A survey of current e-commerce practices

One of the major studies of the current extent of e-commerce and related issues was undertaken by KPMG (2001), who surveyed 1253 leading companies in 12 countries. Their major findings included:

- Sixty-two per cent of survey respondents used e-commerce in their business.
- Only 9 per cent of respondents indicated that a security breach had occurred in their organisation within the last 12 months. Although the reported number of instances of electronic fraud and security breaches was low, electronic fraud is a growing problem for companies around the world (see Auditing in the News 17.1 overleaf). Where breaches had occurred, legal action was not always pursued for a variety of reasons, including inadequate legal remedies and a lack of evidence. The existence and use of good computer forensic response guidelines could significantly increase the likelihood of an organisation securing the evidence necessary to

pursue legal action and/or the recovery of misappropriated assets (covered later in this chapter under forensic auditing).

- Respondents indicated overwhelmingly that security of credit card numbers and personal information were by far the most important concerns to their customers. However, less than 35 per cent of respondents reported having security audits (such as SysTrust™ or WebTrust™—discussed in Chapter 14) performed on their e-commerce systems. Only 12 per cent of respondents reported that their web site bears a seal identifying that their e-commerce system has passed a security audit.

- Fifty per cent of businesses identified hackers and the poor implementation of security policies as the greatest threats to their e-commerce systems. Seventy-nine per cent of respondents stated that the highest probability of a breach occurring to their e-commerce system would be through the Internet or other external access. However, it is well documented that a company is at greater risk of being the victim of an internal security breach. The survey results thus illustrate how executives can be misinformed about the actual vulnerabilities of their network systems.

- Survey respondents from the majority of the participating countries stated that the security of their e-commerce system could be most improved by regular system penetration testing (authorised hacking), the use of software specifically designed for security issues in an e-commerce environment, and the increased use of encryption technology.

- Eighty-eight per cent of respondents felt that the public perceives the traditional or established 'bricks and mortar' business as being more secure than e-commerce-based dot.com companies.

AUDITING IN THE NEWS

17.1

Source: 'Online transaction fraud and prevention get more sophisticated— A report by Kenneth Kerr and Avivah Litan', January 2002, GartnerG2.

Merchants lose a higher percentage of sales to fraud online than offline, according to a new report from GartnerG2

Merchants surveyed by GartnerG2, a service from research firm Gartner, reported that they lost 1.14 per cent of all online sales to fraud in 2001, or about $700 million. During that same time period, Visa International and MasterCard reported that about 0.06 per cent of physical world sales were lost to fraud, said Avivah Litan, research director at GartnerG2 …

Fraud rates were up only slightly from 2000, when merchants reported 1.13 per cent, but merchants said the problem was becoming more difficult to deal with, Litan said.

Merchants were rejecting around 5 per cent of Internet transactions, on average, as 'suspicious', Litan said. And for large retailers that sell more than 25 per cent of their goods and services online, the figure was up to 7 per cent.

'It's much easier to commit fraud online because you're not authenticating the buyer. You don't have someone walking into a store and signing a receipt', Litan said, adding that there are programs out there that can enter fake numbers, without even a person behind them.

Quick review

1. Electronic commerce is the use of telecommunications to exchange goods and services, and is becoming increasingly popular.
2. Electronic commerce differs from traditional EDI in that it has a lower entry cost, covers a broader market and does not require a pre-existing relationship between parties.
3. Security of credit card details and other personnel details (privacy) are of major concern to e-commerce customers.

BUSINESS RISK ASSESSMENTS AND CONTROL CONSIDERATIONS IN ELECTRONIC COMMERCE

From the auditor's perspective as well as the company's perspective, there are a number of differences between a B2B e-commerce system and a B2C e-commerce system. A lot of this has to do with the control environment, having a small group of other businesses (in most cases known to you) that you are transacting with versus transacting with the world at large. Many B2B e-commerce systems operate through an exchange which can restrict access to only appropriately authorised entities. A B2B exchange (also called a marketplace or hub) is a web site where many companies can buy from and sell to each other using a common technology platform. Many exchanges also offer additional services, such as payment or logistics services, that help members complete a transaction. Exchanges may also support other activities, like distributing industry news, sponsoring online discussions and providing research on customer demand or industry forecasts for components and raw materials.

A client's involvement in e-commerce may impact heavily on the auditors' business risk analysis. If a client is considering entering e-commerce relationships there will be associated risks. If e-commerce applications are not placed in the proper business context and the strategy aligned with the business's overall business strategy, then the e-commerce application is likely to fail. New business models are necessary that integrate e-commerce initiatives with overall business goals. There will also be risks of potential loss of market if the organisation does not embrace e-commerce but its competitors do.

The auditor's knowledge of the business (see AUS 402/ISA 315) is fundamental to assessing the significance of e-commerce to the entity's business activities and its impact on audit risk. The auditor must obtain a sufficient knowledge of the entity's e-commerce activities to enable the auditor to identify and understand the events, transactions and practices that may have a significant impact on the financial report, the audit and/or the audit report. The auditor may engage the services of an expert in order to fulfil the objectives of the audit engagement where e-commerce activities are deemed significant (see AUS 606/ISA 620).

In January 2000 the AUASB issued *Audit and Assurance Alert No. 8*, entitled 'Electronic Commerce and its Impacts on Audits'. Within this document they identified the potential impact of e-commerce on the business environment of the entity, including, for example:

- customer–supplier relationships in the value chain;
- the verification of electronic identities of customers;
- the integrity of transactions;
- the integration of business operations and financial reporting, including the use of **Enterprise Resource Planning (ERP) software** such as Oracle, Peoplesoft or SAP; and
- disaster recovery planning when entities have a high dependence on the technology.

Under each of these impacts there are both business and control risk considerations.

Audit and Assurance Alert No. 8 was a precursor to AGS 1056/IAPS 1013. The guidance is intended to increase auditor awareness of the potential business risks associated with e-commerce and their impact on audit risk and resultant audit procedures. The potential audit risks associated with an entity's e-commerce activities will depend on the level of such activities, the nature and extent of controls over such activities and the auditor's assessment of risk. E-commerce codes of conduct for business practice are still evolving, hence risks may be large and outcomes unknown.

Business risk considerations

The implementation of e-commerce introduces new business risks. The auditor is concerned with e-commerce business risks insofar as they may impact on audit risk.

E-commerce business risks for consideration (AGS 1056.33/IAPS 1013.33) include:

- risks arising through the nature of relationships with e-commerce trading partners;
- risks related to the recording and processing of e-commerce transactions;
- pervasive e-commerce security risks, including privacy issues;
- fraud risks; and
- risks of systems failures or 'crashes'.

These risks must be addressed by management through the implementation of appropriate security controls and authorisation processes.

An entity's e-commerce activities may impact on all aspects of the audit depending on the extent of activities, the nature and extent of controls and the auditor's risk assessment. E-commerce operations may be outsourced to a third party (e.g. an ISP). The auditor must evaluate the outsourcing arrangements and identify how the client entity manages the control risks that arise from such outsourcing (see AUS 404/IAS 402). The auditor must consider the business continuity plans and service level agreement included in the outsourcing arrangements that support the e-commerce activities.

Inherent and control risk considerations

The auditor must assess the control framework applied by an entity to its e-commerce activities to ensure that appropriate consideration has been given to inherent risks arising from the technology used. An appropriate client IT strategy can provide controls which mitigate many of the risks identified. An IT security infrastructure and systems controls can help manage these risks even though some residual risk will always be present. These factors will have a direct bearing on the security, completeness and reliability of financial information, thereby impacting on the auditor's assessment of inherent and control risk.

The way an entity uses its web site for e-commerce determines the nature of risks to be addressed by its security infrastructure. The auditor must consider the entity's e-commerce business model to assess the adequacy of its security and controls over data integrity.

Controls

An entity engaged in e-commerce should implement controls designed to:

- establish security to prevent fraud and error and to maintain privacy of customer information;
- ensure transaction integrity; and
- monitor internal controls.

Security involves a consideration of logical and physical measures, internal and external security, user profiles, information protection and privacy issues. Risks associated with the recording and processing of e-commerce transactions will be addressed by the entity's security infrastructure and system controls. The auditor needs to consider:

- the security infrastructure: firewalls (software or hardware that aids security by channelling all network connections through control gateways), encryption (transforming a standard message into a coded message) and other security practices;
- security controls incorporated in the system's design;

- controls where systems are interfaced;
- controls over systems development; and
- the monitoring of security controls.

The auditor is concerned with the manner in which an entity addresses transaction integrity, as this may have a direct bearing on accounting entries. Transaction integrity in an e-commerce environment will generally depend on the reliability of systems used for information capture and execution. System controls should be in place to ensure the accuracy, validity and completeness of e-commerce transactions. These system controls will include programmed controls (e.g. field tests and reasonableness tests, described in Chapter 8) to ensure that before a transaction is accepted for processing:

- all transaction details have been entered by the customer;
- the customer is authentic;
- the product is available for supply;
- the order is reasonable (e.g. an unusually large quantity has not been input in error; the order has not been duplicated);
- the pricing structure has been applied (including delivery costs where appropriate); and
- the method of payment or credit-worthiness of the customer has been established.

The auditor must also consider how an entity's web site is linked to the entity's internal reporting system (referred to as process alignment) as this will impact on the auditor's assessment of the completeness and accuracy of transaction recording, revenue recognition and the recognition of disputed transactions. The auditor must also consider whether an entity's security infrastructure and security controls are adequate to prevent unauthorised access or changes to the internal financial records.

Impact on financial report assertions

The auditor will also have to identify the impact of the e-commerce transactions on the assertions contained in the financial report. When e-commerce occurs via public networks like the Internet, three fundamental problems arise:

1 How do the parties to a transaction establish each other's *identity and authenticity*?
2 How do the parties to a transaction protect the *privacy* of their dealings?
3 How do the parties to a transaction effect a *secure exchange* of money for any goods and services provided?

Thus, with e-commerce transactions the assertions of existence, occurrence, completeness, measurement, valuation and rights and obligations must be carefully considered, in particular for the accounts associated with the sales and purchases cycles.

It is possible that matters arising from the use of e-commerce may impact on many stages of the audit, including planning, knowledge of the business, risk assessment, control evaluation, sampling, analytical procedures, use of an expert or legal considerations (AGS 1056/IAPS 1013). Reflecting the growth in this area, the auditing profession is looking at providing assurance services for both the entity and the entity's clients. These assurance services products are, for business to business transactions, SysTrust™, and for business to customer transactions, WebTrust™.

Quick review

1 Electronic commerce is changing the way firms do business, and hence impacting on the audit strategy. The audit objectives remain the same, but the timing and methods of audit work may change.

Continued...

2 Significant business risks are associated with e-commerce systems. These include:
- risks arising through the nature of relationships with e-commerce trading partners;
- risks related to the recording and processing of e-commerce transactions;
- pervasive e-commerce security risks, including privacy issues;
- fraud risks; and
- risks of systems failures or 'crashes'.

3 An entity engaged in e-commerce should address the following controls:
- establish security and controls to prevent fraud and error and to maintain privacy;
- ensure transaction integrity; and
- monitor internal controls.

EVIDENCE-GATHERING IN AN E-COMMERCE ENVIRONMENT

In this section of the chapter the evidence-gathering steps used by the auditor are considered. What must clearly be remembered is that the audit objectives do not change in an e-commerce environment. Thus the auditor addresses objectives such as existence, occurrence, completeness, valuation, measurement and rights and obligations for the associated transactions and account balances.

Tests of controls in an e-commerce environment

With the emphasis on controls in e-commerce environments, there is a view that the auditor will never completely understand the risks in clients if they don't test the controls, and therefore the auditor should not automatically assess control risk as high and undertake a purely substantive approach.

Controls are different in a business-to-business e-commerce environment compared with a business-to-consumer environment. In a business-to-business e-commerce environment, there are normally a limited number of customers with whom the client is transacting. There is usually an authorisation system that permits e-commerce transactions between the two business partners. Testing of the authorisation system will be part of the general control review. If the authorisation involves the entering of computer codes, then the auditor may use test data techniques to check that only valid authorisation codes are entered. Authorisation of business-to-consumer transactions is different, and the authorisation of transactions is on many occasions established through the payment system. It involves entry of a credit card and checking the details of this credit card. For programmed controls (such as a reasonableness test of amount or a test that all fields are completed) the auditor will use test data techniques (described in Chapter 9) to test the programmed controls.

The auditor will also be interested in checking controls associated with ensuring that, for valid transactions, the details are accurate, and transactions have not been added to or lost. Authentication techniques, encryption, acknowledgments and audit trails decrease the risk of the client accepting an invalid transaction. Acknowledgments are a common form of authentication, and can verify all details of the transactions as well as include specific information such as time, message size, and status of transactions. This process also provides audit evidence as to the occurrence, measurement and completeness of transactions. Other audit evidence that the auditor may seek for completeness would include evidence of sequential control of transactions with exception reporting for missing numbers, duplicated numbers or out-of-sequence messages.

Substantive testing in an e-commerce environment

In a financial report audit there should be evidence to support the figures contained in the financial report. The auditor can substantively verify these figures. So for example, for receivables, there should be a list of receivables that supports the receivables figure contained in the financial report. The auditor can then undertake their audit procedures on these figures, such as confirmations or review of subsequent receipts. If inventory is reported on the financial report, the auditor can undertake their evidence-gathering procedures for existence and valuation of inventory.

There are assertions to which the auditor may have to pay closer attention. For example, under rights and obligations, does inventory meet the tests for classification as an asset? With regards revenue recognition, at what time does title change for the recording of a sale?

In the year 2000 version of AGS 1056 (at that stage there was no equivalent IAPS), caution was expressed against reliance on the use of analytical procedures in an e-commerce environment. It was argued that as e-commerce changes the competitive environment and the integrity of relationships, traditional relationships between financial reporting account balances may no longer be appropriate. This matter has a significant impact on the use of analytical procedures as an audit procedure.

Areas where it can have a significant effect are:

- inventory held;
- accounts payable;
- accounts receivable;
- ratio analysis;
- forecasts and budgets; and
- going concern considerations.

The auditor needs to carefully consider what are appropriate benchmarks to assess the 'reasonableness' of results of analytical procedures.

The extent of substantive testing will depend upon the extent to which tests of controls are undertaken, as is normal in any audit. However, it can be argued that it is necessary for the auditor to undertake an evaluation of controls (thus they shouldn't evaluate control risk as high by default) because the controls are so important in gaining an understanding of the business and assessing the risk of misstatement in these environments.

The use of CAATs in an e-commerce environment

In order to gather evidence in an e-commerce environment, the auditor may require the use of computer-assisted audit techniques (CAATs). The need for CAATs is likely to increase with the level of integration of the e-commerce systems with other operating systems, the complexities of the systems in use, the assessment of risk and the availability of audit trails. In particular the auditor should ensure that there is access to all data in the database.

As to which CAATs are likely to be used, there does not seem to be wide agreement at this time. Some advocate the use of test data techniques for specific programmed controls, while others caution against their use in the more complex systems. With the emphasis on program controls, it appears that the auditor should very carefully consider the use of the test data techniques. There appears to be agreement that the use of audit software to interrogate client's files is of benefit in most cases. Also, CAATs to aid evidence collection in e-commerce environments continue to be developed. In the next section, the development of software tools that have implications for audit (such as XBRL) is discussed. It is expected that there will be increased use of these techniques in the future.

Quick review

1 There is a view that auditors need to understand control systems in e-commerce environments and should therefore not undertake a purely substantive approach to the audit.

2 As controls are very important, there will usually be an increased emphasis on testing controls in an e-commerce environment.

3 For substantive testing, certain assertions such as rights and obligations may become more important.

4 Because financial relationships are not as clear cut, the auditor is cautioned in their use of analytical procedures.

CONTINUOUS ASSURANCE

Continuous reporting, and hence **continuous assurance**, is perceived to be the natural evolution of information needs in the marketplace. The demand for high-quality decision-making information is already far greater than the need for reliable historical cost-based financial reports.

Rapid advances in information technology enable information to be made available to users on a more timely basis. Eventually, information may be provided in real time or simultaneously with the occurrence of events underlying the reports (see Auditing in the News 17.2). If decision-makers need continuous information on which to base their decisions, it is likely that they will also need independent assurance on the reliability of that information (see Figure 17.1).

In 1996, as a first step in the evolution of continuous assurance services, the CICA's Auditing Standards Board (now the Assurance Standards Board) commissioned a research report to discuss the viability of such engagements and the significant issues that assurance providers would be likely to encounter when performing them. The AICPA supported the need for such a project and appointed members to the Study Group. In addition, the AUASB formed a working group to review and provide comments on the material being developed, and provided input at various stages during the development of the report. In 1999 the AUASB issued *Audit and Assurance Alert No. 5*, entitled 'Electronic Reporting and Continuous Assurance Engagements'.

The report defines a continuous audit as 'a methodology that enables independent assurance providers to provide written assurance on a subject matter using a series of audit reports issued simultaneously with, or a short period of time after, the occurrence of events underlying the subject matter'. It discusses the feasibility of immediate reporting by independent assurance providers and recognises a number of prerequisite conditions for this type of assurance service. In particular, these prerequisites include the requirement for entities to employ highly automated, reliable systems to produce timely and relevant data. Also, assurance providers will be required to have a high level of expertise in various aspects of information technology. Figure 17.1, from *Audit and Assurance Alert No. 5*, outlines the conditions necessary for continuous assurance to occur.

FIGURE **17.1** Conditions necessary for a continuous audit

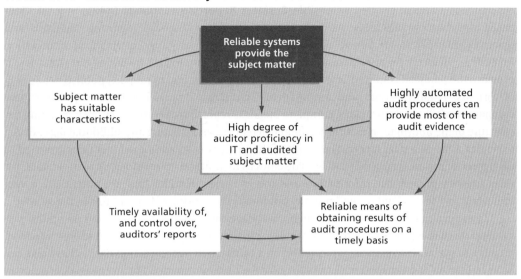

Source: Adapted from *Audit and Assurance Alert No. 5.* Reproduced with the permission of The Institute of Chartered Accountants in Australia and CPA Australia.

Continuous assurance may be required in relation to either financial or non-financial information (including systems and controls). Examples of continuous assurance scenarios include:

- specific financial information required by debt covenants;
- an entity's compliance with stated policies and practices with regard to e-commerce transactions;
- completeness and accuracy of frequently updated key information provided publicly on a web site;
- financial reports available on demand; and
- effective operation of controls over specified systems or publicly accessible databases.

Continuous assurance engagements are seen as a long-term goal which will evolve through the use of enhanced audit techniques in financial report audits and the provision of new assurance services such as assurance provided to trading partners and service providers, and web site assurance. However, the viability of continuous reporting and assurance thereon is dependent on the entity implementing highly automated, reliable systems and controls, and the assurance provider's increasing use of highly automated audit procedures, such as **SCARF**, **snapshots** and **audit hooks**, which were outlined in Chapter 9.

AUDITING IN THE NEWS

Continuous assurance

Every aspect of the accounting profession is being pervasively affected by advances in information technology (IT). IT shifts power from producers (such as accountants and auditors) to consumers (such as investors, creditors, and other information users). Present and potential users of accounting and auditing services have increasing needs for relevant, reliable, and timely information, and IT provides the means to meet them. But responding to these needs will require changes in virtually every aspect of auditing—where it is applied and how it is produced and distributed, for example, as well as the profession's relations with assurance users.

SNIPPET 17.2

Source: Elliott, R. (2002) 'Twenty-first century assurance', *Auditing: A Journal of Practice & Theory*, Vol. 21, No. 1, March, 139–46.

A new technology that appears to be giving increased emphasis to the concept of continuous assurance is a system entitled **eXtensible Business Reporting Language (XBRL)**. It is an XML-based specification (discussed earlier) that uses accepted financial reporting standards and practices in order to encourage the standardisation and exchange of financial information (including financial reports) across all software and technologies, including the Internet. It provides the financial community with a standards-based method to prepare, publish in a variety of formats, reliably extract and automatically exchange financial reports of publicly held companies. XBRL works by taking company business reporting data (transactions), mapping the structure of the information to XBRL for financial reports, and creating any additional tags needed to render a full financial report. The result of the process is an additional identifier attached to each piece of business data that can provide clues as to its origin, its relationship to other data, the rules used to prepare the information and more. These identifier tags are potentially a very important tool for the auditor and permit continuous monitoring of key controls in the system.

The expectation is that assurance clients will have their financial information up on the web site, and this will be updated fairly continuously, possibly daily or weekly. Theoretically it would be possible to update the financial information on a transaction by transaction basis. These tags can be as numerous and varied as necessary to make the data informative. For any given data point an assurance tag may have a variety of values (e.g. it may indicate that the information is a product of an information system with SysTrust™ assurance, or that the information has been subjected to key controls). The assurance service provider can review these tags at any stage to determine the origin of information, and the controls that the information has been subject to.

Q u i c k   r e v i e w

1 A current professional initiative is the development of guidelines for continuous assurance. These are designed to enable the assurance provider to provide assurance on a subject matter very shortly after the occurrence of the underlying events.

2 The technology XBRL assists this process by being able to take transactions and map these to financial reports, while providing an audit trail for each transaction.

FORENSIC AUDITING

In many cases forensic auditors (often referred to as forensic accountants) are called upon when there have been large systems or corporate failures, or when fraud is suspected. Forensic auditors can be engaged in public practice (the big accounting firms each offer forensic accounting or assurance services) or can be employed by private institutions such as insurance companies, banks and police forces. Over the last 10 years forensic auditing has been one of the fastest growing areas for the public accounting firms (see Auditing in the News 17.3 on page 729).

A forensic auditor can be of assistance in various ways, including:

Investigative engagements

The major types of investigative engagements involve business/employee fraud investigations and business economic loss analysis. Business investigations can involve funds tracing, asset identification and recovery and forensic intelligence gathering. Employee fraud investigations often involve procedures to determine the existence, nature and extent of fraud and may concern attempting to establish the identity of a fraud perpetrator. These investigations often entail interviews of personnel who had access to the funds and a detailed review of the documentary evidence. Examples of assignments involving business economic losses include contract disputes, construction claims, product liability claims, trademark and patent infringements, and losses stemming from breaches of trade agreements.

Litigation support

In these cases a client may be either considering or involved in litigation proceedings. At the early stages, the forensic auditor may undertake a review of the relevant evidence in order to form an initial assessment of the case and to identify areas of loss. They may also assist in obtaining the relevant evidence necessary to support or refute a claim.

Involvement in litigation proceedings may include:

- Assistance with early legal proceedings, including the formulation of questions to be asked regarding the financial evidence.
- Attendance at early legal proceedings to review the testimony, assist with understanding the financial issues and to formulate additional questions to be asked.
- Review of the opposing expert's damages report and reporting on both the strengths and weaknesses of the positions taken.
- Assistance with settlement discussions and negotiations.
- Attendance at trial to hear the testimony of the opposing expert and to provide assistance with the cross-examination.

In order to properly perform these services a forensic auditor must be familiar with legal concepts and procedures, accounting issues, assurance processes, and information technology concepts.

What would be a typical approach to a forensic auditing assignment?

Each forensic auditing assignment is unique and accordingly the actual approach adopted and the procedures performed would be specific to it. However, in general, many forensic auditing assignments would include the following steps:

Planning meeting with the client

It is always important to meet with the client in order to obtain an understanding of the important facts, players and issues at hand.

Perform an engagement acceptance check

An engagement acceptance check should be carried out as soon as the relevant parties are established, in order to try to identify whether there are any reasons why the engagement should not be accepted.

Perform a preliminary investigation

It is often useful to carry out a preliminary investigation prior to the development of a detailed plan of action. This will allow the subsequent planning to be based upon a more complete understanding of the issues.

Develop an action plan

This plan will take into account the knowledge gained through the meeting with the client and the initial investigation and will set out the objectives to be achieved, the evidence to be acquired, and the methods to be used for obtaining the evidence.

Obtain the relevant evidence

Depending on the nature of the case this may involve locating documents, assets, collecting background information about another person or company, or attempting to find information to prove the occurrence of an event. The types of procedures used to gather evidence will include those that were outlined in Chapters 9 and 10.

Evaluate the evidence

The actual analysis performed by the forensic auditor will be dependent upon the nature of the assignment and may involve:

- undertaking statistical analysis using computer modelling techniques, regression-style analysis and sensitivity analysis;
- performing present value calculations utilising appropriate discount rates;
- summarising large numbers of transactions;
- tracing assets; and
- performing loss of income calculations.

Prepare the report

In most circumstances a fairly detailed report will be prepared by the forensic auditor. This may include sections on the nature of the assignment, scope of the investigation, approach utilised, limitations of scope and findings and/or opinions. The report will include schedules and graphics necessary to properly support and explain the findings.

Is a forensic audit an assurance service?

A forensic audit is not necessarily an assurance service. The type of engagement should be clearly established and stated in the engagement letter. If it is an assurance engagement, the auditing and assurance standards will apply. However, if it is set up as a consulting or an agreed-upon procedures engagement rather than an assurance engagement then these standards will not apply.

The other test to see whether such an engagement is an assurance engagement is to look at the steps undertaken in the engagement and the form of the report. If the steps undertaken are intended to provide a level of assurance, or the form of the report does provide a level of assurance, then by definition the engagement will be an assurance engagement, and all the requirements outlined in this book will be applicable to that engagement.

Quick review

1. Forensic auditing is a very fast-growing professional service. It involves investigation and analysis of financial evidence, and is usually called upon where corporations or large systems have failed, or there is a suspicion of fraud.

2. A forensic audit may or may not be an assurance service.

AUDITING IN THE NEWS

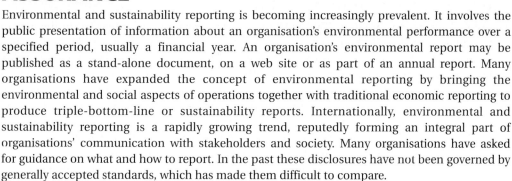

Forensic accounting is hot job

With a virtual media cottage industry blooming on the corpse of bankrupt Enron and its complicated array of alleged financial shenanigans, could it be just a matter of time before some television executive plots a new drama starring ... forensic accountants?

You can almost hear the pitch now: 'It's like Quincy, only with balance sheets instead of cadavers!'

OK, maybe you won't see droves of shows portraying financial detectives wooing beautiful women aboard a boat à la the opening montage from the 70s NBC hit about a medical examiner named Quincy, starring Jack Klugman.

But forensic accountants are becoming the rising stars of their profession as more and more companies seek to avoid becoming the next Enron.

Like detectives in green eye shades, forensic accountants bring a healthy dose of suspicion to their jobs, along with a willingness to look beyond normal channels to get to the bottom of a situation. Forensic accountants might have to do everything from sorting through computer files to detecting falsified records. In short, anything that can help detect financial wrongdoing.

S N I P P E T 17.3

Source:
<http://ABCNews.com>, 10/4/2002.

ENVIRONMENTAL AND SUSTAINABILITY ASSURANCE

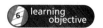
6 learning objective

Environmental and sustainability reporting is becoming increasingly prevalent. It involves the public presentation of information about an organisation's environmental performance over a specified period, usually a financial year. An organisation's environmental report may be published as a stand-alone document, on a web site or as part of an annual report. Many organisations have expanded the concept of environmental reporting by bringing the environmental and social aspects of operations together with traditional economic reporting to produce triple-bottom-line or sustainability reports. Internationally, environmental and sustainability reporting is a rapidly growing trend, reputedly forming an integral part of organisations' communication with stakeholders and society. Many organisations have asked for guidance on what and how to report. In the past these disclosures have not been governed by generally accepted standards, which has made them difficult to compare.

Providing **assurance on environmental and sustainability reports** is one way to mitigate the scepticism with which they are often received. Indeed, it has been commonly argued that this will be the 'next step' in the evolution of corporate environmental reporting. In fact, the IAASB has identified this as one of two 'other' (than historical financial information) assurance areas that it will be concentrating on in 2005–2006 (the other being assurance on reports on internal control effectiveness—discussed in Chapter 14). The importance of assurance engagements in relation to environmental reports is reflected in recent developments in the regulatory sphere.

International developments

There are a number of current international initiatives in the area of environmental and sustainability assurance. This section will provide an overview of these initiatives.

IAASB

As outlined earlier, the IAASB has determined that the area of environmental and sustainability assurance will be one of two 'other' (than historical financial information) assurance areas that it will be concentrating on in 2005–2006 (the other being assurance on reports on internal control effectiveness—discussed in Chapter 14). The provision of environmental and sustainability assurance services has been aided since 2004 by the issuing of the assurance framework (AUS 108/International Framework for Assurance Services) and related standards (AUS 110/ISAE 3000), which have been very beneficial in providing standards and guidance on how such engagements should be undertaken.

One of the major difficulties in providing such assurances services has been the lack of suitable generally accepted criteria for such engagements. As one of its initiatives over 2005–2006 the IAASB has set up a panel of experts to aid it in working with the Global Reporting Initiative (GRI) in its efforts to develop criteria that can be used for these engagements. This is discussed further in what follows. This panel of experts will also monitor other developments in the area of environmental and sustainability assurance.

Fédération des Experts Comptables Européens (FEE)

The Fédération des Experts Comptables Européens (FEE) is the representative organisation for the accountancy profession in Europe. FEE's membership consists of 41 professional institutes of accountants from 29 countries. FEE member bodies represent more than 500 000 accountants in Europe. In relation to providing assurance on such engagements, FEE produced a publication called 'FEE Call for Action: Assurance for Sustainability (2004)'. In this publication FEE outlined its belief that independent assurance is central to building the credibility of environmental and sustainability reports. Urgent action is required if environmental and sustainability reporting is to attain the same level of investor recognition as that accorded high quality financial reporting.

Global Reporting Initiative (GRI)

The **Global Reporting Initiative (GRI)** (2005) represents organisations interested in the area of sustainability reporting. The GRI was convened by the Coalition for Environmentally Responsible Economies (CERES) in partnership with the United Nations Environment Programme (UNEP). It involves the active participation of corporations (e.g. General Motors), non-governmental organisations, accounting organisations (e.g. the UK Association of Chartered Certified Accountants and the Canadian Institute of Chartered Accountants), business associations and other stakeholders from around the world (GRI, 2002). One of its initiatives has been to produce detailed Sustainability Reporting Guidelines (SRG). It is claimed that these guidelines represent the first global framework for comprehensive sustainability reporting, encompassing the 'triple bottom line' of economic, environmental and social issues. It is the GRI guidelines that are most commonly adopted for environmental and sustainability reports. A revised version of the GRI guidelines is due to be released in 2006. The IAASB's panel of experts, discussed above, will liaise with the GRI in an effort to have these guidelines accepted by the auditing profession as suitable criteria.

While the GRI's mission statement does not specifically address needs for or practices in verification (independent assurance) regarding sustainability reports, the GRI does encourage the development and adoption of principles for verification, as this can enhance the quality, usefulness and credibility of information used within the reporting organisation and the underlying management systems and processes. The GRI recognises that the verification of sustainability reports is at an early stage in its evolution. It therefore encourages the development and use of principles and guidelines for verification practices.

Institute of Social and Ethical Accountability (AccountAbility)

Established in 1995, AccountAbility is an international non-profit institute that draws its membership from a wide and diverse cross-section of society. It has quickly developed a significant profile in the environmental and sustainability assurance area. The Institute has developed standards in the assurance area, with its 'AA 1000 Assurance Standard' (AA1000AS), issued in March 2003. AA1000AS is the assurance component of AccountAbility's 1999 AA 1000 framework. This assurance standard has become very broadly used, not only by groups outside the accounting profession that are providing assurance, but also by some members of the accounting profession. As such, it is a standard that is effectively in competition with the assurance standard AUS 110 (ISAE 3000) in providing standards and guidance on how environmental and sustainability assurance engagements should be undertaken. However, AA1000AS provides guidance rather than requiring specific action, so has drawn the criticism that any assurance service, irrespective of its quality, could be argued to have been carried out in accordance with this standard. One issue it does tackle, however, which is not covered in AUS 110 (ISAE 3000), is the issue of stakeholder engagement. This is seen as important by many groups, including the GRI. As the GRI guidelines note: 'Compared with financial reporting, which is targeted at one key stakeholder—the shareholder—sustainability reporting has a large and diverse audience. Stakeholder engagement plays an important role in helping ensure that a report achieves its primary purpose: providing information that meets the needs of the organisation's stakeholders...' The GRI therefore outlines a process that helps identify stakeholders and their needs.

International Organisation for Standardisation (ISO) 14 000 series

At the international level, the ISO developed a suite of 20 standards in the field of environmental management (the ISO 14 000 series). This series was first published in 1994. In terms of environmental auditing, the ISO has a range of standards that are applicable, including:

1 ISO 14 011–1, Guidelines for Environmental Auditing—Audit Procedures. Part 1: Auditing of Environmental Management Systems

2 ISO 14 011–2, Guidelines for Environmental Auditing—Audit Procedures. Part 2: Compliance Audits

3 ISO 14 011–3, Guidelines for Environmental Auditing—Audit Procedures: Part 3: Audit of an Environmental Statement.

4 ISO 14 031, Environmental Management—Environmental Performance Evaluation—Guidelines.

In addition, ISO 14 001 contains a requirement for organisations to maintain programs and procedures for periodic environmental management system audits. The purpose of an environmental management system audit is to determine whether an organisation's environmental management system conforms to the ISO 14001 specification, and whether it has been properly implemented and maintained. However, while these standards have been prepared mainly for systems certification only, they are occasionally being cited in assurance reports on environmental and sustainability reports.

CPA Australia

CPA Australia has adopted environmental and sustainability reporting as a major initiative. CPA Australia's first initiative was to investigate environmental and sustainability reporting assurance practices in organisations worldwide. In 2003–2005 CPA Australia undertook a comprehensive analysis of assurance reports that had been issued on environmental and sustainability (triple-bottom-line) reports. The project 'Triple bottom line—a study of assurance statements worldwide' has resulted in a database of over 380 companies that release TBL reports accompanied by assurance statements. The database is a resource to assist in the application of TBL reporting and assurance practices. This research aims to provide a better understanding of the differences in assurance statements and of the value placed on environmental and sustainability reporting principles by both stakeholders and users. The standard of reporting was found to be deficient and a number of suggestions were made for improvement. The executive summary of CPA Australia's initial report is contained in Auditing in the News 17.4.

SNIPPET

17.4

Source:
<http://www.
cpaaustralia.com.
au/cps/rde/xbcr/
SID-3F57FEDE-
F4E366A2/cpa/
summary_report.
pdf> (accessed
January 2005).

AUDITING IN THE NEWS

Corporate sustainability reporting and verification

Triple bottom line—a study of assurance statements worldwide provides an analysis of triple bottom line (TBL) report assurance statements ('TBL assurance statements') on a geographical basis. Specifically, the analysis covered four groups comprising Australia, United Kingdom, Europe, and Japan.

A TBL report is defined as 'a publicly released document that provides information about the social, environmental and economic performance of the reporting organisation'. The study was commissioned by CPA Australia and investigated current practice for TBL report assurance statements. The research was conducted by RMIT University's school of Accounting and Law. In undertaking the analysis, a database was constructed of over 160 companies releasing TBL reports and assurance statements. The database provides a detailed analysis of each of the assurance statements and is the basis of the information used to compile this report.

In summary, the study found that assurance statements provided by third parties are a necessary component in adding credibility to the TBL reporting process. For there to be value in the assurance process, the assurance provider must be qualified to undertake the assurance engagement and be independent of the organisation to which the TBL report belongs. Further, the contents of the assurance statement need to be unambiguous.

TBL report assurance activities are an important component of enhancing the transparency and accountability of an entity's social and environmental performance. It is intended that research such as this will stimulate more effort aimed at improving TBL report assurance practices.

Specifically, the report argues that:
- sound approaches to undertaking TBL report assurance engagements ('TBL assurance engagements') are essential in enhancing the credibility of TBL reports;
- there are no generally accepted frameworks for undertaking TBL assurance engagements; and
- there is considerable scope for improving current TBL assurance statements.

The main recommendation is that assurance providers need to present clear information about items such as:
- the objectives of the assurance engagement (e.g. to give an opinion on all or a part of the TBL report, to assess controls and systems in place, to assess performance against targets or codes, to assess the processes used to identify, collect and report data);
- the coverage of the assurance statement (e.g. content of the report generally, environmental, social and/or economic data, management systems, performance indicators);
- the reporting criteria against which the reports are assessed (e.g. AA 1000, GRI, ISO 14001, relevant statutory requirements);
- the nature, timing, and extent of assurance procedures employed;
- the standards used that govern the work of the assurance provider (e.g. International Standards on Assurance Engagements, International Standards on Auditing);

- whether experts were used in the assurance engagement; and
- whether any restrictions were imposed by management on the scope of the assurance work.

The report also suggests that TBL assurance statement practice be improved internationally. Improvement could be achieved through organisations capable of providing authoritative guidance.

Such guidance needs to be accepted more broadly by the accounting profession.

The current practice of providing assurance on environmental and sustainability reports

As the concept of environmental and sustainability reporting has continued to grow, providing assurance on these reports has become more common in practice. In its 2002 survey of corporate sustainability reporting, KPMG observed a significant rise in the number of companies issuing such reports (45 per cent in 2002, compared with 35 per cent in 1999), and a large increase in the proportion of those reporting being independently assured (27 per cent in 2002 compared with 19 per cent in 1999). The major accounting firms performed the majority of these verifications (65 per cent).

These findings are supported by the CPA Australia study discussed earlier in this learning objective. This study, while roughly in agreement with the above statistics for reports prepared in Europe as a whole, shows a marked variation from region to region with respect to who provides assurance reports. In the four regions looked at in the CPAA Report, accounting firms provided 87 per cent of reports in Japan, 60 per cent in continental Europe, 23 per cent in the UK, and 15 per cent in Australia. It is acknowledged that few such assurance reports are issued in the USA and Canada, although the numbers in these markets are also increasing.

With respect to suitable criteria, the survey showed that only 40 per cent of assurance reports refer to the reporting criteria used (that is criteria against which the assuror has evaluated the sustainability report). The criteria that are mentioned most frequently are the GRI guidelines (11 per cent), followed by the AA 1000 framework.

With respect to the assurance standards that were being followed, it was found that 66 per cent of all reports (accounting firms: 55 per cent) do not mention any standards in accordance with which the assurance engagement has been performed. In fact, a common statement in sustainability assurance reports, including ones prepared by accounting firms, is that there are no generally accepted assurance standards for such engagements. The standard with the highest degree of recognition was AccountAbility's 'AA 1000 Assurance Standard' (AA1000AS), discussed earlier. However, with the issuing of AUS 110 (ISAE 3000) in 2004, it is expected that this standard will become prevalent, especially for use by the accounting firms.

Undertaking an environmental assurance engagement

Under assurance standards AUS 110 (ISAE 3000), an assurance engagement cannot be undertaken unless there are suitable criteria. It is debatable at the moment whether there are internationally recognised suitable criteria. The GRI clearly suggests that suitable criteria can be devised on a case by case basis for specific assurance engagements. These criteria should be developed jointly by the assurance provider and the reporting organisation. The communication of results can be done in a report, statement, or other formats such as symbols. The aim is to communicate the findings/conclusions reached relative to the objectives of the assignment.

The November 2000 GRI Symposium included a session on 'Verifying GRI Reports'. The discussion focused on three principal themes:

1 Verification of GRI reports is likely to evolve incrementally over time, with progress requiring multidisciplinary co-operation, based on verifier-community dialogue with report users and preparers about their expectations.
2 Verification and verifiers need to be multidisciplinary, innovative, adaptive and credible.
3 The role of the GRI is to assist in this process in practical, consensus-building ways, without itself being a verifier, accrediting verifiers or setting detailed standards for verification.

The GRI has recently expanded its involvement in the assurance of sustainability reporting through the formation of the Verification Working Group. This group aims to create a forum for discussing needs, expectations and best practice in sustainability reporting verification. Its role involves, among other things:

- encouraging the standardisation of verification methodologies;
- pushing for the recognition of legitimacy and competence of assurance providers;
- creating a forum for report preparers, users and verifiers to reach mutual understandings; and
- being a source of tools to facilitate understanding between interested parties.

One such tool is the 'Overarching Principles for Providing Independent Assurance on Sustainability Reports'. Figure 17.2 sets out the overarching principles of the GRI for providing independent assurance on sustainability reports. As can be seen from Figure 17.2, developing the business case includes consideration and determination of at least the following elements:

- **Goals and expectations:** 'The reporting organisation identifies and states its goals and expectations as to how independent assurance about the sustainability report will contribute to advancing strategic objectives and strengthening stakeholder relations.'
- **Scope:** 'The reporting organisation decides the scope and nature of the subject matter within the sustainability report for which independent assurance is to be provided. This may be the report as a whole or specific parts of it, and may depend upon the objectives for the assignment. The extent or level and nature of assurance that can be provided therefore varies with the type of reported information in question, which in turn affects the objectives of the assurance-providing assignment.'
- **Objectives:** 'The reporting organisation determines the exact purpose and objective of the assurance-providing assignment relative to the scope and subject matter.'
- **Benefits and costs:** 'The reporting organisation identifies the benefits that it can expect to gain as a result of the assurance-providing process.'

Environment Australia notes that there are four primary levels of assurance services currently provided by assurance providers. These are:

1 **Level 1:** Data verification—the checking of randomly selected data trails, focusing on ensuring that data and statements included in the report are accurate and fair.
2 **Level 2:** Verification of completeness of reporting—assessing the level of reporting against the organisation's policy, aspects and impacts, and objectives and targets, to assess the completeness of reporting against identified significant environmental impacts.
3 **Level 3:** Report verification, including site level compliance auditing—incorporating the level of compliance of operations at the site level into the verification process, to assess the accuracy of the report in representing the actual performance of the organisation.
4 **Level 4:** Report verification incorporating re-sampling and analysis—including re-sampling and analysis of data streams as part of the verification process to determine the accuracy of the data from site level.

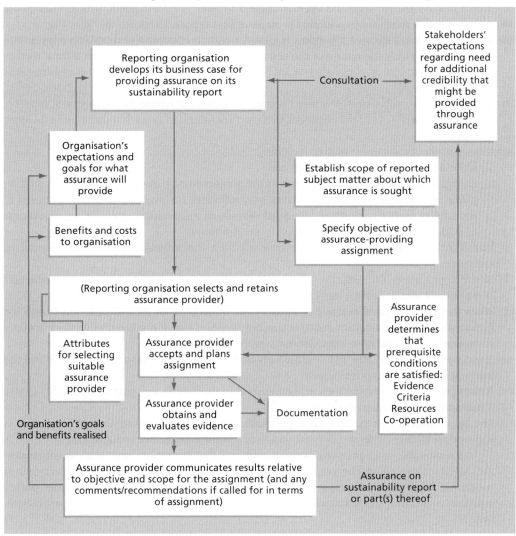

Source: Global Reporting Initiative (2002) 'Overarching principles of the GRI for providing independent assurance on sustainability reports' (working paper). Reprinted with permission of the Global Reporting Initiative. For the full guidelines please visit <www.globalreporting.org <http://www.globalreporting.org>>, accessed January 2005.

Environment Australia goes on to mention that all four levels of verification would generally require site visits by the verifiers. A combination of these processes can be used to suit the organisation's verification requirements. In general, Level 1 is considered appropriate for first-time reporters, whereas a combination of Levels 1 and 2 is considered good practice. Inclusion of Level 3 is considered useful if no separate site audits are undertaken. Level 4 is generally only recommended for the largest clients with significant potential for stakeholder scrutiny.

Reporting considerations

The CPA research report referred to earlier identified a deficiency in the assurance reports on environmental and sustainability reports. These included lack of detail about the suitable criteria, a lack of detail about the assurance standards followed, imprecision in the disclosure of the evidence-gathering procedures that were undertaken, and difficulty determining the level of assurance being provided. This has been addressed by AUS 110 (ISAE 3000), which outlines the basic elements that need to be contained in an assurance report. These are the following:

(a) A title that clearly indicates the report is an independent engagement report: an appropriate title helps to identify the nature of the engagement report, and to distinguish it from reports issued by others, such as those who do not have to comply with the same ethical requirements as the practitioner.

(b) An addressee: an addressee identifies the party or parties to whom the engagement report is directed. All addressees of the engagement report are intended users, but there could be other intended users.

(c) A description of the subject matter, including:
   (i) identification of the subject matter; and
   (ii) an explanation of the characteristics of the subject matter the intended users should be aware of, and how such characteristics may influence the evaluation or measurement of the subject matter against the identified criteria, or the persuasiveness or conclusiveness of evidence supporting the evaluation or measurement.

(d) Identification of the suitable criteria against which the subject matter was evaluated or measured.

(e) Where appropriate, a description of any inherent limitations associated with the evaluation of the subject matter against that criteria.

(f) When the criteria used to evaluate or measure the subject matter are available only to specific intended users, or are relevant only to a specific purpose, a statement restricting the use of the engagement report to those intended users or that purpose.

(g) A statement to identify the responsible party and to describe the responsible party's and the assurance provider's responsibilities.

(h) A statement to the effect that the engagement was performed in accordance with AUSs/ ISAEs.

(i) A summary of the work performed.

(j) The practitioner's conclusion: each conclusion must be expressed in the form that is appropriate to either a reasonable-assurance or a limited-assurance engagement.

In a reasonable-assurance engagement, and only that kind of engagement, the conclusion should be expressed in the positive form. For example: 'In our opinion subject matter conforms, in all material respects, with criteria.' or 'In our opinion, responsible party's assertion concerning subject matter's conformity, in all material respects, with criteria is fairly stated.'

In a limited-assurance engagement, the conclusion should be expressed in the negative form. For example, 'Nothing has come to our attention that causes us to believe that subject matter does not conform, in all material respects, with criteria.' or 'Nothing has come to our attention that causes us to believe the responsible party has not fairly asserted subject matter's conformity, in all material respects, with criteria.'

An engagement report expressing a qualified conclusion should clearly describe the reasons for the qualification.

(k) The assurance report date: this informs the intended users that the practitioner has considered the effect on the subject matter and on the engagement report of events that occurred up to that date.

(l) The name of the firm or the assurance provider, and the specific location at which the practitioner maintains the office that bears the responsibility for the engagement: This informs the intended users of the individual or firm assuming responsibility for the engagement.

Considering environmental matters in a financial report

The discussion up to this point has been about providing assurance on separate environmental and sustainability reports. There also needs to be some consideration of relevant environmental matters in financial reports. AGS 1036 (IAPS 1010) provides some practical assistance concerning the impact of such factors as pollution, hazardous waste, compliance with environmental laws and regulations on financial report accruals, and the impairment of assets. When forming an opinion on the financial report, the auditor needs to consider whether the effects of environmental matters are adequately treated or disclosed in accordance with accounting standards. Because comments about environmental and sustainability issues are frequently contained in the annual report, outside the financial report, the auditor needs to read this other information carefully in order to identify any misstatements of fact or material inconsistencies regarding environmental matters.

Quick review

1 There is an increasing demand for organisations to show that they are environmentally aware and are acting in a socially responsible manner.

2 There is increased disclosure of environmental and sustainability information, which information is being verified increasingly by an independent expert. On many occasions, for larger clients, the assurance service provider is one of the larger public accounting firms.

3 A number of groups are producing standards in the areas of environmental and sustainability reporting and assurance. These include the Global Reporting Initiative, the International Organisation for Standardisation, and the IAASB.

4 It is debatable whether there are internationally recognised suitable criteria at this time.

5 Reporting formats for environmental and sustainability assurance engagements are evolving over time.

Summary

This chapter has provided coverage on some of the advanced topics in assurance services. In particular it has provided an overview of auditing implications associated with e-commerce systems. The business and control risks associated with e-commerce systems, as well as the major evidence-gathering techniques, were discussed. The topics of continuous assurance and forensic audit were also introduced. Finally, the chapter concluded with a review of the current status of environmental and sustainability audits.

Key terms

Audit hooks	745	Enterprise Resource Planning (ERP) software	739
Business-to-business e-commerce (B2B)	737	eXtensible Business Reporting Language (XBRL)	746
Business-to-consumer e-commerce (B2C)	737	eXtensible Markup Language (XML)	737
Continuous assurance	744	Global Reporting Initiative (GRI)	750
E-commerce	736	Snapshots	745
Electronic data interchange (EDI)	736	Systems control audit review file (SCARF)	745
Environmental and sustainability reports (assurance on)	749		

References

Adam, M. (1999) *Driving Forces on the New Silk Road: The Use of Electronic Commerce by Australian Businesses*, AGPS, Canberra.

Australian Society of Certified Practising Accountants (1994) *EDI—a Business Perspective*, Melbourne.

Beets, D.S. and Souther, C.C. (1999) 'Corporate environmental reports: The need for standards and an environmental assurance service', *Accounting Horizons*, June, 129–45.

Bennet, C. and Sylph, J. (1998) 'The trust business: assurance services and e-commerce', *Australian CPA*, Vol. 68, No. 2, 43–4.

CPA Australia 'Triple bottom line: A Summary of Assurance Statements Worldwide' http://www.cpaaustralia.com.au (accessed January 2005).

Deegan, C. and Rankin, M. (1999) 'The Environmental Reporting Expectations Gap: Australian Evidence', *British Accounting Review*, Vol. 31, No. 3, 313–46.

Environment Australia (2000) *A Framework for Public Environmental Reporting: An Australian Approach*, National Heritage Trust, Environment Australia, March 2002, Canberra.

Fédération des Experts Comptables Européens (FEE) (2004) 'FEE Call for Action: Assurance for Sustainability' http://www.fee.be/publications.main.htm (accessed January 2005).

Global Reporting Initiative (2005) http://www.globalreporting.org (accessed January 2005)

Gray, R. (2000) 'Current developments and trends in social and environmental auditing, reporting and attestation', *International Journal of Auditing*, November, 247–68.

Greenstein, M. and Fanman, T.M. (2000) *Electronic Commerce: Security, Risk Management and Control*, McGraw-Hill, Boston.

KPMG (2001) 2001 Global e.fraud survey, KPMG Forensic and Litigation Services, Ireland, http://www.kpmg.ie/services/irm/publications/pub_4.html

Muysken, J. (1998) 'Web trust: assurance and e-commerce'. *Australian CPA*, Vol. 68, No. 7, 56–7.

Pace, D. (1999) 'Assurance in the electronic commerce environment', *Pennsylvania CPA Journal*, Fall, 21–5.

Vahtera, P. (1991) 'Electronic data interchange: The auditor's slant', *EDPACS*, November, 1–14.

Vasarhelyi, M.A. and Halper, F.B. (1991) 'The continuous audit of online systems', *Auditing: A Journal of Practice and Theory*, Spring, 110–25.

Wallage, P. (2000) 'Assurance on sustainability reporting: an auditor's view', *Auditing: A Journal of Practice and Theory*, Vol. 19 (Supplement), 53–65.

Weber, R. (1999) *Information Systems Control and Audit*, Prentice-Hall, New Jersey.

(MaxMARK) Assignments

MAXIMISE YOUR MARKS! There are approximately 30 interactive questions on advanced topics in assurance services available online at www.mhhe.com/au/gay3e

Additional assignments for this chapter are contained in Appendix A of this book, page 775.

REVIEW QUESTIONS

17.1 **(a)** Which of the following business risks are not increased by the introduction of an e-commerce environment?

 A Risks arising through the nature of relationships with trading partners
 B Risks relating to the recording and processing of transactions
 C Fraud risks
 D Product obsolescence risks

 (b) Which of the following assurance services are intended to provide specific assurance for business-to-business e-commerce?

 A WebTrust™
 B SysTrust™
 C business sustainability audits
 D financial reporting audits

 (c) Which of the following assurance services are intended to provide specific assurance for business-to-consumer e-commerce?

 A WebTrust™
 B SysTrust™
 C business sustainability audits
 D financial reporting audits

E-commerce environments

17.2 What are the major fundamental problems which arise when e-commerce is undertaken?

17.3 What are the audit implications of a client processing transactions by an EDI system?

17.4 What are the major differences in risks for an auditor confronted with a business-to-business e-commerce system versus a business-to-consumer e-commerce system?

17.5 What are the major concerns of consumers with regard to transacting in a business-to-business e-commerce environment?

Risk assessment in e-commerce environments

17.6 What risks does an organisation face in verifying the authenticity and integrity of e-commerce trading partners?

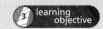

Substantive procedures in e-commerce environments

17.7 To what extent can CAATs be used in an e-commerce environment? Consider the use of both test data and audit software.

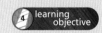

Continuous assurance

17.8 What are the major steps in a continuous assurance engagement?

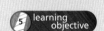

Forensic auditing

17.9 Outline the major steps in undertaking a forensic audit engagement.

Environmental and sustainability assurance services

17.10 What would you regard as suitable criteria for an environmental assurance engagement?

DISCUSSION PROBLEMS AND CASE STUDIES

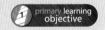

E-commerce environments

17.11 Moderate Your client, Khalifa Ltd, a local sporting goods company, has asked your firm for assistance in setting up its web site. Sally Wright, the CEO, is concerned that potential customers will be reluctant to place orders over the Internet to a relatively unknown entity. She recently heard about companies finding ways to provide assurance to customers about secure web sites, and Wright has asked to meet with you about this issue.

Required
Prepare answers to each of the following questions that may be asked by Wright.

(a) Why are customers reluctant to engage in e-commerce?

(b) Discuss whether you believe either the WebTrust™ or SysTrust™ assurance services (discussed in Chapter 14) are beneficial in providing assurance for these circumstances.

Risk assessment in e-commerce environments

17.12 Complex You have just completed the 30 June 2000 audit of UT Pty Ltd (UT), a retailer of exclusive hand-made children's toys. During the close-out meeting with the client, one of the directors mentions that, from 1 October, the company will be moving into electronic commerce. UT's information technology staff are currently putting the finishing touches on UT's web site, which will include colour photos of all product lines, prices and an electronic order form. It is hoped the web site will allow UT to expand its market beyond Australia without the need to establish stores overseas. Based on conservative projections, UT estimates that 5–10% of sales will come via the web site by 30 June 2001.

In order to purchase goods online, customers will follow these broad steps:

1 The customer enters the web site and navigates to find information about UT's products.

2 The customer searches for the exact product required, either by scrolling through the entire catalogue or by performing a search for a specific item (for example, the customer could specifically search for 'rocking horse').

3 The customer places the product/s chosen into an online 'shopping trolley'.

4 The customer then proceeds to the 'check out', and confirms the purchase of the items in the 'trolley'. Prices are automatically displayed, and the site calculates the total amount due, including freight and insurance costs. The customer is then asked to input their name, address and credit card details, and the order is sent.

5 The web site confirms that the order has been received; the order is recorded along with all others made that day, for later printing by UT's sales staff.

6 Once the day's sales are printed, the order details are checked and the orders recorded on the system in the same way as 'non web' sales. Banking is organised through an online banking facility. The product is then shipped to the customer, usually within seven days.

For the next few months, UT intends to manually handle web sales and keep them separate from normal retail sales. However, from 1 February 2001, it is envisaged that web sales will directly interface with UT's existing ledger and inventory systems.

In previous years, you have placed reliance on UT's internal control system to reduce the level of substantive testing performed.

Required

(a) What risks does UT Pty Ltd face as a result of its move into electronic commerce?

(b) What issues does UT Pty Ltd's move into electronic commerce raise for your firm, as auditors? What action could your firm take to deal with these issues?

(c) Give examples of the controls you would expect UT Pty Ltd to implement to control the online ordering function. Include brief details of how you might test these controls.

Source: This question was adapted from the CA Programme of The Institute of Chartered Accountants in Australia—2000 Accounting 2 Module.

17.13 Moderate You are an audit senior at Carroll & Co. and have been assigned to a new client of your firm, Solomon's Mines Limited. You are aware of the increasing pressure on mining companies to be environmentally responsible, but are unsure how the various laws and regulations will affect the Solomon's Mines audit.

You are due to have a planning meeting with the client next week and want to gain an understanding of how environmental issues are likely to affect the Solomon's Mines audit.

Required

Using Appendix 1 of AGS 1036, develop a list of five key questions you will ask at the meeting.

Source: This question was adapted from the CA Programme of The Institute of Chartered Accountants in Australia—2002 Financial Reporting and Assurance Module.

17.14 Moderate Fernanda Ltd recently implemented a business-to-business electronic commerce system. Your audit partner has indicated that she would like to be able to determine the reliance that can be placed on the internal controls. However, she has limited knowledge of how, in such an IT environment, you can test controls sufficiently to justify relying upon them.

Required

Prepare a memo for the partner outlining the audit implications of the business-to-business e-commerce systems and discuss the CAATs that might be appropriate to aid the testing of the controls. You should also address any strengths and weaknesses of the CAATs that you discuss.

Continuous assurance

17.15 Moderate Your audit partner has heard about a revolutionary reporting language, XBRL. However, she is not sure whether it has any benefit for a proposed engagement where the client wants to report and also have independent assurance on key performance indicators, updated on their web site every week.

Required

Outline in a memorandum to the audit partner the potential uses of XBRL in providing continuous assurance in this engagement.

Forensic auditing

17.16 Moderate Your client, Amy Ltd, has discovered a fairly sophisticated e-commerce fraud in the inventory/accounts payable area. This has involved collusion between those authorising approved suppliers and those receiving goods. A bogus supplier was approved, bogus goods received notes were created in the receiving area, and these were matched to approved suppliers' orders, resulting in inventory records being updated. The payment was electronically transferred to a bank account in the name of the supplier that could be accessed by the colluding employers although the goods were never received. On undertaking the stocktake, the inventory shortfall was recognised, the inventory records updated, and the shortfall written off to a stock loss account.

Required

The CEO of Amy Ltd wishes to know:
(i)   why this fraud was not picked up by the external auditors;
(ii) how management can gain confidence that there are no other frauds in existence; and
(iii) whether they can develop a case against the colluding employees in order to recover the lost monies.

Write a letter to management advising them on these issues.

Environmental and sustainability assurance services

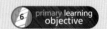

17.17 Moderate The accounting profession is concerned about whether companies are in compliance with various federal and state environmental laws and regulations and whether they have reported environmental liabilities in their financial statements. *Environmental auditing* typically refers to the process of assessing compliance with environmental laws and regulations, as well as compliance with company policies and procedures. It is possible for an auditor to perform agreed-upon procedures to assist users in evaluating management's written assertions about (1) the entity's compliance with specified requirements, (2) the effectiveness of the entity's internal control over compliance, or (3) both.

Required

(a) Discuss how a practitioner would conduct an agreed-upon procedures engagement to evaluate an entity's written assertion that it was in compliance with its state's environmental laws and regulations.

(b) Assume that this same entity maintained an internal control system that monitored the entity's compliance with its state's environmental laws and regulations. Discuss how a practitioner would evaluate the effectiveness of the entity's internal control over compliance.

CHAPTER 1

1.31 Basic The AUASB (IAASB) has recently issued two new overarching standards. These are AUS 108 (International Framework for Assurance Engagements), and AUS 110 (ISAE 3000).

Required

To what extent do these standards apply to:

(a) a financial report audit; and

(b) an assurance engagement on environmental and sustainability information.

1.32 Basic The following are essential elements of an assurance engagement and are discussed in this chapter:

(a) a three-party relationship

(b) an appropriate subject matter

(c) suitable criteria

Required

Outline how these elements relate to a financial report audit.

CHAPTER 2

2.31 Basic Do you believe that the AUASB should simply adopt international auditing standards indiscriminately, use international standards as a basis for Australian standards or develop its own auditing standards? Why?

2.32 Basic Quality control procedures are considered essential in ensuring auditors meet their responsibilities. Do you believe there is any one procedure that is more necessary than any other?

CHAPTER 3

3.31 Basic Indicate the statutory rights that enhance auditor independence.

3.32 Basic Tania Hollis, a retired partner of your audit firm, has just been appointed to the board of directors of Zilker Ltd, your firm's client. Hollis is also a member of your firm's income tax committee, which meets monthly to discuss income tax problems of the firm's clients. The audit firm pays Hollis $500 for each committee meeting she attends and a monthly retirement benefit of $2000.

Discuss the effect of Hollis's appointment to the board of directors of Zilker Ltd on your audit firm's independence in expressing an opinion on Zilker Ltd's financial report.

Source: AICPA adapted

3.33 Moderate Asian Foods Ltd was formed on 1 October 20X0, and its fiscal year will end on 30 September 20X1. You audited the company's opening balance sheet and rendered an unqualified opinion on it. A month after rendering your report you are offered the position of secretary of the company because of the need for a complete set of officers and for the sake of convenience in signing various documents. You will have no financial interest in the company through share ownership or otherwise, will receive no salary, will not keep the books and will not have any influence on its financial matters other than occasional advice on income tax matters and similar advice normally given a client by an accountant.

(a) Assume that you accept the offer but plan to resign the position prior to conducting your annual audit, with the intention of resuming the office after rendering an opinion on the financial report. Discuss.

(b) Assume that you accept the offer on a temporary basis until the company gets on its feet and can employ a secretary. In any event, you would permanently resign the position before conducting your annual audit. Can you render an independent opinion on the financial report? Discuss.

Source: AICPA adapted

3.34 **Complex** In each of the following unrelated circumstances, explain what course of action an auditor should follow in order to discharge their professional and ethical responsibilities.

(a) Lisa Nobles is employed by a firm of accountants practising in a small town. Early in 20X2, she reviews with the principal shareholder the draft of the audited 20X1 financial report of Builders Pty Ltd, building contractors. Nobles notes that the company's deteriorating cash position is so serious that she believes the company is facing bankruptcy.

Nobles subsequently reviews the draft of the audited 20X1 financial report of Patton Pty Ltd, also a client, and notes that the company has a large overdue account receivable from Builders Pty Ltd, against which no provision for doubtful accounts has been provided. When Nobles questions the owner of Patton Pty Ltd on the collectability of the account, she is convinced that the owner is not aware of the actual financial condition of Builders Pty Ltd.

(b) Brenda George, an accountant, is in charge of the audit of Portland Ltd, a public company. George is asked by an economist who is doing research for a thesis on the financial operations of firms in the same industry as Portland if she would contribute any information or views on the financial operations of Portland. The economist promises to keep confidential any information received from George.

(c) Singing Mines Pty Ltd is a small mining company whose principal shareholders are actively promoting the company's shares. Peter Dunn, the auditor of the company for several years, is in the company's offices conducting interim audit tests before the year-end when he discovers a copy of a set of third-quarter financial reports recently prepared and apparently sent to the company's bank. These were prepared by the company's accounting staff without Dunn's knowledge. They are clearly marked 'unaudited', and Dunn's name does not appear on them. A quick scrutiny reveals that the report appears to overstate net profit by a material amount.

Source: CICA adapted

CHAPTER 4

4.31 **Basic** What legislative actions have been taken to reduce the extent of auditor liability? Why?

4.32 **Moderate** Sarah Williams, an auditor, was engaged by Jackson Financial Development Company to audit the financial report of Apex Construction Company. Williams was told when she was engaged that Jackson Financial needed a reliable financial report, which would be used to determine whether or not to purchase a substantial amount of Apex's debentures at the price asked by the estate of one of Apex's former directors.

Williams performed her examination in a negligent manner. As a result of her negligence, she failed to discover substantial defalcations by Raymond Leong, the Apex finance director. Jackson Financial purchased the debentures, but would not have if the defalcations had been discovered. After discovery of the fraud, Jackson Financial promptly sold the debentures for the highest price offered in the market at a $70 000 loss.

(a) What liability does Williams have to Jackson Financial? Explain.

(b) If Apex also sues Williams for negligence, what are the probable legal defences that her solicitor would raise? Explain.

(c) Will the negligence of the auditor, as described above, prevent her from recovering on a liability insurance policy covering the practice of her profession? Explain.

Source: AICPA adapted

CHAPTER 5

5.31 Basic Explain why it is necessary to obtain corroborating evidence for inquiries of client personnel and management.

5.32 Basic In this chapter there is an illustration of specific audit objectives developed from the broad categories of assertions for inventory. For the account balance of *accounts payable*, develop one specific audit objective for each of the broad categories of assertions. Which audit objective do you believe will be the most difficult to achieve?

5.33 Moderate You have been assigned to the audit of inventory at XY Limited, a distributor of hardware to retailers throughout Australia. While planning for the audit, you have obtained the following information:

1 XY has 50 warehouses located throughout Australia. Warehouses are used on a short-term basis depending on regional demand. The marketing manager has indicated that the hardware market is highly competitive and the ability to deliver product quickly is essential.

2 A follow up on inventory counts has indicated that at least three warehouses were not included in the final stocktake procedure as the financial controller was not informed of their existence until after the balance date. The inventory omitted comprised approximately 4 per cent of total inventory.

3 Significant problems were experienced during stocktakes in New South Wales and Queensland as the client's staff were relatively new and were confused by the stocktake instructions sent out by head office.

4 Stock is commonly moved between warehouses in order to cater for stronger demand in areas owing to seasonal fluctuations.

Required

Identify and discuss the financial report assertions for the audit of inventory at XY that you believe would be assessed as high risk. Provide reasons for your decisions.

5.34 Moderate You are the auditor in charge of a medical research company, MR Pty Limited. The company researches and produces specialised equipment for use in the nuclear medicine area. At present you are considering the audit of MR's intangible assets. These assets include a patent over one of its 'breakthrough' products. The asset is material.

Required

For each of the key financial report assertions in relation to the asset indicate the audit evidence you would require, assuming a substantive approach is used.

5.35 Complex You have been assigned to the audit of Faraway Limited, a large listed company with diverse operations. During the audit you become aware of the following:

(i) Faraway Limited has a $6 million investment in Siberia Pty Limited, a controlled entity based in Russia. This company imports and sells Australian wool and cotton to Russian manufacturers. With the devaluation of the rouble, sales have plummeted and many customers are unable to settle their accounts. By year-end, Siberia Pty Limited expects to have incurred losses of over $5 million.

(ii) Faraway Limited's trade receivables are recorded in a ledger that is produced weekly. Lately accounting staff have been having difficulties with the ledger as it has reached the maximum permissible number of debtor accounts. Management have approved an upgrade of the system, but in the meantime staff are having to keep extensive manual records in order to derive accurate receivables figures.

(iii) One of Faraway Limited's divisions, IC, manufactures soft drinks. Part of IC's agreement with its distributors is that IC will supply a fridge complete with advertising signs for the distributor's use, providing IC's products are stocked exclusively. These fridges are rented out to the distributors at a nominal rent and recorded as fixed assets in the books of IC (and therefore Faraway Limited). Most distributors are either service stations or corner shops.

(iv) In line with many other businesses, Faraway Limited is finding it extremely difficult to recruit and retain skilled factory staff. Accordingly, it has been decided that staff in the most difficult to retain award categories will be rewarded with annual bonuses. These are calculated using a relatively complex formula that takes into account employees' length of service, award rate, seniority and estimated contribution to profit.

Required

For each independent item (i) to (iv) above:

(a) Identify up to two key audit assertion(s) and link these to the relevant balance sheet/income statement account.

(b) Recommend the audit procedures you would perform to gather sufficient, appropriate audit evidence on each assertion.

This question was adapted from the CA Program of The Institute of Chartered Accountants in Australia—2002 Financial Reporting and Assurance Module

CHAPTER 6

6.31 Basic What is the purpose of an auditor communicating with the previous auditor, and what information would the auditor be seeking?

6.32 Moderate NS Pty Limited was incorporated on 1 January 20X0 and has a 31 December year-end. NS's only product is a new form of sunscreen for which it has a worldwide patent pending. This sunscreen is reputedly effective for eight hours in the sun without requiring reapplication, and includes an in-built insect repellent. NS's product is the first such sunscreen on the market.

NS leases factory premises where plastic tubes are filled with the sunscreen, labelled and boxed ready for shipment. The tubes themselves are supplied by a subcontractor. To date, NS has only one major customer, a pharmacy chain, which receives significant volume discounts on purchases. NS expects to gain more customers as the weather warms up.

One of NS's major assets is research and development costs carried forward. These relate to expenses incurred in developing and testing the sunscreen and applying for patents.

NS's two executive directors are Mr Arbutt and Ms Bonnici. Ms Bonnici was previously a director of GJ Pty Limited, a company which is being prosecuted for misleading claims relating to one of its products, a slimming tea. Mr Arbutt was previously the finance director of YO Pty Limited. YO is being prosecuted by the Australian Securities and Investments Commission for offences related to the preparation of annual financial reports, offences which allegedly took place while Mr Arbutt was employed there.

As a newcomer in the sunscreen market, NS's competitors include large multinational pharmaceutical companies as well as the 'house brands' of certain supermarket and pharmacy chains.

Your firm, KJ Partners, has been approached by a shareholder of NS to carry out the annual audit. There are no previous auditors.

Required
(a) What factors might lead you to conclude that this is a high-risk engagement?
(b) What are the risks to your firm in accepting this engagement?
(c) What further information would you seek prior to deciding whether to accept or reject this engagement?
(d) Assume the company offers to indemnify KJ Partners against possible claims that may be made against it in its role as auditor. How would you respond to this offer?

This question was adapted from the Professional Year Programme of The Institute of Chartered Accountants in Australia—1998 Accounting 2 Module

6.33 Complex FNU Limited is a large public company whose year-end is 30 June 20X0. FNU operates three divisions: entertainment, hospitality, and tourism and leisure. Each division is run as a separate business, with its own accounting system and management team.

While planning the audit of FNU, you become aware of the following independent and material situations.

Entertainment division
(i) The entertainment division owns the largest chain of cinemas in Australia. Owing to changes in technology in the USA, movie distributors will shortly begin releasing films using a recording system that is incompatible with the movie projectors used by FNU. Approximately 70 per cent of the movies the entertainment division screens are sourced from the USA. The movie projectors currently have an estimated useful life of four years. FNU has sufficient financial resources to purchase and install new movie projectors without interrupting cinema operations.
(ii) In March 20X0 the entertainment division introduced a new general ledger system. Apart from a few teething problems the system seems to be functioning well and now produces a range of management reports that were not previously available. Owing to an oversight by your firm's computer audit division, no audit staff were present during the conversion process.

Hospitality division
(iii) The hospitality division is involved in a luxury hotel development on an island in Indonesia. The project is currently around 60 per cent complete, and FNU is carrying around $70 million of work –in progress related to the project in its balance sheet. The Asian economic crisis has cast doubts on the future of the project, with estimates of hotel patronage and revenue falling on a weekly basis.
(iv) Under the terms of its bank loan the hospitality division must maintain three key financial ratios at set levels or risk the loan being immediately recalled. Owing to the downturn in the hospitality industry, the division is currently in breach of two of these ratios. The directors are currently negotiating the loan terms with the bank, arguing that although the hospitality division is in breach, overall FNU's ratios are within set limits.

Tourism and leisure division
(v) The tourism and leisure division manages three ski lodges in Victoria on behalf of a private investor. In March 20X0 unusually heavy rains caused land slippage, which badly affected the foundations of these lodges. Preliminary reports suggest that the lodges will have to be demolished and rebuilt. The private investor is taking legal action against FNU, claiming that a lack of proper maintenance work caused the slippage.

(vi) Approximately 30 per cent of the division's revenue comes from organising and selling tour packages to travel agents. The tour packages are tailored to the needs of tourists from Korea, Japan and Thailand. Selected travel agents are given a certain number of packages, which they allocate to customers once a deposit is paid. On account of the economic downturn in Asia, travel agencies are experiencing late cancellation rates of around 50 per cent. Although the customers are liable for the full cost of the tour for cancelling on short notice, FNU has found it is unable to collect most of the money owing as the customers simply lack the capacity to pay.

Required

For each of the situations (i) to (vi):

(a) How will the situation affect your audit plan?

(b) What further information would you seek prior to finalising your audit program?

This question was adapted from the Professional Year Programme of The Institute of Chartered Accountants in Australia—1998 Accounting 2 Module

6.34 **Moderate** Your client has recently completed an MBA. Full of enthusiasm, she has been calculating ratios based on some of her competitors' financial reports to gain a better perspective of her own company's performance. She suggests that this ratio analysis often leads to some very conflicting signals. She provides you with the ratio analysis of Competitor A and asks you to explain the apparent conflicting signals in these ratios.

	Competitor A	
	20X1	20X0
Return on equity	14%	12%
Return on assets	9%	11%
Assets turnover	.45	.55
Profit margin	20%	20%
Debt/Total assets	60%	40%
Current ratio	2:1	1.4:1
Quick asset ratio	1.1:1	1.2:1
Days in receivables	48 days	44 days
Days in inventory	40 days	35 days

Required

Outline to the client a possible scenario that could explain these changes in ratios.

This question was adapted from the Professional Year Programme of The Institute of Chartered Accountants in Australia—1998 Accounting 2 Module

CHAPTER 7

7.26 **Basic** Explain the relationship between inherent risk and business risk

7.27 **Basic** Explain the different rules of thumb for planning material and explain why you might use them.

7.28 **Basic** Why does AUS 210 specifically require the auditor to consider manipulation of revenue and override of controls in relation to fraud?

CHAPTER 8

8.31 **Basic** Explain the impact of the new audit risk standards on the evaluation of internal control.

8.32 Basic Many auditors use flowcharts as an auditing technique, in conjunction with internal control questionnaires.

(a) Outline the disadvantages and problems with the use of an internal control questionnaire that can be minimised if they are used in conjunction with flowcharts.

(b) What benefits are obtained from the use of flowcharts that are not available from internal control questionnaires alone?

Source: CICA

8.33 Moderate Phil King has now completed his review of the internal control of Q Pty Ltd. His supervisor was so impressed that he has asked him to determine a preliminary assessment of control risk for certain key accounts. An extract of Phil's narrative account of the payroll area follows:

General

The payroll process is a predominantly manual process with a PC program used for routine functions such as addition and summarisation only. There are two people employed within the payroll area. These people and their duties are:

- Joe Leung: Payroll supervisor. Joe is responsible for maintaining personnel details, including current position, rates of pay and leave taken and owing. In addition, Joe is responsible for approving the weekly pay.
- Josie Black: Pay clerk. Josie is responsible for processing the weekly payroll. This includes calculation of any overtime or leave loading. Josie is also responsible for dispensing pays.

Procedures

The payroll processing procedures are as follows:

- On Monday of each week Josie prepares a report of amounts due to employees for the week just completed. In the main, employees are on a salary and receive a constant payment. However, some employees are paid for overtime and Josie calculates the amount of overtime payment based on timesheets sent to the payroll department each week by the supervisor of each section and the rates of pay contained in personnel files. Once the report is completed, Josie gives it to Joe to review.
- Joe advises Josie weekly of any new or terminated employees.
- Joe reviews the report and authorises Josie to prepare payments.
- Josie then draws an appropriate amount of cash from the bank, prepares pay envelopes and distributes wages to each of the employees. At the completion of this process Josie signs the payroll report as evidence that all cash has been distributed.
- Any envelopes that are not distributed (owing to employee absence) are returned to Joe, who locks the envelopes in the safe. Employees can then receive their pay envelope by visiting the payroll area. Employees must sign for their payment.
- Josie then prepares a journal sheet detailing the journal required to record the wages payment and passes it, together with the payroll report, to Joe to authorise. Once authorised, Josie keys in the journal and files the journal and report in date order.

Required

Assume that you are Phil and determine your preliminary assessment of control risk for Q. Provide reasons for your decision.

8.34 Moderate You are the auditor of Community Sports Enterprises Inc. (CSE), a community-based organisation that supplies sporting equipment and apparel to the local community at cost price. The manager of CSE has asked you to perform a review of the internal controls within the payments area of CSE. From your discussions with management and staff you ascertain the following facts:

1 The accounts payable clerk receives all supplier invoices. The clerk then checks the invoices to relevant delivery notes. If a discrepancy is found the clerk will telephone

the supplier to rectify the problem. No payment is made until the clerk is satisfied the problem has been rectified. Little if any documentation is kept by the clerk to indicate how problems are resolved.

2   If there are no discrepancies between the supplier invoice and the delivery note, the clerk prepares a cheque requisition for the amount indicated on the supplier invoice and signs the cheque requisition as evidence of matching the invoice to the delivery notes. She then files the supplier invoice with the relevant delivery note. The only markings made on the invoice are a series of 'ticks' indicating the invoice has been matched to the delivery note.

3   The completed cheque requisition is forwarded to the banking clerk, who prepares a manual cheque and posts an appropriate journal entry.

4   Once completed, the banking clerk forwards the cheque requisition and unsigned cheque to the manager director, who signs the cheque. All signed cheques are returned to the banking clerk for mailing.

Required

Identify the strengths and weaknesses in CSE's internal control for the payments area.

8.35 Moderate You are the audit senior on FMG Pty Limited, a distributor of kitchenware products. The company operates on a national basis and uses an online network system. The company is highly computerised, with all major accounting functions being processed within the system. The IT department operates out of the Brisbane head office and comprises 30 people. The system has been fully developed and maintained by the IT department, and the current system, apart from minor changes, has been in use for three years. Each location is responsible for processing its own transactions.

Required

(a) In what ways does the use of an IT system alter the audit assertions that are required to be achieved by the auditor? In what ways does the type of audit evidence change?

(b) You have been asked by the audit manager to prepare a memorandum detailing what types of controls you would expect to see in both the general and application control environment in a company like FMG Pty Limited. The memorandum is to be used as the basis of a system review to be performed in relation to the audit for the year ended 31 December 20X0.

(c) Assume you have completed your review and found the application controls to be very efficient but the general controls to be lacking in some areas. What would be the impact of the review on your audit approach?

This question was adapted from the Professional Year Programme of The Institute of Chartered Accountants in Australia—1994 Accounting 2 Module

CHAPTER 9

9.29 Basic The revised audit risk standards outline the circumstances in which the auditor is required to undertake testing of controls.

Required

What are these circumstances?

9.30 Moderate You have been assigned to perform tests of controls on the sales system at EDB Pty Limited as part of the 30 June 20X1 audit. EDB is a wholesaler of bathroom supplies such as vanities, toilets, taps and sinks. During testing, you noted the following errors:

(i) Invoice number 54922, issued on 12 December 20X0, was entered twice. The error was discovered when the customer rang to complain about being charged double the agreed amount.

(ii) Invoice number 51839, issued on 25 September 20X0, contained incorrect prices. Three vanity units were charged at $453 instead of $543 each and five sinks were charged at $231 instead of $312 each. The error was discovered when the salesperson complained about not receiving their full commission entitlement for the month.

(iii) No prices were entered on invoice number 56329, issued on 24 January 20X1, resulting in a zero dollar invoice being issued. The error was discovered when accounts receivable staff queried the zero amount appearing on the accounts receivable ledger.

(iv) Invoice number 59328, issued on 18 March 20X1, matched the customer's order. However, the order was only partially filled owing to a lack of stock in the warehouse, with the result that items were included in the invoice that were never delivered. The error was discovered when the customer rang to complain about being overcharged.

(v) Invoice number 61348, issued on 7 May 20X1, was sent to the wrong address. Apparently the invoice had the correct address on it, but a typing error occurred on the envelope. The error was discovered when the customer rang to complain about the overdue notice they received, stating they had never received an invoice in the first place.

(vi) Invoice number 62875, issued on 29 June 20X1, was not processed through the usual channels. Although the invoice details were correct, certain procedures, such as a formal credit check, were not documented. The invoice was a special order for a large building project and amounted to around ten times the value of EDB's average invoices. The sale was personally handled by one of the directors and the invoice prepared by his assistant.

Required

Treating each of the above errors independently:

(a) Describe application controls (both manual and IT) that would have either prevented or detected the error.

(b) What further work would you perform in relation to the error?

(c) What are the implications of the error for your substantive testing of accounts receivable?

This question was adapted from the Professional Year Programme of The Institute of Chartered Accountants in Australia—1999 Accounting 2 Module

CHAPTER 10

10.35 Basic For each of the following material transactions describe:

    (a) what the transaction represents;

    (b) the assertions contained in the transaction that would be of prime interest to the auditor; and

    (c) the evidence the auditor will seek in order to verify these assertions.

Transaction 1		
Dr Accumulated depreciation	100 000	
Dr Debtors-associated entity	4 900 000	
Cr Buildings		2 600 000
Cr Profit on sale of buildings		2 400 000
Transaction 2		
Dr Sales returns and allowances	2 000 000	
Dr Inventory	1 000 000	
Cr Accounts receivable		2 000 000
Cr Cost of goods sold		1 000 000

10.36 Moderate You have been assigned to the audit of property, plant and equipment at W Ltd. Some of the main components of W's property, plant and equipment are personal computers (PCs) and associated network hardware. You have some concerns as to the best way to audit the PCs and have approached the information technology manager at W to determine the nature and extent of equipment held. The manager has told you the following:

- All PCs are compulsorily retired after three years. At this point they are scrapped; however, the IT department keeps a small number for spare parts (e.g. monitors, keyboards).
- On installation each PC is barcoded and the details given to the accounting area. He understands that each section manager is responsible for ensuring all barcodes are accounted for annually.
- Network installation and equipment is added to, retired and repaired as necessary. Each time a new piece of equipment is purchased, the purchase is organised by the accounting section with the record of purchase held in that area. Periodically the IT manager will notify the fixed assets clerk of equipment that has been scrapped.

  As a result of the last comment you have some concern about the validity of the balances recorded for network equipment and you asked the fixed assets clerk to explain how he knows everything is accounted for.

  The fixed assets clerk said: 'To be honest with you I have no real idea what is still in that area; I know what we purchased but I just rely on the IT manager to tell me what to write off.'

Required

Assuming the value of components associated with the network is material, identify three procedures you could use to audit the computer equipment held by W. For each procedure indicate the assertion tested.

CHAPTER 11

11.31 Basic The following is a list of audit procedures that might be applied to property, plant and equipment. Identify the procedures that might be applied using audit sampling.
(a) Inquire about procedures followed to ensure that retirements are recorded.
(b) Review capital budgets for the period and compare to accounting records.
(c) Vouch additions by inspecting supporting documents.
(d) Tour the plant and note the existence and appearance of new equipment.
(e) Scan repair and maintenance expense and inspect supporting documents for large disbursements.

11.32 Moderate An audit assistant has been asked to complete testing of controls in the revenue and receipts cycle. The assistant reviews the audit program and notes that a sample of 50 sales invoices is required for testing and that a statistical sampling approach has been adopted. The required confidence level has been set at 95% and the tolerable error is 10%. After requesting access to copies of invoices, she selects 10 sequential invoices from each of the months of January, February, October, November and December for her testing. The company processes approximately 500 invoices per year.

The assistant completes her testing and finds only one error. Using a statistical table (Table 11.6 on p. 532), she determines that the actual deviation rate does not exceed the expected number of deviations. She concludes: 'this control appears to be operating as anticipated'.

Required

Do you agree with the assistant's conclusion? Provide reasons for your opinion.

CHAPTER 12

12.31 Basic In an examination of Cotter Pty Ltd as at 31 December 20X0, you have learned of the following situation.

During the year 20X0, Cotter was named as a defendant in a suit for damages by Bixby Pty Ltd for breach of contract. A decision adverse to Cotter was rendered, and Bixby was awarded $40 000 damages. At the time of the audit, the case was under appeal to a higher court. No entry in this regard has been made in the accounting records. What entry would you recommend, and what disclosure, if any, would you make of this situation in the financial report for 31 December 20X0?

Source: AICPA adapted

12.32 Moderate You are the audit senior on the audit of an Australian company that retails computers and other high technology electronic equipment. During the year the company has expanded rapidly both locally and overseas, particularly in the United Kingdom, the United States of America and Eastern European countries. As a result of the rapid expansion, accounts receivable and inventories have increased considerably.

Required

Outline the auditing procedures you would undertake in order to obtain the necessary assurance that all subsequent events had been identified and considered before finalisation and signing of the financial report and audit report.

12.33 Complex Consider each of the following independent and material situations. In each case:
- the balance date is 31 October 20X4
- the financial report and audit report were signed on 12 December 20X4
- the financial report and audit report were mailed to the members on 20 December 20X4

(i) Your client, MM Mining Ltd, owns a mineral exploration licence in Central Australia. At 31 October this licence was valued by an independent expert at $50 million. This valuation is reflected in the financial report. On 8 December, MM Mining Ltd receives notice that a claim is being lodged under the *Native Titles Act* for land that includes that subject to the exploration licence. If the claim is successful, the exploration licence will be worthless.

(ii) The same facts apply as in (i), but MM Mining Ltd receives the notice on 14 December 20X4.

(iii) Your client, BF Pty Limited, derives approximately 10 per cent of revenues from selling aviary supplies to city-based bird breeders. A government report, leaked to the press and reported on 11 November, recommends that strict limits be placed on the number of birds allowed to be kept in suburban areas. BF estimates that, if the recommendations are enacted, about 70 per cent of its customers will have to cut their flocks by 50 per cent or more. This would affect not only future sales but also their ability to pay existing debts.

(iv) The same facts apply as in (iii), but the legislation has passed through Parliament and will become law on 1 January 20X5.

Required

(a) Identify the period during which the auditor is responsible for identifying subsequent events.

(b) For each of the above events, state the appropriate action A to D for the situation and justify your response. The alternative actions are as follows:

A   Adjust the 31 October 20X4 financial report.
B   Disclose the information in the notes to the 31 October 20X4 financial report.
C   Request the client to recall the 31 October 20X4 financial report for revision.
D   No action is required.

This question was adapted from the Professional Year Programme of The Institute of Chartered Accountants in Australia—1995 Advanced Audit Module

12.34 Complex Consider each of the following independent and material situations. In each case:
- the balance date is 31 October 20X4
- the financial report and audit report were signed on 12 December 20X4
- the financial report and audit report were mailed to the members on 20 December 20X4

    (i)   Your client, GP Ltd, reached an out-of-court settlement on 1 December 20X4 of $300 000. The settlement was in relation to a litigation case dating back to 20X1. A provision of $150 000 was recorded in the 31 October 20X4 financial report.

    (ii)   The same facts apply as in (i), except that the settlement was made on 18 December 20X4.

    (iii)   On 14 December 20X4 you discover a debtor of your client, CP Ltd, was placed in provisional liquidation on 8 December. The debtor owed $600 000 as at 31 October; a specific provision of $300 000 of this amount was made at this date. On very preliminary information, the likely payout to unsecured creditors is zero.

    (iv)   The same facts apply as in (iii), but you do not find out about the provisional liquidation of 8 December until 21 December 20X4.

    (v)   A flood occurred in the warehouse of your client, PP Ltd, on 2 November 20X4. Inventory valued at $2 million was destroyed. The directors believe only half of this value will be recovered from the insurers.

    (vi)   The same facts apply as in (v), but the insurance company decides to replace all the inventory destroyed. The new inventory is at PP's premises on 6 December 20X4.

Required
(a) Identify the period during which the auditor is responsible for identifying subsequent events.
(b) For each of the above events, state the appropriate action A to D for the situation and justify your response. The alternative actions are as follows:
    A   Adjust the 31 October 20X4 financial report.
    B   Disclose the information in the notes to the 31 October 20X4 financial report.
    C   Request the client to recall the 31 October 20X4 financial report for revision.
    D   No action is required.

This question was adapted from the Professional Year Programme of The Institute of Chartered Accountants in Australia—1995 Advanced Audit Module

CHAPTER 13

13.31 Basic The consolidated profit of Y Ltd and its subsidiaries for the year ended 30 June 20X0 is $490 000. During the audit of X Ltd, one of the subsidiaries, the auditor, CA, notices that there is $5000 of intercompany profit in the inventory. The net profit of X Ltd for the year ended 30 June 20X0 is $25 000. There was no adjustment on any of the entity's financial reports for this profit, and management refuses to allow any change in the reports.

Required

Indicate the opinions, with reasons, CA would issue on:

(a) X Ltd

(b) Y Ltd and its subsidiaries

Source: CICA

13.32 **Moderate** The 30 June 20X0 audit of X Ltd (X) has now been completed. A number of difficulties were experienced during the audit, including significant disagreements over the valuation of X's investment property holdings. The audit partner had suggested the property value was overstated by $10 million, a figure which was twice the level of materiality set for the audit. As a result of discussions with the audit committee, the CEO of X agreed to revise the valuations downward by $8 million. All other issues were resolved to the satisfaction of the audit partner, resulting in an overall misstatement of the accounts of $2 million. The audit partner is now considering the effect of the misstatement on the audit report.

Required

Discuss the effect of the misstatement on the audit report.

CHAPTER 14

14.31 **Basic** 'The accounting profession should encourage public companies to present a budgeted financial report for the forthcoming year in the same detail and following the same rules as those used in preparing historical financial reports. The audit report should be required to encompass both the historical and budgeted statements.'

From the accounting and auditing points of view, what are the advantages and disadvantages of this proposal?

14.32 **Basic** The following are essential elements of an assurance engagement:

(a) a three-party relationship

(b) an appropriate subject matter

(c) suitable criteria

Required

Outline how these elements relate to an assurance engagement on reporting on internal control.

CHAPTER 15

No additional questions.

CHAPTER 16

No additional questions.

CHAPTER 17

17.18 **Basic** The following are essential elements of an assurance engagement:

(a) a three-party relationship

(b) an appropriate subject matter

(c) suitable criteria

Required

Outline how these elements relate to an assurance engagement on environmental and sustainability information.

17.19 Basic The research undertaken by CPA Australia identified a number of deficiencies in the area of assurance engagements being provided on environmental and sustainability reports.

Required
What deficiencies were identified, and what corrective actions are being undertaken to address these deficiencies?

A

Access controls Procedures designed to restrict access to online terminal devices, programs and data. Access controls consist of 'user authentication' and 'user authorisation'. 'User authentication' typically attempts to identify a user through unique log-on identifications, passwords, access cards or biometric data. 'User authorisation' consists of access rules to determine the computer resources each user may access.

Accountability matter A matter for which the governing body of an entity: is responsible and is obliged to report on, and/or be subject to an examination on, pursuant to an accountability relationship between two or more parties internal or external to the entity.

Accounting estimate An approximation of the amount of an item in the absence of a precise means of measurement.

Accounting system *See* Information system.

Accrual accounting The method of making an economically meaningful and comprehensive measurement of performance and position by recognising economic events regardless of when cash transactions happen, as opposed to the simpler cash basis of accounting. Under this method, revenues and expenses (and related assets and liabilities) are reflected in the accounts in the period to which they relate.

Actual independence The achievement of actual freedom from bias, personal interest, prior commitment to an interest, or susceptibility to undue influence or pressure.

Adverse opinion The subject matter taken as a whole is misleading or of little use to the addressee of the audit report. This type of opinion will be expressed when the effects of a disagreement with management or conflict with an accepted framework are of great magnitude or pervasive or fundamental to the subject matter.

Agency theory Investors, as principals in a relationship, entrust their resources to managers, who act as their agents or stewards of the resources. This gives rise to a demand for assurance to ensure that the agents have acted in the interests of the principals. This theory is also known as the 'stewardship hypothesis'.

Agreed-upon procedures engagement A service where the auditor's objective is to issue a report of factual findings to those parties that have agreed to the procedures to be performed, in which no conclusion is communicated and therefore no assurance is expressed, but which provides the user with information to meet a particular need, and from which the user can draw conclusions and derive assurance as a result of the auditor's procedures.

Allowable risk of over-reliance The risk the auditor is willing to accept that a sample supports a planned level of reliance when the true deviation rate does not justify such a low level.

Analytical procedures The investigation and analysis of fluctuations and relationships to determine whether there are inconsistencies with other relevant information or deviations from predicted amounts.

Analytical procedures risk The risk that analytical procedures will not detect the misstatements in an assertion.

Another auditor (using the work of) This occurs in the audit of group accounts where another auditor is appointed to audit part of that group.

Application controls Controls over the processing of transactions within a specific accounting application, such as invoicing customers, paying suppliers and preparing payroll.

Appropriateness of audit evidence The measure of the quality of audit evidence, its relevance to particular assertions, and its reliability.

Assertions Representations made by a responsible party in an accountability arrangement that pertains to economic actions and events. *See also* Financial report assertions.

Assessing control risk The process of evaluating the effectiveness of the design and operation of an entity's internal controls in preventing or detecting material misstatements in the financial report.

Assistants Personnel involved in an individual audit other than the auditor signing the audit report; includes an expert employed by the auditor.

Assurance The satisfaction as to the reliability of information provided. The degree of satisfaction achieved is determined by the nature, extent and timing of procedures performed by the auditor, the results of the procedures and the objectivity of the evidence obtained.

Assurance engagement An engagement in which a practitioner expresses a conclusion designed to enhance the degree of confidence of the intended users other than the responsible party about the outcome of the evaluation or measurement of a subject matter against criteria. The outcome of the evaluation or measurement of a subject matter is the information that results from applying the criteria (*see also* Subject matter information). Under the 'International Framework for Assurance Engagements' there are two types of assurance engagement a practitioner is permitted to perform: a reasonable assurance engagement and a limited assurance engagement.

Assurance services *See* Assurance engagement.

Attest engagement The issue of a positive expression of an opinion that enhances the credibility of a written assertion(s) about an accountability matter ('attest audit').

Attribute sampling A statistical sampling technique involving examining documents for particular attributes and providing a given level of confidence on these attributes.

Attribute standards Set of standards issued by the Institute of Internal Auditors, outlining the personal standards and qualities to be maintained by internal auditors.

Audit A service where the auditor's objective is to provide a high level of assurance through the issue of a positive expression of opinion that enhances the credibility of an assertion about an accountability matter.

Audit and Assurance Alerts Notifications issued by the AUASB to bring matters considered to be of significant and immediate concern to the attention of members of the profession.

Audit committee A committee of directors (usually predominantly non-executive) responsible for overseeing external financial reporting and liaising with the external and internal audit functions.

Audit evidence The information obtained by the auditor in arriving at the conclusions on which the audit opinion is based. Audit evidence will comprise source documents and accounting records underlying the financial report, and corroborating information from other sources. Audit evidence is gathered through all stages of an audit.

Audit hooks Exit points provided in computer application programs that allow the auditor to insert commands for special processing.

Audit mandate An authority to undertake an audit and provide a report. The mandate may prescribe the nature of the audit and the type of report expected.

Audit opinion A positive written expression within a specified framework, indicating the auditor's overall conclusion based upon audit evidence obtained that provides a reasonable level of assurance (high but not absolute assurance).

Audit plan A description of the expected scope and conduct of the audit with sufficient detail to guide the audit and aid the development of the audit program.

Audit procedures Methods and techniques used by the auditor to gather and evaluate audit evidence.

Audit program Sets out the nature, timing and extent of planned audit procedures required to implement the overall audit plan. The audit program serves as a set of instructions to assistants involved in the audit, and as a means to control and record the proper execution of the work.

Audit-related services The range of engagements that:
(a) involve a systematic examination for which audit-based skills, which includes such skills as analysis of financial information, knowledge of internal control, problem solving, risk assessment, sample selection, knowledge of accounting standards and other aspects of reporting, are required;
(b) can be applied to an accountability matter that is capable of evaluation against reasonable criteria; and
(c) result in an independent, written report that provides assurance or information from which the user can derive assurance.

These services comprise audit, review and agreed-upon procedures.

Audit report A report issued by the auditor that expresses a high level of assurance about an accountability matter that is capable of evaluation against an identified framework.

Audit risk The risk that the auditor gives an inappropriate audit opinion when the financial report is materially misstated. Audit risk has three components; inherent risk, control risk and detection risk.

Audit sampling involves the application of audit procedures to less than 100 per cent of items within an account balance or class of transactions such that all sampling units have a chance of selection.

Audit software Use of computer programs to aid the audit in interrogating the audit client's data and files.

Audit strategy The planning process to develop an efficient and effective audit which includes making decisions in relation to the scope of the audit, the general evidence requirements for the forming of an opinion, and the initial choice as to the nature, timing and extent of audit procedures to make efficient use of resources.

Audit trail A chain of evidence provided by coding, cross-references and documentation that connects account balances and other summary results with original transaction data.

Auditing Guidance Statements Statements approved and issued by the AUASB that provide guidance on procedural matters or on entity- or industry-specific issues, or clarify and explain principles in an AUS but do not establish new principles and do not amend existing standards.

Auditing standards Standards issued by professional accounting organisations. These standards prescribe the basic principles and essential procedures, together with the related guidance, which govern the professional conduct of an auditor.

Auditor The person with final responsibility for the audit or audit-related service engagement. *See* Engagement partner.

B

Back-up Plans made by the entity to obtain access to comparable hardware, software and data in the event of their system's failure, loss or destruction.

Balance sheet approach An audit approach which concentrates on verifying the assets and liabilities of the entity.

Balanced scorecard A report that provides a balance of financial and non-financial measures that focus on both short-term and long-term performance and support the entity's competitive strategy.

Bank confirmation requests Requests to banks to provide independent confirmation of audit client's account balances and other information held by the bank on behalf of the client.

Bank transfer schedule A schedule of all transfers between the audit client's bank accounts (usually around balance dates) and the dates of recording on the books and bank statements.

Basic bound Maximum monetary misstatement that would exist in a population when no monetary misstatements are found in a sample.

Batch entry/batch processing An input and processing method whereby data are accumulated by classes of transactions and are entered and processed in batches.

Black lettering Bold words used in the auditing standard to highlight basic principles and essential procedures.

Block selection Sample selection method where the auditor selects all items of a specified type processed on a particular day or week or otherwise stored in a block.

Business performance measurement Assurance service which evaluates whether a client's performance measurement system contains relevant or reliable measures for assessing the degree to which the client's objectives are achieved, or how its performance compares to competitors.

Business risk Risk that an entity's business objectives will not be attained as a result of external and internal factors, pressures and forces brought to bear on the entity.

Business risk approach A modification to the financial risk analysis approach to auditing. The auditor must understand the business risks faced by the client in addition to understanding the risks that affect the traditional processing and recording of transactions.

Business-to-business e-commerce (B2B) Electronic commercial transactions between businesses.

Business-to-consumer e-commerce (B2C) Electronic commercial transactions between businesses and consumers.

C

Check digit A redundant digit added to a computer code to check accuracy of other characters in the code.

Classic disbursements fraud The preparation of fraudulent supporting documents that are used to obtain an authorised cheque.

Code of ethics A formal and systematic statement of rules, principles, regulations or laws, developed by a community to promote its well-being and to exclude or punish any undermining behaviour.

Common-size statement method A technique of analysing financial statements in which income statement figures are expressed in percentages of revenue and balance sheet accounts are expressed in percentages of total assets.

Compilation engagement In a compilation engagement, the accountant is engaged to use accounting expertise as opposed to auditing expertise to collect, classify and/or summarise financial information.

Complete inventory count A process by which operating activity largely stops and all inventory on hand is counted at one time.

Completeness An assertion that all transactions and accounts have been presented in the financial report.

Compliance audit An audit that involves obtaining and examining evidence to determine whether certain financial and operating activities of an entity conform to specified conditions, rules or regulations.

Comfort letter A letter issued by a parent entity to support a subsidiary that is in financial difficulty.

Comprehensive audit Audit that involves a range of audit and audit-related services within an audit mandate for a client. It encompasses the elements of a financial report audit, a compliance audit and a performance audit.

Computation Checking the arithmetical accuracy of source documents and accounting records, or performing independent calculations.

Computer-assisted audit techniques (CAATs) Techniques that involve the auditor using the computer in the performance of the audit. It can involve the use of either audit software or test data techniques.

Computer service bureau An external service centre where computerised accounting applications are processed.

Conclusive evidence Decisive, convincing evidence.

Concurring partner A partner, other than the audit engagement partner, who reviews the audit files as part of an audit firm's quality control procedures.

Confidentiality Information relating to an entity or party is not made available or disclosed to unauthorised individuals, entities, or processes.

Confirmation The response to an inquiry to corroborate information contained in the accounting record.

Continuing professional development A quality control requirement that involves all members of the professional accounting bodies undertaking a minimum number of hours of education each year.

Continuous assurance An assurance service provided in an ongoing manner so that any new information collected and stored within a system is validated continuously.

Contributory negligence The failure of the plaintiff to meet certain required standards of care.

Control activities Those activities in addition to the control environment that management has established to ensure, as far as possible, that specific entity objectives will be achieved.

Control environment The overall attitude, awareness and actions of management regarding internal control and its importance in the entity.

Control risk The risk that misstatements that could occur in an account balance or class of transactions and that could be material, individually or when aggregated with the misstatements in other balances or classes, will not be prevented or detected on a timely basis by the internal control.

Control totals The adding of a set of transactions or account balances, to provide reasonable assurance of the occurrence, completeness and measurement of data processed by the computer.

Corporate governance The framework of how directors and management perform their respective duties to add and create shareholder value.

Corroborating evidence Evidence obtained by an auditor that supports the conclusions reached from other evidence-gathering procedures.

Criminal liability The possibility of being found guilty under criminal law; auditors may be convicted of a criminal offence if they are found to have defrauded a person through knowing involvement with false financial reports.

Criteria The benchmarks used to evaluate or measure the subject matter, including, where relevant, benchmarks for presentation and disclosure. *See also* Suitable criteria.

Current ratio Current assets divided by current liabilities.

Current working paper file A file that contains corroborating information pertaining to the execution of the current year's audit program.

Cutoff tests Tests performed on transactions each side of year-end, designed to ensure that transactions are recorded in the correct period.

Cycle count (of inventory) Periodic counts of selected inventory items are made during the year, with all items counted at least once each year.

D

Database A collection of data that is shared and used by many users for different purposes. Each user may not necessarily be aware of all the data stored in the database or of the ways that the data may be used for multiple purposes. Generally, individual users are aware only of the data that they use and may view the data as computer files utilised by their applications.

Database management system (DBMS) The software that is used to create, maintain and operate the database. Together with the operating system, the DBMS facilitates the physical storage of the data, maintains the interrelationships among the data, and makes the data available to application programs.

Database systems Principally comprised of two components: the database and the database management system (DBMS).

Date of audit report The date on which the audit is completed. It should not be a date earlier than that of the directors' declaration, and must be included on the audit report.

Days in inventory How long inventory is held on average, in days. This is calculated by dividing 365 by the inventory turnover, which is the cost of goods sold/inventory assets.

Days in receivables This indicates how many days it takes, on average, to collect a day's sales revenue.

Debt to equity ratio Total liabilities divided by total equity.

Deontological theories State that actions and motivations are inspired by a sense of moral obligations. They are based on duties and rights which are set down in rules which must be followed regardless of the consequences. Also called non-consequential theories.

Detection risk The risk that an auditor's substantive procedures will not detect a material misstatement that exists in an account balance or class of transactions that could be material, individually or when aggregated with misstatements in other balances or classes.

Difference estimation A sampling approach involving the calculation of the difference between the audited value and book value of each item in the population.

Direct reporting engagements The provision of relevant and reliable information and a positive expression of opinion about an accountability matter where the party responsible for the matter does not make a written assertion(s).

Directors' assurance Assurance service which gives assurance on whether the information considered by directors at their regular meetings is appropriate and reliable for their consideration.

Disciplinary provisions Provisions for imposing penalties for substandard performance, to regulate the auditing profession.

Disclaimer *See* Inability to form an opinion.

Disclosure An assertion that the account balances and classes of transactions are properly described and identified in the correct section of the financial report.

Discovery sampling An attribute sampling approach that is used to identify a specified probability of finding at least one example of a deviation in a population.

Documentation The material (working papers) prepared by, and for, or obtained and retained by, the auditor in connection with the performance of the assurance service.

Dollar-unit sampling (DUS) Sampling technique where sample units are individual dollars rather than physical units.

Dual-purpose tests Audit tests that are specifically planned to provide direct evidence of both controls and substantive matters.

Due diligence An assurance service commonly involved with an acquisition of a business; aimed at identifying significant issues concerned with valuing the business and determining the purchase price.

Due professional care Planning and performing an assurance service and issuing an opinion with the skill and competence expected of a reasonably competent and cautious auditor, having regard to the needs of users.

E

E-commerce Commercial transactions conducted by electronic means, including through the Internet.

Earnings management Earnings management occurs when judgment in financial reporting and in structuring transactions is used to alter financial reports to influence the perceptions of stakeholders about the underlying economic performance of the entity and/or to influence outcomes that depend on reported accounting numbers.

Economy With regard to economy audits, assurance about the acquisition of the appropriate quantity and quality of resources at the appropriate time and at the lowest cost.

Effectiveness With regard to effectiveness audits, assurance about the achievement of the objectives of the activities.

Efficiency With regard to efficiency audits, assurance about the use of resources such that output is maximised for any given set of resource inputs.

Egoism The habit of valuing everything only in reference to one's personal interest.

ElderCare An assurance service designed to ensure that the medical, financial and household needs of the elderly are being met.

Electronic Data Interchange (EDI) The electronic transmission of documents between or within organisations.

Embedded audit modules Procedures written directly into the program of specific computer applications enabling auditor intervention to capture or process data for audit purposes.

'Emphasis of matter' section A paragraph at the end of an auditor's report that draws attention to or highlights a matter that is relevant to the users of the audit report but it is not of such a nature that it affects the audit opinion. An emphasis of matter section may only be used in certain limited circumstances.

Encryption (cryptography) The process of transforming programs and information into a form that cannot be understood without access to specific decoding algorithms (cryptographic keys). Encryption can provide an effective control for protecting confidential or sensitive programs and information from unauthorised access or modification.

Engagement letter A letter that documents and confirms the auditor's acceptance of the appointment, the objective and scope of the audit, the extent of the auditor's responsibilities to the entity and the form of any reports.

Engagement partner The partner or other person in the firm who is responsible for the engagement and its performance, and for the report that is issued on behalf of the firm, and who, where required, has the appropriate authority from a professional, legal or regulatory body.

Engagement quality control review A process designed to provide an objective evaluation, before the report is issued, of the significant judgments the engagement team made and the conclusions they reached in formulating the report.

Engagement quality control reviewer A partner, other person in the firm, suitably qualified external person or a team made up of such individuals with sufficient and appropriate experience and authority to objectively evaluate, before the report is issued, the significant judgments the engagement team made and the conclusions they reached in formulating the report.

Engagement risk Auditor's exposure to loss or injury to the professional practice from litigation, adverse publicity or other events arising in connection with an assurance engagement. This risk is increased when the client entity is in a weak financial position.

Enterprise Resource Planning (ERP) software Software that integrates business operations and financial report.

Environmental and sustainability reports (assurance on) Providing assurance on reports relating to the environmental and social aspects of operations.

Error An unintentional misstatement in financial reports, including the omission of an amount or a disclosure. For example: a mistake in gathering or processing data from which the financial report is prepared; an incorrect accounting estimate arising from oversight or misinterpretation of facts; or a mistake in the application of accounting principles relating to measurement, recognition, classification, presentation, or disclosure.

Estimation sampling Sampling method where the auditor creates an estimate of the amount and compares it to the amount recorded by the client.

Ethical decision models Models that have been developed to assist in sound ethical decision making.

Ethical pronouncements Series of ethical statements set out by the auditing profession. In Australia, ethical pronouncements are contained in the Joint Code of Professional Conduct (CPC).

'Except for' opinion An 'except for' opinion indicates that certain circumstances exist, which in the auditor's opinion are material or are likely to be material; however, they are not of such magnitude or so pervasive or fundamental as to affect the subject matter as a whole.

Executive management *See* Operational management.

Existence An assertion pertaining to a financial report that assets or liabilities exist at a given date.

Expectation gap The gap that exists between what users expect of an auditor and the actual service that auditors provide. This gap may be due to unreasonable expectations of users or to the inadequate performance of auditors.

Expected error The error the auditor expects to find in the population.

Expert systems Computer systems that incorporate the knowledge of human experts to assist decision-making processes.

External auditor An auditor independent from the entity, appointed to express an opinion on an accountability matter.

External confirmation The process of obtaining and evaluating audit evidence through a direct communication from a third party in response to a request for information about a particular item affecting assertions made by management in the financial report.

External file labels Printed or handwritten adhesive labels on diskettes or magnetic tape reels.

eXtensible Business Reporting Language (XBRL) XML-based language that uses accepted financial reporting standards and practices in order to encourage the standardisation and exchange of financial information across all software and technologies, including the Internet.

eXtensible Markup Language (EML) Grammatical rules for describing data on the web, which provide a standard language for data exchange.

F

Field test A logic test based on the characteristics that data in particular fields should exhibit. For example, characters should be alphabetic or numeric (alpha-numeric test); the field should have a specified size (for example, a field contains 5 characters, not 4 or 6).

File controls Control activities that ensure that the proper versions of files are used in processing.

Financial modelling A complex analytical procedure which involves the identification of a key input variable (such as sales revenues) from which values of other accounts (such as expenses and profits) can be calculated.

Financial report The financial statements, notes, supplementary schedules and explanatory material that are intended to be read with the financial statements.

Financial report assertions Assertions made by management, explicit or otherwise, that are embodied in the financial report. These are (*see also* the entries for these terms): Existence; Rights and obligations; Occurrence; Completeness; Valuation; Measurement; and Disclosure.

Financial risk analysis approach An audit approach where an auditor adopts a risk analysis approach to determine the audit program for the operating cycles of a business.

Financial totals The totals of field amounts (in dollars) for all the records in a batch or group of transactions that are normally computed as a result of processing.

Flowcharts Schematic diagrams using standardised symbols, interconnecting flow lines and annotations that portray the steps involved in processing information through the information system.

Footing Adding up a sequence of numbers such as journal entries.

Forecast Prospective financial information prepared on the basis of assumptions as to future events which management expects to take place and the actions management expects to take as of the date the information is prepared (best-estimate assumptions).

Forensic audit Audit assurance services to establish the validity of forensic evidences related to fraud and white-collar crimes.

Fraud An intentional act by one or more individuals among management, those charged with governance, employees, or third parties, involving the use of deception to obtain an unjust or illegal advantage. Fraudulent financial reporting involves intentional misstatements or omissions of amounts or disclosures in the financial report to deceive financial report users. Misappropriation of assets involves the theft of an entity's assets.

G

General controls in computer information systems Manual and computer controls affecting the overall computer information system, to provide a reasonable level of assurance that the overall objectives of internal control are achieved.

General-purpose financial report A financial report intended to meet the information needs common to users who are unable to command the preparation of reports tailored so as to satisfy, specifically, all of their information needs.

Generalised audit software (GAS) Audit software that is capable of being used for a number of data organisation and processing methods.

Global Reporting Initiative (GRI) Coalition of organisations interested in promoting the issue of environmental and sustainability reporting.

Globalisation Process of increasing the connectivity and mobility of the world's markets and businesses.

Going concern basis The accounting basis whereby in the preparation of the financial report the reporting entity is viewed as a going concern. That is, the entity is expected to be able to pay its debts as and when they fall due; and continue in operation without any intention or necessity to liquidate or otherwise wind up its operations.

Governance The role of persons entrusted with the supervision, control and direction of an entity. Those charged with governance ordinarily are accountable for ensuring that the entity achieves its objectives. *See also* Governing body.

Governing body An entity's board of directors, trustees or governors, or other equivalent body or person. *See also* Governance; Management.

Grandfather–father–son concept Retaining three generations of a particular master file and the related transaction files, where the current version of the master file is the son file and the two previous versions are the father and grandfather.

Gross profit ratio Provides an indication of the company's product pricing and product mix. Calculated as (sales − cost of goods sold) / sales.

H

Haphazard selection Auditor selects sample items without a conscious bias.

Hash total A control total that has no meaning in itself other than for control, e.g. total of customer numbers.

High (but not absolute) level of assurance Commonly referred to as reasonable level of assurance provided through an audit by issuing a positive expression of opinion that enhances the credibility of a written assertion(s) or by providing relevant and reliable information and a positive expression of opinion about an accountability matter.

I

Illegal acts Acts that involve non-compliance with laws and regulations.

Imprest fund Petty cash fund maintained at a constant level via replenishment of the value of vouchers paid out of the fund.

Inability to form an opinion The auditor is unable to express an opinion on the subject matter as a whole. This may occur if a scope limitation exists, where sufficient appropriate audit evidence cannot be reasonably obtained and the possible effects of any adjustments might be of great magnitude or pervasive or fundamental to the subject matter.

Independence Ability to withstand pressure from management influence when conducting an audit or providing audit-related services, so that one's professional integrity is not compromised. To add true value to the assurance function, this requires both independence in appearance and independence of mind.

Independence in appearance Belief of financial report users that independence has been achieved by auditors. Also called perceived independence.

Independence of mind An auditor's independent attitude of mind that actual independence has been achieved. Factors contributing to this independence are integrity, objectivity and strength of character. Also called independence of fact.

Industry specialisation Having extensive knowledge and experience of a particular industry in order to provide better service to clients in that industry.

Information hypothesis Posits that the demand for auditing is a result of investors wanting reliable information that can be used effectively in decision making. Unlike agency theory, the emphasis is not so much on the agent as on the reliability of information.

Information system The methods and records established to identify, assemble, analyse, calculate, classify, record and report the transactions and other events that affect an entity, and to maintain accountability for assets, liabilities, revenues and expenditures.

Inherent limitations of internal control The reasons (such as cost versus benefit and management override) that an entity's internal control can provide only reasonable assurance to management and the board of directors regarding the achievement of an entity's objectives.

Inherent risk A component of audit risk relating to the susceptibility of an account balance or class of transactions to misstatement that could be material, individually or when aggregated with misstatements in other balances or classes, assuming there were no related internal controls.

Inherent uncertainty The potential for a matter to affect the financial report that is not so remote as to make its disclosure irrelevant; however, at the date of signing the audit report the outcome is contingent upon future events and cannot be reasonably measured.

Input controls Procedures that provide assurance that data received for processing have been properly authorised, that they are complete and that they have been correctly converted into machine-readable form.

Inquiry Audit evidence-gathering technique that seeks appropriate information from knowledgeable persons inside or outside the entity. Inquiries range from written inquiries addressed to third parties, to informal oral inquiries addressed to persons inside the entity.

Inspection Audit evidence-gathering technique that consists of examining records, documents, or tangible assets.

Insurance hypothesis A view that posits that managers and professional participants in financial activities seek to use an auditor as a means of insurance — that is, as a means of shifting financial responsibility if any losses are expected from litigation.

Integrated test facility (ITF) A type of test of control that requires using a fictitious entity and entering fictitious transactions for that entity with the regular transactions, and then comparing the result with the expected output.

Integrity Consistent adherence to an ethical code. If client management lacks integrity, the auditor must be more sceptical than usual.

Interim work Audit work performed prior to balance date. Typically this involves performing tests of control and tests of details of transactions.

Internal audit/auditing An independent appraisal function established within an organisation to examine and evaluate the activities of the entity as a service to the entity. From the perspective of the external auditor, internal auditing is a component of the control environment.

Internal control The process designed and effected by those charged with governance, management and other personnel to provide reasonable assurance about the achievement of the entity's objectives with regard to reliability of financial reporting, effectiveness and efficiency of operations and compliance with applicable laws and regulations.
Internal control consists of the following components:
(a) the control environment;
(b) the entity's risk assessment process;
(c) the information system, including the related business processes, relevant to financial reporting, and communication;
(d) control activities; and
(e) monitoring of controls.

Internal control questionnaires A series of questions about accounting and control policies and procedures that the auditor considers necessary to prevent material misstatements in the financial report.

Internal file labels Computer-readable data that are actually part of the file. They identify the data and content of the file.

Internal review In-house audit firm procedures to ensure quality of work. Auditors may have their engagements periodically reviewed by another auditor from within the same firm or office.

Irregularities Actions that comprise fraud and other illegal acts, acts that contravene the constitution of the entity, intentional (but not fraudulent) misstatements, and unintentional errors.

IT controls Controls related to information technology (IT) environment. They may be 'General controls' that relate to all or many computerised accounting applications or 'Application controls' that relate to specific individual computerised accounting applications.

IT (information technology) environment The policies and procedures that the entity implements and the IT infrastructure (hardware, operating systems, etc.) and application software that it uses to support business operations and achieve business strategies.

J

Joint and several liability An obligation of two or more persons. Each is liable severally and all are liable jointly.

Judgmental selection Sample selection method where the auditor applies judgment in the selection of the sampling units to be tested.

K

Key entry validation A general term for tests to detect inaccurate or incomplete data. Computer equipment has logic capabilities that permit data validation, and exclude invalid responses.

Key verification A duplicate keying of data to detect errors of entry. As key verification is expensive, it is usually confined to critical data fields on source documents.

Kickbacks Illegal, secret payments made in return for a referral which resulted in a transaction or contract.

Kiting An irregularity overstating the cash balance by intentionally recording a bank transfer as a deposit in the receiving bank while failing to show a deduction from the bank account on which the transfer cheque is drawn.

Knowledge of the client's business The auditor's level of knowledge for an engagement, including a general knowledge of the economy and the industry within which the entity operates, and a more particular knowledge of how the entity operates.

L

Lapping An irregularity concealing the misappropriation of cash by using subsequent cash receipts to conceal the original misappropriation.

Lead partner *See* Engagement partner.

Lead schedule A summary working sheet for each area of the audit that is supported by individual working papers.

Legal structure The way a company handles its taxes, constitution, contracts, by-laws and the rights and duties of shareholders and provisions relating to the holding of meetings and election of directors.

Letter of subordination A form of comfort letter issued by a parent entity to support a subsidiary that is in financial difficulty. States that the parent entity agrees not to demand repayment of debts the subsidiary owes.

Letter of support A form of comfort letter issued by a parent entity to support a subsidiary that is in financial difficulty. States that the parent entity agrees to provide financial support to a subsidiary for a fixed period.

Limit or reasonableness test Computer program control designed to ensure that transactions or accounts balances do not exceed a particular limit (e.g. credit limit) or are not unreasonably large or small for the circumstances.

Limitation on scope A limitation on scope of an auditor's work exists when sufficient appropriate audit evidence on which to base an unqualified opinion does or did exist, or could reasonably be expected to have existed, but is not available to the auditor.

Limited assurance engagement The objective of a limited assurance engagement is a reduction in assurance engagement risk to a level that is acceptable in the circumstances of the engagement, but where that risk is greater than for a reasonable assurance engagement, as the basis for a negative form of expression of the practitioner's conclusion.

Local area networks (LANs) Networks that connect computer equipment, data files, software and peripheral equipment within a local area, such as a single building or small cluster of buildings for intra-company communications.

Low-balling A practice whereby a bid price of an audit service is quoted at an unreasonably low level so as to win the bid, with any 'losses' subsequently recovered through other means.

M

Management Comprises officers and others who also perform senior managerial functions. Management includes those charged with governance only in those instances when they perform such functions.

Management controls Controls performed by one or more managers.

Management letter A letter written to the management of an entity by an auditor at the completion of the audit. It contains recommendations to management for improved control systems or efficiency and effectiveness of operations that were noticed during the audit. *See also* Report to management.

Management representation letter A letter signed by management that contains representations made by management to an auditor during the course of an audit.

Management representations Representations made by management to the auditor during the course of the audit, either solicited or unsolicited or in response to specific inquiries.

Material inconsistency When other information contradicts information contained in the audited financial report. A material inconsistency may raise doubt about the audit conclusions drawn from audit evidence previously obtained and, possibly, about the basis for the auditor's opinion on the financial report.

Material misstatement of fact Misstatement of fact in other information exists when such information, not related to matters appearing in the audited financial report, is incorrectly stated or presented.

Material weakness A weakness in internal control that could have a material effect on the financial statements.

Materiality Information which if omitted, misstated or not disclosed separately has the potential to adversely affect decisions about the allocation of scarce resources made by users of the financial report or the discharge of accountability by the management including the governing body of the entity.

Mean-per-unit estimation Sample technique involving calculation of the average value (mean) of the sample, multiplying by the number of items in the population and comparing to the recorded balance.

Measurement An assertion that a transaction or event is recorded in the proper amount and in the proper period.

Misstatement A mistake in financial information which would arise from fraud, error or non-compliance with laws and regulations.

Moderate level of assurance Provided in a review engagement by issuing a statement of negative assurance that enhances the credibility of a written assertion(s) or by providing relevant and reliable information and a statement of negative assurance about an accountability matter. It is a lower level of assurance than that provided by an Audit.

Modified audit report An audit report that contains a qualified opinion and/or an emphasis of matter.

Monetary-unit sampling *See* Dollar-unit sampling.

N

Narrative memorandum Written description of internal control policies and procedures.

Negative assurance A moderate level of assurance, being a lower level of assurance than that provided in an audit. The auditor states whether anything has come to the auditor's attention that the information is not presented fairly in accordance with identified criteria.

Negative form of debtors' confirmation A request to a debtor which outlines the amount owing, asking them to respond if there is disagreement with the amount owing.

Negligence Not exercising due professional care.

Net profit ratio The net profit ratio, net profit/net sales, (usually measured after interest and taxes) measures the entity's profitability after all expenses are considered.

Non-routine transactions Transactions, such as the estimates of the doubtful debts provisions, that involve managerial discretion rather than rules (and thus can be more easily manipulated).

Non-sampling risk The component of audit risk that is not due to examining only a portion of the data, such as through the use of inappropriate procedures or the misinterpretation of evidence.

Non-statistical sampling All sampling approaches that do not have all the characteristics of statistical sampling (being random sample selection and use of probability theory to evaluate sample results).

O

Objectivity The notion that the information in financial reports must be as free from bias as possible, in order that all user groups can have confidence in it. Objectivity from the perspective of the assurance provider involves maintaining an impartial approach.

Observation An audit evidence-gathering technique that consists of looking at a process or procedure being performed by others. For example, the auditor may observe the counting of inventories by entity personnel or the performance of control activities that leave no audit trail.

Occurrence An assertion, pertaining to financial information, that transactions did in fact take place.

Online computer systems Enable users to access data and programs directly through terminal devices.

Operating cash flow ratio A short-term liquidity ratio that indicates the entity's ability to meet its current obligations. It measures the entity's ability to cover its current liabilities with cash generated from operations and is calculated as cash flow from operations/current liabilities.

Operation of internal control Design of the control environment, information system and control activities maintained by management to assist in ensuring that the conduct of the business is orderly and efficient.

Operational audit/auditing A systematic process of evaluating an organisation's effectiveness, efficiency and economy of operations under management's control, and then reporting to appropriate persons the results of the evaluations.

Operational management Those persons with responsibility for supervision of the day-to-day activities of the entity. *See also* Management.

Operational structure Includes types of products and services, locations, and methods of production, distribution and compensation.

Opinion shopping A practice whereby an audit client invites another firm of accountants to offer a second opinion on a disagreement the client's management has with the auditor over a proposed accounting treatment. This action can pressure the auditor to issue an unqualified audit report so as not to lose the audit to the second firm.

Organisational structure Division of tasks between individual employees, groups or departments and locations. To control the work of an entity, procedural methods and measures are adopted which provide evidence that the tasks specified by the organisational structure have been carried out.

Other auditor An auditor other than the principal auditor, who has responsibility for reporting on the financial information of part of an entity (such as a subsidiary) which is included in the financial report audited by the principal auditor. Other auditors include affiliated firms, whether using the same name or not, and correspondents, as well as unrelated auditors.

Other information Other financial or non-financial information (such as the directors' report) contained in a document which includes the audited financial report.

Output controls Controls over computer output that provide assurance that the processing result is correct and that only authorised personnel receive the output.

P

Package programs Programs written by a software provider that is usually independent of the entity and the auditor.

Parallel simulation A computer-assisted audit technique for testing computer controls, where actual entity data are processed using auditor-controlled software.

Peer review Independent periodic reviews of the quality of an auditor's audit procedures by other firms of public accountants.

Perceived independence *See* Independence in appearance.

Performance audit An audit of all or part of an entity's or entities' activities to assess economy and/or efficiency and/or effectiveness. It includes any audit directed to the adequacy of an internal control system or specific internal controls, including those intended to safeguard assets and to ensure due regard for economy, efficiency and effectiveness; the extent to which resources have been managed economically and efficiently; and the extent to which activities have been effective.

Performance review Management control activities that independently check the performance of individuals or processes.

Performance standards Set of standards issued by the Institute of Internal Auditors, outlining the work and performance standards and qualities to be maintained by internal auditors.

Periodic rotation of auditors Rotating partners and staff on audit engagements to bring fresh views to the audits, aid professional scepticism and promote independence.

Permanent file Contains information useful in an audit of a particular client, such as a client's history. It is carried forward and updated for each audit.

Persuasive evidence Evidence that has the power to influence. Most audit evidence is persuasive, but not conclusive.

PEST analysis Management and audit tool used to define the impact of political, economic, social and technological forces on an entity.

Physical inventory count (stocktake) Inventory items are counted, listed and the results are compared to accounting records.

Planning The development of a general strategy and a detailed approach for the expected nature, timing and extent of the audit engagement.

Population In relation to sampling, the entire set of data from which a sample is selected and about which the auditor wishes to draw conclusions.

Positive assurance *See* Reasonable assurance.

Positive form of debtors' confirmation Confirmation of amount owing by debtor, asking debtor whether or not they agree with the information on the request.

Presentation and disclosure An assertion that the components of a financial report are properly classified and described, and disclosed in accordance with the financial reporting framework.

'Presents fairly' Used in the audit opinion to express the auditor's view that there is no material misstatement from the reporting framework, such as applicable accounting standards, and that this reporting framework has been consistently applied. *See also* 'True and fair'.

Previous auditor The auditor who was previously the auditor of an entity and who has been replaced by another auditor.

Principal auditor The principal auditor is the auditor with responsibility for reporting on the financial report of an entity when that financial report includes financial information of one or more components audited by another auditor.

Privity letter A letter addressed to an auditor by a third party in an attempt to establish a duty of care owed by the auditor to the third party.

Probability proportionate to size sampling (PPS) *See* dollar-unit sampling.

Processing controls Controls that provide an assurance that computer processing has been performed as intended for a particular application.

Professional accountants Those persons, whether in public practice (including a sole practitioner, partnership or corporate body), industry, commerce, the public sector or education, who are members of a recognised accounting body.

Professional scepticism An attitude that includes a questioning mind and a critical assessment of evidence. Without an attitude of professional scepticism, the professional accountant may not be alert to circumstances that lead to a suspicion, and may draw inappropriate conclusions from the evidence obtained.

Program code review Where an auditor reviews the client's program documentation and the source code and considers whether the processing steps and control procedures are properly coded and logically correct.

Program library management software A specialised systems software that protects application programs that are stored online.

Projection Prospective financial information prepared on the basis of hypothetical assumptions about future events and management actions which are not necessarily expected to take place, such as when some entities are in a start-up phase or are considering a major change in the nature of operations; or a mixture of best-estimate and hypothetical assumptions.

Proportionate liability An arrangement whereby the plaintiff's loss is divided among the defendants according to their share of responsibility.

Prospective financial information Financial information based on assumptions about events that may occur in the future and on possible actions by an entity.

Proximity Closeness in space, time or relationships, where the occurrence of reliance on the auditor's work is foreseeable.

Purpose-written programs Computer programs written to achieve a specific audit purpose.

Q

Qualified opinion Indicates that an auditor is not satisfied in all material respects that the subject matter is in accordance with an identified framework. The following represent the types of qualified opinion that may be expressed by the auditor (*see also* the entries for these terms): 'Except for' opinion; Adverse opinion; Inability to form an opinion.

Quality assurance Quality checks and reporting mechanisms to ensure adherence to standards of quality.

Quality control Those policies and procedures adopted by an audit firm to ensure that all audits and audit-related service engagements are conducted in accordance with professional standards.

Quick asset ratio This is also called the acid test and is calculated as (current assets – inventory)/current liabilities. This is a more demanding version of the current ratio and indicates whether current liabilities could be paid without having to sell the inventory.

R

Random selection A sampling method where every item in the population has a known chance of selection. The person selecting the sample cannot bias the selection of items either consciously or unconsciously.

Ratio analysis Numbers produced by dividing one figure by another figure; for example, the working capital ratio is the total current assets figure divided by the total current liabilities figure. Standard ratios are used to assess aspects of a firm, particularly profitability, solvency and liquidity.

Ratio estimation A sampling method where the auditor calculates a ratio by dividing the sum of the audited values by the sum of the sample book value. The ratio is multiplied by the recorded total book value for the account balance, to create the estimated audited value.

Reasonable assurance A high but not absolute level of assurance on an accountability matter. It is expressed as reasonable assurance in recognition of the fact that absolute assurance is rarely attainable due to such factors as the need for judgment, the use of testing, the inherent limitations on internal control and the fact that much of the evidence available to the auditor is persuasive rather than conclusive in nature.

Reasonable assurance engagement The objective of a reasonable assurance engagement is a reduction in assurance engagement risk to an acceptably low level in the circumstances of the engagement as the basis for a positive form of expression of the practitioner's conclusion.

Reasonable care and skill Professionalism, or the due professional care and competence reasonably expected of a professional person (as opposed to a lay person) under the circumstances of the case. The professional is expected to have considered all facts (and their reliability) to arrive at a responsible and well-informed opinion of the matter.

Reasonable foreseeability A test used in third-party liability which requires evaluation of whether the auditors could reasonably foresee that the third party would rely on their work.

Reasonable person test Tests whether a reasonable person having access to all the facts would consider that the auditor was independent.

Receivables turnover ratio Calculated by dividing credit sales by trade debtors. It indicates how many times accounts receivable are turned over during a year. Also known as the debtors turnover.

Reconciliation A schedule establishing agreement between separate sources of information, such as accounting records reconciled with the source documents.

Record totals The totals of the number of logical or physical records in a batch, or file.

Regression analysis Estimates the relationship between a dependent variable (for example, sales) and one or more independent variables (for example, cost of sales or shipping costs). Provides a line of best fit for the data points.

Regulatory audits Audits undertaken with the aim of ensuring regulations have been fulfilled.

Related services *See* Audit-related services.

Reliability factor Statistical factor extracted from supporting tables to aid in calculation of sample size and evaluation of sample results.

Reperformance The auditor's independent execution of procedures or controls that were originally performed as part of the entity's internal controls, either manually or through the use of CAATs.

Report of factual findings The report issued by the auditor flowing from an agreed-upon procedures engagement.

Report to management A communication, excluding the audit report, to management on matters arising from the audit of an entity's financial report. *See also* Management letter.

Representation letter A letter from management to the auditor, representing that the financial report is fairly presented. The letter is addressed to the external auditor, and dated at the date of the auditor's report. It is signed by members of management whom the auditor believes are responsible for, and knowledgeable about, matters covered (chief executive officer and chief financial officer). *See also* Management representation letter.

Retail inventory method Deducing inventory amounts by using ratios of cost to selling price.

Return on shareholders' equity ratio Net profit divided by shareholders' equity. The most frequently-used ratio for measuring the business's return to owners.

Return on total assets ratio Net profit, before deducting interest expense and tax, divided by total assets. This measures the operating return before the cost of financing.

Review engagement A service where the auditor's objective is to provide a moderate level of assurance, being a lower level of assurance than that provided by an audit.

Review of job (batch) accounting data Auditor reviews the printed log produced for jobs (or batches of transactions) that are run and considers any excessive processing time, error conditions or abnormal halts to identify potential batches of transactions on which they should concentrate their audit attention.

Rights and obligations An assertion that assets are rights of the entity and liabilities are obligations of the entity.

Risk assessment An assurance service identifying the business risks that an organisation faces and the associated risk management policies.

Risk of fraud or error The risk that material misstatements resulting from fraud or error will not be detected.

Risk management The minimisation of exposure to risks in businesses. This involves the techniques of identifying potential risks, estimating the probability of occurrence, minimising damages, and generally managing a business's risk profile.

Routine transactions Common transactions such as sales and cash collections.

Run-to-run control total reconciliation Control totals accumulated during processing are compared to input totals and previous computer-run totals, to ensure that computer processing is complete and accurate.

S

Safeguarding Access to assets and computer records is restricted to authorised personnel by means of physical or computer safeguards, such as fences, vaults, locked doors and appropriate password controls.

Sampling *See* Audit sampling.

Sampling risk The possibility that a properly drawn sample may, by chance, not be representative of the population.

Sampling unit Commonly each of the transactions, account balances or dollars making up the account balance.

Scheduling audit work Preparation of various schedules and analyses of accounts for the auditor's use, usually done by client's personnel.

Scope of an audit The term refers to the audit procedures deemed necessary in the circumstances to achieve the objective of an audit.

Scope limitation *See* Limitation on scope.

Scope paragraph Paragraph in the audit report, identifying the financial report being audited, the responsibilities of the governing body and the auditor. It also indicates the level of assurance provided, and the basis for the opinion.

Service entity An entity that provides services to the client to record, process, execute transactions and/or maintain related accountability for these transactions.

Service entity auditor The auditor engaged to perform an audit on, or provide a written description about, aspects of a service entity and report to the user and/or user auditor.

Significance The relative importance of a matter, taken in context. The significance of a matter is judged by the practitioner in the context in which it is being considered. This might include, for example, the reasonable prospect of its changing or influencing the decisions of intended users of the practitioner's report; or, for example, where the context is a judgment about whether to report a matter to those charged with governance, whether the matter would be regarded as important by them in relation to their duties. Significance can be considered in the context of quantitative and qualitative factors, such as relative magnitude, the nature and effect on the subject matter and the expressed interests of intended users or recipients.

Significant risk A risk that requires special audit consideration.

Simple comparisons Simple analytical procedures used in preliminary planning. These help the auditor identify account balances that have changed significantly, simply by comparing the amounts for the current and previous year on the working trial balance in the working papers.

Snapshot An audit log generated by an application program which encounters a tagged transaction and writes the details—the transaction data, date and time of occurrence, the application program involved and the point in the program at which it was generated.

Solicitor's representation letter A letter or audit enquiry to a solicitor as a means of obtaining corroborating information about management's assertion concerning the status of litigation, claims and unrecorded or contingent liabilities.

Special relationship Relationship in which a person occupying a position of skill and care professes or offers advice to another person and the advice is given at the direct request of the recipient, or the adviser knows or ought to have known that the advice being given would be relied on by a person such as that recipient in the relevant circumstances.

Standard costing system A method of determining manufactured inventory costs that uses expected normal production costs rather than actual costs.

Statistical sampling Any approach to sampling that uses random sample selection, and also uses probability theory to evaluate sample results, including measurement of sampling risk.

Stocktake *See* Physical inventory count.

Stratification Process of dividing a population into discrete sub-populations, for example by monetary value, in order to reduce variation in the population and direct the auditor's attention to sampling units of interest.

Subject matter information The outcome of the evaluation or measurement of a subject matter. It is the subject matter information about which the practitioner gathers sufficient appropriate evidence to provide a reasonable basis for expressing a conclusion in an assurance report.

Subsequent events For audit purposes, subsequent events refers to events occurring between reporting period end and the date of the audit report, and also to facts discovered after the date of the audit report.

Substantive procedures Tests performed to obtain audit evidence to detect material misstatements in the financial report. These involve tests of details (transactions and balances) and analytical procedures.

Substantive tests of details risk The risk that detailed substantive tests of transactions and account balances will fail to detect a material misstatement.

Sufficiency The measure of the quantity of audit evidence obtained from tests of controls and substantive procedures.

Sufficient appropriate audit evidence A measure of the quantity and quality of audit evidence. The independent auditor's objective is to obtain sufficient competent evidence to provide a reasonable basis for forming an opinion. *See also* Sufficiency; Appropriateness of audit evidence.

Suitable criteria Standards or benchmarks considered appropriate for the evaluation and measurement of the subject matter of an assurance engagement.

Summarised financial report An abridged report for the purpose of informing users interested in the highlights of the entity's performance and financial position.

SWOT analysis A management tool that helps identify the internal strengths and weaknesses of an organisation and the external opportunities and threats.

Systematic selection Sampling procedure where sampling units are selected from a population at regular intervals, the regular interval being determined by dividing the number of units in the population by the sample size.

Systems control audit review file (SCARF) An embedded audit facility that enables auditors to specify parameters of interest, such as transactions meeting specified criteria, which are then recorded on a special audit file for subsequent review by the auditors.

Systems management software Software that aids the running of the computer system and controls access to application programs and data files.

SysTrust™ An assurance service aimed at establishing whether management has maintained effective controls over systems.

T

Teleological theories Deal with the consequences or outcomes of actions. They state that actions are right or wrong only in terms of their ability to bring about desired ends. Also called consequential theories.

Tendering The calling by audit clients for competitive bids for audit appointments.

Test data Simulated transactions that can be used to test processing logic, computations and controls actually programmed in computer applications.

Tests of controls Tests performed to obtain audit evidence about the suitability of design and effective operation of the internal control.

Time budget The estimated amount of time required at each staff level (partner, manager, senior and staff) to complete each part of the assurance service.

Time of completion The date at which the auditor signs the audit report.

Time series analysis A simple analytical procedure which is a predictive technique involving the extrapolation of past values of an item of financial information into the current audit period. For example, the past values of sales are examined to identify some trend which can be used to predict the level of the current audit balances.

Time series models Complex analytical procedures which aim to forecast what the current level of various financial report items should be, based on the pattern of past amounts of different variables.

Times interest earned ratio Indicates the ability of current operations to pay the interest that is due on the entity's debt obligations. Calculated by dividing net profit by interest expense. The more times that interest is earned, the better the entity's ability to service the interest on long-term debt.

Tolerable error The total error the auditor is willing to accept in a population before concluding that the population is materially misstated.

Tracing Testing from supporting documents to recorded amounts.

Transaction logs Reports that are designed to create an audit trail for each online transaction. Such reports often document the source of a transaction (terminal, time and user) as well as the transaction's details.

Transactions cycle approach An audit approach that involves testing the controls operating within transactions cycles. These transactions cycles include: sales– accounts receivable–cash receipts cycle, purchases– inventory– creditors–cash payments cycle, payroll–cash payments cycle, and other purchases–cash payments cycle.

Trend statements Statements that disclose trends by comparison of account balances by month, within the year and between years, and by year with those of previous years. Each number in a trend statement is expressed as a percentage of its own level calculated from some base year. The focus is on the trend rather than the absolute magnitude of dollar changes.

'True and fair view' Used in the audit opinion of *Corporations Act* audits to express the auditor's view that there is no material misstatement from the reporting framework, such as applicable accounting standards, and that this reporting framework has been consistently applied. *See also* 'Presents fairly'.

Type 1 or adjusting event After balance date events which relate to conditions existing at balance date. The effects of these events should be used to determine appropriate account balances in the financial report.

Type 2 or disclosing event After balance date events which do not relate to a condition existing at Balance date. If significant, they should be disclosed in the notes to the accounts.

U

Uncertainty *See* Inherent uncertainty.

Unqualified opinion Indicates that an auditor is satisfied in all material respects that the subject matter is in accordance with an identified framework.

User controls Manual control activities established and maintained by departments whose processing is performed by computer.

Utilitarianism A doctrine that holds that actions should be directed towards providing the greatest good for the greatest number of people.

V

Valid code test A logic test in which a code field in a record is compared to a table of valid codes stored online.

Valuation An assertion that assets and liabilities are recorded at appropriate carrying value.

Value-chain approach A chain of activities within a composite function that, when put together, adds value for the users.

Value-for-money auditing *See* Performance audit.

Value-weighted selection *See* Dollar-unit sampling.

Variables sampling Used to determine the value of a population, involving comparing audited and recorded values using the properties of the normal distribution.

Virtue ethics Emphasises the personal qualities of the auditor that allow them to identify and undertake ethically desirable acts.

Voucher system A type of expenditures accounting system which is designed to improve control over disbursements by establishing a sequential prenumbered record of suppliers' invoices, and to improve efficiency by eliminating inessential record keeping and facilitating timing of payments.

Vouching Testing from recorded amounts back to supporting documents.

W

Walk-through The tracing of selected transactions through the accounting system to determine that controls are in place.

WebTrust™ An assurance service examining the integrity, security and adherence to disclosed business practices for a business-to-consumer e-commerce environment.

Whistleblowing Disclosure of information, made in good faith and in the public interest, showing objectionable misconduct which is not otherwise known or visible.

Wide Area Network (WAN) A communications network that transmits information across an expanded area such as between plant sites, cities and nations. WANs allow for on-line access to applications from remote terminals. Several LANs can be interconnected in a WAN.

Working papers *See* Documentation.

INDEX

identification tags for non-current
assets, 486
'if not, why not?' obligation, 94
IFAC *see* International Federation of
Accountants
IFAD *see* International Forum on
Accountancy Development
IFSA *see* Investment and Financial
Services Association
IIA *see* Institute of Internal Auditors
IIA Code of Ethics, 693
IIA Standards, 688, 690–5
IIAC Code of Ethics, 688
illegal acts *see also* fraud
in accounts payable, 425
forensic audits, 35–6
inherent risk of, 307–8
reporting on, 169
ImClone, 7
implementation stage (performance
audit), 723–5
implementation standards
for internal auditing, 691
imprest fund, 426
imprisonment, 161
inability to form an opinion, 615–16
income statement
assertions and audit procedures, 455
income statement accounts
accounting principle changes, 492
discontinued operations, 492
substantiation of, 491–2
income statement items
evaluating materiality, 314
inconsistent other information, 618
incorporation of auditors, 165
independence, 5, 10, 29, 67, 86, 100–5
of AASB and AUASB, 52
in appearance, 105
ethical requirements, 105
financial and business relationships,
111–12
in internal auditing, 375, 689, 692,
696
of mind, 105
need for, 21
public sector auditing, 717
recent developments, 105–9
specified in reports, 607, 610
standards for, 119
threats and safeguards, 106–7
independence declaration, 101
Independent Expert Reports, 115
indexing working papers, 215
industry conditions *see also* operating
environment
factors affecting risk, 298–9
knowledge of required, 257–9
specialised audit software, 495
industry data
and ratio analysis, 267
industry specialists, 69, 208
informal norms, 255

information *see also* data
highlight information, 669–70
inconsistencies in audit report, 618
statistical, 669–70
used in analytical procedures, 273–4
information about the entity, 252–7
information hypothesis, 21–2
information processing control
activities, 345
information systems, 344–5
assurance on reliability, 673–4
auditor's understanding of, 352–3
flowcharts of, 357–9
information technology *see* computer
systems; computerised systems;
IT controls; IT risk
inherent risk, 200, 202, 204, 296–302,
at assertion level, 301–2
in e-commerce systems, 740
at financial report level, 297–300
sample sizes and, 521–3
inherent uncertainties, 617–18
input controls, 368–9, 409–10
inquiry from individuals, 194
in accounts payable, 480
in accounts receivable, 464–8
in inventory audits, 474
in performance audits, 725
regarding non-current liabilities, 489
regarding property, plant and
equipment, 483
inquiry of management
in reviews, 656
insolvency
see also going concern basis
assessing, 311–12
concerns about, 581
due to subsequent events, 618
services offered by auditing firms, 67
inspection of records and assets, 194
Institute of Chartered Accountants of
Australia (ICAA), 56
Institute of Internal Auditors (IIA), 39,
689–90
Institute of Social and Ethical
Accountability (AccountAbility),
750–1
insurance *see* professional indemnity
insurance
insurance hypothesis, 22
insurance industry, 310
insurance payments, 428
intangible assets, 488
integrated test facilities, 429, 430
integrity, 17, 84, 86, 343
Interactive Data Extraction and
Analysis (IDEA), 216
interest expense, 427–8
interim period, 398
interim work, 243, 245
internal auditing, 39–40, 348–9,
688–700
conflicts of interest in, 115

considering the work of internal
auditor, 374–6
current practice of, 695–6
definition of, 688–9
and external auditors, 698
future of, 696
general review of, 376
management of the department,
693
nature of work, 694
offered by auditing firms, 67
operational auditing, 696
outsourcing of, 696, 698
performance of, 694
and specialist audit groups, 696
internal auditors
using work of, 251
internal control
see also tests of controls
accounts receivable, 408–9
assurance services for, 666, 667–9
and audit strategy, 336–8
auditor's consideration of, 349–62
auditor's interest in, 189–90
auditor's knowledge of, 243–4
auditor's understanding of, 351
characteristics of satisfactory
control, 341
computer service bureaus, 372–3
for computerised systems, 362–74,
673–4
control activities, 345–8
criteria for evaluating, 667–8
database systems, 370–1
design effectiveness, 668–9
details in permanent file, 212
documenting auditor's
understanding of, 355–9
e-commerce systems, 739
effectiveness against fraud, 303, 306
evidence of consideration, 248
five elements of, 342
on information provided by
management, 675–6
inherent limitations of, 338–9
internal auditing and, 688, 697,
698–700
inventory management, 417–25
LANs and other networks, 372
and level of control risk, 200
limited assurance engagements on,
658
monitoring of, 348–9, 355
notifying managers of flaws, 581
objectives of, 339–42
operating effectiveness, 668–9
performance audits, 723
questionnaires testing, 27, 355–6
reasonable assurance concept, 339
and reliability of evidence, 196
reperformance, 195
reporting on, 5
responsibility for, 338

record totals, 368
records
　effective information systems, 344–5
　fraud indicators, 305
　right of access to, 104
recovery from back-up, 367
'red flags' indicating fraud, 303–5
regional and local audit firms, 66–7
registration of auditors, 55–6
regression analysis, 273
regularity audits
　see also compliance audits
　public sector, 726–8
regulation of auditing, 52–6
　see also legislation; self-regulation
　regulative codes, 51
regulative codes (professional), 51
related parties and related party
　　transactions, 257, 308–9, 580
related transactions and balances
indirect testing, 491
relative risk, 27
relevance of evidence, 196
relevance of information, 20
reliability
　of audit report, 611
　of data, 273
　of evidence, 196–8
　of financial information, 20
reliability factor
　sample sizes and, 530
remittance advice, 406
remoteness of parties, 21
removal of auditors, 103–4
rent payments, 428
repair costs, 484
reperformance, 195
　for testing internal controls, 668
report on the effectiveness of internal
　　control, 667–9
reports, 18
　see also financial reports; qualified
　　reports
　on agreed-upon procedure
　　engagements, 659–61
　attest reporting, 14
　direct reporting, 14
　of factual findings, 13, 15
　to managers, 627–8
　of performance audits, 725
　on prospective financial
　　information, 666–7
　in public sector auditing, 716
　in public sector auditing, 716
　review reports, 656–8
　unqualified, 607–11
representation letters, 569–77
representations see assertions;
　　management representation
　　letters
resignation of auditors, 103–4
respect, 87
response to assessed risks, 265

responsibilities
　assignment of, 343
　internal auditing, 692
　for internal control, 338
　segregation of, 341–2
responsibility, 18
retail inventory method, 470
retirements from fixed assets, 484–5
return on shareholders' equity ratio,
　　271
return on total assets ratio, 270–10
revaluations, 483, 485
revenues, 404–12
review engagements, 654, 655–8
review of audit, 245
review procedures
　on prospective financial
　　information, 666–7
reviews, 11, 12
　of audits, 562–4
　definition of, 12
　of internal auditing, 693
　level of assurance in, 12–13
revised financial reports, 618–19
rights of the reporting entity
　accounts payable, 479
　accounts receivable, 465
　cash balances, 460
　inventory audits, 473
　investments and intangibles, 487
　management assertions about, 451,
　　456, 460
　non-current liabilities, 490
　property, plant and equipment, 484
　verification of, 191, 196
rigour, 18
risk advisory, 671
Risk Advisory Services Task Force,
　　671–2
risk assessment
　assurance services on, 671–2
risk assessment process
　auditor's understanding of, 352
risk management see also specific risks
　　(eg, audit risk; control risk)
　internal auditing and, 689, 694, 697,
　　698–700
　relation to internal control, 339
risk of fraud or error, 302–5
risk of incorrect acceptance, 541
risk of incorrect rejection, 541
roll-forward procedures, 564
routine transactions, 408
Royal British Bank case, 167
rules of thumb
　for planning materiality, 315–16
run-to-run control total reconciliation,
　　370

S
SAC 2
　on accountability, 708
　legal implications, 156

safeguarding controls
　inventory, 477
safeguards
　of auditor independence, 106–7, 114
　for working papers, 213–14
sales
　documents, 404–8
　expenditures cycle compared,
　　416–17
　inventory area compared, 469–72
　tests of, 462–9
　tests of controls, 410–12
sampling see audit sampling
sampling risk, 201, 203, 514–6, 521
sampling unit, 520
SAP, 739
Sarbanes-Oxley Act 2002 (US), 107–8,
　　667
　criminal penalties, 161
　on non-auditing services, 118
　prompted by earnings management,
　　307
　Public Company Accounting
　　Oversight Board, 120
　requires audit committees, 120
　retention of working papers, 214
　rotation of auditors, 121
SAS (specialised audit software), 495
scanning documents
　accounts payable, 480
　accounts receivable, 464
　inventory audits, 474
　property, plant and equipment, 483
SCARF, 432, 745
SCAS (US), 670–1
scepticism, 18
　earnings management, 317
scheduling audit work, 251–2
scope of a review, 656
scope of audit
　environmental assurance
　　engagement, 754
　limitation of, 621
　scope section, 607–10
　tests of controls, 397–9
scope of special purpose report, 662–3
scope of work
　internal auditing activity, 692
Scott Group case, 153–4
securities, 486
Securities and Exchange Commission
　　(US), 307
security audits
　and e-commerce, 738
　protective security audits (public
　　sector), 715
Segenhoe case, 148
segment data
　and ratio analysis, 268
segregation of duties, 341–2, 346
　accounts payable, 418, 421
　accounts receivable, 408–9
　in computerised systems, 364–5